FAMILY LAW CODE, SELECTED STATES AND ALI PRINCIPLES

ASPEN PUBLISHERS

FAMILY LAW CODE, SELECTED STATES AND ALI PRINCIPLES

WITH COMMENTARY

2008

D. Kelly Weisberg

Professor of Law
Hastings College of the Law
University of California

Law & Business

AUSTIN BOSTON CHICAGO NEW YORK THE NETHERLANDS

http://lawschool.aspenpublishers.com

Printed in the United States of America.

1 2 3 4 5 6 7 8 9 0

ISBN: 978-0-7355-7302-4

ISSN: 1546-1920

About Wolters Kluwer Law & Business

Wolters Kluwer Law & Business is a leading provider of research information and workflow solutions in key specialty areas. The strength of the individual brands of Aspen Publishers, CCH, Kluwer Law International and Loislaw are aligned within Wolters Kluwer Law & Business to provide comprehensive, in-depth solutions and expert-authored content for the legal, professional and education markets.

CCH was founded in 1913 and has served more than four generations of business professionals and their clients. The CCH products in the Wolters Kluwer Law & Business group are highly regarded electronic and print resources for legal, securities, antitrust and trade regulation, government contracting, banking, pension, payroll, employment and labor, and healthcare reimbursement and compliance professionals.

Aspen Publishers is a leading information provider for attorneys, business professionals and law students. Written by preeminent authorities, Aspen products offer analytical and practical information in a range of specialty practice areas from securities law and intellectual property to mergers and acquisitions and pension/benefits. Aspen's trusted legal education resources provide professors and students with high-quality, up-to-date and effective resources for successful instruction and study in all areas of the law.

Kluwer Law International supplies the global business community with comprehensive English-language international legal information. Legal practitioners, corporate counsel and business executives around the world rely on the Kluwer Law International journals, loose-leafs, books and electronic products for authoritative information in many areas of international legal practice.

Loislaw is a premier provider of digitized legal content to small law firm practitioners of various specializations. Loislaw provides attorneys with the ability to quickly and efficiently find the necessary legal information they need, when and where they need it, by facilitating access to primary law as well as state-specific law, records, forms and treatises.

Wolters Kluwer Law & Business, a unit of Wolters Kluwer, is headquartered in New York and Riverwoods, Illinois. Wolters Kluwer is a leading multinational publisher and information services company.

SUMMARY OF CONTENTS

CONTENTS

PART II
SELECTED FEDERAL STATUTES

PART III
SELECTED UNIFORM ACTS

PART IV
AMERICAN LAW INSTITUTE, PRINCIPLES OF THE LAW OF FAMILY DISSOLUTION: ANALYSIS AND RECOMMENDATIONS

PREFACE

Family Law Code, Selected States and ALI Principles, With Commentary, provides an authoritative guide to family law tailored to the unique needs of the law student. The book furnishes explanations of fundamental legal principles, commentary on selected statutes, notations on important case law developments, citations to recent law review articles, and a glossary explaining key terminology. It illustrates legal principles by reference to the law of several states (i.e., California, Hawaii, Massachusetts, New York, Texas, and Vermont). The book also elucidates current legal developments in the cutting-edge areas of domestic partnerships and reproductive privacy. Designed for use in both basic and advanced family law courses, this Code also is recommended for courses in marital property law and children and the law.

This book, however, goes far beyond the study of state law to illuminate important federal statutes, constitutional issues (both federal and state), and uniform legislation on many areas of family law. Part I includes a selective presentation of pertinent family law statutes from a variety of state codes. Part II focuses on selected federal statutes, and Part III presents various Uniform Acts (with selected commentary).

Part IV highlights major provisions of the American Law Institute's *Principles of the Law of Family Dissolution* (with selected commentary) on the topics of child custody, child support, division of property upon dissolution and compensatory spousal payments, domestic partners, and premarital agreements. The ALI Principles were drafted by an influential group of lawyers, law professors, and judges and constitute the culmination of a 10-year law reform project to clarify underlying principles and make policy recommendations.

This book is intended to be especially user-friendly. Unlike traditional Codes, which are targeted to practitioners with some knowledge of the underlying substantive law and its statutory provisions, this Code is written for students. It assumes that the readers have little or no prior knowledge of the field and therefore provides essential explanations, commentary, and definitions.

In addition, it is organized topically, rather than chronologically, enabling readers to find a given statute easily. All statutes addressing a given topic are included in one location. Thus, if a reader is interested in learning about the legal regulation of bigamy or incest, he or she will quickly be able to locate all pertinent statutory provisions from civil and criminal statutes—set forth in the same place. Headings of the statutes distill the content of the provisions, and legislative histories include essential information. A Table of Cases, a Table of Statutes, and a detailed Index also help students navigate the material.

Equally important, the substantive material is presented in a logical progression. That is, the framework of this Code reflects the same theoretical structure as the basic family law course—from marriage, divorce, and nontraditional families, to child-related topics. Thus, the coverage of Part I begins with premarital issues and moves on to marital rights and duties before it turns to divorce and its financial incidents (spousal support and property rights).

The Code then explores the law's response to nontraditional families, including the traditional and modern responses. It focuses on aspects of new domestic partnership legislation. The last few chapters of Part I turn to children's issues: child support, child custody, adoption, procreation, child abuse and neglect, and the parent-child relationship in special contexts.

In the preparation of this book, I would like to acknowledge the helpful assistance of Derek Deavenport, Kristen Driscoll, and Kenny Jue, of Hastings College of the Law.

I invite you to contact me at weisberg@uchastings.edu with any comments, criticisms, and suggestions.

D. Kelly Weisberg
Hastings College of the Law
University of California

FAMILY LAW CODE, SELECTED STATES AND ALI PRINCIPLES

PART I

FAMILY LAW CODE

I.

THE MARRIAGE PROCESS: PREPARING TO MARRY

This chapter explores the law that governs the individual's decision to marry: the validity of premarital agreements, the resolution of premarital controversies, substantive and procedural restrictions on entry into marriage, procedural variations, and finally, informal marriages and curative devices. Massachusetts law provides an illustration of these topics.

A. COURTSHIP

1. Premarital Agreements

Premarital agreements (sometimes called "antenuptial agreements" or "prenuptial agreements") are agreements between prospective spouses made in contemplation of marriage. Such agreements typically require a party to limit or relinquish certain rights (e.g., rights regarding property or spousal support) that the party would have acquired by reason of the marriage.

Premarital agreements in Massachusetts are governed by Massachusetts General Laws, ch. 209, §§25, 26. They permit a marital party to keep his or her property separate during the marriage (and thereby preclude the property being divisible upon divorce) and also limit a spouse's claims on the other's estate. Mass. Gen. Laws ch. 209, §25. The agreement must be in writing. *Id.* Also, it must contain an annexed schedule with a sufficiently clear description to identify the pertinent property. Mass. Gen. Laws ch. 209, §26. To be binding on the creditors of either party, the agreement must be recorded. Failure to do so renders the agreement void as to creditors, although it is still binding on the parties, their heirs, and personal representatives.

Early Massachusetts case law, similar to that of many jurisdictions, held that a premarital agreement was void as against public policy. French v. McAnarney, 290 Mass. 544 (Mass. 1935). Subsequent case law enforced premarital agreements as to the rights of the parties upon death (Rosenberg v. Lipnick, 389 N.E.2d 385 (Mass. 1979)). Finally, in Osborne v. Osborne, 428 N.E.2d 810 (1981), the Supreme Judicial Court held that premarital contracts settling the alimony or property rights of the parties in the event of divorce are not per se against public policy and may be specifically enforced.

According to Massachusetts case law, premarital agreements must be fair and reasonable at the time of execution and at enforcement (*Osborne, supra*; DeMatteo v. DeMatteo, 762 N.E.2d 797 (Mass. 2002)). The agreement must be free from fraud or overreaching (*Rosenberg, supra*), and contain full and fair disclosure of the parties' net worth (or the contesting party must have had independent knowledge of the other's net worth) (*id.*). See also Austin v. Austin, 839 N.E.2d 837 (Mass. 2005) (holding valid a premarital agreement waiving alimony, reasoning that at the time of enforcement, the wife had suffered no physical or mental deterioration and was left with sufficient property to support herself); Biliouris v. Biliouris, 852 N.E.2d 687 (Mass. App. Ct. 2006) (holding that pregnancy is not sufficient to raise a defense of duress in signing a premarital agreement).

Unlike many other states and the Uniform Premarital Agreement Act (UPAA), which has been adopted in 25 states and the District of Columbia, Massachusetts does not adhere to the stricter standard that the agreement be unconscionable. (Massachusetts has not adopted the UPAA.) See also *DeMatteo, supra* (holding that antenuptial agreement was valid at time of execution despite the wife's alleged lack of sophistication and potential entitlement to a significantly larger share of marital estate in absence of the agreement).

The UPAA (promulgated in 1983) supports a wide latitude of permissible matters as the subject for premarital agreements. Agreements must be in writing and signed by both parties. Such agreements are not enforceable if not entered voluntarily by the party against whom enforcement is sought. They require that a spouse fairly and reasonably disclose property holdings and financial obligations absent a voluntary and express waiver of disclosure rights. If disclosure is lacking, actual knowledge by the other spouse at the time of agreement still permits enforcement. Also, if disclosure is lacking, the agreement must also be unconscionable to preclude enforcement. A valid agreement that meets the requirements for voluntariness and fair disclosure may still be set aside (provided that the agreement affects support upon separation or dissolution) if a spouse becomes eligible for welfare. The UPAA is set forth in Part III of this Code *infra*.

Under rules approved by the American Law Institute (ALI), premarital agreements must meet standards of procedural fairness (i.e., informed consent and disclosure) and substantive fairness. A rebuttable presumption arises that the agreement satisfies the informed consent requirement if (1) it was executed at least 30 days prior to the marriage; (2) both parties had, or were advised to obtain, counsel and had the opportunity to do so; and (3) if one of the parties did not have counsel, the agreement contained understandable information about the parties' rights and the adverse nature of their interests. ALI, Principles of the Law of Family Dissolution: Analysis and Recommendations §7.04(3)(a)(b) & (c) (2002) [hereafter ALI Principles]. In addition, the court must undertake a review of substantive fairness at the time of enforcement, specifically regarding whether enforcement would work a "substantial injustice" based on the passage of time, the presence of children, or changed circumstances that were unanticipated and would have a significant impact on the parties or their children. *Id.* at §7.05. The ALI Principles, including those on premarital agreements, are set forth in Part IV *infra*.

On premarital agreements generally, see Developments in the Law, Marriage as Contract and Marriage as Partnership: The Future of Antenuptial Agreement Law, 116 Harv. L. Rev. 2075 (2003). On premarital agreements in Massachusetts, see Charles P. Kindregan, Jr. & Monroe L. Inker, Mass. Prac. Series, Family Law and Practice, Chapter 20 (3d ed. 2003 & Supp.) [hereafter Kindregan & Inker].

Massachusetts General Laws

Ch. 209

§25. Prospective marital parties may make antenuptial agreements

At any time before marriage, the parties may make a written contract providing that, after the marriage is solemnized, the whole or any designated part of the real or personal property or any right of action, of which either party may be seized or possessed at the time of the marriage, shall remain or become the property of the husband or wife, according to the terms of the contract. Such contract may limit to the husband or wife an estate in fee or for life in the whole or any part of the property, and may designate any other lawful limitations. All such limitations shall take effect at the time of the marriage in like manner as if they had been contained in a deed conveying the property limited.

(Stat. 1845, ch. 208,§1; G.S. 1860, ch. 108, §27; P.S. 1882, ch. 147, §26; R.L. 1902, ch. 153, §26.)

§26. Premarital agreement that is recorded and contains property description is binding on third parties

A schedule of the property intended to be affected, containing a sufficiently clear description thereof to enable a creditor of the husband or wife to distinguish it from other property, shall be annexed to such contract; and such contract and schedule shall, either before the marriage or within ninety days thereafter, be recorded in the registry of deeds for the county or district where the husband resides at the time of the record, or, if he is not a resident of this commonwealth, then in the registry of deeds for the county or district where the wife resides at the time of the record, if it is made before the marriage, or where she last resided, if made after the marriage. If the contract is not so recorded, it shall be void except as between the parties thereto and their heirs and personal representatives. It shall also be recorded in the registry of deeds for every county or district where there is land to which it relates.

(Stat. 1845, ch. 208, §2; G.S. 1860, ch. 108, §28; Stat. 1867, ch. 248; P.S. 1882, ch. 147, §27; R.L. 1902, ch. 153, §27.)

B. PREMARITAL CONTROVERSIES

1. Breach of Promise to Marry

Only a few states currently permit a "heart balm" action for breach of promise to marry. The clear trend is toward abolition. See Gilbert v. Barkes, 987 S.W.2d 772 (Ky. 1999) (pointing out that 28 states have abolished the action either legislatively or judicially).

Under a cause of action for breach of promise to marry, A can recover damages from B if B terminates the engagement. English common law courts entertained such actions, which reflect Roman, Germanic, and canon law influences, as early as 1576. Criticisms of the action culminated in a movement in the United States in the 1930s when many states enacted statutes ("anti-heart balm" legislation) to eliminate the action.

Although Massachusetts recognized claims for breach of contract to marry at common law, the state legislature abrogated the action in 1938. See MacCleave v. Merchant, 2002 WL 31480307 (Mass. Super. 2002) (slip op.) (refusing to recognize breach of contract action based on defendant's breach of agreement to marry plaintiff, reasoning that the action was abolished by statute). But cf. Sutton v. Valois, 846 N.E.2d 1171 (Mass. App. Ct. 2006) (holding that a promise to marry is sufficient consideration to enforce agreements made between cohabiting partners)

Massachusetts General Laws

Ch. 207

§47A. No claim may be maintained for breach of contract to marry

Breach of contract to marry shall not constitute an injury or wrong recognized by law, and no action, suit or proceeding shall be maintained therefore.

(Stat. 1938, ch. 350, §1.)

2. Gifts in Contemplation of Marriage

During an engagement, the parties may give gifts to each other (commonly, an engagement ring). Many courts hold that an engagement ring is a conditional gift. Under this theory, A's gift to B of an engagement ring is conditioned on B's performance of an act (getting married). If the condition is not fulfilled (i.e., the marriage does not take place), then A may recover the gift.

At common law, fault barred recovery or retention of the engagement ring. Thus, the man could recover the ring if the woman unjustifiably ended the engagement or if the couple mutually dissolved it, but not if he unjustifiably terminated the engagement. In some states today, whether a party must return such a gift depends on who was responsible (at fault) for terminating the engagement. The fault-based rule is the majority rule.

See Brian L. Kruckenberg, Comment, "I Don't": Determining Ownership of the Engagement Ring When the Engagement Terminates; (Herman v. Parrish, 942 P.2d 631 (Kan. 1997)), 37 Washburn L.J. 425, 434 (1998).

However, according to the modern trend, fault is irrelevant. See Estate of Church v. Tubbs, 2006 WL 568335 (E.D. Mich. 2006); Meyer v. Mitnick, 625 N.W.2d 136 (Mich. Ct. App. 2001); Benassi v. Back and Neck Pain Clinic, 629 N.W.2d 475 (Minn. Ct. App. 2001).

Massachusetts case law holds that a suit to recover an engagement ring is not barred by the statutory abolition of actions for breach of promise to marry. Rather, such gifts may be recovered under principles of equitable restitution (De Cicco v. Barker, 159 N.E.2d 534 (Mass. 1959)). Massachusetts appears to follow the fault-based rule: "If the contract to marry is terminated without fault on the part of the donor, the [donor] may recover the ring" (*De Cicco*, 159 N.E.2d at 535). See generally Rebecca Tushnet, Rules of Engagement, 107 Yale L.J. 2583 (1998); Barbara Frazier, Comment, "But I Can't Marry You": Who Is Entitled to the Engagement Ring When the Conditional Performance Falls Short of the Altar?, 17 J. Am. Acad. Matrim. L. 419 (2001).

C. RESTRICTIONS ON ENTRY INTO MARRIAGE

1. Constitutional Limitations on Regulation of the Right to Marry

All states have restrictions on who may marry. Beginning in 1967, the United States Supreme Court invalidated several state restrictions on marriage. The Court held that racial restrictions on marriage are unconstitutional in Loving v. Virginia, 388 U.S. 1 (1967). *Loving* also declared that marriage is a fundamental right, subject to the highest level of constitutional protection. Later, the Supreme Court upheld the right to marry in the prison context (Turner v. Safley, 482 U.S. 78 (1987)).

In addition, the United States Supreme Court invalidated a restriction on the right to marry based on poverty (specifically, for persons with unpaid court-ordered child support obligations). Zablocki v. Redhail, 434 U.S. 374 (1978), examined the constitutionality of a Wisconsin statute that provided that those noncustodial parents with unpaid court-ordered support obligations could not marry. The Supreme Court declared the statute unconstitutional, holding that the restriction violated equal protection. *Zablocki* established different degrees of scrutiny for regulations infringing the right to marry; that is, rigorous scrutiny for those restrictions that are "direct" and "substantial," but minimal scrutiny for "reasonable regulations that do not significantly interfere with decisions to enter into the marital relationship."

Subsequent to *Zablocki*, many courts invalidated similar statutes denying marriage licenses to applicants with delinquent support obligations. See Cooper v. Utah, 684 F. Supp. 1060 (C.D. Utah 1987); Miller v. Morris, 386 N.E.2d 1203 (Ind. 1979).

For a recent case involving the constitutional right to marry, see Buck v. Stankovic, 2007 WL 1258615 (M.D. Pa. 2007).(holding that a policy requiring an alien seeking to marry a U.S. citizen to produce certain forms of identification violates the parties' fundamental right to marry because, based on strict scrutiny review, the policy significantly interferes with their right to marry by placing a direct legal obstacle in their path).

2. Substantive Regulations: Capacity

All states have substantive restrictions on who may marry. Substantive regulations generally require that the parties have capacity to marry and the requisite state of mind.

Capacity requires that the parties (1) be above the statutorily defined age, (2) be of opposite sexes (except in Massachusetts, which is the only state that currently permits same-sex marriage), (3) not be related, and (4) be married to only one spouse at a time. State of mind restrictions (discussed *infra*) require that the parties have sufficient understanding to be able to make a valid contract and that they marry without fraud or duress.

a. Age

All states establish minimum ages for marriage. Most states, including Massachusetts, establish 18 years as the requisite minimum age at which a person can validly consent to marriage (Mass. Gen. Laws ch. 207, §§7, 24). See also Uniform Marriage and Divorce Act (UMDA) §§203, 208.

According to Massachusetts statute, an authorized official must not solemnize a marriage involving a party under age 18 (Mass. Gen. Laws ch. 207, §7); nor may the clerk or registrar receive a notice of the intention to marry from a person under age 18 (Mass. Gen. Laws ch. 207, §24). (All persons who intend to marry in the state must file a written notice of their intention to marry with the clerk or registrar of the town or city and pay the statutory fee.) If the clerk or registrar has reasonable cause to doubt that the applicant is age 18, the official may require documentary proof of age (Mass. Gen. Laws ch. 207, §33A). See also Solemnization, Section D3, *infra*.

A minor under the requisite age may still marry in Massachusetts, but he or she must first secure parental written consent and judicial consent (Mass. Gen. Laws ch. 207, §25). Parental consent is not required if a parent has deserted the family, is incapable of consent, or is otherwise unfit. *Id.* Courts have upheld the constitutionality of parental consent requirements. See, e.g., Moe v. Dinkins, 533 F. Supp. 623 (S.D.N.Y. 1981), aff'd, 669 F.2d 67 (2d Cir.), *cert. denied*, 459 U.S. 827 (1982).

Defects of nonage render a marriage voidable upon the petition of the underage party, thereby providing a ground for annulment (Mass. Gen. Laws ch. 207, §16). A void marriage is one that is invalid, even if never annulled. In contrast, a voidable marriage is presumed valid until it is annulled. See also Annulment, Section C, *infra*.

Several states recently enacted legislation raising the minimum age for marriage in response to well-publicized cases of underage marriages in their respective states. For example, Kansas raised the minimum age to 16 for minors to marry with parental consent, and 15 with judicial consent. (Kansas formerly had no minimum age for marriage provided that a parent or judge agreed.) David Klepper, Kansas Acts to Protect Teens: Marriage Age Bill Is Sent to Sebelius, Kan. City Star, May 5, 2006, at B2. Calls for reform also followed a Colorado case ruling allowing a 15-year-old girl to enter a common law marriage with a felon. In response to the case of In re Marriage of J.M.H. & Rouse, 143 P.3d 1116 (Colo. Ct. App. 2006), the Colorado legislature raised the minimum age for common law marriage to 18, or 16 with parental and judicial approval (S.B. 6, eff. Sept, 1, 2006) — the same ages as for marriage generally in the state. April M. Washington, Colo. Marriages Now Have Law in Common, Minimum Age of 18 Now Applies Across Matrimonial Board, Rocky Mtn. News, July 19, 2006, at 4A.

Massachusetts General Laws

Ch. 207

§7. Requirements for solemnization of marriage of minor

A magistrate or minister shall not solemnize a marriage if he has reasonable cause to believe that a party to the intended marriage is under eighteen unless the provisions of sections twenty-four and twenty-five have been satisfied.

(Stat. 1692-3, ch. 25, §1; Stat. 1695-6, ch. 2, §4; Stat. 1786, ch. 3, §3; Stat. 1834, ch. 177, §2; R.S. 1836, ch. 75, §15; G.S. 1860, ch. 106, §13; P.S. 1882, ch. 145, §6; R.L. 1902, ch. 151, §7; Stat, 1941, ch. 270, §1; Stat. 1971, ch. 255, §1; Stat. 1981, ch. 684, §13.)

§24. Clerk or registrar shall not receive notice of intention to marry from a minor

The clerk or registrar shall not, except as provided in the following section, receive a notice of the intention of marriage of a person under eighteen.

(Stat. 1894, ch. 401, §1; R.L. 1902, ch. 151, §19; Stat. 1977, ch. 581, §2.)

§25. Requirements for the marriage of minors

The probate court for the county where, or a district court within the judicial district of which, a minor under the age specified in the preceding section resides may, after hearing, make an order allowing the marriage of such minor, if the parents or surviving parent of such minor, or, if only one such parent resides in the commonwealth, that parent, or, if neither such parent is alive and a resident thereof, or if the parent or parents qualified as aforesaid to consent are disqualified as hereinafter provided, a legal guardian with custody of the person of such minor has consented to such order. If a parent has deserted his family, or if found to be incapacitated by reason of mental illness and incapable of consent, or if found unfit under the provisions of section five of chapter two hundred and one to have custody of such minor, it shall not be necessary to obtain his consent to such order. If a parent whose consent would be required if living in the commonwealth lives outside thereof and the address of such parent is known, such notice of the proceedings shall be given him as the probate or district court may order. Said court may also after hearing make such order in the case of a person whose age is alleged to exceed that specified in the preceding section, but who is unable to produce an official record of birth, whereby the reasonable doubt of the clerk or registrar, as exercised under section thirty-five, may be removed. Upon receipt of a certified copy of such order by the clerk or registrar of the town where such minor resides, he shall receive the notice required by law and issue a certificate as in other cases.

(Stat. 1894, ch 401, §2; Stat. 1899, ch. 197; R.L .1902, ch. 151, §20; Stat. 1907, ch. 159; Stat. 1922, ch. 98; Stat. 1923, ch. 305, §1; Stat. 1931, ch. 212; Amended by Stat. 1987, ch. 522, §10.)

§33A. Clerk or registrar may require proof of age

If it appears from the statements made in the written notice of intention of marriage that a party to such intended marriage is under eighteen, the clerk or registrar shall not, except as required under section twenty-five, issue a certificate under section twenty-eight before receiving proof of the age of the parties. Such proof shall be contained in any of the following documents, graded and taking precedence in the order named: (1) an original or certified copy of a record of birth; (2) an original or certified copy of a baptismal record; (3) a passport; (4) a life insurance policy; (5) an employment certificate; (6) a school record; (7) an immigration record; (8) a naturalization record; or (9) a court record. Documentary evidence of a lower grade as aforesaid shall not be received by the clerk or registrar unless he is satisfied that evidence of a higher grade is not readily procurable. If no such documentary proof of age is procurable, the consent of the parent shall be sufficient. If the clerk or registrar has reasonable cause to believe that a party to an intended marriage represented to be eighteen or over is under such age, he shall, before issuing such certificate, require documentary proof of age as aforesaid.

(Stat. 1931, ch. 264; Stat. 1971, ch. 255, §3.)

b. Opposite Sex

In 2003, Massachusetts became the first state (and still is the only state) to permit same-sex marriage. Yet, the movement toward legalization of same-sex marriage accelerated a decade before, in 1993, when Hawaii became the first jurisdiction to rule favorably on same-sex marriage (Baehr v. Lewin, 852 P.2d 44 (Haw. 1993)) (holding that the denial of marriage licenses to three same-sex couples implicates the state constitution's Equal Protection Clause that explicitly bars sex-based discrimination). However, the Hawaii legislature subsequently nullified that decision by enacting legislation recognizing "reciprocal beneficiaries." For a comparative treatment of domestic partnership legislation in different states, see Chapter VI, *infra*.

Following *Baehr*, Congress and a number of states acted to undermine the impact of the decision. In 1996, Congress passed the Defense of Marriage Act (DOMA), 1 U.S.C. §7, which for the first time provides a heterosexual definition for the terms "marriage" and "spouse" for purposes of federal benefits and also specifies that states are not required to give effect to same-sex marriages under the Full Faith and Credit Clause of the U.S. Constitution. DOMA is included in Part II of this Code *infra*.

Many states followed by enacting state legislation or state constitutional amendments (sometimes referred to as "baby" or "mini" DOMAs) that adopt a definition of marriage as a union between a man and a woman. Currently, only five states (Massachusetts, New Jersey, New Mexico, New York, and Rhode Island) have neither a statute nor a constitutional provision prohibiting same-sex marriage. Alliance Defense Fund, DOMA Watch, available at www.domawatch.org (last visited Oct. 3, 2007). (However, New York has case law prohibiting same-sex marriage, discussed *infra*.) Massachusetts extended marriage to same-sex couples in Goodridge v. Department of Public Health, 798 N.E.2d 941 (Mass. 2003). Seven same-sex couples who were denied marriage licenses challenged the state statutory scheme. The state supreme court held that the limitation of protections, benefits, and obligations of civil marriage to individuals of opposite sexes lacks a rational basis and violates state constitutional equal protection principles.

Extremely influential in the *Goodridge* decision was the landmark case of Lawrence v. Texas, 539 U.S. 558 (2003), in which the United States Supreme Court declared unconstitutional a Texas statute (Texas Penal Code §21.06(a)) making it a crime for two persons of the same sex to engage in sodomy. The Supreme Court held that the statute violated the petitioners' interests in liberty and privacy protected by the Due Process Clause.

The Supreme Judicial Court stayed the entry of judgment in *Goodridge* for 180 days to enable the legislature "to take such action as it may deem appropriate in light of this opinion." *Id.* at 970. In response, the legislature solicited the court's opinion on the constitutionality of proposed legislation that would prohibit same-sex marriage but allow civil unions providing all the benefits of marriage. Ruling that the civil union bill contained the same defects as the ban on same-sex marriage, the state supreme court condemned the bill's "choice of language that reflects a demonstrable assigning of same-sex, largely homosexual, couples to second-class status." Opinions of the Justices to the Senate, 802 N.E.2d 565, 570 (Mass. 2004). Upon expiration of the stay on May 17, 2004, Massachusetts began permitting same-sex couples to marry.

A subsequent attempt by a Massachusetts citizen and several state legislators to prevent implementation of *Goodridge (*claiming that the state supreme court had usurped the legislature's authority to define marriage) was unsuccessful. In Largess v. Massachusetts Supreme Judicial Court, 373 F.3d 219, 229 (1st Cir. 2004), the U.S. Circuit Court of Appeals for the First Circuit rejected plaintiffs' argument, pointing out that voters and legislators had an alternative method of "preserving the republican government [that] the constitution mandates" by resort to the state constitutional amendment process.

As the 180-day deadline (imposed by *Goodridge*) approached, then-Massachusetts Governor Mitt Romney restricted the availability of same-sex marriage to *state residents* by requiring proof of residency pursuant to state statutes adopting the Uniform Marriage Evasion Act (Mass. Gen. Laws ch. 207 §§11 & 12). In Cote-Whiteacre v. Department of Public Health, 844 N.E.2d 623 (Mass. 2006), the Massachusetts Supreme Judicial Court upheld the constitutionality of the state's marriage evasion statutes (Mass. Gen. Laws ch. 207, §§11, 12) prohibiting the contracting of marriage by, or issuance of a marriage license to, nonresidents intending to continue living in jurisdictions in which same-sex marriage is banned. However, the court permitted nonresident members of same-sex couples from those few states without express bans on same-sex marriage to proceed to trial in Massachusetts to present evidence to rebut the claim that their home states would prohibit same-sex marriage. Specifically, the court remanded the cases of three couples from Rhode Island and New York for a determination whether same-sex marriage was prohibited in those states.

In September 2006, in Cote-Whitacre v. Department of Public Health, 2006 WL 3208758 (Mass. Super. Ct. 2006), a trial court judge (Judge Thomas Connolly) determined that same-sex marriage was prohibited in New York (as a result of Hernandez v. Robles, 821 N.Y.S.2d 770 (N.Y. 2006), discussed *infra*) but not in Rhode Island because the latter state did not have an express prohibition. (Whether Rhode Island will honor these marriages is still unclear.) However, Judge Connolly's ruling did not answer the question of the validity of the marriages of *New Yorkers* who were married in Massachusetts *after* same-sex marriage became legal there but *before Hernandez* was decided in July 2006. In May 2007, the same judge addressed that issue and ruled that those marriages were valid. See Denise Lavoie, Unions Valid for Gays Who Wed Before N.Y. Ban; Mass. Judge Backs 170 Marriages, N.J. Record, May 18, 2007, at A20.

In June 2007, the fate of same-sex marriage in Massachusetts hung by a thread. The state legislature faced a highly contentious effort to amend the state constitution to overturn *Goodridge.* In order to amend the Massachusetts constitution, an amendment must pass two consecutive legislative sessions before it goes before the voters in a referendum. In legislative sessions in March 2004 and September 2005, the state legislature considered a measure to define marriage as a heterosexual relationship and to replace same-sex marriage with civil unions. That measure was ultimately defeated in the second required vote.

In response, opponents of same-sex marriage formulated a *new* ballot initiative to ban same-sex marriages by a constitutional amendment that would enact a heterosexual definition of marriage, this time with no provision for civil unions, but without invalidating the marriage licenses already issued to same-sex couples. Supporters of same-sex marriage immediately challenged the amendment based on a provision in the Massachusetts Constitution (Art. 48, Sec. 2), that prohibits the use of an initiative petition for "reversal of a judicial decision." In July 2006, the Massachusetts Supreme Judicial Court ruled that the proposed amendment did not "reverse" a judicial decision because the initiative petition was not seeking to vacate *Goodridge* so as to affect the rights of the parties to that case, but instead was seeking to amend the state constitution prospectively. Schulman v. Attorney General, 850 N.E.2d 505 (Mass. 2006). That judicial decision thereby permitted the issue to go before the voters if the measure was passed by a minimum of 50 votes in each of two consecutive sessions.

The first vote on the proposed amendment was scheduled for November 2006 but was delayed by the legislature until January 2, in large part to wait until after state elections. In response, then-Massachusetts Governor Mitt Romney submitted a petition for certification to the state supreme court, asking the court to order the initiative to be placed on the ballot in the event that the legislature failed to vote on the last day of the session as required by the state constitution (Art. 48). On December 27, 2006, the court agreed with the former governor that the state constitution requires a vote before the end of the legislative session. When the legislature took the first vote, the measure passed. However, in the second vote, on June 14, 2007, Massachusetts legislators, by a razor-thin margin, defeated the measure by a 151 to 45 vote. (The margin was "razor-thin" because the proposal needed a minimum of 50 favorable votes to advance it to the voters and the measure fell short by 5 votes). See Pam Belluck, Massachusetts Gay Marriage Referendum Is Rejected, N.Y. Times, June 15, 2007, at A13.

In 2006, three state supreme courts (in New Jersey, New York, and Washington) upheld their respective bans on same-sex marriage. See Lewis v. Harris, 908 A.2d 196 (N.J. 2006); Hernandez v. Robles, 821 N.Y.S.2d 770 (N.Y. 2006); Andersen v. King County, 138 P.3d 963 (Wash. 2006). The setback in Washington State led a coalition of gay legislators there to propose gay marriage legislation and, in the alternative, domestic partnership legislation. Washington Governor Christine Gregoire signed the ensuing domestic partnership bill (SB 5336) on April 21, 2007. The law took effect July 21, 2007.

Same-sex marriage cases are still pending in California and Connecticut. See, e.g., In re Marriage Cases [Six Consolidated Appeals], 49 Cal. Rptr. 3d 675 (Ct. App.), *rev. granted*, In re Marriage Cases, 149 P.3d 737 (Cal. 2006); Kerrigan & Mock v. Conn. Dept. of Public Health, No. NNH-CV-04-4001813-S (filed September 28, 2004).

Courts in Iowa and Maryland currently are split on the issue. In Varnum v. Brien, No. CV5965 (Iowa Dist. Ct., Polk County, Aug. 30, 2007), an Iowa trial court declared that that state's ban violated the state constitutional right to equal protection and due process. The ruling was stayed pending appeal to the Iowa Supreme Court. However, in September 2007, Maryland's highest court upheld that state's ban on same-sex marriage. In Conaway v. Deane, 2007 WL 2702132 (Md. 2007), the court held that the ban was rationally related to the legitimate governmental interests in fostering procreation and encouraging the traditional family structure. Same-sex marriage advocates in that state plan to introduce legislation to establish civil unions.

To date, nine states and the District of Columbia have enacted domestic partnership legislation. New laws in New Hampshire and Oregon take effect on January 1, 2008. Seven other jurisdictions (California, Connecticut, the District of Columbia, Hawaii, Maine, New Jersey, and Vermont) offer domestic partnership benefits. Four of these states call their partnerships "civil unions" (Connecticut, New Hampshire, New Jersey, Vermont).

On the international level, Belgium, Canada, the Netherlands, South Africa, and Spain have legalized same-sex marriage. Eleven countries currently offer some form of domestic partnership legislation granting a range of rights to same-sex partners. These countries include: Denmark, Finland, France, Germany, Hungary, Iceland, Israel, Norway, Portugal, Sweden, Switzerland and the United Kingdom (except for Scotland). Human Rights Campaign Foundation, Domestic Partnerships, available at www.hrc.org (last visited Oct. 3, 2007).

c. Incest

All states regulate the degrees of kinship within which persons may marry. States have both civil restrictions and criminal sanctions. Civil restrictions require that prospective spouses not be granted marriage licenses if the parties are related to each other within certain prohibited degrees of kinship. Such restrictions provide that marriages between persons who are related within prohibited degrees of kinship are void. States also have criminal provisions imposing criminal penalties on marital parties in an incestuous relationship as well as those authorized officials who knowingly solemnize such relationships.

In terms of civil restrictions, all states restrict marriages by *consanguinity* (i.e., blood relationships), such as those between parent and child, brother and sister, uncle and niece, and aunt and nephew. Although restrictions based on consanguinity are widespread, fewer states restrict marriages between parties who are related by *affinity* (i.e., relationships established by law, such as marriage with step relatives, or relatives by adoption).

Massachusetts law restricts marriage by those persons related by consanguinity (Mass. Gen. Laws ch. 207, §1) as well as by affinity (Mass. Gen. Laws ch. 207, §2 (step relatives)). Such marriages are void (Mass. Gen. Laws ch. 207, §8).

Criminal penalties for incest traditionally have been harsh. See, e.g., Mass. Gen. Laws ch. 272, §17 (maximum 20 years in state prison). The interaction between civil and criminal statutes is illustrated in Commonwealth v. Rahim, 805 N.E.2d 13 (Mass. 2004) (holding that the state incest statute punishes those relationships, including step relationships, that are listed as prohibited relationships in the state marriage statutes).

The constitutionality of state incest prohibitions recently arose in Muth v. Frank, 412 F.3d 808 (7th Cir. 2005). Washington State officials terminated the parental rights of a couple based on their incestuous marriage and then charged them with criminal liability for incest. Following their conviction, the husband argues that the state incest statute is unconstitutional because it criminalizes a sexual relationship between consenting adults in violation of Lawrence v. Texas, 539 U.S. 558 (2003) (invalidating sodomy statutes). The U.S. Court of Appeals for the Seventh Circuit refuses to read *Lawrence* so broadly as to create a fundamental right to engage in all forms of private sexual intimacy, reasoning that *Lawrence* had a limited focus on homosexual sodomy and also that it failed to apply strict scrutiny review.

Massachusetts General Laws

Ch. 207

§1. Man may not marry certain relatives

No man shall marry his mother, grandmother, daughter, granddaughter, sister, stepmother, grandfather's wife, grandson's wife, wife's mother, wife's grandmother, wife's daughter, wife's granddaughter, brother's daughter, sister's daughter, father's sister or mother's sister.

(C.L. 102, §5; Stat. 1695-6, ch. 2, §1; Stat. 1785, ch. 69, §1; R.S. 1836, ch. 75, §1; G.S. 1860, ch. 106, §1; P.S. 1882, ch. 145, §1; R.L. 1902, ch. 151, §1; Stat. 1983, ch. 277.)

§2. Woman may not marry certain relatives

No woman shall marry her father, grandfather, son, grandson, brother, stepfather, grandmother's husband, daughter's husband, granddaughter's husband, husband's grandfather, husband's son, husband's grandson, brother's son, sister's son, father's brother or mother's brother.

(Stat. 1785, ch. 69, §1; R.S. 1836, ch. 75, §2; G.S. 1860, 106, §2; P.S. 1882, ch. 145, §2; R.L. 1902, ch. 151, §2; 1983, ch. 277.)

§3. Dissolution, death, or divorce has no effect on marriage prohibitions

The prohibition of the two preceding sections shall continue notwithstanding the dissolution, by death or divorce, of the marriage by which the affinity was created, unless the divorce was granted because such marriage was originally unlawful or void.

(R.S. 1836, ch. 75, §3; G.S. 1860, ch. 106, §3; P.S. 1882, ch. 145, §3; R.L. 1902, ch. 151, §3.)

§8. Void marriage does not require judicial declaration

A marriage solemnized within the commonwealth which is prohibited by reason of consanguinity or affinity between the parties, or of either of them having a former wife or husband living, shall be void without a judgment of divorce or other legal process.

(Stat. 1695-6, ch. 2, §1; Stat. 1785, ch. 69, §2; R.S. 1836, ch. 76, §1; G.S. 1860, ch. 107, §1; P.S. 1882, ch. 145, §7; R.L. 1902, ch. 151, §8; Stat. 1975, ch. 400, §1.)

Ch. 272

§17. Penalty for incestuous marriage or incestuous sexual activities

Persons within degrees of consanguinity within which marriages are prohibited or declared by law to be incestuous and void, who intermarry or have sexual intercourse with each other, or who engage in sexual activities with each other, including but not limited to, oral or anal intercourse, fellatio, cunnilingus, or other penetration of a part of a person's body, or insertion of an object into the genital or anal opening of another person's body, or the manual manipulation of the genitalia of another person's body, shall be punished by imprisonment in the state prison for not more than 20 years or in the house of correction for not more than 2 1/2 years.

(Stat. 1695-6, ch. 2, §2; R.S. 1836, ch. 130, §13. G.S. 1860, ch. 165, §7; P.S. 1882, ch. 207, §7; R.L. 1902, ch. 212, §13; Stat. 1918, ch. 257, §464; Stat. 1919, ch. 5; Stat. 1920, ch. 2; Stat. 2002, ch. 13.)

---

d. Bigamy/Polygamy

All states refuse to permit marriages that are bigamous (i.e., having two spouses at the same time) or polygamous (i.e., having more than two spouses at the same time). Civil restrictions provide that a person may not marry if he or she already has a spouse. If a party to a marriage is still validly married to a prior living spouse, then the subsequent marriage is void. States also make bigamy and polygamy criminal offenses (Mass. Gen. Laws ch. 272, §15). To impose criminal sanctions, modern courts require intent (i.e., that the defendant enter into a second marriage with the knowledge that the first marriage is still valid). The United States Supreme Court has held that freedom of religion is not a valid defense to the crime of bigamy. Reynolds v. United States, 98 U.S. 145 (1878).

Under Massachusetts law, bigamous or polygamous marriages are void, that is, invalid from inception (Mass. Gen. Laws ch. 107, §4) without the necessity for the parties to secure a divorce or judgment of nullity (Mass. Gen. Laws ch. 107, §8). However, a statutory exception applies in some cases if a person enters into a subsequent marriage in good faith during the existence of a former marriage. Thus, if a person marries in the belief that the former spouse was dead or that the former marriage ended in divorce or without knowledge of the former marriage, then the subsequent marriage shall be valid after removal of the impediment if the parties continue to live together (in good faith on the part of one of them), and their issue shall be considered legitimate (Mass. Gen. Laws ch. 207, §6).

Furthermore, a divorced spouse may not remarry until the divorce becomes final. According to Massachusetts General Laws ch. 208, §21, judgments of divorce shall be in the first instance judgments *nisi* and become absolute only 90 days later. Any remarriage contracted during the interval between a judgment *nisi* and the absolute judgment is void (because the party then would have two spouses at the same time) (Ross v. Ross, 430 N.E.2d 815, 819 (Mass. 1982)). On Annulments, see also Section C, Annulment, *infra*.

To address the problem of child sexual exploitation associated with the practice of polygamy, the Utah legislature enacted a Child Bigamy Law in 2003 (Utah Code Ann. §76-7-101.5). The Act increases the penalties for bigamy involving underage brides, by providing that marriage or cohabitation with a person under age 18, while the actor is validly married to another, constitutes a second-degree felony punishable by up to 15 years in prison.

In 2006, the Utah Supreme Court examined the issue of whether polygamy laws were invalid based on Lawrence v. Texas. In State v. Holm, 137 P.3d 726 (Utah 2006), the court upheld the conviction of a polygamist who challenged the constitutionality of the state bigamy statute. The court rejected the defendant's argument that his conduct (marrying two wives while he was already married) was protected as a fundamental liberty interest based on *Lawrence*. The court distinguished *Lawrence* by reasoning that (1) the present case implicates the institution of marriage (rather than mere private consensual sexual conduct) because the state has an interest in preventing the formation of marital forms it deems harmful, and (2) the present case involves a minor (and sexual conduct involving minors is outside the scope of *Lawrence*).

Also, in 2006, Warren Jeffs, renown leader of a fundamentalist Mormon sect, was arrested during a routine traffic stop in Las Vegas after he evaded authorities for several years. He was subsequently convicted of being an accomplice to rape involving an arranged marriage between a 14-year-old church follower and her 19-year-old cousin. John Dougherty & Kirk Johnson, Sect Leader Is Convicted as an Accomplice to Rape, N.Y. Times, Sept. 26, 2007, at A18.

For recent legal commentary on polygamy, see Shayna M. Sigman, Everything Lawyers Know About Polygamy Is Wrong, 16 Cornell J.L. & Pub. Pol'y 101 (2006) (arguing that polygamy should be decriminalized because legal policy is based on faulty assumptions and misconceptions); Anne Taylor, Case Note: In re Kingsston Children: The Best Interests of Polygamous Children, 8 J.L. & Fam. Stud. 427 (2006) (case note exploring the role of polygamy in the determination of the best interests of children in custody disputes).

Massachusetts General Laws

Ch. 207

§4. Polygamous marriage is void

A marriage contracted while either party thereto has a former wife or husband living, except as provided in section six and in chapter two hundred and eight, shall be void.

(Stat. 1784, ch. 40, §2; Stat. 1785, ch. 69, §2; R.S. 1836, ch. 75, §4; G.S. 1860, ch. 106, §4; P.S. 1882, ch. 145, §4; R.L. 1902, ch. 151, §4.)

§6. Validity of a subsequent marriage entered into in good faith during existence of former marriage

If a person, during the lifetime of a husband or wife with whom the marriage is in force, enters into a subsequent marriage contract with due legal ceremony and the parties thereto live together thereafter as husband and wife, and such subsequent marriage contract was entered into by one of the parties in good faith, in the full belief that the former husband or wife was dead, that the former marriage had been annulled by a divorce, or without knowledge of such former marriage, they shall, after the impediment to their marriage has been removed by the death or divorce of the other party to the former marriage, if they continue to live together as husband and wife in good faith on the part of one of them, be held to have been legally married from and after the removal of such impediment, and the issue of such subsequent marriage shall be considered as the legitimate issue of both parents.

(Stat. 1895, ch. 427; Stat. 1896, ch. 499; R.L. 1902, ch. 151, §6.)

§8. Void marriage does not require judicial declaration

A marriage solemnized within the commonwealth which is prohibited by reason of consanguinity or affinity between the parties, or of either of them having a former wife or husband living, shall be void without a judgment of divorce or other legal process.

(Stat. 1695-6, ch. 2, §1; Stat. 1785, ch. 69, §2; R.S. 1836, ch. 76, §1; G.S. 1860, ch. 107, §1; P.S. 1882, ch. 145, § 7; R.L. 1902, ch. 151, §8; Stat. 1975, ch. 400, §1.)

Massachusetts General Laws

Ch. 272

§15. Penalty for polygamy

Whoever, having a former husband or wife living, marries another person or continues to cohabit with a second husband or wife in the commonwealth shall be guilty of polygamy, and be punished by imprisonment in the state prison for not more than five years or in jail for not more than two and one half years or by a fine of not more than five hundred dollars; but this section shall not apply to a person whose husband or wife has continually remained beyond sea, or has voluntarily withdrawn from the other and remained absent, for seven consecutive years, the party marrying again not knowing the other to be living within that time, nor to a person who has been legally divorced from the bonds of matrimony.

(Stat. 1694-5, ch. 5, §§3 to 5; Stat. 1698, ch. 19; Stat. 1784, ch. 40, §2; R.S. 1836, ch. 130, §§2, 3; G.S. 1860, ch. 165, §§4, 5; P.S. 1882, ch. 207, §§4, 5; R.L. 1902, ch. 212, §11; Stat. 1918, ch. 257, §464; Stat. 1919, ch. 5; Stat. 1920, ch. 2; Stat. 1969, ch. 301.)

3. State of Mind Restrictions

All states have substantive restrictions regarding the requisite state of mind for entering into marriage. A majority of states provide that fraud or duress provides grounds to annul a marriage. The existence of fraud or duress vitiates consent and makes the marriage voidable at the request of the injured party.

Because of the public policy in favor of preserving a marriage whenever possible, many courts apply the strict test for fraud, requiring that the misrepresentation go to the "essentials" to render the marriage voidable. "Essentials" generally include ability and willingness to engage in sexual relations and childbearing. Other states require only that the fraud be material, that is, the plaintiff would not have married the defendant but for the fraud. When considering fraud to annul marriage, courts traditionally distinguished between consummated and unconsummated marriages, sometimes requiring a high standard for the former.

To support an annulment in Massachusetts on grounds of fraud, the fraud must meet the strictest standard. That is, it must affect the "essence" or "essentials" of the relationship (Reynolds v. Reynolds, 85 Mass. (3 Allen) 605 (1862) (granting an annulment when wife was pregnant by another man at time of marriage because her concealment of pregnancy and false statement as to her chastity go directly to the essentials of the marriage contract)). See also Symonds v. Symonds, 432 N.E.2d 700 (Mass. 1982) (abrogating rule that man who has had premarital sexual relations with a woman may not obtain annulment on ground that he was fraudulently induced to marry a woman who asserted that he was the father of her unborn child or that she was not pregnant).

D. ANNULMENT

An annulment declares that no marriage occurred because some impediment existed at the time of the ceremony. In contrast, divorce terminates a valid marriage.

Annulments were utilized more frequently when divorce was difficult to obtain. In England until the Matrimonial Causes Act of 1857, a divorce that enabled the parties to remarry was almost impossible to secure. Discontented marital partners, however, might secure an annulment for fraud, duress, or nonage. Following divorce reform, the importance of annulment decreased.

Different procedural rules govern annulment and divorce. First, annulment jurisdiction generally exists at either party's domicile, the state where the marriage was celebrated, or any state with personal jurisdiction over the spouses. In contrast, divorce jurisdiction rests on domicile. Second, spousal support, child support, and division of property did not follow typically from an invalid marriage. Today, many states, by equitable remedies or statute, assimilate the financial consequences of annulment to those of divorce. Third, the "relation back" doctrine is applicable only to annulments. Because a decree of annulment establishes that a marriage never existed, benefits lost by virtue of the marriage may be reinstated. See Haacke v. Glenn, 814 P.2d 1157 (Utah Ct. App. 1991) (granting wife an annulment stemming from her husband's concealment of his status as a convicted felon and thereby eliminating wife-attorney's conflict of interest with her employer—Department of Corrections).

In Massachusetts, either spouse may bring an action to annul the marriage (Mass. Gen. Laws ch. 207, §14). Incestuous or bigamous marriages are void without the necessity of a judicial declaration (Mass. Gen. Laws ch. 207, §8 *supra*). If a marriage is declared void on the specific grounds of nonage or mental capacity, any issue are deemed legitimate descendants of the parent who is capable of contracting the marriage (Mass. Gen. Laws ch. 207, §16). Following an annulment, a court may issue orders concerning child custody and child support (Mass. Gen. Laws ch. 207, §18).

Massachusetts General Laws

Ch. 207

§14. Either party may institute an action to annul a marriage

If the validity of a marriage is doubted, either party may institute an action for annulling such marriage, or if it is denied or doubted by either party, the other party may institute an action for affirming the marriage. Such action shall be commenced in the same manner as an action for divorce, and all the provisions of chapter two hundred and eight relative to actions for divorce shall, so far as appropriate, apply to actions under this section. Upon proof of the validity or nullity of the marriage, it shall be affirmed or declared void by a judgment of the court, and such judgment of nullity may be made although the marriage was solemnized out of the commonwealth, if at that time and also when the action was commenced the plaintiff had his domicile in the commonwealth, of if he had resided in this commonwealth for five years last preceding the commencement of said action, unless the court finds that he has removed into this commonwealth for the purpose of obtaining said judgment.

The register of probate shall, within two days after the expiration of the appeal period following the entry of a judgment annulling a marriage, or if an appeal was taken within two days after entry of final judgment pursuant to a rescript of the appellate court, send an attested copy thereof to the commissioner of public health, the clerk or registrar of the

city or town in the commonwealth where the marriage was solemnized, and the clerk or the registrar of each city and town in the commonwealth where a party to the marriage dwelt at the time of the marriage. The commissioner of public health and every clerk or registrar to whom such an attested copy is sent shall, forthwith upon receipt of such copy, enter upon the margin of his record of the marriage a note of reference to the judgment of annulment.
(Stat. 1951, ch. 469; Stat. 1975, ch. 400, §3; Stat. 1976, ch. 486, §19; Stat. 1986, ch. 462, §1.)

§16. Issue of some void marriages shall be legitimate

The issue of a marriage declared void by reason of nonage, insanity or idiocy of either party shall be the legitimate issue of the parent who was capable of contracting the marriage.
(R.S. 1836, ch. 76, §22; G.S. 1860, ch. 107, §29; P.S. 1882, ch. 145, §13; R.L. 1902, ch. 151, §13.)

§18. Post-annulment orders of custody and support

Upon or after a judgment of nullity, the court shall have like power to make orders relative to the care, custody and maintenance of the minor children of the parties as upon a judgment of divorce.
(Stat. 1820, ch. 56, §1; R.S.1836, ch. 76, §26; G.S.1860, ch. 107, §33; P.S.1882, ch. 145, §15; R.L. 1902, ch. 151, §15; Amended by Stat. 1975, ch. 400, §5.)

E. MARRIAGE PROCEDURE: PROCEDURAL REGULATIONS

All states regulate marriage procedure. Such regulation is intended to promote the stability of marriage and to facilitate the collection of vital statistics.

Massachusetts requires that the parties consent to marry, procure a marriage license, and have the marriage solemnized by an authorized person who must sign the marriage certificate and submit it to the county clerk. The clerk or registrar then registers the marriage so that the marriage becomes part of the public record.

1. Consent

Early Massachusetts case law held that a person who lacks sufficient mental capacity to consent cannot validly marry. See Inhabitants of Middleborough v. Inhabitants of Rochester, 12 Mass. 363 (Mass. 1815) (holding that a marriage with a person who had been judicially declared non compos mentis was void)). But cf. Bradford v. Parker, 99 N.E.2d 537 (Mass. 1951) (holding that a widow was entitled to family allowance from her husband's estate because his status as conservatee did not prevent him from contracting a valid marriage).

2. Licensure

States require that the parties procure a marriage license, often by applying to a county clerk. The clerk may refuse to issue the license if the information provided by the parties reveals that they are ineligible to marry.

Parties who wish to marry in Massachusetts must file an application ("notice of their intent to marry") with the clerk or registrar of the city or town at least three days prior to the marriage and pay the statutory fee (Mass. Gen. Laws ch. 207, §19). Many states, similar to Massachusetts, have waiting periods between the application and issuance of the marriage license, the purpose of which is to deter hasty marriages. (Note that Section 204 of the Uniform Marriage and Divorce Act (UMDA) also requires a three-day waiting period.)

A judge may waive the waiting period in an emergency (Mass. Gen. Laws ch. 207, §30). The requisite notice must be in writing, under oath, and contain a statement that there is no legal impediment to the marriage (Mass. Gen. Laws ch. 207, §20). After the three-day waiting period (but no later than 60 days afterward), the clerk or registrar issues to the parties a certificate (marriage license) that they shall give to the solemnizing official (Mass. Gen. Laws ch. 207, §28).

Marriages performed in Massachusetts are not valid if a party resides and intends to continue to reside in another jurisdiction and if such a marriage would be void if contracted in that jurisdiction (Mass. Gen Laws ch. 207, §11). Additionally, licensing officials must make sure that such a person is not prohibited from intermarrying by the laws of the jurisdiction where he or she resides (Mass. Gen Laws ch. 207, §12). See Cote-Whiteacre v. Department of Public Health, 844 N.E.2d 623 (Mass. 2006) (interpreting Mass Gen. Laws ch. 207, §§11, 12 to have the combined effect of prohibiting all nonresident same-sex couples from marrying in Massachusetts, except to the extent that such marriages are not prohibited in their states of domicile).

Many states require that before the clerk issues the license, the parties file a health certificate, signed by a physician, stating that the applicants have undergone a physical examination (including blood tests) and are free from communicable venereal disease.

Premarital blood tests for venereal disease arose out of concern with the nascent eugenics movement in the first few decades of the twentieth century and also with the concern regarding the double standard (i.e., the notion that young men, who had engaged in sex with unchaste women before marriage, would then marry and infect an innocent woman). See Allan M. Brandt, No Magic Bullet: A Social History of Venereal Disease in the United States Since 1880, 19-21, 147 (1987).

Massachusetts law previously required that the parties submit to the clerk or registrar a health certificate that certifies that each is free from syphilis and that the woman either has received an immunization for rubella or else is immune from the disease (Mass. Gen. Laws ch. 207, §28A). However, this statutory requirement was repealed in 2005.

The clerk may refuse to issue the marriage license if he has reasonable cause to believe that the parties have made false representations in their application (Mass. Gen. Laws ch. 207, §35).

Massachusetts General Laws

Ch. 207

§10. Validity of marriages contracted elsewhere to circumvent marriage laws of the commonwealth

If any person residing and intending to continue to reside in this commonwealth is disabled or prohibited from contracting marriage under the laws of this commonwealth and goes into another jurisdiction and there contracts a marriage prohibited and declared void by the laws of this commonwealth, such marriage shall be null and void for all purposes in this commonwealth with the same effect as though such prohibited marriage had been entered into in this commonwealth.

(R.S. 1836, ch. 75, §6; G.S. 1860, ch. 106, §6; P.S. 1882, ch. 145, §10; R.L. 1902, ch. 151, §10; Stat. 1913, ch. 360, §1.)

§11. Validity of marriages contracted in commonwealth to circumvent marriage laws elsewhere

No marriage shall be contracted in this commonwealth by a party residing and intending to continue to reside in another jurisdiction if such marriage would be void if contracted in such other jurisdiction, and every marriage contracted in this commonwealth in violation hereof shall be null and void.

(Stat. 1913, ch. 360, §2.)

§12. Licensing official must ascertain ability of nonresidents to marry

Before issuing a license to marry a person who resides and intends to continue to reside in another state, the officer having authority to issue the license shall satisfy himself, by requiring affidavits or otherwise, that such person is not prohibited from intermarrying by the laws of the jurisdiction where he or she resides.

(Stat. 1913, ch. 360, §3.)

§13. Construction to effect uniformity of laws

The three preceding sections shall be so interpreted and construed as to effectuate their general purpose to make uniform the law of those states which enact like legislation.

(Stat. 1913, ch. 360, §5.)

§19. Parties must file notice of intention to marry three days before marriage and pay fee

Persons intending to be joined in marriage in the commonwealth shall, not less than three days before their marriage, jointly cause notice of their intention to be filed in the office of the clerk or registrar of any city or town in the commonwealth, and pay the fee provided by clause (42) of section thirty-four of chapter two hundred and sixty-two. In computing the three day period specified in this section and in determining the third day referred to in section twenty-eight, Sundays and holidays shall be counted.

(C.L. 101, §2; Stat. 1695-6, ch. 2, §4; Stat. 1727-8, ch. 11; Stat. 1786, ch. 3, §3; Stat. 1834, ch. 177, §2; R.S. 1836, ch. 75, §7; Stat. 1850, ch. 121, §1; G.S. 1860, ch. 106, §7; Stat. 1867, ch. 58, §1; P.S. 1882, ch. 145, §16; R.L. 1902, ch. 151, §16; Stat. 1911, ch. 736, §1; Stat. 1930, ch. 141; Stat. 1948, ch. 550, §41; Stat. 1959, ch. 118, §1; Stat. 1969, ch. 80; Stat. 1979, ch. 718, §1.)

§20. Requirements of notice of intention to marry

The clerk shall require written notice of intention of marriage, on forms furnished by the state registrar of vital records and statistics, containing such information as is required by law and also a statement of absence of any legal impediment to the marriage, to be given before such town clerk under oath by both of the parties to the intended marriage; provided, that if a registered physician makes affidavit to the satisfaction of the town clerk that a party is unable, by reason of illness, to appear, such notice may be given on behalf of such party, by his or her parent or legal guardian, or, in case there is no parent or legal guardian competent to act or by the other party. Said forms containing the parties' written notice of intent to marry shall constitute a public record. In addition to such forms, the town clerk shall also require the parties to furnish information required for a separate report to be transmitted to the state registrar, including the social security number and residence address of both parties and such other information as may be required by state or federal law. A copy of said report shall not be retained by the town clerk nor shall it constitute a public record. The state registrar may make the information contained in said separate report available to the IV-D agency as set forth in chapter 119A and to such other state or federal agencies as may be required by state or federal law. In case of persons, one or both of whom are in the armed forces, such notice may be given by either party, provided that one is domiciled within the commonwealth. In the case of persons, one of whom is incarcerated in a county house of correction, or a state correctional facility, such notice shall be given by either party to the intended marriage. The oath or affirmation to such notice shall be to the truth of all the statements contained therein whereof the party subscribing the same could have knowledge, and may be given before the town clerk or before a regularly employed clerk in his office designated by him in writing and made a matter of record in the office. No fee shall be charged for administering such oath or affirmation. In towns having an assistant town clerk, he may administer the oath.

(Stat. 1853, ch. 335, §2; G.S. 1860, ch. 106, §10; P.S. 1882, ch. 145, §19; Stat. 1894, ch. 409, §1; R.L. 1902, ch. 151, §§17, 27; Stat. 1912, ch. 120, §1; Stat. 1913, ch. 752, §2; Stat. 1914, ch. 121, §1; Stat. 1931, ch. 237; Stat. 1933, ch. 127; Stat. 1943, ch. 561, §3; Stat. 1976, ch. 486, §20; Stat. 1979, ch. 718, §1; Stat. 1989, ch. 635; amended by Stat. 1998, ch. 64, §§189-192, approved with emergency

preamble, March 31, 1998; Stat. 1998, ch. 463, §172, approved with emergency preamble, January 14, 1999.)

§23. Clerk or registrar need not receive notice on holidays

The clerk or registrar need not receive notices of intention of marriage on Sunday or a legal holiday, nor at any place except his office.

(Stat. 1894, ch. 409, §3; R.L. 1902, ch. 151, §18.)

§24. Clerk or registrar shall not receive notice of intention to marry from minors

The clerk or registrar shall not, except as provided in the following section, receive a notice of the intention of marriage of a person under eighteen.

(Stat. 1894, ch. 401, §1; R.L. 1902, ch. 151, §19; Stat. 1977, ch. 581, §2.)

§26. Notice of intention to marry shall not be given without parties' consent

Whoever, without the consent of both parties to an intended marriage, gives the notice of their intention of marriage required by law shall be liable in damages to either of such parties whose name was so used without such consent. The superior court, upon petition of either party alleged to intend marriage in such a notice given without the consent of both parties, and not followed by their intermarriage, may, after notice and a hearing, order that such notice of intention be cancelled in the town records.

(Stat. 1894, ch. 409, §§6, 7; R.L. 1902, ch. 151, §21.)

§27. Notice of intention to marry by adopted persons

A party to an intended marriage who has been legally adopted shall, in the notice of intention thereof, give the names of his parents by adoption; and the names of his parents may also be added. The consent of a parent by adoption to the marriage of a minor shall be sufficient if the consent of a parent of a minor is required by law as a preliminary to marriage. If the natural parents of a minor have been divorced and the consent of one of them is required by law, preliminary to the marriage of such minor, the consent of the parent having the custody of such minor shall be sufficient.

(Stat. 1897, ch. 424, §4; R.L. 1902, ch. 151, §22.)

§28. Clerk or registrar shall deliver marriage license to parties

On or after the third day from the filing of notice of intention of marriage, except as otherwise provided, but not in any event later than sixty days after such filing, the clerk or registrar shall deliver to the parties a certificate signed by him, specifying the date when notice was filed with him and all facts relative to the marriage which are required by law to be ascertained and recorded, except those relative to the person by whom the marriage is to be solemnized. Such certificate shall be delivered to the minister or magistrate before whom the marriage is to be contracted, before he proceeds to solemnize the same. If such certificate is not sooner used, it shall be returned to the office issuing it within sixty days after the date when notice of intention of marriage was filed.

(Stat. 1727-8, ch. 11; Stat. 1786, ch. 3, §3; Stat. 1834, ch. 177, §2; R.S. 1836, ch. 75, §9; Stat. 1850, ch. 121, §2; G.S. 1860, ch. 106, §8; Stat. 1867, ch. 58, §1; P.S. 1882, ch. 145, §17; R.L. 1902, ch. 151, §23; Stat. 1911, ch. 736, §2; Stat. 1912, ch. 463, §1; Stat. 1914, ch. 428, §1; Stat. 1930, ch. 51, §1; Stat. 1941, ch. 601, §2; Stat. 1959, ch. 118, §2.)

§29. Notice and marriage license for immigrants

If either of the parties to an intended marriage has arrived as an immigrant from a foreign country within five days, the notice of intention may be filed at any time before the marriage, and the certificate required by the preceding section shall be issued at any time after the filing of such intention.

(Stat. 1911, ch. 736, §6.)

§30. Judge may waive waiting period in emergency

Upon application by both of the parties to an intended marriage, when both parties are residents of the commonwealth or both parties are non-residents, or upon application of the party residing within the commonwealth when one of the parties is a resident and the other a non-resident, a judge of probate or a justice of a district court, or a special judge of probate and insolvency or special justice of a district court, may, after hearing such evidence as is presented, grant a certificate stating that in his opinion it is expedient that the intended marriage be solemnized without delay. Upon presentation of such a certificate, or, in extraordinary or emergency cases when the death of either party is imminent, upon the authoritative request of a minister, clergyman, priest, rabbi, authorized representative of a Spiritual Assembly of the Baha'is or attending physician, the clerk or registrar of the town where the notice of intention has been filed shall at once issue the certificate prescribed in section twenty-eight.

(Stat. 1911, ch. 736, §4; Stat. 1912, ch. 463, §2; Stat. 1937, ch. 11, §1; Stat. 1945, ch. 214, §1; Stat. 1946, ch. 197, §1; Stat. 1968, ch. 81, §1.)

§31. Prohibition on alteration of application

No alteration or erasure shall be made by any person on the certificate under section twenty-eight until it has been returned to the clerk or registrar, and then only in such form and to such extent as he may prescribe. Any such certificate may be recorded after correction in accordance herewith.

(Stat. 1897, ch. 424, §1; R.L. 1902, ch. 151, §24.)

§33A. Clerk or registrar may require proof of age

If it appears from the statements made in the written notice of intention of marriage that a party to such intended marriage is under eighteen, the clerk or registrar shall not, except as required under section twenty-five, issue a certificate under section twenty-eight before receiving proof of the age of the parties. Such proof shall be contained in

any of the following documents, graded and taking precedence in the order named: (1) an original or certified copy of a record of birth; (2) an original or certified copy of a baptismal record; (3) a passport; (4) a life insurance policy; (5) an employment certificate; (6) a school record; (7) an immigration record; (8) a naturalization record; or (9) a court record. Documentary evidence of a lower grade as aforesaid shall not be received by the clerk or registrar unless he is satisfied that evidence of a higher grade is not readily procurable. If no such documentary proof of age is procurable, the consent of the parent shall be sufficient. If the clerk or registrar has reasonable cause to believe that a party to an intended marriage represented to be eighteen or over is under such age, he shall, before issuing such certificate, require documentary proof of age as aforesaid.
(Stat. 1931, ch. 264; Stat. 1971, ch. 255, §3.)

§34. Minors who give notice in two towns need duplicate copies of parental consent

If it is necessary to give notice in two towns of the intention of marriage of a minor, the clerk or registrar who first takes the consent of the parent or guardian shall take it in duplicate, retaining one copy and delivering the other duly attested by him to the person obtaining the certificate, to be given to the clerk or registrar issuing the second certificate; and no fee shall be charged for such consent or copy.
(Stat. 1894, ch. 409, §4; R.L. 1902, ch.151, §26.)

§35. Clerk or registrar may refuse to issue marriage license

The clerk or registrar may refuse to issue a certificate if he has reasonable cause to believe that any of the statements contained in the notice of intention of marriage are incorrect; but he may, in his discretion, accept depositions under oath, made before him, which shall be sufficient proof of the facts therein stated to authorize the issuing of a certificate. He may also dispense with the statement of any facts required by law to be given in a notice of intention of marriage, if they do not relate to or affect the identification or age of the parties, or a former marriage of either party, if he is satisfied that the same cannot with reasonable effort be obtained.
(Stat. 1894, ch. 409, §2; R.L. 1902, ch. 151, §28.)

§36. Residents who were married elsewhere may file certificate in commonwealth

Any resident of this commonwealth who marries outside the commonwealth and thereafter resides within the United States or any of its territories or possessions, or the spouse or heirs-at-law of such a person, may personally present to the town clerk or registrar of the town where such person was domiciled at the time of said marriage an original certificate, declaration or other written evidence of the same, or a photostatic copy thereof. The clerk or registrar may file such certificate, declaration, written evidence or photostatic copy as evidence establishing such marriage, or may make a copy thereof, which he shall attest as a true copy, and which he may then file as such evidence.

If such certificate, declaration, written evidence, photostatic copy or attested copy is not, in the opinion of the clerk or registrar, sufficient to establish such marriage, and he refuses to file the same, a judge of probate in the county wherein such town lies may, on petition and after a hearing, at which the clerk shall have an opportunity to be heard, order him to receive such certificate, declaration, written evidence, photostatic copy or attested copy as sufficient evidence to establish such marriage, whereupon such clerk or registrar shall file the same.
(Stat. 1850, ch. 121, §3; G.S. 1860, ch. 106, §12; P.S. 1882, ch. 145, §21; R.L. 1902, ch. 151, §29; Stat. 1946, ch. 273, §1; Stat. 1965, ch. 12, §4.)

§37. Clerk or registrar shall post list of legal impediments to marriage

The commissioner of public health shall furnish to the clerk or registrar of every town a printed list of all legal impediments to marriage, and the clerk or registrar shall forthwith post and thereafter maintain it in a conspicuous place in his office.
(Stat. 1913, ch. 752, §1; Stat. 1976, ch. 486, §21.)

3. Solemnization

All states require solemnization of the marriage by an authorized person before witnesses. However, no specific form of ceremony is prescribed. Massachusetts General Laws ch. 207, §38 specifies the persons who are authorized to perform the ceremony. The governor may designate additional persons and revoke such designations (Mass. Gen. Laws ch. 207, §39).

a. Authorized Persons

Massachusetts General Laws

Ch. 207

§38. Persons who are authorized to perform the ceremony

A marriage may be solemnized in any place within the commonwealth by the following persons who are residents of the commonwealth: a duly ordained minister of the gospel in good and regular standing with his church or denomination, including an ordained deacon in The United Methodist Church or in the Roman Catholic Church; a commissioned cantor or duly ordained rabbi of the Jewish faith; by a justice of the peace if he is also clerk or assistant clerk of a city or town, or a registrar or assistant registrar, or a clerk or assistant clerk of a court, or a clerk or assistant clerk of the senate or house of representatives, by a justice of the peace if he has been designated as provided in the following section and has received a certificate of designation and has qualified thereunder; an authorized representative of a Spiritual Assembly of the Baha'is in accordance with the usage of their community; a priest or minister of the Buddhist religion; a minister in fellowship with the Unitarian Universalist Association and ordained by a local church; a leader of an Ethical Culture Society which is duly established in the commonwealth and recognized by the American Ethical Union and who is duly appointed and in good and regular standing with the American Ethical Union; the Imam of the Orthodox Islamic religion; and, it may be solemnized in a regular or special meeting for worship conducted by or under the oversight of a Friends or Quaker Monthly Meeting in accordance with the usage of their Society; and, it may be solemnized by a duly ordained nonresident minister of the gospel if he is a pastor of a church or denomination duly established in the commonwealth and who is in good and regular standing as a minister of such church or denomination, including an ordained deacon in The United Methodist Church or in the Roman Catholic Church; and, it may be solemnized according to the usage of any other church or religious organization which shall have complied with the provisions of the second paragraph of this section.

Churches and other religious organizations shall file in the office of the state secretary information relating to persons recognized or licensed as aforesaid, and relating to usages of such organizations, in such form and at such times as the secretary may require.

(C.L. 102, §5; Stat. 1692-3, ch. 25, §1; Stat. 1695-6, ch. 2, §4; Stat. 1716-17, ch. 16, §1; Stat. 1762-3, ch. 28; Stat. 1772-3, ch. 31, §1, 2; Stat. 1786, ch. 3, §§1, 2, 8; Stat. 1817, 141; Stat. 1820, ch. 55; Stat. 1834, ch. 177, §§1, 6; R.S. 1836, ch. 75, §§16, 22; Stat. 1850, ch. 121, §5; G.S. 1860, ch. 106, §§14, 15; Stat. 1867, ch. 58, §2; P.S. 1882, ch. 145, §§22, 23; Stat. 1893, ch. 461, §1; Stat. 1894, ch. 409, §5; Stat. 1896, ch. 306, §4; Stat. 1899, ch. 387, §1; R.L. 1902, ch. 151, §30; Stat. 1929, ch. 169; Stat. 1932, ch. 162; Stat. 1946, ch. 197, §2; Stat. 1949, ch. 249; Stat. 1965, ch. 11, §1; Stat. 1968, ch. 81, §2; Stat. 1970, ch. 668; Stat. 1972, ch. 186, §5; Stat. 1973, ch. 1201; Stat. 1975, ch. 464, §1; Stat. 1976, ch. 51; Stat. 1981, ch. 521, §1; Stat. 1982 ch. 379; 1982, ch. 486; Stat. 1986, ch. 702, §1; Stat. 1991, ch. 419, approved December 27, 1991, effective 90 days thereafter; amended by Stat. 1998, ch. 476, §1, effective April 15, 1999.)

§39. Governor may designate additional persons to solemnize marriage

The governor may in his discretion designate a justice of the peace in each town and such further number, not exceeding one for every five thousand inhabitants of a city or town, as he considers expedient, to solemnize marriages, and may for a cause at any time revoke such designation. The state secretary, upon payment of twenty-five dollars to him by a justice of the peace so designated, who is also a clerk or an assistant clerk of a city or town or upon the payment of fifty dollars by any other such justice, shall issue to him a certificate of such designation.

The state secretary may authorize, subject to such conditions as he may determine, the solemnization of any specified marriage anywhere within the commonwealth by the following nonresidents: a minister of the gospel in good and regular standing with his church or denomination; a commissioned cantor or duly ordained rabbi of the Jewish faith; an authorized representative of a Spiritual Assembly of the Baha'is in accordance with the usage of their community; the Imam of the Orthodox Islamic religion; a duly ordained priest or minister of the Buddhist religion; a minister in fellowship with the Unitarian Universalist Association and ordained by a local church; a leader of an Ethical Culture Society which is recognized by the American Ethical Union and who is duly appointed and in good and regular standing with the American Ethical Union; a justice of a court or a justice of the peace authorized to solemnize a marriage by virtue of their office within their state of residence; and, it may be solemnized in a regular or special meeting for worship conducted by or under the oversight of a Friends or Quaker Monthly Meeting in accordance with the usage of their Society. A nonresident may solemnize a marriage according to the usage of any church or religious organization which shall have complied with the provisions of the second paragraph of section 38. A certificate of such authorization shall be issued by the state secretary and shall be attached to the certificate issued under section twenty-eight and filed with the appropriate city or town clerk. If one of the nonresidents enumerated above solemnizes a specified marriage anywhere within the commonwealth without having obtained a certificate under this section, the state secretary, upon application of such person, may issue a certificate validating such person's acts. The certificate of validation shall be filed with the certificate issued under section twenty-eight of chapter two hundred and seven.

In addition to the foregoing, the governor may designate any other person to solemnize a particular marriage on a particular date and in a particular city or town, and may for cause at any time revoke such designation. The state secretary, upon the payment to him of twenty-five dollars by said other person, shall issue to said person a certificate of such designation. Such certificate shall expire upon completion of such solemnization.

(Stat. 1899, ch. 387, §§2, 3; R.L. 1902, ch. 151, §31; Stat. 1926, ch. 102; Stat. 1958, ch. 438; Stat. 1965, ch. 54; Stat. 1968, ch. 81, §3; Stat. 1975, ch. 464, §2; Stat. 1983, ch. 112, §1; Stat. 1984, ch. 440, §1; Stat. 1986, ch. 702, §2; Stat. 1989, ch. 711, §1; Stat. 1991, ch. 249, effective by act of Governor, October 8, 1991, amended by Stat. 1998, ch. 476, §§2, 3, effective April 15, 1999.)

b. Duties of Persons Solemnizing Marriages

Massachusetts General Laws

Ch. 207

§40. Persons who solemnize marriage must keep records and return authenticated license

Every justice of the peace, minister of the gospel, minister of the Unitarian Universalist Association, rabbi, secretary of a Spiritual Assembly of the Baha'is, leader of an Ethical Culture Society, duly ordained priest or minister of the Buddhist religion, Imam of the Orthodox Islamic religion, clerk or keeper of the records of a meeting wherein marriages among Friends or Quakers are solemnized, nonresident justice of a court and any person authorized to solemnize marriages according to the usage of any other church or religious organization which shall have complied with the provisions of the second paragraph of section thirty-eight shall make and keep a record of each marriage solemnized by him, or in such meeting, and of all facts relative to the marriage required to be recorded by section one of chapter forty-six. He shall also return each certificate issued under section twenty-eight no later than the tenth day of the month following each month in which marriages are solemnized by him to the clerk or registrar who issued the same. Each certificate and copy so returned shall contain a statement giving the place and date of marriage, attested by the signature of the person who solemnized the same, or of said secretary of a Spiritual Assembly of the Baha'is or of said leader of an Ethical Culture Society, or of said duly ordained priest or minister of the Buddhist religion, or Imam of the Orthodox Islamic religion, or of said clerk or keeper of the records of a Friends or Quaker Monthly Meeting or any person authorized to solemnize marriages according to the usage of any other church or religious organization which shall have complied with the provisions of the second paragraph of section thirty-eight. The person who solemnized the marriage shall add the title of the office by virtue of which the marriage was solemnized, as "justice of the peace", "minister of the gospel", "clergyman", "priest", "rabbi", "authorized representative of a Spiritual Assembly", "leader of an Ethical Culture Society", or "duly ordained priest or minister of the Buddhist religion", or "Imam of the Orthodox Islamic religion", or other appropriate title, and his residence. All certificates or copies so returned shall be recorded by the clerk or registrar receiving them.

(C.L. 130, §2; Stat. 1692-3, ch. 25, §3; Stat. 1695-6, ch. 2, §§4, 6; Stat. 1716-17, ch. 16, §3; Stat. 1786, ch. 3, §§6, 8; Stat. 1795, ch. 7; Stat. 1817, ch. 61; Stat. 1834, ch. 177, §§5, 6; R.S. 75, §§17, 23; Stat. 1844, ch. 159, §3; G.S. 106, §16; Stat. 1879, ch. 116, §1; Stat. 1881, ch. 11, §1; P.S. 145, §24; Stat. 1887, ch. 202, §3; Stat. 1892, ch. 300; Stat. 1897, ch. 424, §5; R.L. 151, §32; Stat. 1946, ch. 197, §3; Stat. 1965, ch. 11, §2; Stat. 1968, ch. 81, §4; Stat. 1979, ch. 718, §2; Stat. 1983, ch. 112, §2; Stat. 1984, ch. 440, §2; Stat. 1986, ch. 702, §3.)

§41. Clerk shall have errors corrected in authenticated licenses

If a certificate of marriage is found, upon its return to the clerk or registrar, to have been incorrectly filled out by the person who solemnized a marriage under it, the clerk or registrar shall have it corrected and shall enforce the penalties provided by law relative thereto. Such imperfect certificates shall be recorded and indexed by the clerk or registrar.

(Stat. 1897, ch. 424, §2; R.L. 1902, ch. 151, §33.)

§42. Validity of marriage that is improperly solemnized

A marriage solemnized by a person professing to have the authority to solemnize marriages under section thirty-eight or thirty-nine shall not be void, nor shall the validity thereof be in any way affected by want of authority in such person or society, or by an omission or by informality in the manner of filing the notice of intention, if the marriage is in other respects lawful and is consummated with a full belief of either of the persons so married that they have been lawfully married.

(Stat. 1834, ch. 177, §7; R.S. 1836, ch. 75, §24; G.S. 1860, ch. 106, §20; Stat. 1881, ch. 11, §2; P.S. 1882, ch. 145, §27; Stat. 1893, ch. 461, §2; R.L. 1902, ch. 151, §34; Stat. 1946, ch. 197, §4; Stat. 1965, ch. 11, §3; Stat. 1968, ch. 81, §5; Stat. 1983, ch. 112, §3; Stat. 1984, ch. 440, §3; Stat. 1986, ch. 702, §4.)

§43. Validity of marriage solemnized in foreign country

Marriages solemnized in a foreign country by a consul or diplomatic agent of the United States shall be valid in this commonwealth.

(G.S. 1860, ch. 106, §23; P.S. 1882, ch. 145, §28; R.L. 1902, ch. 151, §35.)

§44. Fees payable upon receipt of certificate of solemnization

A city by ordinance and a town by vote may authorize its clerk or registrar to pay on demand, in his office, twenty-five cents to any person who has legally solemnized a marriage in the commonwealth, after the receipt by such clerk or registrar of the certificate in legal form of the solemnization of such marriage. A city or town which passes such ordinance or vote shall annually appropriate the money necessary therefor, and the clerk or registrar thereof shall file quarterly with the treasurer or other proper financial officer of said city or town proper vouchers for all such payments.

(Stat. 1897, ch. 424, §3; R.L. 1902, ch. 151, §36.)

§45. Solemnizing official shall keep record of marriage

The record of a marriage made and kept as provided by law by the person by whom the marriage was solemnized, or by the clerk or registrar, or a copy thereof duly certified, shall be prima facie evidence of such marriage.

(R.S. 1836, ch. 75, §25; G.S. 1860, ch. 106, §21; P.S. 1882, ch. 145, §29; R.L. 1902, ch. 151, §37.)

§46. Certificate of consul shall be prima facie evidence

A copy of the record of a marriage solemnized by a consul or diplomatic agent of the United States or a certificate from such consul or agent shall be prima facie evidence of such marriage.

(G.S. 1860, ch. 106, §23; P.S. 1882, ch. 145, §30; R.L. 1902, ch. 151, §38.)

c. Noncompliance with Procedural Requirements

Statutes provide for penalties for persons (i.e., authorized officials) who fail to comply with the procedural requirements, such as by solemnizing marriage without authority (Mass. Gen. Laws ch. 207, §48); marrying persons who have not procured a marriage license (Mass. Gen. Laws ch. 207, §49); issuing licenses to, or solemnizing marriages of, persons who are attempting to evade the statutory requirements of the home state (Mass. Gen. Laws ch. 207, §50); issuing a license to a minor without securing the requisite consent (Mass. Gen. Laws ch. 207, §53); illegally altering a marriage license (Mass. Gen. Laws ch. 207, §54); and so on.

A marriage that is performed by persons who do not have the proper authority (or in cases in which there are certain errors in the marriage application) is nonetheless valid if the marriage is otherwise lawful, is consummated, and the parties believe that they are lawfully married (Mass. Gen. Laws ch. 207, §42).

Massachusetts General Laws

Ch. 207

§42. Validity of marriages that are improperly solemnized

A marriage solemnized by a person professing to have the authority to solemnize marriages under section thirty-eight or thirty-nine shall not be void, nor shall the validity thereof be in any way affected by want of authority in such person or society, or by an omission or by informality in the manner of filing the notice of intention, if the marriage is in other respects lawful and is consummated with a full belief of either of the persons so married that they have been lawfully married.

(Stat. 1834, ch. 177, §7; R.S. 1836, ch. 75, §24; G.S. 1860, ch. 106, §20; Stat. 1881, ch. 11, §2; P.S. 1882, ch. 145, §27; Stat. 1893, ch. 461, §2; R.L. 1902, ch. 151, §34; Stat. 1946, ch. 197, §4; Stat. 1965, ch. 11, §3; Stat. 1968, ch. 81, §5; Stat. 1983, ch. 112, §3; Stat. 1984, ch. 440, §3; Stat. 1986, ch. 702, §4.)

§48. Penalty for solemnizing marriage without due authority

Whoever, not being duly authorized by the laws of the commonwealth, undertakes to join persons in marriage therein shall be punished by a fine of not more than five hundred dollars or by imprisonment for not more than one year, or both.

(Stat. 1786, ch. 3, §5; Stat. 1834, ch. 177, §4; R.S. 1836, ch. 75, §20; G.S. 1860, ch. 106, §19; P.S. 1882, ch. 145, §26; Stat. 1896, ch. 306, §2; R.L. 1902, ch. 151, §40.)

§49. Penalty for marrying persons who have not procured marriage license

Whoever, being duly authorized to solemnize marriages in the commonwealth, joins in marriage persons who have not complied with the laws relative to procuring certificates of notice of intention of marriage shall be punished by a fine of not more than five hundred dollars.

(Stat. 1695-6, ch. 2, §4; Stat. 1772-3, ch. 31, §3; Stat. 1786, ch. 3, §5; Stat. 1834, ch. 177, §§4, 9; R.S. 1836, ch. 75, §19; G.S. 1860, ch. 106, §18; Stat. 1867, ch. 58, §3; P.S. 1882, ch. 145, §25; Stat. 1896, ch. 306, §1; R.L. 1902, ch. 151, §41.)

§50. Penalty for issuing license or solemnizing marriage if parties are evading laws of another state

Any official issuing a certificate of notice of intention of marriage knowing that the parties are prohibited by section eleven from intermarrying, and any person authorized to solemnize marriage who shall solemnize a marriage knowing that the parties are so prohibited, shall be punished by a fine of not less than one hundred or more than five hundred dollars or by imprisonment for not more than one year, or both.

(Stat. 1913, ch. 360, §4.)

§51. Penalty for violating certain provisions

Violations of any provision of section seven, twenty-six or thirty-four, shall, upon complaint made within one year thereafter, be punished by a fine of not more than five hundred dollars or by imprisonment for not more than one year, or both.

(Stat. 1894, ch. 409, §8; R.L. 1902, ch. 151, §43.)

§52. Penalty for violating law regarding application or making false statements

Whoever violates any provision of section twenty, and whoever falsely swears or affirms in making any statement required under section twenty, shall be punished by a fine of not more than one hundred dollars.

(Stat. 1857, Ch. 34; G.S. 1860, ch. 106, §11; P.S. 1882, ch. 145, §20; Stat. 1894, ch. 409, §8; R.L. 1902, ch. 151, §§43, 44; Stat. 1913, ch. 752, §3; Stat. 1943, ch. 312, §1.)

§53. Penalty for issuing license to minor in violation of law

A clerk or registrar issuing a certificate of intention of marriage contrary to section thirty-three shall forfeit not more than one hundred dollars.

(Stat. 1853, ch. 335, §1; G.S. 1860, ch. 106, §9; P.S. 1882, ch. 145, §18; R.L. 1902, ch. 151, §25; Stat. 1911, ch. 736, §3.)

§54. Penalty for illegal alteration of marriage license

Whoever makes an illegal alteration or erasure on a certificate of intention of marriage shall be punished by a fine of not more than one hundred dollars.
(Stat. 1897, ch. 424, §1; R.L. 1902, ch. 151, §42.)

§56. Penalty for failure to make record and return authenticated certificate

Whoever neglects to make the record and returns required by section forty shall forfeit not less than twenty nor more than one hundred dollars.
(Stat. 1834, ch. 177, §§5, 6; R.S. 1836, ch. 75, §§18, 23; Stat. 1844, ch. 159, §3; G.S. 1860, ch. 106, §17; Stat. 1879, ch. 116, §2; P.S. 1882, ch. 145, §24; Stat. 1892, ch. 300; R.L. 1902, ch. 151, §32.)

§57. Penalty for solemnizing marriage based on expired license

Whoever performs a ceremony of marriage upon a certificate more than sixty days after the filing of the notice of intention of marriage as set forth in such certificate, and whoever having taken out such certificate and not having used it fails to return it, within sixty days after such filing, to the office issuing the same, shall be punished by a fine of not more than ten dollars.
(Stat. 1914, ch. 428, §2; Stat. 1930, ch. 51, §2; Stat. 1941, ch. 601, §3.)

§58. Penalty for violating law regarding advertising to perform marriages

A justice of the peace or other person authorized to solemnize marriages may advertise his name or any trade name, business address, telephone number, rate of compensation as provided by law, regular hours of availability and any ability in a second language and any present or former professional affiliation, in any newspaper, magazine, telephone directory or other publication of general circulation. Whoever advertises to perform or to procure the performance of a marriage ceremony by any other means shall be punished by a fine of not less than ten nor more than one hundred dollars; provided, however, that this section shall not be construed to prohibit the use of a business card by a justice of the peace or other person authorized to perform marriage ceremonies; and provided, further, that if a justice of the peace uses a business card said card shall not display the seal of the commonwealth.
(Stat. 1902, ch. 249; Stat. 1985, ch. 250; Stat. 1989, ch. 711, §2.)

F. PROCEDURAL VARIATIONS: PROXY MARRIAGES

Proxy marriages are permitted by some jurisdictions. In a proxy marriage, at least one party is represented at the ceremony by an agent or proxy. Marriage by proxy was once the exclusive province of European royalty. The practice was valid in England until the mid-nineteenth century, when Parliament enacted legislation that required the presence of both parties at the ceremony. Comment, Persons—Marriage—Validity of Proxy Marriages, 25 S. Cal. L. Rev. 181, 182 (1952). In modern law, the practice has been utilized by military personnel, prisoners, and political refugees. Marriage by proxy was particularly visible during the twentieth century in times of war, frequently to legitimize children.

Massachusetts permits the limited use of a proxy for *applications* to marry. Whereas normally both parties must give the oath and written notice of intention to marry, only one party may do so if one or both are in the military or one is incarcerated. However, the statute does not permit the use of a proxy at the ceremony (Mass. Gen. Laws ch. 207, §20).

Massachusetts General Laws

Ch. 207

§20. Requirements of notice of intention to marry; proxies permitted in some cases

The clerk shall require written notice of intention of marriage, on forms furnished by the state registrar of vital records and statistics, containing such information as is required by law and also a statement of absence of any legal impediment to the marriage, to be given before such town clerk under oath by both of the parties to the intended marriage; provided, that if a registered physician makes affidavit to the satisfaction of the town clerk that a party is unable, by reason of illness, to appear, such notice may be given on behalf of such party, by his or her parent or legal guardian, or, in case there is no parent or legal guardian competent to act or by the other party. Said forms containing the parties' written notice of intent to marry shall constitute a public record. In addition to such forms, the town clerk shall also require the parties to furnish information required for a separate report to be transmitted to the state registrar, including the social security number and residence address of both parties and such other information as may be required by state or federal law. A copy of said report shall not be retained by the town clerk nor shall it constitute a public record. The state registrar may make the information contained in said separate report available to the IV-D agency as set forth in chapter 119A and to such other state or federal agencies as may be required by state or federal law. In case of persons, one or both of whom are in the armed forces, such notice may be given by either party, provided that one is domiciled within the commonwealth. In the case of persons, one of whom is incarcerated in a county house of correction, or a state correctional facility, such notice shall be given by either party to the intended marriage. The oath or affirmation to such notice shall be to the truth of all the statements contained therein whereof the party subscribing the same could have knowledge, and may be given before the town clerk or before a regularly employed clerk in his office designated by him in writing and made a matter of record in

the office. No fee shall be charged for administering such oath or affirmation. In towns having an assistant town clerk, he may administer the oath.
(Stat. 1853, ch. 335, §2; G.S. 1860, ch. 106, §10; P.S. 1882, ch. 145, §19; Stat. 1894, ch. 409, §1; R.L. 1902, ch. 151, §§17, 27; Stat. 1912, ch. 120, §1; Stat. 1913, ch. 752, §2; Stat. 1914, ch. 121, §1; Stat. 1931, ch. 237; Stat. 1933, ch. 127; Stat. 1943, ch. 561, §3; Stat. 1976, ch. 486, §20; Stat. 1979, ch. 718, §1; Stat. 1989, ch. 635; amended by Stat. 1998, ch. 64, §§189-192, approved with emergency preamble, March 31, 1998; Stat. 1998, ch. 463, §172, approved with emergency preamble, January 14, 1999.)

G. INFORMAL MARRIAGES AND CURATIVE DEVICES

1. Common Law Marriage

Common law marriage is a form of informal marriage (without solemnization) that is recognized in a few states. Ariela R. Dubler, Wifely Behavior: A Legal History of Acting Married, 100 Colum. L. Rev. 957, 1011 (2000) (noting 11 states and the District of Columbia). Common law marriage has four elements: The parties must have capacity to enter a marital contract, presently agree to be married, cohabit, and hold themselves out to the community as husband and wife.

Massachusetts has never recognized common law marriage. However, Massachusetts does confer recognition on those relationships that were validly contracted in other jurisdictions where such marriages are legal, based on the rule of lex loci (a marriage valid where performed is valid everywhere). Boltz v. Boltz, 92 N.E.2d 365 (Mass. 1950) (recognizing a common law marriage that was validly contracted in New York). See Kindregan & Inker, *supra*, at §18.13.

For legal commentary on common law marriage, see Henry Baskin, Important Changes in the Law During the 20th Century: The Abolition of Common Law Marriage, 79 Mich. B.J. 176 (2000); Hon. John B. Crawley, Is the Honeymoon Over for Common-Law Marriage? A Consideration of the Continued Viability of the Common-Law Marriage Doctrine, 29 Cumb. L. Rev. 399 (1998-1999); Sonya C. Garza, Common Law Marriage: A Proposal for the Revival of a Dying Doctrine, 40 New Eng. L. Rev. 541 (2006).

2. Putative Spouses

The "putative spouse doctrine" is a curative device that was created to protect the rights of a person who enters into a marital relationship that was defectively solemnized. To qualify as a putative spouse, a party must have a good faith belief that a valid marriage exists (i.e., not be aware of the legal impediment to the marriage).

By case law and statute, a few jurisdictions (e.g., California and Texas) protect the putative spouse's rights to property upon dissolution or death. Note that nonmarital heterosexual cohabitants (commonly referred to as "unmarried couples") differ from putative spouses.

Massachusetts recognizes a limited form of putative marriage in the case of polygamous marriages (Mass. Gen. Laws ch. 207, §6). Kindregan & Inker, *supra*, at §§18.5, 18.13. That is, if a person marries in the belief that the former spouse was dead or that the former marriage ended in divorce or without knowledge of the former marriage, then the subsequent marriage shall be valid after removal of the impediment if the parties continue to live together (in good faith on the part of one of them) and their issue shall be considered legitimate (Mass. Gen. Laws ch. 207, §6).

Massachusetts General Laws

Ch. 207

§6. Validity of a subsequent marriage entered into in good faith during existence of former marriage

If a person, during the lifetime of a husband or wife with whom the marriage is in force, enters into a subsequent marriage contract with due legal ceremony and the parties thereto live together thereafter as husband and wife, and such subsequent marriage contract was entered into by one of the parties in good faith, in the full belief that the former husband or wife was dead, that the former marriage had been annulled by a divorce, or without knowledge of such former marriage, they shall, after the impediment to their marriage has been removed by the death or divorce of the other party to the former marriage, if they continue to live together as husband and wife in good faith on the part of one of them, be held to have been legally married from and after the removal of such impediment, and the issue of such subsequent marriage shall be considered as the legitimate issue of both parents.
(Stat. 1895, ch. 427; Stat. 1896, ch. 499; R.L. 1902, ch. 151, §6.)

II.
BEING MARRIED: MARITAL RIGHTS AND DUTIES

This chapter addresses the legal regulation of marital roles and responsibilities. It examines the duty of support, rights regarding surnames, discrimination against married persons, parenting issues, crimes and torts regarding spouses and third parties (including domestic violence), and evidentiary privileges based on the marital relationship. Massachusetts law provides an illustration of these rules.

A. Duty of Support

At common law, the husband had a duty to support his wife which included a duty to provide "necessaries" (i.e., necessary goods and services). A wife had a correlative duty to render services to her husband. Today, many states provide that the spouses share the duty of support while they are living together.

Criminal liability exists for nonsupport of children and often spouses as well. Statutes generally provide that criminal nonsupport of a spouse is committed only when the spouse is left destitute, i.e., without necessary food, clothing, or shelter. On spousal support obligations, see Homer H. Clark, Jr., Law of Domestic Relations in the United States, 250-258, 265-266, 269-274 (2d ed. 1988).

The Massachusetts provisions below address the spousal duty of support, parental duty of support, and the duty of adult children to support parents. According to Massachusetts General Laws ch. 273, §1, a husband incurs criminal liability for abandoning his spouse and/or child; leaving the state without making reasonable provision for them; entering the state without making reasonable provision for a spouse and/or child who is domiciled in another state; or willfully failing to comply with an order or judgment for support while having the financial ability to do so.

A wife may be jointly liable with the husband (up to a maximum of $100 per debt) for necessaries furnished to her or her family with her knowledge or consent, provided that she has separate property in the amount of $2,000 or more (Mass. Gen. Laws ch. 209, §7).

1. During the Marriage

Massachusetts General Laws

Ch. 273

§1. Spouse's duty of support

A spouse or parent shall be guilty of a felony and shall be subject to the penalties set forth in section fifteen A if: (1) he abandons his spouse or minor child without making reasonable provisions for the support of his spouse or minor child or both of them; or (2) he leaves the commonwealth and goes into another state without making reasonable provisions for the support of his spouse or minor child or both of them; or

(3) he enters the commonwealth from another state without making reasonable provisions for the support of his spouse or minor child, or both of them, domiciled in another state; or

(4) wilfully and while having the financial ability or earning capacity to have complied, he fails to comply with an order or judgment for support which has been entered pursuant to chapter one hundred and nineteen, two hundred and seven, two hundred and eight, two hundred and nine, two hundred and nine C, or two hundred and seventy-three, or received, entered or registered pursuant to chapter two hundred and nine D, or entered pursuant to similar laws of other states. No civil proceeding in any court shall be held to be a bar to a prosecution hereunder but the court shall not enter any order pursuant to section fifteen A which would directly or indirectly result in a decrease in the amount paid for current support pursuant to an order or judgment on behalf of the child or spouse to who, or on whose behalf, support is owed.

In a prosecution hereunder a decree or judgment of a probate court in a proceeding in which the defendant or spouse appeared or was personally served with process, establishing the right of his spouse to live apart or the freedom of such spouse to convey and deal with property, or the right to the custody of the children, shall be admissible and shall be prima facie evidence of such right.

(Stat. 1882, ch. 270, §4; Stat. 1884, ch. 210, §1; Stat. 1885, ch. 176, §1; Stat. 1893, ch. 262; Stat. 1899, ch. 309, §1; R.L. 1902, ch. 212, §45; Stat. 1905, ch. 307; Stat. 1906, ch. 501, §1; Stat. 1907, ch. 563, §26; Stat. 1908, ch. 104; Stat. 1909, ch. 180; Stat. 1911, ch. 456, §1; Stat. 1925, ch. 126; Stat. 1929, ch. 258, §1; Stat. 1931, ch. 226; Stat. 1939, ch. 177, §1; Stat. 1954, ch. 539; Stat. 1957, ch. 49; Stat. 1971, ch. 276; Stat. 1971, ch. 762; Stat. 1977, ch. 848, §2; Stat. 1986, ch. 310, §22; Stat. 1993, ch. 340, §3; Stat. 1993, ch. 460, §88; Stat. 1995, ch. 5, §§97, 98.)

§15A. Penalty for abandonment and nonsupport

(1) The penalty for violation of sections one and fifteen of this chapter shall be by fine or by imprisonment or by both fine and imprisonment as specified below.

(2) A person who abandons his spouse or minor child without making reasonable provisions for the support of either or both of them or who is subject to an order or judgment for support pursuant to chapters one hundred and nineteen, two hundred and seven, two hundred and eight, two hundred and nine, two hundred and nine C, two hundred and seventy-three, or two hundred and nine D, or pursuant to similar laws of other states, who, wilfully and while having the financial ability or earning capacity to have complied, fails to comply with that order or judgment, shall be punished by imprisonment in the state prison for not more than five years or by imprisonment in jail or the house of correction for not more than two and one-half years, or by a fine of not more

than five thousand dollars, or by both such fine and imprisonment.

(3) A person who leaves the commonwealth and goes into another state without making reasonable provisions for the support of a spouse or child, or who enters the commonwealth from another state without making reasonable provision for the support of a spouse or child domiciled in another state, shall be punished by imprisonment in the state prison for not more than ten years or by imprisonment in jail or the house of correction for not more than two and one-half years, or by a fine of not more than ten thousand dollars, or by both such fine and imprisonment.

(4) In a prosecution under this chapter, the court may, upon conviction of the defendant, provide for alternative sentencing including (a) the suspension of the sentence upon and during the compliance by the defendant with any order for the support as already made or as thereafter modified, or (b) notwithstanding the provision of section six of chapter two hundred and seventy-nine, the imprisonment of the defendant only on designated weekends, evenings or holidays, provided, that such defendant retains employment and complies with such support orders.

(5) In a prosecution under this chapter the defendant may be ordered to make restitution to the spouse or the custodial parent or to the person or agency, including the department of public welfare, who is supporting or has supported the spouse or child for all sums expended on behalf of such spouse or child, provided that if the defendant establishes a lesser ability to have provided support, the amount of any liability imposed by this section shall be consistent with the defendant's prior ability to have paid support.

(Stat. 1986, ch. 310, §26; Stat. 1993, ch. 460, §§92 to 95; Stat. 1995, ch. 5, §§101 to 104.)

Massachusetts General Laws

Ch. 209

§7. Wife's liability for necessaries

A married woman shall not be liable for her husband's debts, nor shall her property be liable to be taken on an execution against him. But a married woman shall be liable jointly with her husband for debts due, to the amount of one hundred dollars in each case, for necessaries furnished with her knowledge or consent to herself or her family, if she has property to the amount of two thousand dollars or more.

(Stat. 1855, ch. 304, §§1, 6.; G.S.1860, ch. 108, §§1, 7; P.S. 1882, ch. 147, §8; R.L. 1902, ch. 153, §7; Stat. 1910, ch. 576; Stat. 1974, ch. 147, §1.)

§8. Husband's liability for certain debts of wife

A husband shall not be liable upon a cause of action which originated against his wife prior to their marriage, or to pay a judgment recovered against her.

(Stat. 1855, ch. 304, §2; G.S.1860, ch. 108, §8; Stat. 1871, ch. 312; P.S. 1882, ch. 147, §9; R.L. 1902, ch. 153, §8; Stat. 1974, ch. 147, §2.)

§9. Husband's liability on wife's contracts concerning her separate property

Contracts made by a married woman relative to her separate property, trade, business, labor or services shall not bind her husband or render him or his property liable therefor; but she and her separate property shall be liable on such contracts in the same manner as if she were sole.

(Stat. 1855, ch. 304, §7; Stat. 1857, ch. 249, §6; G.S. 1860, ch. 108, §5; P.S. 1882, ch. 147, §10; R.L. 1902, ch. 153, §9; Stat. 1974, ch. 147, §3.)

---

2. Support of Parents

At common law, states imposed a duty upon adult children to support an indigent parent or parents. These "filial responsibility laws" or "relative responsibility laws" originated in the Elizabethan period and specified the relatives who were liable for support obligations, although the enumerated relatives varied from state to state.

Filial responsibility laws declined in the twentieth century based on a number of societal changes, including changes in the American family (i.e., increases in the elderly population, a decreased fertility rate, adult children who were more resistant to shouldering the financial burden of caring for elderly parents), the reluctance of prosecutors to prosecute violators, and constitutional attacks on filial support laws. See Usha Narayanan, Note, The Government's Role in Fostering the Relationship Between Adult Children and Their Elder Parents: From Filial Responsibility Laws to . . . What? A Cross-Cultural Perspective, 4 Elder L.J. 369 (1996). See also Shannon Frank Edelstone, Filial Responsibility: Can the Legal Duty to Support Our Parents Be Effectively Enforced?, 36 Fam. L.Q. 501 (2002).

Massachusetts law imposes a duty on an adult child to support a parent "when such parent through misfortune or without fault of his own is destitute of means of sustenance and unable by reason of old age, infirmity or illness to support and maintain himself" (Mass. Gen. Laws ch. 273, §20). The adult child will not incur liability for refusing to support the parent if the parent failed to support that child during the latter's minority or if the adult child is one of several adult children who has "made proper and reasonable contribution" to the parent's support. *Id.*

Massachusetts General Laws

Ch. 273

§20. Adult child's duty to support parent

Any person, over eighteen, who, being possessed of sufficient means, unreasonably neglects or refuses to provide for the support and maintenance of his parent, whether father or mother, residing in the commonwealth, when such parent through misfortune and without fault of his own is destitute of means of sustenance and unable by reason of old age, infirmity or illness to support and maintain himself, shall be punished by a fine of not more than two hundred dollars or by imprisonment for not more than one year, or both. No such neglect or refusal shall be deemed unreasonable as to a child who shall not during his minority have been reasonably supported by such parent, if such parent was charged with the duty so to do, nor as to a child who, being one of two or more children, has made proper and reasonable contribution toward the support of such parent.

(Stat. 1915, ch. 163, §1; amended by Stat. 1973, ch. 925, §80.)

B. Names in the Family

At common law, a married woman assumed her husband's surname based on custom, not operation of law. Today, a married woman may retain her maiden name. Two methods of name change currently exist: the common law method of consistent, nonfraudulent use, and also a statutorily prescribed judicial procedure. Upon marriage, most women change their name by the common law method above.

The first Massachusetts statute permitting a name change by judicial decree, enacted in 1851, provided that no lawful name change could be made except for sufficient reason, consistent with the public interest and subject to the court's satisfaction. Massachusetts statute now omits the latter requirement that the proposed change be satisfactory to the court. Francis T. Talty et al., 5A Mass. Prac. Methods of Practice §24:4 (4th ed. 2003). See also Petition of Rusconi, 167 N.E.2d 847 (1960) (reversing denial of name change because judge thought the change was "un-American," reasoning that court may not inquire into motives for name change unless they are dishonest or unlawful).

Massachusetts is among the few states (as well as Georgia, Hawaii, Iowa, Louisiana, New York, and North Dakota) that currently allow a husband to assume his wife's surname. Matthew Yi, Bill Would Simplify Changing Names for Partners, Men, S.F. Chron., May 31, 2007, at A17.

The Massachusetts statute currently provides that a spouse may (1) retain his or her surname, (2) adopt the surname of the other spouse, (3) adopt a hyphenated name or (4) resume use of a former name (Mass. Gen. Laws ch. 46, §1D). If a married woman retains her maiden name upon marriage, she may register to vote with that name (Mass. Gen. Laws ch. 51, §2). Statute also permits women to resume their maiden names (or that of a former husband) when they divorce (Mass. Gen. Laws ch. 208, §23).

Generally, American children who are born in wedlock are given their father's name. In response to the women's movement, however, case law or statutory law increasingly give parents the right to choose the father's name, the mother's birth name, or a hyphenated surname. Currently, in name disputes between the parents, courts usually apply one of three standards: a custodial parent presumption, a presumption favoring the status quo, or the best interests of the child. See Merle H. Weiner, We Are Family: Valuing Associationalism in Disputes Over Children's Surnames, 75 N.C. L. Rev. 1625, 1692 (1997).

Massachusetts, based on case law, adheres to the best interests standard in parental disputes regarding marital, as well as nonmarital, children. See Mark v. Kahn, 131 N.E.2d 758, 762 (Mass. 1956) (holding that the lack of findings regarding whether the children's name change to that of stepfather was in their best interests required reversal of decree for husband); Petition of an Adult and Two Minors for Name Change, 750 N.E.2d 522 (Mass. App. Ct. 2001) (unpublished opinion) (affirming denial of children's surname change from former husband's surname to mother's maiden name based on conclusion that name change was not in children's best interests); Jones v. Roe, 604 N.E.2d 45, 46 (Mass. App. Ct. 1992) (applying best-interests-of-child standard to disputes involving nonmarital child and finding that father had not established that change to paternal surname would be in child's best interests); Petition of Two Minors for Change of Name, 517 N.E.2d 1291 (Mass. App. Ct. 1988) (holding that court's findings that name change of nonmarital children from that of their father to their mother would not be in their best interest was supported by record).

See generally Linda D. Elrod & Robert G. Spector, A Review of the Year in Family Law: State Courts React to *Troxel*, 35 Fam. L. Q. 577, 625 (Chart 9: Child's Name Change) (2002); Michael Rosensaft, Comment, The Right of Men to Change Their Names Upon Marriage, 5 U. Pa. J. Const. L. 186 (2002).

Massachusetts General Laws

Ch. 46

§1D. Choice of surname upon marriage

Each party to a marriage may adopt any surname, including but not limited to the present or birth-given surname of either party, may retain or resume use of a present or birth-given surname, or may adopt any hyphenated combination thereof.

(Stat. 1977, ch. 869, §2.)

Massachusetts General Laws

Ch. 51

§2. Name change of registered voter

A registered voter who chooses to adopt a new name shall continue to be registered in his former name until June first of the following year at which time the voter shall be registered in his new name; provided, however, that if such voter appears in person prior to the close of registration for any preliminary, primary, or election to notify the registrars of such adoption of a new name, the registrars shall correct the current annual register so that such voter shall be registered in his new name.

If a voter does not choose to adopt a new name as a result of marriage, the registrars shall make no change in the name of such voter entered in the current annual register.

(Stat. 1933, ch. 254, §3; Stat. 1945, ch. 310; Stat. 1962, ch. 437, §4; Stat. 1966, ch. 666; Stat. 1975, ch. 367, §1; Stat. 1981, ch. 198; Stat. 1985, ch. 477, §5.)

Massachusetts General Laws

Ch. 208

§23. Wife's resumption of former name upon divorce

The court granting a divorce may allow a woman to resume her maiden name or that of a former husband.

(Stat. 1849, ch. 141; G.S. 1860, ch. 107, §23; P.S. 1882, ch. 146, §21; R.L. 1902, ch. 152, §20; Stat. 1973, ch. 379.)

Ch. 210

§12. Petition for name change

A petition for the change of name of a person may be heard by the probate court in the county where the petitioner resides. The change of name of a person shall be granted unless such change is inconsistent with the public interests.

(Stat. 1977, ch. 869, §3.)

§13. Procedure for name change

The court shall, before decreeing a change of name, request a report from the commissioner of probation on the person filing the petition and, except for good cause shown, require public notice of the petition to be given and any person may be heard thereon, and, upon entry of a decree, the name as established thereby shall be the legal name of the petitioner, and the register may issue a certificate, under the seal of the court, of the name as so established.

No decree shall be entered, however, until there has been filed in the court a copy of the birth record of the person whose name is sought to be changed and, in case such person's name has previously been changed by decree of court or at marriage pursuant to section one D of chapter forty-six, either a copy of the record of his birth amended to conform to the previous decree changing his name, a copy of such decree, or a copy of the record of marriage; provided, that the filing of any such copy may be dispensed with if the judge is satisfied that it cannot be obtained.

(Stat. 1943, ch. 155, §2; Stat. 1948, ch. 247; Stat. 1966, ch. 342, §1; Stat. 1977, ch. 869, §4.)

§14. Annual report of name changes

Each register of probate shall annually, in December, make a return to the commissioner of public health and the commissioner of probation of all changes of name made in his court.

(Stat. 1851, ch. 256, §4; G.S. 1860, ch. 110, §14; P.S. 1882, ch. 148, §14; Stat. 1897, ch. 89; R.L. 1902, ch. 154, §14.)

C. Parenting

1. Family and Medical Leave

The entrance into the workplace of an increasing number of women with children prompted calls for enhanced protection against employment discrimination. In the 1970s, such claims included constitutional challenges to mandatory maternity leave policies that required employees to leave their employment when they became pregnant. See, e.g., Cleveland Board of Education v. LaFleur, 414 U.S. 632 (1974) (holding that school boards' mandatory maternity leave policy violates school teachers' right to due process).

Also, plaintiffs challenged public and private disability programs that provided partial wage replacement to disabled employees but excluded pregnancy-related claims. In 1974 in Geduldig v. Aiello, 417 U.S. 484 (1974), the United States Supreme Court upheld such a state disability fund scheme and eliminated the Equal Protection Clause as a means for challenging legislation singling out pregnancy for special treatment. Two years later, the Supreme Court upheld a private employer's disability insurance plan that excluded pregnancy, by interpreting Title VII as it had the Equal Protection Clause, to hold that discrimination on the basis of pregnancy was not sex discrimination.

In response to *Geduldig* and *Gilbert*, Congress passed the Pregnancy Discrimination Act (PDA), 42 U.S.C. §2000e(k), in 1978 as an amendment to Title VII to require employers to treat pregnancy similarly to other physical conditions in terms of leave and other employment benefits. Following enactment of the PDA, a question arose as to the effect of the PDA on state statutes that affirmatively provided for employment-related pregnancy benefits. In California Federal Savings & Loan Association v. Guerra, 479 U.S. 272 (1987), the United States Supreme Court held that state maternity leave legislation was not preempted by Title VII because it was not inconsistent with the purposes of Title VII.

A public outcry for federal family leave (rather than maternity leave) legislation began in the 1970s. Legislation was first proposed in 1985 and was finally enacted in 1993. The Family and Medical Leave Act (FMLA), 29 U.S.C. §§2601 et seq., requires employers of 50 or more to provide eligible employees with unpaid leave for up to three months because of birth, adoption, or to care for a family member with a "serious health condition."

In 2002, California became the first state to offer paid family leave, providing workers up to six weeks paid time off to care for a sick parent, spouse, domestic partner, or child or to bond with a new child. The legislation (S.B. 1661), which amended Cal. Unemployment Insurance Code §§984, 2116, 2601, 2613, 2708, and 3254, and added Chapter 7 (commencing with §3300) to Part 2 of Division 1 of that Code, relating to disability compensation, enables eligible employees to receive up to 55 percent of their salary, up to a maximum of $738 per week. Employers may require employees to utilize up to two weeks of earned but unused vacation leave prior to receipt of these additional benefits. Legislative Counsel's Digest, S.B. 1661. See also Lynda Gledhill, Davis OK's Paid Leave to Care for Family, S.F. Chron. Sept. 24, 2002, at A1.

In May 2007, the governor of Washington signed legislation making Washington the second state (after California) to offer paid leave. The new policy begins in October 2009. Amy Roe, Making Motherhood Visible, Seattle Times, May 19, 2007, at B2. Also, New York's Governor Eliot Spitzer is supporting a measure that would offer paid leave (up to 12 weeks per year, with a maximum of $170 per week). In comparison, California offers 6 weeks of paid leave, with a maximum of $882 per week, and Washington offers 5 weeks at $250 per week. The New York plan thus would offer longer leaves but lower benefits, and also would be more expansive because it would cover care for grandchildren, foster parents, and parents-in-law (not merely newborns, newly adopted children, or seriously ill children). Steven Greenhouse, Spitzer Pushes a Plan for Paid Leave to Care for Relatives, N.Y. Times, June 2, 2007, at B1.

New Jersey is also considering a bill to provide partial paid leave to any employee (up to 10 weeks to care for a sick family member, newborn, or newly adopted child, and up to a maximum of $488 per week), but employers could require employees to take 2 weeks of vacation before qualifying. Business groups oppose the measure, saying it would be too costly. Tangible Family Values, N.Y. Times, June 10, 2007, at 19.

In Nevada Department of Human Resources v. Hibbs, 538 U.S. 721 (2003), the United States Supreme Court held that state employees could recover money damages in federal court in the event of the employer's violation of the FMLA, notwithstanding the Eleventh Amendment. The Court reasoned that Congress had made its intention to abrogate Eleventh Amendment immunity unmistakably clear in the language of the FMLA by enabling employees to seek damages "against any employer (including a public agency) in any Federal or State court of competent jurisdiction." 29 U.S.C. §2617(a)(2).

Massachusetts enacted maternity leave legislation in 1972 (Mass. Gen. Laws ch. 149, §105D). The Massachusetts law provides eight weeks of maternity leave for eligible female employees who work for employers with six or more employees. The Act provides maternity leave, regardless of disability, either for giving birth or for adopting a child under age 18 or a disabled child under age 23. Employers may provide paid or unpaid leave. An employee returning to work must be restored to her former position or to a similar position without loss of benefits. As originally enacted, the law only provided for maternity leave for the purpose of childbirth; however, a 1984 amendment permitted leave for adoption of a child under three years of age (Stat. 1984, ch. 423), and a 1989 amendment permitted adoptions of children up to age 18 or those under age 23 if mentally or physically disabled (Stat. 1989, ch. 318). Unlike pre-PDA federal law, Massachusetts case law held that pregnancy discrimination constituted sex-based discrimination. Massachusetts Elec. Co. v. Massachusetts Comm'n Against Discrim., 375 N.E.2d 1192 (Mass. 1978). In addition to the FMLA and state-based provisions for maternity leave, Massachusetts also provides unpaid leave for certain family-related educational or medical reasons. In 1998, the state legislature enacted the Small Necessities Leave Act (Mass. Gen. Laws ch. 149, §52D). That Act, applicable to state employees covered by the FMLA, provides 24 hours of unpaid leave annually to bring a child or elderly relative to a doctor or dentist, or to participate in school activities related to the educational advancement of a child or the employee.

In 2006, the Massachusetts legislature considered legislation (S.113/114) that would provide families with paid family and medical leave. The bill would apply to all employees who have worked for at least a year, for at least 1,250 hours, and all employers with six or more employees. It would guarantee employees a stipend of 80 percent of their wages for up to 12 weeks, subject to a $750 per week cap. The bill was referred to the Committee on Children, Families and Persons with Disabilities. See National Partnership for Women & Families, States and Cities Taking on Paid Leave in 2007, available at http://www.nationalpartnership.org (last updated Oct. 3, 2007). Legislation on paid family and medical leave was also introduced in 2007 in Illinois, Oregon, and Texas. *Id.*

On the interplay between the federal family leave legislation, and Massachusetts legislation, see Sally L. Adams et al., Interrelationships Between the ADA, the FMLA, G.L. C. 151B, and G.L. C. 149 §52D, Mass. Emp. Law (MA-CLE) §16-1 (Supp. 2006).

Massachusetts General Laws

Ch. 149

§52D. Small Necessities Leave Act

(a) As used in this section, terms shall have the meanings assigned to them by the federal act, notwithstanding any contrary provision of section 1 of this chapter. In addition, the following terms shall have the following meanings:

"Elderly relative", an individual of at least 60 years of age who is related by blood or marriage to the employee, including a parent.

"Federal act", sections 101 to 105, inclusive, of the Family and Medical Leave Act of 1993, 29 U.S.C. sections 2611 to 2615, inclusive, as it may be amended.

"School", a public or private elementary or secondary school; a Head Start program assisted under the Head Start Act, 42 U.S.C. sections 9831 et seq.; and a children's day care facility licensed under chapter 28A.

(b) An eligible employee shall be entitled to a total of 24 hours of leave during any 12-month period, in addition to leave available under the federal act, to:

(1) participate in school activities directly related to the educational advancement of a son or daughter of the employee, such as parent-teacher conferences or interviewing for a new school;

(2) accompany the son or daughter of the employee to routine medical or dental appointments, such as check-ups or vaccinations; and

(3) accompany an elderly relative of the employee to routine medical or dental appointments or appointments for other professional services related to the elder's care, such as interviewing at nursing or group homes.

(c) Unless this section provides otherwise, the terms of the federal act shall apply to leave under this section. As provided in section 102(d)(2)(A) of the federal act, 29 U.S.C. section 2612(d)(2)(A), an eligible employee may elect, or an employer may require the employee, to substitute any of the accrued paid vacation leave, personal leave, or medical or sick leave of the employee for any of the leave provided under this section, but nothing in this section shall require an employer to provide paid sick leave or paid medical leave in any situation in which the employer would not normally provide any such paid leave. Leave under this section may be taken intermittently or on a reduced leave schedule.

(d) If the necessity for leave under this section is foreseeable, the employee shall provide the employer with not less than seven days' notice before the date the leave is to begin. If the necessity for leave is not foreseeable, the employee shall provide such notice as is practicable.

(e) An employer may require that a request for leave under this section be supported by a certification issued at such time and in such manner as the attorney general may by regulation require.

(f) The attorney general shall enforce this section, and may obtain injunctive or declaratory relief for this purpose. Violation of this section shall be subject to the second paragraph of section 150 and to section 180.

(Stat. 1998, ch. 109.)

§105D. Maternity leave rights and benefits

A female employee who has completed the initial probationary period set by the terms of her employment or, if there is no such probationary period, has been employed by the same employer for at least three consecutive months as a full-time employee, who is absent from such employment for a period not exceeding eight weeks for the purpose of giving birth or for adopting a child under the age of eighteen or for adopting a child under the age of twenty-three if the child is mentally or physically disabled, said period to be hereinafter called maternity leave, and who shall give at least two weeks' notice to her employer of her anticipated date of departure and intention to return, shall be restored to her previous, or a similar, position with the same status, pay, length of service credit and seniority, wherever applicable, as of the date of her leave. Said maternity leave may be with or without pay at the discretion of the employer.

Such employer shall not be required to restore an employee on maternity leave to her previous or a similar position if other employees of equal length of service credit and status in the same or similar position have been laid off due to economic conditions or other changes in operating conditions affecting employment during the period of such maternity leave; provided, however, that such employee on maternity leave shall retain any preferential consideration for another position to which she may be entitled as of the date of her leave.

Such maternity leave shall not affect the employee's right to receive vacation time, sick leave, bonuses, advancement, seniority, length of service credit, benefits, plans or programs for which she was eligible at the date of her leave, and any other advantages or rights of her employment incident to her employment position; provided, however, that such maternity leave shall not be included, when applicable, in the computation of such benefits, rights, and advantages; and provided, further, that the employer need not provide for the cost of any benefits, plans, or programs during the period of maternity leave unless such employer so provides for all employees on leave of absence. Nothing in this section shall be construed to affect any bargaining agreement or company policy which provides for greater or additional benefits than those required under this section.

A notice of this provision shall be posted in every establishment in which females are employed.

For the purposes of this section, an "employer" shall be defined as in subsection 5 of section one of chapter one hundred and fifty-one B.

(Stat. 1972, ch. 790, §1; Stat. 1984, ch. 423; Stat. 1989, ch. 318.)

2. Marital Status Discrimination

In 1946, Massachusetts enacted a comprehensive antidiscrimination law prohibiting employment discrimination (Mass. Gen. Laws ch. 151B, §4). The original grounds covered race, color, religious creed, national origin or ancestry. In 1950, the legislature amended the statute to include age (i.e., a person older than 40). Subsequent prohibitions encompassed housing discrimination (1957), and employment discrimination based on sex (1965), handicap (1983), and sexual orientation (1989). That is, employers may not refuse to hire, discharge, or discriminate against individuals in compensation or in the terms, conditions, or privileges of employment on these prohibited grounds (unless based upon a bona fide occupational qualification). In 2000, the legislature added a prohibition against employment discrimination based on a person's genetic information. In 2004, another prohibition was added making it unlawful for an employer to discriminate against a person who is a veteran. Howard J. Alperin & Lawrence D. Subow, 14 Mass. Prac. Summary of Basic Law §5.11 (3d ed. 2003).

Specific statutory provisions prohibit discrimination on the basis of marital status or parenting. The housing discrimination provisions prohibit discrimination in the sale or lease of housing on the basis of gender and marital status (*inter alia*) (Mass. Gen. Laws ch. 151B, §§4(6)-4(8)). Section 4(11) adds prohibitions in the sale or rental of housing because the applicant has a child.

The Massachusetts legislature considered (but did not enact) legislation (S.B. 2328) in 2006 that would have prohibited housing discrimination against victims of domestic violence, rape, sexual assault, or stalking. The bill would also have created a defense to eviction if a landlord attempted to evict a tenant because the tenant had been a victim of one of the aforementioned crimes. Further, if a tenant notified a landlord that he or she was a victim of such crimes (and had a valid order of protection, had notified a law enforcement officer, or had consulted service providers), then the tenant would have had the right to terminate a rental agreement without further obligation. See Legal Momentum, State Law Guide: Housing Protections for Victims of Domestic and Sexual Violence, http://legalmomentum.org/legalmomentum/files/housingaug2007.pdf (last updated Aug. 2007) (last visited Oct. 3, 2007).

Also, Massachusetts law (Mass. Gen. Laws. ch. 151B, §4(15)) prohibits discrimination based on sex or marital status in the use of a surname. Different statutory provisions protect teachers and other full-time school employees from being dismissed because of marital status (Mass. Gen. Laws ch. 71, §42); and prohibit discrimination on the basis of sex, children, or marital status (*inter alia*) by insurers in the provision of homeowners' insurance (Mass. Gen. Laws ch. 175, §4C) and by insurers who refuse to issue, renew, or execute as surety motor vehicle liability policies on the basis of sex or marital status (Mass. Gen. Laws ch. 175, §22E).

A plaintiff alleging gender-based discrimination is entitled to a jury trial under the state constitution. See Dean v. City of Springfield, 645 N.E.2d 39 (Mass. App. Ct. 1995); Dalis v. Buyer Advertising, Inc., 636 N.E.2d 212 (Mass. 1994).

Furthermore, Massachusetts has enacted an Equal Rights Amendment (*infra*) that prohibits discrimination based on sex (*inter alia*) but not marital status. Several states have constitutions providing that equality of rights shall not be denied on account of sex or which otherwise prohibit discrimination based on sex. Paul Benjamin Linton, Same-Sex "Marriage" Under State Equal Rights Amendments, 46 St. Louis U. L.J. 909, 910 (2002) (finding that 19 states have adopted equal rights or antidiscrimination provisions). Massachusetts case law has held that a statutory classification based upon sex is subject to strict judicial scrutiny under the state equal rights amendment. Lowell v. Kowalski, 405 N.E.2d 135, 139 (Mass. 1980); Op. of Justices to House of Reps., 371 N.E.2d 426, 428 (Mass. 1977).

Massachusetts Constitution

Art. I (Equal Rights Amendment)

All people are born free and equal and have certain natural, essential and unalienable rights; among which may be reckoned the right of enjoying and defending their lives and liberties; that of acquiring, possessing and protecting property; in fine, that of seeking and obtaining their safety and happiness. Equality under the law shall not be denied or abridged because of sex, race, color, creed, or national origin.

Massachusetts General Laws

Ch. 71

§42. Teachers cannot be dismissed based on their marital status

A principal may dismiss or demote any teacher or other person assigned full-time to the school, subject to the review and approval of the superintendent; and subject to the provisions of this section, the superintendent may dismiss any employee of the school district. In the case of an employee whose duties require him to be assigned to more than one school, and in the case of teachers who teach in more than one school, those persons shall be considered to be under the supervision of the superintendent for all decisions relating to dismissal or demotion for cause.

A teacher who has been teaching in a school system for at least ninety calendar days shall not be dismissed unless he has been furnished with written notice of intent to dismiss and with an explanation of the grounds for the dismissal in sufficient detail to permit the teacher to respond and documents relating to the grounds for dismissal, and, if he so requests, has been given a reasonable opportunity within ten school days after receiving such written notice to review the decision with the principal or superintendent, as the case may be, and to present information pertaining to the basis for the decision and to the teacher's status. The teacher receiving such notice may be represented by an attorney or other representative at such a meeting with the principal or superintendent. Teachers without professional teacher status shall otherwise be deemed employees at will.

A teacher with professional teacher status, pursuant to section forty-one, shall not be dismissed except for inefficiency, incompetency, incapacity, conduct unbecoming a teacher, insubordination or failure on the part of the teacher to satisfy teacher performance standards developed pursuant to section thirty-eight of this chapter or other just cause.

A teacher with professional teacher status may seek review of a dismissal decision within thirty days after receiving notice of his dismissal by filing a petition for arbitration with the commissioner. The commissioner shall forward to the parties a list of three arbitrators provided by the American Arbitration Association. Each person on the list shall be accredited by the National Academy of Arbitrators. The parties each shall have the right to strike one of the three arbitrators' names if they are unable to agree upon a single arbitrator from amongst the three. The arbitration shall be conducted in accordance with the rules of the American Arbitration Association to be consistent with the provisions of this section. The parties each shall have the right to strike one of the three arbitrators' names if they are unable to agree upon a single arbitrator from amongst the three. The board of education shall determine the process for selecting arbitrators for the pool. The fee for the arbitration shall be split equally between the two parties involved in the arbitration.

At the arbitral hearing, the teacher and the school district may be represented by an attorney or other representative, present evidence, and call witnesses and the school district shall have the burden of proof. In determining whether the district has proven grounds for dismissal consistent with this section, the arbitrator shall consider the best interests of the pupils in the district and the need for elevation of performance standards.

The arbitrator's decision shall be issued within one month from the completion of the arbitral hearing, unless all parties involved agree otherwise, and shall contain a detailed statement of the reasons for the decision. Upon a finding that the dismissal was improper under the standards set forth in this section, the arbitrator may award back pay, benefits, reinstatement, and any other appropriate non-financial relief or any combination thereof. Under no circumstances shall the arbitrator award punitive, consequential, or nominal damages, or compensatory damages other than back pay, benefits or reinstatement. In the event the teacher is reinstated, the period between the dismissal and reinstatement shall be considered to be time served for purposes of employment. The arbitral decision shall be subject to judicial review as provided in chapter one hundred and fifty C. With the exception of other remedies provided by statute, the remedies provided hereunder shall be the exclusive remedies available to teachers for wrongful termination. The rules governing this arbitration procedure shall be the rules of the American Arbitration Association as pertains to arbitration.

Neither this section nor section forty-one shall affect the right of a superintendent to lay off teachers pursuant to reductions in force or reorganization resulting from declining enrollment or other budgetary reasons. No teacher with professional teacher status shall be laid off pursuant to a reduction in force or reorganization if there is a teacher without such status for whose position the covered employee is currently certified. No teacher with such status shall be displaced by a more senior teacher with such status in accordance with the terms of a collective bargaining agreement or otherwise unless the more senior teacher is currently qualified pursuant to section thirty-eight G for the junior teacher's position.

(Stat. 1934, ch. 123; Stat. 1946, ch. 195; Stat. 1947, ch. 597, §2; Stat. 1953, ch. 244; Stat. 1956, ch. 132, §2; Stat. 1966, ch. 185, §§1, 2; Stat. 1970, ch. 388, §1; Stat. 1972, ch. 464, §2; Stat. 1985, ch. 188, §18; Stat. 1988, ch. 153, §§4 to 6; Stat. 1993, ch. 71, §44.)

Massachusetts General Laws

Ch. 151B

§4. Unlawful employment practices

It shall be an unlawful practice:

1. For an employer, by himself or his agent, because of the race, color, religious creed, national origin, sex, sexual orientation, which shall not include persons whose sexual orientation involves minor children as the sex object, genetic information, or ancestry of any individual to refuse to hire or employ or to bar or to discharge from employment such individual or to discriminate against such individual in compensation or in terms, conditions or privileges of employment, unless based upon a bona fide occupational qualification.

1A. It shall be unlawful discriminatory practice for an employer to impose upon an individual as a condition of obtaining or retaining employment any terms or conditions, compliance with which would require such individual to violate, or forego the practice of, his creed or religion as required by that creed or religion including but not limited to the observance of any particular day or days or any portion thereof as a sabbath or holy day and the employer shall make reasonable accommodation to the religious needs of such individual. No individual who has given notice as hereinafter provided shall be required to remain at his place of employment during any day or days or portion thereof that, as a requirement of his religion, he observes as his sabbath or other holy day, including a reasonable time prior and subsequent thereto for travel between his place of employment and his home, provided, however, that any employee intending to be absent from work when so required by his or her creed or religion shall notify his or her employer not less than ten days in advance of each absence, and that any such absence from work shall, wherever practicable in the judgment of the employer, be made up by an equivalent amount of time at some other mutually convenient time. Nothing under this subsection shall be deemed to require an employer to compensate an employee for such absence. "Reasonable Accommodation", as used in this subsection shall mean such accommodation to an employee's or prospective employee's religious observance or practice as shall not cause undue hardship in the conduct of the employer's business. The employee shall have the burden of proof as to the required practice of his creed or religion. As used in this subsection, the words "creed or religion" mean any sincerely held religious beliefs, without regard to whether such beliefs are approved, espoused, prescribed or required by an established church or other religious institution or organization.

Undue hardship, as used herein, shall include the inability of an employer to provide services which are required by and in compliance with all federal and state laws, including regulations or tariffs promulgated or required by any regulatory agency having jurisdiction over such services or where the health or safety of the public would be unduly compromised by the absence of such employee or employees, or where the employee's presence is indispensable to the orderly transaction of business and his or her work cannot be performed by another employee of substantially similar qualifications during the period of absence, or where the employee's presence is needed to alleviate an emergency situation. The employer shall have the burden of proof to show undue hardship.

1B. For an employer in the private sector, by himself or his agent, because of the age of any individual, to refuse to hire or employ or to bar or to discharge from employment such individual, or to discriminate against such individual in compensation or in terms, conditions or privileges of employment, unless based upon a bona fide occupational qualification.

1C For the commonwealth or any of its political subdivisions, by itself or its agent, because of the age of any individual, to refuse to hire or employ or to bar or discharge from employment such individual in compensation or in terms, conditions or privileges of employment unless pursuant to any other general or special law.

1D. For an employer, an employment agency, the commonwealth or any of its political subdivisions, by itself or its agents, to deny initial employment, reemployment, retention in employment, promotion or any benefit of employment to a person who is a member of, applies to perform, or has an obligation to perform, service in a uniformed military service of the United States, including the National Guard, on the basis of that membership, application or obligation.

2. For a labor organization, because of the race, color, religious creed, national origin, sex, sexual orientation, which shall not include persons whose sexual orientation involves minor children as the sex object, age, genetic information, or ancestry of any individual, or because of the handicap of any person alleging to be a qualified handicapped person, to exclude from full membership rights or to expel from its membership such individual or to discriminate in any way against any of its members or against any employer or any individual employed by an employer unless based upon a bona fide occupational qualification.

3. For any employer or employment agency to print or circulate or cause to be printed or circulated any statement, advertisement or publication, or to use any form of application for employment or to make any inquiry or record in connection with employment, which expresses, directly or indirectly, any limitation, specification or discrimination as to the race, color, religious creed, national origin, sex, sexual orientation, which shall not include persons whose sexual orientation involves minor children as the sex object, age, genetic information or ancestry, or the handicap of a qualified handicapped person or any intent to make any such limitation, specification or discrimination, or to discriminate in any way on the ground of race, color, religious creed, national origin, sex, sexual orientation, age, genetic information, ancestry or the handicap of a qualified handicapped person, unless based upon a bona fide occupational qualification.

3A. For any person engaged in the insurance or bonding business, or his agent, to make any inquiry or record of any person seeking a bond or surety bond conditioned upon faithful performance of his duties or to use any form of application in connection with the furnishing of such bond, which seeks information relative to the race, color, religious creed, national origin, sex, sexual orientation, which shall not include persons whose sexual orientation involves minor children as the sex object, genetic information, or ancestry of the person to be bonded.

3B. For any person whose business includes granting mortgage loans or engaging in residential real estate-related transactions to discriminate against any person in the granting of any mortgage loan or in making available such a transaction, or in the terms or conditions of such a loan or transaction, because of race, color, religion, sex, sexual orientation which shall not include persons whose sexual orientation involves minor children as the sex object, children, national origin, genetic information, ancestry, age or handicap. Such transactions shall include, but not be limited to:

(1) the making or purchasing of loans or the provision of other financial assistance for purchasing, constructing, improving, repairing, or maintaining a dwelling; or the making or purchasing of loans or the provision of other financial assistance secured by residential real estate; or

(2) the selling, brokering, or appraising of residential real estate.

In the case of age, the following shall not be an unlawful practice:

(1) an inquiry of age for the purpose of determining a pertinent element of credit worthiness;

(2) the use of an empirically derived credit system which considers age; provided, however, that such system is based on demonstrably and statistically sound data; and provided, further, that such system does not assign a negative factor or score to any applicant who has reached age sixty-two;

(3) the offering of credit life insurance or credit disability insurance, in conjunction with any mortgage loan, to a limited age group;

(4) the failure or refusal to grant any mortgage loan to a person who has not attained the age of majority;

(5) the failure or refusal to grant any mortgage loan the duration of which exceeds the life expectancy of the applicant as determined by the most recent Individual Annuity Mortality Table.

Nothing in this subsection prohibits a person engaged in the business of furnishing appraisals of real property from taking into consideration factors other than those hereinabove proscribed.

3C. For any person to deny another person access to, or membership or participation in, a multiple listing service, real estate brokers' organization, or other service, organization, or facility relating to the business of selling or renting dwellings, or to discriminate against such person in the terms or conditions of such access, membership, or participation, on account of race, color, religion, sex, sexual orientation which shall not include persons whose sexual orientation involves minor children as the sex object, children, national origin, genetic information, ancestry, age, or handicap.

4. For any person, employer, labor organization or employment agency to discharge, expel or otherwise discriminate against any person because he has opposed any practices forbidden under this chapter or because he has filed a complaint, testified or assisted in any proceeding under section five.

4A. For any person to coerce, intimidate, threaten, or interfere with another person in the exercise or enjoyment of any right granted or protected by this chapter, or to coerce, intimidate, threaten or interfere with such other person for having aided or encouraged any other person in the exercise or enjoyment of any such right granted or protected by this chapter.

5. For any person, whether an employer or an employee or not, to aid, abet, incite, compel or coerce the doing of any of the acts forbidden under this chapter or to attempt to do so.

6. For the owner, lessee, sublessee, licensed real estate broker, assignee or managing agent of publicly assisted or multiple dwelling or contiguously located housing accommodations or other person having the right of ownership or possession or right to rent or lease, or sell or negotiate for the sale of such accommodations, or any agent or employee of such a person, or any organization of unit owners in a condominium or housing cooperative:

(a) to refuse to rent or lease or sell or negotiate for sale or otherwise to deny to or withhold from any person or group of persons such accommodations because of the race, religious creed, color, national origin, sex, sexual orientation, which shall not include persons whose sexual orientation involves minor children as the sex object, age, genetic information, ancestry, or marital status of such person or persons or because such person is a veteran or member of the armed forces, or because such person is blind, or hearing impaired or has any other handicap;

(b) to discriminate against any person because of his race, religious creed, color, national origin, sex, sexual orientation, which shall not include persons whose sexual orientation involves minor children as the sex object, age, ancestry, or marital status or because such person is a veteran or member of the armed forces, or because such person is blind, or hearing impaired or has any other handicap in the terms, conditions or privileges of such accommodations or the acquisitions thereof, or in the furnishings of facilities and services in connection therewith, or because such a person possesses a trained dog guide as a consequence of blindness, or hearing impairment;

(c) to cause to be made any written or oral inquiry or record concerning the race, religious creed, color, national origin, sex, sexual orientation, which shall not include persons whose sexual orientation involves minor children as the sex object, age, genetic information, ancestry or marital status of the person seeking to rent or lease or buy any such accommodation, or concerning the fact that such person is a veteran or a member of the armed forces or because such person is blind or hearing impaired or has any other handicap. The word "age" as used in this subsection shall not apply to persons who are minors nor to residency in state-aided or federally-aided housing developments for the elderly nor to residency in housing developments assisted under the federal low income housing tax credit and intended for use as housing for persons 55 years of age or over or 62 years of age or over, nor to residency in communities consisting of either a structure or structures constructed expressly for use as housing for persons 55 years of age or over or 62 years of age or over, on 1 parcel or on contiguous parcels of land, totaling at least 5 acres in size. For the purpose of this subsection, housing intended for occupancy by persons fifty-five or over and sixty-two or over shall comply with the provisions set forth in 42 USC 3601 et seq.

For purposes of this subsection, discrimination on the basis of handicap includes, but is not limited to, in connection with the design and construction of:

(1) all units of a dwelling which has three or more units and an elevator which are constructed for first occupancy after March thirteenth, nineteen hundred and ninety-one; and

(2) all ground floor units of other dwellings consisting of three or more units which are constructed for first occupancy after March thirteenth, nineteen hundred and ninety-one, a failure to design and construct such dwellings in such a manner that

(i) the public use and common use portions of such dwellings are readily accessible to and usable by handicapped persons;

(ii) all the doors are designed to allow passage into and within all premises within such dwellings and are sufficiently wide to allow passage by handicapped persons in wheelchairs; and

(iii) all premises within such dwellings contain the following features of adaptive design;

(a) an accessible route into and through the dwelling;

(b) light switches, electrical outlets, thermostats, and other environmental controls in accessible locations;

(c) reinforcements in bathroom walls to allow later installation of grab bars; and

(d) usable kitchens and bathrooms such that an individual in a wheelchair can maneuver about the space.

7. For the owner, lessee, sublessee, real estate broker, assignee or managing agent of other covered housing accommodations or of land intended for the erection of any housing accommodation included under subsection 10, 11, 12, or 13 of section one, or other person having the right of ownership or possession or right to rent or lease or sell, or negotiate for the sale or lease of such land or accommodations, or any agent or employee of such a person or any organization of unit owners in a condominium or housing cooperative:

(a) to refuse to rent or lease or sell or negotiate for sale or lease or otherwise to deny or withhold from any person or group of persons such accommodations or land because of race, color, religious creed, national origin, sex, sexual orientation, which shall not include persons whose sexual orientation involves minor children as the sex object, age, genetic information, ancestry, or marital status, veteran status or membership in the armed forces, blindness, hearing impairment, or because such person possesses a trained dog guide as a consequence of blindness or hearing impairment or other handicap of such person or persons;

(b) to discriminate against any person because of his race, color, religious creed, national origin, sex, sexual orientation, which shall not include persons whose sexual orientation involves minor children as the sex object, age, genetic information, ancestry, or marital status, veteran status or membership in the armed services, blindness, or hearing impairment or other handicap, or because such person possesses a trained dog guide as a consequence of blindness or hearing impairment in the terms, conditions or privileges of such accommodations or land or the acquisition thereof, or in the furnishing of facilities and services in the connection therewith or

(c) to cause to be made any written or oral inquiry or record concerning the race, color, religious creed, national origin, sex, sexual orientation, which shall not include persons whose sexual orientation involves minor children as the sex object, age, genetic information, ancestry, marital status, veteran status or membership in the armed services, blindness, hearing impairment or other handicap or because such person possesses a trained dog guide as a consequence of blindness or hearing impairment, of the person seeking to rent or lease or buy any such accommodation or land; provided, however, that this subsection shall not apply to the leasing of a single apartment or flat in a two family dwelling, the other occupancy unit of which is occupied by the owner as his residence. The word "age" as used in this subsection shall not apply to persons who are minors nor to residency in state-aided or federally-aided housing developments for the elderly nor to residency in housing developments assisted under the federal low income housing tax credit and intended for use as housing for persons 55 years of age or over or 62 years of age or over, nor to residency in communities consisting of either a structure or structures constructed expressly for use as housing for persons 55 years of age or over or 62 years of age or over, on 1 parcel or on contiguous parcels of land, totaling at least 5 acres in size. For the purpose of this subsection, housing intended for occupancy by persons fifty-five or over and sixty-two or over shall comply with the provisions set forth in 42 USC 3601 et seq.

7A. For purposes of subsections 6 and 7 discrimination on the basis of handicap shall include but not be limited to:

(1) a refusal to permit or to make, at the expense of the handicapped person, reasonable modification of existing premises occupied or to be occupied by such person if such modification is necessary to afford such person full enjoyment of such premises; provided, however, that, in the case of publicly assisted housing, multiple dwelling housing consisting of ten or more units, or contiguously located housing consisting of ten or more units, reasonable modification shall be at the expense of the owner or other person having the right of ownership; provided, further, that, in the case of public ownership of such housing units the cost of such reasonable modification shall be subject to appropriation; and provided, further, that, in the case of a rental, the landlord may, where the modification to be paid for by the handicapped person will materially alter the marketability of the housing, condition permission for a modification on the tenant agreeing to restore or pay for the cost of restoring, the interior of the premises to the condition that existed prior to such modification, reasonable wear and tear excepted;

(2) a refusal to make reasonable accommodations in rules, policies, practices, or services, when such accommodations may be necessary to afford a handicapped person equal opportunity to use and enjoy a dwelling; and

(3) discrimination against or a refusal to rent to a person because of such person's need for reasonable modification or accommodation.

Reasonable modification shall include, but not be limited to, making the housing accessible to mobility-impaired, hearing-impaired and sight-impaired persons including installing raised numbers which may be read by a sight-impaired person, installing a door bell which flashes a light for a hearing-impaired person, lowering a cabinet, ramping a front entrance of five or fewer vertical steps, widening a doorway, and installing a grab bar; provided, however, that for purposes of this subsection, the owner or other person having the right of ownership shall not be required to pay for ramping a front entrance of more than five steps or for installing a wheelchair lift.

Notwithstanding any other provisions of this subsection, an accommodation or modification which is paid for by the owner or other person having the right of ownership is not considered to be reasonable if it would impose an undue hardship upon the owner or other person having the right of ownership and shall therefore not be required. Factors to be considered shall include, but not be limited to, the nature and cost of the accommodation or modification needed, the extent to which the accommodation or modification would materially alter the marketability of the housing, the overall size of the housing business of the owner or other person having the right of ownership, including but not limited to, the number and type of housing units, size of budget and available assets, and the ability of the owner or other person having the right of ownership to recover the cost of the accommodation or modification through a federal tax deduction. Ten percent shall be the maximum number of units for which an owner or other person having the right of ownership shall be required to pay for a modification in order to make units fully accessible to persons using a wheelchair pursuant to the requirements of this subsection.

In the event a wheelchair accessible unit becomes or will become vacant, the owner or other person having the right of ownership shall give timely notice to a person who has, within the previous twelve months, notified the owner or person having the right of ownership that such person is in need of a unit which is wheelchair accessible, and the owner or other person having the right of ownership shall give at least fifteen days notice of the vacancy to the Massachusetts rehabilitation commission, which shall maintain a central registry of accessible apartment housing under the provisions of section seventy-nine of chapter six. During such fifteen day notice period, the owner or other person having the right of ownership may lease or agree to lease the unit only if it is to be occupied by a person who is in need of wheelchair accessibility.

Notwithstanding any general or special law, by-law or ordinance to the contrary, there shall not be established or imposed a rent or other charge for such handicap-accessible housing which is higher than the rent or other charge for comparable nonaccessible housing of the owner or other person having the right of ownership.

7B. For any person to make print, or publish, or cause to be made, printed, or published any notice, statement or advertisement, with respect to the sale or rental of multiple dwelling, contiguously located, publicly assisted or other covered housing accommodations that indicates any preference, limitation, or discrimination based on race, color, religion, sex, sexual orientation which shall not include persons whose sexual orientation involves minor children as the sex object, national origin, genetic information, ancestry, children, marital status, public assistance recipiency, or handicap or an intention to make any such preference, limitation or discrimination except where otherwise legally permitted.

8. For the owner, lessee, sublessee, or managing agent of, or other person having the right of ownership or possession of or the right to sell, rent or lease, commercial space:

(1) To refuse to sell, rent, lease or otherwise deny to or withhold from any person or group of persons such commercial space because of race, color, religious creed, national origin, sex, sexual orientation, which shall not include persons whose sexual orientation involves minor children as the sex object, age, genetic information, ancestry handicap or marital status of such person or persons.

(2) To discriminate against any person because of his race, color, religious creed, national origin, sex, sexual orientation, which shall not include persons whose sexual orientation involves minor children as the sex object, age, genetic information, ancestry, handicap or marital status in the terms, conditions or privileges of the sale, rental or lease of any such commercial space or in the furnishing of facilities or services in connection therewith.

(3) To cause to be made any written or oral inquiry or record concerning the race, color, religious creed, national origin, sex, sexual orientation, which shall not include persons whose sexual orientation involves minor children as the sex object, age, genetic information, ancestry, handicap or marital status of a person seeking to rent or lease or buy any such commercial space. The word "age" as used in this subsection shall not apply to persons who are minors, nor to residency in state-aided or federally-aided housing developments for the elderly nor to residency in self-contained retirement communities constructed expressly for use by the elderly and which are at least twenty acres in size and have a minimum age requirement for residency of at least fifty-five years.

9. For an employer, himself or through his agent, in connection with an application for employment, or the terms, conditions, or privileges of employment, or the transfer, promotion, bonding, or discharge of any person, or in any other matter relating to the employment of any person, to request any information, to make or keep a record of such information, to use any form of application or application blank which requests such information, or to exclude, limit or otherwise discriminate against any person by reason of his or her failure to furnish such information through a written application or oral inquiry or otherwise regarding:

(i) an arrest, detention, or disposition regarding any violation of law in which no conviction resulted, or

(ii) a first conviction for any of the following misdemeanors: drunkenness, simple assault, speeding, minor traffic violations, affray, or disturbance of the peace, or

(iii) any conviction of a misdemeanor where the date of such conviction or the completion of any period of incarceration resulting therefrom, whichever date is later, occurred five or more years prior to the date of such application for employment or such request for information, unless such person has been convicted of any offense within five years immediately preceding the date of such application for employment or such request for information.

No person shall be held under any provision of any law to be guilty of perjury or of otherwise giving a false statement by reason of his failure to recite or acknowledge such information as he has a right to withhold by this subsection.

Nothing contained herein shall be construed to affect the application of section thirty-four of chapter ninety-four C, or of chapter two hundred and seventy-six relative to the sealing of records.

9A. For an employer himself or through his agent to refuse, unless based upon a bonafide occupational qualification, to hire or employ or to bar or discharge from employment any person by reason of his or her failure to furnish information regarding his or her admission, on one or more occasions, voluntarily or involuntarily, to any public or private facility for the care and treatment of mentally ill persons, provided that such person has been discharged from such facility or facilities and can prove by a psychiatrist's certificate that he is mentally competent to perform the job or the job for which he is applying. No application for employment shall contain any questions or requests for information regarding the admission of an applicant, on one or more occasions, voluntarily or involuntarily, to any public or private facility for the care and treatment of mentally ill persons, provided that such applicant has been discharged from such public or private facility or facilities and is no longer under treatment directly related to such admission.

10. For any person furnishing credit, services or rental accommodations to discriminate against any individual who is a recipient of federal, state, or local public assistance, including medical assistance, or who is a tenant receiving federal, state, or local housing subsidies, including rental assistance or rental supplements, because the individual is such a recipient, or because of any requirement of such public assistance, rental assistance, or housing subsidy program.

11. For the owner, sublessees, real estate broker, assignee or managing agent of publicly assisted or multiple dwelling or contiguously located housing accommodations or other covered housing accommodations, or other person having the right of ownership or possession or right to rent or lease or sell such accommodations, or any agent or employee of such person or organization of unit owners in a condominium or housing cooperative, to refuse to rent or lease or sell or otherwise to deny to or withhold from any person such accommodations because such person has a child or children who shall occupy the premises with such person or to discriminate against any person in the terms, conditions, or privileges of such accommodations or the acquisition thereof, or in the furnishing of facilities and services in connection therewith, because such person has a child or children who occupy or shall occupy the premises with such person; provided, however, that nothing herein shall limit the applicability of any local, state, or federal restrictions regarding the maximum number of persons permitted to occupy a dwelling. When the commission or a court finds that discrimination in violation of this paragraph has occurred with respect to a residential premises containing dangerous levels of lead in paint, plaster, soil, or other accessible material, notification of such finding shall be sent to the director of the childhood lead poisoning prevention program.

This subsection shall not apply to:

(1) Dwellings containing three apartments or less, one of which apartments is occupied by an elderly or infirm person for whom the presence of children would constitute a hardship. For purposes of this subsection, an "elderly person" shall mean a person sixty-five years of age or over, and an "infirm person" shall mean a person who is disabled or suffering from a chronic illness.

(2) The temporary leasing or temporary subleasing of a single family dwelling, a single apartment, or a single unit of a condominium or housing cooperative, by the owner of such dwelling, apartment, or unit, or in the case of a subleasing, by the sublessor thereof, who ordinarily occupies the dwelling, apartment, or unit as his or her principal place of residence. For purposes of this subsection, the term "temporary leasing" shall mean leasing during a period of the owner's or sublessor's absence not to exceed one year.

(3) The leasing of a single dwelling unit in a two family dwelling, the other occupancy unit of which is occupied by the owner as his residence.

11A. For an employer, by himself or his agent, to refuse to restore certain female employees to employment following their absence by reason of a maternity leave taken in accordance with section one hundred and five D of chapter one hundred and forty-nine or to otherwise fail to comply with the provisions of said section, or for the commonwealth and any of its boards, departments and commissions to deny vacation credit to any female employee for the fiscal year during which she is absent due to a maternity leave taken in accordance with said section or to impose any other penalty as a result of a maternity leave of absence.

12. For any retail store which provides credit or charge account privileges to refuse to extend such privileges to a customer solely because said customer had attained age sixty-two or over.

13. For any person to directly or indirectly induce, attempt to induce, prevent, or attempt to prevent the sale, purchase, or rental of any dwelling or dwellings by:

(a) implicit or explicit representations regarding the entry or prospective entry into the neighborhood of a person or persons of a particular age, race, color, religion, sex, national or ethnic origin, or economic level or a handicapped person, or a person having a child, or implicit or explicit representations regarding the effects or consequences of any such entry or prospective entry;

(b) unrequested contact or communication with any person or persons, initiated by any means, for the purpose of so inducing or attempting to induce the sale, purchase, or rental of any dwelling or dwellings when he knew or, in the exercise of reasonable care, should have known that such unrequested solicitation would reasonably be associated by the persons solicited with the entry into the neighborhood of a person or persons of a particular age, race, color, religion, sex, national or ethnic origin, or economic level or a handicapped person, or a person having a child;

(c) implicit or explicit false representations regarding the availability of suitable housing within a particular neighborhood or area, or failure to disclose or offer to show all properties listed or held for sale or rent within a requested price or rental range, regardless of location; or

(d) false representations regarding the listing, prospective listing, sale, or prospective sale of any dwelling.

14. For any person furnishing credit or services to deny or terminate such credit or services or to adversely affect an individual's credit standing because of such individual's sex, marital status, age or sexual orientation, which shall not include persons whose sexual orientation involves minor children as the sex object; provided that in the case of age the following shall not be unlawful practices:

(1) an inquiry of age for the purpose of determining a pertinent element of creditworthiness;

(2) the use of empirically derived credit systems which consider age, provided such systems are based on demonstrably and statistically sound data and provided further that such systems do not assign a negative factor or score to any applicant who has reached age sixty-two;

(3) the offering of credit life insurance or credit disability insurance, in conjunction with any credit or services, to a limited age group;

(4) the denial of any credit or services to a person who has not attained the age of majority;

(5) the denial of any credit or services the duration of which exceeds the life expectancy of the applicant as determined by the most recent Individual Annuity Mortality Table; or

(6) the offering of more favorable credit terms to students, to persons aged eighteen to twenty-one, or to persons who have reached the age of sixty-two.

Any person who violates the provisions of this subsection shall be liable in an action of contract for actual damages; provided, however, that, if there are no actual damages, the court may assess special damages to the aggrieved party not to exceed one thousand dollars; and provided further, that any person who has been found to violate a provision of this subsection by a court of competent jurisdiction shall be assessed the cost of reasonable legal fees actually incurred.

15. For any person responsible for recording the name of or establishing the personal identification of an individual for any purpose, including that of extending credit, to require such individual to use, because of such individual's sex or marital status, any surname other than the one by which such individual is generally known.

16. For any employer, personally or through an agent, to dismiss from employment or refuse to hire, rehire or advance in employment or otherwise discriminate against, because of his handicap, any person alleging to be a qualified handicapped person, capable of performing the essential functions of the position involved with reasonable accommodation, unless the employer can demonstrate that the accommodation required to be made to the physical or mental limitations of the person would impose an undue hardship to the employer's business. For purposes of this subsection, the word employer shall include an agency which employs individuals directly for the purpose of furnishing part-time or temporary help to others.

In determining whether an accommodation would impose an undue hardship on the conduct of the employer's business, factors to be considered include:—

(1) the overall size of the employer's business with respect to the number of employees, number and type of facilities, and size of budget or available assets;

(2) the type of the employer's operation, including the composition and structure of the employer's workforce; and

(3) the nature and cost of the accommodation needed.

Physical or mental job qualification requirement with respect to hiring, promotion, demotion or dismissal from employment or any other change in employment status or responsibilities shall be functionally related to the specific job or jobs for which the individual is being considered and shall be consistent with the safe and lawful performance of the job.

An employer may not make preemployment inquiry of an applicant as to whether the applicant is a handicapped individual or as to the nature or severity of the handicap, except that an employer may condition an offer of employment on the results of a medical examination conducted solely for the purpose of determining whether the employee, with reasonable accommodation, is capable of performing the essential functions of the job, and an employer may invite applicants to voluntarily disclose their handicap for purposes of assisting the employer in its affirmative action efforts.

16A. For an employer, personally or through its agents, to sexually harass any employee.

17. Notwithstanding any provision of this chapter, it shall not be an unlawful employment practice for any person, employer, labor organization or employment agency to:

(a) observe the terms of a bona fide seniority system or any bona fide employee benefit plan such as a retirement, pension, or insurance plan, which is not a subterfuge to evade the purposes of this section, except that no such employee benefit plan shall excuse the failure to hire any person, and no such seniority system or employee benefit plan shall require or permit the involuntary retirement of any person because of age except as permitted by paragraph (b).

(b) require the compulsory retirement of any person who has attained the age of sixty-five and who, for the two year period immediately before retirement, is employed in a bona fide executive or high policymaking position, if such person [is] entitled to an immediate nonforfeitable annual retirement benefit from a pension, profit-sharing, savings or deferred compensation plan, or any combination of such plans, of the employer, which equals, in the aggregate, at least forty-four thousand dollars.

(c) require the retirement of any employee who has attained seventy years of age and who is serving under a contract of unlimited tenure or similar arrangement providing for unlimited tenure at an independent institution of higher education, or to limit the employment in a faculty capacity of such an employee, or another person who has attained seventy years of age who was formerly employed under a contract of unlimited tenure or similar arrangement, to such terms and to such a period as would serve the present and future needs of the institution, as determined by it; provided, however, that in making such a determination, no institution shall use as a qualification for employment or reemployment, the fact that the individual is under any particular age.

18. For the owner, lessee, sublessee, licensed real estate broker, assignee, or managing agent of publicly assisted or multiple dwelling or contiguously located housing accommodations or other covered housing accommodations, or other person having the right of ownership or possession, or right to rent or lease, or sell or negotiate for the sale of such accommodations, or any agent or employee of such person or any organization of unit owners in a condominium or housing cooperative to sexually harass any tenant, prospective tenant, purchaser or prospective purchaser of property.

Notwithstanding the foregoing provisions of this section, it shall not be an unlawful employment practice for any person, employer, labor organization or employment agency to inquire of an applicant for employment or membership as to whether or not he or she is a veteran or a citizen.

Notwithstanding the provisions of any general or special law nothing herein shall be construed to bar any religious or denominational institution or organization, or any organization operated for charitable or educational purposes, which is operated, supervised or controlled by or in connection with a religious organization, from limiting admission to or giving preference to persons of the same religion or denomination or from taking any action with respect to matters of employment, discipline, faith, internal organization, or ecclesiastical rule, custom, or law which are calculated by such organization to promote the religious principles for which it is established or maintained.

Notwithstanding the foregoing provisions of this section, (a) every employer, every employment agency, including the division of employment and training, and every labor organization shall make and keep such records relating to race, color or national origin as the commission may prescribe from time to time by rule or regulation, after public hearing, as reasonably necessary for the purpose of showing compliance with the requirements of this chapter, and

(b) every employer and labor organization may keep and maintain such records and make such reports as may from time to time be necessary to comply, or show compliance with, any executive order issued by the President of the United States or any rules or regulations issued thereunder prescribing fair employment practices for contractors and subcontractors under contract with the United States, or, if not subject to such order, in the manner prescribed therein and subject to the jurisdiction of the commission. Such requirements as the commission may, by rule or regulation, prescribe for the making and keeping of records under clause (a) shall impose no greater burden or requirement on the employer, employment agency or labor organization subject thereto, than the comparable requirements which could be prescribed by Federal rule or regulation so long as no such requirements have in fact been prescribed, or which have in fact been prescribed for an employer, employment agency or labor organization under the authority of the Civil Rights Act of 1964 [42 U.S.C.A. §2000a] from time to time amended. This paragraph shall apply only to employers who on each working day in each of twenty or more calendar weeks in the annual period ending with each date set forth below, employed more employees than the number set forth beside such date, and to labor organizations which have more members on each such working day during such period.

Period Ending	*Minimum Employees or Members*
June 30, 1965	100
June 30, 1966	75
June 30, 1967	50
June 30, 1968 and thereafter	25

Nothing contained in this chapter or in any rule or regulation issued by the commission shall be interpreted as requiring any employer, employment agency or labor organization to grant preferential treatment to any individual or to any group because of the race, color, religious creed, national origin, sex, sexual orientation, which shall not include persons whose sexual orientation involves minor children as the sex object, age, genetic information or ancestry of such individual or group because of imbalance which may exist between the total number or percentage of persons employed by any employer, referred or classified for employment by any employment agency or labor organization, admitted to membership or classified by any labor organization or admitted to or employed in, any apprenticeship or other training program, and the total number or percentage of persons of such race, color, religious creed, national origin, sex, sexual orientation, which shall not include persons whose sexual orientation involves minor children as the sex object, age, genetic information or ancestry in the commonwealth or in any community, section or other area therein, or in the available work force in the commonwealth or in any of its political subdivisions.

19. (a) It shall be unlawful discrimination for any employer, employment agency, labor organization, or licensing agency to

(1) refuse to hire or employ, represent, grant membership to, or license a person on the basis of that person's genetic information;

(2) collect, solicit or require disclosure of genetic information from any person as a condition of employment, or membership, or of obtaining a license;

(3) solicit submission to, require, or administer a genetic test to any person as a condition of employment, membership, or obtaining a license;

(4) offer a person an inducement to undergo a genetic test or otherwise disclose genetic information;

(5) question a person about their genetic information or genetic information concerning their family members, or inquire about previous genetic testing;

(6) use the results of a genetic test or other genetic information to affect the terms, conditions, compensation or privileges of a person's employment, representation, membership, or the ability to obtain a license;

(7) terminate or refuse to renew a per-son's employment, representation, membership, or license on the basis of a genetic test or other genetic information; or

(8) otherwise seek, receive, or maintain genetic information for non-medical purposes.

(Stat. 1946, ch. 368, §4; Stat. 1947, ch. 424; Stat. 1950, ch. 697, §§6 to 8; Stat. 1955, ch. 274; Stat. 1957, ch. 426, §§2, 3; Stat. 1959, ch. 239, §2; Stat. 1960, ch. 163, §2; Stat. 1961, ch. 128; Stat. 1963, ch. 197, §2; Stat. 1965, ch. 213, §2; Stat. 1965, ch. 397, §§4 to 6; Stat. 1966, ch. 361; Stat. 1969, ch. 90; Stat. 1969, ch. 314; Stat. 1971, ch. 661; Stat. 1971, ch. 726; Stat. 1971, ch. 874, §§1 to 3; Stat. 1972, ch. 185; Stat. 1972, ch. 428; Stat. 1972, ch. 542; Stat. 1972, ch. 786, §2; Stat. 1972, ch. 790, §2; Stat. 1973, ch. 168; Stat. 1973, ch. 187, §§1 to 3; Stat. 1973, ch. 325; Stat. 1973, ch. 701, §1; Stat. 1973, ch. 929; Stat. 1973, ch. 1015, §§1 to 3; Stat. 1974, ch. 531; Stat. 1975, ch. 84; Stat. 1975, ch. 367, §3; Stat. 1975, ch. 637, §§1, 2; Stat. 1978, ch. 89; Stat. 1978, ch. 288, §§1, 2; Stat. 1979, ch. 710, §2; Stat. 1980, ch. 343; Stat. 1983, ch. 533, §§4 to 6; Stat. 1983, ch. 585, §7; Stat. 1983, ch. 628, §§1 to 3; Stat. 1984, ch. 266, §§5 to 7; Stat. 1985, ch. 239; Stat. 1986, ch. 588, §3; Stat. 1987, ch. 270, §§1, 2; Stat. 1987, ch. 773, §11; Stat. 1989, ch. 516, §§4 to 7 and 9 to 14; Stat. 1989, ch. 544; Stat. 1989, ch. 722, §§13 to 23; Stat. 1990, ch. 177, §341; Stat. 1990, ch. 283, §§1, 2; Stat. 1996, ch. 262; Stat. 1997, ch. 2, §2; Stat. 1997, ch. 19, §§105, 106; Stat. 1998, ch. 161, §532; Stat. 2000, ch. 254, §§6 to 23A; Stat. 2001, ch. 11, §§1, 2.)

Massachusetts General Laws

Ch. 175

§4C. Insurers may not discriminate in provision of homeowners insurance

No insurer licensed to write and engaged in the writing of homeowners insurance in this commonwealth nor the joint underwriting association, formed pursuant to the provisions of chapter one hundred and seventy-five C, shall take into consideration when deciding whether to provide, renew, or cancel homeowners insurance the race, color, religious creed, national origin, sex, age, ancestry, sexual orientation, children, marital status, veteran status, the receipt of public assistance or disability of the applicant or insured. Nothing herein shall preempt any existing remedy provided by law for any action that constitutes a violation of this section.
(Stat. 1996, ch. 93, §3.)

§22E. Insurers may not discriminate in provision of motor vehicle liability policy

No insurance company, and no officer or agent thereof in its behalf, shall refuse to issue, renew or execute as surety a motor vehicle liability policy or bond, or any other insurance based on the ownership or operation of a motor vehicle because of age, sex, race, occupation, marital status, or principal place of garaging of the vehicle. A particular company may make a general reduction in volume of automobile insurance in the commonwealth if such a reduction is determined by the commissioner not to be an attempt to circumvent the purposes of this section and that the company's refusal to write motor vehicle liability policies or bonds is not contrary to the public interest by disrupting the market for said insurance in the commonwealth. Any company which does not intend to issue a renewal policy shall give written notice of its intent not to issue a policy for the ensuing policy period in accordance with the provisions of section one hundred and thirteen F and such notice shall specify the reasons for such nonrenewal.
(Stat. 1970, ch. 670, §8; Stat. 1970, ch. 744, §1; Stat. 1973, ch. 551, §2; Stat. 1976, ch. 266, §9; Stat. 1983, ch. 241, §9; Stat. 1983, ch. 596, §2.)

D. Tort and Criminal Law

1. Tort Actions Involving Third Parties

a. Generally

The common law imposed many legal disabilities on a married woman. These disabilities stemmed from the principle, as stated by Blackstone, that the husband and wife became one upon marriage. 1 William Blackstone, Commentaries 442-445.

Among these disabilities, the wife's personal property became the property of her husband (he also acquired an estate in the wife's real property for the duration of the marriage); she could not make contracts; she could not sue or be sued without joining her husband; she could not make a will or enter into contracts except as her husband's agent; and the husband was liable for the wife's premarital debts as well as for torts she committed before or during the marriage. Married women's legal status changed in the mid- to late-nineteenth century when many states passed "married women's property acts." See generally Mary Lynn Salmon, Women and the Law of Property in Early America (1986).

The Massachusetts' married women's property legislation dates from 1845. According to that legislation, a married woman may sue and be sued in her own right. However, the provision authorizes interspousal suits only in limited circumstances. See also Tort Actions Between Spouses, Section D2, *infra*.

Massachusetts General Laws

Ch. 209

§6. A married woman may sue and be sued

A married woman may sue and be sued in the same manner as if she were sole; but this section shall not authorize suits between husband and wife except in connection with contracts entered into pursuant to the authority contained in section two.
(Stat. 1845, ch. 208, §5; Stat. 1855, ch. 304, §§2, 4; Stat. 1857, ch. 249, §3; G.S. 1860, ch. 108, §8; Stat. 1871, ch. 312; Stat. 1874, ch. 184, §3; P.S. 1882, ch. 147, §7; R.L. 1902, ch. 153, §6; Stat. 1963, ch. 765, §2.)

b. Torts for Interference with the Marital Relationship

The common law made interference with the marital relationship remediable by tort actions (such as for alienation of affection and criminal conversation). Alienation of affection requires: a valid marriage, wrongful conduct by the defendant with the plaintiff's spouse, the loss of affection or consortium, and a causal connection between the defendant's conduct and the deprivation of affection. Restatement (Second) of Torts §683 (1977). Unlike alienation of affection, criminal conversation requires sexual intercourse. *Id.* at §685.

Many jurisdictions have abolished these tort actions by anti-heart balm legislation. Massachusetts abolished recovery for alienation of affection and criminal conversation by statute in 1985 (Mass. Gen. Laws ch. 207, §47B). Only seven states continue to recognize the former claim (Hawaii, Illinois, Mississippi, New Mexico, North Carolina, South Dakota, and Utah). See Helsel v. Noellsch, 107 S.W.3d 231, 235 (Mo. 2003) (invalidating Missouri statute and surveying jurisdictions).

The law also recognizes tort claims for loss of consortium arising out of familial relationships. Consortium includes companionship, affection, society, and (between spouses) sexual relations. Massachusetts recognizes several types of consortium claims: (1) a spouse has a claim for loss of consortium arising from injury to the other spouse caused by a third party's negligence, (2) a spouse has a claim for loss of consortium arising from injury to the other spouse caused by a third party's intentional misconduct, (3) a parent of a minor or adult dependent child has a claim for loss of consortium, (4) a minor dependent child has a claim for loss of consortium for injury to a parent, (5) a disabled adult dependent child living in the injured parent's home has a consortium claim caused by a third party's negligent injury to the child's parent, (6) a viable or non-viable fetus (provided that the fetus is subsequently born alive) has a consortium claim for a parent's subsequent injury caused by a third party's negligence, and (7) a child born after a parent's wrongful death has a claim for loss of consortium. Kindregan & Inker, *supra*, at §16.7 (citing authority).

However, a surviving spouse has no claim against the deceased spouse's estate for loss of consortium if the decedent's death was caused by the decedent's negligence. *Id.* See also Comeau v. Currier, 616 N.E.2d 1091 (Mass. App. Ct. 1993) (holding that husband's degree of negligence should not be considered in wife's consortium claim because the latter's claim was independent of the injured spouse's claim) (cited in Kindregan & Inker, *supra*).

Massachusetts General Laws

Ch. 207

§47B. Abolition of claims for alienation of affection and criminal conversation

Alienation of affection and criminal conversation shall not constitute an injury or wrong recognized by law, and no action, suit or proceeding shall be maintained therefor.
(Stat. 1985, ch. 274, §1.)

2. Tort Actions Between Spouses

Common law recognized the doctrine of interspousal immunity based on the legal fiction that husband and wife share the same identity in law. According to the interspousal immunity doctrine, spouses could not maintain tort actions against each other. The history of this doctrine reflects a century of primarily judicial, rather than legislative, reform. The movement for abrogation occurred first for intentional acts and, subsequently, for negligence. See generally Carl Tobias, Interspousal Tort Immunity in America, 23 Ga. L. Rev. 359 (1989).

Massachusetts courts abolished the interspousal immunity doctrine initially in the context of motor vehicle accidents (Lewis v. Lewis, 351 N.E.2d 526 (1976)). Later, the doctrine was abolished for negligence claims (Brown v. Brown, 409 N.E.2d 717 (1980)), and subsequently for the intentional tort of assault and battery (Knobel-Aronova v. Knobel, 1987 Mass. App. Div. 75 (1987)). See Howard J. Alperin & Lawrence D. Shubow, 14C Mass. Prac. Summary of Basic Law §20.269 (3d ed. 2003).

On tort actions in the context of domestic violence, see Section G, Domestic Violence, *infra*.

Massachusetts General Laws

Ch. 209

§2. A married woman may make contracts

A married woman may make contracts, oral and written, sealed and unsealed, in the same manner as if she were sole, and may make such contracts with her husband.
(Stat. 1976, ch. 765, §1.)

§6. A married woman may sue and be sued

A married woman may sue and be sued in the same manner as if she were sole; but this section shall not authorize suits between husband and wife except in connection with contracts entered into pursuant to the authority contained in section two.
(Stat. 1845, ch. 208, §5; Stat. 1855, ch.304, §§2, 4; Stat. 1857, ch. 249, §3; G.S. 1860, ch. 108, §8; 1871, ch. 312; Stat. 1874, ch. 184, §3; P.S. 1882, ch. 147, §7; R.L. 1902, ch. 153, §6; Stat. 1963, ch. 765, §2.)

§9. Husband's liability regarding wife's contracts relative to her separate property

Contracts made by a married woman relative to her separate property, trade, business, or labor or services shall not bind her husband or render him or his property liable therefore; but she and her separate property shall be liable on such contracts in the same manner as if she were sole.
(Stat. 1974, ch. 147, §3.)

3. Crime of Marital Rape

Marital rape is a form of domestic violence. Historically, a husband could not be convicted of raping his own wife based on the marital rape exemption. This common law rule rested on three theories: (1) the implied consent of a wife to sexual intercourse with her husband (Lord Matthew Hale's opinion in his treatise, Pleas of the Crown (1847)), (2) the property theory (the wife was considered the property of the husband to do with as he wished), and (3) the merger theory (husband and wife were one, and a husband could not be convicted of raping himself). Steven A. Morley & Jay Shapiro, Prosecution and Defense of Spouse Abuse and Marital Rape, in The Prosecution and Defense of Sex Crimes §12.03 (Anthony B. Molosco ed., Supp. 2001).

Feminist calls for reform in the 1970s led to significant changes in rape law. Most states reformed their marital rape laws by statute rather than case law. But cf. Warren v. State, 336 S.E.2d 221 (Ga. 1985), *on remand*, 363 S.E.2d 357 (Ga. Ct. App. 1987); People v. Liberta, 474 N.E.2d 567 (N.Y. 1984), *cert. denied*, 471 U.S. 1020 (1985). One commentator criticizes the reform movement by suggesting that, despite the law reform movement, most states still retain some form of special treatment for marital rapists. Jill Elaine Hasday, Contest and Consent: A Legal History of Marital Rape, 88 Calif. L. Rev. 1373, 1375 (2000).

Massachusetts became the first state to recognize the marital rape exemption in Commonwealth v. Fogerty, 74 Mass. 489, 491 (1857). See Esther M.

Bixler, The Legal Effects of the Massachusetts Abuse Prevention Act, the Stalking Statute, and the Marital Rape Exemption on Victims of Domestic Abuse, 2 Suffolk J. Trial & App. Advoc. 79, 80 (1997).

Massachusetts abolished the marital rape exemption judicially in Commonwealth v. Chretien, 417 N.E.2d 1203 (Mass. 1981) (allowing prosecution of husband for raping wife during separation period after judgment *nisi*, reasoning that the rape law reform of 1974 abandoned the common law spousal exemption and finding legislative intent in the 1978 enactment of the Domestic Violence Act (Mass. Gen. Laws ch. 209, §3) which defined abuse to include marital rape).

Massachusetts General Laws

Ch. 265

§22. Rape defined

(a) Whoever has sexual intercourse or unnatural sexual intercourse with a person, and compels such person to submit by force and against his will, or compels such person to submit by threat of bodily injury and if either such sexual intercourse or unnatural sexual intercourse results in or is committed with acts resulting in serious bodily injury, or is committed by a joint enterprise, or is committed during the commission or attempted commission of an offense defined in section fifteen A, fifteen B, seventeen, nineteen or twenty-six of this chapter, section fourteen, fifteen, sixteen, seventeen or eighteen of chapter two hundred and sixty-six or section ten of chapter two hundred and sixty-nine shall be punished by imprisonment in the state prison for life or for any term of years.

No person serving a sentence for a second or subsequent such offense shall be eligible for furlough, temporary release, or education, training or employment programs established outside a correctional facility until such person shall have served two-thirds of such minimum sentence or if such person has two or more sentences to be served otherwise than concurrently, two-thirds of the aggregate of the minimum terms of such several sentences.

(b) Whoever has sexual intercourse or unnatural sexual intercourse with a person and compels such person to submit by force and against his will, or compels such person to submit by threat of bodily injury, shall be punished by imprisonment in the state prison for not more than twenty years; and whoever commits a second or subsequent such offense shall be punished by imprisonment in the state prison for life or for any term [of] years.

Whoever commits any offense described in this section while being armed with a firearm, rifle, shotgun, machine-gun or assault weapon, shall be punished by imprisonment in the state prison for not less than ten years. Whoever commits a second or subsequent such offense shall be punished by imprisonment in the state prison for life or for any term of years, but not less than 15 years.

No person serving a sentence for a second or subsequent such offense shall be eligible for furlough, temporary release, or education, training or employment programs established outside a correctional facility until such person shall have served two-thirds of such minimum sentence or if such person has two or more sentences to be served otherwise than concurrently, two-thirds of the aggregate of the minimum terms of such several sentences.

For the purposes of prosecution, the offense described in subsection (b) shall be a lesser included offense to that described in subsection (a).

(C.L. 15, §15; Stat. 1697, ch. 18; Stat. 1784, ch. 68; Stat. 1805, ch. 97, §1; R.S. 1836, ch. 125, §18; Stat. 1852, ch. 259, §2; G.S. 1860, ch. 160, §26; Stat. 1871, ch. 55; P.S. 1882, ch. 202, §27; Stat. 1886, ch. 305; Stat. 1888, ch. 391; Stat. 1893, ch. 466, §1; R.L. 1902, ch. 207, §22; Stat. 1974, ch. 474, §1; Stat. 1980, ch. 459, §6; Stat. 1998, ch. 180, §59.)

4. Wiretapping

Spouses sometimes conduct unauthorized eavesdropping to discover evidence of a spouse's extramarital affair. In such situations, two primary legal issues arise: (1) interspousal civil and/or criminal liability under federal or state law; and (2) the admissibility of the illegally obtained evidence in any ensuing dissolution proceedings. The latter issue has receded in importance with the advent of no-fault divorce (although admissibility issues may still surface in the custody context).

At the federal level, Title III of the Omnibus Crime Control Act, 18 U.S.C. §§2510 et seq., was enacted to protect individuals from nonconsensual interception of wire or oral communications. With various exceptions (i.e., law enforcement orders by court order and agents of the communications common carrier to protect the property rights of the carrier), the Act imposes civil and criminal liability by the creation of a new tort, a new crime, and evidentiary rules excluding use of the contents. The Act entitles an injured party to recover actual damages of a minimum of $100 per day for each day of violation or $10,000, whichever is greater, plus punitive damages, reasonable attorneys' fees, and litigation costs. For the provisions of the federal Act, see Part II of this Code *infra*.

A majority of the federal courts of appeal (i.e., Fourth, Sixth, Eighth, Tenth, and Eleventh Circuits) apply Title III to impose liability for spousal wiretapping. See Pritchard v. Pritchard, 732 F.2d 372 (4th Cir. 1984); United States v. Jones, 542 F.2d 661 (6th Cir. 1976); Kempf v. Kempf, 868 F.2d 970 (8th Cir. 1989); Heggy v. Heggy, 944 F.2d 1537 (10th Cir. 1991); Glazner v. Glazner, 347 F.3d 1212 (11th Cir. 2003). But cf. Anonymous v. Anonymous, 558 F.2d 677 (2nd Cir. 1977).

Many states have wiretapping acts that are modeled on the federal Act. The Massachusetts legislation is set forth at Massachusetts General Laws §99 *infra*. Some state statutes provide an exception to the wiretapping statute in cases of domestic violence. For example, at the request of a victim of domestic violence who is seeking a restraining order, California statute provides that a judge may permit the victim to record communications that the abuser makes to the victim (Cal. Penal Code §633.6).

Parental wiretapping is a controversial issue: the right of a parent to intercept a child's telephone conversations with the other parent. The issue often arises in the context of custody disputes when one parent tries to gather adverse evidence about the other parent's parenting abilities. Parental wiretapping first surfaced in Anonymous v. Anonymous, 558 F.2d 677 (2d Cir. 1977) (holding that a custodial father who recorded his children's conversations with their mother was exempt from liability under the extension exemption of the federal Wiretap Act based on the reasoning that the use of an extension phone in one's home is "certainly . . . in the 'ordinary course of (the user's) business.' " *Id.* at 678-679 (citation omitted). See also Pollock v. Pollock, 154 F.3d 601, 607 (6th Cir. 1998) (holding that guardian who has good faith belief that recording child's telephone conversations is in child's best interests may vicariously consent to recording on child's behalf but that genuine issue of material fact as to whether mother was motivated by child's best interests precluded summary judgment).

See generally Laura S. Killian, Note, Concerned or Just Plain Nosy? The Consequences of Parental Wiretapping Under the Federal Wiretap Act in Light of Pollock v. Pollock, 104 Dick. L. Rev. 561 (2000); Deana A. Labriola, Comment, Parent-Child Wiretapping: Is Title III Enough?, 50 Cath. U. L. Rev. 429 (2001).

Massachusetts General Laws

Ch. 272

§99. Interception of wire and oral communications: Wiretap legislation

Interception of wire and oral communications.—

(Stat. 1992, ch. 31; Stat. 1996, ch. 298, §§11, 12; Stat. 1997, ch. 238, §§1, 2.)

A. Preamble.

The general court finds that organized crime exists within the commonwealth and that the increasing activities of organized crime constitute a grave danger to the public welfare and safety. Organized crime, as it exists in the commonwealth today, consists of a continuing conspiracy among highly organized and disciplined groups to engage in supplying illegal goods and services. In supplying these goods and services organized crime commits unlawful acts and employs brutal and violent tactics. Organized crime is infiltrating legitimate business activities and depriving honest businessmen of the right to make a living.

The general court further finds that because organized crime carries on its activities through layers of insulation and behind a wall of secrecy, government has been unsuccessful in curtailing and eliminating it. Normal investigative procedures are not effective in the investigation of illegal acts committed by organized crime. Therefore, law enforcement officials must be permitted to use modern methods of electronic surveillance, under strict judicial supervision, when investigating these organized criminal activities.

The general court further finds that the uncontrolled development and unrestricted use of modern electronic surveillance devices pose grave dangers to the privacy of all citizens of the commonwealth. Therefore, the secret use of such devices by private individuals must be prohibited. The use of such devices by law enforcement officials must be conducted under strict judicial supervision and should be limited to the investigation of organized crime.

B. Definitions. As used in this section—

1. The term "wire communication" means any communication made in whole or in part through the use of facilities for the transmission of communications by the aid of wire, cable, or other like connection between the point of origin and the point of reception.

2. The term "oral communication" means speech, except such speech as is transmitted over the public air waves by radio or other similar device.

3. The term "intercepting device" means any device or apparatus which is capable of transmitting, receiving, amplifying, or recording a wire or oral communication other than a hearing aid or similar device which is being used to correct subnormal hearing to normal and other than any telephone or telegraph instrument, equipment, facility, or a component thereof,

(a) furnished to a subscriber or user by a communications common carrier in the ordinary course of its business under its tariff and being used by the subscriber or user in the ordinary course of its business; or

(b) being used by a communications common carrier in the ordinary course of its business.

4. The term "interception" means to secretly hear, secretly record, or aid another to secretly hear or secretly record the contents of any wire or oral communication through the use of any intercepting device by any person other than a person given prior authority by all parties to such communication; provided that it shall not constitute an interception for an investigative or law enforcement officer, as defined in this section, to record or transmit a wire or oral communication if the officer is a party to such communication or has been given prior authorization to record or transmit the communication by such a party and if recorded or transmitted in the course of an investigation of a designated offense as defined herein.

5. The term "contents", when used with respect to any wire or oral communication, means any information concerning the identity of the parties to such communication or the existence, contents, substance, purport, or meaning of that communication.

6. The term "aggrieved person" means any individual who was a party to an intercepted wire or oral communication or who was named in the warrant authorizing the interception, or who would otherwise have standing to complain that his personal or property interest or privacy was invaded in the course of an interception.

7. The term "designated offense" shall include the following offenses in connection with organized crime as defined in the preamble: arson, assault and battery with a dangerous weapon, extortion, bribery, burglary, embezzlement, forgery, gaming in violation of section seventeen of chapter two hundred and seventy-one of the general laws, intimidation of a witness or juror, kidnapping, larceny, lending of money or things of value in violation of the general laws, mayhem, murder, any offense involving the possession or sale of a narcotic or harmful drug, perjury, prostitution, robbery, subornation of perjury, any violation of this section, being an accessory to any of the foregoing offenses and conspiracy or attempt or solicitation to commit any of the foregoing offenses.

8. The term "investigative or law enforcement officer" means any officer of the United States, a state or a political subdivision of a state, who is empowered by law to

conduct investigations of, or to make arrests for, the designated offenses, and any attorney authorized by law to participate in the prosecution of such offenses.

9. The term "judge of competent jurisdiction" means any justice of the superior court of the commonwealth.

10. The term "chief justice" means the chief justice of the superior court of the commonwealth.

11. The term "issuing judge" means any justice of the superior court who shall issue a warrant as provided herein or in the event of his disability or unavailability any other judge of competent jurisdiction designated by the chief justice.

12. The term "communication common carrier" means any person engaged as a common carrier in providing or operating wire communication facilities.

13. The term "person" means any individual, partnership, association, joint stock company, trust, or corporation, whether or not any of the foregoing is an officer, agent or employee of the United States, a state, or a political subdivision of a state.

14. The terms "sworn" or "under oath" as they appear in this section shall mean an oath or affirmation or a statement subscribed to under the pains and penalties of perjury.

15. The terms "applicant attorney general" or "applicant district attorney" shall mean the attorney general of the commonwealth or a district attorney of the commonwealth who has made application for a warrant pursuant to this section.

16. The term "exigent circumstances" shall mean the showing of special facts to the issuing judge as to the nature of the investigation for which a warrant is sought pursuant to this section which require secrecy in order to obtain the information desired from the interception sought to be authorized.

17. The term "financial institution" shall mean a bank, as defined in section 1 of chapter 167, and an investment bank, securities broker, securities dealer, investment adviser, mutual fund, investment company or securities custodian as defined in section 1.165-12(c)(1) of the United States Treasury regulations.

18. The term "corporate and institutional trading partners" shall mean financial institutions and general business entities and corporations which engage in the business of cash and asset management, asset management directed to custody operations, securities trading, and wholesale capital markets including foreign exchange, securities lending, and the purchase, sale or exchange of securities, options, futures, swaps, derivatives, repurchase agreements and other similar financial instruments with such financial institution.

C. Offenses.

1. Interception, oral communications prohibited.

Except as otherwise specifically provided in this section any person who—

willfully commits an interception, attempts to commit an interception, or procures any other person to commit an interception or to attempt to commit an interception of any wire or oral communication shall be fined not more than ten thousand dollars, or imprisoned in the state prison for not more than five years, or imprisoned in a jail or house of correction for not more than two and one half years, or both so fined and given one such imprisonment.

Proof of the installation of any intercepting device by any person under circumstances evincing an intent to commit an interception, which is not authorized or permitted by this section, shall be prima facie evidence of a violation of this subparagraph.

2. Editing of tape recordings in judicial proceeding prohibited.

Except as otherwise specifically provided in this section any person who willfully edits, alters or tampers with any tape, transcription or recording of oral or wire communications by any means, or attempts to edit, alter or tamper with any tape, transcription or recording of oral or wire communications by any means with the intent to present in any judicial proceeding or proceeding under oath, or who presents such recording or permits such recording to be presented in any judicial proceeding or proceeding under oath, without fully indicating the nature of the changes made in the original state of the recording, shall be fined not more than ten thousand dollars or imprisoned in the state prison for not more than five years or imprisoned in a jail or house of correction for not more than two years or both so fined and given one such imprisonment.

3. Disclosure or use of wire or oral communications prohibited.

Except as otherwise specifically provided in this section any person who—

a. willfully discloses or attempts to disclose to any person the contents of any wire or oral communication, knowing that the information was obtained through interception; or

b. willfully uses or attempts to use the contents of any wire or oral communication, knowing that the information was obtained through interception, shall be guilty of a misdemeanor punishable by imprisonment in a jail or a house of correction for not more than two years or by a fine of not more than five thousand dollars or both.

4. Disclosure of contents of applications, warrants, renewals, and returns prohibited.

Except as otherwise specifically provided in this section any person who—

willfully discloses to any person, any information concerning or contained in, the application for, the granting or denial of orders for interception, renewals, notice or return on an ex parte order granted pursuant to this section, or the contents of any document, tape, or recording kept in accordance with paragraph N, shall be guilty of a misdemeanor punishable by imprisonment in a jail or a house of correction for not more than two years or by a fine of not more than five thousand dollars or both.

5. Possession of interception devices prohibited.

A person who possesses any intercepting device under circumstances evincing an intent to commit an interception not permitted or authorized by this section, or a person who permits an intercepting device to be used or employed for an interception not permitted or authorized by this section, or a person who possesses an intercepting device knowing that the same is intended to be used to commit an interception not permitted or authorized by this section, shall be guilty of a misdemeanor punishable by imprisonment in a jail or house of correction for not more than two years or by a fine of not more than five thousand dollars or both.

The installation of any such intercepting device by such person or with his permission or at his direction shall be prima facie evidence of possession as required by this subparagraph.

6. Any person who permits or on behalf of any other person commits or attempts to commit, or any person who participates in a conspiracy to commit or to attempt to commit, or any accessory to a person who commits a violation of subparagraphs 1 through 5 of paragraph C of this section shall be punished in the same manner as is provided for the respective offenses as described in subparagraphs 1 through 5 of paragraph C.

D. Exemptions.

1. Permitted interception of wire or oral communications.

It shall not be a violation of this section—

a. for an operator of a switchboard, or an officer, employee, or agent of any communication common carrier, whose facilities are used in the transmission of a wire communication, to intercept, disclose, or use that communication in the normal course of his employment while engaged in any activity which is a necessary incident to the rendition of service or to the protection of the rights or property of the carrier of such communication, or which is necessary to prevent the use of such facilities in violation of section fourteen A of chapter two hundred and sixty-nine of the general laws; provided, that said communication common carriers shall not utilize service observing or random monitoring except for mechanical or service quality control checks.

b. for persons to possess an office intercommunication system which is used in the ordinary course of their business or to use such office intercommunication system in the ordinary course of their business.

c. for investigative and law enforcement officers of the United States of America to violate the provisions of this section if acting pursuant to authority of the laws of the United States and within the scope of their authority.

d. for any person duly authorized to make specified interceptions by a warrant issued pursuant to this section.

e. for investigative or law enforcement officers to violate the provisions of this section for the purposes of ensuring the safety of any law enforcement officer or agent thereof who is acting in an undercover capacity, or as a witness for the commonwealth; provided, however, that any such interception which is not otherwise permitted by this section shall be deemed unlawful for purposes of paragraph P.

f. for a financial institution to record telephone communications with its corporate or institutional trading partners in the ordinary course of its business; provided, however, that such financial institution shall establish and maintain a procedure to provide semi-annual written notice to its corporate and institutional trading partners that telephone communications over designated lines will be recorded.

2. Permitted disclosure and use of intercepted wire or oral communications.

a. Any investigative or law enforcement officer, who, by any means authorized by this section, has obtained knowledge of the contents of any wire or oral communication, or evidence derived therefrom, may disclose such contents or evidence in the proper performance of his official duties.

b. Any investigative or law enforcement officer, who, by any means authorized by this section has obtained knowledge of the contents of any wire or oral communication, or evidence derived therefrom, may use such contents or evidence in the proper performance of his official duties.

c. Any person who has obtained, by any means authorized by this section, knowledge of the contents of any wire or oral communication, or evidence derived therefrom, may disclose such contents while giving testimony under oath or affirmation in any criminal proceeding in any court of the United States or of any state or in any federal or state grand jury proceeding.

d. The contents of any wire or oral communication intercepted pursuant to a warrant in accordance with the provisions of this section, or evidence derived therefrom, may otherwise be disclosed only upon a showing of good cause before a judge of competent jurisdiction.

e. No otherwise privileged wire or oral communication intercepted in accordance with, or in violation of, the provisions of this section shall lose its privileged character.

E. Warrants: when issuable:

A warrant may issue only:

1. Upon a sworn application in conformity with this section; and

2. Upon a showing by the applicant that there is probable cause to believe that a designated offense has been, is being, or is about to be committed and that evidence of the commission of such an offense may thus be obtained or that information which will aid in the apprehension of a person who the applicant has probable cause to believe has committed, is committing, or is about to commit a designated offense may thus be obtained; and

3. Upon a showing by the applicant that normal investigative procedures have been tried and have failed or reasonably appear unlikely to succeed if tried.

F. Warrants: application.

1. Application. The attorney general, any assistant attorney general specially designated by the attorney general, any district attorney, or any assistant district attorney specially designated by the district attorney may apply ex parte to a judge of competent jurisdiction for a warrant to intercept wire or oral communications. Each application ex parte for a warrant must be in writing, subscribed and sworn to by the applicant authorized by this subparagraph.

2. The application must contain the following:

a. A statement of facts establishing probable cause to believe that a particularly described designated offense has been, is being, or is about to be committed; and

b. A statement of facts establishing probable cause to believe that oral or wire communications of a particularly described person will constitute evidence of such designated offense or will aid in the apprehension of a person who the applicant has probable cause to believe has committed, is committing, or is about to commit a designated offense; and

c. That the oral or wire communications of the particularly described person or persons will occur in a particularly described place and premises or over particularly described telephone or telegraph lines; and

d. A particular description of the nature of the oral or wire communications sought to be overheard; and

e. A statement that the oral or wire communications sought are material to a particularly described investigation or prosecution and that such conversations are not legally privileged; and

f. A statement of the period of time for which the interception is required to be maintained. If practicable, the application should designate hours of the day or night during which the oral or wire communications may be reasonably expected to occur. If the nature of the investigation is such that the authorization for the interception should not automatically terminate when the described oral or wire communications have been first obtained, the application must specifically state facts establishing probable cause to believe that additional oral or wire communications of the same nature will occur thereafter; and

g. If it is reasonably necessary to make a secret entry upon a private place and premises in order to install an intercepting device to effectuate the interception, a statement to such effect; and

h. If a prior application has been submitted or a warrant previously obtained for interception of oral or wire communications, a statement fully disclosing the date, court, applicant, execution, results, and present status thereof; and

i. If there is good cause for requiring the postponement of service pursuant to paragraph L, subparagraph 2, a description of such circumstances, including reasons for the applicant's belief that secrecy is essential to obtaining the evidence or information sought.

3. Allegations of fact in the application may be based either upon the personal knowledge of the applicant or upon information and belief. If the applicant personally knows the facts alleged, it must be so stated. If the facts establishing such probable cause are derived in whole or part from the statements of persons other than the applicant, the sources of such information and belief must be either disclosed or described; and the application must contain facts establishing the existence and reliability of any informant and the reliability of the information supplied by him. The application must also state, so far as possible, the basis of the informant's knowledge or belief. If the applicant's information and belief is derived from tangible evidence or recorded oral evidence, a copy or detailed description thereof should be annexed to or included in the application. Affidavits of persons other than the applicant may be submitted in conjunction with the application if they tend to support any fact or conclusion alleged therein. Such accompanying affidavits may be based either on personal knowledge of the affiant or information and belief, with the source thereof, and reason therefor, specified.

G. Warrants: application to whom made.

Application for a warrant authorized by this section must be made to a judge of competent jurisdiction in the county where the interception is to occur, or the county where the office of the applicant is located, or in the event that there is no judge of competent jurisdiction sitting in said county at such time, to a judge of competent jurisdiction sitting in Suffolk County; except that for these purposes, the office of the attorney general shall be deemed to be located in Suffolk County.

H. Warrants: application how determined.

1. If the application conforms to paragraph F, the issuing judge may examine under oath any person for the purpose of determining whether probable cause exists for the issuance of the warrant pursuant to paragraph E. A verbatim transcript of every such interrogation or examination must be taken, and a transcription of the same, sworn to by the stenographer, shall be attached to the application and be deemed a part thereof.

2. If satisfied that probable cause exists for the issuance of a warrant the judge may grant the application and issue a warrant in accordance with paragraph I. The application and an attested copy of the warrant shall be retained by the issuing judge and transported to the chief justice of the superior court in accordance with the provisions of paragraph N of this section.

3. If the application does not conform to paragraph F, or if the judge is not satisfied that probable cause has been shown sufficient for the issuance of a warrant, the application must be denied.

I. Warrants: form and content.

A warrant must contain the following:

1. The subscription and title of the issuing judge; and

2. The date of issuance, the date of effect, and termination date which in no event shall exceed thirty days from the date of effect. The warrant shall permit interception of oral or wire communications for a period not to exceed fifteen days. If physical installation of a device is necessary, the thirty- day period shall begin upon the date of installation. If the effective period of the warrant is to terminate upon the acquisition of particular evidence or information or oral or wire communication, the warrant shall so provide; and

3. A particular description of the person and the place, premises or telephone or telegraph line upon which the interception may be conducted; and

4. A particular description of the nature of the oral or wire communications to be obtained by the interception including a statement of the designated offense to which they relate; and

5. An express authorization to make secret entry upon a private place or premises to install a specified intercepting device, if such entry is necessary to execute the warrant; and

6. A statement providing for service of the warrant pursuant to paragraph L except that if there has been a finding of good cause shown requiring the postponement of such service, a statement of such finding together with the basis therefor must be included and an alternative direction for deferred service pursuant to paragraph L, subparagraph 2.

J. Warrants: renewals.

1. Any time prior to the expiration of a warrant or a renewal thereof, the applicant may apply to the issuing judge for a renewal thereof with respect to the same person, place, premises or telephone or telegraph line. An application for renewal must incorporate the warrant

sought to be renewed together with the application therefor and any accompanying papers upon which it was issued. The application for renewal must set forth the results of the interceptions thus far conducted. In addition, it must set forth present grounds for extension in conformity with paragraph F, and the judge may interrogate under oath and in such an event a transcript must be provided and attached to the renewal application in the same manner as is set forth in subparagraph 1 of paragraph H.

2. Upon such application, the judge may issue an order renewing the warrant and extending the authorization for a period not exceeding fifteen (15) days from the entry thereof. Such an order shall specify the grounds for the issuance thereof. The application and an attested copy of the order shall be retained by the issuing judge to be transported to the chief justice in accordance with the provisions of subparagraph N of this section. In no event shall a renewal be granted which shall terminate later than two years following the effective date of the warrant.

K. Warrants: manner and time of execution.

1. A warrant may be executed pursuant to its terms anywhere in the commonwealth.

2. Such warrant may be executed by the authorized applicant personally or by any investigative or law enforcement officer of the commonwealth designated by him for the purpose.

3. The warrant may be executed according to its terms during the hours specified therein, and for the period therein authorized, or a part thereof. The authorization shall terminate upon the acquisition of the oral or wire communications, evidence or information described in the warrant. Upon termination of the authorization in the warrant and any renewals thereof, the interception must cease at once, and any device installed for the purpose of the interception must be removed as soon thereafter as practicable. Entry upon private premises for the removal of such device is deemed to be authorized by the warrant.

L. Warrants: service thereof.

1. Prior to the execution of a warrant authorized by this section or any renewal thereof, an attested copy of the warrant or the renewal must, except as otherwise provided in subparagraph 2 of this paragraph, be served upon a person whose oral or wire communications are to be obtained, and if an intercepting device is to be installed, upon the owner, lessee, or occupant of the place or premises, or upon the subscriber to the telephone or owner or lessee of the telegraph line described in the warrant.

2. If the application specially alleges exigent circumstances requiring the postponement of service and the issuing judge finds that such circumstances exist, the warrant may provide that an attested copy thereof may be served within thirty days after the expiration of the warrant or, in case of any renewals thereof, within thirty days after the expiration of the last renewal; except that upon a showing of important special facts which set forth the need for continued secrecy to the satisfaction of the issuing judge, said judge may direct that the attested copy of the warrant be served on such parties as are required by this section at such time as may be appropriate in the circumstances but in no event may he order it to be served later than three (3) years from the time of expiration of the warrant or the last renewal thereof. In the event that the service required herein is postponed in accordance with this paragraph, in addition to the requirements of any other paragraph of this section, service of an attested copy of the warrant shall be made upon any aggrieved person who should reasonably be known to the person who executed or obtained the warrant as a result of the information obtained from the interception authorized thereby.

3. The attested copy of the warrant shall be served on persons required by this section by an investigative or law enforcement officer of the commonwealth by leaving the same at his usual place of abode, or in hand, or if this is not possible by mailing the same by certified or registered mail to his last known place of abode. A return of service shall be made to the issuing judge, except, that if such service is postponed as provided in subparagraph 2 of paragraph L, it shall be made to the chief justice. The return of service shall be deemed a part of the return of the warrant and attached thereto.

M. Warrant: return.

Within seven days after termination of the warrant or the last renewal thereof, a return must be made thereon to the judge issuing the warrant by the applicant therefor, containing the following:

a. a statement of the nature and location of the communications facilities, if any, and premise or places where the interceptions were made; and

b. the periods of time during which such interceptions were made; and

c. the names of the parties to the communications intercepted if known; and

d. the original recording of the oral or wire communications intercepted, if any; and

e. a statement attested under the pains and penalties of perjury by each person who heard oral or wire communications as a result of the interception authorized by the warrant, which were not recorded, stating everything that was overheard to the best of his recollection at the time of the execution of the statement.

N. Custody and secrecy of papers and recordings made pursuant to a warrant.

1. The contents of any wire or oral communication intercepted pursuant to a warrant issued pursuant to this section shall, if possible, be recorded on tape or wire or other similar device. Duplicate recordings may be made for use pursuant to subparagraphs 2 (a) and (b) of paragraph D for investigations. Upon examination of the return and a determination that it complies with this section, the issuing judge shall forthwith order that the application, all renewal applications, warrant, all renewal orders and the return thereto be transmitted to the chief justice by such persons as he shall designate. Their contents shall not be disclosed except as provided in this section. The application, renewal applications, warrant, the renewal order and the return or any one of them or any part of them may be transferred to any trial court, grand jury proceeding of any jurisdiction by any law enforcement or investigative officer or court officer designated by the chief justice and a trial justice may allow them to be disclosed in accordance with paragraph D, subparagraph 2, or paragraph O or any other applicable provision of this section.

The application, all renewal applications, warrant, all renewal orders and the return shall be stored in a secure place which shall be designated by the chief justice, to which access shall be denied to all persons except the chief justice or such court officers or administrative personnel of the court as he shall designate.

2. Any violation of the terms and conditions of any order of the chief justice, pursuant to the authority granted in this paragraph, shall be punished as a criminal contempt of court in addition to any other punishment authorized by law.

3. The application, warrant, renewal and return shall be kept for a period of five (5) years from the date of the issuance of the warrant or the last renewal thereof at which time they shall be destroyed by a person designated by the chief justice. Notice prior to the destruction shall be given to the applicant attorney general or his successor or the applicant district attorney or his successor and upon a showing of good cause to the chief justice, the application, warrant, renewal, and return may be kept for such additional period as the chief justice shall determine but in no event longer than the longest period of limitation for any designated offense specified in the warrant, after which time they must be destroyed by a person designated by the chief justice.

O. Introduction of evidence.

1. Notwithstanding any other provisions of this section or any order issued pursuant thereto, in any criminal trial where the commonwealth intends to offer in evidence any portions of the contents of any interception or any evidence derived therefrom the defendant shall be served with a complete copy of each document and item which make up each application, renewal application, warrant, renewal order, and return pursuant to which the information was obtained, except that he shall be furnished a copy of any recording instead of the original. The service must be made at the arraignment of the defendant or, if a period in excess of thirty (30) days shall elapse prior to the commencement of the trial of the defendant, the service may be made at least thirty (30) days before the commencement of the criminal trial. Service shall be made in hand upon the defendant or his attorney by any investigative or law enforcement officer of the commonwealth. Return of the service required by this subparagraph including the date of service shall be entered into the record of trial of the defendant by the commonwealth and such return shall be deemed prima facie evidence of the service described therein. Failure by the commonwealth to make such service at the arraignment, or if delayed, at least thirty days before the commencement of the criminal trial, shall render such evidence illegally obtained for purposes of the trial against the defendant; and such evidence shall not be offered nor received at the trial notwithstanding the provisions of any other law or rules of court.

2. In any criminal trial where the commonwealth intends to offer in evidence any portions of a recording or transmission or any evidence derived therefrom, made pursuant to the exceptions set forth in paragraph B, subparagraph 4, of this section, the defendant shall be served with a complete copy of each recording or a statement under oath of the evidence overheard as a result of the transmission. The service must be made at the arraignment of the defendant or if a period in excess of thirty days shall elapse prior to the commencement of the trial of the defendant, the service may be made at least thirty days before the commencement of the criminal trial. Service shall be made in hand upon the defendant or his attorney by any investigative or law enforcement officer of the commonwealth. Return of the service required by this subparagraph including the date of service shall be entered into the record of trial of the defendant by the common-wealth and such return shall be deemed prima facie evi-dence of the service described therein. Failure by the common-wealth to make such service at the arraignment, or if delayed at least thirty days before the commencement of the criminal trial, shall render such service illegally obtained for purposes of the trial against the defendant and such evi-dence shall not be offered nor received at the trial notwith-standing the provisions of any other law or rules of court.

P. Suppression of evidence.

Any person who is a defendant in a criminal trial in a court of the commonwealth may move to suppress the contents of any intercepted wire or oral communication or evidence derived therefrom, for the following reasons:

1. That the communication was unlawfully intercepted.

2. That the communication was not intercepted in accordance with the terms of this section.

3. That the application or renewal application fails to set forth facts sufficient to establish probable cause for the issuance of a warrant.

4. That the interception was not made in conformity with the warrant.

5. That the evidence sought to be introduced was illegally obtained.

6. That the warrant does not conform to the provisions of this section.

Q. Civil remedy.

Any aggrieved person whose oral or wire communications were intercepted, disclosed or used except as permitted or authorized by this section or whose personal or property interests or privacy were violated by means of an interception except as permitted or authorized by this section shall have a civil cause of action against any person who so intercepts, discloses or uses such communications or who so violates his personal, property or privacy interest, and shall be entitled to recover from any such person—

1. actual damages but not less than liquidated damages computed at the rate of $100 per day for each day of violation or $1000, whichever is higher;

2. punitive damages; and

3. a reasonable attorney's fee and other litigation disburse-ments reasonably incurred. Good faith reliance on a warrant issued under this section shall constitute a complete defense to an action brought under this paragraph.

R. Annual report of interceptions of the general court.

On the second Friday of January, each year, the attorney general and each district attorney shall submit a report to the general court stating

(1) the number of applications made for warrants during the previous year,

(2) the name of the applicant,

(3) the number of warrants issued,

(4) the effective period for the warrants,

(5) the number and designation of the offenses for which those applications were sought, and for each of the designated offenses the following:

(a) the number of renewals,

(b) the number of interceptions made during the previous year,

(c) the number of indictments believed to be obtained as a result of those interceptions,

(d) the number of criminal convictions obtained in trials where interception evidence or evidence derived therefrom was introduced. This report shall be a public document and be made available to the public at the offices of the attorney general and district attorneys. In the event of failure to comply with the provisions of this paragraph any person may compel compliance by means of an action of mandamus.

(Amended by Stat. 1959, ch. 449, §1; Stat. 1968, ch. 738, §1; Stat. 1986, ch. 557, §199; Stat. 1993, ch. 432, §13; Stat. 1998, ch. 163, §§7, 8.)

E. Evidentiary Privileges

Married persons are entitled to assert two evidentiary privileges. First, they may assert a privilege against disclosing adverse spousal testimony (so that one spouse will not be called as a witness against the other spouse or required to testify against the other spouse). Second, they may avoid the disclosure of confidential marital communications, i.e., private communications between husband and wife. Note that those communications made to the spouse in the presence of *third parties* do not merit the same protection as those between husband and wife. In Trammel v. United States, 445 U.S. 40 (1980), the United States Supreme Court held that the privilege to prevent communications made to the spouse in the presence of third parties was vested in the witness spouse. *Trammel* applies to criminal proceedings in the federal courts.

Massachusetts statute includes an *adverse spousal testimony privilege*. That statute provides that the spouse of a criminal defendant has a privilege not to be compelled to testify against the defendant (Mass. Gen. Laws ch. 233, §20). Certain exceptions exist, i.e., in child abuse proceedings (including incest) or in prosecutions for abandonment and nonsupport under Massachusetts General Laws ch. 273, §7. The privilege not to testify belongs to the spouse-witness. Thus, the spouse-witness may waive her privilege not to testify. Commonwealth v. Szczuka, 464 N.E.2d 38 (Mass. 1984) (holding that defendant was without standing to complain that waiver by his wife of a spousal privilege in testifying was not knowing). See also Kindregan & Inker, *supra*, at §16.4.

Note that many states include a "spousal-crime exception" to the adverse spousal testimony privilege. In domestic violence prosecutions, for example, such an exception would bar a defendant-husband from preventing his victim-wife from testifying against him. As of 2006, however, Massachusetts was one of a handful of states that do not include such an exception to the privilege. See R. Michael Cassidy, Reconsidering Spousal Privileges After *Crawford*, 33 Am. J. Crim. L. 339, 367-368 (2006).

A Massachusetts *rule of marital disqualification* prevents introduction of evidence of the contents of *private conversations between a husband and wife* (Mass. Gen. Laws ch. 233, §20). The Massachusetts doctrine is termed a rule of disqualification rather than privilege. Gallagher v. Goldstein, 524 N.E.2d 53 (Mass. 1988) (holding that husband was disqualified from testifying as to substance of private conversations with wife in a malpractice action against physician for failure to diagnose her stroke). Evidence of the contents of private conversations is inadmissible even if both spouses wish the evidence to be received. Anderson v. Barrera, 6 Mass. L. Rptr. 481 (Mass. Super. Ct. 1997) (refusing to apply the rule to a business transaction between a nurse-wife and her physician-husband regarding treatment of a patient).

Some *exceptions* to the marital disqualification rule exist. That is, spouses may testify as to conversations in proceedings regarding contracts made by a wife with her husband (Mass. Gen. Laws ch. 233, §20), and in actions for desertion and criminal nonsupport of a spouse or child (*id.*; Mass. Gen. Laws ch. 272, §1 (set forth *supra* in Section A1)); Mass. Gen. Laws ch. 273, §7). See also Commonwealth v. Sugrue, 607 N.E.2d 1045 (Mass. App. Ct. 1993) (holding that evidence of a private conversation between defendant and his wife in which defendant threatened to obtain custody of children in the event of divorce was admissible in prosecution for indecent assault and battery; defendant's constitutional rights of confrontation and cross-examination and his right to fair trial outweighed application of marital disqualification, where credible showing was made that conversation was material to presentation of defendant's case inasmuch as it provided motive for wife to lie about incident which gave rise to charges), *review denied*, 616 N.E.2d 469 (1993)).

Additional types of spousal communications are not disqualified. For example, spouses' *written* communications are not disqualified. Commonweath v. Szczuka, 464 N.E.2d 38, 46 (Mass. 1984) (finding no merit in defendant's claim that evidence in four letters to his wife should not have been admitted into evidence). Moreover, the disqualification does not apply to conversations in the presence of third parties. Commonwealth v. O'Brien, 388 N.E.2d 658 (Mass. 1979) (holding that statute did not exclude testimony by attorney who was present during conversation between husband and wife). Kindregan & Inker, Mass. Prac. Series Family Law and Practice, *supra*, at §16.5. Finally, declarations of a deceased person are admissible as hearsay or as private conversations between spouses (Mass. Gen. Laws ch. 233, §65).

The court in *Anderson*, *supra*, explains five historical and policy reasons for the rule of marital disqualification: (1) the husband and wife were considered one entity at common law, (2) a marital couple has only one interest and thus nothing could be gained by allowing a spouse to testify for or against the other, (3) a spouse would be biased and not testify truthfully, (4) allowing testimony would disturb marital peace, and (5) allowing a wife as a witness and subjecting her to cross-examination would result in marital disharmony. *Anderson*, *supra*.

See generally Katherine O. Eldred, "Every Spouse's Evidence": Availability of the Adverse Spousal Testimonial Privilege in Federal Civil Trials, 69 U. Chi. L. Rev. 1319 (2002); Christopher Mason, Recent Development, Brown v. State: Spousal Privilege Allows for the Confidentiality of Marital Communications By Bestowing a Privilege, Waivable Upon the Spouse Making the Communication, 31 U. Balt. L.F. 53 (2000).

Massachusetts General Laws

Ch. 233

§20. Competency of witnesses; adverse spousal testimony privilege

Any person of sufficient understanding, although a party, may testify in any proceeding, civil or criminal, in court or before a person who has authority to receive evidence, except as follows:

First, Except in a proceeding arising out of or involving a contract made by a married woman with her husband, a proceeding under chapter two hundred and nine D and in a prosecution begun under sections one to ten, inclusive, of chapter two hundred and seventy-three, any criminal proceeding in which one spouse is a defendant alleged to have committed a crime against the other spouse or to have violated a temporary or permanent vacate, restraining, or no-contact order or judgment issued pursuant to section eighteen, thirty-four B or thirty-four C of chapter two hundred and eight, section thirty-two of chapter two hundred and nine, section three, three B, three C, four, or five of chapter two hundred and nine A, or sections fifteen or twenty of chapter two hundred and nine C, or a similar protection order issued by another jurisdiction, obtained by the other spouse, and except in a proceeding involving abuse of a person under the age of eighteen, including incest, neither husband nor wife shall testify as to private conversations with the other.

Second, Except as otherwise provided in section seven of chapter two hundred and seventy-three and except in any proceeding relating to child abuse, including incest, neither husband nor wife shall be compelled to testify in the trial of an indictment, complaint or other criminal proceeding against the other;

Third, The defendant in the trial of an indictment, complaint or other criminal proceeding shall, at his own request, but not otherwise, be allowed to testify; but his neglect or refusal to testify shall not create any presumption against him.

Fourth, An unemancipated, minor child, living with a parent, shall not testify before a grand jury, trial of an indictment, complaint or other criminal proceeding, against said parent, where the victim in such proceeding is not a member of said parent's family and who does not reside in the said parent's household. For the purposes of this clause the term "parent" shall mean the natural or adoptive mother or father of said child.

(Stat. 1851, ch. 233, §97; Stat. 1851, ch. 255, §3; Stat. 1852, ch. 312, §60; Stat. 1856, ch. 188; Stat. 1857, ch. 305, §1; Stat. 1859, ch. 230; G.S.1860, ch. 131, §§13, 14, 16; Stat. 1864, ch. 304, §1; Stat. 1865, ch. 207, §2; Stat. 1866, ch. 148, §5; Stat. 1866, ch. 260; Stat. 1870, ch. 393, §1; P.S. 1882, ch. 169, §18; R.L. 1902, ch. 175, §20; Stat. 1911, ch. 456, §7; Stat. 1951, ch. 657, §3; Stat. 1963, ch. 765, §3; Stat. 1983, ch. 145; Stat. 1986, ch. 145; Stat. 1995, ch. 5, §94; Stat. 1996, ch. 298, §10.)

§65. Exception to marital disqualification rule: declaration of a deceased person

In any action or other civil judicial proceeding, a declaration of a deceased person shall not be inadmissible in evidence as hearsay or as private conversation between husband and wife, as the case may be, if the court finds that it was made in good faith and upon the personal knowledge of the declarant.

(Stat. 1898, ch. 535; R.L. 1902, ch. 175, §66; Stat. 1941, ch. 363, §1; Stat. 1943, ch. 105, §1; Stat. 1943, ch. 232, §1.)

Massachusetts General Laws

Ch. 273

§7. Disqualification of confidential communications between husband and wife; exceptions

No other or greater evidence shall be required to prove the marriage of the husband and wife, or that the alleged father is the parent of the child, than may be required to prove the same facts in a civil action. In any prosecution begun under section one [for abandonment and non-support], both husband and wife shall be competent witnesses to testify against each other to any relevant matters, including the fact of their marriage and the parentage of the child; provided, that neither shall be compelled to give evidence incriminating himself. Proof of the desertion of the spouse or child, or of the neglect or refusal to make reasonable provision for their support and maintenance, shall be prima facie evidence that such desertion, neglect or refusal is wilful and without just cause. In no prosecution under sections one to ten, inclusive, shall any existing statute or rule of law prohibiting the disclosure of confidential communications between husband and wife apply.

(Stat. 1893, ch. 262, §1; R.L. 1902, ch. 212, §45; Stat. 1905, ch. 307; Stat. 1906, ch. 501, §1; Stat. 1907, ch. 563, §26; Stat. 1908, ch. 104; Stat. 1909, ch. 180; Stat. 1911, ch. 456, §7; Stat. 1977, ch. 848, §4.)

F. Domestic Violence

In 1978 Massachusetts became one of the first states to enact a statutory scheme providing relief to victims of domestic violence. The Abuse Prevention Act (APA) (codified as Massachusetts General Laws ch. 209A) defines "abuse" broadly to cover: "attempting to cause or causing physical harm" (Mass. Gen. Laws ch. 209A, §1(a)); "placing another in fear of imminent serious physical harm" (*id.* at §1(b)); as well as marital rape ("causing another to engage involuntarily in sexual relations by force, threat of force or duress") (*id.* at §1(c)).

The APA also defines broadly the class of possible complainants. Included are: (1) married persons, (2) persons residing in the same household, (3) persons related by blood or marriage, (4) those having a child in common (whether married or unmarried parents), and (5) those involved in "substantive dating or engagement relationships" with persons of the same or opposite sex (Mass. Gen. Laws ch. 209A, §1). For an example of what constitutes a "substantive dating or engagement relationship, see C.O. v. M.M., 815 N.E.2d 582 (Mass. 2004)(holding that plaintiff failed to sustain her burden of showing a "substantial dating" relationship where there existed evidence of limited past dating activity between the parties). The legislation applies to male and female victims, minor as well as adult plaintiffs and defendants, and to heterosexual and same-sex disputes.

The Act provides a wide range of remedies. Under Massachusetts General Laws ch. 209A, §3, a court may enjoin the defendant from committing abuse, compel a defendant to vacate and remain away from a household or workplace, grant a temporary custody or support order, and reimburse the victim for losses caused by the abuse. For a case clarifying the meaning of "vacate," see Commonwealth v. Gordon, 553 N.E.2d 915 (Mass. 1990) (holding that the abuse prevention statute criminalizing violation of protective order requiring defendant to "vacate" marital residence did not require defendant only to surrender occupancy of residence, but also required that he remain away). In addition, the APA requires that when a court issues a protective order, the defendant must surrender firearms, firearms identification cards, and firearm licenses (Mass. Gen. Laws ch. 209A, §3B). The statute expressly states that proceedings under chapter 209A shall not preclude any other available civil or criminal remedies (Mass. Gen. Laws ch. 209A, §3).

Victims seek relief by filing a complaint, requesting the court's protection by means of various court orders. The court may issue a temporary order in an ex parte proceeding if the complainant demonstrates a substantial likelihood of immediate danger of abuse. The court gives the defendant notice of the order which may be in effect for no more than ten business days. The court then conducts an adversarial hearing to determine if relief should be granted. The court may extend the temporary order or issue a permanent order for a period of time up to one year. At the expiration of the court order, the court may determine again the plaintiff's need for protection.

A court order in an abuse prevention action is a civil order. However, violation of that order may be enforced via a criminal proceeding and is punishable by a fine or imprisonment or both. The court may order an abuser to participate in a treatment program.

In 1991, Massachusetts added further protection for victims by criminalizing stalking (Mass. Gen. Laws ch. 265, §43). The crime of stalking consists of: willfully or maliciously engaging in a knowing pattern of conduct directed at a specific person that seriously alarms or annoys that person and would cause a reasonable person to suffer substantial emotional distress, and making a threat with the intent to place the person in imminent fear of death or bodily injury. *Id.* In Commonwealth v. Kwiatkowski, 637 N.E.2d 854 (Mass. 1994), a defendant who was convicted of stalking and violating a restraining order challenged the constitutionality of the statute. The Supreme Judicial Court held that (1) the defendant preserved a facial vagueness challenge to the statute; (2) the harassment portion of the stalking statute was unconstitutionally vague because terms could be construed to require proof of repeated, rather than single, patterns of conduct or series of acts; and (3) the ambiguous word "repeatedly" would be removed from the harassment-based offense under the stalking statute. In response to *Kwiatkowski*, the legislature adopted the Supreme Judicial Court's language in an amendment (Mass. Gen. Laws ch. 265, §43(b)).

The federal Violence Against Women Act (VAWA), Title II, enacted in 1994, requires that each jurisdiction give full faith and credit to protective orders issued by courts in other states. Pub. L. 103-322, 108 Stat. 1796 (2000). In response, the Massachusetts legislature enacted an amendment to the APA in 1996 providing for recognition or enforcement of restraining orders granted in other jurisdictions (Mass. Gen. Laws ch. 209A, §5A). Kindregan & Inker, *supra*, at §59.1.

In United States v. Morrison, 529 U.S. 598 (2000), the United States Supreme Court invalidated VAWA's Title III, creating a federal civil rights remedy for victims of gender-motivated violent crimes, as an unconstitutional exercise of Congress's power under both Section 5 of the Fourteenth Amendment and the Commerce Clause. Although Title III is no longer a remedy, other VAWA provisions continue to provide financial incentives for states to address domestic violence (via education, prevention, and support programs). See generally Jennifer R. Hagan, Can We Lose the Battle and Still Win the War?: The Fight Against Domestic Violence After the Death of Title III of the Violence Against Women Act, 50 DePaul L. Rev. 919 (2001).

A statewide registry contains information on protection orders issued by Massachusetts state courts as well as those filed in state courts by victims who have been granted protective orders by other jurisdictions (Mass. Gen. Laws ch. 209A, §5A). Thus, law enforcement officers are able to learn whether an individual is the subject of a protective order by consulting the registry.

Finally, Massachusetts statutory and case law establish that the battered women's defense is available in criminal cases (Mass. Gen. Laws ch. 233, §23E; Commonwealth v. Rodriquez, 633 N.E.2d 1039 (1994)). The battered women's defense permits the introduction of expert testimony on issues of self-defense in criminal prosecutions of an abuse victim for harming or killing her abuser. On the battered women's defense, see generally Elizabeth M. Schneider, Battered Women and Feminist Lawmaking (2000).

Massachusetts General Laws

Ch. 209A

§1. "Abuse" defined

As used in this chapter the following words shall have the following meanings:

"Abuse", the occurrence of one or more of the following acts between family or household members:

(a) attempting to cause or causing physical harm;

(b) placing another in fear of imminent serious physical harm;

(c) causing another to engage involuntarily in sexual relations by force, threat or duress.

"Court", the superior, probate and family, district or Boston municipal court departments of the trial court, except when the petitioner is in a dating relationship when "Court" shall mean district, probate, or Boston municipal courts.

"Family or household members", persons who:

(a) are or were married to one another;

(b) are or were residing together in the same household;

(c) are or were related by blood or marriage;

(d) having a child in common regardless of whether they have ever married or lived together; or

(e) are or have been in a substantive dating or engagement relationship, which shall be adjudged by district, probate or Boston municipal courts consideration of the following factors:

(1) the length of time of the relationship;

(2) the type of relationship;

(3) the frequency of interaction between the parties; and

(4) if the relationship has been terminated by either person, the length of time elapsed since the termination of the relationship.

"Law officer", any officer authorized to serve criminal process.

"Protection order issued by another jurisdiction", any injunction or other order issued by a court of another state, territory or possession of the United States, the Commonwealth of Puerto Rico, or the District of Columbia, or tribal court that is issued for the purpose of preventing violent or threatening acts or harassment against, or contact or communication with or physical proximity to another person, including temporary and final orders issued by civil and criminal courts filed by or on behalf of a person seeking protection.

"Vacate order", court order to leave and remain away from a premises and surrendering forthwith any keys to said premises to the plaintiff. The defendant shall not damage any of the plaintiff's belongings or those of any other occupant and shall not shut off or cause to be shut off any utilities or mail delivery to the plaintiff. In the case where the premises designated in the vacate order is a residence, so long as the plaintiff is living at said residence, the defendant shall not interfere in any way with the plaintiff's right to possess such residence, except by order or judgment of a court of competent jurisdiction pursuant to appropriate civil eviction proceedings, a petition to partition real estate, or a proceeding to divide marital property. A vacate order may include in its scope a household, a multiple family dwelling and the plaintiff's workplace. When issuing an order to vacate the plaintiff's workplace, the presiding justice must consider whether the plaintiff and defendant work in the same location or for the same employer.

(Stat. 1978, ch. 447, §2; Stat. 1983, ch. 678, §2; Stat. 1986, ch. 310, §15; Stat. 1990, ch. 403, §2; Stat. 1996, ch. 298, §1, effective November 7, 1996; Stat. 1996, ch. 450, §232, approved, with emergency preamble, December 27, 1996.)

§2. Venue

Proceedings under this chapter shall be filed, heard and determined in the superior court department or the Boston municipal court department or respective divisions of the probate and family or district court departments having venue over the plaintiff's residence. If the plaintiff has left a residence or household to avoid abuse, such plaintiff shall have the option of commencing an action in the court having venue over such prior residence or household, or in the court having venue over the present residence or household.

(Stat. 1978, ch. 447, §2; Stat. 1983, ch. 678, §3.)

§3. Victims of abuse may seek wide range of relief

A person suffering from abuse from an adult or minor family or household member may file a complaint in the court requesting protection from such abuse, including, but not limited to, the following orders:

(a) ordering the defendant to refrain from abusing the plaintiff, whether the defendant is an adult or minor;

(b) ordering the defendant to refrain from contacting the plaintiff, unless authorized by the court, whether the defendant is an adult or minor;

(c) ordering the defendant to vacate forthwith and remain away from the household, multiple family dwelling, and workplace. Notwithstanding the provisions of section thirty-four B of chapter two hundred and eight, an order to vacate shall be for a fixed period of time, not to exceed one year, at the expiration of which time the court may extend any such order upon motion of the plaintiff, with notice to the defendant, for such additional time as it deems necessary to protect the plaintiff from abuse;

(d) awarding the plaintiff temporary custody of a minor child; provided, however, that in any case brought in the probate and family court a finding by such court by a preponderance of the evidence that a pattern or serious incident of abuse, as defined in section 31A of chapter 208, toward a parent or child has occurred shall create a rebuttable presumption that it is not in the best interests of the child to be placed in sole custody, shared legal custody or shared physical custody with the abusive parent. Such presumption may be rebutted by a preponderance of the evidence that such custody award is in the best interests of the child. For the purposes of this section, an "abusive parent" shall mean a parent who has committed a pattern of abuse or a serious incident of abuse.

For the purposes of this section, the issuance of an order or orders under chapter 209A shall not in and of itself constitute a pattern or serious incident of abuse; nor shall an order or orders entered ex parte under said chapter 209A be admissible to show whether a pattern or serious incident of abuse has in fact occurred; provided, however, that an order or orders entered ex parte under said chapter 209A may be admissible for other purposes as the court may determine, other than showing whether a pattern or serious incident of abuse has in fact occurred; provided further, that the underlying facts upon which an order or orders under said chapter 209A was based may also form the basis for a finding by the probate and family court that a pattern or serious incident of abuse has occurred.

If the court finds that a pattern or serious incident of abuse has occurred and issues a temporary or permanent custody order, the court shall within 90 days enter written findings of fact as to the effects of the abuse on the child, which findings demonstrate that such order is in the furtherance of the child's best interests and provides for the safety and well-being of the child.

If ordering visitation to the abusive parent, the court shall provide for the safety and well-being of the child and the safety of the abused parent. The court may consider:

(a) ordering an exchange of the child to occur in a protected setting or in the presence of an appropriate third party;

(b) ordering visitation supervised by an appropriate third party, visitation center or agency;

(c) ordering the abusive parent to attend and complete, to the satisfaction of the court, a certified batterer's treatment program as a condition of visitation;

(d) ordering the abusive parent to abstain from possession or consumption of alcohol or controlled substances during the visitation and for 24 hours preceding visitation;

(e) ordering the abusive parent to pay the costs of supervised visitation;

(f) prohibiting overnight visitation;

(g) requiring a bond from the abusive parent for the return and safety of the child;

(h) ordering an investigation or appointment of a guardian ad litem or attorney for the child; and

(i) imposing any other condition that is deemed necessary to provide for the safety and well-being of the child and the safety of the abused parent.

Nothing in this section shall be construed to affect the right of the parties to a hearing under the rules of domestic relations procedure or to affect the discretion of the probate and family court in the conduct of such hearing.

(e) ordering the defendant to pay temporary support for the plaintiff or any child in the plaintiff's custody or both, when the defendant has a legal obligation to support such a person. In determining the amount to be paid, the court shall apply the standards established in the child support guidelines. Each judgment or order of support which is issued, reviewed or modified pursuant to this chapter shall conform to and shall be enforced in accordance with the provisions of section 12 of chapter 119A;

(f) ordering the defendant to pay the person abused monetary compensation for the losses suffered as a direct result of such abuse. Compensatory losses shall include, but not be limited to, loss of earnings or support, costs for restoring utilities, out-of-pocket losses for injuries sustained, replacement costs for locks or personal property removed or destroyed, medical and moving expenses and reasonable attorney's fees;

(g) ordering information in the case record to be impounded in accordance with court rule;

(h) ordering the defendant to refrain from abusing or contacting the plaintiff's child, or child in plaintiff's care or custody, unless authorized by the court;

(i) the judge may recommend to the defendant that the defendant attend a batterer's intervention program that is certified by the department of public health.

No filing fee shall be charged for the filing of the complaint. Neither the plaintiff nor the plaintiff's attorney shall be charged for certified copies of any orders entered by the court, or any copies of the file reasonably required for future court action or as a result of the loss or destruction of plaintiff's copies.

Any relief granted by the court shall be for a fixed period of time not to exceed one year. Every order shall on its face state the time and date the order is to expire and shall include the date and time that the matter will again be heard. If the plaintiff appears at the court at the date and time the order is to expire, the court shall determine whether or not to extend the order for any additional time reasonably necessary to protect the plaintiff or to enter a permanent order. When the expiration date stated on the order is on a weekend day or holiday, or a date when the court is closed to business, the order shall not expire until the next date that the court is open to business. The plaintiff may appear on such next court business day at the time designated by the order to request that the order be extended. The court may also extend the order upon motion of the plaintiff, for such additional time as it deems necessary to protect from abuse the plaintiff or any child in the plaintiff's care or custody. The fact that abuse has not occurred during the pendency of an order shall not, in itself, constitute sufficient ground for denying or failing to extend the order, of allowing an order to expire or be vacated, or for refusing to issue a new order.

The court may modify its order at any subsequent time upon motion by either party. When the plaintiff's address is inaccessible to the defendant as provided in section 8 of this chapter and the defendant has filed a motion to modify the court's order, the court shall be responsible for notifying the plaintiff. In no event shall the court disclose any such inaccessible address.

No order under this chapter shall in any manner affect title to real property.

No court shall compel parties to mediate any aspect of their case. Although the court may refer the case to the family service office of the probation department or victim/witness advocates for information gathering purposes, the court shall not compel the parties to meet together in such information gathering sessions.

A court shall not deny any complaint filed under this chapter solely because it was not filed within a particular time period after the last alleged incident of abuse.

A court may issue a mutual restraining order or mutual no-contact order pursuant to any abuse prevention action only if the court has made specific written findings of fact. The court shall then provide a detailed order, sufficiently specific to apprise any law officer as to which party has violated the order, if the parties are in or appear to be in violation of the order.

Any action commenced under the provisions of this chapter shall not preclude any other civil or criminal remedies. A party filing a complaint under this chapter shall be required to disclose any prior or pending actions involving the parties for divorce, annulment, paternity, custody or support, guardianship, separate support or legal separation, or abuse prevention.

If there is a prior or pending custody support order from the probate and family court department of the trial court, an order issued in the superior, district or Boston municipal court departments of the trial court pursuant to this chapter may include any relief available pursuant to this chapter except orders for custody or support.

If the parties to a proceeding under this chapter are parties in a subsequent proceeding in the probate and family court department for divorce, annulment, paternity, custody or support, guardianship or separate support, any custody or support order or judgment issued in the subsequent proceeding shall supersede any prior custody or support order under this chapter.

(Stat. 1978, ch. 447, §2; Stat. 1983, 678, §4; Stat. 1990, 403, §3; Stat. 1998, ch. 64, §204, approved with emergency preamble, March 31, 1998; Stat. 1998, ch. 179, §5, effective October 20, 1998; Stat. 1999, ch. 127, §155, approved with emergency preamble, November 16, 1999, by §390, effective July 1, 1999; Stat. 2000, ch. 236, §§22, 23, approved with emergency preamble, August 10, 2000, by §101, effective September 28, 2000; Stat. 2002, ch. 184, §113, approved with emergency preamble, July 9, 2002, by §247, effective July 1, 2002.)

§3A. Complainant shall be given information regarding proceedings and orders

Upon the filing of a complaint under this chapter, a complainant shall be informed that the proceedings hereunder are civil in nature and that violations of orders issued hereunder are criminal in nature. Further, a complainant shall be given information prepared by the appropriate district attorney's office that other criminal proceedings may be available and such complainant shall be instructed by such district attorney's office relative to the procedures required to initiate criminal proceedings including, but not limited to, a complaint for a violation of section forty-three of chapter two hundred and sixty-five. Whenever possible, a complainant shall be provided with such information in the complainant's native language.

(Stat. 1992, ch. 188, §3, approved with emergency preamble, September 18, 1992.)

§3B. Upon issuance of temporary order, court shall order suspension of firearm license and surrender of firearms

Upon issuance of a temporary or emergency order under section four or five of this chapter, the court shall, if the plaintiff demonstrates a substantial likelihood of immediate danger of abuse, order the immediate suspension and surrender of any license to carry firearms and or firearms identification card which the defendant may hold and order the defendant to surrender all firearms, rifles, shotguns, machine guns and ammunition which he then controls, owns or possesses in accordance with the provisions of this chapter and any license to carry firearms or firearms identification cards which the defendant may hold shall be surrendered to the appropriate law enforcement officials in accordance with the provisions of this chapter and, said law enforcement official may store, transfer or otherwise dispose of any such weapon in accordance with the provisions of section 129D of chapter 140; provided however, that nothing herein shall authorize the transfer of any weapons surrendered by the defendant to anyone other than a licensed dealer. Notice of such suspension and ordered surrender shall be appended to the copy of abuse prevention order served on the defendant pursuant to section seven. Law enforcement officials, upon the service of said orders, shall immediately take possession of all firearms, rifles, shotguns, machine guns, ammunition, any license to carry firearms and any firearms identification cards in the control, ownership, or possession of said defendant. Any violation of such orders shall be punishable by a fine of not more than five thousand dollars, or by imprisonment for not more than two and one-half years in a house of correction, or by both such fine and imprisonment.

Any defendant aggrieved by an order of surrender or suspension as described in the first sentence of this section may petition the court which issued such suspension or surrender order for a review of such action and such petition shall be heard no later than ten court business days after the receipt of the notice of the petition by the court. If said license to carry firearms or firearms identification card has been suspended upon the issuance of an order issued pursuant to section four or five, said petition may be heard contemporaneously with the hearing specified in the second sentence of the second paragraph of section four. Upon the filing of an affidavit by the defendant that a firearm, rifle, shotgun, machine gun or ammunition is required in the performance of the defendant's employment, and upon a request for an expedited hearing, the court shall order said hearing within two business days of receipt of such affidavit and request but only on the issue of surrender and suspension pursuant to this section.

(Stat. 1994, ch. 24, §6, approved May 25, 1994, by §11, effective July 1, 1994; Stat. 1996, ch. 298, §2, effective November 7, 1996; Stat. 1998, ch. 180, §48, approved July 23, 1998.)

§3C. Upon continuation or modification of order, court shall order suspension or surrender of firearm license, firearms identification card and surrender of all firearms

Upon the continuation or modification of an order issued pursuant to section 4 or upon petition for review as described in section 3B, the court shall also order or continue to order the immediate suspension and surrender of a defendant's license to carry firearms, including a Class A or Class B license, and firearms identification card and the surrender of all firearms, rifles, shotguns, machine guns or ammunition which such defendant then controls, owns or possesses if the court makes a determination that the return of such license to carry firearms, including a Class A or Class B license, and firearm identification card or firearms, rifles, shotguns, machine guns or ammunition presents a likelihood of abuse to the plaintiff. A suspension and surrender order issued pursuant to this section shall continue so long as the restraining order to which it relates is in effect; and, any law enforcement official to whom such weapon is surrendered may store, transfer or otherwise dispose of any such weapon in accordance with the provisions of section 129D of chapter 140; provided, however, that nothing herein shall authorize the transfer of any weapons surrendered by the defendant to anyone other than a licensed dealer. Any violation of such order shall be punishable by a fine of not more than $5,000 or by imprisonment for not more than two and one-half years in a house of correction or by both such fine and imprisonment.

(Stat. 1994, ch. 24, §6, approved May 25, 1994, by §11, effective July 1, 1994; Stat. 1996, ch. 450, §233, approved, with emergency preamble, December 27, 1996; Stat. 1998, ch. 180, §49, effective October 21, 1998.)

§4. Court may enter temporary orders ex parte

Upon the filing of a complaint under this chapter, the court may enter such temporary orders as it deems necessary to protect a plaintiff from abuse, including relief as provided in section three. Such relief shall not be contingent upon the filing of a complaint for divorce, separate support, or paternity action.

If the plaintiff demonstrates a substantial likelihood of immediate danger of abuse, the court may enter such temporary relief orders without notice as it deems necessary to protect the plaintiff from abuse and shall immediately thereafter notify the defendant that the temporary orders have been issued. The court shall give the defendant an opportunity to be heard on the question of continuing the temporary order and of granting other relief as requested by the plaintiff no later than ten court business days after such orders are entered.

Notice shall be made by the appropriate law enforcement agency as provided in section seven.

If the defendant does not appear at such subsequent hearing, the temporary orders shall continue in effect without further order of the court.
(Stat. 1978, ch. 447, §2; Stat. 1983, ch. 678, §4; Stat. 1984, ch. 189, §152; Stat. 1990, ch. 403, §4.)

§5. Relief may be granted by telephone when courts are closed

When the court is closed for business or the plaintiff is unable to appear in court because of severe hardship due to the plaintiff's physical condition, any justice of the superior, probate and family, district or Boston municipal court departments may grant relief to the plaintiff as provided under section four if the plaintiff demonstrates a substantial likelihood of immediate danger of abuse. In the discretion of the justice, such relief may be granted and communicated by telephone to an officer or employee of an appropriate law enforcement agency, who shall record such order on a form of order promulgated for such use by the chief administrative justice and shall deliver a copy of such order on the next court day to the clerk-magistrate of the court having venue and jurisdiction over the matter. If relief has been granted without the filing of a complaint pursuant to this section of this chapter, then the plaintiff shall appear in court on the next available business day to file said complaint. If the plaintiff in such a case is unable to appear in court without severe hardship due to the plaintiff's physical condition, then a representative may appear in court on the plaintiff's behalf and file the requisite complaint with an affidavit setting forth the circumstances preventing the plaintiff from appearing personally. Notice to the plaintiff and defendant and an opportunity for the defendant to be heard shall be given as provided in said section four.

Any order issued under this section and any documentation in support thereof shall be certified on the next court day by the clerk-magistrate or register of the court issuing such order to the court having venue and jurisdiction over the matter. Such certification to the court shall have the effect of commencing proceedings under this chapter and invoking the other provisions of this chapter but shall not be deemed necessary for an emergency order issued under this section to take effect.
(Stat. 1978, ch. 447, §2; Stat. 1983, ch. 678, §4; Stat. 1990, ch. 403, §§5, 6; Stat. 1996, ch. 298, §§3, 4, effective November 7, 1996.)

§5A. Massachusetts courts must give full faith and credit to protective orders issued in other jurisdictions

Any protection order issued by another jurisdiction, as defined in section one, shall be given full faith and credit throughout the commonwealth and enforced as if it were issued in the commonwealth for as long as the order is in effect in the issuing jurisdiction.

A person entitled to protection under a protection order issued by another jurisdiction may file such order in the superior court department or the Boston municipal court department or any division of the probate and family or district court departments by filing with the court a certified copy of such order which shall be entered into the statewide domestic violence record keeping system established pursuant to the provisions of section seven of chapter one hundred and eighty-eight of the acts of nineteen hundred and ninety-two and maintained by the office of the commissioner of probation. Such person shall swear under oath in an affidavit, to the best of such person's knowledge, that such order is presently in effect as written. Upon request by a law enforcement agency, the register or clerk of such court shall provide a certified copy of the protection order issued by the other jurisdiction.

A law enforcement officer may presume the validity of, and enforce in accordance with section six, a copy of a protection order issued by another jurisdiction which has been provided to the law enforcement officer by any source; provided, however, that the officer is also provided with a statement by the person protected by the order that such order remains in effect. Law enforcement officers may rely on such statement by the person protected by such order.
(Stat. 1996, ch. 298, §5, effective November 7, 1996.)

§6. Duties of law enforcement personnel

Whenever any law officer has reason to believe that a family or household member has been abused or is in danger of being abused, such officer shall use all reasonable means to prevent further abuse. The officer shall take, but not be limited to the following action:

(1) remain on the scene of where said abuse occurred or was in danger of occurring as long as the officer has reason to believe that at least one of the parties involved would be in immediate physical danger without the presence of a law officer. This shall include, but not be limited to remaining in the dwelling for a reasonable period of time;

(2) assist the abused person in obtaining medical treatment necessitated by an assault, which may include driving the victim to the emergency room of the nearest hospital, or arranging for appropriate transportation to a health care facility, notwithstanding any law to the contrary;

(3) assist the abused person in locating and getting to a safe place; including but not limited to a designated meeting place for a shelter or a family member's or friend's residence. The officer shall consider the victim's preference in this regard and what is reasonable under all the circumstances;

(4) give such person immediate and adequate notice of his or her rights. Such notice shall consist of handing said person a copy of the statement which follows below and reading the same to said person. Where said person's native language is not English, the statement shall be then provided in said person's native language whenever possible.

"You have the right to appear at the Superior, Probate and Family, District or Boston Municipal Court, if you reside within the appropriate jurisdiction, and file a complaint requesting any of the following applicable orders:

(a) an order restraining your attacker from abusing you;

(b) an order directing your attacker to leave your household, building or workplace;

(c) an order awarding you custody of a minor child;

(d) an order directing your attacker to pay support for you or any minor child in your custody, if the attacker has a legal obligation of support; and

(e) an order directing your attacker to pay you for losses suffered as a result of abuse, including medical and moving expenses, loss of earnings or support, costs for restoring utilities and replacing locks, reasonable attorney's fees and other out-of-pocket losses for injuries and property damage sustained.

For an emergency on weekends, holidays, or weeknights the police will refer you to a justice of the superior, probate and family, district, or Boston municipal court departments.

You have the right to go to the appropriate district court or the Boston municipal court and seek a criminal complaint for threats, assault and battery, assault with a deadly weapon, assault with intent to kill or other related offenses.

If you are in need of medical treatment, you have the right to request that an officer present drive you to the nearest hospital or otherwise assist you in obtaining medical treatment.

If you believe that police protection is needed for your physical safety, you have the right to request that the officer present remain at the scene until you and your children can leave or until your safety is otherwise ensured. You may also request that the officer assist you in locating and taking you to a safe place, including but not limited to a designated meeting place for a shelter or a family member's or a friend's residence, or a similar place of safety.

You may request a copy of the police incident report at no cost from the police department."

The officer shall leave a copy of the foregoing statement with such person before leaving the scene or premises.

(5) assist such person by activating the emergency judicial system when the court is closed for business;

(6) inform the victim that the abuser will be eligible for bail and may be promptly released; and

(7) arrest any person a law officer witnesses or has probable cause to believe has violated a temporary or permanent vacate, restraining, or no-contact order or judgment issued pursuant to section eighteen, thirty-four B or thirty-four C of chapter two hundred and eight, section thirty-two of chapter two hundred and nine, section three, three B, three C, four or five of this chapter, or sections fifteen or twenty of chapter two hundred and nine C or similar protection order issued by another jurisdiction. When there are no vacate, restraining, or no-contact orders or judgments in effect, arrest shall be the preferred response whenever an officer witnesses or has probable cause to believe that a person:

(a) has committed a felony;

(b) has committed a misdemeanor involving abuse as defined in section one of this chapter;

(c) has committed an assault and battery in violation of section thirteen A of chapter two hundred and sixty-five.

The safety of the victim and any involved children shall be paramount in any decision to arrest. Any officer arresting both parties must submit a detailed, written report in addition to an incident report, setting forth the grounds for dual arrest.

No law officer investigating an incident of domestic violence shall threaten, suggest, or otherwise indicate the arrest of all parties for the purpose of discouraging requests for law enforcement intervention by any party.

No law officer shall be held liable in any civil action regarding personal injury or injury to property brought by any party to a domestic violence incident for an arrest based on probable cause when such officer acted reasonably and in good faith and in compliance with this chapter and the statewide policy as established by the secretary of public safety.

Whenever any law officer investigates an incident of domestic violence, the officer shall immediately file a written incident report in accordance with the standards of the officer's law enforcement agency and, wherever possible, in the form of the National Incident-Based Reporting System, as defined by the Federal Bureau of Investigation. The latter information may be submitted voluntarily by the local police on a monthly basis to the crime reporting unit of the criminal history systems board.

The victim shall be provided a copy of the full incident report at no cost upon request to the appropriate law enforcement department.

When a judge or other person authorized to take bail bails any person arrested under the provisions of this chapter, he shall make reasonable efforts to inform the victim of such release prior to or at the time of said release.

When any person charged with or arrested for a crime involving abuse under this chapter is released from custody, the court or the emergency response judge shall issue, upon the request of the victim, a written no-contact order prohibiting the person charged or arrested from having any contact with the victim and shall use all reasonable means to notify the victim immediately of release from custody. The victim shall be given at no cost a certified copy of the no-contact order.

(Stat. 1978, ch. 447, §2; Stat. 1983, ch. 678, §4; Stat. 1987, ch. 761; Stat. 1990, ch. 403, §7; amended by Stat. 1996, ch. 298, §§6, 7, effective November 7, 1996.)

§7. Statewide registry of civil restraining orders

When considering a complaint filed under this chapter, a judge shall cause a search to be made of the records contained within the statewide domestic violence record keeping system maintained by the office of the commissioner of probation and shall review the resulting data to determine whether the named defendant has a civil or criminal record involving domestic or other violence. Upon receipt of information that an outstanding warrant exists against the named defendant, a judge shall order that the appropriate law enforcement officials be notified and shall order that any information regarding the defendant's most recent whereabouts shall be forwarded to such officials. In all instances where an outstanding warrant exists, a judge shall make a finding, based upon all of the circumstances, as to whether an imminent threat of bodily injury exists to the petitioner. In all instances where such an imminent threat of bodily injury is found to exist, the judge shall notify the appropriate law enforcement officials of such finding and such officials shall take all necessary actions to execute any such outstanding warrant as soon as is practicable.

Whenever the court orders under sections eighteen, thirty-four B, and thirty-four C of chapter two hundred and eight, section thirty-two of chapter two hundred and nine, sections three, four and five of this chapter, or sections fifteen and twenty of chapter two hundred and nine C, the defendant to vacate, refrain from abusing the plaintiff or to have no contact with the plaintiff or the plaintiff's minor child, the register or clerk-magistrate shall transmit two certified copies of each such order and one copy of the complaint and summons forthwith to the appropriate law enforcement agency which, unless otherwise ordered by the court, shall serve one copy of each order upon the defendant, together with a copy of the complaint, order and summons and notice of any suspension or surrender ordered pursuant to section three B of this chapter. The law enforcement agency shall promptly make its return of service to the court.

Law enforcement officers shall use every reasonable means to enforce such abuse prevention orders. Law enforcement agencies shall establish procedures adequate to insure that an officer on the scene of an alleged violation of such order may be informed of the existence and terms of such order. The court shall notify the appropriate law enforcement agency in writing whenever any such order is vacated and shall direct the agency to destroy all record of such vacated order and such agency shall comply with that directive.

Each abuse prevention order issued shall contain the following statement: VIOLATION OF THIS ORDER IS A CRIMINAL OFFENSE.

Any violation of such order or a protection order issued by another jurisdiction shall be punishable by a fine of not more than five thousand dollars, or by imprisonment for not more than two and one-half years in a house of correction, or by both such fine and imprisonment. In addition to, but not in lieu of, the forgoing penalties and any other sentence, fee or assessment, including the victim witness assessment in section 8 of chapter 258B, the court shall order persons convicted of a crime under this statute to pay a fine of $25 that shall be transmitted to the treasurer for deposit into the General Fund. For any violation of such order, the court shall order the defendant to complete a certified batterer's intervention program unless, upon good cause shown, the court issues specific written findings describing the reasons that batterer's intervention should not be ordered or unless the batterer's intervention program determines that the defendant is not suitable for intervention. The court shall not order substance abuse or anger management treatment or any other form of treatment as a substitute for certified batterer's intervention. If a defendant ordered to undergo treatment has received a suspended sentence, the original sentence shall be reimposed if the defendant fails to participate in said program as required by the terms of his probation. If the court determines that the violation was in retaliation for the defendant being reported by the plaintiff to the department of revenue for failure to pay child support payments or for the establishment of paternity, the defendant shall be punished by a fine of not less than one thousand dollars and not more than ten thousand dollars and by imprisonment for not less than sixty days; provided, however, that the sentence shall not be suspended, nor shall any such person be eligible for probation, parole, or furlough or receive any deduction from his sentence for good conduct until he shall have served sixty days of such sentence.

When a defendant has been ordered to participate in a treatment program pursuant to this section, the defendant shall be required to regularly attend a certified or provisionally certified batterer's treatment program. To the extent permitted by professional requirements of confidentiality, said program shall communicate with local battered women's programs for the purpose of protecting the victim's safety. Additionally, it shall specify the defendant's attendance requirements and keep the probation department informed of whether the defendant is in compliance.

In addition to, but not in lieu of, such orders for treatment, if the defendant has a substance abuse problem, the court may order appropriate treatment for such problem. All ordered treatment shall last until the end of the probationary period or until the treatment program decides to discharge the defendant, whichever comes first. When the defendant is not in compliance with the terms of probation, the court shall hold a revocation of probation hearing. To the extent possible, the defendant shall be responsible for paying all costs for court ordered treatment.

In each instance where there is a violation of an abuse prevention order or a protection order issued by another jurisdiction, the court may order the defendant to pay the plaintiff for all damages including, but not limited to, cost for shelter or emergency housing, loss of earnings or support, out-of-pocket losses for injuries sustained or property damaged, medical expenses, moving expenses, cost for obtaining an unlisted telephone number, and reasonable attorney's fees.

Any such violation may be enforced in the superior, the district or Boston municipal court departments. Criminal remedies provided herein are not exclusive and do not preclude any other available civil or criminal remedies. The superior, probate and family, district and Boston municipal court departments may each enforce by civil contempt procedure a violation of its own court order.

The provisions of section eight of chapter one hundred and thirty-six shall not apply to any order, complaint or summons issued pursuant to this section.

(Stat. 1983, ch. 678, §5; Stat. 1987, ch. 213; Stat. 1990, ch. 403, §8; Stat. 1992, ch. 188, §4, approved, with emergency preamble, September 18, 1992; Stat. 1994, ch. 24, §7, approved May 25, 1994, by §11, effective July 1, 1994; Stat. 1995, ch. 5, §81, approved February 10, 1995, by §143, effective upon passage; Stat. 1996, ch. 298, §8, effective November 7, 1996; Stat. 2002, ch. 184, §114, approved with emergency preamble, July 9, 2002, by §247, effective July 1, 2002.)

§8. Records shall be confidential

The records of cases arising out of an action brought under the provisions of this chapter where the plaintiff or defendant is a minor shall be withheld from public inspection except by order of the court; provided, that such records shall be open, at all reasonable times, to the inspection of the minor, said minor's parent, guardian, attorney, and to the plaintiff and the plaintiff's attorney, or any of them.

The plaintiff's residential address, residential telephone number and workplace name, address and telephone number, contained within the court records of cases arising out of an action brought by a plaintiff under the provisions of this chapter, shall be confidential and withheld from public inspection, except by order of the court, except that the plaintiff's residential address and workplace address shall appear on the court order and [be] accessible to the defendant and the defendant's attorney unless the plaintiff specifically requests that this information be withheld from the order. All confidential portions of the records shall be accessible at all reasonable times to the plaintiff and plaintiff's attorney, to others specifically authorized by the plaintiff to obtain such information, and to prosecutors, victim-witness advocates as defined in section 1 of chapter 258B, domestic violence victim's counselors as defined in section 20K of chapter 233, sexual assault counselors as defined in section 20J of chapter 233, and law enforcement officers, if such access is necessary in the performance of their duties. The provisions of this paragraph shall apply to any protection order issued by another jurisdiction, as defined in section 1, that is filed with a court of the commonwealth pursuant to section 5A. Such

confidential portions of the court records shall not be deemed to be public records under the provisions of clause twenty-sixth of section 7 of chapter 4.
(Stat. 1983, ch. 678, §5; Stat. 1996, ch. 298, §9; Stat. 1999, ch. 127, §156; Stat. 2000, ch. 236, §24.)

§9. Plaintiff can file complaint without the assistance of counsel

The administrative justices of the superior court, probate and family court, district court, and the Boston municipal court departments shall jointly promulgate a form of complaint for use under this chapter which shall be in such form and language to permit a plaintiff to prepare and file such complaint *pro se*.
(Stat. 1983, ch. 678, §5.)

§10. Assessments against persons referred to certified batterers' treatment program as condition of probation

The court shall impose an assessment of three hundred and fifty dollars against any person who has been referred to a certified batterers' treatment program as a condition of probation. Said assessment shall be in addition to the cost of the treatment program. In the discretion of the court, said assessment may be reduced or waived when the court finds that the person is indigent or that payment of the assessment would cause the person, or the dependents of such person, severe financial hardship. Assessments made pursuant to this section shall be in addition to any other fines, assessments, or restitution imposed in any disposition. All funds collected by the court pursuant to this section shall be transmitted monthly to the state treasurer, who shall deposit said funds in the General Fund.
(Stat. 1993, ch. 110, §217; Stat. 1993, ch. 151, §49; Stat. 1996, ch. 151, §466.)

Massachusetts General Laws

Ch. 265

§43. Criminal liability for stalking

(a) Whoever

(1) willfully and maliciously engages in a knowing pattern of conduct or series of acts over a period of time directed at a specific person which seriously alarms or annoys that person and would cause a reasonable person to suffer substantial emotional distress, and

(2) makes a threat with the intent to place the person in imminent fear of death or bodily injury, shall be guilty of the crime of stalking and shall be punished by imprisonment in the state prison for not more than five years or by a fine of not more than one thousand dollars, or imprisonment in the house of correction for not more than two and one-half years or both. Such conduct, acts or threats described in this paragraph shall include, but not be limited to, conduct, acts or threats conducted by mail or by use of a telephonic or telecommunication device including, but not limited to, electronic mail, internet communications and facsimile communications.

(b) Whoever commits the crime of stalking in violation of a temporary or permanent vacate, restraining, or no-contact order or judgment issued pursuant to sections eighteen, thirty-four B, or thirty-four C of chapter two hundred and eight; or section thirty-two of chapter two hundred and nine; or sections three, four, or five of chapter two hundred and nine A; or sections fifteen or twenty of chapter two hundred and nine C or a protection order issued by another jurisdiction; or a temporary restraining order or preliminary or permanent injunction issued by the superior court, shall be punished by imprisonment in a jail or the state prison for not less than one year and not more than five years. No sentence imposed under the provisions of this subsection shall be less than a mandatory minimum term of imprisonment of one year.

A prosecution commenced hereunder shall not be placed on file or continued without a finding, and the sentence imposed upon a person convicted of violating any provision of this subsection shall not be reduced to less than the mandatory minimum term of imprisonment as established herein, nor shall said sentence of imprisonment imposed upon any person be suspended or reduced until such person shall have served said mandatory term of imprisonment.

A person convicted of violating any provision of this subsection shall not, until he shall have served the mandatory minimum term of imprisonment established herein, be eligible for probation, parole, furlough, work release or receive any deduction from his sentence for good conduct under sections one hundred and twenty-nine, one hundred and twenty-nine C and one hundred and twenty-nine D of chapter one hundred and twenty-seven; provided, however, that the commissioner of correction may, on the recommendation of the warden, superintendent, or other person in charge of a correctional institution, grant to said offender a temporary release in the custody of an officer of such institution for the following purposes only: to attend the funeral of next of kin or spouse; to visit a critically ill close relative or spouse; or to obtain emergency medical services unavailable at said institution. The provisions of section eighty-seven of chapter two hundred and seventy-six relating to the power of the court to place certain offenders on probation shall not apply to any person seventeen years of age or over charged with a violation of this subsection. The provisions of section thirty-one of chapter two hundred and seventy-nine shall not apply to any person convicted of violating any provision of this subsection.

(c) Whoever, after having been convicted of the crime of stalking, commits a second or subsequent such crime shall be punished by imprisonment in a jail or the state prison for not less than two years and not more than ten years. No sentence imposed under the provisions of this subsection shall be less than a mandatory minimum term of imprisonment of two years.

A prosecution commenced hereunder shall not be placed on file or continued without a finding, and the sentence imposed upon a person convicted of violating any provision of this subsection shall not be reduced to less than the mandatory minimum term of imprisonment as established herein, nor shall said sentence of imprisonment imposed upon any person be suspended or reduced until such person shall have served said mandatory term of imprisonment.

A person convicted of violating any provision of this subsection shall not, until he shall have served the mandatory minimum term of imprisonment established herein, be eligible for probation, parole, furlough, work release or receive any deduction from his sentence for good conduct under sections one hundred and twenty-nine, one hundred and twenty-nine C and one hundred and twenty-nine D of chapter one hundred and twenty-seven; provided, however, that the commissioner of correction may, on the recommendation of the warden, superintendent, or other person in charge of a correctional institution, grant to said offender a temporary release in the custody of an officer of such institution for the following purposes only: to attend the funeral of next of kin or spouse; to visit a critically ill close relative or spouse; or to obtain emergency medical services unavailable at said institution. The provisions of section eighty-seven of chapter two hundred and seventy-six relating to the power of the court to place certain offenders on probation shall not apply to any person seventeen years of age or over charged with a violation of this subsection. The provisions of section thirty-one of chapter two hundred and seventy-nine shall not apply to any person convicted of violating any provision of this section.

III. DIVORCE

This chapter addresses: (1) alternatives to divorce (i.e., annulment and legal separation), (2) the grounds for dissolution or legal separation, (3) principles of jurisdiction applicable to proceedings for dissolution or legal separation, (4) procedures for obtaining a dissolution or legal separation, and (5) the role of counsel in the divorce context. The law of New York (Domestic Relations Law (DRL), Family Court Act (FCA), and related provisions) provides an illustration of these topics.

New York uses special nomenclature for its court system. The highest court in the state of New York is called the Court of Appeals. The Appellate Division of the Supreme Court rules on appeals from trial courts. Those trial courts include the Supreme Court, Surrogate's Court, County Court, Family Court, and Court of Claims. The Supreme Court has a branch in each county. Its jurisdiction is derived from the New York Constitution (Art. VI, §7, see Chapter V, Section C, *infra*).

The Supreme Court and the Family Court share jurisdiction over support, custody, and visitation. However, the Supreme Court has sole jurisdiction over annulment, divorce, and separation actions (although it may transfer issues of support in such actions to the Family Court). The Supreme Court also may transfer to the Family Court proceedings brought for support or the enforcement of a prior support or alimony decree. See Douglas J. Besharov, Practice Commentaries (commentary following FCA §411).

A. ALTERNATIVES TO DIVORCE

1. Annulment

Spouses may terminate a marriage either by dissolution (commonly called divorce) or an annulment. In contrast to a dissolution, which terminates a valid marriage, an annulment declares that no valid marriage occurred because of certain reasons (discussed *infra*) that existed at the time of the marriage.

Annulments, historically, enjoyed popularity prior to the adoption of no-fault divorce when divorce was difficult to obtain. Today, parties may resort to annulment (rather than divorce) for religious reasons, jurisdictional reasons (i.e., some states have longer residency requirements for divorce than for annulment), or to reinstate benefits that were lost upon marriage.

A marriage may be characterized as void or voidable. A *void* marriage is invalid from inception. Strictly speaking, no legal action is required to declare its invalidity (although such action nonetheless may be advisable). However, a *voidable* marriage is valid from inception and requires that one of the parties take judicial action to establish its invalidity. If neither party acts to disaffirm the marriage, the marriage remains valid. The difference between a void and voidable marriage may be attributed to the fact that the state has a greater interest in invalidating certain marriages.

New York's Domestic Relations Law §140 makes a distinction between actions (1) to declare the *nullity* of a *void* marriage and (2) to *annul* a *voidable* marriage. (In some states, a spouse may petition for a "judgment of nullity" regarding either a void or voidable marriage, e.g., Cal. Fam. Code §2250.)

Void marriages in New York are those that are incestuous (DRL §5), bigamous (DRL §6), or solemnized by unauthorized officials (DRL §11). Marriages that are voidable are those in which a party (or parties) is underage (under age 18); lacks sufficient understanding to consent; has a physical incapacity; manifests force, duress, or fraud to secure consent; or has an incurable mental illness for at least five years (DRL §7).

DRL §140 sets forth the requisite grounds for actions to declare the nullity of a void marriage and for annulment of a voidable marriage, as well as the parties who are authorized to maintain these actions. Pursuant to that statute, either party (as well as the former spouse) may maintain an action during the lifetime of the other in cases of bigamy (DRL §140(a)); a minor, parent, or guardian may maintain an action in cases of underage marriages (DRL §140(b)); a relative of a mentally retarded person "who has an interest to avoid the marriage" may maintain an action in cases of mental retardation (DRL §140(c)); a mentally ill person may maintain an action in cases of mental illness "at any time after restoration to a sound mind" or "any relative of the mentally ill person who has an interest to avoid the marriage" may maintain the action during the continuance of the mental illness, during the life of the other party, or even after the death of the mentally ill person (DRL §140(c)); either spouse may maintain an action in cases of physical incapacity (before a period of five years has expired) (DRL §140(d)); the aggrieved spouse in cases of fraud, duress, or force, or the parent, guardian, or any relative of the aggrieved party "who has an interest to avoid the marriage" (DRL §140(e)); or either party or someone on their behalf in cases of incurable mental illness for five years or more (DRL §140(f)).

In cases of underage marriages, the spouse who has attained the age of consent may not maintain the action; and neither party may maintain the action if the couple cohabits following the underage spouse's attainment of the age of majority (DRL §140(b)). In cases of duress or force, the aggrieved spouse may not obtain an annulment if he or she cohabited with the wrongdoer or, in cases of fraud, cohabited with the wrongdoer after learning of the fraud (*id.*).

To obtain an annulment on the ground of fraud, New York case law requires that the fraud be *material*. That is, the fraud need not meet the strictest standard of "relating to the essentials of the marriage" (e.g., procreation or sexual intercourse). Annulment of Marriage, 18A Carmody-Wait, 2d N.Y. Prac. §113:23 (2002). Fraud is material where the plaintiff relied on the representations such that, had such representations not been made, he or she would not have consented to the marriage. Murray v. Murray, 706 N.Y.S.2d 164 (N.Y. App. Div. 2000) (holding that the wife's fraudulent representations concerning her prior marital status, age, and child rendered marriage void). See also Lawrence Drew Borten, Sex, Procreation, and the State Interest in Marriage, 102 Colum. L. Rev. 1089, 1096-1097 & n.33 (2002) (attributing New York's liberal "material fraud standard of contract law" to the strict legal policy regarding divorce; also pointing out that seven states adhere to the strict essentials standard).

According to New York law, an annulment requires that the plaintiff prove the facts on which the annulment is sought (e.g., no cohabitation or, in cases of mental illness, the continuation of the mental illness) (DRL §144). Thus, an annulment may not be granted upon default, consent of the parties, or by either party's declaration of the facts (*id.*). These strict evidentiary requirements date back to the days of fault-based divorce when courts did not want to enable petitioners to evade the divorce restrictions requirements by resort to annulments. See also Joseph A. Ranney, Anglicans, Merchants, and Feminists: A Comparative Study of the Evolution of Married Women's Rights in Virginia, New York, and Wisconsin, 6 Wm. & Mary J. Women & L. 493, 530 (2000) (explaining that the grounds for annulment were influenced by the social pressure to end bad marriages in a society in which divorce was extremely difficult to obtain).

Residency requirements for actions to annul a marriage or to declare the nullity of a void marriage are specified in DRL §230 and are discussed *infra*.

New York Domestic Relations Law

§5. Incestuous marriage is void; prohibited relationships

A marriage is incestuous and void whether the relatives are legitimate or illegitimate between either:

1. An ancestor and a descendant;

2. A brother and sister of either the whole or the half blood;

3. An uncle and niece or an aunt and nephew.

If a marriage prohibited by the foregoing provisions of this section be solemnized it shall be void, and the parties thereto shall each be fined not less than fifty nor more than one hundred dollars and may, in the discretion of the court in addition to said fine, be imprisoned for a term not exceeding six months. Any person who shall knowingly and willfully solemnize such marriage, or procure or aid in the solemnization of the same, shall be deemed guilty of a misdemeanor and shall be fined or imprisoned in like manner.

(L. 1909, ch. 19.)

§6. Bigamous marriage is void; exceptions

A marriage is absolutely void if contracted by a person whose husband or wife by a former marriage is living, unless either:

1. Such former marriage has been annulled or has been dissolved for a cause other than the adultery of such person; provided, that if such former marriage has been dissolved for the cause of the adultery of such person, he or she may marry again in the cases provided for in section eight of this chapter [section eight no longer contains any restriction on remarriage after the granting of divorce on the ground of adultery] and such subsequent marriage shall be valid;

[2. Repealed.]

3. Such former marriage has been dissolved pursuant to section seven-a [repealed] of this chapter.

(L. 1909, ch. 19; L. 1915, ch. 266, §1; L. 1922, ch. 279, §1; L. 1950, ch. 144, §3; L. 1967, ch. 680, §20; L. 1981, ch. 118, §2.)

§7. Marriage is void in some cases from time a court declares its nullity

A marriage is void from the time its nullity is declared by a court of competent jurisdiction if either party thereto:

1. Is under the age of legal consent, which is eighteen years, provided that such nonage shall not of itself constitute an absolute right to the annulment of such marriage, but such annulment shall be in the discretion of the court which shall take into consideration all the facts and circumstances surrounding such marriage;

2. Is incapable of consenting to a marriage for want of understanding;

3. Is incapable of entering into the married state from physical cause;

4. Consent to such marriage by reason of force, duress or fraud;

5. Has been incurably mentally ill for a period of five years or more.

(L. 1909, ch. 19; L. 1922, ch. 279, §2; L. 1922, ch. 313, §1; L. 1924, ch. 165, §1; L. 1928, ch. 589, §1; L. 1929, ch. 537, §1; L. 1945, ch. 686, §1; L. 1948, ch. 362, §1; L. 1958, ch. 804, §1; L. 1962, ch. 313, §1; L. 1978, ch. 550, §14.)

§11. Persons authorized to solemnize a marriage

No marriage shall be valid unless solemnized by either:

1. A clergyman or minister of any religion, or by the senior leader, or any of the other leaders, of The Society for Ethical Culture in the city of New York, having its principal office in the borough of Manhattan, or by the leader of The Brooklyn Society for Ethical Culture, having its principal office in the borough of Brooklyn of the city of New York, or of the Westchester Ethical Society, having its principal office in Westchester county, or of the Ethical Culture Society of Long Island, having its principal office in Nassau county, or of the Riverdale-Yonkers Ethical Society having its principal office in Bronx county, or by the leader of any other Ethical Culture Society affiliated with the American Ethical Union.

2. A mayor of a village, a county executive of a county, or a mayor, recorder, city magistrate, police justice or police magistrate of a city, a former mayor or the city clerk of a city of the first class of over one million inhabitants or any of his or her deputies or not more than four regular clerks, designated by him or her for such purpose as provided in section eleven-a of this chapter, except that in cities which contain more than one hundred thousand and less than one million inhabitants, a marriage shall be solemnized by the mayor, or police justice, and by no other officer of such city,

except as provided in subdivisions one and three of this section.

3. A judge of the federal circuit court of appeals for the second circuit, a judge of a federal district court for the northern, southern, eastern or western district of New York, a judge of the United States court of international trade, a federal administrative law judge presiding in this state, a justice or judge of a court of the unified court system, a housing judge of the civil court of the city of New York, a retired justice or judge of the unified court system or a retired housing judge of the civil court of the city of New York certified pursuant to paragraph (k) of subdivision two of section two hundred twelve of the judiciary law, the clerk of the appellate division of the supreme court in each judicial department or a county clerk of a county wholly within cities having a population of one million or more; or,

4. A written contract of marriage signed by both parties and at least two witnesses, all of whom shall subscribe the same within this state, stating the place of residence of each of the parties and witnesses and the date and place of marriage, and acknowledged before a judge of a court of record of this state by the parties and witnesses in the manner required for the acknowledgment of a conveyance of real estate to entitle the same to be recorded.

5. Notwithstanding any other provision of this article, where either or both of the parties is under the age of eighteen years a marriage shall be solemnized only by those authorized in subdivision one of this section or by (1) the mayor of a city or village, or county executive of a county, or by (2) a judge of the federal circuit court of appeals for the second circuit, a judge of a federal district court for the northern, southern, eastern or western district of New York, a judge of the United States court of international trade, or a justice or a judge of a court of the unified court system, or by (3) a housing judge of the civil court of the city of New York, or by (4) a former mayor or the clerk of a city of the first class of over one million inhabitants or any of his or her deputies designated by him or her for such purposes as provided in section eleven-a of this chapter.

6. Notwithstanding any other provisions of this article to the contrary no marriage shall be solemnized by a public officer specified in this section, other than a judge of a federal district court for the northern, southern, eastern or western district of New York, a judge of the United States court of international trade, a federal administrative law judge presiding in this state, a judge or justice of the unified court system of this State, a housing judge of the civil court of the city of New York, or a retired judge or justice of the unified court system or a retired housing judge of the civil court certified pursuant to paragraph (k) of subdivision two of section two hundred twelve of the judiciary law, outside the territorial jurisdiction in which he or she was elected or appointed. Such a public officer, however, elected or appointed within the city of New York may solemnize a marriage anywhere within such city.

7. The term "clergyman" or "minister" when used in this article, shall include those defined in section two of the religious corporations law. The word "magistrate," when so used, includes any person referred to in the second or third subdivision.

(L. 1909, ch. 19; L. 1911, ch. 610, §1; L. 1912, ch. 166, §1; L. 1913, ch. 490, §1; L. 1916, ch. 524, §1; L. 1918, ch. 620, §1; L. 1920, ch. 231, §1; L. 1922, ch. 326, §1; L. 1926, ch. 144, §1; L. 1926, ch. 590, §1; L. 1926, ch. 635, §1; L. 1927, ch. 547, §1; L. 1929, ch. 606, §1; L. 1930, ch. 423, §1; L. 1933, ch. 244, §1; L. 1933, ch. 606, §1; L. 1935, ch. 53, §1; L. 1939, ch. 304, §1; L. 1940, ch. 142, §1; L. 1942, ch. 579, §1; L. 1945, ch. 12, §1; L. 1947, ch. 674, §§1, 2; L. 1952, ch. 647, §1; L. 1954, ch. 765, §1; L. 1957, ch. 721, §1; L. 1959, ch. 319, §1; L. 1962, ch. 63, §1; L. 1962, ch. 689, §11; L. 1963, ch. 765, §1; L. 1964, ch. 509, §1; L. 1964, ch. 559, §1; L. 1968, ch. 221, §1; L. 1968, ch. 625, §§1, 2; L. 1968, ch. 723, §1; L. 1970, ch. 378, §1; L. 1971, ch. 321, § 2; L. 1971, ch. 730, §1; L. 1972, ch. 720, §§1, 2; L. 1973, ch. 196, §1; L. 1974, ch. 764, §1; L. 1974, ch. 920, §1; L. 1975, ch. 256, §1; L. 1977, ch. 239, §1; L. 1978, ch. 88, §§1, 2; L. 1978, ch. 615, §1; L. 1981, ch. 149, §1; L. 1983, ch. 484, §1; L. 1985, ch. 321, §§1 to 3; L. 1987, ch. 95, §1; L. 1987, ch. 147, §1; L. 1987, ch. 277, §1; L. 1987, ch. 283, §§ 1, 2; L. 1987, ch. 313, §1; L. 1988, ch. 92, §1; L. 1990, ch. 153, §§1, 2; L. 1991, ch. 39, §1; L. 1992, ch. 404, §§1, 2; L. 1996, ch. 264, §§1, 2.)

§140. Persons who may petition to declare the nullity of a void marriage or annul a voidable marriage

(a) Former husband or wife living. An action to declare the nullity of a void marriage upon the ground that the former husband or wife of one of the parties was living, the former marriage being in force, may be maintained by either of the parties during the life-time of the other, or by the former husband or wife.

(b) Party under age of consent. An action to annul a marriage on the ground that one or both of the parties had not attained the age of legal consent may be maintained by the infant, or by either parent of the infant, or by the guardian of the infant's person; or the court may allow the action to be maintained by any person as the next friend of the infant. But a marriage shall not be annulled under this subdivision at the suit of a party who was of the age of legal consent when it was contracted, or by a party who for any time after he or she attained that age freely cohabited with the other party as husband or wife.

(c) Party a mentally retarded person or mentally ill person. An action to annul a marriage on the ground that one of the parties thereto was a mentally retarded person may be maintained at any time during the life-time of either party by any relative of a mentally retarded person, who has an interest to avoid the marriage. An action to annul a marriage on the ground that one of the parties thereto was a mentally ill person may be maintained at any time during the continuance of the mental illness, or, after the death of the mentally ill person in that condition, and during the life of the other party to the marriage, by any relative of the mentally ill person who has an interest to avoid the marriage. Such an action may also be maintained by the mentally ill person at any time after restoration to a sound mind; but in that case, the marriage should not be annulled if it appears that the parties freely cohabited as husband and wife after the mentally ill person was restored to a sound mind. Where one of the parties to a marriage was a mentally ill person at the time of the marriage, an action may also be maintained by the other party at any time during the continuance of the mental illness, provided the plaintiff did not know of the mental illness at the time of the marriage. Where no relative of the mentally retarded person or mentally ill person brings an action to annul the marriage and the mentally ill person is not restored to sound mind, the court may allow an action for that purpose to be maintained at any time during the life-time of both the parties to the marriage, by any person as the next friend of the mentally retarded person or mentally ill person.

(d) Physical incapacity. An action to annul a marriage on the ground that one of the parties was physically incapable of entering into the marriage state may be maintained by the injured party against the party whose incapacity is alleged; or such an action may be maintained by the party who was incapable against the other party, provided the incapable party was unaware of the incapacity at the time of marriage, or if aware of such incapacity, did not know it was incurable. Such an action can be maintained only where an incapacity continues and is incurable, and must be commenced before five years have expired since the marriage.

(e) Consent by force, duress or fraud. An action to annul a marriage on the ground that the consent of one of the parties thereto was obtained by force or duress may be maintained at any time by the party whose consent was so obtained. An action to annul a marriage on the ground that the consent of one of the parties thereto was obtained by fraud may be maintained by the party whose consent was so obtained within the limitations of time for enforcing a civil remedy of the civil practice law and rules. Any such action may also be maintained during the life-time of the other party by the parent, or the guardian of the person of the party whose consent was so obtained, or by any relative of that party who has an interest to avoid the marriage, provided that in an action to annul a marriage on the ground of fraud the limitation prescribed in the civil practice law and rules has not run. But a marriage shall not be annulled on the ground of force or duress if it appears that, at any time before the commencement of the action, the parties thereto voluntarily cohabited as husband and wife; or on the ground of fraud, if it appears that, at any time before the commencement thereof, the parties voluntarily cohabited as husband and wife, with a full knowledge of the facts constituting the fraud.

(f) Incurable mental illness for five years. An action to annul a marriage upon the ground that one of the parties has been incurably mentally ill for a period of five years or more may be maintained by or on behalf of either of the parties to such marriage.

(L. 1962, ch. 313, §6; L. 1963, ch. 458, §1; L. 1978, ch. 550, §15.)

§141. Procedure for annulment on ground of incurable mental illness

1. If the marriage be annulled on the ground of the mental illness of a spouse, the court may include in the judgment an order providing for his or her suitable support, care and maintenance during life from the property or income of the other spouse. The court shall specify the amount of such support, care and maintenance and, before rendering judgment, may exact security for such support, care and maintenance during life and shall order the filing and recording of the instrument creating such security in the office of the clerk of the county in which the action is brought and the filing of two certified copies thereof with the office of mental health at its Albany office. The provisions of the judgment relating to support, care and maintenance of the mentally ill spouse during his or her life and to security therefore may be modified or amended at any time by the court upon due notice to the other party and other interested parties as the court may direct and in proper case the value of the suitable support, care and maintenance to such spouse during the balance of his or her life based upon appropriate mortality tables may be adjudged and determined by the court in which the estate of a deceased spouse is being administered and the same may be recovered on behalf of the mentally ill spouse from the estate of the deceased spouse. If the mentally ill spouse is maintained in an institution or otherwise under the jurisdiction of the office of mental health, the suitable support, care and maintenance as required in the judgment, unless otherwise directed by the court, shall be the charge established by the commissioner of mental health and such charge may be recovered in the manner provided by law. Such amount shall continue to be so required for the support of the mentally ill spouse in the event of his or her removal from the custody of the office of mental health unless thereafter otherwise directed by the court. Any security exacted for the suitable support, care and maintenance during [the] life of the mentally ill spouse shall be available to that spouse or any person on his or her behalf or to any person or agency providing support, care and maintenance for such spouse in the event that the required payments for such support, care and maintenance have not been made and upon application to the court the other spouse shall be ordered and directed to provide additional or further security.

2. Judgment annulling a marriage on such ground shall not be rendered until, in addition to any other proofs in the case, a thorough examination of the alleged mentally ill party shall have been made by three physicians who are recognized authorities on mental disease, to be appointed by the court, all of whom shall have agreed that such party is incurably mentally ill and shall have so reported to the court. In such action, the testimony of a physician attached to a state hospital in the department of mental hygiene as to information which he acquired in attending a patient in a professional capacity at such hospital, shall be taken before a referee appointed by a judge of the court in which such action is pending if the court in its discretion shall determine that the distance such physician must travel to attend the trial would be a great inconvenience to him or the hospital, or that other sufficient reason exists for the appointment of a referee for such purpose; provided, however, that any judge of such court at any time in his discretion, notwithstanding such deposition, may order that a subpoena issue for the attendance and examination of such physician upon the trial of the action. In such case a copy of the order shall be served together with the subpoena.

3. Except as provided in paragraph five,* when the person alleged to be incurably mentally ill is confined in a state hospital for the mentally ill of this state, one, and one only, of

the physicians so appointed shall be a member of the resident medical staff of such hospital designated by the director thereof. If the alleged incurably mentally ill person is not confined in a state hospital for the mentally ill of this state, one of the examining physicians named in pursuance of this section shall be the director of a state hospital for the mentally ill if the alleged mentally ill person is within this state, or the superintendent or comparable officer of a state hospital for the mentally ill of the state or country where the alleged mentally ill person is present if the alleged mentally ill person is outside of this state. The report of such superintendent or comparable officer of a state hospital for the mentally ill of such other state or country shall not be received in evidence or considered by the court unless he shall be a well educated physician with at least five years of training and experience in the care and treatment of persons suffering from mental disorders.

4. When the plaintiff has been permitted to bring such action or prosecute the same as a poor person and the alleged incurably mentally ill defendant is present within this state, the court shall appoint three physicians who are examining physicians, as defined by section 1.05* of the mental hygiene law, in the employment of the department of mental hygiene. If the alleged mentally ill person be outside of this state, the court may, upon proof thereof, appoint three examining physicians who are qualified under the laws or regulations of the foreign state or country where the alleged mentally ill person is present and who have qualifications comparable to those specified in section 1.05 of the mental hygiene law of the state, provided, however, that one of such examining physicians shall be the superintendent or comparable officer of a state hospital for the mentally ill of such foreign state or country with qualifications as specified in paragraph four.* Such examiners shall make the examination of the alleged mentally ill party present in this state and file with the court a verified report of their findings and conclusions without costs to such plaintiff when the plaintiff is a poor person. Examination of an alleged mentally ill party present outside of this state shall be made at the expense of the plaintiff. Such report shall be received in evidence upon the trial of the action without the personal appearance or testimony of such examiners. If the court shall deem it necessary that the testimony of any such examiners be taken, the court may order the taking of such testimony by deposition only. The examiners so appointed by the court may be members of the resident medical staff of any state hospital, whether or not the alleged mentally ill person is being confined there.

(L. 1962, ch. 313, §6; L. 1966, ch. 572, §1; L. 1973, ch. 195, §17; L. 1978, ch. 550, §16; L. 1980, ch. 281, §§6, 7.)

§142. Court may dismiss the petition for annulment in action by next friend if justice requires

Where the next friend of an infant, mentally retarded person or mentally ill person maintains an action annulling a marriage, the court may dismiss the complaint if justice so requires, although, in a like case, the party to the marriage, if plaintiff, would be entitled to judgment.

(L. 1962, ch. 313, §6; L. 1978, ch. 550, §17.)

§143. Right to jury trial in annulment actions

In an action to annul a marriage, except where it is founded upon an allegation of the physical incapacity of one of the parties thereto, there is a right to trial by a jury of all the issues of fact.

(L. 1962, ch. 313, §6; L. 1963, ch. 685, §1.)

§144. Proof is required in action for annulment

1. In an action to annul a marriage, a final judgment annulling the marriage shall not be rendered by default for want of an appearance or pleading, or by consent, or upon a trial of an issue, without proof of the facts upon which the allegation of nullity is founded. Plaintiff shall prove that there has been no such cohabitation between the parties as would bar a judgment except that in an action under subdivision (c) of section one hundred forty the plaintiff may prove instead that the mental illness still continues.

2. In any action, whether or not contested, brought to annul a marriage, the declaration or confession of either party to the marriage is not alone sufficient as proof, but other satisfactory evidence of the facts must be produced.

(L.1962, c. 313, § 6; L.1978, c. 550, § 18.)

§146. Final judgment is conclusive evidence of the invalidity of the marriage

A final judgment, annulling a marriage rendered during the lifetime of both the parties is conclusive evidence of the invalidity of the marriage in every court of record or not of record, in any action or special proceeding, civil or criminal. Such a judgment rendered after the death of either party to the marriage is conclusive only as against the parties to the action and those claiming under them.

(L. 1962, ch. 313, §6.)

2. Legal Separation

A judicial separation differs from an action for divorce. Whereas a divorce terminates the marriage, a judicial separation relieves the parties from living together but does not formally dissolve the marriage. (Historically, a judicial separation was called *divorce a mensa et thoro* or "divorce from bed and board.") Homer H. Clark, Jr., Law of Domestic Relations in the United States 266-267 (2d ed., 1988).

Judicial separation in New York differs from divorce in additional important ways: (1) a right to jury trial exists in actions for divorce but not separation (DRL §173, included in Section D1 *infra*); (2) there is statutory authorization in a divorce action based on adultery (but not in an action for judicial separation) for a plaintiff or defendant to serve process on a co-respondent who then has the option of contesting the charge (DRL §172); (3) the court may revoke a judgment of separation (but not divorce) upon the parties' joint application and reconciliation, thereby dispensing with the need for the parties to undergo another marriage ceremony (DRL §203); and (4) a divorced husband or wife is not considered a "surviving spouse" for purposes of intestate succession (i.e., inheritance without a will) whereas a husband or wife who is legally separated is still considered a legal spouse under New York's Estates, Powers and Trusts Law (e.g., EPTL §5-1.2) unless the judgment was rendered against the surviving spouse. Alan D. Scheinkman, 11 N.Y. Prac., N.Y. Law of Domestic Relations §11:3 (2005) [hereinafter Scheinkman, *supra*].

New York's Domestic Relations Law specifies grounds for judicial separation in Section 200, and grounds for divorce in Section 170. (On the grounds for divorce, see Section B *infra*.) The parties may obtain a judicial separation in New York on five fault-based grounds: (1) cruelty, (2) abandonment, (3) nonsupport, (4) adultery, and (5) incarceration (DRL §200).

All of the aforementioned grounds (except for nonsupport) also constitute grounds for divorce. However, abandonment must be more serious for divorce purposes than for separation purposes, i.e., it must persist for at least one year. The incarceration of defendant (for both divorce and separation purposes) must persist for three or more consecutive years following the marriage. Nonsupport is a ground for separation but not for divorce. Actions for judicial separation in New York are limited to the aforementioned statutory grounds. Sandra Mulay Casey et al., Separation of Spouses, NY Jur.2d §1907 (2003).

Actions for judicial separation are subject to the fault-based defense of justification. According to DRL §202, a defendant in an action for judicial separation may offer, as justification, the misconduct of the plaintiff. If proven, the defendant is entitled to judgment. See Silverman v. Silverman, 632 N.Y.S.2d 393 (Sup. Ct. 1995) (holding that wife's adultery precluded her from obtaining judgment of separation).

When a plaintiff commences an action for annulment, a defendant may counterclaim for annulment, separation, or divorce. Scheinkman, *supra*, at §10:1. Residency requirements for actions for separation are set forth in DRL §230 and are discussed *infra*.

Note that the spouses may also live separate and apart pursuant to a *written agreement* of separation. See Divorce Grounds and Defenses, Section B *infra*.

New York Domestic Relations Law

§200. Grounds for legal separation

An action may be maintained by a husband or wife against the other party to the marriage to procure a judgment separating the parties from bed and board, forever, or for a limited time, for any of the following causes:

1. The cruel and inhuman treatment of the plaintiff by the defendant such that the conduct of the defendant so endangers the physical or mental well being of the plaintiff as renders it unsafe or improper for the plaintiff to cohabit with the defendant.
2. The abandonment of the plaintiff by the defendant.
3. The neglect or refusal of the defendant-spouse to provide for the support of the plaintiff-spouse where the defendant-spouse is chargeable with such support under the provisions of section thirty-two of this chapter or of section four hundred twelve of the family court act.
4. The commission of an act of adultery by the defendant; except where such offense is committed by the procurement or with the connivance of the plaintiff or where there is voluntary cohabitation of the parties with the knowledge of the offense or where action was not commenced within five years after the discovery by the plaintiff of the offense charged or where the plaintiff has also been guilty of adultery under such circumstances that the defendant would have been entitled, if innocent, to a divorce, provided that adultery for the purposes of this subdivision is hereby defined as the commission of an act of sexual intercourse, oral sexual conduct or anal sexual conduct, voluntarily performed by the defendant, with a person other than the plaintiff after the marriage of plaintiff and defendant. Oral sexual conduct and anal sexual conduct includes, but not limited to, sexual conduct as defined in subdivision two of Section 130.00 and subdivision three of Section 130.20 of the penal law.
5. The confinement of the defendant in prison for a period of three or more consecutive years after the marriage of plaintiff and defendant.

(L. 1962, ch. 313, §8; L. 1966, ch. 254, §5; L. 1968, ch. 702, §1; L. 1981, ch. 300, §1; L. 2003, ch. 264, §54.)

§202. Defenses in action for legal separation

The defendant in an action for separation from bed and board may set up, in justification, the misconduct of the plaintiff; and if that defense is established to the satisfaction of the court, the defendant is entitled to judgment.

(L. 1962, ch. 313, §8.)

§203. Court may revoke judgment of separation

Upon the joint application of the parties, accompanied with satisfactory evidence of their reconciliation, a judgment for a separation, forever, or for a limited period, rendered as prescribed in this article, may be revoked at any time by the court which rendered it, subject to such regulations and restrictions as the court thinks fit to impose.

(L. 1962, ch. 313, §8.)

B. DIVORCE GROUNDS AND DEFENSES

By statute, New York provides six grounds for divorce. The first four are traditional fault-based grounds: (1) cruelty, (2) abandonment, (3) incarceration for more than three years following the marriage, and (4) adultery (DRL §170(1)-(4)). The other two grounds are based on separation: (1) living apart on the basis of a judicial separation, and (2) living apart on the basis of a separation agreement (DRL §170(5)-(6)). Until the state legislature enacted New York's Divorce Reform Law of 1966 (L. 1966, ch. 254, effective 1967), spouses could obtain a divorce only on the ground of adultery. The Divorce Reform Law broadened the bases for divorce to the aforementioned six grounds.

Adultery was the only grounds for divorce in New York from the time the state enacted the first divorce statute in 1787 until 1966. Ranney, *supra*, at 505. From the eighteenth century until the late nineteenth century, reformers made repeated but unsuccessful efforts to expand the permissible grounds for divorce. *Id.* at 529.

As a result, social pressure contributed to three "new outlets" for disgruntled spouses: out-of-state divorces, annulments, and a "widespread but tacit agreement among litigants, lawyers, and many trial judges to accept minimal evidence of adultery as adequate proof in divorce cases." *Id.* at 530. In the early twentieth century, a new lucrative business developed: Agencies provided proof of "adultery" for husbands who desired a divorce by supplying young women to accompany the husband to a hotel where a detective employed by the agency witnessed the "transgression." "Trial courts consistently held this was adequate circumstantial evidence of adultery." *Id.* at 531. Today, proof of adultery may extend to acts that occur post-separation. See, e.g., Golub v. Ganz, 802 N.Y.S.2d 526 (App. Div. 2006) (holding that an act of adultery that begins after the action for divorce commences, but before the divorce is final, establishes a ground for divorce, even if no adultery existed before the original complaint was filed).

Divorce on the ground of cruelty requires cruel and inhuman conduct that "so endangers the physical or mental well being of the plaintiff" as to render cohabitation "unsafe or improper" (DRL §170). See, e.g., Holmes v. Holmes, 807 N.Y.S.2d 217 (App. Div. 2006) (holding that a husband was entitled to divorce on ground of cruel and inhuman treatment where a wife, who was a substance abuser, became aggressive when drunk and purposely pursued husband and rammed his car while he was driving — leading to criminal charges against her and a stay-away order of protection in husband's favor).

The statute thus has two essential elements: the cruel and inhuman treatment and the effect of that treatment on the plaintiff. Therefore, a plaintiff must allege that she or he suffered the requisite degree of physical or mental harm as a result of defendant's cruelty. See, e.g., P.K. v. R.K., N.Y.L.J., June 17, 2006, at 23 (dismissing a wife's counterclaim that her husband's extramarital affair constituted cruelty because she failed to allege that she sustained any harm by virtue of her husband's acts).

Case law rejects an interpretation of cruelty as mere incompatibility. Hessen v. Hessen, 353 N.Y.S.2d 421 (N.Y. 1974); Conrad v. Conrad, 790 N.Y.S.2d 594, 596 (App. Div. 2005). Further, *Hessen* specified that courts must consider certain factors in determining whether cruelty has been established: the ages of the parties, the duration of the marriage, and the effect of a loss of support for the dependent party. *Hessen*, 353 N.Y.S.2d at 411.

New York requires a higher degree of proof of cruelty for divorce from a long-term, compared to short-term, marriage. See, e.g., Pfoltzer v. Pfoltzer, 779 N.Y.S.2d 668 (App. Div. 2004) (holding that evidence was sufficient to support divorce on grounds of cruelty in 19-year marriage despite the high degree of proof required owing to the long duration of the marriage). The rule, reflecting outdated paternalism, expresses a judicial policy that condemns the loss of postdivorce support for a dependent older wife. In addition, according to a recent New York case, cruel and inhuman treatment includes *inter alia* conduct by a spouse who has been involved in a long-term intimate relationship with a third party. P.K. v. R.K., *supra.*

For abandonment, case law specifies that the spouse's departure from the marital residence must be unjustified and without consent. See Myrna Felder, P.K. v. R.K.: When Is Abandonment Justified?, N.Y.L.J., Aug. 14, 2006, at 3 (citing Schine v. Schine, 335 N.Y.S.2d 58 (N.Y. 1972); Johnson v. Johnson, 561 N.Y.S. 2d 1018 (App. Div. 1990)). P.K. v. R.K., *supra*, provides an illustration of the type of conduct that establishes justification for abandonment: The court held that the wife's admission of her long-term affair justified the husband's departure, thereby precluding the wife's counterclaim on the ground of the husband's abandonment. Further, case law also holds that domestic violence can provide justification for a spouse's departure from the marital residence. See Felder, *supra* (citing Del Galdo v. Del Galdo, 379 N.Y.S.2d 479 (App. Div. 1976)).

Note that New York law also provides for divorce on the ground of "absence" of a spouse, requiring that the defendant have absented himself or herself for five successive years, during which time the plaintiff believes the defendant to be dead and has conducted a diligent, unsuccessful search to discover whether the spouse is living (DRL §221).

All states have some form of no-fault divorce. However, "no-fault" does not have the same meaning in all jurisdictions. For example, California adopted no-fault divorce with the enactment of the Family Law Act of 1969 (originally codified as Cal. Civ. Code §4509, now Cal. Fam. Code §2335) that permitted divorce or legal separation on the grounds of "irreconcilable differences" and incurable insanity, and also authorized an equal division of community property without regard to fault. Many states (but not New York) permit no-fault divorce at the request of only one spouse (unilateral divorce) if the parties have lived "separate and apart" for a statutorily prescribed period of time.

New York does not have a pure no-fault ground for divorce, such as "irreconcilable differences" or "incompatibility." Rather, spouses in New York may not obtain a no-fault divorce unless they have lived separate and apart on the basis of a separation agreement for over a year and the party who wishes the divorce has substantially complied with that agreement (DRL §170(6)). Thus, a mutually agreed-upon separation agreement, substantially performed after one year, and one year's separation is the only means whereby a no-fault divorce may be secured under New York law. Absent these circumstances, unilateral divorce in New York can be maintained only on fault grounds. Even if the spouses live separate and apart on the basis of a judicial separation, this circumstance is not sufficient to enable the parties to obtain a no-fault divorce. That is, fault creeps in the back door for parties who wish to prove that they lived apart based on a judicial separation because separation is available in New York only on the grounds of adultery, cruelty, abandonment, nonsupport, or incarceration (DRL §200). Scheinkman, *supra*, at §1:1. See generally Rhona Bork, Note, Taking Fault with New York's Fault-Based Divorce: Is the Law Constitutional?, 16 St. John's J.

Legal Comment, 165 (2002) (considering whether the New York divorce law that requires fault in contested divorce actions may violate constitutional law).

Fault-based defenses are available in some situations under New York law. Traditionally, divorce was awarded to a spouse who was innocent of wrongdoing. As a result, the defendant could introduce certain fault-based defenses that would bar the plaintiff's action. New York still provides for some of these defenses in cases of adultery. Thus, the plaintiff will not be entitled to a divorce based on the defendant's adultery in cases of the plaintiff's connivance or procurement (i.e., participation in, or consent to, the defendant's wrongful conduct); condonation (forgiveness by the wronged spouse, with resumption of sexual relations following knowledge of the wrongdoer's misconduct); or recrimination (both parties' being at fault for adultery) (DRL §171).

Note that these defenses do not apply if the plaintiff's claim is based on the defendant's cruel and inhuman treatment. See, e.g., P.K. v. R.K., *supra* (rejecting the wife's argument that her defense of condonation defeated husband's claim of cruel and inhuman treatment, reasoning that condonation is not a defense to a cause of action for divorce based on cruel and inhuman treatment).

According to the statute of limitations, an action for divorce or separation must be commenced within five years after the plaintiff discovers the wrongdoing (DRL §210).

The New York legislature has been considering divorce reform legislation, particularly liberalizing the rules for no-fault divorce. No-fault divorce has been opposed in New York for many years by a coalition of the Catholic Church and feminist groups. However, in September 2004, the Women's Bar Association of New York (the largest bar association in the country dedicating to advancing the status of women in the legal system) reversed its longstanding policy of opposition to no-fault divorce. The organization changed its policy because of a desire to eliminate the lengthy and expensive trials that are necessary to prove fault under current law. See Women's Bar Calls for No-Fault Divorce Legislation, N.Y. L.J., May 30, 2006, at 2. The Women's Bar Association also was influenced by a concern for the victims of domestic violence who desire to divorce but cannot afford the financial costs of a lengthy trial. In addition, divorce reform was spurred by Chief Judge Judith S. Kaye who, in her State of the Judiciary address in February 2006, advocated the adoption of no-fault divorce. *Id.*

As of 2007, the New York legislature continues to consider enactment of no-fault legislation. Assembly Bill A03027 proposes the Divorce Reform Act of 2007, adding irreconcilable differences as a ground for divorce in Domestic Relations Law §170. Recently, a New York trial court judge made an unusual decision to stay a divorce case in light of the pending divorce reform legislation. In Molinari v. Molinari, 2007 WL 1119894 (N.Y. Sup. Ct. 2007), Justice Robert A. Ross, of the Nassau County Supreme Court, used his ruling to criticize the problems created by the archaic fault-based statute in New York, particularly the significant cost and delay and exacerbation of family tensions. Retaining jurisdiction for a reasonable period of time pending legislative reform, he stated that his decision was "not an abdication of judicial duty, but the fulfillment of a constitutional responsibility." *Id.* at *5.

In response, legislators indicated that approval of the legislation was not guaranteed and commented that they could not recall a judge ever staying a ruling pending passage of legislation. Joel Stashenko, Divorce Ruling Awaits Action in Legislature, 237 N.Y.L.J., Apr. 19, 2007, at 1. A few weeks later, Justice Ross denied Mr. Molinari's petition for divorce, ruling that he failed to prove a prima facie case of constructive abandonment (i.e., the refusal of a spouse to engage in sexual relations for at least a year despite repeated requests from the other spouse). The judge noted that, because Mr. Molinari was the spouse who left the couple's home, his claim of constructive abandonment by the wife was "incredulous." According to the plaintiff's attorney, Mr. Molinari has since moved to New Jersey and is likely to file for divorce in that state. News in Brief, 237 N.Y.L.J., May 3, 2007, at 1.

Although the judge's ruling did not spur passage of the no-fault bill, it may have facilitated passage of a different bill to shorten the necessary period of living apart pursuant to a judicial decree or written agreement of separation (the so-called "conversion divorce") from one year to three months. See generally J. Herbie DiFonzo & Ruth C. Stern, Addicted to Fault: Why Divorce Reform Has Lagged in New York, Pace L. Rev. (forthcoming 2007).

New York Domestic Relations Law

§170. Grounds for divorce

An action for divorce may be maintained by a husband or wife to procure a judgment divorcing the parties and dissolving the marriage on any of the following grounds:

(1) The cruel and inhuman treatment of the plaintiff by the defendant such that the conduct of the defendant so endangers the physical or mental well being of the plaintiff as renders it unsafe or improper for the plaintiff to cohabit with the defendant.

(2) The abandonment of the plaintiff by the defendant for a period of one or more years.

(3) The confinement of the defendant in prison for a period of three or more consecutive years after the marriage of plaintiff and defendant.

(4) The commission of an act of adultery, provided that adultery for the purposes of articles ten, eleven, and eleven-A of this chapter, is hereby defined as the commission of an act of sexual intercourse, oral sexual conduct or anal sexual conduct, voluntarily performed by the defendant, with a person other than the plaintiff after the marriage of plaintiff and defendant. Oral sexual conduct and anal sexual conduct include, but are not limited to, sexual conduct as defined in subdivision two of section 130.00 and subdivision three of section 130.20 of the penal law.

(5) The husband and wife have lived apart pursuant to a decree or judgment of separation for a period of one or more

years after the granting of such decree or judgment, and satisfactory proof has been submitted by the plaintiff that he or she has substantially performed all the terms and conditions of such decree or judgment.

(6) The husband and wife have lived separate and apart pursuant to a written agreement of separation, subscribed by the parties thereto and acknowledged or proved in the form required to entitle a deed to be recorded, for a period of one or more years after the execution of such agreement and satisfactory proof has been submitted by the plaintiff that he or she has substantially performed all the terms and conditions of such agreement. Such agreement shall be filed in the office of the clerk of the county wherein either party resides. In lieu of filing such agreement, either party to such agreement may file a memorandum of such agreement, which memorandum shall be similarly subscribed and acknowledged or proved as was the agreement of separation and shall contain the following information: (a) the names and addresses of each of the parties, (b) the date of marriage of the parties, (c) the date of the agreement of separation and (d) the date of this subscription and acknowledgment or proof of such agreement of separation.

(L. 1966, ch. 254, §2; L. 1967, ch. 648, §1; L. 1968, ch. 700, §§1, 2; L. 1969, ch. 964, §1; L. 1970, ch. 835, §§1, 2; L. 1970, ch. 867, §1; L. 1971, ch. 801, §§1, 2; L. 1972, ch. 719, §1; L. 1974, ch. 920, §7; L. 1974, ch. 1047, §1; L. 1975, ch. 415, §2; L. 2003, c. 264, §53, effective November 1, 2003.)

§171. Defenses to divorce based on adultery

In either of the following cases, the plaintiff is not entitled to a divorce, although the adultery is established:

1. Where the offense was committed by the procurement or with the connivance of the plaintiff.

2. Where the offense charged has been forgiven by the plaintiff. The forgiveness may be proven, either affirmatively, or by the voluntary cohabitation of the parties with the knowledge of the fact.

3. Where there has been no express forgiveness, and no voluntary cohabitation of the parties, but the action was not commenced within five years after the discovery by the plaintiff of the offense charged.

4. Where the plaintiff has also been guilty of adultery under such circumstances that the defendant would have been entitled, if innocent, to a divorce.

(L. 1962, ch. 313, §7.)

§210. Time limitations on actions for divorce and separation

No action for divorce or separation may be maintained on a ground which arose more than five years before the date of the commencement of that action for divorce or separation except where:

(a) In an action for divorce, the grounds therefore are one of those specified in subdivision (2), (4), (5) or (6) of section one hundred seventy of this chapter, or

(b) In an action for separation, the grounds therefore are one of those specified in subdivision 2 or 4 of section two hundred of this chapter.

(L. 1966, ch. 254, §7; L. 1967, ch. 648, §2; L. 1968, ch. 799, §1; L. 1985, ch. 641, §1.)

§220. Requirements to dissolve marriage on ground of absence

A special proceeding to dissolve a marriage on the ground of absence may be maintained in either of the following cases:

1. Where the petitioner is a resident of this state and has been a resident thereof for one year immediately preceding the commencement of the special proceeding.

2. Where the matrimonial domicile at the time of the disappearance of the absent spouse was within the state.

(L. 1962, ch. 313, §9.)

§221. Required allegations in petition for absence

The petition shall allege that the husband or wife of such party has absented himself or herself for five successive years then last past without being known to such party to be living during that time; that such party believes such husband or wife to be dead; and that a diligent search has been made to discover evidence showing that such husband or wife is living, and no such evidence has been found. The court shall thereupon by order require notice of the presentation and object of such petition to be published in a newspaper in the English language designated in the order as most likely to give notice to such absent husband or wife once each week for three successive weeks; such notice shall be directed to the husband or wife who has so absented himself or herself and shall state the time and place of the hearing upon such petition, which time shall be not less than forty days after the completion of the publication of such notice; said notice must be subscribed with the name of the petitioner and with the name of the petitioner's attorney and with his office address, specifying a place within the state where there is a post-office. If in a city, said notice must also set forth the street and street number, if any, of such attorney's office address or other suitable designation of the particular locality in which said office address is located. In addition to the foregoing requirements said notice must be in substantially the following form, the blanks being properly filled: "Supreme court, __________ county. In the matter of the application of __________ for dissolution of his or her marriage with __________.

To__________________________________: Take notice that a petition has been presented to this court by , your husband or wife, for the dissolution of your marriage on the ground that you have absented yourself for five successive years last past without being known to him or her to be living and that he or she believes you to be dead, and that pursuant to an order of said court, entered the day of , 19_, a hearing will be had upon said petition at the said supreme court, term part __, in the _________ county court house, in the state of New York, on the day of , 19_, at __o'clock in the noon. Dated ;" and if the court, after the filing of proof of the proper publication of said notice and after a hearing and proof taken, is satisfied of the truth of all the allegations contained in the petition, it may make a final order dissolving such marriage.

(L. 1962, ch. 313, §9; L. 1971, ch. 161, §1.)

C. JURISDICTION

For divorce purposes, the concept of jurisdiction encompasses issues of subject matter jurisdiction, personal jurisdiction, residency requirements, and constitutional due process concerns. A state has jurisdiction to dissolve a marriage based on the petitioner's domicile in the forum state. Thus, a state's domiciliary requirements, sometimes termed "durational residency requirements" (generally applicable to the divorce petitioner), confer *subject matter jurisdiction* over the marriage upon a given court. Clark, Domestic Relations, *supra*, at 413. In addition, there must be *personal jurisdiction* over the defendant. Jurisdictional rules pertaining to personal jurisdiction over the defendant in the divorce context differ from personal jurisdiction rules in other civil contexts, as explained *infra*. Further, jurisdiction for divorce purposes is "in rem" (i.e., over the marital status).

Personal jurisdiction over the defendant is not required to terminate a marriage if the plaintiff is domiciled in the forum state. This special jurisdictional rule varies from the usual rule in civil actions requiring personal jurisdiction over the defendant. Nevertheless, notice to the defendant in divorce cases that complies with due process is required to inform the defendant of the pendency of the action.

Furthermore, if personal jurisdiction over the defendant is not obtained, then the court may adjudicate only the issue of marital status but not the economic issues (i.e., spousal support, property division). This follows because depriving the defendant of property rights (i.e., regarding support or property division) without due process would violate the Constitution.

The domiciliary requirement assumed considerable importance during the fault era for a spouse who might want to establish domicile elsewhere to evade strict fault-based grounds of the marital forum. Domicile includes the twin elements of physical presence plus intention to remain permanently. Generally, domicile is distinguishable from "residence" because a person may have more than one residence (e.g., a college student) but only one legal domicile.

All states have some form of *residency requirements,* requiring a petitioner to be a state resident for a period of time before maintaining an action for divorce. Some states' durational residency requirements for divorce are construed as indistinguishable from domicile (i.e., some states impose durational residency requirements instead of a domiciliary requirement); other states impose both domicile and residency requirements. The United States Supreme Court upheld the constitutionality of state residency requirements (Sosna v. Iowa, 419 U.S. 393 (1975)). The purpose of such requirements during the fault-based era was to prevent states from becoming "divorce mills."

In 1967 when the New York legislature enacted major divorce reform by expanding divorce grounds, the legislature added the current residency requirements. Scheinkman, *supra*, at §8:18. Three different residency periods are applicable, depending on circumstances: (1) no prior residency period is necessary if both parties were New York residents when the action was commenced and the ground for divorce arose in the state; (2) a one-year continuous residency period is required if only one of the parties is a New York resident, and (a) the parties were married in the state, (b) resided in the state as husband and wife, or (c) the grounds for divorce occurred in the state; or (3) a two-year continuous residency period is required if New York has no other connection to the marriage (DRL §230(5)) (emphasis added). Scheinkman, *supra*, at §8:18. These residency requirements apply not only to actions for divorce, but also to actions to annul a voidable marriage, declare the nullity of a void marriage, or for separation (DRL §230).

According to New York case law, the residency requirements are elements of the cause of action and do not go to the issue of whether the court has subject matter jurisdiction to determine the action. Lacks v. Lacks, 390 N.Y.S.2d 875 (N.Y. 1976) (refusing to grant wife's request for postjudgment relief to set aside a final judgment of divorce on the ground that the husband failed to meet the statutory residency requirements). Scheinkman, *supra*, at §1:2. Courts have held that where the divorce action is dismissed for failure to meet the one-year residency requirement, the court may convert the action into a support proceeding and decide issues of support, maintenance, and expenses under CPLR §103(c). Venizelos v. Venizelos, 629 N.Y.S.2d 218 (App. Div. 1995).

Furthermore, the Full Faith and Credit Clause of the United States Constitution (Article IV, §1) requires that a state give full faith and credit to the decrees of sister states provided that the sister state had jurisdiction. This requirement was interpreted and applied to the divorce context by the United States Supreme Court. Williams v. North Carolina (*Williams I*), 317 U.S. 287 (1942), holds that a state must recognize, under the Full Faith and Credit Clause, a divorce granted to a spouse who is domiciled in a sister state even though the stay-at-home spouse does not appear and is not served with process in the sister state.

A subsequent case, Williams v. North Carolina (*Williams II*), 325 U.S. 226 (1945), clarified that one state's determination of a petitioner's domicile is not binding on another state. That is, the decree-granting state's finding of domicile may be re-examined by another state to determine the bona fides of a petitioner's domicile.

Another New York statute addresses residency of a married woman for purposes of annulment of a voidable marriage, declaration of nullity of a void marriage, divorce, or separation. The determination of residency of a married woman, addressed in DRL §231, attempts to remedy the common law rule that the husband had the right to determine the marital domicile. In the fault-based era, such a rule enabled a husband, by moving to another state, to prevent a wife from obtaining a divorce in her home state. Currently, DRL §231 provides that if a married woman dwells in New York when she commences her divorce action, she is deemed to be a state resident even if her spouse resides elsewhere.

New York law now provides that either spouse may establish the marital domicile. In 1929, the legislature enacted DRL §61, providing that the domicile of a married "woman" for purposes of office holding and voting would be determined by the same facts and legal rules as those applicable to anyone else. The legislature amended the statute in 1976 to make it gender neutral by substituting the phrase "for all purposes without regard to sex" for the phrase "by the same facts and rules of law as that of any other person for the purpose of voting and office-holding."

New York Domestic Relations Law

§61. Married person's domicile

The domicile of a married man or woman shall be established for all purposes without regard to sex.

(L. 1929, ch. 455, §1; L. 1976, ch. 62, §2.)

§230. Residency requirements for annulment, separation, or divorce

An action to annul a marriage, or to declare the nullity of a void marriage, or for divorce or separation may be maintained only when:

1. The parties were married in the state and either party is a resident thereof when the action is commenced and has been a resident for a continuous period of one year immediately preceding, or
2. The parties have resided in this state as husband and wife and either party is a resident thereof when the action is commenced and has been a resident for a continuous period of one year immediately preceding, or
3. The cause occurred in the state and either party has been a resident thereof for a continuous period of at least one year immediately preceding the commencement of the action, or
4. The cause occurred in the state and both parties are residents thereof at the time of the commencement of the action, or
5. Either party has been a resident of the state for a continuous period of at least two years immediately preceding the commencement of the action.

(L. 1962, ch. 313, § 10; L. 1963, ch. 685, §3; L. 1966, ch. 254, §9.)

§231. Residence of married person when spouse resides elsewhere

If a married person dwells within the state when he or she commences an action against his or her spouse for divorce, annulment or separation, such person is deemed a resident thereof, although his or her spouse resides elsewhere.

(L. 1962, ch. 313, §10; L. 1976, ch. 62, §4.)

§232. Notice in action for annulment, divorce or separation

a. In an action to annul a marriage or for divorce or for separation, if the complaint is not personally served with the summons, the summons shall have legibly written or printed upon the face thereof: "Action to annul a marriage", "Action to declare the nullity of a void marriage", "Action for a divorce", or "Action for a separation", as the case may be, and shall specify the nature of any ancillary relief demanded. A judgment shall not be rendered in favor of the plaintiff upon the defendant's default in appearing or pleading, unless either

(1) the summons and a copy of the complaint were personally delivered to the defendant; or

(2) the copy of the summons

(a) personally delivered to the defendant, or

(b) served on the defendant pursuant to an order directing the method of service of the summons in accordance with the provisions of section three hundred eight or three hundred fifteen of the civil practice law and rules, shall contain such notice.

b. An affidavit or certificate proving service shall state affirmatively in the body thereof that the required notice was written or printed on the face of the copy of the summons delivered to the defendant and what knowledge the affiant or officer who executed the certificate had that he was the defendant named and how he acquired such knowledge. The court may require the affiant or officer who executed the affidavit or certificate to appear in court and be examined in respect thereto.

(L. 1962, ch. 313, §10; L. 1963, ch. 685, §4; L. 1969, ch. 712, §1; L. 1974, ch. 765, §1; L. 1978, ch. 528, §6.)

§233. Court may direct sequestration of property in the state if defendant cannot be served

Where in an action for divorce, separation, annulment or declaration of nullity of a void marriage it appears to the court that the defendant is not within the state, or cannot be found therein, or is concealing himself or herself therein, so that process cannot be personally served upon the defendant, the court may at any time and from time to time make any order or orders without notice directing the sequestration of his or her property, both real and personal and whether tangible or intangible, within the state, and may appoint a receiver thereof, or by injunction or otherwise take the same into its possession and control. The property thus sequestered and the income therefrom may be applied in whole or in part and from time to time, under the direction of the court and as justice may require, to the payment of such sum or sums as the court may deem it proper to award, by order or judgment as the case may be, and during the pendency of the action or at the termination thereof, for the education or maintenance of any of the children of a marriage, or for the support of a spouse, or for his or her expenses in bringing and carrying on said action and the proceedings incidental thereto or connected therewith; and if the rents and profits of the real estate, together with the other property so sequestered, be insufficient to pay the sums of money required, the court, upon such terms and conditions as it may prescribe, may direct the mortgage or sale of sufficient of said real estate to pay such sums. The court may appoint the plaintiff spouse receiver or sequestrator in such cases. The court may authorize such spouse to use and occupy, free of any liability for rent or use and occupation or otherwise, any house or other suitable property of the defendant spouse as a

dwelling for himself or herself with or without the children of the marriage, and may likewise turn over to the plaintiff spouse for the use of such spouse with or without the children of the marriage any chattel or chattels of the defendant spouse. The relief herein provided for is in addition to any and every other remedy to which a spouse may be entitled under the law.
(L. 1962, ch. 313, §10; L. 1980, ch. 281, §8.)

§234. Court may determine title to property in action for divorce, separation or annulment

In any action for divorce, for a separation, for an annulment or to declare the nullity of a void marriage, the court may

(1) determine any question as to the title to property arising between the parties, and

(2) make such direction, between the parties, concerning the possession of property, as in the court's discretion justice requires having regard to the circumstances of the case and of the respective parties. Such direction may be made in the final judgment, or by one or more orders from time to time before or subsequent to final judgment, or by both such order or orders and final judgment. Where the title to real property is affected, a copy of such judgment, order or decree, duly certified by the clerk of the court wherein said judgment was rendered, shall be recorded in the office of the recording officer of the county in which such property is situated, as provided by section two hundred ninety-seven-b of the real property law.
(L. 1962, ch. 313, §10; L. 1963, ch. 685, §5.)

New York Civil Practice Laws and Rules

§103. Form of Civil Judicial Proceedings

(a) One form of action. There is only one form of civil action. The distinctions between actions at law and suits in equity, and the forms of those actions and suits, have been abolished.

(b) Action or special proceeding. All civil judicial proceedings shall be prosecuted in the form of an action, except where prosecution in the form of a special proceeding is authorized. Except where otherwise prescribed by law, procedure in special proceedings shall be the same as in actions, and the provisions of the civil practice law and rules applicable to actions shall be applicable to special proceedings.

(c) Improper form. If a court has obtained jurisdiction over the parties, a civil judicial proceeding shall not be dismissed solely because it is not brought in the proper form, but the court shall make whatever order is required for its proper prosecution. If the court finds it appropriate in the interests of justice, it may convert a motion into a special proceeding, or vice-versa, upon such terms as may be just, including the payment of fees and costs.
(L. 1962, ch. 308; amended L. 2002, ch. 593, §1, effective January 1, 2003.)

D. PROCEDURE

A petitioner commences an action for divorce or other matrimonial action in New York (pursuant to DRL §211) by filing (with the county clerk where the action is brought) either a summons with verified complaint (CPLR §304) or a summons with notice (containing the notice required by DRL §232 that sets forth the nature of the action and the requested relief). Service on the defendant must comply with due process requirements. Thus, filing and service of process is required to bring the parties in a matrimonial action within the court's jurisdiction. On jurisdiction generally, see Section C, Jurisdiction, *supra*.

DRL §211 also provides that a matrimonial action cannot be granted by default. A default in appearance by the defendant will not support a default judgment. That is, the plaintiff must submit appropriate proof in support of his or her complaint to obtain relief.

Statutes of limitations exist in New York for maintenance of actions for divorce and separation on some grounds. Thus, DRL §210 provides a five-year period of limitations for maintenance of an action for divorce on the ground of cruelty or incarceration. The statute provides a similar period for an action for separation on the grounds of cruelty, neglect or nonsupport, or incarceration. However, for incarceration, New York has adopted a "continuous wrong" rule, according to which the statute of limitations begins running upon release, rather than at the beginning of imprisonment. Covington v. Walker, 819 N.E.2d 1025 (N.Y. 2004).

Special procedural rules are applicable to divorce actions based on adultery. By statute, a plaintiff or defendant may serve process on a co-respondent who may then appear and defend (DRL §172).

The right to a jury trial on the *grounds* of divorce was accorded by early legislative enactment (i.e., the legislature granted courts the power to decide trial by jury on the question of adultery for divorce purposes by Laws of 1787, ch. 69), and was later codified as DRL §173. See Mandel v. Mandel, 439 N.Y.S.2d 576, 577 (Sup. Ct. 1981) (explaining history). However, there is no right to a jury trial on issues of equitable distribution, child or spousal support, child custody, or exclusive occupancy of the marital dwelling. *Id.* at 577. Nor is there a right to jury trial on issues raised by divorce defenses, such as the defense of condonation. Eliot v. Eliot, 416 N.Y.S.2d 328 (App. Div. 1979) (holding that it was an abuse of discretion to grant jury trial on issue of husband's condonation of wife's adultery).

Courts often require one spouse to pay the other's attorneys' fees and litigation costs. Historically, a gender-based rule, premised on the husband's duty to provide necessaries, prevailed. In Orr v. Orr, 440 U.S. 268 (1979), the United States Supreme Court held that gender-based alimony awards are unconstitutional. That decision led many jurisdictions to impose responsibility for fees and expenses on the spouse in the superior financial position. When the spouses occupy similar financial positions, they now pay their own fees and costs.

According to New York statute, courts may make awards of counsel fees and litigation expenses to either spouse, dependent on the circumstances and financial need (DRL §237). In response to the United States Supreme Court's decision in *Orr, supra*, the New York Supreme Court, Appellate Division, held that statutory provisions, which pertain to counsel fees and expenses, would be construed so as to authorize awards of counsel fees on a gender-neutral, needs basis, and, as so construed, the provisions did not deny equal protection. Childs v. Childs, 419 N.Y.S.2d 533 (N.Y. App. Div. 1979), mandamus denied, 444 U.S. 1010 (1980), appeal dismissed and cert. denied, 446 U.S. 901 (1980). In 1980 the state legislature enacted divorce reform legislation (the Equitable Distribution Law) that (*inter alia*) made many statutes, including DRL §237, gender neutral.

According to (DRL §237(a)), courts may make awards of counsel fees and litigation expenses not only in divorce but also in proceedings for annulment of a voidable marriage, declarations of nullity of a void marriage, separation, or divorce. In addition, the statute provides for fees and expenses to declare the validity or nullity of a judgment of divorce rendered against a spouse who was the defendant in any action outside the state and who did not appear, provided that such spouse asserts the nullity of the foreign judgment; and also to enjoin the prosecution in any other jurisdiction of an action for divorce (*Id.*). The same statute (DRL §237(b)) authorizes fees and expenses to annul or modify an order or judgment for alimony or for custody, visitation, or maintenance of a child, made pursuant to DRL §236 or DRL §240. A different statute (DRL §238) authorizes courts to make awards of counsel fees regarding enforcement proceedings.

Both DRL §237(c) and DRL §238 address awards of counsel fees in enforcement proceedings. Under DRL §238, a court has discretion whether to award such fees. However, under DRL §237(c), the court *must* award counsel fees where it finds that defendant's failure to obey any lawful order compelling the payment of support, maintenance, or a distributive award was willful.

See also Bloch v. Bloch, 746 N.Y.S.2d 15 (N.Y. App. Div. 2002) (holding that there was no justification, on the basis of need or fairness, for an award to wife of $15,000 in interim attorney fees to defend against the husband's appeal of an earlier $35,000 fee award because she had a substantial income and assets and had received a sizable equitable distribution); O'Shea v. O'Shea, 711 N.E.2d 193 (N.Y. 1999) (holding that courts may award counsel fees for legal services that were rendered before the action commenced and for those rendered in connection with a counsel fee hearing).

New York lawyers who represent clients in "domestic relations matters" cannot charge a contingency fee and must put their fee agreements to writing (DR 2-106(C)(2)). Legislative amendments to the New York Lawyers' Code of Professional Responsibility in 1999 clarified the definition of "domestic relations matters" to explain when a lawyer's duties under DR 2-106 are imposed (22 NYCCRR 1200.1 (j)). In addition, DR 2-106(F) states that, in a domestic relations matter, a lawyer must provide a prospective client with a statement of client's rights and responsibilities at an initial conference and prior to the signing of a retainer agreement. Patrick M. Connors, 1998-99 Survey of New York Law: Professional Responsibility, 50 Syracuse L. Rev. 827, 847 (2000). If the attorney fails to comply with the regulation requiring the execution and filing with the court of a retainer agreement that sets forth the compensation and services rendered, the attorney is precluded from seeking fees from the client. Mulcahy v. Mulcahy, 729 N.Y.S.2d 90 (App. Div. 2001).

1. Generally

New York Civil Practice Laws and Rules

§304. Method of commencing civil action

An action is commenced by filing a summons and complaint or summons with notice. A special proceeding is commenced by filing a petition. Where a court finds that circumstances prevent immediate filing, the signing of an order requiring the subsequent filing at a specific time and date not later than five days thereafter shall commence the action. For purposes of this section, and for purposes of sections two hundred three and three hundred six-a of this chapter, filing shall mean the delivery of the summons with notice, summons and complaint or petition to the clerk of the court in the county in which the action or special proceeding is brought or any other person designated by the clerk of the court for that purpose together with any fee required as specified in rule twenty-one hundred two of this chapter for filing. At such time of filing, the original and a copy of such papers shall be date stamped by a court clerk who shall file the original and maintain a record of the date of the filing and who shall immediately return the copy to the party who brought the filing.

(L. 1962, ch. 308; L. 1992, ch. 216, §4; L. 1994, ch. 563, §1; L. 1996, ch. 606, §2; L. 1999, ch. 367, §1, effective July 27, 1999; L. 2001, ch. 473, §1, effective November 21, 2001; L. 2001, ch. 473, §2.)

§315. Service by publication permitted in some cases

The court, upon motion without notice, shall order service of a summons by publication in an action described in section 314 if service cannot be made by another prescribed method with due diligence.

(L. 1962, ch. 308.)

New York Domestic Relations Law

§172. Plaintiff or defendant may serve co-respondent if divorce on ground of adultery

1. In an action brought to obtain a divorce on the ground of adultery the plaintiff or defendant may serve a copy of his

pleading on a co-respondent named therein. At any time within twenty days after such service, the co-respondent may appear to defend such action so far as the issues affect him. If no such service be made, then at any time before the entry of judgment a co-respondent named in any of the pleadings may make a written demand on any party for a copy of a summons and a pleading served by such party, which must be served within ten days thereafter, and he may appear to defend such action so far as the issues affect him.

2. In an action for divorce where a co-respondent has appeared and defended, in case no one of the allegations of adultery controverted by such co-respondent shall be proven, such co-respondent shall be entitled to a bill of costs against the person naming him as such co-respondent, which bill of costs shall consist only of the sum now allowed by law as a trial fee, and disbursements.

(L. 1962, ch. 313, §7.)

§173. Right to jury trial on grounds for divorce

In an action for divorce there is a right to trial by jury of the issues of the grounds for granting the divorce.

(L. 1962, ch. 313, §7; L. 1966, ch. 254, §3.)

§175. Legitimacy of children as affected by judgment of dissolution

1. Where the action for divorce is brought by the wife, the legitimacy of any child of the parties, born or begotten before the commencement of the action, is not affected by the judgment dissolving the marriage.

2. Where the action for divorce is brought by the husband, the legitimacy of a child born or begotten before the commission of the offense charged is not affected by a judgment dissolving the marriage; but the legitimacy of any other child of the wife may be determined as one of the issues in the action. In the absence of proof to the contrary, the legitimacy of all the children begotten before the commencement of the action must be presumed.

(L. 1962, ch. 313, §7.)

§210. Time limitations in actions for divorce and separation

No action for divorce or separation may be maintained on a ground which arose more than five years before the date of the commencement of that action for divorce or separation except where:

(a) In an action for divorce, the grounds therefore are one of those specified in subdivision (2), (4), (5) or (6) of section one hundred seventy of this chapter, or

(b) In an action for separation, the grounds therefore are one of those specified in subdivision 2 or 4 of section two hundred of this chapter.

(L. 1966, ch. 254, §7; L. 1967, ch. 648, §2; L. 1968, ch. 799, §1; L. 1985, ch. 641, §1.)

§211. Commencement of matrimonial action by filing summons and complaint, or summons with notice

A matrimonial action shall be commenced by the filing of a summons with the notice designated in section two hundred thirty-two of this chapter, or a summons and verified complaint as provided in section three hundred four of the civil practice law and rules. A final judgment shall be entered by default for want of appearance or pleading, or by consent, only upon competent oral proof or upon written proof that may be considered on a motion for summary judgment. Where a complaint or counterclaim in an action for divorce or separation charges adultery, the answer or reply thereto may be made without verifying it, except that an answer containing a counterclaim must be verified as to that counterclaim. All other pleadings in a matrimonial action shall be verified.

(L. 1966, ch. 254, §7; L. 1968, ch. 701, §1; L. 1970, ch. 483, §1; L. 1973, ch. 1034, §1; L. 1978, ch. 528, §5; L. 1978, ch. 532, §4; L. 1992, ch. 216, §21.)

§232. Requirements of notice to defendant

a. In an action to annul a marriage or for divorce or for separation, if the complaint is not personally served with the summons, the summons shall have legibly written or printed upon the face thereof: "Action to annul a marriage", "Action to declare the nullity of a void marriage", "Action for a divorce", or "Action for a separation", as the case may be, and shall specify the nature of any ancillary relief demanded. A judgment shall not be rendered in favor of the plaintiff upon the defendant's default in appearing or pleading, unless either

(1) the summons and a copy of the complaint were personally delivered to the defendant; or

(2) the copy of the summons

(a) personally delivered to the defendant, or

(b) served on the defendant pursuant to an order directing the method of service of the summons in accordance with the provisions of section three hundred eight or three hundred fifteen of the civil practice law and rules, shall contain such notice.

b. An affidavit or certificate proving service shall state affirmatively in the body thereof that the required notice was written or printed on the face of the copy of the summons delivered to the defendant and what knowledge the affiant or officer who executed the certificate had that he was the defendant named and how he acquired such knowledge. The court may require the affiant or officer who executed the affidavit or certificate to appear in court and be examined in respect thereto.

(L. 1962, ch. 313, §10; L. 1963, ch. 685, §4; L. 1969, ch. 712, §1; L. 1974, ch. 765, §1; L. 1978, ch. 528, §6.)

§235. Information regarding matrimonial proceedings shall be confidential

1. An officer of the court with whom the proceedings in a matrimonial action or a written agreement of separation or an action or proceeding for custody, visitation or maintenance of a child are filed, or before whom the testimony is taken, or his clerk, either before or after the termination of the suit, shall not permit a copy of any of the pleadings, affidavits, findings of fact, conclusions of law, judgment of dissolution, written agreement of separation or memorandum thereof, or testimony, or any examination or perusal thereof, to be taken

by any other person than a party, or the attorney or counsel of a party, except by order of the court.

2. If the evidence on the trial of such an action or proceeding be such that public interest requires that the examination of the witnesses should not be public, the court or referee may exclude all persons from the room except the parties to the action and their counsel, and in such case may order the evidence, when filed with the clerk, sealed up, to be exhibited only to the parties to the action or proceeding or someone interested, on order of the court.

3. Upon the application of any person to the county clerk or other officer in charge of public records within a county for evidence of the disposition, judgment or order with respect to a matrimonial action, the clerk or other such officer shall issue a "certificate of disposition", duly certifying the nature and effect of such disposition, judgment or order and shall in no manner evidence the subject matter of the pleadings, testimony, findings of fact, conclusions of law or judgment of dissolution derived in any such action.

4. Any county, city, town or village clerk or other municipal official issuing marriage licenses shall be required to accept, as evidence of dissolution of marriage, such "certificate of disposition" in lieu of a complete copy of the findings of fact, conclusions of law and judgment of dissolution.

5. The limitations of subdivisions one, two and three of this section in relation to confidentiality shall cease to apply one hundred years after date of filing, and such records shall thereupon be public records available to public inspection.

(L. 1962, ch. 313, §10; L. 1966, ch. 254, §10; L. 1968, ch. 445, §1; L. 1974, ch. 1027, §1; L. 1978, ch. 438, §1; L. 1979, ch. 121, §1; L. 1979, ch. 122, §1.)

§237. Counsel fees and litigation expenses

(a) In any action or proceeding brought

(1) to annul a marriage or to declare the nullity of a void marriage, or

(2) for a separation, or

(3) for a divorce, or

(4) to declare the validity or nullity of a judgment of divorce rendered against a spouse who was the defendant in any action outside the State of New York and did not appear therein where such spouse asserts the nullity of such foreign judgment, or

(5) to enjoin the prosecution in any other jurisdiction of an action for a divorce, the court may direct either spouse or, where an action for annulment is maintained after the death of a spouse, may direct the person or persons maintaining the action, to pay such sum or sums of money directly to the attorney of the other spouse to enable that spouse to carry on or defend the action or proceeding as, in the court's discretion, justice requires, having regard to the circumstances of the case and of the respective parties. Such direction must be made in the final judgment in such action or proceeding, or by one or more orders from time to time before final judgment, or by both such order or orders and the final judgment; provided, however, such direction shall be made prior to final judgment where it is shown that such order is required to enable the petitioning party to properly proceed. Any applications for counsel fees and expenses may be maintained by the attorney for either spouse in his own name in the same proceeding.

(b) Upon any application to annul or modify an order or judgment for alimony or for custody, visitation, or maintenance of a child, made as in section two hundred thirty-six or section two hundred forty provided, or upon any application by writ of habeas corpus or by petition and order to show cause concerning custody, visitation or maintenance of a child, the court may direct a spouse or parent to pay such sum or sums of money for the prosecution or the defense of the application or proceeding by the other spouse or parent as, in the court's discretion, justice requires, having regard to the circumstances of the case and of the respective parties. With respect to any such application or proceeding, such direction may be made in the order or judgment by which the particular application or proceeding is finally determined, or by one or more orders from time to time before the final order or judgment, or by both such order or orders and the final order or judgment. Any applications for counsel fees and expenses may be maintained by the attorney for either spouse in counsel's own name in the same proceeding. Representation by an attorney pursuant to paragraph (b) of subdivision nine of section one hundred eleven-b of the social services law shall not preclude an award of counsel fees to an applicant which would otherwise be allowed under this section.

(c) In any action or proceeding for failure to obey any lawful order compelling payment of support or maintenance, or distributive award the court shall, upon a finding that such failure was willful, order respondent to pay counsel fees to the attorney representing the petitioner.

(d) The term "expenses" as used in subdivisions (a) and (b) of this section shall include, but shall not be limited to, accountant fees, appraisal fees, actuarial fees, investigative fees and other fees and expenses that the court may determine to be necessary to enable a spouse to carry on or defend an action or proceeding under this section. In determining the appropriateness and necessity of fees, the court shall consider:

1. The nature of the marital property involved;

2. The difficulties involved, if any, in identifying and evaluating the marital property;

3. The services rendered and an estimate of the time involved; and

4. The applicant's financial status.

(L.1962, ch. 313, §10; L.1963, ch. 341, §1; L.1963, ch. 685, §7; L.1978, ch. 444, §1; L.1980, ch. 281, §10; L.1983, ch. 86, §1; L.1983, ch. 287, §1; L.1986, ch. 149, §1; L.1986, ch. 892, §5; L.1987, ch. 482, §1; L.1992, ch. 422, §1.)

§238. Court may require either party to pay expenses in enforcement proceedings

In any action or proceeding to compel the payment of any sum of money required to be paid by a judgment or order entered in an action for divorce, separation, annulment or declaration of nullity of a void marriage, or in any proceeding pursuant to section two hundred forty-three, two hundred forty-four, two hundred forty-five, or two hundred forty-six, the court may in its discretion require either party to pay the expenses of the other in bringing, carrying on, or defending such action or proceeding. In any such action or proceeding, applications for counsel fees and expenses may

be maintained by the attorney for the respective parties in counsel's own name and in counsel's own behalf.
(L. 1962, ch. 313, §10; L. 1963, ch. 685, §8; L. 1978, ch. 529, §1.)

§239. Court may refuse to grant stay in divorce or separation action on default of payment

In an action for divorce or separation the court or the judge thereof may refuse to grant an order to stay proceedings, where the only default is the failure of a spouse to pay alimony, maintenance or counsel fees due to his or her inability to make such payments. In no event shall a spouse who has been imprisoned for contempt of court for failure to pay alimony, maintenance or counsel fees or by virtue of an order of arrest as a provisional remedy under the civil practice law and rules be stayed from proceeding with the prosecution or defense of an action where the only default is the failure of such spouse to pay alimony, maintenance or counsel fees.
(L. 1962, ch. 313, §10; L. 1980, ch. 281, §11.)

§243. Court may direct spouse to give security for payments in action for divorce, separation or annulment

Where a judgment rendered or an order made in an action in this state for divorce, separation or annulment, or for a declaration of nullity of a void marriage, or a judgment rendered in another state for divorce upon any of the grounds provided in section one hundred seventy of this chapter, or for separation or separate support and maintenance for any of the causes specified in section two hundred, or for relief, however designated, granted upon grounds which in this state would be grounds for annulment of marriage or for a declaration of nullity of a void marriage, upon which an action has been brought in this state and judgment rendered therein, requires a spouse to provide for the education or maintenance of any of the children of a marriage, or for the support of his or her spouse, the court, in its discretion, also may direct the spouse from whom maintenance or support is sought to give reasonable security, in such a manner and within such a time as it thinks proper, for the payment, from time to time, of the sums of money required for that purpose. If he or she fails to give the security, or to make any payment required by the terms of such a judgment or order, whether or not security has been given therefore, or to pay any sum of money for the support and maintenance of the children or the support and maintenance of the spouse during the pendency of the action, or for counsel fees and expenses which he or she is required to pay by a judgment or order, the court may cause his or her personal property and the rents and profits of his or her real property to be sequestered, and may appoint a receiver thereof. The rents and profits and other property so sequestered may be applied, from time to time, under the direction of the court, to the payment of any of the sums of money specified in this section, as justice requires; and if the same shall be insufficient to pay the sums of money required, the court, on application of the receiver, may direct the mortgage or sale of such real property by the receiver, under such terms and conditions as it may prescribe, sufficient to pay such sums.
(L. 1962, ch. 313, §10; L. 1980, ch. 281, §11.)

§244. Enforcement by execution of judgment or order

Where a spouse in an action for divorce, separation or annulment, or declaration of nullity of a void marriage, or a person other than a spouse when an action for an annulment is maintained after the death of a spouse, defaults in paying any sum of money as required by the judgment or order directing the payment thereof, or as required by the terms of an agreement or stipulation incorporated by reference in a judgment, such direction shall be enforceable pursuant to section fifty-two hundred forty-one or fifty-two hundred forty-two of the civil practice law and rules. Upon application the court shall make an order directing the entry of judgment for the amount of arrears of child support together with costs and disbursements. The court shall make an order directing the entry of judgment for the amount of arrears of any other payments so directed, together with costs and disbursements, unless the defaulting party shows good cause for failure to make application for relief from the judgment or order directing such payment prior to the accrual of such arrears. The court shall not make an order reducing or cancelling arrears unless the facts and circumstances constituting good cause are set forth in a written memorandum of decision. The application for such order shall be upon such notice to the spouse or other person as the court may direct. Such judgment may be enforced by execution or in any other manner provided by law for the collection of money judgments. The relief herein provided for is in addition to any and every other remedy to which a spouse may be entitled under the law; provided that when a judgment for such arrears or any part thereof shall have been entered pursuant to this section, such judgment shall thereafter not be subject to modification under the discretionary power granted by this section; and after the entry of such judgment the judgment creditor shall not hereafter be entitled to collect by any form of remedy any greater portion of such arrears than that represented by the judgment so entered. Such judgment shall provide for the payment of interest on the amount of any arrears if the default was willful, in that the obligated spouse knowingly, consciously and voluntarily disregarded the obligation under a lawful court order. Such interest shall be computed from the date on which the payment was due, at the prevailing rate of interest on judgments as provided in the civil practice law and rules.
(L.1962, ch. 313, §10; L.1963, ch. 667, §1; L.1963, ch. 685, §12; L.1980, ch. 241, §2; L.1980, ch. 281, §15; L.1980, ch. 645, §5; L.1981, ch. 695, §4; L.1983, ch. 111, §1; L.1985, ch. 809, §8; L.1986, ch. 892, §8; L.1988, ch. 327, §1.)

§244-a. Party may include additional arrears accruing during pendency of enforcement proceeding

In any proceeding for enforcement of payment of any sum of money as required by judgment or order the party seeking enforcement may amend the papers in support of the application for enforcement to include any additional arrears which have accrued since the commencement of such enforcement proceeding at the time of a hearing upon or submission of the matter, provided that written notice of the intention to so amend has been given eight days previously.

(L. 1980, ch. 646, §1; L. 1981, ch. 239, §1.)

§245. Spouse may petition to punish other spouse by contempt proceedings

Where a spouse, in an action for divorce, separation, annulment or declaration of nullity of a void marriage, or for the enforcement in this state of a judgment for divorce, separation, annulment or declaration of nullity of a void marriage rendered in another state, makes default in paying any sum of money as required by the judgment or order directing the payment thereof, and it appears presumptively, to the satisfaction of the court, that payment cannot be enforced pursuant to section two hundred forty-three or two hundred forty-four of this chapter or section fifty-two hundred forty-one or fifty-two hundred forty-two of the civil practice law and rules, the aggrieved spouse may make application pursuant to the provisions of section seven hundred fifty-six of the judiciary law to punish the defaulting spouse for contempt, and where the judgment or order directs the payment to be made in installments, or at stated intervals, failure to make such single payment or installment may be punished as therein provided, and such punishment, either by fine or commitment, shall not be a bar to a subsequent proceeding to punish the defaulting spouse as for a contempt for failure to pay subsequent installments, but for such purpose such spouse may be proceeded against under the said order in the same manner and with the same effect as though such installment payment was directed to be paid by a separate and distinct order, and the provisions of the civil rights law are hereby superseded so far as they are in conflict therewith. Such application may also be made without any previous sequestration or direction to give security where the court is satisfied that they would be ineffecttual. No demand of any kind upon the defaulting spouse shall be necessary in order that he or she be proceeded against and punished for failure to make any such payment or to pay any such installment; personal service upon the defaulting spouse of an uncertified copy of the judgment or order under which the default has occurred shall be sufficient.

(L. 1962, ch. 313, §10; amended L. 1975, ch. 497, §1; L. 1977, ch. 437, §11; L. 1980, ch. 281, §16; L. 1985, ch. 809, §9.)

§246. Persons financially unable to comply with orders or judgments may petition for relief

1. Any person who, by an order or judgment made or entered in an action for divorce, separation, annulment or declaration of the nullity of a void marriage or an action for the enforcement in this state of a judgment for divorce, separation or annulment or declaring the nullity of a void marriage rendered in another state, is directed to make payment of any sum or sums of money and against whom an order to punish for a contempt of court has been made pursuant to the provisions of section two hundred forty-five of this chapter or the judiciary law may, if financially unable to comply with the order or judgment to make such payment, upon such notice to such parties as the court may direct, make application to the court for an order relieving him from such payment and such contempt order. The court, upon the hearing of such application, if satisfied from the proofs and evidence offered and submitted that the applicant is financially unable to make such payment may, upon a showing of good cause, until further order of the court, modify the order or judgment to make such payment and relieve him from such contempt order. No such modification shall reduce or annul unpaid sums or installments accrued prior to the making of such application unless the defaulting party shows good cause for failure to make application for relief from the judgment or order directing such payment prior to the accrual of such arrears. Such modification may increase such support nunc pro tunc based on newly discovered evidence.

2. Whenever, upon application to the court by an interested party, it appears to the satisfaction of the court that any person, who has been relieved totally or partially from making any such payment pursuant to the provisions of this section, is no longer financially [able] to comply with the order or judgment to make such payment, then the court may, upon a showing of good cause, modify or revoke its order relieving him totally or partially from making such payment.

3. Any person may assert his financial inability to comply with the directions contained in an order or judgment made or entered in an action for divorce, separation, annulment or declaration of the nullity of a void marriage or an action for the enforcement in this state of a judgment for divorce, separation or annulment or declaring the nullity of a void marriage rendered in another state, as a defense in a proceeding instituted against him under section two hundred forty-five or under the judiciary law to punish him for his failure to comply with such directions and, if the court, upon the hearing of such contempt proceeding, is satisfied from the proofs and evidence offered and submitted that the defendant is financially unable to comply with such order or judgment, it may, in its discretion, until further order of the court, make an order modifying such order or judgment and denying the application to punish the defendant for contempt. No such modification shall reduce or annul arrears accrued prior to the making of such application unless the defaulting party shows good cause for failure to make application for relief from the judgment or order directing such payment prior to the accrual of such arrears. Such modification may increase such support nunc pro tunc as of the date of the application based on newly discovered evidence. Any retroactive amount of support due shall be paid in one sum or periodic sums, as the court shall direct, taking into account any amount of temporary support which has been paid.

(L. 1962, ch 313, §10; amended L. 1963, ch 685, §13; L. 1977, ch 516, §25; L. 1980, ch 645, §6; L. 1981, ch 695, §5.)

§247. Obligation for alimony or maintenance is suspended during incarceration for contempt

Notwithstanding any inconsistent provision of this article, the provision of any judgment or order rendered or made in an action for divorce, separation, annulment or declaration of nullity of a void marriage, requiring the payment of moneys by one spouse for the support of the other shall be suspended and inoperative so far as punishment for contempt is concerned during the period in which the defaulting spouse shall be imprisoned pursuant to any order adjudging him or her in contempt for failure to comply with any provision in such order.

(L. 1962, ch. 313, §10; L. 1980, ch. 281, §17.)

§248. Modification of judgment or order in action for divorce or annulment

Where an action for divorce or for annulment or for a declaration of the nullity of a void marriage is brought by a husband or wife, and a final judgment of divorce or a final judgment annulling the marriage or declaring its nullity has been rendered, the court, by order upon the application of the husband on notice, and on proof of the marriage of the wife after such final judgment, must modify such final judgment and any orders made with respect thereto by annulling the provisions of such final judgment or orders, or of both, directing payments of money for the support of the wife. The court in its discretion upon application of the husband on notice, upon proof that the wife is habitually living with another man and holding herself out as his wife, although not married to such man, may modify such final judgment and any orders made with respect thereto by annulling the provisions of such final judgment or orders or of both, directing payment of money for the support of such wife.

(L. 1962, ch. 313, §10; amended L. 1975, ch. 604, §1.)

§249. Court may give trial preference in matrimonial actions

Upon motion of either party or upon its own motion, the court may direct that any action or proceeding brought

(1) to annul a marriage or to declare the nullity of a void marriage, or

(2) for a separation, or

(3) for a divorce, or

(4) to enjoin the prosecution in any other jurisdiction of an action for divorce, be placed forthwith by the clerk on the supreme court calendar and be entitled to preference in the trial thereof, in accordance with Rule 3403 of the civil practice law and rules, provided that in the courts' discretion, justice so requires. Such direction may be made by separate order or in any order granted in any such action or proceeding upon any application made pursuant to sections two hundred thirty-six, two hundred thirty-seven or two hundred forty of this article.

Such direction, in the event no note of issue has been previously filed with the clerk, may also require either party to file with the clerk proof of service of the summons, two copies of the note of issue and such other data as may be required.

(L. 1965, ch. 296, §1.)

§251. Filing of order in family court

When, in a matrimonial action, the supreme court refers the issues of support, custody or visitation to the family court, the order or judgment shall provide that a copy thereof shall be filed by the plaintiff's attorney, within ten days, with the clerk of the family court therein specified.

(L. 1973, ch. 164, §1.)

New York Civil Practice Laws and Rules

Rule 3403. Trial preferences for civil cases

(a) Preferred cases. Civil cases shall be tried in the order in which notes of issue have been filed, but the following shall be entitled to a preference:

1. an action brought by or against the state, or a political subdivision of the state, or an officer or board of officers of the state or a political subdivision of the state, in his or its official capacity, on the application of the state, the political subdivision, or the officer or board of officers;

2. an action where a preference is provided for by statute; and

. . .

4. in any action upon the application of a party who has reached the age of seventy years.

5. an action to recover damages for medical, dental or podiatric malpractice.

6. an action to recover damages for personal injuries where the plaintiff is terminally ill and alleges that such terminal illness is a result of the conduct, culpability or negligence of the defendant.

(b) Obtaining preference. Unless the court otherwise orders, notice of a motion for preference shall be served with the note of issue by the party serving the note of issue, or ten days after such service by any other party; or thereafter during the pendency of the action upon the application of a party who reaches the age of seventy years, or who is terminally ill.

(L. 1962, ch. 308; L. 1970, ch. 907, §§1, 2; L. 1975, ch. 109, §8; L. 1979, ch. 61, §§1, 2; L. 1985, ch. 760, §4; L. 1986, ch. 485, §5; L. 1990, ch. 670, §§1, 2.)

New York Rules of Court

(Part 1400. Procedure for Attorneys in Domestic Relations Matters)

§1400.3. Written retainer agreement in domestic relations matters

An attorney who undertakes to represent a party and enters into an arrangement for, charges or collects any fee from a client shall execute a written agreement with the client setting forth in plain language the terms of compensation and the nature of services to be rendered. The agreement, and any amendment thereto, shall be signed by both client and attorney, and, in actions in Supreme Court, a copy of the signed agreement shall be filed with the court with the statement of net worth. Where substitution of counsel occurs after the filing of the net worth statement, a signed copy of the attorney's retainer agreement shall be filed with the court within 10 days of its execution. A copy of a signed amendment shall be filed within 15 days of signing. A duplicate copy of the filed agreement and any amendment shall be provided to the client. The agreement shall be subject to the provisions governing confidentiality contained in Domestic Relations Law, section 235(1). The agreement shall contain the following information:

RETAINER AGREEMENT

1. Names and addresses of the parties entering into the agreement;

2. Nature of the services to be rendered;

3. Amount of the advance retainer, if any, and what it is intended to cover;

4. Circumstances under which any portion of the advance retainer may be refunded. Should the attorney withdraw from the case or be discharged prior to the depletion of the advance retainer, the written retainer agreement shall provide how the attorney's fees and expenses are to be determined, and the remainder of the advance retainer shall be refunded to the client;

5. Client's right to cancel the agreement at any time; how the attorney's fee will be determined and paid should the client discharge the attorney at any time during the course of the representation;

6. How the attorney will be paid through the conclusion of the case after the retainer is depleted; whether the client may be asked to pay another lump sum;

7. Hourly rate of each person whose time may be charged to the client; any out-of-pocket disbursements for which the client will be required to reimburse the attorney. Any changes in such rates or fees shall be incorporated into a written agreement constituting an amendment to the original agreement, which must be signed by the client before it may take effect;

8. Any clause providing for a fee in addition to the agreed-upon rate, such as a reasonable minimum fee clause, must be defined in plain language and set forth the circumstances under which such fee may be incurred and how it will be calculated.

9. Frequency of itemized billing, which shall be at least every 60 days; the client may not be charged for time spent in discussion of the bills received;

10. Client's right to be provided with copies of correspondence and documents relating to the case, and to be kept apprised of the status of the case;

11. Whether and under what circumstances the attorney might seek a security interest from the client, which can be obtained only upon court approval and on notice to the adversary;

12. Under what circumstances the attorney might seek to withdraw from the case for nonpayment of fees, and the attorney's right to seek a charging lien from the court.

13. Should a dispute arise concerning the attorney's fee, the client may seek arbitration; the attorney shall provide information concerning fee arbitration in the event of such dispute or upon the client's request.

(Section filed October 11, 1994; amendments filed July 8, 1994, February 24, 1997, January 12, 2001.)

2. Postdissolution Name Restoration

Women often assume their husbands' surname upon marriage. Adoption of the husband's surname, however, is a custom and not a requirement of the common law. New York statute provides that applications for a marriage license in New York must contain a statement informing the parties that: (a) a person's surname does not automatically change upon marriage, (b) neither party must change his or her surname, and (c) the marital parties need not have the same last name (DRL §15(b)(2)).

Statutes often provide for a married woman to resume her birth name (commonly referred to as her "maiden name") upon divorce. Early cases in some jurisdictions wrestled with whether a denial of the wife's request could rest on possible detriment to children from having a different last name. See, e.g., Miller v. Miller, 670 S.W.2d 591 (Mo. Ct. App. 1984) (reversing trial court's refusal to restore a divorced woman's maiden name based on general concern of detriment to the child in having a different name from the parent). New York statute specifically authorizes a divorced spouse to resume use of a former surname (N.Y. Civ. Rts. §65; DRL §240-a).

New York Civil Rights Law

§65. Person may elect to change or resume name upon marriage, divorce or annulment

1. Any person may, upon marriage, elect to assume a new name according to the provisions of paragraph (b) of subdivision one of section fifteen of the domestic relations law.

2. Any person may, upon divorce or annulment, elect to resume the use of a former surname according to the provisions of section two hundred forty-a of the domestic relations law.

3. The effective of the name changes accomplished in the manner prescribed in subdivisions one and two of this section shall be as set forth in section sixty-four of this chapter.

4. Nothing in this article shall be construed to abrogate or alter the common law right of every person, whether married or single, to retain his or her name or to assume a new one so long as the new name is used consistently and without intent to defraud.

5. Notwithstanding any inconsistent provision of law, the state shall not impose any fee, charge, surcharge or assessment solely to change the surname contained on a license, permit, registration or other identifying document for a person who, because of a change in marital status, has assumed a new name or reassumes use of a former surname as provided for in this section.

(L. 1985, ch. 583, §5; L. 1999, ch. 417, §1.)

New York Domestic Relations Law

§15. Duty of town and city clerks

1. (a) It shall be the duty of the town or city clerk when an application for a marriage license is made to him or her to require each of the contracting parties to sign and verify a statement or affidavit before such clerk or one of his or her deputies, containing the following information. From the groom: Full name of husband, place of residence, social security number, age, occupation, place of birth, name of father, country of birth, maiden name of mother, country of birth, number of marriage. From the bride: Full name of bride, place of residence, social security number, age, occupation, place of birth, name of father, country of birth, maiden name of mother, country of birth, number of marriage. The said clerk shall also embody in the statement if either or both of the applicants have been previously married, a statement as to whether the former husband or husbands or the former wife or wives of the respective applicants are living or dead and as to whether either or both of said applicants are divorced persons, if so, when and where and against whom the divorce or divorces were granted and shall also embody therein a statement that no legal impediment exists as to the right of each of the applicants to enter into the marriage state. The town or city clerk is hereby given full power and authority to administer oaths and may require the applicants to produce witnesses to identify them or either of them and may examine under oath or otherwise other witnesses as to any material inquiry pertaining to the issuing of the license, and if the applicant is a divorced person the clerk may also require the production of a certified copy of the decree of the divorce, or proof of an existing marriage of parties who apply for a license to be used for a second or subsequent ceremony; provided, however, that in cities of the first class the verified statements and affidavits may be made before any regular clerk of the city clerk's office designated for that purpose by the city clerk.

(b) Every application for a marriage license shall contain a statement to the following effect:

NOTICE TO APPLICANTS

(1) Every person has the right to adopt any name by which he or she wishes to be known simply by using that name consistently and without intent to defraud.

(2) A person's last name (surname) does not automatically change upon marriage, and neither party to the marriage must change his or her last name. Parties to a marriage need not have the same last name.

(3) One or both parties to a marriage may elect to change the surname by which he or she wishes to be known after the solemnization of the marriage by entering the new name in the space below. Such entry shall consist of one of the following surnames:

(i) the surname of the other spouse; or

(ii) any former surname of either spouse; or

(iii) a name combining into a single surname all or a segment of the premarriage surname or any former surname of each spouse; or

(iv) a combination name separated by a hyphen, provided that each part of such combination surname is the premarriage surname, or any former surname, of each of the spouses.

(4) The use of this option will have the effect of providing a record of the change of name. The marriage certificate, containing the new name, if any, constitutes proof that the use of the new name, or the retention of the former name, is lawful.

(5) Neither the use of, nor the failure to use, this option of selecting a new surname by means of this application abrogates the right of each person to adopt a different name through usage at some future date.

(Optional—Enter new surname above)

2. If it appears from the affidavits and statements so taken, that the persons for whose marriage the license in question is demanded are legally competent to marry, the said clerk shall issue such license except in the following cases. If it shall appear upon an application that the applicant is under eighteen years of age, before the town or city clerk shall issue a license, he shall require documentary proof of age in the form of an original or certified copy of a birth record, a certification of birth issued by the state department of health, a local registrar of vital statistics or other public officer charged with similar duties by the laws of any other state, territory or country, a baptismal record, passport, automobile driver's license, life insurance policy, employment certificate, school record, immigration record, naturalization record or court record, showing the date of birth of such minor. If the town or city clerk shall be in doubt as to whether an applicant claiming to be over eighteen years of age is actually over eighteen years of age, he shall, before issuing such license, require documentary proof as above defined. If it shall appear upon an application of the applicants as provided in this section or upon information required by the clerk that either party is at least sixteen years of age but under eighteen years of age, then the town or city clerk before he shall issue a license shall require the written consent to the marriage from both parents of the minor or minors or such as shall then be living, or if the parents of both are dead, then the written consent of the guardian or guardians of such minor or minors. If one of the parents has been missing and has not been seen or heard from for a period of one year preceding the time of the application for the license, although diligent inquiry has been made to learn the whereabouts of such parent, the town or city clerk may issue a license to such minor upon the sworn statement and consent of the other parent. If the marriage of the parents of such minor has been dissolved by decree of divorce or annulment, the consent of the parent to whom the court which granted the decree has awarded the custody of such minor shall be sufficient. If there is no parent or guardian of the minor or minors living to their knowledge then the town or city clerk shall require the written consent to the marriage of the person under whose care or government the minor or minors may be before a license shall be issued. If a parent of such minor has been adjudicated an incompetent, the town or city clerk may issue a license to such minor upon

the production of a certified copy of such judgment so determining and upon the written consent of the other parent. If there is no other parent whose consent is required by this section, then and in such event, the town or city clerk shall require the written consent of the guardian of such minor or of the person under whose care or government the minor may be before a license shall be issued. The parents, guardians, or other persons whose consent it shall be necessary to obtain and file with the town or city clerk before the license shall issue, shall personally appear and acknowledge or execute the same before the town or city clerk, or some other officer authorized to administer oaths and take acknowledgments provided that where such affidavit or acknowledgment is made before an official other than an officer designated in section two hundred ninety-eight of the real property law as authorized to take such affidavit or acknowledgment if a conveyance of real property were being acknowledged or proved, or if a certificate of authentication would be required by section three hundred ten of the real property law to entitle the instrument to be recorded if it were a conveyance of real property, the consent when filed must have attached thereto a certificate of authentication.

3. If it shall appear upon an application for a marriage license that either party is under the age of sixteen years, the town or city clerk shall require, in addition to any consents provided for in this section, the written approval and consent of a justice of the supreme court or of a judge of the family court, having jurisdiction over the town or city in which the application is made, to be attached to or endorsed upon the application, before the license is issued. The application for such approval and consent shall be heard by the judge at chambers. All papers and records pertaining to any such application shall be sealed by him and withheld from inspection, except by order of a court of competent jurisdiction. Before issuing any licenses herein provided for, the town or city clerk shall be entitled to a fee of thirty dollars, which sum shall be paid by the applicants before or at the time the license is issued. Any town or city clerk who shall issue a license to marry any persons one or both of whom shall not be at the time of the marriage under such license legally competent to marry without first requiring the parties to such marriage to make such affidavits and statements or who shall not require the production of documentary proof of age or the procuring of the approval and consents provided for by this article, which shall show that the parties authorized by said license to be married are legally competent to marry, shall be guilty of a misdemeanor and on conviction thereof shall be fined in the sum of one hundred dollars for each and every offense. On or before the fifteenth day of each month, each town and city clerk, except in the city of New York, shall transmit to the state commissioner of health twenty-two dollars and fifty cents of the amount received for each fee collected, which shall be paid into the vital records management account as provided by section ninety-seven-cccc of the state finance law. In any city the balance of all fees collected for the issuing of a marriage license, or for solemnizing a marriage, so far as collected for services rendered by any officer or employee of such city, shall be paid monthly into the city treasury and may by ordinance be credited to any fund therein designated, and said ordinance, when duly enacted, shall have the force of law in such city. Notwithstanding any other provisions of this article, the clerk of any city with the approval of the governing body of such city is hereby authorized to designate, in writing filed in the city clerk's office, a deputy clerk, if any, and/or other city employees in such office to receive applications for, examine applications, investigate and issue marriage licenses in the absence or inability of the clerk of said city to act, and said deputy and/or employees so designated are hereby vested with all the powers and duties of said city clerk relative thereto. Such deputy and/or employees shall perform said duties without additional compensation.

4. Notwithstanding any other provision of this section, the city clerk of the city of New York, before issuing any licenses herein provided for, shall be entitled to a fee of twenty-five dollars, which sum shall be paid by the applicants before or at the time the license is issued and all such fees so received shall be paid monthly into the city treasury.

(L. 1909, ch. 19; L. 1912, ch. 241, §1; L. 1917, ch. 503, §1; L. 1921, ch. 317, §1; L. 1926, ch. 635, §3; L. 1927, ch. 547, §2; L. 1929, ch. 633, §1; L. 1931, ch. 511, §1; L. 1932, ch. 285, §1; L. 1935, ch. 535, §4; L. 1937, ch. 706, §1; L. 1938, ch. 640, §5; L. 1939, ch. 110, §4; L. 1960, ch. 1026, §1; L. 1962, ch. 689, §14; L. 1964, ch. 168, §1; L. 1965, ch. 102, §1; L. 1965, ch. 142, §1; L. 1972, ch. 561, §1; L. 1974, ch. 920, §4; L. 1980, ch. 356, §1; L. 1981, ch. 103, §115; L. 1984, ch. 126, §3; L. 1985, ch. 583, §2; L. 1989, ch. 61, §265; L. 1990, ch. 424, §2; L. 1997, ch. 398, §30; L. 2003, c. 62 p. W2, §5, effective May 15, 2003.)

§240-a. Judgment or decree; name resumption

In any action or proceeding brought under the provisions of this chapter wherein all or part of the relief granted is divorce or annulment of a marriage any interlocutory or final judgment or decree shall contain, as a part thereof, the social security numbers of the named parties in the action or proceeding, as well as a provision that each party may resume the use of his or her premarriage surname or any other former surname.

(L. 1973, ch. 642, §1; L. 1982, ch. 668, §1; L. 1985, ch. 583, §3; L. 1997, ch. 398, §31.)

---

3. Religious Divorce

New York statute addresses the problem of access to the "Get" or religious divorce. According to Jewish law and practice, the power of divorce rests exclusively with the husband. Without such a divorce, the wife remains an "agunah" (a "tied" woman) and may not remarry in the eyes of Jewish law. If she remarries without obtaining a "Get," she is considered an adulteress, and her subsequent children are considered illegitimate and unable to marry other Jews.

Approximately 15,000 Orthodox Jewish women in New York are civilly divorced but unable to obtain a religious divorce. Heather Lynn Capell, Comment, After the Glass Has Shattered: A Comparative Analysis of Orthodox Jewish Divorce in the United States and Israel, 33 Tex. Int'l L.J. 331, 337 (1998). See also Marc S. Cwik, Note and Comment: The Agunah Problem in

Jewish Society: Exploring the Possibility of an International Law Solution, 17 Wis. Int'l L.J. 109 (1999). The religious doctrine governing the "Get" applies to the Orthodox and Conservative, but not the Reform, branches of Judaism. But cf. Megibow v. Megibow, 612 N.Y.S.2d 758 (Sup. Ct. 1994) (requiring husband to cooperate in obtaining a Jewish religious divorce even though marriage was performed by a Reform rabbi and Reform Judaism may not require that a "Get" be issued, reasoning that withholding of a "Get" by the husband would constitute a "barrier to remarriage" if the wife perceived herself to require a "Get" to remarry).

Many husbands use the threat of denying a "Get" to extract concessions during divorce. For example, in Perl v. Perl, 512 N.Y.S.2d 372, 374 (App. Div. 1987), the husband wanted, in return for giving his wife a "Get," (1) all of the parties' jointly owned securities; (2) payment of $35,000 to compensate him for jointly owned securities she had sold; (3) $30,000 payable in monthly installments of $2,000 with acceleration of the balance due in the event of default, guaranteed by the wife's uncle; (4) a deed conveying her one-half interest in the marital home; (5) title to her automobile; and (6) her engagement ring and other personal jewelry. The Supreme Court, Appellate Division, held that oppressive misuse of religious veto by one spouse subjects the couple's bargain to review and potential revision.

The Israeli Parliament enacted legislation whereby husbands in Israel who deny their wives a religious divorce can be refused employment, a driver's license, or banking privileges. Capell, *supra*, at 334. In the United States, however, the availability of civil divorce increases the husband's bargaining power at the same time it reduces rabbinical leverage.

The New York legislature in 1983 addressed the problem of husbands' withholding Jewish religious divorces by enacting a statute (called the "'Get' statute") that requires if the marriage was "solemnized in a religious ceremony," the party seeking to dissolve the marriage must allege that he or she has taken or will take, prior to entry of judgment, all possible steps to remove any barrier to the defendant's remarriage, or that the defendant has waived, in writing, the statutory requirements (DRL §253(1), (2)). Before the judgment is final, the plaintiff must also file a sworn statement to this effect (DRL §253(3)). A court may not enter a final judgment unless the statements required in both subdivisions 3 and 4 are submitted. The statute applies to actions for both divorce and annulment (DRL §253(2)). Also, pursuant to the statute, a spouse may be prosecuted for alleging falsely that he or she has complied with DRL §253. (DRL §253(8) provides that the knowing submission of a false verified statement constitutes a felony.) Courts have held husbands in contempt after being ordered to deliver a "Get" and failing to do so, and the contempt order may be enforced through imprisonment. Kaplinsky v. Kaplinsky, 603 N.Y.S.2d 574 (App. Div. 1993). See also Kalika v. Stern, 911 F.Supp. 594 (E.D.N.Y. 1995) (holding that attorney, who had probable cause to believe that the husband's verification that he had removed all barriers to his ex-wife's remarriage in his civil divorce proceeding was false and thus in violation of domestic relations law, did not act in bad faith when he informed the district attorney's office about the alleged violation).

Wives sometimes seek to enforce clauses in prenuptial or separation agreements in which the husband agrees to obtain, or to cooperate in obtaining, a religious divorce. Civil courts in several states have enforced such clauses. Compare Avitzur v. Avitzur, 446 N.E.2d 136 (N.Y. 1983); In re Marriage of Goldman, 554 N.E.2d 1016 (Ill. App. Ct. 1990); Scholl v. Scholl, 621 A.2d 808 (Del. Fam. Ct. 1992) (enforcing the agreements) with Victor v. Victor, 866 P.2d 899 (Ariz. Ct. App. 1993); Aflalo v. Aflalo, 685 A.2d 523 (N.J. Super. Ct. Ch. Div. 1996) (denying enforcement).

The New York Get statute (as well as case law enforcing prenuptial and/or separation agreements) raises constitutional issues, that is, whether the law violates the First Amendment's Establishment Clause proscribing the state from advancing religion. See generally Michelle Greenberg-Kobrin, Civil Enforceability of Religious Prenuptial Agreements, 32 Colum. J.L. & Soc. Probs. 359 (1999).

The Get statute was amended in 1984 to address possible constitutional problems. The legislature added an amendment (subdivision 9) (L. 1984, ch. 945, §1, effective August 6, 1984) that eliminated the need for a spouse to consult religious officials to determine whether "barriers to remarriage" exist. Another amendment in 1984 in subdivision 6 defined the term "barrier to marriage" to include "without limitation, any religious or conscientious restraint or inhibition, of which the party required to make the verified statement is aware, that is imposed on a party to a marriage, under the principles held by the clergyman or minister who has solemnized the marriage, by reason of the other party's commission or withholding of any voluntary act" (DRL §253(6)).

A subsequent amendment in 1992 extended the application of the statute, in an attempt to increase its effectiveness, by amending the equitable distribution law to permit a judge to consider the effect of any "barrier to remarriage" in postdivorce decisionmaking regarding property distribution and spousal support (DRL §236B(5)(h)). Unlike DRL §253, the latter statutory provision takes into account the actions of both spouses in regard to removing barriers to remarriage.

Constitutional issues in the application of a Get statute arose in Sieger v. Sieger, 829 N.Y.S.2d 649 (App. Div. 2007), in which a husband complains that he is prepared to comply with the Get statute (N.Y. Dom. Rel. Law §253(3)) but that his wife refuses to accept the Get due to the fact that he obtained an alternative — i.e., a rabbinical court order (a "heter") that permitted him to remarry without giving a Get. The wife claims that, to obtain the "heter," the husband made allegedly defamatory statements about her fitness as a mother in the rabbinical court and, therefore, the "heter" has the practical effect of preventing her remarriage by tarnishing her reputation. She insists that the husband disavow those statements. The appellate court rules that, whereas a court has jurisdiction to require a spouse to remove obstacles to remarriage pursuant to the Get statute, the First Amendment Entanglement

Clause proscribes a review of the couple's religious dispute.

See generally Jeremy Glicksman, Note, Almost, But Not Quite: The Failure of New York's Get Statute, 44 Fam. Ct. Rev. 300 (2006) (proposing amending New York's statute to make it applicable to all divorce proceedings and any barrier to remarriage and apply worldwide).

New York Domestic Relations Law

§236. Special controlling provisions for matrimonial actions

. . .

PART B

NEW ACTIONS OR PROCEEDINGS

Maintenance and distributive award.

1. Definitions. Whenever used in this part, the following terms shall have the respective meanings hereinafter set forth or indicated:

. . .

c. The term "marital property" shall mean all property acquired by either or both spouses during the marriage and before the execution of a separation agreement or the commencement of a matrimonial action, regardless of the form in which title is held, except as otherwise provided in agreement pursuant to subdivision three of this part. Marital property shall not include separate property as hereinafter defined.

d. The term separate property shall mean:

(1) property acquired before marriage or property acquired by bequest, devise, or descent, or gift from a party other than the spouse;

(2) compensation for personal injuries;

(3) property acquired in exchange for or the increase in value of separate property, except to the extent that such appreciation is due in part to the contributions or efforts of the other spouse;

(4) property described as separate property by written agreement of the parties pursuant to subdivision three of this part.

. . .

5. Disposition of property in certain matrimonial actions.

a. Except where the parties have provided in an agreement for the disposition of their property pursuant to subdivision three of this part, the court, in an action wherein all or part of the relief granted is divorce, or the dissolution, annulment or declaration of the nullity of a marriage, and in proceedings to obtain a distribution of marital property following a foreign judgment of divorce, shall determine the respective rights of the parties in their separate or marital property, and shall provide for the disposition thereof in the final judgment.

b. Separate property shall remain such.

c. Marital property shall be distributed equitably between the parties, considering the circumstances of the case and of the respective parties.

d. In determining an equitable disposition of property under paragraph c, the court shall consider:

(1) the income and property of each party at the time of marriage, and at the time of the commencement of the action;

(2) the duration of the marriage and the age and health of both parties;

(3) the need of a custodial parent to occupy or own the marital residence and to use or own its household effects;

(4) the loss of inheritance and pension rights upon dissolution of the marriage as of the date of dissolution;

(5) any award of maintenance under subdivision six of this part;

(6) any equitable claim to, interest in, or direct or indirect contribution made to the acquisition of such marital property by the party not having title, including joint efforts or expenditures and contributions and services as a spouse, parent, wage earner and homemaker, and to the career or career potential of the other party;

(7) the liquid or non-liquid character of all marital property;

(8) the probable future financial circumstances of each party;

(9) the impossibility or difficulty of evaluating any component asset or any interest in a business, corporation or profession, and the economic desirability of retaining such asset or interest intact and free from any claim or interference by the other party;

(10) the tax consequences to each party;

(11) the wasteful dissipation of assets by either spouse;

(12) any transfer or encumbrance made in contemplation of a matrimonial action without fair consideration;

(13) any other factor which the court shall expressly find to be just and proper.

e. In any action in which the court shall determine that an equitable distribution is appropriate but would be impractical or burdensome or where the distribution of an interest in a business, corporation or profession would be contrary to law, the court in lieu of such equitable distribution shall make a distributive award in order to achieve equity between the parties. The court in its discretion, also may make a distributive award to supplement, facilitate or effectuate a distribution of marital property.

f. In addition to the disposition of property as set forth above, the court may make such order regarding the use and occupancy of the marital home and its household effects as provided in section two hundred thirty-four of this chapter, without regard to the form of ownership of such property.

g. In any decision made pursuant to this subdivision, the court shall set forth the factors it considered and the reasons for its decision and such may not be waived by either party or counsel.

h. In any decision made pursuant to this subdivision the court shall, where appropriate, consider the effect of a barrier to remarriage, as defined in subdivision six of section two hundred fifty-three of this article, on the factors enumerated in paragraph d of this subdivision.

. . .

(L. 1962, ch. 313, §10; L. 1963, ch. 685, §6; L. 1968, ch. 699, §1; L. 1980, ch. 281, §9; L. 1980, ch. 645, §§2, 3; L. 1981, ch. 695, §§1, 2; L. 1984, ch. 790, §2; L. 1985, ch. 809, §6; L. 1986, ch. 884, §§1 to 4; L. 1986, ch. 892, §§2 to 4; L. 1987, ch. 815, §§6, 7; L. 1989, ch. 567, §§4, 5; L. 1990, ch. 818, §§4, 5; L. 1992, ch. 41, §§139, 140; L. 1992, ch. 415, §§1, 2; L. 1993, ch. 59, §9; L. 1993, ch. 354, §2; L. 1994, ch. 170, §§359, 360; L. 1997, ch. 398, §§4, 5, effective October 1, 1998; L. 1997, ch. 398, §141, effective January 1, 1998; L. 1997, ch. 436, pt. B, §§105, 106, effective August 20, 1997; L. 1998, ch. 214, §56, effective November 4, 1998; L. 1998, ch. 393, §2, effective July 22, 1998; L. 1999, ch. 275, §2, effective September 18, 1999; L. 2003, c. 595, §1, effective September 22, 2003.)

§253. Removal of barriers to remarriage

1. This section applies only to a marriage solemnized in this state or in any other jurisdiction by a person specified in subdivision one of section eleven of this chapter.

2. Any party to a marriage defined in subdivision one of this section who commences a proceeding to annul the marriage or for a divorce must allege, in his or her verified complaint:

(i) that, to the best of his or her knowledge, that he or she has taken or that he or she will take, prior to the entry of final judgment, all steps solely within his or her power to remove any barrier to the defendant's remarriage following the annulment or divorce; or

(ii) that the defendant has waived in writing the requirements of this subdivision.

3. No final judgment of annulment or divorce shall thereafter be entered unless the plaintiff shall have filed and served a sworn statement:

(i) that, to the best of his or her knowledge, he or she has, prior to the entry of such final judgment, taken all steps solely within his or her power to remove all barriers to the defendant's remarriage following the annulment or divorce; or

(ii) that the defendant has waived in writing the requirements of this subdivision.

4. In any action for divorce based on subdivisions five and six of section one hundred seventy of this chapter in which the defendant enters a general appearance and does not contest the requested relief, no final judgment of annulment or divorce shall be entered unless both parties shall have filed and served sworn statements:

(i) that he or she has, to the best of his or her knowledge, taken all steps solely within his or her power to remove all barriers to the other party's remarriage following the annulment or divorce; or

(ii) that the other party has waived in writing the requirements of this subdivision.

5. The writing attesting to any waiver of the requirements of subdivision two, three or four of this section shall be filed with the court prior to the entry of a final judgment of annulment or divorce.

6. As used in the sworn statements prescribed by this section "barrier to remarriage" includes, without limitation, any religious or conscientious restraint or inhibition, of which the party required to make the verified statement is aware, that is imposed on a party to a marriage, under the principles held by the clergyman or minister who has solemnized the marriage, by reason of the other party's commission or withholding of any voluntary act. Nothing in this section shall be construed to require any party to consult with any clergyman or minister to determine whether there exists any such religious or conscientious restraint or inhibition. It shall not be deemed a "barrier to remarriage" within the meaning of this section if the restraint or inhibition cannot be removed by the party's voluntary act. Nor shall it be deemed a "barrier to remarriage" if the party must incur expenses in connection with removal of the restraint or inhibition and the other party refuses to provide reasonable reimbursement for such expenses. "All steps solely within his or her power" shall not be construed to include application to a marriage tribunal or other similar organization or agency of a religious denomination which has authority to annul or dissolve a marriage under the rules of such denomination.

7. No final judgment of annulment or divorce shall be entered, notwithstanding the filing of the plaintiff's sworn statement prescribed by this section, if the clergyman or minister who has solemnized the marriage certifies, in a sworn statement, that he or she has solemnized the marriage and that, to his or her knowledge, the plaintiff has failed to take all steps solely within his or her power to remove all barriers to the defendant's remarriage following the annulment or divorce, provided that the said clergyman or minister is alive and available and competent to testify at the time when final judgment would be entered.

8. Any person who knowingly submits a false sworn statement under this section shall be guilty of making an apparently sworn false statement in the first degree and shall be punished in accordance with section 210.40 of the penal law.

9. Nothing in this section shall be construed to authorize any court to inquire into or determine any ecclesiastical or religious issue. The truth of any statement submitted pursuant to this section shall not be the subject of any judicial inquiry, except as provided in subdivision eight of this section.

(L. 1983, ch. 979, §1; L. 1984, ch. 945, §1.)

§254. Court may authorize that certain information remain confidential whether or not protection order is sought

1. Notwithstanding any other provision of law, in any proceeding for custody, divorce, separation or annulment, whether or not an order of protection or temporary order of protection is sought or has been sought in the past, the court may, upon its own motion or upon the motion of any party or the law guardian, authorize any party or the child to keep his or her address confidential from any adverse party or the child, as appropriate, in any pleadings or other papers submitted to the court, where the court finds that the disclosure of the address or other identifying information would pose an unreasonable risk to the health or safety of a party or the child. Pending such a finding, any address or

other identifying information of the child or party seeking confidentiality shall be safeguarded and sealed in order to prevent its inadvertent or unauthorized use or disclosure.

2. Notwithstanding any other provision of law, if a party or a child has resided or resides in a residential program for victims of domestic violence as defined in section four hundred fifty-nine-a of the social services law, the present address of the party and the child and the address of the residential program for victims of domestic violence shall not be revealed.

3. Upon authorization as provided in subdivision one of this section, the identifying information shall be sealed and shall not be disclosed in any pleading or other document filed in a proceeding under this article. The court shall designate the clerk of the court or such other disinterested person as it deems appropriate, with consent of such disinterested person, as the agent for service of process for the party whose address is to remain confidential and shall notify the adverse party of such designation in writing. The clerk or disinterested person designated by the court shall, when served with process or other papers on behalf of the party whose address is to remain confidential, promptly notify such party whose address is to remain confidential and forward such process or papers to him or her.

4. In any case in which such a confidentiality authorization is made, the party whose address is to remain confidential shall inform the clerk of the court or disinterested person designated by the court of any change in address for purposes of receipt of service or process [of] any papers.
(L. 2001, ch. 236, §2.)

4. Protective Orders in Matrimonial Matters: Temporary Restraining Orders

In 1977, the New York State legislature enacted legislation to protect battered spouses. DRL §252 authorizes the Supreme Court to issue orders of protection in matrimonial matters and to provide for modification and enforcement of such orders. According to DRL §252(1), either the Supreme Court or the Family Court "shall" entertain the application for a protective order. Amendments in 1995 to DRL §252(1) set forth the precise terms that the Supreme Court can impose in an order of protection. An order of protection provides that the restrained party not harass, menace, recklessly endanger, assault or attempt to assault the petitioner, and refrain from committing a "family offense." The protective order may also include a "stay-away" provision excluding a party from the marital home or directing that the party stay away from the protected party or parties, the party's school, employment, child care, and any other designated locations.

The Family Court Act Article 8 authorizes the Family Court to entertain proceedings for temporary and permanent orders of protection. As originally enacted in 1962, Article 8 emphasized treatment rather than prosecution. Specifically, it gave the Family Court exclusive original jurisdiction over any proceeding concerning acts of family violence. The Act also required that criminal courts transfer domestic violence offenses to the Family Court, and permitted criminal prosecution for these offenses only if a Family Court judge decided to transfer the case to the criminal courts.

However, after a series of legislative hearings in 1977 documenting shortcomings in the responses to domestic violence, the legislature amended Article 8 to pass responsibility for criminal prosecution of the offender from the Family Court judge (who previously had discretion to transfer proceedings to criminal court) to the victim (subject to the authority of the District Attorney). The Act also strengthened the power of the Family Court to issue and enforce (with police assistance) orders of protection (Fam. Ct. Act. §812(2)(a-b)).

Additionally, giving effect to the plain language of the Article, courts have recently gone further, holding that a parent has standing to commence an Article 8 proceeding on behalf of her minor child. Hamm-Jones v. Jones, 788 N.Y.S.2d 690 (App. Div. 2005).

Legislation in 1994 (the Family Protection and Domestic Intervention Act) modified Article 8 to provide victims of domestic violence more flexibility in choosing whether to proceed in criminal court or Family Court (or both) at any time during the statutory time limit, and also created a Statewide Tracking of Orders of Protection (STOP) program to improve the response to domestic violence by enabling law enforcement officials to retrieve information on protective orders and family court arrest warrants through the New York Statewide Police Information Network (NYSPIN).

Upon issuing a protective order (or at any time after an allegation of a violation of a protective order is filed in any court), the court must revoke the respondent's firearms license (and also order a respondent to be ineligible for such a license, order a respondent to surrender any firearms, or suspend a respondent's firearms license) if the court finds that the conduct involved a serious physical injury, use or threatened use of a deadly weapon, constituted any violent felony offense, or constituted a stalking offense (DRL §§240(3), 252(9); FCA §842-a(1)(b), (2)(b), (3)(b); CPL §530.14(1)(b), (2)(b), (3)(b)).

New York Domestic Relations Law

§252. Effect of pendency of matrimonial action on petition for protective order

1. In an action for divorce, separation or annulment or in an action to declare the nullity of a void marriage in the supreme court, the supreme court or the family court shall entertain an application for an order of protection or temporary order of protection by either party. Such an order may require any party:

(a) to stay away from the home, school, business or place of employment of the child, other parent or any other party, and to stay away from any other specific location designated by the court;

(b) to permit a parent, or a person entitled to visitation by a court order or a separation agreement, to visit the child at stated periods;

(c) to refrain from committing a family offense, as defined in subdivision one of section 530.11 of the criminal procedure law, or any criminal offense against such child or against the other parent or against any person to whom custody of the child is awarded or from harassing, intimidating or threatening such persons;

(d) to permit a designated party to enter the residence during a specified period of time in order to remove personal belongings not in issue in a proceeding or action under this chapter or the family court act;

(e) to refrain from acts of commission or omission that create an unreasonable risk to the health, safety or welfare of a child;

(f) to pay the reasonable counsel fees and disbursements involved in obtaining or enforcing the order of the person who is protected by such order if such order is issued or enforced; or

(g) to observe such other conditions as are necessary to further the purposes of protection.

2. An order of protection entered pursuant to this subdivision shall bear in a conspicuous manner, on the front page of said order, the language "Order of protection issued pursuant to section two hundred fifty-two of the domestic relations law". The absence of such language shall not affect the validity of such order. The presentation of a copy of such an order to any peace officer acting pursuant to his or her special duties, or police officer, shall constitute authority, for that officer to arrest a person when that person has violated the terms of such an order, and bring such person before the court and, otherwise, so far as lies within the officer's power, to aid in securing the protection such order was intended to afford.

2-a. If the court that issued an order of protection or temporary order of protection under this section or warrant in connection thereto is not in session when an arrest is made for an alleged violation of the order or upon a warrant issued in connection with such violation, the arrested person shall be brought before a local criminal court in the county of arrest or in the county in which such warrant is returnable pursuant to article one hundred twenty of the criminal procedure law and arraigned by such court. Such local criminal court shall order the commitment of the arrested person to the custody of the sheriff, admit to, fix or accept bail, or release the arrested person on his or her recognizance pending appearance in the court that issued the order of protection, temporary order of protection or warrant. In making such order, such local criminal court shall consider the bail recommendations, if any, made by the supreme or family court as indicated on the warrant or certificate of warrant. Unless the petitioner or complainant requests otherwise, the court, in addition to scheduling further criminal proceedings, if any, regarding such alleged family offense or violation allegation, shall make such matter returnable in the supreme or family court, as applicable, on the next day such court is in session.

3. An order of protection entered pursuant to this subdivision may be made in the final judgment in any matrimonial action, or by one or more orders from time to time before or subsequent to final judgment, or by both such order or orders and the final judgment. The order of protection may remain in effect after entry of a final matrimonial judgment and during the minority of any child whose custody or visitation is the subject of a provision of a final judgment or any order. An order of protection may be entered notwithstanding that the court for any reason whatsoever, other than lack of jurisdiction, refuses to grant the relief requested in the action or proceeding.

4. No order of protection may direct any party to observe conditions of behavior unless: (i) the party requesting the order of protection has served and filed an action, proceeding, counterclaim or written motion and, (ii) the court has made a finding on the record that such party is entitled to issuance of the order of protection which may result from a judicial finding of fact, judicial acceptance of an admission by the party against whom the order was issued or judicial finding that the party against whom the order is issued has given knowing, intelligent and voluntary consent to its issuance. The provisions of this subdivision shall not preclude the court from issuing a temporary order of protection upon the court's own motion or where a motion for such relief is made to the court, for good cause shown.

5. Except with respect to enforcement pursuant to a criminal prosecution under article two hundred fifteen of the penal law, the supreme court may provide in an order made pursuant to this section that the order may be enforced or modified only in the supreme court. If the supreme court so provides, the family court may not entertain an application to enforce or modify such an order of the supreme court.

6. In any such matrimonial action however, the court may not sua sponte consolidate actions or make, vacate or modify orders of protection issued in family court involving the same parties except upon motion and with notice to the non-moving party. Such non-moving party shall be given an opportunity to be heard.

7. A valid order of protection or temporary order of protection issued by a court of competent jurisdiction in another state, territorial or tribal jurisdiction shall be accorded full faith and credit and enforced as if it were issued by a court within the state for as long as the order remains in effect in the issuing jurisdiction in accordance with sections two thousand two hundred sixty-five and two thousand two hundred sixty-six of title eighteen of the United States Code.

(a) An order issued by a court of competent jurisdiction in another state, territorial or tribal jurisdiction shall be deemed valid if:

(i) the issuing court had personal jurisdiction over the parties and over the subject matter under the law of the issuing jurisdiction;

(ii) the person against whom the order was issued had reasonable notice and an opportunity to be heard prior to issuance of the order; provided, however, that if the order was a temporary order of protection issued in the absence of such person, that notice had been given and that an opportunity to be heard had been provided within a reasonable period of time after the issuance of the order; and

(iii) in the case of orders of protection or temporary orders of protection issued against both a petitioner and respondent, the order or portion thereof sought to be enforced was supported by: (A) a pleading requesting such order, including, but not limited to, a petition, cross-petition or counterclaim; and (B) a judicial finding that the requesting party is entitled to the issuance of the order, which may result from a judicial finding of fact, judicial acceptance of an admission by the party against whom the order was issued or judicial finding that the party against whom the order was issued had given knowing, intelligent and voluntary consent to its issuance.

(b) Notwithstanding the provisions of article fifty-four of the civil practice law and rules, an order of protection or temporary order of protection issued by a court of competent jurisdiction in another state, territorial or tribal jurisdiction, accompanied by a sworn affidavit that upon information and belief such order is in effect as written and has not been vacated or modified, may be filed without fee with the clerk of the court, who shall transmit information regarding such order to the statewide registry of orders of protection and warrants established pursuant to section two hundred twenty-one-a of the executive law; provided, however, that such filing and registry entry shall not be required for enforcement of the order.

8. Any party moving for a temporary order of protection pursuant to this subdivision during hours when the court is open shall be entitled to file such motion or pleading containing such prayer for emergency relief on the same day that such person first appears at such court, and a hearing on the motion or portion of the pleading requesting such emergency relief shall be held on the same day or the next day that the court is in session following the filing of such motion or pleading.

9. Upon issuance of an order of protection or temporary order of protection or upon a violation of such order, the court may take an order in accordance with section eight hundred forty-two-a of the family court act directing the surrender of firearms, revoking or suspending a party's firearms license, and/or directing that such party be ineligible to receive a firearms license. Upon issuance of an order of protection pursuant to this section or upon a finding of a violation thereof, the court also may direct payment of restitution in an amount not to exceed ten thousand dollars in accordance with subdivision (e) of section eight hundred forty-one of such act; provided, however, that in no case shall an order of restitution be issued where the court determines that the party against whom the order would be issued has already compensated the injured party or where such compensation is incorporated in a final judgement or settlement of the action.

(L. 1977, ch. 449, § 9; L. 1994, ch. 222, §52; L. 1995, ch. 349, §6; L. 1997, ch. 186, §14; L. 1998, ch. 597, §§3, 4; L. 1999, ch. 606, §2.)

New York Family Court Act

§842. Order of protection

An order of protection under section eight hundred forty-one of this part shall set forth reasonable conditions of behavior to be observed for a period not in excess of two years by the petitioner or respondent or for a period not in excess of five years upon (i) a finding by the court on the record of the existence of aggravating circumstances as defined in paragraph (vii) of subdivision (a) of section eight hundred twenty-seven of this article; or (ii) a finding by the court on the record that the conduct alleged in the petition is in violation of a valid order of protection. Any finding of aggravating circumstances pursuant to this section shall be stated on the record and upon the order of protection. Any order of protection issued pursuant to this section shall specify if an order of probation is in effect. Any order of protection issued pursuant to this section may require the petitioner or the respondent:

(a) to stay away from the home, school, business or place of employment of any other party, the other spouse, the other parent, or the child, and to stay away from any other specific location designated by the court, provided that the court shall make a determination, and shall state such determination in a written decision or on the record, whether to impose a condition pursuant to this subdivision, provided further, however, that failure to make such a determination shall not affect the validity of such order of protection. In making such determination, the court shall consider, but shall not be limited to consideration of, whether the order of protection is likely to achieve its purpose in the absence of such a condition, conduct subject to prior orders of protection, prior incidents of abuse, extent of past or present injury, threats, drug or alcohol abuse, and access to weapons;

(b) to permit a parent, or a person entitled to visitation by a court order or a separation agreement, to visit the child at stated periods;

(c) to refrain from committing a family offense, as defined in subdivision one of section eight hundred twelve of this act, or any criminal offense against the child or against the other parent or against any person to whom custody of the child is awarded, or from harassing, intimidating or threatening such persons;

(d) to permit a designated party to enter the residence during a specified period of time in order to remove personal belongings not in issue in this proceeding or in any other proceeding or action under this act or the domestic relations law;

(e) to refrain from acts of commission or omission that create an unreasonable risk to the health, safety or welfare of a child;

(f) to pay the reasonable counsel fees and disbursements involved in obtaining or enforcing the order of the person who is protected by such order if such order is issued or enforced;

(g) to require the respondent to participate in a batterer's education program designed to help end violent behavior, which may include referral to drug and alcohol counselling, and to pay the costs thereof if the person has the means to do so, provided however that nothing contained herein shall be deemed to require payment of the costs of any such program by the petitioner, the state or any political subdivision thereof; and

(h) to provide, either directly or by means of medical and health insurance, for expenses incurred for medical care and treatment arising from the incident or incidents forming the basis for the issuance of the order.

(i) 1. to refrain from intentionally injuring or killing, without justification, any companion animal the respondent knows to be owned, possessed, leased, kept or held by the petitioner or a minor child residing in the household.

2. "Companion animal", as used in this section, shall have the same meaning as in subdivision five of section three hundred fifty of the agriculture and markets law.

(j) to observe such other conditions as are necessary to further the purposes of protection.

The court may also award custody of the child, during the term of the order of protection to either parent, or to an appropriate relative within the second degree. Nothing in this section gives the court power to place or board out any child or to commit a child to an institution or agency. The court may also upon the showing of special circumstances extend the order of protection for a reasonable period of time.

Notwithstanding the provisions of section eight hundred seventeen of this article, where a temporary order of child support has not already been issued, the court may in addition to the issuance of an order of protection pursuant to this section, issue an order for temporary child support in an amount sufficient to meet the needs of the child, without a showing of immediate or emergency need. The court shall make an order for temporary child support notwithstanding that information with respect to income and assets of the respondent may be unavailable. Where such information is available, the court may make an award for temporary child support pursuant to the formula set forth in subdivision one of section four hundred thirteen of this act. Temporary orders of support issued pursuant to this article shall be deemed to have been issued pursuant to section four hundred thirteen of this act.

Upon making an order for temporary child support pursuant to this subdivision, the court shall advise the petitioner of the availability of child support enforcement services by the support collection unit of the local department of social services, to enforce the temporary order and to assist in securing continued child support, and shall set the support matter down for further proceedings in accordance with article four of this act.

Where the court determines that the respondent has employer-provided medical insurance, the court may further direct, as part of an order of temporary support under this subdivision, that a medical support execution be issued and served upon the respondent's employer as provided for in section fifty-two hundred forty-one of the civil practice law and rules.

Notwithstanding the foregoing provisions, an order of protection, or temporary order of protection where applicable, may be entered against a former spouse and persons who have a child in common, regardless whether such persons have been married or have lived together at any time.

In addition to the foregoing provisions, the court may issue an order, pursuant to section two hundred twenty-seven-c of the real property law, authorizing the party for whose benefit any order of protection has been issued to terminate a lease or rental agreement pursuant to section two hundred twenty-seven-c of the real property law.

(L. 1962, ch. 686; amended L. 1972, ch. 761, §1; L. 1980, ch. 532, §1; L. 1981, ch. 416, §17; L. 1981, ch. 965, §4; L. 1984, ch. 948, §11; L. 1988. ch. 702, §3; L. 1988, ch. 706, §9; L. 1994, ch. 222, §22; L. 1994, ch. 224, §3; L. 1995, ch. 483, §§11, 12; L. 2003, ch. 579, §1, effective October 22, 2003; L. 2006, ch. 253, §6, effective July 26, 2006; L. 2007, ch. 73, §5, effective August 3, 2007.)

New York Criminal Procedure Law

§530.14 Suspension and revocation of a license to carry firearms

1. Mandatory and permissive suspension of firearms license and ineligibility for such a license upon issuance of temporary order of protection. Whenever a temporary order of protection is issued pursuant to subdivision one of section 530.12 or subdivision one of section 530.13 of this article:

(a) the court shall suspend any such existing license possessed by the defendant, order the defendant ineligible for such a license and order the immediate surrender of any or all firearms owned or possessed where the court receives information that gives the court good cause to believe that (i) the defendant has a prior conviction of any violent felony offense as defined in section 70.02 of the penal law; (ii) the defendant has previously been found to have willfully failed to obey a prior order of protection and such willful failure involved (A) the infliction of serious physical injury, as defined in subdivision ten of section 10.00 of the penal law, (B) the use or threatened use of a deadly weapon or dangerous instrument as those terms are defined in subdivisions twelve and thirteen of section 10.00 of the penal law, or (C) behavior constituting any violent felony offense as defined in section 70.02 of the penal law; or (iii) the defendant has a prior conviction for stalking in the first degree as defined in section 120.60 of the penal law, stalking in the second degree as defined in section 120.55 of the penal law, stalking in the third degree as defined in section 120.50 of the penal law or stalking in the fourth degree as defined in section 120.45 of such law; and

(b) the court may where the court finds a substantial risk that the defendant may use or threaten to use a firearm unlawfully against the person or persons for whose protection the temporary order of protection is issued, suspend any such existing license possessed by the defendant, order the defendant ineligible for such a license and order the immediate surrender of any or all firearms owned or possessed.

2. Mandatory and permissive revocation or suspension of firearms license and ineligibility for such a license upon issuance of an order of protection. Whenever an order of protection is issued pursuant to subdivision five of section 530.12 or subdivision four of section 530.13 of this article:

(a) the court shall revoke any such existing license possessed by the defendant, order the defendant ineligible for such a license and order the immediate surrender of any or all firearms owned or possessed where such action is required by section 400.00 of the penal law; and

(b) the court may where the court finds a substantial risk that the defendant may use or threaten to use a firearm unlawfully against the person or persons for whose protection the order of protection is issued, (i) revoke any such existing license possessed by the defendant, order the defendant ineligible for such a license and order the immediate surrender of any or all firearms owned or possessed or (ii) suspend or continue to suspend any such existing license possessed by the defendant, order the defendant ineligible for such a license and order the immediate surrender of any or all firearms owned or possessed.

3. Mandatory and permissive revocation or suspension of firearms license and ineligibility for such a license upon a finding of a willful failure to obey an order of protection. Whenever a defendant has been found pursuant to subdivision eleven of section 530.12 or subdivision eight of section 530.13 of this article to have willfully failed to obey an order of protection issued by a court of competent jurisdiction in this state or another state, territorial or tribal jurisdiction, in addition to any other remedies available pursuant to subdivision eleven of section 530.12 or subdivision eight of section 530.13 of this article:

(a) the court shall revoke any such existing license possessed by the defendant, order the defendant ineligible for such a license and order the immediate surrender of any or all firearms owned or possessed where the willful failure to obey such order involved (i) the infliction of serious physical injury, as defined in subdivision ten of section 10.00 of the penal law, (ii) the use or threatened use of a deadly weapon or dangerous instrument as those terms are defined in subdivisions twelve and thirteen of section 10.00 of the penal law, (iii) behavior constituting any violent felony offense as defined in section 70.02 of the penal law; or (iv) behavior constituting stalking in the first degree as defined in section 120.60 of the penal law, stalking in the second degree as defined in section 120.55 of the penal law, stalking in the third degree as defined in section 120.50 of the penal law or stalking in the fourth degree as defined in section 120.45 of such law; and

(b) the court may where the court finds a substantial risk that the defendant may use or threaten to use a firearm unlawfully against the person or persons for whose protection the order of protection was issued,

(i) revoke any such existing license possessed by the defendant, order the defendant ineligible for such a license and order the immediate surrender of any or all firearms owned or possessed or

(ii) suspend any such existing license possessed by the defendant, order the defendant ineligible for such a license and order the immediate surrender of any or all firearms owned or possessed.

4. Suspension. Any suspension order issued pursuant to this section shall remain in effect for the duration of the temporary order of protection or order of protection, unless modified or vacated by the court.

5. Surrender.

(a) Where an order to surrender one or more firearms has been issued, the temporary order of protection or order of protection shall specify the place where such firearms shall be surrendered, shall specify a date and time by which the surrender shall be completed and, to the extent possible, shall describe such firearms to be surrendered, and shall direct the authority receiving such surrendered firearms to immediately notify the court of such surrender.

(b) The prompt surrender of one or more firearms pursuant to a court order issued pursuant to this section shall be considered a voluntary surrender for purposes of subparagraph (f) of paragraph one of subdivision a of section 265.20 of the penal law. The disposition of any such firearms shall be in accordance with the provisions of subdivision six of section 400.05 of the penal law.

(c) The provisions of this section shall not be deemed to limit, restrict or otherwise impair the authority of the court to order and direct the surrender of any or all pistols, revolvers, rifles, shotguns or other firearms owned or possessed by a defendant pursuant to sections 530.12 or 530.13 of this article.

6. Notice. (a) Where an order of revocation, suspension or ineligibility has been issued pursuant to this section, any temporary order of protection or order of protection issued shall state that such firearm license has been suspended or revoked or that the defendant is ineligible for such license, as the case may be.

(b) The court revoking or suspending the license, ordering the defendant ineligible for such a license, or ordering the surrender of any firearm shall immediately notify the duly constituted police authorities of the locality concerning such action and, in the case of orders of protection and temporary orders of protection issued pursuant to section 530.12 of this article, shall immediately notify the statewide registry of orders of protection.

(c) The court revoking or suspending the license or ordering the defendant ineligible for such a license shall give written notice thereof without unnecessary delay to the division of state police at its office in the city of Albany.

(d) Where an order of revocation, suspension, ineligibility or surrender is modified or vacated, the court shall immediately notify the statewide registry of orders of protection and the duly constituted police authorities of the locality concerning such action and shall give written notice thereof without unnecessary delay to the division of state police at its office in the city of Albany.

7. Hearing. The defendant shall have the right to a hearing before the court regarding any revocation, suspension, ineligibility or surrender order issued pursuant to this section, provided that nothing in this subdivision shall preclude the court from issuing any such order prior to a hearing. Where the court has issued such an order prior to a hearing, it shall commence such hearing within fourteen days of the date such order was issued.

8. Nothing in this section shall delay or otherwise interfere with the issuance of a temporary order of protection or the timely arraignment of a defendant in custody.

(L. 1996, ch. 644, §3; L. 1998, ch. 597, §13; L. 1999, ch. 635, §4; L. 2000, ch. 434, §1.)

E. ROLE OF COUNSEL

1. Conflicts of Interest

The divorce lawyer may face several ethical problems, including conflicts of interest. One area that raises the possibility of conflicts of interest is joint or dual representation. The ABA Model Code of Professional Responsibility (DR 5- 105(C); EC 5-15) and its successor ABA Model Rules of Professional Conduct (Rule 2.2) permit joint representation if the attorney reasonably believes he or she can adequately represent the clients' interests and if both clients consent after full disclosure of the risks of such representation. The Restatement (Third) of the Law Governing Lawyers §128 (2000) reaffirms this rule.

According to the predominant view, lawyers may undertake joint representation with the parties' consent, absent an actual conflict. Debra Lyn Bassett, Three's a Crowd: A Proposal to Abolish Joint Representation, 32 Rutgers L.J. 387, 425 (2001). Despite this view, "the reality is that an inherent conflict exists, particularly when there is property or children." *Id.* at 426.

Unlike some states, New York has no outright prohibition on joint representation. Bassett, *supra*, at 426 & n.173. New York permits dual representation provided that the following conditions are met: (1) the lawyer must make full disclosure to both spouses; (2) both spouses must separately consent to the joint representation after the disclosure; and (3) no serious conflict of interest exists between the spouses. If a conflict later develops, the lawyer must withdraw from representation and cannot represent either party. Association of the Bar of the City of New York, The Committee on Professional and Judicial Ethics, Formal Opinion 2001-01, Conflicts in Corporate and Transactional Matters, 128 PLI/NY 613 (Dec. 2002). See also John S. Dzienkowski, Lawyers as Intermediaries: The Representation of Multiple Clients in the Modern Legal Profession, 1992 U. Ill. L. Rev. 741.

Another common practice is for an attorney to represent both marital parties in negotiations for settlement of property matters. The marital parties often prefer to negotiate their own settlement outside of court and avoid having the court impose property distribution and spousal support provisions. New York case law permits, but disapproves, of joint representation in the context of preparation of a settlement agreement. See Levine v. Levine, 431 N.Y.S.2d 26 (N.Y. 1982) (holding that separation agreements drafted by one attorney who represents both parties are subject to heightened scrutiny); Vandenburgh v. Vandenburgh, 599 N.Y.S.2d 328 (App. Div. 1993) (holding that an agreement drafted by an attorney representing both parties will be set aside if manifestly unfair to one spouse). The practice raises the specter of subsequent challenges by a former spouse to an arrangement drafted by an attorney representing both parties.

Contingent fees also raise potential conflicts of interest between the attorney and client. ABA Model Rule 1.5(d)(1) forbids fees in divorce matters contingent upon "the securing of a divorce or upon the amount of alimony or support or property settlement" achieved. The Rule is based on the public policy concern that a lawyer who charges a contingent fee would place himself or herself in a conflict situation, for by encouraging reconciliation, counsel could lose a fee. New York lawyers who represent clients in "domestic relations matters" cannot charge a contingency fee and must put their fee agreements to writing (DR 2-106(C)(2)), *supra*, Section D. See also the discussion of Fee Disputes in Section E3, *infra*.

2. Sexual Ethics

The issue of attorney-client sexual conduct has prompted considerable debate. The trend has been toward prohibiting sexual relationships between attorneys and clients. Currently, 19 states have some form of prohibition against attorney-client sexual relationships. Jedediah R. Bodger, Revisions to the Rules of Professional Conduct, Nev. Law. 17, 19-20 (Feb. 2004). Some states take the strictest approach, prohibiting all sexual relationships between attorneys and clients. Other states ban attorney-client sexual relations except when the relationship predates the representation. Still other states prohibit only those relationships that negatively affect the practice of law. New York limits the ban to domestic relations attorneys. 22 NYCRR §1200.29-a(b)(3) (*infra*).

In 1991, California became the first state whose bar association approved a rule proscribing attorney-client sexual relationships. Cal. R. Prof. Conduct 3-120. The rule does not apply to sexual relationships predating the initiation of the lawyer-client relationship. Controversial proposed language, eventually eliminated, would have effectuated a presumption that an attorney who engages in sexual relations with a client has violated the rule. See Calif. Sex-with-Clients Rule, 7 Laws. Man. On Prof. Conduct (ABA/BNA) 279, 280 (Sept. 11, 1991).

Until recently, neither the ABA Model Code of Professional Responsibility nor the ABA Model Rules of Professional Conduct explicitly addressed attorney-client sexual conduct. However, in February 2002, the ABA House of Delegates approved Model Rule 1.8(j): "A lawyer shall not have sexual relations with a client unless a consensual sexual relationship existed between them when the client-lawyer relationship commenced."

In New York, attorneys are prohibited from requiring or demanding sexual relations as a condition of representation, or employing coercion, intimidation, or undue influence in entering into sexual relations (Code of Professional Responsibility, DR 5-111 [22 NYCRR §1200.29-a]). Further, attorneys in domestic relations matters are entirely prohibited from having sexual relations with clients unless a sexual relationship already exists when representation commences. *Id.* at §1200.29-a(c) (*infra*). A violation of the disciplinary rule does not give rise to a private cause of action. See Guiles v. Simser, 804 N.Y.S.2d 904 (N.Y. Sup. 2006) (finding that client had no cognizable claim for intentional or negligent infliction of emotional distress, or breach of fiduciary duty for violation of the disciplinary rule prohibiting lawyer-client sexual relations in a domestic relations matter because client failed to show any compensable injury such as misuse of confidential information or detriment to her position).

According to DR 1-102(A)(1), it is misconduct for a lawyer or law firm to violate any of the disciplinary rules in the New York Code of Professional Responsibility. (Disciplinary rules or "DRs" are mandatory, stating the minimum level of conduct below which no lawyer can fall without being subject to disciplinary action. However, an ethical consideration ("EC") is only aspirational and does not constitute misconduct under DR 1-102(A)(1)).

See generally Linda Fitts Mischler, Personal Morals Masquerading as Professional Ethics: Regulations Banning Sex Between Domestic Relations Attorneys and Their Clients, 23 Harv. Women's L.J. 1 (2000); Gretchen M. Staley, Sex and the Divorce Lawyer, 11 J. Contemp. Legal Issues 24 (2000); Florence Vincent, Comment, Regulating Intimacy of Lawyers: Why Is It Needed and How Should It Be Approached?, 33 U. Tol. L. Rev. 645 (2002).

Code of Professional Responsibility

§1200.1. Definitions

(a) "Differing interests" include every interest that will adversely affect either the judgment or the loyalty of a lawyer to a client, whether it be a conflicting, inconsistent, diverse, or other interest.

(b) "Law firm" includes, but is not limited to, a professional legal corporation, a limited liability company or partnership engaged in the practice of law, the legal department of a corporation or other organization and a qualified legal assistance organization.

(c) "Person" includes a corporation, an association, a trust, a partnership, and any other organization or legal entity.

(d) "Professional legal corporation" means a corporation, or an association treated as a corporation, authorized by law to practice law for profit.

(e) "State" includes the District of Columbia, Puerto Rico, and other federal territories and possessions.

(f) "Tribunal" includes all courts, arbitrators and other adjudicatory bodies.

(g) (Repealed.)

(h) "Qualified legal assistance organization" means an office or organization of one of the four types listed in DR 2-103 [1200.8] (D)(1) through (4) inclusive, that meets all the requirements thereof.

(i) "Fraud" does not include conduct, although characterized as fraudulent by statute or administrative rule, which lacks an element of scienter, deceit, intent to mislead, or knowing failure to correct misrepresentations which can be reasonably expected to induce detrimental reliance by another.

(j) "Domestic relations matters" means representation of a client in a claim, action or proceeding, or preliminary to the filing of a claim, action or proceeding, in either Supreme Court or Family Court, or in any court of appellate jurisdiction, for divorce, separation, annulment, custody, visitation, maintenance, child support, or alimony, or to enforce or modify a judgment or order in connection with any such claims, actions or proceedings.

(L. 1909, ch. 35.)

DR 1-102. [22 NYCRR §1200.3] Misconduct

A. A lawyer or law firm shall not:

(1) Violate a Disciplinary Rule.

(2) Circumvent a Disciplinary Rule through actions of another.

(3) Engage in illegal conduct that adversely reflects on the lawyer's honesty, trustworthiness or fitness as a lawyer.

(4) Engage in conduct involving dishonesty, fraud, deceit, or misrepresentation.

(5) Engage in conduct that is prejudicial to the administration of justice.

(6) Unlawfully discriminate in the practice of law, including in hiring, promoting or otherwise determining conditions of employment, on the basis of age, race, creed, color, national origin, sex, disability, marital status, or sexual orientation. Where there is a tribunal with jurisdiction to hear a complaint, if timely brought, other than a Departmental Disciplinary Committee, a complaint based on unlawful discrimination shall be brought before such tribunal in the first instance. A certified copy of a determination by such a tribunal, which has become final and enforceable, and as to which the right to judicial or appellate review has been exhausted, finding that the lawyer has engaged in an unlawful discriminatory practice shall constitute prima facie evidence of professional misconduct in a disciplinary proceeding.

(7) Engage in any other conduct that adversely reflects on the lawyer's fitness as a lawyer.

(L. 1909, ch. 35.)

DR 5-111. [22 NYCRR §1200.29-a] Sexual Relations With Clients

(a). "Sexual relations" means sexual intercourse or the touching of an intimate part of another person for the purpose of sexual arousal, sexual gratification, or sexual abuse.

(b). A lawyer shall not:

(1). Require or demand sexual relations with a client or third party incident to or as a condition of any professional representation.

(2). Employ coercion, intimidation, or undue influence in entering into sexual relations with a client.

(3). In domestic relations matters, enter into sexual relations with a client during the course of the lawyer's representation of the client.

(c). Subdivision (b) of this section shall not apply to sexual relations between lawyers and their spouses or to ongoing consensual sexual relationships that predate the initiation of the lawyer-client relationship.

(d). Where a lawyer in a firm has sexual relations with a client but does not participate in the representation of that client, the lawyers in the firm shall not be subject to discipline under this rule solely because of the occurrence of such sexual relations.

(Section filed July 19, 1999.)

IV.
Spousal Support

This chapter, together with Chapter V, addresses the financial consequences of dissolution. The chapter first explains the duty to support a spouse, including criminal sanctions for nonsupport as well as limitations on that duty in the form of premarital agreements with spousal support waivers. Second, the chapter turns to jurisdiction. Third, it explores the criteria for determining the availability and amount of support. Fourth, it addresses modification and termination of support. Fifth, it explores the enforcement of spousal support orders. Finally, it examines the treatment of spousal support in marital separation agreements. The law of New York (Domestic Relations Law (DRL), Family Court Act (FCA), and related provisions) provides an illustration of these topics.

Spousal support or "maintenance" is an award of future payments to one spouse payable from the future earnings of the other spouse. Formerly, spousal support was termed "alimony." However, the movement toward gender-neutral roles and the desire to remove the stigma from divorce led to a change in nomenclature. In 1980, the New York State legislature reflected this trend with the enactment of the Equitable Distribution Law, which encompassed the theory of marriage as an economic partnership (recognizing the direct and indirect contributions of each spouse, including homemakers) and replaced gender-based terms such as "alimony" with the term "maintenance" (L. 1980, ch. 281, effective July 19, 1980).

Our modern law of spousal support derives from English ecclesiastical law and practice. Until 1857, England permitted only legal separations, not divorce. Neither party was free to remarry. Because wives were economically dependent on their husbands, a separated wife needed a means of support. As a result, courts awarded alimony to a wife, provided that she had not committed any marital misconduct (was free from "fault"). Alimony thus represented a continuation of the husband's marital duty of support.

In a fault-based regime, only the innocent spouse was awarded spousal support. The guilty spouse was "punished" for his or her transgression by having to pay awards of spousal support and property. In New York, former DRL §236 provided that a wife who was guilty of marital misconduct (i.e., conduct that constituted grounds for divorce or legal separation) was precluded from receiving alimony.

The traditional rationales for spousal support were need and fault, as explained earlier. However, the purpose of spousal support has changed today, influenced largely by the women's movement and the acceptability of no-fault divorce. UMDA was influential in the adoption of self-sufficiency as a rationale for awards of spousal support. UMDA provides for awards of spousal support only for those spouses who do not have sufficient property to satisfy their reasonable needs, are unable to support themselves through employment, or have custody of very young children (UMDA §308(a)). Spousal support, thus, is intended as a temporary rehabilitative measure until a spouse becomes self-sufficient. (UMDA aims to provide for a divorced spouse by way of a property settlement rather than spousal support.)

In addition, spousal support is no longer a gender-based award. Orr v. Orr, 440 U.S. 268 (1979) (holding that a statute providing that only husbands pay alimony upon divorce is a violation of equal protection). Further, evidence of the marital misconduct of either spouse is irrelevant today in many jurisdictions (e.g., Cal. Fam. Code §2335). See Role of Fault, Section D1, *infra*. See generally American Bar Association, Chart I: Alimony/Spousal Support Factors, 40 Fam. L.Q. 591 (2007) (listing factors in each state that courts use to determine spousal support).

A. DUTY OF SUPPORT DURING THE MARRIAGE

At common law, the husband had a duty to support his wife and children, which included a duty to provide "necessaries" (i.e., necessary goods and services). The wife had a correlative duty to render services to her husband. Today, the spouses generally share a mutual duty of support while they are living together.

New York has codified the common law duty of support (FCA §§412, 416). Each spouse has a duty to support the other spouse during the marriage (FCA §412). Originally, FCA §412 applied only to the husband. When FCA §412 was enacted, a wife was obligated to support her husband only if he was a recipient of public assistance or likely to become so. The legislature subsequently made FCA §415 gender neutral (as well as many other provisions in Article 4). Douglas J. Besharov, Practice Commentaries, FCA §412 (1998). Specifically, the legislature substituted the term "married person" for the term "husband," the term "spouse" for "wife," and the term "his or her support" for "her support" (L. 1980, ch. 281, §27). Note that, by amendment in November 2001, the legislature rendered the entire state constitution gender neutral.

Four conditions can relieve a party of the spousal duty of support: (1) an invalid marriage (but a respondent may not rely on the invalidity of a prior divorce to avoid support for the spouse of the second marriage; (2) the legal termination of a marriage, unless it was terminated through an ex parte proceeding in a foreign jurisdiction (the right to spousal support under FCA §412 ceases at divorce); (3) a valid separation agreement; and (4) matrimonial fault, at least if it is serious. Besharov, Practice Commentaries, *supra*, §412.

The common law doctrine of necessaries imposed liability on the husband to third-party creditors who provided essential goods and services to family members. The "necessaries doctrine" is codified in Family Court Act §416. As originally enacted (and at common law), the provision applied both to a wife and children; successive amendments to the Family Court Act, Article 4, located most child support provisions elsewhere (e.g., FCA §413). However, FCA §416 still contains rules concerning child support in the form of children's medical and health insurance expenses. Besharov, Practice Commentaries, *supra*, at §416.

Case law interprets the duty of support as measured by station in life. Garlock v. Garlock, 18 N.E.2d 521, 522 (N.Y. 1939). New York courts have held that the scope of a "necessary" (as determined by the parties' station in life) encompasses clothing (Veneri v. Veneri, 336 N.Y.S.2d 474, 475 (App. Div. 1972)); medical insurance, medical and dental expenses, mortgage payments, real estate taxes, water charges, insurance on the parties' home and summer home (Hahn v. Hahn. 336 N.Y.S.2d 500 (App. Div. 1972)); "guidance, care, nursing, and education commensurate with financial ability" (Bentley v. Bentley, 76 N.Y.S.2d 877, 880 (Dom. Rel. Ct., Queens Co., 1948)); toys and books for a sick child (Farah v. Farah, 99 N.Y.S.2d 972, 976 (Dom. Rel. Ct., Kings Co., 1950)); and orthodontia (Bachman v. Carro, 413 N.Y.S.2d 229 (App. Div. 1979); Kelleman v. Kelleman, 475 N.Y.S.2d 583 (App. Div. 1984)). Besharov, Practice Commentaries, *supra*, at §416. Note that case law defines necessaries in the context of child support rather than spousal support. The court also may decide that other "proper and reasonable expenses" (DRL §416) constitute necessaries.

In Medical Business Associates, Inc. v. Steiner, 588 N.Y.S.2d 890 (App. Div. 1992), the Supreme Court, Appellate Division, examined the constitutionality of the common law doctrine of necessaries. In a suit by a medical corporation to recover for medical services provided to a husband and wife, the court held that the doctrine violates the Equal Protection Clause by requiring the husband, but not the wife, to pay for necessary goods and services. Having concluded that the doctrine was unconstitutional, the court faced the choice of abrogating the doctrine or making it gender neutral. The court chose the latter alternative, imposing reciprocal duties on the couple for necessaries incurred by either spouse but ruling that the debtor spouse was primarily liable. See Jill Elaine Hasday, The Cannon of Family Law, 57 Stan. L. Rev. 825, 847 (2004).

Under FCA §415, the duty to support a spouse who is a recipient of public assistance or an institutionalized mental patient has two limitations: (1) the support liability is limited to the amount that would be in the public assistance grant, and (2) the court has discretion to impose liability. Besharov, Practice Commentaries, *supra*, FCA §415. This statutory provision also authorizes a civil suit for reimbursement to the agency.

Some states impose criminal sanctions for nonsupport of certain family members (e.g., spouses, children, elderly parents). New York criminalizes only nonsupport of children.

Family Court Act

§412. Duty to support spouse

A married person is chargeable with the support of his or her spouse and, if possessed of sufficient means or able to earn such means, may be required to pay for his or her support a fair and reasonable sum, as the court may determine, having due regard to the circumstances of the respective parties.

(L. 1962, ch. 686; L. 1980, ch. 281, §27.)

§415. Spouse has duty to support recipient of public assistance or institutionalized mental patient

Except as otherwise provided by law, the spouse or parent of a recipient of public assistance or care or of a person liable to become in need thereof or of a patient in an institution in the department of mental hygiene, if of sufficient ability, is responsible for the support of such person or patient, provided that a parent shall be responsible only for the support of his child or children who have not attained the age of twenty-one years. In its discretion, the court may require any such person to contribute a fair and reasonable sum for the support of such relative and may apportion the costs of such support among such persons as may be just and appropriate in view of the needs of the petitioner and the other circumstances of the case and their respective means. Step-parents shall in like manner be responsible for the support of children under the age of twenty-one years.

(L. 1962, ch. 686; L. 1965, ch. 674, §1; L. 1966, ch. 256, §46; L. 1974, ch. 937, §4; L. 1977, ch. 777, §4.)

§416. Elements of support

(a) The court may include in the requirements for an order for support the providing of necessary shelter, food, clothing, care, medical attention, expenses of confinement, the expense of education, payment of funeral expenses, and other proper and reasonable expenses.

. . .

(L. 1962, ch. 686; L. 1974, ch. 937, §5; L. 1978, ch. 456, §6; L. 1984, ch. 794, §2; L. 1986, ch. 849, §2; L. 1993, ch. 59, §1; L. 1994, ch. 170, §368; L. 1997, ch. 398, §143; L. 1998, ch. 214, §58; L. 1998, ch. 393, §1; L. 2002, ch. 624, §2, effective October 2, 2002.)

B. EFFECT OF PREMARITAL AGREEMENT ON SPOUSAL SUPPORT WAIVERS

Premarital (also "antenuptial" or "prenuptial") agreements generally limit spousal rights to support, property, or both in the event of dissolution and death. Their increasing popularity stems, in part, from the high rate of divorce, delayed marriage age, and a concern with protecting children of a prior marriage. Florence Kaslow, Enter the Prenuptial: A Prelude to Marriage or Remarriage, 9 Behav. Sci. & L. 375-376 (1991).

The law's treatment of premarital agreements represents the interplay of traditional contract principles and family law principles of equitable distribution. Prior to the 1970s, courts held these agreements violative of public policy as an inducement to divorce. Courts also feared that a dependent spouse might become a public charge. Contemporary courts regard such agreements more favorably.

Spouses can agree to limit or waive the right to spousal support postdissolution by means of either a premarital agreement or a separation agreement. The Uniform Premarital Agreement Act (UPAA), promulgated in 1983 by the National Conference of Commissioners on Uniform State Laws (NCCUSL), governs the enforceability of premarital waivers in the 26 jurisdictions that have adopted it. Unif. Premarital Agreement Act, 9C U.L.A. 35 (2001). The UPAA requires a high standard of "unconscionability" to invalidate a premarital agreement. The UPAA is included in Part III of this Code, *infra*.

Under rules approved by the American Law Institute, premarital agreements also must meet standards of procedural unfairness (i.e., informed consent and disclosure) and substantive fairness. A rebuttable presumption arises that the agreement satisfies the informed consent requirement if (1) it was executed at least 30 days prior to the marriage; (2) both parties had, or were advised to obtain, counsel and had the opportunity to do so; and (3) in the event that one of the parties did not have counsel, the agreement contained understandable information about the parties' rights and the adverse nature of their interests. ALI, Principles of the Law of Family Dissolution: Analysis and Recommendations §7.04(3)(a)(b) & (c)(2002). In addition, the court must undertake a review of substantive fairness at the time of enforcement, specifically regarding whether enforcement would work a "substantial injustice" based on the passage of time, presence of children, or changed circumstances that were unanticipated and would have a significant impact on the parties or their children. *Id.* at §7.05. The ALI Principles on premarital agreements are included in Part IV of this Code, *infra*. See generally Paul Bennett Marrow & Kimberly S. Thompson, Drafting Matrimonial Agreements Requires Consideration of Possible Unconscionability Issues, 76 N.Y. St. Bar J. 26 (2004).

New York is not among those states that have adopted the UPAA (*www.nccusl.org*, visited on August 9, 2007). Thus, the requirements for the enforceability of premarital agreements in New York are based on statute and case law.

A premarital agreement or separation agreement (made during the marriage) will be enforceable in New York if the agreement is (1) in writing, (2) subscribed by the parties, and (3) acknowledged or proven in the manner required to entitle a deed to be recorded (DRL §236(B)(3)). Such an agreement is subject to the statutory requirement that it must not relieve either spouse of the liability to support the other in such a manner that the latter becomes incapable of self-support and therefore is likely to become a public charge (Gen. Oblig. Law §5-311). The terms of the agreement must be fair and reasonable at the time of the making of the agreement and not unconscionable at the time of entry of final judgment (DRL §236(B)(3)).

Case law has interpreted the "acknowledgment requirement" (DRL §236(B)(3)) to mean both (1) an oral acknowledgment must be made before an authorized officer and (2) a written certificate of acknowledgment (often prepared by a notary public) must be attached. Caralyn Miller Ross, Separation Agreements, 18B Carmody-Wait 2d, *supra*, at §117:8.

Premarital agreements can affect a spouse's right to temporary, as well as permanent, support. Clanton v. Clanton, 592 N.Y.S.2d 783 (App. Div. 1993) (holding that a broadly worded premarital agreement in which parties renounced all claims against the other in the event of "breakup" "under any circumstances" precluded the wife from seeking maintenance, including maintenance pendente lite). But cf. Solomon v. Solomon, 637 N.Y.S.2d 728 (App. Div. 1996) (holding that while a prenuptial agreement may restrict or waive a spouse's right to support and property, it does not bar temporary relief, such as temporary maintenance, interim counsel fees, and a temporary injunction against disposing of marital property).

The court cannot make an order or judgment contrary to the provisions of the premarital (or separation agreement) if that agreement was fair and in good faith, apparently valid, and has not been breached, set aside by the court, or rescinded by the parties. Romualdo P. Eclavea, Spousal Support, 19 Carmody-Wait 2d, *supra*, at §118:47. On separation agreements, see Section G, Separation Agreements and Spousal Support, *infra*.

Domestic Relations Law

§236. Special controlling provisions

. . .

3. Agreement of the parties. An agreement by the parties, made before or during the marriage, shall be valid and enforceable in a matrimonial action if such agreement is in writing, subscribed by the parties, and acknowledged or proven in the manner required to entitle a deed to be recorded. Notwithstanding any other provision of law, an acknowledgment of an agreement made before marriage may be executed before any person authorized to solemnize a marriage pursuant to subdivisions one, two and three of section eleven of this chapter. Such an agreement may include

(1) a contract to make a testamentary provision of any kind, or a waiver of any right to elect against the provisions of a will;

(2) provision for the ownership, division or distribution of separate and marital property;

(3) provision for the amount and duration of maintenance or other terms and conditions of the marriage relationship, subject to the provisions of section 5-311 of the general obligations law, and provided that such terms were fair and reasonable at the time of the making of the agreement and are not unconscionable at the time of entry of final judgment; and

(4) provision for the custody, care, education and maintenance of any child of the parties, subject to the provisions of section two hundred forty of this article. Nothing in this subdivision shall be deemed to affect the validity of any agreement made prior to the effective date of this subdivision.

. . .

(L. 1962, ch. 313, §10; L. 1963, ch. 685, §6; L. 1968, ch. 699, §1; L. 1980, ch. 281, §9; L. 1980, ch. 645, §§2, 3; L. 1981, ch. 695, §§1, 2; L. 1984, ch. 790, §2; L. 1985, ch. 809, §6; L. 1986, ch. 884, §§1 to 4; L. 1986, ch. 892, §§2 to 4; L. 1987, ch. 815, §§6, 7; L. 1989, ch. 567, §§4, 5; L. 1990, ch. 818, §§4, 5; L. 1992, ch. 41, §§139, 140; L. 1992, ch. 415, §§1, 2; L. 1993, ch. 59, §9; L. 1993, ch. 354, §2; L. 1994, ch. 170, §§359, 360; L. 1997, ch. 398, §§4, 5, effective October 1, 1998; L. 1997, ch. 398, §141, effective January 1, 1998; L. 1997, ch. 436, pt. B, §§105, 106, effective August 20, 1997; L. 1998, ch. 214, §56, effective November 4, 1998; L. 1998, ch. 393, §2, effective July 22, 1998; L. 1999, ch. 275, §2, effective September 18, 1999; L. 2003, ch. 595, §1, effective September 22, 2003.)

General Obligations Law

§3-303. Contracts in contemplation of marriage

A contract made between persons in contemplation of marriage, remains in full force after the marriage takes place.

(L. 1963, ch. 576, §1.)

§5-311. Certain agreements between spouses are void

Except as provided in section two hundred thirty-six of the domestic relations law, a husband and wife cannot contract to alter or dissolve the marriage or to relieve either of his or her liability to support the other in such a manner that he or she will become incapable of self-support and therefore is likely to become a public charge. An agreement, heretofore or hereafter made between a husband and wife, shall not be considered a contract to alter or dissolve the marriage unless it contains an express provision requiring the dissolution of the marriage or provides for the procurement of grounds of divorce.

(L. 1980, ch. 281, §19.)

C. JURISDICTION

In New York State, family-related matters are heard in both the Supreme Court and the Family Court. The Supreme Court is the only court empowered to rule on the marital status of the parties. Scheinkman, 12 N.Y. Prac., *supra*, at §25:3. The Supreme Court is the statewide court of general jurisdiction. It derives its authority from the state constitution (Art. VI, §7(a)), which confers authority on the Supreme Court as a court of "general original jurisdiction in law and equity." That constitutional provision also provides that "the legislature may provide that another court or other courts shall also have jurisdiction and that actions and proceedings of such classes may be originated in such other court or courts." (*Id.* at §7(b).)

The Family Court was established in 1962 and combined jurisdiction from the former Children's Courts and the New York City Domestic Relations Court. Merril Sobie, 10 N.Y. Prac., New York Family Court Practice §1:1 (2002). The Family Court does not have original jurisdiction over matrimonial actions. Scheinkman, 12 N.Y. Prac., *supra*, at §25:3. When the Family Court was established, proponents of the court advocated the inclusion of divorce and annulment jurisdiction (those matters were then heard by the Supreme Court). However, in a legislative compromise, the Supreme Court retained jurisdiction over those matters, but the Family Court was granted concurrent child custody jurisdiction, as well as jurisdiction to determine the financial aspects of marriage dissolution through referral from the Supreme Court. Sobie, *supra*.

The Family Court, a court of limited jurisdiction, possesses only the authority derived from the state constitution and statute. John Kimpflen et al., Jurisdiction of Particular Courts, 1 Carmody-Wait 2d, *supra*, at §2:145. The state constitution (Art. VI, §13(b)) provides that the Family Court has jurisdiction over proceedings involving: (1) minors in need of the court's authority because of neglect, delinquency, or dependency; (2) custody of minors except for custody incidental to actions and proceedings for marital separation, divorce, annulment, and dissolution of marriage; (3) adoption; (4) support of dependents, except where the determination is incidental to actions and proceedings for marital separation, divorce, annulment, or dissolution of marriage; (5) paternity establishment; (6) conciliation of spouses; and (7) guardianship of minors and (8) crimes between family members. Kimpflen et al., 1 Carmody-Wait 2d, *supra*, at §2:143.

The state constitution (Art. VI, §13(c)) also specifies that the Family Court has jurisdiction to determine the following matters *upon referral* from the Supreme Court: habeas corpus proceedings for the minor's custody determinations, and (in actions and proceedings for separation, divorce, annulment of marriage, and dissolution of marriage) applications to fix temporary or permanent support and custody, and applications to enforce or modify judgments and orders of support and of custody. Kimpflen et al., 1 Carmody-Wait 2d, *supra*, at §2:143. The Family Court lacks jurisdiction to enforce divorce judgments or separation agreements to the extent that the provisions at issue do not involve support. Scheinkman, 12 N.Y. Prac., *supra*, at §25:3.

As already explained, the authority of the Family Court derives not only from the state constitution, but also from statute (FCA §§114, 115). The Family Court Act confers exclusive, original jurisdiction (FCA §114) upon the Family Court over abuse and neglect proceedings; support proceedings; proceedings to determine paternity and for the support of nonmarital children; proceedings for termination of parental rights by reason of permanent neglect, mental illness, or the death of both parents; proceedings to determine whether a person is in need of supervision; and delinquency proceedings (FCA §115(a)).

By statute, the Family Court also has jurisdiction over habeas corpus proceedings and over applications for support, maintenance, a distribution of marital property, and custody in matrimonial actions when referred to it by the Supreme Court, conciliation proceedings, and proceedings concerning disabled children (FCA §115(b)). The Family Court also has jurisdiction over support-related proceedings to suspend driving privileges, recreational licenses, and occupational licenses of persons who are delinquent in their child support obligations (or combined child and spousal support obligations) (FCA §115(f)).

One commentator points out that the statute defining the scope of the Family Court's jurisdiction (FCA §115) is somewhat misleading and underinclusive. In reality, other sections of the Family Court Act (e.g., §§641, and 651(b)) specify that the Family Court has original adoption and custody jurisdiction. Besharov, Practice Commentaries, §115. The Family Court also has jurisdiction over other family-related matters pursuant to other code sections. For example, Education Law §3232 gives the Family Court jurisdiction over criminal violations of the compulsory education law; Social Services Law §358-a requires Family Court approval for all foster care placements in which the child is likely to remain in foster care for more than 30 consecutive days; and Social Services Law §392 requires the Family Court to review the status of children who have been in foster care for a continuous period of 24 months. Further, the Uniform Support to Dependents Law (USDL) (formerly DRL Article 3-A, now FCA Article 5-B (L. 1997, ch. 398)) gives the Family Court jurisdiction over support for dependent family members even if a party has moved to another state. The Interstate Compact on Juveniles (New York Unconsolidated Laws, Title 5, Ch. 4) gives the Family Court jurisdiction over runaways from other states, and the Interstate Compact on the Placement of Children (Soc. Serv. Law §374) gives the Family Court power to place delinquent and nondelinquent children in another state and to receive petitions from other states to place children in New York. Besharov, *supra*.

The Family Court has concurrent jurisdiction with criminal courts, the Supreme Court, and the Surrogate's Court, respectively, on a variety of other matters. Thus, the Family Court has concurrent jurisdiction with the criminal court over family offenses, such as battering and child abuse (FCA §115(e)). As explained earlier, the Supreme Court has concurrent jurisdiction with the Family Court over issues of custody and matrimonial proceedings when referred by the Supreme Court and also over issues of support, maintenance, and the distribution of marital property when referred by the Supreme Court. Sobie, 10 N.Y. Prac., New York Family Court Practice §1:7. Moore v. Moore, 725 N.Y.S.2d 821 (Fam. Ct. 2001) (explaining concurrent jurisdiction). In addition, pursuant to FCA §466, the Supreme Court may decide which court (the Supreme Court or the Family Court) should have jurisdiction to enforce *or* modify a support order in a particular matrimonial action. In 1972 the legislature granted the Family Court jurisdiction to determine original custody proceedings (in addition to hearing referrals from the Supreme Court) (FCA §651). And, pursuant to FCA §641, the Family Court has concurrent jurisdiction with the Surrogate's Court over adoption proceedings.

Note that legislative enactment of Article 4 of the Family Court Act in 1962 shifted the focus of support proceedings. Formerly, support proceedings had a criminal emphasis. The Domestic Relations Court (now the Family Court) and the Children's Court (now the Family Court) were empowered to determine charges of nonsupport and to commit a respondent to imprisonment for six months under §33 of the Children's Court Act and for 12 months under §130 of the Domestic Relations Court Act. Article 4, however, treats the proceedings as civil in nature (of course, contempt is still available for failure to obey a court order, such as for support) (FCA §433). Nonsupport of a child remains a criminal matter (N.Y. Penal Law §§260.05 et seq.). Besharov, Practice Commentaries (following FCA §411).

Family Court Act

§115. Jurisdiction of the family court

(a) The family court has exclusive original jurisdiction over

(i) abuse and neglect proceedings, as set forth in article ten;

(ii) support proceedings, as set forth in article four;

(iii) proceedings to determine paternity and for the support of children born out-of-wedlock, as set forth in article five;

(iv) proceedings to permanently terminate parental rights to guardianship and custody of a child:

(A) by reason of permanent neglect, as set forth in part one of article six of this act and paragraph (d) of subdivision four of section three hundred eighty-four-b of the social services law,

(B) by reason of mental illness, mental retardation and severe or repeated child abuse, as set forth in paragraphs (c) and (e) of subdivision four of section three hundred eighty-four-b of the social services law, and

(C) by reason of the death of one or both parents, where no guardian of the person of the child has been lawfully appointed, or by reason of abandonment of the child for a period of six months immediately prior to the filing of the petition, where a child is under the jurisdiction of the family court as a result of a placement in foster care by the family court pursuant to article ten or ten-A of this act or section three hundred fifty-eight-a of the social services law, unless the court declines jurisdiction pursuant to section three hundred eighty-four-b of the social services law;

(v) proceedings concerning whether a person is in need of supervision, as set forth in article seven; and

(vi) proceedings concerning juvenile delinquency as set forth in article three.

(b) The family court has such other jurisdiction as is set forth in this act, including jurisdiction over habeas corpus proceedings and over applications for support, maintenance, a distribution of marital property and custody in matrimonial actions when referred to the family court by the supreme court, conciliation proceedings, and proceedings concerning physically handicapped and mentally defective or retarded children.

(c) The family court has such other jurisdiction as is provided by law, including but not limited to: proceedings concerning adoption and custody of children, as set forth in parts two and three of article six of this act; proceedings concerning the uniform interstate family support act, as set forth in article five-B of this act; proceedings concerning children in foster care and care and custody of children, as set forth in sections three hundred fifty-eight-a and three hundred eighty-four-a of the social services law and article ten-A of this act; proceedings concerning guardianship and custody of children by reason of the death of, or abandonment or surrender by, the parent or parents, as set forth in sections three hundred eighty-three-c, three hundred eighty-four and paragraphs (a) and (b) of subdivision four of section three hundred eighty-four-b of the social services law; proceedings concerning standby guardianship and guardianship of the person as set forth in part four of article six of this act and article seventeen of the surrogate's court procedure act; and proceedings concerning the interstate compact on juveniles as set forth in chapter one hundred fifty-five of the laws of nineteen hundred fifty-five, as amended, the interstate compact on the placement of children, as set forth in section three hundred seventy-four-a of the social services law, and the uniform child custody jurisdiction and enforcement act, as set forth in article five-A of the domestic relations law.

(d) Notwithstanding subdivisions (a) through (c) of this section, jurisdiction of the family court and tribal courts of Indian tribes designated by the Secretary of the Interior over those child custody proceedings provided for in articles three, seven, ten and ten-A of this act and sections three hundred fifty-eight-a and three hundred eighty-four-b of the social services law involving Indian children as defined in subdivision thirty-six of section two of the social services law shall be subject to the terms and conditions set forth in applicable sections of title twenty-five of the United States code;[1] provided that tribal courts of Indian tribes designated as such by the state of New York shall have jurisdiction over such child custody proceedings involving Indian children to the same extent as federally designated Indian tribes upon the approval of the state office of children and family services pursuant to section thirty-nine of the social services law.

(e) The family court has concurrent jurisdiction with the criminal court over all family offenses as defined in article eight of this act.

(f) The family court has jurisdiction to direct the commencement of proceedings to suspend the driving privileges, recreational licenses and permits, and license, permit, registration or authority to practice of persons who are delinquent in their child or combined child and spousal support obligations or persons who have failed, after receiving appropriate notice, to comply with summonses, subpoenas or warrants relating to paternity and child support proceedings as set forth in sections four hundred fifty-eight-a, four hundred fifty-eight-b, four hundred fifty-eight-c, five hundred forty-eight-a, five hundred forty-eight-b, and five[2] forty-eight-c of this act. Such jurisdiction shall include jurisdiction over all boards, departments, authorities or offices of the state for the purposes of implementing such section.

(L. 1962, ch. 686; amended L. 1964, ch. 383, §1; L. 1970, ch. 962, §1; L. 1973, ch. 907, §2; L. 1974, ch. 239, §4; L. 1980, ch. 281, §25; L. 1980, ch. 471, §30; L. 1982, ch. 920, §29; L. 1983, ch. 398, §51; L. 1987, ch. 462 §1; L. 1994, ch. 222, §§3, 4; L. 1994, ch. 384, §2; L. 1995, ch. 81, §200; L. 1997, ch. 398, §108, effective January 1, 1998; L. 2002, ch. 409, §§1, 2, effective August 13, 2002; L. 2005, ch. 3, pt. A, §1, effective December 21, 2005; L. 2006, ch. 185, §1, effective October 24, 2006.)

§411. Jurisdiction

The family court has exclusive original jurisdiction over proceedings for support or maintenance under this article and in proceedings under article five-B of this act, known as the uniform interstate family support act. On its own motion, the court may at any time in the proceedings also direct the filing of a neglect petition in accord with article ten of this act.

(L. 1962, ch. 686; L. 1980, ch. 281, §26; L. 1983, ch. 112, §1; L. 1997, ch. 398, §43, effective January 1, 1998.)

§421. Venue for proceedings to compel support

Proceedings to compel support under this article may be originated in the county in which one of the parties resides or is domiciled at the time of the filing of the petition. Upon application, the family court may change the place of trial of a proceeding in accordance with article five of the civil practice law and rules.

(L. 1962, ch. 686; L. 1965, ch. 305, §1; L. 1980, ch. 281, §30; L. 1986, ch. 892, §11.)

§422. Persons who may bring proceedings

(a) A husband, wife, child, or relative in need of public assistance or care may originate a proceeding under this article to compel a person chargeable with the support to support the petitioner as required by law. A social services official may originate a proceeding under this article if so authorized by section one hundred and two of the social services law. The commissioner of mental health may originate a proceeding under this article when authorized by article forty-three of the mental hygiene law. A parent or guardian, of a child, or other person in loco parentis, or a representative of an incorporated charitable or philanthropic society having a legitimate interest in the petitioner, or, when the petitioner is unable because of his physical or mental condition to file a petition, a guardian ad litem, or a committee, conservator, next friend or other person appointed by the court, may file a petition in behalf of a dependent relative.

(b) Any party to a decree of divorce, separation, or annulment may originate a proceeding to enforce or modify a decree of the supreme court or a court of competent jurisdiction, not of the state of New York, as is provided in part six of this article.

---

[1] 25. U.S.C.A. §1 et seq.

[2] So in original. Inadvertently omitted "hundred."

(L. 1962, ch. 686; L. 1966, ch. 256, §47; L. 1968, ch. 331, §1; L. 1973, ch. 195, §21; L. 1980, ch. 281, §31; L. 1981, ch. 115, §52.)

§423. Proceedings are commenced by filing petition; prior demand for support not required

Proceedings under this article are commenced by the filing of a petition, which may be made on information and belief. The petitioner need not make a demand upon the respondent for support as a condition precedent to the filing of a petition for support. Any such petition for the establishment, modification and/or enforcement of a child support obligation for persons not in receipt of family assistance, which contains a request for child support enforcement services completed in a manner as specified in section one hundred eleven-g of the social services law, shall constitute an application for such services.

(L. 1962, ch. 686; L. 1981, ch. 622, §2; L. 1990, ch. 818, §13; L. 1997, ch. 436, pt. B, §110, effective August 20, 1997.)

§424-a. Compulsory financial disclosure is required in all support proceedings in Family Court

Except as provided herein:

(a) in all support proceedings in family court, there shall be compulsory disclosure by both parties of their respective financial states, provided, however, that this requirement shall not apply to a social services official who is a party in any support proceeding under this act. No showing of special circumstances shall be required before such disclosure is ordered and such disclosure may not be waived by either party or by the court. A sworn statement of net worth shall be filed with the clerk of the court on a date to be fixed by the court, no later than ten days after the return date of the petition. As used in this part, the term "net worth" shall mean the amount by which total assets including income exceed total liabilities including fixed financial obligations. It shall include all income and assets of whatsoever kind and nature and wherever situated and shall include a list of all assets transferred in any manner during the preceding three years, or the length of the marriage, whichever is shorter, provided, however, that transfers in the routine course of business which resulted in an exchange of assets of substantially equivalent value need not be specifically disclosed where such assets are otherwise identified in the statement of net worth. All such sworn statements of net worth shall be accompanied by a current and representative paycheck stub and the most recently filed state and federal income tax returns including a copy of the W-2(s) wage and tax statement(s) submitted with the returns. In addition, both parties shall provide information relating to any and all group health plans available to them for the provision of care or other medical benefits by insurance or otherwise for the benefit of the child or children for whom support is sought, including all such information as may be required to be included in a qualified medical child support order as defined in section six hundred nine of the employee retirement income security act of 1974 (29 USC 1169) including, but not limited to:

(i) the name and last known mailing address of each party and of each dependent to be covered by the order;

(ii) the identification and a description of each group health plan available for the benefit or coverage of the disclosing party and the child or children for whom support is sought;

(iii) a detailed description of the type of coverage available from each group health plan for the potential benefit of each such dependent;

(iv) the identification of the plan administrator for each such group health plan and the address of such administrator;

(v) the identification numbers for each such group health plan; and

(vi) such other information as may be required by the court;

(b) when a respondent fails, without good cause, to file a sworn statement of net worth, a current and representative paycheck stub and the most recently filed state and federal income tax returns, including a copy of the W-2(s) wage and tax statement submitted with the returns, or to provide information relating to all group health plans available for the provision of care or other medical benefits by insurance or otherwise for the benefit of the disclosing party and the child or children for whom support is sought, as provided in subdivision (a) of this section, the court on its own motion or on application shall grant the relief demanded in the petition or shall order that, for purposes of the support proceeding, the respondent shall be precluded from offering evidence as to respondent's financial ability to pay support;

(c) when a petitioner other than a social services official fails, without good cause to file a sworn statement of net worth, a current and representative paycheck stub and the most recently filed state and federal income tax returns, as provided in subdivision (a) of this section, the court may on its own motion or upon application of any party adjourn such proceeding until such time as the petitioner files with the court such statements and tax returns. The provisions of this subdivision shall not apply to proceedings establishing temporary support or proceedings for the enforcement of a support order or support provision of a separation agreement or stipulation.

(L. 1977, ch. 516, §13; L. 1980, ch. 281, §32; L. 1986, ch. 892, §13; L. 1987, ch. 815, §11; L. 1989, ch. 715, §1; L. 1997, ch. 398, §144, effective January 1, 1998; L. 1998, ch. 214, §59, effective November 4, 1998.)

§425. Agreement to support must be reduced to writing and approved by the court

If an agreement for the support of the petitioner is brought about, it must be reduced to writing and submitted to the family court or a support magistrate appointed pursuant to section four hundred thirty-nine of this act for approval. If the court or support magistrate approves it, the court without further hearing may thereupon enter an order for the support of the petitioner by the respondent in accordance with the agreement, which shall be binding upon the respondent and shall in all respects be a valid order as

though made after process had been issued out of the court. The court record shall show that such order was made upon agreement.
(L. 1962, ch. 686; L. 1986, ch. 892, §14 L. 2003, ch. 81, §5, effective June 18, 2003.)

§433. Hearing

(a) Upon the return of the summons or when a respondent is brought before the court pursuant to a warrant, the court shall proceed to hear and determine the case. The respondent shall be informed of the contents of the petition, advised of his right to counsel, and shall be given opportunity to be heard and to present witnesses. The court may exclude the public from the court room in a proper case.

(b) If the initial return of a summons or warrant is before a judge of the court, when support is an issue, the judge must make an immediate order, either temporary or permanent with regard to support. If a temporary order is made, the court shall refer the issue of support to a support magistrate for final determination pursuant to sections four hundred thirty-nine and four hundred thirty-nine-a of this act. Procedures shall be established by the chief administrator of the courts which shall provide for the disposition of all support matters or a referral to a support magistrate prior to the conclusion of a respondent's first appearance before the court. Such procedures shall provide for referral of support issues by appropriate clerical staff of the family court at any time after a petition has been presented to the court.

(c) In any proceeding under this article, the court may permit a party or a witness to be deposed or to testify by telephone, audio-visual means, or other electronic means at a designated family court or other location:

(i) where such party or witness resides in a county other than that of the family court where the case is pending and that of any contiguous county; provided, however, that for the purposes of this section, the five counties of New York city shall be treated as one county;

(ii) where such party or witness is presently incarcerated and will be incarcerated on the date on which the hearing or deposition is scheduled and is not expected to be released within a reasonable period of time after the date on which the hearing or deposition is scheduled; or

(iii) where the court determines that it would be an undue hardship for such party or witness to testify or to be deposed at the family court where the case is pending.

(d) Any such deposition or testimony taken by telephone, audio-visual means or other electronic means in accordance with subdivision (c) of this section shall be recorded and preserved for transcription. Where a party or witness is deposed or testifies by telephone, audio-visual or other electronic means pursuant to this section, documentary evidence referred to by a party or witness or the court may be transmitted by facsimile, telecopier, or other electronic means and may not be excluded from evidence by reason of an objection based on the means of transmission. The chief administrator of the courts shall promulgate rules to facilitate the taking of testimony by telephone, audio-visual means or other electronic means.

(L. 1962, ch. 686; amended L. 1985, ch. 809, §12. As amended L. 2000, ch. 475, §1, effective December 19, 2000; L. 2003, ch. 81, §6, effective June 18, 2003.)

§434-a. Temporary spousal support

The court may make an order for temporary spousal support pending a final determination, notwithstanding that information with respect to income and assets of the respondent may be unavailable.
(L. 1990, ch. 601, §1, effective July 18, 1990.)

§442. Court shall make support order for spouse after hearing under appropriate circumstances

If the court finds after a hearing that a husband or wife is chargeable under section four hundred twelve with the support of his or her spouse and is possessed of sufficient means or able to earn such means, the court shall make an order requiring the husband or wife to pay weekly or at other fixed periods a fair and reasonable sum for or towards the support of the other spouse. The court shall require the spouse chargeable with support to make his or her residence known at all times should he or she move from the address last known to the court by reporting such change to the support collection unit designated by the appropriate social services district. Failure to report such change shall subject him or her to the provisions of section four hundred fifty-four of this act.
(L. 1962, ch. 686; L. 1966, ch. 559, §1; L. 1977, ch. 516, §15; L. 1980, ch. 281, §36.)

§448. Support orders are enforceable by income deduction

Orders of support shall be enforceable pursuant to section fifty-two hundred forty-one or fifty-two hundred forty-two of the civil practice law and rules, or in any other manner provided by law. The family court is hereby authorized to enter an order with respect to an income deduction, in accordance with the provisions of section fifty-two hundred forty-two of the civil practice law and rules, in any support proceeding under the provisions of article five-B of this act under any support order made pursuant to a reference from the supreme court under section two hundred fifty-one of the domestic relations law or in any support proceeding under the provisions of article four, five or five-A of this act.
(L. 1977, ch. 516, §19; L. 1985, ch. 809, §17; L. 1986, ch. 892, §20; L. 1997, ch. 398, §47, effective January 1, 1998.)

§449. Effective date of support order

1. Any order of spousal support made under this article shall be effective as of the date of the filing of the petition therefor, and any retroactive amount of support due shall be paid in one sum or periodic sums, as the court shall direct, to the petitioner, to the custodial parent or to third persons. Any amount of temporary support which has been paid shall be taken into account in calculating any amount of retroactive support due.

2. Any order of child support made under this article shall be effective as of the earlier of the date of the filing of the

petition therefor, or, if the children for whom support is sought are in receipt of public assistance, the date for which their eligibility for public assistance was effective. Any retroactive amount of support due shall be support arrears/past-due support and shall be paid in one sum or periodic sums, as the court shall direct, to the petitioner, to the custodial parent or to third persons. Any amount of temporary support which has been paid shall be taken into account in calculating any amount of retroactive support due. In addition, such retroactive child support shall be enforceable in any manner provided by law including, but not limited to, an execution for support enforcement pursuant to subdivision (b) of section fifty-two hundred forty-one of the civil practice law and rules.
(L. 1981, ch. 695, §6; L. 1992, ch. 41, §143.)

§463. Separation agreement does not preclude order for spousal support of needy spouse

A separation agreement does not preclude the filing of a petition and the making of an order under section four hundred forty-five of this article for support of a spouse who is likely to become in need of public assistance or care.
(L. 1962, ch. 686; L. 1980, ch. 281, §41.)

§464. Court may refer spousal support matter to Family Court

(a) In a matrimonial action in the supreme court, the supreme court on its own motion or on motion of either spouse may refer to the family court an application for temporary or permanent support, or for maintenance or a distribution of marital property. If the supreme court so refers an application, the family court has jurisdiction to determine the application with the same powers possessed by the supreme court and the family court's disposition of the application is an order of the family court appealable only under article eleven of this act.

(b) In the absence of an order of referral under paragraph (a) of this section and in the absence of an order by the supreme court granting temporary or permanent support or maintenance, the family court during the pendency of such action may entertain a petition and may make an order under section four hundred forty-five of this article for a spouse who is likely to become in need of public assistance or care.
(L. 1962, ch. 686; L. 1963, ch. 809, §17; L. 1980, ch. 281, §42.)

§465. Denial of support in separation action in Supreme Court may lead to Family Court's assertion of jurisdiction

After final adjudication of an action for separation in which the supreme court denies support to a spouse, the family court may entertain a petition and make an order for support of such spouse

(a) under section four hundred forty-two of this article if in the opinion of the family court the circumstances of the parties have changed, or

(b) under section four hundred forty-five of this article if it is shown to the satisfaction of the family court that the petitioner is likely to become in need of public assistance or care.
(L. 1962, ch. 686; L. 1980, ch. 281, §43.)

§466. Supreme Court may provide for enforcement or modification of spousal support by Family Court

(a) The supreme court may provide in an order or decree granting temporary or permanent support or maintenance in an action for divorce, separation or annulment that only the family court may entertain an application to enforce or, upon a showing to the family court that there has been a subsequent change of circumstance and that modification is required, to modify such order or decree. If the supreme court so provides, the family court shall entertain such an application and any disposition by the family court of the application is an order of the family court appealable only under article eleven of this act.

(b) The supreme court may provide in an order or decree granting alimony, maintenance or support in an action for divorce, separation or annulment that the order or decree may be enforced or modified only in the supreme court. If the supreme court so provides, the family court may not entertain an application to enforce or modify an order or decree of the supreme court involving the parties to the action.

(c) If the supreme court enters an order or decree granting alimony, maintenance or support in an action for divorce, separation or annulment and if the supreme court does not exercise the authority given under subdivision (a) or (b) of this section; or if a court of competent jurisdiction not of the state of New York shall enter an order or decree granting alimony, maintenance or support in any such action, the family court may

(i) entertain an application to enforce the order or decree granting alimony or maintenance, or

(ii) entertain an application to modify the order or decree granting alimony or maintenance on the ground that there has been a subsequent change of circumstances and that modification is required.

(L. 1968, ch. 686; L. 1965, ch. 355; L. 1970, ch. 28, §2; L. 1972, ch. 721, §1; L. 1980, ch. 281, §44.)

§641. Jurisdiction over adoption matters

The family court has original jurisdiction concurrent with the surrogate's courts over adoption proceedings under article seven of the domestic relations law.
(L. 1962, ch. 686; L. 1964, ch. 383, §2; L. 1965, ch. 339, §1; L. 1966, ch. 479, §1; L. 1967, ch. 146, §1; L. 1968, ch. 258, §1; L. 1970, ch. 484, §1; L. 1972, ch. 423, §1; L. 1974, ch. 16, §1; L. 1976, ch. 153, §1; L. 1978, ch. 160, §1; L. 1980, ch. 188, §1; L. 1982, ch. 232, §1; L. 1984, ch. 267, §1; L. 1985, ch. 331, §1.)

§651. Jurisdiction over custody and visitation

(a) When referred from the supreme court or county court to the family court, the family court has jurisdiction to determine, in accordance with subdivision one of section two hundred forty of the domestic relations law and with the same powers possessed by the supreme court in addition to its own powers, habeas corpus proceedings and proceedings brought by petition and order to show cause, for the determination of the custody or visitation of minors.

(b) When initiated in the family court, the family court has jurisdiction to determine, in accordance with subdivision one of section two hundred forty of the domestic relations law and with the same powers possessed by the supreme court in addition to its own powers, habeas corpus proceedings and proceedings brought by petition and order to show cause, for the determination of the custody or visitation of minors, including applications by a grandparent or grandparents for visitation or custody rights pursuant to section seventy-two or two hundred forty of the domestic relations law.

(c) When initiated in the family court pursuant to a petition under part eight of article ten of this act or section three hundred fifty-eight-a of the social services law, the family court has jurisdiction to enforce or modify orders or judgments of the supreme court relating to the visitation of minors in foster care, notwithstanding any limitation contained in subdivision (b) of section four hundred sixty-seven of this act.

(d) With respect to applications by a grandparent or grandparents for visitation or custody rights, made pursuant to section seventy-two or two hundred forty of the domestic relations law, with a child remanded or placed in the care of a person, official, agency or institution pursuant to the provisions of article ten of this act, the applicant, in such manner as the court shall prescribe, shall serve a copy of the application upon the social services official having care and custody of such child, and the child's law guardian, who shall be afforded an opportunity to be heard thereon.

(L. 1962, ch. 686; L. 1966, ch. 686, §1; L. 1970, ch. 913, §1; L. 1972, ch. 535, §1; L. 1973, ch. 916, §1; L. 1978, ch. 443, §1; L. 1983, ch. 250, §1; L. 1988, ch. 457, §§2, 3; L. 1996, ch. 85, §6; L. 2003, ch. 657, §3, effective January 5, 2004.)

New York Constitution Art. VI

§7. Jurisdiction of Supreme Court

a. The supreme court shall have general original jurisdiction in law and equity and the appellate jurisdiction herein provided. In the city of New York, it shall have exclusive jurisdiction over crimes prosecuted by indictment, provided, however, that the legislature may grant to the city-wide court of criminal jurisdiction of the city of New York jurisdiction over misdemeanors prosecuted by indictment and to the family court in the city of New York jurisdiction over crimes and offenses by or against minors or between spouses or between parent and child or between members of the same family or household.

b. If the legislature shall create new classes of actions and proceedings, the supreme court shall have jurisdiction over such classes of actions and proceedings, but the legislature may provide that another court or other courts shall also have jurisdiction and that actions and proceedings of such classes may be originated in such other court or courts.

(Adopted Nov. 7, 1961; amended November 8, 1977; amended November 6, 2001, effective January 1, 2002.)

§13. Establishment of Family Court; jurisdiction

a. The family court of the state of New York is hereby established. It shall consist of at least one judge in each county outside the city of New York and such number of additional judges for such counties as may be provided by law. Within the city of New York it shall consist of such number of judges as may be provided by law. The judges of the family court within the city of New York shall be residents of such city and shall be appointed by the mayor of the city of New York for terms of ten years. The judges of the family court outside the city of New York, shall be chosen by the electors of the counties wherein they reside for terms of ten years.

b. The family court shall have jurisdiction over the following classes of actions and proceedings which shall be originated in such family court in the manner provided by law:

(1) the protection, treatment, correction and commitment of those minors who are in need of the exercise of the authority of the court because of circumstances of neglect, delinquency or dependency, as the legislature may determine;

(2) the custody of minors except for custody incidental to actions and proceedings for marital separation, divorce, annulment of marriage and dissolution of marriage;

(3) the adoption of persons;

(4) the support of dependents except for support incidental to actions and proceedings in this state for marital separation, divorce, annulment of marriage or dissolution of marriage;

(5) the establishment of paternity;

(6) proceedings for conciliation of spouses; and

(7) as may be provided by law: the guardianship of the person of minors and, in conformity with the provisions of section seven of this article, crimes and offenses by or against minors or between spouses or between parent and child or between members of the same family or household. Nothing in this section shall be construed to abridge the authority or jurisdiction of courts to appoint guardians in cases originating in those courts.

c. The family court shall also have jurisdiction to determine, with the same powers possessed by the supreme court, the following matters when referred to the family court from the supreme court: habeas corpus proceedings for the determination of the custody of minors; and in actions and proceedings for marital separation, divorce, annulment of marriage and dissolution of marriage, applications to fix temporary or permanent support and custody, or applications to enforce judgments and orders of support and of custody, or applications to modify judgments and orders of support and of custody which may be granted only upon the showing to the family court that there has been a subsequent change of circumstances and that modification is required.

d. The provisions of this section shall in no way limit or impair the jurisdiction of the supreme court as set forth in section seven of this article.

(Adopted November 7, 1961; amended November 6, 1973, effective January 1, 1974; November 6, 2001, effective January 1, 2002.)

D. DETERMINING AVAILABILITY AND AMOUNT OF SUPPORT

Traditionally, the amount of spousal support depended on the parties' needs and their ability to pay (as well as the existence of marital fault in the era before no-fault divorce). Today, the trial court bases its determination on a broad number of factors in light of the couple's marital standard of living (discussed in Section D2, Circumstances to Consider, *infra*).

As explained previously, UMDA was influential in the adoption of self-sufficiency as a rationale for awards of spousal support. UMDA provides for spousal support only for those spouses who do not have sufficient property to provide for their reasonable needs, are unable to support themselves through employment, or have custody of very young children (UMDA §308(a)). Spousal support, thus, according to UMDA, is intended as a temporary rehabilitative measure until a spouse becomes self-sufficient.

Early cases decided after the enactment of New York's Equitable Distribution Law followed this view by limiting maintenance to the period during which the wife could be retrained to join the work force. However, the legislature soon recognized that this approach had shortcomings; that is, some wives could not reenter the workplace (such as those in long-term marriages or with young children).

As a result, the legislature amended the Equitable Distribution Law in 1986 to provide for permanent as well as durational maintenance, changed the basis for awarding maintenance, and expanded the guidelines for setting awards of maintenance (L. 1986, ch. 844, effective August 2, 1986 and September 1, 1986).

The 1986 amendments altered prior law by according priority to the couple's predivorce standard of living in DRL §236, Part B(6)(a). (Formerly, the predivorce standard of living was only one of the enumerated factors.) See also Hartog v. Hartog, 623 N.Y.S.2d 537 (N.Y. 1995) (holding that permanent maintenance was appropriate on the facts given that the wife could not become self-supporting in the context of the marital standard of living). Scheinkman, 11 N.Y. Prac., *supra*, at §§15:1, 15:3.

The Equitable Distribution Law, DRL §236, is set forth in full *infra*. Part A of DRL §236 (omitted) refers to actions or proceedings commenced prior to the effective date of the Act (July 19, 1980), and Part B refers to those actions or proceedings commenced thereafter. Various subsections of DRL §236 are repeated *infra*.

Domestic Relations Act

§236. Equitable Distribution Law: Special controlling provisions

Except as otherwise expressly provided in this section, the provisions of part A shall be controlling with respect to any action or proceeding commenced prior to the date on which the provisions of this section as amended become effective [July 19, 1980] and the provisions of part B shall be controlling with respect to any action or proceeding commenced on or after such effective date.

Any reference to this section or the provisions hereof in any action, proceeding, judgment, order, rule or agreement shall be deemed and construed to refer to either the provisions of part A or part B respectively and exclusively, determined as provided in this paragraph any inconsistent provision of law notwithstanding.

. . .

Part B

NEW ACTIONS OR PROCEEDINGS

Maintenance and distributive award.

1. Definitions. Whenever used in this part, the following terms shall have the respective meanings hereinafter set forth or indicated:

a. The term "maintenance" shall mean payments provided for in a valid agreement between the parties or awarded by the court in accordance with the provisions of subdivision six of this part, to be paid at fixed intervals for a definite or indefinite period of time, but an award of maintenance shall terminate upon the death of either party or upon the recipient's valid or invalid marriage, or upon modification pursuant to paragraph (b) of subdivision nine of section two hundred thirty-six of this part or section two hundred forty-eight of this chapter.

b. The term "distributive award" shall mean payments provided for in a valid agreement between the parties or awarded by the court, in lieu of or to supplement, facilitate or effectuate the division or distribution of property where authorized in a matrimonial action, and payable either in a lump sum or over a period of time in fixed amounts. Distributive awards shall not include payments which are treated as ordinary income to the recipient under the provisions of the United States Internal Revenue Code.

c. The term "marital property" shall mean all property acquired by either or both spouses during the marriage and before the execution of a separation agreement or the commencement of a matrimonial action, regardless of the form in which title is held, except as otherwise provided in agreement pursuant to subdivision three of this part. Marital property shall not include separate property as hereinafter defined.

d. The term separate property shall mean:

(1) property acquired before marriage or property acquired by bequest, devise, or descent, or gift from a party other than the spouse;

(2) compensation for personal injuries;

(3) property acquired in exchange for or the increase in value of separate property, except to the extent that

such appreciation is due in part to the contributions or efforts of the other spouse;

(4) property described as separate property by written agreement of the parties pursuant to subdivision three of this part.

e. The term "custodial parent" shall mean a parent to whom custody of a child or children is granted by a valid agreement between the parties or by an order or decree of a court.

f. The term "child support" shall mean a sum paid pursuant to court order or decree by either or both parents or pursuant to a valid agreement between the parties for care, maintenance and education of any unemancipated child under the age of twenty-one years.

2. Matrimonial actions. Except as provided in subdivision five of this part, the provisions of this part shall be applicable to actions for an annulment or dissolution of a marriage, for a divorce, for a separation, for a declaration of the nullity of a void marriage, for a declaration of the validity or nullity of a foreign judgment of divorce, for a declaration of the validity or nullity of a marriage, and to proceedings to obtain maintenance or a distribution of marital property following a foreign judgment of divorce, commenced on and after the effective date of this part. Any application which seeks a modification of a judgment, order or decree made in an action commenced prior to the effective date of this part shall be heard and determined in accordance with the provisions of part A of this section.

3. Agreement of the parties. An agreement by the parties, made before or during the marriage, shall be valid and enforceable in a matrimonial action if such agreement is in writing, subscribed by the parties, and acknowledged or proven in the manner required to entitle a deed to be recorded. Notwithstanding any other provision of law, an acknowledgment of an agreement made before marriage may be executed before any person authorized to solemnize a marriage pursuant to subdivisions one, two and three of section eleven of this chapter. Such an agreement may include

(1) a contract to make a testamentary provision of any kind, or a waiver of any right to elect against the provisions of a will;

(2) provision for the ownership, division or distribution of separate and marital property;

(3) provision for the amount and duration of maintenance or other terms and conditions of the marriage relationship, subject to the provisions of section 5-311 of the general obligations law, and provided that such terms were fair and reasonable at the time of the making of the agreement and are not unconscionable at the time of entry of final judgment; and

(4) provision for the custody, care, education and maintenance of any child of the parties, subject to the provisions of section two hundred forty of this article. Nothing in this subdivision shall be deemed to affect the validity of any agreement made prior to the effective date of this subdivision.

4. Compulsory financial disclosure. a. In all matrimonial actions and proceedings in which alimony, maintenance or support is in issue, there shall be compulsory disclosure by both parties of their respective financial states. No showing of special circumstances shall be required before such disclosure is ordered. A sworn statement of net worth shall be provided upon receipt of a notice in writing demanding the same, within twenty days after the receipt thereof. In the event said statement is not demanded, it shall be filed with the clerk of the court by each party, within ten days after joinder of issue, in the court in which the proceeding is pending. As used in this part, the term "net worth" shall mean the amount by which total assets including income exceed total liabilities including fixed financial obligations. It shall include all income and assets of whatsoever kind and nature and wherever situated and shall include a list of all assets transferred in any manner during the preceding three years, or the length of the marriage, whichever is shorter; provided, however that transfers in the routine course of business which resulted in an exchange of assets of substantially equivalent value need not be specifically disclosed where such assets are otherwise identified in the statement of net worth. All such sworn statements of net worth shall be accompanied by a current and representative paycheck stub and the most recently filed state and federal income tax returns including a copy of the W-2(s) wage and tax statement(s) submitted with the returns. In addition, both parties shall provide information relating to any and all group health plans available to them for the provision of care or other medical benefits by insurance or otherwise for the benefit of the child or children for whom support is sought, including all such information as may be required to be included in a qualified medical child support order as defined in section six hundred nine of the employee retirement income security act of 1974 (29 USC 1169) including, but not limited to: (i) the name and last known mailing address of each party and of each dependent to be covered by the order; (ii) the identification and a description of each group health plan available for the benefit or coverage of the disclosing party and the child or children for whom support is sought; (iii) a detailed description of the type of coverage available from each group health plan for the potential benefit of each such dependent; (iv) the identification of the plan administrator for each such group health plan and the address of such administrator; (v) the identification numbers for each such group health plan; and (vi) such other information as may be required by the court. Noncompliance shall be punishable by any or all of the penalties prescribed in section thirty-one hundred twenty-six of the civil practice law and rules, in examination before or during trial.

b. As soon as practicable after a matrimonial action has been commenced, the court shall set the date or dates the parties shall use for the valuation of each asset. The valuation date or dates may be anytime from the date of commencement of the action to the date of trial.

5. Disposition of property in certain matrimonial actions.

a. Except where the parties have provided in an agreement for the disposition of their property pursuant to subdivision three of this part, the court, in an action wherein all or part of the relief granted is divorce, or the dissolution, annulment or declaration of the nullity of a marriage, and in proceedings to obtain a distribution of marital property following a foreign judgment of divorce, shall determine the respective rights of the parties in their separate or marital property, and shall provide for the disposition thereof in the final judgment.

b. Separate property shall remain such.

c. Marital property shall be distributed equitably between the parties, considering the circumstances of the case and of the respective parties.

d. In determining an equitable disposition of property under paragraph c, the court shall consider:

(1) the income and property of each party at the time of marriage, and at the time of the commencement of the action;

(2) the duration of the marriage and the age and health of both parties;

(3) the need of a custodial parent to occupy or own the marital residence and to use or own its household effects;

(4) the loss of inheritance and pension rights upon dissolution of the marriage as of the date of dissolution;

(5) any award of maintenance under subdivision six of this part;

(6) any equitable claim to, interest in, or direct or indirect contribution made to the acquisition of such marital property by the party not having title, including joint efforts or expenditures and contributions and services as a spouse, parent, wage earner and homemaker, and to the career or career potential of the other party;

(7) the liquid or non-liquid character of all marital property;

(8) the probable future financial circumstances of each party;

(9) the impossibility or difficulty of evaluating any component asset or any interest in a business, corporation or profession, and the economic desirability of retaining such asset or interest intact and free from any claim or interference by the other party;

(10) the tax consequences to each party;

(11) the wasteful dissipation of assets by either spouse;

(12) any transfer or encumbrance made in contemplation of a matrimonial action without fair consideration;

(13) any other factor which the court shall expressly find to be just and proper.

e. In any action in which the court shall determine that an equitable distribution is appropriate but would be impractical or burdensome or where the distribution of an interest in a business, corporation or profession would be contrary to law, the court in lieu of such equitable distribution shall make a distributive award in order to achieve equity between the parties. The court in its discretion, also may make a distributive award to supplement, facilitate or effectuate a distribution of marital property.

f. In addition to the disposition of property as set forth above, the court may make such order regarding the use and occupancy of the marital home and its household effects as provided in section two hundred thirty-four of this chapter, without regard to the form of ownership of such property.

g. In any decision made pursuant to this subdivision, the court shall set forth the factors it considered and the reasons for its decision and such may not be waived by either party or counsel.

h. In any decision made pursuant to this subdivision the court shall, where appropriate, consider the effect of a barrier to remarriage, as defined in subdivision six of section two hundred fifty-three of this article, on the factors enumerated in paragraph d of this subdivision.

6. Maintenance. a. Except where the parties have entered into an agreement pursuant to subdivision three of this part providing for maintenance, in any matrimonial action the court may order temporary maintenance or maintenance in such amount as justice requires, having regard for the standard of living of the parties established during the marriage, whether the party in whose favor maintenance is granted lacks sufficient property and income to provide for his or her reasonable needs and whether the other party has sufficient property or income to provide for the reasonable needs of the other and the circumstances of the case and of the respective parties. Such order shall be effective as of the date of the application therefor, and any retroactive amount of maintenance due shall be paid in one sum or periodic sums, as the court shall direct, taking into account any amount of temporary maintenance which has been paid. In determining the amount and duration of maintenance the court shall consider:

(1) the income and property of the respective parties including marital property distributed pursuant to subdivision five of this part;

(2) the duration of the marriage and the age and health of both parties;

(3) the present and future earning capacity of both parties;

(4) the ability of the party seeking maintenance to become self-supporting and, if applicable, the period of time and training necessary therefor;

(5) reduced or lost lifetime earning capacity of the party seeking maintenance as a result of having foregone or delayed education, training, employment, or career opportunities during the marriage;

(6) the presence of children of the marriage in the respective homes of the parties;

(7) the tax consequences to each party;

(8) contributions and services of the party seeking maintenance as a spouse, parent, wage earner and homemaker, and to the career or career potential of the other party;

(9) the wasteful dissipation of marital property by either spouse;

(10) any transfer or encumbrance made in contemplation of a matrimonial action without fair consideration; and

(11) any other factor which the court shall expressly find to be just and proper.

b. In any decision made pursuant to this subdivision, the court shall set forth the factors it considered and the reasons for its decision and such may not be waived by either party or counsel.

c. The court may award permanent maintenance, but an award of maintenance shall terminate upon the death of either party or upon the recipient's valid or invalid marriage, or upon modification pursuant to paragraph (b) of subdivision nine of section two hundred thirty-six of this part or section two hundred forty-eight of this chapter.

d. In any decision made pursuant to this subdivision the court shall, where appropriate, consider the effect of a barrier to remarriage, as defined in subdivision six of section two hundred fifty-three of this article, on the factors enumerated in paragraph a of this subdivision.

. . .

8. Special relief in matrimonial actions. a. In any matrimonial action the court may order a party to purchase, maintain or assign a policy of insurance providing benefits for health and hospital care and related services for either spouse or children of the marriage not to exceed such period of time as such party shall be obligated to provide maintenance, child support or make payments of a distributive award. The court may also order a party to purchase, maintain or assign a policy of accident insurance or insurance on the life of either spouse, and to designate in the case of life insurance, either spouse or children of the marriage, or in the case of accident insurance, the insured spouse as irrevocable beneficiaries during a period of time fixed by the court. The obligation to provide such insurance shall cease upon the termination of the spouse's duty to provide maintenance, child support or a distributive award. A copy of such order shall be served, by registered mail, on the home office of the insurer specifying the name and mailing address of the spouse or children, provided that failure to so serve the insurer shall not effect the validity of the order.

b. In any action where the court has ordered temporary maintenance, maintenance, distributive award or child support, the court may direct that a payment be made directly to the other spouse or a third person for real and personal property and services furnished to the other spouse, or for the rental or mortgage amortization or interest payments, insurances, taxes, repairs or other carrying charges on premises occupied by the other spouse, or for both payments to the other spouse and to such third persons. Such direction may be made notwithstanding that the parties continue to reside in the same abode and notwithstanding that the court refuses to grant the relief requested by the other spouse.

c. Any order or judgment made as in this section provided may combine any amount payable to either spouse under this section with any amount payable to such spouse as child support or under section two hundred forty of this chapter.

9. Enforcement and modification of orders and judgments in matrimonial actions.

a. All orders or judgments entered in matrimonial actions shall be enforceable pursuant to section fifty-two hundred forty-one or fifty-two hundred forty-two of the civil practice law and rules, or in any other manner provided by law. Orders or judgments for child support, alimony and maintenance shall also be enforceable pursuant to article fifty-two of the civil practice law and rules upon a debtor's default as such term is defined in paragraph seven of subdivision (a) of section fifty-two hundred forty-one of the civil practice law and rules. The establishment of a default shall be subject to the procedures established for the determination of a mistake of fact for income executions pursuant to subdivision (e) of section fifty-two hundred forty-one of the civil practice law and rules. For the purposes of enforcement of child support orders or combined spousal and child support orders pursuant to section five thousand two hundred forty-one of the civil practice law and rules, a "default" shall be deemed to include amounts arising from retroactive support. The court may, and if a party shall fail or refuse to pay maintenance, distributive award or child support the court shall, upon notice and an opportunity to the defaulting party to be heard, require the party to furnish a surety, or the sequestering and sale of assets for the purpose of enforcing any award for maintenance, distributive award or child support and for the payment of reasonable and necessary attorney's fees and disbursements.

b. Upon application by either party, the court may annul or modify any prior order or judgment as to maintenance or child support, upon a showing of the recipient's inability to be self-supporting or a substantial change in circumstance or termination of child support awarded pursuant to section two hundred forty of this article, including financial hardship. Where, after the effective date of this part, a separation agreement remains in force no modification of a prior order or judgment incorporating the terms of said agreement shall be made as to maintenance without a showing of extreme hardship on either party, in which event the judgment or order as modified shall supersede the terms of the prior agreement and judgment for such period of time and under such circumstances as the court determines. Provided, however, that no modification or annulment shall reduce or annul any arrears of child support which have accrued prior to the date of application to annul or modify any prior order or judgment as to child support. The court shall not reduce or annul any arrears of maintenance which have been reduced to final judgment pursuant to section two hundred forty-four of this chapter. No other arrears of maintenance which have accrued prior to the making of such application shall be subject to modification or annulment unless the defaulting party shows good cause for failure to make application for relief from the judgment or order directing such payment prior to the accrual of such arrears and the facts and circumstances constituting good cause are set forth in a written memorandum of decision. Such modification may increase maintenance or child support nunc pro tunc as of the date of application based on newly discovered evidence. Any retroactive amount of maintenance, or child support due shall, except as provided for herein, be paid in one sum or periodic sums, as the court directs, taking into account any temporary or partial payments which have been made. Any retroactive amount of child support due shall be support arrears/past due support. In addition, such retroactive child support shall be enforceable in any manner provided by law including, but not limited to, an execution for support enforcement pursuant to subdivision (b) of section fifty-two hundred forty-one of the civil practice law and rules. When a child receiving support is a public assistance recipient, or the order of support is being enforced or is to be enforced pursuant to section one hundred eleven-g of the social services law, the court shall establish the amount of retroactive child support and notify the parties that such amount shall be enforced by the support collection unit pursuant to an execution for support enforcement as provided for in subdivision (b) of section fifty-two hundred forty-one of the civil practice law and rules, or in such periodic payments as would have been authorized had such an execution been issued. In such case, the court shall not direct the schedule of repayment of retroactive support. The provisions of this subdivision shall not apply to a separation agreement made prior to the effective date of this part.

c. Notwithstanding any other provision of law, any written application or motion to the court for the modification or enforcement of a child support or combined maintenance and child support order for persons not in receipt of family assistance must contain either a request for child support enforcement services which would authorize the collection of the support obligation by the immediate issuance of an income execution for support enforcement as provided for by this chapter, completed in the manner specified in section one hundred eleven-g of the social services law; or a statement that the applicant has applied for or is in receipt of such services; or a statement that the applicant knows of the availability of such services, has declined them at this time and where support enforcement services pursuant to section one hundred eleven-g of the social services law have been declined that the applicant understands that an income deduction order may be issued pursuant to subdivision (c) of section five thousand two hundred forty-two of the civil practice law and rules without other child support enforcement services and that payment of an administrative fee may be required. The court shall provide a copy of any such request for child support enforcement services to the support collection unit of the appropriate social services district any time it directs payments to be made to such support collection unit. Additionally, the copy of such request shall be accompanied by the name, address and social security number of the parties; the date and place of the parties' marriage; the name and date of birth of the child or children; and the name and address of the employers and income payors of the party ordered to pay child support to the other party. Unless the party receiving child support or combined maintenance and child support has applied for or is receiving such services, the court shall not direct such payments to be made to the support collection unit, as established in section one hundred eleven-h of the social services law.

d. The court shall direct that a copy of any child support or combined child and spousal support order issued by the court on or after the first day of October, nineteen hundred ninety-eight, in any proceeding under this section be provided promptly to the state case registry established pursuant to subdivision four-a of section one hundred eleven-b of the social services law.

(L. 1962, ch. 313, §10; L. 1963, ch. 685, §6; L. 1968, ch. 699, §1; L. 1980, ch. 281, §9; L. 1980, ch. 645, §§2, 3; L. 1981, ch. 695, §§1, 2; L. 1984, ch. 790, §2; L. 1985, ch. 809, §6; L. 1986, ch. 884, §§1 to 4; L. 1986, ch. 892, §§2 to 4; L. 1987, ch. 815, §§6, 7; L. 1989, ch. 567, §§4, 5; L. 1990, ch. 818, §§4, 5; L. 1992, ch. 41, §§139, 140; L. 1992, ch. 415, §§1, 2; L. 1993, ch. 59, §9; L. 1993, ch. 354, §2; L. 1994, ch. 170, §§359, 360; L. 1997, ch. 398, §§4, 5, effective October 1, 1998; L. 1997, ch. 398, §141, effective January 1, 1998; L. 1997, ch. 436, pt. B, §§105, 106, effective August 20, 1997; L. 1998, ch. 214, §56, effective November 4, 1998; L. 1998, ch. 393, §2, effective July 22, 1998; L. 1999, ch. 275, §2, effective September 18, 1999; L. 2003, ch. 595, §1, effective September 22, 2003.)

1. Role of Fault in the Determination of Spousal Support

In the fault-based era, marital misconduct precluded awards of spousal support. As part of divorce law reform, the Uniform Marriage and Divorce Act, ratified by NCCUSL in 1970, provided that marital misconduct was irrelevant to awards of maintenance (UMDA §308). Similarly, when California became the first state to adopt no-fault divorce, the Family Law Act of 1969 provided that alimony was to be awarded without regard for fault. On the history of the California no-fault legislation, see Allen M. Parkman, Good Intentions Gone Awry: No-Fault Divorce and the American Family 72-75, 79-81 (2000).

In 2001, only seven states included considerations of fault in awards of alimony (even though these same states exclude such considerations in property distribution). See Introduction, Principles of the Law of Family Dissolution: Analysis and Recommendations, 8 Duke J. Gender L. & Pol'y 1, 70 (2001) (listing Louisiana, North Carolina, Pennsylvania, South Dakota, Tennessee, Virginia, and West Virginia). However, another 15 states continued to consider fault in both awards of alimony and property distribution. *Id.* at 72 (listing Alabama, Connecticut, Georgia, Maryland, Massachusetts, Michigan, Mississippi, Missouri, New Hampshire, North Dakota, Rhode Island, South Carolina, Texas, Vermont, and Wyoming). See also American Bar Association, Chart I: Alimony/Spousal Support Factors, 40 Fam. L.Q. 591 (2007) (listing factors in each state that courts use to determine spousal support).

In New York, before July 19, 1980, fault triggered a statutorily mandated preclusion of alimony. However, with the enactment of New York's Equitable Distribution Law, marital misconduct no longer automatically precludes an award of maintenance (DRL §236, Part B (5) and (6)). Although fault is no longer a specifically enumerated factor to consider in maintenance awards, a court may consider fault under the broad discretionary category of "any other factor which the court shall expressly find to be just and proper" (DRL §236, Part B(6)(a)(11)).

Most New York state lower courts exclude fault from consideration in alimony determinations. See Introduction, Principles, *supra*, at 69; Campbell v. Campbell, 720 N.Y.S.2d 628 (App. Div. 2001) (holding that the wife's refusal to move to Florida where her husband took another job did not constitute marital fault that was sufficiently serious to justify the diminution or elimination of maintenance). But cf. Bragar v. Bragar, 717 N.Y.S.2d 100 (App. Div. 2000) (holding that a wife's active role in contributing to deterioration of her husband's relationship with his son could be considered in the determination of a maintenance award). Courts will consider economic misconduct, in terms of dissipation of assets or financial disclosure. Wildenstein v. Wildenstein, 674 N.Y.S.2d 665 (App. Div. 1998); Wilbur v. Wilbur, 498 N.Y.S.2d 525 (App. Div. 1986). See also Romualdo P. Eclavea, Spousal Support, 19 Carmody-Wait 2d, *supra*, at §118:56.

Note that marital fault plays no role in awards of child support. According to New York statute, courts are not permitted to consider the misconduct of either party in determining awards of child support (DRL §236(B)). For the role of fault in property division, see Chapter VI, Section E *infra*.

2. Circumstances to Consider

The trial court has discretion to set the amount and duration of spousal support. However, the Equitable Distribution Law of 1980 (DRL §236, Part B(6)(b)) limits that discretion by enumerating 11 specific factors for the trial court to consider. In its order, the court must set forth those factors that it considered, as well as the reasons for its decision. Neither the parties nor counsel may waive this requirement.

On judicial compliance with the statutory mandate to set forth factors and reasons, compare Goldberg v. Goldberg, 531 N.Y.S.2d 318 (App. Div. 1988) (holding that the court failed to state adequately those factors that it considered and the reasons for its determination regarding maintenance where it referred only to husband's income and length of marriage, without indicating whether it considered wife's long-term full-time employment), with Kudela v. Kudela, 716 N.Y.S.2d 231 (App. Div. 2000) (holding that the trial court properly set forth factors that it considered in awarding maintenance to the wife, as well as reasons for its decision, despite its failure to analyze each of the statutory maintenance factors).

Many of the statutorily enumerated factors are economic: (1) the income and property of the respective parties (including distribution of marital property); (2) present and future earning capacity of the parties; (3) ability of party seeking maintenance to become self-supporting; (4) reduced or lost lifetime earning capacity of the party seeking maintenance as a result of foregone opportunities; (5) tax consequences to each party; and (6) contributions and services of the party seeking maintenance as a spouse, parent, wage earner, and homemaker, and to the career or career potential of the other party. Additionally, courts will not reduce maintenance where a party voluntarily decreased his or her income and where there is no loss of earning capacity. Lieberman v. Lieberman, 801 N.Y.S.2d 382 (App. Div. 2005).

Some factors refer to the parties' circumstances (i.e., the age and health of both parties), or features of the marriage: (1) the duration of the marriage and (2) the presence of children of the marriage. Additional factors incorporate vestiges of fault (economic-based): (1) the wasteful dissipation of marital property by either spouse; or (2) any transfer or encumbrance made in contemplation of a matrimonial action without fair consideration. A final factor gives the court broad discretion to consider any other factor that the court finds "just and proper."

Several of the aforementioned factors reflect the "equitable" nature of the award: the duration of the marriage, foregone opportunities, contributions to the other's career or career potential, wasteful dissipation of marital assets or their transfer without fair consideration in contemplation of the marital action, and the "catch-all" factor. Scheinkman, 11 N.Y. Prac., *supra*, at §15:3.

Domestic Relations Law

§236. Special controlling provisions

. . .

6. Maintenance. a. Except where the parties have entered into an agreement pursuant to subdivision three of this part providing for maintenance, in any matrimonial action the court may order temporary maintenance or maintenance in such amount as justice requires, having regard for the standard of living of the parties established during the marriage, whether the party in whose favor maintenance is granted lacks sufficient property and income to provide for his or her reasonable needs and whether the other party has sufficient property or income to provide for the reasonable needs of the other and the circumstances of the case and of the respective parties. Such order shall be effective as of the date of the application therefor, and any retroactive amount of maintenance due shall be paid in one sum or periodic sums, as the court shall direct, taking into account any amount of temporary maintenance which has been paid. In determining the amount and duration of maintenance the court shall consider:

(1) the income and property of the respective parties including marital property distributed pursuant to subdivision five of this part;

(2) the duration of the marriage and the age and health of both parties;

(3) the present and future earning capacity of both parties;

(4) the ability of the party seeking maintenance to become self-supporting and, if applicable, the period of time and training necessary therefor;

(5) reduced or lost lifetime earning capacity of the party seeking maintenance as a result of having foregone or delayed education, training, employment, or career opportunities during the marriage;

(6) the presence of children of the marriage in the respective homes of the parties;

(7) the tax consequences to each party;

(8) contributions and services of the party seeking maintenance as a spouse, parent, wage earner and homemaker, and to the career or career potential of the other party;

(9) the wasteful dissipation of marital property by either spouse;

(10) any transfer or encumbrance made in contemplation of a matrimonial action without fair consideration; and

(11) any other factor which the court shall expressly find to be just and proper.

b. In any decision made pursuant to this subdivision, the court shall set forth the factors it considered and the reasons for its decision and such may not be waived by either party or counsel.

. . .

(L. 1962, ch. 313, §10; L. 1963, ch. 685, §6; L. 1968, ch. 699, §1; L. 1980, ch. 281, §9; L. 1980, ch. 645, §§2, 3; L. 1981, ch. 695, §§1, 2; L. 1984, ch. 790, §2; L. 1985, ch. 809, §6; L. 1986, ch. 884, §§1 to 4; L. 1986, ch. 892, §§2 to 4; L. 1987, ch. 815, §§6, 7; L. 1989, ch. 567, §§4, 5; L. 1990, ch. 818, §§4, 5; L. 1992, ch. 41, §§139, 140; L. 1992, ch. 415, §§1, 2; L. 1993, ch. 59, §9; L. 1993, ch. 354, §2; L. 1994, ch. 170, §§359, 360; L. 1997, ch. 398, §§4, 5, effective October 1, 1998; L. 1997, ch. 398, §141, effective January 1, 1998; L. 1997, ch. 436, pt. B, §§105, 106, effective August 20, 1997; L. 1998, ch. 214, §56, effective November 4, 1998; L. 1998, ch. 393, §2, effective July 22, 1998; L. 1999, ch. 275, §2, effective September 18, 1999; L. 2003, ch. 595, §1, effective September 22, 2003.)

3. Effect of Violence on Spousal Support

A recent trend in the law's response to domestic violence has been recognition of the ramifications of such abuse beyond the imposition of criminal sanctions and restraining orders. Public concern about domestic violence has contributed to the passage of legislation in many states addressing the role of domestic violence in custody disputes and spousal support.

Several states now include domestic violence as a factor in the best interests standard or provide that evidence of domestic violence creates a presumption against awarding custody to the abusive parent. See Amy B. Levin, Comment, Child Witnesses of Domestic Violence: How Should Judges Apply the Best Interests of the Child Standard in Custody and Visitation Cases Involving Domestic Violence, 47 UCLA L. Rev. 813, 827 & nn.31-37 (2000) (state survey).

A finding of domestic violence also can affect orders of spousal support in some jurisdictions. For example, a history of domestic violence is one of the factors that California courts must consider in ordering spousal support (Cal. Fam. Code §4320(i) and (m)). The court also must consider a criminal conviction of the batterer in making a reduction or termination of spousal support. Statute establishes a rebuttable presumption against support to a spouse convicted of domestic violence within five years preceding a marriage dissolution action or at any time thereafter (Cal. Fam. Code §4325). William P. Hogoboom & Donald B. King, 1 Family Law §6:926.20 (Rutter Group, 1994). New York statute does not specifically mention domestic violence as a factor for courts to consider in awarding maintenance (DRL §236, Part B(6)). Theoretically, however, courts may consider such acts based on the catch-all provision "any other factor which the court shall expressly find to be just and proper" (DRL §236, Part B(11)).

E. MODIFICATION OR TERMINATION OF SUPPORT

The trial court has considerable discretion in the determination of whether to modify or terminate spousal support. Under the general rule, a court may modify spousal support upon a showing of a substantial change in circumstances. According to New York's Equitable Distribution Law, a court may modify or terminate ("annul") spousal support upon two grounds: (1) a showing of the obligee's inability to be self-supporting or (2) a substantial change in circumstances (which includes financial hardship) (DRL §236(B)(9)(b)). Thus, a showing of changed circumstances will justify a modification of support. Miller McMillen v. Miller, 790 N.Y.S.2d 556 (2005). Eclavea, 19 Carmody-Wait 2d, *supra*, at §118:324.

1. Generally

Domestic Relations Law

§236. Special controlling provisions

. . .

9. Enforcement and modification of orders and judgments in matrimonial actions.

a. All orders or judgments entered in matrimonial actions shall be enforceable pursuant to section fifty-two hundred forty-one or fifty-two hundred forty-two of the civil practice law and rules, or in any other manner provided by law. Orders or judgments for child support, alimony and maintenance shall also be enforceable pursuant to article fifty-two of the civil practice law and rules upon a debtor's default as such term is defined in paragraph seven of subdivision (a) of section fifty-two hundred forty-one of the civil practice law and rules. The establishment of a default shall be subject to the procedures established for the determination of a mistake of fact for income executions pursuant to subdivision (e) of section fifty-two hundred forty-one of the civil practice law and rules. For the purposes of enforcement of child support orders or combined spousal and child support orders pursuant to section five thousand two hundred forty-one of the civil practice law and rules, a "default" shall be deemed to include amounts arising from retroactive support. The court may, and if a party shall fail or refuse to pay maintenance, distributive award or child support the court shall, upon notice and an opportunity to the defaulting party to be heard, require the party to furnish a surety, or the sequestering and sale of assets for the purpose of enforcing any award for maintenance, distributive award or child support and for the payment of reasonable and necessary attorney's fees and disbursements.

b. Upon application by either party, the court may annul or modify any prior order or judgment as to maintenance or child support, upon a showing of the recipient's inability to be self-supporting or a substantial change in circumstance or termination of child support awarded pursuant to section two hundred forty of this article, including financial hardship. Where, after the effective date of this part, a separation agreement remains in force no modification of a prior order or judgment incorporating the terms of said agreement shall be made as to maintenance without a showing of extreme hardship on either party, in which event the judgment or order as modified shall supersede the terms of the prior agreement and judgment for such period of time and under such circumstances as the court determines. Provided, however, that no modification or annulment shall reduce or annul any arrears of child support which have accrued prior to the date of application to annul or modify any prior order or judgment as to child support. The court shall not reduce or annul any arrears of maintenance which have been reduced to final judgment pursuant to section two hundred forty-four of this chapter. No other arrears of maintenance which have accrued prior to the making of such application shall be subject to modification or annulment unless the defaulting party shows good cause for failure to make application for relief from the judgment or order directing such payment prior to the accrual of such arrears and the facts and circumstances constituting good cause are set forth in a written memorandum of decision. Such modification may increase maintenance or child support nunc pro tunc as of the date of application based on newly discovered evidence. Any retroactive amount of maintenance, or child support due shall, except as provided for herein, be paid in one sum or periodic sums, as the court directs, taking into account any temporary or partial payments which have been made. Any retroactive amount of child support due shall be support arrears/past due support. In addition, such retroactive child support shall be enforceable in any manner provided by law including, but not limited to, an execution for support enforcement pursuant to subdivision (b) of section fifty-two hundred forty-one of the civil practice law and rules. When a child receiving support is a public assistance recipient, or the order of support is being enforced or is to be enforced pursuant to section one hundred eleven-g of the social services law, the court shall establish the amount of retroactive child support and notify the parties that such amount shall be enforced by the support collection unit pursuant to an execution for support enforcement as provided for in subdivision (b) of section fifty-two hundred forty-one of the civil practice law and rules, or in such periodic payments as would have been authorized had such an execution been issued. In such case, the court shall not direct the schedule of repayment of retroactive support. The provisions of this subdivision shall not apply to a separation agreement made prior to the effective date of this part.

c. Notwithstanding any other provision of law, any written application or motion to the court for the modification or enforcement of a child support or combined maintenance and child support order for persons not in receipt of family assistance must contain either a request for child support enforcement services which would authorize the collection of the support obligation by the immediate issuance of an income execution for support enforcement as provided for by this chapter, completed in the manner specified in section one hundred eleven-g of the social services law; or a statement that the applicant has applied for or is in receipt of such services; or a statement that the applicant knows of the availability of such services, has declined them at this time and where support enforcement services pursuant to section one hundred eleven-g of the social services law have been declined that the applicant understands that an income deduction order may be issued pursuant to subdivision (c) of section five thousand two hundred forty-two of the civil practice law and rules without other child support enforcement services and that payment of an administrative fee may be required. The court shall provide a copy of any such request for child support enforcement services to the support collection unit of the appropriate social services district any time it directs payments to be made to such support collection unit. Additionally, the copy of such request shall be accompanied by the name, address and social security number of the parties; the date and place of the parties' marriage; the name and date of birth of the child or children; and the name and address of the employers and income payors of the party ordered to pay child support to the other party. Unless the party receiving child support or combined maintenance and child support has applied for or is receiving such services, the court shall not direct such payments to be made to the support collection unit, as established in section one hundred eleven-h of the social services law.

d. The court shall direct that a copy of any child support or combined child and spousal support order issued by the court on or after the first day of October, nineteen hundred ninety-eight, in any proceeding under this section be provided promptly to the state case registry established pursuant to subdivision four-a of section one hundred eleven-b of the social services law.

(L. 1962, ch. 313, §10; L. 1963, ch. 685, §6; L. 1968, ch. 699, §1; L. 1980, ch. 281, §9; L. 1980, ch. 645, §§2, 3; L. 1981, ch. 695, §§1, 2; L. 1984, ch. 790, §2; L. 1985, ch. 809, §6; L. 1986, ch. 884, §§1 to 4; L. 1986, ch. 892, §§2 to 4; L. 1987, ch. 815, §§6, 7; L. 1989, ch. 567, §§4, 5; L. 1990, ch. 818, §§4, 5; L. 1992, ch. 41, §§139, 140; L. 1992, ch. 415, §§1, 2; L. 1993, ch. 59, §9; L. 1993, ch. 354, §2; L. 1994, ch. 170, §§359, 360; L. 1997, ch. 398, §§4, 5, effective October 1, 1998; L. 1997, ch. 398, §141, effective January 1, 1998; L. 1997, ch. 436, pt. B, §§105, 106, effective August 20, 1997; L. 1998, ch. 214, §56, effective November 4, 1998; L. 1998, ch. 393, §2, effective July 22,

1998; L. 1999, ch. 275, §2, effective September 18, 1999; L. 2003, ch. 595, §1, effective September 22, 2003.)

2. Effect of Subsequent Cohabitation on Spousal Support

Some states permit modification, or even termination, of spousal support when the recipient cohabits with a member of the opposite sex (i.e., the subsequent cohabitation constitutes a sufficient change of circumstances to justify modification of spousal support). The policy rationale appears to be that the cohabitation results in a decrease in the obligee's need for support. Sometimes, the spouses provide for this circumstance by means of a separation agreement.

New York statute (DRL §248) provides that the court has discretion, upon the husband's application (with notice) and upon proof of the wife's cohabitation, to terminate spousal support (i.e., to "annul" a maintenance award). The statute, in gender-based rhetoric, defines cohabitation as "habitually living with another man and holding herself out as his wife, although not married to such man" (*id.*). Case law subsequently construed the statute to be gender neutral. Wood v. Wood, 428 N.Y.S.2d 136 (Fam. Ct., Queens Co., 1980).

Case law has interpreted this requirement to require the following: The obligor must establish that the obligee has (1) a relationship of some duration that constitutes more than an intermittent intimacy (i.e., relationships of six months to five years have satisfied this element); (2) a sexual relationship (more than a mere sharing of a residence); and (3) a relationship with a member of the opposite sex. Pattberg v. Pattberg, 497 N.Y.S.2d 251, 252-253 (Sup. Ct. 1985). But cf. Graev v. Graev, N.Y.L.J., Jan. 13, 2005, at 17 (holding that the presence or absence of sexual intimacy is not dispositive but is one of the factors that courts may consider). See also 19 Carmody-Wait 2d, *supra*, at 118:329.

A spouse also must prove that his or her former spouse is representing himself or herself as the spouse of the person with whom she or he is now living in order to establish that a "holding out" has occurred. *Pattberg*, 497 N.Y.S.2d at 253. See also Szemansco v. Szemansco, 783 N.Y.S.2d 681 (App. Div. 2004) (ruling that "holding out" was not established by wife's reference to her "significant other"); Bliss v. Bliss, 488 N.E.2d 90 (N.Y. 1985) (holding that a wife's 12-year cohabitation did not relieve her husband of obligation to pay spousal support because the wife did not represent herself as married).

By a separation agreement, the parties may agree to mitigate the strict requirements of holding out. Pesa v. Pesa, 646 N.Y.S.2d 558 (App. Div. 1996); Smith v. Smith, 650 N.Y.S.2d 842 (App. Div. 1996). But cf. Famoso v. Famoso, 700 N.Y.S.2d 62 (App. Div. 1999) (holding that information was insufficient to establish that a lover stayed overnight with the ex-wife on requisite number of occasions so as to allow the husband to terminate spousal support under a separation agreement permitting such if wife "resided with" unrelated adult male for 120 days annually).

Constitutional challenges to the termination-of-support-upon-cohabitation provision in New York have not been successful. See *Pattberg*, *supra* (holding that DRL §248 did not violate equal protection on the theory that it was an unconstitutional gender classification because the right to cohabit and hold oneself out as another's spouse was not a fundamental right that would trigger strict scrutiny; also the statute did not use suspect class classifications and served as a rational means to a legitimate state objective); *Wood*, *supra* (construing DRL §248 as gender neutral to preserve its constitutionality); Hall v. Hall, 372 N.Y.S.2d 344 (Fam. Ct., Schenectady Co. 1975), aff'd, 389 N.Y.S.2d 448 (App. Div. 1976) (rejecting constitutional challenge since court can distinguish between persons merely living together in temporary liaison and those living in a more permanent relationship as described in the statute).

Further, according to the statute, because the cohabitation must be with a member of the opposite sex, cohabitation in a lesbian relationship does not result in termination of spousal support. People ex rel. Kenney v. Kenney, 352 N.Y.S.2d 344 (Sup. Ct. 1974). But cf. In re Marriage of Weisbruch, 710 N.E.2d 439 (Ill. Ct. App. 1999) (interpreting gender-neutral statute to hold that ex-spouse's entitlement to maintenance may be terminated by same-sex relationship and that the settlement agreement did not imply that only remarriage could terminate maintenance). See generally Philip M. Longmeyer, Note, Look on the Bright Side: The Prospect of Modifying or Terminating Maintenance Obligations Upon the Homosexual Cohabitation of Your Former Spouse, 36 Brandeis J. Fam. L. 53 (1998).

For a critique of the practice of ending spousal support upon subsequent remarriage or cohabitation, see Cynthia Lee Starnes, One More Time: Alimony, Intuition, and the Remarriage-Termination Rule, 81 Ind. L.J. 971 (2006).

Domestic Relations Law

§248. Effect of cohabitation upon spousal support

Where an action for divorce or for annulment or for a declaration of the nullity of a void marriage is brought by a husband or wife, and a final judgment of divorce or a final judgment annulling the marriage or declaring its nullity has been rendered, the court, by order upon the application of the husband on notice, and on proof of the marriage of the wife after such final judgment, must modify such final judgment and any orders made with respect thereto by annulling the provisions of such final judgment or orders, or of both, directing payments of money for the support of the wife. The court in its discretion upon application of the husband on notice, upon proof that the wife is habitually living with another man and holding herself out as his wife, although not married to such man, may modify such final judgment and any orders made with respect thereto by annulling the provisions of such final judgment or orders or of both, directing payment of money for the support of such wife.

(L. 1962, ch. 313, §10; L. 1975, ch. 604, §1.)

3. Effect of Death or Remarriage

The death of either party or the remarriage of an obligee generally terminates the obligor's obligation to pay spousal support. New York statute has codified these principles in the definitional section of DRL §236(B)1)(a)) and in its provision on permanent maintenance, DRL §236(B)(1)(c)). A different statutory provision sets forth the procedure for terminating the obligee's support upon remarriage. Pursuant to DRL §248, upon the application of a husband (with notice) and upon proof of the wife's remarriage subsequent to a final judgment, the court must terminate spousal support ("must modify such final judgment and any orders made with respect thereto by annuling the provisions of such final judgment or orders, or of both, directing payments of money for the support of the wife"). *Id.* (Note that DRL §248 still retains gender-based language.)

Case law has held that the right to terminate spousal support based on the wife's remarriage is not personal to the husband but may be exercised by his estate. Kirkbridge v. Van Note, 9 N.E.2d 852 (N.Y. 1937). Also, overpayments in support, such as by an obligor-spouse in ignorance of the obligee's remarriage, are not subject to recoupment. Rodgers v. Rodgers, 470 N.Y.S.2d 401 (App. Div. 1983). See generally Scheinkman, Practice Commentaries (following DRL §248).

See also Gold v. Gold, 714 N.Y.S.2d 323 (App. Div. 2000) (holding that it was an error for the trial court to direct that maintenance continue after remarriage or that maintenance be increased if the equitable distribution award was not paid or discharged in bankruptcy, the latter being the proper subject of a request for modification).

Spousal support payments may continue after the obligee's remarriage if the parties so provide by agreement. Hunter v. Annexstein, 529 N.Y.S.2d 785 (App. Div. 1988). Similarly, courts have enforced such spousal agreements that specifically provide for the continuance of maintenance payments after the payor's death (i.e., payable from the estate of the payor-spouse). In re Estate of Donahue, 357 N.Y.S.2d 777 (Surr. Ct., N.Y. County, 1974); Hoeflich v. Chemical Bank, 539 N.Y.S.2d 916 (App. Div. 1989). To protect against the economic hardship that might result from the obligor's death, statute provides that the court may order a party to purchase a policy of insurance on the life of the payor-spouse and to designate the other spouse (or children) as irrevocable beneficiares (DRL §236(B)(8)(a)). Scheinkman, 11 N.Y. Prac., *supra*, at §15:18.

Domestic Relations Law

§236. Special controlling provisions
Part B
New Actions or Proceedings

Maintenance and distributive award. 1. Definitions. Whenever used in this part, the following terms shall have the respective meanings hereinafter set forth or indicated:

a. The term "maintenance" shall mean payments provided for in a valid agreement between the parties or awarded by the court in accordance with the provisions of subdivision six of this part, to be paid at fixed intervals for a definite or indefinite period of time, but an award of maintenance shall terminate upon the death of either party or upon the recipient's valid or invalid marriage, or upon modification pursuant to paragraph (b) of subdivision nine of section two hundred thirty-six of this part or section two hundred forty-eight of this chapter.

. . .

c. The court may award permanent maintenance, but an award of maintenance shall terminate upon the death of either party or upon the recipient's valid or invalid marriage, or upon modification pursuant to paragraph (b) of subdivision nine of section two hundred thirty-six of this part or section two hundred forty-eight of this chapter.

. . .

(L. 1962, ch. 313, §10; L. 1963, ch. 685, §6; L. 1968, ch. 699, §1; L. 1980, ch. 281, §9; L. 1980, ch. 645, §§2, 3; L. 1981, ch. 695, §§1, 2; L. 1984, ch. 790, §2; L. 1985, ch. 809, §6; L. 1986, ch. 884, §§1 to 4; L. 1986, ch. 892, §§2 to 4; L. 1987, ch. 815, §§6, 7; L. 1989, ch. 567, §§4, 5; L. 1990, ch. 818, §§4, 5; L. 1992, ch. 41, §§139, 140; L. 1992, ch. 415, §§1, 2; L. 1993, ch. 59, §9; L. 1993, ch. 354, §2; L. 1994, ch. 170, §§359, 360; L. 1997, ch. 398, §§4, 5; L. 1997, ch. 398, §141; L. 1997, ch. 436, pt. B, §§105, 106; L. 1998, ch. 214, §56; L. 1998, ch. 393, §2; L. 1999, ch. 275, §2; L. 2003, ch. 595, §1, effective September 22, 2003.)

§248. Effect of remarriage upon spousal support

Where an action for divorce or for annulment or for a declaration of the nullity of a void marriage is brought by a husband or wife, and a final judgment of divorce or a final judgment annulling the marriage or declaring its nullity has been rendered, the court, by order upon the application of the husband on notice, and on proof of the marriage of the wife after such final judgment, must modify such final judgment and any orders made with respect thereto by annulling the provisions of such final judgment or orders, or of both, directing payments of money for the support of the wife. The court in its discretion upon application of the husband on notice, upon proof that the wife is habitually living with another man and holding herself out as his wife, although not married to such man, may modify such final judgment and any orders made with respect thereto by annulling the provisions of such final judgment or orders or of both, directing payment of money for the support of such wife.
(L. 1962, ch. 313, §10; L. 1975, ch. 604, §1.)

4. Retention of Jurisdiction

Whereas courts retain jurisdiction over child custody and child support, there is no general rule of retention of jurisdiction over spousal support. Thus, in many jurisdictions, a court cannot make an initial award of spousal support after the dissolution judgment has become final.

However, under the New York statute governing modifications of judgments, orders, or decrees made in actions commenced prior to the effective date of the Equitable Distribution Law (July 19, 1980), the court has the power to amend a judgment of separation or divorce whenever rendered (or any judgment annulling or declaring the nullity of a void marriage rendered on or after September 1, 1940) in order to insert a provision modifying or terminating alimony (DRL §236(A)(1)).

The Equitable Distribution Law confers no specific authority on a court to amend a judgment that contains no provision for maintenance. However, case law has held that a post-Equitable Distribution Law default judgment of divorce against a wife that was silent on the issue of maintenance could be vacated upon a showing of possible overreaching by the husband. Benitez v. Benitez, 577 N.Y.S.2d 862 (App. Div. 1992). Eclavea, 19 Carmody-Wait 2d, *supra*, at §118:320.

F. ENFORCEMENT

Legislation authorizes the Family Court to find respondents liable for the support of their spouses only after a hearing (pursuant to FCA §433, *infra* Section C) or upon stipulation of the parties. Those persons who comply fully with the resulting order of support are discharged from any further financial obligation toward their spouses. The trial court has discretion to require that the obligor provide security for an obligation to pay spousal support.

New York's DRL §236(B)(9)(a) provides that orders or judgments in matrimonial actions shall be enforceable pursuant to Civil Practice Law and Rules (CPLR) §5241 (income execution for support enforcement) and §5242 (income deduction for support enforcement). In addition, the payment of spousal support (and/or child support) may be enforced by the following remedies: (1) security orders (DRL §243); (2) sequestration and receivership (DRL §243); (3) entry of money judgment and execution (DRL §244); (4) contempt proceedings (DRL §245); (5) the state income tax refund intercept program (Soc. Serv. Law §111-y (formerly §111-m)); (6) restraining notice (CPLR §5222); or (7) personal property execution (CPLR §5232); and, (8) real property execution (CPLR §5235). Scheinkman, 12 N.Y. Prac., *supra*, at §24:3.

Domestic Relations Law §246 provides a remedy in cases where contempt either is sought or imposed as an enforcement technique. If the obligor-spouse is unable to comply with the support obligation, the obligee-spouse may petition to hold the obligor in contempt. In a pending contempt proceeding, the obligor may assert inability to pay as a defense (DRL §246(1)).

Domestic Relations Law

§236. Special controlling provisions
Part B

. . .

9. Enforcement and modification of orders and judgments in matrimonial actions.

a. All orders or judgments entered in matrimonial actions shall be enforceable pursuant to section fifty-two hundred forty-one or fifty-two hundred forty-two of the civil practice law and rules, or in any other manner provided by law. Orders or judgments for child support, alimony and maintenance shall also be enforceable pursuant to article fifty-two of the civil practice law and rules upon a debtor's default as such term is defined in paragraph seven of subdivision (a) of section fifty-two hundred forty-one of the civil practice law and rules. The establishment of a default shall be subject to the procedures established for the determination of a mistake of fact for income executions pursuant to subdivision (e) of section fifty-two hundred forty-one of the civil practice law and rules. For the purposes of enforcement of child support orders or combined spousal and child support orders pursuant to section five thousand two hundred forty-one of the civil practice law and rules, a "default" shall be deemed to include amounts arising from retroactive support. The court may, and if a party shall fail or refuse to pay maintenance, distributive award or child support the court shall, upon notice and an opportunity to the defaulting party to be heard, require the party to furnish a surety, or the sequestering and sale of assets for the purpose of enforcing any award for maintenance, distributive award or child support and for the payment of reasonable and necessary attorney's fees and disbursements.

b. Upon application by either party, the court may annul or modify any prior order or judgment as to maintenance or child support, upon a showing of the recipient's inability to be self-supporting or a substantial change in circumstance or termination of child support awarded pursuant to section two hundred forty of this article, including financial hardship. Where, after the effective date of this part, a separation agreement remains in force no modification of a prior order or judgment incorporating the terms of said agreement shall be made as to maintenance without a showing of extreme hardship on either party, in which event the judgment or order as modified shall supersede the terms of the prior agreement and judgment for such period of time and under such circumstances as the court determines. Provided, however, that no modification or annulment shall reduce or annul any arrears of child support which have accrued prior to the date of application to annul or modify any prior order or judgment as to child support. The court shall not reduce or annul any arrears of maintenance which have been reduced to final judgment pursuant to section two hundred forty-four of this chapter. No other arrears of maintenance which have accrued prior to the making of such application shall be subject to modification or annulment unless the defaulting party shows good cause for failure to make application for relief from the judgment or order directing such payment prior to the accrual of such arrears and the facts and circumstances constituting good cause are set forth in a written memorandum of decision. Such modification may increase maintenance or child support nunc pro tunc as of the date of application based on newly discovered evidence. Any retroactive amount of maintenance, or child support due shall, except as provided for herein, be paid in one sum or periodic sums, as the court directs, taking into account any temporary or partial payments which have been made. Any retroactive amount of child support due shall be support arrears/past due support. In addition, such retroactive child support shall be enforceable in any manner provided by law including, but not limited to, an execution for support enforcement pursuant to subdivision (b) of section fifty-two hundred forty-one of the civil practice law and rules. When a child receiving support is a public assistance recipient, or the order of support is being enforced or is to be enforced pursuant to section one hundred eleven-g of the social services law, the court shall establish the amount of retroactive child support and notify the parties that such amount shall be enforced by the support collection unit pursuant to an execution for support enforcement as provided for in subdivision (b) of section fifty-two hundred forty-one of the civil practice law and rules, or in such periodic payments as would have been authorized had such an execution been issued. In such case, the court shall not direct the schedule of repayment of retroactive support. The provisions of this subdivision shall not apply to a separation agreement made prior to the effective date of this part.

c. Notwithstanding any other provision of law, any written application or motion to the court for the modification or enforcement of a child support or combined maintenance and child support order for persons not in receipt of family assistance must contain either a request for child support enforcement services which would authorize the collection of the support obligation by the immediate issuance of an income execution for support enforcement as provided for by this chapter, completed in the manner specified in section one hundred eleven-g of the social services law; or a statement that the applicant has applied for or is in receipt of such services; or a statement that the applicant knows of the availability of such services, has declined them at this time and where support enforcement services pursuant to section one hundred eleven-g of the social services law have been declined that the applicant understands that an income deduction order may be issued pursuant to subdivision (c) of section five thousand two hundred forty-two of the civil practice law and rules without other child support enforcement services and that payment of an administrative fee may be required. The court shall provide a copy of any such request for child support enforcement services to the support collection unit of the appropriate social services district any time it directs payments to be made to such support collection unit. Additionally, the copy of such request shall be accompanied by the name, address and social security number of the parties; the date and place of the parties' marriage; the name and date of birth of the child or children; and the name and address of the employers and income payors of the party ordered to pay child support to the other party. Unless the party receiving child support or combined maintenance and child support has applied for or is receiving such services, the court shall not direct such payments to be made to the support collection unit, as established in section one hundred eleven-h of the social services law.

d. The court shall direct that a copy of any child support or combined child and spousal support order issued by the court on or after the first day of October, nineteen hundred ninety-eight, in any proceeding under this section be provided promptly to the state case registry established pursuant to subdivision four-a of section one hundred eleven-b of the social services law.

(L. 1962, ch. 313, §10; L. 1963, ch. 685, §6; L. 1968, ch. 699, §1; L. 1980, ch. 281, §9; L. 1980, ch. 645, §§2, 3; L. 1981, ch. 695, §§1, 2; L. 1984, ch. 790, §2; L. 1985, ch. 809, §6; L. 1986, ch. 884, §§1 to 4; L. 1986, ch. 892, §§2 to 4; L. 1987, ch. 815, §§6, 7; L. 1989, ch. 567, §§4, 5; L. 1990, ch. 818, §§4, 5; L. 1992, ch. 41, §§139, 140; L. 1992, ch. 415, §§1, 2; L. 1993, ch. 59, §9; L. 1993, ch. 354, §2; L. 1994, ch. 170, §§359, 360; L. 1997, ch. 398, §§4, 5, effective October 1, 1998; L. 1997, ch. 398, §141, effective January 1, 1998; L. 1997, ch. 436, pt. B, §§105, 106, effective August 20, 1997; L. 1998, ch. 214, §56, effective November 4, 1998; L. 1998, ch. 393, §2, effective July 22, 1998; L. 1999, ch. 275, §2, effective September 18, 1999; L. 2003, ch. 595, §1, effective September 22, 2003.)

§243. Court may direct obligor-spouse to give reasonable security in action for divorce, separation or annulment

Where a judgment rendered or an order made in an action in this state for divorce, separation or annulment, or for a declaration of nullity of a void marriage, or a judgment rendered in another state for divorce upon any of the grounds provided in section one hundred seventy of this chapter, or for separation or separate support and maintenance for any of the causes specified in section two hundred, or for relief, however designated, granted upon grounds which in this state would be grounds for annulment of marriage or for a declaration of nullity of a void marriage, upon which an action has been brought in this state and judgment rendered therein, requires a spouse to provide for the education or maintenance of any of the children of a marriage, or for the support of his or her spouse, the court, in its discretion, also may direct the spouse from whom maintenance or support is sought to give reasonable security, in such a manner and within such a time as it thinks proper, for the payment, from time to time, of the sums of money required for that purpose. If he or she fails to give the security, or to make any payment required by the terms of such a judgment or order, whether or not security has been given therefor, or to pay any sum of money for the support and maintenance of the children or the support and maintenance of the spouse during the pendency of the action, or for counsel fees and expenses which he or she is required to pay by a judgment or order, the court may cause his or her personal property and the rents and profits of his or her real property to be sequestered, and may appoint a receiver thereof. The rents and profits and other property so sequestered may be applied, from time to time, under the direction of the court,

to the payment of any of the sums of money specified in this section, as justice requires; and if the same shall be insufficient to pay the sums of money required, the court, on application of the receiver, may direct the mortgage or sale of such real property by the receiver, under such terms and conditions as it may prescribe, sufficient to pay such sums.
(L. 1962, ch. 313, §10; amended L. 1963, ch. 685, §11; L. 1980, ch. 281, §14.)

§244. Enforcement by execution of money judgment in divorce, separation or annulment

Where a spouse in an action for divorce, separation or annulment, or declaration of nullity of a void marriage, or a person other than a spouse when an action for an annulment is maintained after the death of a spouse, defaults in paying any sum of money as required by the judgment or order directing the payment thereof, or as required by the terms of an agreement or stipulation incorporated by reference in a judgment, such direction shall be enforceable pursuant to section fifty-two hundred forty-one or fifty-two hundred forty-two of the civil practice law and rules. Upon application the court shall make an order directing the entry of judgment for the amount of arrears of child support together with costs and disbursements. The court shall make an order directing the entry of judgment for the amount of arrears of any other payments so directed, together with costs and disbursements, unless the defaulting party shows good cause for failure to make application for relief from the judgment or order directing such payment prior to the accrual of such arrears. The court shall not make an order reducing or cancelling arrears unless the facts and circumstances constituting good cause are set forth in a written memorandum of decision. The application for such order shall be upon such notice to the spouse or other person as the court may direct. Such judgment may be enforced by execution or in any other manner provided by law for the collection of money judgments. The relief herein provided for is in addition to any and every other remedy to which a spouse may be entitled under the law; provided that when a judgment for such arrears or any part thereof shall have been entered pursuant to this section, such judgment shall thereafter not be subject to modification under the discretionary power granted by this section; and after the entry of such judgment the judgment creditor shall not hereafter be entitled to collect by any form of remedy any greater portion of such arrears than that represented by the judgment so entered. Such judgment shall provide for the payment of interest on the amount of any arrears if the default was willful, in that the obligated spouse knowingly, consciously and voluntarily disregarded the obligation under a lawful court order. Such interest shall be computed from the date on which the payment was due, at the prevailing rate of interest on judgments as provided in the civil practice law and rules.
(L. 1962, ch. 313, §10; amended L. 1963, ch. 667, §1; L. 1963, ch. 685, §12; L. 1980, ch. 241, §2; L. 1980, ch. 281, §15; L. 1980, ch. 645, §5; L. 1981, ch. 695, §4; L. 1983, ch. 111, §1; L. 1985, ch. 809, §8; L. 1986, ch. 892, §8; L. 1988, ch. 327, §1.)

§244-a. Enforcement of arrears which accrue during pendency of an enforcement proceeding

In any proceeding for enforcement of payment of any sum of money as required by judgment or order the party seeking enforcement may amend the papers in support of the application for enforcement to include any additional arrears which have accrued since the commencement of such enforcement proceeding at the time of a hearing upon or submission of the matter, provided that written notice of the intention to so amend has been given eight days previously.
(L. 1980, ch. 646, §1; amended L. 1981, ch. 239, §1.)

§244-b. Child support proceedings and enforcement of arrears; suspension of driving privileges

(a) In any proceeding for the enforcement of a direction or agreement, incorporated in a judgment or order, to pay any sum of money as child support or combined child and spousal support, if the court is satisfied by competent proof that the respondent has accumulated support arrears equivalent to or greater than the amount of support due pursuant to such judgment or order for a period of four months, the court may order the department of motor vehicles to suspend the respondent's driving privileges, and if such order issues, the respondent may apply to the department of motor vehicles for a restricted use license pursuant to section five hundred thirty of the vehicle and traffic law. The court may at any time upon payment of arrears or partial payment of arrears by the respondent order the department of motor vehicles to terminate the suspension of respondent's driving privileges. For purposes of determining whether a support obligor has accumulated support arrears equivalent to or greater than the amount of support due for a period of four months, the amount of any retroactive support, other than periodic payments of retroactive support which are past due, shall not be included in the calculation of support arrears pursuant to this section.

(b) If the respondent, after receiving appropriate notice, fails to comply with a summons, subpoena or warrant relating to a paternity or child support proceeding, the court may order the department of motor vehicles to suspend the respondent's driving privileges. The court may subsequently order the department of motor vehicles to terminate the suspension of the respondent's driving privileges; however, the court shall order the termination of such suspension when the court is satisfied that the respondent has fully complied with all summonses, subpoenas and warrants relating to a paternity or child support proceeding.

(c) The provisions of subdivision (a) of this section shall not apply to:

(i) respondents who are receiving public assistance or supplemental security income; or

(ii) respondents whose income as defined by subparagraph five of paragraph (b) of subdivision one-b of section two hundred forty of this chapter falls below the self-support reserve as defined by subparagraph six of paragraph (b) of subdivision one-b of section two hundred forty of this chapter; or

(iii) respondents whose income as defined by subparagraph five of paragraph (b) of subdivision one-b of section two hundred forty of this chapter remaining after the payment of the current support obligation would fall below the self- support reserve as defined by subparagraph six of paragraph (b) of subdivision one-b of section two hundred forty of this chapter.

(d) The court's discretionary decision not to suspend driving privileges shall not have any res judicata effect or preclude any other agency with statutory authority to direct the department of motor vehicles to suspend driving privileges.

(L. 1995, ch. 81, §233; amended L. 1997, ch. 398, §§116, 117, effective January 1, 1998. As amended L.2002, ch. 624, §14, effective November 1, 2002.)

§245. Enforcement by contempt proceedings of judgment or order in action for divorce, separation or annulment

Where a spouse, in an action for divorce, separation, annulment or declaration of nullity of a void marriage, or for the enforcement in this state of a judgment for divorce, separation, annulment or declaration of nullity of a void marriage rendered in another state, makes default in paying any sum of money as required by the judgment or order directing the payment thereof, and it appears presumptively, to the satisfaction of the court, that payment cannot be enforced pursuant to section two hundred forty-three or two hundred forty-four of this chapter or section fifty-two hundred forty-one or fifty-two hundred forty-two of the civil practice law and rules, the aggrieved spouse may make application pursuant to the provisions of section seven hundred fifty-six of the judiciary law to punish the defaulting spouse for contempt, and where the judgment or order directs the payment to be made in installments, or at stated intervals, failure to make such single payment or installment may be punished as therein provided, and such punishment, either by fine or commitment, shall not be a bar to a subsequent proceeding to punish the defaulting spouse as for a contempt for failure to pay subsequent installments, but for such purpose such spouse may be proceeded against under the said order in the same manner and with the same effect as though such installment payment was directed to be paid by a separate and distinct order, and the provisions of the civil rights law are hereby superseded so far as they are in conflict therewith. Such application may also be made without any previous sequestration or direction to give security where the court is satisfied that they would be ineffectual. No demand of any kind upon the defaulting spouse shall be necessary in order that he or she be proceeded against and punished for failure to make any such payment or to pay any such installment; personal service upon the defaulting spouse of an uncertified copy of the judgment or order under which the default has occurred shall be sufficient.

(L. 1962, ch. 313, §10; amended L. 1975, ch. 497, §1; L. 1977, ch. 437, §11; L. 1980, ch. 281, §16; L. 1985, ch. 809, §9.)

§246. Persons financially unable to comply with spousal support orders

1. Any person who, by an order or judgment made or entered in an action for divorce, separation, annulment or declaration of the nullity of a void marriage or an action for the enforcement in this state of a judgment for divorce, separation or annulment or declaring the nullity of a void marriage rendered in another state, is directed to make payment of any sum or sums of money and against whom an order to punish for a contempt of court has been made pursuant to the provisions of section two hundred forty-five of this chapter or the judiciary law may, if financially unable to comply with the order or judgment to make such payment, upon such notice to such parties as the court may direct, make application to the court for an order relieving him from such payment and such contempt order. The court, upon the hearing of such application, if satisfied from the proofs and evidence offered and submitted that the applicant is financially unable to make such payment may, upon a showing of good cause, until further order of the court, modify the order or judgment to make such payment and relieve him from such contempt order. No such modification shall reduce or annul unpaid sums or installments accrued prior to the making of such application unless the defaulting party shows good cause for failure to make application for relief from the judgment or order directing such payment prior to the accrual of such arrears. Such modification may increase such support nunc pro tunc based on newly discovered evidence.

2. Whenever, upon application to the court by an interested party, it appears to the satisfaction of the court that any person, who has been relieved totally or partially from making any such payment pursuant to the provisions of this section, is no longer financially unable to comply with the order or judgment to make such payment, then the court may, upon a showing of good cause, modify or revoke its order relieving him totally or partially from making such payment.

3. Any person may assert his financial inability to comply with the directions contained in an order or judgment made or entered in an action for divorce, separation, annulment or declaration of the nullity of a void marriage or an action for the enforcement in this state of a judgment for divorce, separation or annulment or declaring the nullity of a void marriage rendered in another state, as a defense in a proceeding instituted against him under section two hundred forty-five or under the judiciary law to punish him for his failure to comply with such directions and, if the court, upon the hearing of such contempt proceeding, is satisfied from the proofs and evidence offered and submitted that the defendant is financially unable to comply with such order or judgment, it may, in its discretion, until further order of the court, make an order modifying such order or judgment and denying the application to punish the defendant for contempt. No such modification shall reduce or annul arrears accrued prior to the making of such application unless the defaulting party shows good cause for failure to make application for relief from the

judgment or order directing such payment prior to the accrual of such arrears. Such modification may increase such support nunc pro tunc as of the date of the application based on newly discovered evidence. Any retroactive amount of support due shall be paid in one sum or periodic sums, as the court shall direct, taking into account any amount of temporary support which has been paid.
(L. 1962, ch. 313, §10; amended L. 1963, ch. 685, §13; L. 1997, ch. 516, §25; L. 1980, ch. 645, §6; L. 1981, ch. 695, §5.)

Civil Practice Laws and Rules

§5222. Restraining notice

(a) Issuance; on whom served; form; service. A restraining notice may be issued by the clerk of the court or the attorney for the judgment creditor as officer of the court, or by the support collection unit designated by the appropriate social services district. It may be served upon any person, except the employer of a judgment debtor or obligor where the property sought to be restrained consists of wages or salary due or to become due to the judgment debtor or obligor. It shall be served personally in the same manner as a summons or by registered or certified mail, return receipt requested or if issued by the support collection unit, by regular mail, or by electronic means as set forth in subdivision (g) of this section. It shall specify all of the parties to the action, the date that the judgment or order was entered, the court in which it was entered, the amount of the judgment or order and the amount then due thereon, the names of all parties in whose favor and against whom the judgment or order was entered, it shall set forth subdivision (b) and shall state that disobedience is punishable as a contempt of court, and it shall contain an original signature or copy of the original signature of the clerk of the court or attorney or the name of the support collection unit which issued it. Service of a restraining notice upon a department or agency of the state or upon an institution under its direction shall be made by serving a copy upon the head of the department, or the person designated by him or her and upon the state department of audit and control at its office in Albany; a restraining notice served upon a state board, commission, body or agency which is not within any department of the state shall be made by serving the restraining notice upon the state department of audit and control at its office in Albany. Service at the office of a department of the state in Albany may be made by the sheriff of any county by registered or certified mail, return receipt requested, or if issued by the support collection unit, by regular mail.

(b) Effect of restraint; prohibition of transfer; duration. A judgment debtor or obligor served with a restraining notice is forbidden to make or suffer any sale, assignment, transfer or interference with any property in which he or she has an interest, except upon direction of the sheriff or pursuant to an order of the court, until the judgment or order is satisfied or vacated. A restraining notice served upon a person other than the judgment debtor or obligor is effective only if, at the time of service, he or she owes a debt to the judgment debtor or obligor or he or she is in the possession or custody of property in which he or she knows or has reason to believe the judgment debtor or obligor has an interest, or if the judgment creditor or support collection unit has stated in the notice that a specified debt is owed by the person served to the judgment debtor or obligor or that the judgment debtor or obligor has an interest in specified property in the possession or custody of the person served. All property in which the judgment debtor or obligor is known or believed to have an interest then in and thereafter coming into the possession or custody of such a person, including any specified in the notice, and all debts of such a person, including any specified in the notice, then due and thereafter coming due to the judgment debtor or obligor, shall be subject to the notice. Such a person is forbidden to make or suffer any sale, assignment or transfer of, or any interference with, any such property, or pay over or otherwise dispose of any such debt, to any person other than the sheriff or the support collection unit, except upon direction of the sheriff or pursuant to an order of the court, until the expiration of one year after the notice is served upon him or her, or until the judgment or order is satisfied or vacated, whichever event first occurs. A judgment creditor or support collection unit which has specified personal property or debt in a restraining notice shall be liable to the owner of the property or the person to whom the debt is owed, if other than the judgment debtor or obligor, for any damages sustained by reason of the restraint. If a garnishee served with a restraining notice withholds the payment of money belonging or owed to the judgment debtor or obligor in an amount equal to twice the amount due on the judgment or order, the restraining notice is not effective as to other property or money.

(c) Subsequent notice. Leave of court is required to serve more than one restraining notice upon the same person with respect to the same judgment or order.

(d) Notice to judgment debtor or obligor. If a notice in the form prescribed in subdivision (e) has not been given to the judgment debtor or obligor within a year before service of a restraining notice, a copy of the restraining notice together with the notice to judgment debtor or obligor shall be mailed by first class mail or personally delivered to each judgment debtor or obligor who is a natural person within four days of the service of the restraining notice. Such notice shall be mailed to the defendant at his or her residence address; or in the event such mailing is returned as undeliverable by the post office, or if the residence address of the defendant is unknown, then to the defendant in care of the place of employment of the defendant if known, in an envelope bearing the legend "personal and confidential" and not indicating on the outside thereof, by the return address or otherwise, that the communication is from an attorney or concerns a judgment or order; or if neither the residence address nor the place of employment of the defendant is known then to the defendant at any other known address.

(e) Content of notice. The notice required by subdivision (d) shall be in substantially the following form and may be included in the restraining notice:

NOTICE TO JUDGMENT DEBTOR OR OBLIGOR

Money or property belonging to you may have been taken or held in order to satisfy a judgment or order which has been entered against you. Read this carefully.

YOU MAY BE ABLE TO GET YOUR MONEY BACK

State and federal laws prevent certain money or property from being taken to satisfy judgments or orders. Such money or property is said to be "exempt". The following is a partial list of money which may be exempt:

1. Supplemental security income, (SSI);
2. Social security;
3. Public assistance (welfare);
4. Alimony or child support;
5. Unemployment benefits;
6. Disability benefits;
7. Workers' compensation benefits;
8. Public or private pensions; and
9. Veterans benefits.

If you think that any of your money that has been taken or held is exempt, you must act promptly because the money may be applied to the judgment or order. If you claim that any of your money that has been taken or held is exempt, you may contact the person sending this notice.

Also, YOU MAY CONSULT AN ATTORNEY, INCLUDING LEGAL AID IF YOU QUALIFY. The law (New York civil practice law and rules, article four and sections fifty-two hundred thirty-nine and fifty-two hundred forty) provides a procedure for determination of a claim to an exemption.

(f) For the purposes of this section "order" shall mean an order issued by a court of competent jurisdiction directing the payment of support, alimony or maintenance upon which a "default" as defined in paragraph seven of subdivision (a) of section fifty-two hundred forty-one of this article has been established subject to the procedures established for the determination of a "mistake of fact" for income executions pursuant to subdivision (e) of section fifty-two hundred forty-one of this article except that for the purposes of this section only a default shall not be founded upon retroactive child support obligations as defined in paragraph (a) of subdivision one of section four hundred forty of the family court act and subdivision one of section two hundred forty and paragraph b of subdivision nine of section two hundred thirty-six of the domestic relations law.

(g) Restraining notice in the form of magnetic tape or other electronic means. Where such person consents thereto in writing, a restraining notice in the form of magnetic tape or other electronic means, as defined in subdivision (f) of rule twenty-one hundred three of this chapter, may be served upon a person other than the judgment debtor or obligor. A restraining notice in such form shall contain all of the information required to be specified in a restraining notice under subdivision (a), except for the original signature or copy of the original signature of the clerk or attorney who issued the restraining notice. The provisions of this subdivision notwithstanding, the notice required by subdivisions (d) and (e) shall be given to the judgment debtor or obligor in the written form set forth therein.

(L. 1962, ch. 308; amended L. 1963, ch. 544, §1; L. 1968, ch. 743, §2; L. 1969, ch. 1137, §1; L. 1982, ch. 882, §1; L. 1991, ch. 314, §1; L. 1993, ch. 59, §13; L. 1994, ch. 35, §1. As amended L. 2000, ch. 409, §1, effective September 29, 2000.)

§5232. Levy upon personal property

(a) Levy by service of execution. The sheriff or support collection unit designated by the appropriate social services district shall levy upon any interest of the judgment debtor or obligor in personal property not capable of delivery, or upon any debt owed to the judgment debtor or obligor, by serving a copy of the execution upon the garnishee, in the same manner as a summons, except that such service shall not be made by delivery to a person authorized to receive service of summons solely by a designation filed pursuant to a provision of law other than rule 318. In the event the garnishee is the state of New York, such levy shall be made in the same manner as an income execution pursuant to section 5231 of this article. A levy by service of the execution is effective only if, at the time of service, the person served owes a debt to the judgment debtor or obligor or he or she is in the possession or custody of property not capable of delivery in which he or she knows or has reason to believe the judgment debtor or obligor has an interest, or if the judgment creditor or support collection unit has stated in a notice which shall be served with the execution that a specified debt is owed by the person served to the judgment debtor or obligor or that the judgment debtor or obligor has an interest in specified property not capable of delivery in the possession or custody of the person served. All property not capable of delivery in which the judgment debtor or obligor is known or believed to have an interest then in or thereafter coming into the possession or custody of such a person, including any specified in the notice, and all debts of such a person, including any specified in the notice, then due or thereafter coming due to the judgment debtor or obligor, shall be subject to the levy. The person served with the execution shall forthwith transfer all such property, and pay all such debts upon maturity, to the sheriff or to the support collection unit and execute any document necessary to effect the transfer or payment. After such transfer or payment, property coming into the possession or custody of the garnishee, or debt incurred by him, or her shall not be subject to the levy. Until such transfer or payment is made, or until the expiration of ninety days after the service of the execution upon him or her, or of such further time as is provided by any order of the court served upon him or her, whichever event first occurs, the garnishee is forbidden to make or suffer any sale, assignment or transfer of, or any interference with, any such property, or pay over or otherwise dispose of any such debt, to any person other than the sheriff or the support collection unit, except upon direction of the sheriff or the support collection unit or pursuant to an order of the court. At the expiration of ninety days after a levy is made by service of the execution, or of such further time as the court, upon motion of the judgment creditor or support collection unit has provided, the levy shall be void except as to property or debts which have been transferred or paid to the sheriff or to the support collection unit or as to which a proceeding under sections 5225 or 5227 has been brought. A judgment creditor who, or support collection unit which, has specified personal property or debt to be levied upon in a notice served with an execution shall be liable to the owner of the property or the person to whom the debt is owed, if other than the judgment debtor or obligor, for any damages sustained by reason of the levy.

(b) Levy by seizure. The sheriff or support collection unit of the appropriate social services district shall levy upon any interest of the judgment debtor in personal property capable of delivery by taking the property into custody without interfering with the lawful possession of pledgees and lessees. The sheriff or support collection unit shall forthwith serve a copy of the execution in the manner prescribed by subdivision (a) upon the person from whose possession or custody the property was taken.

(c) Notice to judgment debtor or obligor. Where an execution does not state that a notice in the form presented by subdivision (e) of section fifty-two hundred twenty-two of this chapter has been duly served upon the judgment debtor or obligor within a year, the sheriff or support collection unit shall, not later than four days after service of the execution upon any garnishee, mail by first class mail, or personally deliver, to each judgment debtor or obligor who is a natural person, a copy of the execution together with such notice. The sheriff or support collection unit shall specify on the notice to judgment debtor or obligor the name and address of the judgment creditor or the judgment creditor's attorney or the support collection unit. The notice shall be mailed to the judgment debtor or obligor at his or her residence address; and in the event such mailing is returned as undeliverable by the post office, or if the residence address of the judgment debtor or obligor is unknown, then to the judgment debtor or obligor in care of the place of employment of the judgment debtor or obligor if known, in an envelope bearing the legend "personal and confidential" and not indicating on the outside thereof, by the return address or otherwise, that the communication is from a sheriff or support collection unit or concerns a debt; or if neither the residence nor the place of employment of the judgment debtor or obligor is known, then to the judgment debtor or obligor at any other known address.

(d) For the purposes of this section "obligor" shall mean an individual other than a judgment debtor obligated to pay support, alimony or maintenance pursuant to an order of a court of competent jurisdiction who has been found to be in "default" of such order as such term is defined in paragraph seven of subdivision (a) of section fifty-two hundred forty-one of this article and the establishment of such default has been subject to the procedures established for the determination of a "mistake of fact" for income executions pursuant to subdivision (e) of section fifty-two hundred forty-one of this article, except that for the purposes of this section only, a default shall not be founded upon retroactive child support obligations as defined in paragraph (c) of subdivision one of section four hundred forty and subdivision one of section two hundred forty, and paragraph b of subdivision nine of section two hundred thirty-six of the domestic relations law.

(L. 1962, ch. 308, §5231; renumbered 5232, L. 1962, ch. 315, §5; amended L. 1963, ch. 532, §34; L. 1968, ch. 743, §1; L. 1982, ch. 882, §2; L. 1993, ch. 59, §15.)

§5235. Execution upon real property

After the expiration of ten years after the filing of the judgment-roll, the sheriff shall levy upon any interest of the judgment debtor in real property, pursuant to an execution other than one issued upon a judgment for any part of a mortgage debt upon the property, by filing with the clerk of the county in which the property is located a notice of levy describing the judgment, the execution and the property. The clerk shall record and index the notice against the name of the judgment debtor, or against the property, in the same books, and in the same manner as a notice of the pendency of an action.

(L. 1962, ch. 308, §5234; renumbered 5235, L. 1962, ch. 315, §5; amended L. 1963, ch. 532, §35.)

§5241. Income execution for enforcement of support

(a) Definitions. As used in this section and in section fifty-two hundred forty-two of this chapter, the following terms shall have the following meanings:

1. "Order of support" means any temporary or final order, judgment, agreement or stipulation incorporated by reference in such judgment or decree in a matrimonial action or family court proceeding, or any foreign support order, judgment or decree, registered pursuant to article five-B of the family court act which directs the payment of alimony, maintenance, support or child support.

2. "Debtor" means any person directed to make payments by an order of support.

3. "Creditor" means any person entitled to enforce an order of support, including a support collection unit.

4. "Employer" means any employer, future employer, former employer, union or employees' organization.

5. "Income payor" includes:

(i) the auditor, comptroller, trustee or disbursing officer of any pension fund, benefit program, policy of insurance or annuity;

(ii) the state of New York or any political subdivision thereof, or the United States; and

(iii) any person, corporation, trustee, unincorporated business or association, partnership, financial institution, bank, savings and loan association, credit union, stock purchase plan, stock option plan, profit sharing plan, stock broker, commodities broker, bond broker, real estate broker, insurance company, entity or institution.

6. "Income" includes any earned, unearned, taxable or non-taxable income, benefits, or periodic or lump sum payment due to an individual, regardless of source, including wages, salaries, commissions, bonuses, workers' compensation, disability benefits, unemployment insurance benefits , payments pursuant to a public or private pension or retirement program, federal social security benefits as defined in 42 U.S.C. section 662(f) (2), [42 USCA §662(f)(2)] and interest, but excluding public assistance benefits paid pursuant to the social services law and federal supplemental security income. [42 USCA §1381 et seq.]

7. "Default" means the failure of a debtor to remit to a creditor three payments on the date due in the full amount directed by the order of support, or the accumulation of arrears equal to or greater than the amount directed to be paid for one month, whichever first occurs.

8. "Mistake of fact" means an error in the amount of current support or arrears or in the identity of the debtor or that the order of support does not exist or has been vacated.

9. "Support collection unit" means any support collection unit established by a social services district pursuant to the provisions of section one hundred eleven-h of the social services law.

10. "Date of withholding" means the date on which the income would otherwise have been paid or made available to the debtor were it not withheld by the employer or income payor.

11. "Health insurance benefits" means any medical, dental, optical and prescription drugs and health care services or other health care benefits which may be provided for dependents through an employer or organization, including such employers or organizations which are self-insured.

12. "Business day" means a day on which state offices are open for regular business.

(b) Issuance.

(1) When a debtor is in default, an execution for support enforcement may be issued by the support collection unit, or by the sheriff, the clerk of court or the attorney for the creditor as an officer of the court. Where a debtor is receiving or will receive income, an execution for deductions therefrom in amounts not to exceed the limits set forth in subdivision (g) of this section may be served upon an employer or income payor after notice to the debtor. The amount of the deductions to be withheld shall be sufficient to ensure compliance with the direction in the order of support, and shall include an additional amount to be applied to the reduction of arrears. The creditor may amend the execution before or after service upon the employer or income payor to reflect additional arrears or payments made by the debtor after notice pursuant to subdivision (d) of this section, or to conform the execution to the facts found upon a determination made pursuant to subdivision (e) of this section.

(2)(i) Where the court orders the debtor to provide health insurance benefits for specified dependents, an execution for medical support enforcement may, except as provided for herein, be issued by the support collection unit, or by the sheriff, the clerk of court or the attorney for the creditor as an officer of the court; provided, however, that when the court issues an order of child support or combined child and spousal support on behalf of persons other than those in receipt of public assistance or in receipt of services pursuant to section one hundred eleven-g of the social services law, such medical execution shall be in the form of a separate qualified medical child support order as provided by subdivision (f) of section four hundred sixteen of the family court act and paragraph (f) of subdivision one of section two hundred forty of the domestic relations law. Such execution for medical support enforcement may require the debtor's employer, organization or group health plan administrator to purchase on behalf of the debtor and the debtor's dependents such available health insurance benefits. Such execution shall direct the employer, organization or group health plan administrator to provide to the dependents for whom such benefits are required to be provided or such dependents' custodial parent or legal guardian or social services district on behalf of persons applying for or in receipt of public assistance any identification cards and benefit claim forms and to withhold from the debtor's income the employee's share of the cost of such health insurance benefits, and to provide written confirmation of such enrollment indicating the date such benefits were or become available or that such benefits are not available and the reasons therefor to the issuer of the execution. An execution for medical support enforcement shall not require a debtor's employer, organization or group health plan administrator to purchase or otherwise acquire health insurance or health insurance benefits that would not otherwise be available to the debtor by reason of his or her employment or membership. Nothing herein shall be deemed to obligate or otherwise hold any employer, organization or group health plan administrator responsible for an option exercised by the debtor in selecting medical insurance coverage by an employee or member.

(ii) Where the child support order requires the debtor to provide health insurance benefits for specified dependents, and where the debtor provides such coverage and then changes employment, and the new employer provides health care coverage, an amended execution for medical support enforcement may be issued by the support collection unit, or by the sheriff, the clerk of the court or the attorney for the creditor as an officer of the court without any return to court. The issuance of the amended execution shall transfer notice of the requirements of the order and the execution to the new employer, organization or group health plan administrator, and shall have the same effect as the original execution for medical support issued pursuant to this section unless the debtor contests the execution.

(3) Any inconsistent provisions of this title or other law notwithstanding, in any case in which a parent is required by a court order to provide health coverage for a child and the parent is eligible for health insurance benefits as defined in this section through an employer or organization, including those which are self-insured, doing business in the state, such employer or organization must, in addition to implementing the provisions of a medical support execution:

(i) permit such parent to immediately enroll under such health insurance benefit coverage any such dependent who is otherwise eligible for such coverage without regard to any seasonal enrollment restrictions;

(ii) if such a parent is enrolled but fails to make application to obtain coverage of such dependent child, immediately enroll such dependent child under such health benefit coverage upon application by such child's other parent or by the department or social services district furnishing medical assistance to such child, and

(iii) not disenroll, or eliminate coverage of, such a child unless:

(A) the employer or organization is provided with satisfactory written evidence that such court order is no longer in effect, or the child is or will be enrolled in comparable health coverage through another insurer which will take effect not later than the effective date of such disenrollment, or

(B) such employer or organization has eliminated health insurance coverage for all similarly situated employees.

[*(C) Deleted.*]

(c) Execution for support enforcement; form.

(1) The income execution shall contain the caption of the order of support, and specify the date that the order of support was entered, the court in which it was entered, the amount of the periodic payments directed, the amount of arrears, the nature of the default and the names of the debtor and creditor. In addition, the income execution shall include:

(i) the name and address of the employer or income payor from whom the debtor is receiving or will receive income;

(ii) the amount of the deductions to be made therefrom on account of current support, and the amount to be applied to the reduction of arrears;

(iii) a notice that deductions will apply to current and subsequent income;

(iv) a notice that the income execution will be served upon any current or subsequent employer or income payor unless a mistake of fact is shown within fifteen days, a notice of the manner in which a mistake of fact may be asserted, and a notice that, if the debtor claims a mistake of fact, a determination will be made within forty-five days after notice to the debtor as provided in subdivision (d) of this section, and that the debtor will receive written notice whether the income execution will be served and of the time that deductions will begin;

(v) a notice that the employer or income payor must commence deductions no later than the first pay period that occurs after fourteen days following the service of the income execution and that payment must be remitted within seven business days of the date that the debtor paid;

(vi) a notice that the income execution is binding until further notice;

(vii) a notice of the substance of the provisions of section fifty-two hundred fifty-two of this chapter and that a violation thereof is punishable as a contempt of court by fine or imprisonment or both;

(viii) a notice of the limitations upon deductions from wages set forth in subdivision (g) of this section;

(ix) a notice that an employer must notify the issuer promptly when the debtor terminates employment and provide the debtor's last address and the name and address of the new employer, if known;

(x) a notice that when an employer receives an income withholding instrument issued by another state, the employer shall apply the income withholding law of the state of the debtor's principal place of employment in determining:

(A) the employer's fee for processing income withholding;

(B) the maximum amount permitted to be withheld from the debtor's income;

(C) the time periods within which the employer must implement the income withholding and forward the child support payment;

(D) the priorities for withholding and allocating income withheld for multiple child support creditors; and

(E) any withholding terms or conditions not specified in the withholding instrument; and

(xi) a notice that an employer who complies with an income withholding notice that is regular on its face shall not be subject to civil liability to any individual or agency for conduct in compliance with the notice.

(2) The medical support execution shall contain the caption of the order of support and specify the date that the order of support was entered and the court in which it was entered. Such execution shall include the name and address of the employer or organization and shall include:

(i) a notice that the debtor has been ordered by the court to enroll the dependents in any available health insurance benefits and to maintain such coverage for such dependents as long as such benefits remain available;

(ii) a notice inquiring of the employer or organization as to whether such health insurance benefits are presently in effect for the eligible dependents named in the execution, the date such benefits were or become available, or that such benefits are not available and the reasons therefor and directing that the response to such inquiry immediately be forwarded to the issuer of such execution;

(iii) a statement directing the employer or organization to purchase on behalf of the debtor any available health insurance benefits to be made available to the debtor's dependents as directed by the execution, including the enrollment of such eligible dependents in such benefit plans and the provision to the dependents or such dependents' custodial parent or legal guardian or social services district on behalf of persons applying for or in receipt of public assistance of any identification cards and benefit claim forms;

(iv) a statement directing the employer or organization to deduct from the debtor's income such amount which is the debtor's share of the premium, if any, for such health insurance benefits for such dependents who are otherwise eligible for such coverage without regard to any seasonal enrollment restrictions;

(v) a notice that the debtor's employer must notify the issuer promptly at any time the debtor terminates or changes such health insurance benefits;

(vi) a statement that the debtor's employer or organization shall not be required to purchase or otherwise acquire health insurance or health insurance benefits for such dependents that would not otherwise be available to the debtor by reason of his employment or membership;

(vii) a statement that failure to enroll the eligible dependents in such health insurance plan or benefits or failure to deduct from the debtor's income the debtor's share of the premium for such plan or benefits shall make such employer or organization jointly and severally liable for all medical expenses incurred on the behalf of the debtor's dependents named in the execution while such dependents are not so enrolled to the extent of the health insurance benefits that should have been provided under the execution;

(viii) the name and last known mailing address of the debtor and the name and mailing address of the dependents; provided however, that the name and mailing address of a social services official may be substituted on behalf of such dependents;

(ix) a reasonable description of the type of coverage to be provided to each dependent, or the manner in which such type of coverage is to be determined;

(x) the period to which such execution applies; and

(xi) a statement that the debtor's employer or organization shall not be required to provide any type or form of benefit or option not otherwise provided under the group health plan except to the extent necessary to meet the requirements of a law relating to medical child support described in section one thousand three hundred ninety-six-g-1 of title forty-two of the United States Code.

(d) Notice to debtor. The creditor shall serve a copy of the execution upon the debtor by regular mail to the debtor at his last known residence or such other place where he is likely to receive notice, or in the same manner as a summons may be served.

(e) Determination of mistake of fact. Where the execution has been issued by the support collection unit, the debtor may assert a mistake of fact and shall have an opportunity to make a submission in support of the objection within fifteen days from service of a copy thereof. Thereafter, the agency shall determine the merits of the objection, and shall notify the debtor of its determination within forty-five days after notice to the debtor as provided in subdivision (d) of this section. If the objection is disallowed, the debtor shall be notified that the income execution will be served on the employer or income payor, and of the time that deductions will begin. Where the income execution has been issued by an attorney as officer of the court, or by the sheriff, or by the clerk of the court, the debtor may assert a mistake of fact within fifteen days from service of a copy thereof by application to the supreme court or to the family court having jurisdiction in accordance with section four hundred sixty-one of the family court act. If application is made to the family court, such application shall be by petition on notice to the creditor and it shall be heard and determined in accordance with the provisions of section four hundred thirty-nine of the family court act, and a determination thereof shall be made, and the debtor notified thereof within forty-five days of the application. If application is made to the supreme court such application shall be by petition on notice to the creditor and, it shall be heard and determined in accordance with the provisions of article four of the civil practice law and rules, and a determination thereof shall be made, and the debtor notified thereof within forty-five days of the application.

(f) Levy. If a debtor fails to show mistake of fact within fifteen days, or after a determination pursuant to subdivision (e) of this section has been made, or if the creditor is unable to serve the execution upon the debtor, the creditor may levy upon the income that the debtor is receiving or will receive by serving the execution upon the employer or income payor personally in the same manner as a summons or by regular mail, except that such service shall not be made by delivery to a person authorized to receive service of summons solely by a designation filed pursuant to a provision of law other than rule 318.

(g) Deduction from income.

(1) An employer or income payor served with an income execution shall commence deductions from income due or thereafter due to the debtor no later than the first pay period that occurs fourteen days after service of the execution, and shall remit payments to the creditor within seven business days of the date that the debtor is paid. Each payment remitted by an employer or income payor shall include, in addition to the identity and social security number of the debtor, the date and amount of each withholding of the debtor's income included in the payment. If the money due to the debtor consists of salary or wages and his or her employment is terminated by resignation or dismissal at any time after service of the execution, the levy shall thereafter be ineffective, and the execution shall be returned, unless the debtor is reinstated or re-employed within ninety days after such termination. An employer must notify the issuer promptly when the debtor terminates employment and provide the debtor's last address and name and address of the new employer, if known. Where the income is compensation paid or payable to the debtor for personal services, the amount of the deductions to be withheld shall not exceed the following:

(i) Where a debtor is currently supporting a spouse or dependent child other than the creditor, the amount of the deductions to be withheld shall not exceed fifty percent of the earnings of the debtor remaining after the deduction therefrom of any amounts required by law to be withheld ("disposable earnings"), except that if any part of such deduction is to be applied to the reduction of arrears which shall have accrued more than twelve weeks prior to the beginning of the week for which such earnings are payable, the amount of such deduction shall not exceed fifty-five percent of disposable earnings.

(ii) Where a debtor is not currently supporting a spouse or dependent child other than the creditor, the amount of the deductions to be withheld shall not exceed sixty percent of the earnings of the debtor remaining after the deduction therefrom of any amounts required by law to be withheld ("disposable earnings"), except that if any part of such deduction is to be applied to the reduction of arrears which shall have accrued more than twelve weeks prior to the beginning of the week for which such earnings are payable, the amount of such deduction shall not exceed sixty-five percent of disposable earnings.

(2) (A) An employer or income payor served with an income execution in accordance with paragraph one of this subdivision shall be liable to the creditor for failure to deduct the amounts specified. The creditor may commence a proceeding against the employer or income payor for accrued deductions, together with interest and reasonable attorney's fees.

(B) An employer or income payor served with an income execution in accordance with paragraph one of this subdivision shall be liable to the creditor and the debtor for failure to remit any amounts which have been deducted as directed by the income execution. Either party may commence a proceeding against the employer or income payor for accrued deductions, together with interest and reasonable attorney's fees.

(C) The actions of the employer or income payor in deducting or failing to deduct amounts specified by an income execution shall not relieve the debtor of the underlying obligation of support.

(D) In addition to the remedies herein provided and as may be otherwise authorized by law, upon a finding by the family court that the employer or income payor failed to deduct or remit deductions as directed in the income execution, the court shall issue to the employer or income payor an order directing compliance and may direct the payment of a civil penalty not to exceed five hundred dollars for the first instance and one thousand dollars per instance for the second and subsequent instances of employer or income payor noncompliance. The penalty shall be paid to the creditor and may be enforced in the same manner as a civil judgment or in any other manner permitted by law.

(3) If an employer, organization or group health plan administrator is served with an execution for medical support enforcement, such employer, organization or group health plan administrator shall: (i) purchase on behalf of the debtor any health insurance benefits which may be made available to the debtor's dependents as ordered by the execution, including the immediate enrollment of such eligible dependents in such benefit plans; (ii) provide the dependents for whom such benefits are required, or a social services official substituted for such dependents, identification cards and benefit claim forms; (iii) commence deductions from income due or thereafter due to the debtor of such amount which is the debtor's share of the premium, if any, for such health insurance benefits, provided, however, that such deduction when combined with deductions for support does not exceed the limitations set forth in paragraph one of this subdivision and is consistent with the priority provisions set forth in subdivision (h) of this section; and (iv) provide a confirmation of such enrollment indicating the date such benefits were or become available or that such benefits are not available and the reasons therefor to the issuer of the execution. Except as otherwise provided by law, nothing herein shall be deemed to obligate an employer or organization to maintain or continue an employee's or member's health insurance benefits.

(4) If such employer, organization or group health plan administrator shall fail to so enroll such eligible dependents or to deduct from the debtor's income the debtor's share of the premium, such employer, organization or group health plan administrator shall be jointly and severally liable for all medical expenses incurred on behalf of the debtor's dependents named in the execution while such dependents are not so enrolled to the extent of the insurance benefits that should have been provided under such execution. Except as otherwise provided by law, nothing herein shall be deemed to obligate an employer, organization or group health plan administrator to maintain or continue an employee's or member's health insurance benefits.

(h) Priority. A levy pursuant to this section or an income deduction order pursuant to section 5242 of this chapter shall take priority over any other assignment, levy or process. If an employer or income payor is served with more than one execution pursuant to this section, or with an execution pursuant to this section and also an order pursuant to section 5242 of this chapter, and if the combined total amount of the deductions to be withheld exceeds the limits set forth in subdivision (g) of this section, the employer or income payor shall withhold the maximum amount permitted thereby and pay to each creditor that proportion thereof which such creditor's claim bears to the combined total. Any additional deduction authorized by subdivision (g) of this section to be applied to the reduction of arrears shall be applied to such arrears in proportion to the amount of arrears due to each creditor. Deductions to satisfy support obligations, including any additional deductions authorized by subdivision (g) of this section, shall have priority over deductions for the debtor's share of health insurance premiums.

(i) Levy upon money payable by the state. A levy upon money payable directly by a department of the state, or by an institution under its jurisdiction, shall be made by serving the income execution upon the head of the department, or upon a person designated by him, at the office of the department in Albany; a levy upon money payable directly upon the state comptroller's warrant, or directly by a state board, commission, body or agency which is not within any department of the state, shall be made by serving the execution upon the state department of audit and control at its office in Albany. Service at the office of a department or any agency or institution of the state in Albany may be made by registered or certified mail, return receipt requested.

(L. 1985, ch. 809, §2; amended L. 1987, ch. 815, §9; L. 1988, ch. 327, §2; L. 1990, ch. 818, §§1, 2; L. 1993, ch. 59, §§5 to 8; L. 1994, ch. 170, §§369 to 371; L. 1997, ch. 398, §§20 to 28, effective November 11, 1997; L. 1997, ch. 398, §§137 to 140, effective January 1, 1998; L. 1998, ch. 214, §§51 to 55-a, effective November 4, 1998; L. 1998, ch. 214, §79, effective July 7, 1998, deemed effective November 11, 1997; L. 1999, ch. 533, §8, effective September 28, 1999; L. 2006, ch. 335, §1, effective October 24, 2006.)

§5242. Court may enter an income deduction order for support enforcement

(a) Upon application of a creditor, for good cause shown, and upon such terms as justice may require, the court may correct any defect, irregularity, error or omission in an income execution for support enforcement issued pursuant to section 5241 of this article.

(b) Upon application of a creditor, for good cause shown, the court may enter an income deduction order for support enforcement. In determining good cause, the court may take into consideration evidence of the degree of such debtor's past financial responsibility, credit references, credit history, and any other matter the court considers relevant in determining the likelihood of payment in accordance with the order of support. Proof of default establishes a prima facie case against the debtor, which can be overcome only by proof of the debtor's inability to make the payments. Unless the prima facie case is overcome, the court shall enter an income deduction order for support enforcement pursuant to this section.

(c) (1) When the court enters an order of support on behalf of persons other than those in receipt of public assistance or in receipt of services pursuant to section one hundred eleven-g of the social services law, or registers pursuant to article five-B of the family court act an order of support which has been issued by a foreign jurisdiction and which is not to be enforced pursuant to title six-A of article three of the social services law, where the court determines that the respondent earns wages that could be subject to an income deduction order, the court shall issue an income deduction order to obtain payment of the order at the same time it issues or registers the order. The court shall enter the income deduction order unless the court finds and sets forth in writing (i) the reasons that there is good cause not to require immediate income withholding; or (ii) that an agreement providing for an alternative arrangement has been reached between the parties. Such agreement may include a written agreement or an oral stipulation, made on the record, that results in a written order. For purposes of this subdivision, good cause shall mean substantial harm to the debtor. The absence of an arrearage or the mere issuance of an income deduction order shall not constitute good cause. When the court determines that there is good cause not to issue an income deduction order immediately or when the parties agree to an alternative arrangement as provided in this paragraph, the court shall state expressly in the order of support the basis for its decision. In entering the income deduction order, the court shall specify an amount to be withheld by the debtor's employer, which shall be sufficient to ensure compliance with the order of support and also shall include an additional amount to be applied to the reduction of arrears, if any, and shall specify the names, addresses, and social security numbers of the parties to the support proceeding and the mailing address of the unit within the state department of social services designated to receive such deductions. The court shall transmit copies of such order to the parties and to such unit.

(2) An employer served with an income deduction order entered pursuant to this subdivision shall commence deductions from the income due or thereafter due to the debtor no later than the first pay period that occurs fourteen days after service of the income deduction order, and shall remit payments to the state department of social services pursuant to subdivision fourteen of section one hundred eleven-b of the social services law within ten days of the date that the debtor is paid. Each payment remitted by the employer shall be made payable to the creditor named in the order, and shall include the names, addresses, and social security numbers of the debtor and the creditor, and the date and the amount of each withholding of the debtor's income included in the payment. An employer shall be liable to the creditor for failure to deduct the amounts specified in the income deduction order, provided however that deduction by the employer of the amounts specified shall not relieve the debtor of the underlying obligation of support. If an employer shall fail to so pay the creditor, the creditor may commence a proceeding against the employer for accrued deductions, together with interest and reasonable attorney's fees. If the debtor's employment is terminated by resignation or dismissal at any time after service of the income deduction order, the order shall cease to have force and effect unless the debtor is reinstated or re-employed by the same employer. An employer must notify the creditor promptly when the debtor terminates employment and must provide the debtor's last address and the name and address of the debtor's new employer, if known. Where the income is compensation paid or payable to the debtor for personal services, the amount withheld by the employer shall not exceed the following:

(i) Where the debtor currently is supporting a spouse or dependent child other than the creditor's dependent child, the amount withheld shall not exceed fifty percent of the earnings of the debtor remaining after the deduction therefrom of any amounts required by law to be withheld ("disposable earnings"), except that if any part of the deduction is to be applied to the reduction of arrears which shall have accrued more than twelve weeks prior to the beginning of the week for which such earnings are payable, the amount withheld shall not exceed fifty-five percent of disposable earnings.

(ii) Where the debtor currently is not supporting a spouse or dependent child other than the creditor's dependent child, the amount withheld shall not exceed sixty percent of the earnings of the debtor remaining after the deduction therefrom of any amounts required by law to be withheld ("disposable earnings"), except that if any part of the deduction is to be applied to the reduction of arrears which shall have accrued more than twelve weeks prior to the beginning of the week for which such earnings are payable, the amount withheld shall not exceed sixty-five percent of disposable earnings.

(d) An order pursuant to this section shall take priority over any other assignment, levy or process. If an employer or income payor is served with more than one income deduction order pertaining to a single employee pursuant to this section, or with an order issued pursuant to this section and also an execution pursuant to section 5241 of this chapter, and if the combined total amount of the income to be withheld exceeds the limits set forth in subdivision (c) of this section, the employer or income payor shall withhold the maximum amount permitted thereby and pay to each creditor that proportion thereof which such creditor's claim bears to the combined total.

(e) An employer or income payor shall be liable to the creditor for failure to deduct the amounts specified, provided however that deduction of the amounts specified by the employer or income payor shall not relieve the debtor of the underlying obligation of support.

(f) A creditor shall not be required to issue process under section 5241 of this article prior to obtaining relief pursuant to this section.

(g) Where the court issues an income deduction order for support enforcement payable to the support collection unit, as defined in paragraph nine of subdivision (a) of section 5241 of this article, each payment remitted by an employer or income payor shall include, in addition to the identity and social security number of the debtor, the date and amount of each withholding of the debtor's income included in the payment.

(L. 1985, ch. 809, §3; amended L. 1987, ch. 815, §10; L. 1990, ch. 818, §3; L. 1994, ch. 170, §358. As amended L. 1997, ch. 398, §42, effective January 1, 1998.)

Family Court Act

§440. Order of support

1. (a) Any support order made by the court in any proceeding under the provisions of article five-B of this act, pursuant to a reference from the supreme court under section two hundred fifty-one of the domestic relations law or under the provisions of article four, five or five-A of this act

(i) shall direct that payments of child support or combined child and spousal support collected on behalf of persons in receipt of services pursuant to section one hundred eleven-g of the social services law, or on behalf of persons in receipt of public assistance be made to the support collection unit designated by the appropriate social services district, which shall receive and disburse funds so paid; or

(ii) shall be enforced pursuant to subdivision (c) of section five thousand two hundred forty-two of the civil practice law and rules at the same time that the court issues an order of support; and

(iii) shall in either case, except as provided for herein, be effective as of the earlier of the date of the filing of the petition therefor, or, if the children for whom support is sought are in receipt of public assistance, the date for which their eligibility for public assistance was effective. Any retroactive amount of support due shall be support arrears/past due support and shall be paid in one sum or periodic sums, as the court directs, and any amount of temporary support which has been paid to be taken into account in calculating any amount of such retroactive support due. In addition, such retroactive child support shall be enforceable in any manner provided by law including, but not limited to, an execution for support enforcement pursuant to subdivision (b) of section fifty- two hundred forty-one of the civil practice law and rules. When a child receiving support is a public assistance recipient, or the order of support is being enforced or is to be enforced pursuant to section one hundred eleven-g of the social services law, the court shall establish the amount of retroactive child support and notify the parties that such amount shall be enforced by the support collection unit pursuant to an execution for support enforcement as provided for in subdivision (b) of section fifty-two hundred forty-one of the civil practice law and rules, or in such periodic payments as would have been authorized had such an execution been issued. In such case, the court shall not direct the schedule of repayment of retroactive support. Where such direction is for child support and paternity has been established by a voluntary acknowledgment of paternity as defined in section forty-one hundred thirty-five-b of the public health law, the court shall inquire of the parties whether the acknowledgment has been duly filed, and unless satisfied that it has been so filed shall require the clerk of the court to file such acknowledgment with the appropriate registrar within five business days. The court shall not direct that support payments be made to the support collection unit unless the child, who is the subject of the order, is in receipt of public assistance or child support services pursuant to section one hundred eleven-g of the social services law. Any such order shall be enforceable pursuant to section fifty-two hundred forty-one or fifty-two hundred forty-two of the civil practice law and rules, or in any other manner provided by law. Such orders or judgments for child support and maintenance shall also be enforceable pursuant to article fifty-two of the civil practice law and rules upon a debtor's default as such term is defined in paragraph seven of subdivision (a) of section fifty-two hundred forty-one of the civil practice law and rules. The establishment of a default shall be subject to the procedures established for the determination of a mistake of fact for income executions pursuant to subdivision (e) of section fifty-two hundred forty-one of the civil practice law and rules. For the purposes of enforcement of child support orders or combined spousal and child support orders pursuant to section five thousand two hundred forty-one of the civil practice law and rules, a "default" shall be deemed to include amounts arising from retroactive support. Where permitted under federal law and where the record of the proceedings contains such information, such order shall include on its face the social security number and the name and address of the employer, if any, of the person chargeable with support provided, however, that failure to comply with this requirement shall not invalidate such order.

(b) (1) When the court issues an order of child support or combined child and spousal support on behalf of persons in receipt of public assistance or in receipt of services pursuant to section one hundred eleven-g of the social services law, the support collection unit shall issue an income execution immediately for child support or combined spousal and child support, and shall issue an execution for medical support enforcement in accordance with the provisions of the order of support unless:

(i) the court finds and sets forth in writing the reasons that there is good cause not to require immediate income withholding; or

(ii) when the child is not in receipt of public assistance, a written agreement providing for an alternative arrangement has been reached between the parties. Such written agreement may include an oral stipulation made on the record resulting in a written order. For purposes of this paragraph, good cause shall mean substantial harm to the debtor. The absence of an arrearage or the mere issuance of an income execution shall not constitute good cause. When an immediate income execution or an execution for medical support enforcement is issued by the support collection unit, such execution shall be issued pursuant to section five thousand two hundred forty- one of the civil practice law and rules, except that the provisions thereof relating to mistake of fact, default and any other provisions which are not relevant to the issuance of an execution pursuant to this paragraph shall not apply; provided, however, that if the support collection unit makes an error in the issuance of an execution pursuant to this paragraph, and such error is to the detriment of the debtor, the support collection unit shall have thirty days after notification by the debtor to correct the error. Where permitted under federal law and where the record of the proceedings contains such information, such order shall include on its face the social security number and the name and address of the employer, if any, of the person chargeable with support; provided, however, that failure to comply with this requirement shall not invalidate such order. When the court determines that there is good cause not to immediately issue an income execution or when the parties agree to an alternative arrangement as provided in this paragraph, the court shall provide expressly in the order of support that the support collection unit shall not issue an immediate income execution. Notwithstanding any such order, the support collection unit shall issue an income execution for support enforcement when the debtor defaults on the support obligation, as defined in section five thousand two hundred forty-one of the civil practice law and rules. When an income execution for support enforcement is issued pursuant to this paragraph, such income execution shall supersede any income deduction order previously issued for enforcement of the same support order pursuant to subdivision (c) of section five thousand two hundred forty-two of the civil practice law and rules, whereupon such income deduction order shall cease to have further effect.

(2) When the court issues an order of child support or combined child and spousal support on behalf of persons other than those in receipt of public assistance or in receipt of services pursuant to section one hundred eleven-g of the social services law, the court shall issue an income deduction order pursuant to subdivision (c) of section five thousand two hundred forty-two of the civil practice law and rules at the same time at which it issues the order of support. The court shall enter the income deduction order unless the court finds and sets forth in writing: (i) the reasons that there is good cause not to require immediate income withholding; or (ii) that an agreement providing for an alternative arrangement has been reached between the parties. Such agreement may include a written agreement or an oral stipulation, made on the record, that results in a written order. For purposes of this paragraph, good cause shall mean substantial harm to the debtor. The absence of an arrearage or the mere issuance of an income deduction order shall not constitute good cause. Where permitted under federal law and where the record of the proceedings contains such information, the order shall include on its face the social security number and the name and address of the employer, if any, of the person chargeable with support; provided, however, that failure to comply with this requirement shall not invalidate the order. When the court determines that there is good cause not to immediately issue an income deduction order or when the parties agree to an alternative arrangement as provided in this paragraph, the court shall not issue an income deduction order. In addition, the court shall make provisions for health insurance benefits in accordance with the requirements of section four hundred sixteen of this article.

(c) Any order of support issued on behalf of a child in receipt of family assistance or child support enforcement services pursuant to section one hundred eleven-g of the social services law shall be subject to review and adjustment by the support collection unit pursuant to section one hundred eleven-n of the social services law, section two hundred forty-c of the domestic relations law and section four hundred thirteen-a of this article. Such review and adjustment shall be in addition to any other activities undertaken by the support collection unit relating to the establishment, modification, and enforcement of support orders payable to such unit.

2. The court shall require any person chargeable with support under the provisions of article five-B of this act or under any support order made pursuant to a reference from the supreme court under section two hundred fifty- one of the domestic relations law or in any proceeding under the provisions of article four, five or five-A of this act to provide his or her social security number, the name and address of his or her employer and to report any changes of employer or change in employment status affecting compensation received, including rate of compensation or loss of employment, to the support collection unit designated by the appropriate social services district and to keep such support collection unit advised of his or her current employer and current employment status; provided, however, that a social security number may be required only where permitted under federal law.

3. The amount of support determined in accordance with the statewide child support standards, as set forth in section four hundred thirteen of this act, shall constitute prima facie evidence of the ability of any person chargeable with support

in accordance with the provisions of article three-A of the domestic relations law or under any support order made pursuant to a reference from the supreme court under section two hundred fifty-one of the domestic relations law or in any proceeding under the provisions of article four, five or five-A of this chapter to support or contribute such amount towards the support of his or her children.

4. Any support order made by the court in any proceeding under the provisions of article five-B of this act, pursuant to a reference from the supreme court under section two hundred fifty-one of the domestic relations law or under the provisions of article four, five or five-A of this act shall include, on its face, a notice printed or typewritten in a size equal to at least eight point bold type informing the respondent that a willful failure to obey the order may, after court hearing, result in commitment to jail for a term not to exceed six months for contempt of court.

5. The court shall direct that a copy of any child support or combined child and spousal support order issued by the court on or after the first day of October, nineteen hundred ninety-eight, in any proceeding pursuant to a reference from the supreme court under section two hundred fifty-one of the domestic relations law or under the provisions of article four, five, five-A or five-B of this act be provided promptly to the state case registry established pursuant to subdivision four-a of section one hundred eleven-b of the social services law.

6. Any order of support made by the court shall provide for health insurance benefits pursuant to section four hundred sixteen of this article.

(L. 1977, ch. 516, §14; amended L. 1878, ch. 456, §11; L. 1983, ch. 274, §1; L. 1984, ch. 632, §1; L. 1985, ch. 809, §16; L. 1986, ch. 892, §19; L. 1989, ch. 567, §10; L. 1990, ch. 818, §15; L. 1992, ch. 41, §142; L. 1993, ch. 59, §§2, 11, 22; L. 1993, ch. 354, §3; L. 1994, ch. 170, §§364, 365; L. 1997, ch. 398, §7, effective October 1, 1998; L. 1997, ch. 398, §§45, 46, 98, effective January 1, 1998; L. 1998, ch. 214, §59-a, effective November 4, 1998. As amended L. 2002, ch. 624, §3, effective October 2, 2002.)

§454. Powers of the court on violation of a support order

1. If a respondent is brought before the court for failure to obey any lawful order of support and if, after hearing, the court is satisfied by competent proof that the respondent has failed to obey any such order, the court may use any or all of the powers conferred upon it by this part. The court has the power to use any or all enforcement powers in every proceeding brought for violation of a court order under this part regardless of the relief requested in the petition.

2. Upon a finding that a respondent has failed to comply with any lawful order of support:

(a) the court shall enter a money judgment under section four hundred sixty of this article; and

(b) the court may make an income deduction order for support enforcement under section fifty-two hundred forty-two of the civil practice law and rules;

(c) the court may require the respondent to post an undertaking under section four hundred seventy-one of this article;

(d) the court may make an order of sequestration under section four hundred fifty-seven of this article;

(e) the court may suspend the respondent's driving privileges pursuant to section four hundred fifty-eight-a of this article;

(f) the court may suspend the respondent's state professional or business license pursuant to section four hundred fifty-eight-b of this article;

(g) the court may suspend the recreational license or licenses of the respondent pursuant to section four hundred fifty-eight-c of this article;

(h) the court may require the respondent, if the persons for whom the respondent has failed to pay support are applicants for or recipients of public assistance, to participate in work activities as defined in title nine-B of article five of the social services law. Those respondents ordered to participate in work activities need not be applicants for or recipients of public assistance.

3. Upon a finding by the court that a respondent has willfully failed to obey any lawful order of support, the court shall order respondent to pay counsel fees to the attorney representing petitioner pursuant to section four hundred thirty-eight of this act and may in addition to or in lieu of any or all of the powers conferred in subdivision two of this section or any other section of law:

(a) commit the respondent to jail for a term not to exceed six months. For purposes of this subdivision, failure to pay support, as ordered, shall constitute prima facie evidence of a willful violation. Such commitment may be served upon certain specified days or parts of days as the court may direct, and the court may, at any time within the term of such sentence, revoke such suspension and commit the respondent for the remainder of the original sentence, or suspend the remainder of such sentence. Such commitment does not prevent the court from subsequently committing the respondent for failure thereafter to comply with any such order; or

(b) require the respondent to participate in a rehabilitative program if the court determines that such participation would assist the respondent in complying with such order of support and access to such a program is available. Such rehabilitative programs shall include, but not be limited to, work preparation and skill programs, non-residential alcohol and substance abuse programs and educational programs; or

(c) place the respondent on probation under such conditions as the court may determine and in accordance with the provisions of the criminal procedure law.

4. The court shall not deny any request for relief pursuant to this section unless the facts and circumstances constituting the reasons for its determination are set forth in a written memorandum of decision.

5. [Eff. until June 30, 2003, pursuant to L. 1995, ch. 81, §246, subd. 19.] The court may review a support collection unit's denial of a challenge made by a support obligor pursuant to paragraph (d) of subdivision twelve of section one hundred eleven-b of the social services law if objections thereto are filed by a support obligor who has received notice that the department of social services intends to notify the department of motor vehicles that the support obligor's

driving privileges are to be suspended. Specific written objections to a support collection unit's denial may be filed by the support obligor within thirty-five days of the mailing of the notice of the support collection unit's denial. A support obligor who files such objections shall serve a copy of the objections upon the support collection unit, which shall have ten days from such service to file a written rebuttal to such objections and a copy of the record upon which the support collection unit's denial was made, including all documentation submitted by the support obligor. Proof of service shall be filed with the court at the time of filing of objections and any rebuttal. The court's review shall be based upon the record and submissions of the support obligor and the support collection unit upon which the support collection unit's denial was made. Within forty-five days after the rebuttal, if any, is filed, the family court judge shall (i) deny the objections and remand to the support collection unit or (ii) affirm the objections if the court finds the determination of the support collection unit is based upon a clearly erroneous determination of fact or error of law, whereupon the court shall direct the support collection unit not to notify the department of motor vehicles to suspend the support obligor's driving privileges. Provisions set forth herein relating to procedures for appeal to the family court by individuals subject to suspension of driving privileges for failure to pay child support shall apply solely to such cases and not affect or modify any other procedure for review or appeal of administrative enforcement of child support requirements.

(L. 1962, ch. 686; amended L. 1965, ch. 522, §1; L. 1966, ch. 721, §2; L. 1968, ch. 804, §1; L. 1971, ch. 1097, §40; L. 1977, ch. 437, §12; L. 1977, ch. 516, §18; L. 1978, ch. 456, §13; L. 1980, ch. 241, §1; L. 1982, ch. 654, §2; L. 1983, ch. 746, §§1 to 3; L. 1986, ch. 892, §23; L. 1995, ch. 81, §§216, 230; L. 1996, ch. 309, §466; L. 1996, ch. 699, §1; L. 1997, ch. 398, §132, effective January 1, 1998; L. 1998, ch. 214, §63, effective July 7, 1998, deemed effective January 1, 1998.)

Social Services Law

§111-y. Crediting of overpayments of tax to past-due spousal support

1. The department shall provide services for the crediting of overpayments of tax to past-due support, pursuant to section one hundred seventy-one-c of the tax law, which is owed to any current or former spouse entitled to enforce an order of support, who applies to the department for such services, if such spouse is not eligible to receive services pursuant to title six-A of this article. For purposes of this section, "order of support" means any final order, decree or judgment in a matrimonial action or family court proceeding, or any foreign support order, decree or judgment which is registered pursuant to article five-B of the family court act which requires the payment of alimony, maintenance or support.

2. (a) An applicant for services under this section shall provide the department with the following:

(i) a certified transcript of a money judgment for a sum certain for arrears accrued under an order of support;

(ii) a sworn statement that the order of support is no longer subject to appellate judicial review and that the sum set forth as uncollected on the judgment is accurate;

(iii) the name and address of the applicant; and

(iv) the name, last known address and social security number of the person or entity owning [sic] past-due support against whom a judgment has been obtained.

(b) If an application for services is rejected by the department, the department shall inform the applicant in writing of the reason for such rejection.

3. An applicant for services under this section shall receive a pro rata share of the overpayment of tax, based on the amount of past-due support owed to such applicant as certified to the tax commission by the department pursuant to section one hundred seventy-one-c of the tax law, in cases where the individual, estate or trust owing past-due support to such applicant owes past-due support to other persons or entities so certified to the tax commission by the department.

4. The department shall promulgate such regulations as are necessary to carry out the provisions of this section, including regulations as to the date by which an applicant for services under this section shall provide the department with the information and documentation required in subdivision two of this section.

(Formerly §111-m, added L. 1985, ch. 809, §29; renumbered §111-y, L. 1997, ch. 398, §16, effective October 1, 1997; amended L. 1997, ch. 398, §52, effective January 1, 1998.)

Family Court Act

§423. Commencement of proceedings upon filing of petition

Proceedings under this article are commenced by the filing of a petition, which may be made on information and belief. The petitioner need not make a demand upon the respondent for support as a condition precedent to the filing of a petition for support. Any such petition for the establishment, modification and/or enforcement of a child support obligation for persons not in receipt of family assistance, which contains a request for child support enforcement services completed in a manner as specified in section one hundred eleven-g of the social services law, shall constitute an application for such services.

(L. 1962, ch. 686; L. 1981, ch. 622, §2; L. 1990, ch. 818, §13; L. 1997, ch. 436, pt. B, §110, effective August 20, 1997.)

G. SEPARATION AGREEMENTS AND SPOUSAL SUPPORT

Spouses can agree to limit or waive the right to spousal support postdissolution by means of a premarital agreement or a marital separation agreement. (In New York, agreements precluding spousal support or property distribution are sometimes referred to as "opting-out" agreements.) On the effect of premarital agreements on spousal support waivers, see Section A2 *supra*.

A separation agreement, like a premarital agreement, will be enforceable in New York if the agreement is (1) in writing, (2) subscribed by the parties, and (3) acknowledged or proven in the manner required to entitle a deed to be recorded (DRL §236(B)(3)). Case law has interpreted the "acknowledgment requirement" to mean both (1) an oral acknowledgment must be made before an authorized officer and (2) a written certificate of acknowledgment (often prepared by a notary public) must be attached. Matisoff v. Dobi, 681 N.E.2d 376 (N.Y. 1997), on remand to, 663 N.Y.S.2d 526 (App. Div. 1997), leave to appeal denied, 691 N.E.2d 632 (N.Y. 1998) and related reference, 694 N.Y.S.2d 650 (App. Div. 1999) (holding that the parties' postnuptial agreement was invalid where the parties acknowledged in open court the genuineness of their signatures, but no proper certificate of acknowledgment was attached to the agreement). Caralyn Miller Ross, Separation Agreements, 18B Carmody-Wait 2d, *supra*, at §117:8.

Further, although the statute requires that the agreement be in writing, courts are divided about whether an oral stipulation of settlement, which is placed on the record and contemporaneously acknowledged in writing, can constitute a valid agreement. Ross, Separation Agreements, *supra*, at §117:10. *Compare* James v. James, 609 N.Y.S.2d 485 (App. Div. 1994) (holding that such stipulations are not valid given the precise language of the Domestic Relations Law), with Ashcraft v. Ashcraft, 601 N.Y.S.2d 890 (App. Div. 1993), related proceeding, 601 N.Y.S.2d 753 (App. Div. 1993) (holding that an oral stipulation of settlement, placed on the record and contemporaneously acknowledged in writing, was a valid opting-out agreement under DRL 236(B)(3)). See also Hartloff v. Hartloff, 745 N.Y.S.2d 361 (App. Div. 2002) (holding that husband's oral stipulation resolving financial issues was valid).

An agreement between the marital parties in New York may affect: (1) inheritance (DRL §236(B)(3)(1)); (2) distribution of separate and marital property (DRL §236(B)(3)(2)); (3) maintenance and other terms and conditions of the marriage relationship (DRL §236(B)(3)(3)); and (4) child custody and child support (DRL §236(B)(3)(4)). A support order may be modified or terminated, unless the parties agree otherwise in writing.

Separation agreements are subject to the provisions of General Obligations Law (§5-311) prohibiting contracts to alter or dissolve the marriage or to relieve support obligations. Pursuant to that statute, a husband and wife cannot contract to terminate their marriage. For an agreement to "alter or dissolve the marriage," it must contain an express provision requiring dissolution or providing for the procurement of grounds for divorce (*id.*). See also Stephen Lease & John Bourdeau, Grounds for Divorce, 18A Carmody-Wait, *supra*, at §§114:11, 117:1.

Also, for a separation agreement to be valid, the parties must actually be separated at the time they execute the agreement (or immediately thereafter). Klein v. Klein, 676 N.Y.S.2d 69 (App. Div. 1998); Costa v. Costa, 597 N.Y.S.2d 222 (App. Div. 1993); Ross, 18B Carmody-Wait 2d, *supra*, at §117:2. But cf. Thompson v. Thompson, 741 N.Y.S.2d 641 (App. Div. 2002) (slip op.) (refusing to set aside parties' separation agreement even though parties later intermittently lived under same roof, where parties intended to separate and did separate, and maintained separate bedrooms and never had sexual relations, and did not share bank accounts and filed separate tax returns). A spouse may not waive all rights to support if it would result in his or her becoming a public charge (FCA §463; Gen. Oblig. Law §5-311).

The rights and obligations of the parties pursuant to a separation agreement differ from those established by a final decree. An agreement that is incorporated but not merged with a judgment of divorce survives the judgment as a separately enforceable contract. However, the court may incorporate an agreement made by the parties into its judgment in a matrimonial action, thereby making available expansive remedies for the enforcement of marital obligations. Thus, the Family Court does not have jurisdiction to modify a separation agreement that has not been made effective by judicial action. Zamjohn v. Zamjohn, 551 N.Y.S.2d 689 (App. Div. 1990) (holding that the Family Court does not have subject matter jurisdiction to modify or enforce a separation agreement decreasing husband's obligation to pay permanent maintenance because agreement was incorporated but not merged into the divorce judgment). Eclavea, 19 Carmody-Wait 2d, *supra*, at §118:318.

Jurisdictions, increasingly, are extending recognition of cohabitation contracts to same-sex partners. See, e.g., Silver v. Starrett, 674 N.Y.S.2d 915 (Sup. Ct. 1998) (holding that such an agreement was supported by adequate consideration). More recently, in Cannisi v. Walsh, 831 N.Y.S.2d 352 (Sup. Ct. 2006), a New York trial court recognized that contracts between same-sex partners are enforceable (via constructive trusts to prevent unjust enrichment), and also that Hernandez v. Robles, 871 N.Y.S.2d 770 (N.Y. 2006) (upholding New York's limitation on marriage to opposite-sex couples) does not mandate different treatment of the contracts between unmarried same-sex partnerships and those of unmarried heterosexual partners. See also Doe v. Burkland, 808 A.2d 1090 (R.I. 2002) (upholding contract claim between two former same-sex partners). As evidence of a counter movement, however, some state statutes or constitutional amendments prohibiting same-sex marriage take the additional step of prohibiting other legal statuses, such as civil unions or domestic partnerships. See, e.g., Va. Code Ann. §20-45.3 (2005) (refusing to recognize civil unions, including those contracted in other states, and also voiding any contractual arrangements between same-sex couples "purporting to bestow the privileges or obligations of marriage").

Some commentators worry that such laws will prohibit the application of *Marvin* to same-sex couples. See, e.g., Mark Strasser, State Marriage Amendments and Overreaching: On Plain Meaning, Good Public Policy, and Constitutional Limits, 25 Law & Ineq. 59, 98-102 (2007). See also Marsh Garrison, Is Consent Necessary? An Evaluation of the Emerging Law of Cohabitant Obligation, 52 U.C.L.A. L. Rev. 815 (2005).

Family Court Act

§445. Order of support by relative

(a) If the court finds after a hearing that a relative, including a step-parent, should be held responsible under section four hundred fifteen for support [support for recipient of public assistance or welfare or institutionalized mental patient], the court in its discretion may make an order requiring such person to contribute a fair and reasonable sum for the support of such person.

(b) For good cause shown, the court may at any time terminate or modify an order made under this section.

(L. 1962, ch. 686.)

§463. Effect of separation agreement on spousal duty of support

A separation agreement does not preclude the filing of a petition and the making of an order under section four hundred forty-five of this article for support of a spouse who is likely to become in need of public assistance or care.

(L. 1962, ch. 686; L. 1980, ch. 281, §41.)

General Obligations Law

§5-311. Certain agreements between spouses are void

Except as provided in section two hundred thirty-six of the domestic relations law, a husband and wife cannot contract to alter or dissolve the marriage or to relieve either of his or her liability to support the other in such a manner that he or she will become incapable of self-support and therefore is likely to become a public charge. An agreement, heretofore or hereafter made between a husband and wife, shall not be considered a contract to alter or dissolve the marriage unless it contains an express provision requiring the dissolution of the marriage or provides for the procurement of grounds of divorce.

(L. 1980, ch. 281, §19.)

V.
PROPERTY

This chapter (together with Chapter IV) addresses the financial consequences of dissolution. First, the chapter explores background provisions (i.e., effective date of the applicable legislation, the availability of relief, the meaning of an equitable distribution, distributive awards, and the date of valuation). Then, it examines the classification of property (marital versus separate). Next, it focuses on legislative factors that play a role in achieving a fair distribution of assets. It turns to special problems of property distribution (e.g., pensions and employee benefits; degrees, licenses, and enhanced earning capacity; occupancy and possession of the marital home). It concludes with a discussion of the role of fault in the distribution of marital property. The law of New York (Domestic Relations Code (DRL), Family Court Act (FCA), and related provisions) provide an illustration of these topics. (Note that the New York legislature is currently considering the enactment of no-fault legislation. Assembly Bill A03027 proposes the Divorce Reform Act of 2007, adding irreconcilable differences as a ground for divorce in Domestic Relations Law §170.)

A. General Provisions

Property distribution became the subject of widespread divorce reform during the 1960s and 1970s. Reformers urged the abolition of fault as a basis for divorce and as a factor in alimony and property distributions. Many advocated that property distributions should replace alimony as a means of achieving fairness between the spouses. Critics charged that (1) alimony was seldom awarded and infrequently paid, (2) the traditional emphasis on fault and need in setting alimony awards perpetuated notions of women as dependents and failed to recognize the value of the wife's nonmonetary contributions as homemaker and parent; and (3) the idea of lifetime spousal support was outdated because more women were entering the workplace. Reformers urged adoption of the idea of marriage as a partnership with the financial incidents of divorce fashioned accordingly. Marsha Garrison, Good Intentions Gone Awry: The Impact of New York's Equitable Distribution Law on Divorce Outcomes, 57 Brooklyn L. Rev. 621, 629-630 (1991).

Influenced by such criticisms, many states instituted a system of equitable distribution. Most states adopted equitable distribution by statute, modelled after the Uniform Marriage and Divorce Act (UMDA) (discussed below).

1. Effective Date

In 1980, the New York state legislature enacted legislation, commonly referred to as the Equitable Distribution Law (DRL §236), which reflects a modern theory of marriage as an economic partnership (L. 1980, ch. 281, effective July 19, 1980). This major law reform altered the rules that governed the distribution of property upon dissolution and also replaced the concept of alimony with the concept of maintenance. The legislation specified that a maintenance award was a factor in determining a property award, introduced consideration of the marital property distribution into the spousal support decision, provided greater detail in the statutory factors for awarding spousal support, and eliminated fault as a basis for denying spousal support and occupancy of the marital residence. Garrison, *supra*, at 639-640. See also Chapter IV for a discussion of these developments.

Prior to the 1980 legislation, New York awarded property based on the common law scheme of "title theory." At common law, the form of title to property, as evidenced in a deed, for example, determined ownership between the spouses. Property acquired or earned during the marriage belonged to the acquiring or earning spouse, unless that spouse acted to create joint ownership (for example, by purchasing a house titled jointly in the names of both spouses). Upon divorce, the court assigns property to the owner. Before the adoption of New York's equitable distribution law, New York was one of six states (Florida, Mississippi, New York, South Carolina, Virginia, and West Virginia) that awarded property to the titleholder. Garrison, *supra*, at 637, n. 57 (citing Doris J. Freed & Henry H. Foster, Jr., Divorce in the Fifty States: An Overview as of 1978, 13 Fam. L.Q. 105 (1979)).

Reformers severely criticized the title system for its failure to take into account nonmonetary contributions in the division of property and thereby working a hardship on homemaker spouses. In the 1980s, after witnessing the widespread adoption of no-fault grounds and a rising divorce rate, many states abandoned the title system in favor of a system of equitable distribution applicable at the end of marriage. Mississippi was the last state to abandon the title theory. Ferguson v. Ferguson, 639 So. 2d 921 (Miss. 1994) (en banc).

As explained above, most states adopted equitable distribution by statute, influenced by the Uniform Marriage and Divorce Act (UMDA). The 1970 version of UMDA provided that courts should divide marital property "without regard to marital misconduct in just proportions . . . ." according to certain statutorily enumerated factors (UMDA §307(a)) and set forth a presumption that property acquired by either spouse after the marriage was marital property "regardless of whether title is held individually or by the spouses in some form of co-ownership such as joint tenancy, tenancy in common, tenancy by the entirety, and community property" (*id.* at §307(c)). New York adopted equitable distribution by its 1980 legislation.

In enacting the Equitable Distribution Law with its view of marriage as an economic partnership, the New York state legislature provided that property accumulated during the marriage would be distributed equitably based on certain statutory guidelines (discussed *infra*). The guidelines do not fix the amount of each spouse's interest in the marital property. Rather, the statute delineates 13 factors (DRL Section 236B(5)) that guide the court's consideration, with the final factor serving as a discretionary provision. Determinations, thus, are based on the facts of a given case. The applicable legislation has been amended several times since 1980, most notably in 1986 to provide additional relief in the form of long-term maintenance awards for dependent spouses. On spousal support, see Chapter IV.

The statute provides that Part A [omitted] controls any action or proceeding commenced prior to the effective date of the statute (July 19, 1980), and Part B controls any action or proceeding commenced on or after that date.

Domestic Relations Act

§236. Equitable Distribution Law: special controlling provisions

Except as otherwise expressly provided in this section, the provisions of part A shall be controlling with respect to any action or proceeding commenced prior to the date on which the provisions of this section as amended become effective [July 19, 1980] and the provisions of part B shall be controlling with respect to any action or proceeding commenced on or after such effective date.

. . .

(L. 1962, ch. 313, §10; L. 1963, ch. 685, §6; L. 1968, ch. 699, §1; L. 1980, ch. 281, §9; L. 1980, ch. 645, §§2, 3; L. 1981, ch. 695, §§1, 2; L. 1984, ch. 790, §2; L. 1985, ch. 809, §6; L. 1986, ch. 884, §§1 to 4; L. 1986, ch. 892, §§2 to 4; L. 1987, ch. 815, §§6, 7; L. 1989, ch. 567, §§4, 5; L. 1990, ch. 818, §§4, 5; L. 1992, ch. 41, §§139, 140; L. 1992, ch. 415, §§1, 2; L. 1993, ch. 59, §9; L. 1993, ch. 354, §2; L. 1994, ch. 170, §§359, 360; L. 1997, ch. 398, §§4, 5, effective October 1, 1998; L. 1997, ch. 398, §141, effective January 1, 1998; L. 1997, ch. 436, pt. B, §§105, 106, effective August 20, 1997; L. 1998, ch. 214, §56, effective November 4, 1998; L. 1998, ch. 393, §2, effective July 22, 1998; L. 1999, ch. 275, §2, effective September 18, 1999; L. 2003, ch. 595, §1, eff. Sept. 22, 2003.)

2. Availability of Relief

The New York Equitable Distribution statute authorizes a court to award property distributions only when a marriage is terminated (DRL §236(B)(5)(a)). According to statute, [the court] "shall determine the respective rights of the parties in their separate or marital property, and shall provide for the disposition thereof in the final judgment" only in an "action wherein all or part of the relief granted is divorce, or the dissolution, annulment or declaration of the nullity of a marriage, and in proceedings to obtain a distribution of marital property following a foreign judgment of divorce. . . ." Thus, by implication, a court may not provide for a property distribution in cases of legal separation. (However, courts may determine questions of title in separation actions pursuant to DRL §234.) And, the statute (DRL §236(B)(5)) expressly provides that courts may not make property distributions when the parties themselves have entered into a marital settlement agreement that determines their rights to marital property. (Rather, the agreement determines the parties' rights pursuant to DRL §236(B)(3).)

The death of one of the spouses abates the matrimonial proceedings, including those for equitable distribution. Sperber v. Schwartz, 527 N.Y.S.2d 279 (App. Div. 1988) (holding that a claim for equitable distribution abated upon the wife's death in a suit by the administrator of the wife's estate against the husband to obtain equitable distribution of marital property and to recover damages for the wife's wrongful death based on the claim that the husband had murdered wife). See generally Anthony Bologna, Comment, The Impact of the Death of a Party to a Dissolution Proceeding on a Court's Jurisdiction over Property Rights, 16 J. Am. Acad. Matrim. Law. 507 (2000). (Note that a spouse's discharge in bankruptcy does not preclude a court from exercising jurisdiction to determine the parties' respective rights in the marital property. Sinha v. Sinha, 727 N.Y.S.2d 537 (App. Div. 2001).)

In the event of the death of a spouse after the dissolution, any unpaid equitable distribution is the right or responsibility of the deceased ex-spouse's estate. Peterson v. Goldberg, 585 N.Y.S.2d 439 (App. Div. 1992) (cause of action for equitable distribution did not abate upon wife's death where ex parte foreign divorce judgment was granted prior to her death), *lv. dismissed*, 611 N.E.2d 298 (N.Y. 1993).

Domestic Relations Act

§236. Equitable Distribution Law: special controlling provisions

. . .

PART B
NEW ACTIONS OR PROCEEDINGS

. . .

5. Disposition of property in certain matrimonial actions. a. Except where the parties have provided in an agreement for the disposition of their property pursuant to subdivision three of this part, the court, in an action wherein all or part of the relief granted is divorce, or the dissolution, annulment or declaration of the nullity of a marriage, and in proceedings to obtain a distribution of marital property following a foreign judgment of divorce, shall determine the respective rights of the parties in their separate or marital property, and shall provide for the disposition thereof in the final judgment.

. . .

(L. 1962, ch. 313, §10; L. 1963, ch. 685, §6; L. 1968, ch. 699, §1; L. 1980, ch. 281, §9; L. 1980, ch. 645, §§2, 3; L. 1981, ch. 695, §§1, 2; L. 1984, ch. 790, §2; L. 1985, ch. 809, §6; L. 1986, ch. 884, §§1 to 4; L. 1986, ch. 892, §§2 to 4; L. 1987, ch. 815, §§6, 7; L. 1989, ch. 567, §§4, 5; L. 1990, ch. 818, §§4, 5; L. 1992, ch. 41, §§139, 140; L. 1992, ch. 415, §§1, 2; L. 1993, ch. 59, §9; L. 1993, ch. 354, §2; L. 1994, ch. 170, §§359, 360; L. 1997, ch. 398, §§4, 5, effective October 1, 1998; L. 1997, ch. 398, §141,

effective January 1, 1998; L. 1997, ch. 436, pt. B, §§105, 106, effective August 20, 1997; L. 1998, ch. 214, §56, effective November 4, 1998; L. 1998, ch. 393, §2, effective July 22, 1998; L. 1999, ch. 275, §2, effective September 18, 1999.)

3. Meaning of "Equitable" Distribution

Many states, in adopting equitable distribution, followed the approach of UMDA §307. UMDA §307(a) provides that the court shall divide marital property in "just proportions" according to certain factors. Alternative A of UMDA's revised §307 directs an "equitable" apportionment according to various factors.

Community property principles (applicable in the nine community property states), explicitly recognize marriage as a partnership and give each spouse an undivided one-half interest in property acquired by spousal labor during the marriage. Most, but not all, community property states apply a rule or presumption of equal division at divorce. See, e.g., Putterman v. Putterman, 939 P.2d 1047 (Nev. 1997) (equal division absent "compelling reason"). (Note that an equal division contemplates equality in value, not dividing each asset in half.)

The ALI Principles dictate a presumption of equal division of marital property in §4.09. This approach disregards fault, in part to achieve predictability and facilitate settlement. Like UMDA, however, the ALI Principles in §4.10 include an exception for financial misconduct involving marital assets. Unlike other marital misconduct, financial misconduct can be predictably measured, for example, one spouse's gift of $20,000 in marital property to a lover. Under §4.10, the misconduct must occur within a particular time period before serving the dissolution petition, specified in a rule of statewide application. The ALI Principles are set forth in Part IV *infra*.

The New York equitable distribution statute provides that marital property shall be distributed "equitably between the parties, considering the circumstances of the case and of the respective parties" (DRL §236(B)(5)(c)). The law does not require that marital property be divided absolutely equally. Schiffmacher v. Schiffmacher, 801 N.Y.S.2d 848 (App. Div. 2005) (holding that lower court properly considered statutory factors despite awarding wife 70 percent of value of marital savings and investment accounts, and only 20 percent of husband's increased income due to his acquisition of advanced degree).

According to Practice Commentary to DRL §236, when the state legislature was considering the equitable distribution law, women's groups expressed concern that the proposed law vested too much discretion in the courts and preferred an *equal* division for that reason. Although the legislature rejected such a proposal, the legislative record reflects an intent for courts to direct an equal distribution unless circumstances dictate otherwise. The court must set forth the factors considered and the reasoning behind its determination of equitable distribution. Smith v. Smith, 778 N.Y.S.2d 188 (App. Div. 2004). However, the court is not required specifically to cite those factors when the court's factual findings otherwise adequately convey that the relevant factors were considered. Snow v. Snow, 788 N.Y.S.2d 435, 437 (App. Div. 2005). See also Scheinkman, Practice Commentaries (following DRL §236), at C236B:24 (Marital Property to be Distributed "Equitably"). In long-term marriages, courts recognize that the distribution should be as equal as possible. Lipovsky v. Lipovsky, 706 N.Y.S.2d 185, 187 (App. Div. 2000) (holding that in a marriage of long duration where both parties had made significant contributions, the trial court properly made the division of the marital assets as equal as possible).

Domestic Relations Act

§236. Equitable Distribution Law: special controlling provisions

. . .

PART B

NEW ACTIONS OR PROCEEDINGS

. . .

5. Disposition of property in certain matrimonial actions. a. Except where the parties have provided in an agreement for the disposition of their property pursuant to subdivision three of this part, the court, in an action wherein all or part of the relief granted is divorce, or the dissolution, annulment or declaration of the nullity of a marriage, and in proceedings to obtain a distribution of marital property following a foreign judgment of divorce, shall determine the respective rights of the parties in their separate or marital property, and shall provide for the disposition thereof in the final judgment.

b. Separate property shall remain such.

c. Marital property shall be distributed equitably between the parties, considering the circumstances of the case and of the respective parties.

. . .

(L. 1962, ch. 313, §10; L. 1963, ch. 685, §6; L. 1968, ch. 699, §1; L. 1980, ch. 281, §9; L. 1980, ch. 645, §§2, 3; L. 1981, ch. 695, §§1, 2; L. 1984, ch. 790, §2; L. 1985, ch. 809, §6; L. 1986, ch. 884, §§1 to 4; L. 1986, ch. 892, §§2 to 4; L. 1987, ch. 815, §§6, 7; L. 1989, ch. 567, §§4, 5; L. 1990, ch. 818, §§4, 5; L. 1992, ch. 41, §§139, 140; L. 1992, ch. 415, §§1, 2; L. 1993, ch. 59, §9; L. 1993, ch. 354, §2; L. 1994, ch. 170, §§359, 360; L. 1997, ch. 398, §§4, 5, effective October 1, 1998; L. 1997, ch. 398, §141, effective January 1, 1998; L. 1997, ch. 436, pt. B, §§105, 106, effective August 20, 1997; L. 1998, ch. 214, §56, effective November 4, 1998; L. 1998, ch. 393, §2, effective July 22, 1998; L. 1999, ch. 275, §2, effective September 18, 1999.)

4. Form of Relief: Distributive Awards

New York courts may make property distributions and/or distributive awards. According to the Equitable Distribution Law, a distributive award is a payment (or payments) made "in lieu of or to supplement, facilitate or effectuate the division or distribution of property" (DRL §236(B)(1)(b)). Courts award distributive awards when it may be "impracticable or burdensome" (DRL §236(B)(5)(e)) to divide a marital asset, for example, when an asset consists of a spouse's business interest, or when the distribution of an interest (i.e., "in a business, corporation, or profession") would be contrary to law. See *Lipovsky*, *supra*, at 187 (directing distributive award of husband's medical practice). Distributive awards may be court-ordered or pursuant to marital agreements (DRL §236(B)(1)(b)). The awards are payable in a lump sum or over a period of time in fixed amounts.

The statute also attempts to ensure that distributive awards not be considered as spousal support for income tax purposes (DRL §236(B)(1)(b). Nonetheless, the Internal Revenue Service may examine whether a particular award constitutes income rather than a property distribution. Scheinkman, Practice Commentaries, *supra*, at C236B:9 (Distributive Awards).

Domestic Relations Act

§236. Equitable Distribution Law: special controlling provisions

. . .

PART B

NEW ACTIONS OR PROCEEDINGS

Maintenance and distributive award. 1. Definitions. Whenever used in this part, the following terms shall have the respective meanings hereinafter set forth or indicated:

. . .

b. The term "distributive award" shall mean payments provided for in a valid agreement between the parties or awarded by the court, in lieu of or to supplement, facilitate or effectuate the division or distribution of property where authorized in a matrimonial action, and payable either in a lump sum or over a period of time in fixed amounts. Distributive awards shall not include payments which are treated as ordinary income to the recipient under the provisions of the United States Internal Revenue Code.

. . .

5. Disposition of property in certain matrimonial actions.

. . .

e. In any action in which the court shall determine that an equitable distribution is appropriate but would be impractical or burdensome or where the distribution of an interest in a business, corporation or profession would be contrary to law, the court in lieu of such equitable distribution shall make a distributive award in order to achieve equity between the parties. The court in its discretion, also may make a distributive award to supplement, facilitate or effectuate a distribution of marital property.

. . .

(L. 1962, ch. 313, §10; L. 1963, ch. 685, §6; L. 1968, ch. 699, §1; L. 1980, ch. 281, §9; L. 1980, ch. 645, §§2, 3; L. 1981, ch. 695, §§1, 2; L. 1984, ch. 790, §2; L. 1985, ch. 809, §6; L. 1986, ch. 884, §§1 to 4; L. 1986, ch. 892, §§2 to 4; L. 1987, ch. 815, §§6, 7; L. 1989, ch. 567, §§4, 5; L. 1990, ch. 818, §§4, 5; L. 1992, ch. 41, §§139, 140; L. 1992, ch. 415, §§1, 2; L. 1993, ch. 59, §9; L. 1993, ch. 354, §2; L. 1994, ch. 170, §§359, 360; L. 1997, ch. 398, §§4, 5, effective October 1, 1998; L. 1997, ch. 398, §141, effective January 1, 1998; L. 1997, ch. 436, pt. B, §§105, 106, effective August 20, 1997; L. 1998, ch. 214, §56, effective November 4, 1998; L. 1998, ch. 393, §2, effective July 22, 1998; L. 1999, ch. 275, §2, effective September 18, 1999.)

5. Date of Valuation

New York's Equitable Distribution statute does not provide a valuation date for the court to use to determine when marital property is to be valued. The selection of a valuation date is within the discretion of the court and dependent upon the circumstances. According to a 1986 amendment to the Code, the valuation date shall be set by the court "as soon as practicable" after commencement of the matrimonial action, and may be set at "anytime from the date of commencement of the action to the date of trial" (DRL §236(B)(4)(b)). Scheinkman, Practice Commentaries, *supra*, at C236B:26 (Valuation Dates and Proof).

The issue of the date for the valuation of marital property is "one of the most difficult problems created by the Equitable Distribution Law," according to the court in Patelunas v. Patelunas, 527 N.Y.S.2d 325, 326 (App. Div. 1988). Generally, the valuation of marital property is fixed at the time of the commencement of the matrimonial action, unless doing so would be patently inequitable. Lord v. Lord, 508 N.Y.S.2d 676 (App. Div. 1986). For a case which applied the "patently inequitable exception," see *Patelunas*, *supra*, at 326 (holding that in the case of valuation of the marital residence, where six years elapsed between the commencement of the action and trial, accompanied by a six-fold increase in the net value of the asset during that period, the utilization of the commencement-of-the-action date for valuation was patently inequitable).

§236. Equitable Distribution Law: special controlling provisions

. . .

PART B

NEW ACTIONS OR PROCEEDINGS

. . .

4. Compulsory financial disclosure.

. . .

b. As soon as practicable after a matrimonial action has been commenced, the court shall set the date or dates the parties shall use for the valuation of each asset. The valuation date or dates may be anytime from the date of commencement of the action to the date of trial.

. . .

(L. 1962, ch. 313, §10; L. 1963, ch. 685, §6; L. 1968, ch. 699, §1; L. 1980, ch. 281, §9; L. 1980, ch. 645, §§2, 3; L. 1981, ch. 695, §§1, 2; L. 1984, ch. 790, §2; L. 1985, ch. 809, §6; L. 1986, ch. 884, §§1 to 4; L. 1986, ch. 892, §§2 to 4; L. 1987, ch. 815, §§6, 7; L. 1989, ch. 567, §§4, 5; L. 1990, ch. 818, §§4, 5; L. 1992, ch. 41, §§139, 140; L. 1992, ch. 415, §§1, 2; L. 1993, ch. 59, §9; L. 1993, ch. 354, §2; L. 1994, ch. 170, §§359, 360; L. 1997, ch. 398, §§4, 5, effective October 1, 1998; L. 1997, ch. 398, §141, effective January 1, 1998; L. 1997, ch. 436, pt. B, §§105, 106, effective August 20, 1997; L. 1998, ch. 214, §56, effective November 4, 1998; L. 1998, ch. 393, §2,

effective July 22, 1998; L. 1999, ch. 275, §2, effective September 18, 1999.)

B. Classification of Property: Marital Property vs. Separate Property

Two marital property regimes exist in the United States: (1) the common law system ("title theory") and (2) the community property system. In the common law system (followed by most jurisdictions), the husband and wife own all property separately. During the marriage, all property (including earnings, gifts, inheritances) belongs to the spouse who acquires it, unless that spouse chooses another form of ownership. Homer H. Clark, Jr., Law of Domestic Relations in the United States 591 (2d. 1988). Traditionally, the property was divided upon divorce based on these terms of ownership. *Id.* at 591-594. Beginning in the 1980s, in a wave of divorce law reform initiated by the adoption of no fault, most states abandoned the title system in favor of a system of "equitable distribution."

In contrast, the community property system is characterized by the concept of a community of ownership under which the spouses are partners. For this reason, all assets acquired during the marriage through the use of the time, energy, and skill of either spouse are community property (e.g., Cal. Fam. Code §760). All earned assets are equally owned by each spouse, as long as the assets were earned during marriage. Thus, even if one spouse is a homemaker, the wages of the other spouse are equally owned by both spouses and may be equally divided at dissolution. There are nine community property states (Arizona, California, Idaho, Louisiana, Nevada, New Mexico, Texas, Washington, and Wisconsin). See generally William W. DeFuniak & Michael J. Vaughn, Principles of Community Property 114-115, 127-128 (2d ed. 1971). In addition, the community property system respects each spouse's separate property (e.g., Cal. Fam. Code §752). Property that each person brought to the marriage as separate property, remains the property of that spouse. Property acquired by a spouse during the marriage by means of gift or inheritance (as well as the rents, issues, and profits of separate property) also constitutes separate property (e.g., Cal. Fam. Code §770).

Laws following an equitable distribution approach bring common law states much closer to community property states in the treatment of property after divorce. That is, equitable distribution laws in common law states create a "deferred community property" system, with the concept of marital property becoming effective upon divorce. Brett R. Turner, Equitable Distribution of Property §1.02 (2d ed. 1994 & Supp. 2000).

New York previously relied on DRL §50 to empower women to maintain separate property. DeFrance v. Defrance, 710 N.Y.S.2d (App. Div. 2000). However, this policy was partially preempted by the adoption of major divorce reform legislation in 1980. Commonly referred to as the "Equitable Distribution Law," DRL §236, the New York state legislation changed the standards governing the distribution of property at divorce. Before the statute, New York adhered to the "title theory" (discussed above). Upon divorce, when courts assigned property to the spouse who held legal title, homemakers who made nonmonetary contributions to the marriage were at a serious disadvantage.

The Equitable Distribution Law reflected a view of marriage as an economic partnership. However, within a few years of its adoption, several shortcomings of the partnership theory surfaced. Hearings before the State Senate and Assembly Judiciary Committees in 1985 revealed that the new legislation actually led to hardship, based on empirical data demonstrating that women and children suffer an immediate decline in their post-divorce standard of living whereas men enjoy an increased standard of living. As a result, the legislature amended the statute in 1986 to provide additional protection to economically dependent spouses. On the history of New York divorce law reform, see Brooke Grossman, Note, The Evolution of Equitable Distribution in New York, 62 N.Y.U. Ann. Surv. Am. L. 607 (2007).

Property (real or personal) may be classified as marital property or separate property based on provisions of the Domestic Relations Law. According to the statute, marital property is defined as "all property acquired by either or both spouses during the marriage and before the execution of a separation agreement or the commencement of a matrimonial action, regardless of the form in which title is held, except as otherwise provided in agreement . . ." (DRL §236(B)(1)(c)). Marital property does not include separate property. *Id.*

Separate property, as defined by the statute, encompasses: (1) property acquired before marriage or property acquired by gift or inheritance from a party other than the spouse; (2) compensation for personal injuries; (3) property acquired in exchange for or the increase in value of separate property, except to the extent that such appreciation is due in part to contributions or efforts of the other spouse; and (4) property described as separate property by the parties' written agreement. DRL §236(B)(1)(d).

Transmutation refers to the right of married persons to change the classification of property from either separate to marital, from marital to separate, or to transfer one spouse's separate property to the other spouse. All transmutations must be made by express written declaration.

A general presumption exists, based on case law, that all property acquired during a marriage is marital property (provided that it is acquired before the commencement of the matrimonial action and not the subject of a separation agreement). This presumption is rebuttable. A spouse who wants to rebut the pro-marital property presumption must prove that the disputed asset is separate property, for example, by providing proof that the asset was a gift or an inheritance acquired during the marriage. See, e.g., Pelletier v. Pelletier, 662 N.Y.S.2d 64 (App. Div. 1997) (holding that evidence that property transferred to wife from her cousin during marriage was wife's separate property and that all funds used to acquire other real property, to which title was taken solely in wife's name and originated from wife's premarital account, was sufficient to establish that property was wife's separate property). The presumption places the burden of producing evidence on the challenging party who is also the party most likely to have the evidence.

The pro-marital property presumption also applies to commingled funds, i.e., when the spouses mix assets, such as by depositing separate property funds into a joint account or placing separate property in joint names. Commingling results in a rebuttable presumption of gift (to the marital community). Upon dissolution in such cases, the court will give the spouse who contributed the separate property a credit for the amount of funds he or she contributed and then divide the remaining funds (or the appreciated funds). See, e.g., Murphy v. Murphy, 772 N.Y.S.2d 355 (App. Div. 2004) (holding that husband was entitled to a credit of $207,000 for the value of separate property contributed to the creation of a marital residence aquired during the marriage); Zurner v. Zurner, 624 N.Y.S.2d 301 (App. Div. 1995) (holding that the trial court properly credited husband for his separate contribution toward the marital residence but not for the appreciated value of his separate property interest, where both husband and wife contributed physically and financially to the marital household).

DRL §236, Part B, is set forth below in full, along with DRL §50. Various subsections of DRL §236 are repeated throughout this chapter *infra*.

Domestic Relations Act

§236. Equitable Distribution Law: special controlling provisions

Except as otherwise expressly provided in this section, the provisions of part A shall be controlling with respect to any action or proceeding commenced prior to the date on which the provisions of this section as amended become effective [July 19, 1980] and the provisions of part B shall be controlling with respect to any action or proceeding commenced on or after such effective date.

Any reference to this section or the provisions hereof in any action, proceeding, judgment, order, rule or agreement shall be deemed and construed to refer to either the provisions of part A or part B respectively and exclusively, determined as provided in this paragraph any inconsistent provision of law notwithstanding.

. . .

PART B

NEW ACTIONS OR PROCEEDINGS

Maintenance and distributive award.

1. Definitions. Whenever used in this part, the following terms shall have the respective meanings hereinafter set forth or indicated:

a. The term "maintenance" shall mean payments provided for in a valid agreement between the parties or awarded by the court in accordance with the provisions of subdivision six of this part, to be paid at fixed intervals for a definite or indefinite period of time, but an award of maintenance shall terminate upon the death of either party or upon the recipient's valid or invalid marriage, or upon modification pursuant to paragraph (b) of subdivision nine of section two hundred thirty-six of this part or section two hundred forty-eight of this chapter.

b. The term "distributive award" shall mean payments provided for in a valid agreement between the parties or awarded by the court, in lieu of or to supplement, facilitate or effectuate the division or distribution of property where authorized in a matrimonial action, and payable either in a lump sum or over a period of time in fixed amounts. Distributive awards shall not include payments which are treated as ordinary income to the recipient under the provisions of the United States Internal Revenue Code.

c. The term "marital property" shall mean all property acquired by either or both spouses during the marriage and before the execution of a separation agreement or the commencement of a matrimonial action, regardless of the form in which title is held, except as otherwise provided in agreement pursuant to subdivision three of this part. Marital property shall not include separate property as hereinafter defined.

d. The term separate property shall mean:

(1) property acquired before marriage or property acquired by bequest, devise, or descent, or gift from a party other than the spouse;

(2) compensation for personal injuries;

(3) property acquired in exchange for or the increase in value of separate property, except to the extent that such appreciation is due in part to the contributions or efforts of the other spouse;

(4) property described as separate property by written agreement of the parties pursuant to subdivision three of this part.

e. The term "custodial parent" shall mean a parent to whom custody of a child or children is granted by a valid agreement between the parties or by an order or decree of a court.

f. The term "child support" shall mean a sum paid pursuant to court order or decree by either or both parents or pursuant to a valid agreement between the parties for care, maintenance and education of any unemancipated child under the age of twenty-one years.

2. Matrimonial actions. Except as provided in subdivision five of this part, the provisions of this part shall be applicable to actions for an annulment or dissolution of a marriage, for a divorce, for a separation, for a declaration of the nullity of a void marriage, for a declaration of the validity or nullity of a foreign judgment of divorce, for a declaration of the validity or nullity of a marriage, and to proceedings to obtain maintenance or a distribution of marital property following a foreign judgment of divorce, commenced on and after the effective date of this part. Any application which seeks a modification of a judgment, order or decree made in an action commenced prior to the effective date of this part shall be heard and determined in accordance with the provisions of part A of this section.

3. Agreement of the parties. An agreement by the parties, made before or during the marriage, shall be valid and enforceable in a matrimonial action if such agreement is in writing, subscribed by the parties, and acknowledged or proven in the manner required to entitle a deed to be recorded. Such an agreement may include

(1) a contract to make a testamentary provision of any kind, or a waiver of any right to elect against the provisions of a will;

(2) provision for the ownership, division or distribution of separate and marital property;

(3) provision for the amount and duration of maintenance or other terms and conditions of the marriage relationship, subject to the provisions of section 5-311 of the general obligations law, and provided that such terms were fair and reasonable at the time of the making of the agreement and are not unconscionable at the time of entry of final judgment; and

(4) provision for the custody, care, education and maintenance of any child of the parties, subject to the provisions of section two hundred forty of this chapter. Nothing in this subdivision shall be deemed to affect the validity of any agreement made prior to the effective date of this subdivision.

4. Compulsory financial disclosure.

a. In all matrimonial actions and proceedings in which alimony, maintenance or support is in issue, there shall be compulsory disclosure by both parties of their respective financial states. No showing of special circumstances shall be required before such disclosure is ordered. A sworn statement of net worth shall be provided upon receipt of a notice in writing demanding the same, within twenty days after the receipt thereof. In the event said statement is not demanded, it shall be filed with the clerk of the court by each party, within ten days after joinder of issue, in the court in which the proceeding is pending. As used in this part, the term "net worth" shall mean the amount by which total assets including income exceed total liabilities including fixed financial obligations. It shall include all income and assets of whatsoever kind and nature and wherever situated and shall include a list of all assets transferred in any manner during the preceding three years, or the length of the marriage, whichever is shorter; provided, however that transfers in the routine course of business which resulted in an exchange of assets of substantially equivalent value need not be specifically disclosed where such assets are otherwise identified in the statement of net worth. All such sworn statements of net worth shall be accompanied by a current and representative paycheck stub and the most recently filed state and federal income tax returns including a copy of the W-2(s) wage and tax statement(s) submitted with the returns. In addition, both parties shall provide information relating to any and all group health plans available to them for the provision of care or other medical benefits by insurance or otherwise for the benefit of the child or children for whom support is sought, including all such information as may be required to be included in a qualified medical child support order as defined in section six hundred nine of the employee retirement income security act of 1974 (29 USC 1169) including, but not limited to:

(i) the name and last known mailing address of each party and of each dependent to be covered by the order;

(ii) the identification and a description of each group health plan available for the benefit or coverage of the disclosing party and the child or children for whom support is sought;

(iii) a detailed description of the type of coverage available from each group health plan for the potential benefit of each such dependent;

(iv) the identification of the plan administrator for each such group health plan and the address of such administrator;

(v) the identification numbers for each such group health plan; and

(vi) such other information as may be required by the court. Noncompliance shall be punishable by any or all of the penalties prescribed in section thirty-one hundred twenty-six of the civil practice law and rules, in examination before or during trial.

b. As soon as practicable after a matrimonial action has been commenced, the court shall set the date or dates the parties shall use for the valuation of each asset. The valuation date or dates may be anytime from the date of commencement of the action to the date of trial.

5. Disposition of property in certain matrimonial actions.

a. Except where the parties have provided in an agreement for the disposition of their property pursuant to subdivision three of this part, the court, in an action wherein all or part of the relief granted is divorce, or the dissolution, annulment or declaration of the nullity of a marriage, and in proceedings to obtain a distribution of marital property following a foreign judgment of divorce, shall determine the respective rights of the parties in their separate or marital property, and shall provide for the disposition thereof in the final judgment.

b. Separate property shall remain such.

c. Marital property shall be distributed equitably between the parties, considering the circumstances of the case and of the respective parties.

d. In determining an equitable disposition of property under paragraph c, the court shall consider:

(1) the income and property of each party at the time of marriage, and at the time of the commencement of the action;

(2) the duration of the marriage and the age and health of both parties;

(3) the need of a custodial parent to occupy or own the marital residence and to use or own its household effects;

(4) the loss of inheritance and pension rights upon dissolution of the marriage as of the date of dissolution;

(5) any award of maintenance under subdivision six of this part;

(6) any equitable claim to, interest in, or direct or indirect contribution made to the acquisition of such marital property by the party not having title, including joint efforts or expenditures and contributions and services as a spouse, parent, wage earner and homemaker, and to the career or career potential of the other party;

(7) the liquid or non-liquid character of all marital property;

(8) the probable future financial circumstances of each party;

(9) the impossibility or difficulty of evaluating any component asset or any interest in a business, corporation or profession, and the economic desirability of retaining such asset or interest intact and free from any claim or interference by the other party;

(10) the tax consequences to each party;

(11) the wasteful dissipation of assets by either spouse;

(12) any transfer or encumbrance made in contemplation of a matrimonial action without fair consideration;

(13) any other factor which the court shall expressly find to be just and proper.

e. In any action in which the court shall determine that an equitable distribution is appropriate but would be impractical or burdensome or where the distribution of an interest in a business, corporation or profession would be contrary to law, the court in lieu of such equitable distribution shall make a distributive award in order to achieve equity between the parties. The court in its discretion, also may make a distributive award to supplement, facilitate or effectuate a distribution of marital property.

f. In addition to the disposition of property as set forth above, the court may make such order regarding the use and occupancy of the marital home and its household effects as provided in section two hundred thirty-four of this chapter, without regard to the form of ownership of such property.

g. In any decision made pursuant to this subdivision, the court shall set forth the factors it considered and the reasons for its decision and such may not be waived by either party or counsel.

h. In any decision made pursuant to this subdivision the court shall, where appropriate, consider the effect of a barrier to remarriage, as defined in subdivision six of section two hundred fifty-three of this article, on the factors enumerated in paragraph d of this subdivision.

6. Maintenance.

a. Except where the parties have entered into an agreement pursuant to subdivision three of this part providing for maintenance, in any matrimonial action the court may order temporary maintenance or maintenance in such amount as justice requires, having regard for the standard of living of the parties established during the marriage, whether the party in whose favor maintenance is granted lacks sufficient property and income to provide for his or her reasonable needs and whether the other party has sufficient property or income to provide for the reasonable needs of the other and the circumstances of the case and of the respective parties. Such order shall be effective as of the date of the application therefor, and any retroactive amount of maintenance due shall be paid in one sum or periodic sums, as the court shall direct, taking into account any amount of temporary maintenance which has been paid. In determining the amount and duration of maintenance the court shall consider:

(1) the income and property of the respective parties including marital property distributed pursuant to subdivision five of this part;

(2) the duration of the marriage and the age and health of both parties;

(3) the present and future earning capacity of both parties;

(4) the ability of the party seeking maintenance to become self-supporting and, if applicable, the period of time and training necessary therefor;

(5) reduced or lost lifetime earning capacity of the party seeking maintenance as a result of having foregone or delayed education, training, employment, or career opportunities during the marriage;

(6) the presence of children of the marriage in the respective homes of the parties;

(7) the tax consequences to each party;

(8) contributions and services of the party seeking maintenance as a spouse, parent, wage earner and homemaker, and to the career or career potential of the other party;

(9) the wasteful dissipation of marital property by either spouse;

(10) any transfer or encumbrance made in contemplation of a matrimonial action without fair consideration; and

(11) any other factor which the court shall expressly find to be just and proper.

b. In any decision made pursuant to this subdivision, the court shall set forth the factors it considered and the reasons for its decision and such may not be waived by either party or counsel.

c. The court may award permanent maintenance, but an award of maintenance shall terminate upon the death of either party or upon the recipient's valid or invalid marriage, or upon modification pursuant to paragraph (b) of subdivision nine of section two hundred thirty-six of this part or section two hundred forty-eight of this chapter.

d. In any decision made pursuant to this subdivision the court shall, where appropriate, consider the effect of a barrier to remarriage, as defined in subdivision six of section two hundred fifty-three of this article, on the factors enumerated in paragraph a of this subdivision.

. . .

8. Special relief in matrimonial actions.

a. In any matrimonial action the court may order a party to purchase, maintain or assign a policy of insurance providing benefits for health and hospital care and related services for either spouse or children of the marriage not to exceed such period of time as such party shall be obligated to provide maintenance, child support or make payments of a distributive award. The court may also order a party to purchase, maintain or assign a policy of accident insurance or insurance on the life of either spouse, and to designate in the case of life insurance, either spouse or children of the marriage, or in the case of accident insurance, the insured spouse as irrevocable beneficiaries during a period of time fixed by the court. The obligation to provide such insurance shall cease upon the termination of the spouse's duty to provide maintenance, child support or a distributive award. A copy of such order shall be served, by registered mail, on the home office of the insurer specifying the name and mailing address of the spouse or children, provided that failure to so serve the insurer shall not effect the validity of the order.

b. In any action where the court has ordered temporary maintenance, maintenance, distributive award or child support, the court may direct that a payment be made directly to the other spouse or a third person for real and personal property and services furnished to the other spouse, or for the rental or mortgage amortization or interest payments, insurances, taxes, repairs or other carrying charges on premises occupied by the other spouse, or for both payments to the other spouse and to such third persons. Such direction may be made notwithstanding that the parties continue to reside in the same abode and notwithstanding that the court refuses to grant the relief requested by the other spouse.

c. Any order or judgment made as in this section provided may combine any amount payable to either spouse under this section with any amount payable to such spouse as child support or under section two hundred forty of this chapter.

9. Enforcement and modification of orders and judgments in matrimonial actions.

a. All orders or judgments entered in matrimonial actions shall be enforceable pursuant to section fifty-two hundred forty-one or fifty-two hundred forty-two of the civil practice law and rules, or in any other manner provided by law. Orders or judgments for child support, alimony and maintenance shall also be enforceable pursuant to article fifty-two of the civil practice law and rules upon a debtor's default as such term is defined in paragraph seven of subdivision (a) of section fifty-two hundred forty-one of the civil practice law and rules. The establishment of a default shall be subject to the procedures established for the determination of a mistake of fact for income executions pursuant to subdivision (e) of section fifty-two hundred forty-one of the civil practice law and rules. For the purposes of enforcement of child support orders or combined spousal and child support orders pursuant to section five thousand two hundred forty-one of the civil practice law and rules, a "default" shall be deemed to include amounts arising from retroactive support. The court may, and if a party shall fail or refuse to pay maintenance, distributive award or child support the court shall, upon notice and an opportunity to the defaulting party to be heard, require the party to furnish a surety, or the sequestering and sale of assets for the purpose of enforcing any award for maintenance, distributive award or child support and for the payment of reasonable and necessary attorney's fees and disbursements.

b. Upon application by either party, the court may annul or modify any prior order or judgment as to maintenance or child support, upon a showing of the recipient's inability to be self-supporting or a substantial change in circumstance or termination of child support awarded pursuant to section two hundred forty of this article, including financial hardship. Where, after the effective date of this part, a separation agreement remains in force no modification of a prior order or judgment incorporating the terms of said agreement shall be made as to maintenance without a showing of extreme hardship on either party, in which event the judgment or order as modified shall supersede the terms of the prior agreement and judgment for such period of time and under such circumstances as the court determines. Provided, however, that no modification or annulment shall reduce or annul any arrears of child support which have accrued prior to the date of application to annul or modify any prior order or judgment as to child support. The court shall not reduce or annul any arrears of maintenance which have been reduced to final judgment pursuant to section two hundred forty-four of this chapter. No other arrears of maintenance which have accrued prior to the making of such application shall be subject to modification or annulment unless the defaulting party shows good cause for failure to make application for relief from the judgment or order directing such payment prior to the accrual of such arrears and the facts and circumstances constituting good cause are set forth in a written memorandum of decision. Such modification may increase maintenance or child support nunc pro tunc as of the date of application based on newly discovered evidence. Any retroactive amount of maintenance, or child support due shall, except as provided for herein, be paid in one sum or periodic sums, as the court directs, taking into account any temporary or partial payments which have been made. Any retroactive amount of child support due shall be support arrears/past due support. In addition, such retroactive child support shall be enforceable in any manner provided by law including, but not limited to, an execution for support enforcement pursuant to subdivision (b) of section fifty-two hundred forty-one of the civil practice law and rules. When a child receiving support is a public assistance recipient, or the order of support is being enforced or is to be enforced pursuant to section one hundred eleven-g of the social services law, the court shall establish the amount of retroactive child support and notify the parties that such amount shall be enforced by the support collection unit pursuant to an execution for support enforcement as provided for in subdivision (b) of section fifty-two hundred forty-one of the civil practice law and rules, or in such periodic payments as would have been authorized had such an execution been issued. In such case, the court shall not direct the schedule of repayment of retroactive support. The provisions of this subdivision shall not apply to a separation agreement made prior to the effective date of this part.

c. Notwithstanding any other provision of law, any written application or motion to the court for the modification or enforcement of a child support or combined maintenance and child support order for persons not in receipt of family assistance must contain either a request for child support enforcement services which would authorize the collection of the support obligation by the immediate issuance of an income execution for support enforcement as provided for by this chapter, completed in the manner specified in section one hundred eleven-g of the social services law; or a statement that the applicant has applied for or is in receipt of such services; or a statement that the applicant knows of the availability of such services, has declined them at this time and where support enforcement services pursuant to section one hundred eleven-g of the social services law have been declined that the applicant understands that an income deduction order may be issued pursuant to subdivision (c) of section five thousand two hundred forty-two of the civil practice law and rules without other child support enforcement services and that payment of an administrative fee may be required. The court shall provide a copy of any such request for child support enforcement services to the support collection unit of the appropriate social services district any time it directs payments to be made to such support collection unit. Additionally, the copy of such request shall be accompanied by the name, address and social security number of the parties; the date and place of the parties' marriage; the name and date of birth of the child or children; and the name and address of the employers and income payors of the party ordered to pay child support to the other party. Unless the party receiving child support or combined maintenance and child support has applied for or is receiving such services, the court shall not direct such payments to be made to the support collection unit, as established in section one hundred eleven-h of the social services law.

d. The court shall direct that a copy of any child support or combined child and spousal support order issued by the court on or after the first day of October, nineteen hundred ninety-eight, in any proceeding under this section be provided promptly to the state case registry established pursuant to subdivision four-a of section one hundred eleven-b of the social services law.

(L. 1962, ch. 313, §10; L. 1963, ch. 685, §6; L. 1968, ch. 699, §1; L. 1980, ch. 281, §9; L. 1980, ch. 645, §§2, 3; L. 1981, ch. 695, §§1, 2; L. 1984, ch. 790, §2; L. 1985, ch. 809, §6; L. 1986, ch. 884, §§1 to 4; L. 1986, ch. 892, §§2 to 4; L. 1987, ch. 815, §§6, 7; L. 1989, ch. 567, §§4, 5; L. 1990, ch. 818, §§4, 5; L. 1992, ch. 41, §§139, 140; L. 1992, ch. 415, §§1, 2; L. 1993, ch. 59, §9; L. 1993, ch. 354, §2; L. 1994, ch. 170, §§359, 360; L. 1997, ch. 398, §§4, 5, effective October 1, 1998; L. 1997, ch. 398, §141, effective January 1, 1998; L. 1997, ch. 436, pt. B, §§105, 106, effective August 20, 1997; L. 1998, ch. 214, §56, effective November 4, 1998; L. 1998, ch. 393, §2, effective July 22, 1998; L. 1999, ch. 275, §2, effective September 18, 1999.)

§50. Property of married women

Property, real or personal, now owned by a married woman, or hereafter owned by a woman at the time of her marriage, or acquired by her as prescribed in this chapter, and the rents, issues, proceeds and profits thereof, shall continue to be her sole and separate property as if she were unmarried, and shall not be subject to her husband's control or disposal nor liable for his debts.

(L. 1848, ch. 200, §§1, 2; L. 1849, ch. 375, §1; L. 1860. ch. 90, §90, §1; L. 1962, ch. 172).

C. Legislative Factors in Achieving a Fair Distribution

The Uniform Marriage and Divorce Act, as explained above, was influential in the movement to adopt equitable distribution. UMDA §307 limits the relevant factors that courts should consider in making a "just" division of marital property. UMDA §307 provides that the court shall divide the marital property without regard to fault in just proportions considering all relevant factors, including:

(1) contributions of each spouse to acquisition of the marital property, including contribution of a spouse as homemaker;

(2) value of the property set apart to each spouse;

(3) duration of the marriage; and

(4) economic circumstances of each spouse when the division of property is to become effective, including the desirability of awarding the family home or the right to live therein for reasonable periods to the spouse having custody of any children. 9A U.L.A. (pt. I) 289-290 (1998).

Professor Martha Fineman categorizes several factors that are listed by legislatures and courts to guide equitable division either as "contribution" or as "need." Martha I. Fineman, Societal Factors Affecting the Creation of Legal Rules for Distribution of Property of Divorce, 23 Fam. L.Q. 279 (1989). She explains that the co-existence of these factors reflects "the tension between two incompatible contemporary images of marriage — the egalitarian partnership and the dependency models." *Id.* at 290.

New York's Equitable Distribution Statute sets forth 13 factors that courts must consider in determining an equitable distribution of the marital property (DRL §236(B)(5)(d)(1)-(13)). The statute, as originally enacted, listed only nine factors; however, additional factors were added in 1986 (L. 1986, ch. 884, §3). Scheinkman, Practice Commentaries, *supra*, at 236B:25 (Equitable Distribution — The Legislative Factors).

Many of the statutory guidelines in the New York statute clearly reflect the influence of UMDA, such as: the duration of marriage (factor 2), the value of property of each spouse (factor 1), the contributions of the spouses, including their nonmonetary contributions (factor 6), and the economic circumstances of each spouse at time of dissolution, including occupancy and possession of family home (factors 1, 3, and 8).

When UMDA was approved in 1970, its provisions regarding deferral of the sale of the family home were quite innovative. The distribution of marital property often results in the sale of the family home because the marital residence may be the couple's most significant marital asset. That is, if the couple has no asset of comparable value to allocate to the spouse not to be awarded the home, the home must be sold so the proceeds can be shared. Sociologist Lenore Weitman was an early critic of the policy mandating post-dissolution sale of the home, contending that the policy disadvantages children. Lenore J. Weitzman, The Divorce Revolution: The Unexpected Social and Economic Consequences of Divorce 384-387 (1985). In response to such criticisms and influenced by UDMA, many states evidence a reluctance to uproot the children and allow courts to award the family home temporarily to the custodial parent, treating use of the residence as a form of child support. The ALI Principles of the Law of Family Dissolution adhere to this approach, maintaining that child support rules should provide for judicial orders deferring sale of the family home and that a court may make such an order only if it finds that deferral is "economically feasible and would avoid significant detriment to the child." ALI Principles, *supra*, at §3.11.

In addition to the factors influenced by UMDA, the New York statute incorporates several specific factors that UMDA does not cover. These include: the age and health of the parties (factor 2); the income of each party (rather than "the economic circumstances" of the parties) both at the time of the marriage and the matrimonial action (factor 1); loss of inheritance and pension rights (factor 4); awards of maintenance to one spouse (factor 5); the liquidity of the marital property (factor 7); a prediction as to the *future* financial circumstances of the parties (factor 8); the difficulty of evaluating any asset or business interest and the desirability of retaining intact such asset or interest (factor 9); the tax consequences to each party (factor 10); the wasteful dissipation of assets by either spouse (factor 11); or any transfer or encumbrance made in contemplation of a matrimonial action without fair consideration (factor 12). See DRL §236(B)(5)(d)(1)-(13). Finally, the court may consider any other factor that it finds "just and proper" (factor 13). For a discussion of the various statutory factors, see Scheinkman, Practice Commentaries, *supra*, at C236B:27 and C236B:28.

Domestic Relations Act

§236. Equitable Distribution Law: special controlling provisions

. . .

PART B

NEW ACTIONS OR PROCEEDINGS

. . .

5. Disposition of property in certain matrimonial actions.

. . .

c. Marital property shall be distributed equitably between the parties, considering the circumstances of the case and of the respective parties.

d. In determining an equitable disposition of property under paragraph c, the court shall consider:

(1) the income and property of each party at the time of marriage, and at the time of the commencement of the action;

(2) the duration of the marriage and the age and health of both parties;

(3) the need of a custodial parent to occupy or own the marital residence and to use or own its household effects;

(4) the loss of inheritance and pension rights upon dissolution of the marriage as of the date of dissolution;

(5) any award of maintenance under subdivision six of this part;

(6) any equitable claim to, interest in, or direct or indirect contribution made to the acquisition of such marital property by the party not having title, including joint efforts or expenditures and contributions and services as a spouse, parent, wage earner and homemaker, and to the career or career potential of the other party;

(7) the liquid or non-liquid character of all marital property;

(8) the probable future financial circumstances of each party;

(9) the impossibility or difficulty of evaluating any component asset or any interest in a business, corporation or profession, and the economic desirability of retaining such asset or interest intact and free from any claim or interference by the other party;

(10) the tax consequences to each party;

(11) the wasteful dissipation of assets by either spouse;

(12) any transfer or encumbrance made in contemplation of a matrimonial action without fair consideration;

(13) any other factor which the court shall expressly find to be just and proper.

. . .

(L. 1962, ch. 313, §10; L. 1963, ch. 685, §6; L. 1968, ch. 699, §1; L. 1980, ch. 281, §9; L. 1980, ch. 645, §§2, 3; L. 1981, ch. 695, §§1, 2; L. 1984, ch. 790, §2; L. 1985, ch. 809, §6; L. 1986, ch. 884, §§1 to 4; L. 1986, ch. 892, §§2 to 4; L. 1987, ch. 815, §§6, 7; L. 1989, ch. 567, §§4, 5; L. 1990, ch. 818, §§4, 5; L. 1992, ch. 41, §§139, 140; L. 1992, ch. 415, §§1, 2; L. 1993, ch. 59, §9; L. 1993, ch. 354, §2; L. 1994, ch. 170, §§359, 360; L. 1997, ch. 398, §§4, 5, effective October 1, 1998; L. 1997, ch. 398, §141, effective January 1, 1998; L. 1997, ch. 436, pt. B, §§105, 106, effective August 20, 1997; L. 1998, ch. 214, §56, effective November 4, 1998; L. 1998, ch. 393, §2, effective July 22, 1998; L. 1999, ch. 275, §2, effective September 18, 1999.)

D. Special Problems in Property Distribution

1. Pensions and Employee Benefits

Pension and employee benefits plans increasingly play an important role in the division of the property at dissolution. A pension plan is a mechanism by which an employer facilitates an employee's accumulation of savings for retirement. Pension and employee benefits (in addition to the marital home) constitute the most significant marital asset for many couples.

According to the majority rule, nonvested as well as vested (matured) pensions are marital property subject to division upon dissolution. See, e.g., Janssen v. Janssen, 331 N.W.2d 752 (Minn. 1983); Majauskas v. Majauskas, 463 N.E.2d 15 (N.Y. 1984); Grode v. Grode, 543 N.W.2d 795 (S.D. 1996); Cohen v. Cohen, 937 S.W.2d 823 (Tenn. 1996).

The California case In re Marriage of Brown, 544 P.2d 561 (Cal. 1976), established the majority rule. In *Brown*, a couple divorced after a 24-year marriage, but 3 years prior to the husband's eligibility for retirement. The husband argued that his nonvested pension rights were not divisible as a community asset. In ruling for the wife, *Brown* overturned a long line of decisions holding that nonvested pension rights were a "mere expectancy" not subject to division. Justice Tobriner described pension benefits as a form of "deferred compensation" based on the employment contract, a form of property. *Id.* at 565. *Brown* also noted the unfairness of classifying unvested pensions as separate property. Spousal support cannot rectify this unfairness, Tobriner explained, because the spouse "should not be dependent on the discretion of the court . . . to provide her with the equivalent of what should be hers as a matter of absolute right." *Id.* at 567. Courts now use identical analysis to treat unvested stock options as divisible property. See, e.g., DeJesus v. DeJesus, 687 N.E.2d 1319 (N.Y. 1997); Fisher v. Fisher, 769 A.2d 1165 (Pa. 2001).

New York's Equitable Distribution statute expressly refers to pension rights and provides that one of the factors to be considered by the court in determining an equitable distribution of marital property is "the loss of inheritance and pension rights upon dissolution of the marriage as of the date of dissolution" (DRL §236(B)(5)(d)(4). New York adopted the majority rule in *Majauskas, supra.* (See *id.* at 705 (fn.6).) ("The conclusion thus reached accords with that of most out-of-state courts.")

Majauskas applied the statutory factor in light of legislative intent to define marital property broadly and to consider the nonmonetary contribution of the homemaker spouse. The Court of Appeals held that the husband's vested rights in a police department pension plan were marital property to the extent that they were acquired between the date of the marriage and the commencement of the matrimonial action, even though the rights were unmatured at the time the action was begun. (Because the husband had more than 10 years' service with the police department when his divorce action commenced, his rights under the pension plan were vested but he was not then entitled to benefits under the plan.) The court also ruled that distribution of the husband's pension rights did not violate the state constitutional prohibition against diminishment or impairment of benefits derived from the pension system of a civil division of the state.

Majauskas, by declining to allow the ex-wife to share in any *post-divorce* accumulations to a pension plan, also enunciated the principle that assets accumulated either before the marriage or after the commencement of the divorce action are not to be treated as divisible assets because they were not part of the economic partnership that exists only during the marriage.

See also Olivo v. Olivo, 624 N.E.2d 151 (N.Y. 1993) (holding that the wife was not entitled to share in her husband's Social Security bridge payments and a separation (from work) payment awarded to the husband contemporaneously with his accelerated pension, because his right to those payments had arisen entirely after the marriage ended).

In *Majauskas*, because the husband's rights in his pension plan had vested, the court did not reach or consider the status of nonvested pension rights. Subsequent New York case law extended the holding to nonvested pension rights. Burns v. Burns, 618 N.Y.S.2d 761 (N.Y. 1994). In *Burns*, the Court of Appeals recognized the uncertainties associated with the division of nonvested pension rights, but reasoned that such uncertainties did not present an insurmountable barrier to a fair distribution of assets.

> Like their vested counterparts, non-vested pensions often represent deferred compensation for service performed over a number of years. . . . Where that is the case, their value cannot reasonably be deemed to accrue only at the particular point in time when vesting occurs. Rather, the view that the non-vested pension has been earned gradually over a period of time that encompasses the marriage and should be distributed accordingly more appropriately reflects the economic realities. *Id.* at 765.

Note that private pension plans are now regulated by federal law. The Employee Retirement Income Security Act of 1974 (ERISA), 29 U.S.C. §§1001 et seq., protects employee retirement benefits through comprehensive federal regulation of private pension plans. The statute expressly preempts state law. Under ERISA, as originally enacted, a nonemployee spouse (for example, the wife of a covered employee), had limited rights to share in the employee's pension upon dissolution, as the result of an "anti-alienation rule" barring assignment or alienation of pension plan benefits. ERISA §206(d)(1), 29 U.S.C. §1056(d)(1). This protective policy ensures that the participant cannot consume retirement savings before retirement. ERISA made no exceptions for domestic relations claims against an employee's pension plan.

The Retirement Equity Act of 1984 (REA or REAct) sought to remedy this problem experienced primarily by women. REA mandates that ERISA's anti-alienation rule must yield to certain state domestic relations decrees and permits a court to divide pension benefits in the same manner as other marital assets. That is, REA amends ERISA to provide for the enforcement of "qualified domestic relations orders" or QDROs and removes such orders from ERISA's preemption scheme. See ERISA §§206(d)(3), 514(b)(7), 29 U.S.C. §§1056(d)(3), 1144(b)(7)(2000). QDROs facilitate the enforcement of awards of spousal support and child support by authorizing retirement plan administators to make payments directly to a former spouse.

To qualify as a plan beneficiary under a QDRO, the nonemployee spouse must obtain a state court decree (not merely a separation agreement), which specifies the plan participant's liability for pension assets. Note that pension assets can be distributed under a QDRO not only for property division, but also for spousal and child support obligations. Although QDROs facilitate collection of divorce awards by directing retirement plan administrators to make payments directly to the "alternate payee" (former spouse, child, or other dependent of a participant who is recognized by a domestic relations order as having a right to receive all, or a portion of, the benefits payable under a plan with respect to such participant), QDROs have some limitations. The extent of the nonemployee spouse's benefits is governed by those of the employee spouse — that is, the former spouse may not obtain a lump sum distribution, for example, if such an option is not available to the employee spouse. In terms of federal retirement benefit plans, federal legislation now provides that state courts can apply their laws upon divorce to certain of these federal retirement benefits plans (such as military retirement benefits, railroad employee benefits).

2. Degrees, Licenses, and Enhanced Earning Capacity

Some intangible assets of divorcing spouses are career-related assets. These are sometimes referred to as "human capital" to signify the skill, knowledge, and experience acquired through a spouse's investment of time and energy. Such assets often consist of professional licenses or degrees that enhance earning capacity.

States' marital property law characterizes professional licenses and degrees in different ways. Most courts refuse to consider such career assets as marital property to which both spouses have a right. Nor do most courts recognize a spouse's claim to share the other's enhanced earning capacity as a form of spousal support. Alicia Brokars Kelly, The Marital Partnership Pretense and Career Assets: The Ascendancy of Self over the Marital Community, 81 B.U. L. Rev. 59, 80 (2001). New York, however, is the exception to the general rule and is the only state whose court of last resort recognizes a professional license as marital property. Katheryn D. Katz, 2003-2004 Survey of New York Law: Family Law, 55 Syracuse L. Rev. 1053, 1084 (2005).

New York Domestic Relations Law §236B(5)(d)(6) addresses "contributions . . . to the career or career potential of the other party," without specifically mentioning degrees or licenses. However, in interpreting New York's Equitable Distribution Law, New York courts define divisible property more broadly than other state courts. In O'Brien v. O'Brien, 489 N.E.2d 712 (N.Y. 1985), the New York Court of Appeals held that a professional degree or license acquired during the marriage constitutes marital property subject to the state's equitable distribution law. In *O'Brien*, the parties' only significant asset was the husband's newly acquired license to practice medicine. The court examined whether that license was marital property under Domestic Relations Law §236(B)(5). The husband claimed that his medical degree was not property but rather a personal attainment. He relied on prior case law from other jurisdictions and on the view that a license does not satisfy common law concepts of property. The New York Court of Appeals rejected both arguments, reasoning that other state decisions relied principally on their own statutes and legislative history, and opining that the New York legislature deliberately extended traditional property concepts in formulating the Equitable Distribution Law. See, e.g., Holterman v. Holterman, 781 N.Y.S.2d 458 (N.Y. 2004)(upholding wife's award of 35% of husband's enhanced earning capacity as a medical physician in light of wife's contributions to husband's attainment of his medical license).

O'Brien subsequently was extended to a variety of professional licenses, degrees, and certifications that result in increased earnings. See, e.g., Murtha v. Murtha, 694 N.Y.S.2d 382 (App. Div. 1999) (spouse awarded part of the value of a certified financial analyst certification, even though the certification was not strictly necessary for the financial analyst position); Morimando v. Morimando, 536 N.Y.S.2d 701 (App. Div. 1988) (awarding spouse a share of the value of a certification for physician's-assistant-spouse).

Moreover, New York courts have not restricted equitable distribution to those licenses or degrees that are either strictly required for a professional position or those that are traditionally considered to be professional degrees (law, medicine, etc.). See, e.g., McGowan v. McGowan, 535 N.Y.S.2d 990, 992 (App. Div. 1988) (applying equitable distribution law to master's degree in teaching, finding no legal basis for distinguishing between academic and professional degrees); McAlpine v. McAlpine, 539 N.Y.S.2d 680 (Sup. Ct. 1989), *modified*, 574 N.Y.S.2d 385 (App. Div. 1991) (classifying Fellowship in Society of Actuaries as marital property).

Note that the court may require the maintenance recipient to bear a concomitant portion of any student loan debt borrowed to earn the degree or license, and reduce the maintenance awarded by the share of that debt. Chamberlain v. Chamberlain, 808 N.Y.S.2d 352 (App. Div. 2005).

Finally, some cases have held that increased earnings from celebrity status is marital property subject to equitable distribution, particularly where the spouse participated in some way in enhancing the spouse's celebrity status. In Elkus v. Elkus, 572 N.Y.S.2d 901 (App. Div. 1991), the court awarded a husband part of the value of his wife's celebrity status as an opera singer when he had been her opera coach, even though his wife had achieved some degree of success before they married. The *Elkus* court emphasized the nature and extent of the husband's contribution to the wife's career. See also Golub v. Golub, 527 N.Y.S.2d 946 (N.Y. Sup. Ct. 1988) (holding that the increase in the value of a wife's acting and modeling career was marital property; husband was successful entertainment lawyer who represented his wife and other celebrities).

Despite *O'Brien*'s holding that treats a professional license as marital property, New York courts long disagreed about whether the degree merges into the professional practice over time and therefore should not be valued separately. That is, some courts considered the license to have merged with the practice or career when it had been in existence for a number of years and therefore tended to view a separate award as "double recovery." The merger principle was announced in Marcus v. Marcus, 525 N.Y.S.2d 238 (App. Div. 1988) (holding that a professional license should not be assigned an independent value where the licensee has maintained a professional practice for a substantial period of time). Following *Marcus*, lower courts applied the doctrine with varying results. However, in 1995, the New York Court of Appeals abolished the doctrine. See McSparron v. McSparron, 662 N.E.2d 745, 750 (N.Y. 1995) (discussing criticisms of the merger principle, subsequent case law, and suggesting that the merger doctrine should be discarded in favor of a "commonsense approach that recognizes the ongoing independent vitality that a professional license may have and focuses solely on the problem of valuing that asset in a way that avoids duplicative awards").

McSparron provides an alternative to the merger principle in the form of a guide to valuation of an older license or degree. According to *McSparron*,

> [t]he court should ascertain the average annual earnings of the spouse and multiply that average by the number of years remaining in the spouse's work-lifetime. However, the result must be reduced by the remaining work-lifetime earnings that would have been realized without the license or degree. The amount of

> reduction must necessarily be determined by looking to the average annual earnings realized by a college graduate of similar age to the spouse and multiplying that amount by the spouse's remaining work-lifetime. The difference between the spouse's remaining actual earnings and the remaining earnings of a college graduate is then discounted to present value. The result is the remaining enhancement attributable to the license or degree . . . .

Cited in Scheinkman, 11 N.Y. Prac., *supra*, at §14:35 (Special License Valuation Issues — Valuation of Older License or Degree). See also Grunfeld v. Grunfeld, 731 N.E.2d 142 (N.Y. 2000) (discussing methods to use to avoid double-counting the same income stream for practice, license, and maintenance purposes).

Recently, in Keane v. Keane, 861 N.E.2d 98 (N.Y. 2006), the New York Court of Appeals addressed whether to extend the prohibition against double counting (i.e., the principle that in divorce actions a court should not count twice the income associated with a professional license when making distributive and maintenance awards) to the case of the distribution of a tangible income-producing asset. and the subsequent award of maintenance from income derived from that asset. The court refused to extend the prohibition, concluding that consideration of a husband's monthly rental income from a body shop repair business in the computation of an award of maintenance to a wife did not constitute impermissible double counting because the rental property could be readily distinguished from its income-producing capacity.

Consistent with the majority rule, the ALI Principles reject the treatment of earning capacity as divisible property. Instead, they provide for "compensatory payments" to reimburse the supporting spouse for the financial contributions made to the other spouse's education or training. ALI Principles, *supra*, §§4.07, 5.12. The ALI Principles are set forth in Part IV, *infra*. For compensation under §5.12, the education must have been completed in less than a specified number of years (set out in a rule of statewide application) before the filing of the dissolution petition.

The ALI formulation resembles an earlier California statute, which provides for reimbursement of the community "for community contributions to education or training of a party that substantially increases the earning capacity of the party." Cal. Fam. Code §2641(b)(1). This statute contains a rebuttable presumption "that the community has not substantially benefited from community contributions to the education or training made less than 10 years before the commencement of the proceeding, and that the community has substantially benefited from community contributions to the education or training made more than 10 years before the commencement of the proceeding." *Id.* at §2641(c).

With respect to professional goodwill, the majority approach regards it as marital property, but only if the goodwill exists independently of the professional's reputation. *Compare* Thompson v. Thompson, 576 So. 2d 267 (Fla. 1991); Dugan v. Dugan, 457 A.2d 1 (N.J. 1983) (treating professional goodwill as a divisible asset), *with* Powell v. Powell, 648 P.2d 218 (Kan. 1982) (treating professional practice as personal, not divisible).

See generally Laurence J. Cutler & Robin C. Bogan, The Nature of the Beast from Horses to Hedge Funds: Celebrity Goodwill, 25 Fam. Advoc. 20 (2003); Sebastian Weiss, Note, Preventing Inequities in Divorce and Education: The Equitable Distribution of a Career Absent an Advanced Degree or License, 9 Cardozo Women's L.J. 133 (2002).

E. Role of Fault

Fault still plays a limited role in the distribution of marital property in New York. Under the traditional fault-based system, a divorce could be awarded only to the innocent spouse. The "guilty" party was required to pay in the form of property distribution and support, and might also be denied custody of the children.

UMDA, as originally enacted in 1970, was influential in adoption of the rule that courts should divide marital property "without regard to marital misconduct" (UMDA §307(a)).

Nonetheless, as of 2003, approximately 15 states still considered fault in property distribution at dissolution. Introduction, ALI Principles, *supra*, at 72 (listing Alabama, Connecticut, Georgia, Maryland, Massachusetts, Michigan, Mississippi, Missouri, New Hampshire, North Dakota, Rhode Island, South Carolina, Texas, Vermont, and Wyoming).

According to New York *case law*, marital fault may be considered only in extreme cases. In O'Brien v. O'Brien, 489 N.E.2d 712, 719 (N.Y. 1985), the New York Court of Appeals stated:

> Except in egregious cases which shock the conscience of the court, [marital fault] is not a "just and proper" factor for consideration in the equitable distribution of marital property (citations omitted). That is so because marital fault is inconsistent with the underlying assumption that a marriage is in part an economic partnership and upon its dissolution the parties are entitled to a fair share of the marital estate, because fault will usually be difficult to assign and because introduction of the issue may involve the courts in time-consuming procedural maneuvers relating to collateral issues. . . .

Case law has analyzed the type of conduct that is sufficiently egregious to require consideration in the distribution of property. Such egregious conduct includes: attempted murder (Brancovenanu v. Brancovenanu, 535 N.Y.S.2d 86 (App. Div. 1988); Wenzel v. Wenzel, 472 N.Y.S.2d 830 (Sup. Ct. 1984)); rape (Thompson v. Thompson, N.Y.L.J., Jan. 5, 1990, at 22); repeated physical abuse over a 20-year period causing lasting physical damage (Debeny v. Debeny, N.Y.L.J., Jan. 24, 1991, at 21) (cited in Introduction, ALI Principles, *supra,* at 69). See also Havell v. Islam, 718 N.Y.S.2d 807, 811 (Sup. Ct. 2000) (holding that pattern of domestic violence, if properly proven, is just and proper factor to be weighed in equitable distribution of property); Blickstein v. Blickstein, 472 N.Y.S.2d 110, 113 (App. Div. 1984) (stating that occasions in which fault should be considered in property distribution will be rare and will involve situations in which "marital misconduct is so egregious or uncivilized as to bespeak of blatant disregard of marital relationship").

On the other hand, courts have held that the following types of conduct are legally insufficient to merit consideration in the distribution of property: less severe acts of domestic violence (Kellerman v. Kellerman, 590 N.Y.S.2d 570, 571 (App. Div. 1992)); the husband's refusal to have children in violation of a promise (McCann v. McCann, 593 N.Y.S.2d 917 (Sup. 1993)); and the wife's adultery combined with her physical and verbal abuse of husband (Stevens v. Stevens, 484 N.Y.S.2d 708 (App. Div. 1985)).

F. Alteration of Rules by Spousal Agreement

The marital parties may alter their respective rights by spousal agreements executed before or during the marriage. (On premarital agreements, see Chapter I *supra*.) That is, the parties may contract out of the application of the state's equitable distribution law in regard to marital property and spousal support. (For that reason, these agreements are sometimes referred to as "opting-out agreements.")

Separation agreements may govern the parties' rights regarding property (past, present, and future property, including inheritance rights) as well as spousal support, child custody, child support, and child care ("custody, care, education and maintenance of any child of the parties"). DRL §236, Part B(3).

At one time, separation agreements were held to violate public policy because they facilitated divorce by removing uncertainty about how a court would resolve the financial incidents of dissolution. UMDA influenced the increasing acceptance of these agreements. UMDA makes the parties "amicable settlement of disputes" an explicit policy objective. 9A U.L.A. (pt. I) 248-249 (1998). UMDA permits such agreements to govern the disposition of "any property owned by either of them, maintenance of either of them, and support, custody, and visitation of their children." *Id.*

According to New York's Domestic Relations Law, separation may provide a ground for a divorce. That is, based on Domestic Relations Law §170(6), the parties may seek a divorce where they have lived separate and apart for at least one year pursuant to a written separation agreement and where the petitioner has substantially performed all of the terms and conditions of the agreement. The statute requires that the separation agreement must be in writing and subscribed to by the parties and acknowledged in the form required for a deed to be recorded. DRL §170(6).

One limitation on separation agreements is that a spouse may not "contract to alter or dissolve the marriage or to relieve either of his or her liability to support the other in such a manner that he or she will become incapable of self-support and therefore is likely to become a public charge." G.O.L. §5-311. Specifically, the agreement will be void if it contains an "express provision requiring the dissolution of the marriage or provides for the procurement of grounds of divorce." *Id.*

Traditional grounds for setting aside a separation agreement are: unconscionability, overreaching, fraud, duress, and other contractual remedies. Scheinkman, 11 N.Y. Prac., *supra*, at §7:1.

Enforcement of separation agreements depends on whether the agreement was "merged" (with the final decree of divorce) or whether the terms were merely "incorporated" in a final decree. *Id.* That is, a separation agreement can be merged with the judgment and thereby become part of the judgment (i.e., it is no longer a separate contract). Alternatively, the agreement can be incorporated with the judgment but not be merged (i.e., it remains a separate contract).

The difference is important for purposes of enforcement. If the agreement is merged with the final judicial decree, the remedy of contempt may be available in the event that one party does not perform the terms (such as the obligation to pay support). (The remedy of contempt is not available for breach of contract.) See DRL §245 (authorizing the court to invoke the remedy of contempt in limited instances in dissolution actions).

Note that UMDA addresses this issue by creating a presumption of incorporation that the parties seeking to avoid must dispel by a clear statement to the contrary. UMDA §306.

Recently, a New York trial court addressed the issue whether a separation agreement is valid and enforceable even if the couple's marriage is not recognized in the forum. In Gonzalez v. Green, 831 N.Y.S.2d 856 (Sup. Ct. 2006), the court upheld the separation agreement of a same-sex couple from New York who had married in Massachusetts where same-sex marriage is valid. The court also held that Hernandez v. Robles, 821 N.Y.S.2d 770 (N.Y. 2006) (upholding New York's ban on same-sex marriage) did not constitute an impediment to the enforcement of the couple's separation agreement because it did not mandate different treatment of the contracts between unmarried same-sex partners and those of unmarried opposite-sex partners.

Domestic Relations Law

§170. Grounds for divorce

An action for divorce may be maintained by a husband or wife to procure a judgment divorcing the parties and dissolving the marriage on any of the following grounds:

(1) The cruel and inhuman treatment of the plaintiff by the defendant such that the conduct of the defendant so endangers the physical or mental well being of the plaintiff as renders it unsafe or improper for the plaintiff to cohabit with the defendant.

(2) The abandonment of the plaintiff by the defendant for a period of one or more years.

(3) The confinement of the defendant in prison for a period of three or more consecutive years after the marriage of plaintiff and defendant.

(4) The commission of an act of adultery, provided that adultery for the purposes of articles ten, eleven, and eleven-A of this chapter, is hereby defined as the commission of an act of sexual intercourse, oral sexual conduct or anal sexual conduct, voluntarily performed by the defendant, with a person other than the plaintiff after the marriage of

plaintiff and defendant. Oral sexual conduct and anal sexual conduct include, but are not limited to, sexual conduct as defined in subdivision two of Section 130.00 and subdivision three of section 130.20 of the penal law.

(5) The husband and wife have lived apart pursuant to a decree or judgment of separation for a period of one or more years after the granting of such decree or judgment, and satisfactory proof has been submitted by the plaintiff that he or she has substantially performed all the terms and conditions of such decree or judgment.

(6) The husband and wife have lived separate and apart pursuant to a written agreement of separation, subscribed by the parties thereto and acknowledged or proved in the form required to entitle a deed to be recorded, for a period of one or more years after the execution of such agreement and satisfactory proof has been submitted by the plaintiff that he or she has substantially performed all the terms and conditions of such agreement. Such agreement shall be filed in the office of the clerk of the county wherein either party resides. In lieu of filing such agreement, either party to such agreement may file a memorandum of such agreement, which memorandum shall be similarly subscribed and acknowledged or proved as was the agreement of separation and shall contain the following information:

(a) the names and addresses of each of the parties,

(b) the date of marriage of the parties,

(c) the date of the agreement of separation and

(d) the date of this subscription and acknowledgment or proof of such agreement of separation.

(L. 1966, ch. 254, §2; L. 1967, ch. 648, §1; L. 1968, ch. 700, §§1, 2; L. 1969, ch. 964, §1; L. 1970, ch. 835, §§1, 2; L. 1970, ch. 867, §1; L. 1971, ch. 801, §§1, 2; L. 1972, ch. 719, §1; L. 1974, ch. 920, §7; L. 1974, ch. 1047, §1; L. 1975, ch. 415, §2; L. 2003, ch. 264, §53, eff. Nov. 1, 2003.)

§236. Equitable Distribution Law: special controlling provisions

. . .

PART B

NEW ACTIONS OR PROCEEDINGS

. . .

3. Agreement of the parties. An agreement by the parties, made before or during the marriage, shall be valid and enforceable in a matrimonial action if such agreement is in writing, subscribed by the parties, and acknowledged or proven in the manner required to entitle a deed to be recorded. Such an agreement may include

(1) a contract to make a testamentary provision of any kind, or a waiver of any right to elect against the provisions of a will;

(2) provision for the ownership, division or distribution of separate and marital property;

(3) provision for the amount and duration of maintenance or other terms and conditions of the marriage relationship, subject to the provisions of section 5-311 of the general obligations law, and provided that such terms were fair and reasonable at the time of the making of the agreement and are not unconscionable at the time of entry of final judgment; and

(4) provision for the custody, care, education and maintenance of any child of the parties, subject to the provisions of section two hundred forty of this chapter. Nothing in this subdivision shall be deemed to affect the validity of any agreement made prior to the effective date of this subdivision.

. . .

(L. 1962, ch. 313, §10; L. 1963, ch. 685, §6; L. 1968, ch. 699, §1; L. 1980, ch. 281, §9; L. 1980, ch. 645, §§2, 3; L. 1981, ch. 695, §§1, 2; L. 1984, ch. 790, §2; L. 1985, ch. 809, §6; L. 1986, ch. 884, §§1 to 4; L. 1986, ch. 892, §§2 to 4; L. 1987, ch. 815, §§6, 7; L. 1989, ch. 567, §§4, 5; L. 1990, ch. 818, §§4, 5; L. 1992, ch. 41, §§139, 140; L. 1992, ch. 415, §§1, 2; L. 1993, ch. 59, §9; L. 1993, ch. 354, §2; L. 1994, ch. 170, §§359, 360; L. 1997, ch. 398, §§4, 5, effective October 1, 1998; L. 1997, ch. 398, §141, effective January 1, 1998; L. 1997, ch. 436, pt. B, §§105, 106, effective August 20, 1997; L. 1998, ch. 214, §56, effective November 4, 1998; L. 1998, ch. 393, §2, effective July 22, 1998; L. 1999, ch. 275, §2, effective September 18, 1999.)

§245. Availability of contempt proceedings of judgment or order in action for divorce, separation or annulment

Where a spouse, in an action for divorce, separation, annulment or declaration of nullity of a void marriage, or for the enforcement in this state of a judgment for divorce, separation, annulment or declaration of nullity of a void marriage rendered in another state, makes default in paying any sum of money as required by the judgment or order directing the payment thereof, and it appears presumptively, to the satisfaction of the court, that payment cannot be enforced pursuant to section two hundred forty-three or two hundred forty-four of this chapter or section fifty-two hundred forty-one or fifty-two hundred forty-two of the civil practice law and rules, the aggrieved spouse may make application pursuant to the provisions of section seven hundred fifty-six of the judiciary law to punish the defaulting spouse for contempt, and where the judgment or order directs the payment to be made in installments, or at stated intervals, failure to make such single payment or installment may be punished as therein provided, and such punishment, either by fine or commitment, shall not be a bar to a subsequent proceeding to punish the defaulting spouse as for a contempt for failure to pay subsequent installments, but for such purpose such spouse may be proceeded against under the said order in the same manner and with the same effect as though such installment payment was directed to be paid by a separate and distinct order, and the provisions of the civil rights law are hereby superseded so far as they are in conflict therewith. Such application may also be made without any previous sequestration or direction to give security where the court is satisfied that they would be ineffectual. No demand of any kind upon the defaulting spouse shall be necessary in order that he or she be proceeded against and punished for failure to make any such payment or to pay any such installment; personal service upon the defaulting spouse of an uncertified copy of the judgment or order under which the default has occurred shall be sufficient.

(L. 1962, ch. 313, §10; amended L.1975, ch. 497, §1; L. 1977, ch. 437, §11; L. 1980, ch. 281, §16; L. 1985, ch. 809, §9.)

General Obligations Law

§5-311. Invalidity of certain spousal agreements

Except as provided in section two hundred thirty-six of the domestic relations law, a husband and wife cannot contract to alter or dissolve the marriage or to relieve either of his or her liability to support the other in such a manner that he or she will become incapable of self-support and therefore is likely to become a public charge. An agreement, heretofore or hereafter made between a husband and wife, shall not be considered a contract to alter or dissolve the marriage unless it contains an express provision requiring the dissolution of the marriage or provides for the procurement of grounds of divorce.
(L. 1980, ch. 281, §19.)

VI.
NONTRADITIONAL FAMILIES

A. TRADITIONAL RESPONSE: CRIMINAL SANCTIONS

The legal response to extramarital heterosexual and same-sex sexual conduct traditionally was punitive. Many states imposed criminal sanctions for adultery, cohabitation, fornication, and sodomy.

Texas law provides an illustration of the traditional and modern responses to nontraditional families. When the Texas constitution was ratified in 1876, article 392 of the Texas Penal Code of 1857 provided that adultery was a criminal offense punishable by fine. Three years later, the state legislature revised the Penal Code but retained the provision criminalizing adultery (Tex. Penal Code art. 336 (1879)). The prohibition finally was repealed in 1973. See Act of June 14, 1973, 63d Leg., R.S., ch. 399, §3, 1973 Tex. Gen. Laws 883, 992, repealing Tex. Penal Code art. 499 (1925).

Some forms of sexual activity (i.e., oral and anal sexual acts) were prohibited by sodomy statutes. In 1955 (when all states had sodomy prohibitions), the American Law Institute (ALI) recommended decriminalization. Model Penal Code §207.5 (Tent. Draft No. 4, 1955). In response, more than 20 state legislatures repealed their laws. Paula A. Brantner, Note, Removing Bricks from a Wall of Discrimination: State Constitutional Challenges to Sodomy Laws, 19 Hastings Const. L.Q. 495, 498 (1992). Nevertheless, as late as 2001, criminal prohibitions against sodomy continued to exist in 16 states. Diana Hassel, The Use of Criminal Sodomy Laws in Civil Litigation, 79 Tex. L. Rev. 813, 821 (2001).

Texas criminalized same-sex sexual conduct in 1879 with its revision of the Penal Code. In 1973, Texas repealed its prohibition on sodomy, except when performed by persons of the same sex. The U.S. Supreme Court subsequently invalidated this sodomy provision (Tex. Penal Code §21.06) in 2003. Lawrence v. Texas, 539 U.S. 558 (2003). See also Lawrence v. Texas, 41 S.W.3d 349, 361 n.33 (Tex. Crim. App. 2001) (citing Tex. Penal Code art. 342 (1879); Tex. Penal Code art. 364 (1895); Tex. Penal Code art. 507 (1911); and Tex. Penal Code art. 524 (1925)).

In *Lawrence*, because the Texas law targeted only same-sex sexual conduct, the Supreme Court had some basis to strike the law on equal protection grounds. See Justice O'Connor's concurring opinion in *Lawrence*, 539 U.S. at 579 (arguing that the law violated the Equal Protection Clause of the Fourteenth Amendment, failing any rational basis because it targeted a specific class. The Court instead invalidated the law on the basis of the liberty interest under the Due Process Clause of the Fourteenth Amendment, citing Griswold v. Connecticut, 381 U.S. 479 (1965), for the fundamental right to privacy (as well as subsequent cases that held that the privacy right extended to all individuals, not only married persons). See *Lawrence*, 539 U.S. at 564.

Dissenting, Justice Scalia disagreed with the Court's basis for invalidating a morality-based law on due process grounds, stating that laws, particularly laws governing sexuality, are rationally based in traditional morals that courts and legislatures have enforced over an extensive period of time. *Id.* at 589. He noted that such laws should be considered and decided by politically accountable legislatures, not courts. *Id.* Justice Scalia warned that the majority's holding could lead to the end of certain morally based statutes, such as those barring bigamy, incest, and same-sex marriage. *Id.* at 590. See also Michael J. Klarman, *Brown* and *Lawrence* (and *Goodridge*), 104 Mich. L. Rev. 431 (2005); Michael G. Myers, The Polygamist Eye for the Monogamist Guy: Homosexual Sodomy . . . Gay Marriage . . . Is Polygamy Next?, 42 Houston L. Rev. 1451 (2006).

Later that year, the Massachusetts Supreme Court invalidated state laws banning same-sex marriage, reasoning that such laws lacked a rational basis and violated state constitutional equal protection principles. Goodridge v. Department of Public Health, 798 N.E.2d 941, 948 (Mass. 2003). The court cited *Lawrence*, *supra*, noting the court's obligation "to define the liberty of all, not to mandate our own moral code." See *id.* (citing Lawrence v. Texas, 539 U.S. 558, 571 (2003), and quoting Planned Parenthood of Southeastern Pennsylvania v. Casey, 505 U.S. 833, 850 (1992)).

B. CONTRACTS BETWEEN COHABITANTS

The law regulates and protects the rights of the marital parties (e.g., support and property rights) upon dissolution. This legal protection traditionally has been unavailable to members of unmarried couples. This reluctance has been altered somewhat by case law in the past few decades. See, e.g., Marvin v. Marvin, 557 P.2d 106 (Cal. 1976).

Under the traditional rule, courts refuse to enforce agreements between members of unmarried couples (formerly termed "meretricious relationships"). Courts hold such agreements are invalid as contrary to public policy (similar to contracts for prostitution). The rationale for the policy was the deterrence of immorality. Changing sexual mores and increasing attention to the rights of women have contributed to reform.

Jurisdictions have adopted different approaches to contract claims by opposite-sex cohabitants. The majority follow *Marvin, supra*, in recognizing express and implied agreements as well as equitable remedies. However, some jurisdictions recognize only express agreements, whereas others recognize express and implied agreements (but not equitable remedies). Finally, a few jurisdictions (e.g., Georgia, Illinois, Louisiana) refuse to recognize property rights between heterosexual cohabitants on public policy grounds. See Katherine C. Gordon, Note, The Necessity and Enforcement of Cohabitation Agreements: When

Strings Will Attach and How to Prevent Them— A State Survey, 37 Brandeis L.J. 245, 248-254 (1998-1999).

Under the Texas Family Code, an agreement made in consideration of nonmarital cohabitation is not enforceable unless the promise (or a memorandum of that promise) is in writing and signed by the person obligated by the promise or agreement (Tex. Fam. Code §1.108). However, a part performance exception exists to this statute of frauds. See O'Farrill Avila v. Gonzalez, 974 S.W.2d 237, 246 (Tex. App.—San Antonio 1998, pet. denied) (holding sufficient to overcome the statute of frauds evidence that a female domestic partner fully performed her part of the contract by putting an agreed $60,000 downpayment on a house, and the male domestic partner partly performed by making monthly payments for two years). A few jurisdictions recognize the rights of same-sex couples upon termination of their relationships. Massachusetts (the only state presently to recognize gay marriage), of course, treats same-sex partners as marital parties. Nine states (California, Connecticut, Hawaii, Maine, New Hampshire, New Jersey, Oregon, Vermont, and Washington) and the District of Columbia have enacted domestic partnership legislation. However, whereas some of these states equate same-sex couples to spouses for all purposes, other states offer more limited protections.

Texas Family Code

§8.061. Maintenance is not authorized between unmarried cohabitants

An order for maintenance is not authorized between unmarried cohabitants under any circumstances.

(Acts 1997, 75th Leg., ch. 7, §1, effective April 17, 1997. Renumbered from §8.011 by Acts 2001, 77th Leg., ch. 807, §1, effective September 1, 2001.)

Texas Business & Commercial Code

§26.01. Certain agreements must be in writing

(a) A promise or agreement described in Subsection (b) of this section is not enforceable unless the promise or agreement, or a memorandum of it, is

(1) in writing; and

(2) signed by the person to be charged with the promise or agreement or by someone lawfully authorized to sign for him.

(b) Subsection (a) of this section applies to:

(1) a promise by an executor or administrator to answer out of his own estate for any debt or damage due from his testator or intestate;

(2) a promise by one person to answer for the debt, default, or miscarriage of another person;

(3) an agreement made on consideration of marriage or on consideration of nonmarital conjugal cohabitation;

(4) a contract for the sale of real estate;

(5) a lease of real estate for a term longer than one year;

(6) an agreement which is not to be performed within one year from the date of making the agreement;

(7) a promise or agreement to pay a commission for the sale or purchase of:

(A) an oil or gas mining lease;

(B) an oil or gas royalty;

(C) minerals; or

(D) a mineral interest; and

(8) an agreement, promise, contract, or warranty of cure relating to medical care or results thereof made by a physician or health care provider as defined in Section 1.03, Medical Liability and Insurance Improvement Act of Texas. This section shall not apply to pharmacists.

(Acts 1967, 60th Leg., vol. 2, p. 2343, ch. 785, §1. Amended by Acts 1977, 65th Leg., p. 2053, ch. 817, §21.01, effective August 29, 1977; Acts 1987, 70th Leg., ch. 551, §1, effective August 31, 1987; Acts 2005, 79th Leg., ch. 187, §1, effective September 1, 2005.)

Texas Family Code

§1.108. Cohabitation agreement must be in writing

A promise or agreement made on consideration of marriage or nonmarital conjugal cohabitation is not enforceable unless the promise or agreement or a memorandum of the promise or agreement is in writing and signed by the person obligated by the promise or agreement.

(Acts 1997, 75th Leg., ch. 7, §1, effective April 17, 1997.)

C. FAMILY VIOLENCE

All states have civil and criminal legislation addressing family violence. See Chapter III, Section J *supra*. Such legislation often includes provisions for protective orders, such as restraining orders and orders allowing the victim exclusive possession of the dwelling. Many of these statutes include broad definitions that protect cohabitants. For example, the definition of "family" for purposes of the Texas chapter on family violence is quite broad—encompassing "individuals who are the parents of the same child, without regard to marriage" (Tex. Fam. Code §71.003). In addition, current members of the same household, as well as current and former dating partners, are protected under domestic violence laws in Texas (with statutory language that does not specify a dating relationship must be between a man and a woman) (Tex. Fam. Code §§71.0021, 71.005); see also Chapter III, Section J.3.a. *supra*.

Recently, an interesting issue arose in Ohio. In State v. Carswell, 2007 WL 2161508 (Ohio 2007), an unmarried male-cohabitant moved to dismiss a domestic violence charge against him by his girlfriend on the ground that the state domestic violence statute (prohibiting physical harm to a person "living as a spouse") violated the defense of marriage amendment to the state constitution. Rejecting his argument, the state supreme court held that the domestic violence statute did not conflict with the state constitutional amendment. The court reasoned that the statute created a subset of victims rather than bestowing additional rights, duties, or liabilities on a class of persons, and also reasoned that the defendant, and not the state, created the relevant relationship to alleged victim.

---

§71.0021. "Dating violence" defined

(a) "Dating violence" means an act by an individual that is against another individual with whom that person has or has had a dating relationship and that is intended to result in physical harm, bodily injury, assault, or sexual assault or that is a threat that reasonably places the individual in fear of imminent physical harm, bodily injury, assault, or sexual assault, but does not include defensive measures to protect oneself.

(b) For purposes of this title, "dating relationship" means a relationship between individuals who have or have had a continuing relationship of a romantic or intimate nature. The existence of such a relationship shall be determined based on consideration of:

(1) the length of the relationship;

(2) the nature of the relationship; and

(3) the frequency and type of interaction between the persons involved in the relationship.

(c) A casual acquaintanceship or ordinary fraternization in a business or social context does not constitute a "dating relationship" under Subsection (b).

(Acts 2001, 77th Leg., ch. 91, §1, effective September 1, 2001.)

§71.003. "Family" defined

"Family" includes individuals related by consanguinity or affinity, as determined under Sections 573.022 and 573.024, Government Code, individuals who are former spouses of each other, individuals who are the parents of the same child, without regard to marriage, and a foster child and foster parent, without regard to whether those individuals reside together.

(Acts 1997, 75th Leg., ch. 34, §1, effective May 5, 1997. Amended by Acts 2001, 77th Leg., ch. 821, §2.03, effective June 14, 2001.)

§71.005. "Household" defined

"Household" means a unit composed of persons living together in the same dwelling, without regard to whether they are related to each other.

(Acts 1997, 75th Leg., ch. 34, §1, effective May 5, 1997.)

D. TORT

Modern courts often deny cohabitants legal rights in the tort context that are available to members of traditional families. For example, most jurisdictions refuse to permit cohabitants to recover in tort for injuries to each other. That is, an unmarried partner (unlike a legal spouse) does not have a claim either for loss of consortium or for negligent infliction of emotional distress arising from an injury to the other partner. Compare Elden v. Sheldon, 758 P.2d 582 (Cal. 1988) (holding that an unmarried cohabitant may not recover damages to a partner for loss of consortium or negligent infliction of emotional distress) with Graves v. Estabrook, 818 A.2d 1255 (N.H. 2003) (holding that an unmarried cohabitant in a stable, enduring, substantial, and mutually supportive relationship may recover for negligent infliction of emotional distress).Texas courts do not extend tort recovery for relationship injuries to unmarried cohabitants.

E. COMPARATIVE TREATMENT OF SAME-SEX MARRIAGE AND DOMESTIC PARTNERSHIPS

The Texas legislature has barred same-sex marriage. In 2003, Texas became the 37th state to enact a Defense of Marriage Act (DOMA), excluding recognition of same-sex marriages. See Tex. Fam. Code §6.204, *infra*. The Texas legislation was part of a larger trend that began in October 1996, when Congress passed the DOMA, 18 U.S.C. §1738(c), in response to Baehr v. Lewin, 852 P.2d 44 (Haw. 1993) (holding that the denial of marriage licenses to same-sex couples implicates the Hawaii state constitution's Equal Protection Clause that explicitly bars sex-based discrimination).

DOMA provides a federal definition of the terms "marriage" and "spouse" for purposes of federal benefits. The term "spouse" refers only to a person of the opposite sex and "marriage" is defined as a union between a man and a woman. Importantly, DOMA provides that states are not required to give effect to same-sex marriages, based on Congress' Article IV powers to implement the Full Faith and Credit Clause. DOMA is included in Part II of this Code.

In the Texas legislative commentary to Texas Family Code §6.204, the legislature states that other legal means (i.e., designation of guardians, appointment of agents, use of private contracts) provide adequate preservation of the rights for same-sex partners without the need for the state to grant traditional marriage rights to such partners. Note, however, that Texas explicitly bars contracts for alimony to persons in same-sex relationships "under any circumstances" (Tex. Fam. Code §8.061, section B, *supra*). Similarly, Texas law does not extend the right to recovery in tort for relationship injuries to unmarried cohabitants (discussed in Section D, *supra*).

Texas Family Code

§6.204. Same-sex marriage or civil union void

(a) In this section, "civil union" means any relationship status other than marriage that:

(1) is intended as an alternative to marriage or applies primarily to cohabitating persons; and

(2) grants to the parties of the relationship legal protections, benefits, or responsibilities granted to the spouses of a marriage.

(b) A marriage between persons of the same sex or a civil union is contrary to the public policy of this state and is void in this state.

(c) The state or an agency or political subdivision of the state may not give effect to a:

(1) public act, record, or judicial proceeding that creates, recognizes, or validates a marriage between persons of the same sex or a civil union in this state or in any other jurisdiction; or

(2) right or claim to any legal protection, benefit, or responsibility asserted as a result of a marriage between persons of the same sex or a civil union in this state or in any other jurisdiction.

(Acts 2003, 78th Leg., ch. 124, §§2, 3, effective September 1, 2003.)

HISTORICAL AND STATUTORY NOTES

Sections 2 and 3 of Acts 2003, 78th Leg., ch. 124 provide:

Sec. 2: The legislature finds that through the designation of guardians, the appointment of agents, and the use of private contracts persons may adequately and properly appoint guardians and arrange rights relating to hospital visitation, property, and the entitlement to proceeds of life insurance policies without the existence of any legally recognized familial relationship between the persons.

Sec. 3: Ch. 124 applies to a same-sex marriage or civil union regardless of whether the marriage or civil union was entered before, on, or after September 1, 2003.

(Notes, Acts 2003, 78th Leg., ch. 124, §§2, 3, effective September 1, 2003.)

F. THE MODERN RESPONSE: DOMESTIC PARTNERSHIPS

Presently, Massachusetts is the only state to recognize same-sex marriage. However, a small but growing number of states now recognize the rights of same-sex couples through some type of domestic partnership legislation. Nine states (California, Connecticut, Hawaii, Maine, New Hampshire, New Jersey, Oregon, Vermont, and Washington) and the District of Columbia have enacted domestic partnership legislation.

Washington's new law went into effect on July 22, 2007; New Hampshire's legislation will take effect in January 1, 2008, and Oregon's law will also take effect on January 1, 2008.

Some of these state laws refer to "domestic partnerships" whereas other states use the term "civil unions." However, whereas some of the preceding states equate same-sex couples to spouses for all purposes, other states offer more limited protections.

VII. CHILD SUPPORT

This chapter addresses child support. It begins with a general examination of the duty of support. Next, it focuses on determinations of the amount of support (in particular, the statewide uniform guidelines and their application). The chapter then turns to modification and termination of support orders. Finally, it explores enforcement of support and the problems posed by multistate support cases.

A. GENERAL PROVISIONS

Statutes in every state impose a duty on parents to support their minor children. At common law, the father was primarily liable for the support of his children. Now statutes make both the mother and father equally responsible for the support of their children. See, e.g., Tex. Fam. Code §151.001 ("a parent of a child has . . . the duty to support the child"); §154.010 ("The amount of support . . . shall be determined without regard to the sex of the obligor, obligee, or child. . . ").

Traditionally, nonmarital children had a right to support and inheritance only from their mother, not from their father. According to many modern statutes, both parents have the duty to support children regardless of the legitimacy of the children. See, e.g., Tex. Fam. Code §154.010(2) ("The amount of support . . . shall be determined *without regard to . . . the marital status of the parents of the child*") (emphasis added). Further, the United States Supreme Court held in Gomez v. Perez, 409 U.S. 535 (1973), that a state cannot grant only legitimate children a statutory right to paternal support. See also June Carbone, Child Support Comes of Age: An Introduction to the Law of Child Support in Child Support: The Next Frontier 4 (J. Thomas Oldham & Marygold S. Melli, eds., 2000) ("Modern child support practice . . . erases the distinctions between marital and nonmarital births. . . .").

1. Duty of Support

The parent's duty of support includes the duty to provide "clothing, food, shelter, medical and dental care, and education" (Tex. Fam. Code §151.003(a)(3).

Texas Family Code

§151.001. Parental rights and duties

(a) A parent of a child has the following rights and duties:

(1) the right to have physical possession, to direct the moral and religious training, and to establish the residence of the child;

(2) the duty of care, control, protection, and reasonable discipline of the child;

(3) the duty to support the child, including providing the child with clothing, food, shelter, medical and dental care, and education;

(4) the duty, except when a guardian of the child's estate has been appointed, to manage the estate of the child, including the right as an agent of the child to act in relation to the child's estate if the child's action is required by a state, the United States, or a foreign government;

(5) except as provided by Section 264.0111, the right to the services and earnings of the child;

(6) the right to consent to the child's marriage, enlistment in the armed forces of the United States, medical and dental care, and psychiatric, psychological, and surgical treatment;

(7) the right to represent the child in legal action and to make other decisions of substantial legal significance concerning the child;

(8) the right to receive and give receipt for payments for the support of the child and to hold or disburse funds for the benefit of the child;

(9) the right to inherit from and through the child;

(10) the right to make decisions concerning the child's education; and

(11) any other right or duty existing between a parent and child by virtue of law.

(b) The duty of a parent to support his or her child exists while the child is an unemancipated minor and continues as long as the child is fully enrolled in an accredited secondary school in a program leading toward a high school diploma until the end of the school year in which the child graduates.

(c) A parent who fails to discharge the duty of support is liable to a person who provides necessaries to those to whom support is owed.

(d) The rights and duties of a parent are subject to:

(1) a court order affecting the rights and duties;

(2) an affidavit of relinquishment of parental rights; and

(3) an affidavit by the parent designating another person or agency to act as managing conservator.

(e) Only the following persons may use corporal punishment for the reasonable discipline of the child:

(1) a parent or grandparent of the child;

(2) a stepparent of the child who has the duty of control and reasonable discipline of the child; and

(3) an individual who is a guardian of the child and who has the duty of control and reasonable discipline of the child.

(Acts 1995, 74th Leg., ch. 20, §1, effective April 20, 1995. Amended by Acts 1995, 74th Leg., ch. 751, §23, effective September 1, 1995. Renumbered from §151.003 by Acts 2001, 77th Leg., ch. 821, §2.13, effective June 14, 2001. Amended by Acts 2001, 77th Leg., ch. 964, §2, effective September 1, 2001; Acts 2003, 78th Leg., ch. 1036, effective September 1, 2003. Acts 2005, 79th Leg., ch. 924 (H.B 383), §1, effective September 1, 2005.)

§154.010. Court order for support shall not be based on gender or marital status

The amount of support ordered for the benefit of a child shall be determined without regard to:

(1) the sex of the obligor, obligee, or child; or

(2) the marital status of the parents of the child.

(Acts 1995, 74th Leg., ch. 20, §1, effective April 20, 1995.)

2. Duration of Support Duty

Texas law addresses the duration of the support duty. A court may order either or both parents to pay child support until (1) the child reaches 18 or graduates from high school (whichever occurs later), (2) the child is emancipated (by marriage, court order, or operation of law), or (3) the child dies (Tex. Fam. Code §154.001(a)(1), (2), and (3)). However, if the child is disabled, the court may order support indefinitely (*id.* at §154.001(a)(4)). Although the death of the obligor terminates the obligor's support obligation, the death of the obligee parent does not (Tex. Fam. Code §§154.006(a), 154.013(a)). On support of an adult disabled child, see Section A6 *infra*. If a child is in state custody because a parent's rights have been terminated, legislation enacted in 2005 specifies that the parental duty of support continues until a statutorily designated period, such as the child's adoption, attaining age 18 or graduating from high school, emancipation by court order or marriage, or death (Tex. Fam. Code §154.001(a-1).

In 2003, Texas amended the requirements for the support of a child beyond the age of 18. Texas Family Code §154.002 specifies the requirements for continued support of a child who is attending a secondary school leading toward a high school diploma or a joint program for high school and junior college credit. The new legislation added a provision providing that a child may be enrolled in a *private* school leading toward a high school diploma (Tex. Fam. Code §154.002(a)(1)(C)). The child must be attending the school consistently, meeting the minimum attendance requirements set forth either by the private school or by the public school under Texas Education Code §130.008. See Tex. Fam. Code §§154.002(a)(2); 154.006(a)(4)(B).

For cases interpreting the provision that a child must be "fully enrolled" in school for a court to order support past age 18, see In re J.A.B., 13 S.W.3d 813 (Tex. App.—Fort Worth 2000, no writ) (holding that child had been fully enrolled in a program leading toward a high school diploma, and thus was eligible for child support arrearages, despite the fact that the child had too many absences to receive credit for four of six classes); Crocker v. Attorney Gen. of Texas, 3 S.W.3d 650 (Tex. App.—Austin 1999, no writ) (holding that evidence was factually sufficient to support a finding that child was fully enrolled in a program leading to a high school diploma based not on how many hours of class child actually is taking, but on how many hours he would be required to take if seeking to graduate). See also James W. Paulsen, Family Law: Parent and Child, 54 SMU L. Rev. 1417, 1461-1462 (2001). On modification and termination of support, see Section C *infra*.

§154.001. Court may order either or both parents to support child until majority, emancipation, etc.

(a) The court may order either or both parents to support a child in the manner specified by the order:

(1) until the child is 18 years of age or until graduation from high school, whichever occurs later;

(2) until the child is emancipated through marriage, through removal of the disabilities of minority by court order, or by other operation of law;

(3) until the death of the child; or

(4) if the child is disabled as defined in this chapter, for an indefinite period.

(a-1) The court may order a person who is financially able and whose parental rights have been terminated with respect to a child in substitute care for whom the department has been appointed managing conservator to support the child in the manner specified by the order:

(1) until the earliest of:

(A) the child's adoption;

(B) the child's 18th birthday or graduation from high school, whichever occurs later;

(C) removal of the child's disabilities of minority by court order, marriage, or other operation of law; or

(D) the child's death; or

(2) if the child is disabled as defined in this chapter, for an indefinite period.

(b) The court may order either or both parents to make periodic payments for the support of a child in a proceeding in which the Department of Protective and Regulatory Services is named temporary managing conservator. In a proceeding in which the Department of Protective and Regulatory Services is named permanent managing conservator of a child whose parents' rights have not been terminated, the court shall order each parent that is financially able to make periodic payments for the support of the child.

(c) In a Title IV-D case, if neither parent has physical possession or conservatorship of the child, the court may render an order providing that a nonparent or agency having physical possession may receive, hold, or disburse child support payments for the benefit of the child.

(Acts 1995, 74th Leg., ch. 20, §1, effective April 20, 1995. Amended by Acts 1995, 74th Leg., ch. 751, §39, effective September 1, 1995. Amended by Acts 1999, 76th Leg., ch. 556, §8, effective September 1, 1999; Acts 2005, 79th Leg., ch. 268 (S.B. 6), §1.08(a), effective September 1, 2005.)

§154.002. Conditions for post-majority support

(a) The court may render an original support order, or modify an existing order, providing child support past the 18th birthday of the child to be paid only if the child is:

(1) enrolled:

(A) under Chapter 25, Education Code, in an accredited secondary school in a program leading toward a high school diploma;

(B) under Section 130.008, Education Code, in courses for joint high school and junior college credit; or

(C) on a full-time basis in a private secondary school in a program leading toward a high school diploma; and

(2) complying with:

(A) the minimum attendance requirements of Subchapter C, Chapter 25, Education Code; or

(B) the minimum attendance requirements imposed by the school in which the child is enrolled, if the child is enrolled in a private secondary school.

(b) The request for a support order through high school graduation may be filed before or after the child's 18th birthday.

(c) The order for periodic support may provide that payments continue through the end of the month in which the child graduates.

(Acts 1995, 74th Leg., ch. 20, §1, effective April 20, 1995. Amended by Acts 1999, 76th Leg., ch. 506, §1, effective Aug. 30, 1999; Acts 2003, 78th Leg., ch. 38, effective September 1, 2003.)

§154.006. Termination of child support order

(a) Unless otherwise agreed in writing or expressly provided in the order or as provided by Subsection (b), the child support order terminates on:

(1) the marriage of the child;

(2) removal of the child's disabilities for general purposes;

(3) the death of:

(A) the child; or

(B) a parent ordered to pay child support; or

(4) a finding by the court that the child:

(A) is 18 years of age or older; and

(B) has failed to comply with the enrollment or attendance requirements described by Section 154.002(a).

(b) Unless a nonparent or agency has been appointed conservator of the child under Chapter 153, the order for current child support, and any provision relating to conservatorship, possession, or access terminates on the marriage or remarriage of the obligor and obligee to each other.

(Acts 1995, 74th Leg., ch. 20, §1, effective April 20, 1995; Amended by Acts 1999, 76th Leg., ch. 556, §9, effective September 1, 1999; Acts 2003, 78th Leg., ch. 38, effective September 1, 2003.)

§154.013. Child support obligation does not terminate on death of obligee

(a) A child support obligation does not terminate on the death of the obligee but continues as an obligation to the child named in the support order, as required by this section.

(b) Notwithstanding any provision of the Probate Code, a child support payment held by the Title IV-D agency, a local registry, or the state disbursement unit or any uncashed check or warrant representing a child support payment made before, on, or after the date of death of the obligee shall be paid proportionately for the benefit of each surviving child named in the support order and not to the estate of the obligee. The payment is free of any creditor's claim against the deceased obligee's estate and may be disbursed as provided by Subsection (c).

(c) On the death of the obligee, current child support owed by the obligor for the benefit of the child or any amount described by Subsection (b) shall be paid to:

(1) a person, other than a parent, who is appointed as managing conservator of the child;

(2) a person, including the obligor, who has assumed actual care, control, and possession of the child, if a managing conservator or guardian of the child has not been appointed;

(3) the county clerk, as provided by Section 887, Texas Probate Code, in the name of and for the account of the child for whom the support is owed;

(4) a guardian of the child appointed under Chapter XIII, Texas Probate Code, as provided by that code; or

(5) the surviving child, if the child is an adult or has otherwise had the disabilities of minority removed.

(d) On presentation of the obligee's death certificate, the court shall render an order directing payment of child support paid but not disbursed to be made as provided by Subsection (c). A copy of the order shall be provided to:

(1) the obligor;

(2) as appropriate:

(A) the person having actual care, control, and possession of the child;

(B) the county clerk; or

(C) the managing conservator or guardian of the child, if one has been appointed;

(3) the local registry or state disbursement unit and, if appropriate, the Title IV-D agency; and

(4) the child named in the support order, if the child is an adult or has otherwise had the disabilities of minority removed.

(e) The order under Subsection (d) must contain:

(1) a statement that the obligee is deceased and that child support amounts otherwise payable to the obligee shall be paid for the benefit of a surviving child named in the support order as provided by Subsection (c);

(2) the name and age of each child named in the support order; and

(3) the name and mailing address of, as appropriate:

(A) the person having actual care, control, and possession of the child;

(B) the county clerk; or

(C) the managing conservator or guardian of the child, if one has been appointed.

(f) On receipt of the order required under this section, the local registry, state disbursement unit, or Title IV-D agency shall disburse payments as required by the order.

(Acts 2001, 77th Leg., ch. 1023, §6, effective September 1, 2001.

§154.306. Court shall give considerations to designated factors in determining post-majority support

In determining the amount of support to be paid after a child's 18th birthday, the specific terms and conditions of that support, and the rights and duties of both parents with respect to the support of the child, the court shall determine and give special consideration to:

(1) any existing or future needs of the adult child directly related to the adult child's mental or physical disability and the substantial care and personal supervision directly required by or related to that disability;

(2) whether the parent pays for or will pay for the care or supervision of the adult child or provides or will provide substantial care or personal supervision of the adult child;

(3) the financial resources available to both parents for the support, care, and supervision of the adult child; and

(4) any other financial resources or other resources or programs available for the support, care, and supervision of the adult child.

(Acts 1995, 74th Leg., ch. 20, §1, effective April 20, 1995.)

3. Time, Place, and Manner of Payment

Texas law gives courts discretion as to manner of payment of child support (Tex. Fam. Code §154.003), and as to the parent or parents who must pay support (Tex. Fam. Code §154.001 *supra*).

All states, including Texas, use child support guidelines in the determination of child support. On child support guidelines, see Section B *infra*. Also, Texas courts may order retroactive support subject to application of statutory support guidelines (Tex. Fam. Code §154.009(b)). See also In re J.A.G., 18 S.W.3d 772 (Tex. App.—San Antonio, 2000, no writ) (upholding an award of retroactive support against a prison inmate); Paulsen, *supra*, at 1452-1453 (criticizing enforcement of support child judgments on indigent inmates).

§154.003. Manner of payment of child support

The court may order that child support be paid by:

(1) periodic payments;

(2) a lump-sum payment;

(3) an annuity purchase;

(4) the setting aside of property to be administered for the support of the child as specified in the order; or

(5) any combination of periodic payments, lump-sum payments, annuity purchases, or setting aside of property.

(Acts 1995, 74th Leg., ch. 20, §1, effective April 20, 1995.)

§154.004. Court shall order payment of child support to designated state agencies

(a) The court shall order the payment of child support to a local registry, the Title IV-D agency, or the state disbursement unit, as provided by Chapter 234, as added by Chapter 911, Acts of the 75th Legislature, Regular Session, 1997.

(b) In a Title IV-D case, the court or the Title IV-D agency shall order that income withheld for child support be paid to the state disbursement unit of this state, or if appropriate, to the state disbursement unit of another state.

(c) This section does not apply to a child support order that:

(1) was initially rendered by a court before January 1, 1994; and

(2) is not being enforced by the Title IV-D agency.

(Acts 1995, 74th Leg., ch. 20, §1, effective April 20, 1995. Amended by Acts 1999, 76th Leg., ch. 556, §9, effective September 1, 1999; Acts 2003, 78th Leg., ch. 51247, effective September 1, 2003.)

§154.005. Court may order trustees to pay support obligation

(a) The court may order the trustees of a spendthrift or other trust to make disbursements for the support of a child to the extent the trustees are required to make payments to a beneficiary who is required to make child support payments as provided by this chapter.

(b) If disbursement of the assets of the trust is discretionary, the court may order child support payments from the income of the trust but not from the principal.

(Acts 1995, 74th Leg., ch. 20, §1, effective April 20, 1995.)

§154.009. Court may order retroactive child support

(a) The court may order a parent to pay retroactive child support if the parent:

(1) has not previously been ordered to pay support for the child; and

(2) was not a party to a suit in which support was ordered.

(b) In ordering retroactive child support, the court shall apply the child support guidelines provided by this chapter.

(c) Unless the Title IV-D agency is a party to an agreement concerning support or purporting to settle past, present, or future support obligations by prepayment or otherwise, an agreement between the parties does not reduce or terminate retroactive support that the agency may request.

(d) Notwithstanding Subsection (a), the court may order a parent subject to a previous child support order to pay retroactive child support if:

(1) the previous child support order terminated as a result of the marriage or remarriage of the child's parents;

(2) the child's parents separated after the marriage or remarriage; and

(3) a new child support order is sought after the date of the separation.

(e) In rendering an order under Subsection (d), the court may order retroactive child support back to the date of the separation of the child's parents.

(Acts 1995, 74th Leg., ch. 20, §1, effective April 20, 1995. Amended by Acts 2001, 77th Leg., ch. 1023, §4, effective September 1, 2001.)

§154.012. Obligee shall return support paid in excess of support order

(a) If an obligor is not in arrears and the obligor's child support obligation has terminated, the obligee shall return to the obligor a child support payment made by the obligor that exceeds the amount of support ordered, regardless of whether the payment was made before, on, or after the date the child support obligation terminated.

(b) An obligor may file a suit to recover a child support payment under Subsection (a). If the court finds that the obligee failed to return a child support payment under Subsection (a), the court shall order the obligee to pay to the obligor attorney's fees and all court costs in addition to the amount of support paid after the date the child support order terminated. For good cause shown, the court may waive the requirement that the obligee pay attorney's fees and costs if the court states the reasons supporting that finding.

(Acts 1999, 76th Leg., ch. 363, §1, effective September 1, 1999. Amended by Acts 2001, 77th Leg., ch. 1023, §5, effective September 1, 2001.)

§154.014. State agency's role vis à vis obligor's excess payment

(a) If a child support agency or local child support registry receives from an obligor who is not in arrears a child support payment in an amount that exceeds the court-ordered amount, the agency or registry, to the extent possible, shall give effect to any expressed intent of the obligor for the application of the amount that exceeds the court-ordered amount.

(b) If the obligor does not express an intent for the application of the amount paid in excess of the court-ordered amount, the agency or registry shall:

(1) credit the excess amount to the obligor's future child support obligation; and

(2) promptly disburse the excess amount to the obligee.

(c) This section does not apply to an obligee who is a recipient of public assistance under Chapter 31, Human Resources Code.

(Acts 2001, 77th Leg., ch. 1491, §2, effective September 1, 2001. Amended by Acts 2003, 78th Leg., ch 1275, effective September 1, 2003 (renumbered from §154.013)).

4. Relationship of Child Support and Visitation

The general rule is that the right to visitation and the duty of support are not interdependent variables. That is, visitation may not be conditioned on timely payment of child support. Nor may child support be withheld because an ex-spouse denies or interferes with visitation rights. Texas has codified this rule: "[a] court may not render an order that conditions the payment of child support" on whether the custodial parent permits visitation by the other parent" (Tex. Fam. Code §154.011). See also Gani v. Gani, 500 S.W.2d 254 (Tex. Civ. App.—Texarkana 1973) (holding that condition linking father's visitation rights to payment of support, in the absence of findings of a rational relationship between nonpayment and unfitness, was arbitrary and impermissible).

Texas courts have extended this rule to other contexts. Thus, modification of a domicile restriction regarding the mother's residence may not be conditioned on father's payment of child support judgment (Seidel v. Seidel, 10 S.W.3d 365 (Tex. App.—Dallas 1999, no writ)); payment of fees to an attorney ad litem for performing an investigation may not be conditioned on suspension of father's visitation rights (Saxton v. Daggett, 864 S.W.2d 729 (Tex. App.—Houston [1st Dist.] 1993, no writ).

§154.011. Support may not be conditioned on possession or access

A court may not render an order that conditions the payment of child support on whether a managing conservator allows a possessory conservator to have possession of or access to a child.

(Acts 1995, 74th Leg., ch. 751, §40, effective September 1, 1995.)

5. Medical Support

Medical care is among the "necessaries" that a parent must provide to a child. Texas law authorizes a court to order medical support for the child (Tex. Fam. Code §154.008). The statutory child support guidelines take into account this obligation (Tex. Fam. Code §154.064 *infra*). On the statutory child support guidelines, see Section B *infra*.

§154.008. Court shall order medical support

The court shall order medical support for the child as provided by Subchapters B and D.1

(Acts 1995, 74th Leg., ch. 20, §1, effective April 20, 1995. Amended by Acts 2001, 77th Leg., ch. 1023, §3, effective September 1, 2001.)

6. Support for a Disabled Adult Child

Parents generally owe support duties to biological and adopted children, unborn children, and those children conceived by artificial insemination. (On adoption and procreation, see Chapters X and XI *infra*.) In addition, some states require parents to provide support for a disabled adult child. A Texas court may order either or both parents to provide support for a disabled child indefinitely (Tex. Fam. Code §§154.001 *supra*, 154.302). For purposes of this subchapter, a "child" means "a son or daughter of any age" (Tex. Fam. Code §154.301(2)).

Case law has interpreted the Family Code's definition of a disabled child. According to Texas Family Code §154.302(a), a court may order support for a disabled child past age 18 if the child "requires substantial care and personal supervision because of a mental or physical disability and will not be capable of self-support" *and* the disability existed before the child's 18th birthday. In In re M.W.T., 12 S.W.3d 598 (Tex. App.—San Antonio, 2000, review denied), a mother requested that the father's child support and medical support be continued beyond her son's minority because of his Oppositional Defiant Disorder. When the father appealed, the court determined that the evidence was factually and legally sufficient to support the trial court's determination that the child is disabled, needs substantial care and supervision, and is incapable of supporting himself. See also Paulsen, *supra*, at 1458-1460 (criticizing the decision).

Whereas awards of custody and visitation generally pertain only to minors, Texas courts may make awards for "possession" and "access" to an adult disabled child "as appropriate under the circumstances" (Tex. Fam. Code §154.309). If the adult disabled child is mentally competent, however, that disabled adult may refuse custody or visitation (Tex. Fam. Code §154.309(b)).

---

§154.301. Definitions

In this subchapter:

(1) "Adult child" means a child 18 years of age or older.

(2) "Child" means a son or daughter of any age.

(Acts 1995, 74th Leg., ch. 20, §1, effective April 20, 1995.)

§154.302. Court may order support for disabled child

(a) The court may order either or both parents to provide for the support of a child for an indefinite period and may determine the rights and duties of the parents if the court finds that:

(1) the child, whether institutionalized or not, requires substantial care and personal supervision because of a mental or physical disability and will not be capable of self-support; and

(2) the disability exists, or the cause of the disability is known to exist, on or before the 18th birthday of the child.

(b) A court that orders support under this section shall designate a parent of the child or another person having physical custody or guardianship of the child under a court order to receive the support for the child. The court may designate a child who is 18 years of age or older to receive the support directly.

(Acts 1995, 74th Leg., ch. 20, §1, effective April 20, 1995. Amended by Acts 1997, 75th Leg., ch. 1173, §1, effective September 1, 1997.)

§154.303. Standing to sue

(a) A suit provided by this subchapter may be filed only by:

(1) a parent of the child or another person having physical custody or guardianship of the child under a court order; or

(2) the child if the child:

(A) is 18 years of age or older;

(B) does not have a mental disability; and

(C) is determined by the court to be capable of managing the child's financial affairs.

(b) The parent, the child, if the child is 18 years of age or older, or other person may not transfer or assign the cause of action to any person, including a governmental or private entity or agency, except for an assignment made to the Title IV-D agency.

(Acts 1995, 74th Leg., ch. 20, §1, effective April 20, 1995. Amended by Acts 1997, 75th Leg., ch. 1173, §2, effective September 1, 1997.)

§154.304. Substantive and procedural rights and remedies apply to suit filed

Except as otherwise provided by this subchapter, the substantive and procedural rights and remedies in a suit affecting the parent-child relationship relating to the establishment, modification, or enforcement of a child support order apply to a suit filed and an order rendered under this subchapter.

(Acts 1995, 74th Leg., ch. 20, §1, effective April 20, 1995.)

§154.305. Specific procedures for child support actions

(a) A suit under this subchapter may be filed:

(1) regardless of the age of the child; and

(2) as an independent cause of action or joined with any other claim or remedy provided by this code.

(b) If no court has continuing, exclusive jurisdiction of the child, an action under this subchapter may be filed as an original suit affecting the parent-child relationship.

(c) If there is a court of continuing, exclusive jurisdiction, an action under this subchapter may be filed as a suit for modification as provided by Chapter 156.

(Acts 1995, 74th Leg., ch. 20, §1, effective April 20, 1995.)

§154.307. Modification and enforcement of child support orders

An order provided by this subchapter may contain provisions governing the rights and duties of both parents with respect to the support of the child and may be modified or enforced in the same manner as any other order provided by this title.

(Acts 1995, 74th Leg., ch. 20, §1, effective April 20, 1995.)

§154.308. Remedy herein not exclusive

(a) This subchapter does not affect a parent's:

(1) cause of action for the support of a disabled child under any other law; or

(2) ability to contract for the support of a disabled child.

(b) This subchapter does not affect the substantive or procedural rights or remedies of a person other than a parent, including a governmental or private entity or agency, with respect to the support of a disabled child under any other law.

(Acts 1995, 74th Leg., ch. 20, §1, effective April 20, 1995.)

§154.309. Court may render order for possession of or access to adult disabled child

(a) A court may render an order for the possession of or access to an adult disabled child that is appropriate under the circumstances.

(b) Possession of or access to an adult disabled child is enforceable in the manner provided by Chapter 157. An adult disabled child may refuse possession or access if the adult disabled child is mentally competent.

(c) A court that obtains continuing, exclusive jurisdiction of a suit affecting the parent-child relationship involving a disabled person who is a child retains continuing, exclusive jurisdiction of subsequent proceedings involving the person, including proceedings after the person is an adult.

(Acts 1995, 74th Leg., ch. 751, §43, effective September 1, 1995).

B. DETERMINING THE AMOUNT OF SUPPORT

1. Background

Formerly, courts determined child support by the use of discretionary standards. U.S. divorce laws provided only vague guidance in the setting of postdissolution child support by directing courts to set an award that was "just," "reasonable," or "necessary."

Vague standards and judicial discretion resulted in awards that were inadequate, inconsistent, and unpredictable, and led to disrespect for support orders. These difficulties were magnified on the federal level because the welfare system faced increasing burdens in meeting the needs of children left unmet by their parents. Seeking to limit these fiscal burdens, in 1984 Congress mandated that by 1987 states must use child support guidelines as rebuttable presumptions in so-called Title IV-D cases (in which the state seeks to recover from an absent parent payments made to support a needy child). Subsequent legislation, the Family Support Act of 1988 (FSA), 42 U.S.C. §667(a)-(b)(2000), extended the guidelines requirement to all cases. By the FSA, Congress made compliance with the guidelines requirement a condition for receiving federal welfare funds.

In this manner, the regime of judicial discretion gave way to the modern approach: the use of mathematical formulae termed "guidelines." Most jurisdictions adopt guidelines by statute, although some jurisdictions do so by administrative regulations or court rules. Laura W. Morgan, Child Support Guidelines: Interpretation and Application §1.03 (1996 & Supp.). On the history of child support legislation, see generally Andrea H. Beller & John W. Graham, Small Change: The Economics of Child Support (1993); Oldham & Melli, *supra*.

Texas courts adhere to statewide uniform guidelines in adjudicating child support awards (including temporary orders) in any child support proceeding. Awards of child support are based on a percentage of the obligor's "net resources." The Family Code explains the rules applicable in the computation of those net resources available for child support purposes (Tex. Fam. Code §§154.061-154.070).

The statutory guidelines establish a rebuttable presumption of a particular amount of child support. Courts may depart from the guidelines only in special circumstances, which are set forth in the Texas Family Code. Moreover, some considerations are expressly precluded from being taken into account.

2. Computation of Net Resources Available for Support

A parent's "net resources" that are available for support purposes include all wage and salary income and other employment compensation (including self-employment income); interest, dividends, and royalty income; rental income; severance pay; retirement benefits; pensions; trust income; annuities; capital gains, Social Security benefits; unemployment benefits, disability, and workers' compensation benefits; and interest income from notes regardless of the source, gifts and prizes, spousal maintenance, alimony, and any other income actually received (Tex. Fam. Code §154.062(b)).

Certain items are excluded from the determination of "net resources": return of principal or capital, accounts receivable, and certain welfare benefits (Tex. Fam. Code §154.062(c)). Then, the court must make certain deductions after calculating the net resources that are available for child support purposes. Specifically, the court must deduct Social Security taxes, state and federal income tax for a single person claiming one personal exemption, union dues, and expenses for health insurance coverage for the child (*id.* at §154.062(d)).

Some states exclude from consideration the income and needs of the obligor or obligee's subsequent spouses. Texas law provides that the court may not add into the calculation of available net resources those net resources of a spouse of the obligor or obligee, nor may the court subtract the needs of a spouse or dependent of the spouse from the net resources of the obligor or obligee (Tex. Fam. Code §§154.069(a) and (b)).

A frequently litigated issue in many states is the effect of a parent's intentional unemployment or underemployment. Texas law provides that the court may apply the guidelines to the obligor's *earning potential* if the obligor's actual income is "significantly less than what the obligor could earn because of intentional unemployment or underemployment" (Tex. Fam. Code §154.066). That is, the court may hold the obligor liable for child support based on earning potential rather than actual net resources. Compare In re P.J.H., 25 S.W.3d 402 (Tex. App.—Fort Worth 2000, no writ) (affirming trial court finding that former husband, who sought to conceal one of his two jobs from the court, was intentionally underemployed), with Zorilla v. Wahid, 83 S.W.3d 247 (Tex. App.—Corpus Christi 2002, no writ) (holding that trial court acted within its discretion in finding that physician-husband, board-certified in oncology, was not purposefully underemployed in working in the mental health field).

If an obligee is claiming that the obligor is intentionally unemployed or underemployed, "the obligee should present evidence that: (1) the obligor is intentionally unemployed; (2) with the intent to avoid his or her child support obligations; and (3) he or she can earn a specific amount higher than that which is currently being earned." Gagnon et al., Child Support, Tex. Prac. Guide Family Law §12:60.

Texas Family Code

§154.061. Method of computation of gross and net monthly income

(a) Whenever feasible, gross income should first be computed on an annual basis and then should be recalculated to determine average monthly gross income.

(b) The Title IV-D agency shall annually promulgate tax charts to compute net monthly income, subtracting from gross income social security taxes and federal income tax withholding for a single person claiming one personal exemption and the standard deduction.

(Acts 1995, 74th Leg., ch. 20, §1, effective April 20, 1995.)

OFFICE OF THE ATTORNEY GENERAL 2006 TAX CHARTS

Pursuant to §154.061(b) of the Texas Family Code, the Office of the Attorney General of Texas, as the Title IV-D agency, has promulgated the following tax charts to assist courts in establishing the amount of a child support order. These tax charts are applicable to employed and self-employed persons in computing net monthly income.

Instructions for Use

To use these tables, first compute the obligor's annual gross income. Then recompute to determine the obligor's average monthly gross income. These tables provide a method for calculating "monthly net income" for child support purposes, subtracting from monthly gross income the Social Security taxes and the federal income tax withholding for a single person claiming one personal exemption and the standard deduction.

Thereafter, in many cases the guidelines call for a number of additional steps to complete the necessary calculations. For example, §§154.061–154.070 provide for appropriate additions to "income" as that term is defined for federal income tax purposes, and for certain subtractions from monthly net income, to arrive at the net resources of the obligor available for child support purposes. If necessary, one may compute an obligee's net resources using similar steps.

Pursuant to Tex. Fam. Code §154.061(b), attorneys Ted White and John O'Connell, Office of the Attorney General Child Support Division, prepared the following tax charts for 2006. They then forwarded their work product for review to Stephen A. Kuntz, a tax partner at Fulbright & Jaworski L.L.P. Special thanks go to both Stewart Gagnon and Mr. Kuntz for contributing their time and expertise in reviewing the 2006 tax charts to assure that the charts are as accurate as possible.

Employed Persons 2006 Tax Chart
Social Security Taxes

Monthly Gross Wages	Old-Age, Survivors and Disability Insurance Taxes (6.2%)*	Hospital (Medicare) Insurance Taxes (1.45%)*	Federal Income Taxes**	Net Monthly Income
$100	$6.20	$1.45	$0.00	$92.35
200	12.40	2.90	0.00	184.70
300	18.60	4.35	0.00	277.05
400	24.80	5.80	0.00	369.40
500	31.00	7.25	0.00	461.75
600	37.20	8.70	0.00	554.10
700	43.40	10.15	0.00	646.45
800	49.60	11.60	9.58	729.22
892.67***	55.35	12.94	18.85	805.53
900	55.80	13.05	19.58	811.57
1,000	62.00	14.50	29.58	893.92
1,100	68.20	15.95	39.58	976.27
1,200	74.40	17.40	49.58	1,058.62
1,300	80.60	18.85	59.58	1,140.97
1,400	86.80	20.30	72.92	1,219.98
1,500	93.00	21.75	87.92	1,297.33
1,600	99.20	23.20	102.92	1,374.68
1,700	105.40	24.65	117.92	1,452.03
1,800	111.60	26.10	132.92	1,529.38
1,900	117.80	27.55	147.92	1,606.73
2,000	124.00	29.00	162.92	1,684.08
2,100	130.20	30.45	177.92	1,761.43
2,200	136.40	31.90	192.92	1,838.78
2,300	142.60	33.35	207.92	1,916.13
2,400	148.80	34.80	222.92	1,993.48
2,500	155.00	36.25	237.92	2,070.83
2,600	161.20	37.70	252.92	2,148.18
2,700	167.40	39.15	267.92	2,225.53
2,800	173.60	40.60	282.92	2,302.88
2,900	179.80	42.05	297.92	2,380.23
3,000	186.00	43.50	312.92	2,457.58
3,100	192.20	44.95	327.92	2,534.93
3,200	198.40	46.40	342.92	2,612.28
3,300	204.60	47.85	362.08	2,685.47
3,400	210.80	49.30	387.08	2,752.82
3,500	217.00	50.75	412.08	2,820.17
3,600	223.20	52.20	437.08	2,887.52
3,700	229.40	53.65	462.08	2,954.87
3,800	235.60	55.10	487.08	3,022.22
3,900	241.80	56.55	512.08	3,089.57
4,000	248.00	58.00	537.08	3,156.92
4,250	263.50	61.63	599.58	3,325.29
4,500	279.00	65.25	662.08	3,493.67
4,750	294.50	68.88	724.58	3,662.04
5,000	310.00	72.50	787.08	3,830.42
5,250	325.50	76.13	849.58	3,998.79
5,500	341.00	79.75	912.08	4,167.17
5,750	356.50	83.38	974.58	4,335.54
6,000	372.00	87.00	1,037.08	4,503.92
6,250	387.50	90.63	1,099.58	4,672.29
6,500	403.00	94.25	1,162.08	4,840.67
6,750	418.50	97.88	1,224.58	5,009.04
7,000	434.00	101.50	1,290.46	5,174.04
7,500	465.00	108.75	1,430.46	5,495.79
8,000	486.70****	116.00	1,570.46	5,826.84
8,245.44*****	486.70	119.56	1,639.18	6,000.00
8,500	486.70	123.25	1,710.46	6,179.59
9,000	486.70	130.50	1,850.46	6,532.34
9,500	486.70	137.75	1,990.46	6,885.09
10,000	486.70	145.00	2,130.46	7,237.84
10,500	486.70	152.25	2,270.46	7,590.59
11,000	486.70	159.50	2,410.46	7,943.34
11,500	486.70	166.75	2,550.46	8,296.09
12,000	486.70	174.00	2,690.46	8,648.84

12,500	486.70	181.25	2,830.46	9,001.59
13,000	486.70	188.50	2,973.54	9,351.26
13,500	486.70	195.75	3,115.59	9,701.96
14,000	486.70	203.00	3,278.72	10,031.58
14,500	486.70	210.25	3,447.35	10,355.70
15,000	486.70	217.50	3,614.77	10,681.03

FOOTNOTES TO EMPLOYED PERSONS 2006 TAX CHART:

* An employed person not subject to the Old-Age, Survivors and Disability Insurance/Hospital (Medicare) Insurance taxes will be allowed the reductions reflected in these columns, unless it is shown that such person has no similar contributory plan such as teacher retirement, federal railroad retirement, federal civil service retirement, etc.

** These amounts represent one-twelfth (1/12th) of the annual federal income tax calculated for a single taxpayer claiming one personal exemption ($3,300.00, subject to reduction in certain cases, as described in the next paragraph of this footnote) and taking the standard deduction ($5,150.00).

For a single taxpayer with an adjusted gross income in excess of $150,500.00, the deduction for the personal exemption is reduced by two-thirds of two percent (2%) for each $2,500.00 or fraction thereof by which adjusted gross income exceeds $150,500.00. The deduction for the personal exemption is no longer reduced for adjusted gross income in excess of $273,000.00.

For example, monthly gross wages of $15,000.00 times 12 months equals $180,000.00. The excess over $150,500.00 is $29,500.00. $29,500.00 divided by $2,500.00 equals 11.80. The 11.80 amount is rounded up to 2. The reduction percentage is 16.00% (2/3 x 2% x 12 = 16.00%). The $3,300.00 deduction for one personal exemption is reduced by $528.00 ($3,300.00 x 16.00% = $528.00) to $2,772.00 ($3,300.00 – $528.00 = $2,772.00). For annual gross income in excess of $273,000.00 the deduction for the personal exemption is $1,100.00.

*** The amount represents one-twelfth (1/12) of the gross income of an individual earning the federal minimum wage ($5.15 per hour) for a 40-hour week for a full year. $5.15 per hour x 40 hours per week x 52 weeks per year equals $10,712.00 per year. One-twelfth (1/12) of $10,712.00 equals $892.67.

**** For annual gross wages above $94,200.00, this amount represents a monthly average of the Old-Age, Survivors and Disability Insurance tax based on the 2006 maximum Old-Age, Survivors and Disability Insurance tax of $5,840.00 per person (6.2% of the first $94,200.00 of annual gross wages equals $5,840.00). One-twelfth (1/12th) of $5,840.00 equals $486.70.

***** This amount represents the point where the monthly gross wages of an employed individual would result in $6,000.00 of net resources.

References Relating to Employed Persons 2006 Tax Chart:

1. Old-Age, Survivors and Disability Insurance Tax
   (a) Contribution Base
   (1) Social Security Administration's notice dated October 18, 2005, and appearing in 70 Fed. Reg. 61,677 (October 25, 2005)
   (2) Section 3121(a) of the Internal Revenue Code of 1986, as amended (26 U.S.C. §3121(a))
   (3) Section 230 of the Social Security Act, as amended (42 U.S.C. §430)
   (b) Tax Rate
   (1) Section 3101(a) of the Internal Revenue Code of 1986, as amended (26 U.S.C. §3101(a))
2. Hospital (Medicare) Insurance Tax
   (a) Contribution Base
   (1) Section 3121(a) of the Internal Revenue Code of 1986, as amended (26 U.S.C. §3121(a))
   (2) Omnibus Budget Reconciliation Act of 1993, Pub. L. No. 103-66, §13207, 107 Stat. 312, 467-69 (1993)
   (b) Tax Rate
   (1) Section 3101(b) of the Internal Revenue Code of 1986, as amended (26 U.S.C. § 3101(b))
3. Federal Income Tax
   (a) Tax Rate Schedule for 2006 for Single Taxpayers
   (1) Revenue Procedure 2005-70, Section 3.01, Table 3 which appears in Internal Revenue Bulletin 2005-47, dated November 21, 2005
   (2) Section 1(c), (f) and (i) of the Internal Revenue Code of 1986, as amended (26 U.S.C. §1(c), (f) and (i))
   (b) Standard Deduction
   (1) Revenue Procedure 2005-70, Section 3.10(1), which appears in Internal Revenue Bulletin 2005-47, dated November 21, 2005
   (2) Section 63(c) of the Internal Revenue Code of 1986, as amended (26 U.S.C. §63(c))
   (c) Personal Exemption
   (1) Revenue Procedure 2005-70, Section 3.17, which appears in Internal Revenue Bulletin 2005-47, dated November 21, 2005
   (2) Section 151(d) of the Internal Revenue Code of 1986, as amended (26 U.S.C. §151(d)).

Self- Employed Persons 2006 Tax Chart Social Security Taxes

*Monthly Net Earnings From Self-Employment**	*Old-Age, Survivors and Disability Insurance Taxes (12.4%)***	*Hospital (Medicare) Insurance Taxes (2.9%)***	*Federal Income Taxes****	*Net Monthly Income*
$100	$11.45	$2.68	$0.00	$85.87
200	22.90	5.36	0.00	171.74
300	34.35	8.03	0.00	257.62
400	45.81	10.71	0.00	343.48
500	57.26	7.25	0.00	429.35
600	68.71	8.70	0.00	515.22
700	80.16	10.15	0.00	601.09
800	91.61	13.39	3.93	683.03
900	103.06	24.10	13.23	759.61
1,000	114.51	26.78	22.52	836.19
1,100	125.97	29.46	31.81	912.76
1,200	137.42	32.14	41.11	989.33
1,300	148.87	34.82	50.40	1,065.91
1,400	160.32	37.49	59.69	1,142.50
1,500	171.77	40.17	72.02	1,216.04
1,600	183.22	42.85	85.96	1,287.97
1,700	194.67	45.53	99.90	1,359.90
1,800	206.13	48.21	113.84	1,431.82
1,900	217.58	50.88	127.78	1,503.76
2,000	229.03	53.56	141.72	1,575.69

2,100	240.48	56.24	155.66	1,647.62
2,200	251.93	58.92	169.60	1,719.55
2,300	263.38	61.60	183.54	1,791.48
2,400	274.83	64.28	197.48	1,863.41
2,500	286.29	66.95	211.42	1,935.34
2,600	297.74	69.63	225.36	2,007.27
2,700	309.19	72.31	239.30	2,079.20
2,800	320.64	74.99	253.24	2,151.13
2,900	332.09	77.67	267.18	2,223.06
3,000	343.54	80.34	281.13	2,294.99
3,100	354.99	83.02	295.07	2,366.92
3,200	366.44	85.70	309.01	2,438.85
3,300	377.90	88.38	322.95	2,510.77
3,400	389.35	91.06	336.89	2,582.70
3,500	400.80	93.74	350.83	2,654.63
3,600	412.25	96.41	373.50	2,717.84
3,700	423.70	99.09	396.73	2,780.48
3,800	435.15	101.77	419.97	2,843.11
3,900	446.60	104.45	443.20	2,905.75
4,000	458.06	107.13	466.43	2,968.38
4,250	486.68	113.82	524.52	3,124.98
4,500	515.31	120.52	582.60	3,281.57
4,750	543.94	127.21	640.69	3,438.16
5,000	572.57	133.91	698.77	3,594.75
5,250	601.20	140.60	756.86	3,751.34
5,500	629.83	147.30	814.94	3,907.93
5,750	658.46	153.99	873.03	4,064.52
6,000	687.08	160.69	931.11	4,221.12
6,250	715.71	167.38	989.20	4,337.71
6,500	744.34	174.08	1,047.28	4,534.30
6,750	772.97	180.78	1,105.36	4,690.89
7,000	801.60	187.47	1,163.45	4,847.48
7,500	858.86	200.86	1,282.10	5,158.18
8,000	916.11	214.25	1,412.21	5,457.43
8,500	973.37	227.64	1,542.32	5,756.67
8,849.16*****	973.40****	236.99	1,638.77	6,000.00
9,000	973.40	241.03	1,680.44	6,105.13
9,500	973.40	254.42	1,818.56	6,453.62
10,000	973.40	267.82	1,956.69	6,802.09
10,500	973.40	281.21	2,094.81	7,150.58
11,000	973.40	294.60	2,232.94	7,499.06
11,500	973.40	307.99	2,371.06	7,847.55
12,000	973.40	321.38	2,509.19	8,196.03
12,500	973.40	334.77	2,647.31	8,544.52
13,000	973.40	348.16	2,785.44	8,893.00
13,500	973.40	361.55	2,925.62	9,239.43
14,000	973.40	374.94	3,065.80	9,585.86
14,500	973.40	388.33	3,219.03	9,919.24
15,000	973.40	401.72	3,384.25	10,240.63

FOOTNOTES TO SELF-EMPLOYED PERSONS 2006 TAX CHART:

* Determined without regard to Section 1402(a)(12) of the Internal Revenue Code of 1986, as amended (26 U.S.C.) (the "Code").

** In calculating each of the Old-Age, Survivors and Disability Insurance tax and the Hospital (Medicare) Insurance tax, net earnings from self-employment are reduced by the deduction under Section 1402(a)(12) of the Code. The deduction under Section 1402(a)(12) of the Code is equal to net earnings from self-employment (determined without regard to Section 1402(a)(12) of the Code) multiplied by one-half (1/2) of the sum of the Old-Age, Survivors and Disability Insurance tax rate (12.4%) and the Hospital (Medicare) Insurance tax rate (2.9%). The sum of these rates is 15.3% (12.4% + 2.9% = 15.3%). One-half (1/2) of the combined rate is 7.65% (15.3% x 1/2 = 7.65%). The deduction can be computed by multiplying the net earnings from self-employment (determined without regard to Section 1402(a)(12) of the Code) by 92.35%. This gives the same deduction as multiplying the net earnings from self-employment (determined without regard to Section 1402(a)(12) of the Code) by 7.65% and then subtracting the result.

For example, the Social Security taxes imposed on monthly net earnings from self-employment (determined without regard to Section 1402(a)(12) of the Code) of $2,500.00 are calculated as follows:

(i) Old Age, Survivors and Disability Insurance Taxes:

$2,500.00 x 92.35% x 12.4% = $286.29

(ii) Hospital (Medicare) Insurance Taxes:

$2,500.00 x 92.35% x 2.9% = $66.95

*** These amounts represent one-twelfth (1/12) of the annual federal income tax calculated for a single taxpayer claiming one personal exemption ($3,300.00, subject to reduction in certain cases, as described below in this footnote) and taking the standard deduction ($5,150.00).

In calculating the annual federal income tax, gross income is reduced by the deduction under Section 164(f) of the Code. The deduction under Section 164(f) of the Code is equal to one-half (1/2) of the self-employment taxes imposed by Section 1401 of the Code for the taxable year. For example, monthly net earnings from self-employment of $15,000 times 12 months equals $180,000. The Old-Age, Survivors and Disability Insurance taxes imposed by Section 1401 of the Code for the taxable year equal $11,680 ($94,200 x 12.4% = $11,680). The Hospital (Medicare) Insurance taxes imposed by Section 1401 of the Code for the taxable year equal $4,820.67 ($180,000.00 x .9235 x 2.9% = $4,820.67). The sum of the taxes imposed by Section 1401 of the Code for the taxable year equals $16,501.47 ($11,680 + $4,820.67 = $16,501.47). The deduction under Section 164(f) of the Code is equal to one-half (1/2) of $16,501.47 or $8,250.74.

For a single taxpayer with an adjusted gross income in excess of $150,500, the deduction for the personal exemption is reduced by two-thirds (2/3) of two percent (2%) for each $2,500 or fraction thereof by which adjusted gross income exceeds $150,500.00. The deduction for the personal exemption is no longer reduced for adjusted gross income in excess of $273,000. For example, monthly net earnings from self-employment of $15,000.00 times 12 months equals $180,000. The $180,000.00 amount is reduced by $8,250.74 (i.e., the deduction under Section 164(f) of the Code—see the immediately preceding paragraph of this footnote for the computation) to arrive at adjusted gross income of $171,749.26. The excess over $150,500.00 is $21,249.26. $21,249.26 divided by $2,500 equals 8.50. The 8.50 amount is rounded up to 9. The reduction percentage is 12% (2/3 x 2% x 9 = 12%). The $3,300.00 deduction for one personal exemption is reduced by $396 ($3,300 x 12% = $396) to $2,904 ($3,300.00 — $396 = $2,904.00). For adjusted gross income in excess of $273,000.00 the deduction for the personal exemption is $1,100.00.

**** For annual net earnings from self-employment (determined with regard to Section 1402(a)(12) of the Code) above $94,200.00, this amount represents a monthly average of the Old-Age, Survivors and Disability Insurance tax based on the 2006 maximum Old-Age, Survivors and Disability Insurance tax of $11,680.80 per person (12.4% of the first $94,200.00 of net earnings from self-employment (determined with regard to Section 1402(a)(12) of the Code) equals $11,680.80). One-twelfth (1/12) of $11,680.80 equals $973.40.

***** This amount represents the point where the monthly net earnings from self-employment of a self-employed individual would result in $6,000.00 of net resources.

References Relating to Self-Employed Persons 2006 Tax Chart:

1. Old-Age, Survivors and Disability Insurance Tax
   (a) Contribution Base
      (1) Social Security Administration's notice dated October 18, 2005, and appearing in 70 Fed. Reg. 61,677 (October 25, 2005)
      (2) Section 1402(b) of the Internal Revenue Code of 1986, as amended (26 U.S.C. §1402(b))
      (3) Section 230 of the Social Security Act, as amended (42 U.S.C. §430)
   (b) Tax Rate
      (1) Section 1401(a) of the Internal Revenue Code of 1986, as amended (26 U.S.C. §1401(a))
   (c) Deduction Under Section 1402(a)(12)
      (1) Section 1402(a)(12) of the Internal Revenue Code of 1986, as amended (26 U.S.C. §1402(a)(12))
2. Hospital (Medicare) Insurance Tax
   (a) Contribution Base
      (1) Section 1402(b) of the Internal Revenue Code of 1986, as amended (26 U.S.C. §1402(b))
      (2) Omnibus Budget Reconciliation Act of 1993, Pub. L. No. 103-66, §13207, 107 Stat. 312, 467-69 (1993)
   (b) Tax Rate
      (1) Section 1401(b) of the Internal Revenue Code of 1986, as amended (26 U.S.C. §1401(b))
   (c) Deduction Under Section 1402(a)(12)
      (1) Section 1402(a)(12) of the Internal Revenue Code of 1986, as amended (26 U.S.C. §1402(a)(12))
3. Federal Income Tax
   (a) Tax Rate Table for 2006 for Single Taxpayers
      (1) Revenue Procedure 2005-70, Section 3.01, Table 3 which appears in Internal Revenue Bulletin 2005-47, dated November 21, 2005
      (2) Section 1(c), (f) and (i) of the Internal Revenue Code of 1986, as amended (26 U.S.C. §1(c), (f) and (i))
   (b) Standard Deduction
      (1) Revenue Procedure 2005-70, Section 3.10(1), which appears in Internal Revenue Bulletin 2005-47, dated November 21, 2005
      (2) Section 63(c) of the Internal Revenue Code of 1986, as amended (26 U.S.C. §63(c))
   (c) Personal Exemption
      (1) Revenue Procedure 2005-70, Section 3.17, which appears in Internal Revenue Bulletin 2005-47, dated November 21, 2005
      (2) Section 151(d) of the Internal Revenue Code of 1986, as amended (26 U.S.C. §151(d))
   (d) Deduction Under Section 164(f)
      (1) Section 164(f) of the Internal Revenue Code of 1986, as amended (26 U.S.C. § 164(f)).

§154.062. Calculation of net resources

(a) The court shall calculate net resources for the purpose of determining child support liability as provided by this section.

(b) Resources include:

(1) 100 percent of all wage and salary income and other compensation for personal services (including commissions, overtime pay, tips, and bonuses);

(2) interest, dividends, and royalty income;

(3) self-employment income;

(4) net rental income (defined as rent after deducting operating expenses and mortgage payments, but not including noncash items such as depreciation); and

(5) all other income actually being received, including severance pay, retirement benefits, pensions, trust income, annuities, capital gains, social security benefits, unemployment benefits, disability and workers' compensation benefits, interest income from notes regardless of the source, gifts and prizes, spousal maintenance, and alimony.

(c) Resources do not include:

(1) return of principal or capital;

(2) accounts receivable; or

(3) benefits paid in accordance with aid for families with dependent children.

(d) The court shall deduct the following items from resources to determine the net resources available for child support:

(1) social security taxes;

(2) federal income tax based on the tax rate for a single person claiming one personal exemption and the standard deduction;

(3) state income tax;

(4) union dues; and

(5) expenses for health insurance coverage for the obligor's child.

(Acts 1995, 74th Leg., ch. 20, §1, effective April 20, 1995. Amended by Acts 1995, 74th Leg., ch. 751, §41, effective September 1, 1995.)

§154.063. Court shall require party to furnish financial information

The court shall require a party to:

(1) furnish information sufficient to accurately identify that party's net resources and ability to pay child support; and

(2) produce copies of income tax returns for the past two years, a financial statement, and current pay stubs.

(Acts 1995, 74th Leg., ch. 20, §1, effective April 20, 1995.)

§154.064. Support guidelines based on parent's presumptive provision of medical support

The guidelines for support of a child are based on the assumption that the court will order the obligor to provide medical support for the child in addition to the amount of child support calculated in accordance with those guidelines.

(Acts 1995, 74th Leg., ch. 20, §1, effective April 20, 1995. Amended by Acts 2001, 77th Leg., ch. 1023, §7, effective September 1, 2001.)

§154.065. Income from self-employment, defined

(a) Income from self-employment, whether positive or negative, includes benefits allocated to an individual from a business or undertaking in the form of a proprietorship, partnership, joint venture, close corporation, agency, or independent contractor, less ordinary and necessary expenses required to produce that income.

(b) In its discretion, the court may exclude from self-employment income amounts allowable under federal income tax law as depreciation, tax credits, or any other business expenses shown by the evidence to be inappropriate in making the determination of income available for the purpose of calculating child support.

(Acts 1995, 74th Leg., ch. 20, §1, effective April 20, 1995.)

§154.066. Court may apply guidelines to earning potential if obligor is intentionally unemployed or underemployed

If the actual income of the obligor is significantly less than what the obligor could earn because of intentional unemployment or underemployment, the court may apply the support guidelines to the earning potential of the obligor.

(Acts 1995, 74th Leg., ch. 20, §1, effective April 20, 1995.)

§154.067. Court may assign income to non-productive assets

(a) When appropriate, in order to determine the net resources available for child support, the court may assign a reasonable amount of deemed income attributable to assets that do not currently produce income. The court shall also consider whether certain property that is not producing income can be liquidated without an unreasonable financial sacrifice because of cyclical or other market conditions. If there is no effective market for the property, the carrying costs of such an investment, including property taxes and note payments, shall be offset against the income attributed to the property.

(b) The court may assign a reasonable amount of deemed income to income-producing assets that a party has voluntarily transferred or on which earnings have intentionally been reduced.

(Acts 1995, 74th Leg., ch. 20, §1, effective April 20, 1995.)

§154.068. Presumption of federal minimum wage in absence of evidence of party's income

In the absence of evidence of the wage and salary income of a party, the court shall presume that the party has wages or salary equal to the federal minimum wage for a 40 hour week.

(Acts 1995, 74th Leg., ch. 20, §1, effective April 20, 1995.)

§154.069. Net resources of spouse may not be considered

(a) The court may not add any portion of the net resources of a spouse to the net resources of an obligor or obligee in order to calculate the amount of child support to be ordered.

(b) The court may not subtract the needs of a spouse, or of a dependent of a spouse, from the net resources of the obligor or obligee.

(Acts 1995, 74th Leg., ch. 20, §1, effective April 20, 1995.)

§154.070. Court may take into account child support received by obligor

In a situation involving multiple households due child support, child support received by an obligor shall be added to the obligor's net resources to compute the net resources before determining the child support credit or applying the percentages in the multiple household table in this chapter.

(Acts 1995, 74th Leg., ch. 20, §1, effective April 20, 1995.)

---

3. Child Support Guidelines

The policy underling the guidelines is to assist the court in "determining an equitable amount of child support" (Tex. Fam. Code §154.121). An order of child support that conforms to the guidelines is rebuttably presumed to be in the child's best interests (Tex. Fam. Code §154.122(a)).

---

§154.121. Child support guidelines, policy

The child support guidelines in this subchapter are intended to guide the court in determining an equitable amount of child support.

(Acts 1995, 74th Leg., ch. 20, §1, effective April 20, 1995.)

---

a. Best Interests of the Child

§154.122. Child support order conforming to guidelines rebuttably presumed in best interests

(a) The amount of a periodic child support payment established by the child support guidelines in effect in this state at the time of the hearing is presumed to be reasonable, and an order of support conforming to the guidelines is presumed to be in the best interest of the child.

(b) A court may determine that the application of the guidelines would be unjust or inappropriate under the circumstances.

(Acts 1995, 74th Leg., ch. 20, §1, effective April 20, 1995.)

---

b. Deviation from Guidelines Permitted

The court may deviate from the recommended guidelines if "the evidence rebuts the presumption that application of the guidelines is in the best interest of the child and justifies a variance from the guidelines" (Tex. Fam. Code §154.123(a)). The court may consider evidence of 17 specific factors (*id.* at §154.123(b)(17)) in its determination whether application of the guidelines would be "unjust or inappropriate," including "any other reason consistent with the best interest of the child, taking into consideration the circumstances of the parents" (Tex. Fam. Code §154.123(b)(1) – (17)).

§154.123. Court must consider additional factors to determine if guidelines unjust or inappropriate

(a) The court may order periodic child support payments in an amount other than that established by the guidelines if the evidence rebuts the presumption that application of the guidelines is in the best interest of the child and justifies a variance from the guidelines.

(b) In determining whether application of the guidelines would be unjust or inappropriate under the circumstances, the court shall consider evidence of all relevant factors, including:

(1) the age and needs of the child;

(2) the ability of the parents to contribute to the support of the child;

(3) any financial resources available for the support of the child;

(4) the amount of time of possession of and access to a child;

(5) the amount of the obligee's net resources, including the earning potential of the obligee if the actual income of the obligee is significantly less than what the obligee could earn because the obligee is intentionally unemployed or underemployed and including an increase or decrease in the income of the obligee or income that may be attributed to the property and assets of the obligee;

(6) child care expenses incurred by either party in order to maintain gainful employment;

(7) whether either party has the managing conservatorship or actual physical custody of another child;

(8) the amount of alimony or spousal maintenance actually and currently being paid or received by a party;

(9) the expenses for a son or daughter for education beyond secondary school;

(10) whether the obligor or obligee has an automobile, housing, or other benefits furnished by his or her employer, another person, or a business entity;

(11) the amount of other deductions from the wage or salary income and from other compensation for personal services of the parties;

(12) provision for health care insurance and payment of uninsured medical expenses;

(13) special or extraordinary educational, health care, or other expenses of the parties or of the child;

(14) the cost of travel in order to exercise possession of and access to a child;

(15) positive or negative cash flow from any real and personal property and assets, including a business and investments;

(16) debts or debt service assumed by either party; and

(17) any other reason consistent with the best interest of the child, taking into consideration the circumstances of the parents.

(Acts 1995, 74th Leg., ch. 20, §1, effective April 20, 1995.)

c. Application in Special Circumstances

The guidelines apply if the obligor's net resources are $6,000 per month or less (Tex. Fam. Code §154.125(a)). If the obligor's net resources exceed that amount, the guidelines apply only to the first $6,000 of net resources, but the court may order additional support "as appropriate, depending on the income of the parties and the proven needs of the child" (Tex. Fam. Code §154.126).

The court has limited discretion to deviate from the guidelines. If the court decides to deviate from the guidelines, it must make specific findings of fact and conclusions of law (Tex. Fam. Code §154.130). The requisite findings must state that application of the guidelines would be "unjust or inappropriate" (*id.*) and set forth the reasons that the amount varies from the guidelines.

Courts also may vary from the guidelines if the parties have entered into a written agreement for child support (provided that the agreement is in the child's best interest). As of 2003, however, such agreements continue to be enforceable by all remedies generally available for enforcement of judgments, including contempt, but not as contracts. Tex. Fam. Code 154.124(c). Prior law permitted contractual enforcement if the agreement so provided.

In addition, special computations are required if the obligor is liable for child support for children in multiple households (Tex. Fam. Code §154.128), if the obligor is disabled (Tex. Fam. Code §154.132), or if the obligor is receiving Social Security benefits and required to pay support for a child who receives derivative Social Security benefits (Tex. Fam. Code §154.133).

§154.124. Parties may enter into agreement for child support

(a) To promote the amicable settlement of disputes between the parties to a suit, the parties may enter into a written agreement containing provisions for support of the child and for modification of the agreement, including variations from the child support guidelines provided by Subchapter C [§§154.121 et seq.].

(b) If the court finds that the agreement is in the child's best interest, the court shall render an order in accordance with the agreement.

(c) Terms of the agreement in the order may be enforced by all remedies available for enforcement of a judgment, including contempt, but are not enforceable as a contract.

(d) If the court finds the agreement is not in the child's best interest, the court may request the parties to submit a revised agreement or the court may render an order for the support of the child.

(Acts 1995, 74th Leg., ch. 20, §1, effective April 20, 1995. Amended by Acts 2003, 78th Leg., ch. 480, effective September 1, 2003.)

§154.125. Guidelines apply to obligors with monthly net resources of $6,000 or less

(a) The guidelines for the support of a child in this section are specifically designed to apply to situations in which the obligor's monthly net resources are $6,000 or less.

(b) If the obligor's monthly net resources are $6,000 or less, the court shall presumptively apply the following schedule in rendering the child support order:

CHILD SUPPORT GUIDELINES BASED ON THE MONTHLY NET RESOURCES OF THE OBLIGOR

1 child 20% of Obligor's Net Resources
2 children 25% of Obligor's Net Resources
3 children 30% of Obligor's Net Resources
4 children 35% of Obligor's Net Resources
5 children 40% of Obligor's Net Resources
6+ children Not less than the amount for 5 children

(Acts 1995, 74th Leg., ch. 20, §1, effective April 20, 1995.)

§154.126. Presumptive application of guidelines if net resources are more than $6,000 monthly

(a) If the obligor's net resources exceed $6,000 per month, the court shall presumptively apply the percentage guidelines to the first $6,000 of the obligor's net resources. Without further reference to the percentage recommended by these guidelines, the court may order additional amounts of child support as appropriate, depending on the income of the parties and the proven needs of the child.

(b) The proper calculation of a child support order that exceeds the presumptive amount established for the first $6,000 of the obligor's net resources requires that the entire amount of the presumptive award be subtracted from the proven total needs of the child. After the presumptive award is subtracted, the court shall allocate between the parties the responsibility to meet the additional needs of the child according to the circumstances of the parties. However, in no event may the obligor be required to pay more child support than the greater of the presumptive amount or the amount equal to 100 percent of the proven needs of the child.

(Acts 1995, 74th Leg., ch. 20, §1, effective April 20, 1995.)

§154.127. Termination of child support for one child leaves support for remaining child in accordance with guidelines

A child support order for more than one child shall provide that, on the termination of support for a child, the level of support for the remaining child or children is in accordance with the child support guidelines.

(Acts 1995, 74th Leg., ch. 20, §1, effective April 20, 1995.)

§154.128. Computing support for obligor's children in several households

(a) In applying the child support guidelines for an obligor who has children in more than one household, the court shall apply the percentage guidelines in this subchapter by making the following computation:

(1) determine the amount of child support that would be ordered if all children whom the obligor has the legal duty to support lived in one household by applying the schedule in this subchapter;

(2) compute a child support credit for the obligor's children who are not before the court by dividing the amount determined under Subdivision (1) by the total number of children whom the obligor is obligated to support and multiplying that number by the number of the obligor's children who are not before the court;

(3) determine the adjusted net resources of the obligor by subtracting the child support credit computed under Subdivision (2) from the net resources of the obligor; and

(4) determine the child support amount for the children before the court by applying the percentage guidelines for one household for the number of children of the obligor before the court to the obligor's adjusted net resources.

(b) For the purpose of determining a child support credit, the total number of an obligor's children includes the children before the court for the establishment or modification of a support order and any other children, including children residing with the obligor, whom the obligor has the legal duty of support.

(c) The child support credit with respect to children for whom the obligor is obligated by an order to pay support is computed, regardless of whether the obligor is delinquent in child support payments, without regard to the amount of the order.

(Acts 1995, 74th Leg., ch. 20, §1, effective April 20, 1995.)

§154.129. Court may use alternative method of computing support for children in several households

In lieu of performing the computation under the preceding section, the court may determine the child support amount for the children before the court by applying the percentages in the table below to the obligor's net resources:

Multiple Family Adjusted Guidelines (% of Net Resources)

		Number of children before the court						
		1	2	3	4	5	6	7
Number of	0	20.00	25.00	30.00	35.00	40.00	40.00	40.00
other	1	17.50	22.50	27.38	32.20	37.33	37.71	38.00
children for	2	16.00	20.63	25.20	30.33	35.43	36.00	36.44
Whom the	3	14.75	19.00	24.00	29.00	34.00	34.67	35.20
obligor	4	13.60	18.33	23.14	28.00	32.89	33.60	34.18
has a	5	13.33	17.86	22.50	27.22	32.00	32.73	33.33
duty of	6	13.14	17.50	22.00	26.60	31.27	32.00	32.62
support	7	13.00	17.22	21.60	26.09	30.67	31.38	32.00

(Acts 1995, 74th Leg., ch. 20, §1, effective April 20, 1995.)

§154.130. Court shall make requisite findings in child support order

(a) Without regard to Rules 296 through 299, Texas Rules of Civil Procedure, in rendering an order of child support, the court shall make the findings required by Subsection (b) if:

(1) a party files a written request with the court not later than 10 days after the date of the hearing;

(2) a party makes an oral request in open court during the hearing; or

(3) the amount of child support ordered by the court varies from the amount computed by applying the percentage guidelines.

(b) If findings are required by this section, the court shall state whether the application of the guidelines would be unjust or inappropriate and shall state the following in the child support order:

(1) the monthly net resources of the obligor per month are $_____;

(2) the monthly net resources of the obligee per month are $_____;

(3) the percentage applied to the obligor's net resources for child support by the actual order rendered by the court is _____%;

(4) the amount of child support if the percentage guidelines are applied to the first $6,000 of the obligor's net resources is $_____;

(5) if applicable, the specific reasons that the amount of child support per month ordered by the court varies from the amount stated in Subdivision (4) are: ______; and

(6) if applicable, the obligor is obligated to support children in more than one household, and:

(A) the number of children before the court is _____;

(B) the number of children not before the court residing in the same household with the obligor is _____; and

(C) the number of children not before the court for whom the obligor is obligated by a court order to pay support, without regard to whether the obligor is delinquent in child support payments, and who are not counted under Paragraph (A) or (B) is _____."

(c) The application of the guidelines under Section 154.129 does not constitute a variance from the child support guidelines requiring specific findings by the court under this section.

(Acts 1995, 74th Leg., ch. 20, §1, effective April 20, 1995. Amended by Acts 2001, 77th Leg., ch. 1023, §8, effective September 1, 2001.)

§154.132. Application of guidelines if obligor receives disability benefits

In applying the child support guidelines for an obligor who has a disability and who is required to pay support for a child who receives benefits as a result of the obligor's disability, the court shall apply the guidelines by determining the amount of child support that would be ordered under the child support guidelines and subtracting from that total the amount of benefits or the value of the benefits paid to or for the child as a result of the obligor's disability.

(Acts 1999, 76th Leg., ch. 891, §1, effective September 1, 1999.)

§154.133. Application of guidelines if obligor receives social security benefits

In applying the child support guidelines for an obligor who is receiving social security old age benefits and who is required to pay support for a child who receives benefits as a result of the obligor's receipt of social security old age benefits, the court shall apply the guidelines by determining the amount of child support that would be ordered under the child support guidelines and subtracting from that total the amount of benefits or the value of the benefits paid to or for the child as a result of the obligor's receipt of social security old age benefits.

(Acts 2001, 77th Leg., ch. 544, §1, effective September 1, 2001.)

d. Retroactive Support Under the Guidelines

The statutory guidelines are intended to guide courts in the determination of initial awards of child support as well as retroactive awards. In its determination of the amount of retroactive support, the court must consider certain factors relating to both the obligee and the obligor. For example, the court must consider whether the obligee made efforts to notify the obligor of his paternity, as well as whether the obligor had knowledge of his paternity, whether the obligor would suffer undue hardship by an order of retroactive support and has previously provided support (Tex. Fam. Code §154.131(b)).

The court may limit retroactive support to the total support due for the past four years preceding the filing of the petition. Such an order is rebuttably presumed to be "reasonable and in the best interest of the child" (*id.* at §154.131(c)), and the presumption may only be rebutted by evidence that the obligor knew or should have known that he was the father of the child for whom support was sought, *and* sought to avoid the establishment of his support obligation (*id.* at 154.131(d)) (emphasis added).

§154.131. Retroactive child support: factors to consider

(a) The child support guidelines are intended to guide the court in determining the amount of retroactive child support, if any, to be ordered.

(b) In ordering retroactive child support, the court shall consider the net resources of the obligor during the relevant time period and whether:

(1) the mother of the child had made any previous attempts to notify the obligor of his paternity or probable paternity;

(2) the obligor had knowledge of his paternity or probable paternity;

(3) the order of retroactive child support will impose an undue financial hardship on the obligor or the obligor's family; and

(4) the obligor has provided actual support or other necessaries before the filing of the action.

(c) It is presumed that a court order limiting the amount of retroactive child support to an amount that does not exceed the total amount of support that would have been due for the four years preceding the date the petition seeking support was filed is reasonable and in the best interest of the child.

(d) The presumption created under this section may be rebutted by evidence that the obligor:

(1) knew or should have known that the obligor was the father of the child for whom support is sought; and

(2) sought to avoid the establishment of a support obligation to the child.

(e) An order under this section limiting the amount of retroactive support does not constitute a variance from the guidelines requiring the court to make specific findings under Section 154.130.

(Acts 1995, 74th Leg., ch. 20, §1, effective April 20, 1995. Amended by Acts 2001, 77th Leg., ch. 392, §1, effective September 1, 2001; Acts 2001, 77th Leg., ch. 821, §2.14, effective June 14, 2001; Acts 2001, 77th Leg., ch. 1023, §9, effective September 1, 2001.)

4. Medical Support for the Child

The statutory child support guidelines are based on the assumption that the court will order the obligor to provide health insurance coverage as part of the support obligation (Tex. Fam. Code §154.064 *infra*); Gagnon et al., Child Support, Tex. Prac. Guide Family Law §12:45. If a parent fails to provide health insurance coverage as ordered, the parent is liable for the child's necessary medical expenses and the cost of any premiums or contributions paid on behalf of the child (Tex. Fam. Code §154.188).

§154.181. Court shall render medical support order

(a) The court shall render an order for the medical support of the child as provided by this section and Section 154.182 in:

(1) a proceeding in which periodic payments of child support are ordered under this chapter or modified under Chapter 159;

(2) any other suit affecting the parent-child relationship in which the court determines that medical support of the child must be established, modified, or clarified; or

(3) a proceeding under Chapter 159.

(b) Before a hearing on temporary orders or a final order, if no hearing on temporary orders is held, the court shall require the parties to the proceedings to disclose in a pleading or other statement:

(1) if private health insurance is in effect for the child, the identity of the insurance company providing the coverage, the policy number, which parent is responsible for payment of any insurance premium for the coverage, whether the coverage is provided through a parent's employment, and the cost of the premium; or

(2) if private health insurance is not in effect for the child, whether:

(A) the child is receiving medical assistance under Chapter 32, Human Resources Code;

(B) the child is receiving health benefits coverage under the state child health plan under Chapter 62, Health and Safety Code, and the cost of any premium; and

(C) either parent has access to private health insurance at reasonable cost to that parent.

(c) In rendering temporary orders, the court shall, except for good cause shown, order that any health insurance coverage in effect for the child continue in effect pending the rendition of a final order, except that the court may not require the continuation of any health insurance that is not available to the parent at reasonable cost. If there is no health insurance coverage in effect for the child or if the insurance in effect is not available at a reasonable cost and the child is not receiving medical assistance under Chapter 32, Human Resources Code, or coverage under the state child health plan under Chapter 62, Health and Safety Code, the court shall, except for good cause shown, order health care coverage for the child as provided under Section 154.182.

(d) Except for good cause shown, on rendering a final order the court shall require the parent ordered to provide health care coverage for the child as provided under Section 154.182 to produce evidence to the court's satisfaction that the parent has applied for or secured health insurance or has otherwise taken necessary action to provide for health care coverage for the child, as ordered by the court.

(e) In this section, "reasonable cost" means the cost of a health insurance premium that does not exceed 10 percent of the responsible parent's net income in a month.

(Acts 1995, 74th Leg., ch. 20, §1, effective April 20, 1995. Amended by Acts 2001, 77th Leg., ch. 449, §1, effective June 5, 2001; Acts 2003, 78th Leg., ch. 610, effective September 1, 2003.)

§154.182. Court shall consider cost and quality of health insurance coverage

(a) The court shall consider the cost and quality of health insurance coverage available to the parties and shall give priority to health insurance coverage available through the employment of one of the parties.

(b) In determining the manner in which health insurance for the child is to be ordered, the court shall render its order in accordance with the following priorities, unless a party shows good cause why a particular order would not be in the best interest of the child:

(1) if health insurance is available for the child through the obligor's employment or membership in a union, trade association, or other organization at reasonable cost to the obligor, the court shall order the obligor to include the child in the obligor's health insurance;

(2) if health insurance is not available for the child through the obligor's employment but is available for the child at a reasonable cost through the obligee's employment or membership in a union, trade association, or other organization, the court may order the obligee to provide health insurance for the child, and, in such event, shall order the obligor to pay additional child support to be

withheld from earnings under Chapter 158 to the obligee for the actual cost of the health insurance for the child;

(3) if health insurance is not available for the child under Subdivision (1) or (2), the court shall order the obligor to provide health insurance for the child if the court finds that health insurance is available to the obligor for the child from another source and at reasonable cost;

(4) if neither parent has access to private health insurance at a reasonable cost, the court shall order that the custodial parent or, to the extent permitted by law, the noncustodial parent immediately apply on behalf of the child for participation in a medical assistance program under Chapter 32, Human Resources Code, or the state child health plan under Chapter 62, Health and Safety Code, and that the obligor pay additional child support, to be withheld from income under Chapter 158, to the obligee for the actual cost of participation of the child in such program; or

(5) if health coverage is not available for the child under Subdivision (1), (2), (3), or (4), the court shall order the obligor to pay the obligee, in addition to any amount ordered under the guidelines for child support, a reasonable amount each month as medical support for the child to be withheld from earnings under Chapter 158.

(c) In this section, "reasonable cost" has the meaning assigned by Section 154.181(e).

(Acts 1995, 74th Leg., ch. 20, §1, effective April 20, 1995. Amended by Acts 1997, 75th Leg., ch. 550, §2, effective June 2, 1997; Acts 2001, 77th Leg., ch. 449, §2, effective June 5, 2001; Acts 2003, 78th Leg., ch. 610, effective June 5, 2003.)

Notes

A court may not order that coverage be provided to a child through the Texas Healthy Kids Corporation under Section 154.182, Family Code, as amended by 1997 Ch. 550, before the date that corporation first offers coverage under a health benefit plan in the applicable region of the state. Stats. 1997 75th Leg. Sess. Ch. 550 §9.

---

§154.183. Provision of health insurance constitutes additional support duty of obligor

(a) An amount that an obligor is required to pay for health insurance for the child:

(1) is in addition to the amount that the obligor is required to pay for child support under the guidelines for child support;

(2) is a child support obligation; and

(3) may be enforced as a child support obligation.

(b) If the court finds and states in the child support order that the obligee will maintain health insurance coverage for the child at the obligee's expense, the court may increase the amount of child support to be paid by the obligor in an amount not exceeding the total expense to the obligee for maintaining health insurance coverage.

(c) As additional child support, the court shall allocate between the parties, according to their circumstances, the reasonable and necessary health care expenses of a child that are not reimbursed by health insurance.

(Acts 1995, 74th Leg., ch. 20, §1, effective April 20, 1995.)

§154.184. Effect of medical support order shall constitute change in family circumstances

(a) Receipt of a medical support order requiring that health insurance be provided for a child shall be considered a change in the family circumstances of the employee or member, for health insurance purposes, equivalent to the birth or adoption of a child.

(b) If the employee or member is eligible for dependent health coverage, the employer shall automatically enroll the child for the first 31 days after the receipt of the order or notice of the medical support order under Section 154.186 on the same terms and conditions as apply to any other dependent child.

(c) The employer shall notify the insurer of the automatic enrollment.

(d) During the 31 day period, the employer and insurer shall complete all necessary forms and procedures to make the enrollment permanent or shall report in accordance with this subchapter the reasons the coverage cannot be made permanent.

(Acts 1995, 74th Leg., ch. 20, §1, effective April 20, 1995. Amended by Acts 1995, 74th Leg., ch. 341, §4.03, effective September 1, 1995 Amended Acts 1997, 75th Leg., ch. 911, §11, effective September 1, 1997.)

§154.185. Court shall order parent to furnish certain insurance information

(a) The court shall order a parent providing health insurance to furnish to either the obligee, obligor, or child support agency the following information not later than the 30th day after the date the notice of rendition of the order is received:

(1) the social security number of the parent;

(2) the name and address of the parent's employer;

(3) whether the employer is self-insured or has health insurance available;

(4) proof that health insurance has been provided for the child;

(5) if the employer has health insurance available, the name of the health insurance carrier, the number of the policy, a copy of the policy and schedule of benefits, a health insurance membership card, claim forms, and any other information necessary to submit a claim; and

(6) if the employer is self-insured, a copy of the schedule of benefits, a membership card, claim forms, and any other information necessary to submit a claim.

(b) The court shall also order a parent providing health insurance to furnish the obligor, obligee, or child support agency with additional information regarding health insurance coverage not later than the 15th day after the date the information is received by the parent.

(Acts 1995, 74th Leg., ch. 20, §1, effective April 20, 1995. Amended by Acts 2001, 77th Leg., ch. 1023, §10, effective September 1, 2001.)

§154.186. Parent or agency must send employer copy of medical support order

(a) The obligee, obligor, or a child support agency may send to the employer a copy of the order requiring an employee to provide health insurance coverage for a child or may include notice of the medical support order in an order or writ of withholding sent to the employer in accordance with Chapter 158.

(b) In an appropriate Title VI-D case, the Title VI-D agency shall send to the employer the national medical support notice required under Part D, Title IV of the federal Social Security Act (42 U.S.C. Section 651 et. seq.), as amended. The notice may be used in any other suit in which an obligor is ordered to provide health insurance coverage for a child.

(c) The Title IV-D agency by rule shall establish procedures consistent with federal law for use of the national medical support notice and may prescribe forms for the efficient use of notice. The agency shall provide the notice and forms, on request, to obligees, obligors, domestic relations offices, friends of the court, and attorneys.

(Acts 1995, 74th Leg., ch. 20, §1, effective April 20, 1995. Amended by Acts 1995, 74th Leg., ch. 341, §4.04, effective September 1, 1995. Amended Acts 1997, 75th Leg., ch. 911, §12, effective September 1, 1997; 2003, 78th Leg., ch. 120, effective September 1, 2003.)

§154.187. Duties of employer to enroll child in plan

(a) An order or notice under this subchapter to an employer directing that health insurance coverage be provided to a child of an employee or member is binding on a current or subsequent employer on receipt without regard to the date the order was rendered. If the employee or member is eligible for dependent health coverage for the child, the employer shall immediately enroll the child in a health insurance plan regardless of whether the employee is enrolled in the plan. If dependent coverage is not available to the employee or member through the employer's health insurance plan or enrollment cannot be made permanent or if the employer is not responsible or otherwise liable for providing such coverage, the employer shall provide notice to the sender in accordance with Subsection (c).

(b) If additional premiums are incurred as a result of adding the child to the health insurance plan, the employer shall deduct the health insurance premium from the earnings of the employee in accordance with Chapter 158 and apply the amount withheld to payment of the insurance premium.

(c) An employer who has received an order or notice under this subchapter shall provide to the sender, by first class mail not later than the 30th day after the date the employer receives the order or notice, a statement that the child:

(1) has been enrolled in a health insurance plan; or

(2) cannot be enrolled or cannot be enrolled permanently in a health insurance plan and provide the reason why coverage or permanent coverage cannot be provided.

(d) If the employee ceases employment or if the health insurance coverage lapses, the employer shall provide to the sender, by first class mail not later than the 15th day after the date of the termination of employment or the lapse of the coverage, notice of the termination or lapse and of the availability of any conversion privileges.

(e) On request, the employer shall release to the sender information concerning the available health insurance coverage, including the name of the health insurance carrier, the policy number, a copy of the policy and schedule of benefits, a health insurance membership card, and claim forms.

(f) In this section, "sender" means the person sending the order under Section 154.186.

(g) An employer who fails to enroll a child, fails to withhold or remit premiums or cash medical support, or discriminates in hiring or employment on the basis of a medical support order shall be subject to the penalties and fines in Subchapter C, Chapter 158.1.

(h) An employer who receives a national medical support notice under Section 154.186 shall comply with the requirements of the notice.

(Acts 1995, 74th Leg., ch. 20, §1, effective April 20, 1995. Amended by Acts 1995, 74th Leg., ch. 341, §4.05, effective September 1, 1995. Amended Acts 1997, 75th Leg., ch. 911, §13, effective September 1, 1997; Acts 2003, 78th Leg., ch.120, effective September 1, 2003.)

§154.188. Parental liability for failure to provide required health insurance

A parent ordered to provide health insurance who fails to do so is liable for:

(1) necessary medical expenses of the child, without regard to whether the expenses would have been paid if health insurance had been provided; and

(2) the cost of health insurance premiums or contributions, if any, paid on behalf of the child.

(Acts 1995, 74th Leg., ch. 20, §1, effective April 20, 1995. Amended by Acts 2001, 77th Leg., ch. 295, §1, effective September 1, 2001; Acts 2003, 78th Leg., ch. 610, effective September 1, 2003.)

§154.189. Obligor must notify obligee and agency of termination or lapse of insurance coverage

(a) An obligor ordered to provide health insurance coverage for a child must notify the obligee and any child support agency enforcing a support obligation against the obligor of the:

(1) termination or lapse of health insurance coverage for the child not later than the 15th day after the date of a termination or lapse; and

(2) availability of additional health insurance to the obligor for the child after a termination or lapse of coverage not later than the 15th day after the date the insurance becomes available.

(b) If termination of coverage results from a change of employers, the obligor, the obligee, or the child support agency may send the new employer a copy of the order requiring the employee to provide health insurance for a child or notice of the medical support order as provided by this subchapter.

(Acts 1995, 74th Leg., ch. 20, §1, effective April 20, 1995. Amended by Acts 1997, 75th Leg., ch. 911, §14, effective September 1, 1997.)

§154.190. Obligor must re-enroll child for insurance coverage

After health insurance has been terminated or has lapsed, an obligor ordered to provide health insurance coverage for the child must enroll the child in a health insurance plan at the next available enrollment period.

(Acts 1995, 74th Leg., ch. 20, §1, effective April 20, 1995.)

§154.191. Remedies not exclusive

(a) This subchapter does not limit the rights of the obligor, obligee, local domestic relations office, or Title IV-D agency to enforce, modify, or clarify the medical support order.

(b) This subchapter does not limit the authority of the court to render or modify a medical support order containing a provision for payment of uninsured health expenses, health care costs, or health insurance premiums that are in addition to and inconsistent with this subchapter.

(Acts 1995, 74th Leg., ch. 20, §1, effective April 20, 1995.)

§154.192. Employer may not cancel or eliminate coverage of child

(a) Unless the employee or member ceases to be eligible for dependent coverage, or the employer has eliminated dependent health coverage for all of the employer's employees or members, the employer may not cancel or eliminate coverage of a child enrolled under this subchapter until the employer is provided satisfactory written evidence that:

(1) the court order or administrative order requiring the coverage is no longer in effect; or

(2) the child is enrolled in comparable health insurance coverage or will be enrolled in comparable coverage that will take effect not later than the effective date of the cancellation or elimination of the employer's coverage.

(Acts 1995, 74th Leg., ch. 20, §1, effective April 20, 1995. Amended by Acts 1995, 74th Leg., ch. 341, §4.06, effective September 1, 1995.)

§154.193. Tribunal may render medical support order that qualifies for enforcement under federal law

(a) If a plan administrator or other person acting in an equivalent position determines that a medical support order issued under this subchapter does not qualify for enforcement under federal law, the tribunal may, on its own motion or the motion of a party, render an order that qualifies for enforcement under federal law.

(b) The procedure for filing a motion for enforcement of a final order applies to a motion under this section. Service of citation is not required, and a person is not entitled to a jury in a proceeding under this section.

(c) The employer or plan administrator is not a necessary party to a proceeding under this section.

(Acts 1997, 75th Leg., ch. 911, §15, effective September 1, 1997.)

C. MODIFICATION AND TERMINATION OF SUPPORT ORDERS

A "party affected by an order" may petition for an order modifying child support in a court with continuing, exclusive jurisdiction (Tex. Fam. Code §§156.001, 156.002). Any party "whose rights and duties may be affected by a suit for modification" must receive notice of the suit (Tex. Fam. Code §156.003).

The grounds for modification of child support are (1) a material and substantial change (since the date of the order) in the circumstances of the child or a person affected by the order *or* (2) the passage of three years since the order was rendered or last modified *and* the monthly amount under the order differs by either 20 percent or $100 from that mandated by the statutory guidelines (Tex. Fam. Code §156.401) (emphasis added). As of 2005, the "material and substantial changed circumstances" rule also applies to parties who have an agreement as to the amount of child support if that amount differs from the amount specified by the guidelines. Tex. Fam. Code §156.401(a-1).

Release of the obligor from incarceration constitutes a material and substantial change in circumstances if the obligor's child support obligation was reduced or suspended during the incarceration (id. at §156.401(d)). In addition, an order of joint custody does not "in and of itself" constitute grounds for modification of child support (id. at §156.401(c)).

Moreover, the same new spouse rules apply to modification as to the original calculation of obligor's and obligee's net resources. That is, "new-spouse" income is excluded from calculations of the obligor's or obligee's net resources (and, similarly, the needs of a new spouse or new spouse's dependents may not be subtracted from the obligor's or obligee's net resources). Likewise, "new-spouse" income and needs may not be considered in a suit for modification (Tex. Fam. Code §156.404). If the changed circumstances consist of an increase in the obligee's standard of living or lifestyle, such a change does not justify an increase in child support (Tex. Fam. Code §156.405).

A court may terminate child support (unless the parties otherwise agree) on the occurrence of certain events, including the child's marriage, emancipation, or death, and the death of the obligor (Tex. Fam. Code §154.001(a)(1), (2), and (3), §154.006). However, if the child is disabled, the court may order support indefinitely (Tex. Fam. Code §154.001(a)(4)). Although the death of the obligor terminates the obligor's support obligation, the death of the obligee does not (Tex. Fam. Code §§154.006(a), 154.013(a)). In the event of the obligee's death, the obligation continues to the child named in the support order (Tex. Fam. Code §154.013)(a)).

Congress has addressed interstate recognition and enforcement of support orders, and attempted to limit the ability of one state to modify another state's child support order. The Family Support Act of 1988 required states to adopt procedures insuring finality and full faith and credit for all payments or support obligations once due. 42 U.S.C. §666(a)(9)(2000). This federal legislation prohibited retroactive (as distinguished from prospective) modification everywhere.

Congress subsequently enacted the Full Faith and Credit for Child Support Orders Act, 28 U.S.C. §1738B (2000), imposing duties on states to enforce and not modify (except as authorized) child support orders established by other states, consistent with certain requirements. The Act provides for continuing, exclusive jurisdiction by a court that has made an order, so long as the state is the child's state or the residence of any contestant, unless a court in another state has modified the order in accordance with the act. In 1996, Congress amended the legislation to make it consistent with the Uniform Interstate Family Support Act (UIFSA), 9 U.L.A. (pt. 1B) 235 (1999). For discussion of UIFSA, see Section D4 *infra*.

1. Modification

Texas Family Code

§156.001. Court with continuing exclusive jurisdiction may modify order

A court with continuing, exclusive jurisdiction may modify an order that provides for the conservatorship, support, or possession of and access to a child.
(Acts 1995, 74th Leg., ch. 20, §1, effective April 20, 1995.)

§156.002. Standing

(a) A party affected by an order may file a suit for modification in the court with continuing, exclusive jurisdiction.

(b) A person or entity who, at the time of filing, has standing to sue under Chapter 102 may file a suit for modification in the court with continuing, exclusive jurisdiction.
(Acts 1995, 74th Leg., ch. 20, §1, effective April 20, 1995.)

§156.003. Notice

A party whose rights and duties may be affected by a suit for modification is entitled to receive notice by service of citation.
(Acts 1995, 74th Leg., ch. 20, §1, effective April 20, 1995. Amended by Acts 1999, 76th Leg., ch. 178, §9, effective August 30, 1999.)

§156.004. Procedure

The Texas Rules of Civil Procedure applicable to the filing of an original lawsuit apply to a suit for modification under this chapter.
(Acts 1995, 74th Leg., ch. 20, §1, effective April 20, 1995.)

§156.005. Court shall assess attorney's fees in frivolous suit for modification

If the court finds that a suit for modification is filed frivolously or is designed to harass a party, the court shall tax attorney's fees as costs against the offending party.
(Acts 1995, 74th Leg., ch. 20, §1, effective April 20, 1995.)

§156.006. Court may render temporary orders in suit for modification

(a) Except as provided by Subsection (b), the court may render a temporary order in a suit for modification.

(b) While a suit for modification is pending, the court may not render a temporary order that has the effect of changing the designation of the person who has the exclusive right to determine the primary residence of the child under the final order unless:

(1) the order is necessary because the child's present circumstances significantly impair the child's physical health or emotional development;

(2) the person designated in the final order has voluntarily relinquished the primary care and possession of the child for more than six months and the temporary order is in the best interest of the child; or

(3) the child is 12 years of age or older and has filed with the court in writing the name of the person who is the child's preference to have the exclusive right to determine the primary residence of the child and the temporary order designating that person is in the best interest of the child.

(Acts 1995, 74th Leg., ch. 20, §1, effective April 20, 1995. Amended by Acts 1999, 76th Leg., ch. 1390, §15, effective September 1, 1999; Acts 2001, 77th Leg., ch. 1289, §3, effective September 1, 2001; Acts 2003, 78th Leg., ch. 1036, effective September 1, 2003; Acts 2005, 79th Leg., ch. 916 (H.B. 260), effective September 1, 2005.)

§156.103. Court may take into account increased expenses due to change of residence

(a) If a change of residence results in increased expenses for a party having possession of or access to a child, the court may render appropriate orders to allocate those increased expenses on a fair and equitable basis, taking into account the cause of the increased expenses and the best interest of the child.

(b) The payment of increased expenses by the party whose residence is changed is rebuttably presumed to be in the best interest of the child.

(c) The court may render an order without regard to whether another change in the terms and conditions for the possession of or access to the child is made.
(Acts 1995, 74th Leg., ch. 20, §1, effective April 20, 1995. Amended by Acts 2001, 77th Leg., ch. 1289, §7, effective September 1, 2001.)

§156.401. Grounds for modification of child support: material and substantial change of circumstances or passage of time plus deviation from guidelines

(a) Except as provided by Subsection (a-1) or (b), the court may modify an order that provides for the support of a child if:

(1) the circumstances of the child or a person affected by the order have materially and substantially changed since the date of the order's rendition; or

(2) it has been three years since the order was rendered or last modified and the monthly amount of the child support award under the order differs by either 20 percent

or $100 from the amount that would be awarded in accordance with the child support guidelines.

(a-1) If the parties agree to an order under which the amount of child support differs from the amount that would be awarded in accordance with the child support guidelines, the court may modify the order only if the circumstances of the child or a person affected by the order have materially and substantially changed since the date of the order's rendition.

(b) A support order may be modified only as to obligations accruing after the earlier of:

(1) the date of service of citation; or

(2) an appearance in the suit to modify.

(c) An order of joint conservatorship, in and of itself, does not constitute grounds for modifying a support order.

(d) Release of a child support obligor from incarceration is a material and substantial change in circumstances for purposes of this section if the obligor's child support obligation was abated, reduced, or suspended during the period of the obligor's incarceration.

(Acts 1995, 74th Leg., ch. 20, §1, effective April 20, 1995. Amended by Acts 1997, 75th Leg., ch. 911, §16, effective September 1, 1997; Acts 1999, 76th Leg., ch. 43, §1, effective September 1, 1999; Acts 2003, 78th Leg., ch. 1036, effective September 1, 2003. Acts 2005, 79th Leg., ch. 916 (H.B. 260), effective September 1, 2005.)

§156.402. Court may consider guidelines for single and multiple families for modification purposes

(a) The court may consider the child support guidelines for single and multiple families under Chapter 154 to determine whether there has been a material or substantial change of circumstances under this chapter that warrants a modification of an existing child support order if the modification is in the best interest of the child.

(b) If the amount of support contained in the order does not substantially conform with the guidelines for single and multiple families under Chapter 154, the court may modify the order to substantially conform with the guidelines if the modification is in the best interest of the child. A court may consider other relevant evidence in addition to the factors listed in the guidelines.

(Acts 1995, 74th Leg., ch. 20, §1, effective April 20, 1995. Amended by Acts 1999, 76th Leg., ch. 62, §6.22, effective September 1, 1999; Acts 1999, 76th Leg., ch. 556, §12, effective September 1, 1999.)

§156.403. Obligor's voluntary additional support is not reason to increase child support order

A history of support voluntarily provided in excess of the court order does not constitute cause to increase the amount of an existing child support order.

(Acts 1995, 74th Leg., ch. 20, §1, effective April 20, 1995.)

§156.404. Court may not take into account net resources of new spouse

(a) The court may not add any portion of the net resources of a new spouse to the net resources of an obligor or obligee in order to calculate the amount of child support to be ordered in a suit for modification.

(b) The court may not subtract the needs of a new spouse, or of a dependent of a new spouse, from the net resources of the obligor or obligee in a suit for modification.

(Acts 1995, 74th Leg., ch. 20, §1, effective April 20, 1995.)

§156.405. Obligee's change in needs or standard of living does not warrant increased support

An increase in the needs, standard of living, or lifestyle of the obligee since the rendition of the existing order does not warrant an increase in the obligor's child support obligation.

(Acts 1995, 74th Leg., ch. 20, §1, effective April 20, 1995.)

§156.406. Court shall apply percentage guidelines for multiple families

In applying the child support guidelines in a suit under this subchapter, if the obligor has the duty to support children in more than one household, the court shall apply the percentage guidelines for multiple families under Chapter 154.

(Acts 1995, 74th Leg., ch. 20, §1, effective April 20, 1995. Amended by Acts 1999, 76th Leg., ch. 62, §6.23, effective September 1, 1999; Acts 1999, 76th Leg., ch. 556, §13, effective September 1, 1999.)

§156.407. Notice of assignment of child support right

A notice of assignment filed under Chapter 231 does not constitute a modification of an order to pay child support.

(Acts 1995, 74th Leg., ch. 20, §1, effective April 20, 1995.)

§156.408. Court may modify support order rendered by another state as provided

(a) Unless both parties and the child reside in this state, a court of this state may modify an order of child support rendered by an appropriate tribunal of another state only as provided by Chapter 159.

(b) If both parties and the child reside in this state, a court of this state may modify an order of child support rendered by an appropriate tribunal of another state after registration of the order as provided by Chapter 159.

(Acts 1995, 74th Leg., ch. 20, §1, effective April 20, 1995. Amended by Acts 2001, 77th Leg., ch. 1023, §13, effective September 1, 2001.)

§156.409. Court may modify support order if physical possession changes

(a) If the sole managing conservator of a child or the joint managing conservator who has the exclusive right to determine the primary residence of the child has voluntarily relinquished the primary care and possession of the child to another person for at least six months, the court may modify an order providing for the support of the child to provide that the other person having physical possession of the child shall have the right to receive and give receipt for payments of support for the child and to hold or disburse money for the benefit of the child.

(b) Notice of a motion for modification under this section may be served in the manner for serving a notice under Section 157.065.

(Acts 1999, 76th Leg., ch. 556, §14, effective September 1, 1999. Amended by Acts 2001, 77th Leg., ch. 1023, §14, effective September 1, 2001; Acts 2001, 77th Leg., ch. 1289, §10, effective September 1, 2001; Acts 2005, 79th Leg., ch. 261 (H.B. 2231), effective September 1, 2005.)

2. Termination

§154.006. Termination of child support order

(a) Unless otherwise agreed in writing or expressly provided in the order or as provided by Subsection (b), the child support order terminates on:

(1) the marriage of the child,

(2) removal of the child's disabilities for general purposes;

(3) death of :

(A) the child; or

(B) a parent ordered to pay child support; or

(4) a finding by the court that the child:

(A) is 18 years of age or older; and

(B) has failed to comply with the enrollment or attendance requirements described by Section 154.002(a).

(b) Unless a nonparent or agency has been appointed conservator of the child under Chapter 153, the order for current child support, and any provision relating to conservatorship, possession, or access terminates on the marriage or remarriage of the obligor and obligee to each other.

(Acts 1995, 74th Leg., ch. 20, §1, effective April 20, 1995. Amended by Acts 1999, 76th Leg., ch. 556, §9, effective September 1, 1999; Acts 2003, 78th Leg., ch. 38, effective September 1, 2003.)

§154.013. Child support duty continues after death of obligee

(a) A child support obligation does not terminate on the death of the obligee but continues as an obligation to the child named in the support order, as required by this section.

(b) Notwithstanding any provision of the Probate Code, a child support payment held by the Title IV-D agency, a local registry, or the state disbursement unit or any uncashed check or warrant representing a child support payment made before, on, or after the date of death of the obligee shall be paid proportionately for the benefit of each surviving child named in the support order and not to the estate of the obligee. The payment is free of any creditor's claim against the deceased obligee's estate and may be disbursed as provided by Subsection (c).

(c) On the death of the obligee, current child support owed by the obligor for the benefit of the child or any amount described by Subsection (b) shall be paid to:

(1) a person, other than a parent, who is appointed as managing conservator of the child;

(2) a person, including the obligor, who has assumed actual care, control, and possession of the child, if a managing conservator or guardian of the child has not been appointed;

(3) the county clerk, as provided by Section 887, Texas Probate Code, in the name of and for the account of the child for whom the support is owed;

(4) a guardian of the child appointed under Chapter XIII, Texas Probate Code, as provided by that code; or

(5) the surviving child, if the child is an adult or has otherwise had the disabilities of minority removed.

(d) On presentation of the obligee's death certificate, the court shall render an order directing payment of child support paid but not disbursed to be made as provided by Subsection (c). A copy of the order shall be provided to:

(1) the obligor;

(2) as appropriate:

(A) the person having actual care, control, and possession of the child;

(B) the county clerk; or

(C) the managing conservator or guardian of the child, if one has been appointed;

(3) the local registry or state disbursement unit and, if appropriate, the Title IV-D agency; and

(4) the child named in the support order, if the child is an adult or has otherwise had the disabilities of minority removed.

(e) The order under Subsection (d) must contain:

(1) a statement that the obligee is deceased and that child support amounts otherwise payable to the obligee shall be paid for the benefit of a surviving child named in the support order as provided by Subsection (c);

(2) the name and age of each child named in the support order; and

(3) the name and mailing address of, as appropriate:

(A) the person having actual care, control, and possession of the child;

(B) the county clerk; or

(C) the managing conservator or guardian of the child, if one has been appointed.

(f) On receipt of the order required under this section, the local registry, state disbursement unit, or Title IV-D agency shall disburse payments as required by the order.

(Acts 2001, 77th Leg., ch. 1023, §6, effective September 1, 2001.)

D. ENFORCEMENT OF SUPPORT ORDERS

1. General Provisions

Local registries receive and process child support payments. They must promptly forward payments to the appropriate agency or to the obligee (Tex. Fam. Code §154.241). In addition, the obligor may designate (subject to court approval) a special account from which payment will be made by electronic transfer (Tex. Fam. Code §154.242(b)).

Texas Family Code

§154.241. Local registry shall receive and forward payment

(a) A local registry shall receive a court-ordered child support payment or a payment otherwise authorized by law and shall forward the payment, as appropriate, to the Title IV-D agency, local domestic relations office, or obligee within two working days after the date the local registry receives the payment.

(b) A local registry may not require an obligor, obligee, or other party or entity to furnish a certified copy of a court order as a condition of processing child support payments and shall accept as sufficient authority to process the payments a photocopy, facsimile copy, or conformed copy of the court's order.

(c) A local registry shall include with each payment it forwards to the Title IV-D agency the date it received the payment and the withholding date furnished by the employer.

(d) A local registry shall accept child support payments made by personal check, money order, or cashier's check. A local registry may refuse payment by personal check if a pattern of abuse regarding the use of personal checks has been established. Abuse includes checks drawn on insufficient funds, abusive or offensive language written on the check, intentional mutilation of the instrument, or other actions that delay or disrupt the registry's operation.

(e) Subject to Section 154.004, at the request of an obligee, a local registry shall redirect and forward a child support payment to an address and in care of a person or entity designated by the obligee. A local registry may require that the obligee's request be in writing or be made on a form provided by the local registry for that purpose, but may not charge a fee for receiving the request or redirecting the payments as requested.

(f) A local registry may accept child support payments made by credit card, debit card, or automatic teller machine card.

(g) Notwithstanding any other law, a private entity may perform the duties and functions of a local registry under this section either under a contract with a county commissioners court or domestic relations officer executed under Section 204.002 or under an appointment by a court.

(Acts 1995, 74th Leg., ch. 20, §1, effective April 20, 1995. Amended by Acts 1995, 74th Leg., ch. 751, §42, effective September 1, 1995; Acts 2003, 78th Leg., ch. 645, effective September 1, 2003; Acts 2005, 79th Leg., ch. 740 (H.B. 2668), effective September 1, 2005.)

§154.242. Child support payment may be made by electronic funds transfer

(a) A child support payment may be made by electronic funds transfer to:

(1) the Title IV-D agency;

(2) a local registry if the registry agrees to accept electronic payment; or

(3) the state disbursement unit.

(b) A local registry may transmit child support payments to the Title IV-D agency by electronic funds transfer. Unless support payments are required to be made to the state disbursement unit, an obligor may make payments, with the approval of the court entering the order, directly to the bank account of the obligee by electronic transfer and provide verification of the deposit to the local registry. A local registry in a county that makes deposits into personal bank accounts by electronic funds transfer as of April 1, 1995, may transmit a child support payment to an obligee by electronic funds transfer if the obligee maintains a bank account and provides the local registry with the necessary bank account information to complete electronic payment.

(Acts 1995, 74th Leg., ch. 20, §1, effective April 20, 1995. Amended by Acts 1995, 74th Leg., ch. 597, §1, effective January 1, 1996. Amended Acts 1997, 75th Leg., ch. 702, §2, effective January 1, 1998; Acts 1997, 75th Leg., ch. 1053, §2, effective September 1, 1997; Acts 1999, 76th Leg., ch. 556, §10, effective September 1, 1999.)

§154.243. Agency may send child support payment record to court

The Title IV-D agency, a local registry, or the state disbursement unit may comply with a subpoena or other order directing the production of a child support payment record by sending a certified copy of the record or an affidavit regarding the payment record to the court that directed production of the record.

(Acts 1995, 74th Leg., ch. 20, §1, effective April 20, 1995. Amended by Acts 1999, 76th Leg., ch. 556, §10, effective September 1, 1999.)

2. Civil Suits to Enforce Child Support

A number of remedies exist to enforce child support orders. The most common are contempt, income withholding, child support liens, and posting of a bond or other security. In addition, remedies are available under the Uniform Interstate Family Support Act (Tex. Fam. Code §§159.001 et seq.). According to Texas law, a child support agreement is not enforceable under breach-of-contract remedies (Tex. Fam. Code §154.124). A court might order an obligor to execute a bond or post security if the obligor's employer was not subject to the court's jurisdiction or if income withholding was an unworkable or inappropriate remedy (Tex. Fam. Code §157.109(a)(2)).

The traditional method of child support enforcement was a contempt proceeding instituted by the obligee or a representative agency. Both civil and criminal contempt may be used to enforce child support obligations. Courts exercise the contempt power either to punish the contemnor for past misconduct (criminal contempt) or to coerce compliance with a judicial order (civil contempt). Whether the purpose is punitive or remedial determines the criminal versus civil nature and applicable procedural safeguards, such as the standard and burden of proof. See, e.g., Hicks v. Feiock, 485 U.S. 624 (1988).

The obligor's inability to pay precludes the use of imprisonment for civil and criminal contempt to enforce a support award. However, the Child Support Recovery Act (CSRA), 18 U.S.C. §228 (2000), criminalizes the willful failure to pay a past-due support obligation for a child who resides in another state. "Past-due support obligation" means any amount determined by a court order or administrative process to be due for the support and maintenance of a child, or a child and the parent with whom the child is living, if the amount has remained unpaid for more than a year or exceeds $5,000.

Congress amended the CSRA in 1998, with the enactment of the Deadbeat Parents Punishment Act of 1998, 18 U.S.C. §228(a)(3), which makes willful failure to pay a support obligation for a child living in another state a felony, if the obligation has remained unpaid for over two years or exceeds $10,000 (thereby creating a presumption of willful nonpayment). Courts have rejected ex post facto challenges to the enhanced penalties for accrued arrearages, reasoning that the amendments cover only postenactment willful failures to pay. See United States v. Wilson, 210 F.3d 230 (4th Cir. 2000); United States v. Russell, 186 F.3d 883 (8th Cir. 1999). Moreover, most courts have upheld the CSRA against challenges that it exceeds Congress's authority under the Commerce Clause and the Tenth Amendment, reasoning that the payment of a debt constitutes economic activity and that the difference in the obligor's and obligee's locations necessitates satisfaction of the debt by interstate means. See, e.g., United States v. Faasse, 265 F.3d 475 (6th Cir. 2001); United States v. Mussari, 95 F.3d 787 (9th Cir. 1996), cert. denied sub nom. Schroeder v. United States, 520 U.S. 1203 (1997). See generally Daniel Robert Zmijewski, The Child Support Recovery Act and Its Constitutionality after US v. Morrison, 12 Kan. J.L. & Pub. Pol'y 289 (2003).

a. Procedural Issues

Texas law provides that child support orders may be enforceable by contempt (Tex. Fam. Code §§157.001 et seq.). Both temporary and final orders for child support (as well as the terms of an agreement regarding support contained in the order or those incorporated by reference) may be enforced by contempt. Gagnon et al., Child Support, Tex. Prac. Guide Family Law §12:245. See also Tex. Fam. Code §153.007(c). In 2003, the legislature put a limit on child support enforcement so that courts retain jurisdiction until 10 years after the child becomes an adult or 10 years after the support obligation otherwise terminates. See Tex. Fam. Code §157.005(b).

To find the obligor in contempt, a court must first determine that the obligor has the ability to pay. The Family Code provides several affirmative defenses to a motion for enforcement (Tex. Fam. Code §157.006) that the obligor must prove by a preponderance of the evidence (Tex. Fam. Code §157.006(b)). Specifically, the obligor may argue that he or she lacked the ability to provide the court-ordered support; lacked property that could be sold, mortgaged, or otherwise pledged to raise the necessary funds; attempted unsuccessfully to borrow the necessary funds; and knew of no source from which he or she could borrow or legally obtain the necessary funds (Tex. Fam. Code §157.008(c)).

Inability to pay constitutes a defense to civil contempt, but not to criminal contempt. Requiring proof of inability to pay does not violate due process. Ex parte Jackson, 911 S.W.2d 230 (Tex. App.—Houston [14th Dist.] 1995, no writ); Gagnon et al., Child Support, Tex. Prac. Guide Family Law §12:262.

If a court determines that the obligor may be incarcerated as a result of the proceedings, the court must inform the obligor of the right to be represented by an attorney (Tex. Fam. Code §157.163). If the obligor is indigent, the court must appoint an attorney (*id.* at §157.163(e)).

The obligor who has failed to make child support payments will be ordered to pay the movant's attorney's fees and costs (Tex. Fam. Code §157.167). Under certain circumstances, this requirement may be waived, such as an inability to pay. However, as of 2003, for arrearages of $20,000 or more, the obligor must show that the inability to pay is due to involuntary unemployment or disability. See Tex. Fam. Code §157.167(d).

Texas Family Code

§154.124. Child support agreements: policy, best interests, enforcement

(a) To promote the amicable settlement of disputes between the parties to a suit, the parties may enter into a written agreement containing provisions for support of the child and for modification of the agreement, including variations from the child support guidelines provided by Subchapter C [§§154.121 et seq.].

(b) If the court finds that the agreement is in the child's best interest, the court shall render an order in accordance with the agreement.

(c) Terms of the agreement in the order may be enforced by all remedies available for enforcement of a judgment, including contempt, but are not enforceable as contract terms unless provided by the agreement.

(d) If the court finds the agreement is not in the child's best interest, the court may request the parties to submit a revised agreement or the court may render an order for the support of the child.

(Acts 1995, 74th Leg., ch. 20, §1, effective April 20, 1995. Amended by Acts 2003, 78th Leg., ch. 480, effective September 1, 2003.)

§157.001. Motion for enforcement; availability of contempt

(a) A motion for enforcement as provided in this chapter may be filed to enforce a final order for conservatorship, child support, possession of or access to a child, or other provisions of a final order.

(b) The court may enforce by contempt a final order for possession of and access to a child as provided in this chapter.

(c) The court may enforce a final order for child support as provided in this chapter or Chapter 158.

(d) A motion for enforcement shall be filed in the court of continuing, exclusive jurisdiction.

(Acts 1995, 74th Leg., ch. 20, §1, effective April 20, 1995.)

§157.002. Motion for enforcement must contain certain information

(a) A motion for enforcement must, in ordinary and concise language:

(1) identify the provision of the order allegedly violated and sought to be enforced;

(2) state the manner of the respondent's alleged noncompliance;

(3) state the relief requested by the movant; and

(4) contain the signature of the movant or the movant's attorney.

(b) A motion for enforcement of child support:

(1) must include the amount owed as provided in the order, the amount paid, and the amount of arrearages;

(2) if contempt is requested, must include the portion of the order allegedly violated and, for each date of alleged contempt, the amount due and the amount paid, if any;

(3) may include as an attachment a copy of a record of child support payments maintained by the Title IV-D registry or a local registry; and

(4) if the obligor owes arrearages for a child receiving assistance under Part A of Title IV of the federal Social Security Act (42 U.S.C. Section 601 et seq.), may include a request that:

(A) the obligor pay the arrearages in accordance with a plan approved by the court; or

(B) if the obligor is already subject to a plan and is not incapacitated, the obligor participate in work activities, as defined under 42 U.S.C. Section 607(d), that the court determines appropriate.

(c) A motion for enforcement of the terms and conditions of conservatorship or possession of or access to a child must include the date, place, and, if applicable, the time of each occasion of the respondent's failure to comply with the order.

(d) The movant is not required to plead that the underlying order is enforceable by contempt to obtain other appropriate enforcement remedies.

(e) The movant may allege repeated past violations of the order and that future violations of a similar nature may occur before the date of the hearing.

(Acts 1995, 74th Leg., ch. 20, §1, effective April 20, 1995. Amended by Acts 1997, 75th Leg., ch. 911, §17, effective September 1, 1997.)

§157.003. Party requesting enforcement may join claims and remedies

(a) A party requesting enforcement may join in the same proceeding any claim and remedy provided for in this chapter, other provisions of this title, or other rules of law.

(b) A motion for enforcement does not constitute an election of remedies that limits or precludes:

(1) the use of any other civil or criminal proceeding to enforce a final order; or

(2) a suit for damages under Chapter 42.

(Acts 1995, 74th Leg., ch. 20, §1, effective April 20, 1995. Amended by Acts 1999, 76th Leg., ch. 62, §6.24, effective September 1, 1999.)

§157.005. Time limitations on court's assertion of jurisdiction to render contempt order

(a) The court retains jurisdiction to render a contempt order for failure to comply with the child support order if the motion for enforcement is filed not later than the sixth month after the date:

(1) the child becomes an adult; or

(2) on which the child support obligation terminates under the order or by operation of law.

(b) The court retains jurisdiction to confirm the total amount of child support arrearages and render judgment for past-due child support if a motion for enforcement requesting a money judgment is filed not later than the 10th anniversary after the date:

(1) the child becomes an adult; or

(2) on which the child support obligation terminates under the child support order or by operation of law.

(Acts 1995, 74th Leg., ch. 20, §1, effective April 20, 1995. Amended by Acts 1999, 76th Leg., ch. 556, §15, effective September 1, 1999; Acts 2005, 79th Leg., ch. 916 (H.B. 260), effective September 1, 2005.)

§157.006. Affirmative defense to motion for enforcement: proof by preponderance

(a) The issue of the existence of an affirmative defense to a motion for enforcement does not arise unless evidence is admitted supporting the defense.

(b) The respondent must prove the affirmative defense by a preponderance of the evidence.

(Acts 1995, 74th Leg., ch. 20, §1, effective April 20, 1995.)

§157.008. Affirmative defenses: obligee relinquished control or lack of ability to pay

(a) An obligor may plead as an affirmative defense in whole or in part to a motion for enforcement of child support that the obligee voluntarily relinquished to the obligor actual possession and control of a child.

(b) The voluntary relinquishment must have been for a time period in excess of any court-ordered periods of possession of and access to the child and actual support must have been supplied by the obligor.

(c) An obligor may plead as an affirmative defense to an allegation of contempt or of the violation of a condition of community service requiring payment of child support that the obligor:

(1) lacked the ability to provide support in the amount ordered;

(2) lacked property that could be sold, mortgaged, or otherwise pledged to raise the funds needed;

(3) attempted unsuccessfully to borrow the funds needed; and

(4) knew of no source from which the money could have been borrowed or legally obtained.

(d) An obligor who has provided actual support to the child during a time subject to an affirmative defense under this section may request reimbursement for that support as a counterclaim or offset against the claim of the obligee.

(e) An action against the obligee for support supplied to a child is limited to the amount of periodic payments previously ordered by the court.

(Acts 1995, 74th Leg., ch. 20, §1, effective April 20, 1995.)

§157.061. Court shall set hearing

(a) On filing a motion for enforcement requesting contempt, the court shall set the date, time, and place of the hearing and order the respondent to personally appear and respond to the motion.

(b) If the motion for enforcement does not request contempt, the court shall set the motion for hearing on the request of a party.

(c) The court shall give preference to a motion for enforcement of child support in setting a hearing date and may not delay the hearing because a suit for modification of the order requested to be enforced has been or may be filed.

(Acts 1995, 74th Leg., ch. 20, §1, effective April 20, 1995.)

§157.063. General appearance

A party makes a general appearance for all purposes in an enforcement proceeding if:

(1) the party appears at the hearing or is present when the case is called; and

(2) the party does not object to the court's jurisdiction or the form or manner of the notice of hearing.

(Acts 1995, 74th Leg., ch. 20, §1, effective April 20, 1995.)

§157.066. Effect of failure to appear

If a respondent who has been personally served with notice to appear at a hearing does not appear at the designated time, place, and date to respond to a motion for enforcement of an existing court order, regardless of whether the motion is joined with other claims or remedies, the court may not hold the respondent in contempt but may, on proper proof, grant a default judgment for the relief sought and issue a capias for the arrest of the respondent.

(Acts 1995, 74th Leg., ch. 20, §1, effective April 20, 1995. Amended by Acts 1995, 74th Leg., ch. 751, §50, effective September 1, 1995.)

§157.101. Court shall set appearance bond or security

(a) When the court orders the issuance of a capias as provided in this chapter, the court shall also set an appearance bond or security, payable to the obligee or to a person designated by the court, in a reasonable amount.

(b) An appearance bond or security in the amount of $1,000 or a cash bond in the amount of $250 is presumed to be reasonable. Evidence that the respondent has attempted to evade service of process, has previously been found guilty of contempt, or has accrued arrearages over $1,000 is sufficient to rebut the presumption. If the presumption is rebutted, the court shall set a reasonable bond.

(Acts 1995, 74th Leg., ch. 20, §1, effective April 20, 1995.)

§157.102. Duty of law enforcement officials to treat capias as arrest warrant

Law enforcement officials shall treat the capias in the same manner as an arrest warrant for a criminal offense and shall enter the capias in the computer records for outstanding warrants maintained by the local police, sheriff, and Department of Public Safety. The capias shall be forwarded to and disseminated by the Texas Crime Information Center and the National Crime Information Center.

(Acts 1995, 74th Leg., ch. 20, §1, effective April 20, 1995. Amended by Acts 1997, 75th Leg., ch. 702, §3, effective September 1, 1997; Acts 1999, 76th Leg., ch. 556, §16, effective September 1, 1999.)

§157.109. Conditions for court to order respondent to execute bond or post security

(a) The court may order the respondent to execute a bond or post security if the court finds that the respondent:

(1) has on two or more occasions denied possession of or access to a child who is the subject of the order; or

(2) is employed by an employer not subject to the jurisdiction of the court or for whom income withholding is unworkable or inappropriate.

(b) The court shall set the amount of the bond or security and condition the bond or security on compliance with the court order permitting possession or access or the payment of past-due or future child support.

(c) The court shall order the bond or security payable through the registry of the court:

(1) to the obligee or other person or entity entitled to receive child support payments designated by the court if enforcement of child support is requested; or

(2) to the person who is entitled to possession or access if enforcement of possession or access is requested.

(Acts 1995, 74th Leg., ch. 20, §1, effective April 20, 1995.)

§157.110. Court may forfeit security for failure to comply with order

(a) On the motion of a person or entity for whose benefit a bond has been executed or security deposited, the court may forfeit all or part of the bond or security deposit on a finding that the person who furnished the bond or security:

(1) has violated the court order for possession of and access to a child; or

(2) failed to make child support payments.

(b) The court shall order the registry to pay the funds from a forfeited bond or security deposit to the obligee or person or entity entitled to receive child support payments in an amount that does not exceed the child support arrearages or, in the case of possession of or access to a child, to the person entitled to possession or access.

(c) The court may order that all or part of the forfeited amount be applied to pay attorney's fees and costs incurred by the person or entity bringing the motion for contempt or motion for forfeiture.

(Acts 1995, 74th Leg., ch. 20, §1, effective April 20, 1995.)

§157.111. Forfeiture of bond is not defense to contempt

The forfeiture of bond or security is not a defense in a contempt proceeding.

(Acts 1995, 74th Leg., ch. 20, §1, effective April 20, 1995.)

§157.112. Forfeiture and contempt proceedings may be joined

A motion for enforcement requesting contempt may be joined with a forfeiture proceeding.

(Acts 1995, 74th Leg., ch. 20, §1, effective April 20, 1995.)

§157.113. Application of bond pending writ

If the obligor requests to execute a bond or to post security pending a hearing by an appellate court on a writ, the bond or security on forfeiture shall be payable to the obligee.

(Acts 1995, 74th Leg., ch. 20, §1, effective April 20, 1995.)

§157.114. Conditions for court to order capias

The court may order a capias to be issued for the arrest of the respondent if:

(1) the motion for enforcement requests contempt;

(2) the respondent was personally served; and

(3) the respondent fails to appear.

(Acts 1995, 74th Leg., ch. 20, §1, effective April 20, 1995.)

§157.115. Conditions for court to render default judgment

(a) The court may render a default order for the relief requested if the respondent:

(1) has been personally served, has filed an answer, or has entered an appearance; and

(2) does not appear at the designated time, place, and date to respond to the motion.

(b) If the respondent fails to appear, the court may not hold the respondent in contempt but may order a capias to be issued.

(Acts 1995, 74th Leg., ch. 20, §1, effective April 20, 1995. Amended by Acts 1995, 74th Leg., ch. 751, §51, effective September 1, 1995.)

b. Hearing

§157.161. Record: when required

(a) Except as provided by Subsection (b), a record of the hearing in a motion for enforcement shall be made by a court reporter or as provided by Chapter 201.

(b) A record is not required if:

(1) the parties agree to an order; or

(2) the motion does not request incarceration and the parties waive the requirement of a record at the time of hearing, either in writing or in open court, and the court approves waiver.

(Acts 1995, 74th Leg., ch. 20, §1, effective April 20, 1995.)

§157.162. Court may order other enforcement remedies

(a) The movant is not required to prove that the underlying order is enforceable by contempt to obtain other appropriate enforcement remedies.

(b) A finding that the respondent is not in contempt does not preclude the court from ordering any other enforcement remedy, including rendering a money judgment, posting a bond or other security, or withholding income.

(c) A copy of the payment record attached to the motion is evidence of the facts asserted in the payment record and is admissible to show whether payments were made. The respondent may offer controverting evidence.

(Acts 1995, 74th Leg., ch. 20, §1, effective April 20, 1995.)

§157.163. Appointment of attorney if incarceration is possible result

(a) In a motion for enforcement or motion to revoke community service, the court must first determine whether incarceration of the respondent is a possible result of the proceedings.

(b) If the court determines that incarceration is a possible result of the proceedings, the court shall inform a respondent not represented by an attorney of the right to be represented by an attorney and, if the respondent is indigent, of the right to the appointment of an attorney.

(c) If the court determines that the respondent will not be incarcerated as a result of the proceedings, the court may require a respondent who is indigent to proceed without an attorney.

(d) If the respondent claims indigency and requests the appointment of an attorney, the court shall require the respondent to file an affidavit of indigency. The court may hear evidence to determine the issue of indigency.

(e) Except as provided by Subsection (c), the court shall appoint an attorney to represent the respondent if the court determines that the respondent is indigent.

. . .

(i) The scope of the court appointment of an attorney to represent the respondent is limited to the allegation of contempt or of violation of community supervision contained in the motion for enforcement or motion to revoke community supervision.

(Acts 1995, 74th Leg., ch. 20, §1, effective April 20, 1995.)

§157.164. Attorney entitled to reasonable fee for services

(a) An attorney appointed to represent an indigent respondent is entitled to a reasonable fee for services within the scope of the appointment in the amount set by the court.

(b) The fee shall be paid from the general funds of the county according to the schedule for the compensation of counsel appointed to defend criminal defendants as provided in the Code of Criminal Procedure.

(c) For purposes of this section, a proceeding in a court of appeals or the Supreme Court of Texas is considered the equivalent of a bona fide appeal to the Texas Court of Criminal Appeals.

(Acts 1995, 74th Leg., ch. 20, §1, effective April 20, 1995.)

§157.165. Court may use community supervision or suspend commitment for contempt

The court may place the respondent on community supervision and suspend commitment if the court finds that the respondent is in contempt of court for failure or refusal to obey an order rendered as provided in this title.

(Acts 1995, 74th Leg., ch. 20, §1, effective April 20, 1995. Amended by Acts 1999, 76th Leg., ch. 62, §6.25, effective September 1, 1999.)

§157.166. Enforcement order must include certain information

(a) An enforcement order must include:

(1) in ordinary and concise language the provisions of the order for which enforcement was requested;

(2) the acts or omissions that are the subject of the order;

(3) the manner of the respondent's noncompliance; and

(4) the relief granted by the court.

(b) If the order imposes incarceration or a fine for criminal contempt, an enforcement order must contain findings identifying, setting out, or incorporating by reference the provisions of the order for which enforcement was requested and the date of each occasion when the respondent's failure to comply with the order was found to constitute criminal contempt.

(c) If the enforcement order imposes incarceration for civil contempt, the order must state the specific conditions on which the respondent may be released from confinement.

(Acts 1995, 74th Leg., ch. 20, §1, effective April 20, 1995. Amended by Acts 1999, 76th Leg., ch. 556, §17, effective September 1, 1999.)

§157.167. Court shall order respondent to pay attorney's fees as well as arrearages

(a) If the court finds that the respondent has failed to make child support payments, the court shall order the respondent to pay the movant's reasonable attorney's fees and all court costs in addition to the arrearages. Fees and costs ordered under this subsection may be enforced by any means available for the enforcement of child support, including contempt.

(b) If the court finds that the respondent has failed to comply with the terms of an order providing for the possession of or access to a child, the court shall order the respondent to pay the movant's reasonable attorney's fees and all court costs in addition to any other remedy. If the court finds that the enforcement of the order with which the respondent failed to comply was necessary to ensure the child's physical or emotional health or welfare, the fees and costs ordered under this subsection may be enforced by any means available for the enforcement of child support, including contempt, but not including income withholding.

(c) Except as provided by Subsection (d), for good cause shown, the court may waive the requirement that the respondent pay attorney's fees and costs if the court states the reasons supporting that finding.

(d) If the court finds that the respondent is in contempt of court for failure or refusal to pay child support and that the respondent owes $20,000 or more in child support arrearages, the court may not waive the requirement that the respondent pay attorney's fees and costs unless the court also finds that the respondent:

(1) is involuntarily unemployed or is disabled; and

(2) lacks the financial resources to pay the attorney's fees and costs.

(Acts 1995, 74th Leg., ch. 20, §1, effective April 20, 1995. Amended by Acts 1999, 76th Leg., ch. 556, §18, effective September 1, 1999; Acts 2003, 78th Leg., ch. 1262, effective September 1, 2003; Acts 2005, 79th Leg., ch. 728 (H.B. 2018), effective September 1, 2005.)

---

c. Judgment and Interest

A child support order that is not paid in a timely fashion becomes a final judgment for the amount due and includes interest (Tex. Fam. Code §157.261(a)). The court that issues an order for payment of arrearages retains jurisdiction until the outstanding amount has been paid in full (Tex. Fam. Code §157.269). Courts may not reduce or modify child support arrearages in a contempt proceeding (Tex. Fam. Code §157.262(a)).

---

§157.261. Unpaid child support constitutes final judgment

(a) A child support payment not timely made constitutes a final judgment for the amount due and owing, including interest as provided in this chapter.

(b) For the purposes of this subchapter, interest begins to accrue on the date the judge signs the order for the judgment unless the order contains a statement that the order is rendered on another specific date.

(Acts 1995, 74th Leg., ch. 20, §1, effective April 20, 1995. Amended by Acts 1997, 75th Leg., ch. 702, §5, effective September 1, 1997.)

§157.262. Court may not reduce or modify arrearages but may hold in abeyance

(a) Except as provided by this section, in a contempt proceeding or in rendering a money judgment, the court may not reduce or modify the amount of child support arrearages.

(b) In an enforcement action under this chapter, the court may, with the agreement of the Title IV-D agency, hold in abeyance the enforcement of any arrearages, including interest, assigned to the Title IV-D agency under Section 231.104(a) if, for the period of the court's order of abeyance of enforcement, the obligor:

(1) timely and fully pays the obligor's current child support under a court or administrative order; and

(2) is involved in the life of the child for whom support is ordered through the exercise of the obligor's right of possession of or access to the child.

(c) If the court orders an abeyance of enforcement of arrearages under this section, the court may require the obligor to obtain counseling on parenting skills, work skills, job placement, financial planning, conflict resolution, substance abuse, or other matters causing the obligor to fail to obey the child support order.

(d) If the court finds in a subsequent hearing that the obligor has not met the conditions set by the court's order under this section, the court shall terminate the abeyance of enforcement of the arrearages.

(e) On the expiration of the child support order, the court may, with the agreement of the Title IV-D agency, reduce the amount of the arrearages assigned to the Title IV-D agency under Section 231.104(a) if the court finds that the obligor has complied with the conditions set by the court under this section.

(f) The money judgment for arrearages rendered by the court may be subject to a counterclaim or offset as provided by this subchapter.

(Acts 1995, 74th Leg., ch. 20, §1, effective April 20, 1995. Amended by Acts 2001, 77th Leg., ch. 392, §3, effective September 1, 2001; Acts 2001, 77th Leg., ch. 1023, §15, effective September 1, 2001.)

§157.263. Court shall confirm amount of arrearages and render cumulative money judgment

(a) If a motion for enforcement of child support requests a money judgment for arrearages, the court shall confirm the amount of arrearages and render one cumulative money judgment.

(b) A cumulative money judgment includes:

(1) unpaid child support not previously confirmed;

(2) the balance owed on previously confirmed arrearages or lump sum or retroactive support judgments;

(3) interest on the arrearages; and

(4) a statement that it is a cumulative judgment.

(c) If the amount of arrearages confirmed by the court reflects a credit to the obligor for support arrearages collected from a federal tax refund under 42 U.S.C. Section 664, as amended, and, subsequently, the amount of that credit is reduced because the refund was based on a joint return under which another person was entitled to a share of the refund under 42 U.S.C. Section 664, as amended, the court shall render a new cumulative judgment to include as arrearages an amount equal to the amount by which the credit was reduced.

(Acts 1995, 74th Leg., ch. 20, §1, effective April 20, 1995. Amended by Acts 2003, 78th Leg., ch. 610, effective September 1, 2003.)

§157.264. Manner of enforcement of judgment for child support: income withholding or periodic payments

(a) A money judgment rendered as provided in this subchapter may be enforced by any means available for the enforcement of a judgment for debts.

(b) The court may render an order requiring:

(1) that income be withheld from the disposable earnings of the obligor in an amount sufficient to discharge the judgment in not more than two years; or

(2) if the obligor is not subject to income withholding, that the obligor make periodic payments to the obligee in an amount sufficient to discharge the judgment within a reasonable time.

(Acts 1995, 74th Leg., ch. 20, §1, effective April 20, 1995. Amended by Acts 2001, 77th Leg., ch. 1023, §16, effective September 1, 2001.)

§157.265. Rate of accrual of interest on child support

(a) Interest accrues on the portion of delinquent child support that is greater than the amount of the monthly periodic support obligation at the rate of six percent simple interest per year from the date the support is delinquent until the date the support is paid or the arrearages are confirmed and reduced to money judgment.

(b) Interest accrues on child support arrearages that have been confirmed and reduced to money judgment as provided in this subchapter at the rate of six percent simple interest per year from the date the order is rendered until the date the judgment is paid.

(c) Interest accrues on a money judgment for retroactive or lump-sum child support at the annual rate of six percent simple interest from the date the order is rendered until the judgment is paid.

(d) Subsection (a) applies to a child support payment that becomes due on or after January 1, 2002.

(e) Child support arrearages in existence on January 1, 2002, that were not confirmed and reduced to a money judgment on or before that date accrue interest as follows:

(1) before January 1, 2002, the arrearages are subject to the interest rate that applied to the arrearages before that date; and

(2) on or after January 1, 2002, the cumulative total of arrearages and interest accumulated on those arrearages described by Subdivision (1) is subject to Subsection (a).

(f) Subsections (b) and (c) apply to a money judgment for child support rendered on or after January 1, 2002. A money judgment for child support rendered before that date is governed by law in effect on the date the judgment was rendered, and the former law is continued in effect for that purpose.

(Acts 1995, 74th Leg., ch. 20, §1, effective April 20, 1995. Amended by Acts 1995, 74th Leg., ch. 751, §53, effective September 1, 1995; by Acts 1999, 76th Leg., ch. 943, §1, effective January 1, 2000; Acts 2001, 77th Leg., ch. 1491, §1, effective January 1, 2002; Acts 2005, 79th Leg., ch. 185 (H.B. 678), effective January 1, 2005.)

§157.266. Date of delinquency for child support payment

(a) A child support payment is delinquent for the purpose of accrual of interest if the payment is not received before the 31st day after the payment date stated in the order by:

(1) the local registry, Title IV-D registry, or state disbursement unit; or

(2) the obligee or entity specified in the order, if payments are not made through a registry.

(b) If a payment date is not stated in the order, a child support payment is delinquent if payment is not received by the registry or the obligee or entity specified in the order on the date that an amount equal to the support payable for one month becomes past due.
(Acts 1995, 74th Leg., ch. 20, §1, effective April 20, 1995. Amended by Acts 1999, 76th Leg., ch. 943, §2, effective January 1, 2000.)

§157.267. Enforcement of outstanding accrued interest

Accrued interest is part of the child support obligation and may be enforced by any means provided for the collection of child support.
(Acts 1995, 74th Leg., ch. 20, §1, effective April 20, 1995.)

§157.268. Priority of application of child support payment

Child support collected shall be applied in the following order of priority:

(1) current child support;

(2) non-delinquent child support owed;

(3) interest on the principal amounts specified in Subdivisions (4) and (5);

(4) the principal amount of child support that has not been confirmed and reduced to money judgment;

(5) the principal amount of child support that has been confirmed and reduced to money judgment; and

(6) the amount of any ordered attorney's fees or costs.
(Acts 1995, 74th Leg., ch. 20, §1, effective April 20, 1995. Amended by Acts 2001, 77th Leg., ch. 1023, §17, effective September 1, 2001.)

§157.269. Court retains jurisdiction until payment of current support, medical support, arrearages and interest

A court that renders an order providing for the payment of child support arrearages retains jurisdiction until all current support and medical support and child support arrearages, including interest and any applicable fees and costs, have been paid.
(Acts 1995, 74th Leg., ch. 751, §54, effective September 1, 1995. Amended by Acts 1999, 76th Leg., ch. 556, §19, effective September 1, 1999.)

3. Enforcement by Lien on Property

One common method of securing an obligation to an ex-spouse is to impose a lien on the obligor's property in favor of the obligee. A longstanding state remedy for child support enforcement was the reduction of past-due payments to a money judgment (if accrued installments do not already constitute final judgments), followed by a lien against the obligor's real property.

Under the Personal Responsibility and Work Opportunity Reconciliation Act of 1996, 42 U.S.C. §666(a)(4)(2000), states must impose automatic liens on an obligor's assets. States must institute administrative procedures for imposing liens. *Id.* at §666(a)(2), (c). Administrative liens exemplify the trend from individual enforcement proceedings in favor of an approach that triggers enforcement automatically, without any initiation by the obligee or judicial involvement.

Texas Family Code

§157.311. Definitions

In this subchapter:

(1) "Account" means:

(A) any type of a demand deposit account, checking or negotiable withdrawal order account, savings account, time deposit account, money market mutual fund account, certificate of deposit, or any other instrument of deposit in which an individual has a beneficial ownership either in its entirety or on a shared or multiple party basis, including any accrued interest and dividends; and

(B) a life insurance policy in which an individual has a beneficial ownership or liability insurance against which an individual has filed a claim or counterclaim.

(2) "Claimant" means:

(A) the obligee or a private attorney representing the obligee;

(B) the Title IV-D agency providing child support services;

(C) a domestic relations office or local registry; or

(D) an attorney appointed as a friend of the court.

(3) "Court having continuing jurisdiction" is the court of continuing, exclusive jurisdiction in this state or a tribunal of another state having jurisdiction under the Uniform Interstate Family Support Act or a substantially similar act.

(4) "Financial institution" has the meaning assigned by 42 U.S.C. Section 669a(d)(1) and includes a depository institution, credit union, benefit association, liability or life insurance company, workers' compensation insurer, money market mutual fund, and any similar entity authorized to do business in this state.

(5) "Lien" means a child support lien issued in this or another state.
(Acts 1995, 74th Leg., ch. 20, §1, effective April 20, 1995. Amended by Acts 1997, 75th Leg., ch. 420, §1, effective September 1, 1997; Acts 1997, 75th Leg., ch. 911, §19, effective September 1, 1997; Acts 2001, 77th Leg., ch. 1023, §18, effective September 1, 2001; Acts 2003, 78th Leg., ch. 610, effective September 1, 2003.)

§157.312. Enforcement of child support by a lien

(a) A claimant may enforce child support by a lien as provided in this subchapter.

(b) The remedies provided by this subchapter do not affect the availability of other remedies provided by law.

(c) The lien is in addition to any other lien provided by law.

(d) A child support lien arises by operation of law against real and personal property of an obligor for all amounts of child support due and owing, including any accrued interest, regardless of whether the amounts have been adjudicated or otherwise determined, subject to the requirements of this subchapter for perfection of the lien.

(e) A child support lien arising in another state may be enforced in the same manner and to the same extent as a lien arising in this state.

(f) A foreclosure action under this subchapter is not required as a prerequisite to levy and execution on a judicial or administrative determination of arrearages as provided by Section 157.327.

(g) A child support lien under this subchapter may not be directed to an employer to attach to the disposable earnings of an obligor paid by the employer. [For appropriate means for income withholding through the employer, see *infra*, Tex. Fam. Code §154.007 et seq., and related discussion, Withholding Earnings to Enforce Support.]

(Acts 1995, 74th Leg., ch. 20, §1, effective April 20, 1995. Amended by Acts 1997, 75th Leg., ch. 420, §2, effective September 1, 1997; Acts 1997, 75th Leg., ch. 911, §20, effective September 1, 1997; Acts 2001, 77th Leg., ch. 1023, §19, effective September 1, 2001; Acts 2003, 78th Leg., ch. 610, effective September 1, 2003.)

§157.313. Child support lien notice must contain certain information

(a) Except as provided by Subsection (e), a child support lien notice must contain:

(1) the name and address of the person to whom the notice is being sent;

(2) the style, docket or cause number, and identity of the tribunal of this or another state having continuing jurisdiction of the child support action and, if the case is a Title IV-D case, the case number;

(3) the full name, address, and, if known, the birth date, driver's license number, social security number, and any aliases of the obligor;

(4) the full name and, if known, social security number of the obligee;

(5) the amount of the current or prospective child support obligation, the frequency with which current or prospective child support is ordered to be paid, and the amount of child support arrearages owed by the obligor and the date of the signing of the court order, administrative order, or writ that determined the arrearages or the date and manner in which the arrearages were determined;

(6) the rate of interest specified in the court order, administrative order, or writ or, in the absence of a specified interest rate, the rate provided for by law;

(7) the name and address of the person or agency asserting the lien;

(8) the motor vehicle identification number as shown on the obligor's title if the property is a motor vehicle;

(9) a statement that the lien attaches to all nonexempt real and personal property of the obligor that is located or recorded in the state, including any property specifically identified in the notice;

(10) a statement that any ordered child support not timely paid in the future constitutes a final judgment for the amount due and owing, including interest, and accrues up to an amount that may not exceed the lien amount; and

(11) a statement that the obligor is being provided a copy of the lien notice and that the obligor may dispute the arrearage amount by filing suit under Section 157.323.

(b) A claimant may include any other information that the claimant considers necessary.

(c) The lien notice must be verified.

(d) A claimant must file a notice for each after-acquired motor vehicle.

(e) A notice of a lien for child support under this section may be in the form authorized by federal law or regulation.

(Acts 1995, 74th Leg., ch. 20, §1, effective April 20, 1995. Amended by Acts 1997, 75th Leg., ch. 420, §3, effective September 1, 1997; Acts 1997, 75th Leg., ch. 911, §21, effective September 1, 1997; Acts 2001, 77th Leg., ch. 1023, §20, effective September 1, 2001.)

§157.314. Venue to file lien notice or abstract of judgment for past due support; notice to obligor

(a) A child support lien notice or an abstract of judgment for past due child support may be filed by the claimant with the county clerk of:

(1) any county in which the obligor is believed to own nonexempt real or personal property;

(2) the county in which the obligor resides; or

(3) the county in which the court having continuing jurisdiction has venue of the suit affecting the parent-child relationship.

(b) A child support lien notice may be filed with or delivered to the following, as appropriate:

(1) the clerk of the court in which a claim, counterclaim, or suit by, or on behalf of, the obligor, including a claim or potential right to proceeds from an estate as an heir, beneficiary, or creditor, is pending, provided that a copy of the lien is mailed to the attorney of record for the obligor, if any;

(2) an attorney who represents the obligor in a claim or counterclaim that has not been filed with a court;

(3) any other individual or organization believed to be in possession of real or personal property of the obligor; or

(4) any governmental unit or agency that issues or records certificates, titles, or other indicia of property ownership.

(c) Not later than the 21st day after the date of filing or delivering the child support lien notice, the claimant shall provide a copy of the notice to the obligor by first class or certified mail, return receipt requested, addressed to the obligor at the obligor's last known address. If another person is known to have an ownership interest in the property subject to the lien, the claimant shall provide a copy of the lien notice to that person at the time notice is provided to the obligor.

(d) If a child support lien notice is delivered to a financial institution with respect to an account of the obligor, the institution shall immediately:

(1) provide the claimant with the last known address of the obligor; and

(2) notify any other person having an ownership interest in the account that the account has been frozen in an amount not to exceed the amount of the child support arrearage identified in the notice.

(Acts 1995, 74th Leg., ch. 20, §1, effective April 20, 1995. Amended by Acts 1997, 75th Leg., ch. 420, §4, effective September 1, 1997; Acts 1997, 75th Leg., ch. 911, §22, effective September 1, 1997; Acts 2001, 77th Leg., ch. 1023, §21, effective September 1, 2001.)

§157.3145. Method of service on financial institution

(a) Service of a child support lien notice on a financial institution relating to property held by the institution in the name of, or in behalf of, an obligor is governed by Section 59.008, Finance Code, if the institution is subject to that law, or may be delivered to the registered agent, the institution's main business office in this state, or another address provided by the institution under Section 231.307.

(b) A financial institution doing business in this state shall comply with the notice of lien and levy under this section regardless of whether the institution's corporate headquarters is located in this state.

(Acts 2001, 77th Leg., ch. 1023, §22, effective September 1, 2001; Amended by Acts 2003, 77th Leg., ch. 610, effective September 1, 2003.)

§157.315. County clerk shall record lien

(a) On receipt of a child support lien notice, the county clerk shall immediately record the notice in the county judgment records as provided in Chapter 52, Property Code.

(b) The county clerk may not charge the Title IV-D agency, a domestic relations office, a friend of the court, or any other party a fee for recording the notice of a lien. To qualify for this exemption, the lien notice must be styled "Notice of Child Support Lien" or be in the form authorized by federal law or regulation.

(c) The county clerk may not charge the Title IV-D agency, a domestic relations office, or a friend of the court a fee for recording the release of a child support lien. The lien release must be styled "Release of Child Support Lien."

(Acts 1995, 74th Leg., ch. 20, §1, effective April 20, 1995. Amended by Acts 1999, 76th Leg., ch. 595, §1, effective September 1, 1999; Acts 1999, 76th Leg., ch. 769, §1, effective September 1, 1999; Acts 2001, 77th Leg., ch. 1023, §23, effective September 1, 2001.)

§157.316. Perfection of child support lien; liens on motor vehicles

(a) Except as provided by Subsection (b), a child support lien is perfected when an abstract of judgment for past due child support or a child support lien notice is filed or delivered as provided by Section 157.314.

(b) If a lien established under this subchapter attaches to a motor vehicle, the lien must be perfected in the manner provided by Chapter 501, Transportation Code, and the court or Title IV-D agency that rendered the order of child support shall include in the order a requirement that the obligor surrender to the court or Title IV-D agency evidence of the legal ownership of the motor vehicle against which the lien may attach. A lien against a motor vehicle under this subchapter is not perfected until the obligor's title to the vehicle has been surrendered to the court or Title IV-D agency and the Texas Department of Transportation has issued a subsequent title that discloses on its face the fact that the vehicle is subject to a child support lien under this subchapter.

(Acts 1995, 74th Leg., ch. 20, §1, effective April 20, 1995. Amended by Acts 1997, 75th Leg., ch. 420, §5, effective September 1, 1997; Acts 1997, 75th Leg., ch. 911, §23, effective September 1, 1997; Acts 2001, 77th Leg., ch. 1023, §24, effective September 1, 2001.)

§157.317. Lien attaches to all real and personal property not exempt

(a) A child support lien attaches to all real and personal property not exempt under the Texas Constitution or other law, including:

(1) an account in a financial institution;

(2) a retirement plan, including an individual retirement account; and

(3) the proceeds of a life insurance policy, a claim for negligence, personal injury, or workers' compensation, or an insurance settlement or award for the claim, due to or owned by the obligor.

(a-1) A lien attaches on or after the date the lien notice or abstract of judgment is filed with the county clerk of the county in which the property is located, with the court clerk as to property or claims in litigation, or, as to property of the obligor in the possession or control of a third party, from the date the lien notice is filed with that party.

(b) A lien attaches to all nonhomestead real property of the obligor but does not attach to a homestead exempt under the Texas Constitution or the Property Code.

(Acts 1995, 74th Leg., ch. 20, §1, effective April 20, 1995. Amended by Acts 1997, 75th Leg., ch. 420, §6, effective September 1, 1997; Acts 1997, 75th Leg., ch. 911, §24, effective September 1, 1997; Acts 1999, 76th Leg., ch. 344, §7.007, effective September 1, 1999; Acts 1999, 76th Leg., ch. 556, §20, effective September 1, 1999; Acts 2001, 77th Leg., ch. 1023, §25, effective September 1, 2001; Acts 2003, 78th Leg., ch. 610, effective September 1, 2003.)

§157.318. Lien is effective until full payment of current support, arrearages, interest and fees

(a) A lien is effective until all current support and child support arrearages, including interest and any costs and reasonable attorney's fees, have been paid or the lien is otherwise released as provided by this subchapter.

(b) The lien secures payment of all child support arrearages owed by the obligor under the underlying child support order, including arrearages that accrue after the lien notice was filed or delivered as provided by Section 157.314.

(c) The filing of a lien notice or abstract of judgment with the county clerk is a record of the notice and has the same effect as any other lien notice with respect to real property records.

(Acts 1995, 74th Leg., ch. 20, §1, effective April 20, 1995. Amended by Acts 1997, 75th Leg., ch. 420, §7, effective September 1, 1997; Acts 1997, 75th Leg., ch. 911, §25, effective September 1, 1997; Acts 2001, 77th Leg., ch. 1023, §26, effective September 1, 2001.)

§157.319. Effect of lien notice on possessor of obligor's property

(a) If a person having actual notice of the lien possesses nonexempt personal property of the obligor that may be subject to the lien, the property may not be paid over, released, sold, transferred, encumbered, or conveyed unless:

(1) a release of lien signed by the claimant is delivered to the person in possession; or

(2) a court, after notice to the claimant and hearing, has ordered the release of the lien because arrearages do not exist.

(b) A person having notice of a child support lien who violates this section may be joined as a party to a foreclosure action under this chapter and is subject to the penalties 1 provided by this subchapter.

(c) This section does not affect the validity or priority of a lien of a health care provider, a lien for attorney's fees, or a lien of a holder of a security interest. This section does not affect the assignment of rights or subrogation of a claim under Title XIX of the federal Social Security Act (42 U.S.C. Section 1396 et seq.), as amended.

(Acts 1995, 74th Leg., ch. 20, §1, effective April 20, 1995. Amended by Acts 1997, 75th Leg., ch. 420, §8, effective September 1, 1997; Acts 1997, 75th Leg., ch. 911, §26, effective September 1, 1997; Acts 2001, 77th Leg., ch. 1023, §27, effective September 1, 2001.)

§157.320. Priority of lien as to interest in real property

(a) A lien created under this subchapter does not have priority over a lien or conveyance of an interest in the nonexempt real property recorded before the child support lien notice is recorded in the county where the real property is located.

(b) A lien created under this subchapter has priority over any lien or conveyance of an interest in the nonexempt real property recorded after the child support lien notice is recorded in the county clerk's office in the county where the property of the obligor is located.

(c) A conveyance of real property by the obligor after a lien notice has been recorded in the county where the real property is located is subject to the lien and may not impair the enforceability of the lien against the real property.

(d) A lien created under this subchapter is subordinate to a vendor's lien retained in a conveyance to the obligor.

(Acts 1995, 74th Leg., ch. 20, §1, effective April 20, 1995. Amended by Acts 1997, 75th Leg., ch. 911, §27, effective September 1, 1997.)

§157.321. Conditions for lien claimant to release lien

A child support lien claimant may at any time release a lien on all or part of the property of the obligor or return seized property, without liability, if assurance of payment is considered adequate by the claimant or if the release or return will facilitate the collection of the arrearages. The release or return may not operate to prevent future action to collect from the same or other property owned by the obligor.

(Acts 1995, 74th Leg., ch. 20, §1, effective April 20, 1995. Amended by Acts 1997, 75th Leg., ch. 420, §9, effective September 1, 1997; Acts 1997, 75th Leg., ch. 911, §28, effective September 1, 1997; Acts 2001, 77th Leg., ch. 1023, §28, effective September 1, 2001.)

§157.322. Conditions for mandatory release of child support lien

(a) On payment in full of the amount of child support due, together with any costs and reasonable attorney's fees, the child support lien claimant shall execute and deliver to the obligor or the obligor's attorney a release of the child support lien.

(b) The release of the child support lien is effective when:

(1) filed with the county clerk with whom the lien notice or abstract of judgment was filed; or

(2) delivered to any other individual or organization that may have been served with a lien notice under this subchapter.

(Acts 1995, 74th Leg., ch. 20, §1, effective April 20, 1995. Amended by Acts 1997, 75th Leg., ch. 420, §10, effective September 1, 1997; Acts 1997, 75th Leg., ch. 911, §§29, 97(a), effective September 1, 1997; Acts 2001, 77th Leg., ch. 1023, §29, effective September 1, 2001.)

§157.323. Venue for foreclosure on lien or suit to determine arrearages

(a) In addition to any other remedy provided by law, an action to foreclose a child support lien, to dispute the amount of arrearages stated in the lien, or to resolve issues of ownership interest with respect to property subject to a child support lien may be brought in:

(1) the court in which the lien notice was filed under Section 157. 314(b)(1);

(2) the district court of the county in which the property is or was located and the lien was filed; or

(3) the court of continuing jurisdiction.

(b) The procedures provided by Subchapter B1 apply to a foreclosure action under this section, except that a person or organization in possession of the property of the obligor or known to have an ownership interest in property that is subject to the lien may be joined as an additional respondent.

(c) If arrearages are owed by the obligor, the court shall:

(1) render judgment against the obligor for the amount due, plus costs and reasonable attorney's fees;

(2) order any official authorized to levy execution to satisfy the lien, costs, and attorney's fees by selling any property on which a lien is established under this subchapter; or

(3) order an individual or organization in possession of nonexempt personal property or cash owned by the obligor to dispose of the property as the court may direct.

(d) For execution and sale under this section, publication of notice is necessary only for three consecutive weeks in a newspaper published in the county where the property is located or, if there is no newspaper in that county, in the most convenient newspaper in circulation in the county.

(Acts 1995, 74th Leg., ch. 20, §1, effective April 20, 1995. Amended by Acts 1997, 75th Leg., ch. 420, §11, effective

September 1, 1997; Acts 1997, 75th Leg., ch. 911, §30, effective September 1, 1997; Acts 2001, 77th Leg., ch. 1023, §30, effective September 1, 2001.)

§157.324. Liability for failure to comply with child support lien

A person who knowingly disposes of property subject to a child support lien, who, after a foreclosure hearing, fails to surrender on demand nonexempt personal property as directed by a court or administrative order under this subchapter, or who fails to comply with a notice of levy under this subchapter is liable to the claimant in an amount equal to the arrearages for which the lien, notice of levy, or foreclosure judgment was issued.

(Acts 1995, 74th Leg., ch. 20, §1, effective April 20, 1995. Amended by Acts 1997, 75th Leg., ch. 420, §12, effective September 1, 1997; Acts 1997, 75th Leg., ch. 911, §31, effective September 1, 1997; Acts 2001, 77th Leg., ch. 1023, §31, effective September 1, 2001.)

§157.325. Release of excess funds

(a) If a person has in the person's possession earnings, deposits, accounts, balances, or other funds or assets of the obligor, including the proceeds of a judgment or other settlement of a claim or counterclaim due to the obligor that are in excess of the amount of arrearages specified in the child support lien, the holder of the nonexempt personal property or the obligor may request that the claimant release any excess amount from the lien. The claimant shall grant the request and discharge any lien on the excess amount unless the security for the arrearages would be impaired.

(b) If the claimant refuses the request, the holder of the personal property or the obligor may file suit under this subchapter for an order determining the amount of arrearages and discharging excess personal property or money from the lien.

(Acts 1995, 74th Leg., ch. 20, §1, effective April 20, 1995. Amended by Acts 1997, 75th Leg., ch. 420, §13, effective September 1, 1997; Acts 1997, 75th Leg., ch. 911, §32, effective September 1, 1997; Acts 2001, 77th Leg., ch. 1023, §32, effective September 1, 2001.)

§157.326. Obligor's spouse or another with ownership interest may file suit

(a) A spouse of an obligor or another person having an ownership interest in property that is subject to a child support lien may file suit under Section 157.323 to determine the extent, if any, of the spouse's or other person's interest in real or personal property that is subject to:

(1) a lien perfected under this subchapter; or

(2) an action to foreclose under this subchapter.

(b) After notice to the obligor, the obligor's spouse, any other person alleging an ownership interest, the claimant, and the obligee, the court shall conduct a hearing and determine the extent, if any, of the ownership interest in the property held by the obligor's spouse or other person. If the court finds that:

(1) the property is the separate property of the obligor's spouse or the other person, the court shall order that the lien against the property be released and that any action to foreclose on the property be dismissed;

(2) the property is jointly owned by the obligor and the obligor's spouse, the court shall determine whether the sale of the obligor's interest in the property would result in an unreasonable hardship on the obligor's spouse or family and:

(A) if so, the court shall render an order that the obligor's interest in the property not be sold and that the lien against the property should be released; or

(B) if not, the court shall render an order partitioning the property and directing that the property be sold and the proceeds applied to the child support arrearages; or

(3) the property is owned in part by another person, other than the obligor's spouse, the court shall render an order partitioning the property and directing that the obligor's share of the property be applied to the child support arrearages.

(c) In a proceeding under this section, the spouse or other person claiming an ownership interest in the property has the burden to prove the extent of that ownership interest.

(Acts 1995, 74th Leg., ch. 20, §1, effective April 20, 1995. Amended by Acts 1997, 75th Leg., ch. 420, §14, effective September 1, 1997; Acts 1997, 75th Leg., ch. 911, §33, effective September 1, 1997; Acts 2001, 77th Leg., ch. 1023, §33, effective September 1, 2001.)

§157.327. Claimant may deliver notice of levy to financial institution possessing obligor's funds

(a) Notwithstanding any other provision of law, if a judgment or administrative determination of arrearages has been rendered, a claimant may deliver a notice of levy to any financial institution possessing or controlling assets or funds owned by, or owed to, an obligor and subject to a child support lien, including a lien for child support arising in another state.

(b) The notice under this section must:

(1) identify the amount of child support arrearages owing at the time the amount of arrearages was determined; and

(2) direct the financial institution to pay to the claimant, not earlier than the 15th day or later than the 21st day after the date of delivery of the notice, an amount from the assets of the obligor or from funds due to the obligor that are held or controlled by the institution, not to exceed the amount of the child support arrearages identified in the notice, unless:

(A) the institution is notified by the claimant that the obligor has paid the arrearages or made arrangements satisfactory to the claimant for the payment of the arrearages;

(B) the obligor or another person files a suit under Section 157.323 requesting a hearing by the court; or

(C) if the claimant is the Title IV-D agency, the obligor has requested an agency review under Section 157.328.

(c) A financial institution that receives a notice of levy under this section may not close an account in which the obligor has an ownership interest, permit a withdrawal from any account the obligor owns, in whole or in part, or pay funds to the obligor so that any amount remaining in the account is less than the amount of the arrearages identified in the notice, plus any fees due to the institution and any costs of the levy identified by the claimant.

(d) A financial institution that receives a notice of levy under this section shall notify any other person having an ownership interest in an account in which the obligor has an ownership interest that the account has been levied on in an amount not to exceed the amount of the child support arrearages identified in the notice of levy.

(e) The notice of levy may be delivered to a financial institution as provided by Section 59.008, Finance Code, if the institution is subject to that law or may be delivered to the registered agent, the institution's main business office in this state, or another address provided by the institution under Section 231.307.

(Acts 2001, 77th Leg., ch. 1023, §34, effective September 1, 2001.)

§157.328. Claimant must serve notice of levy on obligor

(a) At the time the notice of levy under Section 157.327 is delivered to a financial institution, the claimant shall serve the obligor with a copy of the notice.

(b) The notice of levy delivered to the obligor must inform the obligor that:

(1) the claimant will not proceed with levy if, not later than the 10th day after the date of receipt of the notice, the obligor pays in full the amount of arrearages identified in the notice or otherwise makes arrangements acceptable to the claimant for the payment of the arrearage amounts; and

(2) the obligor may contest the levy by filing suit under Section 157.323 not later than the 10th day after the date of receipt of the notice.

(c) If the claimant is the Title IV-D agency, the obligor receiving a notice of levy may request review by the agency not later than the 10th day after the date of receipt of the notice to resolve any issue in dispute regarding the existence or amount of the arrearages. The agency shall provide an opportunity for a review, by telephone conference or in person, as appropriate to the circumstances, not later than the fifth business day after the date an oral or written request from the obligor for the review is received. If the review fails to resolve any issue in dispute, the obligor may file suit under Section 157.323 for a hearing by the court not later than the fifth day after the date of the conclusion of the agency review. If the obligor fails to timely file suit, the Title IV-D agency may request the financial institution to release and remit the funds subject to levy.

(d) The notice under this section may be delivered to the last known address of the obligor by first class mail, certified mail, or registered mail.

(Acts 2001, 77th Leg., ch. 1023, §34, effective September 1, 2001.)

§157.329. Financial institution not liable for compliance with notice of levy

A financial institution that possesses or has a right to an obligor's assets for which a notice of levy has been delivered and that surrenders the assets or right to assets to a child support lien claimant is not liable to the obligor or any other person for the property or rights surrendered.

(Acts 2001, 77th Leg., ch. 1023, §34, effective September 1, 2001.)

§157.330. Consequences of failure to comply with notice of levy

A person who possesses or has a right to property that is the subject of a notice of levy delivered to the person and who refuses to surrender the property or right to property to the claimant on demand is liable to the claimant in an amount equal to the value of the property or right to property not surrendered but that does not exceed the amount of the child support arrearages for which the notice of levy has been filed.

(Acts 2001, 77th Leg., ch. 1023, §34, effective September 1, 2001.)

§157.331. Claimant may levy on additional property to satisfy arrearages

If the property or right to property on which a notice of levy has been filed does not produce money sufficient to satisfy the amount of child support arrearages identified in the notice of levy, the claimant may proceed to levy on other property of the obligor until the total amount of child support due is paid.

(Acts 2001, 77th Leg., ch. 1023, §34, effective September 1, 2001.)

4. Uniform Interstate Family Support Act

Child support enforcement, traditionally, presented difficulties when the parties resided in different states. The Uniform Interstate Family Support Act (UIFSA) is the latest in a series of efforts to promote consistency and efficiency in multistate support cases. In 1992 the National Conference of Commissioners on Uniform State Laws (NCCUSL) promulgated UIFSA to replace two earlier uniform acts that addressed interstate support enforcement: the Uniform Reciprocal Enforcement of Support Act (URESA) and its revised version RURESA.

NCCUSAL approved UIFSA in 1992, amended it in 1996, and amended it again in 2001. 9 U.L.A. (pt. 1B) 235, 393 (1999). Although based on URESA and RURESA, UIFSA contains new procedures for establishing, enforcing, and modifying support orders. To assure acceptance by the states, Congress made enactment of UIFSA a condition for federal funding for child support enforcement, under the Personal Responsibility and Work Opportunity Reconciliation Act of 1996, 42 U.S.C. §666(f)(2000). See generally John J. Sampson, Uniform Interstate Family Support Act with Unofficial Annotations, 27 Fam. L.Q. 91 (1993); John J. Sampson, Uniform Interstate Family Support Act (1996),

Statutory Text, Prefatory Note, and Commissioners' Comments (with More Unofficial Annotations), 32 Fam. L.Q. 385 (1998).

Like its predecessors, UIFSA covers both spousal and child support (but not property distribution). See UIFSA §101(21), 9 U.L.A. (pt. 1B) 258 (1999). UIFSA spells out procedures for both the establishment of support orders and their enforcement. UIFSA addresses a number of shortcomings in earlier laws. In particular, UIFSA expands long-arm jurisdiction by its broad provision for asserting long-arm jurisdiction to provide a tribunal in the state of residence of a child entitled to support (or a spouse) with the maximum opportunity to secure personal jurisdiction over an absent respondent (UIFSA §201, Tex. Fam. Code §159.201). This expansion facilitates a one-state proceeding in place of the two-state approach under URESA. Another important feature of UIFSA is its provision for continuing, exclusive jurisdiction and the one-order system. That is, under URESA and RURESA multiple support orders could be in effect in several states. UIFSA establishes the principle of continuing, exclusive jurisdiction in an effort to ensure that only one valid support order may be effective at any one time (UIFSA §§205-207, Tex. Fam. Code §§159.205, 159.206).

Enforcement of a support order of another state begins with the registration of the existing support order in a tribunal of the "responding state." The registered order, however, continues to be the order of the issuing state. See 9 U.L.A. (pt. 1B) 258 (1999), Prefatory Note.

By 1998, all jurisdictions had enacted UIFSA. *Id.* The Texas version of UIFSA is found at Texas Family Code §§159.001 et seq. In 2003, Texas modified some of its child support provisions under §159.001 et seq., adding further definitional detail and requiring (where jurisdiction is in dispute) more detail in court order determinations, concerning the reasons for the court's conclusion as to which state has continuing, exclusive jurisdiction (Tex. Fam. Code §159.207(f)).

a. General Provisions

Texas Family Code

§159.001. Effect of conflicts between provisions

If a provision of this chapter conflicts with a provision of this title or another statute or rule of this state and the conflict cannot be reconciled, this chapter prevails.

(Acts 1995, 74th Leg., ch. 20, §1, effective April 20, 1995.)

§159.102. Definitions

In this chapter:

(1) "Child" means an individual, whether over or under the age of majority, who:

(A) is or is alleged to be owed a duty of support by the individual's parent; or

(B) is or is alleged to be the beneficiary of a support order directed to the parent.

(2) "Child support order" means a support order for a child, including a child who has attained the age of majority under the law of the issuing state.

(3) "Duty of support" means an obligation imposed or imposable by law to provide support for a child, spouse, or former spouse, including an unsatisfied obligation to provide support.

(4) "Home state" means the state in which a child lived with a parent or a person acting as parent for at least six consecutive months preceding the time of filing of a petition or a comparable pleading for support and, if a child is less than six months old, the state in which the child lived with a parent or a person acting as parent from the time of birth. A period of temporary absence of any of them is counted as part of the six-month or other period.

(5) "Income" includes earnings or other periodic entitlements to money from any source and any other property subject to withholding for support under the law of this state.

(6) "Income-withholding order" means an order or other legal process directed to an obligor's employer, as provided in Chapter 158, to withhold support from the income of the obligor.

(7) "Initiating state" means a state from which a proceeding is forwarded or in which a proceeding is filed for forwarding to a responding state under this chapter or a law or procedure substantially similar to this chapter, the Uniform Reciprocal Enforcement of Support Act, or the Revised Uniform Reciprocal Enforcement of Support Act.

(8) "Initiating tribunal" means the authorized tribunal in an initiating state.

(9) "Issuing state" means the state in which a tribunal issues a support order or renders a judgment determining parentage.

(10) "Issuing tribunal" means the tribunal that issues a support order or renders a judgment determining parentage.

(11) "Law" includes decisional and statutory law and rules and regulations having the force of law.

(12) "Obligee" means:

(A) an individual to whom a duty of support is or is alleged to be owed or in whose favor a support order has been issued or a judgment determining parentage has been rendered;

(B) a state or political subdivision to which the rights under a duty of support or support order have been assigned or that has independent claims based on financial assistance provided to an individual obligee; or

(C) an individual seeking a judgment determining parentage of the individual's child.

(13) "Obligor" means an individual or the estate of a decedent:

(A) who owes or is alleged to owe a duty of support;

(B) who is alleged but has not been adjudicated to be a parent of a child; or

(C) who is liable under a support order.

(14) "Person" means an individual, corporation, business trust, estate, trust, partnership, limited liability company, association, joint venture, government, governmental subdivision, agency, instrumentality, public corporation, or any other legal or commercial entity.

(15) "Record" means information that is:

(A) inscribed on a tangible medium or stored in an electronic or other medium; and

(B) retrievable in perceivable form.

(16) "Register" means to file a support order or judgment determining parentage in the registry of foreign support orders.

(17) "Registering tribunal" means a tribunal in which a support order is registered.

(18) "Responding state" means a state in which a proceeding is filed or to which a proceeding is forwarded for filing from an initiating state under this chapter or a law or procedure substantially similar to this chapter, the Uniform Reciprocal Enforcement of Support Act, or the Revised Uniform Reciprocal Enforcement of Support Act.

(19) "Responding tribunal" means the authorized tribunal in a responding state.

(20) "Spousal support order" means a support order for a spouse or former spouse of the obligor.

(21) "State" means a state of the United States, the District of Columbia, Puerto Rico, the United States Virgin Islands, or any territory or insular possession subject to the jurisdiction of the United States. The term includes:

(A) an Indian tribe; and

(B) a foreign jurisdiction that has enacted a law or established procedures for issuance and enforcement of support orders that are substantially similar to the procedures under this chapter, the Uniform Reciprocal Enforcement of Support Act, or the Revised Uniform Reciprocal Enforcement of Support Act.

(22) "Support enforcement agency" means a public official or agency authorized to seek:

(A) enforcement of support orders or laws relating to the duty of support;

(B) establishment or modification of child support;

(C) determination of parentage; or

(D) the location of obligors or their assets.

"Support enforcement agency" does not include a domestic relations office unless that office has entered into a cooperative agreement with the Title IV-D agency to perform duties under this chapter.

(23) "Support order" means a judgment, decree, or order, whether temporary, final, or subject to modification, for the benefit of a child, a spouse, or a former spouse that provides for monetary support, health care, arrearages, or reimbursement and may include related costs and fees, interest, income withholding, attorney's fees, and other relief.

(24) "Tribunal" means a court, administrative agency, or quasi-judicial entity authorized to establish, enforce, or modify support orders or to determine parentage.

(Acts 1995, 74th Leg., ch. 20, §1, effective April 20, 1995. Amended by Acts 1997, 75th Leg., ch. 607, §1, effective September 1, 1997; Acts 2003, 78th Leg., ch. 1247, effective September 1, 2003.)

§159.103. Tribunal

The court is the tribunal of this state.

(Acts 1995, 74th Leg., ch. 20, §1, effective April 20, 1995. Amended by Acts 1997, 75th Leg., ch. 607, §2, effective September 1, 1997; Acts 2003, 78th Leg., ch. 1247, effective September 1, 2003.)

§159.104. Remedies are cumulative; limitations to court jurisdiction under this chapter

(a) Remedies provided in this chapter are cumulative and do not affect the availability of remedies under other law, including the recognition of a support order of a foreign country or political subdivision on the basis of comity.

(b) This chapter does not:

(1) provide the exclusive method of establishing or enforcing a support order under the law of this state; or

(2) grant a tribunal of this state jurisdiction to render a judgment or issue an order relating to child custody or visitation in a proceeding under this chapter.

(Acts 1995, 74th Leg., ch. 20, §1, effective April 20, 1995. Amended by Acts 2003, 78th Leg., ch. 1247, effective September 1, 2003.)

§159.901. Purpose of uniformity of application and construction

In applying and construing this chapter, consideration must be given to the need to promote uniformity of the law with respect to the subject matter of this chapter among states that enact a law similar to this chapter.

(Acts 1995, 74th Leg., ch. 20, §1, effective April 20, 1995. Amended by Acts 2003, 78th Leg., ch. 1247, effective September 1, 2003.)

§159.101. Title

This chapter may be cited as the Uniform Interstate Family Support Act.

(Acts 1995, 74th Leg., ch. 20, §1, effective April 20, 1995. Amended by Acts 2003, 78th Leg., ch. 1247, §3, effective September 1, 2003.)

b. Jurisdiction

Texas Family Code

§159.201. Bases for jurisdiction over nonresident respondent

(a) In a proceeding to establish, enforce, or modify a support order or to determine parentage, a tribunal of this state may exercise personal jurisdiction over a nonresident individual or the individual's guardian or conservator if:

(1) the individual is personally served with citation in this state;

(2) the individual submits to the jurisdiction of this state by consent, by entering a general appearance, or by filing a responsive document having the effect of waiving any contest to personal jurisdiction;

(3) the individual resided with the child in this state;

(4) the individual resided in this state and provided prenatal expenses or support for the child;

(5) the child resides in this state as a result of the acts or directives of the individual;

(6) the individual engaged in sexual intercourse in this state and the child may have been conceived by that act of intercourse;

(7) the individual asserted parentage in the paternity registry maintained in this state by the bureau of vital statistics; or

(8) there is any other basis consistent with the constitutions of this state and the United States for the exercise of personal jurisdiction.

(b) A tribunal of this state may not use the bases of personal jurisdiction listed in Subsection (a) or in any other law of this state to acquire personal jurisdiction to modify a child support order of another state unless the requirements of Section 159.611 or 159.615 are satisfied.

(Acts 1995, 74th Leg., ch. 20, §1, effective April 20, 1995. Amended by Acts 1997, 75th Leg., ch. 561, §5, effective September 1, 1997; Acts 2003, 75th Leg., ch. 1247, effective September 1, 2003.)

§159.203. Tribunal may serve as initiating tribunal and responding tribunal

Under this chapter, a tribunal of this state may serve as an initiating tribunal to forward proceedings to another state and as a responding tribunal for proceedings initiated in another state.

(Acts 1995, 74th Leg., ch. 20, §1, effective April 20, 1995. Amended by Acts 1997, 75th Leg., ch. 607, §3, effective September 1, 1997.)

§159.204. Effect of simultaneous proceedings in another state

(a) A tribunal of this state may exercise jurisdiction to establish a support order if the petition or comparable pleading is filed after a pleading is filed in another state only if:

(1) the petition or comparable pleading in this state is filed before the expiration of the time allowed in the other state for filing a responsive pleading challenging the exercise of jurisdiction by the other state;

(2) the contesting party timely challenges the exercise of jurisdiction in the other state; and

(3) if relevant, this state is the home state of the child.

(b) A tribunal of this state may not exercise jurisdiction to establish a support order if the petition or comparable pleading is filed before a petition or comparable pleading is filed in another state if:

(1) the petition or comparable pleading in the other state is filed before the expiration of the time allowed in this state for filing a responsive pleading challenging the exercise of jurisdiction by this state;

(2) the contesting party timely challenges the exercise of jurisdiction in this state; and

(3) if relevant, the other state is the home state of the child.

(Acts 1995, 74th Leg., ch. 20, §1, effective April 20, 1995. Amended by Acts 2003, 78th Leg., ch. 1247, effective September 1, 2003.)

§159.205. Conditions for continuing, exclusive jurisdiction

(a) A tribunal of this state that has issued a child support order consistent with the law of this state has and shall exercise continuing, exclusive jurisdiction to modify its order if the order is the controlling order and:

(1) at the time a request for modification is filed, this state is the state of residence of the obligor, the individual obligee, or the child for whose benefit the support order is issued; or

(2) the parties consent in a record or in open court that the tribunal of this state may continue to exercise jurisdiction to modify its order.

(b) A tribunal of this state issuing a child support order consistent with the law of this state may not exercise its continuing jurisdiction to modify the order if:

(1) each party who is an individual files consent in a record with the tribunal of this state that a tribunal of another state that has jurisdiction over at least one of the parties who is an individual or that is located in the state of residence of the child may modify the order and assume continuing, exclusive jurisdiction; or

(2) the order is not the controlling order.

(c) A tribunal of this state shall recognize the continuing, exclusive jurisdiction of a tribunal of another state if the tribunal of the other state has issued a child support order that modifies a child support order of a tribunal of this state under a law substantially similar to this chapter.

(d) A tribunal of this state that does not have continuing, exclusive jurisdiction to modify a child support order may serve as an initiating tribunal to request a tribunal of another state to modify a support order issued in that state.

(e) A temporary support order issued ex parte or pending resolution of a jurisdictional conflict does not create continuing, exclusive jurisdiction in the issuing tribunal.

(f) Repealed by Acts 2003, 78th. Leg., ch. 1247, §6.

(Acts 1995, 74th Leg., ch. 20, §1, effective April 20, 1995. Amended by Acts 1997, 75th Leg., ch. 607, §4, effective September 1, 1997; Acts 2003, 78th Leg., ch. 1247, effective September 1, 2003.)

§159.206. Tribunal may serve as initiating tribunal or respondent tribunal to enforce or modify support order; limitations on responding tribunal that lacks continuing, exclusive jurisdiction

(a) A tribunal of this state that has issued a child support order consistent with the law of this state may serve as an initiating tribunal to request a tribunal of another state to enforce:

(1) the order, if the order:

(A) is the controlling order; and

(B) has not been modified by a tribunal of another state that assumed jurisdiction under the Uniform Interstate Family Support Act; or

(2) a money judgment for support arrearages and interest on the order accrued before a determination that an order of another state is the controlling order.

(b) A tribunal of this state having continuing, exclusive jurisdiction over a support order may act as a responding tribunal to enforce the order.

(Acts 1995, 74th Leg., ch. 20, §1, effective April 20, 1995. Amended by Acts 2003, 78th Leg., ch. 1247, effective September 1, 2003.)

§159.207. Rules for recognition of controlling child support order

(a) If a proceeding is brought under this chapter and only one tribunal has issued a child support order, the order of that tribunal controls and must be so recognized.

(b) If a proceeding is brought under this chapter and two or more child support orders have been issued by tribunals of this state or another state with regard to the same obligor and same child, a tribunal of this state having personal jurisdiction over both the obligor and the individual obligee shall apply the following rules to determine by order which order controls:

(1) if only one of the tribunals would have continuing, exclusive jurisdiction under this chapter, the order of that tribunal controls and must be so recognized;

(2) if more than one of the tribunals would have continuing, exclusive jurisdiction under this chapter,:

(A) an order issued by a tribunal in the current home state of the child controls if an order has been issued in the current home state of the child; or

(B) the order most recently issued controls an if an order has not been issued in the current home state of the child; and

(3) if none of the tribunals would have continuing, exclusive jurisdiction under this chapter, the tribunal of this state shall issue a child support order that controls.

(c) If two or more child support orders have been issued for the same obligor and child and if the obligor or the individual obligee resides in this state, a party may request a tribunal of this state to determine which order controls and must be so recognized under Subsection (b). The request may be filed:

(1) with a registration for enforcement or registration for modification under Subchapter G; or

(2) as a separate proceeding.

(d) A request to determine the controlled order must be accompanied by a copy of each child support order in effect and the applicable record of payments. The requesting party shall give notice of the request to each party whose rights may be affected by the determination.

(e) The tribunal that issued the controlling order under Subsection (a), (b), or (c) is the tribunal that has continuing, exclusive jurisdiction under Section 159.205 or 159.206.

(f) The tribunal that issued the controlling order under Subsection (b)(1) or (2) or Subsection (c) or that issues a new controlling order under Subsection (b)(3) shall state in that order:

(1) the basis upon which the tribunal made its determination;

(2) the amount of prospective child support, if any; and

(3) the total amount of consolidated arrearages and accrued interest, if any, under the orders after all payments are credited under Section 159.209.

(g) Within 30 days after issuance of an order determining the identity of the controlling order, the party obtaining the order shall file a certified copy of it with each tribunal that issued or registered an earlier order of child support. A party who obtains the order and fails to file a certified copy is subject to appropriate sanctions by a tribunal in which the issue of failure to file arises. The failure to file does not affect the validity or enforceability of the controlling order.

(h) An order that has been determined to be the controlling order, or a judgment for consolidated support arrearages and interest issued under this section, must be recognized in a proceeding under this chapter.

(Acts 1995, 74th Leg., ch. 20, §1, effective April 20, 1995. Amended by Acts 1997, 75th Leg., ch. 607, §5, effective September 1, 1997; Acts 2003, 78th Leg., ch. 1247, effective September 1, 2003.)

§159.208. Enforcement of multiple child support orders for two or more obligees

In responding to registrations or petitions for enforcement of two or more child support orders in effect at the same time with regard to the same obligor and different individual obligees, at least one of which was issued by a tribunal of another state, a tribunal of this state shall enforce those orders in the same manner as if the multiple orders had been issued by a tribunal of this state.

(Acts 1995, 74th Leg., ch. 20, §1, effective April 20, 1995. Amended by Acts 2003, 78th Leg., ch. 1247, effective September 1, 2003.)

§159.209. Credit for payments under support order issued by tribunal of another state

A tribunal for this state shall credit amounts collected and credited for a particular period under a support order against the amounts owed for the same period under any other child support order issued by a tribunal of this or another state.

(Acts 1995, 74th Leg., ch. 20, §1, effective April 20, 1995. Amended by Acts 2003, 78th Leg., ch. 1247, effective September 1, 2003.)

---

c. Civil Provisions of General Application

Texas Family Code

§159.301. Proceedings under this chapter

(a) Except as otherwise provided in this chapter, this subchapter applies to all proceedings under this chapter.

(b) Repealed by Acts 2003, 78th Leg., ch. 1247, §46.

(c) An individual or a support enforcement agency may commence a proceeding authorized under this chapter by filing a petition in an initiating tribunal for forwarding to a responding tribunal or by filing a petition or a comparable pleading directly in a tribunal of another state that has or that can obtain personal jurisdiction over the respondent.

(Acts 1995, 74th Leg., ch. 20, §1, effective April 20, 1995. Amended by Acts 1997, 75th Leg., ch. 607, §6, effective

September 1, 1997; by Acts 2003, 78th Leg., ch. 1247, effective September 1, 2003.)

§159.302. Minor parent may maintain proceeding for minor's child

A minor parent or a guardian or other legal representative of a minor parent may maintain a proceeding on behalf of or for the benefit of the minor's child.

(Acts 1995, 74th Leg., ch. 20, §1, effective April 20, 1995. Amended by Acts 2003, 78th Leg., ch. 1247, effective September 1, 2003.)

§159.303. Responding tribunal shall apply law of state

Except as otherwise provided in this chapter, a responding tribunal of this state shall:

(1) apply the procedural and substantive law, including the rules on choice of law, generally applicable to similar proceedings originating in this state and may exercise all powers and provide all remedies available in those proceedings; and

(2) determine the duty of support and the amount payable in accordance with the law and support guidelines of this state.

(Acts 1995, 74th Leg., ch. 20, §1, effective April 20, 1995. Amended by Acts 1997, 75th Leg., ch. 607, §7, effective September 1, 1997; Acts 2003, 78th Leg., ch. 1247, effective September 1, 2003.)

§159.304. Duties of initiating tribunal to forward petition and documents

(a) On the filing of a petition authorized by this chapter, an initiating tribunal of this state shall forward three copies of the petition and its accompanying documents:

(1) to the responding tribunal or appropriate support enforcement agency in the responding state; or

(2) if the identity of the responding tribunal is unknown, to the state information agency of the responding state with a request that they be forwarded to the appropriate tribunal and that receipt be acknowledged.

(b) If requested by a responding tribunal, a tribunal of this state shall issue a certificate or other document and make findings required by the law of the responding state. If the responding state is a foreign country or political subdivision, the tribunal shall specify the amount of support sought, convert that amount into the equivalent amount in the foreign currency, under the applicable official or market exchange rate as publicly reported, and provide any other documents necessary to satisfy the requirements of the responding state.

(Acts 1995, 74th Leg., ch. 20, §1, effective April 20, 1995. Amended by Acts 1997, 75th Leg., ch. 607, §8, effective September 1, 1997; Acts 2003, 78th Leg., ch. 1247, effective September 1, 2003.)

§159.305. Duties of responding tribunal to cause petition to be filed and notify petitioner

(a) When a responding tribunal of this state receives a petition or comparable pleading from an initiating tribunal or directly under Section 159.301(c), the responding tribunal shall cause the petition or pleading to be filed and notify the petitioner where and when it was filed.

(b) A responding tribunal of this state, to the extent otherwise authorized by law, may do one or more of the following:

(1) issue or enforce a support order, modify a child support order, or render a judgment to determine parentage;

(2) order an obligor to comply with a support order and specify the amount and the manner of compliance;

(3) order income withholding;

(4) determine the amount of any arrearages and specify a method of payment;

(5) enforce orders by civil or criminal contempt, or both;

(6) set aside property for satisfaction of the support order;

(7) place liens and order execution on the obligor's property;

(8) order an obligor to keep the tribunal informed of the obligor's current residential address, telephone number, employer, address of employment, and telephone number at the place of employment;

(9) issue a bench warrant or capias for an obligor who has failed after proper notice to appear at a hearing ordered by the tribunal and enter the bench warrant or capias in any local and state computer systems for criminal warrants;

(10) order the obligor to seek appropriate employment by specified methods;

(11) award reasonable attorney's fees and other fees and costs; and

(12) grant any other available remedy.

(c) A responding tribunal of this state shall include in a support order issued under this chapter, or in the documents accompanying the order, the calculations on which the support order is based.

(d) A responding tribunal of this state may not condition the payment of a support order issued under this chapter on compliance by a party with provisions for visitation.

(e) If a responding tribunal of this state issues an order under this chapter, the tribunal shall send a copy of the order to the petitioner and the respondent and to the initiating tribunal, if any.

(f) If requested to enforce a support order, arrearages, or a judgment to modify a support order stated in a foreign currency, a responding tribunal of this state shall convert the amount stated in the foreign currency to the equivalent amount in dollars under the applicable official or market exchange rate as publicly reported.

(Acts 1995, 74th Leg., ch. 20, §1, effective April 20, 1995. Amended by Acts 1997, 75th Leg., ch. 607, §9, effective September 1, 1997; Acts 2003, 78th Leg., ch. 1247, effective September 1, 2003.)

§159.306. Receipt of petition by inappropriate tribunal

If a petition or comparable pleading is received by an inappropriate tribunal of this state, that tribunal shall forward the pleading and accompanying documents to an

appropriate tribunal in this state or another state and notify the petitioner where and when the pleading was sent.
(Acts 1995, 74th Leg., ch. 20, §1, effective April 20, 1995. Amended by Acts 1997, 75th Leg., ch. 607, §10, effective September 1, 1997.)

§159.307. Duties of support enforcement agency to provide services to petitioner

(a) A support enforcement agency of this state, on request, shall provide services to a petitioner in a proceeding under this chapter.

(b) A support enforcement agency that provides services to the petitioner as appropriate shall:

(1) take all steps necessary to enable an appropriate tribunal in this state or another state to obtain jurisdiction over the respondent;

(2) request an appropriate tribunal to set a date, time, and place for a hearing;

(3) make a reasonable effort to obtain all relevant information, including information as to income and property of the parties;

(4) not later than the second day, excluding Saturdays, Sundays, and legal holidays, after the date of receipt of a written notice from an initiating, responding, or registering tribunal, send a copy of the notice to the petitioner;

(5) not later than the second day, excluding Saturdays, Sundays, and legal holidays, after the date of receipt of a written communication from the respondent or the respondent's attorney, send a copy of the communication to the petitioner; and

(6) notify the petitioner if jurisdiction over the respondent cannot be obtained.

(c) A support enforcement agency of this state that requests registration of a child support order in this state for enforcement or for modification shall make reasonable efforts to ensure that

(1) the order to be registered is the controlling order; or

(2) a request for a determination of which order is the controlling order is made in a tribunal having jurisdiction to make the determination, if two or more child support orders have been issued and a determination of the controlling order has not been made.

(d) A support enforcement agency of this state that requests registration and enforcement of a support order, arrearages, or a judgment stated in a foreign currency shall convert the amount stated in the foreign currency to the equivalent amount in dollars under the applicable official or market exchange rate as publicly reported.

(1) A support enforcement agency of this state shall issue, or request a tribunal of this state to issue, a child support order and an income-withholding order that redirects payment of current support, arrearages, and interest if requested to do so by a support enforcement agency of another state under Section 159.319.

(f) This chapter does not create or negate a relationship of attorney and client or other fiduciary relationship between a support enforcement agency or the attorney for the agency and the individual being assisted by the agency.
(Acts 1995, 74th Leg., ch. 20, §1, effective April 20, 1995. Amended by Acts 1997, 75th Leg., ch. 607, §11, effective September 1, 1997; Acts 2003, 78th Leg., ch. 1247, effective September 1, 2003.)

§159.308. Duty of attorney general to order agency to perform its duties

(a) If the attorney general determines that the support enforcement agency is neglecting or refusing to provide services to an individual, the attorney general may order the agency to perform its duties under this chapter or may provide those services directly to the individual.

(b) The governor may determine that a foreign country or political subdivision has established a reciprocal arrangement for child support with this state and take appropriate action for notification of the determination.
(Acts 1995, 74th Leg., ch. 20, §1, effective April 20, 1995. Amended by Acts 2003, 78th Leg., ch. 1247, effective September 1, 2003.)

§159.309. Private counsel allowed

An individual may employ private counsel to represent the individual in proceedings authorized by this chapter.
(Acts 1995, 74th Leg., ch. 20, §1, effective April 20, 1995.)

§159.310. Duties of state information agency: maintain register of designated information

(a) The Title IV-D agency is the state information agency under this chapter.

(b) The state information agency shall:

(1) compile and maintain a current list, including addresses, of the tribunals in this state that have jurisdiction under this chapter and any support enforcement agencies in this state and send a copy to the state information agency of every other state;

(2) maintain a register of tribunals and support enforcement agencies received from other states;

(3) forward to the appropriate tribunal in the place in this state where the individual obligee or the obligor resides, or where the obligor's property is believed to be located, all documents concerning a proceeding under this chapter received from an initiating tribunal or the state information agency of the initiating state; and

(4) obtain information concerning the location of the obligor and the obligor's property in this state not exempt from execution, by such means as postal verification and federal or state locator services, examination of telephone directories, requests for the obligor's address from employers, and examination of governmental records, including, to the extent not prohibited by other law, those relating to real property, vital statistics, law enforcement, taxation, motor vehicles, driver's licenses, and social security.
(Acts 1995, 74th Leg., ch. 20, §1, effective April 20, 1995. Amended by Acts 2003, 78th Leg., ch. 1247, effective September 1, 2003.)

§159.311. Contents of pleadings and accompanying documents

(a) A petitioner seeking to establish or modify a support order, to determine parentage, or to register and modify a support order of another state must file a petition. Unless otherwise ordered under Section 159.312, the petition or accompanying documents must provide, so far as known, the name, residential address, and social security numbers of the obligor and the obligee and the name, sex, residential address, social security number, and date of birth of each child for whom support is sought or whose parentage is to be determined. Unless filed at the time of registration, the petition must be accompanied by a certified copy of any support order known to have been issued by another tribunal. The petition may include any other information that may assist in locating or identifying the respondent.

(b) The petition must specify the relief sought. The petition and accompanying documents must conform substantially with the requirements imposed by the forms mandated by federal law for use in cases filed by a support enforcement agency.

(Acts 1995, 74th Leg., ch. 20, §1, effective April 20, 1995. Amended by Acts 2003, 78th Leg., ch. 1247, effective September 1, 2003.)

§159.312. Tribunal may order nondisclosure of information

If a party alleges in an affadavit or pleading under oath that the health, safety, or liberty of a party or child would be unreasonably put at risk by the disclosure of identifying information regarding the party or the child, the identifying information shall be sealed and may not be disclosed to the other party or the public. After a hearing in which a tribunal considers the health, safety, or liberty of the party or the child, the tribunal may order disclosure of information if the tribunal determines that the disclosure serves the interests of justice.

(Acts 1995, 74th Leg., ch. 20, §1, effective April 20, 1995. Amended by Acts 2003, 78th Leg., ch. 1247, effective September 1, 2003.)

§159.313. Assessment of costs and fees

(a) The petitioner may not be required to pay a filing fee or other costs.

(b) If an obligee prevails, a responding tribunal may assess against an obligor filing fees, reasonable attorney's fees, other costs, and necessary travel and other reasonable expenses incurred by the obligee and the obligee's witnesses. The tribunal may not assess fees, costs, or expenses against the obligee or the support enforcement agency of either the initiating state or the responding state, except as provided by other law. Attorney's fees may be taxed as costs and may be ordered paid directly to the attorney, who may enforce the order in the attorney's own name. Payment of support owed to the obligee has priority over fees, costs, and expenses.

(c) The tribunal shall order the payment of costs and reasonable attorney's fees if it determines that a hearing was requested primarily for delay. In a proceeding pursuant to Sections 159.601 through 159.608, a hearing is presumed to have been requested primarily for delay if a registered support order is confirmed or enforced without change.

(Acts 1995, 74th Leg., ch. 20, §1, effective April 20, 1995. Amended by Acts 1997, 75th Leg., ch. 607, §12, effective September 1, 1997.)

§159.314. Petitioner has limited immunity

(a) Participation by a petitioner in a proceeding before a responding tribunal, whether in person, by private attorney, or through services provided by the support enforcement agency, does not confer personal jurisdiction over the petitioner in another proceeding.

(b) A petitioner is not amenable to service of civil process while physically present in this state to participate in a proceeding under this chapter.

(c) The immunity granted by this section does not extend to civil litigation based on acts unrelated to a proceeding under this chapter committed by a party while present in this state to participate in the proceeding.

(Acts 1995, 74th Leg., ch. 20, §1, effective April 20, 1995. Amended by Acts 2003, 78th Leg., ch. 1247, effective September 1, 2003.)

§159.315. Nonparentage is not defense if parentage previously determined

A party whose parentage of a child has been previously determined by or under law may not plead nonparentage as a defense to a proceeding under this chapter.

(Acts 1995, 74th Leg., ch. 20, §1, effective April 20, 1995.)

§159.316. Special jurisdictional rules: petitioner's presence is not required

(a) The physical presence of the petitioner in a responding tribunal of this state is not required for the establishment, enforcement, or modification of a support order or the rendition of a judgment determining parentage.

(b) An affidavit, document substantially complying with federally mandated forms, or a document incorporated by reference in an affidavit or document, that would not be under the hearsay rule if given in person, is admissible in evidence if given under penalty of perjury by a party or witness residing in another state.

(c) A copy of the record of child support payments certified as a true copy of the original by the custodian of the record may be forwarded to a responding tribunal. The copy is evidence of facts asserted in it and is admissible to show whether payments were made.

(d) Copies of bills for testing for parentage and for prenatal and postnatal health care of the mother and child that are furnished to the adverse party not less than 10 days before the date of trial are admissible in evidence to prove the amount of the charges billed and that the charges were reasonable, necessary, and customary.

(e) Documentary evidence sent from another state to a tribunal of this state by telephone, telecopier, or another means that does not provide an original writing may not be excluded from evidence on an objection based on the means of transmission.

(f) In a proceeding under this chapter, a tribunal of this state may permit a party or witness residing in another state to be deposed or to testify by telephone, audiovisual means, or other electronic means at a designated tribunal or other location in that state. A tribunal of this state shall cooperate with a tribunal of another state in designating an appropriate location for the deposition or testimony.

(g) If a party called to testify at a civil hearing refuses to answer on the ground that the testimony may be self-incriminating, the trier of fact may draw an adverse inference from the refusal.

(h) A privilege against disclosure of communications between spouses does not apply in a proceeding under this chapter.

(i) The defense of immunity based on the relationship of husband and wife or parent and child does not apply in a proceeding under this chapter.

(j) A voluntary acknowledgment of paternity, certified as a true copy, is admissible to establish parentage of the child.

(Acts 1995, 74th Leg., ch. 20, §1, effective April 20, 1995. Amended by Acts 2003, 78th Leg., ch. 1247, effective September 1, 2003.)

§159.317. Tribunals in different states may communicate with each other

A tribunal of this state may communicate with a tribunal of another state or of a foreign country or political subdivision in a record, by telephone, or by other means, to obtain information concerning the laws, the legal effect of a judgment, decree, or order of that tribunal, and the status of a proceeding in the other state, foreign country or political subdivision. A tribunal of this state may furnish similar information by similar means to a tribunal of another state or of a foreign country or political subdivision.

(Acts 1995, 74th Leg., ch. 20, §1, effective April 20, 1995. Amended by Acts 2003, 78th Leg., ch. 1247, effective September 1, 2003.)

§159.318. Tribunals may assist another state's tribunal with discovery

A tribunal of this state may:

(1) request a tribunal of another state to assist in obtaining discovery; and

(2) on request, compel a person over whom the tribunal has jurisdiction to respond to a discovery order issued by a tribunal of another state.

(Acts 1995, 74th Leg., ch. 20, §1, effective April 20, 1995.)

§159.319. Agency or tribunal shall promptly disburse payments

(a) A support enforcement agency or tribunal of this state shall disburse promptly any amounts received under a support order, as directed by the order. The agency or tribunal shall furnish to a requesting party or tribunal of another state a certified statement by the custodian of the record of the amounts and dates of all payments received.

(b) If the obligor, the obligee who is an individual, and the child do not reside in this state, on request from the support agency of this state or another state, the support enforcement agency of this state or a tribunal of this state shall:

(1) direct that the support payment be made to the support enforcement agency in the state in which the obligee is receiving services; and

(2) issue and send to the obligor's employer a conforming income-withholding order or an administrative notice of change of payee reflecting the redirected payments.

(c) the support enforcement agency of this state on receiving redirected payments from another state under a law similar to Subsection (b) shall provide to a requesting party or tribunal of the other state a certified statement by the custodian of the record of the amount and dates of all payments received.

(Acts 1995, 74th Leg., ch. 20, §1, effective April 20, 1995. Amended by Acts 2003, 78th Leg., ch. 1247, effective September 1, 2003.)

d. Establishment of Support Order

Texas Family Code

§159.401. Conditions for responding tribunal to issue support order

(a) If a support order entitled to recognition under this chapter has not been issued, a responding tribunal of this state may issue a support order if:

(1) the individual seeking the order resides in another state; or

(2) the support enforcement agency seeking the order is located in another state.

(b) The tribunal may issue a temporary child support order if the tribunal determines that the order is appropriate and the individual ordered to pay is:

(1) the presumed father of the child;

(2) a man petitioning to have his paternity adjudicated;

(3) a man identified as the father of the child through genetic testing;

(4) an alleged father who has declined to submit to genetic testing;

(5) a man shown by clear and convincing evidence to be the father of the child;

(6) an acknowledged father as provided by applicable state law;

(7) the mother of the child; or

(8) an individual who has been ordered to pay child support in a previous proceeding and the order has not been reversed or vacated.

(c) On finding, after notice and an opportunity to be heard, that an obligor owes a duty of support, the tribunal shall issue a support order directed to the obligor and may issue other orders under Section 159.305.

(Acts 1995, 74th Leg., ch. 20, §1, effective April 20, 1995. Amended by Acts 2003, 78th Leg., ch. 1247, effective September 1, 2003.)

e. Enforcement of Order of Another State Without Registration

Texas Family Code

§159.501. Income-withholding order from another state may be sent to obligor's employer

An income-withholding order issued in another state may be sent on behalf of the obligee or by the support enforcement agency to the person defined as the obligor's employer under Chapter 158 without first filing a petition or comparable pleading or registering the order with a tribunal of this state.

(Amended by Acts 1997, 75th Leg., ch. 607, §13, effective September 1, 1997; Acts 2003, 78th Leg., ch. 1247, effective September 1, 2003.)

§159.502. Employer must comply with income-withholding order of another state

(a) On receipt of an income-withholding order, the obligor's employer shall immediately provide a copy of the order to the obligor.

(b) The employer shall treat an income-withholding order issued in another state that appears regular on its face as if the order had been issued by a tribunal of this state.

(c) Except as otherwise provided in Subsection (d) and Section 159.503, the employer shall withhold and distribute the funds as directed in the withholding order by complying with terms of the order that specify:

(1) the duration and amount of periodic payments of current child support, stated as a sum certain;

(2) the person or agency designated to receive payments and the address to which the payments are to be forwarded;

(3) medical support, whether in the form of periodic cash payments, stated as a sum certain, or ordering the obligor to provide health insurance coverage for the child under a policy available through the obligor's employment;

(4) the amount of periodic payments of fees and costs for a support enforcement agency, the issuing tribunal, and the obligee's attorney, stated as sums certain; and

(5) the amount of periodic payments of arrearages and interest on arrearages, stated as sums certain.

(d) An employer shall comply with the law of the state of the obligor's principal place of employment for withholding from income with respect to:

(1) the employer's fee for processing an income-withholding order;

(2) the maximum amount permitted to be withheld from the obligor's income; and

(3) the times within which the employer must implement the withholding order and forward the child support payment.

(Amended by Acts 1997, 75th Leg., ch. 607, §13, effective September 1, 1997; Acts 2003, 78th Leg., ch. 1247, effective September 1, 2003.)

§159.503. Employer's compliance with multiple income-withholding orders

If an obligor's employer receives two or more income-withholding orders with respect to the earnings of the same obligor, the employer satisfies the terms of the orders if the employer complies with the law of the state of the obligor's principal place of employment to establish the priorities for withholding and allocating income withheld for two or more child support obligees.

(Acts 1997, 75th Leg., ch. 607, §13, effective September 1, 1997. Amended by Acts 2003, 78th Leg., ch. 1247, effective September 1, 2003.)

§159.504. Employer has immunity from civil liability

An employer who complies with an income-withholding order issued in another state in accordance with this subchapter is not subject to civil liability to an individual or agency with regard to the employer's withholding of child support from the obligor's income.

(Acts 1997, 75th Leg., ch. 607, §13, effective September 1, 1997.)

§159.505. Penalties for employer's noncompliance

An employer who willfully fails to comply with an income-withholding order issued by another state and received for enforcement is subject to the same penalties that may be imposed for noncompliance with an order issued by a tribunal of this state.

(Acts 1997, 75th Leg., ch. 607, §13, effective September 1, 1997.)

§159.506. Obligor may contest validity of income-withholding order from another state

(a) An obligor may contest the validity or enforcement of an income-withholding order issued in another state and received directly by an employer in this state by registering the order in a tribunal of this state and:

(1) filing a contest to that order under Subchapter G; or

(2) contesting the order in the same manner as if the order had been issued by a tribunal of this state.

(b) The obligor shall give notice of the contest to:

(1) a support enforcement agency providing services to the obligee;

(2) each employer that has directly received an income-withholding order; and

(3) the person or agency designated to receive payments in the income-withholding order or to the obligee, if no person or agency is designated.

(Acts 1997, 75th Leg., ch. 607, §13, effective September 1, 1997. Amended by Acts 2003, 78th Leg., ch. 1247, effective September 1, 2003.)

§159.507. Enforcement of orders by agency of this state

(a) A party seeking to enforce a support order or an income-withholding order, or both, issued by a tribunal of another state may send the documents required for registering the order to a support enforcement agency of this state.

(b) On receipt of the documents, the support enforcement agency, without initially seeking to register the order, shall consider and, if appropriate, use any administrative procedure authorized by the law of this state to enforce a support order or an income-withholding order, or both. If the obligor does not contest administrative enforcement, the order need not be registered. If the obligor contests the validity or administrative enforcement of the order, the support enforcement agency shall register the order under this chapter.
(Acts 1997, 75th Leg., ch. 607, §13, effective September 1, 1997. Amended by Acts 2003, 78th Leg., ch. 1247, effective September 1, 2003.)

f. Enforcement and Modification of Support Order After Registration

Texas Family Code

§159.601. Income-withholding order issued by another state may be registered in this state for enforcement

A support order or income-withholding order issued by a tribunal of another state may be registered in this state for enforcement.
(Acts 1995, 74th Leg., ch. 20, §1, effective April 20, 1995.)

§159.602. Procedure to register support order or income-withholding order for enforcement

(a) A support order or income-withholding order of another state may be registered in this state by sending to the appropriate tribunal in this state:

(1) a letter of transmittal to the tribunal requesting registration and enforcement;

(2) two copies, including one certified copy, of all orders to be registered, including any modification of an order;

(3) a sworn statement by the party seeking registration or a certified statement by the custodian of the records showing the amount of any arrearage;

(4) the name of the obligor and, if known:

(A) the obligor's social security number;

(B) the name and address of the obligor's employer and any other source of income of the obligor; and

(C) a description of and the location of property of the obligor in this state not exempt from execution; and

(5) the name of the obligee and, if applicable, the agency or person to whom support payments are to be remitted.

(b) On receipt of a request for registration, the registering tribunal shall cause the order to be filed as a foreign judgment, together with one copy of the documents and information, regardless of their form.

(c) A petition or comparable pleading seeking a remedy that must be affirmatively sought under other law of this state may be filed at the same time as the request for registration or later. The pleading must specify the grounds for the remedy sought.

(d) If two or more orders are in effect, the person requesting registration shall:

(1) provide to the tribunal a copy of each support order and the documents specified in this section;

(2) identify the order alleged to be the controlling order, if any; and

(3) state the amount of consolidated arrearages, if any.

(e) A request for a determination of which order is the controlling order may be filed separately from or with a request for registration and enforcement or for registration and modification. The person requesting registration shall give notice of the request to each party whose rights may be affected by the determination.
(Acts 1995, 74th Leg., ch. 20, §1, effective April 20, 1995. Amended by Acts 2001, 77th Leg., ch. 296, §3, effective September 1, 2001; Acts 2003, 78th Leg., ch. 1247, effective September 1, 2003.)

§159.603. Effect of registration for enforcement or support order or income-withholding order issued in another state

(a) A support order or income-withholding order issued in another state is registered when the order is filed in the registering tribunal of this state.

(b) A registered order issued in another state is enforceable in the same manner and is subject to the same procedures as an order issued by a tribunal of this state.

(c) Except as otherwise provided in this subchapter, a tribunal of this state shall recognize and enforce, but may not modify, a registered order if the issuing tribunal had jurisdiction.
(Acts 1995, 74th Leg., ch. 20, §1, effective April 20, 1995.)

§159.606. Procedure to contest validity or enforcement of registered order

(a) A nonregistering party seeking to contest the validity or enforcement of a registered order in this state shall request a hearing within 20 days after notice of the registration. The nonregistering party may seek under Section 159.607 to:

(1) vacate the registration;

(2) assert any defense to an allegation of noncompliance with the registered order; or

(3) contest the remedies being sought or the amount of any alleged arrearages.

(b) If the nonregistering party fails to contest the validity or enforcement of the registered order in a timely manner, the order is confirmed by operation of law.

(c) If a nonregistering party requests a hearing to contest the validity or enforcement of the registered order, the registering tribunal shall schedule the matter for hearing and give notice to the parties of the date, time, and place of the hearing.

(Acts 1995, 74th Leg., ch. 20, §1, effective April 20, 1995. Amended by Acts 1997, 75th Leg., ch. 607, §16, effective September 1, 1997.)

§159.607. Party contesting registration or enforcement has burden of proof regarding designated defenses

(a) A party contesting the validity or enforcement of a registered order or seeking to vacate the registration has the burden of proving one or more of the following defenses:

(1) the issuing tribunal lacked personal jurisdiction over the contesting party;

(2) the order was obtained by fraud;

(3) the order has been vacated, suspended, or modified by a later order;

(4) the issuing tribunal has stayed the order pending appeal;

(5) there is a defense under the law of this state to the remedy sought;

(6) full or partial payment has been made;

(7) the statute of limitation under Section 159.604 precludes enforcement of some or all of the arrearages; or

(8) the alleged controlling order is not the controlling order.

(b) If a party presents evidence establishing a full or partial defense under Subsection (a), a tribunal may stay enforcement of the registered order, continue the proceeding to permit production of additional relevant evidence, and issue other appropriate orders. An uncontested portion of the registered order may be enforced by all remedies available under the law of this state.

(c) If the contesting party does not establish a defense under Subsection (a) to the validity or enforcement of the order, the registering tribunal shall issue an order confirming the order.

(Acts 1995, 74th Leg., ch. 20, §1, effective April 20, 1995. Amended by Acts 2003, 78th Leg., ch. 1247, effective September 1, 2003.)

§159.608. Effect of confirmation of registered order

Confirmation of a registered order, whether by operation of law or after notice and hearing, precludes further contest of the order with respect to any matter that could have been asserted at the time of registration.

(Acts 1995, 74th Leg., ch. 20, §1, effective April 20, 1995.)

§159.609. Party seeking to modify or enforce child support order of another state must register that order

A party or support enforcement agency seeking to modify or to modify and enforce a child support order issued in another state shall register that order in this state in the same manner provided in Sections 159.601 and 159.604 if the order has not been registered. A petition for modification may be filed at the same time as a request for registration or later. The pleading must specify the grounds for modification.

(Acts 1995, 74th Leg., ch. 20, §1, effective April 20, 1995.)

§159.611. Conditions for modification of child support order rendered by another state

(a) After a child support order issued in another state has been registered in this state, the responding tribunal of this state may modify the order only if Section 159.613 does not apply and after notice and hearing the tribunal finds that:

(1) the following requirements are met:

(A) the child, the individual obligee, and the obligor do not reside in the issuing state;

(B) a petitioner who is a nonresident of this state seeks modification; and

(C) the respondent is subject to the personal jurisdiction of the tribunal of this state; or

(2) the child, or a party who is an individual, is subject to the personal jurisdiction of the tribunal of this state and all of the parties who are individuals have filed in the issuing tribunal written consents for a tribunal of this state to modify the support order and assume continuing, exclusive jurisdiction over the order; however, for the purposes of this subdivision, if the issuing state is a foreign jurisdiction that has not enacted a law or established procedures substantially similar to the procedures under this chapter, the consent otherwise required of an individual residing in this state is not required for the tribunal to assume jurisdiction to modify the child support order.

(b) Modification of a registered child support order is subject to the same requirements, procedures, and defenses that apply to the modification of an order issued by a tribunal of this state, and the order may be enforced and satisfied in the same manner.

(c) A tribunal of this state may not modify any aspect of a child support order that may not be modified under the law of the issuing state. If two or more tribunals have issued child support orders for the same obligor and child, the order that controls and must be so recognized under Section 159.207 establishes the aspects of the support order that are nonmodifiable.

(d) On issuance of an order modifying a child support order issued in another state, a tribunal of this state becomes the tribunal of continuing, exclusive jurisdiction.

[(e) Repealed by Acts 2001, 77th Leg., ch. 1420, §5.0026, effective September 1, 2001.]

(Acts 1995, 74th Leg., ch. 20, §1, effective April 20, 1995. Amended by Acts 1997, 75th Leg., ch. 607, §17, effective September 1, 1997; Acts 2001, 77th Leg., ch. 1420, §5.0026, effective September 1, 2001; Acts 2003, 78th Leg., ch. 1247, effective September 1, 2003.)

§159.612. Recognition of child support order modified in another state

A tribunal of this state shall recognize a modification of its earlier child support order by a tribunal of another state that assumed jurisdiction under the Uniform Interstate Family Support Act, a tribunal of this state:

(1) may enforce the order that was modified only as to amounts accruing before the modification;

(2) may provide appropriate relief only for violations of the order that occurred before the effective date of the modification; and

(3) recognize the modifying order of the other state, on registration, for the purpose of enforcement.

(Acts 1995, 74th Leg., ch. 20, §1, effective April 20, 1995. Amended by Acts 2003, 78th Leg., ch. 1247, effective September 1, 2003.)

§159.613. Jurisdiction to modify child support order of another state when parties reside here

(a) If all of the parties who are individuals reside in this state and the child does not reside in the issuing state, a tribunal of this state has jurisdiction to enforce and to modify the issuing state's child support order in a proceeding to register that order.

(b) A tribunal of this state exercising jurisdiction under this section shall apply the provisions of Sections 159.101 through 159.209 and 159.601 through 159.614 and the procedural and substantive law of this state to the proceeding for enforcement or modification. Sections 159.301 through 159.507 and 159.701 through 159.802 do not apply.

(Acts 1997, 75th Leg., ch. 607, §18, effective September 1, 1997.)

§159.614. Party obtaining modification shall file certified copy of order with issuing tribunal

Within 30 days after issuance of a modified child support order, the party obtaining the modification shall file a certified copy of the order with the issuing tribunal that had continuing, exclusive jurisdiction over the earlier order and in each tribunal in which the party knows the earlier order has been registered. A party who obtains the order and fails to file a certified copy is subject to appropriate sanctions by a tribunal in which the issue of failure to file arises. The failure to file does not affect the validity or enforceability of the modified order of the new tribunal having continuing, exclusive jurisdiction.

(Acts 1997, 75th Leg., ch. 607, §18, effective September 1, 1997.)

g. Determination of Parentage

Texas Family Code

§159.701. Proceeding to determine parentage

(a) A court of this state may serve as an initiating or responding tribunal in a proceeding to determine parentage brought under this chapter or a law substantially similar to this chapter..

(Acts 1995, 74th Leg., ch. 20, §1, effective April 20, 1995. Amended by Acts 2003, 78th Leg., ch. 1247, effective September 1, 2003.)

h. Interstate Rendition

Texas Family Code

§159.801. Grounds for interstate rendition

(a) In this subchapter, "governor" includes an individual performing the functions of governor or the executive authority of a state covered by this chapter.

(b) The governor of this state may:

(1) demand that the governor of another state surrender an individual found in the other state who is charged criminally in this state with having failed to provide for the support of an obligee; or

(2) on the demand by the governor of another state, surrender an individual found in this state who is charged criminally in the other state with having failed to provide for the support of an obligee.

(c) A provision for extradition of individuals not inconsistent with this chapter applies to the demand even if the individual whose surrender is demanded was not in the demanding state when the crime was allegedly committed and has not fled from that state.

(Acts 1995, 74th Leg., ch. 20, §1, effective April 20, 1995.)

§159.802. Conditions of interstate rendition

(a) In this subchapter, "governor" includes an individual performing the functions or governor of the executive authority of a state covered by this chapter.

(b) The governor of this state may:

(1) demand that the governor of another state surrender an individual charged criminally in this state with having failed to provide for the support of an obligee; or

(2) on the demand of the governor of another state, surrender an individual found in this state who is charged criminally in the other state with having failed to provide for the support of an obligee.

(c) A provision for extradition of individuals not inconsistent with this chapter applies to the demand even if the individual whose surrender is demanded was not in the demanding state when the crime was allegedly committed and has not fled from that state.

(Acts 1995, 74th Leg., ch. 20, §1, effective April 20, 1995. Amended by Acts 2003, 78th Leg., ch. 1247, effective September 1, 2003.)

5. Withholding Earnings to Enforce Support

The Family Support Act of 1988 required states to provide procedures for immediate income withholding for all child support orders issued on or after January 1, 1994, whether or not the child support obligor had fallen in arrears, unless one party shows good cause or the parties have a written agreement providing an alternative. 42 U.S.C. §666(b). The employer becomes liable to the obligee for noncompliance and is subject to penalty for discriminatory hiring or discharge based on such an order. For this reason, parents of supported children are required to provide notice of their current employer.

Child support orders in Texas must include an income withholding order (Tex. Fam. Code §§158.001 et seq.), requiring the employer to divert the obligor's earnings immediately to pay court-ordered support (Tex. Fam. Code §158.001). The court (or the Title IV-D agency) must order wage withholding in proceedings involving initial determinations of child support, modification or enforcement (*id.*). The court may delay issuance or delivery of the wage withholding order to an employer (except in a Title IV-D case), until the obligor has been in arrears more than 30 days, the arrearages amount is equal to or greater than the amount due for a one-month period, or any other violation of the child support order has occurred (Tex. Fam. Code §158.002). The court (or Title IV-D agency) may order wage withholding to cover arrearages, even if the obligor does not owe current child support (Tex. Fam. Code §158.004). The employer is permitted to withhold no more than 50 percent of the obligor's disposable earnings (Tex. Fam. Code §158.009). The obligor may voluntarily request a wage withholding order (Tex. Fam. Code §158.011(a)).

Welfare reform legislation in 1996, the Personal Responsibility and Work Opportunity Reconciliation Act of 1996, strengthens the use of income withholding by establishing a national system to track the employment of delinquent obligors. 42 U.S.C. §653a; 42 U.S.C. §666(b). All employers must report new hires to a designated state agency, which then forwards this information to a national directory for matching with the Federal Case Registry of Child Support Orders.

Texas Family Code

§154.007. Order to withhold child support payments from obligor's income

(a) In a proceeding in which periodic payments of child support are ordered, modified, or enforced, the court or Title IV-D agency shall order that income be withheld from the disposable earnings of the obligor as provided by Chapter 158.

(b) If the court does not order income withholding, an order for support must contain a provision for income withholding to ensure that withholding may be effected if a delinquency occurs.

(c) A child support order must be construed to contain a withholding provision even if the provision has been omitted from the written order.

(d) If the order was rendered or last modified before January 1, 1987, the order is presumed to contain a provision for income withholding procedures to take effect in the event a delinquency occurs without further amendment to the order or future action by the court.

(Acts 1995, 74th Leg., ch. 20, §1, effective April 20, 1995. Amended by Acts 1997, 75th Leg., ch. 911, §10, effective September 1, 1997.)

§158.001. Income withholding generally

In a proceeding in which periodic payments of child support are ordered, modified, or enforced, the court or the Title IV-D agency shall order that income be withheld from the disposable earnings of the obligor as provided by this chapter.

(Acts 1995, 74th Leg., ch. 20, §1, effective April 20, 1995. Amended by Acts 1997, 75th Leg., ch. 911, §34, effective September 1, 1997.)

§158.002. Court may suspend order for income withholding

Except in a Title IV-D case, the court may provide, for good cause shown or on agreement of the parties, that the order withholding income need not be issued or delivered to an employer until:

(1) the obligor has been in arrears for an amount due for more than 30 days;

(2) the amount of the arrearages is an amount equal to or greater than the amount due for a one-month period; or

(3) any other violation of the child support order has occurred.

(Acts 1995, 74th Leg., ch. 20, §1, effective April 20, 1995. Amended by Acts 1997, 75th Leg., ch. 911, §35, effective September 1, 1997.)

§158.003. Income shall be withheld for arrearages as well as current support

(a) In addition to income withheld for the current support of a child, income shall be withheld from the disposable earnings of the obligor to be applied toward the liquidation of any child support arrearages, including accrued interest as provided in Chapter 157.

(b) The additional amount to be withheld for arrearages shall be an amount sufficient to discharge those arrearages in not more than two years or an additional 20 percent added to the amount of the current monthly support order, whichever amount will result in the arrearages being discharged in the least amount of time.

(Acts 1995, 74th Leg., ch. 20, §1, effective April 20, 1995. Amended by Acts 1999, 76th Leg., ch. 556, §21, effective September 1, 1999.)

§158.004. Court or agency shall order withholding for arrearages even if no current support is due

If current support is no longer owed, the court or the Title IV-D agency shall order that income be withheld for arrearages, including accrued interest as provided in Chapter 157, in an amount sufficient to discharge those arrearages in not more than two years.

(Acts 1995, 74th Leg., ch. 20, §1, effective April 20, 1995. Amended by Acts 1999, 76th Leg., ch. 556, §22, effective September 1, 1999.)

§158.005. Court shall order reasonable amount of income be withheld to satisfy judgment for arrearages

In rendering a cumulative judgment for arrearages, the court shall order that a reasonable amount of income be withheld from the disposable earnings of the obligor to be applied toward the satisfaction of the judgment.

(Acts 1995, 74th Leg., ch. 20, §1, effective April 20, 1995.)

§158.0051. Court may order withholding to cover costs and fees

(a) In addition to an order for income to be withheld for child support, including child support and child support arrearages, the court may render an order that income be withheld from the disposable earnings of the obligor to be applied towards the satisfaction of any ordered attorney's fees and costs resulting from an action to enforce child support under this title.

(b) An order rendered under this section is subordinate to an order or writ of withholding for child support under this chapter and is subject to the maximum amount allowed to be withheld under Section 158.009.

(c) The court shall order that amounts withheld for fees and costs under this section be remitted directly to the person entitled to the ordered attorney's fees or costs or be paid through a local registry for disbursement to that person.

(Acts 2001, 77th Leg., ch. 1023, §35, effective September 1, 2001.)

§158.006. Income withholding in Title IV-D cases

In a Title IV-D case, the court or the Title IV-D agency shall order that income be withheld from the disposable earnings of the obligor and may not suspend, stay, or delay issuance of the order or of a judicial or administrative writ of withholding.

(Acts 1995, 74th Leg., ch. 20, §1, effective April 20, 1995. Amended by Acts 1997, 75th Leg., ch. 911, §36, effective September 1, 1997.)

§158.007. Court or agency may extend repayment schedule in case of unreasonable hardship

If the court or the Title IV-D agency finds that the schedule for discharging arrearages would cause the obligor, the obligor's family, or children for whom support is due from the obligor to suffer unreasonable hardship, the court or agency may extend the payment period for a reasonable length of time.

(Acts 1995, 74th Leg., ch. 20, §1, effective April 20, 1995. Amended by Acts 1999, 76th Leg., ch. 556, §22, effective September 1, 1999.)

§158.008. Orders of withholding have priority over other orders affecting earnings

An order or writ of withholding has priority over any garnishment, attachment, execution, or other assignment or order affecting disposable earnings.

(Acts 1995, 74th Leg., ch. 20, §1, effective April 20, 1995.)

§158.009. Order shall specify maximum amount to be withheld from earnings

An order or writ of withholding shall direct that any employer of the obligor withhold from the obligor's disposable earnings the amount specified up to a maximum amount of 50 percent of the obligor's disposable earnings.

(Acts 1995, 74th Leg., ch. 20, §1, effective April 20, 1995. Amended by Acts 1997, 75th Leg., ch. 911, §37, effective September 1, 1997.)

§158.010. Order binding on employer doing business in state

An order or writ of withholding issued under this chapter and delivered to an employer doing business in this state is binding on the employer without regard to whether the obligor resides or works outside this state.

(Acts 1995, 74th Leg., ch. 20, §1, effective April 20, 1995. Amended by Acts 1997, 75th Leg., ch. 911, §38, effective September 1, 1997.)

§158.011. Obligor may file mutual request for voluntary withholding

(a) An obligor may file with the clerk of the court a notarized or acknowledged request signed by the obligor and the obligee for the issuance and delivery to the obligor's employer of a writ of withholding. A notarized or acknowledged request may be filed under this section regardless of whether a writ or order has been served on any party or of the existence or amount of an arrearage.

(b) On receipt of a request under this section, the clerk shall issue and deliver a writ of withholding in the manner provided by this chapter.

(c) An employer that receives a writ of withholding issued under this section may request a hearing in the same manner and according to the same terms provided by Section 158.205.

(d) An obligor whose employer receives a writ of withholding issued under this section may request a hearing in the manner provided by Section 158.309.

(e) An obligee may contest a writ of withholding issued under this section by requesting, not later than the 180th day after the date on which the obligee discovers that the writ has been issued, a hearing in the manner provided by Section 158.309.

(f) A writ of withholding under this section may not reduce the total amount of child support, including arrearages, owed by the obligor.

(Acts 1995, 74th Leg., ch. 751, §55, effective September 1, 1995. Amended by Acts 1997, 75th Leg., ch. 911, §39, effective September 1, 1997.)

§158.101. General procedure for enforcement applies to action for income withholding

Except as otherwise provided in this chapter, the procedure for a motion for enforcement of child support as provided in Chapter 157 applies to an action for income withholding.

(Acts 1995, 74th Leg., ch. 20, §1, effective April 20, 1995.)

§158.102. Order for withholding may be issued until all support, interest and fees paid in full

An order or writ for income withholding under this chapter may be issued until all current support and child support arrearages, interest, and any applicable fees and costs, including ordered attorney's fees and court costs, have been paid.

(Acts 1995, 74th Leg., ch. 20, §1, effective April 20, 1995. Amended by Acts 1997, 75th Leg., ch. 911, §40, effective September 1, 1997; Acts 1999, 76th Leg., ch. 556, §23, effective September 1, 1999.)

§158.103. Order or writ of withholding must contain certain information

An order of withholding or writ of withholding issued under this chapter must contain the information required by the forms prescribed by the Title IV-D agency under Section 158.106.

(Acts 1995, 74th Leg., ch. 20, §1, effective April 20, 1995. Amended by Acts 1997, 75th Leg., ch. 911, §41, effective September 1, 1997; Acts 1999, 76th Leg., ch. 556, §23, effective September 1, 1999; Acts 2001, 77th Leg., ch. 1023, §36, effective September 1, 2001.)

§158.104. Persons or agencies who may request issuance of order or writ of withholding

A request for issuance of an order or judicial writ of withholding may be filed with the clerk of the court by the prosecuting attorney, the Title IV-D agency, the friend of the court, a domestic relations office, the obligor, the obligee, or an attorney representing the obligee or obligor.

(Acts 1995, 74th Leg., ch. 20, §1, effective April 20, 1995. Amended by Acts 1997, 75th Leg., ch. 702, §6, effective September 1, 1997; Acts 1999, 76th Leg., ch. 556, §23, effective September 1, 1999.)

§158.105. Clerk shall cause copy of order or writ to be delivered to obligor's employer

(a) On filing a request for issuance of an order or judicial writ of withholding, the clerk of the court shall cause a certified copy of the order or writ to be delivered to the obligor's current employer or to any subsequent employer of the obligor.

(b) The clerk shall issue and mail the certified copy of the order or judicial writ not later than the fourth working day after the date the order is signed or the request is filed, whichever is later.

(c) An order or judicial writ of withholding shall be delivered to the employer by first class mail or, if requested, by certified or registered mail, return receipt requested, electronic transmission, or by service of citation to:

(1) the person authorized to receive service of process for the employer in civil cases generally; or

(2) a person designated by the employer, by written notice to the clerk, to receive orders or writs of withholding.

(d) The clerk may deliver an order or judicial writ of withholding under Subsection (c) by electronic mail if the employer has an electronic mail address or by facsimile transmission if the employer is capable of receiving documents transmitted in that manner. If delivery is accomplished by electronic mail, the clerk must request acknowledgment of receipt from the employer or use an electronic mail system with a read receipt capability. If delivery is accomplished by facsimile transmission, the clerk's facsimile machine must create a delivery confirmation report.

(Acts 1995, 74th Leg., ch. 20, §1, effective April 20, 1995. Amended by Acts 1997, 75th Leg., ch. 702, §7, effective September 1, 1997; Acts 1999, 76th Leg., ch. 556, §24, effective September 1, 1999; Acts 2001, 77th Leg., ch. 1023, §37, effective September 1, 2001; Acts 2005, 79th Leg., ch. 1113, §37, effective September 1, 2005.)

§158.106. Prescribed forms for income withholding

(a) The Title IV-D agency shall prescribe forms as required by federal law in a standard format entitled order or notice to withhold income for child support.

(b) The Title IV-D agency shall make the appropriate forms available to obligors, obligees, domestic relations offices, friends of the court, and private attorneys.

(c) The Title IV-D agency may prescribe additional forms for the efficient collection of child support and to promote the administration of justice for all parties.

(d) The forms prescribed by the Title IV-D agency under this section may be used to request voluntary withholding under Section 158.011.

(Acts 1995, 74th Leg., ch. 20, §1, effective April 20, 1995. Amended by Acts 1997, 75th Leg., ch. 911, §42, effective September 1, 1997; Acts 1999, 76th Leg., ch. 556, §25, effective September 1, 1999; Acts 2001, 77th Leg., ch. 1023, §38, effective September 1, 2001.)

6. Employers' Liability Regarding Withholding for Child Support

§158.201. Employer not entitled to notice before issuance of writ of withholding

(a) An employer required to withhold income from earnings is not entitled to notice of the proceedings before the order is rendered or writ of withholding is issued.

(b) An order or writ of withholding is binding on an employer regardless of whether the employer is specifically named in the order or writ.

(Acts 1995, 74th Leg., ch. 20, §1, effective April 20, 1995. Amended by Acts 1997, 75th Leg., ch. 911, §43, effective September 1, 1997.)

§158.202. Employer shall withhold income immediately

An employer shall begin to withhold income in accordance with an order or writ of withholding not later than the first pay period following the date on which the order or writ was delivered to the employer and shall continue to withhold income as required by the order or writ as long as the obligor is employed by the employer.

(Acts 1995, 74th Leg., ch. 20, §1, effective April 20, 1995. Amended by Acts 1997, 75th Leg., ch. 911, §44, effective September 1, 1997.)

§158.203. Employer shall remit withheld payments

(a) The employer shall remit the amount to be withheld to the person or office named in the order or writ on each pay date. The payment must include the date on which the withholding occurred.

(b) For payments made by electronic funds transfer or electronic data interchange, the employer shall transmit the amount withheld not later than the second business day after the pay date.

(c) The employer shall include with each payment transmitted:

(1) the number assigned by the Title IV-D agency, if available, and the county identification number, if available;

(2) the name of the county or the county's federal information processing standard code;

(3) the cause number of the suit under which withholding is required;

(4) the payor's name and social security number; and

(5) the payee's name and, if available, social security number, unless the payment is transmitted by electronic funds transfer.

(d) In a case in which an obligor's income is subject to withholding, the employer shall remit the payment of child support directly to a local registry, the Title IV-D agency, or to the state disbursement unit.

(Acts 1995, 74th Leg., ch. 20, §1, effective April 20, 1995. Amended by Acts 1997, 75th Leg., ch. 702, §8, effective Jan. 1, 1998; Acts 1999, 76th Leg., ch. 556, §26, effective September 1, 1999.)

§158.204. Employer may deduct administrative fee from earnings

An employer may deduct an administrative fee of not more than $10 each month from the obligor's disposable earnings in addition to the amount to be withheld as child support.

(Acts 1995, 74th Leg., ch. 20, §1, effective April 20, 1995. Amended by Acts 1999, 76th Leg., ch. 859, §1, effective September 1, 1999.)

§158.205. Employer may request hearing on applicability of order or writ to employer

(a) Not later than the 20th day after the date an order or writ of withholding is delivered, the employer may, as appropriate, file a motion with the court or file a request with the Title IV-D agency for a hearing on the applicability of the order or writ to the employer. The Title IV-D agency by rule shall establish procedures for an agency hearing under this section.

(b) The hearing under this section shall be held not later than the 15th day after the date the motion or request was made.

(c) An order or writ of withholding remains binding and payments shall continue to be made pending further order of the court or, in the case of an administrative writ, action of the Title IV-D agency.

(Acts 1995, 74th Leg., ch. 20, §1, effective April 20, 1995. Amended by Acts 1997, 75th Leg., ch. 911, §45, effective September 1, 1997.)

§158.206. Liability of employer for compliance with order or writ and for noncompliance

(a) An employer receiving an order or a writ of withholding under this chapter, including an order or writ directing that health insurance be provided to a child, who complies with the order or writ is not liable to the obligor for the amount of income withheld and paid as required by the order or writ.

(b) An employer receiving an order or writ of withholding who does not comply with the order or writ is liable:

(1) to the obligee for the amount not paid in compliance with the order or writ, including the amount the obligor is required to pay for health insurance under Chapter 154;

(2) to the obligor for:

(A) the amount withheld and not paid as required by the order or writ; and

(B) an amount equal to the interest that accrues under Section 157.265 on the amount withheld and not paid; and

(3) for reasonable attorney's fees and court costs.

(c) If an obligor has filed a claim for workers' compensation, the obligor's employer shall send a copy of the income withholding order or writ to the insurance carrier with whom the claim has been filed in order to continue the ordered withholding of income.

(Acts 1995, 74th Leg., ch. 20, §1, effective April 20, 1995. Amended by Acts 1995, 74th Leg., ch. 341, §4.07, effective September 1, 1995; by Acts 1997, 75th Leg., ch. 911, §46, effective September 1, 1997; Acts 1999, 76th Leg., ch. 859, §2, effective September 1, 1999; Acts 1999, 76th Leg., ch. 1580, §1, effective September 1, 1999; Acts 2001, 77th Leg., ch. 1023, §39, effective September 1, 2001.)

§158.207. Duty of employer who receives multiple orders or writs

(a) An employer receiving two or more orders or writs for one obligor shall comply with each order or writ to the extent possible.

(b) If the total amount due under the orders or writs exceeds the maximum amount allowed to be withheld under Section 158.009, the employer shall pay an equal amount towards the current support in each order or writ until the employer has complied fully with each current support obligation and, thereafter, equal amounts on the arrearages until the employer has complied with each order or writ, or until the maximum total amount of allowed withholding is reached, whichever occurs first.

(c) An employer who receives more than one order or writ of withholding that combines withholding for child support and spousal maintenance as provided by Section 8.101 shall withhold income and pay the amount withheld in accordance with Section 8.207.

(Acts 1995, 74th Leg., ch. 20, §1, effective April 20, 1995. Amended by Acts 1997, 75th Leg., ch. 911, §47, effective September 1, 1997; Acts 2001, 77th Leg., ch. 807, §2, effective September 1, 2001.)

§158.208. Employer may make single payment to each agency

An employer required to withhold from more than one obligor may combine the amounts withheld and make a single payment to each agency designated if the employer separately identifies the amount of the payment that is attributable to each obligor.

(Acts 1995, 74th Leg., ch. 20, §1, effective April 20, 1995.)

§158.209. Employer may not use employee's delinquency as grounds for discriminatory hiring or discharge

(a) An employer may not use an order or writ of withholding as grounds in whole or part for the termination of employment or for any other disciplinary action against an employee.

(b) An employer may not refuse to hire an employee because of an order or writ of withholding.

(c) If an employer intentionally discharges an employee in violation of this section, the employer continues to be liable to the employee for current wages and other benefits and for reasonable attorney's fees and court costs incurred in enforcing the employee's rights as provided in this section.

(d) An action under this section may be brought by the employee, a friend of the court, the domestic relations office, or the Title IV-D agency.

(Acts 1995, 74th Leg., ch. 20, §1, effective April 20, 1995. Amended by Acts 1997, 75th Leg., ch. 911, §48, effective September 1, 1997.)

§158.210. Employer liable for fines for noncompliance

(a) In addition to the civil remedies provided by this subchapter or any other remedy provided by law, an employer who knowingly violates the provisions of this chapter may be subject to a fine not to exceed $200 for each occurrence in which the employer fails to:

(1) withhold income for child support as instructed in an order or writ issued under this chapter; or

(2) remit withheld income within the time required by Section 158.203 to the payee identified in the order or writ or to the state disbursement unit.

(b) A fine recovered under this section shall be paid to the county in which the obligee resides and shall be used by the county to improve child support services.

(Acts 1995, 74th Leg., ch. 20, §1, effective April 20, 1995. Amended by Acts 1997, 75th Leg., ch. 420, §15, effective September 1, 1997; Acts 1999, 76th Leg., ch. 556, §27, effective September 1, 1999.)

§158.211. Obligor and employer shall provide notice of termination of employment and of new employment

(a) If an obligor terminates employment with an employer who has been withholding income, both the obligor and the employer shall notify the court or the Title IV-D agency and the obligee of that fact not later than the seventh day after the date employment terminated and shall provide the obligor's last known address and the name and address of the obligor's new employer, if known.

(b) The obligor has a continuing duty to inform any subsequent employer of the order or writ of withholding after obtaining employment.

(Acts 1995, 74th Leg., ch. 20, §1, effective April 20, 1995. Amended by Acts 1999, 76th Leg., ch. 556, §28, effective September 1, 1999.)

§158.212. Employer shall remedy improper payment

An employer who remits a payment to an incorrect office or person shall remit the payment to the agency or person identified in the order of withholding not later than the second business day after the date the employer receives the returned payment.

(Acts 1999, 76th Leg., ch. 556, §29, effective September 1, 1999.)

§158.301. Requirements for filing notice of application for writ of withholding

(a) A notice of application for judicial writ of withholding may be filed if:

(1) a delinquency occurs in child support payments in an amount equal to or greater than the total support due for one month; or

(2) income withholding was not ordered at the time child support was ordered.

(b) The notice of application for judicial writ of withholding may be filed in the court of continuing jurisdiction by:

(1) the Title IV-D agency;

(2) the attorney representing the local domestic relations office;

(3) the attorney appointed a friend of the court as provided in Chapter 202;

(4) the obligor or obligee; or

(5) a private attorney representing the obligor or obligee.

(c) The Title IV-D agency may in a Title IV-D case file a notice of application for judicial writ of withholding on request of the obligor or obligee.

(Acts 1995, 74th Leg., ch. 20, §1, effective April 20, 1995. Amended by Acts 1995, 74th Leg., ch. 751, §57, effective September 1, 1995; by Acts 1997, 75th Leg., ch. 911, §50, effective September 1, 1997.)

§158.302. Notice of application for writ of withholding shall contain certain information

The notice of application for judicial writ of withholding shall be verified and:

(1) state the amount of monthly support due, including medical support, the amount of arrearages or anticipated arrearages, including accrued interest, and the amount of wages that will be withheld in accordance with a judicial writ of withholding;

(2) state that the withholding applies to each current or subsequent employer or period of employment;

(3) state that if the obligor does not contest the withholding within 10 days after the date of receipt of the notice, the obligor's employer will be notified to begin the withholding;

(4) describe the procedures for contesting the issuance and delivery of a writ of withholding;

(5) state that if the obligor contests the withholding, the obligor will be afforded an opportunity for a hearing by the court not later than the 30th day after the date of receipt of the notice of contest;

(6) state that the sole ground for successfully contesting the issuance of a writ of withholding is a dispute concerning the identity of the obligor or the existence or amount of the arrearages, including accrued interest;

(7) describe the actions that may be taken if the obligor contests the notice of application for judicial writ of withholding, including the procedures for suspending issuance of a writ of withholding; and

(8) include with the notice a suggested form for the motion to stay issuance and delivery of the judicial writ of withholding that the obligor may file with the clerk of the appropriate court.

(Acts 1995, 74th Leg., ch. 20, §1, effective April 20, 1995. Amended by Acts 1997, 75th Leg., ch. 911, §51, effective September 1, 1997.)

§158.303. Registration of interstate order is sufficient request for income withholding

(a) The registration of a foreign support order as provided in Chapter 159 is sufficient for the filing of a notice of application for judicial writ of withholding.

(b) The notice shall be filed with the clerk of the court having venue as provided in Chapter 159.

(c) Notice of application for judicial writ of withholding may be delivered to the obligor at the same time that an order is filed for registration under Chapter 159.

(Acts 1995, 74th Leg., ch. 20, §1, effective April 20, 1995. Amended by Acts 1995, 74th Leg., ch. 751, §58, effective September 1, 1995; by Acts 1997, 75th Leg., ch. 911, §52, effective September 1, 1997.)

§158.304. Writ of withholding may include additional arrearages

If the notice of application for judicial writ of withholding states that the obligor has repeatedly failed to pay support in accordance with the underlying support order, the judicial writ may include arrearages that accrue between the filing of the notice and the date of the hearing or the issuance of a judicial writ of withholding.

(Acts 1995, 74th Leg., ch. 20, §1, effective April 20, 1995. Amended by Acts 1997, 75th Leg., ch. 911, §53, effective September 1, 1997.)

§158.306. Methods of delivery of notice of application for writ of withholding

(a) A notice of application for judicial writ of withholding may be delivered to the obligor by:

(1) hand delivery by a person designated by the Title IV-D agency or local domestic relations office;

(2) first-class or certified mail, return receipt requested, addressed to the obligor's last known address or place of employment; or

(3) by service of citation as in civil cases generally.

(b) If the notice is delivered by mailing or hand delivery, the party who filed the notice shall file with the court a certificate stating the name, address, and date on which the mailing or hand delivery was made.

(c) Notice is considered to have been received by the obligor:

(1) if hand delivered, on the date of delivery;

(2) if mailed by certified mail, on the date of receipt;

(3) if mailed by first-class mail, on the 10th day after the date the notice was mailed; or

(4) if delivered by service of citation, on the date of service.

(Acts 1995, 74th Leg., ch. 20, §1, effective April 20, 1995. Amended by Acts 1997, 75th Leg., ch. 911, §54, effective September 1, 1997.)

§158.307. Obligor may stay issuance of writ of withholding

(a) The obligor may stay issuance of a judicial writ of withholding by filing a motion to stay with the clerk of court not later than the 10th day after the date the notice of application for judicial writ of withholding was received.

(b) The grounds for filing a motion to stay issuance are limited to a dispute concerning the identity of the obligor or the existence or the amount of the arrearages.

(c) The obligor shall verify that statements of fact in the motion to stay issuance of the writ are true and correct.

(Acts 1995, 74th Leg., ch. 20, §1, effective April 20, 1995. Amended by Acts 1997, 75th Leg., ch. 911, §55, effective September 1, 1997.)

§158.308. Effect of obligor's filing motion to stay: precludes delivery to employer

The filing of a motion to stay by an obligor in the manner provided by Section 158.307 prohibits the clerk of court from delivering the judicial writ of withholding to any employer of the obligor before a hearing is held.

(Acts 1995, 74th Leg., ch. 20, §1, effective April 20, 1995. Amended by Acts 1997, 75th Leg., ch. 911, §56, effective September 1, 1997.)

§158.309. Court shall set hearing on motion to stay

(a) If a motion to stay is filed in the manner provided by Section 158.307, the court shall set a hearing on the motion and the clerk of court shall notify the obligor, obligee, or their authorized representatives, and the party who filed the application for judicial writ of withholding of the date, time, and place of the hearing.

(b) The court shall hold a hearing on the motion to stay not later than the 30th day after the date the motion was filed, except that a hearing may be held later than the 30th day after filing if both the obligor and obligee agree and waive the right to have the motion heard within 30 days.

(c) Upon hearing, the court shall:

(1) render an order for income withholding that includes a determination of the amount of child support arrearages, including medical support and interest; or

(2) grant the motion to stay.

(Acts 1995, 74th Leg., ch. 20, §1, effective April 20, 1995. Amended by Acts 1995, 74th Leg., ch. 751, §59, effective September 1, 1995; by Acts 1997, 75th Leg., ch. 911, §57, effective September 1, 1997.)

§158.310. Obligor waives defect in notice absent special exception in writing

(a) A defect in a notice of application for judicial writ of withholding is waived unless the respondent specially excepts in writing and cites with particularity the alleged defect, obscurity, or other ambiguity in the notice.

(b) A special exception under this section must be heard by the court before hearing the motion to stay issuance.

(c) If the court sustains an exception, the court shall provide the party filing the notice an opportunity to refile and the court shall continue the hearing to a date certain without the requirement of additional service.

(Acts 1995, 74th Leg., ch. 20, §1, effective April 20, 1995. Amended by Acts 1997, 75th Leg., ch. 911, §58, effective September 1, 1997.)

§158.311. Payment of arrearages is not sufficient basis for court to refuse to order withholding

(a) Payment of arrearages after receipt of notice of application for judicial writ of withholding may not be the sole basis for the court to refuse to order withholding.

(b) The court shall order that a reasonable amount of income be withheld to be applied toward the liquidation of arrearages, even though a judgment confirming arrearages has been rendered against the obligor.

(Acts 1995, 74th Leg., ch. 20, §1, effective April 20, 1995. Amended by Acts 1997, 75th Leg., ch. 911, §59, effective September 1, 1997.)

§158.312. Petitioner shall file request for issuance and delivery of writ of withholding: time limit

(a) If a notice of application for judicial writ of withholding is delivered and a motion to stay is not filed within the time limits provided by Section 158.307, the party who filed the notice shall file with the clerk of the court a request for issuance of the writ of withholding stating the amount of current support, including medical support, the amount of arrearages, and the amount to be withheld from the obligor's income.

(b) The request for issuance may not be filed before the 11th day after the date of receipt of the notice of application for judicial writ of withholding by the obligor.

(Acts 1995, 74th Leg., ch. 20, §1, effective April 20, 1995. Amended by Acts 1997, 75th Leg., ch. 911, §60, effective September 1, 1997; Acts 1999, 76th Leg., ch. 556, §30, effective September 1, 1999.)

§158.313. Clerk shall issue writ of withholding

(a) On the filing of a request for issuance of a writ of withholding, the clerk of the court shall issue the writ.

(b) The writ shall be delivered as provided by Subchapter B.1

(c) The clerk shall issue and mail the writ not later than the second working day after the date the request is filed.

(Acts 1995, 74th Leg., ch. 20, §1, effective April 20, 1995.)

§158.314. Writ of withholding must direct employer to withhold income

The judicial writ of income withholding issued by the clerk must direct that the employer or a subsequent employer withhold from the obligor's disposable income for current child support, including medical support, and child support arrearages an amount that is consistent with the provisions of this chapter regarding orders of withholding.

(Acts 1995, 74th Leg., ch. 20, §1, effective April 20, 1995. Amended by Acts 1997, 75th Leg., ch. 911, §61, effective September 1, 1997.)

§158.315. Petitioner may extend repayment schedule for arrearages based on hardship

If the party who filed the notice of application for judicial writ of withholding finds that the schedule for repaying arrearages would cause the obligor, the obligor's family, or the children for whom the support is due from the obligor to suffer unreasonable hardship, the party may extend the payment period in the writ.

(Acts 1995, 74th Leg., ch. 20, §1, effective April 20, 1995. Amended by Acts 1997, 75th Leg., ch. 911, §62, effective September 1, 1997.)

§158.316. Amount to be withheld shall be paid to designated person or agency on pay date

The amount to be withheld shall be paid to the person or office named in the writ on each pay date and shall include with the payment the date on which the withholding occurred.

(Acts 1995, 74th Leg., ch. 20, §1, effective April 20, 1995.)

§158.317. Obligor may claim failure to receive notice of application for writ of withholding

(a) Not later than the 30th day after the date of the first pay period following the date of delivery of the writ of withholding to the obligor's employer, the obligor may file an affidavit with the court that a motion to stay was not timely filed because the notice of application for judicial writ of withholding was not received by the obligor and that grounds exist for a motion to stay.

(b) Concurrently with the filing of the affidavit, the obligor may file a motion to withdraw the writ of withholding and request a hearing on the applicability of the writ.

(c) Income withholding may not be interrupted until after the hearing at which the court renders an order denying or modifying withholding.

(Acts 1995, 74th Leg., ch. 20, §1, effective April 20, 1995. Amended by Acts 1997, 75th Leg., ch. 911, §63, effective September 1, 1997.)

§158.319. Party may issue and deliver writ of withholding to subsequent employer

(a) After the issuance of a judicial writ of withholding by the clerk, a party authorized to file a notice of application for judicial writ of withholding under this subchapter may issue the judicial writ of withholding to a subsequent employer of the obligor by delivering to the employer by certified mail a copy of the writ.

(b) The judicial writ of withholding must include the name, address, and signature of the party and clearly indicate that the writ is being issued to a subsequent employer.

(c) The party shall file a copy of the judicial writ of withholding with the clerk not later than the third working day following delivery of the writ to the subsequent employer. The party shall pay the clerk a fee of $15 at the time the copy of the writ is filed.

(d) The party shall file the postal return receipt from the delivery to the subsequent employer not later than the third working day after the party receives the receipt.

(Acts 1995, 74th Leg., ch. 751, §60, effective September 1, 1995. Amended by Acts 1997, 75th Leg., ch. 911, §64, effective September 1, 1997.)

§158.401. Agency shall establish procedures for modification or termination of withholding

(a) The Title IV-D agency shall establish procedures for the reduction in the amount of or termination of withholding from income on the liquidation of an arrearages or the termination of the obligation of support in Title IV-D cases. The procedures shall provide that the payment of overdue support may not be used as the sole basis for terminating withholding.

(b) At the request of the Title IV-D agency, the clerk of the court shall issue a judicial writ of withholding to the obligor's employer reflecting any modification or changes in the amount to be withheld or the termination of withholding.

(Acts 1995, 74th Leg., ch. 20, §1, effective April 20, 1995. Amended by Acts 1997, 75th Leg., ch. 911, §65, effective September 1, 1997.)

§158.402. Parties may agree to reduce or terminate withholding upon occurrence of certain events

(a) An obligor and obligee may agree on a reduction in or termination of income withholding for child support on the occurrence of one of the following contingencies stated in the order:

(1) the child becomes 18 years of age or is graduated from high school, whichever is later;

(2) the child's disabilities of minority are removed by marriage, court order, or other operation of law; or

(3) the child dies.

(b) The obligor and obligee may file a notarized or acknowledged request with the clerk of the court under Section 158.011 for a revised judicial writ of withholding, including the termination of withholding.

(c) The clerk shall issue and deliver to an employer of the obligor a judicial writ of withholding that reflects the agreed revision or termination of withholding.

(d) An agreement by the parties under this section does not modify the terms of a support order.

(Acts 1995, 74th Leg., ch. 751, §61, effective September 1, 1995. Amended by Acts 1997, 75th Leg., ch. 911, §66, effective September 1, 1997.)

§158.403. Modification or termination of withholding for obligors who initiate voluntary withholding

(a) If an obligor initiates voluntary withholding under Section 158.011, the obligee or an agency providing child support services may file with the clerk of the court a notarized request signed by the obligor and the obligee or agency, as appropriate, for the issuance and delivery to the obligor of a:

(1) modified writ of withholding that reduces the amount of withholding; or

(2) notice of termination of withholding.

(b) On receipt of a request under this section, the clerk shall issue and deliver a modified writ of withholding or notice of termination in the manner provided by Section 158.402.

(c) The clerk may charge a reasonable fee not to exceed $15 for filing the request.

(d) An obligee may contest a modified writ of withholding or notice of termination issued under this section by requesting a hearing in the manner provided by Section 158.309 not later than the 180th day after the date the obligee discovers that the writ or notice has been issued.

(Acts 1995, 74th Leg., ch. 751, §61, effective September 1, 1995.)

§158.404. Any person or agency may deliver to employer an order of reduction or termination of withholding

If a court has rendered an order that reduces the amount of child support to be withheld or terminates withholding for child support, any person or governmental entity may deliver to the employer a certified copy of the order without the requirement that the clerk of the court deliver the order.

(Acts 1995, 74th Leg., ch. 20, §1, effective April 20, 1995. Renumbered from §158.402 by Acts 1995, 74th Leg., ch. 751, §61, effective September 1, 1995.)

§158.405. Liability of employers extends to orders for modification or termination of withholding

The provisions of this chapter regarding the liability of employers for withholding apply to an order that reduces or terminates withholding.

(Acts 1995, 74th Leg., ch. 20, §1, effective April 20, 1995. Renumbered from §158.403 by Acts 1995, 74th Leg., ch. 751, §61, effective September 1, 1995.)

§158.501. Agency may issue administrative writ of withholding for enforcement of existing order

(a) The Title IV-D agency may initiate income withholding by issuing an administrative writ of withholding for the enforcement of an existing order as authorized by this subchapter.

(b) Except as provided by Subsection (d), the Title IV-D agency is the only entity that may issue an administrative writ under this subchapter.

(c) The Title IV-D agency may use the procedures authorized by this subchapter to enforce a support order rendered by a tribunal of another state regardless of whether the order has been registered under Chapter 159.

(d) A domestic relations office may issue an administrative write of withholding under this chapter in a proceeding in which the office is providing child support enforcement services. A reference in this code to the Title IV-D agency that relates to an administrative writ includes a domestic relations office, except that the writ must be in the form prescribed by the Title IV-D agency under Section 158.504.

(Acts 1997, 75th Leg., ch. 911, §67, effective September 1, 1997. Amended by Acts 1999, 76th Leg., ch. 556, §31, effective September 1, 1999; Acts 2001, 77th Leg., ch. 1023, §40, effective September 1, 2001; Acts 2005, 79th Leg., ch. 199, §§3, 4, effective September 1, 2005.)

§158.502. Agency may issue administrative writ at any time until all support has been paid in full

(a) An administrative writ of withholding under this subchapter may be issued by the Title IV-D agency at any time until all current support, including medical support, and child support arrearages have been paid. The writ issued under this subsection may be based on an obligation in more than one support order.

(b) The Title IV-D agency may issue an administrative writ of withholding that directs that an amount be withheld for an arrearage or adjusts the amount to be withheld for an arrearage. An administrative writ issued under this subsection may be contested as provided by Section 158.506.

(c) The Title IV-D agency may issue an administrative writ of withholding as a reissuance of an existing withholding order on file with the court of continuing jurisdiction or a tribunal of another state. The administrative writ under this subsection is not subject to the contest provisions of Sections 158.505(a)(2) and 158.506.

(d) The Title IV-D agency may issue an administrative writ of withholding to direct child support payments to the state disbursement unit of another state.

(Acts 1997, 75th Leg., ch. 911, §67, effective September 1, 1997. Amended by Acts 1999, 76th Leg., ch. 556, §31, effective September 1, 1999; Acts 2001, 77th Leg., ch. 1023, §41, effective September 1, 2001; Acts 2003, 78th Leg., ch. 1247, effective September 1, 2003.)

§158.503. Method of delivery of administrative writ to employer

(a) An administrative writ of withholding issued under this subchapter may be delivered to an obligor, obligee, and employer by mail or by electronic transmission.

(b) Not later than the third business day after the date of delivery of the administrative writ of withholding to an employer, the Title IV-D agency shall file a copy of the writ, together with a signed certificate of service, in the court of continuing jurisdiction. The certificate of service may be signed electronically. This subsection does not apply to the enforcement under Section 158.501(c) of a support order rendered by a tribunal of another state.

(c) The copy of the administrative writ of withholding filed with the clerk of court must include:

(1) the name, address, and signature of the authorized attorney or individual that issued the writ;

(2) the name and address of the employer served with the writ; and

(3) a true copy of the information provided to the employer.

(d) The clerk of the court may charge a reasonable fee not to exceed $15 for filing an administrative writ under this section.

(Acts 1997, 75th Leg., ch. 911, §67, effective September 1, 1997. Amended by Acts 1999, 76th Leg., ch. 556, §32, effective September 1, 1999; Acts 2001, 77th Leg., ch. 116, §1, effective September 1, 2001; Acts 2001, 77th Leg., ch. 1023, §42, effective September 1, 2001.)

§158.504. Administrative writ of withholding must contain certain information

(a) The administrative writ of withholding must be in the form prescribed by the Title IV-D agency as required by this chapter and in a standard format authorized by the United States Department of Health and Human Services.

(b) An administrative writ of withholding issued under this subchapter may contain only the information that is necessary for the employer to withhold income for child support and medical support and shall specify the place where the withheld income is to be paid.

(Acts 1997, 75th Leg., ch. 911, §67, effective September 1, 1997. Amended by Acts 1999, 76th Leg., ch. 556, §33, effective September 1, 1999; Acts 2001, 77th Leg., ch. 1023, §43, effective September 1, 2001.)

§158.505. Agency shall provide notice to obligor

(a) On issuance of an administrative writ of withholding, the Title IV-D agency shall send the obligor:

(1) notice that the withholding has commenced, including, if the writ is issued as provided by Section 158.502(b), the amount of the arrearages, including accrued interest;

(2) except as provided by Section 158.502(c), notice of the procedures to follow if the obligor desires to contest withholding on the grounds that the identity of the obligor or the existence or amount of arrearages is incorrect; and

(3) a copy of the administrative writ, including the information concerning income withholding provided to the employer.

(b) The notice required under this section may be sent to the obligor by:

(1) personal delivery by a person designated by the Title IV-D agency;

(2) first-class mail or certified mail, return receipt requested, addressed to the obligor's last known address; or

(3) service of citation as in civil cases generally.

[(c) Repealed by Acts 1999, 76th Leg., ch. 556, §81, effective September 1, 1999.]

(Acts 1997, 75th Leg., ch. 911, §67, effective September 1, 1997. Amended by Acts 1999, 76th Leg., ch. 556, §§34, 81, effective September 1, 1999; Acts 2001, 77th Leg., ch. 1023, §44, effective September 1, 2001.)

§158.506. Obligor may contest administrative writ of withholding

(a) Except as provided by Section 158.502(c), an obligor receiving the notice under Section 158.505 may request a review by the Title IV-D agency to resolve any issue in dispute regarding the identity of the obligor or the existence or amount of arrearages. The Title IV-D agency shall provide an opportunity for a review, by telephonic conference or in person, as may be appropriate under the circumstances.

(b) After a review under this section, the Title IV-D agency may issue a new administrative writ of withholding to the employer, including a writ modifying the amount to be withheld or terminating withholding.

(c) If a review under this section fails to resolve any issue in dispute, the obligor is entitled to the remedies provided by Section 158.317 for cases in which a notice of an application for judicial writ of withholding was not received. The obligor may file a motion with the court to withdraw the administrative writ and request a hearing with the court not later than the 30th day after receiving notice of the agency's determination. Income withholding may not be interrupted pending a hearing by the court.

(Acts 1997, 75th Leg., ch. 911, §67, effective September 1, 1997. Amended by Acts 1999, 76th Leg., ch. 556, §35, effective September 1, 1999.)

§158.507. Agency may deliver writ to terminate withholding when all support has been paid

An administrative writ to terminate withholding may be issued and delivered to an employer by the Title IV-D agency when all current support, including medical support, and child support arrearages have been paid.

(Acts 1997, 75th Leg., ch. 911, §67, effective September 1, 1997.)

VIII.
CHILD CUSTODY

This chapter examines child custody, primarily in the context of dissolution. After some general provisions, it explores the standards applicable for selecting the custodial parent. Then, it explores the rights of the noncustodial parent and also the rights of non-biological parents (including same-sex partners). Next, it focuses on the role of third parties (i.e., the child, counsel, experts). It turns to the standard for modification and issues of jurisdiction and enforcement. Finally, it addresses the dispute resolution process.

A. GENERAL PROVISIONS

An award of custody, in general, encompasses two concepts: legal custody and physical custody. Legal custody confers responsibility for significant and long-range decisions regarding upbringing, health, welfare, and education. Physical custody determines the child's residence and confers responsibility for day-to-day decisions regarding physical care. Compare the ALI Principles' attempt to clarify these terms by use of "decisionmaking responsibility" for legal custody and "custodial responsibility" for physical custody (ALI Principles, Chapter 2 "The Allocation of Custodial and Decisionmaking Responsibility for Children"). For the ALI Principles, see Part IV *infra*.

Traditional awards of sole custody vest one parent with legal control and permanent physical custody; the noncustodial parent has only temporary physical custody during specified visitation periods. Almost all jurisdictions now permit some form of joint custody. In an award of joint custody (more accurately termed joint legal custody), each parent shares responsibility for major child-rearing decisionmaking irrespective of which parent has physical custody.

1. Definitions

California Family Code

§3000. Application of definitions

Unless the provision or context otherwise requires, the definitions in this chapter govern the construction of this division.

(Stats. 1992 (A.B. 2650), ch. 162, §10, effective January 1, 1994.)

§3002. "Joint custody"

"Joint custody" means joint physical custody and joint legal custody.

(Stats. 1992 (A.B. 2650), ch. 162, §10, effective January 1, 1994.)

§3003. "Joint legal custody"

"Joint legal custody" means that both parents shall share the right and the responsibility to make the decisions relating to the health, education, and welfare of a child.

(Stats. 1992 (A.B. 2650), ch. 162, §10, effective January 1, 1994.)

§3004. "Joint physical custody"

"Joint physical custody" means that each of the parents shall have significant periods of physical custody. Joint physical custody shall be shared by the parents in such a way so as to assure a child of frequent and continuing contact with both parents, subject to Sections 3011 and 3020.

(Stats. 1992 (A.B. 2650), ch. 162, §10, effective January 1, 1994. Amended by Stats. 1997 (A.B. 200) ch. 849, §1.)

§3006. "Sole legal custody"

"Sole legal custody" means that one parent shall have the right and the responsibility to make the decisions relating to the health, education, and welfare of a child.

(Stats. 1992 (A.B. 2650), ch. 162, §10, effective January 1, 1994.)

§3007. "Sole physical custody"

"Sole physical custody" means that a child shall reside with and be under the supervision of one parent, subject to the power of the court to order visitation.

(Stats. 1992 (A.B. 2650), ch. 162, §10, effective January 1, 1994.)

§3022. Court may make order for custody as necessary or proper

The court may, during the pendency of a proceeding or at any time thereafter, make an order for the custody of a child during minority that seems necessary or proper.

(Formerly §3021, added by Stats. 1992 (A.B. 2650), ch. 162, §10, effective January 1, 1994. Renumbered §3022 and amended by Stats. 1993 (A.B. 1500), ch. 219, §116.12.)

§3023. Custody issues shall be given preference for trial

(a) If custody of a minor child is the sole contested issue, the case shall be given preference over other civil cases, except matters to which special precedence may be given by law, for assigning a trial date and shall be given an early hearing.

(b) If there is more than one contested issue and one of the issues is the custody of a minor child, the court, as to the issue of custody, shall order a separate trial. The separate trial shall be given preference over other civil cases, except matters to which special precedence may be given by law, for assigning a trial date.

(Stats. 1992 (A.B. 2650), ch. 162, §10, effective January 1, 1994. Amended by Stats. 1993 (A.B. 1500) ch. 219, §116.14.)

§3025. Noncustodial parent shall not be denied access to records

Notwithstanding any other provision of law, access to records and information pertaining to a minor child, including, but not limited to, medical, dental, and school records, shall not be denied to a parent because that parent is not the child's custodial parent.

(Stats. 1992 (A.B. 2650), ch. 162, §10, effective January 1, 1994.)

§3026. Family reunification services shall not be ordered

Family reunification services shall not be ordered as a part of a child custody or visitation rights proceeding. Nothing in this section affects the applicability of Section 16507 of the Welfare and Institutions Code.

(Stats. 1992 (A.B. 2650), ch. 162, §10, effective January 1, 1994. Amended Stats. 1993 (A.B. 1500) ch. 219, §116.16.)

§3029. Custody order shall include order for support if custodial parent on public assistance

An order granting custody to a parent who is receiving, or in the opinion of the court is likely to receive, assistance pursuant to the Family Economic Security Act of 1982 (Chapter 2 (commencing with Part 3) of Division 9 of the Welfare and Institutions Code) for the maintenance of the child shall include an order pursuant to Chapter 2 (commencing with Section 4000) of Part 2 of Division 9 of this code, directing the noncustodial parent to pay any amount necessary for the support of the child, to the extent of the noncustodial parent's ability to pay.

(Stats. 1993 (A.B. 1500), ch. 219, §116.19.)

§3043. Court shall give due weight to nomination of guardian by parent

In determining the person or persons to whom custody should be granted under paragraph (2) or (3) of subdivision (a) of Section 3040, the court shall consider and give due weight to the nomination of a guardian of the person of the child by a parent under Article 1 (commencing with Section 1500) of Chapter 1 of Part 2 of Division 4 of the Probate Code.

(Stats. 1993, ch. 219 (A.B. 1500), §116.50.)

2. Temporary Custody During Proceedings

The court's decision on temporary custody is often determinative of the permanent custody arrangement. Because of the child's need for stability, courts are often reluctant to change the status quo.

§3060. Temporary custody petition

A petition for a temporary custody order, containing the statement required by Section 3409, may be included with the initial filing of the petition or action or may be filed at any time after the initial filing.

(Stats. 1992 (A.B. 2650), ch. 162, §10, effective January 1, 1994. Amended Stats. 1993 (A.B. 1500), ch. 219, §116.60.)

§3061. Court shall grant temporary custody in accordance with parties' agreement

If the parties have agreed to or reached an understanding on the custody or temporary custody of their children, a copy of the agreement or an affidavit as to their understanding shall be attached to the petition or action. As promptly as possible after this filing, the court shall, except in exceptional circumstances, enter an order granting temporary custody in accordance with the agreement or understanding or in accordance with any stipulation of the parties.

(Stats. 1992 (A.B. 2650), ch. 162, §10, effective January 1, 1994. Amended Stats. 1993 (A.B. 1500) ch. 219, §116.61.)

§3062. Court may enter ex parte temporary custody order and issue order to show cause

(a) In the absence of an agreement, understanding, or stipulation, the court may, if jurisdiction is appropriate, enter an ex parte temporary custody order, set a hearing date within 20 days, and issue an order to show cause on the responding party. If the responding party does not appear or respond within the time set, the temporary custody order may be extended as necessary, pending the termination of the proceedings.

(b) If, despite good faith efforts, service of the ex parte order and order to show cause has not been effected in a timely fashion and there is reason to believe, based on an affidavit, or other manner of proof made under penalty of perjury, by the petitioner, that the responding party has possession of the minor child and seeks to avoid the jurisdiction of the court or is concealing the whereabouts of the child, then the hearing date may be reset and the ex parte order extended up to an additional 90 days. After service has been effected, either party may request ex parte that the hearing date be advanced or the ex parte order be dissolved or modified.

(Stats. 1992 (A.B. 2650), ch. 162, §10, effective January 1, 1994.)

B. STANDARDS FOR SELECTING THE CUSTODIAL PARENT

1. Presumptions

Some states invoke presumptions to adjudicate child custody disputes. Historically, the tender years presumption provided that the natural mother of a young child was entitled to custody unless the mother was found to be unfit. "Tender years" generally was defined to include preschool children. Beginning in the 1980's, several courts invalidated the tender years presumption as a violation of equal protection. See, e.g., Devine v. Devine, 398 So. 2d 686 (Ala. 1981).

In response to constitutional challenges, states abolished that presumption. Courts now assume that both parents are capable of caring for a child. The California Family Code specifically provides that the courts "shall not prefer a parent as custodian because of that parent's sex" (Cal. Fam. Code §3040(a)(1)).

In 1969, the Family Law Act (establishing no-fault divorce) eliminated that preference. In 1972, the state legislature repealed the tender years presumption. This latter statutory development led to adoption of the twin principles that both parents have equal rights to custody and that the child's best interests are paramount. In 1979, the legislature reaffirmed parents' equal rights to custody by adding the statutory prohibition on custody awards based on the parent's gender (now Cal. Fam. Code §3010(a)(1)). Raye et al., *supra*, at §4.65.

Many states (including California) have presumptions against awarding custody to a parent who has committed domestic violence. See §B3 *infra*.

§3010. Both parents are equally entitled to custody

(a) The mother of an unemancipated minor child and the father, if presumed to be the father under Section 7611, are equally entitled to the custody of the child.

(b) If one parent is dead, is unable or refuses to take custody, or has abandoned the child, the other parent is entitled to custody of the child.

(Stats. 1993 (A.B. 1500), ch. 219, §115.5.)

§3040. Court shall grant custody in order of preference according to best interests

(a) Custody should be granted in the following order of preference according to the best interest of the child as provided in Sections 3011 and 3020:

(1) To both parents jointly pursuant to Chapter 4 (commencing with Section 3080) or to either parent. In making an order granting custody to either parent, the court shall consider, among other factors, which parent is more likely to allow the child frequent and continuing contact with the noncustodial parent, consistent with Section 3011 and 3020, and shall not prefer a parent as custodian because of that parent's sex. The court, in its discretion, may require the parents to submit to the court a plan for the implementation of the custody order.

(2) If to neither parent, to the person or persons in whose home the child has been living in a wholesome and stable environment.

(3) To any other person or persons deemed by the court to be suitable and able to provide adequate and proper care and guidance for the child.

(b) This section establishes neither a preference nor a presumption for or against joint legal custody, joint physical custody, or sole custody, but allows the court and the family the widest discretion to choose a parenting plan that is in the best interest of the child.

(Stats. 1993 (A.B. 1500), ch. 219, §116.50. Amended Stats. 1997 (A.B. 200), ch. 849, §4.)

2. Best Interests of the Child

The prevailing standard in custody determinations is the best interests of the child. Despite its widespread adoption, the standard has been criticized as highly discretionary and imprecise. As a result, many legislatures have attempted to define the factors for consideration more precisely. In the determination of the best interests, California courts must consider four factors but may consider any relevant factors. The mandatory factors are: (1) the health, safety, and welfare of the child; (2) domestic violence; (3) contact with both parents; and (4) substance abuse (Cal. Fam. Code §3011).

The legislature has declared the dual public policies of the state to assure "that the health, safety, and welfare of children shall be the court's primary concern" (Cal. Fam. Code §3020(a)) and also "to assure that children have frequent and continuing contact with both parents" post-dissolution (Cal. Fam. Code §3020(b)). In cases in which the two policies conflict, the former shall prevail.

Courts have broad discretion to consider many relevant factors. In this determination,

racial considerations may not be determinative, based on Palmore v. Sidoti, 466 U.S. 429 (1984);

courts may not base a custody or visitation determination on a parent's religious beliefs and practices (because of constitutional concerns regarding the First Amendment's Free Exercise Clause) absent a showing that these beliefs or practices are detrimental to the child (In re Marriage of Murga, 163 Cal. Rptr. 79 (1980); In re Marriage of Weiss, 49 Cal. Rptr. 2d 339 (1996));

a parent's sexual misconduct is irrelevant to a custody decision absent evidence of adverse effect (In re Marriage of Slayton, 103 Cal. Rptr. 2d 545 (Cal. 2001));

a parent's sexual orientation may not be grounds for denial of custody absent evidence that it negatively affects the child's best interests (Nadler v. Superior Court, 63 Cal. Rptr. 352 (Ct. App. 1967));

a court may not deny custody based on a parent's physical or mental disability unless the condition will have a substantial and lasting adverse effect on the child's welfare (Marriage of Lewin, 162 Cal. Rptr. 757 (Ct. App. 1980); In re Jamie M., 184 Cal. Rptr. 778 (Ct. App. 1982)). Hogoboom & King, *supra*, at §7:400 to 7:406.

On parental agreements regarding children's religious upbringing, see In re Marriage of Weiss, 49 Cal. Rptr. 2d 339, 346-347 (Ct. App. 1996) (antenuptial agreement violates mother's right to free exercise which includes the right to change her religious beliefs). See also Hogoboom & King, *supra*, at §7:403.

The American Law Institute has been involved in a project since 1989 to reform family law by clarifying its underlying principles and making policy recommendations. The ALI's recommendations on child custody reject the best-interests-of-the-child standard because of its subjectivity and lack of predictability. Instead, the ALI emphasizes "private ordering," i.e., parental agreements. See ALI Principles of the Law of Family Dissolution: Analysis and Recommendations §§2.06, 2.11-2.12 (2002) (parenting agreements and limiting and prohibited factors for such plans) Part IV *infra*. A number of states now provide for parenting plans. Some jurisdictions require such plans in all cases, whereas other states require such plans only before entering a joint custody order. In other states, the court has discretion to require parenting plans. Mary Kay Kisthardt, The AAML Model for a Parenting Plan, 19 J. Am. Acad. Matrim. Law. 223, 226 (2005).

According to the ALI Principles, if the parents agree, the court should enforce their agreement unless the agreement is not voluntary or would be harmful to the child (§2.06(1)(a) & (b)). However, if the parents are unable to agree, the court should award custody based on the allocation of caretaking responsibility prior to the separation (§2.08(1)). The objective is to replicate the division of responsibility that was followed when the family was intact (thereby giving deference to the arrangements on which the parties once agreed). The ALI rule may be rebutted by specific factors such as a prior parental agreement, the child's preference, the need to keep siblings together, harm to the child's welfare (based on emotional attachment to a parent and the parent's ability/availability to meet the child's needs), avoidance of custodial arrangements that would be impractical or interfere with the child's need for stability, and the need to deal with parental relocation (§2.08(1)(a) to (g)).

In determining custody arrangements, the ALI Principles prohibit courts from considering:

the gender of either the parent or the child (§2.12(1)(b);

the race or ethnicity of the child, parent, or other member of the household (§2.12(1)(a));

the "religious practices" of either the parent or the child except if (a) the religious practices present "severe and almost certain harm" to the child (and then a court may limit the practices only to the minimum degree necessary to protect the child), or (b) if necessary to protect the child's ability to practice a religion "that has been a significant part of the child's life" (§2.12(1)(c));

either the sexual orientation or the extramarital sexual conduct of a parent except upon a showing that such conduct causes harm to the child (§2.12(1)(d) (sexual orientation))(e) (extramarital sexual conduct); and

parents' relative earning capacities or financial circumstances unless the parents' combined financial resources "set practical limits on the custodial arrangements" (§2.12(1)(f)).

Further, the ALI Principles provide that placement of a child in day care does not constitute sufficient changed circumstances to warrant custody modification (§2.15(3)(c)). For discussion of the ALI Principles on domestic violence, see §B3 *infra*.

Courts do not generally like to separate siblings in custody decisionmaking. However, courts will separate siblings if the court finds that such an award is in the child's best interests and if exceptional circumstances are present. For example, in In re Marriage of Steiner, 11 Cal. Rptr.3d 671 (Ct. App. 2004), a court awarded sole legal and physical custody of a younger son to his father in order to prevent the mother from "poisoning" his relationship with his father as she allegedly had done with the older son. And, in In re Marriage of Heath, 18 Cal. Rptr.3d 760 (Ct. App. 2004), an appellate court held that the trial court erred by splitting custody of two brothers on the assumption that one would be harmed by the other's autism.

§3011. Court shall consider certain factors in determining best interests of child

In making a determination of the best interest of the child in a proceeding described in Section 3021, the court shall, among any other factors it finds relevant, consider all of the following:

(a) The health, safety, and welfare of the child.

(b) Any history of abuse by one parent or any other person seeking custody against any of the following:

(1) Any child to whom he or she is related by blood or affinity or with whom he or she has had a caretaking relationship, no matter how temporary.

(2) The other parent.

(3) A parent, current spouse, or cohabitant, of the parent or person seeking custody, or a person with whom the parent or person seeking custody has a dating or engagement relationship.

As a prerequisite to the consideration of allegations of abuse, the court may require substantial independent corroboration, including, but not limited to, written reports by law enforcement agencies, child protective services or other social welfare agencies, courts, medical facilities, or other public agencies or private nonprofit organizations providing services to victims of sexual assault or domestic violence. As used in this subdivision, "abuse against a child" means "child abuse" as defined in Section 11165.6 of the Penal Code and abuse against any of the other persons described in paragraph (2) or (3) means "abuse" as defined in Section 6203 of this code.

(c) The nature and amount of contact with both parents, except as provided in Section 3046.

(d) The habitual or continual illegal use of controlled substances or habitual or continual abuse of alcohol by either parent. Before considering these allegations, the court may first require independent corroboration, including, but not limited to, written reports from law enforcement agencies, courts, probation departments, social welfare agencies, medical facilities, rehabilitation facilities, or other public agencies or nonprofit organizations providing drug and alcohol abuse services. As used in this subdivision, "controlled substances" has the same meaning as defined in the California Uniform Controlled Substances Act, Division 10 (commencing with Section 11000) of the Health and Safety Code.

(e)(1) Where allegations about a parent pursuant to subdivision (b) or (d) have been brought to the attention of the court in the current proceeding, and the court makes an order for sole or joint custody to that parent, the court shall state its reasons in writing or on the record. In these circumstances, the court shall ensure that any order regarding custody or visitation is specific as to time, day, place, and manner of transfer of the child as set forth in subdivision (b) of Section 6323.

(2) The provisions of this subdivision shall not apply if the parties stipulate in writing or on the record regarding custody or visitation.

(Stats. 1993 (A.B. 1500), ch. 219, §115.5. Amended Stats. 1996 (A.B. 2474), ch. 835, §1 (S.B. 384), ch. 836, §1.5; Stats. 1997 (A.B. 200), ch. 849, §2; Stats. 1999 (A.B. 1671), ch. 980, §4.)

§3020. Legislative findings and public policy

(a) The Legislature finds and declares that it is the public policy of this state to assure that the health, safety, and welfare of children shall be the court's primary concern in determining the best interest of children when making any orders regarding the physical or legal custody or visitation of children. The Legislature further finds and declares that the perpetration of child abuse or domestic violence in a household where a child resides is detrimental to the child.

(b) The Legislature finds and declares that it is the public policy of this state to assure that children have frequent and continuing contact with both parents after the parents have separated or dissolved their marriage, or ended their relationship, and to encourage parents to share the rights and responsibilities of child rearing in order to effect this policy, except where the contact would not be in the best interest of the child, as provided in Section 3011.

(c) Where the policies set forth in subdivisions (a) and (b) of this section are in conflict, any court's order regarding physical or legal custody or visitation shall be made in a manner that ensures the health, safety, and welfare of the child and the safety of all family members.

(Stats. 1992 (A.B. 2650), ch. 162, §10, effective January 1, 1994. Amended Stats. 1993 (A.B. 1500), ch. 219, §116; Stats. 1997 (A.B. 200), ch. 849, §3; Stats. 1999 (A.B. 1671), ch. 980, §5.)

3. Role of Domestic Violence in Custody Decisionmaking

Public concern about battering has contributed to the passage of legislation addressing the role of domestic violence in custody disputes. States take two approaches, either including domestic violence as a factor in the best interests standard or providing that evidence of domestic violence creates a rebuttable presumption against awarding custody (often including joint custody) to the abusive parent.

Currently, 24 states provide for a rebuttable presumption against an award of custody to a batterer. Some of these states apply the presumption in any custodial situation whereas others apply it only to awards of joint custody. Annette M. Gonzalez & Linda M. Rio Reichmann, Representing Children in Civil Cases Involving Domestic Violence, 39 Fam. L.Q. 197, 198 (2005). States have different requirements about the proof that is necessary to trigger the presumption and to rebut it. Many states (including California) have "friendly parent provisions" mandating courts to favor a custody award to the parent most likely to maintain the child's relationship with the other parent. Nancy Ver Steegh, Differentiating Types of Domestic Violence: Implications for Child Custody, 65 La. L. Rev. 1379, 1421 (2005) (noting that 28 states have such provisions). Such statutes, enacted during the 1980s when policy shifted toward encouraging post-divorce involvement of both parents in children's lives, pose special risks for victims of domestic violence. See Margaret K. Dore, The "Friendly Parent" Concept: A Flawed Factor for Child Custody, 6 Loy. J. Pub. Int. L. 41, 42 (2004).

California enacted legislation in 1999 providing for a rebuttable presumption (in terms of awarding sole or joint physical or legal custody) against a parent who has perpetrated domestic violence against the other parent, the child or the child's siblings within the previous five years (Cal. Fam. Code §3044(a)). This presumption may be rebutted by a preponderance of the evidence. In determining whether the presumption has been rebutted, the court must consider such factors as (*inter alia*): the perpetrator's completion of a treatment program, substance abuse counseling, or parenting classes (Cal. Fam. Code §3044(b)).

In the first year that California's statutory presumption was in effect, several difficulties arose, including: what types of evidence constitute a finding of domestic violence under Cal. Fam. Code §3044, whether the issuance of a civil protective order against an alleged batterer can trigger the presumption, and whether judges will be reluctant to issue civil protective orders if these orders have res judicata effect on §3044 determinations. See Lois A. Weithorn, Protecting Children From Exposure to Domestic Violence: The Use and Abuse of Child Maltreatment, 53 Hastings L.J. 1, 16 n.46 (2001)

Additionally, some states (including California) provide protection for battered spouses in custody mediation (see §H2f *infra*).

The ALI also addresses the role of domestic violence in custody decisionmaking. According to the ALI Principles, parents and the court share the burden of discovery: Parents must disclose battering in the parenting plan submitted to the court; the court also must have a process to identify abuse. ALI Principles §§2.06, 2.11. Batterers may not receive custodial responsibility unless the court orders appropriate measures in order to ensure the protection of the child and the other parent (e.g., by mandated counseling). *Id.* at §2.11(2)(i). In addition, the Principles broadly define abuse for purposes of custody determinations (i.e., any physical injury or creation of a reasonable fear thereof on the part of a parent, child, or any member of household). *Id.* at §2.03(7). Finally, the Principles suggest that courts be aware that the abuser might try to use custody or visitation rights to harass the victim-spouse. *Id.* at §2.11(c) cmt. See the ALI Principles in Part IV *infra*.

Note that California law (Cal. Fam. Code §4325) also provides for a rebuttable presumption against awards of spousal support to a spouse who has been convicted of domestic violence. See In re Marriage of

Cauley, 41 Cal. Rptr.3d 902 (Ct. App. 2006) (holding that a nonmodifiable spousal support provision in a settlement agreement, strictly limiting modifiability to cases of cohabitation or loss of income, was unenforceable as a violation of the public policy against domestic violence).

§3011. Role of domestic violence in determining best interests of child

In making a determination of the best interest of the child in a proceeding described in Section 3021, the court shall, among any other factors it finds relevant, consider all of the following:

. . .

(b) Any history of abuse by one parent or any other person seeking custody against any of the following:

(1) Any child to whom he or she is related by blood or affinity or with whom he or she has had a caretaking relationship, no matter how temporary.

(2) The other parent.

(3) A parent, current spouse, or cohabitant, of the parent or person seeking custody, or a person with whom the parent or person seeking custody has a dating or engagement relationship.

As a prerequisite to the consideration of allegations of abuse, the court may require substantial independent corroboration, including, but not limited to, written reports by law enforcement agencies, child protective services or other social welfare agencies, courts, medical facilities, or other public agencies or private nonprofit organizations providing services to victims of sexual assault or domestic violence. As used in this subdivision, "abuse against a child" means "child abuse" as defined in Section 11165.6 of the Penal Code and abuse against any of the other persons described in paragraph (2) or (3) means "abuse" as defined in Section 6203 of this code.

. . .

(e)(1) Where allegations about a parent pursuant to subdivision (b) [regarding domestic violence] or (d) [regarding substance abuse] have been brought to the attention of the court in the current proceeding, and the court makes an order for sole or joint custody to that parent, the court shall state its reasons in writing or on the record. In these circumstances, the court shall ensure that any order regarding custody or visitation is specific as to time, day, place, and manner of transfer of the child as set forth in subdivision (b) of Section 6323.

(Stats. 1993 (A.B. 1500), ch. 219, §115.5. Amended Stats. 1996 (A.B. 2474), ch. 835, §1, (S.B. 384), ch. 836, §1.5 ; Stats. 1997 (A.B. 200), ch. 849, §2; Stats. 1999 (A.B. 1671), ch. 980, §4.)

§3020. Legislative findings: role of domestic violence in custody

(a) The Legislature finds and declares that it is the public policy of this state to assure that the health, safety, and welfare of children shall be the court's primary concern in determining the best interest of children when making any orders regarding the physical or legal custody or visitation of children. The Legislature further finds and declares that the perpetration of child abuse or domestic violence in a household where a child resides is detrimental to the child.

(b) The Legislature finds and declares that it is the public policy of this state to assure that children have frequent and continuing contact with both parents after the parents have separated or dissolved their marriage, or ended their relationship, and to encourage parents to share the rights and responsibilities of child rearing in order to effect this policy, except where the contact would not be in the best interest of the child, as provided in Section 3011.

(c) Where the policies set forth in subdivisions (a) and (b) of this section are in conflict, any court's order regarding physical or legal custody or visitation shall be made in a manner that ensures the health, safety, and welfare of the child and the safety of all family members.

(Stats. 1992 (A.B. 2650), ch. 162, §10, effective January 1, 1994. Amended Stats. 1993 (A.B. 1500), ch. 219, §116; Stats. 1997 (A.B. 200), ch. 849, §3; Stats. 1999 (A.B. 1671), ch. 980, §5.)

§3021. Application to various proceedings

This part applies in any of the following:

(a) A proceeding for dissolution of marriage.

(b) A proceeding for nullity of marriage.

(c) A proceeding for legal separation of the parties.

(d) An action for exclusive custody pursuant to Section 3120.

(e) A proceeding to determine physical or legal custody or for visitation in a proceeding pursuant to the Domestic Violence Prevention Act (Division 10 (commencing with Section 6200)).

In an action under Section 6323, nothing in this subdivision shall be construed to authorize physical or legal custody, or visitation rights, to be granted to any party to a Domestic Violence Prevention Act proceeding who has not established a parent and child relationship pursuant to paragraph (2) of subdivision (a) of Section 6323.

(f) A proceeding to determine physical or legal custody or visitation in an action pursuant to the Uniform Parentage Act (Part 3 (commencing with Section 7600) of Division 12).

(g) A proceeding to determine physical or legal custody or visitation in an action brought by the district attorney pursuant to Section 17404.

(Stats. 1993 (A.B. 1500), ch. 219, §116.11. Amended Stats. 1996 (S.B. 1444), ch. 1075, §9; Stats. 1997 (S.B. 564), ch. 396, §1; Stats. 1999 (A.B. 1671), ch. 980, §6; Stats. 2000 (A.B. 2539), ch 135, §58.)

§3022.5. Court shall grant motion for reconsideration if other parent convicted of false accusation of child abuse

A motion by a parent for reconsideration of an existing child custody order shall be granted if the motion is based on the fact that the other parent was convicted of a crime in connection with falsely accusing the moving parent of child abuse.

(Stats. 1995 (S.B. 558), ch. 406, §1.)

§3027. Court may take steps to protect child victim of sexual abuse during custody proceedings

(a) If allegations of child sexual abuse are made during a child custody proceeding and the court has concerns regarding the child's safety, the court may take any reasonable, temporary steps as the court, in its discretion, deems appropriate under the circumstances to protect the child's safety until an investigation can be completed. Nothing in this section shall affect the applicability of Section 16504 or 16506 of the Welfare and Institutions Code.

(b) If allegations of child sexual abuse are made during a child custody proceeding, the court may request that the local child welfare services agency conduct an investigation of the allegations pursuant to Section 328 of the Welfare and Institutions Code. Upon completion of the investigation, the agency shall report its findings to the court.

(Stats. 2000 (S.B. 1716) ch. 926, §3.)

§3027.1. Court may impose monetary sanction for false accusation of abuse or neglect

(a) If a court determines, based on the investigation described in Section 3027 or other evidence presented to it, that an accusation of child abuse or neglect made during a child custody proceeding is false and the person making the accusation knew it to be false at the time the accusation was made, the court may impose reasonable money sanctions, not to exceed all costs incurred by the party accused as a direct result of defending the accusation, and reasonable attorney's fees incurred in recovering the sanctions, against the person making the accusation. For the purposes of this section, "person" includes a witness, a party, or a party's attorney.

(b) On motion by any person requesting sanctions under this section, the court shall issue its order to show cause why the requested sanctions should not be imposed. The order to show cause shall be served on the person against whom the sanctions are sought and a hearing thereon shall be scheduled by the court to be conducted at least 15 days after the order is served.

(c) The remedy provided by this section is in addition to any other remedy provided by law.

(Stats. 1992 (A.B. 2650), ch. 162, §10, effective January 1, 1994, as Fam. Code, §3027. Amended Stats. 1993 (A.B. 1500), ch. 219, §116.17; Stats. 1994 (A.B. 2845), ch. 688, §1. Amended and renumbered Stats. 2000 (S.B. 1716), ch. 926, §2.)

§3030. Presumption against custody for registered sex offender, parent convicted of rape or murder of child's other parent

(a)(1) No person shall be granted physical or legal custody of, or unsupervised visitation with, a child if the person is required to be registered as a sex offender under Section 290 of the Penal Code where the victim was a minor, or if the person has been convicted under Section 273a, 273d, or 647.6 of the Penal Code, unless the court finds that there is no significant risk to the child and states its reasons in writing or on the record.

(2) No person shall be granted physical or legal custody of, or unsupervised visitation with, a child if anyone residing in the person's household is required, as a result of a felony conviction in which the victim was a minor, to register as a sex offender under Section 290 of the Penal Code, unless the court finds there is no significant risk to the child and states its reasons in writing or on the record.

(3) The fact that a child is permitted unsupervised contact with a person who is required, as a result of a felony conviction in which the victim was a minor, to be registered as a sex offender under Section 290 of the Penal Code, shall be prima facie evidence that the child is at significant risk. When making a determination regarding significant risk to the child, the prima facie evidence shall constitute a presumption affecting the burden of producing evidence. However, this presumption shall not apply if there are factors mitigating against its application, including whether the party seeking custody or visitation is also required, as the result of a felony conviction in which the victim was a minor, to register as a sex offender under Section 290 of the Penal Code.

(b) No person shall be granted custody of, or visitation with, a child if the person has been convicted under Section 261 of the Penal Code and the child was conceived as a result of that violation.

(c) No person shall be granted custody of, or unsupervised visitation with, a child if the person has been convicted of murder in the first degree, as defined in Section 189 of the Penal Code, and the victim of the murder was the other parent of the child who is the subject of the order, unless the court finds that there is no risk to the child's health, safety, and welfare, and states the reasons for its finding in writing or on the record. In making its finding, the court may consider, among other things, the following:

(1) The wishes of the child, if the child is of sufficient age and capacity to reason so as to form an intelligent preference.

(2) Credible evidence that the convicted parent was a victim of abuse, as defined in Section 6203, committed by the deceased parent. That evidence may include, but is not limited to, written reports by law enforcement agencies, child protective services or other social welfare agencies, courts, medical facilities, or other public agencies or private nonprofit organizations providing services to victims of domestic abuse.

(3) Testimony of an expert witness, qualified under Section 1107 of the Evidence Code, that the convicted parent experiences intimate partner battering.

Unless and until a custody or visitation order is issued pursuant to this subdivision, no person shall permit or cause the child to visit or remain in the custody of the convicted parent without the consent of the child's custodian or legal guardian.

(d) The court may order child support that is to be paid by a person subject to subdivision (a), (b), or (c) to be paid through the local child support agency, as authorized by Section 4573 of the Family Code and Division 17 (commencing with Section 17000) of this code.

(e) The court shall not disclose, or cause to be disclosed, the custodial parent's place of residence, place of

employment, or the child's school, unless the court finds that the disclosure would be in the best interest of the child.
(Stats. 1993 (A.B. 1500), ch. 219, §116.2. Amended Stats. 1st Ex. Sess. 1993-94 (S.B. 25X), ch. 5, §1, effective November 30, 1994; Stats. 1997 (A.B. 1222), ch. 594, §1; Stats. 1998 (A.B. 1645), ch. 131, §1 (A.B. 2803), ch. 485, §64 (A.B. 2745), ch. 704, §1.5 (A.B. 2386), ch. 705, §1.5; Stats. 2000 (A.B. 1358), ch. 808, §26, effective September 28, 2000; Stats. 2005 (A.B. 220), ch. 215, §2; Stats. 2005 (S.B 594), ch. 483, §2.5.)

§3031. Court is encouraged not to make custody or visitation order that is inconsistent with emergency protective order

(a) Where the court considers the issue of custody or visitation the court is encouraged to make a reasonable effort to ascertain whether or not any emergency protective order, protective order, or other restraining order is in effect that concerns the parties or the minor. The court is encouraged not to make a custody or visitation order that is inconsistent with the emergency protective order, protective order, or other restraining order, unless the court makes both of the following findings:

(1) The custody or visitation order cannot be made consistent with the emergency protective order, protective order, or other restraining order.

(2) The custody or visitation order is in the best interest of the minor.

(b) Whenever custody or visitation is granted to a parent in a case in which domestic violence is alleged and an emergency protective order, protective order, or other restraining order has been issued, the custody or visitation order shall specify the time, day, place, and manner of transfer of the child for custody or visitation to limit the child's exposure to potential domestic conflict or violence and to ensure the safety of all family members. Where the court finds a party is staying in a place designated as a shelter for victims of domestic violence or other confidential location, the court's order for time, day, place, and manner of transfer of the child for custody or visitation shall be designed to prevent disclosure of the location of the shelter or other confidential location.

(c) When making an order for custody or visitation in a case in which domestic violence is alleged and an emergency protective order, protective order, or other restraining order has been issued, the court shall consider whether the best interest of the child, based upon the circumstances of the case, requires that any custody or visitation arrangement shall be limited to situations in which a third person, specified by the court, is present, or whether custody or visitation shall be suspended or denied.
(Stats. 1993 (A.B. 1500), ch. 219, §116.30. Amended Stats. 1994 (A.B. 356), ch. 320, §1.)

§3044. Rebuttable presumption that award of custody to abuser is detrimental

(a) Upon a finding by the court that a party seeking custody of a child has perpetrated domestic violence against the other party seeking custody of the child or against the child or the child's siblings within the previous five years, there is a rebuttable presumption that an award of sole or joint physical or legal custody of a child to a person who has perpetrated domestic violence is detrimental to the best interest of the child, pursuant to Section 3011. This presumption may only be rebutted by a preponderance of the evidence.

(b) In determining whether the presumption set forth in subdivision (a) has been overcome, the court shall consider all of the following factors:

(1) Whether the perpetrator of domestic violence has demonstrated that giving sole or joint physical or legal custody of a child to the perpetrator is in the best interest of the child. In determining the best interest of the child, the preference for frequent and continuing contact with both parents, as set forth in subdivision (b) of Section 3020, or with the noncustodial parent, as set forth in paragraph (1) of subdivision (a) of Section 3040, may not be used to rebut the presumption, in whole or in part.

(2) Whether the perpetrator has successfully completed a batterer's treatment program that meets the criteria outlined in subdivision (c) of Section 1203.097 of the Penal Code.

(3) Whether the perpetrator has successfully completed a program of alcohol or drug abuse counseling if the court determines that counseling is appropriate.

(4) Whether the perpetrator has successfully completed a parenting class if the court determines the class to be appropriate.

(5) Whether the perpetrator is on probation or parole, and whether he or she has complied with the terms and conditions of probation or parole.

(6) Whether the perpetrator is restrained by a protective order or restraining order, and whether he or she has complied with its terms and conditions.

(7) Whether the perpetrator of domestic violence has committed any further acts of domestic violence.

(c) For purposes of this section, a person has "perpetrated domestic violence" when he or she is found by the court to have intentionally or recklessly caused or attempted to cause bodily injury, or sexual assault, or to have placed a person in reasonable apprehension of imminent serious bodily injury to that person or to another, or to have engaged in any behavior involving, but not limited to, threatening, striking, harassing, destroying personal property or disturbing the peace of another, for which a court may issue an ex parte order pursuant to Section 6320 to protect the other party seeking custody of the child or to protect the child and the child's siblings.

(d) (1) For purposes of this section, the requirement of a finding by the court shall be satisfied by, among other things, and not limited to, evidence that a party seeking custody has been convicted within the previous five years, after a trial or a plea of guilty or no contest, of any crime against the other party that comes within the definition of domestic violence contained in Section 6211 and of abuse contained in Section 6203, including, but not limited to, a crime described in subdivision (e) of Section 243 of, or Section 261, 262, 273.5, 422, or 646.9 of, the Penal Code.

(2) The requirement of a finding by the court shall also be satisfied if any court, whether that court hears or has heard the child custody proceedings or not, has made a finding pursuant to subdivision (a) based on conduct occurring within the previous five years.

(e) When a court makes a finding that a party has perpetrated domestic violence, the court may not base its findings solely on conclusions reached by a child custody evaluator or on the recommendation of the Family Court Services staff, but shall consider any relevant, admissible evidence submitted by the parties.

(f) In any custody or restraining order proceeding in which a party has alleged that the other party has perpetrated domestic violence in accordance with the terms of this section, the court shall inform the parties of the existence of this section and shall give them a copy of this section prior to any custody mediation in the case.

(Stats. 1999 (A.B. 840), ch. 445, §1. Amended by Stats. 2003 (S.B. 265), ch. 243, §1.)

§3046. Court shall not consider absence from family residence as factor if due to threat of violence

(a) If a party is absent or relocates from the family residence, the court shall not consider the absence or relocation as a factor in determining custody or visitation in either of the following circumstances:

(1) The absence or relocation is of short duration and the court finds that, during the period of absence or relocation, the party has demonstrated an interest in maintaining custody or visitation, the party maintains, or makes reasonable efforts to maintain, regular contact with the child, and the party's behavior demonstrates no intent to abandon the child.

(2) The party is absent or relocates because of an act or acts of actual or threatened domestic or family violence by the other party.

(b) The court may consider attempts by one party to interfere with the other party's regular contact with the child in determining if the party has satisfied the requirements of subdivision (a).

(c) This section does not apply to the following:

(1) A party against whom a protective or restraining order has been issued excluding the party from the dwelling of the other party or the child, or otherwise enjoining the party from assault or harassment against the other party or the child, including, but not limited to, orders issued under Part 4 (commencing with Section 6300) of Division 10, orders preventing civil harassment or workplace violence issued pursuant to Section 527.6 or 527.8 of the Code of Civil Procedure, and criminal protective orders issued pursuant to Section 136.2 of the Penal Code.

(2) A party who abandons a child as provided in Section 7822.

(Stats. 1999 (A.B. 1671), ch. 980, §7.)

§3064. Court shall not make ex parte custody order absent showing of immediate harm

The court shall refrain from making an order granting or modifying a custody order on an ex parte basis unless there has been a showing of immediate harm to the child or immediate risk that the child will be removed from the State of California. "Immediate harm to the child" includes having a parent who has committed acts of domestic violence, where the court determines that the acts of domestic violence are of recent origin or are a part of a demonstrated and continuing pattern of acts of domestic violence.

(Stats. 1992 (A.B. 2650), ch. 162, §10, effective January 1, 1994.)

§3113. Parties shall meet with investigator separately in cases of domestic violence

Where there has been a history of domestic violence between the parties, or where a protective order as defined in Section 6218 is in effect, at the request of the party alleging domestic violence in a written declaration under penalty of perjury or at the request of a party who is protected by the order, the parties shall meet with the court-appointed investigator separately and at separate times.

(Stats. 1993 (A.B. 1500), ch. 219, §116.81.)

§3118. Court shall require evaluation in custody cases involving allegations of sexual abuse

(a) In any contested proceeding involving child custody or visitation rights, where the court has appointed a child custody evaluator or has referred a case for a full or partial court-connected evaluation, investigation, or assessment, and the court determines that there is a serious allegation of child sexual abuse, the court shall require an evaluation, investigation, or assessment pursuant to this section. When the court has determined that there is a serious allegation of child sexual abuse, any child custody evaluation, investigation, or assessment conducted subsequent to that determination shall be considered by the court only if the evaluation, investigation, or assessment is conducted in accordance with the minimum requirements set forth in this section in determining custody or visitation rights, except as specified in paragraph (1). For purposes of this section, a serious allegation of child sexual abuse means an allegation of child sexual abuse, as defined in Section 11165.1 of the Penal Code, that is based in whole or in part on statements made by the child to law enforcement, a child welfare services agency investigator, any person required by statute to report suspected child abuse, or any other court-appointed personnel, or that is supported by substantial independent corroboration as provided for in subdivision (b) of Section 3011. When an allegation of child abuse arises in any other circumstances in any proceeding involving child custody or visitation rights, the court may require an evaluator or investigator to conduct an evaluation, investigation, or assessment pursuant to this section. The order appointing a child custody evaluator or investigator pursuant to this section shall provide that the evaluator or investigator have access to all juvenile court records pertaining to the child who is the subject of the evaluation, investigation, or assessment. The order shall also provide that any juvenile court records or information gained from those records remain confidential and shall only be released as specified in Section 3111.

(1) This section does not apply to any emergency court-ordered partial investigation that is conducted for the purpose of assisting the court in determining what immediate temporary orders may be necessary to protect and meet the immediate needs of a child. This section does apply when the emergency is resolved and the court is considering permanent child custody or visitation orders.

(2) This section does not prohibit a court from considering evidence relevant to determining the safety and protection needs of the child.

(3) Any evaluation, investigation, or assessment conducted pursuant to this section shall be conducted by an evaluator or investigator who meets the qualifications set forth in Section 3110.5.

(b) The evaluator or investigator shall, at a minimum, do all of the following:

(1) Consult with the agency providing child welfare services and law enforcement regarding the allegations of child sexual abuse, and obtain recommendations from these professionals regarding the child's safety and the child's need for protection.

(2) Review and summarize the child welfare services agency file. No document contained in the child welfare services agency filemay be photocopied, but a summary of the information in the file, including statements made by the children and the parents, and the recommendations made or anticipated to be made by the child welfare services agency to the juvenile court, may be recorded by the evaluator or investigator, except for the identity of the reporting party. The evaluator's or investigator's notes summarizing the child welfare services agency information shall be stored in a file separate from the evaluator's or investigator's file and may only be released to either party under order of the court.

(3) Obtain from a law enforcement investigator all available information obtained from criminal background checks of the parents and any suspected perpetrator that is not a parent, including information regarding child abuse, domestic violence, or substance abuse.

(4) Review the results of a multidisciplinary child interview team (hereafter MDIT) interview if available, or if not, or if the evaluator or investigator believes the MDIT interview is inadequate for purposes of the evaluation, investigation, or assessment, interview the child or request an MDIT interview, and shall wherever possible avoid repeated interviews of the child.

(5) Request a forensic medical examination of the child from the appropriate agency, or include in the report required by paragraph (6) a written statement explaining why the examination is not needed.

(6) File a confidential written report with the clerk of the court in which the custody hearing will be conducted and which shall be served on the parties or their attorneys at least 10 days prior to the hearing. This reportmay not be made available other than as provided in this subdivision. This report shall include, but is not limited to, the following:

(A) Documentation of material interviews, including any MDIT interview of the child or the evaluator or investigator, written documentation of interviews with both parents by the evaluator or investigator, and interviews with other witnesses who provided relevant information.

(B) A summary of any law enforcement investigator's investigation, including information obtained from the criminal background check of the parents and any suspected perpetrator that is not a parent, including information regarding child abuse, domestic violence, or substance abuse.

(C) Relevant background material, including, but not limited to, a summary of a written report from any therapist treating the child for suspected child sexual abuse, excluding any communication subject to Section 1014 of the Evidence Code, reports from other professionals, and the results of any forensic medical examination and any other medical examination or treatment that could help establish or disprove whether the child has been the victim of sexual abuse.

(D) The written recommendations of the evaluator or investigator regarding the therapeutic needs of the child and how to ensure the safety of the child.

(E) A summary of the following information: whether the child and his or her parents are or have been the subject of a child abuse investigation and the disposition of that investigation; the name, location, and telephone number of the children's services worker; the status of the investigation and the recommendations made or anticipated to be made regarding the child's safety; and any dependency court orders or findings that might have a bearing on the custody dispute.

(F) Any information regarding the presence of domestic violence or substance abuse in the family that has been obtained from a child protective agency in accordance with paragraphs (1) and (2), a law enforcement agency, medical personnel or records, prior or currently treating therapists, excluding any communication subject to Section 1014 of the Evidence Code, or from interviews conducted or reviewed for this evaluation, investigation, or assessment.

(G) Which, if any, family members are known to have been deemed eligible for assistance from the Victims of Crime Program due to child abuse or domestic violence.

(H) Any other information the evaluator or investigator believes would be helpful to the court in determining what is in the best interests of the child.

(c) If the evaluator or investigator obtains information as part of a family court mediation, that information shall be maintained in the family court file, which is not subject to subpoena by either party. If, however, the members of the family are the subject of an ongoing child welfare services investigation, or the evaluator or investigator has made a child welfare services referral, the evaluator or investigator shall so inform the family law judicial officer in writing and this information shall become part of the family law file. This subdivision may not be construed to authorize or require a mediator to disclose any information not otherwise authorized or required by law to be disclosed.

(d) In accordance with subdivision (d) of Section 11167 of the Penal Code, the evaluator or investigator may not disclose any information regarding the identity of any person making a report of suspected child abuse. Nothing in this section is intended to limit any disclosure of information by any agency that is otherwise required by law or court order.

(e) The evaluation, investigation, or assessment standards set forth in this section represent minimum requirements of evaluation and the court shall order further evaluation beyond these minimum requirements when necessary to determine the safety needs of the child.

(f) If the court orders an evaluation, investigation, or assessment pursuant to this section, the court shall consider whether the bestinterests of the child require that a temporary order be issued that limits visitation with the parent against whom the allegations have been made to situations in which a third person specified by the court is present or whether visitation will be suspended or denied in accordance with Section 3011.

(g) An evaluation, investigation, or assessment pursuant to this section shall be suspended if a petition is filed to declare the child a dependent child of the juvenile court pursuant to Section 300 of the Welfare and Institutions Code, and all information gathered by the evaluator or investigator shall be made available to the juvenile court.

(h) This section may not be construed to authorize a court to issue any orders in a proceeding pursuant to this division regarding custody or visitation with respect to a minor child who is the subject of a dependency hearing in juvenile court or to otherwise supersede Section 302 of the Welfare and Institutions Code.

(Stats. 2000 (S.B. 1716), ch. 926, §6.)

§3192. Court may order parties to participate in separate counseling in cases of domestic violence

In a proceeding in which counseling is ordered pursuant to this chapter, where there has been a history of abuse by either parent against the child or by one parent against the other parent and a protective order as defined in Section 6218 is in effect, the court may order the parties to participate in counseling separately and at separate times. Each party shall bear the cost of his or her own counseling separately, unless good cause is shown for a different apportionment. The costs associated with a minor child participating in counseling shall be apportioned in accordance with Section 4062.

(Stats. 1992 (A.B. 2650), ch. 162, §10, effective January 1, 1994. Amended Stats. 1993 (A.B. 1500), ch. 219, §116.92; Stats. 1994 (A.B. 2208), ch. 1269, §31.)

---

4. Joint Custody

"Joint custody," as defined in California Family Code §3002, means joint physical (residential) custody and joint legal custody. "Joint legal custody" (Cal. Fam. Code §3003) means that both parents share decisionmaking authority regarding the child's health, education and welfare. Courts may award joint legal custody without awarding joint physical custody. That is, in an award of joint legal custody, both parents share responsibility for major childrearing decisions. In such an award, both parents may share physical custody or only one parent may be the actual physical custodian. Thus, joint custody is distinguishable from the traditional award of sole custody which gave one parent (normally the mother) both legal control and physical custody while the other parent (normally the father) had visitation rights.

Joint custody is based on the belief that the child benefits from frequent and continuing contact with both parents. A nascent fathers' rights movement spearheaded the passage of joint custody legislation in the 1970's. See Herbert Jacob, The Silent Revolution: The Transformation of Divorce Law in the United States 136-143 (1988). Currently, all states permit some form of joint custody. States adopt different approaches to joint custody. Some create a presumption of joint custody; others create a preference for joint custody; and still others make it a factor in the best interests determination.

California was one of the first states to recognize joint custody in 1980 (Cal. Fam. Code §3080, formerly Cal. Civ. Code §4600.5(a)). The recognition of joint custody was based on the public policy consideration that children should have "frequent and continuing contact with both parents after the parents have separated or dissolved their marriage" (Cal. Fam. Code §3020(b).

California Family Code §3040 prescribes an order of preference in awarding custody. Although the California statute places joint custody first in the order of priority (Cal. Fam. Code §3040(a)), a subsequent provision of the same statute (Cal. Fam. Code §3040(b)) makes it clear that the statute creates neither a preference nor a presumption for or against joint legal custody, joint physical custody, or sole custody.

However, if both parents *agree* to joint custody, California Family Code §3080 expressly specifies that there shall be a presumption affecting the burden of proof that joint custody is in the best interests of a minor, subject to consideration of the relevant factors that enter into the best interests determination pursuant to California Family Code §3011. Even if the parents do not agree, a court has discretion to order joint custody subject to the best interests of the child (Cal. Fam. Code §3081).

When awarding joint (or sole) custody, the court *may* require the parents to submit a "parenting plan" (Cal. Fam. Code §3040(a)(1)) to implement the custody order. In this plan, parents specify caretaking and decisionmaking authority for their children and the manner in which future disputes are to be resolved.

In 2005, the California legislation considered A.B. 1307 calling for a presumption in favor of joint custody. In May 3, 2005, the bill was defeated in the Assembly Judiciary Committee. The bill was opposed by women's groups who argued that a presumption for joint custody is particularly harmful in cases of domestic violence.

§3011. Court shall consider certain factors in determining best interests of child

In making a determination of the best interest of the child in a proceeding described in Section 3021, the court shall, among any other factors it finds relevant, consider all of the following:

(a) The health, safety, and welfare of the child.

(b) Any history of abuse by one parent or any other person seeking custody against any of the following:

(1) Any child to whom he or she is related by blood or affinity or with whom he or she has had a caretaking relationship, no matter how temporary.

(2) The other parent.

(3) A parent, current spouse, or cohabitant, of the parent or person seeking custody, or a person with whom the parent or person seeking custody has a dating or engagement relationship.

As a prerequisite to the consideration of allegations of abuse, the court may require substantial independent corroboration, including, but not limited to, written reports by law enforcement agencies, child protective services or other social welfare agencies, courts, medical facilities, or other public agencies or private nonprofit organizations providing services to victims of sexual assault or domestic violence. As used in this subdivision, "abuse against a child" means "child abuse" as defined in Section 11165.6 of the Penal Code and abuse against any of the other persons described in paragraph (2) or (3) means "abuse" as defined in Section 6203 of this code.

(c) The nature and amount of contact with both parents, except as provided in Section 3046.

(d) The habitual or continual illegal use of controlled substances or habitual or continual abuse of alcohol by either parent. Before considering these allegations, the court may first require independent corroboration, including, but not limited to, written reports from law enforcement agencies, courts, probation departments, social welfare agencies, medical facilities, rehabilitation facilities, or other public agencies or nonprofit organizations providing drug and alcohol abuse services. As used in this subdivision, "controlled substances" has the same meaning as defined in the California Uniform Controlled Substances Act, Division 10 (commencing with Section 11000) of the Health and Safety Code.

(e)(1) Where allegations about a parent pursuant to subdivision (b) or (d) have been brought to the attention of the court in the current proceeding, and the court makes an order for sole or joint custody to that parent, the court shall state its reasons in writing or on the record. In these circumstances, the court shall ensure that any order regarding custody or visitation is specific as to time, day, place, and manner of transfer of the child as set forth in subdivision (b) of Section 6323.

(2) The provisions of this subdivision shall not apply if the parties stipulate in writing or on the record regarding custody or visitation.

(Stats. 1993 (A.B. 1500), ch. 219, §115.5. Amended Stats. 1996 (A.B. 2474), ch. 835, §1 (S.B. 384), ch. 836, §1.5; Stats. 1997 (A.B. 200), ch. 849, §2; Stats. 1999 (A.B. 1671), ch. 980, §4.)

§3020. Legislative findings: joint custody

(a) The Legislature finds and declares that it is the public policy of this state to assure that the health, safety, and welfare of children shall be the court's primary concern in determining the best interest of children when making any orders regarding the physical or legal custody or visitation of children. The Legislature further finds and declares that the perpetration of child abuse or domestic violence in a household where a child resides is detrimental to the child.

(b) The Legislature finds and declares that it is the public policy of this state to assure that children have frequent and continuing contact with both parents after the parents have separated or dissolved their marriage, or ended their relationship, and to encourage parents to share the rights and responsibilities of child rearing in order to effect this policy, except where the contact would not be in the best interest of the child, as provided in Section 3011.

(c) Where the policies set forth in subdivisions (a) and (b) of this section are in conflict, any court's order regarding physical or legal custody or visitation shall be made in a manner that ensures the health, safety, and welfare of the child and the safety of all family members.

(Stats. 1992 (A.B. 2650), ch. 162, §10, effective January 1, 1994. Amended Stats. 1993 (A.B. 1500), ch. 219, §116; Stats. 1997 (A.B. 200), ch. 849, §3; Stats. 1999 (A.B. 1671), ch. 980, §5.)

§3040. Custody preferences; court has widest discretion

(a) Custody should be granted in the following order of preference according to the best interest of the child as provided in Sections 3011 and 3020:

(1) To both parents jointly pursuant to Chapter 4 (commencing with Section 3080) or to either parent. In making an order granting custody to either parent, the court shall consider, among other factors, which parent is more likely to allow the child frequent and continuing contact with the noncustodial parent, consistent with Section 3011 and 3020, and shall not prefer a parent as custodian because of that parent's sex. The court, in its discretion, may require the parents to submit to the court a plan for the implementation of the custody order.

(2) If to neither parent, to the person or persons in whose home the child has been living in a wholesome and stable environment.

(3) To any other person or persons deemed by the court to be suitable and able to provide adequate and proper care and guidance for the child.

(b) This section establishes neither a preference nor a presumption for or against joint legal custody, joint physical custody, or sole custody, but allows the court and the family the widest discretion to choose a parenting plan that is in the best interest of the child.

(Stats. 1993 (A.B. 1500), ch. 219, §116.50. Amended by Stats. 1997 (A.B. 200), ch. 849, §4.)

§3080. Presumption for joint custody if parents agree

There is a presumption, affecting the burden of proof, that joint custody is in the best interest of a minor child, subject to Section 3011, where the parents have agreed to joint custody or so agree in open court at a hearing for the purpose of determining the custody of the minor child.

(Stats. 1992 (A.B. 2650), ch. 162, §10, effective January 1, 1994. Amended by Stats. 1993 (A.B. 1500) ch. 219, §116.70.)

§3081. Court may grant joint custody absent parental agreement

On application of either parent, joint custody may be ordered in the discretion of the court in cases other than those described in Section 3080, subject to Section 3011. For the purpose of assisting the court in making a determination whether joint custody is appropriate under this section, the court may direct that an investigation be conducted pursuant to Chapter 6 (commencing with Section 3110).

(Stats. 1992 (A.B. 2650), ch. 162, §10, effective January 1, 1994. Amended by Stats. 1993 (A.B. 1500), ch. 219, §116.71.)

§3082. Court shall state reasons for grant or denial of joint custody request

When a request for joint custody is granted or denied, the court, upon the request of any party, shall state in its decision the reasons for granting or denying the request. A statement that joint physical custody is, or is not, in the best interest of the child is not sufficient to satisfy the requirements of this section.

(Stats. 1992 (A.B. 2650), ch. 162, §10, effective January 1, 1994.)

§3083. Court shall specify situations requiring mutual consent and consequences of failure to obtain it

In making an order of joint legal custody, the court shall specify the circumstances under which the consent of both parents is required to be obtained in order to exercise legal control of the child and the consequences of the failure to obtain mutual consent. In all other circumstances, either parent acting alone may exercise legal control of the child. An order of joint legal custody shall not be construed to permit an action that is inconsistent with the physical custody order unless the action is expressly authorized by the court.

(Stats. 1992 (A.B. 2650), ch. 162, §10, effective January 1, 1994.)

§3084. Court shall specify parent's rights to facilitate enforcement of laws on child abduction

In making an order of joint physical custody, the court shall specify the rights of each parent to physical control of the child in sufficient detail to enable a parent deprived of that control to implement laws for relief of child snatching and kidnapping.

(Stats. 1992 (A.B. 2650), ch. 162, §10, effective January 1, 1994.)

§3085. Court may grant joint legal custody without joint physical custody

In making an order for custody with respect to both parents, the court may grant joint legal custody without granting joint physical custody.

(Stats. 1992 (A.B. 2650), ch. 162, §10, effective January 1, 1994. Amended by Stats. 1993 (A.B. 1500), ch. 219, §116.72.)

§3086. Court may designate one parent as primary caretaker of child for public assistance purposes

In making an order of joint physical custody or joint legal custody, the court may specify one parent as the primary caretaker of the child and one home as the primary home of the child, for the purposes of determining eligibility for public assistance.

(Stats. 1992 (A.B. 2650), ch. 162, §10, effective January 1, 1994.)

C. VISITATION

Traditionally, an award of sole custody to one parent was accompanied by an award of visitation rights to the other parent. Some modern custody awards continue to mirror this traditional arrangement. An increasing number of jurisdictions now permit nonparents to petition for visitation rights. See §C5 *infra*.

1. Generally

§3100. Visitation rights generally

(a) In making an order [granting custody of a minor] pursuant to Chapter 4 (commencing with Section 3080), the court shall grant reasonable visitation rights to a parent unless it is shown that the visitation would be detrimental to the best interest of the child. In the discretion of the court, reasonable visitation rights may be granted to any other person having an interest in the welfare of the child.

. . .

(Stats. 1992 (A.B. 2650), ch. 162, §10, effective January 1, 1994. Amended by Stats. 1993 (A.B. 1500), ch. 219, §116.74; Stats. 1994 (A.B. 356) ch. 320, §2; Stats. 2005 (A.B.118), ch. 465, §1.)

2. Denial of Visitation

Courts deny visitation reluctantly because of concerns about constitutional protection of the parent-child relationship (Meyer v. Nebraska, 262 U.S. 390 (1923); Pierce v. Soc'y of Sisters, 268 U.S. 510 (1925)). However, some courts make exceptions to this general policy in cases of severe physical abuse or sexual abuse. For example, visitation will be denied when a party seeking visitation rights is a registered sex offender whose victim was a minor; a person convicted of endangering, injuring, or molesting a child; a parent convicted of rape with respect to the child's conception, or guilty of first degree murder of the child's parent. (See Cal. Fam. Code §3030 in §B3 *supra*.) Case law also supports denial of visitation to a parent who sexually abused a child (Cheeseman v. Cheeseman, 278 P. 242 (Cal. 1929)).

Generally, however, courts prefer supervised visitation to complete denials. The California legislature encouraged the development of standards for supervised visitation centers. California Family Code §3200 (omitted) authorizes the Judicial Council to develop and present to the legislature standards for supervised visitation providers.

§3100. Visitation rights generally: supervised, suspended or denied

. . .

(b) If a protective order, as defined in Section 6218, has been directed to a parent, the court shall consider whether the best interest of the child requires that any visitation by that parent shall be limited to situations in which a third person, specified by the court, is present, or whether visitation shall be suspended or denied. The court shall include in its deliberations a consideration of the nature of the acts from which the parent was enjoined and the period of time that has elapsed since that order. A parent may submit to the court the name of a person that the parent deems suitable to be present during visitation. . . .

(Stats. 1992 (A.B. 2650), ch. 162, §10, effective January 1, 1994. Amended by Stats. 1993 (A.B. 1500), ch. 219, §116.74; Stats. 1994 (A.B. 356), ch. 320, §2; Stats. 2005 (A.B.118), ch. 465, §1.)

3. Conditions on Visitation

Based on courts' wide discretion in fashioning visitation orders, courts may specify the time, place and circumstances of visitation, including placing conditions on visitation by the noncustodial parent. Procedurally, if a parent requests the court to order restrictions on visitation, that parent bears the burden of proof on the need for that restriction.

A court may not place conditions on visitation rights that would infringe a parent's constitutional rights. For example, a court may not place restrictions on visitation (e.g., overnight visitation in the presence of another homosexual) that are premised on a parent's sexual preferences (In re Marriage of Birdsall, 243 Cal. Rptr. 287 (Cal. 1988)). Similarly, a court cannot order a parent to refrain from engaging the child in religious activities or religious discussions during visitation (In re Marriage of Mentry, 190 Cal. Rptr. 843 (Ct. App. 1983)).

In cases of domestic violence, courts are encouraged not to make custody or visitation orders that are "inconsistent" with restraining orders (Cal. Fam. Code §3031(a)). If custody or visitation is granted to a parent in a domestic violence case, the order must specify "the time, day, place and manner of transfer" of the child in order to limit the child's exposure to violence and to ensure the safety of all family members (Cal. Fam. Code §3031(b)). On the role of domestic violence in custody decisionmaking, see also §B3 *supra*.

A recent statutory amendment (Cal. Fam. Code §3041.5). authorizes drug and alcohol testing for a parent who is seeking custody or visitation if the court finds, by a preponderance of the evidence, that the parent uses illegal drugs or alcohol habitually or continually.

§3027.5. Visitation and custody implications of parent's actions regarding suspicion of sexual abuse

(a) No parent shall be placed on supervised visitation, or be denied custody of or visitation with his or her child, and no custody or visitation rights shall be limited, solely because the parent (1) lawfully reported suspected sexual abuse of the child, (2) otherwise acted lawfully, based on a reasonable belief, to determine if his or her child was the victim of sexual abuse, or (3) sought treatment for the child from a licensed mental health professional for suspected sexual abuse.

(b) The court may order supervised visitation or limit a parent's custody or visitation if the court finds substantial evidence that the parent, with the intent to interfere with the other parent's lawful contact with the child, made a report of child sexual abuse, during a child custody proceeding or at any other time, that he or she knew was false at the time it was made. Any limitation of custody or visitation, including an order for supervised visitation, pursuant to this subdivision, or any statute regarding the making of a false child abuse report, shall be imposed only after the court has determined that the limitation is necessary to protect the health, safety, and welfare of the child, and the court has considered the state's policy of assuring that children have frequent and continuing contact with both parents as declared in subdivision (b) of Section 3020.

(Stats. 1999 (S.B. 792), ch. 985, §1.)

§3041.5. Substance abuse testing for persons seeking child custody or visitation

(a) In any custody or visitation proceeding bought under this part, as described in Section 3021, or any guardianship proceeding brought under the Probate Code, the court may order any person who is seeking custody of, or visitation with, a child who is the subject of the proceeding to undergo testing for the illegal use of controlled substances and the use of alcohol if there is a judicial determination based upon a preponderance of evidence that there is the habitual, frequent, or continual illegal use of controlled substances or the habitual or continual abuse of alcohol by the parent, legal custodian, parent seeking guardianship, or person seeking visitation in a guardianship. This evidence may include, but may not be limited to, a conviction within the last five years for the illegal use or possession of a controlled substance. . . . The parent, legal custody, person seeking guardianship, or person seeking visitation in a guardianship who has undergone drug testing shall have the right to a hearing, if requested, to challenge a positive test result. A positive test result, even if challenged and upheld, shall not, by itself, constitute grounds for an adverse custody or guardianship decision.. . . . The results of this testing shall be confidential, shall be maintained as a sealed record in the court file, and may not be released to any person except the court, the parties, their attorneys, the Judicial Council (until completion of its authorized study of the testing process) and any person to whom the court expressly grants access bywritten order made with prior notice to all parties. . . .

(b)This section shall remain in effect only until January 1, 2008, and as of that date is repealed, unless a later enacted statute, that is enacted before January 1,2008, deletes or extends that date.

(Stats. 2004, ch. 19 (A.B. 1108),, §1, effective February 23, 2004. Amended by Stats. 2005, ch. 302 (A.B. 541), §1.)

§3100. Visitation rights generally: conditions in cases of domestic violence

. . .

(c) If visitation is ordered in a case in which domestic violence is alleged and an emergency protective order, protective order, or other restraining order has been issued, the visitation order shall specify the time, day, place, and manner of transfer of the child, so as to limit the child's exposure to potential domestic conflict or violence and to ensure the safety of all family members. If a criminal protective order has been issued pursuant to Section 136.2 of the Penal Code, the visitation order shall make reference to, and acknowledge the precedence of enforcement of, any appropriate criminal protective order.

(d) If the court finds a party is staying in a place designated as a shelter for victims of domestic violence or other confidential location, the court's order for time, day, place, and manner of transfer of the child for visitation shall be designed to prevent disclosure of the location of the shelter or other confidential location.

(Stats. 1992 (A.B. 2650), ch. 162, §10, effective January 1, 1994. Amended by Stats. 1993 (A.B. 1500), ch. 219, §116.74; Stats. 1994 (A.B. 356), ch. 320, §2; Stats. 2005 (A.B.118), ch. 465, §1.)

4. Relationship Between Visitation and Child Support

According to the general rule, visitation normally will not be conditioned on payment of child support. Nor may support be withheld because an ex-spouse interferes with visitation. See Camacho v. Camacho, 218 Cal. Rptr. 810 (Ct. App. 1985) (court cannot condition visitation on the noncustodial parent's timely payment of child support). See also Chapter VIII, §A5 *supra*.

§3556. Child support duty unaffected by failure or refusal to implement custody or visitation rights

The existence or enforcement of a duty of support owed by a noncustodial parent for the support of a minor child is not affected by a failure or refusal by the custodial parent to implement any rights as to custody or visitation granted by a court to the noncustodial parent.

(Stats 1992 (A.B. 2650), ch. 162, §10, effective January 1, 1994.)

5. Nonparental Visitation Rights

Courts have discretion to grant visitation rights to nonparents who have an interest in the child's welfare. Courts may award visitation rights to a stepparent (Cal. Fam. Code §3101(a)); grandparent (Cal. Fam. Code § 3103(a)); or to children, siblings, parents, or grandparents of a deceased parent (Cal. Fam. Code §3102).

The United States Supreme Court examined the issue of grandparents' visitation rights. Troxel v. Granville, 530 U.S. 57 (2000), held that a broad third-party visitation statute was unconstitutional, as applied, on due process grounds.

California's statutory scheme differs from the statute at issue in *Troxel* in several ways: (1) it is not as broad (i.e., it does not permit "any person" to petition for visitation rights "at any time" and that the petition will be granted if an award is in the child's best interests, see Wash. Rev. Code §26.10.160 (3) (2005)), and also (2) the California statute creates a rebuttable presumption that grandparent visitation is contrary to the best interests of the child when both parents agree (Cal. Fam. Code §§3103(d), 3104(e)).

In the wake of *Troxel*, California courts examined third-party visitation in several situations. See Herbst v. Swan, 125 Cal. Rptr. 2d 836 (Ct. App. 2002) (holding that statute was unconstitutional as applied to authorize visitation by a half-sibling when one of the child's parents was deceased because it infringed on mother's liberty to select those with whom child should associate); Zasueta v. Zasueta, 126 Cal. Rptr. 2d 245 (Ct. App. 2002) (holding that application of visitation statute without due deference to fit mother's decision not to allow visitation with grandparents violated mother's fundamental parenting rights); Punsly v. Ho, 105 Cal. Rptr. 2d 139 (Ct. App. 2001)(holding that statute authorizing visitation for certain relatives of a deceased person if it was in child's best interest, as applied, unconstitutionally infringed on mother's fundamental rights.

More recently, the California Supreme Court examined the issue in In re Marriage of Harris, 96 P.3d 141 (Cal. 2004) . Following a divorce, a mother was awarded sole legal and physical custody of the couple's infant daughter while the father was awarded supervised visitation pending his completion of various therapeutic programs (drug testing, substance abuse, and psychotherapy). The paternal grandparents also were awarded visitation.When the child was five years old and living with her mother and adoptive father in Utah, the father joined with the paternal grandparents to petition for increased visitation. The mother subsequently challenged the trial court order expanding the visitation because it would have necessitated the child's flying, unaccompanied, from Utah.

The California Supreme Court held that the statute (Cal. Fam. Code §3104) was constitutional on its face and as applied, and that no judicial precedent holds that an order of grandparent visitation supported by one of the parents violates the other parent's parental rights. However, because the mother had been granted sole custody and objected to the grandparent visitation, the state supreme court ruled that the trial court should have applied the rebuttable presumption in California Family Code §3104(f) that grandparent visitation was not in the child's best interest. The court remanded the case to permit the trial court to reconsider its order in light of this statutory presumption.

California law provides that a court may grant reasonable visitation to a grandparent if the court finds that there is a preexisting grandparent-child relationship that "engendered a bond such that visitation is in the best interest of the child" and also balances the child's interest in visitation with the grandparent against the parents' right to exercise their authority (Cal. Fam. Code §3104(a)(1), (2)). In addition, a grandparent has no standing to petition for visitation as against married natural or adoptive parents unless one or more of the following occurs: (1) the parents are separated, (2) one parent has departed for more than one month without informing the other parent of his or her whereabouts, or (3) the child is not residing with either parent (*id.* at §3104(b)(1), (2), (4)). Alternatively, a grandparent will have standing if one of the parents joins in the grandparent's petition (*id.* at §3104(b)(3)). Finally, there is a rebuttable presumption that visitation is not in the child's best interests if: (a) the parents (natural or adoptive) do not wish to permit visitation or b) a parent who has sole custody objects (*id.* at §3104(e), (f)).

For *custody* rights of non-biological parents (including discussion of the rights of same-sex parents), see §D *infra*.

See generally Joan Catherine Bohl, That Thorny Issue Redux: California Grandparent Visitation Law in the Wake of Troxel v. Granville, 36 Golden Gate U. L. Rev. 121 (2006).

§3101. Court may grant reasonable visitation to a stepparent

(a) Notwithstanding any other provision of law, the court may grant reasonable visitation to a stepparent, if visitation by the stepparent is determined to be in the best interest of the minor child.

(b) If a protective order, as defined in Section 6218, has been directed to a stepparent to whom visitation may be granted pursuant to this section, the court shall consider whether the best interest of the child requires that any visitation by the stepparent be denied.

(c) Visitation rights may not be ordered under this section that would conflict with a right of custody or visitation of a birth parent who is not a party to the proceeding.

(d) As used in this section:

(1) "Birth parent" means "birth parent" as defined in Section 8512.

(2) "Stepparent" means a person who is a party to the marriage that is the subject of the proceeding, with respect to a minor child of the other party to the marriage.

(Stats. 1993 (A.B. 1500) ch. 219, §116.76.)

§3102. Visitation rights of close relatives if parent is deceased

(a) If either parent of an unemancipated minor child is deceased, the children, siblings, parents, and grandparents of the deceased parent may be granted reasonable visitation with the child during the child's minority upon a finding that the visitation would be in the best interest of the minor child.

(b) In granting visitation pursuant to this section to a person other than a grandparent of the child, the court shall consider the amount of personal contact between the person and the child before the application for the visitation order.

(c) This section does not apply if the child has been adopted by a person other than a stepparent or grandparent of the child. Any visitation rights granted pursuant to this section before the adoption of the child automatically terminate if the child is adopted by a person other than a stepparent or grandparent of the child.

(Stats. 1992 (A.B. 2650), ch. 162, §10, effective January 1, 1994. Amended by Stats. 1993 (A.B. 1500), ch. 219, §116.77; Stats. 1994 (A.B. 3042), ch. 164, §1.)

§3103. Court may grant reasonable visitation to a grandparent

(a) Notwithstanding any other provision of law, in a proceeding described in Section 3021 [set forth in §A3 *supra*], the court may grant reasonable visitation to a grandparent of a minor child of a party to the proceeding if the court determines that visitation by the grandparent is in the best interest of the child.

(b) If a protective order as defined in Section 6218 [set forth in Chapter III §G1 *supra*] has been directed to the grandparent during the pendency of the proceeding, the court shall consider whether the best interest of the child requires that visitation by the grandparent be denied.

(c) The petitioner shall give notice of the petition to each of the parents of the child, any stepparent, and any person who has physical custody of the child, by certified mail, return receipt requested, postage prepaid, to the person's last known address, or to the attorneys of record of the parties to the proceeding.

(d) There is a rebuttable presumption affecting the burden of proof that the visitation of a grandparent is not in the best interest of a minor child if the child's parents agree that the grandparent should not be granted visitation rights.

(e) Visitation rights may not be ordered under this section if that would conflict with a right of custody or visitation of a birth parent who is not a party to the proceeding.

(f) Visitation ordered pursuant to this section shall not create a basis for or against a change of residence of the child, but shall be one of the factors for the court to consider in ordering a change of residence.

(g) When a court orders grandparental visitation pursuant to this section, the court in its discretion may, based upon the relevant circumstances of the case:

(1) Allocate the percentage of grandparental visitation between the parents for purposes of the calculation of child support pursuant to the statewide uniform guideline (Article 2 (commencing with Section 4050) of Chapter 2 of Part 2 of Division 9).

(2) Notwithstanding Sections 3930 [no duty to support grandchild, set forth in Chapter VIII §B6 *supra*] and 3951 [no duty to relative absent agreement, set forth in Chapter VIII §B6 *supra*], order a parent or grandparent to pay to the other, an amount for the support of the child or grandchild. For purposes of this paragraph, "support" means costs related to visitation such as any of the following:

(A) Transportation.

(B) Provision of basic expenses for the child or grandchild, such as medical expenses, day care costs, and other necessities.

(h) As used in this section, "birth parent" means "birth parent" as defined in Section 8512.

(Stats. 1993 (A.B. 1500), ch. 219, §116.78. Amended by Stats. 1993 (S.B. 306), ch. 832, §1.)

§3104. Necessary findings for grant of visitation to grandparent

(a) On petition to the court by a grandparent of a minor child, the court may grant reasonable visitation rights to the grandparent if the court does both of the following:

(1) Finds that there is a preexisting relationship between the grandparent and the grandchild that has engendered a bond such that visitation is in the best interest of the child.

(2) Balances the interest of the child in having visitation with the grandparent against the right of the parents to exercise their parental authority.

(b) A petition for visitation under this section may not be filed while the natural or adoptive parents are married, unless one or more of the following circumstances exist:

(1) The parents are currently living separately and apart on a permanent or indefinite basis.

(2) One of the parents has been absent for more than one month without the other spouse knowing the whereabouts of the absent spouse.

(3) One of the parents joins in the petition with the grandparents.

(4) The child is not residing with either parent.

At any time that a change of circumstances occurs such that none of these circumstances exist, the parent or parents may move the court to terminate grandparental visitation and the court shall grant the termination.

(c) The petitioner shall give notice of the petition to each of the parents of the child, any stepparent, and any person who has physical custody of the child, by personal service pursuant to Section 415.10 of the Code of Civil Procedure.

(d) If a protective order as defined in Section 6218 has been directed to the grandparent during the pendency of the proceeding, the court shall consider whether the best interest of the child requires that any visitation by that grandparent should be denied.

(e) There is a rebuttable presumption that the visitation of a grandparent is not in the best interest of a minor child if the natural or adoptive parents agree that the grandparent should not be granted visitation rights.

(f) There is a rebuttable presumption affecting the burden of proof that the visitation of a grandparent is not in the best interest of a minor child if the parent who has been awarded sole legal and physical custody of the child in another proceeding or with whom the child resides if there is currently no operative custody order objects to visitation by the grandparent.

(g) Visitation rights may not be ordered under this section if that would conflict with a right of custody or visitation of a birth parent who is not a party to the proceeding.

(h) Visitation ordered pursuant to this section shall not create a basis for or against a change of residence of the child, but shall be one of the factors for the court to consider in ordering a change of residence.

(i) When a court orders grandparental visitation pursuant to this section, the court in its discretion may, based upon the relevant circumstances of the case:

(1) Allocate the percentage of grandparental visitation between the parents for purposes of the calculation of child support pursuant to the statewide uniform guideline (Article 2 (commencing with Section 4050) of Chapter 2 of Part 2 of Division 9).

(2) Notwithstanding Sections 3930 and 3951, order a parent or grandparent to pay to the other, an amount for the support of the child or grandchild. For purposes of this paragraph, "support" means costs related to visitation such as any of the following:

(A) Transportation.

(B) Provision of basic expenses for the child or grandchild, such as medical expenses, day care costs, and other necessities.

(j) As used in this section, "birth parent" means "birth parent" as defined in Section 8512.

(Stats. 1993 (S.B. 306), ch. 832, §2.)

§8512. "Birth parent" defined

"Birth parent" means the biological parent or, in the case of a person previously adopted, the adoptive parent.

(Stats.1992, ch. 162 (A.B. 2650), §10, effective January 1, 1994.)

---

6. Interference with Custody or Visitation Rights

Some states recognize (either by case law or statute) a tort action for custodial interference. Criminal liability for custodial interference also exists in some jurisdictions. See, e.g., N.Y. Penal Law §135.45 (2000). See generally Ann M. Haralambie, Handling Child Custody, Abuse and Adoption Cases §19.18 (1993 & Supp.) (discussing liability). Recognition of such a tort is highly controversial. See, e.g., Zaharias v. Gammill, 844 P.2d 137, 139-140 (Okla. 1992) (noting the policy concerns implicating in recognizing a tort of custodial interference).

California provides that a parent who is the victim of custodial interference may be awarded financial compensation, i.e., "reasonable expenses" to compensate for the other parent's failure to assume caretaking or for interfering with the parent's visitation rights (Cal. Fam. Code §3028(b)).

§3028. Court may order compensation for custodial interference

(a) The court may order financial compensation for periods when a parent fails to assume the caretaker responsibility or when a parent has been thwarted by the other parent when attempting to exercise custody or visitation rights contemplated by a custody or visitation order, including, but not limited to, an order for joint physical custody, or by a written or oral agreement between the parents.

(b) The compensation shall be limited to (1) the reasonable expenses incurred for or on behalf of a child, resulting from the other parent's failure to assume caretaker responsibility or (2) the reasonable expenses incurred by a parent for or on behalf of a child, resulting from the other parent's thwarting of the parent's efforts to exercise custody or visitation rights. The expenses may include the value of caretaker services but are not limited to the cost of services provided by a third party during the relevant period.

(c) The compensation may be requested by noticed motion or an order to show cause, which shall allege, under penalty of perjury, (1) a minimum of one hundred dollars ($100) of expenses incurred or (2) at least three occurrences of failure to exercise custody or visitation rights or (3) at least three occurrences of the thwarting of efforts to exercise custody or visitation rights within the six months before filing of the motion or order.

(d) Attorney's fees shall be awarded to the prevailing party upon a showing of the nonprevailing party's ability to pay as required by Section 270.

(Stats. 1992 (A.B. 2650), ch. 162, §10, effective January 1, 1994. Amended by Stats. 1993 (A.B. 1500), ch. 219, §116.18.)

D. CUSTODY RIGHTS OF THIRD PARTIES

In disputes between a nonparent and parent, the nonparent traditionally had to prove (by clear and convincing evidence) that an award to the parent would be detrimental to the child and that granting custody to the nonparent is in the child's best interests (Cal. Fam. Code §3041). This is termed the "natural parent presumption." See also In re Guardianship of Phillip B., 188 Cal. Rptr. 781 (Ct. App. 1983) (holding that the evidence was sufficient to overcome the natural parent presumption because the natural parents' retention of custody of a child with Downs Syndrome, who had been institutionalized since birth, had caused and would continue to cause serious detriment to child).

The custody/visitation rights of same-sex parents has been the subject of considerable recent case law and legislation in California. The California Supreme Court recently examined the issue of second-parent custody/visitation rights in two cases. In Kristine H. v. Lisa R., 117 P.3d 690, a biological mother filed a motion against her former same-sex partner to set aside a stipulated judgment declaring that both women were the child's joint legal parents. The state supreme court ruled that fairness dictated that the biological mother was estopped from challenging the validity of the pre-birth stipulated judgment because (1) the trial court had had subject matter jurisdiction to determine the parentage of the unborn child pursuant to the Uniform Parentage Act (Cal. Fam. Code §7600 et seq.), and (2) the biological mother had invoked that jurisdiction in stipulating to issuance of the judgment and (3) the biological mother had enjoyed the benefits of the judgment for two years while the child resided with the two parents.

In K.M. v. E.G., 117 P.3d 673 (Cal. 2005). a woman donated her eggs to her registered domestic partner so that the latter could bear a child. When the couple separated, the egg donor filed a petition to establish a parental relationship with the couple's twins. The California Supreme Court held that both women were legal parents of the children and that the statute (Cal. Fam. Code §7613) providing that the law treats a sperm donor as if he were not the natural father of a child so conceived did not apply in this situation.

California's new domestic partnership law, A.B. 205, vastly expands the rights and responsibilities of registered domestic partners. It expressly grants such domestic partners "the same rights, protections, and benefits," and imposed upon them "the same responsibilities, obligations, and duties . . . as a granted to and imposed upon spouses." (Cal. Fam. Code §297.5(a)). In addition, it makes former or surviving domestic partners legally equivalent to former or surviving spouses, and with respect to a child of either partner, it makes domestic partners subject to the same rights and obligations as spouses (Cal. Fam. Code §297.5(b), (c) and (d)).

On grandparents' visitation rights, see §C5 *supra*.

California Family Code

§297.5. Registered domestic partners shall have the same rights and responsibilities as spouses

(a) Registered domestic partners shall have the same rights, protections, and benefits, and shall be subject to the same responsibilities, obligations, and duties under law, whether they derive from statutes, administrative regulations, court rules, government policies, common law, or any other provisions or sources of law, as are granted to and imposed upon spouses.

(b) Former registered domestic partners shall have the same rights, protections, and benefits, and shall be subject to the same responsibilities, obligations, and duties under law, whether they derive from statutes, administrative regulations, court rules, government policies, common law, or any other provisions or sources of law, as are granted to and imposed upon former spouses.

(c) A surviving registered domestic partner, following the death of the other partner, shall have the same rights, protections, and benefits, and shall be subject to the same responsibilities, obligations, and duties under law, whether they derive from statutes, administrative regulations, court rules, government policies, common law, or any other provisions or sources of law, as are granted to and imposed upon a widow or a widower.

(d) The rights and obligations of registered domestic partners with respect to a child of either of them shall be the same as those of spouses. The rights and obligations of former or surviving registered domestic partners with respect to a child of either of them shall be the same as those of former or surviving spouses.

(e) To the extent that provisions of California law adopt, refer to, or rely upon, provisions of federal law in a way that otherwise would cause registered domestic partners to be treated differently than spouses, registered domestic partners shall be treated by California law as if federal law recognized a domestic partnership in the same manner as California law.

(f) Registered domestic partners shall have the same rights regarding nondiscrimination as those provided to spouses.

(g) Notwithstanding this section, in filing their state income tax returns, domestic partners shall use the same filing status as is used on their federal income tax returns, or that would have been used had they filed federal income tax returns. Earned income may not be treated as community property for state income tax purposes.

(h) No public agency in this state may discriminate against any person or couple on the ground that the person is a registered domestic partner rather than a spouse or that the couple are registered domestic partners rather than spouses, except that nothing in this section applies to modify eligibility for long-term care plans pursuant to Chapter 15 (commencing with Section 21660) of Part 3 of Division 5 of Title 2 of the Government Code.

(i) This act does not preclude any state or local agency from exercising its regulatory authority to implement statutes providing rights to, or imposing responsibilities upon, domestic partners.

(j) This section does not amend or modify any provision of the California Constitution or any provision of any statute that was adopted by initiative.

(k) This section does not amend or modify federal laws or the benefits, protections, and responsibilities provided by those laws.

(l) Where necessary to implement the rights of registered domestic partners under this act, gender-specific terms referring to spouses shall be construed to include domestic partners.

(m) (1) For purposes of the statutes, administrative regulations, court rules, government policies, common law, and any other provision or source of law governing the rights, protections, and benefits, and the responsibilities, obligations, and duties of registered domestic partners in this state, as effectuated by this section, with respect to community property, mutual responsibility for debts to third parties, the right in particular circumstances of either partner to seek financial support from the other following the dissolution of the partnership, and other rights and duties as between the partners concerning ownership of property, any reference to the date of a marriage shall be deemed to refer to the date of registration of a domestic partnership with the state.

(2) Notwithstanding paragraph (1), for domestic partnerships registered with the state before January 1, 2005, an agreement between the domestic partners that the partners intend to be governed by the requirements set forth in Sections 1600 to 1620, inclusive, and which complies with those sections, except for the agreement's effective date, shall be enforceable as provided by Sections 1600 to 1620, inclusive, if that agreement was fully executed and in force as of June 30, 2005.

(Enacted Stats. 2003 (A.B. 205), ch. 421, §4, effective January 1, 2005. Amended Stats. 2004 (A.B. 2580), ch. 947, §2.)

§3041. Natural parent presumption and the standard of detriment to the child

(a) Before making an order granting custody to a person or persons other than a parent, over the objection of a parent, the court shall make a finding that granting custody to a parent would be detrimental to the child and that granting custody to the nonparent is required to serve the best interest of the child. Allegations that parental custody would be detrimental to the child, other than a statement of that ultimate fact, shall not appear in the pleadings. The court may, in its discretion, exclude the public from the hearing on this issue.

(b) Subject to subdivision (d), a finding that parental custody would be detrimental to the child shall be supported by clear and convincing evidence.

(c) As used in this section, "detriment to the child" includes the harm of removal from a stable placement of a child with a person who has assumed, on a day-to-day basis, the role of his or her parent, fulfilling both the child's physical needs and the child's psychological needs for care and affection, and who has assumed that role for a substantial period of time. A finding of detriment does not require any finding of unfitness of the parents.

(d) Notwithstanding subdivision (b), if the court finds by a preponderance of the evidence that the person to whom custody may be given is a person described in subdivision (c), this finding shall constitute a finding that the custody is in the best interest of the child and that parental custody would be detrimental to the child absent a showing by a preponderance of the evidence to the contrary.

(Stats. 1993, ch. 219 (A.B. 1500), §116.50. Amended by Stats. 2002, ch. 1118 (A.B.1938), §3.)

E. SPECIAL PARTICIPANTS IN CUSTODY DETERMINATION

1. Child's Preference

Most states have statutes that call for consideration of the child's wishes, including (a) those modeled after the Uniform Marriage and Divorce Act (UMDA), which requires consideration of the child's wishes; (b) those that require consideration of the child's preference after a preliminary finding of maturity; (c) those that require deference to the child's preference for children of a specified age (usually 12 to 14 years); and (d) those that give judges complete discretion as to whether to consider children's wishes. Kathleen Nemecheck, Note, Child Preference in Custody Decisions: Where We Have Been, Where We are Now, Where We Should Go, 83 Iowa L. Rev. 437, 445-460 (1998).

California's approach, modeled after the second of the above approaches, provides that the court "shall consider and give due weight" to the wishes of those children of "sufficient age and capacity to reason so as to form an intelligence preference" (Cal. Fam. Code §3042(a)). Thus, the court must make a threshold determination as to the child's maturity. Also, the court must give "due weight" to the child's preference but is not required to follow the child's wishes.

Note the special situation involving a parent convicted of murder the other parent. According to statute, the child's wishes are relevant in the determination of custody and/or visitation in such circumstances (Cal. Fam. Code §3030(c)(1)).

The child's preference may be expressed by other persons, such as appointed counsel or a mediator. For example, if a child is represented by appointed counsel, counsel may orally state the child's wishes for the court's consideration unless that information is a privileged communication (Cal. Fam. Code §3151(b)). Or, the court may rely on the mediator's report to ascertain the child's wishes (see In re Marriage of Slayton, 103 Cal. Rptr. 2d 545 (Ct. App. 2001)).

A child's preference is entitled to greater consideration in a modification proceeding than in an initial award of custody. In re Marriage of Rosson, 224 Cal. Rptr. 250 (Cal. 1986) (disapproved on other grounds in In re Marriage of Burgess, 51 Cal. Rptr. 2d 444 (Cal. 1996)).

In ascertaining the child's preference, the court must protect the child's best interests. With this objective in mind, the court may preclude calling the child as a witness and permit expression of the child's preference by alternative means (e.g., on the parties' stipulation, private interview in chambers, perhaps with the assistance of a counselor from family court services; or through a mediator's or custody evaluator's interviews with the child). Hogoboom & King, *supra*, at §7:325.5.

§3042. Court shall consider preference of child of sufficient age and capacity; method of obtaining child's preference

(a) If a child is of sufficient age and capacity to reason so as to form an intelligent preference as to custody, the court shall consider and give due weight to the wishes of the child in making an order granting or modifying custody.

(b) In addition to the requirements of subdivision (b) of Section 765 of the Evidence Code, the court shall control the examination of the child witness so as to protect the best interests of the child. The court may preclude the calling of the child as a witness where the best interests of the child so dictate and may provide alternative means of obtaining information regarding the child's preferences.

(Stats. 1993 (A.B. 1500), ch. 219, §116.50. Amended by Stats. 1994 (S.B. 1700), ch. 596, §1; Stats. 1995 (S.B. 975), ch. 91, §38.)

2. Counsel for the Child

Despite considerable support by commentators and practitioners for mandatory representation for children in custody and visitation disputes, appointment of the child's representative in custody disputes is generally at the court's discretion. Only one state mandates representation in contested cases. Wis. Stat. Ann. §767.045 (West 1993 & Supp. 2000).

In California, a court-appointed investigator or a mediator may recommend that counsel be appointed for the child. If either individual recommends appointment of counsel, the investigator or mediation must specify the reasons for the recommendation (Cal. Fam. Code §§3114, 3184 [both set forth in §H2 *infra*]).

§1003. Court may appoint guardian ad litem to represent designated persons

(a) The court may, on its own motion or on request of a personal representative, guardian, conservator, trustee, or other interested person, appoint a guardian ad litem at any stage of a proceeding under this code to represent the interest of any of the following persons, if the court determines that representation of the interest otherwise would be inadequate:

(1) A minor.

(2) An incapacitated person.

(3) An unborn person.

(4) An unascertained person.

(5) A person whose identity or address is unknown.

(6) A designated class of persons who are not ascertained or are not in being.

(b) If not precluded by a conflict of interest, a guardian ad litem may be appointed to represent several persons or interests.

(c) The reasonable expenses of the guardian ad litem, including compensation and attorney's fees, shall be determined by the court and paid as the court orders, either out of the property of the estate involved or by the petitioner or from such other source as the court orders.

(Stats. 1990 (A.B. 759), ch. 79, §14, effective July 1, 1991.)

§3114. Investigator may recommend appointment of counsel for minor child

Nothing in this chapter prohibits a court-appointed investigator from recommending to the court that counsel be appointed pursuant to Chapter 10 (commencing with Section 3150) to represent the minor child. In making that recommendation, the court-appointed investigator shall inform the court of the reasons why it would be in the best interest of the child to have counsel appointed.

(Stats. 1993 (A.B. 1500), ch. 219, §116.81.)

§3150. Court may appoint private counsel to represent child in custody or visitation proceeding

(a) If the court determines that it would be in the best interest of the minor child, the court may appoint private counsel to represent the interests of the child in a custody or visitation proceeding.

(b) Upon entering an appearance on behalf of a child pursuant to this chapter, counsel shall continue to represent that child unless relieved by the court upon the substitution of other counsel by the court or for cause.

(Stats. 1992 (A.B. 2650), ch. 162, §10, effective January 1, 1994. Amended by Stats. 1993 (A.B. 1500), ch. 219, §116.85.)

§3151. Counsel has specified duties in representing child's best interests

(a) The child's counsel appointed under this chapter is charged with the representation of the child's best interests. The role of the child's counsel is to gather facts that bear on the best interests of the child, and present those facts to the court, including the child's wishes when counsel deems it appropriate for consideration by the court pursuant to Section 3042. The counsel's duties, unless under the circumstances it is inappropriate to exercise the duty, include interviewing the child, reviewing the court files and all accessible relevant records available to both parties, and making any further investigations as the counsel considers necessary to ascertain facts relevant to the custody or visitation hearings.

(b) At the court's request, counsel shall prepare a written statement of issues and contentions setting forth the facts that bear on the best interests of the child. The statement shall set forth a summary of information received by counsel, a list of the sources of information, the results of the counsel's investigation, and such other matters as the court may direct. The statement of issues and contentions shall not contain any communication subject to Section 954 of the Evidence Code. The statement of issues and contentions shall be filed with the court and submitted to the parties or their attorneys of record at least 10 days before the hearing, unless the court orders otherwise. At the court's request, counsel may orally state the wishes of the child if that information is not a privileged communication subject to Section 954 of the Evidence Code, for consideration by the court pursuant to Section 3042 [set forth in §E1 *supra*]. Counsel shall not be called as a witness in the proceeding. Counsel may introduce and examine counsel's own witnesses, present arguments to the court concerning the child's welfare, and participate further in the proceeding to the degree necessary to represent the child adequately. In consultation with representatives of the Family Law Section of the State Bar and the Senate and Assembly Judiciary Committees, the Judicial Council may specify standards for the preparation of the statement of issues and contentions and may promulgate a model statement of issues and contentions, which shall include simple instructions regarding how to subpoena a witness, and a blank subpoena form.

(c) The child's counsel shall have the following rights :

(1) Reasonable access to the child .

(2) Standing to seek affirmative relief on behalf of the child.

(3) Notice of any proceeding, and all phases of that proceeding, including a request for examination affecting the child.

(4) The right to take any action that is available to a party to the proceeding, including, but not limited to, the following: filing pleadings, making evidentiary objections, and presenting evidence and being heard in the proceeding, which may include, but shall not be limited to, presenting motions and orders to show cause, and participating in settlement conferences, trials, seeking writs, appeals, and arbitrations.

(5) Access to the child's medical, dental, mental health, and other health care records, school and educational records, and the right to interview school personnel, caretakers, health care providers, mental health professionals, and others who have assessed the child or provided care to the child. The release of this information to counsel shall not constitute a waiver of the confidentiality of the reports, files, and any disclosed communications. Counsel may interview mediators; however, the provisions of Sections 3177 [confidentially, set forth in §H2d *infra*] and 3182 [mediator may exclude counsel, set forth in §H2e *infra*] shall apply.

(6) The right to reasonable advance notice of and the right to refuse any physical or psychological examination or evaluation, for purposes of the proceeding, which has not been ordered by the court.

(7) The right to assert or waive any privilege on behalf of the child .

(8) The right to seek independent psychological or physical examination or evaluation of the child for purposes of the pending proceeding, upon approval by the court.

(Stats. 1992 (A.B. 2650), ch. 162, §10, effective January 1, 1994. Amended by Stats. 1997 (A.B. 1526), ch. 449, §1.)

§3151.5. Court shall consider counsel's statement of issues and contentions; attorney shall not be called as witness

If a child is represented by court appointed counsel, at every hearing in which the court makes a judicial determination regarding custody or visitation the court shall consider any statement of issues and contentions of the child's counsel. Any party may subpoena as a witness any person listed in the statement of issues and contentions as having provided information to the attorney, but the attorney shall not be called as a witness.

(Stats. 1997 (A.B. 1526), ch. 449, §2.)

§3152. Release to counsel of reports and files of child protective agency

(a) The child's counsel may, upon noticed motion to all parties and the local child protective services agency, request the court to authorize release of relevant reports or files, concerning the child represented by the counsel, of the relevant local child protective services agency.

(b) The court shall review the reports or files in camera in order to determine whether they are relevant to the pending action and whether and to what extent they should be released to the child's counsel.

(c) Neither the review by the court nor the release to counsel shall constitute a waiver of the confidentiality of the reports and files. Counsel shall not disclose the contents or existence of the reports or files to anyone unless otherwise permitted by law.

(Stats. 1992 (A.B. 2650), ch. 162, §10, effective January 1, 1994.)

§3153. Appointed counsel shall receive compensation

(a) If the court appoints counsel under this chapter to represent the child, counsel shall receive a reasonable sum for compensation and expenses, the amount of which shall be determined by the court. Except as provided in subdivision (b), this amount shall be paid by the parties in the proportions the court deems just.

(b) Upon its own motion or that of a party, the court shall determine whether both parties together are financially unable to pay all or a portion of the cost of counsel appointed pursuant to this chapter, and the portion of the cost of that counsel which the court finds the parties are unable to pay shall be paid by the county. The Judicial Council shall adopt guidelines to assist in determining financial eligibility for county payment of counsel appointed by the court pursuant to this chapter.

(Stats. 1992 (A.B. 2650), ch. 162, §10, effective January 1, 1994.)

3. Court-Appointed Investigator

In contested custody proceedings (involving either custody or visitation disputes), the court may appoint an investigator to conduct an evaluation if such appointment would be in the best interests of the child (Cal. Fam. Code §3111(a)). Authority for the appointment of a psychiatric examination in any custody and/or visitation proceeding exists under California Evidence Code §730. Custody investigators are exempt from liability for publications made in judicial proceedings under California Civil Code §47(b). See also Howard v. Drapkin, 271 Cal. Rptr. 893 (Ct. App. 1990) (holding that statutory privilege and common law quasi-judicial immunity protect custody investigators).

§3110. "Court-appointed investigator"

As used in this chapter, "court-appointed investigator" means a probation officer, domestic relations investigator, or court-appointed evaluator directed by the court to conduct an investigation pursuant to this chapter.

(Stats. 1993 (A.B. 1500) ch. 219, §116.81.)

§3110.5. Qualifications of child custody evaluator

(a) No person may be a court-connected or private child custody evaluator under this chapter unless the person has completed the domestic violence and child abuse training program described in Section 1816 and has complied with Rules 5.220 and 5.230 of the California Rules of Court.

(b) (1) On or before January 1, 2002, the Judicial Council shall formulate a statewide rule of court that establishes education, experience, and training requirements for all child custody evaluators appointed pursuant to this chapter, Section 730 of the Evidence Code, or Chapter 15 (commencing with Section 2032.010) of Title 4 of Part 4 of the Code of Civil Procedure.

(A) The rule shall require a child custody evaluator to declare under penalty of perjury that he or she meets all of the education, experience, and training requirements specified in the rule and, if applicable, possesses a license in good standing. The Judicial Council shall establish forms to implement this section. The rule shall permit court-connected evaluators to conduct evaluations if they meet all of the qualifications established by the Judicial Council. The education, experience, and training requirements to be specified for court-connected evaluators shall include, but not be limited to, knowledge of the psychological and developmental needs of children and parent-child relationships.

(B) The rule shall require all evaluators to utilize comparable interview, assessment, and testing procedures for all parties that are consistent with generally accepted clinical, forensic, scientific, diagnostic, or medical standards. The rule shall also require evaluators to inform each adult party of the purpose, nature, and method of the evaluation.

(C) The rule may allow courts to permit the parties to stipulate to an evaluator of their choosing with the approval of the court under the circumstances set forth in subdivision (d). The rule may require courts to provide general information about how parties can contact qualified child custody evaluators in their county.

(2) On or before January 1, 2004, the Judicial Council shall include in the statewide rule of court created pursuant to this section a requirement that all court-connected and private child custody evaluators receive training in the nature of child sexual abuse. The Judicial Council shall develop standards for this training that shall include, but not be limited to, the following:

(A) Children's patterns of hiding and disclosing sexual abuse occurring in a family setting.

(B) The effects of sexual abuse on children.

(C) The nature and extent of child sexual abuse.

(D) The social and family dynamics of child sexual abuse.

(E) Techniques for identifying and assisting families affected by child sexual abuse.

(F) Legal rights, protections, and remedies available to victims of child sexual abuse.

(c) In addition to the education, experience, and training requirements established by the Judicial Council pursuant to subdivision (b), on or after January 1, 2005, no person may be a child custody evaluator under this chapter, Section 730 of the Evidence Code, or Chapter 15 (commencing with Section 2032.010) of Title 4 of Part 4 of the Code of Civil Procedure unless the person meets one of the following criteria:

(1) He or she is licensed as a physician under Chapter 5 (commencing with Section 2000) of Division 2 of the Business and Professions Code and either is a board certified psychiatrist or has completed a residency in psychiatry.

(2) He or she is licensed as a psychologist under Chapter 6.6 (commencing with Section 2900) of Division 2 of the Business and Professions Code.

(3) He or she is licensed as a marriage and family therapist under Chapter 13 (commencing with Section 4980) of Division 2 of the Business and Professions Code.

(4) He or she is licensed as a clinical social worker under Article 4 (commencing with Section 4996) of Chapter 14 of Division 2 of the Business and Professions Code.

(5) He or she is a court-connected evaluator who has been certified by the court as meeting all of the qualifications for court-connected evaluators as specified by the Judicial Council pursuant to subdivision (b).

(d) Subdivision (c) does not apply in any case where the court determines that there are no evaluators who meet the criteria of subdivision (c) who are willing and available, within a reasonable period of time, to perform child custody evaluations. In those cases, the parties may stipulate to an individual who does not meet the criteria of subdivision (c), subject to approval by the court.

(e) A child custody evaluator who is licensed by the Medical Board of California, the Board of Psychology, or the Board of Behavioral Sciences shall be subject to disciplinary action by that board for unprofessional conduct, as defined in the licensing law applicable to that licensee.

(f) On or after January 1, 2005, a court-connected or private child custody evaluator may not evaluate, investigate, or mediate an issue of child custody in a proceeding pursuant to this division unless that person has completed child sexual abuse training as required by this section.

(Stats. 1999 (S.B. 433), ch. 932, §1. Amended by Stats. 2000 (S.B. 1716), ch. 926, §4; Stats. 2004 (A.B. 3079), ch. 811, §1, effective until July 1, 2005; Stats. 2004 (A.B. 3081), ch. 811, §1.5, effective until July 1, 2005 (ch. 811 prevails).)

§3111. Court may appoint child custody evaluator if in child's best interests

(a) In any contested proceeding involving child custody or visitation rights, the court may appoint a child custody evaluator to conduct a child custody evaluation in cases where the court determines it is in the best interests of the child. The child custody evaluation shall be conducted in accordance with the standards adopted by the Judicial Council pursuant to Section 3117, and all other standards adopted by the Judicial Council regarding child custody evaluations. If directed by the court, the court-appointed child custody evaluator shall file a written confidential report on his or her evaluation. At least 10 days before any hearing regarding custody of the child, the report shall be filed with the clerk of the court in which the custody hearing will be conducted and served on the parties or their attorneys, and any other counsel appointed for the child pursuant to Section 3150. The report may be considered by the court.

(b) The report shall not be made available other than as provided in subdivision (a), or as described in Section 204 of the Welfare and Institutions Code or Section 1514.5 of the Probate Code. Any information obtained from access to a juvenile court case file, as defined in subdivision (e) of Section 827 of the Welfare and Institutions Code, is confidential and shall only be disseminated as provided by paragraph (4) of subdivision (a) of Section 827 of the Welfare and Institutions Code.

(c) The report may be received in evidence on stipulation of all interested parties and is competent evidence as to all matters contained in the report.

(Stats. 1999 (A.B. 1500), ch. 219, §116.81. Amended by Stats. 1996 (S.B. 1995), ch. 761, §1; Stats. 1999 (S.B. 433), ch. 932, §2; Stats. 2002 (A.B. 3028), ch. 1008, §16; Stats. 2004 (A.B. 2228), ch. 574, §1; Stats. 2005 (S.B. 1108), ch. 22, §62.)

§3112. Court may order parent to repay expenses for custody investigation or evaluation

(a) Where a court-appointed investigator is directed by the court to conduct a custody investigation or evaluation pursuant to this chapter or to undertake visitation work, including necessary evaluation, supervision, and reporting, the court shall inquire into the financial condition of the parent, guardian, or other person charged with the support of the minor. If the court finds the parent, guardian, or other person able to pay all or part of the expense of the investigation, report, and recommendation, the court may make an order requiring the parent, guardian, or other person to repay the court the amount the court determines proper.

(b) The repayment shall be made to the court. The court shall keep suitable accounts of the expenses and repayments and shall deposit the collections as directed by the Judicial Council.

(Stats. 1993 (A.B. 1500), ch. 219, §116.81. Amended by Stats. 2000 (S.B. 1716), ch. 926, §5.)

§3113. Parties shall meet with custody investigator separately in cases of domestic violence

Where there has been a history of domestic violence between the parties, or where a protective order as defined in Section 6218 [set forth in Chapter III §G1 *supra*] is in effect, at the request of the party alleging domestic violence in a written declaration under penalty of perjury or at the request of a party who is protected by the order, the parties shall meet with the court-appointed investigator separately and at separate times.

(Stats. 1993 (A.B. 1500), ch. 219, §116.81.)

§3115. Waiver of right to cross-examine investigator

No statement, whether written or oral, or conduct shall be held to constitute a waiver by a party of the right to cross-examine the court-appointed investigator, unless the statement is made, or the conduct occurs, after the report has been received by a party or his or her attorney.

(Stats. 1993 (A.B. 1500), ch. 219, §116.81. Amended by Stats. 1996 (S.B. 1995), ch. 761, §2.)

§3116. No limitation on investigator's duty to assist court

Nothing in this chapter limits the duty of a court-appointed investigator to assist the appointing court in the transaction of the business of the court.

(Stats. 1993 (A.B. 1500), ch. 219, §116.81.)

§3117. Standards for custody evaluations, procedural guidelines for cross-examination

The Judicial Council shall, by January 1, 1999, do both of the following:

(a) Adopt standards for full and partial court-connected evaluations, investigations, and assessments related to child custody.

(b) Adopt procedural guidelines for the expeditious and cost-effective cross-examination of court-appointed investigators, including, but not limited to, the use of electronic technology whereby the court-appointed investigator may not need to be present in the courtroom. These guidelines shall in no way limit the requirement that the court-appointed investigator be available for the purposes of cross-examination. These guidelines shall also provide for written notification to the parties of the right to cross-examine these investigators after the parties have had a reasonable time to review the investigator's report.

(Stats. 1996 (S.B. 1995), ch. 761, §3.)

§3118. Court shall require evaluation in custody cases involving allegations of sexual abuse

(a) In any contested proceeding involving child custody or visitation rights, where the court has appointed a child custody evaluator or has referred a case for a full or partial court-connected evaluation, investigation, or assessment, and the court determines that there is a serious allegation of child sexual abuse, the court shall require an evaluation, investigation, or assessment pursuant to this section. When the court has determined that there is a serious allegation of child sexual abuse, any child custody evaluation, investigation, or assessment conducted subsequent to that determination shall be considered by the court only if the evaluation, investigation, or assessment is conducted in accordance with the minimum requirements set forth in this section in determining custody or visitation rights, except as specified in paragraph (1). For purposes of this section, a serious allegation of child sexual abuse means an allegation of child sexual abuse, as defined in Section 11165.1 of the Penal Code, that is based in whole or in part on statements made by the child to law enforcement, a child welfare services agency investigator, any person required by statute to report suspected child abuse, or any other court-appointed personnel, or that is supported by substantial independent corroboration as provided for in subdivision (b) of Section 3011. When an allegation of child abuse arises in any other circumstances in any proceeding involving child custody or visitation rights, the court may require an evaluator or investigator to conduct an evaluation, investigation, or assessment pursuant to this section. The order appointing a child custody evaluator or investigator pursuant to this section shall provide that the evaluator or investigator have access to all juvenile court records pertaining to the child who is the subject of the evaluation, investigation, or assessment. The order shall also provide that any juvenile court records or information gained from those records remain confidential and shall only be released as specified in Section 3111.

(1) This section does not apply to any emergency court-ordered partial investigation that is conducted for the purpose of assisting the court in determining what immediate temporary orders may be necessary to protect and meet the immediate needs of a child. This section does apply when the emergency is resolved and the court is considering permanent child custody or visitation orders.

(2) This section does not prohibit a court from considering evidence relevant to determining the safety and protection needs of the child.

(3) Any evaluation, investigation, or assessment conducted pursuant to this section shall be conducted by an evaluator or investigator who meets the qualifications set forth in Section 3110.5.

(b) The evaluator or investigator shall, at a minimum, do all of the following:

(1) Consult with the agency providing child welfare services and law enforcement regarding the allegations of child sexual abuse, and obtain recommendations from these professionals regarding the child's safety and the child's need for protection.

(2) Review and summarize the child welfare services agency file. No document contained in the child welfare services agency filemay be photocopied, but a summary of the information in the file, including statements made by the children and the parents, and the recommendations made or anticipated to be made by the child welfare services agency to the juvenile court, may be recorded by the evaluator or investigator, except for the identity of the reporting party. The evaluator's or investigator's notes summarizing the child welfare services agency information shall be stored in a file separate from the evaluator's or investigator's file and may only be released to either party under order of the court.

(3) Obtain from a law enforcement investigator all available information obtained from criminal background checks of the parents and any suspected perpetrator that is not a parent, including information regarding child abuse, domestic violence, or substance abuse.

(4) Review the results of a multidisciplinary child interview team (hereafter MDIT) interview if available, or if not, or if the evaluator or investigator believes the MDIT interview is inadequate for purposes of the evaluation, investigation, or assessment, interview the child or request an MDIT interview, and shall wherever possible avoid repeated interviews of the child.

(5) Request a forensic medical examination of the child from the appropriate agency, or include in the report required by paragraph (6) a written statement explaining why the examination is not needed.

(6) File a confidential written report with the clerk of the court in which the custody hearing will be conducted and which shall be served on the parties or their attorneys at least 10 days prior to the hearing. This reportmay not be made available other than as provided in this subdivision. This report shall include, but is not limited to, the following:

(A) Documentation of material interviews, including any MDIT interview of the child or the evaluator or investigator, written documentation of interviews with both parents by the evaluator or investigator, and interviews with other witnesses who provided relevant information.

(B) A summary of any law enforcement investigator's investigation, including information obtained from the criminal background check of the parents and any suspected perpetrator that is not a parent, including information regarding child abuse, domestic violence, or substance abuse.

(C) Relevant background material, including, but not limited to, a summary of a written report from any therapist treating the child for suspected child sexual abuse, excluding any communication subject to Section 1014 of the Evidence Code, reports from other professionals, and the results of any forensic medical examination and any other medical examination or treatment that could help establish or disprove whether the child has been the victim of sexual abuse.

(D) The written recommendations of the evaluator or investigator regarding the therapeutic needs of the child and how to ensure the safety of the child.

(E) A summary of the following information: whether the child and his or her parents are or have been the subject of a child abuse investigation and the disposition of that investigation; the name, location, and telephone number of the children's services worker; the status of the investigation and the recommendations made or anticipated to be made regarding the child's safety; and any dependency court orders or findings that might have a bearing on the custody dispute.

(F) Any information regarding the presence of domestic violence or substance abuse in the family that has been obtained from a child protective agency in accordance with paragraphs (1) and (2), a law enforcement agency, medical personnel or records, prior or currently treating therapists, excluding any communication subject to Section 1014 of the Evidence Code, or from interviews conducted or reviewed for this evaluation, investigation, or assessment.

(G) Which, if any, family members are known to have been deemed eligible for assistance from the Victims of Crime Program due to child abuse or domestic violence.

(H) Any other information the evaluator or investigator believes would be helpful to the court in determining what is in the best interests of the child.

(c) If the evaluator or investigator obtains information as part of a family court mediation, that information shall be maintained in the family court file, which is not subject to subpoena by either party. If, however, the members of the family are the subject of an ongoing child welfare services investigation, or the evaluator or investigator has made a child welfare services referral, the evaluator or investigator shall so inform the family law judicial officer in writing and this information shall become part of the family law file. This subdivision may not be construed to authorize or require a mediator to disclose any information not otherwise authorized or required by law to be disclosed.

(d) In accordance with subdivision (d) of Section 11167 of the Penal Code, the evaluator or investigator may not disclose any information regarding the identity of any person making a report of suspected child abuse. Nothing in this section is intended to limit any disclosure of information by any agency that is otherwise required by law or court order.

(e) The evaluation, investigation, or assessment standards set forth in this section represent minimum requirements of evaluation and the court shall order further evaluation beyond these minimum requirements when necessary to determine the safety needs of the child.

(f) If the court orders an evaluation, investigation, or assessment pursuant to this section, the court shall consider whether the bestinterests of the child require that a temporary order be issued that limits visitation with the parent against whom the allegations have been made to situations in which a third person specified by the court is present or whether visitation will be suspended or denied in accordance with Section 3011.

(g) An evaluation, investigation, or assessment pursuant to this section shall be suspended if a petition is filed to declare the child a dependent child of the juvenile court pursuant to Section 300 of the Welfare and Institutions Code, and all information gathered by the evaluator or investigator shall be made available to the juvenile court.

(h) This section may not be construed to authorize a court to issue any orders in a proceeding pursuant to this division regarding custody or visitation with respect to a minor child who is the subject of a dependency hearing in juvenile court or to otherwise supersede Section 302 of the Welfare and Institutions Code.

(Stats. 2000 (S.B. 1716), ch. 926, §6. Amended by Stats. 2002 (S.B.1704), ch. 305, §1; Stats. 2003 (S.B. 600), ch. 62, §87.)

4. Court-Ordered Counselors

Courts may require parents, children and "any other party involved in a custody or visitation dispute" to participate in counseling (Cal. Fam. Code §3190(a)). Such counseling may include mental health or substance abuse services (but is not limited to such services) (*id.*). Before the court may require such counseling, the court must find both of the following conditions: (1) the dispute poses a substantial danger to the best interests of the child, and (2) the counseling is in the child's best interests (Cal. Fam. Code §3190(a)(1) & (2)). To determine the meaning of "substantial danger," the court must consider any history of domestic violence, as well as any other factors the court considers relevant (Cal. Fam. Code §3190(b)).

§3190. Court may order parents to participate in counseling

(a) The court may require parents or any other party involved in a custody or visitation dispute, and the minor child, to participate in outpatient counseling with a licensed mental health professional, or through other community programs and services that provide appropriate counseling, including, but not limited to, mental health or substance abuse services, for not more than one year, provided that the program selected has counseling available for the designated period of time, if the court finds both of the following:

(1) The dispute between the parents, between the parent or parents and the child, between the parent or parents and another party seeking custody or visitation rights with the child, or between a party seeking custody or visitation rights and the child, poses a substantial danger to the best interest of the child.

(2) The counseling is in the best interest of the child.

(b) In determining whether a dispute, as described in paragraph (1) of subdivision (a), poses a substantial danger to the best interest of the child, the court shall consider, in addition to any other factors the court determines relevant, any history of domestic violence, as defined in Section 6211, within the past five years between the parents, between the parent or parents and the child, between the parent or parents and another party seeking custody or visitation rights with the child, or between a party seeking custody or visitation rights and the child.

(c) Subject to Section 3192, if the court finds that the financial burden created by the order for counseling does not otherwise jeopardize a party's other financial obligations, the court shall fix the cost and shall order the entire cost of the services to be borne by the parties in the proportions the court deems reasonable.

(d) The court, in its finding, shall set forth reasons why it has found both of the following:

(1) The dispute poses a substantial danger to the best interest of the child and the counseling is in the best interest of the child.

(2) The financial burden created by the court order for counseling does not otherwise jeopardize a party's other financial obligations.

(e) The court shall not order the parties to return to court upon the completion of counseling. Any party may file a new order to show cause or motion after counseling has been completed, and the court may again order counseling consistent with this chapter.

(Stats. 1992 (A.B. 2650), ch. 162, §10, effective January 1, 1994. Amended by Stats. 1993 (A.B. 1500), ch. 219, §116.90, (A.B. 197), ch. 301, §1, (S.B. 1068), ch. 876, §15.4, effective January 1, 1994; Stats. 1994 (A.B. 2208), ch. 1269, §30; Stats. 1998 (A.B. 1837), ch. 229, §1.)

§3191. Purpose of counseling

The counseling pursuant to this chapter shall be specifically designed to facilitate communication between the parties regarding their minor child's best interest, to reduce conflict regarding custody or visitation, and to improve the quality of parenting skills of each parent.

(Stats. 1992 (A.B. 2650), ch. 162, §10, effective January 1, 1994. Amended by Stats. 1993 (A.B. 1500), ch. 219, §116.91.)

§3192. Court may order separate counseling in cases of domestic violence

In a proceeding in which counseling is ordered pursuant to this chapter, where there has been a history of abuse by either parent against the child or by one parent against the other parent and a protective order as defined in Section 6218 [set forth in Chapter III §G1 *supra*] is in effect, the court may order the parties to participate in counseling separately and at separate times. Each party shall bear the cost of his or her own counseling separately, unless good cause is shown for a different apportionment. The costs associated with a minor child participating in counseling shall be apportioned in accordance with Section 4062.

(Stats. 1992 (A.B. 2650), ch. 162, §10, effective January 1, 1994. Amended by Stats. 1993 (A.B. 1500), ch. 219, §116.92; Stats. 1994 (A.B. 2208), ch. 1269, §31.)

§3200. Standards for supervised visitation providers

The Judicial Council shall develop standards for supervised visitation providers in accordance with the guidelines set forth in this section. On or before April 1, 1997, the Judicial Council shall report the standards developed and present an implementation plan to the Legislature. For the purposes of the development of these standards, the term "provider" shall include any individual who functions as a visitation monitor, as well as supervised visitation centers. Provisions shall be made within the standards to allow for the diversity of supervised visitation providers.

(a) When developing standards, the Judicial Council shall consider all of the following issues:

(1) The provider's qualifications, experience, and education.

(2) Safety and security procedures, including ratios of children per supervisor.

(3) Any conflict of interest.

(4) Maintenance and disclosure of records, including confidentiality policies.

(5) Procedures for screening, delineation of terms and conditions, and termination of supervised visitation services.

(6) Procedures for emergency or extenuating situations.

(7) Orientation to and guidelines for cases in which there are allegations of domestic violence, child abuse, substance abuse, or special circumstances.

(8) The legal obligations and responsibilities of supervisors.

(b) The Judicial Council shall consult with visitation centers, mothers' groups, fathers' groups, judges, the State Bar of California, children's advocacy groups, domestic violence prevention groups, Family Court Services, and other groups it regards as necessary in connection with these standards.

(c) It is the intent of the Legislature that the safety of children, adults, and visitation supervisors be a precondition to providing visitation services. Once safety is assured, the best interest of the child is the paramount consideration at all stages and particularly in deciding the manner in which supervision is provided.

(Stats. 1996 (S.B. 1643), ch. 387, §1.)

§3201. Administration of court-imposed supervised visitation

Any supervised visitation maintained or imposed by the court shall be administered in accordance with Section 26.2 of the California Standards of Judicial Administration recommended by the Judicial Council.

(Stats. 1999 (S.B. 792), ch. 985, §2.)

For another section with the same number, see §3201 *post.*

§3201. Administration of parenting education programs

(a) The programs described in this chapter shall be administered by the family law division of the superior court in the county.

(b) For purposes of this chapter, "education about protecting children during family disruption" includes education on parenting skills and the impact of parental conflict on children, how to put a parenting agreement into effect, and the responsibility of both parents to comply with custody and visitation orders.

(Stats. 1999 (A.B. 673), ch. 1004, §2.)

§3202. Supervised visitation programs shall comply with state requirements

(a) All supervised visitation and exchange programs funded pursuant to this chapter shall comply with all requirements of the Uniform Standards of Practice for Providers of Supervised Visitation set forth in Section 26.2 of the Standards of Judicial Administration as amended. The family law division of the superior court may contract with eligible providers of supervised visitation and exchange services, education, and group counseling to provide services under this chapter.

(b) As used in this section, "eligible provider" means:

(1) For providers of supervised visitation and exchange services, a local public agency or nonprofit entity that satisfies the Uniform Standards of Practice for Providers of Supervised Visitation.

(2) For providers of group counseling, a professional licensed to practice psychotherapy in this state, including, but not limited to, a licensed psychiatrist, licensed psychologist, licensed clinical social worker, or licensed marriage and family therapist; or a mental health intern working under the direct supervision of a professional licensed to practice psychotherapy.

(3) For providers of education, a professional with a bachelor's or master's degree in human behavior, child development, psychology, counseling, family-life education, or a related field, having specific training in issues relating to child and family development, substance abuse, child abuse, domestic violence, effective parenting, and the impact of divorce and interparental conflict on children; or an intern working under the supervision of that professional.

(Stats. 1999 (A.B. 673), ch. 1004, §3.)

§3203. Establishment of parent education and counseling programs by family law division

Subject to the availability of federal funding for the purposes of this chapter, the family law division of the superior court in each county may establish and administer a supervised visitation and exchange program, programs for education about protecting children during family disruption, and group counseling programs for parents and children under this chapter. The programs shall allow parties and children to participate in supervised visitation between a custodial party and a noncustodial party or joint custodians, and to participate in the education and group counseling programs, irrespective of whether the parties are or are not married to each other or are currently living separately and apart on a permanent or temporary basis.

(Stats. 1999 (A.B. 673), ch. 1004, §4.)

§3204. Application for federal funds

(a) The Judicial Council shall annually submit an application to the federal Administration for Children and Families, pursuant to Section 669B of the "1996 Federal Personal Responsibility and Work Opportunity Recovery Act" (PRWORA), for a grant to fund child custody and visitation programs pursuant to this chapter.

The Judicial Council shall be charged with the administration of the grant funds.

(b)(1) It is the intention of the Legislature that, effective October 1, 2000, the grant funds described in subdivision (a) shall be used to fund the following three types of programs: supervised visitation and exchange services, education about protecting children during family disruption, and group counseling for parents and children, as set forth in this chapter. Contracts shall follow a standard request for proposal procedure, that may include multiple year funding. Requests for proposals shall meet all state and federal requirements for receiving access and visitation grant funds.

(2) The grant funds shall be awarded with the intent of approving as many requests for proposals as possible while assuring that each approved proposal would provide beneficial services and satisfy the overall goals of the program under this chapter. The Judicial Council shall determine the final number and amount of grants. Requests for proposals shall be evaluated based on the following criteria:

(A) Availability of services to a broad population of parties.

(B) The ability to expand existing services.

(C) Coordination with other community services.

(D) The hours of service delivery.

(E) The number of counties or regions participating.

(F) Overall cost effectiveness.

(G) The purpose of the program to promote and encourage healthy parent and child relationships between noncustodial parents and their children, while ensuring the health, safety, and welfare of the children.

(3) Special consideration for grant funds shall be given to proposals that coordinate supervised visitation and exchange services, education, and group counseling with existing court-based programs and services.

(c) The family law division of the superior court in each county shall approve sliding scale fees that are based on the ability to pay for all parties, including low-income families, participating in a supervised visitation and exchange, education, and group counseling programs under this chapter.

(d) The Judicial Council shall, on March 1, 2002, and on the first day of March of each subsequent year, report to the Legislature on the programs funded pursuant to this chapter

and whether and to what extent those programs are achieving the goal of promoting and encouraging healthy parent and child relationships between noncustodial or joint custodial parents and their children while ensuring the health, safety, and welfare of children, and the other goals described in this chapter.
(Stats. 1999 (A.B. 673), ch. 1004, §5.)

F. MODIFICATION OF CUSTODY AGREEMENTS

1. Standard Generally

The paramount concern with child welfare gives courts continuing power to modify custody orders. The standard for modification is higher than for initial awards of custody in order to ensure stability for the child.

According to the prevailing standard, the plaintiff has the burden of showing by a preponderance of the evidence that conditions since the dissolution decree have so materially and substantially changed that the children's best interests require a change of custody. A few states have adopted a more liberal requirement that modification serve the best interests of the child (regardless of a change in circumstances).

Several states have more stringent rules, influenced by UMDA §409(b), 9A U.L.A. 439 (1998), requiring endangerment for nonconsensual changes. Absent serious endangerment, UMDA §409(a) provides for a two-year waiting period following the initial decree.

In California, several Family Code sections authorize custody modification, e.g., Cal. Fam. Code §§3022 [court may make order for custody as "necessary or proper" during the pendency of a proceeding or at any time thereafter, in §A1 *supra*], 3042 [court shall consider child's wishes in initial award or modification, in §E1 *supra*], 3087 *infra*, and 3088 *infra*. Family courts have such authority even without express statutory authority. Raye et al., *supra*, at §18:44. Based on California case law, modification requires a showing that there has been a substantial change of circumstances such that modification is essential for the child's welfare. Hogoboom & King, *supra*, at §7:322. The burden of proof is on the party seeking the modification. *id.*; Raye et al., *supra*, at §18:47.

The changed circumstances rule applies after a final or permanent judicial custody or visitation determination. Final custody orders obtained by stipulation are treated similarly. Hogoboom & King, *supra*, at §7:322.2. (Note that the rule does not apply in joint custody move-away cases in which the trial court must determine de novo what custody arrangement is in the children's best interests.) *Id.* at 322.10.

California appellate courts differ on whether a showing of changed circumstances is required to revise a coparenting residential agreement under a joint custody order where the provisions of the prior order for joint custody otherwise remained unchanged. Compare In re Marriage of Birnbaum, 260 Cal. Rptr. 210 (Ct. App. 1989) (holding that no changed circumstances need be shown to modify existing order for joint physical custody by changing dates on which children lived with former husband and wife and dates of visitation because modification was not "change of custody" but merely change in "coparenting residential arrangement") with In re Marriage of Congdon, 82 Cal. Rptr. 2d 686 (Ct. App. 2000) (holding that parent with joint physical custody who wishes to modify a custody decree by placing two younger children on same schedule as two older children is required to show a change in circumstances justifying the modification).

See also In re Marriage of Dunn, 126 Cal. Rptr. 2d 636 (Ct. App. 2002) (holding that a formal hearing is required for a custody modification order limiting the new spouse's participation in the children's school activities).

§3087. Order for joint custody may be modified or terminated subject to best interests

An order for joint custody may be modified or terminated upon the petition of one or both parents or on the court's own motion if it is shown that the best interest of the child requires modification or termination of the order. If either parent opposes the modification or termination order, the court shall state in its decision the reasons for modification or termination of the joint custody order.
(Stats. 1992 (A.B. 2650), ch. 162, §10, effective January 1, 1994.)

§3088. Custody order may be modified to joint custody order

An order for the custody of a minor child entered by a court in this state or any other state may, subject to the jurisdictional requirements in Sections 3403 and 3414, be modified at any time to an order for joint custody in accordance with this chapter.
(Stats. 1992 (A.B. 2650), ch. 162, §10, effective January 1, 1994. Amended by Stats. 1993 (A.B. 1500), ch. 219, §116.73.)

2. Relocation Controversies (Move-Away Cases)

Relocation controversies frequently arise when a separated or divorced parent decides to relocate for reasons such as remarriage, employment or educational opportunities, or the promise of moral or economic support from relatives. Such disputes may arise because a decree or statute requires a custodial parent to seek permission to leave the jurisdiction. Absent statute or decree, the noncustodial parent may petition to enjoin the move. Alternatively, when faced with an impending move, a noncustodial parent may request a custody modification. The current trend in relocation cases is a shift away from a strong presumption favoring such relocations toward a case-by-case evaluation.

The California Supreme Court has addressed several move-away cases in recent years. In re Marriage of Burgess, 51 Cal. Rptr. 2d 444 (Cal. 1996), involved an initial custody determination in which a mother with temporary physical custody desired to move 40 miles away in order to take a better job. In rejecting the father's motion for a change of custody, the California Supreme Court held that the trial court did not abuse its discretion in concluding that the mother should retain sole physical custody in the face of the move. The court also ruled that in an initial custody determination (and stated, by way of dictum, after a custody order is in place) based on the child's best interests, the parent seeking to relocate does not bear the burden of establishing that the move is "necessary" as a condition of custody.

Burgess thereby recognized a presumptive right of the custodial parent to relocate with a child provided that the move would not prejudice the child's welfare. The California legislature codified the result in *Burgess* in California Family Code §7501.

Subsequently, In re Marriage of LaMusga, 88 P.3d 81 (Cal. 2004), weakened the presumption favoring the custodial parent's right to relocate. In *LaMusga*, the California Supreme attempted to clarify the standard applicable to a noncustodial parent who opposes a custodial parent's desire to relocate.

LaMusga involved a mother who desired to move to Ohio. The mother had been awarded joint legal custody but primary physical custody of two children. The trial court ordered a transfer of physical custody to the father if the mother moved. The court of appeals reversed. Reversing, the California Supreme Court held that if the proposed move would cause detriment, then a court must determine whether a change of custody is in the child's best interests. The state supreme court then examined the burden on the noncustodial parent in move-away cases. The court pointed out that "just as a custodial parent does not have to establish that a planned move is 'necessary,' neither does the noncustodial parent have to establish that a change of custody is 'essential' to prevent detriment to the children from the planned move." Id. at 84. The court concluded that the trial court order was not an abuse of discretion because the court properly considered the effect that the move would have on the tenuous relationship between the children and their father.

The case thereby weakened the custodial parent's right to relocate by permitting consideration of such factors as the effect of the move on the noncustodial parent's relationship with the child as a possible detriment to the child's welfare.

The National Conference of Commissioners on Uniform State Laws is presently considering adoption of a uniform law on relocation. Stephanie Francis Ward, Move is Not Enough for Custody Hearing, 7 A.B.A. J. E.-Report 5 (Feb. 17, 2006).

See generally Tricia Kelly, Presumptions, Burdens, and Standards, Oh My: In re Marriage of *LaMusga*'s Search for a Solution to Relocation Disputes, 74 U. Cin. L. Rev. 213, 215 n.16 (2005).

In a subsequent case, In re Marriage of Brown and Yana, 127 P.3d 28 (Cal. 2006), the California Supreme Court held that a trial court has discretion to deny a modification request in a relocation case without holding an evidentiary hearing if the noncustodial parent fails to make a legally sufficient threshold showing of detriment. In this case, the court found that the father failed to make the requisite showing.

§3024. Court may specify that a parent shall notify the other parent of change of residence

In making an order for custody, if the court does not consider it inappropriate, the court may specify that a parent shall notify the other parent if the parent plans to change the residence of the child for more than 30 days, unless there is prior written agreement to the removal. The notice shall be given before the contemplated move, by mail, return receipt requested, postage prepaid, to the last known address of the parent to be notified. A copy of the notice shall also be sent to that parent's counsel of record. To the extent feasible, the notice shall be provided within a minimum of 45 days before the proposed change of residence so as to allow time for mediation of a new agreement concerning custody. This section does not affect orders made before January 1, 1989.

(Stats. 1992 (A.B. 2650), ch. 162, §10, effective January 1, 1994.)

§3063. Court shall enter order restraining removal of child from state pending notice

In conjunction with any ex parte order seeking or modifying an order of custody, the court shall enter an order restraining the person receiving custody from removing the child from the state pending notice and a hearing on the order seeking or modifying custody.

(Stats. 1992 (A.B. 2650), ch. 162, §10, effective January 1, 1994.)

§7501. Custodial parent has right to determine residence of child

(a) A parent entitled to the custody of a child has a right to change the residence of the child, subject to the power of the court to restrain a removal that would prejudice the rights or welfare of the child.

(b) It is the intent of the Legislature to affirm the decision in In re Marriage of Burgess (1996) 13 Cal.4th 25, and to declare that ruling to be the public policy and law of this state.

(Stats. 1993 (A.B. 1500), ch. 219, §164; Amended by Stats. 2003 (S.B. 156), ch. 674, §1.)

G. JURISDICTION AND ENFORCEMENT

1. Generally

Several provisions of the California Family Code pertain to jurisdiction. California Family Code §2010 provides for jurisdiction generally over a number of family law matters. California Family Code §3120 authorizes an action for sole custody without the need for filing a petition for dissolution or separation. In addition, California's version of the Uniform Child Custody Jurisdiction and Enforcement Act is found at California Family Code §§3400 et seq., *infra*.

§2010. Jurisdiction for divorce, annulment and legal separation

In a proceeding for dissolution of marriage, for nullity of marriage, or for legal separation of the parties, the court has jurisdiction to inquire into and render any judgment and make orders that are appropriate concerning the following:

(a) The status of the marriage.

(b) The custody of minor children of the marriage.

(c) The support of children for whom support may be ordered, including children born after the filing of the initial petition or the final decree of dissolution.

(d) The support of either party.

(e) The settlement of the property rights of the parties.

(f) The award of attorney's fees and costs.

(Stats. 1992 (A.B. 2650), ch. 162, §10, effective January 1, 1994. Amended by Stats. 1993 (A.B. 1500), ch. 219, §103. Amended by Stats. 1994 (A.B. 2208), ch. 1269, §12.5.)

§3120. Parent may request exclusive custody without need for petition for divorce or separation

Without filing a petition for dissolution of marriage or legal separation of the parties, the husband or wife may bring an action for the exclusive custody of the children of the marriage. The court may, during the pendency of the action, or at the final hearing thereof, or afterwards, make such order regarding the support, care, custody, education, and control of the children of the marriage as may be just and in accordance with the natural rights of the parents and the best interest of the children. The order may be modified or terminated at any time thereafter as the natural rights of the parties and the best interest of the children may require.

(Stats. 1992 (A.B. 2650), ch. 162, §10, effective January 1, 1994.)

2. Uniform Child Custody Jurisdiction and Enforcement Act

Prior to the 1960's, a state could assert jurisdiction over child custody if it had a "substantial interest" in the case. This vague standard often led to concurrent assertions of jurisdictions by different states. In addition, because of judicial willingness to reopen custody decisions at the behest of a state resident, decrees were freely modifiable in other states. Supreme Court decisions left unclear whether custody decisions were entitled to the protection of the Full, Faith and Credit Clause. Leonard Ratner, Child Custody in a Federal System 62 Mich. L. Rev. 795, 808 (1964).

The Uniform Child Custody Jurisdiction Act (UCCJA) was drafted in 1968 to reduce jurisdictional competition and confusion, as well as to deter parents from forum shopping to re-litigate custody. The Act applies to both initial custody decisions as well as modifications. The UCCJA provided four alternate bases for a state to assert jurisdiction, and attempted to prevent competing assertions of jurisdiction by its prohibition against simultaneous proceedings.

In 1980, Congress enacted the Parental Kidnapping Prevention Act (PKPA), Pub. L. No. 96-611, §6 (1980) (codified as amended in 42 U.S.C. §1073 and 28 U.S.C. §1738A). Despite its title, the PKPA is also relevant in cases involving jurisdiction over child custody. The PKPA was drafted (1) to provide rules that would apply in all states, even those that might never enact the UCCJA, and (2) to make jurisdictional rules uniform because some state legislatures had changed the UCCJA provisions in their enactments and some state courts interpreted the UCCJA provisions differently. Russell M. Coombs, Nuts and Bolts of the PKPA, 22 Colo. Law. 2397 (1993).

In 1997 the National Conference of Commissioners on Uniform State Laws revised the UCCJA by drafting the Uniform Child Custody Jurisdiction and Enforcement Act (UCCJEA). The UCCJEA, which replaces the UCCJA, was intended to harmonize some of the differences between the UCCJA and the PKPA.

The UCCJEA differs from its predecessor UCCJA in several ways. Whereas the UCCJA did not prioritize among the four bases of jurisdiction, the UCCJEA follows the PKPA in giving priority to "home state" jurisdiction. In addition, the UCCJEA goes further than either the UCCJA or PKPA by eliminating the "best interests" language and severely restricting the use of emergency jurisdiction to the issuance of temporary orders. Also the UCCJEA provides strict requirements for modification, providing that a court cannot exercise modification jurisdiction if another state has "exclusive continuing jurisdiction." That is, a state that makes the initial custody determination has continuing exclusive jurisdiction so long as any party to the original custody determination remains in that state. (Continuing exclusive jurisdiction is a feature of the PKPA but not the original UCCJA.)

The UCCJEA is the exclusive authority for determinations of subject matter jurisdiction in child custody cases in California (Cal. Fam. Code §§3400 et seq.). The jurisdictional requirements for initial custody awards are specified in California Family Code §3421; additional requirements apply to modifications in California Family Code §3423. Note that the child's or parent's presence in California is not necessary to confer jurisdiction for custody determinations. (Of course, the out-of-state parent must be given notice and an opportunity to be heard.)

Child custody awards, if they meet the jurisdictional requirements under the Code, will be accorded full faith and credit in other states. As explained above, the UCCJEA limits the ability of a court to modify an award made in another state except in cases of temporary emergency jurisdiction. However, temporary emergency jurisdiction has been severely restricted; it no longer includes cases of "neglected or dependent" (i.e., abused) (Cal. Fam. Code §3424(a)).

Currently, 43 states (including California) and the District of Columbia have adopted the UCCJEA. See Child Custody Jurisdiction and Enforcement Act, Legislative Fact Sheet, available at http://nccusl.org/Update/ActSearch Results.aspx (last visited on June 3, 2006).

a. General Provisions

§3400. Title

This part may be cited as the Uniform Child Custody Jurisdiction and Enforcement Act.
(Stats. 1999 (S.B. 668), ch. 867, §3.)

§3402. Definitions

As used in this part:

(a) "Abandoned" means left without provision for reasonable and necessary care or supervision.

(b) "Child" means an individual who has not attained 18 years of age.

(c) "Child custody determination" means a judgment, decree, or other order of a court providing for the legal custody, physical custody, or visitation with respect to a child. The term includes a permanent, temporary, initial, and modification order. The term does not include an order relating to child support or other monetary obligation of an individual.

(d) "Child custody proceeding" means a proceeding in which legal custody, physical custody, or visitation with respect to a child is an issue. The term includes a proceeding for dissolution of marriage, legal separation of the parties, neglect, abuse, dependency, guardianship, paternity, termination of parental rights, and protection from domestic violence, in which the issue may appear. The term does not include a proceeding involving juvenile delinquency, contractual emancipation, or enforcement under Chapter 3 (commencing with Section 3441).

(e) "Commencement" means the filing of the first pleading in a proceeding.

(f) "Court" means an entity authorized under the law of a state to establish, enforce, or modify a child custody determination.

(g) "Home state" means the state in which a child lived with a parent or a person acting as a parent for at least six consecutive months immediately before the commencement of a child custody proceeding. In the case of a child less than six months of age, the term means the state in which the child lived from birth with any of the persons mentioned. A period of temporary absence of any of the mentioned persons is part of the period.

(h) "Initial determination" means the first child custody determination concerning a particular child.

(i) "Issuing court" means the court that makes a child custody determination for which enforcement is sought under this part.

(j) "Issuing state" means the state in which a child custody determination is made.

(k) "Modification" means a child custody determination that changes, replaces, supersedes, or is otherwise made after a previous determination concerning the same child, whether or not it is made by the court that made the previous determination.

(l) "Person" means an individual, corporation, business trust, estate, trust, partnership, limited liability company, association, joint venture, or government; governmental subdivision, agency, or instrumentality; public corporation; or any other legal or commercial entity.

(m) "Person acting as a parent" means a person, other than a parent, who: (1) has physical custody of the child or has had physical custody for a period of six consecutive months, including any temporary absence, within one year immediately before the commencement of a child custody proceeding; and (2) has been awarded legal custody by a court or claims a right to legal custody under the law of this state.

(n) "Physical custody" means the physical care and supervision of a child.

(o) "State" means a state of the United States, the District of Columbia, Puerto Rico, the United States Virgin Islands, or any territory or insular possession subject to the jurisdiction of the United States.

(p) "Tribe" means an Indian tribe or band, or Alaskan Native village, that is recognized by federal law or formally acknowledged by a state.

(q) "Warrant" means an order issued by a court authorizing law enforcement officers to take physical custody of a child.
(Stats. 1999 (S.B. 668), ch. 867, §3.)

§3403. Inapplicable to adoption proceedings and authorization of emergency medical care

This part does not govern an adoption proceeding or a proceeding pertaining to the authorization of emergency medical care for a child.
(Stats. 1999 (S.B. 668), ch. 867, §3.)

§3404. Inapplicable to custody proceedings involving Indian children

(a) A child custody proceeding that pertains to an Indian child as defined in the Indian Child Welfare Act (25 U.S.C. Secs. 1901 et seq.) is not subject to this part to the extent that it is governed by the Indian Child Welfare Act.

(b) A court of this state shall treat a tribe as if it were a state of the United States for the purpose of applying this chapter and Chapter 2 (commencing with Section 3421).

(c) A child custody determination made by a tribe under factual circumstances in substantial conformity with the jurisdictional standards of this part must be recognized and enforced under Chapter 3 (commencing with Section 3441).
(Stats. 1999 (S.B. 668), ch. 867, §3.)

§3405. Custody determinations of foreign country

(a) A court of this state shall treat a foreign country as if it were a state of the United States for the purpose of applying this chapter and Chapter 2 (commencing with Section 3421).

(b) Except as otherwise provided in subdivision (c), a child custody determination made in a foreign country under factual circumstances in substantial conformity with the jurisdictional standards of this part must be recognized and enforced under Chapter 3 (commencing with Section 3441 [set forth in §G2c *infra*]).

(c) A court of this state need not apply this part if the child custody law of a foreign country violates fundamental principles of human rights.
(Stats. 1999 (S.B. 668), ch. 867, §3.)

§3406. Child custody determination is binding and conclusive

A child custody determination made by a court of this state that had jurisdiction under this part binds all persons who have been served in accordance with the laws of this state or notified in accordance with Section 3408 or who have submitted to the jurisdiction of the court, and who have been given an opportunity to be heard. As to those persons, the determination is conclusive as to all decided issues of law and fact except to the extent the determination is modified.

(Stats. 1999 (S.B. 668), ch. 867, §3.)

§3407. Challenges to jurisdiction have priority on calendar

If a question of existence or exercise of jurisdiction under this part is raised in a child custody proceeding, the question, upon request of a party, must be given priority on the calendar and handled expeditiously.

(Stats. 1999 (S.B. 668), ch. 867, §3.)

§3408. Requirements for notice to person outside state

(a) Notice required for the exercise of jurisdiction when a person is outside this state may be given in a manner prescribed by the law of this state for service of process or by the law of the state in which the service is made. Notice must be given in a manner reasonably calculated to give actual notice but may be by publication if other means are not effective.

(b) Proof of service may be made in the manner prescribed by the law of this state or by the law of the state in which the service is made.

(c) Notice is not required for the exercise of jurisdiction with respect to a person who submits to the jurisdiction of the court.

(Stats. 1999 (S.B. 668), ch. 867, §3.)

§3409. Court's exercise of personal jurisdiction is limited

(a) A party to a child custody proceeding, including a modification proceeding, or a petitioner or respondent in a proceeding to enforce or register a child custody determination, is not subject to personal jurisdiction in this state for another proceeding or purpose solely by reason of having participated, or of having been physically present for the purpose of participating, in the proceeding.

(b) A person who is subject to personal jurisdiction in this state on a basis other than physical presence is not immune from service of process in this state. A party present in this state who is subject to the jurisdiction of another state is not immune from service of process allowable under the laws of that state.

(c) The immunity granted by subdivision (a) does not extend to civil litigation based on acts unrelated to the participation in a proceeding under this part committed by an individual while present in this state.

(Stats. 1999 (S.B. 668), ch. 867, §3.)

§3410. Court may communicate with court in another state concerning proceeding

(a) A court of this state may communicate with a court in another state concerning a proceeding arising under this part.

(b) The court may allow the parties to participate in the communication. If the parties are not able to participate in the communication, they must be given the opportunity to present facts and legal arguments before a decision on jurisdiction is made.

(c) Communication between courts on schedules, calendars, court records, and similar matters may occur without informing the parties. A record need not be made of the communication.

(d) Except as otherwise provided in subdivision (c), a record must be made of a communication under this section. The parties must be informed promptly of the communication and granted access to the record.

(e) For the purposes of this section, "record" means information that is inscribed on a tangible medium or that is stored in an electronic or other medium and is retrievable in perceivable form.

(Stats. 1999 (S.B. 668), ch. 867, §3.)

§3411. Party may offer testimony of witnesses located in another state by deposition

(a) In addition to other procedures available to a party, a party to a child custody proceeding may offer testimony of witnesses who are located in another state, including testimony of the parties and the child, by deposition or other means allowable in this state for testimony taken in another state. The court, on its own motion, may order that the testimony of a person be taken in another state and may prescribe the manner in which and the terms upon which the testimony is taken.

(b) A court of this state may permit an individual residing in another state to be deposed or to testify by telephone, audiovisual means, or other electronic means before a designated court or at another location in that state. A court of this state shall cooperate with courts of other states in designating an appropriate location for the deposition or testimony.

(c) Documentary evidence transmitted from another state to a court of this state by technological means that do not produce an original writing may not be excluded from evidence on an objection based on the means of transmission.

(Stats. 1999 (S.B. 668), ch. 867, §3.)

§3412. Court may request hearings or evaluations in another state

(a) A court of this state may request the appropriate court of another state to do all of the following:

(1) Hold an evidentiary hearing.

(2) Order a person to produce or give evidence pursuant to procedures of that state.

(3) Order that an evaluation be made with respect to the custody of a child involved in a pending proceeding.

(4) Forward to the court of this state a certified copy of the transcript of the record of the hearing, the evidence

otherwise presented, and any evaluation prepared in compliance with the request.

(5) Order a party to a child custody proceeding or any person having physical custody of the child to appear in the proceeding with or without the child.

(b) Upon request of a court of another state, a court of this state may hold a hearing or enter an order described in subdivision (a).

(c) Travel and other necessary and reasonable expenses incurred under subdivisions (a) and (b) may be assessed against the parties according to the law of this state.

(d) A court of this state shall preserve the pleadings, orders, decrees, records of hearings, evaluations, and other pertinent records with respect to a child custody proceeding until the child attains 18 years of age. Upon appropriate request by a court or law enforcement official of another state, the court shall forward a certified copy of those records.

(Stats. 1999 (S.B. 668), ch. 867, §3.)

§3461. Need to promote uniformity of law

In applying and construing this Uniform Child Custody Jurisdiction and Enforcement Act, consideration shall be given to the need to promote uniformity of the law with respect to its subject matter among states that enact it.

(Stats. 1999 (S.B. 668), ch. 867, §3.)

§3462. Invalid provision is severable

If any provision of this part or its application to any person or circumstance is held invalid, the invalidity does not affect other provisions or applications of this part that can be given effect without the invalid provision or application, and to this end the provisions of this part are severable.

(Stats. 1999 (S.B. 668), ch. 867, §3.)

§3465. Governing law in effect at time of request

A motion or other request for relief made in a child custody proceeding or to enforce a child custody determination that was commenced before the effective date of this part is governed by the law in effect at the time the motion or other request was made.

(Stats 1999 (S.B. 668), ch. 867, §3.)

---

b. Jurisdiction

§3421. Conditions for exercise of jurisdiction for custody determinations

(a) Except as otherwise provided in Section 3424, a court of this state has jurisdiction to make an initial child custody determination only if any of the following are true:

(1) This state is the home state of the child on the date of the commencement of the proceeding, or was the home state of the child within six months before the commencement of the proceeding and the child is absent from this state but a parent or person acting as a parent continues to live in this state.

(2) A court of another state does not have jurisdiction under paragraph (1), or a court of the home state of the child has declined to exercise jurisdiction on the grounds that this state is the more appropriate forum under Section 3427 or 3428, and both of the following are true:

(A) The child and the child's parents, or the child and at least one parent or a person acting as a parent, have a significant connection with this state other than mere physical presence.

(B) Substantial evidence is available in this state concerning the child's care, protection, training, and personal relationships.

(3) All courts having jurisdiction under paragraph (1) or (2) have declined to exercise jurisdiction on the ground that a court of this state is the more appropriate forum to determine the custody of the child under Section 3427 or 3428.

(4) No court of any other state would have jurisdiction under the criteria specified in paragraph (1), (2), or (3).

(b) Subdivision (a) is the exclusive jurisdictional basis for making a child custody determination by a court of this state.

(c) Physical presence of, or personal jurisdiction over, a party or a child is not necessary or sufficient to make a child custody determination.

(Stats. 1999 (S.B. 668), ch. 867, §3.)

§3422. Court has exclusive and continuing jurisdiction

(a) Except as otherwise provided in Section 3424, a court of this state that has made a child custody determination consistent with Section 3421 or 3423 has exclusive, continuing jurisdiction over the determination until either of the following occurs:

(1) A court of this state determines that neither the child, nor the child and one parent, nor the child and a person acting as a parent have a significant connection with this state and that substantial evidence is no longer available in this state concerning the child's care, protection, training, and personal relationships.

(2) A court of this state or a court of another state determines that the child, the child's parents, and any person acting as a parent do not presently reside in this state.

(b) A court of this state that has made a child custody determination and does not have exclusive, continuing jurisdiction under this section may modify that determination only if it has jurisdiction to make an initial determination under Section 3421.

(Stats. 1999 (S.B. 668), ch. 867, §3.)

§3423. Court's ability to modify determination made by another state

Except as otherwise provided in Section 3424, a court of this state may not modify a child custody determination made by a court of another state unless a court of this state has jurisdiction to make an initial determination under paragraph (1) or (2) of subdivision (a) of Section 3421 and either of the following determinations is made:

(a) The court of the other state determines it no longer has exclusive, continuing jurisdiction under Section 3422 or that a court of this state would be a more convenient forum under Section 3427.

(b) A court of this state or a court of the other state determines that the child, the child's parents, and any person acting as a parent do not presently reside in the other state.
(Stats. 1999 (S.B. 668), ch. 867, §3.)

§3424. Conditions of exercise of temporary emergency jurisdiction

(a) A court of this state has temporary emergency jurisdiction if the child is present in this state and the child has been abandoned or it is necessary in an emergency to protect the child because the child, or a sibling or parent of the child, is subjected to, or threatened with, mistreatment or abuse.

(b) If there is no previous child custody determination that is entitled to be enforced under this part and a child custody proceeding has not been commenced in a court of a state having jurisdiction under Sections 3421 to 3423, inclusive, a child custody determination made under this section remains in effect until an order is obtained from a court of a state having jurisdiction under Sections 3421 to 3423, inclusive. If a child custody proceeding has not been or is not commenced in a court of a state having jurisdiction under Sections 3421 to 3423, inclusive, a child custody determination made under this section becomes a final determination, if it so provides and this state becomes the home state of the child.

(c) If there is a previous child custody determination that is entitled to be enforced under this part, or a child custody proceeding has been commenced in a court of a state having jurisdiction under Sections 3421 to 3423, inclusive, any order issued by a court of this state under this section must specify in the order a period that the court considers adequate to allow the person seeking an order to obtain an order from the state having jurisdiction under Sections 3421 to 3423, inclusive. The order issued in this state remains in effect until an order is obtained from the other state within the period specified or the period expires.

(d) A court of this state that has been asked to make a child custody determination under this section, upon being informed that a child custody proceeding has been commenced in, or a child custody determination has been made by, a court of a state having jurisdiction under Sections 3421 to 3423, inclusive, shall immediately communicate with the other court. A court of this state which is exercising jurisdiction pursuant to Sections 3421 to 3423, inclusive, upon being informed that a child custody proceeding has been commenced in, or a child custody determination has been made by, a court of another state under a statute similar to this section shall immediately communicate with the court of that state to resolve the emergency, protect the safety of the parties and the child, and determine a period for the duration of the temporary order.

(e) It is the intent of the Legislature in enacting subdivision (a) that the grounds on which a court may exercise temporary emergency jurisdiction be expanded. It is further the intent of the Legislature that these grounds include those that existed under Section 3403 of the Family Code as that section read on December 31, 1999, particularly including cases involving domestic violence.
(Stats. 1999 (S.B. 668), ch. 867, §3.)

§3425. Notice and opportunity to be heard in custody determinations

(a) Before a child custody determination is made under this part, notice and an opportunity to be heard in accordance with the standards of Section 3428 must be given to all persons entitled to notice under the law of this state as in child custody proceedings between residents of this state, any parent whose parental rights have not been previously terminated, and any person having physical custody of the child.

(b) This part does not govern the enforceability of a child custody determination made without notice or an opportunity to be heard.

(c) The obligation to join a party and the right to intervene as a party in a child custody proceeding under this part are governed by the law of this state as in child custody proceedings between residents of this state.
(Stats. 1999 (S.B. 668), ch. 867, §3.)

§3426. Prohibition on simultaneous proceedings in different states

(a) Except as otherwise provided in Section 3424, a court of this state may not exercise its jurisdiction under this chapter if, at the time of the commencement of the proceeding, a proceeding concerning the custody of the child has been commenced in a court of another state having jurisdiction substantially in conformity with this part, unless the proceeding has been terminated or is stayed by the court of the other state because a court of this state is a more convenient forum under Section 3427.

(b) Except as otherwise provided in Section 3424, a court of this state, before hearing a child custody proceeding, shall examine the court documents and other information supplied by the parties pursuant to Section 3429. If the court determines that a child custody proceeding has been commenced in a court in another state having jurisdiction substantially in accordance with this part, the court of this state shall stay its proceeding and communicate with the court of the other state. If the court of the state having jurisdiction substantially in accordance with this part does not determine that the court of this state is a more appropriate forum, the court of this state shall dismiss the proceeding.

(c) In a proceeding to modify a child custody determination, a court of this state shall determine whether a proceeding to enforce the determination has been commenced in another state. If a proceeding to enforce a child custody determination has been commenced in another state, the court may do any of the following:

(1) Stay the proceeding for modification pending the entry of an order of a court of the other state enforcing, staying, denying, or dismissing the proceeding for enforcement.

(2) Enjoin the parties from continuing with the proceeding for enforcement.

(3) Proceed with the modification under conditions it considers appropriate.
(Stats. 1999 (S.B. 668), ch. 867, §3.)

§3427. Court may decline to exercise jurisdiction subject to determination of inconvenient forum

(a) A court of this state that has jurisdiction under this part to make a child custody determination may decline to exercise its jurisdiction at any time if it determines that it is an inconvenient forum under the circumstances and that a court of another state is a more appropriate forum. The issue of inconvenient forum may be raised upon motion of a party, the court's own motion, or request of another court.

(b) Before determining whether it is an inconvenient forum, a court of this state shall consider whether it is appropriate for a court of another state to exercise jurisdiction. For this purpose, the court shall allow the parties to submit information and shall consider all relevant factors, including:

(1) Whether domestic violence has occurred and is likely to continue in the future and which state could best protect the parties and the child.

(2) The length of time the child has resided outside this state.

(3) The distance between the court in this state and the court in the state that would assume jurisdiction.

(4) The degree of financial hardship to the parties in litigating in one forum over the other.

(5) Any agreement of the parties as to which state should assume jurisdiction.

(6) The nature and location of the evidence required to resolve the pending litigation, including testimony of the child.

(7) The ability of the court of each state to decide the issue expeditiously and the procedures necessary to present the evidence.

(8) The familiarity of the court of each state with the facts and issues in the pending litigation.

(c) If a court of this state determines that it is an inconvenient forum and that a court of another state is a more appropriate forum, it shall stay the proceedings upon condition that a child custody proceeding be promptly commenced in another designated state and may impose any other condition the court considers just and proper.

(d) A court of this state may decline to exercise its jurisdiction under this part if a child custody determination is incidental to an action for dissolution of marriage or another proceeding while still retaining jurisdiction over the dissolution of marriage or other proceeding.

(e) If it appears to the court that it is clearly an inappropriate forum, the court may require the party who commenced the proceeding to pay, in addition to the costs of the proceeding in this state, necessary travel and other expenses, including attorney's fees, incurred by the other parties or their witnesses. Payment is to be made to the clerk of the court for remittance to the proper party.

(Stats. 1999 (S.B. 668), ch. 867, §3.)

§3428. Court must decline jurisdiction on ground of unjustifiable conduct

(a) Except as otherwise provided in Section 3424 or by any other law of this state, if a court of this state has jurisdiction under this part because a person seeking to invoke its jurisdiction has engaged in unjustifiable conduct, the court shall decline to exercise its jurisdiction unless one of the following are true:

(1) The parents and all persons acting as parents have acquiesced in the exercise of jurisdiction.

(2) A court of the state otherwise having jurisdiction under Sections 3421 to 3423, inclusive, determines that this state is a more appropriate forum under Section 3427.

(3) No court of any other state would have jurisdiction under the criteria specified in Sections 3421 to 3423, inclusive.

(b) If a court of this state declines to exercise its jurisdiction pursuant to subdivision (a), it may fashion an appropriate remedy to ensure the safety of the child and prevent a repetition of the unjustifiable conduct, including staying the proceeding until a child custody proceeding is commenced in a court having jurisdiction under Sections 3421 to 3423, inclusive.

(c) If a court dismisses a petition or stays a proceeding because it declines to exercise its jurisdiction pursuant to subdivision (a), it shall assess against the party seeking to invoke its jurisdiction necessary and reasonable expenses including costs, communication expenses, attorney's fees, investigative fees, expenses for witnesses, travel expenses, and child care during the course of the proceedings, unless the party from whom fees are sought establishes that the assessment would be clearly inappropriate. The court may not assess fees, costs, or expenses against this state unless authorized by law other than this part.

(d) In making a determination under this section, a court shall not consider as a factor weighing against the petitioner any taking of the child, or retention of the child after a visit or other temporary relinquishment of physical custody, from the person who has legal custody, if there is evidence that the taking or retention of the child was a result of domestic violence against the petitioner, as defined in Section 6211.

(Stats. 1999 (S.B. 668), ch. 867, §3.)

§3429. Confidentiality of information provided to court in cases of domestic violence

(a) In a child custody proceeding, each party, in its first pleading or in an attached affidavit, shall give information, if reasonably ascertainable, under oath as to the child's present address or whereabouts, the places where the child has lived during the last five years, and the names and present addresses of the persons with whom the child has lived during that period. However, where there are allegations of domestic violence or child abuse, any addresses of the party alleging violence or abuse and of the child which are unknown to the other party are confidential and may not be disclosed in the pleading or affidavit. The pleading or affidavit must state whether the party:

(1) Has participated, as a party or witness or in any other capacity, in any other proceeding concerning the custody of, or visitation with, the child and, if so, identify the court, the case number, and the date of the child custody determination, if any.

(2) Knows of any proceeding that could affect the current proceeding, including proceedings for enforcement and proceedings relating to domestic violence, protective orders, termination of parental rights, and adoptions and, if

so, identify the court, the case number, and the nature of the proceeding.

(3) Knows the names and addresses of any person not a party to the proceeding who has physical custody of the child or claims rights of legal custody or physical custody of, or visitation with, the child and, if so, the names and addresses of those persons.

(b) If the information required by subdivision (a) is not furnished, the court, upon motion of a party or its own motion, may stay the proceeding until the information is furnished.

(c) If the declaration as to any of the items described in paragraphs (1) to (3), inclusive, of subdivision (a) is in the affirmative, the declarant shall give additional information under oath as required by the court. The court may examine the parties under oath as to details of the information furnished and other matters pertinent to the court's jurisdiction and the disposition of the case.

(d) Each party has a continuing duty to inform the court of any proceeding in this or any other state that could affect the current proceeding.

(Stats. 1999 (S.B. 668), ch. 867, §3.)

§3430. Court may order party to appear with or without child

(a) In a child custody proceeding in this state, the court may order a party to the proceeding who is in this state to appear before the court in person with or without the child. The court may order any person who is in this state and who has physical custody or control of the child to appear in person with the child.

(b) If a party to a child custody proceeding whose presence is desired by the court is outside this state, the court may order that a notice given pursuant to Section 3408 include a statement directing the party to appear in person with or without the child and informing the party that failure to appear may result in a decision adverse to the party.

(c) The court may enter any orders necessary to ensure the safety of the child and of any person ordered to appear under this section.

(d) If a party to a child custody proceeding who is outside this state is directed to appear under subdivision (b) or desires to appear personally before the court with or without the child, the court may require another party to pay reasonable and necessary travel and other expenses of the party so appearing and of the child.

(Stats. 1999 (S.B. 668), ch. 867, §3.)

c. Enforcement

§3441. "Petitioner" and "Respondent"

In this chapter:

(a) "Petitioner" means a person who seeks enforcement of an order for return of a child under the Hague Convention on the Civil Aspects of International Child Abduction or enforcement of a child custody determination.

(b) "Respondent" means a person against whom a proceeding has been commenced for enforcement of an order for return of a child under the Hague Convention on the Civil Aspects of International Child Abduction or enforcement of a child custody determination.

(Stats. 1999 (S.B. 668), ch. 867, §3.)

§3442. Court may enforce order under Hague Convention on Child Abduction

Under this chapter, a court of this state may enforce an order for the return of a child made under the Hague Convention on the Civil Aspects of International Child Abduction as if it were a child custody determination.

(Stats. 1999 (S.B. 668), ch. 867, §3.)

§3443. Court may recognize and enforce another state's custody determination

(a) A court of this state shall recognize and enforce a child custody determination of a court of another state if the latter court exercised jurisdiction in substantial conformity with this part or the determination was made under factual circumstances meeting the jurisdictional standards of this part and the determination has not been modified in accordance with this part.

(b) A court of this state may utilize any remedy available under other laws of this state to enforce a child custody determination made by a court of another state. The remedies provided in this chapter are cumulative and do not affect the availability of other remedies to enforce a child custody determination.

(Stats. 1999 (S.B. 668), ch. 867, §3.)

§3444. Court lacking jurisdiction to modify may still issue temporary order

(a) A court of this state which does not have jurisdiction to modify a child custody determination may issue a temporary order enforcing either:

(1) A visitation schedule made by a court of another state.

(2) The visitation provisions of a child custody determination of another state that does not provide for a specific visitation schedule.

(b) If a court of this state makes an order under paragraph (2) of subdivision (a), it shall specify in the order a period that it considers adequate to allow the petitioner to obtain an order from a court having jurisdiction under the criteria specified in Chapter 2 (commencing with Section 3421). The order remains in effect until an order is obtained from the other court or the period expires.

(Stats. 1999 (S.B. 668), ch. 867, §3.)

§3445. Method of registering determination by court of another state

(a) A child custody determination issued by a court of another state may be registered in this state, with or without a simultaneous request for enforcement, by sending all of the following to the appropriate court in this state:

(1) A letter or other document requesting registration.

(2) Two copies, including one certified copy, of the determination sought to be registered, and a statement under penalty of perjury that to the best of the knowledge

and belief of the person seeking registration the order has not been modified.

(3) Except as otherwise provided in Section 3429, the name and address of the person seeking registration and any parent or person acting as a parent who has been awarded custody or visitation in the child custody determination sought to be registered.

(b) On receipt of the documents required by subdivision (a), the registering court shall do both of the following:

(1) Cause the determination to be filed as a foreign judgment, together with one copy of any accompanying documents and information, regardless of their form.

(2) Serve notice upon the persons named pursuant to paragraph (3) of subdivision (a) and provide them with an opportunity to contest the registration in accordance with this section.

(c) The notice required by paragraph (2) of subdivision (b) shall state all of the following:

(1) That a registered determination is enforceable as of the date of the registration in the same manner as a determination issued by a court of this state.

(2) That a hearing to contest the validity of the registered determination must be requested within 20 days after service of the notice.

(3) That failure to contest the registration will result in confirmation of the child custody determination and preclude further contest of that determination with respect to any matter that could have been asserted.

(d) A person seeking to contest the validity of a registered order must request a hearing within 20 days after service of the notice. At that hearing, the court shall confirm the registered order unless the person contesting registration establishes any of the following:

(1) That the issuing court did not have jurisdiction under Chapter 2 (commencing with Section 3421).

(2) That the child custody determination sought to be registered has been vacated, stayed, or modified by a court having jurisdiction to do so under Chapter 2 (commencing with Section 3421).

(3) That the person contesting registration was entitled to notice, but notice was not given in accordance with the standards of Section 3408, in the proceedings before the court that issued the order for which registration is sought.

(e) If a timely request for a hearing to contest the validity of the registration is not made, the registration is confirmed as a matter of law and the person requesting registration and all persons served shall be notified of the confirmation.

(f) Confirmation of a registered order, whether by operation of law or after notice and hearing, precludes further contest of the order with respect to any matter that could have been asserted at the time of registration.

(Stats. 1999 (S.B. 668), ch. 867, §3.)

§3446. Court may grant relief to enforce a registered determination by another state

(a) A court of this state may grant any relief normally available under the law of this state to enforce a registered child custody determination made by a court of another state.

(b) A court of this state shall recognize and enforce, but may not modify, except in accordance with Chapter 2 (commencing with Section 3421), a registered child custody determination of a court of another state.

(Stats. 1999 (S.B. 668), ch. 867, §3.)

§3447. Contemporaneous enforcement proceedings in more than one state

If a proceeding for enforcement under this chapter is commenced in a court of this state and the court determines that a proceeding to modify the determination is pending in a court of another state having jurisdiction to modify the determination under Chapter 2 (commencing with Section 3421), the enforcing court shall immediately communicate with the modifying court. The proceeding for enforcement continues unless the enforcing court, after consultation with the modifying court, stays or dismisses the proceeding.

(Stats. 1999 (S.B. 668), ch. 867, §3.)

§3448. Requirements for petition

(a) A petition under this chapter must be verified. Certified copies of all orders sought to be enforced and of any order confirming registration must be attached to the petition. A copy of a certified copy of an order may be attached instead of the original.

(b) A petition for enforcement of a child custody determination must state all of the following:

(1) Whether the court that issued the determination identified the jurisdictional basis it relied upon in exercising jurisdiction and, if so, what the basis was.

(2) Whether the determination for which enforcement is sought has been vacated, stayed, or modified by a court whose decision must be enforced under this part and, if so, identify the court, the case number, and the nature of the proceeding.

(3) Whether any proceeding has been commenced that could affect the current proceeding, including proceedings relating to domestic violence, protective orders, termination of parental rights, and adoptions and, if so, identify the court, the case number, and the nature of the proceeding.

(4) The present physical address of the child and the respondent, if known.

(5) Whether relief in addition to the immediate physical custody of the child and attorney's fees is sought, including a request for assistance from law enforcement officials and, if so, the relief sought.

(6) If the child custody determination has been registered and confirmed under Section 3445, the date and place of registration.

(c) Upon the filing of a petition, the court shall issue an order directing the respondent to appear in person with or without the child at a hearing and may enter any order necessary to ensure the safety of the parties and the child. The hearing must be held on the next judicial day after service of the order unless that date is impossible. In that event, the court shall hold the hearing on the first judicial day possible. The court may extend the date of hearing at the request of the petitioner.

(d) An order issued under subdivision (c) must state the time and place of the hearing and advise the respondent that, at the hearing, the court will order that the petitioner may take immediate physical custody of the child and the payment of fees, costs, and expenses under Section 3452, and may schedule a hearing to determine whether further relief is appropriate, unless the respondent appears and establishes either of the following:

(1) That the child custody determination has not been registered and confirmed under Section 3445 and all of the following are true:

(A) The issuing court did not have jurisdiction under Chapter 2 (commencing with Section 3421).

(B) The child custody determination for which enforcement is sought has been vacated, stayed, or modified by a court having jurisdiction to do so under Chapter 2 (commencing with Section 3421).

(C) The respondent was entitled to notice, but notice was not given in accordance with the standards of Section 3408, in the proceedings before the court that issued the order for which enforcement is sought.

(2) That the child custody determination for which enforcement is sought was registered and confirmed under Section 3444, but has been vacated, stayed, or modified by a court of a state having jurisdiction to do so under Chapter 2 (commencing with Section 3421).

(Stats. 1999 (S.B. 668), ch. 867, §3.)

§3449. Service of petition and order upon respondent and custodian

Except as otherwise provided in Section 3451, the petition and order shall be served, by any method authorized by the law of this state, upon the respondent and any person who has physical custody of the child.

(Stats. 1999 (S.B. 668), ch. 867, §3.)

§3450. Court shall order petitioner to take immediate physical custody

(a) Unless the court issues a temporary emergency order pursuant to Section 3424, upon a finding that a petitioner is entitled to immediate physical custody of the child, the court shall order that the petitioner may take immediate physical custody of the child unless the respondent establishes either of the following:

(1) That the child custody determination has not been registered and confirmed under Section 3445 and one of the following is true:

(A) The issuing court did not have jurisdiction under Chapter 2 (commencing with Section 3421).

(B) The child custody determination for which enforcement is sought has been vacated, stayed, or modified by a court of a state having jurisdiction to do so under Chapter 2 (commencing with Section 3421).

(C) The respondent was entitled to notice, but notice was not given in accordance with the standards of Section 3408, in the proceedings before the court that issued the order for which enforcement is sought.

(2) That the child custody determination for which enforcement is sought was registered and confirmed under Section 3445 but has been vacated, stayed, or modified by a court of a state having jurisdiction to do so under Chapter 2 (commencing with Section 3421).

(b) The court shall award the fees, costs, and expenses authorized under Section 3452 and may grant additional relief, including a request for the assistance of law enforcement officials, and set a further hearing to determine whether additional relief is appropriate.

(c) If a party called to testify refuses to answer on the ground that the testimony may be self-incriminating, the court may draw an adverse inference from the refusal.

(d) A privilege against disclosure of communications between spouses and a defense of immunity based on the relationship of husband and wife or parent and child may not be invoked in a proceeding under this chapter.

(Stats. 1999 (S.B. 668), ch. 867, §3.)

§3451. Petitioner may apply for issuance of warrant to take physical custody of child

(a) Upon the filing of a petition seeking enforcement of a child custody determination, the petitioner may file a verified application for the issuance of a warrant to take physical custody of the child if the child is imminently likely to suffer serious physical harm or be removed from this state.

(b) If the court, upon the testimony of the petitioner or other witness, finds that the child is imminently likely to suffer serious physical harm or be removed from this state, it may issue a warrant to take physical custody of the child. The petition must be heard on the next judicial day after the warrant is executed unless that date is impossible. In that event, the court shall hold the hearing on the first judicial day possible. The application for the warrant must include the statements required by subdivision (b) of Section 3448.

(c) A warrant to take physical custody of a child must do all of the following:

(1) Recite the facts upon which a conclusion of imminent serious physical harm or removal from the jurisdiction is based.

(2) Direct law enforcement officers to take physical custody of the child immediately.

(3) Provide for the placement of the child pending final relief.

(d) The respondent must be served with the petition, warrant, and order immediately after the child is taken into physical custody.

(e) A warrant to take physical custody of a child is enforceable throughout this state. If the court finds on the basis of the testimony of the petitioner or other witness that a less intrusive remedy is not effective, it may authorize law enforcement officers to enter private property to take physical custody of the child. If required by exigent circumstances of the case, the court may authorize law enforcement officers to make a forcible entry at any hour.

(f) The court may impose conditions upon placement of a child to ensure the appearance of the child and the child's custodian.

(Stats. 1999 (S.B. 668), ch. 867, §3.)

§3452. Court shall award costs and expenses for prevailing party

(a) The court shall award the prevailing party, including a state, necessary and reasonable expenses incurred by or on behalf of the party, including costs, communication expenses, attorney's fees, investigative fees, expenses for witnesses, travel expenses, and child care during the course of the proceedings, unless the party from whom fees or expenses are sought establishes that the award would be clearly inappropriate.

(b) The court may not assess fees, costs, or expenses against a state unless authorized by law other than this part.
(Stats. 1999 (S.B. 668), ch. 867, §3.)

§3453. Full faith and credit to orders issued by another state

A court of this state shall accord full faith and credit to an order issued by another state, and consistent with this part, enforce a child custody determination by a court of another state unless the order has been vacated, stayed, or modified by a court having jurisdiction to do so under Chapter 2 (commencing with Section 3421).
(Stats. 1999 (S.B. 668), ch. 867, §3.)

§3454. Appeal procedures

An appeal may be taken from a final order in a proceeding under this chapter in accordance with expedited appellate procedures in other civil cases. Unless the court enters a temporary emergency order under Section 3424, the enforcing court may not stay an order enforcing a child custody determination pending appeal.
(Stats. 1999 (S.B. 668), ch. 867, §3.)

§3455. District attorney's authority in cases of international child abduction

(a) In a case arising under this part or involving the Hague Convention on the Civil Aspects of International Child Abduction, a district attorney is authorized to proceed pursuant to Chapter 8 (commencing with Section 3130) of Part 2.

(b) A district attorney acting under this section acts on behalf of the court and may not represent any party.
(Stats. 1999 (S.B. 668), ch. 867, §3.)

§3456. Law enforcement officer may assist in finding child or any party

At the request of a district attorney acting under Section 3455, a law enforcement officer may take any lawful action reasonably necessary to locate a child or a party and assist the district attorney with responsibilities under Section 3455.
(Stats. 1999 (S.B. 668), ch. 867, §3.)

§3457. Court may assess costs and expenses incurred by district attorney

The court may assess all direct expenses and costs incurred by a district attorney under Section 3455 or 3456 pursuant to the provisions of Section 3134.
(Stats. 1999 (S.B. 668), ch. 867, §3.)

3. Parental Abduction

Parental abduction is an increasingly serious problem. Traditional remedies in cases of parental abduction include civil contempt proceedings and the writ of habeas corpus. California legislation currently authorizes the court and district attorney to take certain actions to locate and return children who have been taken in violation of a custody or visitation order. See, e.g., Cal. Fam. Code §3131 (district attorney must take "all actions necessary"); Cal. Fam. Code §3133 (court may make a temporary custody order to facilitate the return of the child); Cal. Fam. Code §3134.5 (court may issue a protective custody warrant to secure the recovery of the child).

The Hague Convention on the Civil Aspects of International Child Abduction governs international abductions. The United States implemented the Convention by enabling legislation, the International Child Abduction Remedies Act (ICARA), 42 U.S.C. §§11601-11610 (2000). In 2002, the Ninth Circuit Court of Appeals held that, in light of the Hague Convention's policy encouraging signatory countries to return children expeditiously and through any appropriate remedy, a federal district court erred by staying a parent's petition for the return of his children until the parent's state court custody proceedings were resolved. Holder v. Holder, 305 F.3d 854 (9th Cir. 2002). See also Gonzalez v. Gutierrez, 311 F.3d 942 (9th Cir. 2002) (holding that *ne exeat* clause in foreign divorce agreement, which prohibited mother from taking children out of the country without father's permission, did not grant father right to determine his children's place of residence, such that father had "custodial rights" under Hague Convention when he possessed only access rights to children).

Congress has also addressed international child abduction. In 1993 Congress enacted the International Parental Kidnapping Act (IPKA), 18 U.S.C. §1204 (2000). Unlike the Hague Convention, IPKA imposes criminal sanctions. IPKA makes it a federal felony for a parent wrongfully to remove or retain a child outside the United States. IPKA's affirmative defenses differ from those in the Hague Convention: if the defendant has been granted custody or visitation by a court acting pursuant to the UCCJA; is fleeing from domestic violence; or had court-ordered custody and failed to return the child because of circumstances beyond the defendant's control, provided that the defendant made reasonable attempts to notify the other parent.

See generally Barbara Lubin, Note, International Parental Child Abduction: Conceptualizing New Remedies Through Application of the Hague Convention4 Wash. U. Global Stud. L. Rev. 415 (2005).

In 2002 the California legislature enacted new legislation (Cal. Fam. Code §3048) to deter child abductions. If a court makes a finding that the child is at risk, it must consider taking certain measures to prevent the child's abduction. (Cal. Fam. Code §3048(b)(2).) See generally Deborah M. Zawadski, Note, The Role of Courts in Preventing International Child Abduction, 13 Cardozo J. Int'l & Comp. L. 353 (2005).

§3048. Synclair-Cannon Child Abduction Prevention Act; required contents for custody or visitation orders

(a) Notwithstanding any other provision of law, in any proceeding to determine child custody or visitation with a child, every custody or visitation order shall contain all of the following:

(1) The basis for the court's exercise of jurisdiction.

(2) The manner in which notice and opportunity to be heard were given.

(3) A clear description of the custody and visitation rights of each party.

(4) A provision stating that a violation of the order may subject the party in violation to civil or criminal penalties, or both.

(5) Identification of the country of habitual residence of the child or children.

(b) (1) In cases in which the court becomes aware of facts which may indicate that there is a risk of abduction of a child, the court shall, either on its own motion or at the request of a party, determine whether measures are needed to prevent the abduction of the child by one parent. To make that determination, the court shall consider the risk of abduction of the child, obstacles to location, recovery, and return if the child is abducted, and potential harm to the child if he or she is abducted. To determine whether there is a risk of abduction, the court shall consider the following factors:

(A) Whether a party has previously taken, enticed away, kept, withheld, or concealed a child in violation of the right of custody or of visitation of a person

(B) Whether a party has previously threatened to take, entice away, keep, withhold, or conceal a child in violation of the right of custody or of visitation of a person.

(C) Whether a party lacks strong ties to this state.

(D) Whether a party has strong familial, emotional, or cultural ties to another state or country, including foreign citizenship. This factor shall be considered only if evidence exists in support of another factor specified in this section.

(E) Whether a party has no financial reason to stay in this state, including whether the party is unemployed, is able to work anywhere, or is financially independent.

(F) Whether a party has engaged in planning activities that would facilitate the removal of a child from the state, including quitting a job, selling his or her primary residence, terminating a lease, closing a bank account, liquidating other assets, hiding or destroying documents, applying for a passport, applying to obtain a birth certificate or school or medical records, or purchasing airplane or other travel tickets, with consideration given to whether a party is carrying out a safety plan to flee from domestic violence.

(G) Whether a party has a history of a lack of parental cooperation or child abuse, or there is substantiated evidence that a party has perpetrated domestic violence.

(H) Whether a party has a criminal record.

(2) If the court makes a finding that there is a need for preventative measures after considering the factors listed in paragraph (1), the court shall consider taking one or more of the following measures to prevent the abduction of the child:

(A) Ordering supervised visitation.

(B) Requiring a parent to post a bond in an amount sufficient to serve as a financial deterrent to abduction, the proceeds of which may be used to offset the cost of recovery of the child in the event there is an abduction.

(C) Restricting the right of the custodial or noncustodial parent to remove the child from the county, the state, or the country.

(D) Restricting the right of the custodial parent to relocate with the child, unless the custodial parent provides advance notice to, and obtains the written agreement of, the noncustodial parent, or obtains the approval of the court, before relocating with the child.

(E) Requiring the surrender of passports and other travel documents.

(F) Prohibiting a parent from applying for a new or replacement passport for the child.

(G) Requiring a parent to notify a relevant foreign consulate or embassy of passport restrictions and to provide the court with proof of that notification.

(H) Requiring a party to register a California order in another state as a prerequisite to allowing a child to travel to that state for visits, or to obtain an order from another country containing terms identical to the custody and visitation order issued in the United States (recognizing that these orders may be modified or enforced pursuant to the laws of the other country), as a prerequisite to allowing a child to travel to that county for visits.

(I) Obtaining assurances that a party will return from foreign visits by requiring the traveling parent to provide the court or the other parent or guardian with any of the following:

(i) The travel itinerary of the child.

(ii) Copies of round trip airline tickets.

(iii) A list of addresses and telephone numbers where the child can be reached at all times.

(iv) An open airline ticket for the left-behind parent in case the child is not returned.

(J) Including provisions in the custody order to facilitate use of the Uniform Child Custody Jurisdiction and Enforcement Act (Part 3 (commencing with Section 3400)) and the Hague Convention on the Civil Aspects of International Child Abduction (implemented pursuant to 42 U.S.C. Sec. 11601 et seq.), such as identifying California as the home state of the child or otherwise defining the basis for the California court's exercise of jurisdiction under Part 3 (commencing with Section 3400), identifying the United States as the country of habitual residence of the child pursuant to the Hague Convention, defining custody rights pursuant to the Hague Convention, obtaining the express agreement of the parents that the United States is the country of habitual residence of the child, or that California or the United States is the most appropriate forum for addressing custody and visitation orders.

(K) Authorizing the assistance of law enforcement.

(3) If the court imposes any or all of the conditions listed in paragraph (2), those conditions shall be specifically noted on the minute order of the court proceedings.

(4) If the court determines there is a risk of abduction that is sufficient to warrant the application of one or more of the prevention measures authorized by this section, the court shall inform the parties of the telephone number and address of the Child Abduction Unit in the office of the district attorney in the county where the custody or visitation order is being entered.

(c) The Judicial Council shall make the changes to its child custody order forms that are necessary for the implementation of subdivision (b). This subdivision shall become operative on July 1, 2003.

(d) Nothing in this section affects the applicability of Section 278.7 of the Penal Code.

(Stats. 2002, ch. 856 (A.B. 2441), §2, effective January 1, 2003. Amended by Stats. 2003 (A.B. 1516), ch. 52, §1, effective July 14, 2003 (ch. 52 prevails); Stats 2003 (S.B. 600), ch. 62, §86.)

§3130. District attorney shall take all necessary actions to locate missing party and child and procure compliance with order to appear

If a petition to determine custody of a child has been filed in a court of competent jurisdiction, or if a temporary order pending determination of custody has been entered in accordance with Chapter 3 (commencing with Section 3060), and the whereabouts of a party in possession of the child are not known, or there is reason to believe that the party may not appear in the proceedings although ordered to appear personally with the child pursuant to Section 3411, the district attorney shall take all actions necessary to locate the party and the child and to procure compliance with the order to appear with the child for purposes of adjudication of custody. The petition to determine custody may be filed by the district attorney.

(Stats. 1992 (A.B. 2650), ch. 162, §10, effective January 1, 1994.)

§3131. District attorney shall take all necessary actions if child taken in violation of custody or visitation order

If a custody or visitation order has been entered by a court of competent jurisdiction and the child is taken or detained by another person in violation of the order, the district attorney shall take all actions necessary to locate and return the child and the person who violated the order and to assist in the enforcement of the custody or visitation order or other order of the court by use of an appropriate civil or criminal proceeding.

(Stats. 1992 (A.B. 2650), ch. 162, §10, effective January 1, 1994.)

§3132. District attorney shall not represent any party

In performing the functions described in Sections 3130 and 3131, the district attorney shall act on behalf of the court and shall not represent any party to the custody proceedings.

(Stats. 1992 (A.B. 2650), ch. 162, §10, effective January 1, 1994.)

§3133. Court may issue temporary custody order upon request of district attorney

If the district attorney represents to the court, by a written declaration under penalty of perjury, that a temporary custody order is needed to recover a child who is being detained or concealed in violation of a court order or a parent's right to custody, the court may issue an order, placing temporary sole physical custody in the parent or person recommended by the district attorney to facilitate the return of the child to the jurisdiction of the court, pending further hearings. If the court determines that it is not in the best interest of the child to place temporary sole physical custody in the parent or person recommended by the district attorney, the court shall appoint a person to take charge of the child and return the child to the jurisdiction of the court.

(Stats. 1992 (A.B. 2650), ch. 162, §10, effective January 1, 1994.)

§3134. Court shall allocate liabliity for payment of district attorney's expenses

(a) When the district attorney incurs expenses pursuant to this chapter, including expenses incurred in a sister state, payment of the expenses may be advanced by the county subject to reimbursement by the state, and shall be audited by the Controller and paid by the State Treasury according to law.

(b) The court in which the custody proceeding is pending or which has continuing jurisdiction shall, if appropriate, allocate liability for the reimbursement of actual expenses incurred by the district attorney to either or both parties to the proceedings, and that allocation shall constitute a judgment for the state for the funds advanced pursuant to this section. The county shall take reasonable action to enforce that liability and shall transmit all recovered funds to the state.

(Stats. 1992 (A.B. 2650), ch. 162, §10, effective January 1, 1994.)

§3134.5. Court may issue protective custody warrant to recover child

(a) Upon request of the district attorney, the court may issue a protective custody warrant to secure the recovery of an unlawfully detained or concealed child. The request by the district attorney shall include a written declaration under penalty of perjury that a warrant for the child is necessary in order for the district attorney to perform the duties described in Sections 3130 and 3131. The protective custody warrant for the child shall contain an order that the arresting agency shall place the child in protective custody, or return the child as directed by the court. The protective custody warrant may be served in any county in the same manner as a warrant of arrest and may be served at any time of the day or night.

(b) Upon a declaration of the district attorney that the child has been recovered or that the warrant is otherwise no longer required, the court may dismiss the warrant without further court proceedings.
(Stats. 1996 (A.B. 2936), ch. 988, §1.5.)

§3135. Uniform Child Custody Jurisdiction and Enforcement Act does not limit authority of district attorney

Part 3 (commencing with Section 3400) does not limit the authority of a district attorney or arresting agency to act pursuant to this chapter, Section 279.6 of the Penal Code, or any other applicable law.
(Stats. 1999 (S.B. 668), ch. 867, §1.)

§3140. Court shall require submission of birth certificate to court if parent has not appeared

(a) Subject to subdivisions (b) and (c), before granting or modifying a custody order in a case in which one or both parents of the child have not appeared either personally or by counsel, the court shall require the parent, petitioner, or other party appearing in the case to submit a certified copy of the child's birth certificate to the court. The court or its designee shall forward the certified copy of the birth certificate to the local police or sheriff's department which shall check with the National Crime Information Center Missing Person System to ascertain whether the child has been reported missing or is the victim of an abduction and shall report the results of the check to the court.

(b) If the custody matter before the court also involves a petition for the dissolution of marriage or the adjudication of paternity rights or duties, this section applies only to a case in which there is no proof of personal service of the petition on the absent parent.

(c) For good cause shown, the court may waive the requirements of this section.
(Stats. 1992 (A.B. 2650), ch. 162, §10, effective January 1, 1994.)

4. Indian Child Welfare Act

Congress enacted the Indian Child Welfare Act of 1978 (ICWA), 25 U.S.C. §§1900 et seq. (2000), §1915(a) (1994), in the mid-1970's stemming from concerns about the consequences to Native American children, families, tribes and culture, of child welfare practices that resulted in the separation of Indian children from their families and tribes through adoption or foster care placement in non-Indian homes. As a result, federal law makes ethnic background decisive for placement of Native American children under the ICWA.

Under the ICWA, preference is given (absent good cause) to placement with: (1) a member of the child's extended family, (2) other members of the Indian child's tribe, or (3) other Indian families. See also Mississippi Band of Choctaw Indians v. Holyfield, 490 U.S. 30 (1989) (holding that state courts lack authority to permit adoption of Indians by non-Indians even when natural parents leave the reservation to give up the children). But cf. In re Bridget R., 41 Cal. App. 4th 1483 (Ct. App. 1996), *cert. denied sub nom.* Cindy R. v. James R., 519 U.S. 1060 (1997) (holding that the ICWA does not apply if the natural parents are "fully assimilated into non-Indian culture").

California's version of the Indian Child Welfare Act directs courts to comply with the ICWA in "all child custody proceedings" affecting Indian children (Cal. Fam. Code §7810) as defined in the federal ICWA. Under federal law, the term "child custody proceeding" is defined broadly to include: (1) "foster care placement," (2) "termination of parental rights," (3) "preadoptive placement" and (4) "adoptive placement." 25 U.S.C. §1903(1). However, the term does not include "a placement based upon an act which, if committed by an adult, would be deemed a crime or upon an award, in a divorce proceeding, of custody to one of the parents." *Id.*

California courts have examined the notice requirements of the ICWA in dependency proceedings involving termination of parental rights. According to the ICWA, tribes have the right to intervene at any point in state court dependency proceedings (25 U.S.C. §1911(c)). However, for the tribe to intervene, the tribe must have notice that an action is pending. To implement the notice requirement, ICWA provides that where the court knows or has reason to know that an Indian child is involved, the party seeking the foster care placement of, or termination of parental rights to, an Indian child shall notify the parent or Indian custodian and the Indian child's tribe, by registered mail with return receipt requested, of the pending proceedings and their right of intervention (25 U.S.C. §1912(a)). Compliance requires the completion of a preprinted form.

In Dwayne P. v. Superior Court, 126 Cal. Rptr. 2d 639 (Ct. App. 2002), a California court of appeal held that the juvenile court was required to comply with the notice provisions of the ICWA prior to terminating the parents' rights and that the notice requirement was triggered once the father stated he might have Cherokee Indian heritage. Thus, the Indian status of a child need not be certain to invoke the notice requirement of the ICWA. See also In re Antoinette S., 129 Cal. Rptr. 2d 15 (Ct. App. 2002) (holding that father's suggestion that child "might" be an Indian child was sufficient to trigger ICWA's notice requirement but that social service agency's failure to comply with notice requirement was harmless error).

A more recent case, In re Francisco W., 2006 WL 1350302 (Ct. App. 2006), addressed an appellate practice of limited reversals of judgments for correction of ICWA notice defects (providing for automatic reinstatement of the prior termination order if the tribe failed to intervene). The court of appeal held that the practice was proper as comporting with the public policy of the child dependency scheme and did not violate a parent's substantive due process rights.

§7810. Legislative findings regarding Indian child custody proceedings

(a) The Legislature finds and declares the following:

(1) There is no resource that is more vital to the continued existence and integrity of recognized Indian

tribes than their children, and the State of California has an interest in protecting Indian children who are members of, or are eligible for membership in, an Indian tribe.

(2) It is in the interest of an Indian child that the child's membership in the child's Indian tribe and connection to the tribal community be encouraged and protected.

(b) In all Indian child custody proceedings, as defined in the federal Indian Child Welfare Act (25 U.S.C. Secs. 1901 et seq.), the court shall consider all of the findings contained in subdivision (a), strive to promote the stability and security of Indian tribes and families, comply with the federal Indian Child Welfare Act, and seek to protect the best interest of the child.

(c) A determination by an Indian tribe that an unmarried person, who is under the age of 18 years, is either

(1) a member of an Indian tribe or

(2) eligible for membership in an Indian tribe and a biological child of a member of an Indian tribe shall constitute a significant political affiliation with the tribe and shall require the application of the federal Indian Child Welfare Act (25 U.S.C. Sec. 1901 et seq.) to the proceedings.

(Stats.1999 (A.B. 65), ch. 275, §1, effective September 1, 1999. Amended by Stats. 2003 (S.B. 947), ch. 469, §2.)

H. PROCESS TO RESOLVE DISPUTES

1. Conciliation Courts

California courts offered court-connected conciliation services as early as 1939. These services consisted of marriage counseling with the aim of reconciliation. However, with the adoption of no-fault divorce, the focus shifted from reconciliation to divorce counseling. The focus shifted again in 1981 when California enacted legislation requiring custody mediation (formerly Cal. Civ. Code §4607, now Cal. Fam. Code §3170). That statute reformed California's system of family conciliation courts to provide mediation services. See Jay Folberg, A Mediation Overview: History and Dimensions of Practice, 1 Mediation Q. 3, 6 (1983).

§3089. Court or parties may consult with conciliation court

In counties having a conciliation court, the court or the parties may, at any time, pursuant to local rules of court, consult with the conciliation court for the purpose of assisting the parties to formulate a plan for implementation of the custody order or to resolve a controversy which has arisen in the implementation of a plan for custody.

(Stats. 1992 (A.B. 2650), ch. 162, §10, effective January 1, 1994.)

2. Mandatory Mediation

In 1981, California became the first state to require custody mediation. Mandatory mediation was intended to facilitate parental agreements for joint custody. According to the statute, before the parties can proceed to a hearing, mediation is required in all cases in which custody and/or visitation is contested. See generally Alana Dunnigan, Note, Restoring Power to the Powerless: The Need to Reform California's Mandatory Mediation for Victims of Domestic Violence, 37 U.S.F. L. Rev. 1031 (2003) (listing twelve states that have mandatory mediation, including California, Delaware, Florida, Hawaii, Idaho, Kentucky, Maine, Nevada, North Carolina, Oklahoma, South Dakota, and Wisconsin). On the history of child custody mediation, see Andrew Schepard, The Evolving Judicial Role in Child Custody Disputes: From Fault Finder to Conflict Manager to Differential Case Management, 22 U. Ark. Little Rock L. Rev. 395, 407-408 (2000).

If mediation is unsuccessful, the mediator must inform the court in writing. The court then sets the matter for hearing on the contested issues (Cal. Fam. Code §3185(a)). Note that mediation is not limited to disputes between parents. Visitation disputes involving stepparents or grandparents also involve mediation (Cal. Fam. Code §3171(a)).

Statutes delineate the role of the child in mediation. The mediator has a duty to assess the children's needs and interests. Also, the mediator may interview the child if the mediator believes such an interview would be "appropriate or necessary" (Cal. Fam. Code §3180(a)). The mediator also is authorized to recommend the appointment of counsel for the child but must inform the courts of the reasons for that recommendation (Cal. Fam. Code §3184).

The ABA Model Standards for Mediators leave the determination of children's role in custody mediation to parents. The Standards provide that children should not participate (except in extraordinary circumstances) absent consent by parents and the court-appointed representative of the child. The Standards suggest that the mediator should inform parents about the range of options concerning the manner of children's participation. See Andrew Schepard, Note: Model Standards of Practice for Family and Divorce Mediation: The Symposium on Standards of Practice, 39 Fam. Ct. Rev. 121, 128 (2001).

In cases of custody disputes involving domestic violence, the California Family Code provides special protections. In contested custody or visitation cases, California Family Code §3181 [set forth in §H2f *infra*] provides for separate mediation sessions (with the mediator) upon the written request of the party alleging domestic violence. Furthermore, a victim of domestic violence may bring a support person to mediation (Cal. Fam. Code §6303 [set forth in §H2f *infra*]).

a. Generally

§3160. Each superior court must make mediator available

Each superior court shall make a mediator available. The court is not required to institute a family conciliation court in order to provide mediation services.

(Stats. 1993 (A.B. 1500) ch. 219, §116.87.)

§3161. Purpose of family mediation

The purposes of a mediation proceeding are as follows:

(a) To reduce acrimony that may exist between the parties.

(b) To develop an agreement assuring the child close and continuing contact with both parents that is in the best interest of the child, consistent with Sections 3011 and 3020.

(c) To effect a settlement of the issue of visitation rights of all parties that is in the best interest of the child.

(Stats. 1993 (A.B. 1500), ch. 219, §116.87. Amended by Stats. 1997 (A.B. 200), ch. 849, §5.)

§3163. Courts shall develop local rules on mediation

Courts shall develop local rules to respond to requests for a change of mediators or to general problems relating to mediation.

(Stats. 1993 (A.B. 1500), ch. 219, §116.87.)

§3170. Court shall set all contested custody and visitation issues for mediation

(a) If it appears on the face of a petition, application, or other pleading to obtain or modify a temporary or permanent custody or visitation order that custody, visitation, or both are contested, the court shall set the contested issues for mediation.

(b) Domestic violence cases shall be handled by Family Court Services in accordance with a separate written protocol approved by the Judicial Council. The Judicial Council shall adopt guidelines for services, other than services provided under this chapter, that counties may offer to parents who have been unable to resolve their disputes. These services may include, but are not limited to, parent education programs, booklets, videotapes, or referrals to additional community resources.

(Stats. 1993 (A.B. 1500), ch. 219, §116.87. Amended by Stats. 1996 (S.B. 1995), ch. 761, §5.)

§3171. Court shall set disputes for mediation involving stepparents or grandparents

(a) If a stepparent or grandparent has petitioned, or otherwise applied, for a visitation order pursuant to Chapter 5 (commencing with Section 3100), the court shall set the matter for mediation.

(b) A natural or adoptive parent who is not a party to the proceeding is not required to participate in the mediation proceeding, but failure to participate is a waiver of that parent's right to object to a settlement reached by the other parties during mediation or to require a hearing on the matter.

(Stats. 1993 (A.B. 1500), ch. 219, §116.87.)

§3172. Paternity disputes may be set for mediation

Mediation shall not be denied to the parties on the basis that paternity is at issue in a proceeding before the court.

(Stats. 1993 (A.B. 1500), ch. 219, §116.87.)

§3173. Mediation of dispute relating to existing order for custody and/or visitation

(a) Upon the adoption of a resolution by the board of supervisors authorizing the procedure, a petition may be filed pursuant to this chapter for mediation of a dispute relating to an existing order for custody, visitation, or both.

(b) The mediation of a dispute concerning an existing order shall be set not later than 60 days after the filing of the petition.

(Stats. 1993 (A.B. 1500), ch. 219, §116.87.)

§3175. Mediation shall be set before or concurrent with hearing

If a matter is set for mediation pursuant to this chapter, the mediation shall be set before or concurrent with the setting of the matter for hearing.

(Stats. 1993 (A.B. 1500), ch. 219, §116.87.)

§3176. Persons eligible to receive notice of mediation or hearing

(a) Notice of mediation and of any hearing to be held pursuant to this chapter shall be given to the following persons:

(1) Where mediation is required to settle a contested issue of custody or visitation, to each party and to each party's counsel of record.

(2) Where a stepparent or grandparent seeks visitation rights, to the stepparent or grandparent seeking visitation rights, to each parent of the child, and to each parent's counsel of record.

(b) Notice shall be given by certified mail, return receipt requested, postage prepaid, to the last known address.

(c) Notice of mediation pursuant to Section 3188 shall state that all communications involving the mediator shall be kept confidential between the mediator and the disputing parties.

(Stats. 1993, ch. 219 (A.B. 1500), §116.87. Amended by Stats. 2002, ch. 1077 (S.B. 174), §1.)

§3178. Scope of mediation agreements

An agreement reached by the parties as a result of mediation shall be limited as follows:

(a) Where mediation is required to settle a contested issue of custody or visitation, the agreement shall be limited to the resolution of issues relating to parenting plans, custody, visitation, or a combination of these issues.

(b) Where a stepparent or grandparent seeks visitation rights, the agreement shall be limited to the resolution of issues relating to visitation.

(Stats. 1993 (A.B. 1500), ch. 219, §116.87.)

§3179. Custody or visitation agreement may be modified at court's discretion

A custody or visitation agreement reached as a result of mediation may be modified at any time at the discretion of the court, subject to Chapter 1 (commencing with Section 3020), Chapter 2 (commencing with Section 3040), Chapter

4 (commencing with Section 3080), and Chapter 5 (commencing with Section 3100).
(Stats. 1993 (A.B. 1500), ch. 219, §116.87.)

§3180. Mediator has duty to assess child's needs and interests

(a) In mediation proceedings pursuant to this chapter, the mediator has the duty to assess the needs and interests of the child involved in the controversy, and is entitled to interview the child where the mediator considers the interview appropriate or necessary.

(b) The mediator shall use his or her best efforts to effect a settlement of the custody or visitation dispute that is in the best interest of the child, as provided in Section 3011.
(Stats. 1993 (A.B. 1500), ch. 219, §116.87.)

§3185. Mediator informs court of unresolved issues and court shall set matter for hearing; stepparent or grandparent visitation hearings

(a) If issues that may be resolved by agreement pursuant to Section 3178 are not resolved by an agreement of all the parties who participate in mediation, the mediator shall inform the court in writing and the court shall set the matter for hearing on the unresolved issues.

(b) Where a stepparent or grandparent requests visitation, each natural or adoptive parent and the stepparent or grandparent shall be given an opportunity to appear and be heard on the issue of visitation.
(Stats. 1993 (A.B. 1500), ch. 219, §116.87.)

§3186. Agreement may be confirmed if both parties assent

(a) An agreement reached by the parties as a result of mediation shall be reported to counsel for the parties by the mediator on the day set for mediation or as soon thereafter as practical, but before the agreement is reported to the court.

(b) An agreement may not be confirmed or otherwise incorporated in an order unless each party, in person or by counsel of record, has affirmed and assented to the agreement in open court or by written stipulation.

(c) An agreement may be confirmed or otherwise incorporated in an order if a party fails to appear at a noticed hearing on the issue involved in the agreement.
(Stats. 1993 (A.B. 1500), ch. 219, §116.87.)

---

b. Qualifications

Mediation may be provided by publicly funded court services or by mediators in private practice. Early in the development of mediation, many states failed to specify minimum qualifications for mediators. Now statutes often provide for qualifications for court-connected mediators but leave mediators in the private sector unregulated.

§3164. Qualifications of a mediator

(a) The mediator may be a member of the professional staff of a family conciliation court, probation department, or mental health services agency, or may be any other person or agency designated by the court.

(b) The mediator shall meet the minimum qualifications required of a counselor of conciliation as provided in Section 1815.
(Stats. 1993 (A.B. 1500), ch. 219, §116.87.)

§3165. Continuing education requirements for supervisors, investigators and mediators

Any person, regardless of administrative title, hired on or after January 1, 1998, who is responsible for clinical supervision of evaluators, investigators, or mediators or who directly supervises or administers the Family Court Services evaluation or mediation programs shall meet the same continuing education requirements specified in Section 1816 for supervising and associate counselors of conciliation.
(Stats. 1996 (S.B. 1995), ch. 761, §4.)

---

c. Standards of Practice

In the early years of mediation, standards of conduct for professional mediators did not exist. To address this shortcoming, the American Bar Association (ABA) Family Law Section adopted the ABA Standards of Practice in 1984 to provide guidelines to lawyers who wished to serve as family mediators but were concerned about complying with professional responsibility requirements. Schepard, Model Standards of Practice for Family and Divorce Mediation, *supra*, at 121.

The House of Delegates adopted Model Standards of Practice for Family and Divorce Mediation in 2001 applying to mediators in public and private practice, to lawyers and therapists, and in all types of custody and visitation disputes (such as grandparent visitation disputes, child protection mediation, etc.). A major innovation is the Standards' approach to domestic violence, requiring mediators to have special training, to screen for abuse, to shape mediation to assure the safety of the participants and children, to inform participants (before mediation begins) of reporting requirements, and to suspend mediation if a participant is threatened. *Id.* at 20-23. For the Standards, see 2001 Model Standards of Practice for Family and Divorce Mediation, 35 Fam. L.Q. 27 (2001).

§3162. Uniform standards of practice for custody mediation

(a) Mediation of cases involving custody and visitation concerning children shall be governed by uniform standards of practice adopted by the Judicial Council.

(b) The standards of practice shall include, but not be limited to, all of the following:

(1) Provision for the best interest of the child and the safeguarding of the rights of the child to frequent and continuing contact with both parents, consistent with Sections 3011 and 3020.

(2) Facilitation of the transition of the family by detailing factors to be considered in decisions concerning the child's future.

(3) The conducting of negotiations in such a way as to equalize power relationships between the parties.

(c) In adopting the standards of practice, the Judicial Council shall consider standards developed by recognized associations of mediators and attorneys and other relevant standards governing mediation of proceedings for the dissolution of marriage.

(d) The Judicial Council shall offer training with respect to the standards to mediators.

(Stats. 1993 (A.B. 1500), ch. 219, §116.87. Amended by Stats. 1997 (A.B. 200), ch. 849, §6.)

---

d. Confidentiality

Confidentiality is central to the mediation process. However, California law permits the mediator in some locales to make a recommendation to the court if mediation proves unsuccessful. In McLaughlin v. Superior Court, 189 Cal. Rptr. 479 (Ct. App. 1983), the California Supreme Court examined such a local court rule that prohibited cross-examination of the mediator by the parties. The court held that this requirement, exempting mediators from cross-examination, violates due process. As a result, the parties must be allowed to cross-examine the mediator as to the basis for his or her recommendation.

No other state permits this practice of mediator recommendations upon the failure of mediation. A coalition of family lawyers sought legislation (S.B. 2124) eliminating this practice. The bill's author, Senator Liz Figueroa, abandoned the effort because of opposition from the judiciary and mediators in her home district of Alameda County (a recommending county). See Hugh McIsaac, Confidentiality Revised California Style, 39 Fam. Ct. Rev. 405, 405 (2001).

Mediator McIsaac argues that when the mediator makes a recommendation, mediation becomes an adversarial process, the parties lose their trust in the mediator, the mediator's role changes to evaluator rather than facilitator, mediators have less time to spend resolving disputes because of their involvement in court proceedings, the parties feel more pressured to reach an agreement, and the parties are more likely to re-litigate. He adds that the practice is opposed by major national mediation organizations as well as by the Uniform Mediation Act. *Id.* at 408. The Uniform Mediation Act, a joint effort of the National Conference of Commissioners on Uniform State Laws and the ABA's Dispute Resolution Section, was adopted by NCCUSL in August 2001.

§3177. Mediation proceedings shall be confidential

Mediation proceedings pursuant to this chapter shall be held in private and shall be confidential. All communications, verbal or written, from the parties to the mediator made in the proceeding are official information within the meaning of Section 1040 of the Evidence Code.

(Stats. 1993 (A.B. 1500), ch. 219, §116.87.)

§3183. Mediator may make recommendation to court subject to local court rules

(a) Except as provided in Section 3188, the mediator may, consistent with local court rules, submit a recommendation to the court as to the custody of or visitation with the child.

(b) Where the parties have not reached agreement as a result of the mediation proceedings, the mediator may recommend to the court that an investigation be conducted pursuant to Chapter 6 (commencing with Section 3110) or that other services be offered to assist the parties to effect a resolution of the controversy before a hearing on the issues.

(c) In appropriate cases, the mediator may recommend that restraining orders be issued, pending determination of the controversy, to protect the well being of the child involved in the controversy.

(Stats. 1993, ch. 219 (A.B. 1500), §116.87. Amended by Stats. 1996, ch. 761 (S.B. 1995), §6; Stats. 2002, ch. 1077 (S.B. 174), §2.)

California Family Code §3188 *infra* will not become effective until the appropriation of sufficient funds and then will be operative only in four or more counties selected by the Judicial Council that allow mediators to make custody recommendations.

---

§3188. Court may adopt a confidential mediation program

(a) Any court selected by the Judicial Council under subdivision (c) may voluntarily adopt a confidential mediation program that provides for all of the following:

(1) The mediator may not make a recommendation as to custody or visitation to anyone other than the disputing parties, except as otherwise provided in this section.

(2) If total or partial agreement is reached in mediation, the mediator may report this fact to the court. If both parties consent in writing, where there is a partial agreement, the mediator may report to the court a description of the issues still in dispute, without specific reference to either party.

(3) In making the recommendation described in Section 3184, the mediator may not inform the court of the reasons why it would be in the best interest of the minor child to have counsel appointed.

(4) If the parties have not reached agreement as a result of the initial mediation, this section does not prohibit the court from requiring subsequent mediation that may result in a recommendation as to custody or visitation with the child if the subsequent mediation is conducted by a different mediator with no prior involvement with the case or knowledge of any communications, as defined in Section 1040 of the Evidence Code, with respect to the initial mediation. The court, however, shall inform the parties that the mediator will make a recommendation to the court regarding custody or visitation in the event that the parties cannot reach agreement on these issues.

(5) If an initial screening or intake process indicates that the case involves serious safety risks to the child, such as domestic violence, sexual abuse, or serious substance abuse, the court may provide an initial emergency assessment service that includes a recommendation to the court concerning temporary custody or visitation orders in order to expeditiously address those safety issues.

(b) This section shall become operative upon the appropriation of funds in the annual Budget Act sufficient to implement this section.

(c) This section shall apply only in four or more counties selected by the Judicial Council that currently allow a mediator to make custody recommendations to the court and have more than 1,000 family law case filings per year. The Judicial Council may also make this section applicable to additional counties that have fewer than 1,000 family law case filings per year.

(Stats. 2002, ch. 1077 (S.B. 174), §4.)

e. Counsel

§3182. Mediator may exclude counsel from participation in mediation proceedings

(a) The mediator has authority to exclude counsel from participation in the mediation proceedings pursuant to this chapter if, in the mediator's discretion, exclusion of counsel is appropriate or necessary.

(b) The mediator has authority to exclude a domestic violence support person from a mediation proceeding as provided in Section 6303.

(Stats. 1993 (A.B. 1500), ch. 219, §116.87.)

§3184. Mediator may recommend that counsel be appointed for child

Except as provided in Section 3188 [set forth in §H2d *supra*], nothing in this chapter prohibits the mediator from recommending to the court that counsel be appointed, pursuant to Chapter 10 (commencing with Section 3150), to represent the minor child. In making this recommendation, the mediator shall inform the court of the reasons why it would be in the best interest of the minor child to have counsel appointed.

(Stats. 1993, ch. 219 (A.B. 1500), §116.87. Amended by Stats. 2002, ch. 1077 (S.B.174), §3.)

f. Special Provisions in Cases of Domestic Violence

§3181. Mediator shall meet with parties separately in cases of domestic violence

(a) In a proceeding in which mediation is required pursuant to this chapter, where there has been a history of domestic violence between the parties or where a protective order as defined in Section 6218 is in effect, at the request of the party alleging domestic violence in a written declaration under penalty of perjury or protected by the order, the mediator appointed pursuant to this chapter shall meet with the parties separately and at separate times.

(b) Any intake form that an agency charged with providing family court services requires the parties to complete before the commencement of mediation shall state that, if a party alleging domestic violence in a written declaration under penalty of perjury or a party protected by a protective order so requests, the mediator will meet with the parties separately and at separate times.

(Stats. 1993 (A.B. 1500), ch. 219, §116.87.)

§3182. Mediator may exclude domestic violence support person

. . .

(b) The mediator has authority to exclude a domestic violence support person from a mediation proceeding as provided in Section 6303.

(Stats. 1993 (A.B. 1500), ch. 219, §116.87.)

§6303. Victim of domestic violence may select support person to attend proceedings

(a) It is the function of a support person to provide moral and emotional support for a person who alleges he or she is a victim of domestic violence. The person who alleges that he or she is a victim of domestic violence may select any individual to act as a support person. No certification, training, or other special qualification is required for an individual to act as a support person. The support person shall assist the person in feeling more confident that he or she will not be injured or threatened by the other party during the proceedings where the person and the other party must be present in close proximity. The support person is not present as a legal adviser and shall not give legal advice.

(b) A support person shall be permitted to accompany either party to any proceeding to obtain a protective order, as defined in Section 6218. Where the party is not represented by an attorney, the support person may sit with the party at the table that is generally reserved for the party and the party's attorney.

(c) Notwithstanding any other provision of law to the contrary, if a court has issued a protective order, a support person shall be permitted to accompany a party protected by the order during any mediation orientation or mediation session, including separate mediation sessions, held pursuant to a proceeding described in Section 3021. The agency charged with providing family court services shall advise the party protected by the order of the right to have a support person during mediation. A mediator may exclude a support person from a mediation session if the support person participates in the mediation session, or acts as an advocate, or the presence of a particular support person is disruptive or disrupts the process of mediation. The presence of the support person does not waive the confidentiality of the mediation, and the support person is bound by the confidentiality of the mediation.

(d) In a proceeding subject to this section, a support person shall be permitted to accompany a party in court where there are allegations or threats of domestic violence and, where the party is not represented by an attorney, may sit with the party at the table that is generally reserved for the party and the party's attorney.

(e) Nothing in this section precludes a court from exercising its discretion to remove a person from the courtroom when it would be in the interest of justice to do so, or when the court believes the person is prompting, swaying, or influencing the party protected by the order.

(Stats. 1993 (A.B. 1500), ch. 219, §154. Amended by Stats. 1996 (S.B. 1995), ch. 761 §7.)

IX.
ADOPTION

This chapter examines the adoption process that creates a new parent-child relationship. First, it presents definitions and general provisions, prohibitions on baby selling, and the legal consequences of adoption. Second, the chapter identifies the selection standards for adoptive parents (including such factors as race, ethnicity, sexual orientation, etc.). Third, it explores issues of parental consent. Fourth, it examines placement procedures by agencies and independent intermediaries. Fifth, it addresses special types of adoption, such as adoption of children with special needs (subsidized adoption), open adoption, equitable adoption, interstate adoption, international adoption, and adult adoption. Sixth, it explores the rights of adoptees to search for their birth parents. Finally, it examines adoption failure (i.e., abrogation and revocation).

A. INTRODUCTION

Adoption is the legal process of creating a parent-child relationship. By adoption, an individual acquires a new parent or parents. The adoption process terminates the legal rights and responsibilities (e.g., custody and support) of the natural parent or parents (Cal. Fam. Code §§8617, 9306). Simultaneously, an adoption creates new legal rights and responsibilities (e.g., custody and support) in the adoptive parents or parents (Cal. Fam. Code §§8616, 9305). See §A4 infra.

The termination of the natural parent's or natural parents' rights may be voluntary or involuntary. On the one hand, a biological parent may choose to relinquish a child for adoption. On the other hand, a biological parent may have his or her parental rights terminated judicially because of some act of misconduct (e.g., abuse, neglect, nonsupport, abandonment). However, this provision can be waived by the parties and is not required for a valid adoption. See Sharon S. v. Superior Ct. of San Diego Cty., 2 Cal. Rptr. 3d 699 (Cal. 2003).

Adoption was not recognized at common law. This policy stemmed from British emphasis on the importance of the bloodline. U.S. adoption law and practice is a comparatively recent development and is entirely statutory. Massachusetts adopted the first adoption statute in 1851. Model legislation consists of the Uniform Adoption Act, 9 U.L.A. 11 (rev. 1971) and the revised Uniform Adoption Act, 9 U.L.A. 1 (1994) (approved by the ABA in 1995). California has adopted neither of the Uniform Adoption Acts. For the Revised Uniform Adoption Act, see Part III, infra.

1. Definitions

California Family Code

§8500. Application of definitions

Unless the provision or context otherwise requires, the definitions in this part govern the construction of this division.

(Stats. 1992 (A.B. 2650), ch. 162, §10, effective January 1, 1994.)

§8502. "Adoption service provider"

(a) "Adoption service provider" means any of the following:

(1) A licensed private adoption agency.

(2) An individual who has presented satisfactory evidence to the department that he or she is a licensed clinical social worker who also has a minimum of five years of experience providing professional social work services while employed by a licensed California adoption agency or the department.

(3) In a state other than California, or a country other than the United States, an adoption agency licensed or otherwise approved under the laws of that state or country, or an individual who is licensed or otherwise certified as a clinical social worker under the laws of that state or country.

(4) An individual who has presented satisfactory evidence to the department that he or she is a licensed marriage and family therapist who has a minimum of five years of experience providing professional adoption casework services while employed by a licensed California adoption agency or the department. The department shall review the qualifications of each individual to determine if he or she has performed professional adoption casework services for five years as required by this section while employed by a licensed California adoption agency or the department.

(b) If, in the case of a birth parent located in California, at least three adoption service providers are not reasonably available, or, in the case of a birth parent located outside of California or outside of the United States who has contacted at least three potential adoption service providers and been unsuccessful in obtaining the services of an adoption service provider who is reasonably available and willing to provide services, independent legal counsel for the birth parent may serve as an adoption service provider pursuant to subdivision (e) of Section 8801.5 [delineating the duties of an adoption service provider]. "Reasonably available" means that an adoption service provider is all of the following:

(1) Available within five days for an advisement of rights pursuant to Section 8801.5, or within 24 hours for the signing of the placement agreement pursuant to paragraph (3) of subdivision (b) of Section 8801.3.

(2) Within 100 miles of the birth mother.

(3) Available for a cost not exceeding five hundred dollars ($500) to make an advisement of rights and to witness the signing of the placement agreement.

(c) Where an attorney acts as an adoption service provider, the fee to make an advisement of rights and to witness the signing of the placement agreement shall not exceed five hundred dollars ($500).

(Stats. 1993 (S.B. 792), ch. 758, §3, effective January 1, 1995. Amended Stats. 1994 (A.B. 3336), ch. 585, §1,

effective January 1, 1995; Stats. 1997 (S.B. 1121), ch. 559, §1. Amended by Stats. 2002 (S.B. 2026), ch. 1013, §81. Amended by Stats. 2004 (S.B. 1357), ch. 858, §3.)

§8503. "Adoptive parent"

"Adoptive parent" means a person who has obtained an order of adoption of a minor child or, in the case of an adult adoption, an adult.

(Stats. 1992 (A.B. 2650), ch. 162, §10, effective January 1, 1994.)

§8506. "Agency adoption"

"Agency adoption" means the adoption of a minor, other than an intercountry adoption, in which the department or a licensed adoption agency is a party to, or joins in, the adoption petition.

(Stats. 1992 (A.B. 2650), ch. 162, §10, effective January 1, 1994.)

§8518. "Department"

"Department" means the State Department of Social Services.

(Stats. 1992 (A.B. 2650), ch. 162, §10, effective January 1, 1994.)

§8521. "Full-service adoption agency"

(a) "Full-service adoption agency" means a licensed entity engaged in the business of providing adoption services, which does all of the following:

(1) Assumes care, custody, and control of a child through relinquishment of the child to the agency or involuntary termination of parental rights to the child.

(2) Assesses the birth parents, prospective adoptive parents, or child.

(3) Places children for adoption.

(4) Supervises adoptive placements.

(b) Private full-service adoption agencies shall be organized and operated on a nonprofit basis.

(Stats. 1992 (A.B. 2650), ch. 162, §10, effective January 1, 1994.)

§8524. "Independent adoption"

"Independent adoption" means the adoption of a child in which neither the department nor an agency licensed by the department is a party to, or joins in, the adoption petition.

(Stats. 1992 (A.B. 2650), ch. 162, §10, effective January 1, 1994.)

§8527. "Intercountry adoption"

"Intercountry adoption" means the adoption of a foreign-born child for whom federal law makes a special immigration visa available. Intercountry adoption includes completion of the adoption in the child's native country or completion of the adoption in this state.

(Stats. 1992 (A.B. 2650), ch. 162, §10, effective January 1, 1994.)

§8533. "Noncustodial adoption agency"

(a) "Noncustodial adoption agency" means any licensed entity engaged in the business of providing adoption services, which does all of the following:

(1) Assesses the prospective adoptive parents.

(2) Cooperatively matches children freed for adoption, who are under the care, custody, and control of a licensed adoption agency, for adoption, with assessed and approved prospective adoptive parents.

(3) Cooperatively supervises adoptive placements with a full-service adoption agency, but does not disrupt a placement or remove a child from a placement.

(b) Private noncustodial adoption agencies shall be organized and operated on a nonprofit basis.

(Stats. 1992 (A.B. 2650), ch. 162, §10, effective January 1, 1994.)

§8539. "Place for adoption"

Place for adoption" means, in the case of an independent adoption, the selection of a prospective adoptive parent or parents for a child by the birth parent or parents and the completion of an adoptive placement agreement on a form prescribed by the department by the birth parent or parents placing the child with prospective adoptive parents.

(Stats. 1993 (S.B. 792), ch. 758, §4, effective January 1, 1995.)

§8543. "Qualified court investigator"

"Qualified court investigator" means a superior court investigator with the same minimum qualifications as a probation officer or county welfare worker designated to conduct stepparent adoption investigations in stepparent adoption proceedings and proceedings to declare a minor free from parental custody and control.

(Stats. 1993 (A.B. 1500), ch. 219, §185.)

§8545. "Special-needs child"

"Special-needs child" means a child whose adoption without financial assistance would be unlikely because of adverse parental background, ethnic background, race, color, language, membership in a sibling group that should remain intact, mental, physical, medical, or emotional handicaps, or age of three years or more.

(Stats. 1992 (A.B. 2650), ch. 162, §10, effective January 1, 1994.)

§8548. "Stepparent adoption"

"Stepparent adoption" means an adoption of a child by a stepparent where one birth parent retains custody and control of the child.

(Stats. 1992 (A.B. 2650), ch. 162, §10, effective January 1, 1994.)

2. General Provisions

Prospective adoptive parents are required to execute an agreement stating that they agree to treat the adoptee in all respects as their lawful child (Cal. Fam. Code §8612(b)). The court enters an order of adoption after if it is satisfied that the adoption will promote the child's interest (Cal. Fam. Code §8612(c)). At the proceeding, the court examines all persons appearing before it (Cal. Fam. Code §8612(a)). Adoption proceedings generally are closed to the public (Cal. Fam. Code §8611).

At the request of the adoptive parents (or the child), the county clerk issues a "certificate of adoption" containing the following information: the date and place of adoption, names of the adoptive parents, and the name that the child has taken. Only in cases of a relative or stepparent adoption may the certificate state the name of the child's biological parents (Cal. Fam. Code §8614).

§8600. Eligibility of unmarried minors for adoption

An unmarried minor may be adopted by an adult as provided in this part.

(Stats. 1992 (A.B. 2650), ch. 162, §10, effective January 1, 1994.)

§8607. Infant-release forms to noncustodians must delineate types of adoptions

All forms adopted by the department authorizing the release of an infant from a health facility to the custody of persons other than the person entitled to custody of the child pursuant to Section 3010 and authorizing these other persons to obtain medical care for the infant shall contain a statement in boldface type delineating the various types of adoptions available, the birth parents' rights with regard thereto, including, but not limited to, rights with regard to revocation of consent to adoption, and a statement regarding the authority of the court under Part 4 (commencing with Section 7800) of Division 12 to declare the child abandoned by the birth parent or parents.

(Stats. 1992 (A.B. 2650), ch. 162, §10, effective January 1, 1994.)

§8608. Regulations concern form and content of medical reports

(a) The department shall adopt regulations specifying the form and content of the reports required by Sections 8706, 8817, and 8909. In addition to any other material that may be required by the department, the form shall include inquiries designed to elicit information on any illness, disease, or defect of a genetic or hereditary nature.

(b) All licensed adoption agencies shall cooperate with and assist the department in devising a plan that will effectuate the effective and discreet transmission to adoptees or prospective adoptive parents of pertinent medical information reported to the department or the licensed adoption agency, upon the request of the person reporting the medical information.

(Stats. 1992 (A.B. 2650), ch. 162, §10, effective January 1, 1994.)

§8609. Advertising by unlicensed person or agency is prohibited

(a) Any person or organization that, without holding a valid and unrevoked license to place children for adoption issued by the department, advertises in any periodical or newspaper, by radio, or other public medium, that he, she, or it will place children for adoption, or accept, supply, provide, or obtain children for adoption, or that causes any advertisement to be published in or by any public medium soliciting, requesting, or asking for any child or children for adoption is guilty of a misdemeanor.

(b) Any person, other than a birth parent, or any organization, association, or corporation that, without holding a valid and unrevoked license to place children for adoption issued by the department, places any child for adoption is guilty of a misdemeanor.

(Stats. 1992 (A.B. 2650), ch. 162, §10, effective January 1, 1994.)

§8610. Petitioners shall file accounting of all disbursements

(a) The petitioners in a proceeding for adoption of a child shall file with the court a full accounting report of all disbursements of anything of value made or agreed to be made by them or on their behalf in connection with the birth of the child, the placement of the child with the petitioners, any medical or hospital care received by the child's birth mother or by the child in connection with the child's birth, any other expenses of either birth parent, or the adoption. The accounting report shall be made under penalty of perjury and shall be submitted to the court on or before the date set for the hearing on the adoption petition, unless the court grants an extension of time.

(b) The accounting report shall be itemized in detail and shall show the services relating to the adoption or to the placement of the child for adoption that were received by the petitioners, by either birth parent, by the child, or by any other person for whom payment was made by or on behalf of the petitioners. The report shall also include the dates of each payment, the names and addresses of each attorney, physician and surgeon, hospital, licensed adoption agency, or other person or organization who received any funds of the petitioners in connection with the adoption or the placement of the child with them, or participated in any way in the handling of those funds, either directly or indirectly.

(c) This section does not apply to an adoption by a stepparent where one birth parent or adoptive parent retains custody and control of the child.

(Stats. 1992 (A.B. 2650), ch. 162, §10, effective January 1, 1994.)

§8611. Adoption proceedings shall be closed

All court hearings in an adoption proceeding shall be held in private, and the court shall exclude all persons except the officers of the court, the parties, their witnesses, counsel, and

representatives of the agencies present to perform their official duties under the law governing adoptions.
(Stats. 1992 (A.B. 2650), ch. 162, §10, effective January 1, 1994.)

§8612. Court shall examine all persons; adoptive parents must agree to treat child as their child

(a) The court shall examine all persons appearing before it pursuant to this part. The examination of each person shall be conducted separately but within the physical presence of every other person unless the court, in its discretion, orders otherwise.

(b) The prospective adoptive parent or parents shall execute and acknowledge an agreement in writing that the child will be treated in all respects as their lawful child.

(c) If satisfied that the interest of the child will be promoted by the adoption, the court may make and enter an order of adoption of the child by the prospective adoptive parent or parents.
(Stats. 1992 (A.B. 2650), ch. 162, §10, effective January 1, 1994.)

§8613. Counsel may appear for adoptive parent in military, charitable, or religious service

(a) If the prospective adoptive parent is commissioned or enlisted in the military service, or auxiliary thereof, of the United States, or of any of its allies, or is engaged in service on behalf of any governmental entity of the United States, or in the American Red Cross, or in any other recognized charitable or religious organization, so that it is impossible or impracticable, because of the prospective adoptive parent's absence from this state, or otherwise, to make an appearance in person, and the circumstances are established by satisfactory evidence, the appearance may be made for the prospective adoptive parent by counsel. . . .

(c) Where the prospective adoptive parent is permitted to appear by counsel, or otherwise, the court may, in its discretion, cause an examination of the prospective adoptive parent, other interested person, or witness to be made upon deposition, as it deems necessary. . . .

(f) Where, pursuant to this section, neither prospective adoptive parent need appear before the court, the child proposed to be adopted need not appear. . . .

(g) Where none of the parties appears, the court may not make an order of adoption until after a report has been filed with the court pursuant to Section 8715, 8807, 8914, or 9001.
(Stats. 1992 (A.B. 2650), ch. 162, §10, effective January 1, 1994. Amended Stats. 1993 (S.B. 1152) ch. 1158, §1. Amended by Stats. 2002 (S.B. 1316), ch. 784, §109.)

§8614. County clerk may issue certificate of adoption; birth parents' names omitted except in stepparent adoption

Upon the request of the adoptive parents or the adopted child, a clerk of the superior court may issue a certificate of adoption that states the date and place of adoption, the birthday of the child, the names of the adoptive parents, and the name the child has taken. Unless the child has been adopted by a stepparent or by a relative, as defined in subdivision (c) of Section 8616.5, the certificate shall not state the name of the birth parents of the child.
(Stats. 1992 (A.B. 2650), ch. 162, §10, effective January 1, 1994. Amended Stats. 1997 (A.B. 1544) ch. 793, §2. Amended by Stats. 2002 (S.B. 1316), ch. 784, §110. Amended by Stats. 2003 (S.B. 182), ch. 251, §5.)

§8714. Adoption petition and order; attached postadoption contact agreement

(a) A person desiring to adopt a child may for that purpose file a petition in the county in which the petitioner resides, or, if the petitioner is not a resident of this state, in the county in which the birth parent or birth parents resided when the relinquishment of parental rights for the purpose of adoption was signed. Where a child has been adjudged to be a dependent of the juvenile court pursuant to Section 300 of the Welfare and Institutions Code, and has thereafter been freed for adoption by the juvenile court, the petition may be filed either in the county where the petitioner resides or in the county where the child was freed for adoption.

(b) The court clerk shall immediately notify the department at Sacramento in writing of the pendency of the proceeding and of any subsequent action taken.

(c) If the petitioner has entered into a postadoption contact agreement with the birth parent as set forth in Section 8616.5, the agreement, signed by the participating parties, shall be attached to and filed with the petition for adoption under subdivision (a).

(d) The caption of the adoption petition shall contain the names of the petitioners, but not the child's name. The petition shall state the child's sex and date of birth. The name the child had before adoption shall appear in the joinder signed by the licensed adoption agency.

(e) If the child is the subject of a guardianship petition, the adoption petition shall so state and shall include the caption and docket number or have attached a copy of the letters of the guardianship or temporary guardianship. The petitioners shall notify the court of any petition for guardianship or temporary guardianship filed after the adoption petition. The guardianship proceeding shall be consolidated with the adoption proceeding.

(f) The order of adoption shall contain the child's adopted name, but not the name the child had before adoption.
(Stats. 1992 (A.B. 2650), ch. 162, §10, effective January 1, 1994. Amended Stats. 1993 (A.B. 1500), ch. 219, §190; Stats. 2000 (A.B. 2921), ch. 910, §2, (S.B. 2157), ch. 930, §1. Amended by Stats. 2002 (A.B. 746), ch. 1112, §1. Amended by Stats. 2003 (S.B. 182), ch. 251, §6.)

§8716. Agency may require petitioners to pay fee

Where a petition is filed for the adoption of a child who has been placed for adoption by a licensed county adoption agency or the department, the agency or department may, at the time of filing a favorable report with the court, require the petitioners to pay to the agency, as agent of the state, or to the department, a fee of five hundred dollars ($500). The agency or department may defer, waive, or reduce the fee if its payment would cause economic hardship to the prospective adoptive parents detrimental to the welfare of the adopted child, if the child has been in the foster care of the prospective

adoptive parents for at least one year, or if necessary for the placement of a special-needs child.
(Stats. 1992 (A.B. 2650), ch. 162, §10, effective January 1, 1994.)

3. Prohibition on Baby Selling

Baby selling statutes in all jurisdictions forbid compensation in connection with an adoption or termination of parental rights. See also Cal. Fam. Code §8609 (*supra* §A2) (prohibiting advertising by unlicensed persons or organizations that they will obtain or place children for adoption).

California Penal Code

§273. Payment for adoption is prohibited except for payment of maternity expenses

(a) It is a misdemeanor for any person or agency to pay, offer to pay, or to receive money or anything of value for the placement for adoption or for the consent to an adoption of a child. This subdivision shall not apply to any fee paid for adoption services provided by the State Department of Social Services, a licensed adoption agency, adoption services providers, as defined in Section 8502 of the Family Code, or an attorney providing adoption legal services.

(b) This section shall not make it unlawful to payor receive the maternity-connected medical or hospital and necessary living expenses of the mother preceding and during confinement as an act of charity, as long as the payment is not contingent upon placement of the child for adoption, consent to the adoption, or cooperation in the completion of the adoption.

(c) It is a misdemeanor punishable by imprisonment in a county jail not exceeding one year or by a fine not exceeding two thousand five hundred dollars ($2,500) for any parent to obtain the financial benefits set forth in subdivision (b) with the intent to receive those financial benefits where there is an intent to do either of the following:

(1) Not complete the adoption.

(2) Not consent to the adoption.

(d) It is a misdemeanor punishable by imprisonment in a county jail not exceeding one year or by a fine not exceeding two thousand five hundred dollars ($2,500) for any parent to obtain the financial benefits set forth in subdivision (b) from two or more prospective adopting families or persons, if either parent does both of the following:

(1) Knowingly fails to disclose to those families or persons that there are other prospective adopting families or persons interested in adopting the child, with knowledge that there is an obligation to disclose that information.

(2) Knowingly accepts the financial benefits set forth in subdivision (b) if the aggregate amount exceeds the reasonable maternity-connected medical or hospital and necessary living expenses of the mother preceding and during the pregnancy.

(e) Any person who has been convicted previously of an offense described in subdivision (c) or (d), who is separately tried and convicted of a subsequent violation of subdivision (c) or (d), is guilty of a public offense punishable by imprisonment in a county jail or in the state prison.

(f) Nothing in this section shall be construed to prohibit the prosecution of any person for a misdemeanor or felony pursuant to Section 487 or any other provision of law in lieu of prosecution pursuant to this section.
(Stats. 1967, ch. 1088, §1; Stats. 1990 (A.B. 4288), ch. 1492, §1; Stats. 1993 (S.B. 244), ch. 377, §1; Stats. 1997 (S.B. 122) ch. 185, §1.)

4. Legal Consequences of Adoption

As explained above, adoption creates the legal relationship of parent and child. It creates the same rights and obligations (i.e., custody, support, etc.) that exist between a biological parent and child. Among the other legal consequences, adoption implicates inheritance rights. In addition, adoption may give rise to subsequent claims by third parties (such as grandparents) for visitation rights. On grandparents' visitation rights, see Chapter IX §C5 *supra*.

California Family Code

§8616. Parent-child relationship between adopted child and adoptive parents

After adoption, the adopted child and the adoptive parents shall sustain towards each other the legal relationship of parent and child and have all the rights and are subject to all the duties of that relationship.
(Stats. 1992 (A.B. 2650), ch. 162, §10, effective January 1, 1994.)

§8617. Relationship between adopted child and birth parents terminated

The birth parents of an adopted child are, from the time of the adoption, relieved of all parental duties towards, and all responsibility for, the adopted child, and have no right over the child.
(Stats. 1992 (A.B. 2650), ch. 162, §10, effective January 1, 1994.)

§8618. Adopted child may take adoptive parent's surname

A child adopted pursuant to this part may take the family name of the adoptive parent.
(Stats. 1992 (A.B. 2650), ch. 162, §10, effective January 1, 1994.)

§9305. Rights and duties of adoptive relationship

After adoption, the adoptee and the adoptive parent or parents shall sustain towards each other the legal relationship of parent and child and have all the rights and are subject to all the duties of that relationship.

(Stats. 1992 (A.B. 2650), ch. 162, §10, effective January 1, 1994.)

§9306. Birth parents are relieved of all parental duties and responsibilities

(a) Except as provided in subdivision (b), the birth parents of a person adopted pursuant to this part are, from the time of the adoption, relieved of all parental duties towards, and all responsibility for, the adopted person, and have no right over the adopted person.

(b) Where an adult is adopted by the spouse of a birth parent, the parental rights and responsibilities of that birth parent are not affected by the adoption.

(Stats. 1992 (A.B. 2650), ch. 162, §10, effective January 1, 1994. Amended Stats. 1993 (S.B. 970), ch. 266, §2.)

B. SELECTION STANDARDS FOR ADOPTIVE PARENTS

The primary consideration in determining issues regarding adoption (similar to the standard for determinations of custody and visitation) is the best interest of the child. See Cal. Fam. Code §8612(c) *supra*.

The revised Uniform Adoption Act §2-104 (which California has not adopted) lists in order of preference several factors that an agency should consider in determining a child's best interests in the selection of adoptive parents: the previous adoption of a sibling, characteristics requested by the minor's birth parent or guardian, custody of the minor for 6 months within the preceding 24 months or half the child's life, and status as a relative with whom the child has established a positive emotional relationship by one who makes a written adoption request. After considering these possibilities, the agency can consider other individuals. 9 U.L.A. (pt. IA) 33-34 (1999). Alternatively, the child's parent or guardian can select an adoptive family and place the child directly. UAA §2-102, *id.* at 12. Under the Act, most adopters must have a favorable preplacement evaluation. UAA §§2-102, 2-104, 7-101, *id.* at 30-31, 33-34, 124. All placements require an evaluation before the adoption becomes final. UAA §§3-601 through 3-603, *id.* at 91-92.

1. Race, Color, Religion, National Origin

Several factors are relevant in the determination of the best interests of the child. The United States Supreme Court has not yet addressed the issue of the relevance of race in the adoption context. However, the Court has held that race may not be the determinative factor in a custody determination (Palmore v. Sidoti, 466 U.S. 429 (1984)).

Congress has legislated "removal of barriers to inter-ethnic adoption" by providing that no state or state entity receiving federal funds can "deny to any individual the opportunity to become an adoptive or a foster parent, on the basis of the race, color, or national origin of the individual, or of the child, involved" or "delay or deny" placements on these bases. 42 U.S.C. §1996b (2000). An earlier law, the Multiethnic Placement Act (now repealed), reflected political compromise by allowing consideration of "the cultural, ethnic or racial background of the child and the capacity of the prospective foster or adoptive parents to meet [the child's needs] as one of a number of factors used to determine [the child's] best interests." 42 U.S.C. §5115a.

Prior to 2003, California law allowed adoption agencies to consider the race, ethnicity and cultural background of a child (as well as "the capacity of the prospective adoptive parent to meet the needs of a child of this background") as factors in the determination of the best interests of the child. These sections were repealed in 2003, leaving the child's religious background as the only suitable demographic factor to be considered (Cal. Fam. Code §8709). However, religion may not be determinative. See Scott v. Family Ministries, 135 Cal. Rptr. 430 (Ct. App. 1976) (applying constitutional protection to adoptions arranged by the state as well as private agencies). Just as race, ethnicity and cultural background are not acceptable criteria for placement of a child, they also cannot be factors tending to disqualify potential adoptive parents (Cal. Fam. Code. §8708).

See generally Solangel Maldonado, Discouraging Racial Preferences in Adoptions, 39 U.C. Davis. L. Rev. 1415 (2006).

Special regulations govern the relinquishment of children of Native American ancestry (Cal. Fam. Code §8619). California law directs courts to comply with the Indian Child Welfare Act of 1978 (ICWA), 25 U.S.C. §1915(a) (2000), in "all child custody proceedings" affecting Indian children (Cal. Fam. Code §7810) as defined by the federal ICWA. Under federal law, the term "child custody proceeding" is defined broadly to include: (1) "foster care placement," (2) "termination of parental rights," (3) "preadoptive placement" and (4) "adoptive placement." 25 U.S.C. §1903(1). Under the ICWA, preference is given (absent good cause) to placement with: (1) a member of the child's extended family, (2) other members of the Indian child's tribe, or (3) other Indian families. See Dwayne P. v. Superior Court, 126 Cal. Rptr.2d 639 (Ct. App. 2002) (holding that juvenile court was required to secure compliance with the notice provisions of the ICWA prior to terminating parental rights once father stated he might have Cherokee Indian heritage and mother agreed). See also the discussion of Native American rights in Chapter IX §G4 supra.

§8619. Information for children of Indian ancestry

The department shall adopt rules and regulations it determines are reasonably necessary to ensure that the birth parent or parents of Indian ancestry, seeking to relinquish a child for adoption, provide sufficient information to the department or to the licensed adoption agency so that a certificate of degree of Indian blood can be obtained from the Bureau of Indian Affairs. The department shall immediately request a certificate of degree of Indian blood from the Bureau of Indian Affairs upon obtaining the information. A copy of all documents pertaining to the degree of Indian blood and tribal enrollment, including a copy of the certificate of degree of Indian blood, shall become a permanent record in the adoption files and shall be housed in a central location and made available to authorized personnel from the Bureau of Indian Affairs when required to determine the adopted person's eligibility to receive services or benefits because of the adopted person's status as an Indian. This information shall be made available to the adopted person upon reaching the age of majority.

(Stats. 1992 (A.B. 2650), ch. 162, §10, effective January 1, 1994.)

§8708. Prohibition on discrimination in adoption or placement

(a) Neither the department nor a licensed adoption agency to which a child has been freed for adoption by either relinquishment or termination of parental rights may do any of the following:

(1) Deny to any person the opportunity to become an adoptive parent on the basis of the race, color, or national origin of the person or the child involved.

(2) Delay or deny the placement of a child for adoption on the basis of the race, color, or national origin of the adoptive parent or the child involved.

(3) Delay or deny the placement of a child for adoption solely because the prospective, approved adoptive family resides outside the jurisdiction of the department or the licensed adoption agency. For purposes of this paragraph, an approved adoptive family means a family approved pursuant to the California adoptive applicant assessment standards. If the adoptive applicant assessment was conducted in another state according to that state's standards, the California placing agency shall determine whether the standards of the other state substantially meet the standards and criteria established in California adoption regulations.

(b) This section shall not be construed to affect the application of the Indian Child Welfare Act (25 U.S.C. Sec. 1901 and following).

(Stats. 1995 (A.B. 1743), ch. 884, §4. Amended Stats. 1998 (A.B. 2773), ch. 1056, §3. Amended by Stats. 2003 (S.B. 984), ch. 323, §2.)

§8709. Role of religion in custody decisionmaking

(a) The department or licensed adoption agency to which a child has been freed for adoption by either relinquishment or termination of parental rights may consider the child's religious background in determining an appropriate placement.

(b) This section shall not be construed to affect the application of the Indian Child Welfare Act (25 U.S.C. Sec. 1901 and following).

(Stats. 1995 (A.B. 1743), ch. 884, §6. Amended by Stats. 2003 (S.B. 984), ch. 323, §3.)

2. Relatives, Stepparents, and Foster Parents

The legislature has enacted certain provisions to facilitate the adoption of children by relative caregivers, stepparents, domestic partners and foster parents. Many states, including California (Cal. Fam. Code §8710), give preference to relatives. Foster parents also receive preferential treatment in some cases: if no relative is available, relative placement is not in the child's best interests, or relative placement would separate siblings; and if the child has been in foster care for more than 4 months, the child has "substantial emotional ties" to the foster parents, the child's removal from the foster home would be "seriously detrimental" to the child's well-being and the foster parents have requested in writing to be considered as adoptive parents (Cal. Fam. Code §8710).

The procedure for adoption by a stepparent is governed by California Family Code §§9000 et seq. The stepparent files a petition to adopt the child or his or her spouse. Various designated persons or agencies then conduct an investigation, file a report and make a recommendation to the court. After consideration of the report and recommendation, the court makes an order of adoption (Cal. Fam. Code §9001(a)). However, a home study is not required in a stepparent adoption (Cal. Fam. Code §9001(b)). A domestic partner may petition to adopt the child of his or her partner using the stepparent adoption procedure of California Family Code §9000.

For additional provisions on adoption by stepparents and domestic partners, see §C3 *infra*.

§8616.5. Kinship adoption agreement: terms, consent, warning, etc.

(a) The Legislature finds and declares that some adoptive children may benefit from either direct or indirect contact with birth relatives, including the birth parent or parents, after being adopted. Postadoption contact agreements are intended to ensure children of an achievable level of continuing contact when contact is beneficial to the children and the agreements are voluntarily entered into by birth relatives, including the birth parent or parents, and adoptive parents.

(b)(1) Nothing in the adoption laws of this state shall be construed to prevent the adopting parent or parents, the birth relatives, including the birth parent or parents, and the child from voluntarily entering into a written agreement to permit continuing contact between the birth relatives, including the birth parent or parents, and the child if the agreement is found by the court to have been entered into voluntarily and to be in the best interests of the child at the time the adoption petition is granted.

(2) Except as provided in paragraph (3), the terms of any postadoption contact agreement executed under this section shall be limited to, but need not include, all of the following:

(A) Provisions for visitation between the child and a birth parent or parents and other birth relatives, including siblings, and the child's Indian tribe if the case is governed by the Indian Child Welfare Act (25 U.S.C. Sec. 1901 et seq.).

(B) Provisions for future contact between a birth parent or parents or other birth relatives, including siblings, or both, and the child or an adoptive parent, or both, and in cases governed by the Indian Child Welfare Act, the child's Indian tribe.

(C) Provisions for the sharing of information about the child in the future.

(3) The terms of any postadoption contact agreement shall be limited to the sharing of information about the child, unless the child has an existing relationship with the birth relative.

(c) At the time an adoption decree is entered pursuant to a petition filed pursuant to Section 8714, 8714.5, 8802, 8912, or 9000, the court entering the decree may grant postadoption privileges if an agreement for those privileges has been entered into, including agreements entered into pursuant to subdivision (f) of Section 8620.

(d) The child who is the subject of the adoption petition shall be considered a party to the postadoption contact agreement. The written consent to the terms and conditions of the postadoption contact agreement and any subsequent modifications of the agreement by a child who is 12 years of age or older is a necessary condition to the granting of privileges regarding visitation, contact, or sharing of information about the child, unless the court finds by a preponderance of the evidence that the agreement, as written, is in the best interests of the child. Any child who has been found to come within Section 300 of the Welfare and Institutions Code or who is the subject of a petition for jurisdiction of the juvenile court under Section 300 of the Welfare and Institutions Code shall be represented by an attorney for purposes of consent to the postadoption contact agreement.

(e) A postadoption contact agreement shall contain the following warnings in bold type:

(1) After the adoption petition has been granted by the court, the adoption cannot be set aside due to the failure of an adopting parent, a birth parent, a birth relative, or the child to follow the terms of this agreement or a later change to this agreement.

(2) A disagreement between the parties or litigation brought to enforce or modify the agreement shall not affect the validity of the adoption and shall not serve as a basis for orders affecting the custody of the child.

(3) A court will not act on a petition to change or enforce this agreement unless the petitioner has participated, or attempted to participate, in good faith in mediation or other appropriate dispute resolution proceedings to resolve the dispute.

(f) Upon the granting of the adoption petition and the issuing of the order of adoption of a child who is a dependent of the juvenile court, juvenile court dependency jurisdiction shall be terminated. Enforcement of the postadoption contact agreement shall be under the continuing jurisdiction of the court granting the petition of adoption. The court may not order compliance with the agreement absent a finding that the party seeking the enforcement participated, or attempted to participate, in good faith in mediation or other appropriate dispute resolution proceedings regarding the conflict, prior to the filing of the enforcement action, and that the enforcement is in the best interests of the child. Documentary evidence or offers of proof may serve as the basis for the court's decision regarding enforcement. No testimony or evidentiary hearing shall be required. The court shall not order further investigation or evaluation by any public or private agency or individual absent a finding by clear and convincing evidence that the best interests of the child may be protected or advanced only by that inquiry and that the inquiry will not disturb the stability of the child's home to the detriment of the child.

(g) The court may not award monetary damages as a result of the filing of the civil action pursuant to subdivision (e) of this section.

(h) A postadoption contact agreement may be modified or terminated only if either of the following occurs:

(1) All parties, including the child if the child is 12 years of age or older at the time of the requested termination or modification, have signed a modified postadoption contact agreement and the agreement is filed with the court that granted the petition of adoption.

(2) The court finds all of the following:

(A) The termination or modification is necessary to serve the best interests of the child.

(B) There has been a substantial change of circumstances since the original agreement was executed and approved by the court.

(C) The party seeking the termination or modification has participated, or attempted to participate, in good faith in mediation or other appropriate dispute resolution proceedings prior to seeking court approval of the proposed termination or modification.

Documentary evidence or offers of proof may serve as the basis for the court's decision. No testimony or evidentiary hearing shall be required. The court shall not order further investigation or evaluation by any public or private agency or individual absent a finding by clear and convincing evidence that the best interests of the child may be protected or advanced only by that inquiry and that the inquiry will not disturb the stability of the child's home to the detriment of the child.

(i) All costs and fees of mediation or other appropriate dispute resolution proceedings shall be borne by each party, excluding the child. All costs and fees of litigation shall be borne by the party filing the action to modify or enforce the agreement when no party has been found by the court as failing to comply with an existing postadoption contact agreement. Otherwise, a party, other than the child, found by the court as failing to comply without good cause with an existing agreement shall bear all the costs and fees of litigation.

(j) The Judicial Council shall adopt rules of court and forms for motions to enforce, terminate, or modify postadoption contact agreements.

(k) The court shall not set aside a decree of adoption, rescind a relinquishment, or modify an order to terminate parental rights or any other prior court order because of the

failure of a birth parent, adoptive parent, birth relative, or the child to comply with any or all of the original terms of, or subsequent modifications to, the postadoption contact agreement.
(Stats. 1997 (A.B. 1544), ch. 793, §5. Amended Stats. 2000 (A.B. 2921), ch. 910, §4, (S.B. 2157), ch. 930, §3. Amended and Renumbered Cal. Fam. Code §8616.5 by Stats. 2003 (S.B. 182), ch. 251, §8. Amended by Stats. 2004 (S.B. 1357), ch. 858, §4.)

§8710. Relative preference for adoption placement

Where a child is being considered for adoption, the department or licensed adoption agency shall first consider adoptive placement in the home of a relative. However, if a relative is not available, if placement with an available relative is not in the child's best interest, or if placement would permanently separate the child from other siblings who are being considered for adoption or who are in foster care and an alternative placement would not require the permanent separation, the foster parent or parents of the child shall be considered with respect to the child along with all other prospective adoptive parents where all of the following conditions are present:

(a) The child has been in foster care with the foster parent or parents for a period of more than four months.

(b) The child has substantial emotional ties to the foster parent or parents.

(c) The child's removal from the foster home would be seriously detrimental to the child's well-being.

(d) The foster parent or parents have made a written request to be considered to adopt the child.

This section does not apply to a child who has been adjudged a dependent of the juvenile court pursuant to Section 300 of the Welfare and Institutions Code.
(Stats. 1995 (A.B. 1743), ch. 884, §8.)

§8714.5. Procedures to expedite adoptions by relatives

(a) The Legislature finds and declares the following:

(1) It is the intent of the Legislature to expedite legal permanency for children who cannot return to their parents and to remove barriers to adoption by relatives of children who are already in the dependency system or who are at risk of entering the dependency system.

(2) This goal will be achieved by empowering families, including extended families, to care for their own children safely and permanently whenever possible, by preserving existing family relationships, thereby causing the least amount of disruption to the child and the family, and by recognizing the importance of sibling and half-sibling relationships.

(b) A relative desiring to adopt a child may for that purpose file a petition in the county in which the petitioner resides. Where a child has been adjudged to be a dependent of the juvenile court pursuant to Section 300 of the Welfare and Institutions Code, and thereafter has been freed for adoption by the juvenile court, the petition may be filed either in the county where the petitioner resides or in the county where the child was freed for adoption.

(c) Upon the filing of a petition for adoption by a relative, the clerk of the court shall immediately notify the State Department of Social Services in Sacramento in writing of the pendency of the proceeding and of any subsequent action taken.

(d) If the adopting relative has entered into a post adoption contact agreement with the birth parent as set forth in Section 8616.5, the agreement, signed by the participating parties, shall be attached to and filed with the petition for adoption under subdivision (b).

(e) The caption of the adoption petition shall contain the name of the relative petitioner. The petition shall state the child's name, sex, and date of birth.

(f) If the child is the subject of a guardianship petition, the adoption petition shall so state and shall include the caption and docket number or have attached a copy of the letters of the guardianship or temporary guardianship. The petitioner shall notify the court of any petition for adoption. The guardianship proceeding shall be consolidated with the adoption proceeding.

(g) The order of adoption shall contain the child's adopted name and, if requested by the adopting relative, or if requested by the child who is 12 years of age or older, the name the child had before adoption.

(h) For purposes of this section, "relative" means an adult who is related to the child or the child's half-sibling by blood or affinity, including all relatives whose status is preceded by the words "step," "great," "great-great," or "grand," or the spouse of any of these persons, even if the marriage was terminated by death or dissolution.
(Stats. 1997 (A.B. 1544), ch. 793, §4. Amended Stats. 2000 (A.B. 2921), ch. 910, §3, (S.B. 2157), ch. 930, §2. Amended by Stats. 2002 (S.B. 1316), ch. 784, §112. Amended by Stats. 2003 (S.B. 182), ch. 251, §7.)

§8730. Limited assessment in cases of adoptions sought by foster parent or relative caregiver

If the prospective adoptive parent of a child is a foster parent with whom the child has lived for a minimum of six months or a relative caregiver who has had an ongoing and significant relationship with the child, an assessment or home study of the prospective adoptive parent may, at the discretion of the department or a licensed adoption agency, or unless the court with jurisdiction over the child orders otherwise, require only the following:

(a) A criminal records check of the relative caregiver or foster parent, as provided in subdivision (a) of Section 8712 [set forth in §B5 infra].

(b) A determination that the relative caregiver or foster parent has sufficient financial stability to support the child and ensure that any adoption assistance program payment or other government assistance to which the child is entitled is used exclusively to meet the child's needs. In making this determination, the experience of the relative caregiver or foster parent only while the child was in his or her care shall be considered. For purposes of this section, the relative caregiver or foster parent shall be required to provide verification of employment records or income or both.

(c) A determination that the relative caregiver or foster parent has not abused or neglected the child while the child has been in his or her care and has fostered the healthy growth and development of the child. This determination shall include a review of the disciplinary practices of the relative caregiver or foster parent to ensure that the practices are age appropriate and do not physically or emotionally endanger the child.

(d) A determination that there is not a likelihood that the relative caregiver or foster parent will abuse or neglect the child in the future, that the caregiver or foster parent can protect the child, ensure necessary care and supervision, and foster the child's healthy growth and development.

(e) A determination that the relative caregiver or foster parent can address racial and cultural issues that may affect the child's well-being.

(f) An interview with the relative caregiver or foster parent, an interview with each individual residing in the home and an interview with the child to be adopted.

(Stats. 1998 (A.B. 2286), ch. 983, §3.)

§8731. Time of assessment in cases of adoption by foster parent

If the prospective adoptive parent of a child is a foster parent, the assessment or home study described in Section 8730 shall not be initiated until the child to be adopted has resided in the home of the foster parent for at least six months.

(Stats. 1998 (A.B. 2286), ch. 983, §3.)

§8732. Assessment shall include medical exam in cases of adoption by foster parent

A report of a medical examination of the foster parent with whom the child has lived for a minimum of six months or the relative caregiver who has had an ongoing and significant relationship with the child shall be included in the assessment of each applicant unless the department or licensed adoption agency determines that, based on other available information, this report is unnecessary. The assessment shall require certification that the applicant and each adult residing in the applicant's home has received a test for communicable tuberculosis.

(Stats. 1998 (A.B. 2286), ch. 983, §3.)

§8733. Adoptive parent shall receive information regarding special needs of adoptee

The department or licensed adoption agency shall require the adoptive parent to be provided with information related to the specific needs of the child to be adopted, that, as determined by the licensed adoption agency, may include information regarding the following: issues surrounding birth parents, the effects of abuse and neglect on children, cultural and racial issues, sexuality, contingency planning for children in the event of the parents' death or disability, financial assistance for adopted children, common childhood disabilities, including, but not limited to, emotional disturbances, attention deficit disorder, learning disabilities, speech and hearing impairment, and dyslexia, the importance of sibling and half-sibling relationships, and other issues related to adoption and child development and the availability of counseling to deal with these issues.

(Stats. 1998 (A.B. 2286), ch. 983, §3.)

§8735. Denial of adoption approval must be conveyed to foster care agencies

The department shall require adoption agencies to inform the agency responsible for the foster care placement when a relative caregiver or foster parent has been denied approval to adopt based on an inability of the relative caregiver or foster parent to provide for the mental and emotional health, safety, and security of the child and to recommend either that the relative caregiver or foster parent be provided with additional support and supervision or that the child be removed from the home of the relative caregiver or foster parent.

(Stats. 1998 (A.B. 2286), ch. 983, §3.)

§9000. Procedure for stepparent adoption; availability to domestic partner

(a) A stepparent desiring to adopt a child of the stepparent's spouse may for that purpose file a petition in the county in which the petitioner resides.

(b) A domestic partner, as defined in Section 297, desiring to adopt a child of his or her domestic partner may for that purpose file a petition in the county in which the petitioner resides.

(c) The caption of the adoption petition shall contain the names of the petitioners, but not the child's name. The petition shall state the child's sex and date of birth and the name the child had before adoption.

(d) If the child is the subject of a guardianship petition, the adoption petition shall so state and shall include the caption and docket number or have attached a copy of the letters of the guardianship or temporary guardianship. The petitioners shall notify the court of any petition for guardianship or temporary guardianship filed after the adoption petition. The guardianship proceeding shall be consolidated with the adoption proceeding.

(e) The order of adoption shall contain the child's adopted name, but not the name the child had before adoption.

(f) If the petitioner has entered into a postadoption contact agreement with the birth parent as set forth in Section 8616.5, the agreement, signed by the participating parties, shall be attached to and filed with the petition for adoption.

(g) For the purposes of this chapter, stepparent adoption includes adoption by a domestic partner, as defined in Section 297.

(Stats. 1992 (A.B. 2650), ch. 162, §10, effective January 1, 1994. Amended Stats. 2001 (A.B. 25), ch. 893, §5. Amended by Stats. 2004 (S.B. 1357), ch. 858, §7.)

3. Sexual Orientation

Although most state statutes are silent on the issue of the role of sexual orientation in adoption, some courts interpret their adoption statutes to permit adoptions by gays and lesbians in either joint adoption or second-parent situations. However, other courts deny such adoptions based either on the best- interests-of-the-child standard or by application of parental termination statutes (holding that termination of the parental rights of one parent is required in order to permit adoption by another parent of the same sex).

California is among the few states that expressly permit adoption by same-sex partners (Cal. Fam. Code §§9000(b)(2003)).

A few states expressly restrict adoption by same-sex couples. See Fla. Stat. Ann. §63.042(3) (West 2003) (no person may adopt if a homosexual); Miss. Code Ann. §93-17-3(2) (1999) (prohibiting adoption by couples of the same gender). See also Utah Code Ann. §78-30-1(3)(6)(2002) (prohibiting adoption by a person who is cohabiting in a relationship that is not a valid marriage under state law). Cf. N.H. Rev. Stat. Ann. §170-B:4 (Supp. 2000) (revising statute to remove prohibition).

Florida was the first state to ban adoptions by same-sex couples in 1977. Lofton v. Kearney, 157 F. Supp.2d 1372, 1374 n.1 (S.D. Fla. 2001) (holding that Florida ban on gay adoptions did not violate Equal Protection Clause and reasoning that foster parent-child relationship did not create liberty interest entitled to protection under Due Process Clause). See also Cox v. Florida Dept. of Health & Rehabilitative Servs., 656 So. 2d 902 (Fla. 1995) (holding that Florida ban on gay adoptions did not violate *state* constitutional protection against privacy or due process and was not unconstitutionally vague but failing to reach the equal protection issue because of insufficient record).

According to legislation in California, domestic partners may utilize the stepparent adoption procedure governed by California Family Code §§9000 et seq. (The complete version of California Family Code §9000 is given in §B2 *supra.*)

§9000. Availability to domestic partner of procedure for stepparent adoption

(a) A stepparent desiring to adopt a child of the stepparent's spouse may for that purpose file a petition in the county in which the petitioner resides.

(b) A domestic partner, as defined in Section 297, desiring to adopt a child of his or her domestic partner may for that purpose file a petition in the county in which the petitioner resides.

. . .

(g) For the purposes of this chapter, stepparent adoption includes adoption by a domestic partner, as defined in Section 297.

(Stats. 1992 (A.B. 2650), ch. 162, §10, effective January 1, 1994. Amended Stats. 2001 (A.B. 25), ch. 893, §5. Amended by Stats. 2004 (S.B. 1357), ch. 858, §7.)

4. Age

According to California law, a prospective adoptive parent (or parents) must be at least 10 years older than the child (Cal. Fam. Code §8601(a)). However, a court may dispense with this requirement in cases of adoption by relatives if the adoption is "in the best interest of the parties and is in the public interest" (Cal. Fam. Code §8601(b)).

§8601. Prospective adoptive parent shall be at least 10 years older than adoptee

(a) Except as otherwise provided in subdivision (b), a prospective adoptive parent or parents shall be at least 10 years older than the child.

(b) If the court is satisfied that the adoption of a child by a stepparent, or by a sister, brother, aunt, uncle, or first cousin and, if that person is married, by that person and that person's spouse, is in the best interest of the parties and is in the public interest, it may approve the adoption without regard to the ages of the child and the prospective adoptive parent or parents.

(Stats. 1992 (A.B. 2650), ch. 162, §10, effective January 1, 1994.)

5. Criminal History

Several states, including California, require that adoption agencies must investigate whether a prospective adoptive parent has a criminal record. See, e.g., Cal. Fam. Code §8712.

§8712. Adoption agencies must investigate criminal history of prospective adoptive parents

(a) The department or licensed adoption agency shall require each person filing an application for adoption to be fingerprinted and shall secure from an appropriate law enforcement agency any criminal record of that person to determine whether the person has ever been convicted of a crime other than a minor traffic violation. The department or licensed adoption agency may also secure the person's full criminal record, if any.

(b) The criminal record, if any, shall be taken into consideration when evaluating the prospective adoptive parent, and an assessment of the effects of any criminal history on the ability of the prospective adoptive parent to provide adequate and proper care and guidance to the child shall be included in the report to the court.

(c) Any fee charged by a law enforcement agency for fingerprinting or for checking or obtaining the criminal record of the applicant shall be paid by the applicant. The department or licensed adoption agency may defer, waive, or reduce the fee when its payment would cause economic hardship to prospective adoptive parents detrimental to the welfare of the adopted child, when the child has been in the foster care of the prospective adoptive parents for at least one year, or if necessary for the placement of a special-needs child.

(Stats. 1992 (A.B. 2650), ch. 162, §10, effective January 1, 1994.)

C. CONSENT

State statutes generally require consent of biological parents before an adoption may take place. If a child is born in wedlock, consent from both parents is required absent a showing of abandonment or unfitness. If a child is born out of wedlock, the United States Supreme Court has held that courts may dispense with the father's consent if he has not indicated sufficient "indicia" of parenthood (Lehr v. Robertson, 463 U.S. 248 (1983); Caban v. Mohammed, 442 U.S. 380 (1979); Quilloin v. Walcott, 434 U.S. 246 (1978), *reh'g denied*, 435 U.S. 918 (1978)).

The California statutory scheme creates three classifications of parents: mothers, biological fathers who are "presumed fathers," and biological fathers who are not presumed fathers. Consent is required of a mother and a presumed father, absent a showing by clear and convincing evidence of that parent's unfitness. The biological father who is not a presumed father is treated differently: his consent is not required. Therefore, an unwed father's rights depend on whether he is "presumed father." See discussion in §C(2) *infra*.

1. Mother's Consent

In an agency adoption, the birth parent begins the adoption process with the relinquishment of the child to the Department of Social Services or a licensed adoption agency (depending on the county) by executing a written statement of relinquishment (Cal. Fam. Code §8700(a) *infra* §D1(b)). Relinquishment by the parent (like a judicial termination of parental rights) serves to vest care, custody and control of the child in the department or agency until the court grants an order of adoption (Cal. Fam. Code §8704(a)).

If a birth parent refuses to give consent (or subsequently withdraws his or her consent), the court must order the child restored to the birth parent's care and custody (Cal. Fam. Code 8804(c), *infra* §D2.

§7660. Mother's relinquishment or consent; notice to presumed father of adoption proceeding

If a mother relinquishes for or consents to, or proposes to relinquish for or consent to, the adoption of a child who has a presumed father under Section 7611, the father shall be given notice of the adoption proceeding and have the rights provided under Part 2 (commencing with Section 8600) of Division 13, unless the father's relationship to the child has been previously terminated or determined by a court not to exist or the father has voluntarily relinquished for or consented to the adoption of the child.

(Stats. 1992 (A.B. 2650), ch. 162, §10, effective January 1, 1994. Amended Stats. 2000 (A.B. 2433), ch. 937, §1.)

§8604. Requirement of birth parents' consent

(a) Except as provided in subdivision (b), a child having a presumed father under Section 7611 may not be adopted without the consent of the child's birth parents, if living. The consent of a presumed father is not required for the child's adoption unless he became a presumed father as described in Chapter 1 (commencing with Section 7540) or Chapter 3 (commencing with Section 7570) of Part 2 of Division 12, or subdivision (a), (b), or (c) of Section 7611 before the mother's relinquishment or consent becomes irrevocable or before the mother's parental rights have been terminated.

(b) If one birth parent has been awarded custody by judicial order, or has custody by agreement of both parents, and the other birth parent for a period of one year willfully fails to communicate with and to pay for the care, support, and education of the child when able to do so, then the birth parent having sole custody may consent to the adoption, but only after the birth parent not having custody has been served with a copy of a citation in the manner provided by law for the service of a summons in a civil action that requires the birth parent not having custody to appear at the time and place set for the appearance in court under Section 8718, 8823, 8913, or 9007.

(c) Failure of a birth parent to pay for the care, support, and education of the child for the period of one year or failure of a birth parent to communicate with the child for the period of one year is prima facie evidence that the failure was willful and without lawful excuse.

(Stats. 1992 (A.B. 2650), ch. 162, §10, effective January 1, 1994. Amended by Stats. 2005 (S.B. 302), ch. 627, §3.)

§8605. Consent of mother required if child does not have presumed father

A child not having a presumed father under Section 7611 may not be adopted without the consent of the child's mother, if living.

(Stats. 1992 (A.B. 2650), ch. 162, §10, effective January 1, 1994.)

---

2. Consent by the Unmarried Father

An unwed father's rights in an adoption proceeding are governed by California statute and the Fourteenth Amendment. In California, an unwed father's rights depend on whether he qualifies as a "presumed father" under state law. California statute creates a category of "presumed father" whose consent is required prior to a child's adoption. In its treatment of a presumed father, California law mirrors that of the original Uniform Parentage Act. A father is presumed to be the natural father of a child if he meets the conditions provided in California Family Code §7611 *infra*. When the presumption is established, it can be rebutted by clear and convincing evidence to the contrary (Cal. Fam. Code §7612(a)). However, the presumption is absolutely rebutted by a judgment that actual paternity exists from another man. (Cal. Fam. Code §7612(c)). When there is more than one person for whom the presumption applies, the standard is a preponderence of the evidence as to which man is the legally recognized presumptive father (Cal. Fam. Code §7612(b)).

In Adoption of Kelsey S., 4 Cal. Rptr. 2d 615 (1992), the California Supreme Court held that California Family Code §§7611 and 7664 are unconstitutional insofar as they allow a mother unilaterally to prevent a man from becoming a "presumed father" and then allow the state to terminate his parental rights based merely upon a showing of the best interests of the child. According to *Kelsey S.*, the parental rights of an unwed father who demonstrates full commitment to his parental responsibilities may only be terminated by a showing of parental unfitness. (The natural father filed an action two days after the child's birth to establish his parental relationship with the child and to obtain custody of the child but his efforts were thwarted by the child's mother.)

In re Jerry P., 116 Cal. Rptr. 2d 123 (Ct. App. 2002) held that *Kelsey* applies to dependency proceedings, and therefore California Family Code §7611 and the related dependency scheme violate the constitutional rights of a nonbiological father who was seeking presumed father status to the extent that the statutes permit a mother unilaterally to deny him that status by preventing him from receiving the child into his home.

See also Adoption of Michael H., 898 P.2d 891 (Cal. 1995) (holding that an unwed father has no federal constitutional right to withhold consent to adoption unless he shows that he promptly came forward and demonstrated as full a commitment to his parental responsibilities as the biological mother allowed and circumstances permitted within a short time after he learned or should have learned that biological mother was pregnant); In re Ariel H., 86 Cal. Rptr. 2d 125 (Cal. 1999) (holding that unwed 15-year-old biological father's rights to equal protection rights and due process were not violated for purposes of consent to adoption, where the trial court found father's unfitness based on his failure to timely demonstrate a full commitment to his parental responsibilities before or after the child's birth); In re N.S., 2002 WL 31270246 (Ct. App. 2002) (slip opinion) (holding that unwed biological father's due process rights were violated by failing to find him a presumed father because he provided a home for child on occasion, held out child as his, and never disputed mother's decision to name him on birth certificate).

In 2002, the California Supreme Court examined the application of the presumption of paternity to a nonbiological father. In In re Nicholas H., 46 P.3d 932 (Cal. 2002), the state supreme court held that a presumed father's admission that he was not the child's biological father does not necessarily rebut the paternity presumption under California Family Code §7611 that arose by his receiving the child into his home and openly holding the child out as his natural child.

Nicholas H. is an example of recent California case law that gives increased weight to the claims of nonbiological fathers for recognition of parental status , particularly in cases in which the biological father was not married to the mother and had not established a relationship with the child. See also In re Jerusa V., 85 P.3d 205 (Cal. 2004); In re Raphael P., 118 Cal. Rptr.2d 610 (Ct. App. 2002).

§7610. Parent-child relationship: method of establishment

The parent and child relationship may be established as follows:

(a) Between a child and the natural mother, it may be established by proof of her having given birth to the child, or under this part.

(b) Between a child and the natural father, it may be established under this part.

(c) Between a child and an adoptive parent, it may be established by proof of adoption.

(Stats. 1992 (A.B. 2650), ch. 162, §10, effective January 1, 1994.)

§7611. Conditions for presumed fatherhood

A man is presumed to be the natural father of a child if he meets the conditions provided in Chapter 1 (commencing with Section 7540) or Chapter 3 (commencing with Section 7570) of Part 2 or in any of the following subdivisions:

(a) He and the child's natural mother are or have been married to each other and the child is born during the marriage, or within 300 days after the marriage is terminated by death, annulment, declaration of invalidity, or divorce, or after a judgment of separation is entered by a court.

(b) Before the child's birth, he and the child's natural mother have attempted to marry each other by a marriage solemnized in apparent compliance with law, although the attempted marriage is or could be declared invalid, and either of the following is true:

(1) If the attempted marriage could be declared invalid only by a court, the child is born during the attempted marriage, or within 300 days after its termination by death, annulment, declaration of invalidity, or divorce.

(2) If the attempted marriage is invalid without a court order, the child is born within 300 days after the termination of cohabitation.

(c) After the child's birth, he and the child's natural mother have married, or attempted to marry, each other by a marriage solemnized in apparent compliance with law, although the attempted marriage is or could be declared invalid, and either of the following is true:

(1) With his consent, he is named as the child's father on the child's birth certificate.

(2) He is obligated to support the child under a written voluntary promise or by court order.

(d) He receives the child into his home and openly holds out the child as his natural child.

(e) If the child was born and resides in a nation with which the United States engages in an Orderly Departure Program or successor program, he acknowledges that he is the child's father in a declaration under penalty of perjury, as specified in Section 2015.5 of the Code of Civil Procedure. This subdivision shall remain in effect only until January 1, 1997, and on that date shall become inoperative.

(f) The child is in utero after the death of the decedent and the conditions set forth in Section 249.5 of the Probate Code are satisfied.

(Stats. 1992 (A.B. 2650), ch. 162, §10, effective January 1, 1994. Amended by Stats. 1993 (A.B. 1500), ch. 219, §176. Amended by Stats. 1994 (A.B. 2208), ch. 1269, §53. Amended by Stats. 2004 (A.B. 1910), ch. 775, §1.)

§7611.5. Conditions for presumption against natural father status

Where Section 7611 does not apply, a man shall not be presumed to be the natural father of a child if either of the following is true:

(a) The child was conceived as a result of an act in violation of Section 261 of the Penal Code and the father was convicted of that violation.

(b) The child was conceived as a result of an act in violation of Section 261.5 of the Penal Code, the father was convicted of that violation, and the mother was under the age of 15 years and the father was 21 years of age or older at the time of conception.

(Stats. 1993 (A.B. 1500), ch. 219, §177.)

§7612. Presumption as natural father is rebuttable; case of conflicting presumptions

(a) Except as provided in Chapter 1 (commencing with Section 7540) and Chapter 3 (commencing with Section 7570) of Part 2 or in Section 20102, a presumption under Section 7611 is a rebuttable presumption affecting the burden of proof and may be rebutted in an appropriate action only by clear and convincing evidence.

(b) If two or more presumptions arise under Section 7611 which conflict with each other, the presumption which on the facts is founded on the weightier considerations of policy and logic controls.

(c) The presumption under Section 7611 is rebutted by a judgment establishing paternity of the child by another man.

(Stats. 1992 (A.B. 2650), ch. 162, §10, effective January 1, 1994. Amended by Stats. 1993 (A.B. 1500), ch. 219, §178. Amended by Stats. 1994 (A.B. 2208), ch. 1269, §54.)

§7661. Father's relinquishment or consent; notice to mother of adoption proceeding

If a father relinquishes for or consents to, or proposes to relinquish for or consent to, the adoption of a child, the mother shall be given notice of the adoption proceeding and have the rights provided under Part 2 (commencing with Section 8600) of Division 13, unless the mother's relationship to the child has been previously terminated by a court or the mother has voluntarily relinquished for or consented to the adoption of the child.

(Stats. 1992 (A.B. 2650), ch. 162, §10, effective January 1, 1994.)

§7662. Mother or agency may file proceeding to terminate father's parental rights

(a) If a mother relinquishes for or consents to, or proposes to relinquish for or consent to, the adoption of a child who does not have a presumed father under Section 7611, or if a child otherwise becomes the subject of an adoption proceeding and the alleged father, if any, has not, in writing, denied paternity, waived his right to notice, or voluntarily relinquished for or consented to the adoption, the agency or person to whom the child has been or is to be relinquished, or the mother or the person having physical or legal custody of the child, or the prospective adoptive parent, shall file a petition to terminate the parental rights of the father, unless either of the following occurs:

(1) The father's relationship to the child has been previously terminated or determined not to exist by a court.

(2) The father has been served as prescribed in Section 7666 with a written notice alleging that he is or could be the natural father of the child to be adopted or placed for adoption and has failed to bring an action for the purpose of declaring the existence of the father and child relationship pursuant to subdivision (c) of Section 7630 within 30 days of service of the notice or the birth of the child, whichever is later.

(b) All proceedings affecting a child under Divisions 8 (commencing with Section 3000) to 11 (commencing with Section 6500), inclusive, and Parts 1 (commencing with Section 7500) to 3 (commencing with Section 7600), inclusive, of this division, other than an action brought pursuant to this section, shall be stayed pending final determination of proceedings to terminate the parental rights of the father pursuant to this section.

(c) Nothing in this section may limit the jurisdiction of the court pursuant to Part 3 (commencing with Section 6240) and Part 4 (commencing with Section 6300) of Division 10 with respect to domestic violence orders.

(Stats. 1992 (A.B. 2650), ch. 162, §10, effective January 1, 1994. Amended Stats. 2000 (A.B. 2433), ch. 937, §2; Stats. 2003 (S.B. 182), ch. 251, §3.)

§7663. Court shall make effort to identify natural father

(a) In an effort to identify the natural father, the court shall cause inquiry to be made of the mother and any other appropriate person by any of the following:

(1) The State Department of Social Services.

(2) A licensed county adoption agency.

(3) The licensed adoption agency to which the child is to be relinquished.

(4) In the case of a stepparent adoption, at the option of the board of supervisors, a licensed county adoption agency, the county department designated by the board of supervisors to administer the public social services program, or the county probation department.

(b) The inquiry shall include all of the following:

(1) Whether the mother was married at the time of conception of the child or at any time thereafter.

(2) Whether the mother was cohabiting with a man at the time of conception or birth of the child.

(3) Whether the mother has received support payments or promises of support with respect to the child or in connection with her pregnancy.

(4) Whether any man has formally or informally acknowledged or declared his possible paternity of the child.

(c) The department or the licensed adoption agency shall report the findings to the court.

(Stats. 1992 (A.B. 2650), ch. 162, §10, effective January 1, 1994.)

§7664. Court shall give notice to possible natural father and make determination of parentage

(a) If, after the inquiry, the natural father is identified to the satisfaction of the court, or if more than one man is identified as a possible father, each shall be given notice of the proceeding in accordance with Section 7666, unless he has been served with a written notice alleging that he is or could be the natural father of the child to be adopted or placed or relinquished for adoption and has failed to bring an action pursuant to subdivision (c) of Section 7630 to declare the existence of the father and child relationship within 30 days after service of the notice or the birth of the child, whichever is later. If any of them fails to appear or, if appearing, fails to claim parental rights, his parental rights with reference to the child shall be terminated.

(b) If the natural father or a man representing himself to be the natural father claims parental rights, the court shall determine if he is the father. The court shall then determine if it is in the best interest of the child that the father retain his parental rights, or that an adoption of the child be allowed to proceed. The court, in making that determination, may consider all relevant evidence, including the efforts made by the father to obtain custody, the age and prior placement of the child, and the effects of a change of placement on the child. If the court finds that it is in the best interest of the child that the father should be allowed to retain his parental rights, it shall order that his consent is necessary for an adoption. If the court finds that the man claiming parental rights is not the father, or that if he is the father it is in the child's best interest that an adoption be allowed to proceed, it shall order that that person's consent is not required for an adoption. This finding terminates all parental rights and responsibilities with respect to the child. Section 3041 does not apply to a proceeding under this chapter.

(c) Nothing in this part changes the rights of a presumed father under Section 7611.

(Stats. 1992 (A.B. 2650), ch. 162, §10, effective January 1, 1994.)

§7665. Court shall terminate rights of unknown natural father

If, after the inquiry, the court is unable to identify the natural father or any possible natural father and no person has appeared claiming to be the natural father and claiming custodial rights, the court shall enter an order terminating the unknown natural father's parental rights with reference to the child.

(Stats. 1992 (A.B. 2650), ch. 162, §10, effective January 1, 1994.)

§7666. Manner of giving notice to all possible fathers

(a) Except as provided in subdivision (b), notice of the proceeding shall be given to every person identified as the natural father or a possible natural father in accordance with the Code of Civil Procedure for the service of process in a civil action in this state at least 10 days before the date stated in the notice of the proceeding, except that publication or posting of the notice of the proceeding is not required. Proof of giving the notice shall be filed with the court before the petition is heard.

(b) If a person identified as the natural father or possible natural father cannot be located or his whereabouts are unknown or cannot be ascertained, the court may issue an order dispensing with notice to that person.

(Stats. 1992 (A.B. 2650), ch. 162, §10, effective January 1, 1994. Amended by Stats. 2002 (S.B. 1512), ch. 260, §1.)

3. Stepparents' and Domestic Partners' Consent

A stepparent initiates the procedure for adoption of his or her spouse's child by filing an adoption petition. After consideration of a report and a recommendation by the Department of Social Services or a licensed adoption agency, the court makes an order of adoption (Cal. Fam. Code §9001(a)) (see §C3 supra). A domestic partner may petition to adopt the child of his or her partner by using the stepparent adoption procedure of California Family Code §9000 (see §C3 supra).

§9002. Adoptive parent is liable for costs of stepparent adoption

In a stepparent adoption, the prospective adoptive parent is liable for all reasonable costs incurred in connection with the stepparent adoption, including, but not limited to, costs incurred for the investigation required by Section 9001, up to a maximum of seven hundred dollars ($700). The court, probation officer, qualified court investigator, or county welfare department may defer, waive, or reduce the fee if its payment would cause economic hardship to the prospective adoptive parent detrimental to the welfare of the adopted child.

(Stats.1992 (A.B. 2650), ch. 162, §10, effective January 1, 1994. Amended by Stats.1993 (A.B. 1500), ch. 219, §205; Stats.1993 (A.B. 1430), ch. 494, §1. Amended by Stats. 2001 (A.B. 25), ch. 893, §6.)

§9003. Procedure for consent of birth parents to stepparent adoption

(a) In a stepparent adoption, the consent of either or both birth parents shall be signed in the presence of a notary public, court clerk, probation officer, qualified court investigator, or county welfare department staff member of any county of this state. The county clerk, probation officer, qualified court investigator, or county welfare department staff member before whom the consent is signed shall immediately file the consent with the clerk of the court where the adoption petition is filed. The clerk shall immediately notify the probation officer or, at the option of the board of supervisors, the county welfare department of that county.

(b) If the birth parent of a child to be adopted is outside this state at the time of signing the consent, the consent may be signed before a notary or other person authorized to perform notarial acts.

(c) The consent, when reciting that the person giving it is entitled to sole custody of the child and when acknowledged before the notary public, court clerk, probation officer, qualified court investigator, or county welfare department staff member, is prima facie evidence of the right of the person signing the consent to the sole custody of the child and that person's sole right to consent.

(d) A birth parent who is a minor has the right to sign a consent for the adoption of the birth parent's child and the consent is not subject to revocation by reason of the minority.
(Stats. 1992 (A.B. 2650), ch. 162, §10, effective January 1, 1994. Amended Stats. 1993 (A.B. 1500), ch. 219, §206. Amended by Amended Stats. 2005 (S.B. 302), ch. 627, §4.)

§9004. Birth parent consent form

In a stepparent adoption, the form prescribed by the department for the consent of the birth parent shall contain substantially the following notice:

"Notice to the parent who gives the child for adoption: If you and your child lived together at any time as parent and child, the adoption of your child through a stepparent adoption does not affect the child's right to inherit your property or the property of other blood relatives."
(Stats. 1992 (A.B. 2650), ch. 162, §10, effective January 1, 1994. Amended Stats. 2001 (A.B. 25), ch. 893, §7.)

§9005. Birth parents may not withdraw consent except with court approval

(a) Consent of the birth parent to the adoption of the child through a stepparent adoption may not be withdrawn except with court approval. . . .

(b) The court clerk shall set the matter for hearing and shall give notice thereof to the probation officer, qualified court investigator, or county welfare department, to the prospective adoptive parent, and to the birth parent or parents by certified mail, return receipt requested, to the address of each as shown in the proceeding, at least 10 days before the time set for hearing.

(c) The probation officer, qualified court investigator, or county welfare department shall, before the hearing of the motion or petition for withdrawal, file a full report with the court and shall appear at the hearing to represent the interests of the child.

(d) At the hearing, the parties may appear in person or with counsel. The hearing shall be held in chambers, but the court reporter shall report the proceedings and, on court order, the fee therefor shall be paid from the county treasury. If the court finds that withdrawal of the consent to adoption is reasonable in view of all the circumstances and that withdrawal of the consent is in the child's best interest, the court shall approve the withdrawal of the consent. Otherwise the court shall withhold its approval. Consideration of the child's best interest shall include, but is not limited to, an assessment of the child's age, the extent of bonding with the prospective adoptive parent, the extent of bonding or the potential to bond with the birth parent, and the ability of the birth parent to provide adequate and proper care and guidance to the child. If the court approves the withdrawal of consent, the adoption proceeding shall be dismissed.

(e) A court order granting or withholding approval of a withdrawal of consent to an adoption may be appealed in the same manner as an order of the juvenile court declaring a person to be a ward of the juvenile court.
(Stats. 1992 (A.B. 2650), ch. 162, §10, effective January 1, 1994. Amended Stats. 1993 (A.B. 1500), ch. 219, §207; Stats. 2001 (A.B. 25), ch. 893, §8.)

§9006. Court clerk shall give notice of withdrawal of petition; court shall dismiss if consent refused

(a) If the petitioner moves to withdraw the adoption petition or to dismiss the proceeding, the court clerk shall immediately notify the probation officer, qualified court investigator, or county welfare department of the action.

(b) If a birth parent has refused to give the required consent, the adoption petition shall be dismissed.
(Stats. 1992 (A.B. 2650), ch. 162, §10, effective January 1, 1994. Amended Stats. 1993 (A.B. 1500), ch. 219, §208.)

4. Consent of Adoptee

A child over the age of 12 must give consent to his or her adoption (Cal. Fam. Code §8602).

§8602. Child must give consent to adoption if child is over 12 years old

The consent of a child, if over the age of 12 years, is necessary to the child's adoption.
(Stats. 1992 (A.B. 2650), ch. 162, §10, effective January 1, 1994

5. Circumstances Where Birth Parents' Consent Is Unnecessary

State law dispenses with the consent of the birth parent or parents in some cases, such as for children who are abused, neglected, abandoned, or for parents whose rights previously have been judicially terminated. On consent of unwed fathers, see §C2 supra.

§8606. Birth parents' consent not required in some circumstances

Notwithstanding Sections 8604 and 8605, the consent of a birth parent is not necessary in the following cases:

(a) Where the birth parent has been judicially deprived of the custody and control of the child (1) by a court order declaring the child to be free from the custody and control of either or both birth parents pursuant to Part 4 (commencing with Section 7800) of Division 12 of this code, or Section 366.25 or 366.26 of the Welfare and Institutions Code, or (2) by a similar order of a court of another jurisdiction, pursuant to a law of that jurisdiction authorizing the order.

(b) Where the birth parent has, in a judicial proceeding in another jurisdiction, voluntarily surrendered the right to the custody and control of the child pursuant to a law of that jurisdiction providing for the surrender.

(c) Where the birth parent has deserted the child without provision for identification of the child.

(d) Where the birth parent has relinquished the child for adoption as provided in Section 8700.

(e) Where the birth parent has relinquished the child for adoption to a licensed or authorized child-placing agency in another jurisdiction pursuant to the law of that jurisdiction.
(Stats. 1992 (A.B. 2650), ch. 162, §10, effective January 1, 1994.)

6. Consent of Adopter's Spouse

Consent of a married adopter's spouse is required unless the spouses are legally separated (Cal. Fam. Code §8603).

§8603. A married person must secure consent of his or her spouse to an adoption

A married person, not lawfully separated from the person's spouse, may not adopt a child without the consent of the spouse, provided that the spouse is capable of giving that consent.
(Stats. 1992 (A.B. 2650), ch. 162, §10, effective January 1, 1994.)

D. PLACEMENT PROCEDURE

There are two procedures for adoptions: agency adoptions and independent (private) adoptions. Both usually require that the natural parents' rights be extinguished, either by consent or by termination.

In an agency adoption, a social agency acts as an intermediary between the birth mother and the adoptive family. Often after counseling, the mother relinquishes her parental rights and consents to having the agency place the child for adoption. The agency chooses an adoptive family from applicants, after investigation and evaluation. After placing the child in its new home, the agency provides counseling services, may evaluate the family's adjustment, and will assist in completing the legal adoption. Should the adoption fail for some reason, the agency will take the child back. Some adoption agencies are state agencies whereas others are private, often sectarian organizations, licensed by the state.

Generally, parents may relinquish children to either public or private agencies, but subject to the juvenile court's ability to limit a parent's control over a child. See Teresa J. v. Superior Court, 125 Cal. Rptr. 2d 506 (Ct. App. 2002) (reversing a juvenile court order that a birth mother of a dependent child must relinquish the child only to a public adoption agency, construing California Family Code §8700 infra).

An independent adoption is one in which the child is not placed with its new family by an adoption agency. Instead, the birth parent(s) may place the child directly with the adoptive family; or some nonagency intermediary (e.g., a friend, relative, doctor, lawyer, or spiritual adviser) may act as a go-between and place the child. Private adoptions account for a significant number of domestic adoptions annually. Although independent adoptions are legal in most states, recent years have witnessed increasing regulation of such adoptions.

1. Agency's Role

a. Generally

§8621. Department shall adopt regulations for provision of adoption services

The department shall adopt regulations regarding the provision of adoption services by the department, licensed adoption agencies and other adoption service providers, and shall monitor the provision of those services by licensed adoption agencies and other adoption providers. The department shall report violations of regulations to the appropriate licensing authority.
(Stats. 1993 (S.B. 792), ch. 758, §6, effective January 1, 1995.)

§8622. Adoption agency must inform parents of limited target population

A licensed private adoption agency whose services are limited to a particular target population shall inform all birth parents and prospective adoptive parents of its service limitations before commencing any services, signing any documents or agreements, or accepting any fees.
(Stats. 1993 (S.B. 792), ch. 758, §6.2, effective January 1, 1995.)

b. Relinquishment of Child to Agency

§8700. Either birth parent may relinquish child to department or licensed adoption agency

(a) Either birth parent may relinquish a child to the department or a licensed adoption agency for adoption by a written statement signed before two subscribing witnesses and acknowledged before an authorized official of the department or agency. The relinquishment, when reciting that the person making it is entitled to the sole custody of the child and acknowledged before the officer, is prima facie evidence of the right of the person making it to the sole custody of the child and the person's sole right to relinquish.

(b) A relinquishing parent who is a minor has the right to relinquish his or her child for adoption to the department or a licensed adoption agency, and the relinquishment is not subject to revocation by reason of the minority.

(c) If a relinquishing parent resides outside this state and the child is being cared for and is or will be placed for adoption by the department or a licensed adoption agency, the relinquishing parent may relinquish the child to the department or agency by a written statement signed by the relinquishing parent before a notary on a form prescribed by the department, and previously signed by an authorized official of the department or agency, that signifies the willingness of the department or agency to accept the relinquishment.

(d) If a relinquishing parent and child reside outside this state and the child will be cared for and will be placed for adoption by the department or a licensed adoption agency, the relinquishing parent may relinquish the child to the department or agency by a written statement signed by the relinquishing parent, after that parent has satisfied the following requirements:

(1) Prior to signing the relinquishment, the relinquishing parent shall have received, from a representative of an agency licensed or otherwise approved to provide adoption services under the laws of the relinquishing parent's state of residence, the same counseling and advisement services as if the relinquishing parent resided in this state.

(2) The relinquishment shall be signed before a representative of an agency licensed or otherwise approved to provide adoption services under the laws of the relinquishing parent's state of residence whenever possible or before a licensed social worker on a form prescribed by the department, and previously signed by an authorized official of the department or agency, that signifies the willingness of the department or agency to accept the relinquishment.

(e) The relinquishment authorized by this section has no effect until a certified copy is sent to, and filed with, the department. The licensed adoption agency shall send that copy by certified mail, return receipt requested, or by overnight courier or messenger, with proof of delivery, to the department no earlier than the end of the business day following the signing thereof. The relinquishment shall be final within 10 business days after receipt of the filing by the department, unless a longer period of time is necessary due to a pending court action or some other cause beyond the control of the department. After the relinquishment is filed and final, it may be rescinded only by the mutual consent of the department or licensed adoption agency to which the child was relinquished and the birth parent or parents relinquishing the child.

(f) The relinquishing parent may name in the relinquishment the person or persons with whom he or she intends that placement of the child for adoption be made by the department or licensed adoption agency.

(g) Notwithstanding subdivision (e), if the relinquishment names the person or persons with whom placement by the department or licensed adoption agency is intended and the child is not placed in the home of the named person or persons or the child is removed from the home prior to the granting of the adoption, the department or agency shall mail a notice by certified mail, return receipt requested, to the birth parent signing the relinquishment within 72 hours of the decision not to place the child for adoption or the decision to remove the child from the home.

(h) The relinquishing parent has 30 days from the date on which the notice described in subdivision (g) was mailed to rescind the relinquishment.

(1) If the relinquishing parent requests rescission during the 30-day period, the department or licensed adoption agency shall rescind the relinquishment.

(2) If the relinquishing parent does not request rescission during the 30-day period, the department or licensed adoption agency shall select adoptive parents for the child.

(3) If the relinquishing parent and the department or licensed adoption agency wish to identify a different person or persons during the 30-day period with whom the child is intended to be placed, the initial relinquishment shall be rescinded and a new relinquishment identifying the person or persons completed.

(i) If the parent has relinquished a child, who has been found to come within Section 300 of the Welfare and Institutions Code or is the subject of a petition for jurisdiction of the juvenile court under Section 300 of the Welfare and Institutions Code, to the department or a licensed adoption agency for the purpose of adoption, the department or agency accepting the relinquishment shall provide written notice of the relinquishment within five court days to all of the following:

(1) The juvenile court having jurisdiction of the child.

(2) The child's attorney, if any.

(3) The relinquishing parent's attorney, if any.

(j) The filing of the relinquishment with the department terminates all parental rights and responsibilities with regard to the child, except as provided in subdivisions (g) and (h).

(k) The department shall adopt regulations to administer the provisions of this section.

(Stats. 1992 (A.B. 2650), ch. 162, §10, effective January 1, 1994. Amended Stats. 1993 (A.B. 1500), ch. 219, §189; Stats. 1994 (A.B. 2208), ch. 1269, §56; Stats. 1997, (A.B. 1544), ch. 793, §3; Stats. 1998 (A.B. 2773), ch. 1056, §1. Amended by Stats. 2004 (A.B. 2674), ch. 306, §1.)

§8701. Birth parents have right to request information on status of adoption

At or before the time a relinquishment is signed, the department or licensed adoption agency shall advise the birth parent signing the relinquishment, verbally and in writing, that the birth parent may, at any time in the future, request from the department or agency all known information about the status of the child's adoption, except for personal, identifying information about the adoptive family. The birth parent shall be advised that this information includes, but is not limited to, all of the following:

(a) Whether the child has been placed for adoption.

(b) The approximate date that an adoption was completed.

(c) If the adoption was not completed or was vacated, for any reason, whether adoptive placement of the child is again being considered.

(Stats.1992 (A.B. 2650), ch. 162, §10, effective January 1, 1994.)

§8702. Birth parents must be advised to keep department or agency informed

(a) The department shall adopt a statement to be presented to the birth parents at the time a relinquishment is signed and to prospective adoptive parents at the time of the home study. The statement shall, in a clear and concise manner and in words calculated to ensure the confidence of the birth parents in the integrity of the adoption process, communicate to the birth parents of a child who is the subject of an adoption petition all of the following facts:

(1) It is in the child's best interest that the birth parent keep the department or licensed adoption agency to whom the child was relinquished for adoption informed of any

health problems that the parent develops that could affect the child.

(2) It is extremely important that the birth parent keep an address current with the department or licensed adoption agency to whom the child was relinquished for adoption in order to permit a response to inquiries concerning medical or social history.

(3) Section 9203 of the Family Code authorizes a person who has been adopted and who attains the age of 21 years to request the department or the licensed adoption agency to disclose the name and address of the adoptee's birth parents. Consequently, it is of the utmost importance that the birth parent indicate whether to allow this disclosure by checking the appropriate box provided on the form.

(4) The birth parent may change the decision whether to permit disclosure of the birth parent's name and address, at any time, by sending a notarized letter to that effect, by certified mail, return receipt requested, to the department or to the licensed adoption agency that joined in the adoption petition.

(5) The relinquishment will be filed in the office of the clerk of the court in which the adoption takes place. The file is not open to inspection by any persons other than the parties to the adoption proceeding, their attorneys, and the department, except upon order of a judge of the superior court.

(b) The department shall adopt a form to be signed by the birth parents at the time the relinquishment is signed, which shall provide as follows:

"Section 9203 of the Family Code authorizes a person who has been adopted and who attains the age of 21 years to make a request to the State Department of Social Services, or the licensed adoption agency that joined in the adoption petition, for the name and address of the adoptee's birth parents. Indicate by checking one of the boxes below whether or not you wish your name and address to be disclosed:

() YES

() NO

() UNCERTAIN AT THIS TIME; WILL NOTIFY AGENCY AT LATER DATE."

(Stats.1992 (A.B. 2650), ch. 162, §10, effective January 1, 1994. Amended by Stats. 2002 (S.B. 1316), ch. 784, §111.)

§8703. Department or agency shall send written notice to birth parent of advise

When the parental rights of a birth parent are terminated pursuant to Chapter 5 (commencing with Section 7660) of Part 3 of Division 12 or Part 4 (commencing with Section 7800) of Division 12, or pursuant to Section 366.25 or 366.26 of the Welfare and Institutions Code, the department or licensed adoption agency responsible for the adoptive placement of the child shall send a written notice to the birth parent, if the birth parent's address is known, that contains the following statement:

(a) "You are encouraged to keep the department or this agency informed of your current address in order to permit a response to any inquiry concerning medical or social history made by or on behalf of the child who was the subject of the court action terminating parental rights.

(b) Section 9203 of the Family Code authorizes a person who has been adopted and who attains the age of 21 years to make a request to the State Department of Social Services, or the licensed adoption agency, that joined in the adoption petition, for the name and address of the adoptee's birth parents. Indicate by checking one of the boxes below whether or not you wish your name and address to be disclosed:

( ) YES

( ) NO

( ) UNCERTAIN AT THIS TIME; WILL NOTIFY AGENCY AT LATER DATE"

(Stats. 1992 (A.B. 2650), ch. 162, §10, effective January 1, 1994. Amended by Stats. 2000 (A.B. 2921), ch. 910, §1.)

§8704. Department or agency is entitled to exclusive custody until adoption order is granted

(a) The department or licensed adoption agency to which a child has been freed for adoption by either relinquishment or termination of parental rights is responsible for the care of the child, and is entitled to the exclusive custody and control of the child until an order of adoption is granted. Any placement for temporary care, or for adoption, made by the department or a licensed adoption agency may be terminated in its discretion at any time before the granting of an order of adoption. In the event of termination of any placement for temporary care or for adoption, the child shall be returned promptly to the physical custody of the department or licensed adoption agency.

(b) No petition may be filed to adopt a child relinquished to the department or a licensed adoption agency or a child declared free from the custody and control of either or both birth parents and referred to the department or a licensed adoption agency for adoptive placement, except by the prospective adoptive parents with whom the child has been placed for adoption by the department or licensed adoption agency. After the adoption petition has been filed, the department or licensed adoption agency may remove the child from the prospective adoptive parents only with the approval of the court, upon motion by the department or licensed adoption agency after notice to the prospective adoptive parents, supported by an affidavit or affidavits stating the grounds on which removal is sought. If the department or licensed adoption agency refuses to consent to the adoption of a child by the person or persons with whom the department or licensed adoption agency placed the child for adoption, the court may nevertheless order the adoption if it finds that the refusal to consent is not in the child's best interest.

(Stats. 1992 (A.B. 2650), ch. 162, §10, effective January 1, 1994. Amended Stats. 1995 (A.B. 1743), ch. 884, §3.)

c. Duties: Provision of Services

The adoption service provider has certain duties prescribed by statute. Among those duties, California law (similar to that of many other states) requires full disclosure to prospective adoptive parents of the child's medical history (Cal. Fam. Code §§8706 *infra*, 8817 [set forth in §D2 *infra*]). The agency also must advise a birth parent that the parent may at any future time request information about the status of the child's adoption "except for personal, identifying information about the adoptive family" (Cal. Fam. Code §8701 [set forth in §D1b *supra*]).

The UAA §2-106 contains a list of additional background information that must be disclosed to prospective adopters before they accept physical custody of a child, including current medical and psychological history (including prenatal care), genetic diseases or drug addictions by the genetic parent, performance in school, and allegations of parental abuse or neglect. 9 U.L.A. (pt. IA) 36-37 (1999).

---

§8706. Agency may not place child for adoption absent written report on medical background

(a) An agency may not place a child for adoption unless a written report on the child's medical background and, if available, the medical background of the child's biological parents so far as ascertainable, has been submitted to the prospective adoptive parents and they have acknowledged in writing the receipt of the report.

(b) The report on the child's background shall contain all known diagnostic information, including current medical reports on the child, psychological evaluations, and scholastic information, as well as all known information regarding the child's developmental history and family life.

(c)(1) The biological parents may provide a blood sample at a clinic or hospital approved by the State Department of Health Services. The biological parents' failure to provide a blood sample shall not affect the adoption of the child.

(2) The blood sample shall be stored at a laboratory under contract with the State Department of Health Services for a period of 30 years following the adoption of the child.

(3) The purpose of the stored sample of blood is to provide a blood sample from which DNA testing can be done at a later date after entry of the order of adoption at the request of the adoptive parents or the adopted child. The cost of drawing and storing the blood samples shall be paid for by a separate fee in addition to the fee required under Section 8716. The amount of this additional fee shall be based on the cost of drawing and storing the blood samples but at no time shall the additional fee be more than one hundred dollars ($100).

(d)(1) The blood sample shall be stored and released in such a manner as to not identify any party to the adoption.

(2) Any results of the DNA testing shall be stored and released in such a manner as to not identify any party to the adoption.

(Stats. 1992 (A.B. 2650), ch. 162, §10, effective January 1, 1994. Amended by Stats. 1996 (A.B. 3241), ch. 1053, §1.)

§8707. Department shall establish statewide photo-listing service

(a) The department shall establish a statewide photo-listing service to serve all licensed adoption agencies in the state as a means of recruiting adoptive families....

(b) The photo-listing service shall maintain child specific information that, except as provided in this section, contains a photograph and description of each child who has been legally freed for adoption and whose case plan goal is adoption....

(c) The photo-listing service shall be provided to all licensed adoption agencies, adoption support groups, and state, regional, and national photo-listing and exchanges requesting copies of the photo-listing service.

(d) All children legally freed for adoption whose case plan goal is adoption shall be photo-listed, unless deferred....

(e) A child shall be deferred from the photo-listing service when the child's foster parents or other identified individuals who have applied to adopt the child are meeting the licensed adoption agency's requests for required documentation and are cooperating in the completion of a home study being conducted by the agency....

(Stats. 1992 (A.B. 2650), ch. 162, §10, effective January 1, 1994. Amended by Stats. 1998 (A.B. 2773), ch. 1056, §2.)

---

d. Report to Court

The agency also has a duty to submit to the court "a full report of the facts of the case" (Cal. Fam. Code §8715). For children who have been adjudicated under the dependency jurisdiction of juvenile court (for abuse, neglect, etc.), the report shall describe the steps taken to facilitate ongoing sibling contact (*id.* at §8715(b)). And, if the adoptive parents have entered into a postadoption contact agreement with the birth parents, the report must address whether the agreement was entered voluntarily and whether it is in the child's best interests (*id.* at §8715(c)).

---

§8715. Department or agency must submit full report

(a) The department or licensed adoption agency, whichever is a party to, or joins in, the petition, shall submit a full report of the facts of the case to the court.

(b) If the child has been adjudged to be a dependent of the juvenile court pursuant to Section 300 of the Welfare and Institutions Code, and has thereafter been freed for adoption by the juvenile court, the report required by this section shall describe whether the requirements of subdivision (e) of Section 16002 of the Welfare and Institutions Code have been completed and what, if any, plan exists for facilitation of postadoptive contact between the child who is the subject of the adoption petition and his or her siblings and half siblings.

(c) If a petition for adoption has been filed with a postadoption contact agreement pursuant to Section 8616.5, the report shall address whether the postadoption contact agreement has been entered into voluntarily, and whether it is in the best interests of the child who is the subject of the petition.

(d) The department may also submit a report in those cases in which a licensed adoption agency is a party or joins in the adoption petition.

(e) If a petitioner is a resident of a state other than California, an updated and current homestudy report, conducted and approved by a licensed adoption agency or other authorized resource in the state in which the petitioner resides, shall be reviewed and endorsed by the department or licensed adoption agency, if the standards and criteria established for a homestudy report in the other state are substantially commensurate with the homestudy standards and criteria established in California adoption regulations.

(Stats. 1992 (A.B. 2650), ch. 162, §10, effective January 1, 1994. Amended Stats. 1997 (A.B. 1544), ch. 793, §6; Stats. 1998 (A.B. 2196), ch. 1072, §1; Stats. 2000 (A.B. 2921), ch. 910, §4.5, (S.B. 2157), ch. 930, §4. Amended by Stats. 2002 (A.B. 746), ch. 1112, §2. Amended by Stats. 2003 (S.B. 182), ch. 251, §9.)

§8717. Copy of report or findings shall be given to petitioner or petitioner's attorney

When any report or findings are submitted to the court by the department or licensed adoption agency, a copy of the report or findings, whether favorable or unfavorable, shall be given to the petitioner's attorney in the proceeding, if the petitioner has an attorney of record, or to the petitioner.

(Stats. 1992 (A.B. 2650), ch. 162, §10, effective January 1, 1994.)

California Welfare & Institutions Code

§16002. Procedures for sibling group placement

(a) It is the intent of the Legislature to maintain the continuity of the family unit, and ensure the preservation and strengthening of the child's family ties by ensuring that when siblings have been removed from their home, either as a group on one occurrence or individually on separate occurrences, the siblings will be placed in foster care together, unless it has been determined that placement together is not in the best interest of one or more siblings. The Legislature recognizes that in order to ensure the placement of a sibling group in the same foster care placement, placement resources need to be expanded.

(b) The responsible local agency shall make a diligent effort in all out-of- home placements of dependent children, including those with relatives, to develop and maintain sibling relationships. If siblings are not placed together in the same home, the social worker shall explain why the siblings are not placed together and what efforts he or she is making to place the siblings together or why those efforts are not appropriate. When placement of siblings together in the same home is not possible, diligent effort shall be made, and a case plan prepared, to provide for ongoing and frequent interaction among siblings until family reunification is achieved, or, if parental rights are terminated, as part of developing the permanent plan for the child. If the court determines by clear and convincing evidence that sibling interaction is detrimental to a child or children, the reasons for the determination shall be noted in the court order, and interaction shall be suspended.

(c) When there has been a judicial suspension of sibling interaction, the reasons for the suspension shall be reviewed at each periodic review hearing pursuant to Section 366. When the court determines that sibling interaction can be safely resumed, that determination shall be noted in the court order and the case plan shall be revised to provide for sibling interaction.

(d) If the case plan for the child has provisions for sibling interaction, the child, or his or her parent or legal guardian shall have the right to comment on those provisions. If a person wishes to assert a sibling relationship with a dependent child, he or she may file a petition in the juvenile court having jurisdiction over the dependent child pursuant to subdivision (b) of Section 388.

(e) If parental rights are terminated and the court orders a dependent child to be placed for adoption, the licensed county adoption agency or the State Department of Social Services shall take all of the following steps to facilitate ongoing sibling contact, except in those cases provided in subdivision (b) where the court determines by a preponderance of the evidence that sibling interaction is detrimental to the child:

(1) Include in training provided to prospective adoptive parents information about the importance of sibling relationships to the adopted child and counseling on methods for maintaining sibling relationships.

(2) Provide prospective adoptive parents with information about siblings of the child, except the address where the siblings of the children reside. However, this address may be disclosed by court order for good cause shown.

(3) Encourage prospective adoptive parents to make a plan for facilitating postadoptive contact between the child who is the subject of a petition for adoption and any siblings of this child.

(f) Information regarding sibling interaction, contact, or visitation that has been authorized or ordered by the court shall be provided to the foster parent, relative caretaker, or legal guardian of the child as soon as possible after the court order is made, in order to facilitate the interaction, contact, or visitation.

(g) As used in this section, "sibling" means a child related to another person by blood, adoption, or affinity through a common legal or biological parent.

(h) The court documentation on sibling placements required under this section shall not require the modification of existing court order forms until the Child Welfare Services Case Management System is implemented on a statewide basis.

(Stats. 1993 (A.B. 2129), ch. 1089, §32. Amended by Stats. 1994 (S.B. 17), ch. 663, §4; Stats. 1998 (A.B. 2196), ch. 1072, §3; Stats. 2000 (A.B. 1987), ch. 909, §8; Stats. 2003 (S.B. 591), ch. 812, §4.)

---

e. Right to Appeal Unfavorable Recommendation

California Family Code

§8720. Clerk shall set matter for review if unfavorable recommendation

(a) If the department or licensed adoption agency finds that the home of the petitioners is not suitable for the child or that the required agency consents are not available and the department or agency recommends that the petition be denied, or if the petitioners desire to withdraw the petition and the department or agency recommends that the petition be denied, the clerk upon receipt of the report of the department or agency shall immediately refer it to the court for review.

(b) Upon receipt of the report, the court shall set a date for a hearing of the petition and shall give reasonable notice of the hearing to the department or licensed adoption agency, the petitioners, and, if necessary, the birth parents, by certified mail, return receipt requested, to the address of each as shown in the proceeding.

(c) The department or licensed adoption agency shall appear to represent the child.

(Stats. 1992 (A.B. 2650), ch. 162, §10, effective January 1, 1994.)

2. Independent Adoption

California law requires that, in an independent adoption, the birth parent or parents who place(s) the child for adoption must meet with, and be advised of rights by, an adoption service provider (Cal. Fam. Code §8808). The Code specifies that a birth parent must possess certain information in order to place the child in an independent adoption, including the prospective adopting parents' full legal names, religion, race or ethnicity, health, marital status, employment, other household residents, their child support obligations to any other children, and prior criminal record (Cal. Fam. Code §8801(b)). A placing parent has the right to reclaim the child for up to 30 days after giving consent (Cal. Fam. Code §8814.5).

The filing of a petition for adoption by the prospective adoptive parents commences a 180-day period during which the State Department of Social Services or licensed adoption agency investigates "whether the child is a proper subject for adoption and whether the proposed home is suitable" (Cal. Fam. Code §§8806, 8807(a)). The department or agency then submits a report and recommendation to the court (Cal. Fam. Code §8807(a)).

Note that although the adoption service provider owes a very high duty of care to the birth parent being advised, that duty of care does not include a duty to investigate information provided by the parties, their attorneys or agents (Cal. Fam. Code §8801.7).

The prospective adoptive parents may pay the birth mother's (or birth parents') attorney's fees, medical fees and expenses, counseling fees, or living expenses provided that the mother (or parents) request(s) payment in writing and provide(s) receipts (Cal. Fam. Code §8812). The prospective adoptive parents then provide these receipts to the court (*id.*).

Statute cautions that multiple representation in cases of independent adoption should be avoided, whether or not the written consent of the parties has been obtained, "whenever a birth parent displays the slightest reason for the attorney to believe any controversy might arise" (Cal. Fam. Code §8800(c)). If an attorney engages in multiple representation, counsel must obtain written consent to dual representation by all parties, including a notice that the parties have been advised of their respective rights to independent counsel (Cal. Fam. Code §8800(d)). The parties' written consent to dual representation must be filed before the filing of the birth parent's consent to adoption (Cal. Fam. Code §8800(i)).

California Family Code

§8524. "Independent adoption"

"Independent adoption" means the adoption of a child in which neither the department nor an agency licensed by the department is a party to, or joins in, the adoption petition.

(Stats. 1992 (A.B. 2650), ch. 162, §10, effective January 1, 1994.)

§8800. Legislative declaration concerning attorney's potential conflict of interest

(a) The Legislature finds and declares that an attorney's ability to effectively represent his or her client may be seriously impaired when conflict of interest deprives the client of the attorney's undivided loyalty and effort. The Legislature further finds and declares that the relation between attorney and client is a fiduciary relation of the very highest character, and binds the attorney to the most conscientious fidelity.

(b) The Legislature finds that Rule 2-111(A)(2) of the State Bar Rules of Professional Conduct provides that an attorney shall not withdraw from employment until the attorney has taken reasonable steps to avoid foreseeable prejudice to the rights of the client, including giving due notice to the client, allowing time for employment of other counsel, delivering to the client all papers and property to which the client is entitled, and complying with applicable laws and rules.

(c) The Legislature declares that in an independent adoption proceeding, whether or not written consent is obtained, multiple representation by an attorney should be avoided whenever a birth parent displays the slightest reason for the attorney to believe any controversy might arise. The Legislature finds and declares that it is the duty of the attorney when a conflict of interest occurs to withdraw promptly from any case, advise the parties to retain independent counsel, refrain from taking positions in opposition to any of these former clients, and thereafter maintain an impartial, fair, and open attitude toward the new attorneys.

(d) Notwithstanding any other law, it is unethical for an attorney to undertake the representation of both the prospective adoptive parents and the birth parents of a child in any negotiations or proceedings in connection with an adoption unless a written consent is obtained from both parties. The written consent shall include all of the following:

(1) A notice to the birth parents, in the form specified in this section, of their right to have an independent

attorney advise and represent them in the adoption proceeding and that the prospective adoptive parents may be required to pay the reasonable attorney's fees up to a maximum of five hundred dollars ($500) for that representation, unless a higher fee is agreed to by the parties.

(2) A notice to the birth parents that they may waive their right to an independent attorney and may be represented by the attorney representing the prospective adoptive parents.

(3) A waiver by the birth parents of representation by an independent attorney.

(4) An agreement that the attorney representing the prospective adoptive parents shall represent the birth parents.

(e) Upon the petition or motion of any party, or upon motion of the court, the court may appoint an attorney to represent a child's birth parent or parents in negotiations or proceedings in connection with the child's adoption.

(f) The birth parent or parents may have an attorney, other than the attorney representing the interests of the prospective adoptive parents, to advise them fully of the adoption procedures and of their legal rights. The birth parent or parents also may retain an attorney to represent them in negotiations or proceedings in connection with the child's adoption. The court may award attorney's fees and costs for just cause and based upon the ability of the parties to pay those fees and costs.

(g) In the initial communication between the attorney retained by or representing the prospective adoptive parents and the birth parents, or as soon thereafter as reasonable, but before any written consent for dual representation, the attorney shall advise the birth parents of their rights regarding an independent attorney and that it is possible to waive the independent attorney.

(h) The attorney retained by or representing the prospective adoptive parents shall inform the prospective adoptive parents in writing that the birth parent or parents can revoke consent to the adoption pursuant to Section 8814.5 and that any moneys expended in negotiations or proceedings in connection with the child's adoption are not reimbursable. The prospective adoptive parents shall sign a statement to indicate their understanding of this information.

(i) Any written consent to dual representation shall be filed with the court before the filing of the birth parent's consent to adoption.

(Stats. 1992 (A.B. 2650), ch. 162, §10, effective January 1, 1994. Amended Stats. 1993 (S.B. 255), ch. 450, §1, effective until January 1, 1995, (S.B. 255), ch. 450, §2, effective January 1, 1995.)

§8801. Birth parents shall select adoptive parents in independent adoption

(a) The selection of a prospective adoptive parent or parents shall be personally made by the child's birth parent or parents and may not be delegated to an agent. The act of selection by the birth parent or parents shall be based upon his, her, or their personal knowledge of the prospective adoptive parent or parents.

(b) "Personal knowledge" as used in this section includes, but is not limited to, substantially correct knowledge of all of the following regarding the prospective adoptive parents: their full legal names, ages, religion, race or ethnicity, length of current marriage and number of previous marriages, employment, whether other children or adults reside in their home, whether there are other children who do not reside in their home and the child support obligation for these children and any failure to meet these obligations, any health conditions curtailing their normal daily activities or reducing their normal life expectancies, any convictions for crimes other than minor traffic violations, any removals of children from their care due to child abuse or neglect, and their general area of residence or, upon request, their address.

(c) This section shall become operative on January 1, 1995.

(Stats. 1993 (S.B. 792), ch. 758, §6.4, effective January 1, 1995.)

§8801.3. Requisite procedures for placement: advice of rights, execution of placement agreement

A child shall not be considered to have been placed for adoption unless each of the following is true:

(a) Each birth parent placing the child for adoption has been advised of his or her rights, and if desired, has been counseled pursuant to Section 8801.5.

(b) The adoption service provider, each prospective adoptive parent, and each birth parent placing the child have signed an adoption placement agreement on a form prescribed by the department. The signing of the agreement shall satisfy all of the following requirements:

(1) Each birth parent shall have been advised of his or her rights pursuant to Section 8801.5 at least 10 days before signing the agreement, unless the adoption service provider finds exigent circumstances that shall be set forth in the adoption placement agreement.

(2) The agreement may not be signed by either the birth parents or the prospective adoptive parents until the time of discharge of the birth mother from the hospital. However, if the birth mother remains hospitalized for a period longer than the hospitalization of the child, the agreement may be signed by all parties at the time of or after the child's discharge from the hospital but prior to the birth mother's discharge from the hospital if her competency to sign is verified by her attending physician and surgeon before she signs the agreement.

(3) The birth parents and prospective adoptive parents shall sign the agreement in the presence of an adoption service provider.

(4) The adoption service provider who witnesses the signatures shall keep the original of the adoption placement agreement and immediately forward it and supporting documentation as required by the department to the department or delegated county adoption agency.

(5) The child is not deemed to be placed for adoption with the prospective adoptive parents until the adoption placement agreement has been signed and witnessed.

(6) If the birth parent is not located in this state or country, the adoption placement agreement shall be signed

before an adoption service provider or, for purposes of identification of the birth parent only, before a notary or other person authorized to perform notarial acts in the state or country in which the birth parent is located. This paragraph is not applicable to intercountry adoptions, as defined in Section 8527, which shall be governed by Chapter 4 (commencing with Section 8900).

(c) The adoption placement agreement form shall include all of the following:

(1) A statement that the birth parent received the advisement of rights and the date upon which it was received.

(2) A statement that the birth parent understands that the placement is for the purpose of adoption and that if the birth parent takes no further action, on the 31st day after signing the adoption placement agreement, the agreement shall become a permanent and irrevocable consent to the adoption.

(3) A statement that the birth parent signs the agreement having personal knowledge of certain facts regarding the prospective adoptive parents as provided in Section 8801.

(4) A statement that the adoptive parents have been informed of the basic health and social history of the birth parents.

(5) A consent to the adoption that may be revoked as provided by Section 8814.5.

(d) The adoption placement agreement shall also meet the requirements of the Interstate Compact on the Placement of Children in Section 7901.

(e) This section shall become operative on January 1, 1995.

(Stats. 1993 (S.B. 792), ch. 758, §7, effective January 1, 1995. Amended Stats. 1994 (A.B. 3336), ch . 585, §3, effective January 1, 1995; Stats. 2000 (A.B. 2433), ch. 937, §3; Stats. 2001 (S.B. 104), ch. 688, §1.)

§8801.5. Adoption service provider has duties to advise birth parents

(a) Each birth parent placing a child for adoption shall be advised of his or her rights by an adoption service provider.

(b) The birth parent shall be advised of his or her rights in a face-to-face meeting in which the birth parent may ask questions and have questions answered, as provided by Section 8801.3.

(c) The department shall prescribe the format and process for advising birth parents of their rights, the content of which shall include, but not be limited to, the following:

(1) The alternatives to adoption.

(2) The alternative types of adoption, including a description of the full procedures and timeframes involved in each type.

(3) The full rights and responsibilities of the birth parent with respect to adoption, including the need to keep the department informed of his or her current address in case of a medical emergency requiring contact and of providing a full health history.

(4) The right to separate legal counsel paid for by the prospective adoptive parents upon the request of the birth parent, as provided for by Section 8800.

(5) The right to a minimum of three separate counseling sessions, each to be held on different days, to be paid for by the prospective adoptive parents upon the request of the birth parents, as provided for by subdivision (d).

(d) Each person advised pursuant to this section shall be offered at least three separate counseling sessions, to be held on different days. Each counseling session shall be not less than 50 minutes in duration. The counseling may be provided by the adoption service provider who informs the birth parent of his or her rights, or by another adoption service provider, or by a licensed psychotherapist, as defined by Section 1010 of the Evidence Code, as elected by the person, and after having been informed of these choices.

(e) The counselor owes a duty of care to the birth parent being counseled, similar to the duty of care established by a psychotherapist-patient relationship, regardless of who pays the fees of the counselor. No counselor shall have a contractual relationship with the adoptive parents, an attorney for the adoptive parents, or any other individual or an organization performing any type of services for the adoptive parents and for which the adoptive parents are paying a fee, except as relates to payment of the birth parents' fee.

(f) The advisement and counseling fees shall be paid by the prospective adoptive parents at the request of the birth parent.

(g) Failure to fulfill the duties specified in this section shall not be construed as a basis for setting aside the consent or the adoption, but may give rise to a cause of action for malpractice or negligence against those professionals or agencies serving as adoption service providers that are responsible for fulfilling the duties.

(Stats. 1993 (S.B. 792), ch. 758, §8, effective January 1, 1995. Amended Stats. 1994 (A.B. 3336), ch. 585, §4, effective January 1, 1995; Stats. 1997 (S.B. 1121), ch. 559, §2.)

§8801.7. Adoption service provider shall witness signatures and offer to hear concerns of birth parent following placement

(a) An adoption service provider shall also witness the signature of the adoption placement agreement and offer to interview the birth parent after the placement of the child with prospective adoptive parents. The interview shall occur within 10 working days after the placement of the child for adoption and shall include a consideration of any concerns or problems the birth parent has with the placement, a readvisement of the rights of the birth parent, and the taking of the health and social history of the birth parent, if not taken previously.

(b) The adoption service provider shall immediately notify the department or delegated county adoption agency if the birth parent is not interviewed as provided in subdivision (a) or if there are any concerns regarding the placement. If the birth parent wishes to revoke the consent, the adoption service provider shall assist the birth parent in obtaining the return of the child.

(c) The adoption service provider owes a very high duty of care to the birth parent being advised, regardless of who pays the provider's fees. The duty of care specifically does not include a duty to investigate information provided by the birth parents, prospective adoptive parents, or their attorneys or agents. No adoption service provider shall have a contractual relationship with prospective adoptive parents, an attorney or representative for prospective adoptive parents, or any individual or organization providing services of any type to prospective adoptive parents for which the adoptive parents are paying a fee, except as relates to the payment of the fees for the advising and counseling of the birth parents.

(d) This section shall become operative on January 1, 1995.

(Stats. 1993 (S.B. 792), ch. 758, §9, effective January 1, 1995.)

§8802. Adoption petition and order

(a)(1) Any of the following persons who desire to adopt a child may, for that purpose, file a petition in the county in which the petitioner resides or, if the petitioner is not a resident of this state, in the county in which the placing birth parent or birth parents resided when the adoption placement agreement was signed, or the county in which the placing birth parent or birth parents resided when the petition was filed:

(A) An adult who is related to the child or the child's half sibling by blood or affinity, including all relatives whose status is preceded by the words "step," "great," "great-great," or "grand," or the spouse of any of these persons, even if the marriage was terminated by death or dissolution.

(B) A person named in the will of a deceased parent as an intended adoptive parent where the child has no other parent.

(C) A person with whom a child has been placed for adoption.

(D)(i) A legal guardian who has been the child's legal guardian for more than one year.

(ii) If the court has found the child to have been abandoned pursuant to Section 7822, a legal guardian who has been the child's legal guardian for more than six months. The legal guardian may file a petition pursuant to Section 7822 in the same court and concurrently with a petition under this section.

(iii) However, if the parent nominated the guardian for a purpose other than adoption for a specified time period, or if the guardianship was established pursuant to Section 360 of the Welfare and Institutions Code, the guardianship shall have been in existence for not less than three years.

(2) If the child has been placed for adoption, a copy of the adoptive placement agreement shall be attached to the petition. The court clerk shall immediately notify the department at Sacramento in writing of the pendency of the proceeding and of any subsequent action taken.

(3) If the petitioner has entered into a postadoption contact agreement with the birth parent as set forth in Section 8616.5, the agreement, signed by the participating parties, shall be attached to and filed with the petition for adoption.

(b) The petition shall contain an allegation that the petitioners will file promptly with the department or delegated county adoption agency information required by the department in the investigation of the proposed adoption. The omission of the allegation from a petition does not affect the jurisdiction of the court to proceed or the validity of an adoption order or other order based on the petition.

(c) The caption of the adoption petition shall contain the names of the petitioners, but not the child's name. The petition shall state the child's sex and date of birth and the name the child had before adoption.

(d) If the child is the subject of a guardianship petition, the adoption petition shall so state and shall include the caption and docket number or have attached a copy of the letters of the guardianship or temporary guardianship. The petitioners shall notify the court of any petition for guardianship or temporary guardianship filed after the adoption petition. The guardianship proceeding shall be consolidated with the adoption proceeding.

(e) The order of adoption shall contain the child's adopted name, but not the name the child had before adoption.

(Stats. 1993 (S.B. 792), ch. 758, §9.2, effective January 1, 1995. Amended Stats. 1996 (A.B. 2165), ch. 510, §1; Stats. 2000 (A.B. 2433), ch. 937, §4. Amended by Stats. 2002 (A.B. 746), ch. 1112, §3. Amended by Stats. 2003 (S.B. 600), ch. 62, §88, ch. 81 (A.B. 416), §1 (ch. 81 prevails). Amended by Stats. 2004 (S.B. 1357), ch. 858, §5.)

§8803. Child may not be concealed or removed from county

(a) During the pendency of an adoption proceeding:

(1) The child proposed to be adopted may not be concealed within the county in which the adoption proceeding is pending.

(2) The child may not be removed from the county in which the adoption proceeding is pending unless the petitioners or other interested persons first obtain permission for the removal from the court, after giving advance written notice of intent to obtain the court's permission to the department or delegated county adoption agency responsible for the investigation of the proposed adoption. Upon proof of giving notice, permission may be granted by the court if, within a period of 15 days after the date of giving notice, no objections are filed with the court by the department or delegated county adoption agency. If the department or delegated county adoption agency files objections within the 15-day period, upon the request of the petitioners the court shall immediately set the matter for hearing and give to the objector, the petitioners, and the party or parties requesting permission for the removal reasonable notice of the hearing by certified mail, return receipt requested, to the address of each as shown in the records of the adoption proceeding. Upon a finding that the objections are without good cause, the court may grant the requested permission for removal of the child, subject to any limitations that appear to be in the child's best interest.

(b) This section does not apply in any of the following situations:

(1) Where the child is absent for a period of not more than 30 days from the county in which the adoption proceeding is pending, unless a notice of recommendation of denial of petition has been personally served on the petitioners or the court has issued an order prohibiting the child's removal from the county pending consideration of any of the following:

(A) The suitability of the petitioners.

(B) The care provided the child.

(C) The availability of the legally required consents to the adoption.

(2) Where the child has been returned to and remains in the custody and control of the child's birth parent or parents.

(c) A violation of this section is a violation of Section 280 of the Penal Code.

(d) Neither this section nor Section 280 of the Penal Code may be construed to render lawful any act that is unlawful under any other applicable law.

(Stats. 1992 (A.B. 2650), ch. 162, §10, effective January 1, 1994.)

§8804. Clerk of court shall give notice to department of motion to withdraw or dismiss petition

(a) Whenever the petitioners move to withdraw the petition for the adoption or to dismiss the proceeding, the clerk of the court in which the proceeding is pending shall immediately notify the department at Sacramento of the action. The department or the delegated county adoption agency shall file a full report with the court recommending a suitable plan for the child in every case where the petitioners move to withdraw the petition for the adoption or where the department or delegated county adoption agency recommends that the petition for adoption be denied and shall appear before the court for the purpose of representing the child.

(b) Notwithstanding the withdrawal or dismissal of the petition, the court may retain jurisdiction over the child for the purposes of making any order for the child's custody that the court deems to be in the child's best interest.

(c) If a birth parent who did not place a child for adoption as specified in Section 8801.3 has refused to give the required consent, or a birth parent revokes consent as specified in Section 8814.5, the court shall order the child restored to the care and custody of the birth parent or parents subject to the provisions of Section 3041.

(Stats. 1993 (S.B. 792), ch. 758, §10, effective January 1, 1995. Amended by Stats 2002 (A.B. 1938), ch. 1118, §4.)

§8805. Child shall be removed from home of petitioners in cases of denial

At the hearing, if the court sustains the recommendation of the department or delegated county adoption agency that the child be removed from the home of the petitioners because the department or agency recommends denial or if the petitioners move to withdraw the petition or if the court dismisses the petition and does not return the child to the birth parents, the court shall commit the child to the care of the department or delegated county adoption agency, whichever made the recommendation, for the department or agency to arrange adoptive placement or to make a suitable plan. In those counties not served by a delegated county adoption agency, the county welfare department shall act as the agent of the department and shall provide care for the child in accordance with rules and regulations established by the department.

(Stats. 1992 (A.B. 2650), ch. 162, §10, effective January 1, 1994.)

§8806. Department or agency shall ascertain suitability of home

The department or delegated county adoption agency shall accept the consent of the birth parents to the adoption of the child by the petitioners and, before filing its report with the court, shall ascertain whether the child is a proper subject for adoption and whether the proposed home is suitable for the child.

(Stats. 1992 (A.B. 2650), ch. 162, §10, effective January 1, 1994.)

§8807. Department or agency shall investigate and submit full report to the court

(a) Except as provided in subdivisions (b) and (c), within 180 days after the filing of the petition, the department or delegated county adoption agency shall investigate the proposed independent adoption and submit to the court a full report of the facts disclosed by its inquiry with a recommendation regarding the granting of the petition.

(b) If the investigation establishes that there is a serious question concerning the suitability of the petitioners or the care provided the child or the availability of the consent to adoption, the report shall be filed immediately.

(c) In its discretion, the court may allow additional time for the filing of the report, after at least five days' notice to the petitioner or petitioners and an opportunity for the petitioner or petitioners to be heard with respect to the request for additional time.

(d) If a petitioner is a resident of a state other than California, an updated and current homestudy report, conducted and approved by a licensed adoption agency or other authorized resource in the state in which the petitioner resides, shall be reviewed and endorsed by the department or delegated county adoption agency, if the standards and criteria established for a homestudy report in the other state are substantially commensurate with the homestudy standards and criteria established in California adoption regulations.

(Stats. 1992 (A.B. 2650), ch. 162, §10, effective January 1, 1994. Amended by Stats. 2002 (A.B. 746), ch. 1112, §4.)

§8808. Department or agency shall interview all relevant parties

The department or delegated county adoption agency shall interview the petitioners and all persons from whom consent is required and whose addresses are known as soon as possible and, in the case of residents of this state, within 45 working days, excluding legal holidays, after the filing of the adoption petition. The interview with the placing parent or parents shall include, but not be limited to, discussion of any concerns or problems that the parent has with the placement and, if the placing parent was not interviewed as provided in Section 8801.7, the content required in that interview. At the interview, the agency shall give the parent an opportunity to sign either a statement revoking the consent, or a waiver of the right to revoke consent, as provided in Section 8814.5. In order to facilitate these interviews, at the same time the petition is filed with the court, the petitioners shall file with the district office of the department or with the delegated county adoption agency responsible for the investigation of the adoption, a copy of the petition together with the names, addresses, and telephone numbers of all parties to be interviewed, if known.

This section shall become operative on January 1, 1995.

(Stats. 1993 (S.B. 792), ch. 758, §11, effective January 1, 1995.)

§8810. Petitioner shall pay fees

(a) Except as otherwise provided in this section, whenever a petition is filed under this chapter for the adoption of a child, the petitioner shall pay a nonrefundable fee to the department or to the delegated county adoption agency for the cost of investigating the adoption petition. Payment shall be made to the department or delegated county adoption agency, within 40 days of the filing of the petition, for an amount as follows:

(1) For petitions filed on and after July 1, 2003, two thousand nine hundred fifty dollars ($ 2,950).

(2) For petitioners who have a valid replacement evaluation at the time of filing a petition pursuant to Section 8811.5, seven hundred seventy-five dollars ($ 775) for a postplacement evaluation pursuant to Sections 8806 and 8807.

(b) Revenues produced by fees collected by the department pursuant to subdivision (a) shall be used, when appropriated by the Legislature, to fund only the direct costs associated with the state program for independent adoptions. Revenues produced by fees collected by the delegated county adoption agency pursuant to subdivision (a) shall be used by the county to fund the county program for independent adoptions.

(c) The department or delegated county adoption agency may only waive, or reduce the fee when the prospective adoptive parents are low income, according to the income limits published by the Department of Housing and Community Development, and making the required payment would be detrimental to the welfare of an adopted child. The department shall develop additional guidelines to determine the financial criteria for waiver or reduction of the fee under this subdivision.

(Stats. 1993 (S.B. 1152), ch. 1158, §2, effective until January 1, 1999. Amended Stats. 1996 (A.B. 2165), ch. 510, §2. Amended by Stats. 2003 (A.B. 1752), ch. 225, §2, effective August 11, 2003.)

§8811. Department or agency shall require criminal investigation of prospective adoptive parents

(a) The department or delegated county adoption agency shall require each person filing an adoption petition to be fingerprinted and shall secure from an appropriate law enforcement agency any criminal record of that person to determine whether the person has ever been convicted of a crime other than a minor traffic violation. The department or delegated county adoption agency may also secure the person's full criminal record, if any.

(b) The criminal record, if any, shall be taken into consideration when evaluating the prospective adoptive parent, and an assessment of the effects of any criminal history on the ability of the prospective adoptive parent to provide adequate and proper care and guidance to the child shall be included in the report to the court.

(c) Any fee charged by a law enforcement agency for fingerprinting or for checking or obtaining the criminal record of the petitioner shall be paid by the petitioner. The department or delegated county adoption agency may defer, waive, or reduce the fee when its payment would cause economic hardship to the prospective adoptive parents detrimental to the welfare of the adopted child, when the child has been in the foster care of the prospective adoptive parents for at least one year, or if necessary for the placement of a special-needs child.

(Stats. 1992 (A.B. 2650), ch. 162, §10, effective January 1, 1994.)

§8811.5. Agency may certify prospective adoptive parents

(a) A licensed private or public adoption agency of the state of the petitioner's residency may certify prospective adoptive parents by a replacement evaluation that contains a finding that an individual is suited to be an adoptive parent.

(b) The replacement evaluation shall include an investigation pursuant to standards included in the regulations governing independent adoption investigations established by the department. Fees for the investigation shall be commensurate with those fees charged for a comparable investigation conducted by the department or by a delegated licensed county adoption agency.

(c) The replacement evaluation, whether it is conducted for the purpose of initially certifying prospective adoptive parents or for renewing that certification, shall be completed no more than one year prior to the signing of an adoption placement agreement. The cost for renewal of that certification shall be in proportion to the extent of the work required to prepare the renewal that is attributable to changes in family circumstances.

(Stats. 1996 (A.B. 2165), ch. 510, §3. Amended by Stats. 2004 (A.B. 2492), ch. 128, §1.)

§8812. Birth parent may request payment of fees by prospective adoptive parents

Any request by a birth parent or birth parents for payment by the prospective adoptive parents of attorney's fees, medical fees and expenses, counseling fees, or living expenses of the birth mother shall be in writing. The birth parent or parents shall, by first-class mail or other agreed upon means to ensure receipt, provide the prospective adoptive parents written

receipts for any money provided to the birth parent or birth parents. The prospective adoptive parents shall provide the receipts to the court when the accounting report required pursuant to Section 8610 is filed.
(Stats. 1993 (S.B. 255), ch. 450, §3.)

§8813. Birth parents have right to request information on status of adoption

At or before the time a consent to adoption is signed, the department or delegated county adoption agency shall advise the birth parent signing the consent, verbally and in writing, that the birth parent may, at any time in the future, request from the department or agency, all known information about the status of the child's adoption, except for personal, identifying information about the adoptive family. The birth parent shall be advised that this information includes, but is not limited to, all of the following:

(a) Whether the child has been placed for adoption.

(b) The approximate date that an adoption was completed.

(c) If the adoption was not completed or was vacated, for any reason, whether adoptive placement of the child is again being considered.
(Stats. 1992 (A.B. 2650), ch. 162, §10, effective January 1, 1994.)

§8814. Procedure for executing consent of birth parents to adoption

(a) Except as provided in Section 7662, the consent of the birth parent or parents who did not place the child for adoption, as described in Section 8801.3, to the adoption shall be signed in the presence of an agent of the department or of a delegated county adoption agency on a form prescribed by the department. The consent shall be filed with the clerk of the appropriate superior court.

(b) The consent described in subdivision (a), when reciting that the person giving it is entitled to the sole custody of the child and when acknowledged before that agent, is prima facie evidence of the right of the person making it to the sole custody of the child and that person's sole right to consent.

(c) If the birth parent described in subdivision (a) is located outside this state for an extended period of time unrelated to the adoption at the time of signing the consent, the consent may be signed before a notary or other person authorized to perform notarial acts, and in that case the consent of the department or of the delegated county adoption agency is also necessary.

(d) A birth parent who is a minor has the right to sign a consent for the adoption of the birth parent's child and the consent is not subject to revocation by reason of minority.

(e) This section shall become operative on January 1, 1995.
(Stats. 1993 (S.B. 792), ch. 758, §12, effective January 1, 1995. Amended Stats. 1994 (A.B. 3336), ch. 585, §5, effective January 1, 1995; Stats. 1996 (A.B. 2165), ch. 510, §4.)

§8814.5. Birth parents' right to revocation of consent

(a) After a consent to the adoption is signed by the birth parent or parents pursuant to Section 8801.3 or 8814, the birth parent or parents signing the consent shall have 30 days to take one of the following actions:

(1) Sign and deliver to the department or delegated county adoption agency a written statement revoking the consent and requesting the child to be returned to the birth parent or parents. After revoking consent, in cases where the birth parent or parents have not regained custody, or the birth parent or parents have failed to make efforts to exercise their rights under subdivision (b) of Section 8815, a written notarized statement reinstating the original consent may be signed and delivered to the department or delegated county adoption agency, in which case the revocation of consent shall be void and the remainder of the original 30-day period shall commence. After revoking consent, in cases in which the birth parent or parents have regained custody or made efforts to exercise their rights under subdivision (b) of Section 8815 by requesting the return of the child, upon the delivery of a written notarized statement reinstating the original consent to the department or delegated county adoption agency, the revocation of consent shall be void and a new 30-day period shall commence. The birth mother shall be informed of the operational timelines associated with this section at the time of signing of the statement reinstating the original consent.

(2)(A) Sign a waiver of the right to revoke consent on a form prescribed by the department in the presence of a representative of the department or delegated county adoption agency. If neither a representative of the department nor a representative of a delegated county adoption agency is reasonably available, the waiver of the right to revoke consent may be signed in the presence of a judicial officer of a court of record if the birth parent is represented by independent legal counsel. "Reasonably available" means that a representative from either the department or the delegated county adoption agency is available to accept the signing of the waiver within 10 days and is within 100 miles of the location of the birth mother.

(B) An adoption service provider may assist the birth parent or parents in any activity where the primary purpose of that activity is to facilitate the signing of the waiver with the department, a delegated county agency, or a judicial officer. The adoption service provider or another person designated by the birth parent or parents may also be present at any interview conducted pursuant to this section to provide support to the birth parent or parents.

(C) The waiver of the right to revoke consent may not be signed until an interview has been completed by the department or delegated county adoption agency unless the waiver of the right to revoke consent is signed in the presence of a judicial officer of a court of record as specified in this section, in which case the interview and the witnessing of the signing of the waiver shall be conducted by the judicial officer. Within 10 working days of a request made after the department, the delegated county adoption agency, or the court has received a copy of the petition for the adoption and the names and addresses of the persons to be interviewed, the department, the delegated county adoption agency, or the court shall interview, at the department or agency office or the court, any birth parent requesting to be interviewed. However, the interview, and the witnessing of the signing of a waiver of the right to revoke consent of a birth parent residing outside of California or located outside of California for an extended period of time unrelated to the adoption may be conducted in the state where the birth parent is located, by any of the following:

(i) A representative of a public adoption agency in that state.

(ii) A judicial officer in that state where the birth parent is represented by independent legal counsel.

(iii) An adoption service provider.

(3) Allow the consent to become a permanent consent on the 31st day after signing.

(b) The consent may not be revoked after a waiver of the right to revoke consent has been signed or after 30 days, beginning on the date the consent was signed or as provided in paragraph (1) of subdivision (a), whichever occurs first.

(Stats. 1993 (S.B. 792), ch. 758, §13, effective January 1, 1995. Amended Stats. 1994 (A.B. 3336), ch. 585, §6, effective January 1, 1995; Stats. 1996 (A.B. 2165), ch. 510, §5; Stats. 2000 (A.B. 2433), ch. 937, §5; Stats. 2001 (S.B. 104), ch. 688, §2. Amended by Stats. 2002 (A.B. 3034), ch. 664, §79. Amended by Stats. 2003 (S.B. 182), ch. 251, §10.)

§8815. Irrevocability of consent to adoption

(a) Once the revocable consent to adoption has become permanent as provided in Section 8814.5, the consent to the adoption by the prospective adoptive parents may not be withdrawn.

(b) Before the time when the revocable consent becomes permanent as provided in Section 8814.5, the birth parent or parents may request return of the child. In such a case the child shall immediately be returned to the birth parent or parents so requesting.

(c) If the person or persons with whom the child has been placed have concerns that the birth parent or parents requesting return of the child are unfit or present a danger of harm to the child, that person's or those persons' only option is to report their concerns to the investigating adoption agency and the appropriate child welfare agency. These concerns shall not be a basis for failure to immediately return the child.

(d) This section shall become operative on January 1, 1995.

(Stats. 1993 (S.B. 792), ch. 758, §16, effective January 1, 1995.)

§8816. Consent of agency or department when birth parents' consent is unnecessary

In an independent adoption where the consent of the birth parent or parents is not necessary, the department or delegated county adoption agency shall, before the hearing of the petition, file its consent to the adoption with the clerk of the court in which the petition is filed. The consent may not be given unless the child's welfare will be promoted by the adoption.

(Stats. 1992 (A.B. 2650), ch. 162, §10, effective January 1, 1994.)

§8817. Department or agency shall prepare medical report on child and biological parents

(a) A written report on the child's medical background, and if available, the medical background of the child's biological parents so far as ascertainable, shall be made by the department or delegated county adoption agency as part of the study required by Section 8806.

(b) The report on the child's background shall contain all known diagnostic information, including current medical reports on the child, psychological evaluations, and scholastic information, as well as all known information regarding the child's developmental history and family life.

(c) The report shall be submitted to the prospective adoptive parents who shall acknowledge its receipt in writing.

(d)(1) The biological parents may provide a blood sample at a clinic or hospital approved by the State Department of Health Services. The biological parents' failure to provide a blood sample shall not affect the adoption of the child.

(2) The blood sample shall be stored at a laboratory under contract with the State Department of Health Services for a period of 30 years following the adoption of the child.

(3) The purpose of the stored sample of blood is to provide a blood sample from which DNA testing can be done at a later date after entry of the order of adoption at the request of the adoptive parents or the adopted child. The cost of drawing and storing the blood samples shall be paid for by a separate fee in addition to the fee required under Section 8810. The amount of this additional fee shall be based on the cost of drawing and storing the blood samples but at no time shall the additional fee be more than one hundred dollars ($100).

(e)(1) The blood sample shall be stored and released in such a manner as to not identify any party to the adoption.

(2) Any results of the DNA testing shall be stored and released in such a manner as to not identify any party to the adoption.

(Stats. 1992 (A.B. 2650), ch. 162, §10, effective January 1, 1994. Amended Stats. 1996 (A.B. 3241), ch. 1053, §2.)

§8818. Department shall adopt statement to present to birth parents at time of consent

(a) The department shall adopt a statement to be presented to the birth parents at the time the consent to adoption is signed and to prospective adoptive parents at the time of the home study. The statement shall, in a clear and concise manner and in words calculated to ensure the confidence of the birth parents in the integrity of the adoption process, communicate to the birth parent of a child who is the subject of an adoption petition all of the following facts:

(1) It is in the child's best interest that the birth parents keep the department informed of any health problems that the parent develops that could affect the child.

(2) It is extremely important that the birth parent keep an address current with the department in order to permit a response to inquiries concerning medical or social history.

(3) Section 9203 of the Family Code authorizes a person who has been adopted and who attains the age of 21 years to request the department to disclose the name and address of the adoptee's birth parents. Consequently, it is of the utmost importance that the birth parent indicate whether to allow this disclosure by checking the appropriate box provided on the form.

(4) The birth parent may change the decision whether to permit disclosure of the birth parent's name and address, at any time, by sending a notarized letter to that effect, by certified mail, return receipt requested, to the department.

(5) The consent will be filed in the office of the clerk of the court in which the adoption takes place. The file is not open to inspection by any persons other than the parties to the adoption proceeding, their attorneys, and the department, except upon order of a judge of the superior court.

(b) The department shall adopt a form to be signed by the birth parents at the time the consent to adoption is signed, which shall provide as follows: "Section 9203 of the Family Code authorizes a person who has been adopted and who attains the age of 21 years to make a request to the State Department of Social Services, or the licensed adoption agency that joined in the adoption petition, for the name and address of the adoptee's birth parents. Indicate by checking one of the boxes below whether or not you wish your name and address to be disclosed:

[ ] YES

[ ] NO

[ ] UNCERTAIN AT THIS TIME;

WILL NOTIFY AT AGENCY AT LATER DATE."

(Stats. 1992 (A.B. 2650), ch. 162, §10, effective January 1, 1994. Amended by Stats. 2002 (S.B. 1316), ch. 784, §113.)

§8819. Department or agency shall send notice to birth parent on termination of parental rights

When the parental rights of a birth parent are terminated pursuant to Chapter 5 (commencing with Section 7660) of Part 3 of Division 12 or Part 4 (commencing with Section 7800) of Division 12, the department or delegated county adoption agency shall send a written notice to the birth parent, if the birth parent's address is known, that contains the following statement:

"You are encouraged to keep the department or this agency informed of your current address in order to permit a response to any inquiry concerning medical or social history made by or on behalf of the child who was the subject of the court action terminating parental rights."

(Stats. 1992 (A.B. 2650), ch. 162, §10, effective January 1, 1994.)

§8820. Birth parents' right to appeal

(a) The birth parent or parents or the petitioner may appeal in either of the following cases:

(1) If for a period of 180 days from the date of filing the adoption petition or upon the expiration of any extension of the period granted by the court, the department or delegated county adoption agency fails or refuses to accept the consent of the birth parent or parents to the adoption.

(2) In a case where the consent of the department or delegated county adoption agency is required by this chapter, if the department or agency fails or refuses to file or give its consent to the adoption.

(b) The appeal shall be filed in the court in which the adoption petition is filed. The court clerk shall immediately notify the department or delegated county adoption agency of the appeal and the department or agency shall, within 10 days, file a report of its findings and the reasons for its failure or refusal to consent to the adoption or to accept the consent of the birth parent or parents.

(c) After the filing of the report by the department or delegated county adoption agency, the court may, if it deems that the welfare of the child will be promoted by that adoption, allow the signing of the consent by the birth parent or parents in open court or, if the appeal is from the refusal of the department or delegated county adoption agency to consent thereto, grant the petition without the consent.

(Stats. 1992 (A.B. 2650), ch. 162, §10, effective January 1, 1994.)

§8821. Copy of favorable or unfavorable report or findings must be given to petitioner or attorney

When any report or findings are submitted to the court by the department or a delegated county adoption agency, a copy of the report or findings, whether favorable or unfavorable, shall be given to the petitioner's attorney in the proceeding, if the petitioner has an attorney of record, or to the petitioner.

(Stats. 1992 (A.B. 2650), ch. 162, §10, effective January 1, 1994.)

§8822. Unfavorable recommendation by department or agency leads to court review

(a) If the findings of the department or delegated county adoption agency are that the home of the petitioners is not suitable for the child or that the required consents are not available and the department or agency recommends that the petition be denied, or if the petitioners desire to withdraw the petition and the department or agency recommends that the petition be denied, the clerk upon receipt of the report of the department or agency shall immediately refer it to the court for review.

(b) Upon receipt of the report, the court shall set a date for a hearing of the petition and shall give reasonable notice of the hearing to the department or delegated county adoption agency, the petitioners, and the birth parents by certified mail, return receipt requested, to the address of each as shown in the proceeding.

(c) The department or delegated county adoption agency shall appear to represent the child.

(Stats. 1992 (A.B. 2650), ch. 162, §10, effective January 1, 1994.)

§8823. Required appearances of prospective adoptive parents and child

The prospective adoptive parents and the child proposed to be adopted shall appear before the court pursuant to Sections 8612 and 8613.

(Stats. 1992 (A.B. 2650), ch. 162, §10, effective January 1, 1994.)

E. SUBSIDIZED ADOPTION

Adoption of children with special needs has risen to constitute almost half of all domestic adoptions by nonrelatives. National Council for Adoption, Adoption Factbook III 27 (1999). Prospective adoptees who are hard to place (often called "children with special needs") include older children, children of color, sibling groups, and children with handicaps, including HIV infection.

To encourage such adoptions, state and federal law provide financial assistance to prospective adoptive parents. The Adoption and Safe Families Act of 1997 attempts to promote the adoption of children with special needs by requiring states to seek termination of parental rights after a limited period of foster care (42 U.S.C. §675(5) (2000); provides financial incentives for states to increase adoptions of children in foster care and those with special needs (id. at §673b); and requires state plans to provide for health insurance for special needs children covered by adoption assistance agreements (id. at §671(a)). States are eligible for federal funds provided that they have a plan that complies with federal requirements (42 U.S.C. §671).

In addition, UAA, §2-105 requires agencies receiving federal funds to make diligent efforts to recruit adopters for children with special needs. 9 U.L.A. (pt. IA) 35-36 (1999).

California provides for adoption subsidies by means of its Adoption Assistance Program (Welf. & Inst. Code §§16115 et seq.). Legislation specifies the responsibilities of the department administering the program (Cal. Welf. & Inst. Code §16118), and conditions for eligibility (Cal. Welf. & Inst. Code §16120(a)).

California Welfare and Institutions Code

§16115. Title

Aid under this chapter shall be known as the Adoption Assistance Program.

(Stats. 1968, ch. 1322, §1, effective January 1, 1969. Amended Stats. 1982, ch. 977, §18, effective September 13, 1982, effective October 1, 1982.)

§16115.5. Legislative intent to benefit children in foster homes

It is the intent of the Legislature in enacting this chapter to benefit children residing in foster homes by providing the stability and security of permanent homes, and in so doing, achieve a reduction in foster home care. It is not the intent of this chapter to increase expenditures but to provide for payments to adoptive parents to enable them to meet the needs of children who meet the criteria established in Sections 16116, 16120, and 16121.

(Stats. 1976, ch. 504, §21, effective August 20, 1976. Amended Stats. 1978, ch. 380, §184; Stats. 1982, ch. 977, §19, effective October 1, 1982; Stats. 1986, ch. 767, §3, ch. 1517, §1, effective September 30, 1986; Stats. 1993 (A.B. 930), ch. 1087, §1, effective October 10, 1993.)

§16118. Departmental responsibilities

(a) The department shall establish and administer the program to be carried out by the department or the county pursuant to this chapter. The department shall adopt any regulations necessary to carry out the provisions of this chapter.

(b) The department shall keep any records necessary to evaluate the program's effectiveness in encouraging and promoting the adoption of children eligible for the Adoption Assistance Program.

(c) The department or the county responsible for providing financial aid in the amount determined in Section 16120 shall have responsibility for certifying that the child meets the eligibility criteria and for determining the amount of financial assistance needed by the child and the adopting family.

(d) The department shall actively seek and make maximum use of federal funds that may be available for the purposes of this chapter. All gifts or grants received from private sources for the purpose of this chapter shall be used to offset public costs incurred under the program established by this chapter.

(e) For purposes of this chapter, the county responsible for determining the child's Adoption Assistance Program eligibility status and for providing financial aid in the amount determined in Sections 16120 and 16120.1 shall be the county that at the time of the adoptive placement would otherwise be responsible for making a payment pursuant to Section 11450 under the CalWORKs program or Section 11461 under the Aid to Families with Dependent Children-Foster Care program if the child were not adopted. When the child has been voluntarily relinquished for adoption prior to a determination of eligibility for such a payment, the responsible county shall be the county in which the relinquishing parent resides. The responsible county for all other eligible children shall be the county where the child is physically residing prior to placement with the adoptive family. The responsible county shall certify eligibility on a form prescribed by the department.

(Stats. 1968, ch. 1322, §1, effective January 1, 1969. Amended Stats. 1969, ch. 261, §2; Stats. 1971, ch. 123, §3, ch. 1724, §3, effective December 14, 1971; Stats. 1982, ch. 977, §22, effective October 1, 1982; Stats. 1986, ch. 767, §5, ch. 1517, §3, effective September 30, 1986; Stats. 1992 (S.B. 485), ch. 722, §130, effective October 1, 1992; Stats. 1993 (A.B. 930), ch. 1087, §3, effective October 10, 1993; Stats. 1999 (S.B. 966), ch. 83, §207, (A.B. 390), ch. 547, §1.)

§16119. Department or agency shall provide information on availability of program benefits

(a) At the time application for adoption of a child who is potentially eligible for Adoption Assistance Program benefits is made, and at the time immediately prior to the finalization of the adoption decree, the department or the licensed adoption agency, whichever is appropriate, shall provide the prospective adoptive family with information, in writing, on the availability of Adoption Assistance Program benefits, with an explanation of the difference between these benefits and foster care payments. . . .

(c) The department or the county, whichever is responsible for determining the child's eligibility for the Adoption Assistance Program, shall assess the needs of the child and the circumstances of the family.

(d)(1) The amount of an adoption assistance cash benefit, if any, shall be a negotiated amount based upon the needs of the child and the circumstances of the family . There shall be no means test used to determine an adoptive family's eligibility for the Adoption Assistance Program. . . .

(2) For purposes of paragraph (1), "circumstances of the family" includes the family's ability to incorporate the child into the household in relation to the lifestyle, standard of living, and future plans and to the overall capacity to meet the immediate and future plans and needs, including education, of the child.

. . .

(f) The department or the licensed adoption agency shall inform the prospective adoptive family that the adoptive parents will continue to receive benefits in the agreed upon amount unless one of the following occurs:

(1) The department determines that the adoptive parents are no longer legally responsible for the support of the child.

(2) The department determines that the child is no longer receiving support from the adoptive family.

(3) The adoption assistance payment exceeds the amount that the child would have been eligible for in a licensed foster home.

(4) The adoptive parents demonstrate a need for an increased payment.

(5) The adoptive parents voluntarily reduce or terminate payments.

(6) The adopted child has an extraordinary need that was not anticipated at the time the amount of the adoption assistance was originally negotiated.

(Stats. 1968, ch. 1322, §1, effective January 1, 1969. Amended Stats. 1971, ch. 123, §4, ch. 1724, §4, effective December 14, 1971; Stats. 1986, ch. 767, §6; Stats. 1987, ch. 978, §1; Stats. 1989, ch. 1376, §1; Stats. 1992 (S.B. 485), ch. 722, §131, effective October 1, 1992; Stats. 1993 (A.B. 930), ch. 1087, §4, effective October 10, 1993; Stats. 1999 (A.B. 390), ch. 547, §2, (A.B. 1225), ch. 905, §1, effective until January 1, 2000 , (A.B. 1225), §2, effective January 1, 2000.)

§16120. Eligibility conditions for payment of benefits

A child shall be eligible for Adoption Assistance Program benefits if all of the conditions specified in subdivisions (a) through (g), inclusive, are met or if the conditions specified in subdivision (h) are met.

(a) The child has at least one of the following characteristics that are barriers to his or her adoption:

(1) Adoptive placement without financial assistance is unlikely because of membership in a sibling group that should remain intact or by virtue of race, ethnicity, color, language, age of three years or older, or parental background of a medical or behavioral nature that can be determined to adversely affect the development of the child.

(2) Adoptive placement without financial assistance is unlikely because the child has a mental, physical, emotional, or medical disability that has been certified by a licensed professional competent to make an assessment and operating within the scope of his or her profession. This paragraph shall also apply to children with a developmental disability as defined in subdivision (a) of Section 4512, including those determined to require out-of-home nonmedical care as described in Section 11464.

(b) The need for adoption subsidy is evidenced by an unsuccessful search for an adoptive home to take the child without financial assistance, as documented in the case file of the prospective adoptive child. The requirement for this search shall be waived when it would be against the best interest of the child because of the existence of significant emotional ties with prospective adoptive parents while in the care of these persons as a foster child.

(c) The child meets either of the following criteria:

(1) At the time a petition for an agency adoption, as defined in Section 8506 of the Family Code, or an independent adoption, as defined in Section 8524 of the Family Code, is filed, the child has met the requirements to receive federal supplemental security income benefits pursuant to Subchapter 16 (commencing with Section 1381) of Chapter 7 of Title 42 of the United States Code, as determined and documented by the federal Social Security Administration.

(2) The child is the subject of an agency adoption as defined in Section 8506 of the Family Code and was any of the following:

(A) Under the supervision of a county welfare department as the subject of a legal guardianship or juvenile court dependency.

(B) Relinquished for adoption to a licensed California private or public adoption agency, or the department, and would have otherwise been at risk of dependency as certified by the responsible public child welfare agency.

(C) Committed to the care of the department pursuant to Section 8805 or 8918 of the Family Code.

(d) The child is under 18 years of age, or under 21 years of age and has a mental or physical handicap that warrants the continuation of assistance.

(e) The adoptive family is responsible for the child pursuant to the terms of an adoptive placement agreement or a final decree of adoption and has signed an adoption assistance agreement.

(f) The adoptive family is legally responsible for the support of the child and the child is receiving support from the adoptive parent.

(g) The department or the county responsible for determining the child's Adoption Assistance Program eligibility status and for providing financial aid, and the prospective adoptive parent, prior to or at the time the adoption decree is issued by the court, have signed an adoption assistance agreement that stipulates the need for, and the amount of, Adoption Assistance Program benefits.

(h) A child shall be eligible for Adoption Assistance Program benefits if the child received Adoption Assistance Program benefits with respect to a prior adoption and the child is again available for adoption because the prior adoption was dissolved and the parental rights of the adoptive parents were terminated or because the child's adoptive parents died.

(Stats. 1993 (A.B. 930), ch. 1087, §6, effective October 10, 1993. Amended Stats. 1998 (A.B. 2773), ch. 1056, §26; Stats. 2003 (S.B. 984), ch. 323, §5.)

§16120.05. Scope of adoption assistance agreement

The adoption assistance agreement shall, at a minimum, specify the amount and duration of assistance. The date for reassessment of the child's needs shall be set at the time of the initial negotiation of the adoption assistance agreement, and shall, thereafter be set at each subsequent reassessment. The interval between any reassessments may not exceed two years.

The adoption assistance agreement shall also specify the responsibility of the adopting family for reporting changes in circumstances that might negatively affect their ability to provide for the identified needs of the child.

(Stats. 1993 (A.B. 930), ch. 1087, §7, effective October 10, 1993. Amended Stats. 1999 (A.B. 390), ch. 547, §3.)

§16120.1. County shall reimburse eligible individuals

Upon the authorization of the department or, where appropriate, the county responsible for determining the child's Adoption Assistance Program eligibility status and for providing financial aid, the responsible county shall directly reimburse eligible individuals for reasonable nonrecurring expenses, as defined by the department, incurred as a result of the adoption of a child eligible for the Adoption Assistance Program. The state shall provide payment to the county for the reimbursement. . . .

(Stats. 1989, ch. 1376, §2, effective until January 1, 1992. Amended Stats. 1991 (S.B. 700), ch. 987, §1, effective until January 1, 1994; Stats. 1992, ch. 722, §133, effective until January 1, 1994; Stats. 1993 (A.B. 930), ch. 1087, §8, effective October 10, 1993 (A.B. 2129) ch. 1089, §33.)

§16121.05. Department shall develop regulations to recoup overpayments

(a) The department may recover any overpayments of financial assistance under the Adoption Assistance Program, and shall develop regulations that establish the means to recoup them, including an appropriate notice of action and appeal rights, when the department determines either of the following applies:

(1) The adoptive parents are no longer legally responsible for the support of the child.

(2) The child is no longer receiving support from the adoptive family.

(3) The adoptive family has committed fraud in its application for, or reassessment of, the adoption assistance.

. . .

(Stats. 1993 (A.B. 930), ch. 1087, §11, effective October 10, 1993. Amended Stats. 1999 (A.B. 390), ch. 547, §4. Amended by Stats. 2004 (A.B. 3082), ch. 183, §392.)

§16122. Compensation of private adoption agencies for otherwise unreimbursed placement costs

(a) It is the intent of the Legislature in enacting this chapter to provide children who would otherwise remain in long-term foster care with permanent adoptive homes. It is also the intent of this Legislature to encourage private adoption agencies to continue placing these children, and in so doing, to achieve a substantial savings to the state in foster care costs.

(b) From any funds appropriated for this purpose, the state shall compensate private adoption agencies licensed pursuant to Chapter 3 (commencing with Section 1500) of Division 2 of the Health and Safety Code for costs of placing for adoption children eligible for Adoption Assistance Program benefits pursuant to Section 16120. . . .

(c) Effective July 1, 1999, the maximum amount of reimbursement pursuant to subdivision (b) shall be five thousand dollars ($ 5,000).

(Stats. 1982, ch. 977, §30, effective October 1, 1982. Amended Stats. 1984, ch. 1116, §10, effective September 13, 1984; Stats. 1986, ch. 767, §8, ch. 1517, §5, effective September 30, 1986; Stats. 1988, ch. 160, §195; Stats. 1996 (A.B. 1524), ch. 1083, §8; Stats. 1999 (A.B. 1225), ch. 905, §3, effective October 10, 1999.)

§16123. Continuing payments dependent on receipt of federal funds; exception

The provisions of Section 16120, permitting the payment of adoption assistance until a child attains the age of 18 or 21 if the child has mental or physical handicaps, shall be effective as long as federal funds are available under Title IV-E of the federal Social Security Act (Part E (commencing with Section 670) of Subchapter 4 of Chapter 7 of Title 42 of the United States Code). When those funds cease to be available the maximum length for payment of the Adoption Assistance Program shall be five years except in instances in which there is a continuing need, related to a chronic health condition of the child which necessitated the initial financial assistance. In those cases, a parent may, until October 1, 1992, petition the department or licensed adoption agency to continue financial assistance up to age of majority. On and after October 1, 1992, the parent may petition the department or the

responsible county to continue financial assistance up to the age of majority.
(Stats. 1982, ch. 977, §31, effective October 1, 1982. Amended Stats. 1992 (S.B. 485), ch. 722, §136, effective September 14, 1992.)

§16135. Purpose of chapter

The purpose of this chapter is to establish a program for special training and services to facilitate the adoption of children who are HIV positive, or born to a substance-abusing mother. This program shall be available to any county that requests participation pursuant to procedures established by the department to the extent funds are appropriated through the annual Budget Act. Nothing in this chapter shall authorize the use of state funds appropriated for any other purpose to be used in this program.
(Stats. 1998 (A.B. 2779), ch. 329, §29, effective August 21, 1998 (A.B. 2198), ch. 1014, §2.)

§16135.1. Definitions

(a) "Eligible child" means any child who meets the requirements of paragraph (1) or (2), and paragraph (3).

(1) Any child who has a condition or symptoms resulting from, or are suspected as resulting from, alcohol or substance abuse by the mother.

(2) Any child who is HIV positive.

(3) Any child who meets the requirements of either paragraph (1) or (2) and who meets all of the following requirements:

(A) The child is a dependent child of the court.

(B) The child has an adoption case plan and resides with a preadoptive or adoptive caregiver, or the plan is to transition and move the child to a preadoptive or adoptive caregiver.

(b) "TIES for Adoption" means Training, Intervention, Education, and Services for Adoption, a training project developed and implemented by the Adoptions Division of the Los Angeles County Department of Children's Services, the UCLA Center for Healthier Children, Families, and Communities, and the UCLA Psychology Department, a demonstration project funded by the Federal Adoption Opportunities Program from September 30, 1995, to December 31, 1997, inclusive.

(c) "HIV positive" means having a human immunodeficiency virus infection.

(d) "Specialized in-home health care" means, but is not limited to, those services identified by the child's primary physician as appropriately administered by a prospective adoptive parent who has been trained by mental health or health care professionals.
(Stats. 1998 (A.B. 2779), ch. 329, §29, effective August 21, 1998 (A.B. 2198), ch. 1014, §2.)

§16135.10. Promotion of adoption of substance and alcohol-exposed dependent children

(a) In order to promote successful adoptions of substance and alcohol exposed court dependent children, the department shall establish a program of specialized training and supportive services to families adopting court dependent children who are either HIV positive or assessed as being prenatally exposed to alcohol or a controlled substance.

(b) Notwithstanding any other provision of law, respite services, if offered, shall be funded with a 30 percent nonfederal county share consistent with the normal sharing ratio for child welfare services. This county share may be provided with county general funds, in-kind contributions, or other funds not appropriated by the State Budget Act. The source of the county share shall meet all applicable state and federal requirements and provide counties with maximum flexibility.
(Stats. 1998 (A.B. 2779), ch. 329, §29, effective August 21, 1998.)

§16135.13. County shall provide special training

(a) A participating county shall provide special training to recruited adoptive parents to care for eligible children. The training curriculum shall include, but is not limited to:

(1) Orientation.

(2) Effect of alcohol and controlled substances on the fetus and children.

(3) Normal and abnormal infant and early childhood development.

(4) Special medical needs and disabilities.

(5) Recovery from addiction to alcohol and controlled substances.

(6) Self-care for the caregiver.

(7) HIV/AIDS in children.

(8) Issues in parenting and providing lifelong permanency and substance abuse prevention to, children with prenatal alcohol and other controlled substances exposure.

(9) Issues specific to caring for a child who tests HIV positive.

(b) Participating counties may provide the same special training to relative caretakers in the process of adopting program-eligible children.
(Stats. 1998 (A.B. 2779), ch. 329, §29, effective August 21, 1998.)

§16135.14. County shall determine eligibility for services

(a) The county shall determine whether a child is eligible for services pursuant to this section.

(b) A participating county shall select a specialized prospective adoptive home for the child.

(c) If an eligible child's adoptive placement changes from one participating county to another participating county, the child shall remain eligible for services.
(Stats. 1998 (A.B. 2779), ch. 329, §29, effective August 21, 1998 (A.B. 2198), ch. 1014, §2.)

§16135.16. Counties shall submit plan as condition to funding

(a) In order to receive funding, all participating counties shall submit and have an approved plan that is in compliance with the policies and procedures established by the department.

(b) The requirements of this section may be met by the implementation of the TIES for Adoption program as defined in subdivision (b) of Section 16135.1.
(Stats. 1998 (A.B. 2779), ch. 329, §29, effective August 21, 1998 (A.B. 2198), ch. 1014, §2.)

F. OPEN ADOPTION

An open adoption signifies a degree of openness in the relationship between the birth parent and the adopting parent. In an open adoption, the birth parents of a child who is placed for adoption are aware of the identity of the adoptive parents. Similarly, the adopted child is aware of the identity of the birth parents. The biological and adoptive parents may enter into an agreement regarding the adoption such that the birth parent(s) continue(s) to play some role (visitation perhaps) in the child's life.

The rise of open adoption is attributable to several developments. First, an increasing number of older children, with established bonds to their birth families, have been freed for adoption. Second, because of the decreased availability of infants following the legalization of abortion, birth parents can demand conditions in placement such as open adoption. Finally, experts claim that an open system avoids the harmful effects of anonymity for adoptees, birth parents and adopters. Annette Ruth Appell, The Move Toward Legally Sanctioned Cooperative Adoption: Can It Survive the Uniform Adoption Act?, 30 Fam. L.Q. 483, 483 (1996). The majority of these adoptions are by relatives and stepparents. *Id.* at 488-489.

According to California law, the birth parent or parents must have substantial information about the prospective adoptive parents in an independent adoption (Cal. Fam. Code §8801 [set forth in §D2 *supra*]). Therefore, independent adoptions tend to be open adoptions to some extent (see Independent Adoptions §D2 *supra*).

The California legislature (effective January 1, 1998) provided for openness in certain circumstances in order to remove barriers to adoption by relatives of those children who are in (or at risk of entering) the dependency system. In a kinship adoption agreement, the adoptive parent(s), birth relatives, and the child enter into a written agreement to permit continuing contact between the birth relatives and the child, if the court finds such an agreement would be in the child's best interests. The kinship adoption agreement may include visitation provisions between the child and birth parent(s) and other birth relatives (including siblings) and provisions for the future sharing of information (Cal. Fam. Code §8616.5(a)). The kinship adoption agreement is filed with the adoption petition (Cal. Fam. Code §8714.5(d)). If the child is 12 years old or older, he or she is a necessary party to the kinship adoption agreement (Cal. Fam. Code §8616.5(d)). Modification or termination of the agreement is permitted upon agreement of all parties, if necessary to serve the child's best interests, a substantial change of circumstances has occurred, and the petitioner has participated in mediation (Cal. Fam. Code §8616.5(h)).

The Uniform Adoption Act [included in Part III infra] authorizes stepparent adoption as the preferred context for openness in adoptive placements. UAA §4-113 expressly provides for judicial enforcement of visitation agreements in stepparent adoptions. 9 U.L.A. (pt. IA) 110-112 (1999). Otherwise, it permits "mutually agreed-upon communication between birth and adoptive families" without making such agreements enforceable. See id. at 15 (Prefatory Note 9).

California Family Code

§8616.5. Scope of kinship adoption agreement

(a) The Legislature finds and declares that some adoptive children may benefit from either direct or indirect contact with birth relatives, including the birth parent or parents, after being adopted. Postadoption contact agreements are intended to ensure children of an achievable level of continuing contact when contact is beneficial to the children and the agreements are voluntarily entered into by birth relatives, including the birth parent or parents, and adoptive parents.

(b)(1) Nothing in the adoption laws of this state shall be construed to prevent the adopting parent or parents, the birth relatives, including the birth parent or parents, and the child from voluntarily entering into a written agreement to permit continuing contact between the birth relatives, including the birth parent or parents, and the child if the agreement is found by the court to have been entered into voluntarily and to be in the best interests of the child at the time the adoption petition is granted.

(2) Except as provided in paragraph (3), the terms of any postadoption contact agreement executed under this section shall be limited to, but need not include, all of the following:

(A) Provisions for visitation between the child and a birth parent or parents and other birth relatives, including siblings, and the child's Indian tribe if the case is governed by the Indian Child Welfare Act (25 U.S.C. Sec. 1901 et seq.).

(B) Provisions for future contact between a birth parent or parents or other birth relatives, including siblings, or both, and the child or an adoptive parent, or both, and in cases governed by the Indian Child Welfare Act, the child's Indian tribe.

(C) Provisions for the sharing of information about the child in the future.

(3) The terms of any postadoption contact agreement shall be limited to the sharing of information about the child, unless the child has an existing relationship with the birth relative.

(c) At the time an adoption decree is entered pursuant to a petition filed pursuant to Section 8714, 8714.5, 8802, 8912, or 9000, the court entering the decree may grant postadoption privileges if an agreement for those privileges has been entered into, including agreements entered into pursuant to subdivision (f) of Section 8620.

(d) The child who is the subject of the adoption petition shall be considered a party to the postadoption contact agreement. The written consent to the terms and conditions of the postadoption contact agreement and any subsequent modifications of the agreement by a child who is 12 years of age or older is a necessary condition to the granting of privileges regarding visitation, contact, or sharing of information about the child, unless the court finds by a preponderance of the evidence that the agreement, as written, is in the best interests of the child. Any child who has been found to come within Section 300 of the Welfare and Institutions Code or who is the subject of a petition for jurisdiction of the juvenile court under Section 300 of the Welfare and Institutions Code shall be represented by an attorney for purposes of consent to the postadoption contact agreement.

(e) A postadoption contact agreement shall contain the following warnings in bold type:

(1) After the adoption petition has been granted by the court, the adoption cannot be set aside due to the failure of an adopting parent, a birth parent, a birth relative, or the child to follow the terms of this agreement or a later change to this agreement.

(2) A disagreement between the parties or litigation brought to enforce or modify the agreement shall not affect the validity of the adoption and shall not serve as a basis for orders affecting the custody of the child.

(3) A court will not act on a petition to change or enforce this agreement unless the petitioner has participated, or attempted to participate, in good faith in mediation or other appropriate dispute resolution proceedings to resolve the dispute.

(f) Upon the granting of the adoption petition and the issuing of the order of adoption of a child who is a dependent of the juvenile court, juvenile court dependency jurisdiction shall be terminated. Enforcement of the postadoption contact agreement shall be under the continuing jurisdiction of the court granting the petition of adoption. The court may not order compliance with the agreement absent a finding that the party seeking the enforcement participated, or attempted to participate, in good faith in mediation or other appropriate dispute resolution proceedings regarding the conflict, prior to the filing of the enforcement action, and that the enforcement is in the best interests of the child. Documentary evidence or offers of proof may serve as the basis for the court's decision regarding enforcement. No testimony or evidentiary hearing shall be required. The court shall not order further investigation or evaluation by any public or private agency or individual absent a finding by clear and convincing evidence that the best interests of the child may be protected or advanced only by that inquiry and that the inquiry will not disturb the stability of the child's home to the detriment of the child.

(g) The court may not award monetary damages as a result of the filing of the civil action pursuant to subdivision (e) of this section.

(h) A postadoption contact agreement may be modified or terminated only if either of the following occurs:

(1) All parties, including the child if the child is 12 years of age or older at the time of the requested termination or modification, have signed a modified postadoption contact agreement and the agreement is filed with the court that granted the petition of adoption.

(2) The court finds all of the following:

(A) The termination or modification is necessary to serve the best interests of the child.

(B) There has been a substantial change of circumstances since the original agreement was executed and approved by the court.

(C) The party seeking the termination or modification has participated, or attempted to participate, in good faith in mediation or other appropriate dispute resolution proceedings prior to seeking court approval of the proposed termination or modification.

Documentary evidence or offers of proof may serve as the basis for the court's decision. No testimony or evidentiary hearing shall be required. The court shall not order further investigation or evaluation by any public or private agency or individual absent a finding by clear and convincing evidence that the best interests of the child may be protected or advanced only by that inquiry and that the inquiry will not disturb the stability of the child's home to the detriment of the child.

(i) All costs and fees of mediation or other appropriate dispute resolution proceedings shall be borne by each party, excluding the child. All costs and fees of litigation shall be borne by the party filing the action to modify or enforce the agreement when no party has been found by the court as failing to comply with an existing postadoption contact agreement. Otherwise, a party, other than the child, found by the court as failing to comply without good cause with an existing agreement shall bear all the costs and fees of litigation.

(j) The Judicial Council shall adopt rules of court and forms for motions to enforce, terminate, or modify postadoption contact agreements.

(k) The court shall not set aside a decree of adoption, rescind a relinquishment, or modify an order to terminate parental rights or any other prior court order because of the failure of a birth parent, adoptive parent, birth relative, or the child to comply with any or all of the original terms of, or subsequent modifications to, the postadoption contact agreement.

(Stats. 1997 (A.B. 1544), ch. 793, §5. Amended Stats. 2000 (A.B. 2921), ch. 910, §4, (S.B. 2157), ch. 930, §3. Amended and Renumbered Cal. Fam. Code §8616.5 by Stats. 2003 (S.B. 182), ch. 251, §8. Amended by Stats. 2004 (S.B. 1357), ch. 858, §4.)

G. EQUITABLE ADOPTION

By resort to the remedy of equitable adoption, courts effectuate an adoption (or effectuate the consequences of an adoption) in cases in which a legal adoption never occurred. The process is sometimes referred to as "virtual adoption." Many cases arise when an adoptive parent dies and the adoptee seeks a determination of inheritance rights. Courts generally apply equitable adoption by resort to either contract theory or estoppel theory.

Although recognized by statute (Cal. Prob. Code §6455), the doctrine is of judicial origin in California. See In re Estate of Wilson, 111 Cal. App. 3d 242 (Ct. App. 1980).

In In re Estate of Ford, 82 P.3d 747 (Cal. 2004), a claimant filed an action against the decedent's niece and nephew for a share of the decedent's intestate estate, alleging that he was an equitably adopted son. Rejecting his claim, the California Supreme Court held that the claimant failed to prove the decedent's intent to adopt him by clear and convincing evidence despite evidence showing that he had a close enduring relationship with the decedent's family after he was taken into their home as a foster child.

California Probate Code

§6455. Equitable adoption

Nothing in this chapter affects or limits application of the judicial doctrine of equitable adoption for the benefit of the child or the child's issue. See also Estate of Furia, 126 Cal. Rptr. 2d. 384 (Ct. App. 2002) (affirming the denial of an equitably adopted step-granddaughter to inherit from her testate "grandmother" and reasoning that the equitable adoption doctrine does not convey to the equitable child all the right of an heir).

(Stats. 1993 (A.B. 1137), ch 529, §5.)

H. INTERSTATE ADOPTION

Children from one state often are placed in adoptive homes in another state. Interstate adoption is now encouraged by social work standards and by the Interstate Compact on the Placement of Children (ICPC) which has been enacted in all states. For California's version, see California Family Code §§7900 et seq.

The Interstate Compact on the Placement of Children was drafted in 1960 in response to concerns raised at an informal meeting of social service administrators in the 1950s regarding problems of interstate adoptive placement. See Bernadette W. Hartfield, The Role of the Interstate Compact on the Placement of Children in Interstate Adoption, 68 Neb. L. Rev. 292, 295 (1989). In particular, the social workers lamented the powerlessness of the sending state to ensure that proper care and supervision were provided in the receiving state. The ICPC was drafted under the auspices of the New York State Legislative Committee on Interstate Cooperation, and New York was the first state to enact its provisions in 1960. Id. at 295.

The ICPC attempts to ensure that a child receives proper care following transfer from a sending state to a home in a receiving state. To accomplish that purpose, the ICPC requires the sending agency to comply with certain requirements (e.g., provide information to appropriate public authorities in the receiving state about the child and prospective adoptive parents) and to require the receiving state also to fulfill certain requirements (e.g., conduct a home study).

Controversy exists regarding whether the ICPC applies when a child is placed out-of-state with the other biological parent. See Kimberly M. Butler, Child Welfare Outside the Interstate Compact on the Placement of Children — Placement of a Child With a Natural Parent, McComb v. Wambaugh, 37 Villanova L. Rev. 896, 903, n.51 (1992) (explaining that several states favor application of the ICPC to the placement of a child with a natural parent). Compare Green v. Division of Fam. Servs., 864 A.2d 921 (Del. 2004) (holding that ICPC does apply to non-resident noncustodial parents in some circumstances and that application of ICPC to sch fathers did not violate their due process rights), with McComb v. Wambaugh, 934 F.2d 474 (3d. 1991) (holding that the ICPC does not apply to out-of-state placements with a biological parent).

On international adoptions, see §I infra.

California Rules of Court

Rule 1428. Implementation of Interstate Compact on the Placement of Children

(a) [Applicability of Rule (Fam. Code §§7900 et seq.)] This rule implements the purposes and provisions of the Interstate Compact on the Placement of Children (Compact). California juvenile courts shall apply this rule when placing children who are dependents or wards of the juvenile court and for whom placement is indicated in any other state, the District of Columbia, or the U.S. Virgin Islands. The rule applies to the placement in California of children who are dependents or wards of the juvenile court in any of the above-named jurisdictions. This rule also applies to priority placements as described below in subdivision (b)(2). This rule does not apply to placements made pursuant to the Interstate Compact on Juveniles (Welf. & Inst. Code, §§1300 et seq.).

(b) [Definitions]

(1) "Placement" is defined in Article II(d) of the Compact. It includes placements with a stepparent, a grandparent, an adult brother or sister, an adult aunt or uncle, a nonagency guardian of the child, a placement recipient who is not related to the child, a residential institution, a group home, or a treatment facility. A court directing or making an award of custody to a parent of the child is not a placement within the meaning of this rule, unless the sending court retains dependency jurisdiction over the child or the order or award requests or provides for supervision or other services or places some other condition or restriction on the conduct of the parent. Except in cases in which a child is placed with a parent and jurisdiction has been terminated or in cases in which dependency is maintained only to provide services to, or conditions imposed on, the noncustodial parent remaining in the sending jurisdiction, an order causing a child to be sent or brought to another party compact jurisdiction without a specific date of return to the sending jurisdiction, or with a return date more than 30 days from the start of the visit or beyond the ending date of a school vacation period, constitutes a placement, and the Compact shall be applied.

(2) "Priority placement" means a placement or placement request made by a court with specific findings of one or more of the following circumstances:

(A) The proposed placement recipient is a relative belonging to a class of persons who, under Article VIII(a) of the Compact, could receive the child from another person belonging to such a class, without complying with the Compact; if the child was not under the jurisdiction of the court; and if:

(i) The child is under two years of age; or

(ii) The child is in an emergency shelter; or

(iii) The court finds that the child has spent a substantial period of time in the home of the proposed placement recipient.

(B) The receiving Compact Administrator has been in possession of a properly completed interstate compact placement request form and supporting documentation for over 30 business days, but the sending agency has not received a notice under Article III(d) of the Compact determining whether or not the child may be placed.

(c) [Compact Requirements (Fam. Code §7901)] Whenever the juvenile court makes a placement in another jurisdiction included in the Compact or reviews a placement plan, the court shall adhere to the provisions and regulations of the compact.

(d) [Notice of Intention; Authorization (Fam. Code §7901)] A sending jurisdiction shall provide to the designated receiving jurisdiction written notice of intention to place the child, using an interstate compact placement request form.

(1) The representative of the receiving jurisdiction may request and receive additional information as the representative deems necessary.

(2) The child shall not be placed until the receiving jurisdiction has determined that the placement is not contrary to the interest of the child and has so notified the sending jurisdiction in writing.

(e) [Placement of Delinquent Children in Institutional Care] A child declared a ward of the court under Welfare & Institutions Code section 602 may be placed in an institution in another jurisdiction under the Compact only when:

(1) Prior to the placement, the court has held a hearing at which the child and the parent or guardian have had an opportunity to be heard;

(2) The court has found that equivalent facilities for the child are not available in the sending jurisdiction; and

(3) Institutional care in the other jurisdiction is in the best interest of the child and will not produce undue hardship for the child.

(f) [Priority Placement] A court in a sending jurisdiction may designate placement as a priority placement and utilize expedited procedures as described in Regulation 7 of the Compact.

(1) The court may designate a priority placement upon express findings that:

(A) The Compact Administrator of the receiving jurisdiction has had possession of a properly completed interstate compact placement request form and supporting documents for over 30 business days, and the sending jurisdiction agency has not received a notice indicating whether or not placement in the receiving jurisdiction is contrary to the interest of the child; or

(B) The proposed placement recipient is a parent, stepparent, grandparent, adult sibling, adult uncle or aunt, or guardian of the child; and

(i) The child is under two years of age; or

(ii) The child is in an emergency shelter; or

(iii) The court finds that the child has spent a substantial period of time in the home of the proposed placement recipient.

(2) Upon the findings of the court under subdivision (f)(1) that a proposed priority placement is necessary, the court shall proceed as follows:

(A) The findings shall be noted in a written order using Judicial Council form ICPC Priority — Findings and Orders (JV-567), which shall include the name, address, telephone number, and fax number of the court and the judicial officer.

(B) The order shall be transmitted to the sending agency of the court's jurisdiction within two business days.

(C) The sending agency shall be ordered to transmit to the Compact Administrator of the sending jurisdiction within three business days the following:

(i) A copy of the completed Judicial Council form ICPC Priority—Findings and Orders (JV-567); and

(ii) A completed interstate compact placement request form and supporting documentation as noted on that form.

(D) Within two business days the Compact Administrator of the sending jurisdiction shall transmit by overnight mail the documents described in (C)(i) and (C)(ii) above to the Compact Administrator of the receiving jurisdiction with a notice that the request is entitled to priority placement.

(3) The Compact Administrator of the receiving jurisdiction shall determine immediately, and no later than 20 business days after receipt, whether or not the placement is acceptable and shall transmit the completed interstate compact placement request form by fax to the Compact Administrator of the sending jurisdiction.

(4) If the Compact Administrator of the receiving jurisdiction fails to comply with subdivision (f)(3) within the required time limit, the sending court may inform an appropriate court in the receiving jurisdiction that the Compact Administrator in that jurisdiction has not complied with the Compact, provide the receiving jurisdiction court with relevant documents, including Judicial Council form Findings and Request for Assistance Under ICPC (JV-565), and request assistance.

(5) The receiving jurisdiction court that receives notification may render appropriate assistance and may issue orders to secure compliance with the Compact and regulations.

(6) The time limits for a single case may be modified by written agreement between the sending court, the sending agency, and the Compact Administrators of the sending and receiving jurisdictions.

(7) To fulfill its obligations under the Compact, a jurisdiction, its local agencies, and the court are required to process interstate cases as quickly as intrastate cases and to devote equal efforts to interstate and intrastate hardship cases. If in doing so a receiving jurisdiction's Compact Administrator finds that extraordinary circumstances make compliance within the time requirements impossible, strict compliance may be excused. However, the receiving jurisdiction Compact Administrator shall immediately notify the sending jurisdiction Compact Administrator via fax of the inability to comply and shall designate a date on or before which there will be compliance. The notice shall contain a full identification and explanation of the extraordinary circumstances that are delaying compliance.

(g) [Ongoing Jurisdiction] If a child is placed in another jurisdiction under the terms of the Compact, the sending court shall not terminate its jurisdiction until the child is adopted, reaches majority, or is emancipated, or the dependency is terminated with the concurrence of the receiving state authority.

(Adopted, effective January 1, 1999.)

California Family Code

§7900. Adoption of Interstate Compact

The Interstate Compact on Placement of Children as set forth in Section 7901 is hereby adopted and entered into with all other jurisdictions joining therein.

(Stats. 1992 (A.B. 2650), ch. 162, §10, effective January 1, 1994.)

§7901. Provisions

The provisions of the interstate compact referred to in Section 7900 are as follows:

INTERSTATE COMPACT ON THE PLACEMENT OF CHILDREN

Article 1. Purpose and Policy

It is the purpose and policy of the party states to cooperate with each other in the interstate placement of children to the end that:

(a) Each child requiring placement shall receive the maximum opportunity to be placed in a suitable environment and with persons or institutions having appropriate qualifications and facilities to provide a necessary and desirable degree and type of care.

(b) The appropriate authorities in a state where a child is to be placed may have full opportunity to ascertain the circumstances of the proposed placement, thereby promoting full compliance with applicable requirements for the protection of the child.

(c) The proper authorities of the state from which the placement is made may obtain the most complete information on the basis on which to evaluate a projected placement before it is made.

(d) Appropriate jurisdictional arrangements for the care of children will be promoted.

Article 2. Definitions

As used in this compact:

(a) "Child" means a person who, by reason of minority, is legally subject to parental, guardianship, or similar control.

(b) "Sending agency" means a party state, or officer or employee thereof; subdivision of a party state, or officer or employee thereof; a court of a party state; a person, corporation, association, charitable agency, or other entity which sends, brings, or causes to be sent or brought any child to another party state.

(c) "Receiving state" means the state to which a child is sent, brought, or caused to be sent or brought, whether by public authorities or private persons or agencies, and whether for placement with state or local public authorities or for placement with private agencies or persons.

(d) "Placement" means the arrangement for the care of a child in a family free or boarding home or in a child-caring agency or institution but does not include any institution caring for the mentally ill, mentally defective or epileptic or any institution primarily educational in character, and any hospital or other medical facility.

Article 3. Conditions for Placement

(a) No sending agency shall send, bring, or cause to be sent or brought into any other party state any child for placement in foster care or as a preliminary to a possible adoption unless the sending agency shall comply with each and every requirement set forth in this article and with the applicable laws of the receiving state governing the placement of children therein.

(b) Before sending, bringing, or causing any child to be sent or brought into a receiving state for placement in foster care or as a preliminary to a possible adoption, the sending agency shall furnish the appropriate public authorities in the receiving state written notice of the intention to send, bring, or place the child in the receiving state. The notice shall contain:

(1) The name, date, and place of birth of the child.

(2) The identity and address or addresses of the parents or legal guardian.

(3) The name and address of the person, agency, or institution to or with which the sending agency proposes to send, bring, or place the child.

(4) A full statement of the reasons for the proposed action and evidence of the authority pursuant to which the placement is proposed to be made.

(c) Any public officer or agency in a receiving state which is in receipt of a notice pursuant to paragraph (b) of this article may request of the sending agency, or any other appropriate officer or agency of or in the sending agency's state, and shall be entitled to receive therefrom, supporting or additional information as it may deem necessary under the circumstances to carry out the purpose and policy of this compact.

(d) The child shall not be sent, brought, or caused to be sent or brought into the receiving state until the appropriate public authorities in the receiving state shall notify the sending agency, in writing, to the effect that the proposed placement does not appear to be contrary to the interests of the child.

Article 4. Penalty for Illegal Placement

The sending, bringing, or causing to be sent or brought into any receiving state of a child in violation of the terms of this compact shall constitute a violation of the laws respecting the placement of children of both the state in which the sending agency is located or from which it sends or brings the child and of the receiving state. A violation may be punished or subjected to penalty in either jurisdiction in accordance with its laws. In addition to liability for any punishment or penalty, any violation shall constitute full and sufficient grounds for the suspension or revocation of any license, permit, or other legal authorization held by the sending agency which empowers or allows it to place, or care for children.

Article 5. Continuing Jurisdiction

(a) The sending agency shall retain jurisdiction over the child sufficient to determine all matters in relation to the custody, supervision, care, treatment, and disposition of the child which it would have had if the child had remained in the sending agency's state, until the child is adopted, reaches majority, becomes self-supporting, or is discharged with the concurrence of the appropriate authority in the receiving state. That jurisdiction shall also include the power to effect or cause the return of the child or its transfer to another location and custody pursuant to law. The sending agency shall continue to have financial responsibility for support and maintenance of the child during the period of the placement. Nothing contained herein shall defeat a claim of jurisdiction by a receiving state sufficient to deal with an act of delinquency or crime committed therein.

(b) When the sending agency is a public agency, it may enter into an agreement with an authorized public or private agency in the receiving state providing for the performance of one or more services in respect of that case by the latter as agent for the sending agency.

(c) Nothing in this compact shall be construed to prevent a private charitable agency authorized to place children in the receiving state from performing services or acting as agent in that state for a private charitable agency of the sending state; nor to prevent the agency in the receiving state from discharging financial responsibility for the support and maintenance of a child who has been placed on behalf of the sending agency without relieving the responsibility set forth in paragraph (a) of this article.

Article 6. Institutional Care of Delinquent Children

A child adjudicated delinquent may be placed in an institution in another party jurisdiction pursuant to this compact but no such placement shall be made unless the child is given a court hearing on notice to the parent or guardian with opportunity to be heard, before being sent to the other party jurisdiction for institutional care and the court finds that both of the following exist:

(a) Equivalent facilities for the child are not available in the sending agency's jurisdiction.

(b) Institutional care in the other jurisdiction is in the best interest of the child and will not produce undue hardship.

Article 7. Compact Administrator

The executive head of each jurisdiction party to this compact shall designate an officer who shall be general coordinator of activities under this compact in his or her jurisdiction and who, acting jointly with like officers of other party jurisdictions, shall have power to promulgate rules and regulations to carry out more effectively the terms and provisions of this compact.

Article 8. Limitations

This compact shall not apply to:

(a) The sending or bringing of a child into a receiving state by his or her parent, stepparent, grandparent, adult brother or sister, adult uncle or aunt, or his or her guardian and leaving the child with any such relative or nonagency guardian in the receiving state.

(b) Any placement, sending or bringing of a child into a receiving state pursuant to any other interstate compact to which both the state from which the child is sent or brought and the receiving state are party, or to any other agreement between said states which has the force of law.

Article 9. Enactment and Withdrawal

This compact shall be open to joinder by any state, territory, or possession of the United States, the District of Columbia, the Commonwealth of Puerto Rico, and, with the consent of Congress, the government of Canada or any province thereof. It shall become effective with respect to any of these jurisdictions when that jurisdiction has enacted the same into law. Withdrawal from this compact shall be by the enactment of a statute repealing the same, but shall not take effect until two years after the effective date of the statute and until written notice of the withdrawal has been given by the withdrawing state to the Governor of each other party jurisdiction. Withdrawal of a party state shall not affect the rights, duties, and obligations under this compact of any sending agency therein with respect to a placement made before the effective date of withdrawal.

Article 10. Construction and Severability

The provisions of this compact shall be liberally construed to effectuate the purposes thereof. The provisions of this compact shall be severable and if any phrase, clause, sentence, or provision of this compact is declared to be contrary to the constitution of any party state or of the United States or the applicability thereof to any government, agency, person, or circumstance is held invalid, the validity of the remainder of this compact and the applicability thereof to any government, agency, person, or circumstance shall not be affected thereby. If this compact shall be held contrary to the constitution of any state party thereto, the compact shall remain in full force and effect as to the remaining states and in full force and effect as to the state affected as to all severable matters.

(Stats. 1992 (A.B. 2650), ch. 162, §10, effective January 1, 1994. Amended by Stats. 2002 (S.B. 1512), ch. 260, §6.)

§7902. Determination of financial responsibility for child placed pursuant to compact

Financial responsibility for a child placed pursuant to the Interstate Compact on the Placement of Children shall be determined in accordance with Article 5 of the compact in the first instance. However, in the event of partial or complete default of performance thereunder, the provisions of other state laws also may be invoked.

(Stats. 1992 (A.B. 2650), ch. 162, §10, effective January 1, 1994.)

§7903. "Appropriate public authorities"

The phrase "appropriate public authorities" as used in Article 3 of the Interstate Compact on the Placement of Children means, with reference to this state, the State Department of Social Services, and that department shall receive and act with reference to notices required by Article 3 of the compact.

(Stats. 1992 (A.B. 2650), ch. 162, §10, effective January 1, 1994.)

§7904. "Appropriate authority in receiving state"

The phrase "appropriate authority in receiving state" as used in paragraph (a) of Article 5 of the Interstate Compact on the Placement of Children, with reference to this state, means the State Department of Social Services.

(Stats. 1992 (A.B. 2650), ch. 162, §10, effective January 1, 1994.)

§7905. State officers and agencies have authority to enter into agreements with party states

The officers and agencies of this state and its subdivisions having authority to place children are hereby empowered to enter into agreements with appropriate officers or agencies of or in other party states pursuant to paragraph (b) of Article 5 of the Interstate Compact on the Placement of Children. Any such agreement which contains a financial commitment or imposes a financial obligation on this state or subdivision or agency thereof is not binding unless it has the approval in writing of the Controller in the case of the state and of the chief local fiscal officer in the case of a subdivision of the state.

(Stats. 1992 (A.B. 2650), ch. 162, §10, effective January 1, 1994.)

§7906. Requirements for visitation, inspection or supervision of children in another state

Any requirements for visitation, inspection, or supervision of children, homes, institutions, or other agencies in another party state which may apply under the law of this state shall be deemed to be met if performed pursuant to an agreement entered into by appropriate officers or agencies of this state or a subdivision thereof as contemplated by paragraph (b) of Article 5 of the Interstate Compact on the Placement of Children.

(Stats. 1992 (A.B. 2650), ch. 162, §10, effective January 1, 1994.)

§7907. Inapplicability of laws restricting out-of-state placements

No provision of law restricting out-of-state placement of children for adoption shall apply to placements made pursuant to the Interstate Compact on the Placement of Children.

(Stats. 1992 (A.B. 2650), ch. 162, §10, effective January 1, 1994.)

§7908. Court may place delinquent child in institution in another state

A court having jurisdiction to place delinquent children may place a delinquent child in an institution in another state pursuant to Article 6 of the Interstate Compact on the Placement of Children and shall retain jurisdiction as provided in Article 5 of the compact.

(Stats. 1992 (A.B. 2650), ch. 162, §10, effective January 1, 1994.)

§7909. "Executive head"

"Executive head" as used in Article 7 of the Interstate Compact on the Placement of Children means the Governor. The Governor shall appoint a compact administrator in accordance with the terms of Article 7 of the compact.

(Stats. 1992 (A.B. 2650), ch. 162, §10, effective January 1, 1994.)

§7910. Approval of interstate placement shall not be granted in violation of state law

Approval of an interstate placement of a child for adoption shall not be granted by the compact administrator if the placement is in violation of either Section 8801 of this code or Section 273 of the Penal Code.

(Stats. 1992 (A.B. 2650), ch. 162, §10, effective January 1, 1994.)

§7911. Legislative declaration

The Legislature finds and declares all of the following:

(a) The health and safety of California children placed by a county social services agency or probation department out of state pursuant to the provisions of the Interstate Compact on the Placement of Children are a matter of statewide concern.

(b) The Legislature therefore affirms its intention that the State Department of Social Services has full authority to require an assessment and placement recommendation by a county multidisciplinary team prior to placement of a child in an out-of-state group home, to investigate allegations of child abuse or neglect of minors so placed, and to ensure that out-of-state group homes, accepting California children, meet all California group home licensing standards.

(c) This section is declaratory of existing law with respect to the Governor's designation of the State Department of Social Services to act as the compact administrator and of that department to act as the single state agency charged with supervision of public social services under Section 10600 of the Welfare and Institutions Code.

(Stats. 1998 (S.B. 933), ch. 311, §9, effective August 19, 1998. Amended by Stats. 1999 (A.B. 1659), ch. 881, §1, effective October 10, 1999.)

§7911.1. State department shall investigate out-of-state placements

(a) Notwithstanding any other provision of law, the State Department of Social Services or its designee shall investigate any threat to the health and safety of children placed by a California county social services agency or probation department in an out-of-state group home pursuant to the provisions of the Interstate Compact on the Placement of Children. This authority shall include the authority to interview children or staff in private or review their file at the out-of-state facility or wherever the child or files may be at the time of the investigation. Notwithstanding any other provisions of law, the State Department of Social Services or its designee shall require certified out-of- state group homes to comply with the reporting requirements applicable to group homes licensed in California pursuant to Title 22 of the California Code of Regulations for each child in care regardless of whether he or she is a California placement, by submitting a copy of the required reports to the Compact Administrator within regulatory timeframes. The Compact Administrator within one business day of receiving a serious events report shall verbally notify the appropriate placement agencies and within five working days of receiving a written report from the out-of-state group home, forward a copy of the written report to the appropriate placement agencies.

(b) Any contract, memorandum of understanding, or agreement entered into pursuant to paragraph (b) of Article 5 of the Interstate Compact on the Placement of Children regarding the placement of a child out of state by a California county social services agency or probation department shall include the language set forth in subdivision (a).

(c) The State Department of Social Services or its designee shall perform initial and continuing inspection of out-of-state group homes in order to either certify that the out-of-state group home meets all licensure standards required of group homes operated in California or that the department has granted a waiver to a specific licensing standard upon a finding that there exists no adverse impact to health and safety. Any failure by an out-of-state group home facility to make children or staff available as required by subdivision (a) for a private interview or make files available for review shall be grounds to deny or discontinue the certification. The State Department of Social Services shall grant or deny an initial certification or a waiver under this subdivision to an out-of-state group home facility that has more than six California children placed by a county social services agency or probation department by August 19, 1999. The department shall grant or deny an initial certification or a waiver under this subdivision to an out-of-state group home facility that has six or fewer California children placed by a county social services agency or probation department by February 19, 2000. Certifications made pursuant to this subdivision shall be reviewed annually.

(d) Within six months of the effective date of this section, a county shall be required to obtain an assessment and placement recommendation by a county multidisciplinary team for each child in an out-of-state group home facility. On or after March 1, 1999, a county shall be required to obtain an assessment and placement recommendation by a county multidisciplinary team prior to placement of a child in an out-of-state group home facility.

(e) Any failure by an out-of-state group home to obtain or maintain its certification as required by subdivision (c) shall preclude the use of any public funds, whether county, state, or federal, in the payment for the placement of any child in that out-of-state group home, pursuant to the Interstate Compact on the Placement of Children.

(f)(1) A multidisciplinary team shall consist of participating members from county social services, county mental health, county probation, county superintendents of schools, and other members as determined by the county.

(2) Participants shall have knowledge or experience in the prevention, identification, and treatment of child abuse and neglect cases, and shall be qualified to recommend a broad range of services related to child abuse or neglect.

(g)(1) The department may deny, suspend, or discontinue the certification of the out-of-state group home if the department makes a finding that the group home is not operating in compliance with the requirements of subdivision (c).

(2) Any judicial proceeding to contest the department's determination as to the status of the out-of-state group home certificate shall be held in California pursuant to Section 1085 of the Code of Civil Procedure.

(h) This section shall not impact placements made pursuant to Chapter 26.5 (commencing with Section 7570) of Division 7 of Title 1 of the Government Code relating to seriously emotionally disturbed children.

(i) Only an out-of-state group home authorized by the Compact Administrator to receive state funds for the placement by a county social services agency or probation department of any child in that out-of-state group home from the effective date of this section shall be eligible for public funds pending the department's certification under this section.

(Stats. 1998 (S.B. 933), ch. 311, §10, effective August 19, 1998. Amended by Stats. 1999 (A.B. 1659), ch. 881, §2, effective October 10, 1999.)

§7912. Rights of children in out-of-state placements

(a) The Legislature finds and declares that the health and safety of children in out-of-state group home care pursuant to the Interstate Compact on the Placement of Children is a matter of statewide concern. The Legislature therefore affirms its intention that children placed by a county social services agency or probation department in out-of-state group homes be accorded the same personal rights and safeguards of a child placed in a California group home. This section is in clarification of existing law.

(b) The Compact Administrator may temporarily suspend any new placements in an out-of-state group home, for a period not to exceed 100 days, pending the completion of an investigation, pursuant to subdivision (a) of Section 7911.1, regarding a threat to the health and safety of children in care. During any suspension period the department or its designee shall have staff daily onsite at the out-of-state group home.

(Stats. 1998 (S.B. 933), ch. 311, §11, effective August 19, 1998.)

I. INTERNATIONAL ADOPTIONS

A shortage of babies, as well as agency restrictions on adoptions, has led many people to seek children from abroad. International adoptions account for almost 20 percent of all nonrelative domestic adoptions. National Council for Adoption, Adoption Factbook III 27 (1999) (based on 1996 figures).

Several bodies of law apply to international adoptions: federal immigration laws, state adoption standards, and the foreign country's relinquishment requirements. Sometimes a child must be adopted in the country of origin in order to travel to the United States and then again in the jurisdiction where the adoptive parents live because decrees from foreign countries are not entitled to full faith and credit.

In 2000, the United States ratified and enacted implementing legislation for the Hague Convention on Protection of Children and Cooperation in Respect of Intercountry Adoption. The Intercountry Adoption Act, 42 U.S.C. §§14901-14954 (2004). This Convention (32 I.L.M. 1134 (1993), which applies when both countries are signatories, is designed to regularize international adoptions by requiring a finding that the child is adoptable and a determination that the adoption would serve the child's best interests. Also, federal legislation now provides that, when certain statutory conditions are met, children adopted from abroad by U.S. citizens automatically become U.S. citizens. 8 U.S.C. §1431(b) (2004).

See generally Cynthia Ellen Szejner, Note, Intercountry Adoptions: Are the Biological Parents' Rights Protected, 5 Wash. U. Global Stud. L. Rev. 211 (2006).

California Family Code

§8900. Private adoption agencies shall be exclusive provider of intercountry adoption services

Intercountry adoption services described in this chapter shall be exclusively provided by private adoption agencies licensed by the department specifically to provide these services.

(Stats. 1992 (A.B. 2650), ch. 162, §10, effective January 1, 1994.)

§8901. Department shall adopt regulations

The department shall adopt regulations to administer the intercountry adoption program.

(Stats. 1992 (A.B. 2650), ch. 162, §10, effective January 1, 1994.)

§8902. Agency services for intercountry adoptions

For intercountry adoptions that will be finalized in this state, the licensed adoption agency shall provide all of the following services:

(a) Assessment of the suitability of the applicant's home.

(b) Placement of the foreign-born child in an approved home.

(c) Postplacement supervision.

(d) Submission to the court of a report on the intercountry adoptive placement with a recommendation regarding the granting of the petition.

(e) Services to applicants seeking to adopt related children living in foreign countries. The Legislature recognizes that these children have an impelling need for adoptive placement with their relatives.

(Stats. 1992 (A.B. 2650), ch. 162, §10, effective January 1, 1994.)

§8903. Agency shall assume care, custody, and control of child in intercountry adoptions

(a) For each intercountry adoption finalized in this state, the licensed adoption agency shall assume all responsibilities for the child including care, custody, and control as if the child had been relinquished for adoption in this state from the time the child left the child's native country.

(b) Notwithstanding subdivision (a), if the child's native country requires and has given full guardianship to the prospective adoptive parents, the prospective adoptive parents shall assume all responsibilities for the child including care, custody, control, and financial support.

(c) If the licensed adoption agency or prospective adoptive parents fail to meet the responsibilities under subdivision (a) or (b) and the child becomes a dependent of the court pursuant to Section 300 of the Welfare and Institutions Code, the state shall assume responsibility for the cost of care for the child. When the child becomes a dependent of the court and if, for any reason, is ineligible for AFDC under Section 14005.1 of the Welfare and Institutions Code and loses Medi-Cal eligibility, the child shall be deemed eligible for Medi-Cal under Section 14005.4 of the Welfare and Institutions Code and the State Director of Health Services has authority to provide payment for the medical services to the child that are necessary to meet the child's needs.

(Stats. 1992 (A.B. 2650), ch. 162, §10, effective January 1, 1994.)

§8904. Agency shall provide certain services for intercountry adoptions that will be finalized elsewhere

For an intercountry adoption that will be finalized in a foreign country, the licensed adoption agency shall provide all of the following services:

(a) Assessment of the suitability of the applicant's home.

(b) Certification to the Immigration and Naturalization Service that this state's intercountry adoption requirements have been met.

(c) Readoption services as required by the Immigration and Naturalization Service.

(Stats. 1992 (A.B. 2650), ch. 162, §10, effective January 1, 1994. Amended Stats. 1993 (A.B. 1500), ch. 219, §202.)

§8905. Licensed agencies may work only with certain domestic and foreign adoption agencies

Licensed adoption agencies may work only with domestic and foreign adoption agencies with whom they have written agreements that specify the responsibilities of each. The agreements may not violate any statute or regulation of the United States or of this state.

(Stats. 1992 (A.B. 2650), ch. 162, §10, effective January 1, 1994.)

§8906. License agency may enter into agreement to share or transfer financial responsibility

Nothing in this chapter may be construed to prohibit the licensed adoption agency from entering into an agreement with the prospective adoptive parents to share or transfer financial responsibility for the child.

(Stats. 1992 (A.B. 2650), ch. 162, §10, effective January 1, 1994.)

§8907. Agency may charge fees to cover costs

The costs incurred by a licensed adoption agency pursuant to programs established by this chapter shall be funded by fees charged by the agency for services required by this chapter. The agency's fee schedule is required to be approved by the department initially and whenever it is altered.

(Stats. 1992 (A.B. 2650), ch. 162, §10, effective January 1, 1994.)

§8908. Agency shall conduct criminal Investigation of prospective adoptive parents

(a) A licensed adoption agency shall require each person filing an application for adoption to be fingerprinted and shall secure from an appropriate law enforcement agency any criminal record of that person to determine whether the person has ever been convicted of a crime other than a minor traffic violation. The licensed adoption agency may also secure the person's full criminal record, if any.

(b) The criminal record, if any, shall be taken into consideration when evaluating the prospective adoptive parent, and an assessment of the effects of any criminal history on the ability of the prospective adoptive parent to provide adequate and proper care and guidance to the child shall be included in the report to the court.

(c) Any fee charged by a law enforcement agency for fingerprinting or for checking or obtaining the criminal record of the applicant shall be paid by the applicant. The licensed adoption agency may defer, waive, or reduce the fee when its payment would cause economic hardship to the prospective adoptive parents detrimental to the welfare of the adopted child.

(Stats. 1992 (A.B. 2650), ch. 162, §10, effective January 1, 1994.)

§8909. Agency must submit medical report to prospective adoptive parents

(a) An agency may not place a child for adoption unless a written report on the child's medical background and, if available, the medical background of the child's biological parents so far as ascertainable, has been submitted to the prospective adoptive parents and they have acknowledged in writing the receipt of the report.

(b) The report on the child's background shall contain all known diagnostic information, including current medical reports on the child, psychological evaluations, and scholastic information, as well as all known information regarding the child's developmental history and family life.

(c)(1) The biological parents may provide a blood sample at a clinic or hospital approved by the State Department of Health Services. The biological parents' failure to provide a blood sample shall not affect the adoption of the child.

(2) The blood sample shall be stored at a laboratory under contract with the State Department of Health Services for a period of 30 years following the adoption of the child.

(3) The purpose of the stored sample of blood is to provide a blood sample from which DNA testing can be done at a later date after entry of the order of adoption at the request of the adoptive parents or the adopted child. The cost of drawing and storing the blood samples shall be paid for by a separate fee in addition to any fee required under Section 8907. The amount of this additional fee shall be based on the cost of drawing and storing the blood samples but at no time shall the additional fee be more than one hundred dollars ($100).

(d)(1) The blood sample shall be stored and released in such a manner as to not identify any party to the adoption.

(2) Any results of the DNA testing shall be stored and released in such a manner as to not identify any party to the adoption.

(Stats. 1992 (A.B. 2650), ch. 162, §10, effective January 1, 1994. Amended Stats. 1996 (A.B. 3241), ch. 1053, §3.)

§8910. Child may not be concealed or removed from county

(a) In no event may a child who has been placed for adoption be removed from the county in which the child was placed, by any person who has not petitioned to adopt the child, without first obtaining the written consent of the licensed adoption agency responsible for the child.

(b) During the pendency of an adoption proceeding:

(1) The child proposed to be adopted may not be concealed within the county in which the adoption proceeding is pending.

(2) The child may not be removed from the county in which the adoption proceeding is pending unless the petitioners or other interested persons first obtain permission for the removal from the court, after giving advance written notice of intent to obtain the court's permission to the licensed adoption agency responsible for the child. Upon proof of giving notice, permission may be granted by the court if, within a period of 15 days after the date of giving notice, no objections are filed with the court by the licensed adoption agency responsible for the child. If the licensed adoption agency files objections within the 15-day period, upon the request of the petitioners the court shall immediately set the matter for hearing and give to the objector, the petitioners, and the party or parties requesting permission for the removal reasonable notice of the

hearing by certified mail, return receipt requested, to the address of each as shown in the records of the adoption proceeding. Upon a finding that the objections are without good cause, the court may grant the requested permission for removal of the child, subject to any limitations that appear to be in the child's best interest.

(c) This section does not apply in any of the following situations:

(1) Where the child is absent for a period of not more than 30 days from the county in which the adoption proceeding is pending, unless a notice of recommendation of denial of petition has been personally served on the petitioners or the court has issued an order prohibiting the removal of the child from the county pending consideration of any of the following:

(A) The suitability of the petitioners.

(B) The care provided the child.

(C) The availability of the legally required agency consents to the adoption.

(2) Where the child has been returned to and remains in the custody and control of the child's birth parent or parents.

(3) Where written consent for the removal of the child is obtained from the licensed adoption agency responsible for the child.

(d) A violation of this section is a violation of Section 280 of the Penal Code.

(e) Neither this section nor Section 280 of the Penal Code may be construed to render lawful any act that is unlawful under any other applicable law.

(Stats. 1992 (A.B. 2650), ch. 162, §10, effective January 1, 1994.)

§8911. Prospective adoptive parents shall file petition within 30 days of placement

As a condition of placement, the prospective adoptive parents shall file a petition to adopt the child under Section 8912 within 30 days of placement.

(Stats. 1992 (A.B. 2650), ch. 162, §10, effective January 1, 1994.)

§8912. Contents of adoption petition

(a) A person desiring to adopt a child may for that purpose file a petition in the county in which the petitioner resides. The court clerk shall immediately notify the department at Sacramento in writing of the pendency of the proceeding and of any subsequent action taken.

(b) The caption of the adoption petition shall contain the names of the petitioners, but not the child's name. The petition shall state the child's sex and date of birth. The name the child had before adoption shall appear in the joinder signed by the licensed adoption agency.

(c) If the child is the subject of a guardianship petition, the adoption petition shall so state and shall include the caption and docket number or have attached a copy of the letters of the guardianship or temporary guardianship. The petitioners shall notify the court of any petition for guardianship or temporary guardianship filed after the adoption petition. The guardianship proceeding shall be consolidated with the adoption proceeding.

(d) The order of adoption shall contain the child's adopted name, but not the name the child had before adoption.

(e) If the petitioner has entered into a postadoption contact agreement with the birth parent as set forth in Section 8616.5, the agreement, signed by the participating parties, shall be attached to and filed with the petition for adoption.

(Stats. 1992 (A.B. 2650), ch. 162, §10, effective January 1, 1994. Amended by Stats. 2004 (S.B. 1357), ch. 858, §6.)

§8913. Prospective adoptive parents and child shall appear

The prospective adoptive parents and the child proposed to be adopted shall appear before the court pursuant to Sections 8612 and 8613.

(Stats. 1992 (A.B. 2650), ch. 162, §10, effective January 1, 1994.)

§8914. Agency shall submit full report

If the licensed adoption agency is a party to or joins in the adoption petition, it shall submit a full report of the facts of the case to the court. The department may also submit a report.

(Stats. 1992 (A.B. 2650), ch. 162, §10, effective January 1, 1994.)

§8915. Copy of report or findings must go to petitioner or petitioner's attorney

When any report or findings are submitted to the court by a licensed adoption agency, a copy of the report or findings, whether favorable or unfavorable, shall be given to the petitioner's attorney in the proceeding, if the petitioner has an attorney of record, or to the petitioner.

(Stats. 1992 (A.B. 2650), ch. 162, §10, effective January 1, 1994.)

§8916. Clerk shall notify department of motion to withdraw or dismiss

(a) If the petitioners move to withdraw the adoption petition or to dismiss the proceeding, the court clerk shall immediately notify the department at Sacramento of the action. The licensed adoption agency shall file a full report with the court recommending a suitable plan for the child in every case where the petitioners desire to withdraw the adoption petition or where the licensed adoption agency recommends that the adoption petition be denied and shall appear before the court for the purpose of representing the child.

(b) Notwithstanding the petitioners' withdrawal or dismissal, the court may retain jurisdiction over the child for the purpose of making any order for the child's custody that the court deems to be in the child's best interest.

(Stats. 1992 (A.B. 2650), ch. 162, §10, effective January 1, 1994.)

§8917. Clerk shall refer unfavorable recommendation to court for review

(a) If the licensed adoption agency finds that the home of the petitioners is not suitable for the child or that the required agency consents are not available and the agency recommends that the petition be denied, or if the petitioners desire to withdraw the petition and the agency recommends that the petition be denied, the clerk upon receipt of the report of the licensed adoption agency shall immediately refer it to the court for review.

(b) Upon receipt of the report, the court shall set a date for a hearing of the petition and shall give reasonable notice of the hearing to the licensed adoption agency and the petitioners by certified mail, return receipt requested, to the address of each as shown in the proceeding.

(c) The licensed adoption agency shall appear to represent the child.

(Stats. 1992 (A.B. 2650), ch. 162, §10, effective January 1, 1994.)

§8918. Court shall transfer child to care of agency if unfavorable recommendation is sustained

At the hearing, if the court sustains the recommendation that the child be removed from the home of the petitioners because the licensed adoption agency has recommended denial or the petitioners desire to withdraw the petition or the court dismisses the petition and does not return the child to the child's parents, the court shall commit the child to the care of the licensed adoption agency for the agency to arrange adoptive placement or to make a suitable plan.

(Stats. 1992 (A.B. 2650), ch. 162, §10, effective January 1, 1994.)

§8919. Readoption of children adopted through intercountry adoption; obtaining birth certificate

(a) Each state resident who adopts a child through an intercountry adoption that is finalized in a foreign country shall readopt the child in this state if it is required by the Immigration and Naturalization Service. The readoption shall include, but is not limited to, at least one postplacement in-home visit, the filing of the adoption petition pursuant to Section 8912, the intercountry adoption court report, accounting reports, and the final adoption order. No readoption order shall be granted unless the court receives a report from an adoption agency authorized to provide intercountry adoption services pursuant to Section 8900.

(b) Each state resident who adopts a child through an intercountry adoption that is finalized in a foreign country may readopt the child in this state. The readoption shall meet the standards described in subdivision (a).

(c) In addition to the requirement or option of the readoption process set forth in this section, each state resident who adopts a child through an intercountry adoption which is finalized in a foreign country may obtain a birth certificate in the State of California in accordance with the provisions of Section 103450 of the Health and Safety Code.

(Stats. 1993 (A.B. 1500), ch. 219, §203. Amended Stats. 2001 (A.B. 538), ch. 353, §2.)

J. ADULT ADOPTION

Many states, although not all, permit adult adoption. If permitted, adult adoption creates a legally recognized family relationship that facilitates: (1) establishment of inheritance rights, (2) access to information limited to family members (such as for purposes of medical decisionmaking), (3) evasion of housing and zoning restrictions, (4) access to insurance and unemployment benefits, and (5) immigration into the United States. Peter N. Fowler, Comment, Adult Adoption: A "New" Legal Tool for Lesbians and Gay Men, 14 Golden Gate U. L. Rev. 667, 679-688 (1984).

Adult adoption is regulated by California Family Code §§9300 et seq. In an adult adoption, both parties (the adoptee and adopter) must execute a written adoption agreement, and the court must approve that agreement (Cal. Fam. Code §9320(a), (b)). No agency investigation or report is necessary (Cal. Fam. Code §9325). According to California law, an adult may only adopt another adult if the adoptee is younger (Cal. Fam. Code §9320(a)), although no particular age difference is required. Further, the adoption statutes limit the number of unrelated adults that one may adopt, i.e., a person may not adopt more than one adult within 1 year of the adoption of another adult (unless the proposed adoptee is a sibling of a person previously adopted or is disabled) (Cal. Fam. Code §9303(a)).

An adult adoption requires spousal consent. That is, both the spouse of the adoptee (Cal. Fam. Code §9301(a)) and of the adopter (Cal. Fam. Code §9301) must consent to the adoption. However, consent of the parents of the prospective adoptee is not required (Cal. Fam. Code §9302(b)). Note that, in California, an adult may not adopt his or her spouse (Cal. Fam. Code §9320(a)).

Adult adoption has been often used by same sex-couples. Fowler, *supra.* In California, prior to the enactment of domestic partnership legislation, approximately 200 to 300 adult adoptions occurred each year, of which 30 to 40 percent involved lesbians or gay men. *Id.* at 702. See also Mandi Rae Urban, The History of Adult Adoption in California, 11 J. Contemp. Legal Issues 612 (2000).

California Family Code

§9300. Adult may adopt another adult

(a) An adult may be adopted by another adult, including a stepparent, as provided in this part.

(b) A married minor may be adopted in the same manner as an adult under this part.

(Stats. 1992 (A.B. 2650), ch. 162, §10, effective January 1, 1994. Amended Stats. 1993 (S.B. 970), ch. 266, §1.)

§9301. Married person must secure consent of his or her spouse to adopt

A married person who is not lawfully separated from the person's spouse may not adopt an adult without the consent of

the spouse, provided that the spouse is capable of giving that consent.
(Stats. 1992 (A.B. 2650), ch. 162, §10, effective January 1, 1994.)

§9302. Adoptee must secure consent of his or her spouse

(a) A married person who is not lawfully separated from the person's spouse may not be adopted without the consent of the spouse, provided that the spouse is capable of giving that consent.

(b) The consent of the parents of the proposed adoptee, of the department, or of any other person is not required.
(Stats. 1992 (A.B. 2650), ch. 162, §10, effective January 1, 1994.)

§9303. Limitation on number of adoptions annually by one person

(a) A person may not adopt more than one unrelated adult under this part within one year of the person's adoption of an unrelated adult, unless the proposed adoptee is the biological sibling of a person previously adopted pursuant to this part or unless the proposed adoptee is disabled or physically handicapped.

(b) A person may not adopt an unrelated adult under this part within one year of an adoption of another person under this part by the prospective adoptive parent's spouse, unless the proposed adoptee is a biological sibling of a person previously adopted pursuant to this part.
(Stats. 1992 (A.B. 2650), ch. 162, §10, effective January 1, 1994.)

§9304. Adoptee may take surname of adoptive parent

A person adopted pursuant to this part may take the family name of the adoptive parent.
(Stats. 1992 (A.B. 2650), ch. 162, §10, effective January 1, 1994.)

§9305. Parent-child relationship between adoptee and adoptive parents

After adoption, the adoptee and the adoptive parent or parents shall sustain towards each other the legal relationship of parent and child and have all the rights and are subject to all the duties of that relationship.
(Stats. 1992 (A.B. 2650), ch. 162, §10, effective January 1, 1994.)

§9306. Birth parents are relieved from parental duties

(a) Except as provided in subdivision (b), the birth parents of a person adopted pursuant to this part are, from the time of the adoption, relieved of all parental duties towards, and all responsibility for, the adopted person, and have no right over the adopted person.

(b) Where an adult is adopted by the spouse of a birth parent, the parental rights and responsibilities of that birth parent are not affected by the adoption.
(Stats. 1992 (A.B. 2650), ch. 162, §10, effective January 1, 1994. Amended Stats. 1993 (S.B. 970), ch. 266, §2.)

§9307. Court has discretion regarding public nature of hearing

A hearing with regard to adoption under Chapter 2 (commencing with Section 9320) or termination of a parent and child relationship under Chapter 3 (commencing with Section 9340) may, in the discretion of the court, be open and public.
(Stats. 1992 (A.B. 2650), ch. 162, §10, effective January 1, 1994.)

§9320. Contents of agreement to adopt adult

(a) An adult may adopt another adult who is younger, except the spouse of the prospective adoptive parent, by an adoption agreement approved by the court, as provided in this chapter.

(b) The adoption agreement shall be in writing, executed by the prospective adoptive parent and the proposed adoptee, and shall state that the parties agree to assume toward each other the legal relationship of parent and child and to have all of the rights and be subject to all of the duties and responsibilities of that relationship.
(Stats. 1992 (A.B. 2650), ch. 162, §10, effective January 1, 1994.)

§9321. Contents of petition for approval of adoption

(a) The prospective adoptive parent and the proposed adoptee may file in the county in which either person resides a petition for approval of the adoption agreement.

(b) The petition for approval of the adoption agreement shall state all of the following:

(1) The length and nature of the relationship between the prospective adoptive parent and the proposed adoptee.

(2) The degree of kinship, if any.

(3) The reason the adoption is sought.

(4) A statement as to why the adoption would be in the best interest of the prospective adoptive parent, the proposed adoptee, and the public.

(5) The names and addresses of any living birth parents or adult children of the proposed adoptee.

(6) Whether the prospective adoptive parent or the prospective adoptive parent's spouse has previously adopted any other adult and, if so, the name of the adult, together with the date and place of the adoption.

(Stats. 1992 (A.B. 2650), ch. 162, §10, effective January 1, 1994.)

§9322. County clerk shall set matter for hearing

When the petition for approval of the adoption agreement is filed, the court clerk shall set the matter for hearing.
(Stats. 1992 (A.B. 2650), ch. 162, §10, effective January 1, 1994.)

§9323. Court may require notice to and appearance by interested persons

The court may require notice of the time and place of the hearing to be served on any other interested person and any interested person may appear and object to the proposed adoption.

(Stats. 1992 (A.B. 2650), ch. 162, §10, effective January 1, 1994.)

§9324. Both adoptive parent and adoptee shall appear

Both the prospective adoptive parent and the proposed adoptee shall appear at the hearing in person, unless an appearance is impossible, in which event an appearance may be made for either or both of the persons by counsel, empowered in writing to make the appearance.

(Stats. 1992 (A.B. 2650), ch. 162, §10, effective January 1, 1994.)

§9325. Neither investigation nor report is required for adult adoption

No investigation or report to the court by any public officer or agency is required, but the court may require the county probation officer or the department to investigate the circumstances of the proposed adoption and report thereon with recommendations, to the court before the hearing.

(Stats. 1992 (A.B. 2650), ch. 162, §10, effective January 1, 1994.)

§9326. Notice of hearing for adoption of developmentally disabled adult

The prospective adoptive parent shall mail or personally serve notice of the hearing and a copy of the petition to the director of the regional center for the developmentally disabled, established pursuant to Chapter 5 (commencing with Section 4620) of Division 4.5 of the Welfare and Institutions Code, and to any living birth parents or adult children of the proposed adoptee, at least 30 days before the day of the hearing on an adoption petition in any case in which both of the following conditions exist:

(a) The proposed adoptee is an adult with developmental disabilities.

(b) The prospective adoptive parent is a provider of board and care, treatment, habilitation, or other services to persons with developmental disabilities or is a spouse or employee of a provider.

(Stats. 1992 (A.B. 2650), ch. 162, §10, effective January 1, 1994.)

§9327. Report concerning proposed adoptee with developmental disability

If the prospective adoptive parent is a provider of board and care, treatment, habilitation, or other services to persons with developmental disabilities, or is a spouse or employee of a provider, and seeks to adopt an unrelated adult with developmental disabilities, the regional center for the developmentally disabled notified pursuant to Section 9326 shall file a written report with the court regarding the suitability of the proposed adoption in meeting the needs of the proposed adoptee and regarding any known previous adoption by the prospective adoptive parent.

(Stats. 1992 (A.B. 2650), ch. 162, §10, effective January 1, 1994.)

§9328. Hearing and order

(a) At the hearing the court shall examine the parties, or the counsel of any party not present in person.

(b) If the court is satisfied that the adoption will be in the best interests of the persons seeking the adoption and in the public interest and that there is no reason why the petition should not be granted, the court shall approve the adoption agreement and make an order of adoption declaring that the person adopted is the child of the adoptive parent. Otherwise, the court shall withhold approval of the agreement and deny the petition.

(c) In determining whether or not the adoption of any person pursuant to this part is in the best interests of the persons seeking the adoption or the public interest, the court may consider evidence, oral or written, whether or not it is in conformity with the Evidence Code.

(Stats. 1992 (A.B. 2650), ch. 162, §10, effective January 1, 1994.)

§9340. Adoptee may file petition to terminate parent-child relationship

(a) Any person who has been adopted under this part may, upon written notice to the adoptive parent, file a petition to terminate the relationship of parent and child. The petition shall state the name and address of the petitioner, the name and address of the adoptive parent, the date and place of the adoption, and the circumstances upon which the petition is based.

(b) If the adoptive parent consents in writing to the termination, an order terminating the relationship of parent and child may be issued by the court without further notice.

(c) If the adoptive parent does not consent in writing to the termination, a written response shall be filed within 30 days of the date of mailing of the notice, and the matter shall be set for hearing. The court may require an investigation by the county probation officer or the department.

(Stats. 1992 (A.B. 2650), ch. 162, §10, effective January 1, 1994.)

K. ADOPTEE'S RIGHT TO KNOW ORIGINS

Secrecy traditionally shrouded the adoption process to avoid the stigma associated with illegitimate births, eliminate the fear that birth parents would intrude in adoptive families, and to facilitate the child's adjustment (in the belief that adoptive families should imitate biological families). Statutes provide for the issuance of a new birth certificate when a child is adopted, changing the name of the adoptee to that of the adoptive parents. The original birth certificate is then sealed. Disclosure is permitted only by court order based on good cause. Courts are generally more willing to find good cause for medical than psychological reasons. Many states permit access to "nonidentifying information," such as medical histories, while requiring good cause or consent of all parties for identifying information. Some states have special provisions for access to medical information and history. (Of course, the practice of secrecy contrasts with independent adoption in which the adoptive parents and child often know the identity of the birth parents.)

While the tradition of confidentiality is still honored in many states, there is a growing movement toward allowing for an exchange of information between the adopted child and the birth parents. Some states have created voluntary registries that provide information when the birth family member and adoptee have registered. Voluntary matching is also possible over the Internet. Other states have statutes under which an intermediary will contact one party to obtain consent to release information once the other party has registered. Still other states (such as California) have enacted laws honoring a party's request for information in the absence of a veto registered by the other party.

Two states, Alaska and Kansas, have long allowed adult adoptees to view their birth records. Alaska Stat. §18.50.500 (Michie 2000); Kan. Stat. Ann. §65-2423 (Supp. 2004). See generally Elizabeth J. Samuels, The Idea of Adoption: An Inquiry Into the History of Adult Adoptee Access to Birth Records, 53 Rutgers L. Rev. 367 (2001).

In California, the child's birth certificate does not state the name of the birth parents unless the child has been adopted by a stepparent or relative (Cal. Fam. Code §8614). Adoption records may not be disclosed except by court order "in exceptional circumstances and for good cause approaching the necessitous" (Cal. Fam. Code §9200). Medical information may be provided to an adoptee who is 18 or older or to an adoptive parent of a minor (Cal. Fam. Code §§9202, 9203). The adoptive parent may have a copy of the agency's medical report upon request (Cal. Fam. Code 9202) and may receive the name and address (that found in the records) of the birth parent in case of a medical necessity or other "extraordinary circumstances" (Cal. Fam. Code §9203)).

California law also permits disclosure of identities at the request of an adoptee who is 21 or older, or at the request of a birth parent of an adoptee who has attained age 21 (Cal. Fam. Code §9203(a)). The Department of Social Services must respond promptly to such requests (Cal. Fam. Code §9203(d)) (either by reply within 20 working days or forwarding the request to the agency involved). However, by statute, disclosure is not permitted if either a birth parent or adoptee has registered a veto (Cal. Fam. Code §9203(c).

See generally Rosemary Cabellero, Open Records Adoption: Finding the Missing Piece, 30 So. Ill. U. L. Rev. 291 (2006).

California Family Code

§8614. County clerk may issue certificate of adoption

Upon the request of the adoptive parents or the adopted child, a clerk of the superior court may issue a certificate of adoption that states the date and place of adoption, the birthday of the child, the names of the adoptive parents, and the name the child has taken. Unless the child has been adopted by a stepparent or by a relative, as defined in subdivision (c) of Section 8616.5, the certificate shall not state the name of the birth parents of the child.

(Stats. 1992 (A.B. 2650), ch. 162, §10, effective January 1, 1994. Amended Stats. 1997 (A.B. 1544), ch. 793, §2. Amended by Stats. 2002 (S.B. 1316), ch. 784, §110. Amended by Stats. 2003 (S.B. 182), ch. 251, §5.)

§9200. Records shall be confidential

(a) The petition, relinquishment or consent, agreement, order, report to the court from any investigating agency, and any power of attorney and deposition filed in the office of the clerk of the court pursuant to this part is not open to inspection by any person other than the parties to the proceeding and their attorneys and the department, except upon the written authority of the judge of the superior court. A judge of the superior court may not authorize anyone to inspect the petition, relinquishment or consent, agreement, order, report to the court from any investigating agency, or power of attorney or deposition or any portion of any of these documents, except in exceptional circumstances and for good cause approaching the necessitous. The petitioner may be required to pay the expenses for preparing the copies of the documents to be inspected.

(b) Upon written request of any party to the proceeding and upon the order of any judge of the superior court, the clerk of the court shall not provide any documents referred to in this section for inspection or copying to any other person, unless the name of the child's birth parents or any information tending to identify the child's birth parents is deleted from the documents or copies thereof.

(c) Upon the request of the adoptive parents or the child, a clerk of the court may issue a certificate of adoption that states the date and place of adoption, the child's birth date, the names of the adoptive parents, and the name the child has taken. Unless the child has been adopted by a stepparent, the certificate shall not state the name of the child's birth parents.

(Stats. 1992 (A.B. 2650), ch. 162, §10, effective January 1, 1994. Amended by Stats 2002 (S.B. 1316), ch. 784, §114.)

§9201. Department and agency shall not release information identifying persons who receive services

(a) Except as otherwise permitted or required by statute, neither the department nor a licensed adoption agency shall release information that would identify persons who receive, or have received, adoption services.

(b) Employees of the department and licensed adoption agencies shall release to the department at Sacramento any requested information, including identifying information, for the purposes of recordkeeping and monitoring, evaluation, and regulation of the provision of adoption services.

(c) Prior to the placement of a child for adoption, the department or licensed adoption agency may, upon the written request of both a birth and a prospective adoptive parent, arrange for contact between these birth and prospective adoptive parents that may include the sharing of identifying information regarding these parents.

(d) The department and any licensed adoption agency may, upon written authorization for the release of specified information by the subject of that information, share information regarding a prospective adoptive parent or birth parent with other social service agencies, including the department and other licensed adoption agencies, or providers of health care as defined in Section 56.05 of the Civil Code.

(e) Notwithstanding any other law, the department and any licensed adoption agency may furnish information relating to an adoption petition or to a child in the custody of the department or any licensed adoption agency to the juvenile court, county welfare department, public welfare agency, private welfare agency licensed by the department, provider of foster care services, potential adoptive parent, or provider of health care as defined in Section 56.05 of the Civil Code, if it is believed the child's welfare will be promoted thereby.

(f) The department and any licensed adoption agency may make adoptions case records, including identifying information, available for research purposes, provided that the research will not result in the disclosure of the identity of the child or the parties to the adoption to anyone other than the entity conducting the research.

(Stats. 1992 (A.B. 2650), ch. 162, §10, effective January 1, 1994. Amended Stats. 2000 (A.B. 2921), ch. 910, §5.)

§9202. Copy of medical report

(a) Notwithstanding any other law, the department or licensed adoption agency that made a medical report required by Section 8706, 8817, or 8909 shall provide a copy of the medical report, in the manner the department prescribes by regulation, to any of the following persons upon the person's request:

(1) A person who has been adopted pursuant to this part and who has attained the age of 18 years or who presents a certified copy of the person's marriage certificate.

(2) The adoptive parent of a person under the age of 18 years who has been adopted pursuant to this part.

(b) A person who is denied access to a medical report pursuant to regulations adopted pursuant to this section may petition the court for review of the reasonableness of the department's or licensed adoption agency's decision.

(c) The names and addresses of any persons contained in the report shall be removed unless the person requesting the report has previously received the information.

(Stats. 1992 (A.B. 2650), ch. 162, §10, effective January 1, 1994. Amended Stats. 2000 (A.B. 2921), ch. 910, §6.)

§9202.5. Limited access to blood samples

(a) Notwithstanding any other law, the laboratory that is storing a blood sample pursuant to Section 8706, 8817, or 8909 shall provide access to the blood sample to only the following persons upon the person's request:

(1) A person who has been adopted pursuant to this part.

(2) The adoptive parent of a person under the age of 18 years who has been adopted pursuant to this part. The adoptive parent may receive access to the blood sample only after entry of the order of adoption.

(b) The birth parent or parents shall be given access to any DNA test results related to the blood sample on request.

(c) Except as provided in subdivision (b), no person other than the adoptive parent and the adopted child shall have access to the blood sample or any DNA test results related to the blood sample, unless the adoptive parent or the child authorizes another person or entity to have that access.

(Stats. 1996 (A.B. 3241), ch. 1053, §4.)

§9203. Department or agency may disclose identity of birth parents

(a) The department or a licensed adoption agency shall do the following:

(1) Upon the request of a person who has been adopted pursuant to this part and who has attained the age of 21 years, disclose the identity of the person's birth parent or parents and their most current address shown in the records of the department or licensed adoption agency, if the birth parent or parents have indicated consent to the disclosure in writing.

(2) Upon the request of the birth parent of a person who has been adopted pursuant to this part and who has attained the age of 21 years, disclose the adopted name of the adoptee and the adoptee's most current address shown in the records of the department or licensed adoption agency, if the adult adoptee has indicated in writing, pursuant to the registration program developed by the department, that the adult adoptee wishes the adult adoptee's name and address to be disclosed.

(3) Upon the request of the adoptive parent of a person under the age of 21 years who has been adopted pursuant to this part, disclose the identity of a birth parent and the birth parent's most current address shown in the records of the department or licensed adoption agency if the department or licensed adoption agency finds that a medical necessity or other extraordinary circumstances justify the disclosure.

(b) The department shall prescribe the form of the request required by this section. The form shall provide for an affidavit to be executed by the requester that to the best of the requester's knowledge the requester is an adoptee, the adoptee's birth parent, or the adoptee's adoptive parent. The department may adopt regulations requiring any additional means of identification from a requester that it deems necessary. The request shall advise an adoptee that if the adoptee consents, the adoptee's adoptive parents will be notified of the filing of the request before the release of the name and address of the adoptee's birth parent.

(c) Subdivision (a) is not applicable if a birth parent or an adoptee has indicated that he or she does not wish his or her name or address to be disclosed.

(d) Within 20 working days of receipt of a request for information pursuant to this section, the department shall either respond to the request or forward the request to a licensed adoption agency that was a party to the adoption.

(e) Notwithstanding any other law, the department shall announce the availability of the present method of arranging contact among an adult adoptee, the adult adoptee's birth parents, and adoptive parents authorized by Section 9204 utilizing a means of communication appropriate to inform the public effectively.

(f) The department or licensed adoption agency may charge a reasonable fee in an amount the department establishes by regulation to cover the costs of processing requests for information made pursuant to subdivision (a). The department or licensed adoption agency shall waive fees authorized by this section for any person who is receiving public assistance pursuant to Part 3 (commencing with Section 11000) of Division 9 of the Welfare and Institutions Code. The revenue resulting from the fees so charged shall be utilized by the department or licensed adoption agency to increase existing staff as needed to process these requests. Fees received by the department shall be deposited in the Adoption Information Fund. This revenue shall be in addition to any other funds appropriated in support of the state adoption program.

(g) This section applies only to adoptions in which the relinquishment for or consent to adoption was signed or the birth parent's rights were involuntarily terminated by court action on or after January 1, 1984.

(Stats. 1992 (A.B. 2650), ch. 162, §10, effective January 1, 1994. Amended Stats. 2000 (A.B. 2921), ch. 910, §7.)

§9204. Department or agency may arrange for contact subject to parties' filing mutual consents

(a) Notwithstanding any other law, if an adult adoptee and the adult adoptee's birth parents have each filed a written consent with the department or licensed adoption agency, the department or licensed adoption agency may arrange for contact between those persons. Neither the department nor a licensed adoption agency may solicit, directly or indirectly, the execution of a written consent.

(b) The written consent authorized by this section shall be in a form prescribed by the department.

(Stats. 1992 (A.B. 2650), ch. 162, §10, effective January 1, 1994.)

§9205. Department or agency shall disclose names of siblings subject to mutual consent

(a) Notwithstanding any other law, the department or adoption agency that joined in the adoption petition shall release the names and addresses of biological siblings to one another if both of the siblings have attained the age of 21 years and have filed the following with the department or agency:

(1) A current address.

(2) A written request for contact with any biological sibling whose existence is known to the person making the request.

(3) A written waiver of the person's rights with respect to the disclosure of the person's name and address to the sibling, if the person is an adoptee.

(b) Upon inquiry and proof that a person is the biological sibling of an adoptee who has filed a waiver pursuant to this section, the department or agency may advise the sibling that a waiver has been filed by the adoptee. The department or agency may charge a reasonable fee, not to exceed fifty dollars ($50), for providing the service required by this section.

(c) An adoptee may revoke a waiver filed pursuant to this section by giving written notice of revocation to the department or agency.

(d) The department shall adopt a form for the request authorized by this section. The form shall provide for an affidavit to be executed by a person seeking to employ the procedure provided by this section that, to the best of the person's knowledge, the person is an adoptee or biological sibling of an adoptee. The form also shall contain a notice of an adoptee's rights pursuant to subdivision (c) and a statement that information will be disclosed only if there is a currently valid waiver on file with the department or agency. The department may adopt regulations requiring any additional means of identification from a person making a request pursuant to this section as it deems necessary, and for obtaining the consent of the birth parents of the adoptee and the sibling in order to make the disclosure authorized by this section in any case in which the sibling remained in the custody and control of the birth parents until the age of 18 years.

(e) The department or agency may not solicit the execution of a waiver authorized by this section. However, the department shall announce the availability of the procedure authorized by this section, utilizing a means of communication appropriate to inform the public effectively.

(Stats. 1992 (A.B. 2650), ch. 162, §10, effective January 1, 1994.)

§9206. Department or agency shall release items of personal property upon written request

(a) Notwithstanding any other law, the department or licensed adoption agency shall release any letters, photographs, or other items of personal property in its possession to an adoptee, birth parent, or adoptive parent, upon written request. The material may be requested by any of the following persons:

(1) The adoptee, if the adoptee has attained the age of 18 years.

(2) The adoptive parent or parents, on behalf of an adoptee under the age of 18 years, as long as instructions to the contrary have not been made by the depositor.

(3) The birth parent or parents.

(b) Notwithstanding any other law, all identifying names and addresses shall be deleted from the letters, photographs, or items of personal property before delivery to the requester.

(c) Letters, photographs, and other items of personal property deposited on or after January 1, 1985, shall be accompanied by a release form or similar document signed by the person depositing the material, specifying to whom the material may be released. At its discretion, the department or licensed adoption agency may refuse for deposit items of personal property that, because of value or bulk, would pose storage problems.

(d) Notwithstanding subdivisions (a) and (b), only the following photographs deposited before January 1, 1985, shall be released:

(1) Photographs of the adoptee that have been requested by the adoptee.

(2) Photographs that have been deposited by the adoptee, the adoptive parent or parents, or the birth parent or parents, and for which there is a letter or other document on file indicating that person's consent to the release of the photographs.

(e) The department and licensed adoption agencies may charge a fee to cover the actual costs of any services required by this section in excess of normal postadoptive services provided by the department or agency. The department shall develop a fee schedule that shall be implemented by the department and licensed adoption agencies in assessing charges to the person who deposits the material or the person to whom the material is released. The fee may be waived by the department or licensed adoption agencies in cases in which it is established that a financial hardship exists.

(f) "Photograph" as used in this section means a photograph of the person depositing the photograph or the person making the request for the release.

(Stats. 1992 (A.B. 2650), ch. 162, §10, effective January 1, 1994.)

L. ADOPTION FAILURE

Most states have laws that permit an adoption to be abrogated even after a child is placed with the adoptive family. First, a birth parent may reclaim his or her child in some circumstances, e.g., if the birth mother demonstrates that her relinquishment of parental rights was induced by duress, if the birth parent's consent was not obtained or there was failure to give notice to a birth parent. Many states have statutes of limitations that bar attacks on adoption decrees after a certain period of time, typically ranging from six months to three years. See Cal. Fam. Code §9102 (one-year statute of limitations after entry of an order of adoption absent fraud).

Second, in some states, an adoption can be abrogated by the adoptive parents in certain circumstances. These circumstances include: fraud, misrepresentation, and undue influence, as well as on procedural grounds such as lack of compliance with statutory requirements. Most cases involving petitions for abrogation by adoptive parents stem from two common situations: (1) the adoptive parents seek abrogation due to some abnormality or defect in the child; and (2) adoptive fathers seek abrogation, usually after divorce, to avoid child support obligations.

In California, the adoptive parents may petition to set aside an adoption in some cases of an agency adoption (but not an independent adoption) (Cal. Fam. Code §9100). To vacate an adoption, the child must show evidence of a "developmental disability or mental illness as a result of conditions existing before the adoption to an extent that the child cannot be relinquished to an adoption agency on the grounds that the child is considered unadoptable" (id.).

In response to the problems of misrepresentation by adoption agencies, states increasingly are recognizing a new remedy of wrongful adoption. This cause of action does not seek annulment of the adoption but rather damages from the agency for the extraordinary expenses and emotional distress associated with caring for the child. See, e.g., Michael J. v. Los Angeles County of Adoptions, 247 Cal. Rptr. 504 (Ct. App. 1988) (holding that cause of action exists against county adoption agency for misrepresentation in adoption process).

California Family Code

§9100. Adoptive parents may petition to set aside adoption in some circumstances

(a) If a child adopted pursuant to the law of this state shows evidence of a developmental disability or mental illness as a result of conditions existing before the adoption to an extent that the child cannot be relinquished to an adoption agency on the grounds that the child is considered unadoptable, and of which conditions the adoptive parents or parent had no knowledge or notice before the entry of the order of adoption, a petition setting forth those facts may be filed by the adoptive parents or parent with the court that granted the adoption petition. If these facts are proved to the satisfaction of the court, it may make an order setting aside the order of adoption.

(b) The petition shall be filed within five years after the entry of the order of adoption.

(c) The court clerk shall immediately notify the department at Sacramento of the petition. Within 60 days after the notice, the department shall file a full report with the court and shall appear before the court for the purpose of representing the adopted child.

(Stats. 1992 (A.B. 2650), ch. 162, §10, effective January 1, 1994.)

§9101. Consequences of setting aside adoption for child

(a) If an order of adoption is set aside as provided in Section 9100, the court making the order shall direct the district attorney, the county counsel, or the county welfare department to take appropriate action under the Welfare and Institutions Code. The court may also make any order relative to the care, custody, or confinement of the child pending the proceeding the court sees fit.

(b) The county in which the proceeding for adoption was had is liable for the child's support until the child is able to support himself or herself.

(Stats. 1992 (A.B. 2650), ch. 162, §10, effective January 1, 1994.)

§9102. Limitation on order to set aside adoption

(a) An action or proceeding of any kind to vacate, set aside, or otherwise nullify an order of adoption on any ground, except fraud, shall be commenced within one year after entry of the order.

(b) An action or proceeding of any kind to vacate, set aside, or nullify an order of adoption, based on fraud, shall be commenced within three years after entry of the order.

(Stats. 1992 (A.B. 2650), ch. 162, §10, effective January 1, 1994. Amended Stats. 1995 (A.B. 898), ch. 567, §1; Stats. 2000 (A.B. 2433), ch. 937, §6.)

X.
PROCREATION

This chapter explores issues of reproductive freedom and reproductive control. Specifically, it addresses reproductive rights in the contexts of contraception, abortion, restrictions on the rights of pregnant women, and new reproductive technologies.

A. CONTRACEPTION

1. Generally

Harsh restrictions on contraceptives date from the 1870s. In 1873, a vice crusader and ex-dry goods salesman, Anthony Comstock, spearheaded passage of federal legislation (known as the "Comstock law") that banned the circulation and importation through the mail of obscene materials (defined to include contraceptives and abortifacients). See generally Nicola Beisel, Imperiled Innocents: Anthony Comstock and Family Reproduction in Victorian America (1997).

Many states enacted similar legislation. As a result, physicians were unable to prescribe birth control devices and disseminate information about contraception. Courts upheld the constitutionality of such state legislation as a valid exercise of the police power until the United States Supreme Court invalidated the Connecticut law in Griswold v. Connecticut, 381 U.S. 479 (1965).

In *Griswold*, the Supreme Court held that the Connecticut restriction on the use of contraception was an unconstitutional interference with the right of marital privacy. The Court based its holding on the recognition of a constitutional right to privacy that encompassed intimate decisionmaking by marital partners about contraception. The Court subsequently determined that the right of access to contraception does not depend on marital status. Eisenstadt v. Baird, 405 U.S. 438 (1972) (holding that the denial of contraceptives to single persons violates the Equal Protection Clause by providing different treatment for persons who are similarly situated).

2. Minors' Rights to Contraception

The United States Supreme Court also has examined the issue of minors' right to contraception. In Carey v. Population Services, 431 U.S. 678 (1977), the Court extended the constitutional right to privacy to minors' contraceptive choices. However, the Court in *Carey* also makes clear that the scope of permissible state regulation is broader with respect to minors than adults.

At common law, parental consent is required for medical treatment of a minor. Some states have adopted "a mature minor rule" as an exception to the common law that permits a minor to give effective consent if she or he is capable of appreciating the nature, extent, and consequences of the treatment. Some states adopt the mature minor rule for medical care related specifically to substance abuse, venereal disease, and pregnancy, excluding abortion.

A few states specifically authorize a minor to consent, on her own behalf, for contraceptives. See, e.g., Cal. Fam. Code §6925 (West 2004) (minor may consent to medical care related to "the prevention or treatment of pregnancy"). However, Texas permits minors to consent to their own medical treatment (i.e., without the need to secure parental consent) only in limited circumstances. Tex. Fam. Code §32.002. These circumstances include *inter alia* minors who are on active duty in the military, who are emancipated, and those who are unmarried and pregnant who may consent to "hospital, medical, or surgical treatment, other than abortion, related to the pregnancy" (Tex. Fam. Code §32.003(a)(4)). As a result, the Texas Family Code does not appear to give minors the right to consent to contraceptives or other prescription birth control devices, signifying that parental consent is required for such services. See also Harris County Medical Society, Consent for Treatment of Minors, at http://www.hcms.org/Template.aspx?id=66#minors (last visited Sept. 6, 2006). Furthermore, Texas law gives parents the duty of providing medical and dental care to their children. That statutory authority also implies that parents have a right to consent to that treatment (including the provision of contraceptive information) and the right to access a child's health information to make treatment decisions. See *id.* Minors do not need parental consent for their own medical treatment if they are on Medicaid or request services from a Title X (family planning)-funded facility. See Planned Parenthood (Houston), Facts About Minor Consent About Medical Treatment, at http://www.pphouston.org/site/PageServer?pagename=TitleXlocations (last visited April 1, 2003).

a. Access Generally

Texas Family Code

§32.003. Child may consent to treatment in limited cases

(a) A child may consent to medical, dental, psychological, and surgical treatment for the child by a licensed physician or dentist if the child:

(1) is on active duty with the armed services of the United States of America;

(2) is:

(A) 16 years of age or older and resides separate and apart from the child's parents, managing conservator, or guardian, with or without the consent of the parents, managing conservator, or guardian and regardless of the duration of the residence; and

(B) managing the child's own financial affairs, regardless of the source of the income;

(3) consents to the diagnosis and treatment of an infectious, contagious, or communicable disease that is required by law or a rule to be reported by the licensed physician or dentist to a local health officer or the Texas Department of Health, including all diseases within the scope of Section 81.041, Health and Safety Code;

(4) is unmarried and pregnant and consents to hospital, medical, or surgical treatment, other than abortion, related to the pregnancy;

(5) consents to examination and treatment for drug or chemical addiction, drug or chemical dependency, or any other condition directly related to drug or chemical use; or

(6) is unmarried, is the parent of a child, and has actual custody of his or her child and consents to medical, dental, psychological, or surgical treatment for the child.

(b) Consent by a child to medical, dental, psychological, and surgical treatment under this section is not subject to disaffirmance because of minority.

(c) Consent of the parents, managing conservator, or guardian of a child is not necessary in order to authorize hospital, medical, surgical, or dental care under this section.

(d) A licensed physician, dentist, or psychologist may, with or without the consent of a child who is a patient, advise the parents, managing conservator, or guardian of the child of the treatment given to or needed by the child.

(e) A physician, dentist, psychologist, hospital, or medical facility is not liable for the examination and treatment of a child under this section except for the provider's or the facility's own acts of negligence.

(f) A physician, dentist, psychologist, hospital, or medical facility may rely on the written statement of the child containing the grounds on which the child has capacity to consent to the child's medical treatment.

(Amended by Acts 1995, 74th Leg., ch. 20, §1, effective April 20, 1995; Acts 1995, 74th Leg., ch. 751, §6, effective September 1, 1995. Amended Acts 2001, 77th Leg., ch. 821, §2.01, effective June 14, 2001.)

§151.001. Parental rights and duties

(a) A parent of a child has the following rights and duties:

(1) the right to have physical possession, to direct the moral and religious training, and to designate the residence of the child;

(2) the duty of care, control, protection, and reasonable discipline of the child;

(3) the duty to support the child, including providing the child with clothing, food, shelter, medical and dental care, and education;

(4) the duty, except when a guardian of the child's estate has been appointed, to manage the estate of the child, including the right as an agent of the child to act in relation to the child's estate if the child's action is required by a state, the United States, or a foreign government;

(5) except as provided by Section 264.0111, the right to the services and earnings of the child;

(6) the right to consent to the child's marriage, enlistment in the armed forces of the United States, medical and dental care, and psychiatric, psychological, and surgical treatment;

(7) the right to represent the child in legal action and to make other decisions of substantial legal significance concerning the child;

(8) the right to receive and give receipt for payments for the support of the child and to hold or disburse funds for the benefit of the child;

(9) the right to inherit from and through the child;

(10) the right to make decisions concerning the child's education; and

(11) any other right or duty existing between a parent and child by virtue of law.

(b) The duty of a parent to support his or her child exists while the child is an unemancipated minor and continues as long as the child is fully enrolled in an accredited secondary school in a program leading toward a high school diploma until the end of the school year in which the child graduates.

(c) A parent who fails to discharge the duty of support is liable to a person who provides necessaries to those to whom support is owed.

(d) The rights and duties of a parent are subject to:

(1) a court order affecting the rights and duties;

(2) an affidavit of relinquishment of parental rights;

(3) an affidavit by the parent designating another person or agency to act as managing conservator.

(e) Only the following persons may use corporal punishment for the reasonable discipline of a child:

(1) a parent or grandparent of the child;

(2) a stepparent of the child who has the duty of control and reasonable discipline of the child; and

(3) an individual who is a guardian of the child and who has the duty of control and reasonable discipline of the child.

(Added by Acts 1995, 74th Leg., ch. 20, §1, effective April 20, 1995. Amended by Acts 1995, 74th Leg., ch. 751, §23, effective September 1, 1995. Renumbered from §51.003 by Acts 2001, 77th Leg., ch. 821, §2.13, effective June 14, 2001; Acts 2001, 77th Leg., ch. 964, §2, effective September 1, 2001; Acts 2003, 78th Leg., ch. 1036, § 3, effective September 1, 2003; Acts 2005, 79th Leg., ch. 924, §1, effective September 1, 2005.)

b. Sex Education in Public Schools

Public school districts often require that students take classes in sex education. Courses provide information primarily about contraception and the prevention of sexually transmitted diseases. In the past few years, many state lawmakers have enacted legislation making abstinence the focus of such courses.

Abstinence-based sex education received a boost from federal welfare reform legislation, the Personal Responsibility Work Opportunity Reconciliation Act (PRWORA), Pub. L. No. 104-193, 110 Stat. 2105 (codified in scattered sections of 7, 8, 21, 15 and 42 U.S.C.A.) that was enacted in 1996. In an effort to reduce teen pregnancy, PRWORA allocates money ($50 million in each of fiscal years 1998 through 2002) to states that adopt abstinence education programs. "Abstinence education" is defined as a program that has as its "exclusive purpose" the teaching of abstinence from sexual activity until marriage, 42 U.S.C. §710(b)(2)(A).

The topic of sex education in Texas public schools is included in "health education" classes (Tex. Educ. Code §28.004). In addition to instruction on human sexuality, the curriculum of such courses "may" include information on the prevention of obesity, cardiovascular disease, Type II diabetes, and the use of tobacco (Tex. Educ. Code §28.004(2)). These classes must emphasize abstinence "as the only completely reliable method of avoiding unwanted teenage pregnancy and sexually transmitted diseases" (Tex. Health & Safety Code §163.002(1)). School districts must notify parents about the classes and give parents the opportunity to request that their children not attend (Tex. Educ. Code §28.004(i)(2)). Parents have the opportunity to inspect all curriculum materials used in such classes (Tex. Educ. Code §28.004(j)). The school districts may not distribute condoms (Tex. Educ. Code §28.004(f)) as part of such courses. Further, the courses should emphasize "in a factual manner and from a public health perspective, that homosexuality is not a lifestyle acceptable to the general public and that homosexual conduct is a criminal offense [under Penal Code §21.06]" (Tex. Health & Safety Code §163.002(8)). (Note that Texas Penal Code §21.06 was subsequently declared unconstitutional in Lawrence v. Texas, 539 U.S. 558 (2003)).

On the constitutionality of condom distribution programs generally, see Curtis v. School Committee of Falmouth, 652 N.E.2d 580 (1st Cir. 1995); Parents United for Better Public Schools, Inc. v. School Dist. of Phila., 148 F.3d 260 (3rd Cir. 1998).

Texas Education Code

§28.004. Health education instruction: curriculum, condoms, notice to parents

(a) The board of trustees of each school district shall establish a local school health education advisory council to assist the district in ensuring that local community values are reflected in the district's health education instruction.

(b) A school district must consider the recommendations of the local school health education advisory council before changing the district's health education curriculum or instruction.

(c) The local school health education advisory council's duties include recommending:

(1) the number of hours of instruction to be provided in health education;

(2) health education curriculum appropriate for specific grade levels that may include a coordinated health education program designed to prevent obesity, cardiovascular disease, and Type II diabetes through coordination of:

(A) health education;

(B) physical education;

(C) nutritional services;

(D) parental involvement; and

(E) instruction to prevent the use of tobacco; and

(3) appropriate grade levels and methods of instruction for human sexuality instruction; and

(4) strategies for integrating the curriculum components specified by Subdivision (2) with the following elements in a coordinated school health program for the district:

(A) school health services;

(B) counseling and guidance services;

(C) a safe and healthy school environment; and

(D) school employee wellness.

(d) The board of trustees shall appoint members to the local school health education advisory council. A majority of the members must be persons who are parents of students enrolled in the district and who are not employed by the district. The board of trustees also may appoint one or more persons from each of the following groups or a representative from a group other than a group specified under this subsection:

(1) public school teachers;

(2) public school administrators;

(3) district students;

(4) health care professionals;

(5) the business community;

(6) law enforcement;

(7) senior citizens;

(8) the clergy; and

(9) nonprofit health organizations.

(e) Any course materials and instruction relating to human sexuality, sexually transmitted diseases, or human immunodeficiency virus or acquired immune deficiency syndrome shall be selected by the board of trustees with the advice of the local school health education advisory council and must:

(1) present abstinence from sexual activity as the preferred choice of behavior in relationship to all sexual activity for unmarried persons of school age;

(2) devote more attention to abstinence from sexual activity than to any other behavior;

(3) emphasize that abstinence from sexual activity, if used consistently and correctly, is the only method that is 100 percent effective in preventing pregnancy, sexually transmitted diseases, infection with human immunodeficiency virus or acquired immune deficiency syndrome, and the emotional trauma associated with adolescent sexual activity;

(4) direct adolescents to a standard of behavior in which abstinence from sexual activity before marriage is the most effective way to prevent pregnancy, sexually transmitted diseases, and infection with human immunodeficiency virus or acquired immune deficiency syndrome; and

(5) teach contraception and condom use in terms of human use reality rates instead of theoretical laboratory rates, if instruction on contraception and condoms is included in curriculum content.

(f) A school district may not distribute condoms in connection with instruction relating to human sexuality.

(g) A school district that provides human sexuality instruction may separate students according to sex for instructional purposes.

(h) The board of trustees shall determine the specific content of the district's instruction in human sexuality, in accordance with Subsections (e), (f), and (g).

(i) A school district shall notify a parent of each student enrolled in the district of:

(1) the basic content of the district's human sexuality instruction to be provided to the student; and

(2) the parent's right to remove the student from any part of the district's human sexuality instruction.

(j) A school district shall make all curriculum materials used in the district's human sexuality instruction available for reasonable public inspection.

(k) A school district shall publish in the student handbook and post on the district's Internet website, if the district has an Internet website:

(1) a statement of the policies adopted to ensure that elementary school, middle school, and junior high school students engage in at least 30 minutes per school day or 135 minutes per school week of physical activity; and

(2) a statement of:

(A) the number of times during the preceding year the district's school health advisory council has met;

(B) whether the district has adopted and enforces policies to ensure that district campuses comply with agency vending machine and food service guidelines for restricting student access to vending machines; and

(C) whether the district has adopted and enforces policies and procedures that prescribe penalties for the use of tobacco products by students and others on school campuses or at school-sponsored or school-related activities.

(Acts 1995, 74th Leg., ch. 260, §1, effective May 30, 1995. Amended by Acts 2001, 77th Leg., ch. 907, §2, effective June 14, 2001; Acts 2003, 78th Leg., ch. 944, §1, effective September 1, 2003; Acts 2005, 79th Leg., ch. 784, §2, effective June 17, 2005.)

Texas Health & Safety Code

§163.002. Sex education courses should emphasize abstinence

Course materials and instruction relating to sexual education or sexually transmitted diseases should include:

(1) an emphasis on sexual abstinence as the only completely reliable method of avoiding unwanted teenage pregnancy and sexually transmitted diseases;

(2) an emphasis on the importance of self-control, responsibility, and ethical conduct in making decisions relating to sexual behavior;

(3) statistics, based on the latest medical information, that indicate the efficacy of the various forms of contraception;

(4) information concerning the laws relating to the financial responsibilities associated with pregnancy, childbirth, and child rearing;

(5) information concerning the laws prohibiting sexual abuse and the legal and counseling options available to victims of sexual abuse;

(6) information on how to cope with and rebuff unwanted physical and verbal sexual advances, as well as the importance of avoiding the sexual exploitation of other persons;

(7) psychologically sound methods of resisting unwanted peer pressure; and

(8) emphasis, provided in a factual manner and from a public health perspective, that homosexuality is not a lifestyle acceptable to the general public and that homosexual conduct is a criminal offense under Section 21.06, Penal Code.

(Acts 1991, 72nd Leg., ch. 14, §51, effective September 1, 1991.)

3. Misrepresentation of Contraceptive Use

Courts are reluctant to grant tort recovery for misrepresentation of contraceptive use but will permit recovery in limited cases in which physical injury results. Barbara A. v. John G., 193 Cal. Rptr. 422 (Ct. App. 1983) (holding that woman may maintain a cause of action for damages sustained during an ectopic pregnancy after man misrepresented that he was sterile).

However, according to the general rule, misrepresentation about contraceptive use will not provide a parent with a defense to a claim for child support. See Wallis v. Smith, 22 P.3d 682 (N.M. Ct. App. 3002). In Piatt v. Schultz, 1998 WL 476725 (Tex. App.—Austin 1998, no writ) (not designated for publication), a woman misrepresented to her lover that she was taking oral contraceptives. After she gave birth, he filed a petition to terminate his parent-child relationship. The court determined that the child's best interests would be served by maintaining the parent-child relationship and ordered him to pay child support.

B. ABORTION

1. Woman's Right to an Abortion

Early American proscriptions against abortion date from the 1820s. The anti-abortion movement escalated in the second half of the nineteenth century when many states enacted restrictive abortion regulations. Physicians spearheaded legislative restrictions in an effort to end the lucrative abortion practices of nonmedical practitioners. The anti-abortion movement also benefited from the nineteenth century "social purity" campaign supporting the Comstock laws' restriction of access to contraceptives. See generally Beisel, *supra*; David Garrow, Liberty and Sexuality: The Right to Privacy and the Making of Roe v. Wade (1994).

Reform began in the 1960s when a number of states adopted the American Law Institute (ALI)'s Model Penal Code abortion provisions liberalizing abortion for pregnancies resulting from rape or incest, those involving a deformed fetus, and those whose continuation would impair the mother's mental or physical health (i.e., "therapeutic abortions"). The women's movement also contributed to abortion reform.

The United States Supreme Court decided in Roe v. Wade, 410 U.S. 113 (1973), that a woman has a constitutionally protected right to an abortion. The Court based this protection in the right to privacy situated in the Fourteenth Amendment's concept of personal liberty.

In Roe v. Wade, Jane Roe, an unmarried pregnant woman who desired an abortion, sought a declaratory judgment against Henry Wade (the district attorney of Dallas County) that the Texas criminal abortion statute was unconstitutional. The statute made abortion illegal except for the purpose of saving the life of the mother. *Roe* holds that the right to an abortion is fundamental and, therefore, should be subject to strict scrutiny (i.e., states must have a compelling interest in restricting abortion and the statute must be narrowly tailored to effectuate that interest).

The state offers three possible governmental interests for restricting abortion: (1) to discourage illicit sexual conduct, (2) to protect mothers from the hazardous nature of the abortion procedure, and (3) to protect the state's interest in potential life. Although dismissing the first governmental interest, the Court accepts the remaining interests as compelling. The Court determines that the mother's right to an abortion is not absolute and must be balanced again these competing interests.

Roe reaches an accommodation of these competing interests by adopting a trimester framework. In the first trimester, the woman has an unqualified right to an abortion that may not be infringed by the state. After the first trimester and until the point of viability, the state may regulate abortion in the interest of maternal health. After viability, the state's interest in protecting potential life justifies the state in regulating, and even proscribing, abortion except when necessary for the preservation of the life or health of the mother.

The Supreme Court subsequently reaffirmed Roe v. Wade but retreated from *Roe's* guarantee of abortion freedom. In Planned Parenthood of Southeastern Pennsylvania v. Casey, 505 U.S. 833 (1992), the Court examined the constitutionality of a Pennsylvania statute that provides for informed consent, a 24-hour waiting period, spousal notification, parental consent for a minor's abortion, a medical emergency exception, and reporting requirements for abortion facilities. In upholding all of the restrictions except spousal notification, the Court rejected *Roe's* trimester framework and announced a new standard by which to scrutinize abortion restrictions. *Casey* recognizes that the state has a substantial interest in potential life throughout the pregnancy (*id.* at 876), demotes abortion from a "fundamental right" to a liberty interest, and holds that only those regulations that impose an "undue burden" on the woman's abortion decision will be subject to strict scrutiny. See also Stenberg v. Carhart, 530 U.S. 914 (2000) (holding Nebraska statute banning "partial birth abortion" was unconstitutional because it lacked any exception for preservation of health of the mother).

A state may not require a spouse's prior written consent to an abortion (Planned Parenthood v. Danforth, 428 U.S. 52 (1976)), or spousal notification (*Casey, supra*, at 907-908).

Many states regulate the medical facilities that perform abortions. In Women's Medical Center of Northwest Houston v. Bell, 248 F.3d 411 (5th Cir. 2001), physicians challenged the constitutionality of certain amendments to, and regulations of, the Texas Abortion Facility Reporting and Licensing Act (Tex. Health & Safety Code §§245.001-245.022) that exempted physicians' offices from licensing requirements if their offices performed only a limited number of abortions. The Fifth Circuit Court of Appeals affirmed the district court's ruling that the regulations were unconstitutionally vague, but reversed the holding that the amendments violated equal protection. See generally Thomas William Mayo, Health Care Law, 55 S.M.U. L. Rev. 1113 (2002) (summarizing case law).

Texas Health & Safety Code

§170.001. Definitions

In this chapter:

(1) "Abortion" means an act involving the use of an instrument, medicine, drug, or other substance or device developed to terminate the pregnancy of a woman if the act is done with an intention other than to:

(A) increase the probability of a live birth of the unborn child of the woman;

(B) preserve the life or health of the child; or

(C) remove a dead fetus.

(2) "Physician" means an individual licensed to practice medicine in this state.

(3) "Viable" means the stage of fetal development when, in the medical judgment of the attending physician based on the particular facts of the case, an unborn child possesses the capacity to live outside its mother's womb after its premature birth from any cause. The term does not include a fetus whose biparietal diameter is less than 60 millimeters.

(Acts 1999, 76th Leg., ch. 388, §5, effective September 1, 1999. Amended by Acts 2001, 77th Leg., ch. 1420, §10.001, effective September 1, 2001.)

§170.002. Prohibited acts; exemption

(a) Except as provided by Subsection (b), a person may not intentionally or knowingly perform an abortion on a woman who is pregnant with a viable unborn child during the third trimester of the pregnancy.

(b) Subsection (a) does not prohibit a person from performing an abortion if at the time of the abortion the person is a physician and concludes in good faith according to the physician's best medical judgment that:

(1) the fetus is not a viable fetus and the pregnancy is not in the third trimester;

(2) the abortion is necessary to prevent the death or a substantial risk of serious impairment to the physical or mental health of the woman; or

(3) the fetus has a severe and irreversible abnormality, identified by reliable diagnostic procedures.

(c) A physician who performs an abortion that, according to the physician's best medical judgment at the time of the abortion, is to abort a viable unborn child during the third trimester of the pregnancy shall certify in writing to the department, on a form prescribed by the department, the medical indications supporting the physician's judgment that the abortion was authorized by Subsection (b)(2) or (3). The certification must be made not later than the 30th day after the date the abortion was performed.
(Acts 1999, 76th Leg., ch. 388, §5, effective September 1, 1999.)

2. Minor's Right to an Abortion

A minor's right to an abortion is more limited than an adult's. A majority of states mandate parental consent or notification when minors seek an abortion. According to the United States Supreme Court, parental consent and notification requirements are constitutional so long as they include provisions for a judicial bypass as an alternative. Bellotti v. Baird, 443 U.S. 622 (1979)) (holding that if a state requires one or both parents' consent, the state must provide either a judicial or administrative alternative procedure whereby the minor can obtain authorization); Hodgson v. Minnesota, 497 U.S. 417 (1990) (holding that the existence of an alternative means for a minor to obtain an abortion mitigates the constitutional defect of a two-parent notification provision); Planned Parenthood of Southeastern Pennsylvania v. Casey, 505 U.S. 833 (1992) (upholding a one-parent consent requirement with judicial bypass).

The United States Supreme Court recently addressed minors' abortion rights in Ayotte v. Planned Parenthood of Northern New England, 126 S. Ct. 961 (2006). A group of abortion providers brought a §1983 action seeking to have New Hampshire's parental notification act declared unconstitutional. A federal district court found the law unconstitutional because it failed to contain an exception allowing a minor toobtain an abortion without notice to her parents when necessary to preserve her health. The Supreme Court vacated and remanded the case for reconsideration of the remedy, specifically whether the law could be applied in such a manner as to prohibit only its unconstitutional applications without invalidating the entire statute.

A minor's right to abortion in Texas is regulated by the Family Code (the Parental Notification Act), the Occupations Code, and Parental Notification Rules adopted by the Texas Supreme Court. The Parental Notification Act (Chapter 33 of the Texas Family Code), was enacted in 1999. The Act requires parental notification (48 hours before the procedure) or judicial approval before a physician can perform an abortion on a minor (Tex. Fam. Code §33.002). In enacting the Act, the legislature "intended to protect parents' rights by encouraging minors to involve their parents in the profound decision to proceed with or terminate a pregnancy." In re Jane Doe, 19 S.W.3d 346, 350 (Tex. 2000).

Recent legislation passed in 2005 strengthened the law by requiring not merely parental notification but also parental *consent* before an unmarried minor under age 18 may obtain an abortion. Similar to the parental notification law, the parental consent law provides for judicial bypass proceedings in designated circumstances. The recent legislation was enacted as an amendment to Texas Occupations Code §164.052(a)(19) to provide that it shall be a prohibited practice for a physician to perform an abortion on an unemancipated minor without parental consent. The Texas Medical Board in September 2006 adopted administrative rules requiring that the written parental consent forms must also be notarized. Jan Jarvis, Notarized OK Needed for Minors, Fort Worth-Star Telegram, Sept. 2, 2006.

A minor who wishes to have an abortion without notifying one of her parents (or without securing a parent's consent) may petition the court, as an alternative, for an order authorizing the abortion (Tex. Fam. Code §33.003(a)). Her petition, which must be filed under oath, may be filed in any county court, probate court, or district court (including a family district court) (Tex. Fam. Code §33.003(a)(c)). The court must appoint a guardian ad litem and an attorney (who may be the same person) (Tex. Fam. Code §33.003(e)). The hearing must be expedited and confidential (Tex. Fam. Code §33.003(h)(k)(l)).

Based on a preponderance of the evidence, the trial court can grant the minor's application on three possible bases: (1) if the minor is "mature and sufficiently well informed" to make the abortion decision without notification; (2) if notification would not be in her best interests; or (3) if notification might lead to physical, sexual, or emotional abuse (Tex. Fam. Code §33.003(i)). Once the court makes the requisite determination, the court "must" enter an order authorizing consent without notification (Tex. Fam. Code §33.003(i)).

The Texas Supreme Court clarified the statutory requirements in several cases involving pregnant minors' appeals of a trial court denial of the minors' application for a court order authorizing consent to abortion without notifying the minors' parents. In In re Jane Doe, 19 S.W.3d 249 (Tex. 2000), the Texas Supreme Court set forth the factors relevant in the determination of the first prong (that the minor be mature and sufficiently well-informed). The state supreme court said that the trial court should take into account the "totality of the circumstances" and that the minor must make three showings: (1) she has obtained information about the health risks of an abortion and that she understands those risks; (2) she understands the alternatives to abortion (adoption, keeping the baby) and their implications; and (3) she is aware of the psychological and emotional aspects of undergoing an abortion (*id.* at 256-257).

In re Jane Doe 2, 19 S.W.3d 278 (Tex. 2000), clarified the second requirement above. The Texas Supreme Court noted that the proper inquiry under the statute is whether notification *would not* be in the best interests of the minor (rather than whether notification would be in the minor's best interests) (*id.* at 282).

Further, the state supreme court developed factors relevant to determining the minor's best interests: (1) her emotional or physical needs; (2) the possibility of emotional or physical danger to the minor; (3) the stability of the minor's home and whether notification would cause serious, lasting harm to the family structure; and (4) the relationship between the parent and the minor and the effect of notification on that relationship (*id.*). See also In re Jane Doe 4, 19 S.W.3d 337 (Tex. 2000) (holding that minor did not meet her burden of proof that she was sufficiently well informed or that notification would not be in her best interests).

In re Jane Doe 3, 19 S.W.3d 300 (Tex. 2000), addressed the third prong above (notification might lead to abuse). The minor argued that she had established as a matter of law that notification would lead to emotional abuse. An examination of the meaning of "abuse" in various contexts (child abuse, elder abuse) led the state supreme court to conclude that emotional abuse contemplates "unreasonable conduct causing serious emotional injury" (*id.* at 304). The court set aside the trial court's denial of the minor's petition and remanded, advising that the minor's application may not merely "parrot" terms from the statute or forms but must reveal evidence establishing that notification may lead to serious emotional injury (*id.* at 305).

See also Jane Doe 2, *supra*, at 283 (rejecting trial court's finding that adolescent's testimony provided no evidence that notification might lead to abuse; advising trial court to determine whether a preponderance of the evidence supports a finding that notification may lead to abuse and suggesting that, for meaningful appellate review, the trial court must make specific findings concerning the potential for abuse or determining that the minor's testimony about potential abuse is not credible); In re Doe 10, 78 S.W.3d 338 (2002) (reversing trial court's denial of minor's application for judicial bypass to have an abortion without parental notification because minor presented some evidence that, regardless of which parent she notified, notification might lead to her physical or emotional abuse); In re Doe 11, 92 S.W.3d 511 (2002) (affirming appellate court's dismissal of minor's appeal because the trial court's failure to rule on the minor's application for a judicial bypass to have an abortion without parental notification was deemed to be granted under §33.003(h)).

The constitutionality of Family Code Chapter 33 was at issue in In re Jane Doe 2, 19 S.W.3d 278 (Tex. 2000). The Texas Supreme Court refused to review the trial court's determination that Family Code Chapter 33 was unconstitutional, saying that the trial court erred by raising the issue sua sponte without benefit of argument or briefing. *Id.* at 284.

The Parental Notification Act also required that the Texas Supreme Court "shall issue promptly such rules as may be necessary in order that the process established by Sections 33.003 and 33.004, Family Code, as added by this Act, may be conducted in a manner that will ensure confidentiality and sufficient precedence over all other pending matters to ensure promptness of disposition." In January 2000, the Texas Supreme Court enacted Texas Parental Notification Rules to provide relevant procedures. Those court rules are set forth below.

Texas Family Code

§33.001. Definitions

In this chapter:

(1) "Abortion" means the use of any means to terminate the pregnancy of a female known by the attending physician to be pregnant, with the intention that the termination of the pregnancy by those means will with reasonable likelihood cause the death of the fetus. This definition, as applied in this chapter, applies only to an unemancipated minor known by the attending physician to be pregnant and may not be construed to limit a minor's access to contraceptives.

(2) "Fetus" means an individual human organism from fertilization until birth.

(3) "Guardian" means a court-appointed guardian of the person of the minor.

(4) "Physician" means an individual licensed to practice medicine in this state.

(5) "Unemancipated minor" includes a minor who:

(A) is unmarried; and

(B) has not had the disabilities of minority removed under Chapter 31.

(Acts 1999, 76th Leg., ch. 395, §1, effective September 1, 1999.)

§33.002. Physician must give prior notice to parents before performing abortion on minor

(a) A physician may not perform an abortion on a pregnant unemancipated minor unless:

(1) the physician performing the abortion gives at least 48 hours actual notice, in person or by telephone, of the physician's intent to perform the abortion to:

(A) a parent of the minor, if the minor has no managing conservator or guardian; or

(B) a court-appointed managing conservator or guardian;

(2) the judge of a court having probate jurisdiction, the judge of a county court at law, the judge of a district court, including a family district court, or a court of appellate jurisdiction issues an order authorizing the minor to consent to the abortion as provided by Section 33.003 or 33.004;

(3) a probate court, county court at law, district court, including a family district court, or court of appeals, by its inaction, constructively authorizes the minor to consent to the abortion as provided by Section 33.003 or 33.004; or

(4) the physician performing the abortion:

(A) concludes that on the basis of the physician's good faith clinical judgment, a condition exists that complicates the medical condition of the pregnant minor and necessitates the immediate abortion of her pregnancy to avert her death or to avoid a serious risk of substantial and irreversible impairment of a major bodily function; and

(B) certifies in writing to the Texas Department of Health and in the patient's medical record the medical indications supporting the physician's judgment that the circumstances described by Paragraph (A) exist.

(b) If a person to whom notice may be given under Subsection (a)(1) cannot be notified after a reasonable effort, a physician may perform an abortion if the physician gives 48 hours constructive notice, by certified mail, restricted delivery, sent to the last known address, to the person to whom notice may be given under Subsection (a)(1). The period under this subsection begins when the notice is mailed. If the person required to be notified is not notified within the 48-hour period, the abortion may proceed even if the notice by mail is not received.

(c) The requirement that 48 hours actual notice be provided under this section may be waived by an affidavit of:

(1) a parent of the minor, if the minor has no managing conservator or guardian; or

(2) a court-appointed managing conservator or guardian.

(d) A physician may execute for inclusion in the minor's medical record an affidavit stating that, according to the best information and belief of the physician, notice or constructive notice has been provided as required by this section. Execution of an affidavit under this subsection creates a presumption that the requirements of this section have been satisfied.

(e) The Texas Department of Health shall prepare a form to be used for making the certification required by Subsection (a)(4).

(f) A certification required by Subsection (a)(4) is confidential and privileged and is not subject to disclosure under Chapter 552, Government Code, or to discovery, subpoena, or other legal process. Personal or identifying information about the minor, including her name, address, or social security number, may not be included in a certification under Subsection (a)(4). The physician must keep the medical records on the minor in compliance with the rules adopted by the Texas State Board of Medical Examiners under Section 153.003, Occupations Code.

(g) A physician who intentionally performs an abortion on a pregnant unemancipated minor in violation of this section commits an offense. An offense under this subsection is punishable by a fine not to exceed $10,000. In this subsection, "intentionally" has the meaning assigned by Section 6.03(a), Penal Code.

(h) It is a defense to prosecution under this section that the minor falsely represented her age or identity to the physician to be at least 18 years of age by displaying an apparently valid governmental record of identification such that a reasonable person under similar circumstances would have relied on the representation. The defense does not apply if the physician is shown to have had independent knowledge of the minor's actual age or identity or failed to use due diligence in determining the minor's age or identity. In this subsection, "defense" has the meaning and application assigned by Section 2.03, Penal Code.

(i) In relation to the trial of an offense under this section in which the conduct charged involves a conclusion made by the physician under Subsection (a)(4), the defendant may seek a hearing before the Texas State Board of Medical Examiners on whether the physician's conduct was necessary to avert the death of the minor or to avoid a serious risk of substantial and irreversible impairment of a major bodily function. The findings of the Texas State Board of Medical Examiners under this subsection are admissible on that issue in the trial of the defendant. Notwithstanding any other reason for a continuance provided under the Code of Criminal Procedure or other law, on motion of the defendant, the court shall delay the beginning of the trial for not more than 30 days to permit a hearing under this subsection to take place.

(Acts 1999, 76th Leg., ch. 395, §1, effective September 1, 1999. Amended by Acts 2001, 77th Leg., ch. 1420, §14.741, effective September 1, 2001.)

§33.003. Pregnant minor may request bypass proceeding without parental notification; procedure

(a) A pregnant minor who wishes to have an abortion without notification to one of her parents, her managing conservator, or her guardian may file an application for a court order authorizing the minor to consent to the performance of an abortion without notification to either of her parents or a managing conservator or guardian.

(b) The application may be filed in any county court at law, court having probate jurisdiction, or district court, including a family district court, in this state.

(c) The application must be made under oath and include:

(1) a statement that the minor is pregnant;

(2) a statement that the minor is unmarried, is under 18 years of age, and has not had her disabilities removed under Chapter 31;

(3) a statement that the minor wishes to have an abortion without the notification of either of her parents or a managing conservator or guardian; and

(4) a statement as to whether the minor has retained an attorney and, if she has retained an attorney, the name, address, and telephone number of her attorney.

(d) The clerk of the court shall deliver a courtesy copy of the application made under this section to the judge who is to hear the application.

(e) The court shall appoint a guardian ad litem for the minor. If the minor has not retained an attorney, the court shall appoint an attorney to represent the minor. If the guardian ad litem is an attorney admitted to the practice of law in this state, the court may appoint the guardian ad litem to serve as the minor's attorney.

(f) The court may appoint to serve as guardian ad litem:

(1) a person who may consent to treatment for the minor under Sections 32.001(a)(1) (3);

(2) a psychiatrist or an individual licensed or certified as a psychologist under Chapter 501, Occupations Code;

(3) an appropriate employee of the Department of Protective and Regulatory Services;

(4) a member of the clergy; or

(5) another appropriate person selected by the court.

(g) The court shall fix a time for a hearing on an application filed under Subsection (a) and shall keep a record of all testimony and other oral proceedings in the action. The court shall enter judgment on the application immediately after the hearing is concluded.

(h) The court shall rule on an application submitted under this section and shall issue written findings of fact and conclusions of law not later than 5 p.m. on the second business day after the date the application is filed with the court. On request by the minor, the court shall grant an extension of the period specified by this subsection. If a request for an extension is made, the court shall rule on an application and shall issue written findings of fact and conclusions of law not later than 5 p.m. on the second business day after the date the minor states she is ready to proceed to hearing. If the court fails to rule on the application and issue written findings of fact and conclusions of law within the period specified by this subsection, the application is deemed to be granted and the physician may perform the abortion as if the court had issued an order authorizing the minor to consent to the performance of the abortion without notification under Section 33.002. Proceedings under this section shall be given precedence over other pending matters to the extent necessary to assure that the court reaches a decision promptly.

(i) The court shall determine by a preponderance of the evidence whether the minor is mature and sufficiently well informed to make the decision to have an abortion performed without notification to either of her parents or a managing conservator or guardian, whether notification would not be in the best interest of the minor, or whether notification may lead to physical, sexual, or emotional abuse of the minor. If the court finds that the minor is mature and sufficiently well informed, that notification would not be in the minor's best interest, or that notification may lead to physical, sexual, or emotional abuse of the minor, the court shall enter an order authorizing the minor to consent to the performance of the abortion without notification to either of her parents or a managing conservator or guardian and shall execute the required forms.

(j) If the court finds that the minor does not meet the requirements of Subsection (i), the court may not authorize the minor to consent to an abortion without the notification authorized under Section 33.002(a)(1).

(k) The court may not notify a parent, managing conservator, or guardian that the minor is pregnant or that the minor wants to have an abortion. The court proceedings shall be conducted in a manner that protects the anonymity of the minor. The application and all other court documents pertaining to the proceedings are confidential and privileged and are not subject to disclosure under Chapter 552, Government Code, or to discovery, subpoena, or other legal process. The minor may file the application using a pseudonym or using only her initials.

(l) An order of the court issued under this section is confidential and privileged and is not subject to disclosure under Chapter 552, Government Code, or discovery, subpoena, or other legal process. The order may not be released to any person but the pregnant minor, the pregnant minor's guardian ad litem, the pregnant minor's attorney, another person designated to receive the order by the minor, or a governmental agency or attorney in a criminal or administrative action seeking to assert or protect the interest of the minor. The supreme court may adopt rules to permit confidential docketing of an application under this section.

(m) The clerk of the supreme court shall prescribe the application form to be used by the minor filing an application under this section.

(n) A filing fee is not required of and court costs may not be assessed against a minor filing an application under this section.

(Acts 1999, 76th Leg., ch. 395, §1, effective September 1, 1999. Amended by Acts 2001, 77th Leg., ch. 1420, §14.742, effective September 1, 2001.)

§33.004. Minor has right to appeal denial of authorization for abortion

(a) A minor whose application under Section 33.003 is denied may appeal to the court of appeals having jurisdiction over civil matters in the county in which the application was filed. On receipt of a notice of appeal, the clerk of the court that denied the application shall deliver a copy of the notice of appeal and record on appeal to the clerk of the court of appeals. On receipt of the notice and record, the clerk of the court of appeals shall place the appeal on the docket of the court.

(b) The court of appeals shall rule on an appeal under this section not later than 5 p.m. on the second business day after the date the notice of appeal is filed with the court that denied the application. On request by the minor, the court shall grant an extension of the period specified by this subsection. If a request for an extension is made, the court shall rule on the appeal not later than 5 p.m. on the second business day after the date the minor states she is ready to proceed. If the court of appeals fails to rule on the appeal within the period specified by this subsection, the appeal is deemed to be granted and the physician may perform the abortion as if the court had issued an order authorizing the minor to consent to the performance of the abortion without notification under Section 33.002. Proceedings under this section shall be given precedence over other pending matters to the extent necessary to assure that the court reaches a decision promptly.

(c) A ruling of the court of appeals issued under this section is confidential and privileged and is not subject to disclosure under Chapter 552, Government Code, or discovery, subpoena, or other legal process. The ruling may not be released to any person but the pregnant minor, the pregnant minor's guardian ad litem, the pregnant minor's attorney, another person designated to receive the ruling by the minor, or a governmental agency or attorney in a criminal or administrative action seeking to assert or protect the interest of the minor. The supreme court may adopt rules to permit confidential docketing of an appeal under this section.

(d) The clerk of the supreme court shall prescribe the notice of appeal form to be used by the minor appealing a judgment under this section.

(e) A filing fee is not required of and court costs may not be assessed against a minor filing an appeal under this section.

(f) An expedited confidential appeal shall be available to any pregnant minor to whom a court of appeals denies an order authorizing the minor to consent to the performance of an abortion without notification to either of her parents or a managing conservator or guardian.

(Acts 1999, 76th Leg., ch. 395, §1, effective September 1, 1999.)

§33.005. Physician may execute affidavit and perform abortion

(a) A physician may execute for inclusion in the minor's medical record an affidavit stating that, after reasonable inquiry, it is the belief of the physician that:

(1) the minor has made an application or filed a notice of an appeal with a court under this chapter;

(2) the deadline for court action imposed by this chapter has passed; and

(3) the physician has been notified that the court has not denied the application or appeal.

(b) A physician who in good faith has executed an affidavit under Subsection (a) may rely on the affidavit and may perform the abortion as if the court had issued an order granting the application or appeal.

(Acts 1999, 76th Leg., ch. 395, §1, effective September 1, 1999.)

§33.006. Guardian ad litem has immunity

A guardian ad litem appointed under this chapter and acting in the course and scope of the appointment is not liable for damages arising from an act or omission of the guardian ad litem committed in good faith. The immunity granted by this section does not apply if the conduct of the guardian ad litem is committed in a manner described by Sections 107.003(b)(1) (4).

(Acts 1999, 76th Leg., ch. 395, §1, effective September 1, 1999.)

§33.007. Court may require state to pay costs

(a) A court acting under Section 33.003 or 33.004 may issue an order requiring the state to pay:

(1) the cost of any attorney ad litem and any guardian ad litem appointed for the minor;

(2) notwithstanding Sections 33.003(n) and 33.004(e), the costs of court associated with the application or appeal; and

(3) any court reporter's fees incurred.

(b) An order issued under Subsection (a) must be directed to the comptroller, who shall pay the amount ordered from funds appropriated to the Texas Department of Health.

(Acts 1999, 76th Leg., ch. 395, §1, effective September 1, 1999.)

§33.011. Health Department shall provide information about judicial bypass

The Texas Department of Health shall produce and distribute informational materials that explain the rights of a minor under this chapter. The materials must explain the procedures established by Sections 33.003 and 33.004 and must be made available in English and in Spanish. The material provided by the department shall also provide information relating to alternatives to abortion and health risks associated with abortion.

(Acts 1999, 76th Leg., ch. 395, §1, effective September 1, 1999.)

---

a. Texas Parental Notification Rules

The Texas Supreme Court adopted Parental Notification Rules, effective January 1, 2000, that further regulate minors' abortion procedures. The Rules provide that all proceedings must be expeditious (Rule 1.2, Rule 3.3), confidential (Rule 1.4), and protect the minor's anonymity (Rule 1.3). The minor has the right to appeal a denial of her application (Rule 3.1). To facilitate the minor's application, she may file in any county, regardless of her residence or the location of the abortion provider (Rule 2.1(a)), and she shall not be assessed fees or costs (Rule 1.9). The Rules were adopted without any determination whether the Parental Notification Act or any of its provisions are constitutional under the federal or state constitution.

Texas Parental Notification Rules

Rule 1.1 Applicability of rules

These rules govern proceedings for obtaining a court order authorizing a minor to consent to an abortion without notice to either of her parents or a managing conservator or guardian under Chapter 33, Family Code (or as amended). Other Texas court rules — including the Rules of Civil Procedure, Rules of Evidence, Rules of Appellate Procedure, Rules of Judicial Administration, and local rules approved by the Supreme Court — also apply, but when the application of another rule would be inconsistent with the general framework or policy of Chapter 33, Family Code, or these rules, these rules control.

(Adopted December 22, 1999, effective January 1, 2000. Amended November 8, 2000, effective March 1, 2001.)

Rule 1.2 Proceedings have precedence

(a) Proceedings. A court must give proceedings under these rules precedence over all other pending matters to the extent necessary to assure that applications and appeals are adjudicated as soon as possible and within the time required by Rules 2.4(a), 2.5(d), and 3.3(c).

(b) Prompt Actual Notice Required. Without compromising the confidentiality and anonymity required by statute and these rules, courts and clerks must serve orders, decisions, findings, and notices required under these rules in a manner designed to give prompt actual notice in order that the deadlines imposed by Chapter 33, Family Code, can be met.

(c) Instanter. "Instanter" means immediately, without delay. An action required by these rules to be taken instanter should be done at the first possible time and with the most expeditious means available.

(Adopted December 22, 1999, effective January 1, 2000. Amended November 8, 2000, effective March 1, 2001.)

Rule 1.3 Anonymity of minor

(a) Generally. Proceedings under these rules must be conducted in a way that protects the anonymity of the minor.

(b) No Reference to Minor's Identity in Proceeding. With the exception of the verification page required under Rule

2.1(c)(2) and the communications required under Rule 2.2(e), no reference may be made in any order, decision, finding, or notice, or on the record, to the name of the minor, her address, or other information by which she might be identified by persons not participating in the proceedings. Instead, the minor must be referred to as "Jane Doe" in a numbered cause.

(c) Notice Required to Minor's Attorney. With the exception of orders and rulings released under Rule 1.4(b), all service and communications from the court to the minor must be directed to the minor's attorney. This requirement takes effect when an attorney appears for the minor, or when the clerk has notified the minor of the appointment of an attorney.

(Adopted December 22, 1999, effective January 1, 2000. Amended November 8, 2000, effective March 1, 2001.)

Rule 1.4 Confidentiality of proceedings

(a) Generally. All officials and court personnel involved in the proceedings must ensure that the minor's contact with the clerk and court is confidential and expeditious. Except as permitted by law, no officials or court personnel involved in the proceedings may ever disclose to anyone outside the proceedings — including the minor's parent, managing conservator, or legal guardian — that the minor is or has ever been pregnant, or that she wants or has ever wanted an abortion.

(b) Documents and information pertaining to the proceeding. As required by Chapter 33, Family Code, the application and all other court documents and information pertaining to the proceedings are confidential and privileged and are not subject to disclosure under Chapter 552, Government Code, or to discovery, subpoena, or other legal process. But documents and information may be disclosed when expressly authorized by these rules, and an order, ruling, opinion, or clerk's certificate may be released to:

(1) the minor;

(2) the minor's guardian ad litem;

(3) the minor's attorney;

(4) a person designated in writing by the minor to receive the order, ruling, opinion, or certificate;

(5) a governmental agency or governmental attorney, in connection with a criminal or administrative action seeking to assert or protect the minor's interests; or

(6) another court, judge, or clerk in the same or related proceedings.

(c) Filing of Court Reporter's Notes Permitted. To assure confidentiality, court reporter notes, in whatever form, may be filed with other court documents in the proceeding.

(d) Duty to Report Possible Sexual Abuse. A court, guardian ad litem, or attorney ad litem who reasonably believes, based on information obtained in the proceeding, that a violation of Section 22.011, 22.021, or 25.02, Penal Code, has occurred must report the information to the appropriate officials or agencies as required by Section 33.009, Family Code.

(e) Department of Protective and Regulatory Services to Disclose Certain Information in Proceeding. The Department of Protective and Regulatory Services may disclose to the court, the attorney ad litem, and the guardian ad litem any information obtained under Section 33.008, Family Code, without being ordered to do so. The trial court may order the Department to disclose such information to such persons, and the Department must comply.

(Adopted December 22, 1999, effective January 1, 2000. Amended November 8, 2000, effective March 1, 2001.)

Rule 1.5 Electronic transmission of documents and hearings by remote electronic means

(a) Electronic Filing. Documents may be filed by facsimile or other electronic data transmission. If the sender communicates directly with the clerk the time at which the transmission will occur, the clerk must take all reasonable steps to assure that the confidentiality of the received transmission will be maintained.

(b) Electronic Transmission by Court and Clerk. The court and clerk may transmit orders, rulings, notices, and other documents by facsimile or other electronic data transmission. But before the transmission is initiated, the sender must take all reasonable steps to assure that the confidentiality of the received transmission will be maintained. The time and date of a transmission by the court is the time and date when it was initiated.

(c) Hearings by Electronic Means. Consistent with the anonymity and confidentiality requirements of these rules, with the court's permission, the attorney ad litem, the guardian ad litem, and any witnesses may participate in hearings under these rules by video conferencing, telephone, or other remote electronic means. The minor must appear before the court in person unless the court determines that the minor's appearance by video conferencing will allow the court to view the minor during the hearing sufficiently well to assess her credibility and demeanor.

(d) Record of Hearing Made by Electronic Means if Necessary. If the court determines that a court reporter is unavailable for a hearing, the court may have a record of the hearing made by audio recording or other electronic means. If a notice of appeal is filed, the court must have the recording transcribed if possible. The person transcribing the recording must certify to the accuracy of the transcription. The court must transmit both the recording and the transcription to the court of appeals.

(Adopted December 22, 1999, effective January 1, 2000. Amended November 8, 2000, effective March 1, 2001.)

Rule 1.6 Disqualification, recusal, or objection to a judge

(a) Time for filing and ruling. An objection to a trial judge, or a motion to recuse or disqualify a trial judge, must be filed before 10:00 a.m. of the first business day after an application is filed or promptly after the assignment of a judge to hear the case is made known to the minor or her attorney, whichever is later. An objection to an appellate judge, or a motion to recuse or disqualify an appellate judge must be filed before 10 a.m. of the first business day after a notice of appeal is filed. A judge who chooses to recuse voluntarily must do so instanter. An objection to a judge or a motion to disqualify or recuse does not extend the deadline for ruling on the minor's application.

(b) Voluntary Disqualification or Recusal, or Objection. A judge to whom objection is made under Chapter 74,

Government Code, or a judge or justice who voluntarily does not sit, must notify instanter the appropriate authority for assigning another judge by local rules or by statute. That authority must instanter assign a judge or justice to the proceeding.

(c) Involuntary Disqualification or Recusal. A judge or justice who refuses to remove himself or herself voluntarily from a proceeding in response to a motion must instanter refer the motion to the appropriate judge or justice, pursuant to local rule, rule, or statute, for determination. The judge or justice to whom the motion is referred must rule on it as soon as possible and may do so with or without a hearing. If the motion is granted, the judge or justice to whom the motion was referred must instanter assign a judge or justice to the proceeding.

(d) Only One Objection or Motion to Recuse Permitted. A minor who objects to a judge assigned to the proceeding may not thereafter file a motion to recuse or disqualify, and a minor who files a motion to recuse or disqualify a judge may not thereafter object to a judge assigned to the proceeding.

(e) Issues on Appeal. Any error in the denial of a motion to recuse or disqualify, or any error in the disallowance of an objection, or any challenge to a judge that a minor is precluded from making by subsections (a) or (d), may be raised only on appeal from the court's denial of the application. 1.7 Rules and Forms to be Made Available. A copy of these rules, and a copy of the attached forms in English and Spanish, must be made available to any person without charge in the clerk's offices of all courts in which applications or appeals may be filed under these rules, on the Texas Judiciary Internet site at www.courts.state.tx.us, and by the Office of Court Administration upon request. A copy of a court's local rules relating to proceedings under Chapter 33, Family Code, must be made available to any person without charge in the office of the clerk for that court where applications may be filed. Rules and forms may be copied.

(Adopted December 22, 1999, effective January 1, 2000. Amended November 8, 2000, effective March 1, 2001.)

Rule 1.8 Duties of attorneys ad litem

An attorney ad litem must represent the minor in the trial court in the proceeding in which the attorney is assigned, and in any appeal under these rules to the court of appeals or the Supreme Court. But an attorney ad litem is not required to represent the minor in any other court or any other proceeding.

(Adopted December 22, 1999, effective January 1, 2000. Amended November 8, 2000, effective March 1, 2001.)

Rule 1.9 Fees and costs

(a) No fees or costs charged to minor. No filing fee or court cost may be assessed against a minor for any proceeding in a trial or appellate court.

(b) State ordered to pay fees and costs.

(1) Fees and costs that may be paid. The State may be ordered to pay the reasonable and necessary fees and expenses of the attorney ad litem, the reasonable and necessary fees and expenses of the guardian ad litem, the court reporter's fee as certified by the court reporter, and trial court filing fees and costs as certified by the clerk. Court costs include the expenses of an interpreter (Form 2H) but do not include the fees or expenses of a witness. Court costs do not include fees which must be remitted to the state treasury.

(2) To whom order directed and sent. The order must be directed to the Comptroller of Public Accounts but should be sent by the clerk to the Director, Fiscal Division, of the Texas Department of Health.

(3) Form and contents of the order. The order must state the amounts to be awarded the attorney ad litem and the guardian ad litem. The order must be separate from any other order in the proceeding and must not address any subject other than the assessment of costs. A trial court may use Forms 2F and 2G, but it is not required to do so.

(4) Time for signing and sending order. To be valid, the order must be signed by the judge and sent by the clerk to the Department of Health not later than the ninetieth day after the date of the final ruling in a proceeding, whether the application is granted, deemed granted, or denied, or the proceeding is dismissed or nonsuited.

(c) Motion to reconsider; time for filing. Within thirty days of actual receipt of the order, the Comptroller or any other person adversely affected by the order may file a motion in the trial court to reconsider the assessment of costs. The trial court retains jurisdiction of the case to hear and determine any timely filed motion to reconsider.

(d) Appeal. The Comptroller or any other person adversely affected by the order may appeal from the trial court's ruling on the motion to reconsider as from any other final judgment of the court.

(e) Report to the Office of Court Administration. The Department of Health must transmit to the Office of Court Administration a copy of every order assessing costs in a proceeding under Chapter 33, Family Code. Such orders are not subject to the Amended Order of the Supreme Court of Texas, dated September 21, 1994, in Misc. Docket No. 94-9143, regarding mandatory reports of judicial appointments and fees.

(f) Confidentiality. When transmitting an order awarding costs to the Department of Health, the clerk must take reasonable steps to preserve its confidentially. The confidentiality of an order awarding costs — as prescribed by Chapter 33, Family Code—is not affected by its transmission to the Comptroller, Texas Department of Health, or the Office of Court Administration, nor is the order subject to public disclosure in response to a request under any statute, rule or other law. But these rules do not preclude the Comptroller, Texas Department of Health, and the Office of Court Administration from disclosing summary information from orders assessing costs for statistical or other such purposes.

(Adopted December 22, 1999, effective January 1, 2000. Amended November 8, 2000, effective March 1, 2001.)

Rule 1.10 Amicus briefs

Amicus briefs may be submitted and received by a court—but not filed—under either of the following procedures.

(a) Confidential, Case-Specific Briefs. A non-party who is authorized to attend or participate in a particular proceeding under Chapter 33, Family Code may submit an amicus brief addressing matters, including confidential matters, specific to the proceeding. The brief and the manner in which it is submitted must comply with Rules 1.3 and 1.4 and be directed to the court in which the proceeding is pending. The person must submit the original brief and the same number of copies required for other submissions to the court, and must serve a copy of the brief on the minor's attorney. The court to which the brief is submitted must maintain the brief as part of the confidential case file in accordance with Rule 1.4.

(b) Public or General Briefs. Any person may submit a brief addressing any matter relating to proceedings under Chapter 33, Family Code. Such a brief must not contain any information in violation of Rules 1.3 and 1.4. The person must submit the original brief and the same number of copies required for other submissions to the court. If the brief is submitted to a court of appeals, the original and eleven copies of the brief, plus a computer disk containing the brief, must also be submitted to the Supreme Court of Texas. When an appeal of a proceeding is filed, the clerk of the court of appeals or the Supreme Court must notify the parties to the appeal of the existence of any brief filed under this subsection and must make the brief available for inspection and copying. Upon submission, the Clerk of the Supreme Court must, as soon as practicable, have the brief posted on the Texas Judiciary Internet site and make it available to the public for inspection and copying.

(Adopted December 22, 1999, effective January 1, 2000. Amended November 8, 2000, effective March 1, 2001.)

Rule 2.1 Counties and courts in which to file application; transfer; application form

(a) Counties in Which an Application May Be Filed. An application for an order under Section 33.003, Family Code, may be filed in any county, regardless of the minor's residence or where the abortion sought is to be performed.

(b) Courts in Which an Application May Be Filed; Assignment and Transfer.

(1) Courts with Jurisdiction. An application may be filed in a district court (including a family district court), a county court-at-law, or a court having probate jurisdiction.

(2) Application Filed With District or County Clerk. An application must be filed with either the district clerk or the county clerk, who will assign the application to a court as provided by local rule or these rules. The clerk to whom the application is tendered cannot refuse to accept it because of any local rule or other rule or law that provides for filing and assignment of such applications but must accept the application and transfer it instanter to the proper clerk, advising the person tendering the application where it is being transferred.

(3) Court Assignment and Transfer by Local Rule. The courts in a county that have jurisdiction to hear applications may determine by local rule how applications will be assigned between or among them. A local rule must be approved by the Supreme Court under Rule 3a, Texas Rules of Civil Procedure.

(4) Initial Court Assignment if No Local Rule. Absent a local rule, the clerk that files an application — whether the district clerk or the county clerk — must assign it as follows:

(i) to a district court, if the active judge of the court, or a judge assigned to it, is then present in the county;

(ii) if the application cannot be assigned under (i), then to a statutory county or probate court, if the active judge of the court, or a judge assigned to it, is then present in the county;

(iii) if the application cannot be assigned under (i) or (ii), then to the constitutional county court, if it has probate jurisdiction, and if the active judge of the court, or a judge assigned to it, is then present in the county;

(iv) if the application cannot be assigned under (i), (ii), or (iii), then to the district court.

(5) Judges Who May Hear and Determine Applications. An application may be heard and determined

(i) by the active judge of the court to which the application is assigned, or

(ii) by any judge authorized to sit for the active judge, or

(iii) by any judge who may be assigned to the court in which the application is pending. An application may not be heard or determined, or any proceedings under these rules conducted, by a master or magistrate.

(c) Application Form. An application consists of two pages: a cover page and a separate verification page.

(1) Cover Page. The cover page may be submitted on Form 2A, but use of the form is not required. The cover page must be styled "In re Jane Doe" and must not disclose the name of the minor or any information from which the minor's identity could be derived. The cover page must state:

(A) that the minor is pregnant;

(B) that the minor is unmarried, is under 18 years of age, and has not had her disabilities removed under Chapter 31, Family Code;

(C) that the minor wishes to have an abortion without notifying either of her parents or a managing conservator or guardian, and the statutory ground or grounds on which she relies;

(D) whether the minor has retained an attorney, and if so, the attorney's name, address, and telephone number;

(E) whether the minor requests the court to appoint a particular person as her guardian ad litem; and

(F) whether, concerning her current pregnancy, the minor has previously filed an application that was denied, and if so, where the application was filed.

(2) Verification Page. The verification page may be submitted on Form 2B, but use of the form is not required. The verification page must be separate from the cover page, must be signed under oath by the person completing the application, and must state:

(A) the minor's full name and date of birth;

(B) the name, address, telephone number, and relationship to the minor of any person the minor requests the court to appoint as her guardian ad litem;

(C) a telephone or pager number — whether that of the minor or someone else (such as a physician, friend, or relative) — at which the minor may be contacted immediately and confidentially until an attorney is appointed to represent her; and

(D) that all information contained in the application, including both the cover page and the verification page, is true.

(d) Time of Filing. An application is filed when it is actually received by the district or county clerk.

(Adopted December 22, 1999, effective January 1, 2000.)

Rule 2.2 Clerk's duties

(a) Assistance in Filing. The clerk must give prompt assistance — in a manner designed to protect the minor's confidentiality and anonymity — to persons seeking to file an application. If requested, the clerk must administer the oath required for the verification page or provide a person authorized to do so. The clerk should also redact from the cover page any information identifying the minor. The clerk should ensure that both the cover page and the separate verification page are completed in full.

(b) Filing Procedure. The clerk must assign the application a cause number and affix it to both the cover page and the verification page. The clerk must then provide a certified copy of the verification page to the person filing the application. The clerk must file the verification page under seal in a secure place where access is limited to essential court personnel.

(c) Distribution. When an application is filed, the clerk must distribute the cover page and verification page, or a copy of them, to the appropriate court instanter. If appointment of a specific person as guardian ad litem has been requested, the clerk must also communicate the information to the appropriate court instanter.

(d) If Judge of Assigned Court Not Present in County. The clerk must determine instanter whether the judge of the court to which the application is assigned is present in the county. If that judge is not present in the county, the clerk must instanter notify the local administrative judge or judges and the presiding judge of the administrative judicial region and must send them any information requested, including the cover page and verification page.

(e) Notice of Hearing and Appointments. When the clerk is advised by the court of a time for hearing or an appointment of a guardian ad litem or attorney ad litem, the clerk must instanter give notice — as directed in the verification page and to each appointee — of the hearing time or appointment. A court coordinator or other court personnel may give notice instead of the clerk.

(f) Orders. The clerk must provide the minor and the attorney ad litem with copies of all court orders, including findings of fact and conclusions of law.

(g) Certificate of Court's Failure to Rule Within Time Prescribed by Statute. If the court fails to rule on an application within the time required by Section 33.002(g) and (h), Family Code, upon the minor's request, the clerk must instanter issue a certificate to that effect, stating that the application is deemed by statute to be granted. The clerk may use Form 2E but is not required to do so.

(Adopted December 22, 1999, effective January 1, 2000.)

Rule 2.3 Duties of court to appoint representatives and set hearing

Upon receipt of an application from the clerk, the court must promptly:

(a) appoint a qualified person to serve as guardian ad litem for the minor;

(b) appoint an attorney for the minor, who may be the same person appointed guardian ad litem if that person is an attorney admitted to practice law in Texas and there is no conflict of interest in the same person serving as attorney ad litem and guardian ad litem;

(c) set a hearing on the application in accordance with Rule 2.4(a); and

(d) advise the clerk of the appointment or appointments and the hearing time.

(Adopted December 22, 1999, effective January 1, 2000.)

Rule 2.4 Hearing

(a) Time. The court must conduct a hearing in time to rule on the application as required by Rule 2.5(d). But the minor may postpone the hearing by written request to the clerk when the application is filed or thereafter. The request may be submitted on Form 2C, but use of the form is not required. The request must either specify a date on which the minor will be ready for the hearing, or state that the minor will later provide a date on which she will be ready for the hearing. Once the minor determines when she will be ready for the hearing, she must notify the clerk of that time in writing. The postponed hearing must be conducted in time for the court to rule on the application as required by Rule 2.5(d).

(b) Place. The hearing should be held in a location, such as a judge's chambers, that will assure confidentiality. The hearing may be held away from the courthouse.

(c) Persons Attending. Hearings must be closed to the public. Only the judge, the court reporter and any other essential court personnel, the minor, her attorney, her guardian ad litem, and witnesses on the minor's behalf may be present.

(d) Record. If the minor appeals, or if there is evidence of past or potential abuse of the minor, the hearing must be transcribed instanter.

(e) Hearing to Be Informal. The court should attempt to rule on the application without regard to technical defects in the application or the evidence. Affidavits of persons other than applicants are admissible. Statements in the application cannot be offered as evidence to support the application. If necessary, the court may assist the minor in remedying technical defects in the application and in presenting relevant and material facts.

(Adopted December 22, 1999, effective January 1, 2000.)

Rule 2.5 Ruling

(a) Form of Ruling. The court's ruling on the application must include a signed order and written findings of fact and conclusions of law. The findings and conclusions may be included in the order. The court may use Form 2D, but it is not required to do so.

(b) Grounds for Granting Application. The court must grant the application if the minor establishes, by a preponderance of the evidence, that:

(1) the minor is mature and sufficiently well informed to make the decision to have an abortion performed without notifying either of the minor's parents, the minor's managing conservator, or the minor's legal guardian, as the case may be;

(2) notifying either of the minor's parents, the minor's managing conservator, or the minor's legal guardian, as the case may be, would not be in the minor's best interest; or

(3) notifying either of the minor's parents, the minor's managing conservator, or the minor's legal guardian, as the case may be, may lead to physical, sexual, or emotional abuse of the minor.

(c) Grounds for Denying Application. If the minor can establish none of the grounds in Rule 2.5(b) by a preponderance of the evidence, the court must deny the application. If the court, the guardian ad litem, or the attorney ad litem are unable to contact the minor before the hearing despite diligent attempts to do so, or if the minor does not attend the hearing, the court must deny the application without prejudice.

(d) Time for Ruling. The court must rule on an application as soon as possible after it is filed, subject to any postponement requested by the minor, and immediately after the hearing is concluded. Section 33.003(h), Family Code, states that a court must rule on an application by 5:00 p.m. on the second business day after the day the application is filed, or if the minor requests a postponement, after the date the minor states she is ready for the hearing, and that if the court does not rule within this time, the application is deemed to be granted.

(e) Notification of Right to Appeal. If the court denies the application, it must inform the minor of her right to appeal under Rule 3 and furnish her with the notice of appeal form, Form 3A.

(Adopted December 22, 1999, effective January 1, 2000.)

b. Parental Consent Provisions

Texas Occupations Code

§164.052. Prohibited practices by physicians

(a) A physician or an applicant for a license to practice medicine commits a prohibited practice if that person:

(1) submits to the board a false or misleading statement, document, or certificate in an application for a license;

(2) presents to the board a license, certificate, or diploma that was illegally or fraudulently obtained;

(3) commits fraud or deception in taking or passing an examination;

(4) uses alcohol or drugs in an intemperate manner that, in the board's opinion, could endanger a patient's life;

(5) commits unprofessional or dishonorable conduct that is likely to deceive or defraud the public, as provided by Section 164.053, or injure the public;

(6) uses an advertising statement that is false, misleading, or deceptive;

(7) advertises professional superiority or the performance of professional service in a superior manner if that advertising is not readily subject to verification;

(8) purchases, sells, barters, or uses, or offers to purchase, sell, barter, or use, a medical degree, license, certificate, or diploma, or a transcript of a license, certificate, or diploma in or incident to an application to the board for a license to practice medicine;

(9) alters, with fraudulent intent, a medical license, certificate, or diploma, or a transcript of a medical license, certificate, or diploma;

(10) uses a medical license, certificate, or diploma, or a transcript of a medical license, certificate, or diploma that has been:

(A) fraudulently purchased or issued;

(B) counterfeited; or

(C) materially altered;

(11) impersonates or acts as proxy for another person in an examination required by this subtitle for a medical license;

(12) engages in conduct that subverts or attempts to subvert an examination process required by this subtitle for a medical license;

(13) impersonates a physician or permits another to use the person's license or certificate to practice medicine in this state;

(14) directly or indirectly employs a person whose license to practice medicine has been suspended, canceled, or revoked;

(15) associates in the practice of medicine with a person:

(A) whose license to practice medicine has been suspended, canceled, or revoked; or

(B) who has been convicted of the unlawful practice of medicine in this state or elsewhere;

(16) performs or procures a criminal abortion, aids or abets in the procuring of a criminal abortion, attempts to perform or procure a criminal abortion, or attempts to aid or abet the performance or procurement of a criminal abortion;

(17) directly or indirectly aids or abets the practice of medicine by a person, partnership, association, or corporation that is not licensed to practice medicine by the board;

(18) performs an abortion on a woman who is pregnant with a viable unborn child during the third trimester of the pregnancy unless:

(A) the abortion is necessary to prevent the death of the woman;

(B) the viable unborn child has a severe, irreversible brain impairment; or

(C) the woman is diagnosed with a significant likelihood of suffering imminent severe, irreversible brain damage or imminent severe, irreversible paralysis; or

(19) performs an abortion on an unemancipated minor without the written consent of the child's parent, managing conservator, or legal guardian or without a court order, as

provided by Section 33.003 or 33.004, Family Code, authorizing the minor to consent to the abortion, unless the physician concludes that on the basis of the physician's good faith clinical judgment, a condition exists that complicates the medical condition of the pregnant minor and necessitates the immediate abortion of her pregnancy to avert her death or to avoid a serious risk of substantial impairment of a major bodily function and that there is insufficient time to obtain the consent of the child's parent, managing conservator, or legal guardian.

(b) For purposes of Subsection (a)(12), conduct that subverts or attempts to subvert the medical licensing examination process includes, as prescribed by board rules, conduct that violates:

(1) the security of the examination materials;

(2) the standard of test administration; or

(3) the accreditation process.

(c) The board shall adopt the forms necessary for physicians to obtain the consent required for an abortion to be performed on an unemancipated minor under Subsection (a). The form executed to obtain consent or any other required documentation must be retained by the physician until the later of the fifth anniversary of the date of the minor's majority or the seventh anniversary of the date the physician received or created the documentation for the record.

(Acts 1999, 76th Leg., ch. 388, §1, effective September 1, 1999. Amended by Acts 2005, 79th Leg., ch. 269, §1.42, effective September 1, 2005.)

3. Abortion Funding

The abortion funding cases arose in the context of challenges to certain federal legislation pertaining to funding of medical care. A federal statute, Title XIX of the Social Security Act, established a joint federal-state Medicaid program to assist indigents with medical costs. Prior to 1976, a significant percentage of legal abortions were funded by the Medicaid program. Since then, many state legislatures have restricted public abortion funding in an effort to limit the number of abortions.

Although the United States Supreme Court has ruled that a woman has a constitutionally protected right to an abortion, the Court has also held that the government is under no obligation to provide funds for abortion (Harris v. McRae, 448 U.S. 297 (1980)) (holding that the Hyde Amendment prohibiting expenditure of Medicaid funds for abortion unless the mother's life is endangered or she is a victim of reported rape or incest does not violate due process or equal protection).

Many states, including Texas, limit Medicaid funds for abortion. The Texas Medicaid program (termed the "Medical Assistance Program") is codified at Texas Human Resources Code §§32.001-.052 and covers all "health care and related services and benefits authorized or provided under federal law for needy individuals of this state." Tex. Hum. Res. Code §32.003. Services are limited, however, to those for which the State can receive federal matching funds. See *id.* at §32.024(e). The Texas Medical Assistance Program thereby adopts the limits set forth by the Hyde Amendment (federal legislation preventing states from receiving federal matching funds for most abortion services)—reimbursing physicians with Medicaid funds only for abortions necessary to save the woman's life or when the pregnancy has resulted from rape or incest. As a result, all reproductive health services provided by a doctor under the Texas Medical Assistance Program, except abortion, are reimbursed if "medically necessary."

In Low-Income Women of Texas v. Bost, 38 S.W.3d 689 (Tex. App.—Austin 2000, no writ), medical personnel challenged these funding restrictions as a violation of the state Equal Rights Amendment and the rights of privacy and equal protection under the state constitution. The court of appeals, although declining to reach the plaintiffs' privacy and equal protection arguments, found that the state's failure to provide for abortion funding for all medically necessary procedures violates the Equal Rights Amendment. The court concluded that the state did not offer any explanation why the state of being pregnant justified funding restrictions with respect to medically necessary abortions but not with respect to any other health care services. In Bell v. Low Income Women of Texas, 95 S.W.3d 253 (Tex. 2002), the Texas Supreme Court overturned the appellate court's ruling, concluding that because all other pregnancy-related treatments are funded, the restriction is directed at abortion as a medical treatment and not directed at women as a class.

Texas Health & Safety Code

§32.005. Funds may not be used for abortion services unless mother's life in danger

Notwithstanding any other provision of this chapter, funds administered under this chapter [maternal and infant health improvement program] may not be used to provide abortion services unless the mother's life is in danger.

(Acts 1989, 71st Leg., ch. 678, § 1, effective September 1, 1989.)

Texas Human Resources Code

§32.024. Scope of Program

(a) The department shall provide medical assistance to all persons who receive financial assistance from the state under Chapter 31 of this code and to other related groups of persons if the provision of medical assistance to those persons is required by federal law and rules as a condition for obtaining federal matching funds for the support of the medical assistance program.

(b) The department may provide medical assistance to other persons who are financially unable to meet the cost of medical services if federal matching funds are available for that purpose. The department shall adopt rules governing the eligibility of those persons for the services.

(c) The department shall establish standards governing the amount, duration, and scope of services provided under the medical assistance program. The standards may not be lower than the minimum standards required by federal law and rule as a condition for obtaining federal matching funds for support of the program, and may not be lower than the standards in effect on August 27, 1967. Standards or payments for the vendor drug program may not be lower than those in effect on January 1, 1973.

(d) The department may establish standards that increase the amount, duration, and scope of the services provided only if federal matching funds are available for the optional services and payments and if the department determines that the increase is feasible and within the limits of appropriated funds. The department may establish and maintain priorities for the provision of the optional medical services.

(e) The department may not authorize the provision of any service to any person under the program unless federal matching funds are available to pay the cost of the service....
(Acts 1979, 66th Leg., p. 2350, ch. 842, art. 1, §1, effective September 1, 1979. Amended by Acts 1989, 71st Leg., ch. 1027, §11, effective September 1, 1989; Acts 1989, 71st Leg., ch. 1085, §3, effective September 1, 1989; Acts 1989, 71st Leg., ch. 1107, §1, effective September 1, 1989; Acts 1989, 71st Leg., ch. 1219, §1, effective September 1, 1989; Acts 1990, 71st Leg., 6th C.S., ch. 12, §2(11) to (13), effective September 6, 1990; Acts 1991, 72nd Leg., ch. 690, §1, effective August 26, 1991; Acts 1995, 74th Leg., ch. 6, §3, effective March 23, 1995; Acts 1997, 75th Leg., ch. 1153, §§2.01(a), 2.02(a), effective June 20, 1997; Acts 1999, 76th Leg., ch. 766, §1, effective September 1, 1999; Acts 1999, 76th Leg., ch. 1333, §1, effective September 1, 1999; Acts 1999, 76th Leg., ch. 1347, §3, effective September 1, 1999; Acts 1999, 76th Leg., ch. 1505, §1.06, effective September 1, 1999; Acts 2001, 77th Leg., ch. 220, §1, effective September 1, 2001; Acts 2001, 77th Leg., ch. 348, §1, effective September 1, 2001; Acts 2001, 77th Leg., ch. 974, §1, effective September 1, 2001; Acts 2001, 77th Leg., ch. 1420, §21.001(81), effective September 1, 2001; Acts 2003, 78th Leg., ch. 198, §§2.96, 2.97(a), 2.207(a), effective September 1, 2003; Acts 2003, 78th Leg., ch. 215, §1, effective June 18, 2003; Acts 2003, 78th Leg., ch. 1251, §6, effective June 20, 2003; Acts 2003, 78th Leg., ch. 1275, §2(97), effective September 1, 2003; Acts 2005, 79th Leg., ch. 728, §23.001(57), effective September 1, 2005; Acts 2005, 79th Leg., ch. 349, §22, effective September 1, 2005; Acts 2005, 79th Leg., ch. 1314, §1, effective September 1, 2005.)

Texas Labor Code

§21.107. Employer is not required to pay benefits for abortion unless mother's life in danger

This chapter [employment discrimination] does not:

(1) require an employer to pay for health insurance benefits for abortion unless the life of the mother would be endangered if the fetus were carried to term;

(2) preclude an employer from providing abortion benefits; or

(3) affect a bargaining agreement relating to abortion.
(Acts 1993, 73rd Leg., ch. 269, §1, effective September 1, 1993.)

Texas Tax Code

§11.183. Association is entitled to property tax exemption if it does not provide abortion services

(a) An association is entitled to an exemption from taxation of the property it owns and uses exclusively for the purposes for which the association is organized if the association:

(1) is exempt from federal income taxation under Section 501(a), Internal Revenue Code of 1986, as an organization described by Section 501(c)(3) of that code;

(2) complies with the criteria for a charitable organization under Sections 11.18(e) and (f);

(3) except as provided by Subsection (b), engages exclusively in providing assistance to ambulatory health care centers that provide medical care to individuals without regard to the individuals' ability to pay, including providing policy analysis, disseminating information, conducting continuing education, providing research, collecting and analyzing data, or providing technical assistance to the health care centers;

(4) is funded wholly or partly, or assists ambulatory health care centers that are funded wholly or partly, by a grant under Section 330, Public Health Service Act (42 U.S.C. Section 254b), and its subsequent amendments; and

(5) does not perform abortions or provide abortion referrals or provide assistance to ambulatory health care centers that perform abortions or provide abortion referrals.

(b) Use of the property by a person other than the association does not affect the eligibility of the property for an exemption authorized by this section if the use is incidental to use by the association and limited to activities that benefit:

(1) the ambulatory health care centers to which the association provides assistance; or

(2) the individuals to whom the health care centers provide medical care.

(c) Performance of noncharitable functions by the association does not affect the eligibility of the property for an exemption authorized by this section if those other functions are incidental to the association's charitable functions.
(Acts 1999, 76th Leg., ch. 675, §1, effective January 1, 2000.)

Texas Insurance Code

§1454.001. Definitions

In this chapter:

(1) "Health care provider" means a home health aide, hospital, nurse practitioner, nurse midwife, outpatient care center, physician assistant, registered nurse, or surgery center.

(2) "Physician" has the meaning assigned by Section 151.002, Occupations Code.
(Acts 2003, 78th Leg., ch. 1274, §3, effective April 1, 2005.)

§1454.002. Applicability of this chapter

This chapter applies only to a health benefit plan that provides benefits for medical or surgical expenses incurred as a result of a health condition, accident, or sickness, including an individual, group, blanket, or franchise insurance policy or insurance agreement, a group hospital service contract, or an individual or group evidence of coverage or similar coverage document that is offered by:

(1) an insurance company;

(2) a group hospital service corporation operating under Chapter 842;

(3) a fraternal benefit society operating under Chapter 885;

(4) a stipulated premium company operating under Chapter 884;

(5) a reciprocal exchange operating under Chapter 942;

(6) a health maintenance organization operating under Chapter 843;

(7) a multiple employer welfare arrangement that holds a certificate of authority under Chapter 846;

(8) an approved nonprofit health corporation that holds a certificate of authority under Chapter 844; or

(9) a small employer health benefit plan written under Chapter 1501.

(Acts 2003, 78th Leg., ch. 1274, §3, effective April 1, 2005.)

§1454.051. Reimbursement for reproductive health services

A health benefit plan issuer that reimburses a physician or health care provider for reproductive health or oncology services provided to women must reimburse the physician or provider in an amount at least equal to the annual average compensation per hour or unit that would be paid in the service area to a physician or provider for the same medical, surgical, hospital, pharmaceutical, nursing, or other similar resources used to provide the services if the resources would be used to provide health services exclusively to men or to the general population.
(Acts 2003, 78th Leg., ch. 1274, §3, effective April 1, 2005.)

§1454.052. Health benefit plan not required to reimburse for abortion

This chapter does not require a health benefit plan issuer to provide reimbursement for an abortion, as defined by the Family Code, or for a service related to an abortion.
(Acts 2003, 78th Leg., ch. 1274, §3, effective April 1, 2005.)

4. Abortion Counseling

The Texas abortion counseling law (*infra*), enacted in 2003, mandates that a physician or physician's agent must secure the woman's "informed consent"—by informing the woman (at least 24 hours before the abortion) of the probable gestational age of the fetus, fetal physiological characteristics, and of the availability of benefits for prenatal care, childbirth, and neonatal care; offering women written materials containing a list of adoption agencies; telling women that their infant's father is liable for child support; and warning women of the potential danger to a subsequent pregnancy and of infertility and the possibility that abortion can increase the risk of breast cancer. This last claim is disputed by physicians' organizations. Scott Gold, Texas OKs Rigid Abortion-Counseling Law, S.F. Chron., May 22, 2003, at A5.

Texas Health & Safety Code

§171.001. Title

This chapter may be called the Woman's Right to Know Act.
(Acts 2003, 78th Leg., ch. 999, §1, effective September 1, 2003.)

§171.002. Definition

In this chapter, "abortion" means the use of any means to terminate the pregnancy of a female known by the attending physician to be pregnant with the intention that the termination of the pregnancy by those means will, with reasonable likelihood, cause the death of the fetus.
(Acts 2003, 78th Leg., ch. 999, §1, effective September 1, 2003.)

§171.003. Licensed physician to perform

An abortion may be performed only by a physician licensed to practice medicine in this state.
(Acts 2003, 78th Leg., ch. 999, §1, effective September 1, 2003.)

§171.004. Abortion of fetus age 16 weeks or more

An abortion of a fetus age 16 weeks or more may be performed only at an ambulatory surgical center or hospital licensed to perform the abortion.
(Acts 2003, 78th Leg., ch. 999, §1, effective September 1, 2003.)

§171.005. Department to enforce

The department shall enforce this chapter.
(Acts 2003, 78th Leg., ch. 999, §1, effective September 1, 2003.)

§171.011. Informed consent required

A person may not perform an abortion without the voluntary and informed consent of the woman on whom the abortion is to be performed.
(Acts 2003, 78th Leg., ch. 999, §1, effective September 1, 2003.)

§171.012. Voluntary and informed consent

(a) Except in the case of a medical emergency, consent to an abortion is voluntary and informed only if:

(1) the physician who is to perform the abortion or the referring physician informs the woman on whom the abortion is to be performed of:

(A) the name of the physician who will perform the abortion:

(B) the particular medical risks associated with the particular abortion procedure to be employed, including, when medically accurate:

(i) the risks of infection and hemorrhage;

(ii) the potential danger to a subsequent pregnancy and of infertility; and

(iii) the possibility of increased risk of breast cancer following an induced abortion and the natural protective effect of a completed pregnancy in avoiding breast cancer;

(C) the probable gestational age of the unborn child at the time the abortion is to be performed; and

(D) the medical risks associated with carrying the child to term;

(2) the physician who is to perform the abortion or the physician's agent informs the woman that:

(A) medical assistance benefits may be available for prenatal care, childbirth, and neonatal care;

(B) the father is liable for assistance in the support of the child without regard to whether the father has offered to pay for the abortion;

(C) public and private agencies provide pregnancy prevention counseling and medical referrals for obtaining pregnancy prevention medications or devices, including emergency contraception for victims of rape or incest; and

(D) the woman has the right to review the printed materials described by Section 171.014, that those materials have been provided by the Texas Department of Health and are accessible on an Internet website sponsored by the department, and that the materials describe the unborn child and list agencies that offer alternatives to abortion;

(3) the woman certifies in writing before the abortion is performed that the information described by Subdivisions (1) and (2) has been provided to her and that she has been informed of her opportunity to review the information described by Section 171.014; and

(4) before the abortion is performed, the physician who is to perform the abortion receives a copy of the written certification provided by Subdivision (3).

(b) The information required to be provided under Subsection (a)(1) and (2) must be provided:

(1) orally by telephone or in person; and

(2) at least 24 hours before the abortion is to be performed.

(c) When providing the information under Subsection (a)(2)(D), the physician or the physician's agent must provide the woman with the address of the Internet website on which the printed materials described by Section 171.014 may be viewed as required by Section 171.014(e).

(d) The information provided to the woman under Subsection (a)(2)(B) must include, based on information available from the Office of the Attorney General and the United States Department of Health and Human Services Office of Child Support Enforcement for the three-year period preceding the publication of the information, information regarding the statistical likelihood of collecting child support.

(e) The department is not required to republish informational materials described by Subsection (a)(2)(B) because of a change in information described by Subsection (f) unless the statistical information in the materials changes by five percent or more.

(Acts 2003, 78th Leg., ch. 999, §1, effective September 1, 2003.)

§171.013. Distribution of state materials

(a) If the woman chooses to view the materials described by Section 171.014, the physician or the physician's agent shall furnish copies of the materials to her at least 24 hours before the abortion is to be performed. A physician or the physician's agent may furnish the materials to the woman by mail if the materials are mailed, restricted delivery to addressee, at least 72 hours before the abortion is to be performed.

(b) A physician or the physician's agent is not required to furnish copies of the material if the woman provides the physician with a written statement that she chooses to view the materials on the Internet website sponsored by the department.

(c) The physician and the physician's agent may disassociate themselves from the materials and may choose to comment on the materials or refrain from commenting.

(Acts 2003, 78th Leg., ch. 999, §1, effective September 1, 2003.)

§171.014. Informational materials

(a) The department shall publish informational materials that include:

(1) the information required to be provided under Section 171.012(a)(1)(B) and (D) and (a)(2)(A), (B) and (C); and

(2) the materials required by Sections 171.015 and 171.016.

(b) The materials shall be published in:

(1) English and Spanish;

(2) an easily comprehensible form; and

(3) a typeface large enough to be clearly legible.

(c) The materials shall be available at no cost from the department on request. The department shall provide appropriate quantities of the materials to a person.

(d) The department shall annually review the materials to determine if changes to the contents of the materials are necessary. The department shall adopt rules necessary for considering and making changes to the materials.

(e) The department shall develop and maintain an Internet website to display the information required to be published under this section. In developing and maintaining the website the department shall, to the extent reasonably practicable, safeguard the website against alterations by anyone other than the department and shall monitor the website each day to prevent and correct tampering. The department shall ensure that the website does not collect or maintain information regarding access to the website.

(f) In addition to any organization or entity, the department shall use the American College of Obstetricians and Gynecologists as the resource in developing information required to be provided under Section 171.012 (a)(1)(B) and

(D), Section 171.012 (a)(2)(A), (B), and (C), and Section 171.016, and in maintaining the department's Internet website.

(Acts 2003, 78th Leg., ch. 999, §1, effective September 1, 2003.)

§171.015. Information relating to public and private agencies

The informational materials must include either:

(1) geographically indexed materials designed to inform the woman of public and private agencies and services that:

(A) are available to assist a woman through pregnancy, childbirth, and the child's dependency, including:

(i) a comprehensive list of adoption agencies;

(ii) a description of the services the adoption agencies offer; and

(iii) a description of the manner, including telephone numbers, in which an adoption agency may be contacted;

(B) do not provide abortions or abortion-related services or make referrals to abortion providers; and

(C) are not affiliated with organizations that provide abortions or abortion-related services or make referrals to abortion providers; or

(2) a toll-free, 24-hour telephone number that may be called to obtain an oral list and description of agencies described by Subdivision (1) that are located near the caller and of the services the agencies offer.

(Acts 2003, 78th Leg., ch. 999, §1, effective September 1, 2003.)

§171.016. Information relating to characteristics of unborn child

(a) The informational materials must include materials designed to inform the woman of the probable anatomical and physiological characteristics of the unborn child at two-week gestational increments from the time when a woman can be known to be pregnant to full term, including any relevant information on the possibility of the unborn child's survival.

(b) The materials must include color pictures representing the development of the child at two-week gestational increments. The pictures must contain the dimensions of the unborn child and must be realistic.

(c) The materials provided under this section must be objective and nonjudgmental and be designed to convey only accurate scientific information about the unborn child at the various gestational ages.

(Acts 2003, 78th Leg., ch. 999, §1, effective September 1, 2003.)

§171.017. Periods run concurrently

If the woman is an unemancipated minor subject to Chapter 33, Family Code, the 24-hour periods established under Sections 171.012(b) and 171.013(a) may run concurrently with the period during which actual or constructive notice is provided under Section 33.002, Family Code.

(Acts 2003, 78th Leg., ch. 999, §1, effective September 1, 2003.)

§171.018. Offense

A physician who intentionally performs an abortion on a woman in violation of this subchapter commits an offense. An offense under this section is a misdemeanor punishable by a fine not to exceed $10,000. In this section, "intentionally" has the meaning assigned by Section 6.03(a), Penal Code.

(Acts 2003, 78th Leg., ch. 999, §1, effective September 1, 2003.)

§245.004. Exemptions from licensing requirement

(a) The following facilities need not be licensed under this chapter:

(1) a hospital licensed under Chapter 241 (Texas Hospital Licensing Law);

(2) the office of a physician licensed under Subtitle B, Title 3, Occupations Code, unless the office is used substantially for the purpose of performing abortions; or

(3) an ambulatory surgical center licensed under Chapter 243.

(b) For purposes of this section, a facility is used substantially for the purpose of performing abortions if the facility:

(1) is a provider for performing:

(A) at least 10 abortion procedures during any month; or

(B) at least 100 abortion procedures in a year;

(2) operates less than 20 days in a month and the facility, in any month, is a provider for performing a number of abortion procedures that would be equivalent to at least 10 procedures in a month if the facility were operating at least 20 days in a month;

(3) holds itself out to the public as an abortion provider by advertising by any public means, including advertising placed in a newspaper, telephone directory, magazine, or electronic medium, that the facility performs abortions; or

(4) applies for an abortion facility license.

(c) For purposes of this section, an abortion facility is operating if the facility is open for any period of time during a day and has on site at the facility or on call a physician available to perform abortions.

(Acts 1989, 71st Leg., ch. 678, §1, effective September 1, 1989. Amended by Acts 1999, 76th Leg., ch. 1411, §22.01, effective September 1, 1999. Acts 2001, 77th Leg., ch. 1420, §14.788, effective September 1, 2001; Acts 2003, 78th Leg., ch. 198, §2.63(a), effective September 1, 2003; Acts 2003, 78th Leg., ch. 999, §2, effective September 1, 2003.)

§245.007. Fees

The board shall set fees imposed by this chapter in amounts reasonable and necessary to defray the cost of administering this chapter and Chapter 171.

(Acts 1989, 71st Leg., ch. 678, §1, effective September 1, 1989. Amended by Acts 2003, 78th Leg., ch. 999, §3, effective September 1, 2003.)

§245.010. Minimum Standards

(a) The rules must contain minimum standards to protect the health and safety of a patient of an abortion facility and must contain provisions requiring compliance with the requirements of Subchapter B, Chapter 171.

(b) Only a physician as defined by Subtitle B, Title 3, Occupations Code, may perform an abortion.

(c) The standards may not be more stringent than Medicare certification standards, if any, for:

(1) qualifications for professional and nonprofessional personnel;

(2) supervision of professional and nonprofessional personnel;

(3) medical treatment and medical services provided by an abortion facility and the coordination of treatment and services, including quality assurance;

(4) sanitary and hygienic conditions within an abortion facility;

(5) the equipment essential to the health and welfare of the patients;

(6) clinical records kept by an abortion facility; and

(7) management, ownership, and control of the facility.

(d) This section does not authorize the board to:

(1) establish the qualifications of a licensed practitioner; or

(2) permit a person to provide health care services who is not authorized to provide those services under other laws of this state.

(Acts 1989, 71st Leg., ch. 678, §1, effective September 1, 1989. Amended by Acts 1997, 75th Leg., ch. 23, §1, effective September 1, 1997. Amended by Acts 2001, 77th Leg., ch. 1420, §14.789, effective September 1, 2001; Acts 2003, 78th Leg., ch. 999, §4, effective September 1, 2003.)

C. RESTRICTIONS ON THE RIGHTS OF PREGNANT WOMEN

1. Rights of the Pregnant Terminally Ill

In many states, individuals may declare in advance the wish to withhold or withdraw life-sustaining treatment in the event of a terminal condition. See, e.g., Uniform Rights of the Terminally Ill Act, 9C U.L.A. 318-319 (2001). These instruments are called "advance directives." A "living will" specifies a competent person's wishes regarding medical treatment in the event of incapacity. Individuals also may execute instruments that designate proxy health care decisionmakers who will make treatment decisions if the declarant becomes incapable of doing so.

Some states, however, do not honor provisions in advance directives (living wills and the appointment of proxy health care decisionmakers) for pregnant patients. As a result, a terminally ill or comatose pregnant woman can be kept alive until the fetus can mature, despite the woman's expressed wishes to the contrary. See Bretton H. Horttor, A Survey of Living Will and Advanced Health Care Directives, 74 N.D. L. Rev. 233 (1998) (reporting survey revealing that 36 states prohibit the withdrawal of life support from pregnant women). Texas, similarly, refuses to permit withholding or withdrawal of life-support systems from a pregnant woman (Tex. Health & Safety Code §166.049).

Texas Health & Safety Code

§166.049. Pregnant patients are not able to terminate life support

A person may not withdraw or withhold life-sustaining treatment under this subchapter from a pregnant patient.

(Acts 1989, 71st Leg., ch. 678, §1, effective September 1, 1989. Renumbered from §672.019 and amended by Acts 1999, 76th Leg., ch. 450, §1.03, effective September 1, 1999.)

2. Role of Fetal Abuse in Termination of Parental Rights

Courts and legislatures have wrestled with the issue of whether a mother's prenatal substance abuse constitutes child abuse. Compare State v. McKnight, 576 S.E.2d 168 (S.C. 2003) (holding that conviction of a pregnant woman for "homicide by child abuse" for ingesting cocaine that allegedly resulted in the stillbirth of her infant did not violate her due process rights or right to privacy), with Angela M.W. v. Kruzicki, 561 N.W.2d 729 (Wis. 1997) (holding that the legislature did not intend to include a viable fetus within the definition of the term "child" for purposes of the child welfare statutes).

In many states, a parent's substance abuse is a factor in the termination of parental rights. See, e.g., In re Jamie R., 109 Cal. Rptr. 2d 123, 128 (Cal. Ct. App. 2001) (holding that termination was proper when state provided services to reunite family, children were adoptable, and adoption was least detrimental alternative). Some states explicitly permit termination of parental rights based solely on a newborn infant's addiction. Ellen Marrus, Crack Babies and the Constitution: Ruminations About Addicted Pregnant Women After Ferguson v. City of Charleston, 47 Villanova L. Rev. 299, 333-334 (2002). Texas Family Code §161.001 provides that a court may order termination of parental rights if the court finds by *clear and convincing evidence* that the parent has been the *cause* of the child born addicted to alcohol or a controlled substance (emphasis added).

Texas Family Code

§161.001. Involuntary termination of parental rights for fetal abuse

The court may order termination of the parent-child relationship if the court finds by clear and convincing evidence:

(1) that the parent has:

(R) been the cause of the child being born addicted to alcohol or a controlled substance, other than a controlled substance legally obtained by prescription, as defined by Section 261.001;

. . .

and

(2) that termination is in the best interest of the child.

(Acts 1995, 74th Leg., ch. 20, §1, effective April 20, 1995. Amended by Acts 1995, 74th Leg., ch. 709, §1, effective September 1, 1995; Acts 1995, 74th Leg., ch. 751, §65, effective September 1, 1995; by Acts 1997, 75th Leg., ch. 575, §9, effective September 1, 1997; Acts 1997, 75th Leg., ch. 1022, §60, effective September 1, 1997; Acts 1999, 76th Leg., ch. 1087, §1, effective September 1, 1999; Acts 1999, 76th Leg., ch. 1390, §18, effective September 1, 1999; Acts 2001, 77th Leg., ch. 809, §1, effective September 1, 2001; Acts 2005, 79th Leg., ch. 508, §2, effective September 1, 2005.)

D. ALTERNATIVE REPRODUCTIVE TECHNOLOGY

Medicine and technology offer alternatives to enable childless couples to become parents. Artificial insemination is the most commonly used method of assisted conception. States generally legitimize the resulting offspring of a husband and wife as the product of the marriage. These statutes often require the husband's written consent to the insemination as a prerequisite.

Many statutes are modeled after Section 5 of the 1973 Uniform Parentage Act (UPA) recognizing the husband as the father if he consents in writing to artificial insemination performed by a licensed physician and providing that the sperm donor is not treated as the natural father. Unif. Parentage Act, 9B U.L.A. 377, 407-408 (2001). The revised UPA reaches the same result in §§702 and 704 and adds that the husband's failure to consent to assisted reproduction does not preclude his recognition as father. 9B U.L.A. 355-356 (2001). See also American Law Institute, Principles of the Law of Family Dissolution §§2.03 (parent by estoppel) in Part IV *infra*.

Texas adopted the revised UPA in 2001. The Texas version *infra* of the revised UPA completely replaces former Chapter 160, Determination of Parentage. Current Texas law sets forth the general rule that the sperm donor is not treated as the father (Tex. Fam. Code §160.702) unless the sperm donor is the husband (Tex. Fam. Code §160.703). Alternatively, the husband will be treated as the father if he "consents to assisted reproduction . . . as provided by Section 160.704." Under Texas Family Code §160.704, consent "must be in a record signed by the woman and her husband." Texas law provides that the husband's failure to consent does not preclude his recognition as a father (Tex. Fam. Code §160.704(b)).

Texas law also permits the husband of a child conceived by means of assisted reproduction to challenge paternity. Some husbands must do so before the fourth anniversary of the date on which they learned of the child's birth (Tex. Fam. Code §160.705(a)); other husbands may do so at any time (Tex. Fam. Code §160.705(b)). Statutory provisions also specify the parental status of a spouse who is divorced (Tex. Fam. Code §160.606(a)) or dies before the artificial insemination occurs (Tex. Fam. Code §160.707)).

The issue of parental status of a divorced spouse arose in In re O.G.M., 988 S.W.2d 473 (Tex. Civ. App.—Houston [1st Dist.] 1999, writ dismissed). A couple had three children before the wife underwent a tubal ligation. Subsequently, the couple underwent several unsuccessful attempts at in vitro fertilization in an effort to have another child. In a consent form, they agreed that the pre-embryos would be disposed of according to both their wishes. When they divorced, however, their divorce decree did not address the disposition of the four remaining frozen pre-embryos. Three months postdivorce, the husband accompanied the wife to the IVF clinic where she successfully attempted the procedure again. When the husband filed a paternity action, the wife denied his paternity. The court of appeals found that the evidence supported the summary judgment in favor of the husband. Specifically, the husband was the biological father, he was named on the birth certificate, he filed a statement of paternity, the embryos were conceived during the marriage, the husband consented to implantation, he was present when the procedure took place, he pays child support, the ex-wife was unmarried at the time of the child's birth, no agreement specified the parties' rights and obligations regarding this child, and depriving the husband of paternity would bastardize the child.

On paternity issues generally, see Chapter XIII *infra*.

1. Parental Status Generally

Texas Family Code

§160.701. Application to child conceived by assisted reproduction

This subchapter applies only to a child conceived by means of assisted reproduction.

(Acts 2001, 77th Leg., ch. 821, §1.01, effective June 14, 2001.)

§160.702. Donor is not a parent

A donor is not a parent of a child conceived by means of assisted reproduction.

(Acts 2001, 77th Leg., ch. 821, §1.01, effective June 14, 2001.)

§160.703. Husband is father of child if he provides sperm or consents

If a husband provides sperm for or consents to assisted reproduction by his wife as provided by Section 160.704, he is the father of a resulting child.

(Acts 2001, 77th Leg., ch. 821, §1.01, effective June 14, 2001.)

§160.704. Consent to assisted reproduction by woman; husband's failure to consent does not preclude finding of paternity

(a) Consent by a married woman to assisted reproduction must be in a record signed by the woman and her husband. This requirement does not apply to the donation of eggs by a married woman for assisted reproduction by another woman.

(b) Failure by the husband to sign a consent required by Subsection (a) before or after the birth of the child does not preclude a finding that the husband is the father of a child born to his wife if the wife and husband openly treated the child as their own.

(Acts 2001, 77th Leg., ch. 821, §1.01, eff. June 14, 2001.)

§160.705. Limitation on husband's ability to challenge paternity

(a) Except as otherwise provided by Subsection (b), the husband of a wife who gives birth to a child by means of assisted reproduction may not challenge his paternity of the child unless:

(1) before the fourth anniversary of the date of learning of the birth of the child he commences a proceeding to adjudicate his paternity; and

(2) the court finds that he did not consent to the assisted reproduction before or after the birth of the child.

(b) A proceeding to adjudicate paternity may be maintained at any time if the court determines that:

(1) the husband did not provide sperm for or, before or after the birth of the child, consent to assisted reproduction by his wife;

(2) the husband and the mother of the child have not cohabited since the probable time of assisted reproduction; and

(3) the husband never openly treated the child as his own.

(c) The limitations provided by this section apply to a marriage declared invalid after assisted reproduction.

(Acts 2001, 77th Leg., ch. 821, §1.01, eff. June 14, 2001.)

§160.706. Effect of divorce (prior to fertilization or implantation) on parenthood

(a) If a marriage is dissolved before the placement of eggs, sperm, or embryos, the former spouse is not a parent of the resulting child unless the former spouse consented in a record that if assisted reproduction were to occur after a divorce the former spouse would be a parent of the child.

(b) The consent of a former spouse to assisted reproduction may be withdrawn by that individual in a record at any time before the placement of eggs, sperm, or embryos.

(Acts 2001, 77th Leg., ch. 821, §1.01, eff. June 14, 2001.)

§160.707. Effect of death (prior to fertilization or implantation) on parenthood

If a spouse dies before the placement of eggs, sperm, or embryos, the deceased spouse is not a parent of the resulting child unless the deceased spouse consented in a record that if assisted reproduction were to occur after death the deceased spouse would be a parent of the child.

(Acts 2001, 77th Leg., ch. 821, §1.01, eff. June 14, 2001.)

2. Surrogacy

Surrogacy is a contractual arrangement whereby a woman agrees to be artificially inseminated with the semen of a man whose wife is unable to conceive or bear a child, and then to surrender the ensuing child to the natural father and his wife. The majority of states with legislation on the subject of surrogacy make surrogacy agreements void. However, a few states permit such arrangements subject to state regulation. See, e.g., Ark. Code Ann. §9-10-201 (2002) (declaring that the legal parents of such children are the intended parents); Fla. Stat. Ann. §63.213 (West 2005) (allowing "preplanned adoption agreement" but not for valuable consideration beyond expenses and with opportunity for mother to rescind consent within seven days); N.H. Rev. Stat. Ann. §168-B:16 (2002) (requiring "judicial preauthorization"); Nev. Rev. Stat. §127.287(5) (2000) (exempting surrogacy agreements from the ban on payment in adoptive placements); Va. Code Ann. §§20-160 & 20-162 (West 2005) (prior judicial approval and reformation of contracts not approved by the court to include the designated requirements).

Unable to agree on one approach, the National Conference of Commissioners on Uniform State Laws (NCCUSL) included two alternatives in its model legislation, Uniform Status of Children of Assisted Conception Act (USCACA): Alternative A, which regulated surrogacy arrangements through a preconception adoption proceeding, and Alternative B, which made surrogacy agreements void. See 9C U.L.A. 383 (2001).

The new Uniform Parentage Act (UPA) replaces USCACA, see 9B U.L.A. 297 (2001) (Prefatory Note to UPA). Like Alternative A of USCACA, the new UPA authorizes "gestational agreements," including the payment of consideration (§801); requires a home study of the intended parents and judicial validation of the agreement (§802); and provides for a court order of parentage consistent with the judicially validated agreement upon the child's birth (§806). *Id.* at 360-370. In 2002, NCCUSL eliminated the UPA restriction of surrogacy to married couples. The revised UPA is set forth in Part III *infra* of this Code.

Texas is the only state so far that has adopted the new UPA's Article 8 provisions on gestational agreements. Tex. Fam. Code §160.754. Note that Texas adopted the unamended version of the revised UPA and also that Texas explicitly provides that the gestational mother's eggs may not be used in the procedure. Tex. Fam. Code §160.754(c).

Texas Family Code

§160.751. Definitions

In this subchapter, "gestational mother" means a woman who gives birth to a child conceived under a gestational agreement.

(Acts 2003, 78th Leg., ch. 457, §2, eff. September 1, 2003.)

§160.752. Scope of gestational agreement

(a) Notwithstanding any other provision of this chapter or another law, this subchapter authorizes an agreement between a woman and the intended parents of a child in which the woman relinquishes all rights as a parent of a child conceived by means of assisted reproduction and that provides that the intended parents become the parents of the child.

(b) This subchapter controls over any other law with respect to a child conceived under a gestational agreement under this subchapter.

(Acts 2003, 78th Leg., ch. 457, §2, effective September 1, 2003.)

§160.753. Parent-child relationship exists between nongestational parent and child by adjudication

(a) Notwithstanding any other provision of this chapter or another law, the mother-child relationship exists between a woman and a child by an adjudication confirming the woman as a parent of the child born to a gestational mother under a gestational agreement if the gestational agreement is validated under this subchapter or enforceable under other law, regardless of the fact that the gestational mother gave birth to the child.

(b) The father-child relationship exists between a child and a man by an adjudication confirming the man as a parent of the child born to a gestational mother under a gestational agreement if the gestational agreement is validated under this subchapter or enforceable under other law.

(Acts 2003, 78th Leg., ch. 457, §2, effective September 1, 2003.)

§160.754. Gestational agreement applies to assisted reproduction and not to sexual intercourse

(a) A prospective gestational mother, her husband if she is married, each donor, and each intended parent may enter into a written agreement providing that:

(1) the prospective gestational mother agrees to pregnancy by means of assisted reproduction;

(2) the prospective gestational mother, her husband if she is married, and each donor other than the intended parents, if applicable, relinquish all parental rights and duties with respect to a child conceived through assisted reproduction;

(3) the intended parents will be the parents of the child; and

(4) the gestational mother and each intended parent agree to exchange throughout the period covered by the agreement all relevant information regarding the health of the gestational mother and each intended parent.

(b) The intended parents must be married to each other. Each intended parent must be a party to the gestational agreement.

(c) The gestational agreement must require that the eggs used in the assisted reproduction procedure be retrieved from an intended parent or a donor. The gestational mother's eggs may not be used in the assisted reproduction procedure.

(d) The gestational agreement must state that the physician who will perform the assisted reproduction procedure as provided by the agreement has informed the parties to the agreement of:

(1) the rate of successful conceptions and births attributable to the procedure, including the most recent published outcome statistics of the procedure at the facility at which it will be performed;

(2) the potential for and risks associated with the implantation of multiple embryos and consequent multiple births resulting from the procedure;

(3) the nature of and expenses related to the procedure;

(4) the health risks associated with, as applicable, fertility drugs used in the procedure, egg retrieval procedures, and egg or embryo transfer procedures; and

(5) reasonably foreseeable psychological effects resulting from the procedure.

(e) The parties to a gestational agreement must enter into the agreement before the 14th day preceding the date the transfer of eggs, sperm, or embryos to the gestational mother occurs for the purpose of conception or implantation.

(f) A gestational agreement does not apply to the birth of a child conceived by means of sexual intercourse.

(g) A gestational agreement may not limit the right of the gestational mother to make decisions to safeguard her health or the health of an embryo.

(Acts 2003, 78th Leg., ch. 457, §2, effective September 1, 2003.)

§160.755. Prospective gestational mother or intended parents must reside in state for at least 90 days

(a) The intended parents and the prospective gestational mother under a gestational agreement may commence a proceeding to validate the agreement.

(b) A person may maintain a proceeding to validate a gestational agreement only if:

(1) the prospective gestational mother or the intended parents have resided in this state for the 90 days preceding the date the proceeding is commenced;

(2) the prospective gestational mother's husband, if she is married, is joined as a party to the proceeding; and

(3) a copy of the gestational agreement is attached to the petition.

(Acts 2003, 78th Leg., ch. 457, §2, effective September 1, 2003.)

§160.756. Validation of a gestational agreement

(a) A gestational agreement must be validated as provided by this section.

(b) The court may validate a gestational agreement as provided by Subsection (c) only if the court finds that:

(1) the parties have submitted to the jurisdiction of the court under the jurisdictional standards of this chapter;

(2) the medical evidence provided shows that the intended mother is unable to carry a pregnancy to term and give birth to the child or is unable to carry the pregnancy to term and give birth to the child without unreasonable

risk to her physical or mental health or to the health of the unborn child;

(3) unless waived by the court, an agency or other person has conducted a home study of the intended parents and has determined that the intended parents meet the standards of fitness applicable to adoptive parents;

(4) each party to the agreement has voluntarily entered into and understands the terms of the agreement;

(5) the prospective gestational mother has had at least one previous pregnancy and delivery and carrying another pregnancy to term and giving birth to another child would not pose an unreasonable risk to the child's health or the physical or mental health of the prospective gestational mother; and

(6) the parties have adequately provided for which party is responsible for all reasonable health care expenses associated with the pregnancy, including providing for who is responsible for those expenses if the agreement is terminated.

(c) If the court finds that the requirements of Subsection (b) are satisfied, the court may render an order validating the gestational agreement and declaring that the intended parents will be the parents of a child born under the agreement.

(d) The court may validate the gestational agreement at the court's discretion. The court's determination of whether to validate the agreement is subject to review only for abuse of discretion.

(Acts 2003, 78th Leg., ch. 457, §2, effective September 1, 2003.)

§160.757. Standards of confidentiality under adoption are applied

The proceedings, records, and identities of the parties to a gestational agreement under this subchapter are subject to inspection under the same standards of confidentiality that apply to an adoption under the laws of this state.

(Acts 2003, 78th Leg., ch. 457, §2, effective September 1, 2003.)

§160.759. Termination allowed by written notice before gestational mother becomes pregnant

(a) Before a prospective gestational mother becomes pregnant by means of assisted reproduction, the prospective gestational mother, her husband if she is married, or either intended parent may terminate a gestational agreement validated under Section 160.756 by giving written notice of the termination to each other party to the agreement.

(b) A person who terminates a gestational agreement under Subsection (a) shall file notice of the termination with the court. A person having the duty to notify the court who does not notify the court of the termination of the agreement is subject to appropriate sanctions.

(c) On receipt of the notice of termination, the court shall vacate the order rendered under Section 160.756 validating the gestational agreement.

(d) A prospective gestational mother and her husband, if she is married, may not be liable to an intended parent for terminating a gestational agreement if the termination is in accordance with this section.

(Acts 2003, 78th Leg., ch. 457, §2, effective September 1, 2003.)

§160.760. Validated gestational agreement's effects on parentage

(a) On the birth of a child to a gestational mother under a validated gestational agreement, the intended parents shall file a notice of the birth with the court not later than the 300th day after the date assisted reproduction occurred.

(b) After receiving notice of the birth, the court shall render an order that:

(1) confirms that the intended parents are the child's parents;

(2) requires the gestational mother to surrender the child to the intended parents, if necessary; and

(3) requires the bureau of vital statistics to issue a birth certificate naming the intended parents as the child's parents.

(c) If a person alleges that a child born to a gestational mother did not result from assisted reproduction, the court shall order that scientifically accepted parentage testing be conducted to determine the child's parentage.

(d) If the intended parents fail to file the notice required by Subsection (a), the gestational mother or an appropriate state agency may file the notice required by that subsection. On a showing that an order validating the gestational agreement was rendered in accordance with Section 160.756, the court shall order that the intended parents are the child's parents and are financially responsible for the child.

(Acts 2003, 78th Leg., ch. 457, §2, effective September 1, 2003. Amended by Acts 2005, 79th Leg., ch. 916, §22, effective June 18, 2005.)

§160.761. If gestational mother subsequently marries, validity of gestational agreement is not affected

If a gestational mother is married after the court renders an order validating a gestational agreement under this subchapter:

(1) the validity of the gestational agreement is not affected;

(2) the gestational mother's husband is not required to consent to the agreement; and

(3) the gestational mother's husband is not a presumed father of the child born under the terms of the agreement.

(Acts 2003, 78th Leg., ch. 457, §2, effective September 1, 2003.)

§160.762. Gestational agreements that are not validated are not enforceable

(a) A gestational agreement that is not validated as provided by this subchapter is unenforceable, regardless of whether the agreement is in a record.

(b) The parent-child relationship of a child born under a gestational agreement that is not validated as provided by this subchapter is determined as otherwise provided by this chapter.

(c) A party to a gestational agreement that is not validated as provided by this subchapter who is an intended parent under the agreement may be held liable for the support of a child born under the agreement, even if the agreement is otherwise unenforceable.

(d) The court may assess filing fees, reasonable attorney's fees, fees for genetic testing, other costs, and necessary travel and other reasonable expenses incurred in a proceeding under this section. Attorney's fees awarded by the court may be paid directly to the attorney. An attorney who is awarded attorney's fees may enforce the order in the attorney's own name.

(Acts 2003, 78th Leg., ch. 457, §2, effective September 1, 2003.)

XI.
CHILD ABUSE AND NEGLECT

This chapter concerns the maltreatment of children by their parents. Child abuse forms a basis for state intervention into the family and results in considerable limitations on parental autonomy. The chapter first explores definitions of child abuse (physical, sexual, and emotional) and neglect. Then, it addresses child abuse procedures (i.e., reporting, investigation, etc.). Next, it examines evidentiary issues. The chapter then turns to the forms of intervention (i.e., summary seizure, temporary custody, foster care, and the termination of parental rights). Finally, it examines the state's responsibility to provide services.

A. DEFINING CHILD ABUSE AND NEGLECT

1. Physical Abuse

Children have been abused and neglected from antiquity. Historically, abuse and neglect were attributable, in large part, to the low value placed on children. See Lloyd de Mause, ed., The History of Childhood (1995). Despite a longstanding history, abuse and neglect did not provide a basis for governmental intervention in the family until the sixteenth century in England (i.e., the Elizabethan Poor Law) and the nineteenth century in America (the case of Mary Ellen McCormack in 1874). See Peter Stevens & Marian Eide, The First Chapter of Children's Rights, 42 Am. Heritage 84 (1990).

One of the most common manifestations of child abuse is "the battered child syndrome." The term, now widely accepted in medical literature and case law, signifies a child who manifests multiple fractures in different parts of the body that are in various stages of healing; parental explanations are at odds with clinical findings. Many courts, including the United States Supreme Court, accept battered child syndrome evidence in criminal cases. See Estelle v. McGuire, 502 U.S. 62 (1991).

Civil and criminal liability attaches for physical child abuse. Civil actions include proceedings by a juvenile court to assert jurisdiction over a physically abused child (Tex. Fam. Code §261.001). Criminal sanctions also exist to punish the perpetrator. Sanctions exist for a range of criminal offenses, including "criminal homicide" (Tex. Penal Code §19.01), "capital murder" (for the murder of a child under six years old) (Tex. Penal Code §19.03(a)(8)), and a special offense for injury to a child, disabled, or elderly individual (Tex. Penal Code §22.04).

Texas Family Code

§261.001. Definitions

In this chapter:

(1) "Abuse" includes the following acts or omissions by a person:

. . .

(C) physical injury that results in substantial harm to the child, or the genuine threat of substantial harm from physical injury to the child, including an injury that is at variance with the history or explanation given and excluding an accident or reasonable discipline by a parent, guardian, or managing or possessory conservator that does not expose the child to a substantial risk of harm;

. . .

(I) the current use by a person of a controlled substance as defined by Chapter 481, Health and Safety Code, in a manner or to the extent that the use results in physical, mental, or emotional injury to a child;

(J) causing, expressly permitting, or encouraging a child to use a controlled substance as defined by Chapter 481, Health and Safety Code; . . .

(2) "Department" means the Department of Family and Protective Services.

(3) "Designated agency" means the agency designated by the court as responsible for the protection of children.

. . .

(5) "Person responsible for a child's care, custody, or welfare" means a person who traditionally is responsible for a child's care, custody, or welfare, including:

(A) a parent, guardian, managing or possessory conservator, or foster parent of the child;

(B) a member of the child's family or household as defined by Chapter 71;

(C) a person with whom the child's parent cohabits;

(D) school personnel or a volunteer at the child's school; or

(E) personnel or a volunteer at a public or private child-care facility that provides services for the child or at a public or private residential institution or facility where the child resides.

(6) "Report" means a report that alleged or suspected abuse or neglect of a child has occurred or may occur.

(7) "Board" means the Board of Protective and Regulatory Services.

(8) "Born addicted to alcohol or a controlled substance" means a child:

(A) who is born to a mother who during the pregnancy used a controlled substance, as defined by Chapter 481, Health and Safety Code, other than a controlled substance legally obtained by prescription, or alcohol; and

(B) who, after birth as a result of the mother's use of the controlled substance or alcohol:

(i) experiences observable withdrawal from the alcohol or controlled substance;

(ii) exhibits observable or harmful effects in the child's physical appearance or functioning; or

(iii) exhibits the demonstrable presence of alcohol or a controlled substance in the child's bodily fluids.

(Acts 1995, 74th Leg., ch. 20, §1, effective April 20, 1995. Amended by Acts 1995, 74th Leg., ch. 751, §86, effective September 1, 1995; by Acts 1997, 75th Leg., ch. 575, §10, effective September 1, 1997; Acts 1997, 75th Leg., ch. 1022,

§63, effective September 1, 1997; Acts 1999, 76th Leg., ch. 62, §19.01(26), effective September 1, 1999; Acts 2001, 77th Leg., ch. 59, §1, effective September 1, 2001; Acts 2005, 79th Leg., ch. 268, §1.11, effective September 1, 2005.)

Texas Penal Code

§19.01. Criminal homicide

(a) A person commits criminal homicide if he intentionally, knowingly, recklessly, or with criminal negligence causes the death of an individual.

(b) Criminal homicide is murder, capital murder, manslaughter, or criminally negligent homicide.

(Acts 1973, 63rd Leg., p. 883, ch. 399, §1, effective January 1, 1974. Amended by Acts 1973, 63rd Leg., p. 1123, ch. 426, art. 2, §1, effective January 1, 1974; Acts 1993, 73rd Leg., ch. 900, §1.01, effective September 1, 1994.)

§19.03. Capital murder

(a) A person commits an offense if the person commits murder as defined under Section 19.02(b)(1) and:

(1) the person murders a peace officer or fireman who is acting in the lawful discharge of an official duty and who the person knows is a peace officer or fireman;

(2) the person intentionally commits the murder in the course of committing or attempting to commit kidnapping, burglary, robbery, aggravated sexual assault, arson, obstruction or retaliation, or terroristic threat under Section 22.07(a)(1), (3), (4), (5), or (6);

(3) the person commits the murder for remuneration or the promise of remuneration or employs another to commit the murder for remuneration or the promise of remuneration;

(4) the person commits the murder while escaping or attempting to escape from a penal institution;

(5) the person, while incarcerated in a penal institution, murders another:

(A) who is employed in the operation of the penal institution; or

(B) with the intent to establish, maintain, or participate in a combination or in the profits of a combination;

(6) the person:

(A) while incarcerated for an offense under this section or Section 19.02, murders another; or

(B) while serving a sentence of life imprisonment or a term of 99 years for an offense under Section 20.04, 22.021, or 29.03, murders another;

(7) the person murders more than one person:

(A) during the same criminal transaction; or

(B) during different criminal transactions but the murders are committed pursuant to the same scheme or course of conduct; or

(8) the person murders an individual under six years of age.

(b) An offense under this section is a capital felony.

(c) If the jury or, when authorized by law, the judge does not find beyond a reasonable doubt that the defendant is guilty of an offense under this section, he may be convicted of murder or of any other lesser included offense.

(Acts 1973, 63rd Leg., p. 1123, ch. 426, art. 2, §1, effective January 1, 1974. Amended by Acts 1983, 68th Leg., p. 5317, ch. 977, §6, effective September 1, 1983; Acts 1985, 69th Leg., ch. 44, §1, effective September 1, 1985; Acts 1991, 72nd Leg., ch. 652, §13, effective September 1, 1991; Acts 1993, 73rd Leg., ch. 715, §1, effective September 1, 1993; Acts 1993, 73rd Leg., ch. 887, §1, effective September 1, 1993; Acts 1993, 73rd Leg., ch. 900, §1.01, effective September 1, 1994; Acts 2003, 78th Leg., ch. 388, §1, effective September 1, 2003; Acts 2005, 79th Leg., ch. 428, §1, effective September 1, 2005.)

§22.04. Injury to a child, elderly or disabled person

(a) A person commits an offense if he intentionally, knowingly, recklessly, or with criminal negligence, by act or intentionally, knowingly, or recklessly by omission, causes to a child, elderly individual, or disabled individual:

(1) serious bodily injury;

(2) serious mental deficiency, impairment, or injury; or

(3) bodily injury.

(a-1) A person commits an offense if the person is an owner, operator, or employee of a group home, nursing facility, assisted living facility, intermediate care facility for persons with mental retardation, or other institutional care facility and the person intentionally, knowingly, recklessly, or with criminal negligence by omission causes to a child, elderly individual, or disabled individual who is a resident of that group home or facility:

(1) serious bodily injury;

(2) serious mental deficiency, impairment, or injury;

(3) bodily injury; or

(4) exploitation.

(b) An omission that causes a condition described by Subsection (a)(1), (2), or (3) or (a-1)(1), (2), (3), or (4) is conduct constituting an offense under this section if:

(1) the actor has a legal or statutory duty to act; or

(2) the actor has assumed care, custody, or control of a child, elderly individual, or disabled individual.

(c) In this section:

(1) "Child" means a person 14 years of age or younger.

(2) "Elderly individual" means a person 65 years of age or older.

(3) "Disabled individual" means a person older than 14 years of age who by reason of age or physical or mental disease, defect, or injury is substantially unable to protect himself from harm or to provide food, shelter, or medical care for himself.

(4) "Exploitation" means the illegal or improper use of an individual or of the resources of the individual for monetary or personal benefit, profit, or gain.

(d) For purposes of an omission that causes a condition described by Subsection (a)(1), (2), or (3), the actor has assumed care, custody, or control if he has by act, words, or course of conduct acted so as to cause a reasonable person to conclude that he has accepted responsibility for protection, food, shelter, and medical care for a child, elderly individual, or disabled individual. For purposes of an omission that causes a condition described by Subsection (a-1)(1), (2), (3), or (4), the actor acting during the actor's capacity as owner, operator, or employee of a group home or facility described by Subsection (a-1) is considered to have accepted responsibility for protection, food, shelter, and medical care for the child, elderly individual, or disabled individual who is a resident of the group home or facility.

(e) An offense under Subsection (a)(1) or (2) or (a-1)(1) or (2) is a felony of the first degree when the conduct is committed intentionally or knowingly. When the conduct is engaged in recklessly, the offense is a felony of the second degree.

(f) An offense under Subsection (a)(3) or (a-1)(3) or (4) is a felony of the third degree when the conduct is committed intentionally or knowingly. When the conduct is engaged in recklessly, the offense is a state jail felony.

(g) An offense under Subsection (a) is a state jail felony when the person acts with criminal negligence. An offense under Subsection (a-1) is a state jail felony when the person, with criminal negligence and by omission, causes a condition described by Subsection (a-1)(1), (2), (3), or (4).

(h) A person who is subject to prosecution under both this section and another section of this code may be prosecuted under either or both sections. Section 3.04 does not apply to criminal episodes prosecuted under both this section and another section of this code. If a criminal episode is prosecuted under both this section and another section of this code and sentences are assessed for convictions under both sections, the sentences shall run concurrently.

(i) It is an affirmative defense to prosecution under Subsection (b)(2) that before the offense the actor:

(1) notified in person the child, elderly individual, or disabled individual that he would no longer provide any of the care described by Subsection (d); and

(2) notified in writing the parents or person other than himself acting in loco parentis to the child, elderly individual, or disabled individual that he would no longer provide any of the care described by Subsection (d); or

(3) notified in writing the Department of Protective and Regulatory Services that he would no longer provide any of the care set forth in Subsection (d).

(j) Written notification under Subsection (i)(2) or (i)(3) is not effective unless it contains the name and address of the actor, the name and address of the child, elderly individual, or disabled individual, the type of care provided by the actor, and the date the care was discontinued.

(k) It is a defense to prosecution under this section that the act or omission consisted of:

(1) reasonable medical care occurring under the direction of or by a licensed physician; or

(2) emergency medical care administered in good faith and with reasonable care by a person not licensed in the healing arts.

(l) It is an affirmative defense to prosecution under this section:

(1) that the act or omission was based on treatment in accordance with the tenets and practices of a recognized religious method of healing with a generally accepted record of efficacy;

(2) for a person charged with an act of omission causing to a child, elderly individual, or disabled individual a condition described by Subsection (a)(1), (2), or (3) that:

(A) there is no evidence that, on the date prior to the offense charged, the defendant was aware of an incident of injury to the child, elderly individual, or disabled individual and failed to report the incident; and

(B) the person:

(i) was a victim of family violence, as that term is defined by Section 71.004, Family Code, committed by a person who is also charged with an offense against the child, elderly individual, or disabled individual under this section or any other section of this title;

(ii) did not cause a condition described by Subsection (a)(1), (2), or (3); and

(iii) did not reasonably believe at the time of the omission that an effort to prevent the person also charged with an offense against the child, elderly individual, or disabled individual from committing the offense would have an effect; or

(3) that:

(A) the actor was not more than three years older than the victim at the time of the offense; and

(B) the victim was a child at the time of the offense.

(Acts 1973, 63rd Leg., p. 883, ch. 399, §1, effective January 1, 1974. Amended by Acts 1977, 65th Leg., p. 2067, ch. 819, §1, effective August 29, 1977; Acts 1979, 66th Leg., p. 365, ch. 162, §1, effective August 27, 1979; Acts 1981, 67th Leg., p. 472, ch. 202, §4, effective September 1, 1981; Acts 1981, 67th Leg., p. 2397, ch. 604, §1, effective September 1, 1981; Acts 1989, 71st Leg., ch. 357, §1, effective September 1, 1989; Acts 1991, 72nd Leg., ch. 497, §1, effective September 1, 1991; Acts 1993, 73rd Leg., ch. 900, §1.01, effective September 1, 1994; Acts 1995, 74th Leg., ch. 76, §8.139, effective September 1, 1995; Acts 1999, 76th Leg., ch. 62, §15.02(b), effective September 1, 1999; Acts 2005, 79th Leg., ch. 268, §1.125(a), effective September 1, 2005; Acts 2005, 79th Leg., ch. 949, §46, effective September 1, 2005.)

2. Sexual Abuse

Sexual abuse by family members is another form of child maltreatment. A significant percentage of child molestation is perpetrated by family members. See Andrea J. Sedlak & Diane D. Broadhurst, U.S. Dept. of Health & Human Services, National Center on Child Abuse and Neglect, Executive Summary of the Third National Incidence Study of Child Abuse and Neglect 6.5 (September 1996) (reporting that one-fourth of children are sexually abused by a biological parent and another fourth are abused by other parent substitutes).

Legal responses encompass civil as well as criminal proceedings. Civil actions include proceedings by juvenile courts to assert jurisdiction over a sexually abused child, and also civil lawsuits by victims who seek monetary damages against perpetrators. Criminal sanctions also exist to punish the perpetrator.

Texas law provides for criminal sanctions for a variety of sexual offenses with minors, including "indecency with a child," "sexual assault," "aggravated sexual assault," and "prohibited sexual conduct." An amendment to the Texas Penal Code in 1983 substituted the offense of "sexual assault" for the former offense of "rape" (Tex. Penal Code §19.03). In addition, an amendment to the Texas Penal Code in 1993 substituted the offense of "prohibited sexual conduct" with designated relatives for the formerly named offense of "incest" (Tex. Penal Code §25.02). Another form of prohibited sexual abuse in Texas consists of employing, authorizing, or inducing a minor to engage in sexual conduct or a sexual performance (Tex. Penal Code §43.25 (b)). Texas recently removed the good faith belief that a minor is over 18 as an affirmative defense to sexual performance. (Tex. Penal Code §43.25(f)).

Texas Family Code

§261.001. Definitions

In this chapter:

(1) "Abuse" includes the following acts or omissions by a person:

...

(E) sexual conduct harmful to a child's mental, emotional, or physical welfare, including conduct that constitutes the offense of indecency with a child under Section 21.11, Penal Code, sexual assault under Section 22.011, Penal Code, or aggravated sexual assault under Section 22.021, Penal Code;

(F) failure to make a reasonable effort to prevent sexual conduct harmful to a child;

(G) compelling or encouraging the child to engage in sexual conduct as defined by Section 43.01, Penal Code;

(H) causing, permitting, encouraging, engaging in, or allowing the photographing, filming, or depicting of the child if the person knew or should have known that the resulting photograph, film, or depiction of the child is obscene as defined by Section 43.21, Penal Code, or pornographic; ...

(K) causing, permitting, encouraging, engaging in, or allowing a sexual performance by a child as defined by Section 43.25, Penal Code.

...

(Acts 1995, 74th Leg., ch. 20, §1, effective April 20, 1995. Amended by Acts 1995, 74th Leg., ch. 751, §86, effective September 1, 1995; by Acts 1997, 75th Leg., ch. 575, §10, effective September 1, 1997; Acts 1997, 75th Leg., ch. 1022, §63, effective September 1, 1997; Acts 1999, 76th Leg., ch. 62, §19.01(26), effective September 1, 1999; Acts 2001, 77th Leg., ch. 59, §1, effective September 1, 2001; Acts 2005, 79th Leg., ch. 268, §1.11, effective September 1, 2005.)

Texas Penal Code

§21.11. Indecency with a child

(a) A person commits an offense if, with a child younger than 17 years and not the person's spouse, whether the child is of the same or opposite sex, the person:

(1) engages in sexual contact with the child or causes the child to engage in sexual contact; or

(2) with intent to arouse or gratify the sexual desire of any person:

(A) exposes the person's anus or any part of the person's genitals, knowing the child is present; or

(B) causes the child to expose the child's anus or any part of the child's genitals.

(b) It is an affirmative defense to prosecution under this section that the actor:

(1) was not more than three years older than the victim and of the opposite sex;

(2) did not use duress, force, or a threat against the victim at the time of the offense; and

(3) at the time of the offense:

(A) was not required under Chapter 62, Code of Criminal Procedure, to register for life as a sex offender; or

(B) was not a person who under Chapter 62 had a reportable conviction or adjudication for an offense under this section.

(c) In this section, "sexual contact" means the following acts, if committed with the intent to arouse or gratify the sexual desire of any person:

(1) any touching by a person, including touching through clothing, of the anus, breast, or any part of the genitals of a child; or

(2) any touching of any part of the body of a child, including touching through clothing, with the anus, breast, or any part of the genitals of a person.

(d) An offense under Subsection (a)(1) is a felony of the second degree and an offense under Subsection (a)(2) is a felony of the third degree.

(Acts 1973, 63rd Leg., p. 883, ch. 399, §1, effective January 1, 1974. Amended by Acts 1981, 67th Leg., p. 472, ch. 202, §3, effective September 1, 1981; Acts 1987, 70th Leg., ch. 1028, §1, effective September 1, 1987; Acts 1993, 73rd Leg., ch. 900, §1.01, effective September 1, 1994. Amended by Acts 1999, 76th Leg., ch. 1415, §23, effective September 1, 1999; Acts 2001, 77th Leg., ch. 739, §2, effective September 1, 2001.)

§22.011. Sexual assault

(a) A person commits an offense if the person:

(1) intentionally or knowingly:

(A) causes the penetration of the anus or sexual organ of another person by any means, without that person's consent;

(B) causes the penetration of the mouth of another person by the sexual organ of the actor, without that person's consent; or

(C) causes the sexual organ of another person, without that person's consent, to contact or penetrate the mouth, anus, or sexual organ of another person, including the actor; or

(2) intentionally or knowingly:

(A) causes the penetration of the anus or sexual organ of a child by any means;

(B) causes the penetration of the mouth of a child by the sexual organ of the actor;

(C) causes the sexual organ of a child to contact or penetrate the mouth, anus, or sexual organ of another person, including the actor;

(D) causes the anus of a child to contact the mouth, anus, or sexual organ of another person, including the actor; or

(E) causes the mouth of a child to contact the anus or sexual organ of another person, including the actor.

(b) A sexual assault under Subsection (a)(1) is without the consent of the other person if:

(1) the actor compels the other person to submit or participate by the use of physical force or violence;

(2) the actor compels the other person to submit or participate by threatening to use force or violence against the other person, and the other person believes that the actor has the present ability to execute the threat;

(3) the other person has not consented and the actor knows the other person is unconscious or physically unable to resist;

(4) the actor knows that as a result of mental disease or defect the other person is at the time of the sexual assault incapable either of appraising the nature of the act or of resisting it;

(5) the other person has not consented and the actor knows the other person is unaware that the sexual assault is occurring;

(6) the actor has intentionally impaired the other person's power to appraise or control the other person's conduct by administering any substance without the other person's knowledge;

(7) the actor compels the other person to submit or participate by threatening to use force or violence against any person, and the other person believes that the actor has the ability to execute the threat;

(8) the actor is a public servant who coerces the other person to submit or participate;

(9) the actor is a mental health services provider or a health care services provider who causes the other person, who is a patient or former patient of the actor, to submit or participate by exploiting the other person's emotional dependency on the actor;

(10) the actor is a clergyman who causes the other person to submit or participate by exploiting the other person's emotional dependency on the clergyman in the clergyman's professional character as spiritual adviser; or

(11) the actor is an employee of a facility where the other person is a resident, unless the employee and resident are formally or informally married to each other under Chapter 2, Family Code.

(c) In this section:

(1) "Child" means a person younger than 17 years of age who is not the spouse of the actor.

(2) "Spouse" means a person who is legally married to another.

(3) "Health care services provider" means:

(A) a physician licensed under Subtitle B, Title 3, Occupations Code;

(B) a chiropractor licensed under Chapter 201, Occupations Code;

(C) a physical therapist licensed under Chapter 453, Occupations Code;

(D) a physician assistant licensed under Chapter 204, Occupations Code; or

(E) a registered nurse, a vocational nurse, or an advanced practice nurse licensed under Chapter 301, Occupations Code.

(4) "Mental health services provider" means an individual, licensed or unlicensed, who performs or purports to perform mental health services, including a:

(A) licensed social worker as defined by Section 505.002, Occupations Code;

(B) chemical dependency counselor as defined by Section 504.001, Occupations Code;

(C) licensed professional counselor as defined by Section 503.002, Occupations Code;

(D) licensed marriage and family therapist as defined by Section 502.002, Occupations Code;

(E) member of the clergy;

(F) psychologist offering psychological services as defined by Section 501.003, Occupations Code; or

(G) special officer for mental health assignment certified under Section 1701.404, Occupations Code.

(5) "Employee of a facility" means a person who is an employee of a facility defined by Section 250.001, Health and Safety Code, or any other person who provides services for a facility for compensation, including a contract laborer.

(d) It is a defense to prosecution under Subsection (a)(2) that the conduct consisted of medical care for the child and did not include any contact between the anus or sexual organ of the child and the mouth, anus, or sexual organ of the actor or a third party.

(e) It is an affirmative defense to prosecution under Subsection (a)(2) that:

(1) the actor was not more than three years older than the victim and at the time of the offense:

(A) was not required under Chapter 62, Code of Criminal Procedure, to register for life as a sex offender; or

(B) was not a person who under Chapter 62, Code of Criminal Procedure, had a reportable conviction or adjudication for an offense under this section; and

(2) the victim:

(A) was a child of 14 years of age or older; and

(B) was not a person whom the actor was prohibited from marrying or purporting to marry or with whom the actor was prohibited from living under the appearance of being married under Section 25.01.

(f) An offense under this section is a felony of the second degree, except that an offense under this section is a felony of the first degree if the victim was a person whom the actor was prohibited from marrying or purporting to marry or with whom the actor was prohibited from living under the appearance of being married under Section 25.01.

(Acts 1983, 68th Leg., p. 5312, ch. 977, §3, effective September 1, 1983. Amended by Acts 1985, 69th Leg., ch. 557, §1, effective September 1, 1985; Acts 1987, 70th Leg., ch. 1029, §1, effective September 1, 1987; Acts 1991, 72nd Leg., ch. 662, §1, effective September 1, 1991; Acts 1993, 73rd Leg., ch. 900, §1.01, effective September 1, 1994. Amended by Acts 1995, 74th Leg., ch. 273, §1, effective September 1, 1995; Acts 1995, 74th Leg., ch. 318, §6, effective September 1, 1995; Acts 1997, 75th Leg., ch. 1031, §§1, 2, effective September 1, 1997; Acts 1997, 75th Leg., ch. 1286, §1, effective September 1, 1997; Acts 1999, 76th Leg., ch. 1102, §3, effective September 1, 1999; Acts 1999, 76th Leg., ch. 1415, §24, effective September 1, 1999; Acts 2001, 77th Leg., ch. 1420, §14.829, effective September 1, 2001; Acts 2003, 78th Leg., ch. 155, §§1, 2, effective September 1, 2003; Acts 2003, 78th Leg., ch. 528, §1, effective September 1, 2003; Acts 2003, 78th Leg., ch. 553, §2.017, effective Feb. 1, 2004; Acts 2005, 79th Leg., ch. 268, §4.02, effective September 1, 2005.)

§22.021. Aggravated sexual assault

(a) A person commits an offense:

(1) if the person:

(A) intentionally or knowingly:

(i) causes the penetration of the anus or sexual organ of another person by any means, without that person's consent;

(ii) causes the penetration of the mouth of another person by the sexual organ of the actor, without that person's consent; or

(iii) causes the sexual organ of another person, without that person's consent, to contact or penetrate the mouth, anus, or sexual organ of another person, including the actor; or

(B) intentionally or knowingly:

(i) causes the penetration of the anus or sexual organ of a child by any means;

(ii) causes the penetration of the mouth of a child by the sexual organ of the actor;

(iii) causes the sexual organ of a child to contact or penetrate the mouth, anus, or sexual organ of another person, including the actor;

(iv) causes the anus of a child to contact the mouth, anus, or sexual organ of another person, including the actor; or

(v) causes the mouth of a child to contact the anus or sexual organ of another person, including the actor; and

(2) if:

(A) the person:

(i) causes serious bodily injury or attempts to cause the death of the victim or another person in the course of the same criminal episode;

(ii) by acts or words places the victim in fear that death, serious bodily injury, or kidnapping will be imminently inflicted on any person;

(iii) by acts or words occurring in the presence of the victim threatens to cause the death, serious bodily injury, or kidnapping of any person;

(iv) uses or exhibits a deadly weapon in the course of the same criminal episode;

(v) acts in concert with another who engages in conduct described by Subdivision (1) directed toward the same victim and occurring during the course of the same criminal episode; or

(vi) administers or provides flunitrazepam, otherwise known as rohypnol, gamma hydroxybutyrate, or ketamine to the victim of the offense with the intent of facilitating the commission of the offense;

(B) the victim is younger than 14 years of age; or

(C) the victim is an elderly individual or a disabled individual.

(b) In this section:

(1) "Child" has the meaning assigned by Section 22.011(c).

(2) "Elderly individual" and "disabled individual" have the meanings assigned by Section 22.04(c).

(c) An aggravated sexual assault under this section is without the consent of the other person if the aggravated sexual assault occurs under the same circumstances listed in Section 22.011(b).

(d) The defense provided by Section 22.011(d) applies to this section.

(e) An offense under this section is a felony of the first degree.

(Acts 1983, 68th Leg., p. 5312, ch. 977, §3, effective September 1, 1983. Amended by Acts 1987, 70th Leg., ch. 573, §1, effective September 1, 1987; Acts 1987, 70th Leg., 2nd C.S., ch. 16, §1, effective September 1, 1987; Acts 1993, 73rd Leg., ch. 900, §1.01, effective September 1, 1994. Amended by Acts 1995, 74th Leg., ch. 318, §7, effective September 1, 1995; Acts 1997, 75th Leg., ch. 1286, §2, effective September 1, 1997; Acts 1999, 76th Leg., ch. 417, §1, effective September 1, 1999; Acts 2001, 77th Leg., ch. 459, §5, effective September 1, 2001; Acts 2003, 78th Leg., ch. 528, §2, effective September 1, 2003; Acts 2003, 78th Leg., ch. 896, §1, effective September 1, 2003.)

§25.02. Prohibited sexual conduct with relative

(a) A person commits an offense if the person engages in sexual intercourse or deviate sexual intercourse with another person the actor knows to be, without regard to legitimacy:

(1) the actor's ancestor or descendant by blood or adoption;

(2) the actor's current or former stepchild or stepparent;

(3) the actor's parent's brother or sister of the whole or half blood;

(4) the actor's brother or sister of the whole or half blood or by adoption;

(5) the children of the actor's brother or sister of the whole or half blood or by adoption; or

(6) the son or daughter of the actor's aunt or uncle of the whole or half blood or by adoption.

(b) For purposes of this section:

(1) "Deviate sexual intercourse" means any contact between the genitals of one person and the mouth or anus of another person with intent to arouse or gratify the sexual desire of any person.

(2) "Sexual intercourse" means any penetration of the female sex organ by the male sex organ.

(c) An offense under this section is a felony of the third degree, unless the offense is committed under Subsection (a)(6), in which event the offense is a felony of the second degree.

(Acts 1973, 63rd Leg., p. 883, ch. 399, §1, effective January 1, 1974. Amended by Acts 1993, 73rd Leg., ch. 900, §1.01, effective September 1, 1994.)

§43.01. Definitions

In this subchapter:

(1) "Deviate sexual intercourse" means any contact between the genitals of one person and the mouth or anus of another person.

(2) "Prostitution" means the offense defined in Section 43.02.

(3) "Sexual contact" means any touching of the anus, breast, or any part of the genitals of another person with intent to arouse or gratify the sexual desire of any person.

(4) "Sexual conduct" includes deviate sexual intercourse, sexual contact, and sexual intercourse.

(5) "Sexual intercourse" means any penetration of the female sex organ by the male sex organ.

(Acts 1973, 63rd Leg., p. 883, ch. 399, §1, effective January 1, 1974. Amended by Acts 1979, 66th Leg., p. 373, ch. 168, §2, effective August 27, 1979; Acts 1993, 73rd Leg., ch. 900, §1.01, effective September 1, 1994.)

§43.25. Sexual performance by a child

(a) In this section:

(1) "Sexual performance" means any performance or part thereof that includes sexual conduct by a child younger than 18 years of age.

(2) "Sexual conduct" means sexual contact, actual or simulated sexual intercourse, deviate sexual intercourse, sexual bestiality, masturbation, sado-masochistic abuse, or lewd exhibition of the genitals, the anus, or any portion of the female breast below the top of the areola.

(3) "Performance" means any play, motion picture, photograph, dance, or other visual representation that can be exhibited before an audience of one or more persons.

(4) "Produce" with respect to a sexual performance includes any conduct that directly contributes to the creation or manufacture of the sexual performance.

(5) "Promote" means to procure, manufacture, issue, sell, give, provide, lend, mail, deliver, transfer, transmit, publish, distribute, circulate, disseminate, present, exhibit, or advertise or to offer or agree to do any of the above.

(6) "Simulated" means the explicit depiction of sexual conduct that creates the appearance of actual sexual conduct and during which a person engaging in the conduct exhibits any uncovered portion of the breasts, genitals, or buttocks.

(7) "Deviate sexual intercourse" and "sexual contact" have the meanings assigned by Section 43.01.

(b) A person commits an offense if, knowing the character and content thereof, he employs, authorizes, or induces a child younger than 18 years of age to engage in sexual conduct or a sexual performance. A parent or legal guardian or custodian of a child younger than 18 years of age commits an offense if he consents to the participation by the child in a sexual performance.

(c) An offense under Subsection (b) is a felony of the second degree.

(d) A person commits an offense if, knowing the character and content of the material, he produces, directs, or promotes a performance that includes sexual conduct by a child younger than 18 years of age.

(e) An offense under Subsection (d) is a felony of the third degree.

(f) It is an affirmative defense to a prosecution under this section that:

(1) the defendant was the spouse of the child at the time of the offense;

(2) the conduct was for a bona fide educational, medical, psychological, psychiatric, judicial, law enforcement, or legislative purpose; or

(3) the defendant is not more than two years older than the child.

(g) When it becomes necessary for the purposes of this section or Section 43.26 to determine whether a child who participated in sexual conduct was younger than 18 years of age, the court or jury may make this determination by any of the following methods:

(1) personal inspection of the child;

(2) inspection of the photograph or motion picture that shows the child engaging in the sexual performance;

(3) oral testimony by a witness to the sexual performance as to the age of the child based on the child's appearance at the time;

(4) expert medical testimony based on the appearance of the child engaging in the sexual performance; or

(5) any other method authorized by law or by the rules of evidence at common law.

(Acts 1977, 65th Leg., p. 1035, ch. 381, § 1, effective June 10, 1977. Amended by Acts 1979, 66th Leg., p. 1976, ch. 779, § 1, effective September 1, 1979; Acts 1985, 69th Leg., ch. 530, § 1, effective September 1, 1985; Acts 1993, 73rd Leg., ch. 900, § 1.01, effective September 1, 1994. Amended by Acts 1999, 76th Leg., ch. 1415, § 22(b), effective September 1, 1999.)

---

3. Emotional Abuse

Courts were slow to recognize psychological maltreatment as a form of child abuse. Early definitions were limited to serious physical injuries. See generally J. Robert Shull, Note, Emotional and Psychological Child Abuse: Notes on Discourse, History, and Change, 51 Stan. L. Rev. 1665 (1999).

Texas law prohibits intentional or criminally negligent acts or omissions that cause "serious mental deficiency, impairment, or injury" to a child (Tex. Penal Code §22.04).

Texas Penal Code

§22.04. Injury to a child, elderly or disabled person

(a) A person commits an offense if he intentionally, knowingly, recklessly, or with criminal negligence, by act or intentionally, knowingly, or recklessly by omission, causes to a child, elderly individual, or disabled individual:

(1) serious bodily injury;

(2) serious mental deficiency, impairment, or injury; or

(3) bodily injury.

[The remainder of the statute is reprinted above in the section on Physical Abuse.]

(Acts 1973, 63rd Leg., p. 883, ch. 399, §1, effective January 1, 1974. Amended by Acts 1977, 65th Leg., p. 2067, ch. 819, §1, effective Aug. 29, 1977; Acts 1979, 66th Leg., p. 365, ch. 162, §1, effective Aug. 27, 1979; Acts 1981, 67th Leg., p. 472, ch. 202, §4, effective September 1, 1981; Acts 1981, 67th Leg., p. 2397, ch. 604, §1, effective September 1, 1981; Acts 1989, 71st Leg., ch. 357, §1, effective September 1, 1989; Acts 1991, 72nd Leg., ch. 497, §1, effective September 1, 1991; Acts 1993, 73rd Leg., ch. 900, §1.01, effective September 1, 1994; Acts 1995, 74th Leg., ch. 76, §8.139, effective September 1, 1995; Acts 1999, 76th Leg., ch. 62, §15.02(b), effective September 1, 1999; Acts 2005, 79th Leg., ch. 268, §1.125(a), effective September 1, 2005; Acts 2005, 79th Leg., ch. 949, §46, effective September 1, 2005.)

4. Abandonment or Child Endangerment

States punish child abandonment. The growing number of newborn abandonments has prompted many states (although not Texas) to enact legislation to allow mothers who have given birth to surrender their newborn within the first hours of life to a hospital employee, anonymously, and with impunity. See, e.g., Cal. Health & Safety Code §1255.7 (West 2001). Such laws (called "Baby Moses laws") are addressed primarily to pregnant teens who abandon their newborns because of shame or fear. Texas law provides for special statutory procedures permitting the state to take emergency possession of abandoned infants. See Tex. Fam. Code §§262.301-262.307 in Section C2 *infra*.

Increasingly, states are punishing, as a form of child endangerment, parents who leave children unattended in cars. See, e.g., Tex. Penal Code §22.10.

See also Texas Family Code §161.001(1)(N), which provides for termination of parental rights for constructive abandonment of a child; In the Interest of J.J.O., 131 S.W.3d 618 (Tex. App.—Fort Worth 2004, no pet.) (holding that a mother's failure to visit her child regularly when the child was in state custody and her failure to interact with the child during these visits, when the state had made reasonable efforts to return the child to the mother, constituted evidence of constructive abandonment under Texas Family Code §161.001(1)(N)).

Texas Penal Code

§22.041. Child abandonment or child endangerment

(a) In this section, "abandon" means to leave a child in any place without providing reasonable and necessary care for the child, under circumstances under which no reasonable, similarly situated adult would leave a child of that age and ability.

(b) A person commits an offense if, having custody, care, or control of a child younger than 15 years, he intentionally abandons the child in any place under circumstances that expose the child to an unreasonable risk of harm.

(c) A person commits an offense if he intentionally, knowingly, recklessly, or with criminal negligence, by act or omission, engages in conduct that places a child younger than 15 years in imminent danger of death, bodily injury, or physical or mental impairment.

(c-1) For purposes of Subsection (c), it is presumed that a person engaged in conduct that places a child in imminent danger of death, bodily injury, or physical or mental impairment if the person manufactured the controlled substance methamphetamine in the presence of the child.

(d) Except as provided by Subsection (e), an offense under Subsection (b) is:

(1) a state jail felony if the actor abandoned the child with intent to return for the child; or

(2) a felony of the third degree if the actor abandoned the child without intent to return for the child.

(e) An offense under Subsection (b) is a felony of the second degree if the actor abandons the child under circumstances that a reasonable person would believe would place the child in imminent danger of death, bodily injury, or physical or mental impairment.

(f) An offense under Subsection (c) is a state jail felony.

(g) It is a defense to prosecution under Subsection (c) that the act or omission enables the child to practice for or participate in an organized athletic event and that appropriate safety equipment and procedures are employed in the event.

(h) It is an exception to the application of this section that the actor voluntarily delivered the child to a designated emergency infant care provider under Section 262.302, Family Code.

(Acts 1985, 69th Leg., ch. 791, §1, effective September 1, 1985. Amended by Acts 1989, 71st Leg., ch. 904, §1, effective September 1, 1989; Acts 1993, 73rd Leg., ch. 900, §1.01, effective September 1, 1994; Acts 1997, 75th Leg., ch. 687, §1, effective September 1, 1997; Acts 1999, 76th Leg., ch. 1087, §3, effective September 1, 1999; Acts 2001, 77th Leg., ch. 809, §7, effective September 1, 2001; Acts 2005, 79th Leg., ch. 282, §10, effective August 1, 2005.)

§22.10. Leaving a young child in a motor vehicle

(a) A person commits an offense if he intentionally or knowingly leaves a child in a motor vehicle for longer than five minutes, knowing that the child is:

(1) younger than seven years of age; and

(2) not attended by an individual in the vehicle who is 14 years of age or older.

(b) An offense under this section is a Class C misdemeanor.

(Acts 1984, 68th Leg., 2nd C.S., ch. 24, §1, effective October 2, 1984. Amended by Acts 1993, 73rd Leg., ch. 900, §1.01, effective September 1, 1994.)

5. Failure to Protect

A parent has a duty to provide adequate care to a child. Failure to do so may result in a judicial determination that the child is abused or neglected. Many jurisdictions define child abuse to include acts of omission as well as commission. That is, some statutes make the parental failure to protect children a form of child endangerment.

Considerable controversy exists about the extent of liability if a mother (especially a battered woman) fails to protect her child from an abuser. See, e.g., Nicholson v. Scoppetta, 820 N.E.2d 840 (N.Y. 2004) (avoiding constitutional issues by finding that, based on state law, children's witnessing abuse does not, by itself, presumptively establish neglect by the mother and also that removal requires additional particularized evidence). See generally Justine A. Dunlap, Sometimes I Feel Like a Motherless Child: The Error of Pursuing Battered Mothers for Failure to Protect, 50 Loy. L. Rev. 565 (2004); Evan Stark, A Failure to Protect: Unraveling the "Battered Mother's Dilemma," 27 Western State U. L. Rev. 29 (1999-2000); Jeanne A. Fugate, Note, Who's Failing Whom: A Critical Look at Failure-to-Protect Laws, 76 N.Y.U. L. Rev. 272 (2001).

Texas Family Code

§261.001. Definitions

In this chapter:

(1) "Abuse" includes the following acts or omissions by a person:

. . .

(D) failure to make a reasonable effort to prevent an action by another person that results in physical injury that results in substantial harm to the child;

. . .

(Acts 1995, 74th Leg., ch. 20, §1, effective April 20, 1995. Amended by Acts 1995, 74th Leg., ch. 751, §86, effective September 1, 1995; by Acts 1997, 75th Leg., ch. 575, §10, effective September 1, 1997; Acts 1997, 75th Leg., ch. 1022, §63, effective September 1, 1997; Acts 1999, 76th Leg., ch. 62, §19.01(26), effective September 1, 1999; Acts 2001, 77th Leg., ch. 59, §1, effective September 1, 2001.)

6. Neglect

States impose civil and criminal liability for a parent's failure to provide adequate care for a child. Many state statutes include broad definitions of parental acts of misconduct or omission, allowing room for highly subjective determination of proper parenting.

The Texas statute subjecting the child to jurisdiction of civil courts defines "neglect" with more specificity than many state statutes. The statute provides that neglect encompasses "the failure to provide a child with food, clothing, or shelter necessary to sustain the life or health of the child" (Tex. Fam. Code §261.001(4)(B)(iii)); "failing to seek, obtain, or follow through with medical care for a child" such that the failure results in "substantial risk of death, disfigurement or bodily injury" [or] "observable and material impairment" (*id.* at §261.001(4)(B)(iii)), placing a child in a situation that involves a serious risk of harm (*id.* at §261.001(4)(B)(i) and (iv)), and "placing a child in or failing to remove the child from a situation in which the child would be exposed to acts or omissions that constitute" sexual abuse (*id.* at §261.001(4)(B)(v)). Texas law provides that the refusal to consent to psychiatric treatment for a child is not neglect unless the failure to do so poses a substantial risk to the child (Tax. Fam. Code §261.111).

Criminal felony liability is imposed for a parent's failure to provide financial support for a child (Tex. Penal Code §25.05). However, the parent's financial inability to provide such support constitutes an affirmative defense to criminal liability (*id.* at §25.05 (d)).

Texas Family Code

§261.001. Definitions

In this chapter:

. . .

(4) "Neglect" includes:

(A) the leaving of a child in a situation where the child would be exposed to a substantial risk of physical or mental harm, without arranging for necessary care for the child, and the demonstration of an intent not to return by a parent, guardian, or managing or possessory conservator of the child;

(B) the following acts or omissions by a person:

(i) placing a child in or failing to remove a child from a situation that a reasonable person would realize requires judgment or actions beyond the child's level of maturity, physical condition, or mental abilities and that results in bodily injury or a substantial risk of immediate harm to the child;

(ii) failing to seek, obtain, or follow through with medical care for a child, with the failure resulting in or presenting a substantial risk of death, disfigurement, or bodily injury or with the failure resulting in an observable and material impairment to the growth, development, or functioning of the child;

(iii) the failure to provide a child with food, clothing, or shelter necessary to sustain the life or health of the child, excluding failure caused primarily by financial inability unless relief services had been offered and refused; or

(iv) placing a child in or failing to remove the child from a situation in which the child would be exposed to a substantial risk of sexual conduct harmful to the child; or

(v) placing a child in or failing to remove the child from a situation in which the child would be exposed to acts or omissions that constitute abuse under

Subdivision (1)(E), (F), (G), (H), or (K) committed against another child; or

(C) the failure by the person responsible for a child's care, custody, or welfare to permit the child to return to the child's home without arranging for the necessary care for the child after the child has been absent from the home for any reason, including having been in residential placement or having run away. . . .

(Acts 1995, 74th Leg., ch. 20, §1, effective April 20, 1995. Amended by Acts 1995, 74th Leg., ch. 751, §86, effective September 1, 1995; by Acts 1997, 75th Leg., ch. 575, §10, effective September 1, 1997; Acts 1997, 75th Leg., ch. 1022, §63, effective September 1, 1997; Acts 1999, 76th Leg., ch. 62, §19.01(26), effective September 1, 1999; Acts 2001, 77th Leg., ch. 59, §1, effective September 1, 2001; Acts 2005, 79th Leg., ch. 268, §1.11, effective September 1, 2005.)

§261.111. Refusal to consent to or administer psychiatric treatment is not neglect unless it creates a substantial risk or impairs development of child

(a) In this section, "psychotropic drug" means a substance that is:

(1) used in the diagnosis, treatment, or prevention of a disease or as a component of a medication; and

(2) intended to have an altering effect on perception, emotion, or behavior.

(b) The refusal of a parent, guardian, or managing or possessory conservator of a child to administer or consent to the administration of a psychotropic drug to the child, or to consent to any other psychiatric or psychological treatment of the child, does not by itself constitute neglect of the child unless the refusal to consent:

(1) presents a substantial risk of death, disfigurement, or bodily injury to the child; or

(2) has resulted in an observable and material impairment to the growth, development, or functioning of the child.

(Acts 2003, 78th Leg., ch. 1008, §3, effective June 20, 2003.)

Texas Penal Code

§25.05. Criminal nonsupport

(a) An individual commits an offense if the individual intentionally or knowingly fails to provide support for the individual's child younger than 18 years of age, or for the individual's child who is the subject of a court order requiring the individual to support the child.

(b) For purposes of this section, "child" includes a child born out of wedlock whose paternity has either been acknowledged by the actor or has been established in a civil suit under the Family Code or the law of another state.

(c) Under this section, a conviction may be had on the uncorroborated testimony of a party to the offense.

(d) It is an affirmative defense to prosecution under this section that the actor could not provide support for the actor's child.

(e) The pendency of a prosecution under this section does not affect the power of a court to enter an order for child support under the Family Code.

(f) An offense under this section is a state jail felony.

(Acts 1973, 63rd Leg., p. 883, ch. 399, §1, effective January 1, 1974. Amended by Acts 1987, 70th Leg., 2nd C.S., ch. 73, §13, effective November 1, 1987; Acts 1993, 73rd Leg., ch. 900, §1.01, effective September 1, 1994; Acts 2001, 77th Leg., ch. 375, §1, effective May 25, 2001.)

B. PARENTAL PRIVILEGE TO DISCIPLINE

A threshold issue in many cases is whether a child's injury or injuries resulted from abuse or discipline. At common law, parents have a privilege to discipline their children. Parents also have a constitutionally protected right to raise their children as they see fit, including the privilege to administer reasonable discipline. Meyer v. Nebraska, 262 U.S. 390 (1923); Pierce v. Society of Sisters, 268 U.S. 510 (1925). Thus, the privilege is subject to limitations regarding the amount and type of force that may be used. A parent, stepparent, or person acting in loco parentis must reasonably believe the force is "necessary to discipline the child or to safeguard or promote his welfare" (Tex. Penal Code §9.61). Several cases explore the justifiable force defense. See Goulart v. State, 26 S.W.3d 5 (Tex. App.—Waco 2000, pet. ref'd) (affirming trial court ruling that the level of force used by defendant in disciplining his daughter by whipping her with a dog leash for failing to do the dishes was not justified); Assiter v. State, 58 S.W.3d 743 (Tex. App.—Amarillo 2000, no pet.) (affirming trial court ruling that the defendant's spanking of three children with boat oar exceeded the justifiable force defense). As *Assiter* points out, "The use of force . . . is not justified simply because of a parent's subjective belief that the force is necessary; rather, the use of force is justified only if a reasonable person would have believed the force was necessary to discipline the child or to safeguard or promote the child's welfare." *Id.* at 748.

In 2005, the legislature added a provision limiting the right to use corporal punishment for the "reasonable discipline" of a child to certain designated persons (i.e., a parent, grandparent, stepparent, or guardian) (Tex. Fam. Code §151.001(e)).

Texas Penal Code

§9.61. Parent's justifiable use of force: standard

(a) The use of force, but not deadly force, against a child younger than 18 years is justified:

(1) if the actor is the child's parent or stepparent or is acting in loco parentis to the child; and

(2) when and to the degree the actor reasonably believes the force is necessary to discipline the child or to safeguard or promote his welfare.

(b) For purposes of this section, "in loco parentis" includes grandparent and guardian, any person acting by, through, or under the direction of a court with jurisdiction over the child, and anyone who has express or implied consent of the parent or parents.

(Acts 1973, 63rd Leg., p. 883, ch. 399, §1, effective January 1, 1974. Amended by Acts 1993, 73rd Leg., ch. 900, §1.01, effective September 1, 1994.)

Texas Family Code

§151.001. Parent's rights and duties

(a) A parent of a child has the following rights and duties:

(1) the right to have physical possession, to direct the moral and religious training, and to designate the residence of the child;

(2) the duty of care, control, protection, and reasonable discipline of the child;

(3) the duty to support the child, including providing the child with clothing, food, shelter, medical and dental care, and education;

(4) the duty, except when a guardian of the child's estate has been appointed, to manage the estate of the child, including the right as an agent of the child to act in relation to the child's estate if the child's action is required by a state, the United States, or a foreign government;

(5) except as provided by Section 264.0111, the right to the services and earnings of the child;

(6) the right to consent to the child's marriage, enlistment in the armed forces of the United States, medical and dental care, and psychiatric, psychological, and surgical treatment;

(7) the right to represent the child in legal action and to make other decisions of substantial legal significance concerning the child;

(8) the right to receive and give receipt for payments for the support of the child and to hold or disburse funds for the benefit of the child;

(9) the right to inherit from and through the child;

(10) the right to make decisions concerning the child's education; and

(11) any other right or duty existing between a parent and child by virtue of law.

(b) The duty of a parent to support his or her child exists while the child is an unemancipated minor and continues as long as the child is fully enrolled in an accredited secondary school in a program leading toward a high school diploma until the end of the school year in which the child graduates.

(c) A parent who fails to discharge the duty of support is liable to a person who provides necessaries to those to whom support is owed.

(d) The rights and duties of a parent are subject to:

(1) a court order affecting the rights and duties;

(2) an affidavit of relinquishment of parental rights; and

(3) an affidavit by the parent designating another person or agency to act as managing conservator.

(e) Only the following persons may use corporal punishment for the reasonable discipline of a child:

(1) a parent or grandparent of the child;

(2) a stepparent of the child who has the duty of control and reasonable discipline of the child; and

(3) an individual who is a guardian of the child and who has the duty of control and reasonable discipline of the child.

(Acts 1995, 74th Leg., ch. 20, §1, effective April 20, 1995. Amended by Acts 1995, 74th Leg., ch. 751, §23, effective September 1, 1995. Renumbered from 151.003 by Acts 2001, 77th Leg., ch. 821, §2.13, effective June 14, 2001; Acts 2001, 77th Leg., ch. 964, §2, effective September 1, 2001; Acts 2003, 78th Leg., ch. 1036, §3, effective September 1, 2003; Acts 2005, 79th Leg., ch. 924, §1, effective September 1, 2005.)

C. CHILD ABUSE AND NEGLECT PROCEDURES

1. Reporting Laws

Child abuse reporting statutes, enacted by all states during the 1960s, require designated professionals to report suspected child abuse and neglect. The original purpose of these statutes was to encourage reporting by physicians who might treat a victim for physical injuries. Subsequent revisions expanded the mandated reporters and the types of reportable maltreatment.

Following the general pattern of the enactment of reporting laws, the Texas statute, enacted in 1965, originally applied only to physicians. An amendment in 1969 extended the responsibility for reporting to medical staff of institutions, school teachers, nursery school directors, coroners, social workers, and peace officers. (This history is summarized in State v. Harrod, 81 S.W.3d 904 (Tex. App.—Dallas 2002, no pet. h.)) On the history of reporting statutes generally, see Monrad G. Paulsen, Child Abuse Reporting Laws: The Shape of the Legislation, 67 Colum. L. Rev. 1 (1967).

Texas law requires "professionals" to report physical or sexual abuse by a person responsible for the minor's "care, custody, or welfare" (Tex. Fam. Code §33.008). The term "professional" includes: "teachers, nurses, doctors, day-care employees, employees of a clinic or health care facility that provides reproductive services, juvenile probation officers, and juvenile detention or correctional officers" (Tex. Fam. Code §261.101(b)). The professional may not delegate to others the responsibility to make a report (*id.*). Failure to report results in criminal liability (Tex. Fam. Code §261.109).

The Texas reporting statute now broadly defines both reporters and abusers. Specifically, it mandates reports by: "*A person* having cause to believe that a child's physical or mental health or welfare has been adversely affected by abuse or neglect by *any person*. . . ." (Tex. Fam. Code §261.101(a) (emphasis added)). See also State v. Harrod, 81 S.W.3d 904 (Tex. App.—Dallas 2002, no pet. h.) (holding that mother was not immune from criminal liability for failure to report sexual abuse of her daughters). Moreover, Texas law "encourages" any person witnessing family violence to report it (Tex. Fam. Code §91.002). ("Family violence" includes spousal abuse and child abuse pursuant to the definition in Texas Family Code §71.004.) Statute provides for immunity from civil or criminal liability for reporters who act in good faith (Tex. Fam. Code §261.106(a)).

The reporting requirement applies, without exception, to persons whose communications are normally privileged (including attorneys, clergy, medical practitioners, social workers, mental health professionals, and employees of facilities that provide reproductive services) (Tex. Fam. Code §261.101(c)). In several cases, defendants have argued unsuccessfully that their confessions of abuse to clergy should have been excluded under the clergy-penitent communication privilege. Martinez v. State, 2002 WL 1860301 (Tex. App.—Corpus Christi 2002, no pet. h.) (not designated for publication); Bordman v. State, 56 S.W.3d 63 (Tex. App.—Houston [14th Dist.] 2001, pet ref'd); Almendarez v. State, 153 S.W.3d 727 (Tex. App.—Dallas 2005, no pet.) (holding that family code provisions concerning privilege took precedence over rules of evidence). Note, however, that the attorney-client privilege still applies in "a proceeding regarding the abuse or neglect of a child" (Tex. Fam. Code §261.202 below).

Medical professionals who treat a victim must inform the victim of the nearest family violence shelter and of the fact that family violence is a crime that may be reported to law enforcement (Tex. Fam. Code §91.003).

a. Duty to Report

Texas Family Code

§33.008. Physician has duty to report child abuse

(a) A physician who has reason to believe that a minor has been or may be physically or sexually abused by a person responsible for the minor's care, custody, or welfare, as that term is defined by Section 261.001, shall immediately report the suspected abuse to the Department of Protective and Regulatory Services and shall refer the minor to the department for services or intervention that may be in the best interest of the minor.

(b) The Department of Protective and Regulatory Services shall investigate suspected abuse reported under this section and, if appropriate, shall assist the minor in making an application with a court under Section 33.003.

(Acts 1999, 76th Leg., ch. 395, §1, effective September 1, 1999.)

§33.009. Court or child's representative must make other reports of sexual abuse of a minor

A court or the guardian ad litem or attorney ad litem for the minor shall report conduct reasonably believed to violate Section 22.011[sexual assault], 22.021 [aggravated sexual assault], or 25.02 [prohibited sexual conduct], Penal Code, based on information obtained during a confidential court proceeding held under this chapter to:

(1) any local or state law enforcement agency;

(2) the Department of Protective and Regulatory Services, if the alleged conduct involves a person responsible for the care, custody, or welfare of the child;

(3) the state agency that operates, licenses, certifies, or registers the facility in which the alleged conduct occurred, if the alleged conduct occurred in a facility operated, licensed, certified, or registered by a state agency; or

(4) an appropriate agency designated by the court.

(Acts 1999, 76th Leg., ch. 395, §1, effective September 1, 1999.)

§91.002. Reporting by witnesses is "encouraged"

A person who witnesses family violence is encouraged to report the family violence to a local law enforcement agency.

(*Acts 1997, 75th Leg., ch. 34, §1, effective May 5, 1997.*)

§261.101. Persons who are required to report; professional must report promptly

(a) A person having cause to believe that a child's physical or mental health or welfare has been adversely affected by abuse or neglect by any person shall immediately make a report as provided by this subchapter.

(b) If a professional has cause to believe that a child has been abused or neglected or may be abused or neglected, or that a child is a victim of an offense under Section 21.11, Penal Code, and the professional has cause to believe that the child has been abused as defined by Section 261.001 or 261.401, the professional shall make a report not later than the 48th hour after the hour the professional first suspects that the child has been or may be abused or neglected or is a victim of an offense under Section 21.11, Penal Code. A professional may not delegate to or rely on another person to make the report. In this subsection, "professional" means an individual who is licensed or certified by the state or who is an employee of a facility licensed, certified, or operated by the state and who, in the normal course of official duties or duties for which a license or certification is required, has direct contact with children. The term includes teachers, nurses, doctors, day-care employees, employees of a clinic or health care facility that provides reproductive services, juvenile probation officers, and juvenile detention or correctional officers.

(c) The requirement to report under this section applies without exception to an individual whose personal communications may otherwise be privileged, including an attorney, a member of the clergy, a medical practitioner, a social worker, a mental health professional, and an employee of a clinic or health care facility that provides reproductive services.

(d) Unless waived in writing by the person making the report, the identity of an individual making a report under this chapter is confidential and may be disclosed only:

(1) as provided by Section 261.201; or

(2) to a law enforcement officer for the purposes of conducting a criminal investigation of the report.

(Acts 1995, 74th Leg., ch. 20, §1, effective April 20, 1995. Amended by Acts 1995, 74th Leg., ch. 751, §87, effective September 1, 1995; by Acts 1997, 75th Leg., ch. 162, §1, effective September 1, 1997; Acts 1997, 75th Leg., ch. 575,

§11, effective September 1, 1997; Acts 1997, 75th Leg., ch. 1022, §65, effective September 1, 1997; Acts 1999, 76th Leg., ch. 62, §6.29, effective September 1, 1999; Acts 1999, 76th Leg., ch. 1150, §2, effective September 1, 1999; Acts 1999, 76th Leg., ch. 1390, §21, effective September 1, 1999; Acts 2001, 77th Leg., ch. 1420, §5.003, effective September 1, 2001; Acts 2005, 79th Leg., ch. 949, §27, effective September 1, 2005.)

b. Nature and Contents of Report

§261.102. Report should reflect reporter's belief of present or past abuse

A report should reflect the reporter's belief that a child has been or may be abused or neglected or has died of abuse or neglect.

(Acts 1995, 74th Leg., ch. 20, §1, effective April 20, 1995. Amended by Acts 1995, 74th Leg., ch. 751, §88, effective September 1, 1995.)

§261.104. Report must contain certain information

The person making a report shall identify, if known:

(1) the name and address of the child;

(2) the name and address of the person responsible for the care, custody, or welfare of the child; and

(3) any other pertinent information concerning the alleged or suspected abuse or neglect.

(Acts 1995, 74th Leg., ch. 20, §1, effective April 20, 1995. Amended by Acts 1995, 74th Leg., ch. 751, §90, effective September 1, 1995.)

c. Confidentiality

§33.010. Information is confidential except to prove sexual offense

Notwithstanding any other law, information obtained by the Department of Protective and Regulatory Services or another entity under Section 33.008 or 33.009 is confidential except to the extent necessary to prove a violation of Section 22.011, 22.021, or 25.02, Penal Code.

(Acts 1999, 76th Leg., ch. 395, §1, effective September 1, 1999.)

§261.201. Rules on confidentiality and disclosure

(a) The following information is confidential, is not subject to public release under Chapter 552, Government Code, and may be disclosed only for purposes consistent with this code and applicable federal or state law or under rules adopted by an investigating agency:

(1) a report of alleged or suspected abuse or neglect made under this chapter and the identity of the person making the report; and

(2) except as otherwise provided in this section, the files, reports, records, communications, audiotapes, videotapes, and working papers used or developed in an investigation under this chapter or in providing services as a result of an investigation.

(b) A court may order the disclosure of information that is confidential under this section if:

(1) a motion has been filed with the court requesting the release of the information;

(2) a notice of hearing has been served on the investigating agency and all other interested parties; and

(3) after hearing and an in camera review of the requested information, the court determines that the disclosure of the requested information is:

(A) essential to the administration of justice; and

(B) not likely to endanger the life or safety of:

(i) a child who is the subject of the report of alleged or suspected abuse or neglect;

(ii) a person who makes a report of alleged or suspected abuse or neglect; or

(iii) any other person who participates in an investigation of reported abuse or neglect or who provides care for the child.

(c) In addition to Subsection (b), a court, on its own motion, may order disclosure of information that is confidential under this section if:

(1) the order is rendered at a hearing for which all parties have been given notice;

(2) the court finds that disclosure of the information is:

(A) essential to the administration of justice; and

(B) not likely to endanger the life or safety of:

(i) a child who is the subject of the report of alleged or suspected abuse or neglect;

(ii) a person who makes a report of alleged or suspected abuse or neglect; or

(iii) any other person who participates in an investigation of reported abuse or neglect or who provides care for the child; and

(3) the order is reduced to writing or made on the record in open court.

(d) The adoptive parents of a child who was the subject of an investigation and an adult who was the subject of an investigation as a child are entitled to examine and make copies of any report, record, working paper, or other information in the possession, custody, or control of the state that pertains to the history of the child. The department may edit the documents to protect the identity of the biological parents and any other person whose identity is confidential, unless this information is already known to the adoptive parents or is readily available through other sources, including the court records of a suit to terminate the parent-child relationship under Chapter 161.

(e) Before placing a child who was the subject of an investigation, the department shall notify the prospective adoptive parents of their right to examine any report, record, working paper, or other information in the possession, custody, or control of the state that pertains to the history of the child.

(f) The department shall provide prospective adoptive parents an opportunity to examine information under this section as early as practicable before placing a child.

(f-1) The department shall provide to a relative or other individual with whom a child is placed any information the department considers necessary to ensure that the relative or other individual is prepared to meet the needs of the child. The information required by this subsection may include information related to any abuse or neglect suffered by the child.

(g) Notwithstanding Subsection (b), the department, on request and subject to department rule, shall provide to the parent, managing conservator, or other legal representative of a child who is the subject of reported abuse or neglect information concerning the reported abuse or neglect that would otherwise be confidential under this section if the department has edited the information to protect the confidentiality of the identity of the person who made the report and any other person whose life or safety may be endangered by the disclosure.

(h) This section does not apply to an investigation of child abuse or neglect in a home or facility regulated under Chapter 42, Human Resources Code.

(Acts 1995, 74th Leg., ch. 20, §1, effective April 20, 1995. Amended by Acts 1995, 74th Leg., ch. 751, §93, effective September 1, 1995; by Acts 1997, 75th Leg., ch. 575, §12, effective September 1, 1997; Acts 1997, 75th Leg., ch. 1022, §69, effective September 1, 1997; Acts 1999, 76th Leg., ch. 1150, §3, effective September 1, 1999; Acts 1999, 76th Leg., ch. 1390, §22, effective September 1, 1999; Acts 2003, 78th Leg., ch. 68, §2, effective September 1, 2003; Acts 2005, 79th Leg., ch. 268, §1.15, effective September 1, 2005.)

d. Central Registry

Many states require that some state agency maintain a register of all reported cases of suspected abuse and neglect. Originally, registries were designed to ascertain the incidence of abuse and to assist professionals in keeping track of parents suspected of abuse. More recently, social service agencies and some employers rely on the registries to preclude child abusers from employment in the field of child care. Such registries often contain a high number of unsubstantiated reports of abuse.

§261.002. Central registry of reported cases

(a) The department shall establish and maintain in Austin a central registry of reported cases of child abuse or neglect.

(b) The department may adopt rules necessary to carry out this section. The rules shall provide for cooperation with local child service agencies, including hospitals, clinics, and schools, and cooperation with other states in exchanging reports to effect a national registration system.

(c) The department may enter into agreements with other states to allow for the exchange of reports of child abuse and neglect in other states' central registry systems. The department shall use information obtained under this subsection in performing the background checks required under Section 42.056, Human Resources Code. The department shall cooperate with federal agencies and shall provide information and reports of child abuse and neglect to the appropriate federal agency that maintains the national registry for child abuse and neglect, if a national registry exists.

(Acts 1995, 74th Leg., ch. 20, §1, effective April 20, 1995. Amended by Acts 2005, 79th Leg., ch. 268, §1.12, effective September 1, 2005.)

e. Recipients of Reports

§261.103. Recipients of reports of child abuse

(a) Except as provided by Subsections (b) and (c) and Section 261.405, a report shall be made to:

(1) any local or state law enforcement agency;

(2) the department;

(3) the state agency that operates, licenses, certifies, or registers the facility in which the alleged abuse or neglect occurred; or

(4) the agency designated by the court to be responsible for the protection of children.

(b) A report may be made to the Texas Youth Commission instead of the entities listed under Subsection (a) if the report is based on information provided by a child while under the supervision of the commission concerning the child's alleged abuse of another child.

(c) Notwithstanding Subsection (a), a report, other than a report under Subsection (a)(3) or Section 261.405, must be made to the department if the alleged or suspected abuse or neglect involves a person responsible for the care, custody, or welfare of the child.

(Acts 1995, 74th Leg., ch. 20, §1, effective April 20, 1995. Amended by Acts 1995, 74th Leg., ch. 751, §89, effective September 1, 1995; by Acts 1999, 76th Leg., ch. 1477, §24, effective September 1, 1999; Acts 2001, 77th Leg., ch. 1297, §46, effective September 1, 2001; Acts 2005, 79th Leg., ch. 213, §1, effective September 1, 2005.)

§261.105. Reports shall be referred to Department or law enforcement

(a) All reports received by a local or state law enforcement agency that allege abuse or neglect by a person responsible for a child's care, custody, or welfare shall be referred immediately to the department or the designated agency.

(b) The department or designated agency shall immediately notify the appropriate state or local law enforcement agency of any report it receives, other than a report from a law enforcement agency, that concerns the suspected abuse or neglect of a child or death of a child from abuse or neglect.

(c) In addition to notifying a law enforcement agency, if the report relates to a child in a facility operated, licensed, certified, or registered by a state agency, the department shall refer the report to the agency for investigation.

(d) If the department initiates an investigation and determines that the abuse or neglect does not involve a person responsible for the child's care, custody, or welfare, the department shall refer the report to a law enforcement agency for further investigation. If the department determines that the abuse or neglect involves an employee of a public primary or secondary school, and that the child is a student at the school, the department shall orally notify the superintendent of the school district in which the employee is employed about the investigation.

(e) In cooperation with the department, the Texas Youth Commission by rule shall adopt guidelines for identifying a report made to the commission under Section 261.103(b) that is appropriate to refer to the department or a law enforcement agency for investigation. Guidelines adopted under this subsection must require the commission to consider the severity and immediacy of the alleged abuse or neglect of the child victim.

(Acts 1995, 74th Leg., ch. 20, §1, effective April 20, 1995. Amended by Acts 1997, 75th Leg., ch. 1022, §66, effective September 1, 1997; Acts 1999, 76th Leg., ch. 1477, §25, effective September 1, 1999; Acts 2003, 78th Leg., ch. 374, §3, effective June 18, 2003.)

§261.1055. Notification of suspected abuse or neglect to district attorneys

(a) A district attorney may inform the department or designated agency that the district attorney wishes to receive notification of some or all reports of suspected abuse or neglect of children who were in the county at the time the report was made or who were in the county at the time of the alleged abuse or neglect.

(b) If the district attorney makes the notification under this section, the department or designated agency shall, on receipt of a report of suspected abuse or neglect, immediately notify the district attorney as requested and the department or designated agency shall forward a copy of the reports to the district attorney on request.

(Acts 1997, 75th Leg., ch. 1022, §67, effective September 1, 1997.)

f. Reporters' Liabilities and Immunities

§261.106. Reporters' immunities

(a) A person acting in good faith who reports or assists in the investigation of a report of alleged child abuse or neglect or who testifies or otherwise participates in a judicial proceeding arising from a report, petition, or investigation of alleged child abuse or neglect is immune from civil or criminal liability that might otherwise be incurred or imposed.

(b) Immunity from civil and criminal liability extends to an authorized volunteer of the department or a law enforcement officer who participates at the request of the department in an investigation of alleged or suspected abuse or neglect or in an action arising from an investigation if the person was acting in good faith and in the scope of the person's responsibilities.

(c) A person who reports the person's own abuse or neglect of a child or who acts in bad faith or with malicious purpose in reporting alleged child abuse or neglect is not immune from civil or criminal liability.

(Acts 1995, 74th Leg., ch. 20, §1, effective April 20, 1995. Amended by Acts 1995, 74th Leg., ch. 751, §91, effective September 1, 1995.)

§261.107. Liability for false report of abuse

(a) A person commits an offense if, with the intent to deceive, the person knowingly makes a report as provided in this chapter that is false. An offense under this subsection is a state jail felony unless it is shown on the trial of the offense that the person has previously been convicted under this section, in which case the offense is a felony of the third degree.

(b) A finding by a court in a suit affecting the parent-child relationship that a report made under this chapter before or during the suit was false or lacking factual foundation may be grounds for the court to modify an order providing for possession of or access to the child who was the subject of the report by restricting further access to the child by the person who made the report.

(c) The appropriate county prosecuting attorney shall be responsible for the prosecution of an offense under this section.

(d) The court shall order a person who is convicted of an offense under Subsection (a) to pay any reasonable attorney's fees incurred by the person who was falsely accused of abuse or neglect in any proceeding relating to the false report.

(e) A person who engages in conduct described by Subsection (a) is liable to the state for a civil penalty of $1,000. The attorney general shall bring an action to recover a civil penalty authorized by this subsection.

(Acts 1995, 74th Leg., ch. 20, §1, effective April 20, 1995. Amended by Acts 1995, 74th Leg., ch. 751, §92, effective September 1, 1995; by Acts 1997, 75th Leg., ch. 575, §2, effective September 1, 1997; Acts 1997, 75th Leg., ch. 1022, §68; Acts 1999, 76th Leg., ch. 62, §6.30, effective September 1, 1999; Acts 2005, 79th Leg., ch. 268, §§1.13, 1.14(a), effective September 1, 2005.)

§261.108. Court shall award fees and costs for frivolous claims

(a) In this section:

(1) "Claim" means an action or claim by a party, including a plaintiff, counterclaimant, cross-claimant, or third-party plaintiff, requesting recovery of damages.

(2) "Defendant" means a party against whom a claim is made.

(b) A court shall award a defendant reasonable attorney's fees and other expenses related to the defense of a claim filed against the defendant for damages or other relief arising from reporting or assisting in the investigation of a report under this chapter or participating in a judicial proceeding resulting from the report if:

(1) the court finds that the claim is frivolous, unreasonable, or without foundation because the defendant is immune from liability under Section 261.106; and

(2) the claim is dismissed or judgment is rendered for the defendant.

(c) To recover under this section, the defendant must, at any time after the filing of a claim, file a written motion stating that:

(1) the claim is frivolous, unreasonable, or without foundation because the defendant is immune from liability under Section 261.106; and

(2) the defendant requests the court to award reasonable attorney's fees and other expenses related to the defense of the claim.

(Acts 1995, 74th Leg., ch. 20, §1, effective April 20, 1995.)

§261.109. Liability for failure to report

(a) A person commits an offense if the person has cause to believe that a child's physical or mental health or welfare has been or may be adversely affected by abuse or neglect and knowingly fails to report as provided in this chapter.

(b) An offense under this section is a Class B misdemeanor.

(Acts 1995, 74th Leg., ch. 20, §1, effective April 20, 1995.)

g. Employers' Retaliation

§261.110. Prohibition on employer retaliation

(a) In this section, "professional" has the meaning assigned by Section 261.101(b).

(b) An employer may not suspend or terminate the employment of, or otherwise discriminate against, a person who is a professional and who in good faith:

(1) reports child abuse or neglect to:

(A) the person's supervisor;

(B) an administrator of the facility where the person is employed;

(C) a state regulatory agency; or

(D) a law enforcement agency; or

(2) initiates or cooperates with an investigation or proceeding by a governmental entity relating to an allegation of child abuse or neglect.

(c) A person whose employment is suspended or terminated or who is otherwise discriminated against in violation of this section may sue for injunctive relief, damages, or both.

(d) A plaintiff who prevails in a suit under this section may recover:

(1) actual damages, including damages for mental anguish even if an injury other than mental anguish is not shown;

(2) exemplary damages under Chapter 41, Civil Practice and Remedies Code, if the employer is a private employer;

(3) court costs; and

(4) reasonable attorney's fees.

(e) In addition to amounts recovered under Subsection (d), a plaintiff who prevails in a suit under this section is entitled to:

(1) reinstatement to the person's former position or a position that is comparable in terms of compensation, benefits, and other conditions of employment;

(2) reinstatement of any fringe benefits and seniority rights lost because of the suspension, termination, or discrimination; and

(3) compensation for wages lost during the period of suspension or termination.

(f) A public employee who alleges a violation of this section may sue the employing state or local governmental entity for the relief provided for by this section. Sovereign immunity is waived and abolished to the extent of liability created by this section. A person having a claim under this section may sue a governmental unit for damages allowed by this section.

(g) In a suit under this section against an employing state or local governmental entity, a plaintiff may not recover compensatory damages for future pecuniary losses, emotional pain, suffering, inconvenience, mental anguish, loss of enjoyment of life, and other nonpecuniary losses in an amount that exceeds:

(1) $50,000, if the employing state or local governmental entity has fewer than 101 employees in each of 20 or more calendar weeks in the calendar year in which the suit is filed or in the preceding year;

(2) $100,000, if the employing state or local governmental entity has more than 100 and fewer than 201 employees in each of 20 or more calendar weeks in the calendar year in which the suit is filed or in the preceding year;

(3) $200,000, if the employing state or local governmental entity has more than 200 and fewer than 501 employees in each of 20 or more calendar weeks in the calendar year in which the suit is filed or in the preceding year; and

(4) $250,000, if the employing state or local governmental entity has more than 500 employees in each of 20 or more calendar weeks in the calendar year in which the suit is filed or in the preceding year.

(h) If more than one subdivision of Subsection (g) applies to an employing state or local governmental entity, the amount of monetary damages that may be recovered from the entity in a suit brought under this section is governed by the applicable provision that provides the highest damage award.

(i) A plaintiff suing under this section has the burden of proof, except that there is a rebuttable presumption that the plaintiff's employment was suspended or terminated or that the plaintiff was otherwise discriminated against for reporting abuse or neglect if the suspension, termination, or discrimination occurs before the 61st day after the date on which the person made a report in good faith.

(j) A suit under this section may be brought in a district or county court of the county in which:

(1) the plaintiff was employed by the defendant; or

(2) the defendant conducts business.

(k) It is an affirmative defense to a suit under Subsection (b) that an employer would have taken the action against the employee that forms the basis of the suit based solely on information, observation, or evidence that is not related to the fact that the employee reported child abuse or neglect or initiated or cooperated with an investigation or proceeding relating to an allegation of child abuse or neglect.

(l) A public employee who has a cause of action under Chapter 554, Government Code, based on conduct described by Subsection (b) may not bring an action based on that conduct under this section.

(m) This section does not apply to a person who reports the person's own abuse or neglect of a child or who initiates or cooperates with an investigation or proceeding by a governmental entity relating to an allegation of the person's own abuse or neglect of a child.

(Acts 2001, 77th Leg., ch. 896, §1, effective September 1, 2001.)

h. Statistics

§261.004. Statistics on abused and neglected children

(a) The department shall prepare and disseminate statistics by county relating to the department's activities under this subtitle and include the information specified in Subsection (b) in an annual report available to the public.

(b) The department shall report the following information:

(1) the number of initial phone calls received by the department alleging abuse and neglect;

(2) the number of children reported to the department as having been abused and neglected;

(3) the number of reports received by the department alleging abuse or neglect and assigned by the department for investigation;

(4) of the children to whom Subdivision (2) applies:

(A) the number for whom the report was substantiated;

(B) the number for whom the report was unsubstantiated;

(C) the number for whom the report was determined to be false;

(D) the number who did not receive services from the department under a state or federal program;

(E)the number who received services, including preventative services, from the department under a state or federal program; and

(F)the number who were removed from the child's home during the preceding year;

(5) the number of families in which the child was not removed, but the child or family received services from the department;

(6) the number of children who died during the preceding year as a result of child abuse or neglect;

(7) of the children to whom Subdivision (6) applies, the number who were in foster care at the time of death;

(8) the number of child protective services workers responsible for report intake, assessment, or investigation;

(9) the response time by the department with respect to conducting an initial investigation of a report of child abuse or neglect;

(10) the response time by the department with respect to commencing services to families and children for whom an allegation of abuse or neglect has been made;

(11) the number of children who were returned to their families or who received family preservation services and who, before the fifth anniversary of the date of return or receipt, were the victims of substantiated reports of child abuse or neglect, including abuse or neglect resulting in the death of the child;

(12) the number of cases pursued by the department in each stage of the judicial process, including civil and criminal proceedings and the results of each proceeding; and

(13) the number of children for whom a person was appointed by the court to represent the best interests of the child and the average number of out-of-court contacts between the person and the child.

(c) The department shall compile the information specified in Subsection (b) for the preceding year in a report to be submitted to the legislature and the general public not later than February 1 of each year.

(Acts 1997, 75th Leg., ch. 1022, §64, effective September 1, 1997.)

2. Investigation

The following statutory provisions explain the procedures for investigation of reports of child abuse or neglect. "The primary purpose of the investigation shall be the protection of the child" (Tex. Fam. Code §261.301). The investigation may include home or school visits; interviews with the child and parents; and medical, psychological, or psychiatric examinations (Tex. Fam. Code §261.302). Local law enforcement must accompany caseworkers when responding to a report of "immediate risk of physical or sexual abuse of a child that could result in the death of or serious harm" (Tex. Fam. Code §261.301(f)). The Texas legislature also recently enacted provisions that create a child safety alert check list that would enable the agency to enlist the help of local law enforcement in finding and investigating abused or neglected children placed on the list (Tex. Fam. Code §261.3022).

After the agency completes its investigation, it must file a written report and submit that report to the court, district attorney, or appropriate law enforcement agency if it finds sufficient grounds for filing a suit (Tex. Fam. Code §261.308(a)). On receipt of the agency's recommendations and report, the court may direct the agency to file a petition requesting appropriate relief (*id.* at §261.308(c)).

a. Nature and Conduct of Investigation

§261.301. Department or agency shall promptly investigate report of abuse or neglect

(a) With assistance from the appropriate state or local law enforcement agency as provided by this section, the department or designated agency shall make a prompt and thorough investigation of a report of child abuse or neglect allegedly committed by a person responsible for a child's care, custody, or welfare. The investigation shall be conducted without regard to any pending suit affecting the parent-child relationship.

(b) A state agency shall investigate a report that alleges abuse or neglect occurred in a facility operated, licensed, certified, or registered by that agency as provided by Subchapter E1 In conducting an investigation for a facility operated, licensed, certified, registered, or listed by the department, the department shall perform the investigation as provided by:

(1) Subchapter E; and

(2) the Human Resources Code.

(c) The department is not required to investigate a report that alleges child abuse or neglect by a person other than a person responsible for a child's care, custody, or welfare. The appropriate state or local law enforcement agency shall investigate that report if the agency determines an investigation should be conducted.

(d) The department shall by rule assign priorities and prescribe investigative procedures for investigations based on the severity and immediacy of the alleged harm to the child. The primary purpose of the investigation shall be the protection of the child. The rules must require the department, subject to the availability of funds, to:

(1) immediately respond to a report of abuse and neglect that involves circumstances in which the death of the child or substantial bodily harm to the child would result unless the department immediately intervenes;

(2) respond within 24 hours to a report of abuse and neglect that is assigned the highest priority, other than a report described by Subdivision (1); and

(3) respond within 72 hours to a report of abuse and neglect that is assigned the second highest priority.

(e) As necessary to provide for the protection of the child, the department or designated agency shall determine:

(1) the nature, extent, and cause of the abuse or neglect;

(2) the identity of the person responsible for the abuse or neglect;

(3) the names and conditions of the other children in the home;

(4) an evaluation of the parents or persons responsible for the care of the child;

(5) the adequacy of the home environment;

(6) the relationship of the child to the persons responsible for the care, custody, or welfare of the child; and

(7) all other pertinent data.

(f) An investigation of a report to the department that alleges that a child has been or may be the victim of conduct that constitutes a criminal offense that poses an immediate risk of physical or sexual abuse of a child that could result in the death of or serious harm to the child shall be conducted jointly by a peace officer, as defined by Article 2.12, Code of Criminal Procedure, from the appropriate local law enforcement agency and the department or the agency responsible for conducting an investigation under Subchapter E.

(g) The inability or unwillingness of a local law enforcement agency to conduct a joint investigation under this section does not constitute grounds to prevent or prohibit the department from performing its duties under this subtitle. The department shall document any instance in which a law enforcement agency is unable or unwilling to conduct a joint investigation under this section.

(h) The department and the appropriate local law enforcement agency shall conduct an investigation, other than an investigation under Subchapter E, as provided by this section and Article 2.27, Code of Criminal Procedure, if the investigation is of a report that alleges that a child has been or may be the victim of conduct that constitutes a criminal offense that poses an immediate risk of physical or sexual abuse of a child that could result in the death of or serious harm to the child. Immediately on receipt of a report described by this subsection, the department shall notify the appropriate local law enforcement agency of the report.

(Acts 1995, 74th Leg., ch. 20, §1, effective April 20, 1995. Amended by Acts 1995, 74th Leg., ch. 751, §94, effective September 1, 1995; Acts 1995, 74th Leg., ch. 943, §2, effective September 1, 1995; by Acts 1997, 75th Leg., ch. 1022, §70, effective September 1, 1997; Acts 1997, 75th Leg., ch. 1137, §1, effective September 1, 1997; Acts 1999, 76th Leg., ch. 1150, §4, effective September 1, 1999; Acts 1999, 76th Leg., ch. 1390, §23, effective September 1, 1999; Acts 2003, 78th Leg., ch. 867, §1, effective September 1, 2003; Acts 2005, 79th Leg., ch. 268, §1.16(a), effective September 1, 2005.)

§261.302. Investigation may include certain interviews

(a) The investigation may include:

(1) a visit to the child's home, unless the alleged abuse or neglect can be confirmed or clearly ruled out without a home visit; and

(2) an interview with and examination of the subject child, which may include a medical, psychological, or psychiatric examination.

(b) The interview with and examination of the child may:

(1) be conducted at any reasonable time and place, including the child's home or the child's school;

(2) include the presence of persons the department or designated agency determines are necessary; and

(3) include transporting the child for purposes relating to the interview or investigation.

(b-1) Before the department may transport a child as provided by Subsection (b)(3), the department shall attempt to notify the parent or other person having custody of the child of the transport.

(c) The investigation may include an interview with the child's parents and an interview with and medical, psychological, or psychiatric examination of any child in the home.

(d) If, before an investigation is completed, the investigating agency believes that the immediate removal of a child from the child's home is necessary to protect the child from further abuse or neglect, the investigating agency shall file a petition or take other action under Chapter 262 to provide for the temporary care and protection of the child.

(e) An interview with a child conducted by the department during the investigation stage shall be audiotaped or videotaped. An interview with a child alleged to be a victim of physical abuse or sexual abuse conducted by an investigating agency other than the department shall be audiotaped or videotaped unless the investigating agency determines that good cause exists for not audiotaping or videotaping the interview in accordance with rules of the agency. Good cause may include, but is not limited to, such considerations as the age of the child and the nature and seriousness of the allegations under investigation. Nothing in this subsection shall be construed as prohibiting the investigating agency from audiotaping or videotaping an interview of a child on any case for which such audiotaping or videotaping is not required under this subsection. The fact that the investigating agency failed to audiotape or videotape an interview is admissible at the trial of the offense that is the subject of the interview.

(f) A person commits an offense if the person is notified of the time of the transport of a child by the department and the location from which the transport is initiated and the person is present at the location when the transport is initiated and attempts to interfere with the department's investigation. An offense under this subsection is a Class B misdemeanor. It is an exception to the application of this subsection that the department requested the person to be present at the site of the transport.

(Acts 1995, 74th Leg., ch. 20, §1, effective April 20, 1995. Amended by Acts 1995, 74th Leg., ch. 751, §95, effective September 1, 1995; by Acts 1997, 75th Leg., ch. 575, §§13, 14, effective September 1, 1997; Acts 1997, 75th Leg., ch. 1022, §73, effective September 1, 1997; Acts 2005, 79th Leg., ch. 268, §1.21, effective September 1, 2005.)

§261.3022. Child safety check alert list to help locate families

(a) Subject to the availability of funds, the Department of Public Safety of the State of Texas shall create a child safety check alert list as part of the Texas Crime Information Center to help locate a family for purposes of investigating a report of child abuse or neglect.

(b) If the child safety check alert list is established and the department is unable to locate a family for purposes of investigating a report of child abuse or neglect, after the department has exhausted all means available to the department for locating the family, the department may seek assistance under this section from the appropriate county attorney, district attorney, or criminal district attorney with responsibility for representing the department as provided by Section 264.009.

(c) If the department requests assistance, the county attorney, district attorney, or criminal district attorney, as applicable, may file an application with the court requesting the issuance of an ex parte order requiring the Texas Crime Information Center to place the members of the family the department is attempting to locate on a child safety check alert list. The application must include a summary of:

(1) the report of child abuse or neglect the department is attempting to investigate; and

(2) the department's efforts to locate the family.

(d) If the court determines after a hearing that the department has exhausted all means available to the department for locating the family, the court shall approve the application and order the appropriate law enforcement agency to notify the Texas Crime Information Center to place the family on a child safety check alert list. The alert list must include:

(1) the name of the family member alleged to have abused or neglected a child according to the report the department is attempting to investigate;

(2) the name of the child who is the subject of the report;

(3) a code identifying the type of child abuse or neglect alleged to have been committed against the child;

(4) the family's last known address; and

(5) the minimum criteria for an entry as established by the center.

(Acts 2005, 79th Leg., ch. 268, §1.22, effective September 1, 2005.)

§261.3023. Duty of law enforcement when a child on the child safety check alert list is encountered

(a) If a law enforcement officer encounters a person listed on the Texas Crime Information Center's child safety check alert list who is alleged to have abused or neglected a child, or encounters a child listed on the alert list who is the subject of a report of child abuse or neglect the department is attempting to investigate, the officer shall request information from the person or the child regarding the child's well-being and current residence.

(b) If the law enforcement officer determines that the circumstances described by Section 262.104 exist, the officer may take possession of the child without a court order as authorized by that section if the officer is able to locate the child. If the circumstances described by Section 262.104 do not exist, the officer shall obtain the child's current address and any other relevant information and report that information to the department.

(Acts 2005, 79th Leg., ch. 268, §1.22, effective September 1, 2005.)

§261.3024. Child safety check alert list removal procedures

(a) A law enforcement officer who locates a child listed on the Texas Crime Information Center's child safety check alert list who is the subject of a report of child abuse or neglect the department is attempting to investigate and who reports the child's current address and other relevant information to the department under Section 261.3023 shall report to the Texas Crime Information Center that the child has been located.

(b) If the department locates a child described by Subsection (a) through a means other than information reported by a law enforcement officer under Subsection (a), the department shall report to the Texas Crime Information Center that the child has been located.

(c) On receipt of notice under this section that a child has been located, the Texas Crime Information Center shall remove the child and the child's family from the child safety check alert list.

(Acts 2005, 79th Leg., ch. 268, §1.22, effective September 1, 2005.)

§261.303. Interference with investigation of child abuse or neglect

(a) A person may not interfere with an investigation of a report of child abuse or neglect conducted by the department or designated agency.

(b) If admission to the home, school, or any place where the child may be cannot be obtained, then for good cause shown the court having family law jurisdiction shall order the parent, the person responsible for the care of the children, or the person in charge of any place where the child may be to allow entrance for the interview, examination, and investigation.

(c) If a parent or person responsible for the child's care does not consent to release of the child's prior medical, psychological, or psychiatric records or to a medical, psychological, or psychiatric examination of the child that is requested by the department or designated agency, the court having family law jurisdiction shall, for good cause shown, order the records to be released or the examination to be made at the times and places designated by the court.

(d) A person, including a medical facility, that makes a report under Subchapter B1 shall release to the department or designated agency, as part of the required report under Section 261.103, records that directly relate to the suspected abuse or neglect without requiring parental consent or a court order.

(Acts 1995, 74th Leg., ch. 20, §1, effective April 20, 1995. Amended by Acts 1995, 74th Leg., ch. 751, §96, effective September 1, 1995; by Acts 1999, 76th Leg., ch. 1150, §5, effective September 1, 1999; Acts 1999, 76th Leg., ch. 1390, §24, effective September 1, 1999.)

§261.3031. Department can seek court order if parent fails to cooperate with investigation

If a parent or other person refuses to cooperate with the department's investigation of the alleged abuse or neglect of a child and the refusal poses a risk to the child's safety, the department shall seek assistance from the appropriate county attorney or district attorney or criminal district attorney with responsibility for representing the department as provided by Section 264.009 to obtain a court order as described by Section 261.303.

(Acts 2005, 79th Leg., ch. 268, §1.23, effective September 1, 2005.)

§261.3032. A misdemeanor is committed if a person interferes with investigation by relocating or concealing the child

(a) A person commits an offense if, with the intent to interfere with the department's investigation of a report of abuse or neglect of a child, the person relocates the person's residence, either temporarily or permanently, without notifying the department of the address of the person's new residence or conceals the child and the person's relocation or concealment interferes with the department's investigation.

(b) An offense under this section is a Class B misdemeanor.

(c) If conduct that constitutes an offense under this section also constitutes an offense under any other law, the actor may be prosecuted under this section or the other law.

(Acts 2005, 79th Leg., ch. 268, §1.24, effective September 1, 2005.)

§261.304. Department shall investigate anonymous report of child abuse or neglect

(a) If the department receives an anonymous report of child abuse or neglect by a person responsible for a child's care, custody, or welfare, the department shall conduct a preliminary investigation to determine whether there is any evidence to corroborate the report.

(b) An investigation under this section may include a visit to the child's home and an interview with and examination of the child and an interview with the child's parents. In addition, the department may interview any other person the department believes may have relevant information.

(c) Unless the department determines that there is some evidence to corroborate the report of abuse, the department may not conduct the thorough investigation required by this chapter or take any action against the person accused of abuse.

(Acts 1995, 74th Leg., ch. 20, §1, effective April 20, 1995.)

§261.305. Court may order access to mental health records

(a) An investigation may include an inquiry into the possibility that a parent or a person responsible for the care of a child who is the subject of a report under Subchapter B1 has a history of medical or mental illness.

(b) If the parent or person does not consent to an examination or allow the department or designated agency to have access to medical or mental health records requested by the department or agency, the court having family law jurisdiction, for good cause shown, shall order the examination to be made or that the department or agency be permitted to have access to the records under terms and conditions prescribed by the court.

(c) If the court determines that the parent or person is indigent, the court shall appoint an attorney to represent the parent or person at the hearing. The fees for the appointed attorney shall be paid as provided by Chapter 107.

(d) A parent or person responsible for the child's care is entitled to notice and a hearing when the department or designated agency seeks a court order to allow a medical, psychological, or psychiatric examination or access to medical or mental health records.

(e) This access does not constitute a waiver of confidentiality.

(Acts 1995, 74th Leg., ch. 20, §1, effective April 20, 1995. Amended by Acts 1997, 75th Leg., ch. 575, §15, effective September 1, 1997; Acts 1999, 76th Leg., ch. 1150, §6, effective September 1, 1999; Acts 1999, 76th Leg., ch. 1390, §25, effective September 1, 1999.)

§261.306. Department or agency may file restraining order to prevent removal of child from state

(a) If the department or designated agency has reason to believe that a person responsible for the care, custody, or welfare of the child may remove the child from the state before the investigation is completed, the department or designated agency may file an application for a temporary restraining order in a district court without regard to continuing jurisdiction of the child as provided in Chapter 155.

(b) The court may render a temporary restraining order prohibiting the person from removing the child from the state pending completion of the investigation if the court:

(1) finds that the department or designated agency has probable cause to conduct the investigation; and

(2) has reason to believe that the person may remove the child from the state.

(Acts 1995, 74th Leg., ch. 20, §1, effective April 20, 1995.)

§261.314. Department shall provide testing

(a) The department shall provide testing as necessary for the welfare of a child who the department believes, after an investigation under this chapter, has been sexually abused, including human immunodeficiency virus (HIV) testing of a child who was abused in a manner by which HIV may be transmitted.

(b) Except as provided by Subsection (c), the results of a test under this section are confidential.

(c) If requested, the department shall report the results of a test under this section to:

(1) a court having jurisdiction of a proceeding involving the child or a proceeding involving a person suspected of abusing the child;

(2) a person responsible for the care and custody of the child as a foster parent; and

(3) a person seeking to adopt the child.

(Acts 1995, 74th Leg., ch. 943, §7, effective September 1, 1995.)

---

b. Notice to a Parent

The agency has to provide notice to the suspected abuser regarding information about the investigative procedures (Tex. Fam. Code §261.307); any interviews and examinations with the child (Tex. Fam. Code §261.311); and, at the conclusion of the investigation, the right of expungement if the report of abuse or neglect was not substantiated (Tex. Fam. Code §261.315). The agency does not have to supply notice of interviews and examinations if the agency determines "that the notice is likely to endanger the safety of the child . . . , the person who made the report, or any other person who participates in the investigation of the report" (Tex. Fam. Code §261.311(c)).

---

§261.307. Department shall provide information relating to investigation procedure

(a) As soon as possible after initiating an investigation of a parent or other person having legal custody of a child, the department shall provide to the person:

(1) a summary that:

(A) is brief and easily understood;

(B) is written in a language that the person understands, or if the person is illiterate, is read to the person in a language that the person understands; and

(C) contains the following information:

(i) the department's procedures for conducting an investigation of alleged child abuse or neglect, including:

(a) a description of the circumstances under which the department would request to remove the child from the home through the judicial system; and

(b) an explanation that the law requires the department to refer all reports of alleged child abuse or neglect to a law enforcement agency for a separate determination of whether a criminal violation occurred;

(ii) the person's right to file a complaint with the department or to request a review of the findings made by the department in the investigation;

(iii) the person's right to review all records of the investigation unless the review would jeopardize an ongoing criminal investigation or the child's safety;

(iv) the person's right to seek legal counsel;

(v) references to the statutory and regulatory provisions governing child abuse and neglect and how the person may obtain copies of those provisions; and

(vi) the process the person may use to acquire access to the child if the child is removed from the home;

(2) if the department determines that removal of the child may be warranted, a proposed child placement resources form that:

(A) instructs the parent or other person having legal custody of the child to:

(i) complete and return the form to the department or agency; and

(ii) identify in the form three individuals who could be relative caregivers or designated caregivers, as those terms are defined by Section 264.751; and

(B) informs the parent or other person of a location that is available to the parent or other person to submit the information in the form 24 hours a day either in person or by facsimile machine or e-mail; and

(3) an informational manual required by Section 261.3071.

(b) The child placement resources form described by Subsection (a)(2) must include information on the periods of time by which the department must complete a background check.

(Acts 1995, 74th Leg., ch. 20, §1, effective April 20, 1995. Amended by Acts 2005, 79th Leg., ch. 268, §1.25(a), effective September 1, 2005.)

§261.3071. Informational manuals are to be provided

(a) In this section, "relative caregiver" and "designated caregiver" have the meanings assigned those terms by Section 264.751.

(b) The department shall develop and publish informational manuals that provide information for:

(1) a parent or other person having custody of a child who is the subject of an investigation under this chapter; and

(2) a person who is selected by the department to be the child's relative or designated caregiver.

(c) Information provided in the manuals must be in both English and Spanish and must include, as appropriate:

(1) useful indexes of information such as telephone numbers;

(2) the information required to be provided under Section 261.307(a)(1);

(3) information describing the rights and duties of a relative or designated caregiver; and

(4) information regarding the relative and other designated caregiver program under Subchapter I, Chapter 264.

(Acts 2005, 79th Leg., ch. 268, §1.26, effective September 1, 2005.)

§261.311. Notice of report

(a) When during an investigation of a report of suspected child abuse or neglect a representative of the department or the designated agency conducts an interview with or an examination of a child, the department or designated agency shall make a reasonable effort before 24 hours after the time of the interview or examination to notify each parent of the child and the child's legal guardian, if one has been appointed, of the nature of the allegation and of the fact that the interview or examination was conducted.

(b) If a report of suspected child abuse or neglect is administratively closed by the department or designated agency as a result of a preliminary investigation that did not include an interview or examination of the child, the department or designated agency shall make a reasonable effort before the expiration of 24 hours after the time the investigation is closed to notify each parent and legal guardian of the child of the disposition of the investigation.

(c) The notice required by Subsection (a) or (b) is not required if the department or agency determines that the notice is likely to endanger the safety of the child who is the subject of the report, the person who made the report, or any other person who participates in the investigation of the report.

(d) The notice required by Subsection (a) or (b) may be delayed at the request of a law enforcement agency if notification during the required time would interfere with an ongoing criminal investigation.

(Acts 1995, 74th Leg., ch. 20, §1, effective April 20, 1995. Amended by Acts 1997, 75th Leg., ch. 1022, §74, effective September 1, 1997.)

§261.315. Right to remove certain information from record in cases of unsubstantiated reports

(a) At the conclusion of an investigation in which the department determines that the person alleged to have abused or neglected a child did not commit abuse or neglect, the department shall notify the person of the person's right to request the department to remove information about the person's alleged role in the abuse or neglect report from the department's records.

(b) On request under Subsection (a) by a person whom the department has determined did not commit abuse or neglect, the department shall remove information from the department's records concerning the person's alleged role in the abuse or neglect report.

(c) The board shall adopt rules necessary to administer this section.

(Acts 1997, 75th Leg., ch. 1022, §75, effective September 1, 1997.)

c. Submission of Report

§261.308. Department or agency shall make complete investigation report

(a) The department or designated agency shall make a complete written report of the investigation.

(b) If sufficient grounds for filing a suit exist, the department or designated agency shall submit the report, together with recommendations, to the court, the district attorney, and the appropriate law enforcement agency.

(c) On receipt of the report and recommendations, the court may direct the department or designated agency to file a petition requesting appropriate relief as provided in this title.

(Acts 1995, 74th Leg., ch. 20, §1, effective April 20, 1995. Amended by Acts 1995, 74th Leg., ch. 751, §97, effective September 1, 1995.)

d. Review of Departmental Procedures

§261.309. Department shall establish polices to review Departmental investigations

(a) The department shall by rule establish policies and procedures to resolve complaints relating to and conduct reviews of child abuse or neglect investigations conducted by the department.

(b) If a person under investigation for allegedly abusing or neglecting a child requests clarification of the status of the person's case or files a complaint relating to the conduct of the department's staff or to department policy, the department shall conduct an informal review to clarify the person's status or resolve the complaint. The immediate supervisor of the employee who conducted the child abuse or neglect investigation or against whom the complaint was filed shall conduct the informal review as soon as possible but not later than the 14th day after the date the request or complaint is received.

(c) If, after the department's investigation, the person who is alleged to have abused or neglected a child disputes the department's determination of whether child abuse or neglect occurred, the person may request an administrative review of the findings. A department employee in administration who was not involved in or did not directly supervise the investigation shall conduct the review. The review must sustain, alter, or reverse the department's original findings in the investigation.

(d) Unless a civil or criminal court proceeding or an ongoing criminal investigation relating to the alleged abuse or neglect investigated by the department is pending, the department employee shall conduct the review prescribed by Subsection (c) as soon as possible but not later than the 45th day after the date the department receives the request. If a civil or criminal court proceeding or an ongoing criminal investigation is pending, the department may postpone the review until the court proceeding is completed.

(e) A person is not required to exhaust the remedies provided by this section before pursuing a judicial remedy provided by law.

(f) This section does not provide for a review of an order rendered by a court.
(Acts 1995, 74th Leg., ch. 20, §1, effective April 20, 1995.)\

§261.310. Department shall adopt investigation standards

(a) The department shall by rule develop and adopt standards for persons who investigate suspected child abuse or neglect at the state or local level. The standards shall encourage professionalism and consistency in the investigation of suspected child abuse or neglect.

(b) The standards must provide for a minimum number of hours of annual professional training for interviewers and investigators of suspected child abuse or neglect.

(c) The professional training curriculum developed under this section shall include:

(1) information concerning:

(A) physical abuse and neglect, including distinguishing physical abuse from ordinary childhood injuries;

(B) psychological abuse and neglect;

(C) available treatment resources; and

(D) the incidence and types of reports of child abuse and neglect that are received by the investigating agencies, including information concerning false reports;

(2) law-enforcement-style training, including training relating to forensic interviewing and investigatory techniques and the collection of physical evidence; and

(3) training regarding applicable federal law, including the Adoption and Safe Families Act of 1997 (Pub. L. No. 105-89) and the Child Abuse Prevention and Treatment Act (Pub. L. No. 93-247) and its subsequent amendments by the Keeping Children and Families Safe Act of 2003 (Pub. L. No. 108-36).

(d) The standards shall:

(1) recommend that videotaped and audiotaped interviews be uninterrupted;

(2) recommend a maximum number of interviews with and examinations of a suspected victim;

(3) provide procedures to preserve evidence, including the original recordings of the intake telephone calls, original notes, videotapes, and audiotapes, for one year; and

(4) provide that an investigator of suspected child abuse or neglect make a reasonable effort to locate and inform each parent of a child of any report of abuse or neglect relating to the child.

(e) The department, in conjunction with the Department of Public Safety, shall provide to the department's residential child-care facility licensing investigators advanced training in investigative protocols and techniques.
(Acts 1995, 74th Leg., ch. 20, §1, effective April 20, 1995 Amended by Acts 2005, 79th Leg., ch. 268, §1.27, effective September 1, 2005.)

§261.312. Department shall establish review teams

(a) The department shall establish review teams to evaluate department casework and decision-making related to investigations by the department of child abuse or neglect. The department may create one or more review teams for each region of the department for child protective services. A review team is a citizen review panel or a similar entity for the purposes of federal law relating to a state's child protection standards.

(b) A review team consists of five members who serve staggered two-year terms. Review team members are appointed by the director of the department and consist of community representatives and private citizens who live in the region for which the team is established. Each member must be a parent who has not been convicted of or indicted for an offense involving child abuse or neglect, has not been determined by the department to have engaged in child abuse or neglect, or is not under investigation by the department for child abuse or neglect. A member of a review team is a department volunteer for the purposes of Section 411.114, Government Code.

(c) A review team conducting a review of an investigation may conduct the review by examining the facts of the case as outlined by the department caseworker and law enforcement personnel. A review team member acting in the member's official capacity may receive information made confidential under Section 40.005, Human Resources Code, or Section 261.201.

(d) A review team shall report to the department the results of the team's review of an investigation. The review team's report may not include confidential information. The findings contained in a review team's report are subject to disclosure under Chapter 552, Government Code. This section does not require a law enforcement agency to divulge information to a review team that the agency believes would compromise an ongoing criminal case, investigation, or proceeding.

(e) A member of a review team commits an offense if the member discloses confidential information. An offense under this subsection is a Class C misdemeanor.
(Acts 1995, 74th Leg., ch. 943, §3, effective September 1, 1995. Amended by Acts 1997, 75th Leg., ch. 575, §16, effective September 1, 1997.)

§261.3125. Department shall employ investigations coordinator

(a) The department shall employ in each of the department's administrative regions at least one child safety specialist. The job responsibilities of the child safety specialist must focus on child abuse and neglect investigation issues, including reports of child abuse required by Section 261.101, to achieve a greater compliance with that section, and on assessing and improving the effectiveness of the department in providing for the protection of children in the region.

(b) The duties of a child safety specialist must include the duty to:

(1) conduct staff reviews and evaluations of cases determined to involve a high risk to the health or safety of a child, including cases of abuse reported under Section

261.101, to ensure that risk assessment tools are fully and correctly used;

(2) review and evaluate cases in which there have been multiple referrals to the department of child abuse or neglect involving the same family, child, or person alleged to have committed the abuse or neglect; and

(3) approve decisions and assessments related to investigations of cases of child abuse or neglect that involve a high risk to the health or safety of a child.

(Acts 1999, 76th Leg., ch. 1490, §1, effective September 1, 1999. Amended by Acts 2005, 79th Leg., ch. 268, §1.29, effective September 1, 2005.)

§261.3126. Colocation of investigators with law enforcement

(a) In each county, to the extent possible, the department and the local law enforcement agencies that investigate child abuse in the county shall colocate in the same offices investigators from the department and the law enforcement agencies to improve the efficiency of child abuse investigations. With approval of the local children's advocacy center and its partner agencies, in each county in which a children's advocacy center established under Section 264.402 is located, the department shall attempt to locate investigators from the department and county and municipal law enforcement agencies at the center.

(b) A law enforcement agency is not required to comply with the colocation requirements of this section if the law enforcement agency does not have a full-time peace officer solely assigned to investigate reports of child abuse and neglect.

(c) If a county does not have a children's advocacy center, the department shall work with the local community to encourage one as provided by Section 264.402.

(Acts 2005, 79th Leg., ch. 268, §1.30, effective September 1, 2005.)

§261.316. Department is exempt from fees to obtain medical records

The department is exempt from the payment of a fee otherwise required or authorized by law to obtain a medical record from a hospital or health care provider if the request for a record is made in the course of an investigation by the department.

(Acts 1997, 75th Leg., ch. 575, §17, effective September 1, 1997. Renumbered from §261.315 by Acts 1999, 76th Leg., ch. 62, §19.01(27), effective September 1, 1999.)

---

e. Reports of Abuse of Children Who Are in State Agencies

§261.401. Licensing agency shall make prompt investigation of reports of abuse or neglect

(a) Notwithstanding Section 261.001, in this section:

(1) "Abuse" means an intentional, knowing, or reckless act or omission by an employee, volunteer, or other individual working under the auspices of a facility that causes or may cause emotional harm or physical injury to, or the death of, a child served by the facility as further described by rule or policy.

(2) "Exploitation" means the illegal or improper use of a child or of the resources of a child for monetary or personal benefit, profit, or gain by an employee, volunteer, or other individual working under the auspices of a facility as further described by rule or policy.

(3) "Neglect" means a negligent act or omission by an employee, volunteer, or other individual working under the auspices of a facility, including failure to comply with an individual treatment plan, plan of care, or individualized service plan, that causes or may cause substantial emotional harm or physical injury to, or the death of, a child served by the facility as further described by rule or policy.

(b) A state agency that operates, licenses, certifies, or registers a facility in which children are located shall make a prompt, thorough investigation of a report that a child has been or may be abused, neglected, or exploited in the facility. The primary purpose of the investigation shall be the protection of the child.

(c) A state agency shall adopt rules relating to the investigation and resolution of reports received as provided by this subchapter. The Health and Human Services Commission shall review and approve the rules of agencies other than the Texas Department of Criminal Justice, Texas Youth Commission, or Texas Juvenile Probation Commission to ensure that those agencies implement appropriate standards for the conduct of investigations and that uniformity exists among agencies in the investigation and resolution of reports.

(d) The Texas School for the Blind and Visually Impaired and the Texas School for the Deaf shall adopt policies relating to the investigation and resolution of reports received as provided by this subchapter. The Health and Human Services Commission shall review and approve the policies to ensure that the Texas School for the Blind and Visually Impaired and the Texas School for the Deaf adopt those policies in a manner consistent with the minimum standards adopted by the Health and Human Services Commission under Section 261.407.

(Acts 1995, 74th Leg., ch. 20, §1, effective April 20, 1995. Amended by Acts 1995, 74th Leg., ch. 751, §98, effective September 1, 1995; by Acts 2001, 77th Leg., ch. 355, §2, effective September 1, 2001.)

§261.402. Agency shall prepare investigative reports

(a) A state agency shall prepare and keep on file a complete written report of each investigation conducted by the agency under this subchapter.

(b) A state agency shall immediately notify the appropriate state or local law enforcement agency of any report the agency receives, other than a report from a law enforcement agency, that concerns the suspected abuse, neglect, or exploitation of a child or the death of a child from abuse or neglect. If the state agency finds evidence indicating that a child may have been abused, neglected, or exploited, the agency shall report the evidence to the appropriate law enforcement agency.

(c) A state agency that licenses, certifies, or registers a facility in which children are located shall compile, maintain, and make available statistics on the incidence of child abuse, neglect, and exploitation in the facility.

(d) A state agency shall compile, maintain, and make available statistics on the incidence of child abuse, neglect, and exploitation in a facility operated by the state agency.

(Acts 1995, 74th Leg., ch. 20, §1, effective April 20, 1995. Amended by Acts 1995, 74th Leg., ch. 751, §99, effective September 1, 1995; by Acts 2001, 77th Leg., ch. 355, §3, effective September 1, 2001.)

§261.403. Complaint procedure

(a) If a state agency receives a complaint relating to an investigation conducted by the agency concerning a facility operated by that agency in which children are located, the agency shall refer the complaint to the agency's board.

(b) The board of a state agency that operates a facility in which children are located shall ensure that the procedure for investigating abuse, neglect, and exploitation allegations and inquiries in the agency's facility is periodically reviewed under the agency's internal audit program required by Chapter 2102, Government Code.

(Acts 1995, 74th Leg., ch. 20, §1, effective April 20, 1995. Amended by Acts 2001, 77th Leg., ch. 355, §4, effective September 1, 2001.)

§261.404. Department shall investigate reports of abuse or neglect in mental health facilities

(a) The department shall investigate a report of abuse, neglect, or exploitation of a child receiving services:

(1) in a facility operated by the Texas Department of Mental Health and Mental Retardation;

(2) in or from a community center, a local mental health authority, or a local mental retardation authority; or

(3) through a program providing services to that child by contract with a facility operated by the Texas Department of Mental Health and Mental Retardation, a community center, a local mental health authority, or a local mental retardation authority.

(b) The department shall investigate the report under rules developed jointly between the department and the Texas Department of Mental Health and Mental Retardation.

(c) The definitions of "abuse" and "neglect" prescribed by Section 261.001 do not apply to an investigation under this section.

(d) In this section, "community center," "local mental health authority," and "local mental retardation authority" have the meanings assigned by Section 531.002, Health and Safety Code.

(Acts 1995, 74th Leg., ch. 751, §100, effective September 1, 1995. Amended by Acts 1999, 76th Leg., ch. 907, §39, effective September 1, 1999.)

§261.405. Juvenile Justice Probation Commission shall investigate reports in juvenile justice facilities

(a) In this section:

(1) "Juvenile justice facility" means a facility operated wholly or partly by the juvenile board or by a private vendor under a contract with the juvenile board or county that serves juveniles under juvenile court jurisdiction. The term includes:

(A) a public or private juvenile pre-adjudication secure detention facility, including a holdover facility;

(B) a public or private juvenile post-adjudication secure correctional facility except for a facility operated solely for children committed to the Texas Youth Commission; and

(C) a public or private non-secure juvenile post-adjudication residential treatment facility that is not licensed by the Department of Protective and Regulatory Services or the Texas Commission on Alcohol and Drug Abuse.

(2) "Juvenile justice program" means a program operated wholly or partly by the juvenile board or by a private vendor under a contract with a juvenile board that serves juveniles under juvenile court jurisdiction. The term includes:

(A) a juvenile justice alternative education program; and

(B) a non-residential program that serves juvenile offenders under the jurisdiction of the juvenile court.

(b) A report of alleged abuse, neglect, or exploitation in any juvenile justice program or facility shall be made to the Texas Juvenile Probation Commission and a local law enforcement agency for investigation.

(c) The Texas Juvenile Probation Commission shall conduct an investigation as provided by this chapter if the commission receives a report of alleged abuse, neglect, or exploitation in any juvenile justice program or facility.

(d) In an investigation required under this section, the investigating agency shall have access to medical and mental health records as provided by Subchapter D.1

(e) As soon as practicable after a child is taken into custody or placed in a juvenile justice facility or juvenile justice program, the facility or program shall provide the child's parents with:

(1) information regarding the reporting of suspected abuse, neglect, or exploitation of a child in a juvenile justice facility or juvenile justice program to the Texas Juvenile Probation Commission; and

(2) the commission's toll-free number for this reporting.

(Acts 1995, 74th Leg., ch. 751, §100, effective September 1, 1995. Amended by Acts 1997, 75th Leg., ch. 162, §2; , Acts 1997, 75th Leg., ch. 1374, §8, effective September 1, 1997; Acts 1999, 76th Leg., ch. 1150, §7, effective September 1, 1999; Acts 1999, 76th Leg., ch. 1390, §26, effective September 1, 1999; Acts 1999, 76th Leg., ch. 1477, §26, effective September 1, 1999; Acts 2001, 77th Leg., ch. 1297, §47, effective September 1, 2001; Acts 2003, 78th Leg., ch. 283, §29, effective September 1, 2003; Acts 2005, 79th Leg., ch. 949, §28, effective September 1, 2005.)

§261.406. Department shall investigate reports of abuse or neglect in schools

(a) On receipt of a report of alleged or suspected abuse or neglect of a child in a public or private school under the jurisdiction of the Texas Education Agency, the department shall perform an investigation as provided by this chapter.

(b) The department shall send a written report of the department's investigation, as appropriate, to the Texas Education Agency, the agency responsible for teacher certification, the local school board or the school's governing body, the superintendent of the school district and the school principal or director, unless the principal or director is alleged to have committed the abuse or neglect, for appropriate action. On request, the department shall provide a copy of the report of investigation to the parent, managing conservator, or legal guardian of a child who is the subject of the investigation and to the person alleged to have committed the abuse or neglect. The report of investigation shall be edited to protect the identity of the persons who made the report of abuse or neglect. Section 261.201(b) applies to the release of confidential information relating to the investigation of a report of abuse or neglect under this section and to the identity of the person who made the report of abuse or neglect.

(c) Nothing in this section may prevent a law enforcement agency from conducting an investigation of a report made under this section.

(d) The Board of Protective and Regulatory Services shall adopt rules necessary to implement this section.

(Acts 1995, 74th Leg., ch. 751, §100, effective September 1, 1995. Amended by Acts 1997, 75th Leg., ch. 575, §18, effective September 1, 1997; Acts 1999, 76th Leg., ch. 1150, §8, effective September 1, 1999; Acts 1999, 76th Leg., ch. 1390, §27, effective September 1, 1999; Acts 2005, 79th Leg., ch. 213, §2, effective September 1, 2005.)

§261.407. Minimum standards for investigation

(a) The Health and Human Services Commission by rule shall adopt minimum standards for the investigation under Section 261.401 of suspected child abuse, neglect, or exploitation in a facility.

(b) A rule or policy adopted by a state agency or institution under Section 261.401 must be consistent with the minimum standards adopted by the Health and Human Services Commission.

(c) This section does not apply to a facility under the jurisdiction of the Texas Department of Criminal Justice, Texas Youth Commission, or Texas Juvenile Probation Commission.

(Acts 2001, 77th Leg., ch. 355, §5, effective September 1, 2001.)

§261.408. Uniform procedures for information collection

(a) The Health and Human Services Commission by rule shall adopt uniform procedures for collecting information under Section 261.401, including procedures for collecting information on deaths that occur in facilities.

(b) The department shall receive and compile information on investigations in facilities. An agency submitting information to the department is responsible for ensuring the timeliness, accuracy, completeness, and retention of the agency's reports.

(c) This section does not apply to a facility under the jurisdiction of the Texas Department of Criminal Justice, Texas Youth Commission, or Texas Juvenile Probation Commission.

(Acts 2001, 77th Leg., ch. 355, §5, effective September 1, 2001.)

§261.409. Investigations in facilities under Texas Youth Commission Jurisdiction

The board of the Texas Youth Commission by rule shall adopt standards for:

(1) the investigation under Section 261.401 of suspected child abuse, neglect, or exploitation in a facility under the jurisdiction of the Texas Youth Commission; and

(2) compiling information on those investigations.

(Acts 2001, 77th Leg., ch. 355, §6, effective September 1, 2001.)

§261.410. Abuse by other children is to be reported

(a) In this section:

(1) "Physical abuse" means:

(A) physical injury that results in substantial harm to the child requiring emergency medical treatment and excluding an accident or reasonable discipline by a parent, guardian, or managing or possessory conservator that does not expose the child to a substantial risk of harm; or

(B) failure to make a reasonable effort to prevent an action by another person that results in physical injury that results in substantial harm to the child.

(2) "Sexual abuse" means:

(A) sexual conduct harmful to a child's mental, emotional, or physical welfare; or

(B) failure to make a reasonable effort to prevent sexual conduct harmful to a child.

(b) An agency that operates, licenses, certifies, or registers a facility shall require a residential child-care facility to report each incident of physical or sexual abuse committed by a child against another child.

(c) Using information received under Subsection (b), the agency that operates, licenses, certifies, or registers a facility shall, subject to the availability of funds, compile a report that includes information:

(1) regarding the number of cases of physical and sexual abuse committed by a child against another child;

(2) identifying the residential child-care facility;

(3) regarding the date each allegation of abuse was made;

(4) regarding the date each investigation was started and concluded;

(5) regarding the findings and results of each investigation; and

(6) regarding the number of children involved in each incident investigated.

(Acts 2005, 79th Leg., ch. 268, §1.31, effective September 1, 2005.)

§262.001. Governmental entity may file suit to take custody of child

(a) A governmental entity with an interest in the child may file a suit affecting the parent-child relationship requesting an order or take possession of a child without a court order as provided by this chapter.

(b) In determining the reasonable efforts that are required to be made with respect to preventing or eliminating the need to remove a child from the child's home or to make it possible to return a child to the child's home, the child's health and safety is the paramount concern.

(Acts 1995, 74th Leg., ch. 20, §1, effective April 20, 1995. Amended by Acts 1999, 76th Leg., ch. 1150, §10, effective September 1, 1999; Acts 1999, 76th Leg., ch. 1390, §29, effective September 1, 1999.)

D. REGISTRATION OF SEX OFFENDERS

States require the registration of sex offenders for the protection of the public. Under Texas law, a sex offender must register if the offender has been convicted of, or adjudicated for, the following offenses (among others): indecency with a child, sexual assault, aggravated sexual assault, prohibited sexual conduct, compelling prostitution, sexual performance by a child, possession or promotion of child pornography, or aggravated kidnapping with intent to abuse the victim sexually (Tex. Code Crim. Proc. Art. 62.01(5)). Such information is maintained in a central database (Tex. Code Crim. Proc. Art. 62.08) (omitted). Failure to register is a felony (Tex. Code Crim. Proc. Art. 62.10).

Expiration of the duty to register occurs after 10 years for certain offenses. For more severe offenses or multiple offenses, the duty to register continues for life (Tex. Code Crim. Proc. Art. 62.101).

Other statutory provisions provide for notification of the public when certain sex offenders are released from penal institutions, placed on community supervision or juvenile probation, or move to a new residence in the state (Tex. Code Crim. Proc. Arts. 62.03, 62.045) (omitted).

Texas Code of Criminal Procedure

Article 62.001. Definitions

In this chapter:

. . . [as amended by Acts 2005, 79th Leg., ch. 1008, §1.01]

(5) "Reportable conviction or adjudication" means a conviction or adjudication, including an adjudication of delinquent conduct or a deferred adjudication, that, regardless of the pendency of an appeal, is a conviction for or an adjudication for or based on:

(A) a violation of Section 21.11 (Indecency with a child), 22.011 (Sexual assault), 22.021 (Aggravated sexual assault), or 25.02 (Prohibited sexual conduct), Penal Code;

(B) a violation of Section 43.05 (Compelling prostitution), 43.25 (Sexual performance by a child), or 43.26 (Possession or promotion of child pornography), Penal Code;

(C) a violation of Section 20.04(a)(4) (Aggravated kidnapping), Penal Code, if the actor committed the offense or engaged in the conduct with intent to violate or abuse the victim sexually;

. . .

[as amended by Acts 2005, 79th Leg., ch. 1273, §2]

(5) "Reportable conviction or adjudication" means a conviction or adjudication, regardless of the pendency of an appeal, that is:

(A) a conviction for a violation of Section 21.11 (Indecency with a child), 22.011 (Sexual assault), 22.021 (Aggravated sexual assault), or 25.02 (Prohibited sexual conduct), Penal Code;

(B) a conviction for a violation of Section 43.05 (Compelling prostitution), 43.25 (Sexual performance by a child), or 43.26 (Possession or promotion of child pornography), Penal Code;

(C) a conviction for a violation of Section 20.04(a)(4) (Aggravated kidnapping), Penal Code, if the defendant committed the offense with intent to violate or abuse the victim sexually;

. . .

(H) an adjudication of delinquent conduct:

(i) based on a violation of one of the offenses listed in Paragraph (A), (B), (C), (D), (G), or (N) or, if the order in the hearing contains an affirmative finding that the victim or intended victim was younger than 17 years of age, one of the offenses listed in Paragraph (E); or

(ii) for which two violations of the offense listed in Paragraph (F) are shown;

. . .

(Acts 1991, 72nd Leg., ch. 572, §1, effective September 1, 1991. Amended by Acts 1993, 73rd Leg., ch. 866, §1, effective August 30, 1993; Acts 1995, 74th Leg., ch. 76, §14.62, effective September 1, 1995; Acts 1995, 74th Leg., ch. 258, §1, effective September 1, 1995. Redesignated from Civ. St. Ann. Article 6252-13c.1, §1 and amended by Acts 1997, 75th Leg., ch. 668, §1, effective September 1, 1997. Subd. (3) amended by Acts 1999, 76th Leg., ch. 1415, §7, effective September 1, 1999; Subd. (5) amended by Acts 1999, 76th Leg., ch. 1193, §4, effective September 1, 1999; amended by Acts 1999, 76th Leg., ch. 1415, §8, effective September 1, 1999; Subd. (6) amended by Acts 1999, 76th Leg., ch. 1193, §4, effective September 1, 1999; amended by Acts 1999, 76th Leg., ch. 1415, §8, effective September 1, 1999; Subd. (7) added by Acts 1999, 76th Leg., ch. 1193, §4, effective September 1, 1999; added by Acts 1999, 76th Leg., ch. 1415, §8, effective September 1, 1999; Subd. (5) amended by Acts 2003, 78th Leg., ch. 1005, §8, effective September 1, 2003; Subd. (6) amended by Acts 2003, 78th Leg., ch. 1005, §8, effective September 1, 2003; Subd. (7) amended by Acts 2003, 78th Leg., ch. 1275, §3(4), effective

September 1, 2003; Subd. (8) added by Acts 2003, 78th Leg., ch. 347, §1, effective September 1, 2003; Subsec. (9) added by Acts 2003, 78th Leg., ch. 347, §1, effective September 1, 2003. Subd. (5) amended by Acts 2005, 79th Leg., ch. 1273, §2, effective June 18, 2005. Redesignated from Vernon's Ann.C.C.P. art. 62.01 and amended by Acts 2005, 79th Leg., ch. 1008, §1.01, effective September 1, 2005.)

Article 62.002. Duty to register is terminated only if the appeal or pardon is based on proof of innocence

(a) This chapter applies only to a reportable conviction or adjudication occurring on or after September 1, 1970.

(b) Except as provided by Subsection (c), the duties imposed on a person required to register under this chapter on the basis of a reportable conviction or adjudication, and the corresponding duties and powers of other entities in relation to the person required to register on the basis of that conviction or adjudication, are not affected by:

(1) an appeal of the conviction or adjudication; or

(2) a pardon of the conviction or adjudication.

(c) If a conviction or adjudication that is the basis of a duty to register under this chapter is set aside on appeal by a court or if the person required to register under this chapter on the basis of a conviction or adjudication receives a pardon on the basis of subsequent proof of innocence, the duties imposed on the person by this chapter and the corresponding duties and powers of other entities in relation to the person are terminated.

(Acts 2005, 79th Leg., ch. 1008, §1.01, effective September 1, 2005.)

Article 62.051. Person with reportable conviction or adjudication must register; procedure

(a) A person who has a reportable conviction or adjudication or who is required to register as a condition of parole, release to mandatory supervision, or community supervision shall register or, if the person is a person for whom registration is completed under this chapter, verify registration as provided by Subsection (f), with the local law enforcement authority in any municipality where the person resides or intends to reside for more than seven days. If the person does not reside or intend to reside in a municipality, the person shall register or verify registration in any county where the person resides or intends to reside for more than seven days. The person shall satisfy the requirements of this subsection not later than the later of:

(1) the seventh day after the person's arrival in the municipality or county; or

(2) the first date the local law enforcement authority of the municipality or county by policy allows the person to register or verify registration, as applicable.

(b) The department shall provide the Texas Department of Criminal Justice, the Texas Youth Commission, the Texas Juvenile Probation Commission, and each local law enforcement authority, authority for campus security, county jail, and court with a form for registering persons required by this chapter to register.

(c) The registration form shall require:

(1) the person's full name, each alias, date of birth, sex, race, height, weight, eye color, hair color, social security number, driver's license number, shoe size, and home address;

(2) a recent color photograph or, if possible, an electronic digital image of the person and a complete set of the person's fingerprints;

(3) the type of offense the person was convicted of, the age of the victim, the date of conviction, and the punishment received;

(4) an indication as to whether the person is discharged, paroled, or released on juvenile probation, community supervision, or mandatory supervision;

(5) an indication of each license, as defined by Article 62.005(g), that is held or sought by the person;

(6) an indication as to whether the person is or will be employed, carrying on a vocation, or a student at a particular public or private institution of higher education in this state or another state, and the name and address of that institution; and

(7) any other information required by the department.

(d) The registration form must contain a statement and description of any registration duties the person has or may have under this chapter.

(e) Not later than the third day after a person's registering, the local law enforcement authority with whom the person registered shall send a copy of the registration form to the department and, if the person resides on the campus of a public or private institution of higher education, to any authority for campus security for that institution.

(f) A person for whom registration is completed under this chapter shall report to the applicable local law enforcement authority to verify the information in the registration form received by the authority under this chapter. The authority shall require the person to produce proof of the person's identity and residence before the authority gives the registration form to the person for verification. If the information in the registration form is complete and accurate, the person shall verify registration by signing the form. If the information is not complete or not accurate, the person shall make any necessary additions or corrections before signing the form.

(g) A person who is required to register or verify registration under this chapter shall ensure that the person's registration form is complete and accurate with respect to each item of information required by the form in accordance with Subsection (c).

(h) If a person subject to registration under this chapter does not move to an intended residence by the end of the seventh day after the date on which the person is released or the date on which the person leaves a previous residence, the person shall:

(1) report to the juvenile probation officer, community supervision and corrections department officer, or parole officer supervising the person by not later than the seventh day after the date on which the person is released or the date on which the person leaves a previous residence, as applicable, and provide the officer with the address of the person's temporary residence; and

(2) continue to report to the person's supervising officer not less than weekly during any period of time in which the person has not moved to an intended residence and provide the officer with the address of the person's temporary residence.

(i) If the other state has a registration requirement for sex offenders, a person who has a reportable conviction or adjudication, who resides in this state, and who is employed, carries on a vocation, or is a student in another state shall, not later than the 10th day after the date on which the person begins to work or attend school in the other state, register with the law enforcement authority that is identified by the department as the authority designated by that state to receive registration information. If the person is employed, carries on a vocation, or is a student at a public or private institution of higher education in the other state and if an authority for campus security exists at the institution, the person shall also register with that authority not later than the 10th day after the date on which the person begins to work or attend school.

(Acts 1991, 72nd Leg., ch. 572, §1, effective September 1, 1991. Amended by Acts 1995, 74th Leg., ch. 258, §2, effective September 1, 1995; Acts 1995, 74th Leg., ch. 676, §1, effective September 1, 1995. Redesignated from Vernon's Ann.Civ.St. art. 6252-13c.1, §2 and amended by Acts 1997, 75th Leg., ch. 668, §1, effective September 1, 1997. Subsec. (a) amended by Acts 1999, 76th Leg., ch. 444, §1, effective September 1, 1999; amended by Acts 1999, 76th Leg., ch. 1415, §10, effective September 1, 1999; Subsec. (g) added by Acts 1999, 76th Leg., ch. 1193, §5, effective September 1, 1999; added by Acts 1999, 76th Leg., ch. 1415, §10, effective September 1, 1999; Subsec. (b) amended by Acts 2001, 77th Leg., ch. 932, §1, effective September 1, 2001; Subsecs. (b), (c), and (g) amended by Acts 2003, 78th Leg., ch. 347, §4, effective September 1, 2003; Subsec. (b) amended by Acts 2003, 78th Leg., ch. 1276, §5.003(b), effective September 1, 2003. Redesignated from Vernon's Ann.C.C.P. art. 62.02 and amended by Acts 2005, 79th Leg., ch. 1008, §1.01, effective September 1, 2005.)

Article 62.102. Liability for failure to comply with registration requirements

(a) A person commits an offense if the person is required to register and fails to comply with any requirement of this chapter.

(b) An offense under this article is:

(1) a state jail felony if the actor is a person whose duty to register expires under Article 62.101(b) or (c);

(2) a felony of the third degree if the actor is a person whose duty to register expires under Article 62.101(a) and who is required to verify registration once each year under Article 62.058; and

(3) a felony of the second degree if the actor is a person whose duty to register expires under Article 62.101(a) and who is required to verify registration once each 90-day period under Article 62.058.

(c) If it is shown at the trial of a person for an offense or an attempt to commit an offense under this article that the person has previously been convicted of an offense or an attempt to commit an offense under this article, the punishment for the offense or the attempt to commit the offense is increased to the punishment for the next highest degree of felony.

(Acts 1991, 72nd Leg., ch. 572, §1, effective September 1, 1991. Redesignated from Vernon's Ann.Civ.St. art. 6252-13c.1, §7 and amended by Acts 1997, 75th Leg., ch. 668, §1, effective September 1, 1997. Subsec. (b) amended by Acts 1999, 76th Leg., ch. 444, §9, effective September 1, 1999; amended by Acts 1999, 76th Leg., ch. 1415, §18, effective September 1, 1999; Subsec. (c) amended by Acts 1999, 76th Leg., ch. 444, §9, effective September 1, 1999; amended by Acts 1999, 76th Leg., ch. 1415, §18, effective September 1, 1999. Redesignated from Vernon's Ann.C.C.P. art. 62.10 and amended by Acts 2005, 79th Leg., ch. 1008, §1.01, effective September 1, 2005.)

Article 62.101. When the duty to register expires

(a) Except as provided by Subsection (b) and Subchapter I, the duty to register for a person ends when the person dies if the person has a reportable conviction or adjudication, other than an adjudication of delinquent conduct, for:

(1) a sexually violent offense;

(2) an offense under Section 25.02, 43.05(a)(2), or 43.26, Penal Code;

(3) an offense under Section 21.11(a)(2), Penal Code, if before or after the person is convicted or adjudicated for the offense under Section 21.11(a)(2), Penal Code, the person receives or has received another reportable conviction or adjudication, other than an adjudication of delinquent conduct, for an offense or conduct that requires registration under this chapter;

(4) an offense under Section 20.02, 20.03, or 20.04, Penal Code, if:

(A) the judgment in the case contains an affirmative finding under Article 42.015 or, for a deferred adjudication, the papers in the case contain an affirmative finding that the victim or intended victim was younger than 17 years of age; and

(B) before or after the person is convicted or adjudicated for the offense under Section 20.02, 20.03, or 20.04, Penal Code, the person receives or has received another reportable conviction or adjudication, other than an adjudication of delinquent conduct, for an offense or conduct that requires registration under this chapter; or

(5) an offense under Section 43.23, Penal Code, that is punishable under Subsection (h) of that section.

(b) Except as provided by Subchapter I, the duty to register for a person otherwise subject to Subsection (a) ends on the 10th anniversary of the date on which the person is released from a penal institution or discharges community supervision or the court dismisses the criminal proceedings against the person and discharges the person, whichever date is later, if the person's duty to register is based on a conviction or an order of deferred adjudication in a cause that was transferred to a district court or criminal district court under Section 54.02, Family Code.

(c) Except as provided by Subchapter I, the duty to register for a person with a reportable conviction or adjudication for an offense other than an offense described by Subsection (a) ends:

(1) if the person's duty to register is based on an adjudication of delinquent conduct, on the 10th anniversary of the date on which the disposition is made or the person completes the terms of the disposition, whichever date is later; or

(2) if the person's duty to register is based on a conviction or on an order of deferred adjudication, on the 10th anniversary of the date on which the court dismisses the criminal proceedings against the person and discharges the person, the person is released from a penal institution, or the person discharges community supervision, whichever date is later.

(Acts 2005, 79th Leg., ch. 1008, §1.01, effective September 1, 2005.)

E. EVIDENTIARY ISSUES

1. Competency of Child Witnesses

Texas Rules of Evidence

Rule 601. Competency of witnesses: insane persons, children, etc.

(a) General Rule. Every person is competent to be a witness except as otherwise provided in these rules. The following witnesses shall be incompetent to testify in any proceeding subject to these rules:

(1) Insane persons. Insane persons who, in the opinion of the court, are in an insane condition of mind at the time when they are offered as a witness, or who, in the opinion of the court, were in that condition when the events happened of which they are called to testify.

(2) Children. Children or other persons who, after being examined by the court, appear not to possess sufficient intellect to relate transactions with respect to which they are interrogated.

(b) "Dead Man's Rule" in Civil Actions. In civil actions by or against executors, administrators, or guardians, in which judgment may be rendered for or against them as such, neither party shall be allowed to testify against the others as to any oral statement by the testator, intestate or ward, unless that testimony to the oral statement is corroborated or unless the witness is called at the trial to testify thereto by the opposite party; and, the provisions of this article shall extend to and include all actions by or against the heirs or legal representatives of a decedent based in whole or in part on such oral statement. Except for the foregoing, a witness is not precluded from giving evidence of or concerning any transaction with, any conversations with, any admissions of, or statement by, a deceased or insane party or person merely because the witness is a party to the action or a person interested in the event thereof. The trial court shall, in a proper case, where this rule prohibits an interested party or witness from testifying, instruct the jury that such person is not permitted by the law to give evidence relating to any oral statement by the deceased or ward unless the oral statement is corroborated or unless the party or witness is called at the trial by the opposite party.

(Effective March 1, 1998.)

Texas Family Code

§104.001. Rules of evidence are applicable

Except as otherwise provided, the Texas Rules of Evidence apply as in other civil cases.

(Acts 1995, 74th Leg., ch. 20, §1, effective April 20, 1995. Amended by Acts 2005, 79th Leg., ch. 728, §6.002, effective September 1, 2005.)

§104.002. Admissibility of prerecorded statement of child

If a child 12 years of age or younger is alleged in a suit under this title to have been abused, the recording of an oral statement of the child recorded prior to the proceeding is admissible into evidence if:

(1) no attorney for a party was present when the statement was made;

(2) the recording is both visual and aural and is recorded on film or videotape or by other electronic means;

(3) the recording equipment was capable of making an accurate recording, the operator was competent, and the recording is accurate and has not been altered;

(4) the statement was not made in response to questioning calculated to lead the child to make a particular statement;

(5) each voice on the recording is identified;

(6) the person conducting the interview of the child in the recording is present at the proceeding and available to testify or be cross-examined by either party; and

(7) each party is afforded an opportunity to view the recording before it is offered into evidence.

(Acts 1995, 74th Leg., ch. 20, §1, effective April 20, 1995.)

§104.003. Court may order child's testimony be prerecorded and videotaped

(a) The court may, on the motion of a party to the proceeding, order that the testimony of the child be taken outside the courtroom and be recorded for showing in the courtroom before the court, the finder of fact, and the parties to the proceeding.

(b) Only an attorney for each party, an attorney ad litem for the child or other person whose presence would contribute to the welfare and well-being of the child, and persons necessary to operate the equipment may be present in the room with the child during the child's testimony.

(c) Only the attorneys for the parties may question the child.

(d) The persons operating the equipment shall be placed in a manner that prevents the child from seeing or hearing them.

(e) The court shall ensure that:

(1) the recording is both visual and aural and is recorded on film or videotape or by other electronic means;

(2) the recording equipment was capable of making an accurate recording, the operator was competent, and the recording is accurate and is not altered;

(3) each voice on the recording is identified; and

(4) each party to the proceeding is afforded an opportunity to view the recording before it is shown in the courtroom.

(Acts 1995, 74th Leg., ch. 20, §1, effective April 20, 1995.)

§104.004. Court may order that child's testimony be remotely televised and broadcast

(a) If in a suit a child 12 years of age or younger is alleged to have been abused, the court may, on the motion of a party to the proceeding, order that the testimony of the child be taken in a room other than the courtroom and be televised by closed-circuit equipment in the courtroom to be viewed by the court and the parties.

(b) The procedures that apply to prerecorded videotaped testimony of a child apply to the remote broadcast of testimony of a child.

(Acts 1995, 74th Leg., ch. 20, §1, effective April 20, 1995.)

§104.005. Prerecorded or televised statements substitute for child's in-court testimony

(a) If the testimony of a child is taken as provided by this chapter, the child may not be compelled to testify in court during the proceeding.

(b) The court may allow the testimony of a child of any age to be taken in any manner provided by this chapter if the child, because of a medical condition, is incapable of testifying in open court.

(Acts 1995, 74th Leg., ch. 20, §1, effective April 20, 1995. Amended by Acts 1995, 74th Leg., ch. 751, §11, effective September 1, 1995.)

§104.006. Admissibility of hearsay statement of child abuse victim

In a suit affecting the parent-child relationship, a statement made by a child 12 years of age or younger that describes alleged abuse against the child, without regard to whether the statement is otherwise inadmissible as hearsay, is admissible as evidence if, in a hearing conducted outside the presence of the jury, the court finds that the time, content, and circumstances of the statement provide sufficient indications of the statement's reliability and:

(1) the child testifies or is available to testify at the proceeding in court or in any other manner provided for by law; or

(2) the court determines that the use of the statement in lieu of the child's testimony is necessary to protect the welfare of the child.

(Acts 1997, 75th Leg., ch. 575, §4, effective September 1, 1997.)

§104.007. Court may allow videoconference testimony of professionals

(a) In this section, "professional" has the meaning assigned by Section 261.101(b).

(b) In a proceeding brought by the Department of Protective and Regulatory Services concerning a child who is alleged in a suit to have been abused or neglected, the court may order, with the agreement of the state's counsel and the defendant's counsel, that the testimony of a professional be taken outside the courtroom by videoconference.

(c) In ordering testimony to be taken as provided by Subsection (b), the court shall ensure that the videoconference testimony allows:

(1) the parties and attorneys involved in the proceeding to be able to see and hear the professional as the professional testifies; and

(2) the professional to be able to see and hear the parties and attorneys examining the professional while the professional is testifying.

(d) If the court permits the testimony of a professional by videoconference as provided by this section to be admitted during the proceeding, the professional may not be compelled to be physically present in court during the same proceeding to provide the same testimony unless ordered by the court.

(Acts 2003, 78th Leg., ch. 266, §1, effective September 1, 2003.)

2. Expert Testimony

Texas Rules of Evidence

Rule 702. Admissibility of testimony by experts

If scientific, technical, or other specialized knowledge will assist the trier of fact to understand the evidence or to determine a fact in issue, a witness qualified as an expert by knowledge, skill, experience, training, or education may testify thereto in the form of an opinion or otherwise.

(Effective March 1, 1998.)

3. Child Sexual Abuse Accommodation Syndrome

Child Sexual Abuse Accommodation Syndrome (CSAAS) is a term coined by psychiatrist Dr. Roland Summit to show that certain behavior is characteristic of sexually abused children. See Roland C. Summit, The Child Sexual Abuse Accommodation Syndrome, 7 Child Abuse & Neglect 177 (1983). In judicial proceedings, CSAAS is useful to explain the reason for certain behavior exhibited by sexually abused children (i.e., delay in reporting, half-truths, and recantations) that might lead jurors to question victims' truthfulness. In Texas, a witness who is properly qualified as an expert may give testimony on CSAAS. See Floyd v. State, 959 S.W.2d 706 (Tex. App.—Fort Worth 1998).

4. Anatomically Correct Dolls

Determinations of child sexual abuse increasingly rely on the use of anatomically correct dolls because many victims are young and unable to testify about incidents of abuse. Dolls may be used either to help children communicate better during an interview or to supply a mental health professional with information from which inferences of sexual abuse may be drawn. Texas law allows the use of anatomically correct dolls to convey the substance of a child's testimony in cases of sexual abuse and assault. See Zuniga v. State, 811 S.W.2d 177 (Tex. App.—San Antonio 1991, no writ); Coachman v. State, 692 S.W.2d 940 (Tex. App.—Houston [1st Dist.] 1985, writ ref'd).

5. Right to Confrontation

The Sixth Amendment of the United States Constitution provides that the defendant has the right to confront witnesses against him or her. The Supreme Court has grappled with the requirements of the Sixth Amendment right to confrontation in the child abuse context. See, e.g., Maryland v. Craig, 497 U.S. 836 (1990) (holding that the right of confrontation does not prohibit a procedure by which a child victim testifies via one-way closed-circuit television); Coy v. Iowa, 487 U.S. 102 (1988) (holding that a testimonial procedure involving a screen blocking the defendant from the victim violates the defendant's right to confrontation). Article X of the Texas Constitution (below) mirrors the federal constitutional guarantee of the right to confrontation.

However, the policy of child protection supports the use of special procedures in the abuse context in the event that the child victim testifies and also supports the expansion of exceptions to the hearsay rule so that the child need not testify. Texas permits oral statements of the child to be admitted into evidence in some cases (Tex. Code Crim. Proc. Arts. 2, 5); the child's testimony to be taken outside the courtroom and televised via closed-circuit television in the courtroom (Tex. Code Crim. Proc. Art. 3); and, the child's testimony to be videotaped outside the courtroom and recorded for later showing in the courtroom (Tex. Code Crim. Proc. Art. 4). Other statutes provide that the child need not testify in some circumstances (Tex. Code Crim. Proc. Arts. 6, 7, 8). If a child does testify, the court must take steps to "minimize undue psychological trauma to the child and to minimize the emotional and physical stress to the child caused by relevant factors. . . ." (Tex. Code Crim. Proc. Art. 10). See also the Uniform Child Witness Testimony by Alternative Methods Act in Part III of this Code.

Texas Code of Criminal Procedure

Article 38.071. Testimony of child who is victim of offense

§1

This article applies only to a hearing or proceeding in which the court determines that a child younger than 13 years of age would be unavailable to testify in the presence of the defendant about an offense defined by any of the following sections of the Penal Code:

(1) Section 19.02 (Murder);

(2) Section 19.03 (Capital Murder);

(3) Section 19.04 (Manslaughter);

(4) Section 20.04 (Aggravated Kidnapping);

(5) Section 21.11 (Indecency with a Child);

(6) Section 22.011 (Sexual Assault);

(7) Section 22.02 (Aggravated Assault);

(8) Section 22.021 (Aggravated Sexual Assault);

(9) Section 22.04(e) (Injury to a Child, Elderly Individual, or Disabled Individual);

(10) Section 22.04(f) (Injury to a Child, Elderly Individual, or Disabled Individual), if the conduct is committed intentionally or knowingly;

(11) Section 25.02 (Prohibited Sexual Conduct);

(12) Section 29.03 (Aggravated Robbery); or

(13) Section 43.25 (Sexual Performance by a Child).

§2

(a) The recording of an oral statement of the child made before the indictment is returned or the complaint has been filed is admissible into evidence if the court makes a determination that the factual issues of identity or actual occurrence were fully and fairly inquired into in a detached manner by a neutral individual experienced in child abuse cases that seeks to find the truth of the matter.

(b) If a recording is made under Subsection (a) of this section and after an indictment is returned or a complaint has been filed, by motion of the attorney representing the state or the attorney representing the defendant and on the approval of the court, both attorneys may propound written interrogatories that shall be presented by the same neutral individual who made the initial inquiries, if possible, and recorded under the same or similar circumstances of the original recording with the time and date of the inquiry clearly indicated in the recording.

(c) A recording made under Subsection (a) of this section is not admissible into evidence unless a recording made under Subsection (b) is admitted at the same time if a recording under Subsection (b) was requested prior to the time of the hearing or proceeding.

§3

(a) On its own motion or on the motion of the attorney representing the state or the attorney representing the defendant, the court may order that the testimony of the child be taken in a room other than the courtroom and be televised by closed circuit equipment in the courtroom to be viewed by the court and the finder of fact. To the extent practicable, only the judge, the court reporter, the attorneys for the defendant and for the state, persons necessary to operate the equipment, and any person whose presence would contribute to the welfare and well-being of the child may be present in the room with the child during his testimony. Only the attorneys and the judge may question the child. To the extent practicable, the persons necessary to operate the equipment shall be confined to an adjacent room or behind a screen or mirror that permits them to see and hear the child during his testimony, but does not permit the child to see or hear them. The court shall permit the defendant to observe and hear the testimony of the child and to communicate contemporaneously with his attorney during periods of recess or by audio contact, but the court shall attempt to ensure that the child cannot hear or see the defendant. The court shall permit the attorney for the defendant adequate opportunity to confer with the defendant during cross-examination of the child. On application of the attorney for the defendant, the court may recess the proceeding before or during cross-examination of the child for a reasonable time to allow the attorney for the defendant to confer with defendant.

(b) The court may set any other conditions and limitations on the taking of the testimony that it finds just and appropriate, taking into consideration the interests of the child, the rights of the defendant, and any other relevant factors.

§4

(a) After an indictment has been returned or a complaint filed, on its own motion or on the motion of the attorney representing the state or the attorney representing the defendant, the court may order that the testimony of the child be taken outside the courtroom and be recorded for showing in the courtroom before the court and the finder of fact. To the extent practicable, only those persons permitted to be present at the taking of testimony under Section 3 of this article may be present during the taking of the child's testimony, and the persons operating the equipment shall be confined from the child's sight and hearing as provided by Section 3. The court shall permit the defendant to observe and hear the testimony of the child and to communicate contemporaneously with his attorney during periods of recess or by audio contact but shall attempt to ensure that the child cannot hear or see the defendant.

(b) The court may set any other conditions and limitations on the taking of the testimony that it finds just and appropriate, taking into consideration the interests of the child, the rights of the defendant, and any other relevant factors. The court shall also ensure that:

(1) the recording is both visual and aural and is recorded on film or videotape or by other electronic means;

(2) the recording equipment was capable of making an accurate recording, the operator was competent, the quality of the recording is sufficient to allow the court and the finder of fact to assess the demeanor of the child and the interviewer, and the recording is accurate and is not altered;

(3) each voice on the recording is identified;

(4) the defendant, the attorneys for each party, and the expert witnesses for each party are afforded an opportunity to view the recording before it is shown in the courtroom;

(5) before giving his testimony, the child was placed under oath or was otherwise admonished in a manner appropriate to the child's age and maturity to testify truthfully;

(6) the court finds from the recording or through an in camera examination of the child that the child was competent to testify at the time the recording was made; and

(7) only one continuous recording of the child was made or the necessity for pauses in the recordings or for multiple recordings is established at the hearing or proceeding.

(c) After a complaint has been filed or an indictment returned charging the defendant, on the motion of the attorney representing the state, the court may order that the deposition of the child be taken outside of the courtroom in the same manner as a deposition may be taken in a civil matter. A deposition taken under this subsection is admissible into evidence.

§5

(a) On the motion of the attorney representing the state or the attorney representing the defendant and on a finding by the court that the following requirements have been substantially satisfied, the recording of an oral statement of the child made before a complaint has been filed or an indictment returned is admissible into evidence if:

(1) no attorney or peace officer was present when the statement was made;

(2) the recording is both visual and aural and is recorded on film or videotape or by other electronic means;

(3) the recording equipment was capable of making an accurate recording, the operator of the equipment was competent, the quality of the recording is sufficient to allow the court and the finder of fact to assess the demeanor of the child and the interviewer, and the recording is accurate and has not been altered;

(4) the statement was not made in response to questioning calculated to lead the child to make a particular statement;

(5) every voice on the recording is identified;

(6) the person conducting the interview of the child in the recording is expert in the handling, treatment, and investigation of child abuse cases, present at the hearing or proceeding, called by the state, and subject to cross-examination;

(7) immediately after a complaint was filed or an indictment returned, the attorney representing the state notified the court, the defendant, and the attorney representing the defendant of the existence of the recording;

(8) the defendant, the attorney for the defendant, and the expert witnesses for the defendant were afforded an opportunity to view the recording before it is offered into evidence and, if a proceeding was requested as provided by Subsection (b) of this section, in a proceeding conducted before a district court judge but outside the presence of the jury were afforded an opportunity to cross-examine the child as provided by Subsection (b) of this section from any time immediately following the filing of the complaint or the returning of an indictment charging

the defendant until the date the hearing or proceeding begins;

(9) the recording of the cross-examination, if there is one, is admissible under Subsection (b) of this section;

(10) before giving his testimony, the child was placed under oath or was otherwise admonished in a manner appropriate to the child's age and maturity to testify truthfully;

(11) the court finds from the recording or through an in camera examination of the child that the child was competent to testify at the time that the recording was made; and

(12) only one continuous recording of the child was made or the necessity for pauses in the recordings or for multiple recordings has been established at the hearing or proceeding.

(b) On the motion of the attorney representing the defendant, a district court may order that the cross-examination of the child be taken and be recorded before the judge of that court at any time until a recording made in accordance with Subsection (a) of this section has been introduced into evidence at the hearing or proceeding. On a finding by the court that the following requirements were satisfied, the recording of the cross-examination of the child is admissible into evidence and shall be viewed by the finder of fact only after the finder of fact has viewed the recording authorized by Subsection (a) of this section if:

(1) the recording is both visual and aural and is recorded on film or videotape or by other electronic means;

(2) the recording equipment was capable of making an accurate recording, the operator of the equipment was competent, the quality of the recording is sufficient to allow the court and the finder of fact to assess the demeanor of the child and the attorney representing the defendant, and the recording is accurate and has not been altered;

(3) every voice on the recording is identified;

(4) the defendant, the attorney representing the defendant, the attorney representing the state, and the expert witnesses for the defendant and the state were afforded an opportunity to view the recording before the hearing or proceeding began;

(5) the child was placed under oath before the cross-examination began or was otherwise admonished in a manner appropriate to the child's age and maturity to testify truthfully; and

(6) only one continuous recording of the child was made or the necessity for pauses in the recordings or for multiple recordings was established at the hearing or proceeding.

(c) During cross-examination under Subsection (b) of this section, to the extent practicable, only a district court judge, the attorney representing the defendant, the attorney representing the state, persons necessary to operate the equipment, and any other person whose presence would contribute to the welfare and well-being of the child may be present in the room with the child during his testimony. Only the attorneys and the judge may question the child. To the extent practicable, the persons operating the equipment shall be confined to an adjacent room or behind a screen or mirror that permits them to see and hear the child during his testimony but does not permit the child to see or hear them. The court shall permit the defendant to observe and hear the testimony of the child and to communicate contemporaneously with his attorney during periods of recess or by audio contact, but shall attempt to ensure that the child cannot hear or see the defendant.

(d) Under Subsection (b) of this section the district court may set any other conditions and limitations on the taking of the cross-examination of a child that it finds just and appropriate, taking into consideration the interests of the child, the rights of the defendant, and any other relevant factors.

§6

If the court orders the testimony of a child to be taken under Section 3 or 4 of this article or if the court finds the testimony of the child taken under Section 2 or 5 of this article is admissible into evidence, the child may not be required to testify in court at the proceeding for which the testimony was taken, unless the court finds there is good cause.

§7

In making any determination of good cause under this article, the court shall consider the rights of the defendant, the interests of the child, the relationship of the defendant to the child, the character and duration of the alleged offense, any court finding related to the availability of the child to testify, the age, maturity, and emotional stability of the child, the time elapsed since the alleged offense, and any other relevant factors.

§8

(a) In making a determination of unavailability under this article, the court shall consider relevant factors including the relationship of the defendant to the child, the character and duration of the alleged offense, the age, maturity, and emotional stability of the child, and the time elapsed since the alleged offense, and whether the child is more likely than not to be unavailable to testify because:

(1) of emotional or physical causes, including the confrontation with the defendant; or

(2) the child would suffer undue psychological or physical harm through his involvement at the hearing or proceeding.

(b) A determination of unavailability under this article can be made after an earlier determination of availability. A determination of availability under this article can be made after an earlier determination of unavailability.

§9

If the court finds the testimony taken under Section 2 or 5 of this article is admissible into evidence or if the court orders the testimony to be taken under Section 3 or 4 of this article and if the identity of the perpetrator is a contested issue, the child additionally must make an in-person identification of the defendant either at or before the hearing or proceeding.

§10

In ordering a child to testify under this article, the court shall take all reasonable steps necessary and available to minimize undue psychological trauma to the child and to minimize the emotional and physical stress to the child caused by relevant factors, including the confrontation with the defendant and the ordinary participation of the witness in the courtroom.

§11

In a proceeding under Section 2, 3, or 4 or Subsection (b) of Section 5 of this article, if the defendant is not represented by counsel and the court finds that the defendant is not able to obtain counsel for the purposes of the proceeding, the court shall appoint counsel to represent the defendant at the proceeding.

§12

In this article, "cross-examination" has the same meaning as in other legal proceedings in the state.

§13

The attorney representing the state shall determine whether to use the procedure provided in Section 2 of this article or the procedure provided in Section 5 of this article.

(Acts 1983, 68th Leg., p. 3828, ch. 599, §1, effective August 29, 1983. §3 amended by Acts 1987, 70th Leg., ch. 998, §1, effective August 31, 1987. Amended by Acts 1987, 70th Leg., 2nd C.S., ch. 55, §1, effective October 20, 1987; §3(a) amended by Acts 1991, 72nd Leg., ch. 266, §1, effective September 1, 1991; §1 amended by Acts 1995, 74th Leg., ch. 76, §14.24, effective September 1, 1995; §1 amended by Acts 2001, 77th Leg., ch. 338, § 1, effective September 1, 2001; §2(c) amended by Acts 2001, 77th Leg., ch. 338, §2, effective September 1, 2001; §3(a) amended by Acts 2001, 77th Leg., ch. 338, §3, effective September 1, 2001; §4(a), (b) amended by Acts 2001, 77th Leg., ch. 338, §4, effective September 1, 2001; §5(a), (b) amended by Acts 2001, 77th Leg., ch. 338, §5, effective September 1, 2001; §8(a) amended by Acts 2001, 77th Leg., ch. 338, §6, effective September 1, 2001; §9 amended by Acts 2001, 77th Leg., ch. 338, §7, effective September 1, 2001; §10 amended by Acts 2001, 77th Leg., ch. 338, §8, effective September 1, 2001.)

Article 38.072. Hearsay statement of child abuse victim

§1

This article applies to a proceeding in the prosecution of an offense under any of the following provisions of the Penal Code, if committed against a child 12 years of age or younger:

(1) Chapter 21 (Sexual Offenses) or 22 (Assaultive Offenses);

(2) Section 25.02 (Prohibited Sexual Conduct); or

(3) Section 43.25 (Sexual Performance by a Child).

§2

(a) This article applies only to statements that describe the alleged offense that:

(1) were made by the child against whom the offense was allegedly committed; and

(2) were made to the first person, 18 years of age or older, other than the defendant, to whom the child made a statement about the offense.

(b) A statement that meets the requirements of Subsection (a) of this article is not inadmissible because of the hearsay rule if:

(1) on or before the 14th day before the date the proceeding begins, the party intending to offer the statement:

(A) notifies the adverse party of its intention to do so;

(B) provides the adverse party with the name of the witness through whom it intends to offer the statement; and

(C) provides the adverse party with a written summary of the statement;

(2) the trial court finds, in a hearing conducted outside the presence of the jury, that the statement is reliable based on the time, content, and circumstances of the statement; and

(3) the child testifies or is available to testify at the proceeding in court or in any other manner provided by law.

(Acts 1985, 69th Leg., ch. 590, §1, effective September 1, 1985. Sec. 1 amended by Acts 1995, 74th Leg., ch. 76, §14.25, effective September 1, 1995.)

Texas Constitution

Article X. Rights of defendant in criminal prosecutions

In all criminal prosecutions the accused shall have a speedy public trial by an impartial jury. He shall have the right to demand the nature and cause of the accusation against him, and to have a copy thereof. He shall not be compelled to give evidence against himself, and shall have the right of being heard by himself or counsel, or both, shall be confronted by the witnesses against him and shall have compulsory process for obtaining witnesses in his favor, except that when the witness resides out of the State and the offense charged is a violation of any of the anti-trust laws of this State, the defendant and the State shall have the right to produce and have the evidence admitted by deposition, under such rules and laws as the Legislature may hereafter provide; and no person shall be held to answer for a criminal offense, unless on an indictment of a grand jury, except in cases in which the punishment is by fine or imprisonment, otherwise than in the penitentiary, in cases of impeachment, and in cases arising in the army or navy, or in the militia, when in actual service in time of war or public danger.

(Amended November 5, 1918.)

6. Privileged Communications

Texas Family Code

§261.202. Privileged communications in abuse or neglect proceedings: only attorney-client communications

In a proceeding regarding the abuse or neglect of a child, evidence may not be excluded on the ground of privileged communication except in the case of communications between an attorney and client.

(Acts 1995, 74th Leg., ch. 20, §1, effective April 20, 1995.

F. INTERVENTION

In the child abuse context, state intervention into the family may take two forms: (1) summary seizure or (2) temporary custody. In the former ex parte hearing, the court determines if an emergency exists, that is, if the child is in such immediate danger that the child's welfare dictates immediate removal from the home.

In contrast, at the adversarial hearing on temporary custody, the court determines whether requisite facts exist to find a child within the statutory definition of "abused," "neglected," "dependent," "in need of care," etc. This proceeding is often referred to as a "jurisdictional," "adjudicatory," or "factfinding" hearing. After making such a determination, the court conducts the "dispositional" phase: choosing among various dispositions for the child.

1. Summary Seizure (Emergency Jurisdiction)

Texas Family Code

§261.302. Conduct of investigation: immediate removal from the home

. . .

(d) If, before an investigation is completed, the investigating agency believes that the immediate removal of a child from the child's home is necessary to protect the child from further abuse or neglect, the investigating agency shall file a petition or take other action under Chapter 262 to provide for the temporary care and protection of the child.

. . .

(Acts 1995, 74th Leg., ch. 20, §1, effective April 20, 1995. Amended by Acts 1995, 74th Leg., ch. 751, §95, effective September 1, 1995; by Acts 1997, 75th Leg., ch. 575, §§13, 14, effective September 1, 1997; Acts 1997, 75th Leg., ch. 1022, §73, effective September 1, 1997; Acts 2005, 79th Leg., ch. 268, §1.21, effective September 1, 2005.)

§262.001. Governmental entity may request order for immediate custody

(a) A governmental entity with an interest in the child may file a suit affecting the parent-child relationship requesting an order or take possession of a child without a court order as provided by this chapter.

(b) In determining the reasonable efforts that are required to be made with respect to preventing or eliminating the need to remove a child from the child's home or to make it possible to return a child to the child's home, the child's health and safety is the paramount concern.

(Acts 1995, 74th Leg., ch. 20, §1, effective April 20, 1995. Amended by Acts 1999, 76th Leg., ch. 1150, §10, effective September 1, 1999; Acts 1999, 76th Leg., ch. 1390, §29, effective September 1, 1999.)

§262.002. Jurisdiction

A suit brought by a governmental entity requesting an order under this chapter may be filed in a court with jurisdiction to hear the suit in the county in which the child is found.

(Acts 1995, 74th Leg., ch. 20, §1, effective April 20, 1995. Amended by Acts 1999, 76th Leg., ch. 1150, §11, effective September 1, 1999; Acts 1999, 76th Leg., ch. 1390, §30, effective September 1, 1999.)

§262.003. Immunity from civil liability

A person who takes possession of a child without a court order is immune from civil liability if, at the time possession is taken, there is reasonable cause to believe there is an immediate danger to the physical health or safety of the child.

(Acts 1995, 74th Leg., ch. 20, §1, effective April 20, 1995.)

§262.004. Law enforcement or probation officer may accept voluntary delivery of child

A law enforcement officer or a juvenile probation officer may take possession of a child without a court order on the voluntary delivery of the child by the parent, managing conservator, possessory conservator, guardian, caretaker, or custodian who is presently entitled to possession of the child.

(Acts 1995, 74th Leg., ch. 20, §1, effective April 20, 1995. Amended by Acts 1995, 74th Leg., ch. 751, §101, effective September 1, 1995.)

§262.005. Law enforcement or probation officer must file petition after accepting voluntary delivery of child

When possession of the child has been acquired through voluntary delivery of the child to a law enforcement officer or juvenile probation officer, the law enforcement officer or juvenile probation officer taking the child into possession shall cause a suit to be filed not later than the 60th day after the date the child is taken into possession.

(Acts 1995, 74th Leg., ch. 20, §1, effective April 20, 1995. Amended by Acts 1995, 74th Leg., ch. 751, §102, effective September 1, 1995.)

§262.006. Custody of living child after abortion

(a) An authorized representative of the Department of Protective and Regulatory Services may assume the care, control, and custody of a child born alive as the result of an abortion as defined by Chapter 161.

(b) The department shall file a suit and request an emergency order under this chapter.

(c) A child for whom possession is assumed under this section need not be delivered to the court except on the order of the court.

(Acts 1995, 74th Leg., ch. 20, §1, effective April 20, 1995.)

§262.007. Law enforcement may take possession of missing child

(a) A law enforcement officer who, during a criminal investigation relating to a child's custody, discovers that a child is a missing child and believes that a person may flee with or conceal the child shall take possession of the child and provide for the delivery of the child as provided by Subsection (b).

(b) An officer who takes possession of a child under Subsection (a) shall deliver or arrange for the delivery of the child to a person entitled to possession of the child.

(c) If a person entitled to possession of the child is not immediately available to take possession of the child, the law enforcement officer shall deliver the child to the Department of Protective and Regulatory Services. Until a person entitled to possession of the child takes possession of the child, the department may, without a court order, retain possession of the child not longer than five days after the date the child is delivered to the department. While the department retains possession of a child under this subsection, the department may place the child in foster home care. If a parent or other person entitled to possession of the child does not take possession of the child before the sixth day after the date the child is delivered to the department, the department shall proceed under this chapter as if the law enforcement officer took possession of the child under Section 262.104.

(Acts 1995, 74th Leg., ch. 776, §1, effective September 1, 1995. Amended by Acts 1999, 76th Leg., ch. 685, §6, effective September 1, 1999; Acts 1999, 76th Leg., ch. 1150, §12, effective September 1, 1999; Acts 1999, 76th Leg., ch. 1390, §31, effective September 1, 1999.)

§262.008. Custody of abandoned children

(a) An authorized representative of the Department of Protective and Regulatory Services may assume the care, control, and custody of a child:

(1) who is abandoned without identification or a means for identifying the child; and

(2) whose identity cannot be ascertained by the exercise of reasonable diligence.

(b) The department shall immediately file a suit to terminate the parent-child relationship of a child under Subsection (a).

(c) A child for whom possession is assumed under this section need not be delivered to the court except on the order of the court.

(Acts 1997, 75th Leg., ch. 600, §4, effective January 1, 1998.)

§262.009. Temporary care without a court order

An employee of or volunteer with a law enforcement agency who successfully completes a background and criminal history check approved by the law enforcement agency may assist a law enforcement officer or juvenile probation officer with the temporary care of a child who is taken into possession by a governmental entity without a court order under this chapter until further arrangements regarding the custody of the child can be made.

(Acts 2003, 78th Leg., ch. 970, §1, effective June 20, 2003.)

§262.101. Support by affidavit required in ex parte proceeding by government entity

An original suit filed by a governmental entity that requests permission to take possession of a child without prior notice and a hearing must be supported by an affidavit sworn to by a person with personal knowledge and stating facts sufficient to satisfy a person of ordinary prudence and caution that:

(1) there is an immediate danger to the physical health or safety of the child or the child has been a victim of neglect or sexual abuse and that continuation in the home would be contrary to the child's welfare;

(2) there is no time, consistent with the physical health or safety of the child, for a full adversary hearing under Subchapter C; and

(3) reasonable efforts, consistent with the circumstances and providing for the safety of the child, were made to prevent or eliminate the need for the removal of the child.

(Acts 1995, 74th Leg., ch. 20, §1, effective April 20, 1995. Amended by Acts 1995, 74th Leg., ch. 751, §103, effective September 1, 1995; by Acts 1997, 75th Leg., ch. 752, §1, effective June 17, 1997; Acts 1999, 76th Leg., ch. 1150, §14, effective September 1, 1999; Acts 1999, 76th Leg., ch. 1390, §33, effective September 1, 1999; Acts 2001, 77th Leg., ch. 849, §1, effective September 1, 2001.)

§262.1015. Department shall file petition to remove alleged perpetrator from the home

(a) If the department determines after an investigation that child abuse has occurred and that the child would be protected in the child's home by the removal of the alleged perpetrator of the abuse, the department shall file a petition for the removal of the alleged perpetrator from the residence of the child rather than attempt to remove the child from the residence.

(b) A court may issue a temporary restraining order in a suit by the department for the removal of an alleged perpetrator under Subsection (a) if the department's petition states facts sufficient to satisfy the court that:

(1) there is an immediate danger to the physical health or safety of the child or the child has been a victim of sexual abuse;

(2) there is no time, consistent with the physical health or safety of the child, for an adversary hearing;

(3) the child is not in danger of abuse from a parent or other adult with whom the child will continue to reside in the residence of the child; and

(4) the issuance of the order is in the best interest of the child.

(c) The order shall be served on the alleged perpetrator and on the parent or other adult with whom the child will continue to reside.

(d) A temporary restraining order under this section expires not later than the 14th day after the date the order was rendered.

(e) A temporary restraining order under this section and any other order requiring the removal of an alleged perpetrator from the residence of a child shall require that the parent or other adult with whom the child will continue to reside in the child's home make a reasonable effort to monitor the residence and report to the department and the appropriate law enforcement agency any attempt by the alleged perpetrator to return to the residence.

(f) The court shall order the removal of an alleged perpetrator if the court finds that the child is not in danger of abuse from a parent or other adult with whom the child will continue to reside in the child's residence and that:

(1) the presence of the alleged perpetrator in the child's residence constitutes a continuing danger to the physical health or safety of the child; or

(2) the child has been the victim of sexual abuse and there is a substantial risk that the child will be the victim of sexual abuse in the future if the alleged perpetrator remains in the residence.

(g) A person commits an offense if the person is a parent or other person with whom a child resides, the person is served with an order containing the requirement specified by Subsection (e), and the person fails to make a reasonable effort to monitor the residence of the child or to report to the department and the appropriate law enforcement agency an attempt by the alleged perpetrator to return to the residence. An offense under this section is a Class A misdemeanor.

(h) A person commits an offense if, in violation of a court order under this section, the person returns to the residence of the child the person is alleged to have abused. An offense under this subsection is a Class A misdemeanor, except that the offense is a felony of the third degree if the person has previously been convicted under this subsection.

(Acts 1995, 74th Leg., ch. 943, §4, effective September 1, 1995. Amended by Acts 1997, 75th Leg., ch. 575, §19, effective September 1, 1997.)

§262.102. Standard for emergency order authorizing possession of child: immediate danger

(a) Before a court may, without prior notice and a hearing, issue a temporary restraining order or attachment of a child in a suit brought by a governmental entity, the court must find that:

(1) there is an immediate danger to the physical health or safety of the child or the child has been a victim of neglect or sexual abuse and that continuation in the home would be contrary to the child's welfare;

(2) there is no time, consistent with the physical health or safety of the child and the nature of the emergency, for a full adversary hearing under Subchapter C; and

(3) reasonable efforts, consistent with the circumstances and providing for the safety of the child, were made to prevent or eliminate the need for removal of the child.

(b) In determining whether there is an immediate danger to the physical health or safety of a child, the court may consider whether the child's household includes a person who has:

(1) abused or neglected another child in a manner that caused serious injury to or the death of the other child; or

(2) sexually abused another child.

(c) If, based on the recommendation of or a request by the department, the court finds that child abuse or neglect has occurred and that the child requires protection from family violence by a member of the child's family or household, the court shall render a temporary order under Chapter 71 for the protection of the child. In this subsection, "family violence" has the meaning assigned by Section 71.004.

(Acts 1995, 74th Leg., ch. 20, §1, effective April 20, 1995. Amended by Acts 1995, 74th Leg., ch. 751, §104, effective September 1, 1995; by Acts 1997, 75th Leg., ch. 752, §2, effective June 17, 1997; Acts 1999, 76th Leg., ch. 1150, §15, effective September 1, 1999; Acts 1999, 76th Leg., ch. 1390, §34, effective September 1, 1999; Acts 2001, 77th Leg., ch. 849, §2, effective September 1, 2001; Acts 2003, 78th Leg., ch. 1276, §7.002(m), effective September 1, 2003.)

§262.103. Duration of temporary restraining order: 14 days

A temporary restraining order or attachment of the child issued under this chapter expires not later than 14 days after the date it is issued unless it is extended as provided by the Texas Rules of Civil Procedure.

(Acts 1995, 74th Leg., ch. 20, §1, effective April 20, 1995.)

§262.104. Agency may take possession of child in emergency without court order

(a) If there is no time to obtain a temporary restraining order or attachment before taking possession of a child consistent with the health and safety of that child, an authorized representative of the Department of Family and Protective Services, a law enforcement officer, or a juvenile probation officer may take possession of a child without a court order under the following conditions, only:

(1) on personal knowledge of facts that would lead a person of ordinary prudence and caution to believe that there is an immediate danger to the physical health or safety of the child;

(2) on information furnished by another that has been corroborated by personal knowledge of facts and all of which taken together would lead a person of ordinary prudence and caution to believe that there is an immediate danger to the physical health or safety of the child;

(3) on personal knowledge of facts that would lead a person of ordinary prudence and caution to believe that the child has been the victim of sexual abuse;

(4) on information furnished by another that has been corroborated by personal knowledge of facts and all of which taken together would lead a person of ordinary prudence and caution to believe that the child has been the victim of sexual abuse; or

(5) on information furnished by another that has been corroborated by personal knowledge of facts and all of which taken together would lead a person of ordinary prudence and caution to believe that the parent or person who has possession of the child is currently using a controlled substance as defined by Chapter 481, Health and Safety Code, and the use constitutes an immediate danger to the physical health or safety of the child.

(b) An authorized representative of the Department of Family and Protective Services, a law enforcement officer, or a juvenile probation officer may take possession of a child under Subsection (a) on personal knowledge or information furnished by another, that has been corroborated by personal knowledge, that would lead a person of ordinary prudence and caution to believe that the parent or person who has possession of the child has permitted the child to remain on premises used for the manufacture of methamphetamine.

(Acts 1995, 74th Leg., ch. 20, §1, effective April 20, 1995. Amended by Acts 1997, 75th Leg., ch. 575, §20, effective September 1, 1997; Acts 2005, 79th Leg., ch. 282, §2, effective Aug. 1, 2005.)

§262.1041. Procedure for release of child by law enforcement or probation officer to temporary custody

(a) A law enforcement or juvenile probation officer who takes possession of a child under this chapter may release the child to:

(1) a child-placing agency licensed by the Department of Family and Protective Services under Chapter 42, Human Resources Code, if the agency is authorized by the department to take possession of the child;

(2) the Department of Family and Protective Services; or

(3) any other person authorized by law to take possession of the child.

(b) A child-placing agency or other authorized person who takes possession of a child under this section shall:

(1) immediately notify the Department of Family and Protective Services that the agency or other authorized person has taken possession of the child; and

(2) with the assistance of the law enforcement or juvenile probation officer who releases the child to the agency or other authorized person, complete a form prescribed by the Department of Family and Protective Services that contains basic information regarding the child and the circumstances under which the officer took possession of the child and promptly submit the completed form to the department.

(Acts 2005, 79th Leg., ch. 268, §1.32, effective September 1, 2005; Acts 2005, 79th Leg., ch. 516, §1, effective June 17, 2005.)

§262.105. Agency must file petition after taking possession of child in emergency

(a) When a child is taken into possession without a court order, the person taking the child into possession, without unnecessary delay, shall:

(1) file a suit affecting the parent-child relationship;

(2) request the court to appoint an attorney ad litem for the child; and

(3) request an initial hearing to be held by no later than the first working day after the date the child is taken into possession.

(b) If the Department of Protective and Regulatory Services files a suit affecting the parent-child relationship required under Subsection (a)(1) seeking termination of the parent-child relationship, the department shall file the suit not later than the 45th day after the date the department assumes the care, control, and custody of a child under Section 262.303.

(Acts 1995, 74th Leg., ch. 20, §1, effective April 20, 1995. Amended by Acts 2001, 77th Leg., ch. 809, §2, effective September 1, 2001.)

§262.106. Court shall hold initial hearing promptly after child is taken into possession in emergency without court order

(a) The court in which a suit has been filed after a child has been taken into possession without a court order by a governmental entity shall hold an initial hearing on or before the first working day after the date the child is taken into possession. The court shall render orders that are necessary to protect the physical health and safety of the child. If the court is unavailable for a hearing on the first working day, then, and only in that event, the hearing shall be held no later than the first working day after the court becomes available, provided that the hearing is held no later than the third working day after the child is taken into possession.

(b) The initial hearing may be ex parte and proof may be by sworn petition or affidavit if a full adversary hearing is not practicable.

(c) If the initial hearing is not held within the time required, the child shall be returned to the parent, managing conservator, possessory conservator, guardian, caretaker, or custodian who is presently entitled to possession of the child.

(d) For the purpose of determining under Subsection (a) the first working day after the date the child is taken into possession, the child is considered to have been taken into possession by the Department of Protective and Regulatory Services on the expiration of the five-day period permitted under Section 262.007(c) or 262.110(b), as appropriate.

(Acts 1995, 74th Leg., ch. 20, §1, effective April 20, 1995. Amended by Acts 1999, 76th Leg., ch. 1150, §16, effective September 1, 1999; Acts 1999, 76th Leg., ch. 1390, §35, effective September 1, 1999.)

§262.107. Standard for decision at initial hearing: continuing danger and reasonable efforts unavailing

(a) The court shall order the return of the child at the initial hearing regarding a child taken in possession without a court order by a governmental entity unless the court is satisfied that:

(1) there is a continuing danger to the physical health or safety of the child if the child is returned to the parent, managing conservator, possessory conservator, guardian, caretaker, or custodian who is presently entitled to possession of the child or the evidence shows that the child has been the victim of sexual abuse on one or more occasions and that there is a substantial risk that the child will be the victim of sexual abuse in the future;

(2) continuation of the child in the home would be contrary to the child's welfare; and

(3) reasonable efforts, consistent with the circumstances and providing for the safety of the child, were made to prevent or eliminate the need for removal of the child.

(b) In determining whether there is a continuing danger to the physical health or safety of a child, the court may consider whether the household to which the child would be returned includes a person who has:

(1) abused or neglected another child in a manner that caused serious injury to or the death of the other child; or

(2) sexually abused another child.

(Acts 1995, 74th Leg., ch. 20, §1, effective April 20, 1995. Amended by Acts 1995, 74th Leg., ch. 751, §105, effective September 1, 1995; by Acts 2001, 77th Leg., ch. 849, §3, effective September 1, 2001.)

§262.108. Abused or neglected child may not be held in juvenile detention facilities

When a child is taken into possession under this chapter, that child may not be held in isolation or in a jail, juvenile detention facility, or other secure detention facility.

(Acts 1995, 74th Leg., ch. 20, §1, effective April 20, 1995. Amended by Acts 1997, 75th Leg., ch. 1374, §9, effective September 1, 1997.)

§262.109. Notice to parent of summary seizure

(a) The department or other agency must give written notice as prescribed by this section to each parent of the child or to the child's conservator or legal guardian when a representative of the Department of Protective and Regulatory Services or other agency takes possession of a child under this chapter.

(b) The written notice must be given as soon as practicable, but in any event not later than the first working day after the date the child is taken into possession.

(c) The written notice must include:

(1) the reasons why the department or agency is taking possession of the child and the facts that led the department to believe that the child should be taken into custody;

(2) the name of the person at the department or agency that the parent, conservator, or other custodian may contact for information relating to the child or a legal proceeding relating to the child;

(3) a summary of legal rights of a parent, conservator, guardian, or other custodian under this chapter and an explanation of the probable legal procedures relating to the child; and

(4) a statement that the parent, conservator, or other custodian has the right to hire an attorney.

(d) The written notice may be waived by the court at the initial hearing:

(1) on a showing that:

(A) the parents, conservators, or other custodians of the child could not be located; or

(B) the department took possession of the child under Subchapter D; or

(2) for other good cause.

(Acts 1995, 74th Leg., ch. 20, §1, effective April 20, 1995. Amended by Acts 1997, 75th Leg., ch. 1022, §76, effective January 1, 1998; Acts 1999, 76th Leg., ch. 1150, §17, effective September 1, 1999; Acts 1999, 76th Leg., ch. 1390, §36, effective September 1, 1999; Acts 2001, 77th Leg., ch. 809, §3, effective September 1, 2001.)

§262.110. Agency may take possession without court order in an emergency if purpose was to return child to home

(a) An authorized representative of the Department of Protective and Regulatory Services, a law enforcement officer, or a juvenile probation officer may take temporary possession of a child without a court order on discovery of a child in a situation of danger to the child's physical health or safety when the sole purpose is to deliver the child without unnecessary delay to the parent, managing conservator, possessory conservator, guardian, caretaker, or custodian who is presently entitled to possession of the child.

(b) Until a parent or other person entitled to possession of the child takes possession of the child, the department may retain possession of the child without a court order for not more than five days. On the expiration of the fifth day, if a parent or other person entitled to possession does not take possession of the child, the department shall take action under this chapter as if the department took possession of the child under Section 262.104.

(Acts 1995, 74th Leg., ch. 20, §1, effective April 20, 1995. Amended by Acts 1999, 76th Leg., ch. 1150, §18, effective September 1, 1999; Acts 1999, 76th Leg., ch. 1390, §37, effective September 1, 1999.)

§262.112. Department is entitled to expedited hearing and appeal

(a) The Department of Protective and Regulatory Services is entitled to an expedited hearing under this chapter in any proceeding in which a hearing is required if the department determines that a child should be removed from the child's home because of an immediate danger to the physical health or safety of the child.

(b) In any proceeding in which an expedited hearing is held under Subsection (a), the department, parent, guardian, or other party to the proceeding is entitled to an expedited appeal on a ruling by a court that the child may not be removed from the child's home.

(c) If a child is returned to the child's home after a removal in which the department was entitled to an expedited hearing under this section and the child is the subject of a subsequent allegation of abuse or neglect, the department or any other interested party is entitled to an expedited hearing on the removal of the child from the child's home in the manner provided by Subsection (a) and to an expedited appeal in the manner provided by Subsection (b).

(Acts 1995, 74th Leg., ch. 943, §1, effective September 1, 1995. Renumbered from Family Code §262.111 by Acts 1997, 75th Leg., ch. 165, §31.01(29), effective September 1, 1997.)

2. Temporary Custody After Full Adversary Hearing

§262.113. Government entity must support request for possession if child not presently in custody

An original suit filed by a governmental entity that requests to take possession of a child after notice and a hearing must be supported by an affidavit sworn to by a person with personal knowledge and stating facts sufficient to satisfy a person of ordinary prudence and caution that:

(1) reasonable efforts have been made to prevent or eliminate the need to remove the child from the child's home; and

(2) allowing the child to remain in the home would be contrary to the child's welfare.

(Acts 1999, 76th Leg., ch. 1150, §19, effective September 1, 1999; Acts 1999, 76th Leg., ch. 1390, §38, effective September 1, 1999.)

§262.114. Evaluation of potential caregivers; placement should be in best interest of child

(a) Before a full adversary hearing under Subchapter C, the Department of Family and Protective Services must perform a background and criminal history check of the relatives or other designated individuals identified as a potential relative or designated caregiver, as defined by Section 264.751, on the proposed child placement resources form provided under Section 261.307. The department shall evaluate each person listed on the form to determine the relative or other designated individual who would be the most appropriate substitute caregiver for the child and must complete a home study of the most appropriate substitute caregiver, if any, before the full adversary hearing. Until the department identifies a relative or other designated individual qualified to be a substitute caregiver, the department must continue to explore substitute caregiver options. The time frames in this subsection do not apply to a relative or other designated individual located in another state.

(b) The department may place a child with a relative or other designated individual identified on the proposed child placement resources form if the department determines that the placement is in the best interest of the child. The department may place the child with the relative or designated individual before conducting the background and criminal history check or home study required under Subsection (a). The department shall provide a copy of an informational manual required under Section 261.3071 to the relative or other designated caregiver at the time of the child's placement.

(Added by Acts 2005, 79th Leg., ch. 268, §1.33, effective September 1, 2005.)

§262.201. Court shall hold full adversary hearing within 14 days: return child or issue temporary order

(a) Unless the child has already been returned to the parent, managing conservator, possessory conservator, guardian, caretaker, or custodian entitled to possession and the temporary order, if any, has been dissolved, a full adversary hearing shall be held not later than the 14th day after the date the child was taken into possession by the governmental entity.

(b) At the conclusion of the full adversary hearing, the court shall order the return of the child to the parent, managing conservator, possessory conservator, guardian, caretaker, or custodian entitled to possession unless the court finds sufficient evidence to satisfy a person of ordinary prudence and caution that:

(1) there was a danger to the physical health or safety of the child which was caused by an act or failure to act of the person entitled to possession and for the child to remain in the home is contrary to the welfare of the child;

(2) the urgent need for protection required the immediate removal of the child and reasonable efforts, consistent with the circumstances and providing for the safety of the child, were made to eliminate or prevent the child's removal; and

(3) reasonable efforts have been made to enable the child to return home, but there is a substantial risk of a continuing danger if the child is returned home.

(c) If the court finds sufficient evidence to satisfy a person of ordinary prudence and caution that there is a continuing danger to the physical health or safety of the child and for the child to remain in the home is contrary to the welfare of the child, the court shall issue an appropriate temporary order under Chapter 105. The court shall require each parent, alleged father, or relative of the child before the court to submit the proposed child placement resources form provided under Section 261.307, if the form has not been previously provided, and provide the Department of Family and Protective Services with information necessary to locate any other absent parent, alleged father, or relative of the child. The court shall inform each parent, alleged father, or relative of the child before the court that the person's failure to submit the proposed child placement resources form will not delay any court proceedings relating to the child. The court shall inform each parent in open court that parental and custodial rights and duties may be subject to restriction or to termination unless the parent or parents are willing and able to provide the child with a safe environment. If the court finds that the child requires protection from family violence by a member of the child's family or household, the court shall render a protective order under Title 4 for the child. In this subsection, "family violence" has the meaning assigned by Section 71.004.

(d) In determining whether there is a continuing danger to the physical health or safety of the child, the court may consider whether the household to which the child would be returned includes a person who:

(1) has abused or neglected another child in a manner that caused serious injury to or the death of the other child; or

(2) has sexually abused another child.

(e) The court shall place a child removed from the child's custodial parent with the child's noncustodial parent or with a relative of the child if placement with the noncustodial parent is inappropriate, unless placement with the noncustodial parent or a relative is not in the best interest of the child.

(f) When citation by publication is needed for a parent or alleged or probable father in an action brought under this chapter because the location of the parent, alleged father, or probable father is unknown, the court may render a temporary order without delay at any time after the filing of the action without regard to whether notice of the citation by publication has been published.

(g) For the purpose of determining under Subsection (a) the 14th day after the date the child is taken into possession, a child is considered to have been taken into possession by the department on the expiration of the five-day period permitted under Section 262.007(c) or 262.110(b), as appropriate.

(Acts 1995, 74th Leg., ch. 20, §1, effective April 20, 1995. Amended by Acts 1995, 74th Leg., ch. 751, §107, effective September 1, 1995; by Acts 1997, 75th Leg., ch. 575, §21, effective September 1, 1997; Acts 1997, 75th Leg., ch. 600, §5, effective January 1, 1998; Acts 1997, 75th Leg., ch. 603, §1, effective January 1, 1998; Acts 1997, 75th Leg., ch. 752, §3, effective June 17, 1997; Acts 1997, 75th Leg., ch. 1022, §77, effective January 1, 1998; Acts 1997, 75th Leg., ch. 1022, §78, effective September 1, 1997; Acts 1999, 76th Leg., ch. 62, §6.31, effective September 1, 1999; Acts 1999, 76th Leg., ch. 1150, §20, effective September 1, 1999; Acts 1999, 76th Leg., ch. 1390, §39, effective September 1, 1999; Acts 2001, 77th Leg., ch. 306, §1, effective September 1, 2001; Acts 2001, 77th Leg., ch. 849, §4, effective September 1, 2001; Acts 2005, 79th Leg., ch. 268, §1.34(a), effective September 1, 2005.)

§262.2015. Court may waive service plan and reasonable-efforts requirement in aggravated circumstances

(a) The court may waive the requirement of a service plan and the requirement to make reasonable efforts to return the child to a parent and may accelerate the trial schedule to result in a final order for a child under the care of the department at an earlier date than provided by Subchapter D, Chapter 263, if the court finds that the parent has subjected the child to aggravated circumstances.

(b) The court may find under Subsection (a) that a parent has subjected the child to aggravated circumstances if:

(1) the parent abandoned the child without identification or a means for identifying the child;

(2) the child is a victim of serious bodily injury or sexual abuse inflicted by the parent or by another person with the parent's consent;

(3) the parent has engaged in conduct against the child that would constitute an offense under the following provisions of the Penal Code:

(A) Section 19.02 (murder);

(B) Section 19.03 (capital murder);

(C) Section 19.04 (manslaughter);

(D) Section 21.11 (indecency with a child);

(E) Section 22.011 (sexual assault);

(F) Section 22.02 (aggravated assault);

(G) Section 22.021 (aggravated sexual assault);

(H) Section 22.04 (injury to a child, elderly individual, or disabled individual);

(I) Section 22.041 (abandoning or endangering child);

(J) Section 25.02 (prohibited sexual conduct);

(K) Section 43.25 (sexual performance by a child); or

(L)Section 43.26 (possession or promotion of child pornography);

(4) the parent voluntarily left the child alone or in the possession of another person not the parent of the child for at least six months without expressing an intent to return and without providing adequate support for the child;

(5) the parent's parental rights with regard to another child have been involuntarily terminated based on a finding that the parent's conduct violated Section 161.001(1)(D) or (E) or a substantially equivalent provision of another state's law;

(6) the parent has been convicted for:

(A) the murder of another child of the parent and the offense would have been an offense under 18 U.S.C. Section 1111(a) if the offense had occurred in the special maritime or territorial jurisdiction of the United States;

(B) the voluntary manslaughter of another child of the parent and the offense would have been an offense under 18 U.S.C. Section 1112(a) if the offense had occurred in the special maritime or territorial jurisdiction of the United States;

(C) aiding or abetting, attempting, conspiring, or soliciting an offense under Subdivision (A) or (B); or

(D) the felony assault of the child or another child of the parent that resulted in serious bodily injury to the child or another child of the parent; or

(7) the parent's parental rights with regard to two other children have been involuntarily terminated.

(c) On finding that reasonable efforts to make it possible for the child to safely return to the child's home are not required, the court shall at any time before the 30th day after the date of the finding, conduct an initial permanency hearing under Subchapter D, Chapter 263. Separate notice of the permanency plan is not required but may be given with a notice of a hearing under this section.

(d) The Department of Protective and Regulatory Services shall make reasonable efforts to finalize the permanent placement of a child for whom the court has made the finding described by Subsection (c). The court shall set the suit for trial on the merits as required by Subchapter D, Chapter 263, in order to facilitate final placement of the child.

(Acts 1997, 75th Leg., ch. 1022, §79, effective September 1, 1997. Amended by Acts 1999, 76th Leg., ch. 1150, §21, effective September 1, 1999; Acts 1999, 76th Leg., ch. 1390, §40, effective September 1, 1999; Acts 2001, 77th Leg., ch. 849, §5, effective September 1, 2001; Acts 2005, 79th Leg., ch. 268, §1.35, effective September 1, 2005.)

§262.202. Government agency shall request identification of court with continuing, exclusive jurisdiction

If at the conclusion of the full adversary hearing the court renders a temporary order, the governmental entity shall request identification of a court of continuing, exclusive jurisdiction as provided by Chapter 155.

(Acts 1995, 74th Leg., ch. 20, §1, effective April 20, 1995.)

§262.203. Court must transfer suit

(a) On the motion of a party or the court's own motion, if applicable, the court that rendered the temporary order shall in accordance with procedures provided by Chapter 155:

(1) transfer the suit to the court of continuing, exclusive jurisdiction, if any;

(2) if grounds exist for mandatory transfer from the court of continuing, exclusive jurisdiction under Section 155.201, order transfer of the suit from that court; or

(3) if grounds exist for transfer based on improper venue, order transfer of the suit to the court having venue of the suit under Chapter 103.

(b) Notwithstanding Section 155.204, a motion to transfer relating to a suit filed under this chapter may be filed separately from the petition and is timely if filed while the case is pending.

(c) Notwithstanding Sections 6.407 and 103.002, a court exercising jurisdiction under this chapter is not required to transfer the suit to a court in which a parent has filed a suit for dissolution of marriage before a final order for the protection of the child has been rendered under Subchapter E, Chapter 263.

(Acts 1995, 74th Leg., ch. 20, §1, effective April 20, 1995. Amended by Acts 1997, 75th Leg., ch. 575, §22, effective September 1, 1997; Acts 1999, 76th Leg., ch. 1150, §22, effective September 1, 1999; Acts 1999, 76th Leg., ch. 1390, §41, effective September 1, 1999.)

§262.204. Temporary order is in effect until superseded by court with jurisdiction

(a) A temporary order rendered under this chapter is valid and enforceable until properly superseded by a court with jurisdiction to do so.

(b) A court to which the suit has been transferred may enforce by contempt or otherwise a temporary order properly issued under this chapter.

(Acts 1995, 74th Leg., ch. 20, §1, effective April 20, 1995.)

§262.205. Court may render temporary restraining order when child's not in custody of governmental entity

(a) In a suit requesting possession of a child after notice and hearing, the court may render a temporary restraining order as provided by Section 105.001. The suit shall be promptly set for hearing.

(b) After the hearing, the court may grant the request to remove the child from the parent, managing conservator, possessory conservator, guardian, caretaker, or custodian entitled to possession of the child if the court finds sufficient evidence to satisfy a person of ordinary prudence and caution that:

(1) reasonable efforts have been made to prevent or eliminate the need to remove the child from the child's home; and

(2) allowing the child to remain in the home would be contrary to the child's welfare.

(c) If the court orders removal of the child from the child's home, the court shall:

(1) issue an appropriate temporary order under Chapter 105; and

(2) inform each parent in open court that parental and custodial rights and duties may be subject to restriction or termination unless the parent is willing and able to provide a safe environment for the child.

(d) If citation by publication is required for a parent or alleged or probable father in an action under this chapter because the location of the person is unknown, the court may render a temporary order without regard to whether notice of the citation has been published.

(e) Unless it is not in the best interest of the child, the court shall place a child who has been removed under this section with:

(1) the child's noncustodial parent; or

(2) another relative of the child if placement with the noncustodial parent is inappropriate.

(f) If the court finds that the child requires protection from family violence by a member of the child's family or household, the court shall render a protective order for the child under Title 4.

(Acts 1999, 76th Leg., ch. 1150, §23, effective September 1, 1999; Acts 1999, 76th Leg., ch. 1390, §42, effective September 1, 1999.)

3. Special Procedures for Establishing Jurisdiction Over Abandoned Infants

§262.301. Definitions

In this chapter:

(1) "Designated emergency infant care provider" means:

(A) an emergency medical services provider;

(B) a hospital; or

(C) a child-placing agency licensed by the Department of Protective and Regulatory Services under Chapter 42, Human Resources Code, that:

(i) agrees to act as a designated emergency infant care provider under this subchapter; and

(ii) has on staff a person who is licensed as a registered nurse under Chapter 301, Occupations Code, or who provides emergency medical services under Chapter 773, Health and Safety Code, and who will examine and provide emergency medical services to a child taken into possession by the agency under this subchapter.

(2) "Emergency medical services provider" has the meaning assigned that term by Section 773.003, Health and Safety Code.

(Acts 2001, 77th Leg., ch. 809, §4, effective September 1, 2001.)

§262.302. Infant care provider may accept custody of certain abandoned children

(a) A designated emergency infant care provider shall, without a court order, take possession of a child who appears to be 60 days old or younger if the child is voluntarily delivered to the provider by the child's parent and the parent did not express an intent to return for the child.

(b) A designated emergency infant care provider who takes possession of a child under this section has no legal duty to detain or pursue the parent and may not do so unless the child appears to have been abused or neglected. The designated emergency infant care provider has no legal duty to ascertain the parent's identity and the parent may remain anonymous. However, the parent may be given a form for voluntary disclosure of the child's medical facts and history.

(c) A designated emergency infant care provider who takes possession of a child under this section shall perform any act necessary to protect the physical health or safety of the child. The designated emergency infant care provider is not liable for damages related to the provider's taking possession of, examining, or treating the child, except for damages related to the provider's negligence.

(Acts 2001, 77th Leg., ch. 809, §4, effective September 1, 2001.)

§262.303. Infant care provider shall notify Department of possession of abandoned child

(a) Not later than the close of the first business day after the date on which a designated emergency infant care provider takes possession of a child under Section 262. 302, the provider shall notify the Department of Protective and Regulatory Services that the provider has taken possession of the child.

(b) The department shall assume the care, control, and custody of the child immediately on receipt of notice under Subsection (a).

(Acts 2001, 77th Leg., ch. 809, §4, effective September 1, 2001.)

§262.304. Department shall file emergency petition after accepting possession of abandoned child

A child for whom the Department of Protective and Regulatory Services assumes care, control, and custody under Section 262.303 shall be treated as a child taken into possession without a court order, and the department shall take action as required by Section 262.105 with regard to the child.

(Acts 2001, 77th Leg., ch. 809, §4, effective September 1, 2001.)

§262.305. Department shall report abandoned child to law enforcement as missing child

(a) Immediately after assuming care, control, and custody of a child under Section 262.303, the Department of Protective and Regulatory Services shall report the child to appropriate state and local law enforcement agencies as a potential missing child.

(b) A law enforcement agency that receives a report under Subsection (a) shall investigate whether the child is reported as missing.

(Acts 2001, 77th Leg., ch. 809, §4, effective September 1, 2001.)

§262.306. Infant care provider must post notice that it accepts custody of abandoned children

Each designated emergency infant care provider shall post in a conspicuous location a notice stating that the provider is a designated emergency infant care provider location and will accept possession of a child in accordance with this subchapter.

(Acts 2001, 77th Leg., ch. 809, §4, effective September 1, 2001.)

§262.307. Department shall reimburse infant care provider for care of abandoned child

The department shall reimburse a designated emergency infant care provider that takes possession of a child under Section 262.302 for the cost to the provider of assuming the care, control, and custody of the child.

(Acts 2001, 77th Leg., ch. 809, §4, effective September 1, 2001.)

§262.308. Information related to the abandonment of children to an emergency infant care provider is confidential

(a) All identifying information, documentation, or other records regarding a person who voluntarily delivers a child to a designated emergency infant care provider under this subchapter is confidential and not subject to release to any individual or entity except as provided by Subsection (b).

(b) Any pleading or other document filed with a court under this subchapter is confidential, is not public information for purposes of Chapter 552, Government Code, and may not be released to a person other than to a party in a suit regarding the child, the party's attorney, or an attorney ad litem or guardian ad litem appointed in the suit.

(c) In a suit concerning a child for whom the Department of Family and Protective Services assumes care, control, and custody under this subchapter, the court shall close the hearing to the public unless the court finds that the interests of the child or the public would be better served by opening the hearing to the public.

(d) Unless the disclosure, receipt, or use is permitted by this section, a person commits an offense if the person knowingly discloses, receives, uses, or permits the use of information derived from records or files described by this section or knowingly discloses identifying information concerning a person who voluntarily delivers a child to a designated emergency infant care provider. An offense under this subsection is a Class B misdemeanor.

(Acts 2005, 79th Leg., ch. 620, §1, effective September 1, 2005.)

§262.309. No requirement to search for relatives

The Department of Family and Protective Services is not required to conduct a search for the relatives of a child for whom the department assumes care, control, and custody under this subchapter.

(Acts 2005, 79th Leg., ch. 620, §1, effective September 1, 2005.)

G. DISPOSITIONS

1. Generally

Texas Family Code

§263.001. Definitions

(a) In this chapter:

(1) "Department" means the Department of Family and Protective Services.

(2) "Child's home" means the place of residence of at least one of the child's parents.

(3) "Household" means a unit composed of persons living together in the same dwelling, without regard to whether they are related to each other.

(4) "Substitute care" means the placement of a child who is in the conservatorship of the department or an authorized agency in care outside the child's home. The term includes foster care, institutional care, adoption, or placement with a relative of the child.

(b) In the preparation and review of a service plan under this chapter, a reference to the parents of the child includes both parents of the child unless the child has only one parent or unless, after due diligence by the department in attempting to locate a parent, only one parent is located, in which case the reference is to the remaining parent.

(Acts 1995, 74th Leg., ch. 20, §1, effective April 20, 1995. Amended by Acts 1995, 74th Leg., ch. 751, §108, effective September 1, 1995; Acts 2005, 79th Leg., ch. 268, §1.36, effective September 1, 2005.)

§263.002. Court shall review placements

In a suit affecting the parent-child relationship in which the department or an authorized agency has been appointed by the court or designated in an affidavit of relinquishment of parental rights as the temporary or permanent managing conservator of a child, the court shall hold a hearing to review the conservatorship appointment and substitute care.

(Acts 1995, 74th Leg., ch. 20, §1, effective April 20, 1995. Amended by Acts 1995, 74th Leg., ch. 751, §109, effective September 1, 1995.)

§263.005. Department shall designate personnel to enforce family service plans

The department shall designate existing department personnel to ensure that the parties to a family service plan comply with the plan.

(Acts 1995, 74th Leg., ch. 943, §5, effective September 1, 1995.)

§263.006. Court shall warn parents of risk of termination of parental rights

At the status hearing under Subchapter C1 and at each permanency hearing under Subchapter D2 held after the court has rendered a temporary order appointing the department as temporary managing conservator, the court shall inform each parent in open court that parental and custodial rights and duties may be subject to restriction or to termination unless the parent or parents are willing and able to provide the child with a safe environment.

(Acts 1997, 75th Leg., ch. 600, §6, effective January 1, 1998; Acts 1997, 75th Leg., ch. 603, §2, effective January 1, 1998; Acts 1997, 75th Leg., ch. 1022, §80, effective January 1, 1998.)

2. Service Plan

263.101. Department must file service plan within 45 days

Not later than the 45th day after the date the court renders a temporary order appointing the department as temporary managing conservator of a child under Chapter 262, the department or other agency appointed as the managing conservator of a child shall file a service plan.

(Acts 1995, 74th Leg., ch. 20, §1, effective April 20, 1995. Amended by Acts 1999, 76th Leg., ch. 1150, §24, effective September 1, 1999; Acts 1999, 76th Leg., ch. 1390, §43, effective September 1, 1999.)

§263.1015. Department is not required to file service plan for abandoned child

A service plan is not required under this subchapter in a suit brought by the department for the termination of the parent-child relationship for a child who has been abandoned without identification and whose identity cannot be determined.

(Acts 1997, 75th Leg., ch. 600, §7, effective January 1, 1998.)

§263.102. Service plan must contain certain information

(a) The service plan must:

(1) be specific;

(2) be in writing in a language that the parents understand, or made otherwise available;

(3) be prepared by the department or other agency in conference with the child's parents;

(4) state appropriate deadlines;

(5) state whether the goal of the plan is:

(A) return of the child to the child's parents;

(B) termination of parental rights and placement of the child for adoption; or

(C) because of the child's special needs or exceptional circumstances, continuation of the child's care out of the child's home;

(6) state steps that are necessary to:

(A) return the child to the child's home if the placement is in foster care;

(B) enable the child to remain in the child's home with the assistance of a service plan if the placement is in the home under the department's or other agency's supervision; or

(C) otherwise provide a permanent safe placement for the child;

(7) state the actions and responsibilities that are necessary for the child's parents to take to achieve the plan goal during the period of the service plan and the assistance to be provided to the parents by the department or other authorized agency toward meeting that goal;

(8) state any specific skills or knowledge that the child's parents must acquire or learn, as well as any behavioral changes the parents must exhibit, to achieve the plan goal;

(9) state the actions and responsibilities that are necessary for the child's parents to take to ensure that the child attends school and maintains or improves the child's academic compliance;

(10) state the name of the person with the department or other agency whom the child's parents may contact for information relating to the child if other than the person preparing the plan; and

(11) prescribe any other term or condition that the department or other agency determines to be necessary to the service plan's success.

(b) The service plan shall include the following statement:

TO THE PARENT: THIS IS A VERY IMPORTANT DOCUMENT. ITS PURPOSE IS TO HELP YOU PROVIDE YOUR CHILD WITH A SAFE ENVIRONMENT WITHIN THE REASONABLE PERIOD SPECIFIED IN THE PLAN. IF YOU ARE UNWILLING OR UNABLE TO PROVIDE YOUR CHILD WITH A SAFE ENVIRONMENT, YOUR PARENTAL AND CUSTODIAL DUTIES AND RIGHTS MAY BE RESTRICTED OR TERMINATED OR YOUR CHILD MAY NOT BE RETURNED TO YOU. THERE WILL BE A COURT HEARING AT WHICH A JUDGE WILL REVIEW THIS SERVICE PLAN.

(c) If both parents are available but do not live in the same household and do not agree to cooperate with one another in the development of a service plan for the child, the department in preparing the service plan may provide for the care of the child in the home of either parent or the homes of both parents as the best interest of the child requires.

(d) The department or other authorized entity must write the service plan in a manner that is clear and understandable to the parent in order to facilitate the parent's ability to follow the requirements of the service plan.

(e) Regardless of whether the goal stated in a child's service plan as required under Subsection (a)(5) is to return the child to the child's parents or to terminate parental rights and place the child for adoption, the department shall concurrently provide to the child and the child's family, as applicable:

(1) time-limited family reunification services as defined by 42 U.S.C. Section 629a for a period not to exceed the period within which the court must render a final order in or dismiss the suit affecting the parent-child relationship with respect to the child as provided by Subchapter E; and

(2) adoption promotion and support services as defined by 42 U.S.C. Section 629a.

(Acts 1995, 74th Leg., ch. 20, §1, effective April 20, 1995. Amended by Acts 2005, 79th Leg., ch. 268, §1.38(a), effective September 1, 2005.)

§263.103. Procedure for execution of service plan

(a) Before the service plan is signed, the child's parents and the representative of the department or other agency shall discuss each term and condition of the plan.

(b) The child's parents and the person preparing the service plan shall sign the plan, and the department shall give each parent a copy of the service plan.

(c) If the department or other authorized agency determines that the child's parents are unable or unwilling to sign the service plan, the department may file the plan without the parents' signatures.

(d) The plan takes effect when:

(1) the child's parents and the appropriate representative of the department or other authorized agency sign the plan; or

(2) the department or other authorized agency files the plan without the parents' signatures.

(e) The service plan is in effect until amended by the court.

(Acts 1995, 74th Leg., ch. 20, §1, effective April 20, 1995.)

§263.104. Service plan may be amended

(a) The service plan may be amended at any time.

(b) The amended service plan supersedes the previously filed service plan and takes effect when:

(1) the child's parents and the appropriate representative of the department or other authorized agency sign the plan; or

(2) the department or other authorized agency determines that the child's parents are unable or unwilling to sign the amended plan and files it without the parents' signatures.

(c) The amended service plan remains in effect until amended by the court.

(Acts 1995, 74th Leg., ch. 20, §1, effective April 20, 1995.)

§263.105. Service plan shall be filed and court shall review it

(a) The service plan currently in effect shall be filed with the court.

(b) The court shall review the plan at the next required hearing under this chapter after the plan is filed.

(Acts 1995, 74th Leg., ch. 20, §1, effective April 20, 1995. Amended by Acts 1999, 76th Leg., ch. 1150, §25, effective September 1, 1999; Acts 1999, 76th Leg., ch. 1390, §44, effective September 1, 1999.)

§263.106. Court may render appropriate orders to implement service plan

The court may render appropriate orders to implement or require compliance with an original or amended service plan.

(Acts 1995, 74th Leg., ch. 20, §1, effective April 20, 1995.)

3. Status Hearing

§263.201. Court shall hold hearing to review child's status 60 days after temporary order

(a) Not later than the 60th day after the date the court renders a temporary order appointing the department as temporary managing conservator of a child, the court shall hold a status hearing to review the child's status and the service plan developed for the child.

(b) A status hearing is not required if the court holds an initial permanency hearing under Section 262.2015 before the date a status hearing is required by this section.

(c) The court shall require each parent, alleged father, or relative of the child before the court to submit the proposed child placement resources form provided under Section 261.307 at the status hearing, if the form has not previously been submitted.

(Acts 1995, 74th Leg., ch. 20, §1, effective April 20, 1995. Amended by Acts 1997, 75th Leg., ch. 600, §8, effective January 1, 1998; Acts 1997, 75th Leg., ch. 603, §3, effective January 1, 1998; Acts 1997, 75th Leg., ch. 1022, §81, effective January 1, 1998; Acts 1999, 76th Leg., ch. 1150, §26, effective September 1, 1999; Acts 1999, 76th Leg., ch. 1390, §45, effective September 1, 1999; Acts 2005, 79th Leg., ch. 268, §1.37(a), effective September 1, 2005.)

§263.202. Status hearing: requisite findings, limited to service plan, advice to parties

(a) If all parties entitled to citation and notice under this chapter were not served, the court shall make findings as to whether:

(1) the department or other agency has exercised due diligence to locate all necessary persons; and

(2) each custodial parent, alleged father, or relative of the child before the court has furnished to the department all available information necessary to locate another absent parent, alleged father, or relative of the child through exercise of due diligence.

(b) Except as provided by Subsection (e), a status hearing shall be limited to matters related to the contents and execution of the service plan filed with the court. The court shall review the service plan that the department or other agency filed under this chapter for reasonableness, accuracy, and compliance with requirements of court orders and make findings as to whether:

(1) a plan that has the goal of returning the child to the child's parents adequately ensures that reasonable efforts are made to enable the child's parents to provide a safe environment for the child; and

(2) the child's parents have reviewed and understand the service plan and have been advised that unless the parents are willing and able to provide the child with a safe environment, even with the assistance of a service plan, within the reasonable period of time specified in the plan, the parents' parental and custodial duties and rights may be subject to restriction or to termination under this code or the child may not be returned to the parents.

(c) The court shall advise the parties that progress under the service plan will be reviewed at all subsequent hearings, including a review of whether the parties have acquired or learned any specific skills or knowledge stated in the service plan.

(d) If a service plan with respect to a parent has not been filed with the court, the court shall consider whether to waive the service plan under Section 262.2015.

(e) At the status hearing, the court shall make a finding as to whether the court has identified the individual who has the right to consent for the child under Section 266.003.

(Acts 1995, 74th Leg., ch. 20, §1, effective April 20, 1995. Amended by Acts 1995, 74th Leg., ch. 751, §111, effective September 1, 1995; by Acts 1999, 76th Leg., ch. 1150, §27, effective September 1, 1999; Acts 1999, 76th Leg., ch. 1390, §46, effective September 1, 1999; Acts 2001, 77th Leg., ch. 306, §2, effective September 1, 2001; Acts 2005, 79th Leg., ch. 268, §§1.38(b), 1.39, effective September 1, 2005.)

4. Permanency Hearing

§263.301. Persons entitled to notice of permanency hearing

(a) Notice of a permanency hearing shall be given as provided by Rule 21a, Texas Rules of Civil Procedure, to all persons entitled to notice of the hearing.

(b) The following persons are entitled to at least 10 days' notice of a permanency hearing and are entitled to present evidence and be heard at the hearing:

(1) the department;

(2) the foster parent, preadoptive parent, relative of the child providing care, or director of the group home or institution where the child is residing;

(3) each parent of the child;

(4) the managing conservator or guardian of the child;

(5) an attorney ad litem appointed for the child under Chapter 107;

(6) a volunteer advocate appointed for the child under Chapter 107; and

(7) any other person or agency named by the court to have an interest in the child's welfare.

(c) If a person entitled to notice under Chapter 102 or this section has not been served, the court shall review the department's or other agency's efforts at attempting to locate all necessary persons and requesting service of citation and the assistance of a parent in providing information necessary to locate an absent parent.

(Acts 1995, 74th Leg., ch. 20, §1, effective April 20, 1995. Amended by Acts 1997, 75th Leg., ch. 600, §10, effective January 1, 1998; Acts 1997, 75th Leg., ch. 603, §5, effective January 1, 1998; Acts 1997, 75th Leg., ch. 1022, §83, effective January 1, 1998; Acts 2001, 77th Leg., ch. 849, §6, effective September 1, 2001.)

§263.302. Child shall attend permanency hearing unless excused

The child shall attend each permanency hearing unless the court specifically excuses the child's attendance. Failure by the child to attend a hearing does not affect the validity of an order rendered at the hearing.

(Acts 1995, 74th Leg., ch. 20, §1, effective April 20, 1995. Amended by Acts 1997, 75th Leg., ch. 600, §11, effective January 1, 1998; Acts 1997, 75th Leg., ch. 603, §6, effective January 1, 1998; Acts 1997, 75th Leg., ch. 1022, §84, effective January 1, 1998.)

§263.3025. Department shall prepare permanency plan for each child; relative preference

(a) The department shall prepare a permanency plan for a child for whom the department has been appointed temporary managing conservator. The department shall give a copy of the plan to each person entitled to notice under Section 263.301(b) not later than the 10th day before the date of the child's first permanency hearing.

(b) In addition to the requirements of the department rules governing permanency planning, the permanency plan must contain the information required to be included in a permanency progress report under Section 263.303.

(c) The department shall modify the permanency plan for a child as required by the circumstances and needs of the child.

(d) Repealed by Acts 2005, 79th Leg., 620, §3.

(Acts 1997, 75th Leg., ch. 600, §12, effective January 1, 1998; Acts 1997, 75th Leg., ch. 603, §7, effective January 1, 1998; Acts 1997, 75th Leg., ch. 1022, §85, effective January 1, 1998. Amended by Acts 2001, 77th Leg., ch. 809, §5, effective September 1, 2001; Acts 2005, 79th Leg., ch. 620, §3, effective September 1, 2005.)

§263.303. Department shall file permanency progress report at least 10 days before each hearing

(a) Not later than the 10th day before the date set for each permanency hearing other than the first permanency hearing, the department or other authorized agency shall file with the court and provide to each party, the child's attorney ad litem, the child's guardian ad litem, and the child's volunteer advocate a permanency progress report unless the court orders a different period for providing the report.

(b) The permanency progress report must:

(1) recommend that the suit be dismissed; or

(2) recommend that the suit continue, and:

(A) identify the date for dismissal of the suit under this chapter;

(B) provide:

(i) the name of any person entitled to notice under Chapter 102 who has not been served;

(ii) a description of the efforts by the department or another agency to locate and request service of citation; and

(iii) a description of each parent's assistance in providing information necessary to locate an unserved party;

(C) evaluate the parties' compliance with temporary orders and with the service plan;

(D) evaluate whether the child's placement in substitute care meets the child's needs and recommend other plans or services to meet the child's special needs or circumstances;

(E) describe the permanency plan for the child and recommend actions necessary to ensure that a final order consistent with that permanency plan is rendered before the date for dismissal of the suit under this chapter; and

(F) with respect to a child 16 years of age or older, identify the services needed to assist the child in the transition to adult life.

(c) A parent whose parental rights are the subject of a suit affecting the parent-child relationship, the attorney for that parent, or the child's attorney ad litem or guardian ad litem may file a response to the department's or other agency's report filed under Subsection (b). A response must be filed not later than the third day before the date of the hearing.

(Acts 1995, 74th Leg., ch. 20, §1, effective April 20, 1995. Amended by Acts 1995, 74th Leg., ch. 751, §112, effective September 1, 1995; by Acts 1997, 75th Leg., ch. 600, §13, effective January 1, 1998; Acts 1997, 75th Leg., ch. 603, §8, effective January 1, 1998; Acts 1997, 75th Leg., ch. 1022, §86, effective January 1, 1998; Acts 2005, 79th Leg., ch. 172, §24, effective September 1, 2005.)

§263.304. Initial permanency hearing: 180 days after temporary order

(a) Not later than the 180th day after the date the court renders a temporary order appointing the department as temporary managing conservator of a child, the court shall hold a permanency hearing to review the status of, and permanency plan for, the child to ensure that a final order consistent with that permanency plan is rendered before the date for dismissal of the suit under this chapter.

(b) The court shall set a final hearing under this chapter on a date that allows the court to render a final order before the date for dismissal of the suit under this chapter. Any party to the suit or an attorney ad litem for the child may seek a writ of mandamus to compel the court to comply with the duties imposed by this subsection.

(Acts 1995, 74th Leg., ch. 20, §1, effective April 20, 1995. Amended by Acts 1995, 74th Leg., ch. 751, §113, effective September 1, 1995; by Acts 1997, 75th Leg., ch. 600, §14, effective January 1, 1998; Acts 1997, 75th Leg., ch. 603, §9,

effective January 1, 1998; Acts 1997, 75th Leg., ch. 1022, §87, effective January 1, 1998; Acts 2001, 77th Leg., ch. 1090, §7, effective September 1, 2001.)

§263.305. Subsequent permanency hearings: 120 days after last permanency hearing

A subsequent permanency hearing before entry of a final order shall be held not later than the 120th day after the date of the last permanency hearing in the suit. For good cause shown or on the court's own motion, the court may order more frequent hearings.

(Acts 1995, 74th Leg., ch. 20, §1, effective April 20, 1995. Amended by Acts 1997, 75th Leg., ch. 600, §15, effective January 1, 1998; Acts 1997, 75th Leg., ch. 603, §10, effective January 1, 1998; Acts 1997, 75th Leg., ch. 1022, §88, effective January 1, 1998.)

§263.306. Procedure for permanency hearings

(a) At each permanency hearing the court shall:

(1) identify all persons or parties present at the hearing or those given notice but failing to appear;

(2) review the efforts of the department or another agency in:

(A) attempting to locate all necessary persons;

(B) requesting service of citation; and

(C) obtaining the assistance of a parent in providing information necessary to locate an absent parent, alleged father, or relative of the child;

(3) review the efforts of each custodial parent, alleged father, or relative of the child before the court in providing information necessary to locate another absent parent, alleged father, or relative of the child;

(4) return the child to the parent or parents if the child's parent or parents are willing and able to provide the child with a safe environment and the return of the child is in the child's best interest;

(5) place the child with a person or entity, other than a parent, entitled to service under Chapter 102 if the person or entity is willing and able to provide the child with a safe environment and the placement of the child is in the child's best interest;

(6) evaluate the department's efforts to identify relatives who could provide the child with a safe environment, if the child is not returned to a parent or another person or entity entitled to service under Chapter 102;

(7) evaluate the parties' compliance with temporary orders and the service plan;

(8) determine whether:

(A) the child continues to need substitute care;

(B) the child's current placement is appropriate for meeting the child's needs, including with respect to a child who has been placed outside of the state, whether that placement continues to be in the best interest of the child; and

(C) other plans or services are needed to meet the child's special needs or circumstances;

(9) if the child is placed in institutional care, determine whether efforts have been made to ensure placement of the child in the least restrictive environment consistent with the best interest and special needs of the child;

(10) if the child is 16 years of age or older, order services that are needed to assist the child in making the transition from substitute care to independent living if the services are available in the community;

(11) determine plans, services, and further temporary orders necessary to ensure that a final order is rendered before the date for dismissal of the suit under this chapter; and

(12) determine the date for dismissal of the suit under this chapter and give notice in open court to all parties of:

(A) the dismissal date;

(B) the date of the next permanency hearing; and

(C) the date the suit is set for trial.

(b) The court shall also review the service plan, permanency report, and other information submitted at the hearing to:

(1) determine:

(A) the safety of the child;

(B) the continuing necessity and appropriateness of the placement;

(C) the extent of compliance with the case plan; and

(D) the extent of progress that has been made toward alleviating or mitigating the causes necessitating the placement of the child in foster care; and

(E)whether the department has made reasonable efforts to finalize the permanency plan that is in effect for the child; and

(2) project a likely date by which the child may be returned to and safely maintained in the child's home, placed for adoption, or placed in permanent managing conservatorship.

(Acts 1995, 74th Leg., ch. 20, §1, effective April 20, 1995. Amended by Acts 1995, 74th Leg., ch. 751, §114, effective September 1, 1995; by Acts 1997, 75th Leg., ch. 600, §16, effective January 1, 1998; Acts 1997, 75th Leg., ch. 603, §11, effective January 1, 1998; Acts 1997, 75th Leg., ch. 1022, §89, effective January 1, 1998; Acts 1999, 76th Leg., ch. 1390, §47, effective September 1, 1999; Acts 2001, 77th Leg., ch. 306, §3, effective September 1, 2001; Acts 2001, 77th Leg., ch. 849, §7, effective September 1, 2001.)

§263.307. Factors in determining child's best interest for placement purposes

(a) In considering the factors established by this section, the prompt and permanent placement of the child in a safe environment is presumed to be in the child's best interest.

(b) The following factors should be considered by the court, the department, and other authorized agencies in determining whether the child's parents are willing and able to provide the child with a safe environment:

(1) the child's age and physical and mental vulnerabilities;

(2) the frequency and nature of out-of-home placements;

(3) the magnitude, frequency, and circumstances of the harm to the child;

(4) whether the child has been the victim of repeated harm after the initial report and intervention by the department or other agency;

(5) whether the child is fearful of living in or returning to the child's home;

(6) the results of psychiatric, psychological, or developmental evaluations of the child, the child's parents, other family members, or others who have access to the child's home;

(7) whether there is a history of abusive or assaultive conduct by the child's family or others who have access to the child's home;

(8) whether there is a history of substance abuse by the child's family or others who have access to the child's home;

(9) whether the perpetrator of the harm to the child is identified;

(10) the willingness and ability of the child's family to seek out, accept, and complete counseling services and to cooperate with and facilitate an appropriate agency's close supervision;

(11) the willingness and ability of the child's family to effect positive environmental and personal changes within a reasonable period of time;

(12) whether the child's family demonstrates adequate parenting skills, including providing the child and other children under the family's care with:

(A) minimally adequate health and nutritional care;

(B) care, nurturance, and appropriate discipline consistent with the child's physical and psychological development;

(C) guidance and supervision consistent with the child's safety;

(D) a safe physical home environment;

(E) protection from repeated exposure to violence even though the violence may not be directed at the child; and

(F) an understanding of the child's needs and capabilities; and

(13) whether an adequate social support system consisting of an extended family and friends is available to the child.

(c) In the case of a child 16 years of age or older, the following guidelines should be considered by the court in determining whether to adopt the permanency plan submitted by the department:

(1) whether the permanency plan submitted to the court includes the services planned for the child to make the transition from foster care to independent living; and

(2) whether this transition is in the best interest of the child.

(Acts 1995, 74th Leg., ch. 20, §1, effective April 20, 1995.)

---

5. Final Order

§263.401. Court shall dismiss suit after one year absent final order or extension

(a) Unless the court has rendered a final order or granted an extension under Subsection (b), on the first Monday after the first anniversary of the date the court rendered a temporary order appointing the department as temporary managing conservator, the court shall dismiss the suit affecting the parent-child relationship filed by the department that requests termination of the parent-child relationship or requests that the department be named conservator of the child.

(b) The court may not retain the suit on the court's docket after the time described by Subsection (a) unless the court finds that extraordinary circumstances necessitate the child remaining in the temporary managing conservatorship of the department and that continuing the appointment of the department as temporary managing conservator is in the best interest of the child. If the court makes those findings, the court may retain the suit on the court's docket for a period not to exceed 180 days after the time described by Subsection (a). If the court retains the suit on the court's docket, the court shall render an order in which the court:

(1) schedules the new date for dismissal of the suit not later than the 180th day after the time described by Subsection (a);

(2) makes further temporary orders for the safety and welfare of the child as necessary to avoid further delay in resolving the suit; and

(3) sets a final hearing on a date that allows the court to render a final order before the required date for dismissal of the suit under this subsection.

(c) If the court grants an extension but does not render a final order or dismiss the suit on or before the required date for dismissal under Subsection (b), the court shall dismiss the suit. The court may not grant an additional extension that extends the suit beyond the required date for dismissal under Subsection (b).

(d) For purposes of this section, a final order is an order that:

(1) requires that a child be returned to the child's parent;

(2) names a relative of the child or another person as the child's managing conservator;

(3) without terminating the parent-child relationship, appoints the department as the managing conservator of the child; or

(4) terminates the parent-child relationship and appoints a relative of the child, another suitable person, or the department as managing conservator of the child.

(Acts 1997, 75th Leg., ch. 600, §17, effective September 1, 1997; Acts 1997, 75th Leg., ch. 603, §12, effective January 1, 1998; Acts 1997, 75th Leg., ch. 1022, §90, effective January 1, 1998. Amended by Acts 2001, 77th Leg., ch. 1090, §8, effective September 1, 2001; Acts 2005, 79th Leg., ch. 268, §1.40, effective September 1, 2005.)

§263.402. Parties may not agree to extend deadlines

(a) The parties to a suit under this chapter may not extend the deadlines set by the court under this subchapter by agreement or otherwise.

(b) A party to a suit under this chapter who fails to make a timely motion to dismiss the suit or to make a motion requesting the court to render a final order before the deadline for dismissal under this subchapter waives the right to object to the court's failure to dismiss the suit. A motion to dismiss under this subsection is timely if the motion is made before the department has introduced all of the department's evidence, other than rebuttal evidence, at the trial on the merits.

(Acts 1997, 75th Leg., ch. 600, §17, effective September 1, 1997; Acts 1997, 75th Leg., ch. 603, §12, effective January 1, 1997; Acts 1997, 75th Leg., ch. 1022, §90, effective January 1, 1997. Amended by Acts 1999, 76th Leg., ch. 1390, §48, effective September 1, 1999; Acts 2001, 77th Leg., ch. 1090, §9, effective September 1, 2001.)

§263.403. Court may retain jurisdiction to monitor return of child to parent

(a) Notwithstanding Section 263.401, the court may retain jurisdiction and not dismiss the suit or render a final order as required by that section if the court renders a temporary order that:

(1) finds that retaining jurisdiction under this section is in the best interest of the child;

(2) orders the department to return the child to the child's parent;

(3) orders the department to continue to serve as temporary managing conservator of the child; and

(4) orders the department to monitor the child's placement to ensure that the child is in a safe environment.

(b) If the court renders an order under this section, the court shall:

(1) include in the order specific findings regarding the grounds for the order; and

(2) schedule a new date, not later than the 180th day after the date the temporary order is rendered, for dismissal of the suit.

(c) If a child placed with a parent under this section must be moved from that home by the department before the dismissal of the suit or the rendering of a final order, the court shall, at the time of the move, schedule a new date for dismissal of the suit. The new dismissal date may not be later than the original dismissal date established under Section 263.401 or the 180th day after the date the child is moved under this subsection, whichever date is later.

(d) If the court renders an order under this section, the court must include in the order specific findings regarding the grounds for the order.

(Acts 1997, 75th Leg., ch. 600, §17, effective September 1, 1997; Acts 1997, 75th Leg., ch. 603, §12, effective January 1, 1998; Acts 1997, 75th Leg., ch. 1022, §90, effective January 1, 1998. Renumbered from §263.402 by Acts 2001, 77th Leg., ch. 1090, §9, effective September 1, 2001.)

§263.404. Court may render final order appointing Department as managing conservator without terminating parental rights

(a) The court may render a final order appointing the department as managing conservator of the child without terminating the rights of the parent of the child if the court finds that:

(1) appointment of a parent as managing conservator would not be in the best interest of the child because the appointment would significantly impair the child's physical health or emotional development; and

(2) it would not be in the best interest of the child to appoint a relative of the child or another person as managing conservator.

(b) In determining whether the department should be appointed as managing conservator of the child without terminating the rights of a parent of the child, the court shall take the following factors into consideration:

(1) that the child will reach 18 years of age in not less than three years;

(2) that the child is 12 years of age or older and has expressed a strong desire against termination or being adopted;

(3) that the child has special medical or behavioral needs that make adoption of the child unlikely; and

(4) the needs and desires of the child.

(Acts 1997, 75th Leg., ch. 600, §17, effective September 1, 1997. Renumbered from §263.403 by Acts 2001, 77th Leg., ch. 1090, §9, effective September 1, 2001.)

§263.405. Rules for appeal of final order

(a) An appeal of a final order rendered under this subchapter is governed by the rules of the supreme court for accelerated appeals in civil cases and the procedures provided by this section. The appellate court shall render its final order or judgment with the least possible delay.

(b) Not later than the 15th day after the date a final order is signed by the trial judge, a party intending to appeal the order must file with the trial court a statement of the point or points on which the party intends to appeal. The statement may be combined with a motion for a new trial.

(c) A motion for a new trial, a request for findings of fact and conclusions of law, or any other post-trial motion in the trial court does not extend the deadline for filing a notice of appeal under Rule 26.1(b), Texas Rules of Appellate Procedure, or the deadline for filing an affidavit of indigence under Rule 20, Texas Rules of Appellate Procedure.

(d) The trial court shall hold a hearing not later than the 30th day after the date the final order is signed to determine whether:

(1) a new trial should be granted;

(2) a party's claim of indigence, if any, should be sustained; and

(3) the appeal is frivolous as provided by Section 13.003(b), Civil Practice and Remedies Code.

(e) If a party claims indigency and requests the appointment of an attorney, the court shall require the person to file an affidavit of indigency and shall hear evidence to determine the issue of indigency. If the court does not render a written order denying the claim of indigence or requiring the person to pay partial costs before the 36th day after the date the final order being appealed is signed, the court shall consider the person to be indigent and shall appoint counsel to represent the person.

(f) The appellate record must be filed in the appellate court not later than the 60th day after the date the final order is signed by the trial judge, unless the trial court, after a hearing, grants a new trial or denies a request for a trial court record at no cost.

(g) The appellant may appeal the court's order denying the appellant's claim of indigence or the court's finding that the appeal is frivolous by filing with the appellate court the reporter's record and clerk's record of the hearing held under this section, both of which shall be provided without advance payment, not later than the 10th day after the date the court makes the decision. The appellate court shall review the records and may require the parties to file appellate briefs on the issues presented, but may not hear oral argument on the issues. The appellate court shall render appropriate orders after reviewing the records and appellate briefs, if any.

(h) Except on a showing of good cause, the appellate court may not extend the time for filing a record or appellate brief.

(i) The appellate court may not consider any issue that was not specifically presented to the trial court in a timely filed statement of the points on which the party intends to appeal or in a statement combined with a motion for new trial. For purposes of this subsection, a claim that a judicial decision is contrary to the evidence or that the evidence is factually or legally insufficient is not sufficiently specific to preserve an issue for appeal.

(Acts 2001, 77th Leg., ch. 1090, §9, effective September 1, 2001. Amended by Acts 2005, 79th Leg., ch. 176, §1, effective September 1, 2005.)

§263.407. Rebuttable presumption of consent to terminate parental rights if parent abandons child

(a) There is a rebuttable presumption that a parent who delivers a child to a designated emergency infant care provider in accordance with Subchapter D, Chapter 262:

(1) is the child's biological parent; and

(2) intends to relinquish parental rights and consents to the termination of parental rights with regard to the child.

(a-1) A party that seeks to rebut a presumption in Subsection (a) may do so at any time before the parent-child relationship is terminated with regard to the child.

(b) If a person claims to be the parent of a child taken into possession under Subchapter D, Chapter 262, before the court renders a final order terminating the parental rights of the child's parents, the court shall order genetic testing for parentage determination unless parentage has previously been established. The court shall hold the petition for termination of the parent-child relationship in abeyance for a period not to exceed 60 days pending the results of the genetic testing.

(c) Before filing a petition to terminate the parental rights with regard to a child taken into the department's custody under Section 262.303, the department must:

(1) verify with the National Crime Information Center and state and local law enforcement agencies that the child is not a missing child; and

(2) obtain a certificate of the search of the paternity registry under Subchapter E, Chapter 160, not earlier than the date the department estimates to be the 30th day after the child's date of birth.

(Acts 2001 77th Leg., ch. 809, §6, effective September 1, 2001. Renumbered from V.T.C.A., Family Code §263.405 by Acts 2003, 78th Leg., ch. 1275, §2(54), effective September 1, 2003. Amended by Acts 2005, 79th Leg., ch. 620, §2, effective September 1, 2005.)

§263.406. Information system to track compliance

The Office of Court Administration of the Texas Judicial System shall consult with the courts presiding over cases brought by the department for the protection of children to develop an information system to track compliance with the requirements of this subchapter for the timely disposition of those cases.

(Renumbered from §263.404 by Acts 2001, 77th Leg., ch. 1090, §9, effective September 1, 2001.)

6. Placement Review Hearings

§263.501. Court shall conduct bi-annual placement reviews after final order

(a) If the department has been named as a child's managing conservator in a final order that does not include termination of parental rights, the court shall conduct a placement review hearing at least once every six months until the child becomes an adult.

(b) If the department has been named as a child's managing conservator in a final order that terminates a parent's parental rights, the court shall conduct a placement review hearing at least once every six months until the date the child is adopted or the child becomes an adult.

(c) Notice of a placement review hearing shall be given as provided by Rule 21a, Texas Rules of Civil Procedure, to each person entitled to notice of the hearing.

(d) The following are entitled to not less than 10 days' notice of a placement review hearing:

(1) the department;

(2) the foster parent, preadoptive parent, relative of the child providing care, or director of the group home or institution in which the child is residing;

(3) each parent of the child;

(4) each possessory conservator or guardian of the child;

(5) the child's attorney ad litem and volunteer advocate, if the appointments were not dismissed in the final order; and

(6) any other person or agency named by the court as having an interest in the child's welfare.

(e) The court may dispense with the requirement that the child attend a placement review hearing.

(Acts 1997, 75th Leg., ch. 600, §17, effective September 1, 1997; Acts 1997, 75th Leg., ch. 603, §12, effective January 1, 1998; Acts 1997, 75th Leg., ch. 1022, §90, effective January 1, 1997. Amended by Acts 2001, 77th Leg., ch. 849, §8, effective September 1, 2001.)

§263.502. Department shall file placement review report before placement review hearing

(a) Not later than the 10th day before the date set for a placement review hearing, the department or other authorized agency shall file a placement review report with the court and provide a copy to each person entitled to notice under Section 263.501(d).

(b) For good cause shown, the court may order a different time for filing the placement review report or may order that a report is not required for a specific hearing.

(c) The placement review report must:

(1) evaluate whether the child's current placement is appropriate for meeting the child's needs;

(2) evaluate whether efforts have been made to ensure placement of the child in the least restrictive environment consistent with the best interest and special needs of the child if the child is placed in institutional care;

(3) contain a discharge plan for a child who is at least 16 years of age that identifies the services and specific tasks that are needed to assist the child in making the transition from substitute care to adult living and describes the services that are available through the Preparation for Adult Living Program operated by the department;

(4) evaluate whether the child's current educational placement is appropriate for meeting the child's academic needs;

(5) identify other plans or services that are needed to meet the child's special needs or circumstances; and

(6) describe the efforts of the department or authorized agency to place the child for adoption if parental rights to the child have been terminated and the child is eligible for adoption, including efforts to provide adoption promotion and support services as defined by 42 U.S.C. Section 629a and other efforts consistent with the federal Adoption and Safe Families Act of 1997 (Pub. L. No. 105-89).

(Acts 1997, 75th Leg., ch. 600, §17, effective September 1, 1997; Acts 1997, 75th Leg., ch. 603, §12, effective January 1, 1998; Acts 1997, 75th Leg., ch. 1022, §90, effective January 1, 1998. Amended by Acts 2005, 79th Leg., ch. 268, §1.41(a), effective September 1, 2005.)

§263.503. Procedure for placement review hearings

At each placement review hearing, the court shall determine whether:

(1) the child's current placement is necessary, safe, and appropriate for meeting the child's needs, including with respect to a child placed outside of the state, whether the placement continues to be appropriate and in the best interest of the child;

(2) efforts have been made to ensure placement of the child in the least restrictive environment consistent with the best interest and special needs of the child if the child is placed in institutional care;

(3) the services that are needed to assist a child who is at least 16 years of age in making the transition from substitute care to independent living are available in the community;

(4) other plans or services are needed to meet the child's special needs or circumstances;

(5) the department or authorized agency has exercised due diligence in attempting to place the child for adoption if parental rights to the child have been terminated and the child is eligible for adoption; and

(6) the department or authorized agency has made reasonable efforts to finalize the permanency plan that is in effect for the child.

(Acts 1997, 75th Leg., ch. 600, §17, effective September 1, 1997; Acts 1997, 75th Leg., ch. 603, §12, effective January 1, 1998; Acts 1997, 75th Leg., ch. 1022, §90, effective January 1, 1998. Amended by Acts 2001, 77th Leg., ch. 849, §9, effective September 1, 2001.)

7. Foster Care

Texas Family Code

§102.003. General standing to file suit: person with custody or foster parent

(a) An original suit [to affect the parent child relationship] may be filed at any time by:

. . .

(9) a person, other than a foster parent, who has had actual care, control, and possession of the child for at least six months ending not more than 90 days preceding the date of the filing of the petition; . . .

(12) a person who is the foster parent of a child placed by the Department of Protective and Regulatory Services in the person's home for at least 12 months ending not more than 90 days preceding the date of the filing of the petition; or

. . .

(b) In computing the time necessary for standing under Subsections (a)(9), (11), and (12), the court may not require that the time be continuous and uninterrupted but shall consider the child's principal residence during the relevant time preceding the date of commencement of the suit.

(Acts 1995, 74th Leg., ch. 20, §1, effective April 20, 1995. Amended by Acts 1995, 74th Leg., ch. 751, §8, effective September 1, 1995 Amended Acts 1997, 75th Leg., ch. 575, §3, effective September 1, 1997; Acts 1999, 76th Leg., ch. 1048, §1, effective June 18, 1999; Acts 1999, 76th Leg., ch. 1390, §2, effective September 1, 1999; Acts 2001, 77th Leg., ch. 821, §2.07, effective June 14, 2001; Acts 2003, 78th Leg., ch. 37, §1, effective September 1, 2003; Acts 2003, 78th Leg., ch. 573, §1, effective September 1, 2003.)

§264.101. Requirements for foster care payments

(a) The department may pay the cost of foster care for a child:

(1) for whom the department has initiated a suit and has been named managing conservator under an order rendered under this title, who is a resident of the state, and who has been placed by the department in a foster home or child-care institution, as defined by Chapter 42, Human Resources Code; or

(2) who is under the placement and care of a state agency or political subdivision with which the department has entered into an agreement to reimburse the cost of care and supervision of the child.

(a-1) The department shall continue to pay the cost of foster care for a child for whom the department provides care, including medical care, until the later of:

(1) the date the child attains the age of 18; or

(2) the date the child graduates from high school or ceases to be enrolled in a secondary school in a program leading toward a high school diploma.

(b) The department may not pay the cost of protective foster care for a child for whom the department has been named managing conservator under an order rendered solely under Section 161.001(1)(J).

(c) The payment of foster care, including medical care, for a child as authorized under this subchapter shall be made without regard to the child's eligibility for federally funded care.

(d) The executive commissioner of the Health and Human Services Commission may adopt rules that establish criteria and guidelines for the payment of foster care, including medical care, for a child and for providing care for a child after the child becomes 18 years of age if the child is regularly attending an institution of higher education or a vocational or technical program.

(d-1) The executive commissioner may adopt rules that prescribe the maximum amount of state money that a residential child-care facility may spend on nondirect residential services, including administrative services. The commission shall recover the money that exceeds the maximum amount established under this subsection.

(e) The department may accept and spend funds available from any source to pay for foster care, including medical care, for a child in the department's care.

(f) In this section, "child" means a person who:

(1) is under 22 years of age and for whom the department has been appointed managing conservator of the child before the date the child became 18 years of age; or

(2) is the responsibility of an agency with which the department has entered into an agreement to provide care and supervision of the child.

(Acts 1995, 74th Leg., ch. 20, §1, effective April 20, 1995. Amended by Acts 1997, 75th Leg., ch. 575, §27, effective September 1, 1997; Acts 2005, 79th Leg., ch. 183, §1, effective May 27, 2005; Acts 2005, 79th Leg., ch. 268, §1.45, effective September 1, 2005.)

§264.1015. Child's estate is eligible for costs of foster care

(a) The cost of foster care provided for a child, including medical care, is an obligation of the estate of the child and the estate is liable to the department for the cost of the care.

(b) The department may take action to recover from the estate of the child the cost of foster care for the child.

(Acts 1997, 75th Leg., ch. 575, §28, effective September 1, 1997.)

§264.102. Department may contract to administer funds for eligible children

(a) The department may contract with a county commissioners court to administer the funds authorized by this subchapter for eligible children in the county and may require county participation.

(b) The payments provided by this subchapter do not abrogate the responsibility of a county to provide child welfare services.

(Acts 1995, 74th Leg., ch. 20, §1, effective April 20, 1995.)

§264.103. Department may make direct payments to foster parents if Department does not have contract with that county

The department may make direct payments for foster care to a foster parent residing in a county with which the department does not have a contract authorized by Section 264.102.

(Acts 1995, 74th Leg., ch. 20, §1, effective April 20, 1995.)

§264.104. Parent is liable for costs of foster care

(a) The parent or guardian of a child is liable to the state or to the county for a payment made by the state or county for foster care of a child under this subchapter.

(b) The cost of foster care for a child, including medical care, is a legal obligation of the child's parents, and the estate of a parent of the child is liable to the department for payment of the costs.

(c) The funds collected by the state under this section shall be used by the department for child welfare services.

(Acts 1995, 74th Leg., ch. 20, §1, effective April 20, 1995. Amended by Acts 1997, 75th Leg., ch. 575, §29, effective September 1, 1997.)

§264.105. Department shall maximize federal funds to provide medical services

The department shall attempt to maximize the use of federal funding to provide medical care payments authorized by Section 264.101(c) for children for whom the department has been named managing conservator.

(Acts 1995, 74th Leg., ch. 20, §1, effective April 20, 1995. Amended by Acts 1997, 75th Leg., ch. 575, §30, effective September 1, 1997.)

§264.106. Department shall contract for substitute care services

(a) In this section:

(1) "Case management services" means the provision of case management services to a child for whom the department has been appointed temporary or permanent managing conservator, including caseworker-child visits, family visits, the convening of family group conferences, the development and revision of the case plan, the coordination and monitoring of services needed by the child and family, and the assumption of court-related duties, including preparing court reports, attending judicial hearings and permanency hearings, and ensuring that the child is progressing toward permanency within state and federal mandates.

(2) "Independent administrator" means an independent agency selected through a competitive procurement process to:

(A) secure, coordinate, and manage substitute care services and case management services in a geographically designated area of the state; and

(B) ensure continuity of care for a child referred to the administrator by the department and the child's family from the day a child enters the child protective services system until the child leaves the system.

(3) "Permanency services" means services, other than family-based safety services, provided to secure a child's safety, permanency, and well-being, including substitute care services, family reunification services, adoption and postadoption services, preparation for adult living services, and case management services.

(4) "Substitute care provider" means a child-care institution or a child-placing agency, as defined by Section 42.002, Human Resources Code.

(5) "Substitute care services" means services provided to or for children in substitute care and their families, including the recruitment, training, and management of foster parents, the recruitment of adoptive families, and the facilitation of the adoption process, family preservation, independent living, emergency shelter, residential group care, foster care, therapeutic foster care, and post-placement supervision, including relative placement. The term does not include the regulation of facilities under Subchapter C, Chapter 42, Human Resources Code.

(b) The department shall, in accordance with Section 45.004, Human Resources Code:

(1) assess the need for substitute care and case management services throughout the state;

(2) either contract directly with private agencies as part of regional community-centered networks for the provision of all necessary substitute care and case management services or use an independent administrator to contract for those services;

(3) contract with an independent administrator, if cost beneficial, to coordinate and manage all services needed for children in the temporary or permanent managing conservatorship of the department in a designated geographic area;

(4) monitor the quality of services for which the department and each independent administrator contract under this section; and

(5) ensure that the services are provided in accordance with federal law and the laws of this state, including department rules and rules of the Department of State Health Services and the Texas Commission on Environmental Quality.

(c) An independent administrator may not:

(1) directly provide substitute care services; or

(2) be governed by a board that has a member who has a financial interest in a substitute care or case management provider with whom the independent administrator subcontracts.

(d) Administrative services to be provided by an independent administrator include:

(1) recruiting and subcontracting with community-based substitute care and case management providers to ensure a full array of services in defined geographic areas;

(2) managing placements and making referrals for placement based on department-approved protocols;

(3) monitoring services delivered by subcontractors;

(4) providing training and technical assistance to contract providers;

(5) maintaining data systems that support tracking and reporting key performance and outcome data; and

(6) ensuring accountability for achieving defined client and system outcomes.

(e) In addition to the requirements of Section 40.058(b), Human Resources Code, a contract with an independent administrator must include provisions that:

(1) enable the department to monitor the effectiveness of the services;

(2) specify performance outcomes;

(3) authorize the department to terminate the contract or impose sanctions for a violation of a provision of the contract that specifies performance criteria;

(4) ensure that an independent administrator may not refuse to accept a client who is referred for services or reject a client who is receiving services unless the department has reviewed the independent administrator's decision and approved the decision in writing;

(5) authorize the department, an agent of the department, and the state auditor to inspect all books, records, and files maintained by an independent administrator relating to the contract; and

(6) the department determines are necessary to ensure accountability for the delivery of services and for the expenditure of public funds.

(f) A contract with an independent administrator for substitute care and case management services under Subsection (b)(2) must include department-approved provisions that:

(1) enable the independent administrator and the department to:

(A) monitor the effectiveness of substitute care and case management services; and

(B) specify performance standards and authorize termination of the contract for cause;

(2) describe how performance is linked to reimbursement amounts or schedules to provide incentives for desired results;

(3) require all independent administrators and private contractors to disclose to the department any information that may indicate an actual or potential conflict of interest with the commission, the department, or another health and human services agency, including information regarding actual or potential related-party transactions, relationships, interests, or business history, and any other factor that may indicate an actual or potential conflict of interest;

(4) authorize the independent administrator, an agent of the independent administrator, the department, an agent of the department, and the state auditor to inspect all books, records, and files maintained by a contractor relating to the contract; and

(5) the department determines are necessary to ensure accountability for the delivery of services and for the expenditure of public funds.

(g) In determining whether to contract with a substitute care provider or an independent administrator, the department shall consider the provider's or administrator's performance under any previous contract between the department and the provider or administrator.

(h) A contract under this section does not affect the rights and duties of the department in the department's capacity as the temporary or permanent managing conservator of a child.

(i) Except as provided by Subsections (j) and (k) and notwithstanding any other law, on and after September 1, 2011, the department may not directly provide substitute care and case management services for children for whom the department has been appointed temporary or permanent managing conservator.

(j) On and after September 1, 2011, the department may provide substitute care and case management services in an emergency. The executive commissioner shall adopt rules describing the circumstances in which the department may provide those services.

(k) The department may provide substitute care and case management services as a provider of last resort in any region of the state in which the department or an independent administrator contracting with the department is unable to contract with a private agency to provide those services.

(Acts 1995, 74th Leg., ch. 20, §1, effective April 20, 1995. Amended by Acts 1997, 75th Leg., ch. 1022, §92, effective September 1, 1997; Acts 2005, 79th Leg., ch. 183, §1, effective May 27, 2005; Acts 2005, 79th Leg., ch. 268, §1.45, effective September 1, 2005.)

§264.107. Placement of children: level of care

(a) The department shall use a system for the placement of children in contract residential care, including foster care, that conforms to the levels of care adopted and maintained by the Health and Human Services Commission.

(b) The department shall use the standard application for the placement of children in contract residential care as adopted and maintained by the Health and Human Services Commission.

(c) The contract between the department and an independent administrator or other authorized entity must require, not later than September 1, 2009, the use of real-time technology in the independent administrator's or other authorized entity's placement system to screen possible placement options for a child and match the child's needs with the most qualified providers with vacancies.

(d) The department shall institute a quality assurance system in monitoring the independent administrators or other authorized entities to ensure that placement decisions are reliable and are made in a consistent manner.

(e) In making placement decisions, an independent administrator or other authorized entity shall use clinical protocols to match a child to the most appropriate placement resource.

(f) The department may create a regional advisory council in a region to assist the department and independent administrator or other authorized entity in:

(1) assessing the need for resources in the region; and

(2) locating substitute care services in the region for hard-to-place children.

(Acts 1995, 74th Leg., ch. 20, §1, effective April 20, 1995. Amended by Acts 2005, 79th Leg., ch. 268, §1.48, effective September 1, 2005.)

§264.1075. Department shall use assessment services before placement in substitute care

(a) On removing a child from the child's home, the department shall use assessment services provided by a child-care facility, a child-placing agency, or the child's medical home during the initial substitute care placement. The assessment may be used to determine the most appropriate substitute care placement for the child, if needed.

(b) As soon as possible after a child begins receiving foster care under this subchapter, the department shall assess whether the child has a developmental disability or mental retardation. The commission shall establish the procedures that the department must use in making an assessment under this subsection. The procedures may include screening or participation by:

(1) a person who has experience in childhood developmental disabilities or mental retardation;

(2) a local mental retardation authority; or

(3) a provider in a county with a local child welfare board.

(Acts 1997, 75th Leg., ch. 1022, §93, effective September 1, 1997. Amended by Acts 2005, 79th Leg., ch. 268, §1.49, effective September 1, 2005.)

§264.108. Department may not make placement based on race or ethnicity

(a) The department may not make a foster care placement decision on the presumption that placing a child in a family of the same race or ethnicity as the race or ethnicity of the child is in the best interest of the child.

(b) Unless an independent psychological evaluation specific to a child indicates that placement or continued living with a family of a particular race or ethnicity would be detrimental to the child, the department may not:

(1) deny, delay, or prohibit placement of a child in foster care because the department is attempting to locate a family of a particular race or ethnicity; or

(2) remove a child from foster care with a family that is of a race or ethnicity different from that of the child.

(c) The department may not remove a child from foster care with a family that is of a race or ethnicity different from that of the child for the sole reason that continued foster care with that family may:

(1) strengthen the emotional ties between the child and the family; or

(2) increase the potential of the family's desire to adopt the child because of the amount of time the child and the family are together.

(d) This section does not prevent or limit the department's recruitment of minority families as foster care families, but the recruitment of minority families may not be a reason to delay placement of a child in foster care with an available family of a race or ethnicity different from that of the child.

(e) An employee who violates this section is subject to immediate dismissal.

(f) The department by rule shall define what constitutes a delay under Subsections (b) and (d).

(g) A district court, on the application for an injunction or the filing of a petition complaining of a violation of this section by any person residing in the county in which the court has jurisdiction, shall enforce this section by issuing appropriate orders. An action for an injunction is in addition to any other action, proceeding, or remedy authorized by law. An applicant or petitioner who is granted an injunction or given other appropriate relief under this section is entitled to the costs of the suit, including reasonable attorney's fees.

(Acts 1995, 74th Leg., ch. 20, §1, effective April 20, 1995. Amended by Acts 1995, 74th Leg., ch. 879, §2, effective June 16, 1995.)

§264.109. Placement of child in substitute care constitutes assignment of support rights

(a) The placement of a child in substitute care by the department constitutes an assignment to the state of any support rights attributable to the child as of the date the child is placed in substitute care.

(b) If a child placed by the department in substitute care is entitled under federal law to Title IV-D child support enforcement services without the requirement of an application for services, the department shall immediately refer the case to the Title IV-D agency. If an application for Title IV-D services is required and the department has been named managing conservator of the child, then an authorized representative of the department shall be the designated individual entitled to apply for services on behalf of the child and shall promptly apply for the services.

(c) The department and the Title IV-D agency shall execute a memorandum of understanding for the implementation of the provisions of this section and for the allocation between the department and the agency, consistent with federal laws and regulations, of any child support funds recovered by the Title IV-D agency in substitute care cases. All child support funds recovered under this section and retained by the department or the Title IV-D agency and any federal matching or incentive funds resulting from child support collection efforts in substitute care cases shall be in excess of amounts otherwise appropriated to either the department or the Title IV-D agency by the legislature.

(Acts 1995, 74th Leg., ch. 751, §117, effective September 1, 1995.)

§264.110. Department shall establish registry of foster parents

(a) The department shall establish a registry of persons who are willing to accept foster care placement of a child in the care of the department. The child may be placed temporarily with a person registered under this section pending termination of the parent-child relationship.

(b) A person registered under this section must satisfy requirements adopted by rule by the department.

(c) The department shall maintain a list of persons registered under this section and shall make a reasonable effort to place a child with the first available qualified person on the list if a qualified extended family member is not available for the child.

(d) Before a child may be placed with a person under this section, the person must sign a written statement in which the person agrees to the immediate removal of the child by the department under circumstances determined by the department.

(e) A person registered under this section is not entitled to compensation during the time the child is placed in the person's home but may receive support services provided for the child by the department.

(f) A person registered under this section has the right to be considered first for the adoption of a child placed in the person's home if the parent- child relationship is terminated with regard to the child.

(g) The department may refuse to place a child with a person registered under this section only for a reason permitted under criteria adopted by department rule.

(h) The department shall make the public aware of the existence and benefits of the adoptive parent registry through appropriate existing department communication methods.

(Acts 1995, 74th Leg., ch. 943, §8, effective September 1, 1995. Renumbered from Family Code §264.109 by Acts 1997, 75th Leg., ch. 165, § 31.01(30), effective September 1, 1997.)

§264.111. Department shall maintain central database containing adoption information

(a) The department shall maintain in the department's central database information concerning children placed in the department's custody, including:

(1) for each formal adoption of a child in this state:

(A) the length of time between the date of the permanency plan decision of adoption and the date of the actual placement of the child with an adoptive family;

(B) the length of time between the date of the placement of the child for adoption and the date a final order of adoption was rendered;

(C) if the child returned to the department's custody after the date a final order of adoption was rendered for the child, the time between the date the final adoption order was rendered and the date the child returned to the department's custody; and

(D) for the adoptive family of a child under Paragraph (C), whether the family used postadoption program services before the date the child returned to the department's custody; and

(2) for each placement of a child in substitute care:

(A) the level of care the child was determined to require;

(B) whether the child was placed in an appropriate setting based on the level of care determined for the child;

(C) the number of moves for the child in substitute care and the reasons for moving the child;

(D) the length of stay in substitute care for the child from the date of initial placement to the date of approval of a permanency plan for the child;

(E)the length of time between the date of approval of a permanency plan for the child and the date of achieving the plan;

(F)whether the child's permanency plan was long-term substitute care;

(G) whether the child's achieved permanency plan was placement with an appropriate relative or another person, other than a foster parent, having standing; and

(H) whether the child was adopted by the child's foster parents.

(b) In addition to the information required in Subsection (a), the department shall compile information on:

(1) the number of families that used postadoption program services to assist in maintaining adoptive placements;

(2) the number of children returned to the department's custody after placement with an adoptive family but before a final adoption order was rendered;

(3) the number of children returned to the department's custody after the date a final order of adoption was rendered for the child;

(4) the number of adoptive families who used postadoption program services before the date a child placed with the family returned to the department's custody;

(5) the percentage of children who were placed in an appropriate setting based on the level of care determined for the child;

(6) the percentage of children placed in a department foster home;

(7) the percentage of children placed in a private child-placing agency;

(8) the number of children whose permanency plan was long-term substitute care;

(9) the number of children whose achieved permanency plan was placement with an appropriate relative or another person, other than a foster parent, having standing;

(10) the number of children adopted by the child's foster parents; and

(11) the number of children whose achieved permanency plan was removal of the disabilities of minority.

(c) The department shall make the information maintained under this section, other than information that is required by law to be confidential, available to the public by computer.

(Acts 1997, 75th Leg., ch. 600, §18, effective September 1, 1997.)

§264.112. Department shall report status of children in substitute care

(a) The department shall report the status for children in substitute care to the Board of Protective and Regulatory Services at least once every 12 months.

(b) The report shall analyze the length of time each child has been in substitute care and the barriers to placing the child for adoption or returning the child to the child's parent or parents.

(Acts 1997, 75th Leg., ch. 600, §18, effective September 1, 1997.)

§264.113. Recruitment of foster parents through religious organizations

(a) In this section, "faith-based organization" means a religious or denominational institution or organization, including an organization operated for religious, educational, or charitable purposes and operated, supervised, or controlled, in whole or in part, by or in connection with a religious organization.

(b) The department shall develop a program to recruit and retain foster parents from faith-based organizations. As part of the program, the department shall:

(1) collaborate with faith-based organizations to inform prospective foster parents about the department's need for foster parents, the requirements for becoming a foster parent, and any other aspect of the foster care program that is necessary to recruit foster parents;

(2) provide training for prospective foster parents recruited under this section; and

(3) identify and recommend ways in which faith-based organizations may support persons as they are recruited, are trained, and serve as foster parents.

(Acts 2003, 78th Leg., ch. 957, §1, effective June 20, 2003.)

§264.114. Religious organizations immune from liability

(a) A faith-based organization, including the organization's employees and volunteers, that participates in a program under this chapter is subject to civil liability as provided by Chapter 84, Civil Practice and Remedies Code.

(b) A faith-based organization that provides financial or other assistance to a foster parent or to a member of the foster parent's household is not liable for damages arising out of the conduct of the foster parent or a member of the foster parent's household.

(Acts 2003, 78th Leg., ch. 957, §1, effective June 20, 2003.)

§264.115. Child must return to school within three days if feasible

(a) If the department takes possession of a child under Chapter 262 during the school year, the department shall ensure that the child returns to school not later than the third school day after the date an order is rendered providing for possession of the child by the department, unless the child has a physical or mental condition of a temporary and remediable nature that makes the child's attendance infeasible.

(b) If a child has a physical or mental condition of a temporary and remediable nature that makes the child's attendance in school infeasible, the department shall notify the school in writing that the child is unable to attend school. If the child's physical or mental condition improves so that the child's attendance in school is feasible, the department shall ensure that the child immediately returns to school.

(Acts 2003, 78th Leg., ch. 234, §1, effective September 1, 2003. Renumbered from V.T.C.A., Family Code §264.113 by Acts 2005, 79th Leg., ch. 728, §23.001(25), effective September 1, 2005.)

§264.117. Attorney ad litem for a child is given notice of each event that is reported in child's case file

(a) The department shall notify the attorney ad litem for a child in the conservatorship of the department about each event involving the child that the department reports in the child's case file.

(b) The department shall give a child's attorney ad litem written notice at least 48 hours before the date the department changes the child's residential care provider. The department may change the child's residential care provider without notice if the department determines that an immediate change is necessary to protect the child.

(Acts 2005, 79th Leg., ch. 268, §1.50(a), effective September 1, 2005.)

§264.116. Recruitment of senior citizens as mentors for foster children

(a) The department shall make the active recruitment and inclusion of senior citizens a priority in ongoing mentoring initiatives.

(b) An individual who volunteers as a mentor is subject to state and national criminal background checks in accordance with Sections 411.087 and 411.114, Government Code.

(c) The department shall require foster parents or employees of residential child-care facilities to provide appropriate supervision over individuals who serve as mentors during their participation in the mentoring initiative.

(d) Chapter 2109, Government Code, applies to the mentoring initiative described by this section.

(Acts 2005, 79th Leg., ch. 268, §1.50(a), effective September 1, 2005.)

§264.121. Foster children are to be prepared for adult living

(a) The department shall address the unique challenges facing foster children in the conservatorship of the department who must transition to independent living by:

(1) expanding efforts to improve discharge planning and increasing the availability of transitional family group decision-making to all youth age 16 or older in the department's permanent managing conservatorship;

(2) coordinating with the Health and Human Services Commission to obtain authority, to the extent allowed by federal law, the state Medicaid plan, the Title IV-E state plan, and any waiver or amendment to either plan, necessary to:

(A) extend foster care eligibility and transition services for youth up to age 21 and develop policy to permit eligible youth to return to foster care as necessary to achieve the goals of the Preparation for Adult Living Program; and

(B) extend Medicaid coverage for foster care youth and former foster care youth up to age 21 with a single application at the time the youth leaves foster care; and

(3) entering into cooperative agreements with the Texas Workforce Commission and local workforce development boards to further the objectives of the Preparation for Adult Living Program. The department, the Texas Workforce Commission, and the local workforce development boards shall ensure that services are prioritized and targeted to meet the needs of foster care and former foster care children and that such services will include, where feasible, referrals for short-term stays for youth needing housing.

(b) In this section "local workforce development board" means a local workforce development board created under Chapter 2308, Government Code.

(Acts 2005, 79th Leg., ch. 268, §1.51, effective September 1, 2005.)

§264.751. Definitions for the caregiver placement program

In this subchapter:

(1) "Designated caregiver" means an individual who has a longstanding and significant relationship with a child for whom the department has been appointed managing conservator and who:

(A) is appointed to provide substitute care for the child, but is not licensed or certified to operate a foster home, foster group home, agency foster home, or agency foster group home under Chapter 42, Human Resources Code; or

(B) is subsequently appointed permanent managing conservator of the child after providing the care described by Paragraph (A).

(2) "Relative" means a person related to a child by consanguinity as determined under Section 573.022, Government Code.

(3) "Relative caregiver" means a relative who:

(A) provides substitute care for a child for whom the department has been appointed managing conservator, but who is not licensed or certified to operate a foster home, foster group home, agency foster home, or agency foster group home under Chapter 42, Human Resources Code; or

(B) is subsequently appointed permanent managing conservator of the child after providing the care described by Paragraph (A).

(Acts 2005, 79th Leg., ch. 268, §1.62(a), effective September 1, 2005.)

§264.752. Caregiver program to place children with relatives

(a) The department shall develop and procure a program to:

(1) promote continuity and stability for children for whom the department is appointed managing conservator by placing those children with relative or other designated caregivers; and

(2) facilitate relative or other designated caregiver placements by providing assistance and services to those caregivers in accordance with this subchapter and rules adopted by the executive commissioner.

(b) To the extent permitted by federal law, the department shall use federal funds available under Title IV-E, Social Security Act (42 U.S.C. Section 670 et seq.), to administer the program under this subchapter.

(c) The executive commissioner shall adopt rules necessary to implement this subchapter. The rules must include eligibility criteria for receiving assistance and services under this subchapter.

(Acts 2005, 79th Leg., ch. 268, §1.62(a), effective September 1, 2005.)

§264.753. Child should be placed with caregiver as soon as possible

The department or other authorized entity shall expedite the completion of the background and criminal history check, the home study, and any other administrative procedure to ensure that the child is placed with a qualified relative or caregiver as soon as possible after the date the caregiver is identified.

(Acts 2005, 79th Leg., ch. 268, §1.62(a), effective September 1, 2005.)

§264.754. Placement must be in child's best interest

Before placing a child with a proposed relative or other designated caregiver, the department must conduct an investigation to determine whether the proposed placement is in the child's best interest.

(Acts 2005, 79th Leg., ch. 268, §1.62(a), effective September 1, 2005.)

§264.755. Caregiver will be given monetary assistance

(a) The department shall, subject to the availability of funds, enter into a caregiver assistance agreement with each relative or other designated caregiver to provide monetary assistance and additional support services to the caregiver. The monetary assistance and support services shall be based on a family's need, as determined by rules adopted by the executive commissioner.

(b) Monetary assistance provided under this section must include a one-time cash payment of not more than $1,000 to the caregiver on the initial placement of a child or a sibling group. The cash payment must be provided on the initial placement of each child with the caregiver and is provided to assist the caregiver in purchasing essential child-care items such as furniture and clothing.

(c) Monetary assistance and additional support services provided under this section may include:

(1) case management services and training and information about the child's needs until the caregiver is appointed permanent managing conservator;

(2) referrals to appropriate state agencies administering public benefits or assistance programs for which the child, the caregiver, or the caregiver's family may qualify;

(3) family counseling not provided under the Medicaid program for the caregiver's family for a period not to exceed two years from the date of initial placement;

(4) if the caregiver meets the eligibility criteria determined by rules adopted by the executive commissioner, reimbursement of all child-care expenses incurred while the child is under 13 years of age, or under 18 years of age if the child has a developmental disability, and while the department is the child's managing conservator;

(5) if the caregiver meets the eligibility criteria determined by rules adopted by the executive commissioner, reimbursement of 50 percent of child-care expenses incurred after the caregiver is appointed permanent managing conservator of the child while the child is under 13 years of age, or under 18 years of age if the child has a developmental disability; and

(6) reimbursement of other expenses, as determined by rules adopted by the executive commissioner, not to exceed $500 per year for each child.

(Acts 2005, 79th Leg., ch. 268, §1.62(a), effective September 1, 2005.)

§264.756. Department will assist caregivers with making placement permanent

The department shall collaborate with the State Bar of Texas and local community partners to identify legal resources to assist relatives and other designated caregivers in obtaining conservatorship, adoption, or other permanent legal status for the child.

(Acts 2005, 79th Leg., ch. 268, §1.62(a), effective September 1, 2005.)

§264.757. Department will coordinate with other agencies

The department shall coordinate with other health and human services agencies, as defined by Section 531.001, Government Code, to provide assistance and services under this subchapter.

(Acts 2005, 79th Leg., ch. 268, §1.62(a), effective September 1, 2005.)

§264.758. Program will seek federal funds

The department and other state agencies shall actively seek and use federal funds available for the purposes of this subchapter.

(Acts 2005, 79th Leg., ch. 268, §1.62(a), effective September 1, 2005.)

8. Termination of Parental Rights

After making a determination that a child falls within the statutory definition of an abused or neglected child, the state must select a disposition for the child (e.g., return to the family with conditions and/or services; foster care; termination of parental rights, etc.).

Generally, the state may terminate the parent-child relationship only when the child is subjected to real physical or emotional harm and less drastic measures are unavailing. The United States Supreme Court has held that due process requires that the standard of proof for termination of parental rights proceedings must be, at a minimum, clear and convincing evidence. Santosky v. Kramer, 455 U.S. 745 (1982). By statute, Texas adopts this standard of proof for termination of parental rights (Tex. Fam. Code §161.001). See also Section d. "Standard of Proof," *infra*.

a. Grounds

Termination of parental rights may be involuntary or voluntary. According to Texas law, a court may order involuntary termination based on a number of grounds, including abandonment of a child or the child's mother during the pregnancy, lack of support, placing the child in conditions of harm or engaging in conduct harmful to the child, refusing to submit to a court order or failing to meet the conditions of a court order (e.g., for return of the child), failing to enroll the child in school, causing the child to be absent from the home without parental consent, being convicted or placed on community supervision for the death of or serious injury to a child, having had parental rights terminated with respect to another child, using a controlled substance in a manner that is harmful to the child or that causes a child to be born addicted, murdering the other parent of the child, and being incarcerated for more than two years (Tex. Fam. Code §161.001).

Texas Family Code

§161.001. Grounds for involuntary termination of parental rights

The court may order termination of the parent-child relationship if the court finds by clear and convincing evidence:

(1) that the parent has:

(A) voluntarily left the child alone or in the possession of another not the parent and expressed an intent not to return;

(B) voluntarily left the child alone or in the possession of another not the parent without expressing an intent to return, without providing for the adequate support of the child, and remained away for a period of at least three months;

(C) voluntarily left the child alone or in the possession of another without providing adequate support of the child and remained away for a period of at least six months;

(D) knowingly placed or knowingly allowed the child to remain in conditions or surroundings which endanger the physical or emotional well-being of the child;

(E) engaged in conduct or knowingly placed the child with persons who engaged in conduct which endangers the physical or emotional well-being of the child;

(F) failed to support the child in accordance with the parent's ability during a period of one year ending within six months of the date of the filing of the petition;

(G) abandoned the child without identifying the child or furnishing means of identification, and the child's identity cannot be ascertained by the exercise of reasonable diligence;

(H) voluntarily, and with knowledge of the pregnancy, abandoned the mother of the child beginning at a time during her pregnancy with the child and continuing through the birth, failed to provide adequate support or medical care for the mother during the period of abandonment before the birth of the child, and remained apart from the child or failed to support the child since the birth;

(I) contumaciously refused to submit to a reasonable and lawful order of a court under Subchapter D, Chapter 261;

(J) been the major cause of:

(i) the failure of the child to be enrolled in school as required by the Education Code; or

(ii) the child's absence from the child's home without the consent of the parents or guardian for a substantial length of time or without the intent to return;

(K) executed before or after the suit is filed an unrevoked or irrevocable affidavit of relinquishment of parental rights as provided by this chapter;

(L) been convicted or has been placed on community supervision, including deferred adjudication community supervision, for being criminally responsible for the death or serious injury of a child under the following sections of the Penal Code or adjudicated under Title 3 for conduct that caused the death or serious injury of a child and that would constitute a violation of one of the following Penal Code sections:

(i) Section 19.02 (murder);

(ii) Section 19.03 (capital murder);

(iii) Section 19.04 (manslaughter);

(iv) Section 21.11 (indecency with a child);

(v) Section 22.01 (assault);

(vi) Section 22.011 (sexual assault);

(vii) Section 22.02 (aggravated assault);

(viii) Section 22.021 (aggravated sexual assault);

(ix) Section 22.04 (injury to a child, elderly individual, or disabled individual);

(x) Section 22.041 (abandoning or endangering child);

(xi) Section 25.02 (prohibited sexual conduct);

(xii) Section 43.25 (sexual performance by a child); and

(xiii) Section 43.26 (possession or promotion of child pornography);

(M) had his or her parent-child relationship terminated with respect to another child based on a finding that the parent's conduct was in violation of Paragraph (D) or (E) or substantially equivalent provisions of the law of another state;

(N) constructively abandoned the child who has been in the permanent or temporary managing conservatorship of the Department of Family and Protective Services or an authorized agency for not less than six months, and:

(i) the department or authorized agency has made reasonable efforts to return the child to the parent;

(ii) the parent has not regularly visited or maintained significant contact with the child; and

(iii) the parent has demonstrated an inability to provide the child with a safe environment;

(O) failed to comply with the provisions of a court order that specifically established the actions necessary for the parent to obtain the return of the child who has been in the permanent or temporary managing conservatorship of the Department of Family and Protective Services for not less than nine months as a result of the child's removal from the parent under Chapter 262 for the abuse or neglect of the child;

(P) used a controlled substance, as defined by Chapter 481, Health and Safety Code, in a manner that endangered the health or safety of the child, and:

(i) failed to complete a court-ordered substance abuse treatment program; or

(ii) after completion of a court-ordered substance abuse treatment program, continued to abuse a controlled substance;

(Q) knowingly engaged in criminal conduct that has resulted in the parent's:

(i) conviction of an offense; and

(ii) confinement or imprisonment and inability to care for the child for not less than two years from the date of filing the petition;

(R) been the cause of the child being born addicted to alcohol or a controlled substance, other than a controlled substance legally obtained by prescription, as defined by Section 261.001;

(S) voluntarily delivered the child to a designated emergency infant care provider under Section 262.302 without expressing an intent to return for the child; or

(T) been convicted of the murder of the other parent of the child under Section 19.02 or 19.03, Penal Code, or under a law of another state, federal law, the law of a foreign country, or the Uniform Code of Military Justice that contains elements that are substantially similar to the elements of an offense under Section 19.02 or 19.03, Penal Code; and

(2) that termination is in the best interest of the child.

(Acts 1995, 74th Leg., ch. 20, §1, effective April 20, 1995. Amended by Acts 1995, 74th Leg., ch. 709, §1, effective September 1, 1995; Acts 1995, 74th Leg., ch. 751, §65, effective September 1, 1995; by Acts 1997, 75th Leg., ch. 575, §9, effective September 1, 1997; Acts 1997, 75th Leg., ch. 1022, §60, effective September 1, 1997; Acts 1999, 76th Leg., ch. 1087, §1, effective September 1, 1999; Acts 1999, 76th Leg., ch. 1390, §18, effective September 1, 1999; Acts 2001, 77th Leg., ch. 809, §1, effective September 1, 2001; Acts 2005, 79th Leg., ch. 508, §2, effective September 1, 2005.)

§161.002. Grounds for termination of rights of an alleged biological father

(a) The procedural and substantive standards for termination of parental rights apply to the termination of the rights of an alleged father.

(b) The rights of an alleged father may be terminated if:

(1) after being served with citation, he does not respond by timely filing an admission of paternity or a counterclaim for paternity under Chapter 160;

(2) he has not registered with the paternity registry under Chapter 160,1 and after the exercise of due diligence by the petitioner:

(A) his identity and location are unknown; or

(B) his identity is known but he cannot be located; or

(3) he has registered with the paternity registry under Chapter 160, but the petitioner's attempt to personally serve citation at the address provided to the registry and at any other address for the alleged father known by the petitioner has been unsuccessful, despite the due diligence of the petitioner.

(c) The termination of the rights of an alleged father under Subsection (b)(2) rendered on or after January 1, 1998, does not require personal service of citation or citation by publication on the alleged father.

(d) The termination of rights of an alleged father under Subsection (b)(3) does not require service of citation by publication on the alleged father.

(e) The court shall not render an order terminating parental rights under Subsection (b)(2) unless the court, after reviewing the petitioner's sworn affidavit describing the petitioner's effort to identify and locate the alleged father and considering any evidence submitted by the attorney ad litem for the alleged father, has found that the petitioner exercised due diligence in attempting to identify and locate the alleged father. The order shall contain specific findings regarding due diligence of the petitioner.

(f) The court shall not render an order terminating parental rights under Subsection (b)(3) unless the court, after reviewing the petitioner's sworn affidavit describing the petitioner's effort to obtain personal service of citation on the alleged father and considering any evidence submitted by the attorney ad litem for the alleged father, has found that the petitioner exercised due diligence in attempting to obtain service on the alleged father. The order shall contain specific findings regarding the exercise of due diligence of the petitioner.

(Acts 1995, 74th Leg., ch. 20, §1, effective April 20, 1995. Amended by Acts 1995, 74th Leg., ch. 751, §66, effective September 1, 1995; by Acts 1997, 75th Leg., ch. 561, §7, effective September 1, 1997; Acts 2001, 77th Leg., ch. 821, §2.16, effective June 14, 2001; Acts 2001, 77th Leg., ch. 1090, §1, effective September 1, 2001.)

§161.003. Grounds for involuntary termination: inability to care for child

(a) The court may order termination of the parent-child relationship in a suit filed by the Department of Protective and Regulatory Services if the court finds that:

(1) the parent has a mental or emotional illness or a mental deficiency that renders the parent unable to provide for the physical, emotional, and mental needs of the child;

(2) the illness or deficiency, in all reasonable probability, proved by clear and convincing evidence, will continue to render the parent unable to provide for the child's needs until the 18th birthday of the child;

(3) the department has been the temporary or sole managing conservator of the child of the parent for at least six months preceding the date of the hearing on the termination held in accordance with Subsection (c);

(4) the department has made reasonable efforts to return the child to the parent; and

(5) the termination is in the best interest of the child.

(b) Immediately after the filing of a suit under this section, the court shall appoint an attorney ad litem to represent the interests of the parent against whom the suit is brought.

(c) A hearing on the termination may not be held earlier than 180 days after the date on which the suit was filed.

(d) An attorney appointed under Subsection (b) shall represent the parent for the duration of the suit unless the parent, with the permission of the court, retains another attorney.

(Acts 1995, 74th Leg., ch. 20, §1, effective April 20, 1995. Amended by Acts 1995, 74th Leg., ch. 751, §67, effective September 1, 1995; by Acts 2001, 77th Leg., ch. 496, §1, effective September 1, 2001; Acts 2001, 77th Leg., ch. 1090, §2, effective September 1, 2001.)

§161.004. Court may terminate parental rights even after previous refusal of termination

(a) The court may terminate the parent-child relationship after rendition of an order that previously denied termination of the parent-child relationship if:

(1) the petition under this section is filed after the date the order denying termination was rendered;

(2) the circumstances of the child, parent, sole managing conservator, possessory conservator, or other party affected by the order denying termination have materially and substantially changed since the date that the order was rendered;

(3) the parent committed an act listed under Section 161.001 before the date the order denying termination was rendered; and

(4) termination is in the best interest of the child.

(b) At a hearing under this section, the court may consider evidence presented at a previous hearing in a suit for termination of the parent-child relationship of the parent with respect to the same child.

(Acts 1995, 74th Leg., ch. 20, §1, effective April 20, 1995.)

§161.005. Parent may request termination of other parent's rights

(a) A parent may file a suit for termination of the petitioner's parent-child relationship. The court may order termination if termination is in the best interest of the child.

(b) If the petition designates the Department of Protective and Regulatory Services as managing conservator, the department shall be given service of citation. The court shall notify the department if the court appoints the department as the managing conservator of the child.

(Acts 1995, 74th Leg., ch. 20, §1, effective April 20, 1995. Amended by Acts 1995, 74th Leg., ch. 751, §68, effective September 1, 1995.)

§161.006. Court may order termination after failed abortion

(a) A petition requesting termination of the parent-child relationship with respect to a parent who is not the petitioner may be granted if the child was born alive as the result of an abortion.

(b) In this code, "abortion" means an intentional expulsion of a human fetus from the body of a woman induced by any means for the purpose of causing the death of the fetus.

(c) The court or the jury may not terminate the parent-child relationship under this section with respect to a parent who:

(1) had no knowledge of the abortion; or

(2) participated in or consented to the abortion for the sole purpose of preventing the death of the mother.

(Acts 1995, 74th Leg., ch. 20, §1, effective April 20, 1995.)

§161.007. Court may order termination when pregnancy results from parent's criminal act

The court may order the termination of the parent-child relationship of a parent and a child if the court finds that:

(1) the parent has been convicted of an offense committed under Section 22.011, 22.021, or 25.02, Penal Code;

(2) as a direct result of the commission of the offense by the parent, the victim of the offense became pregnant with the parent's child; and

(3) termination is in the best interest of the child.

(Acts 1997, 75th Leg., ch. 561, §8, effective September 1, 1997.)

---

b. Termination Procedures

§161.101. Necessary allegations in petition for termination of parental rights

A petition for the termination of the parent-child relationship is sufficient without the necessity of specifying the underlying facts if the petition alleges in the statutory language the ground for the termination and that termination is in the best interest of the child.

(Acts 1995, 74th Leg., ch. 20, §1, effective April 20, 1995.)

§161.102. Suit for termination may be filed before child's birth

(a) A suit for termination may be filed before the birth of the child.

(b) If the suit is filed before the birth of the child, the petition shall be styled "In the Interest of an Unborn Child." After the birth, the clerk shall change the style of the case to conform to the requirements of Section 102.008.

(Acts 1995, 74th Leg., ch. 20, §1, effective April 20, 1995.)

§161.103. Affidavit of voluntary relinquishment of parental rights: signed, witnessed, contents

(a) An affidavit for voluntary relinquishment of parental rights must be:

(1) signed after the birth of the child, but not before 48 hours after the birth of the child, by the parent, whether or not a minor, whose parental rights are to be relinquished;

(2) witnessed by two credible persons; and

(3) verified before a person authorized to take oaths.

(b) The affidavit must contain:

(1) the name, address, and age of the parent whose parental rights are being relinquished;

(2) the name, age, and birth date of the child;

(3) the names and addresses of the guardians of the person and estate of the child, if any;

(4) a statement that the affiant is or is not presently obligated by court order to make payments for the support of the child;

(5) a full description and statement of value of all property owned or possessed by the child;

(6) an allegation that termination of the parent-child relationship is in the best interest of the child;

(7) one of the following, as applicable:

(A) the name and address of the other parent;

(B) a statement that the parental rights of the other parent have been terminated by death or court order; or

(C) a statement that the child has no presumed father and that an affidavit of status of the child has been executed as provided by this chapter;

(8) a statement that the parent has been informed of parental rights and duties;

(9) a statement that the relinquishment is revocable, that the relinquishment is irrevocable, or that the relinquishment is irrevocable for a stated period of time;

(10) if the relinquishment is revocable, a statement in boldfaced type concerning the right of the parent signing the affidavit to revoke the relinquishment only if the revocation is made before the 11th day after the date the affidavit is executed;

(11) if the relinquishment is revocable, the name and address of a person to whom the revocation is to be delivered; and

(12) the designation of a prospective adoptive parent, the Department of Protective and Regulatory Services, if the department has consented in writing to the designation, or a licensed child-placing agency to serve as managing conservator of the child and the address of the person or agency.

(c) The affidavit may contain:

(1) a waiver of process in a suit to terminate the parent-child relationship filed under this chapter or in a suit to terminate joined with a petition for adoption; and

(2) a consent to the placement of the child for adoption by the Department of Protective and Regulatory Services or by a licensed child-placing agency.

(d) A copy of the affidavit shall be provided to the parent at the time the parent signs the affidavit.

(e) The relinquishment in an affidavit that designates the Department of Protective and Regulatory Services or a licensed child-placing agency to serve as the managing conservator is irrevocable. A relinquishment in any other affidavit of relinquishment is revocable unless it expressly provides that it is irrevocable for a stated period of time not to exceed 60 days after the date of its execution.

(f) A relinquishment in an affidavit of relinquishment of parental rights that fails to state that the relinquishment is irrevocable for a stated time is revocable as provided by Section 161.1035.

(g) To revoke a relinquishment under Subsection (e) the parent must sign a statement witnessed by two credible persons and verified before a person authorized to take oaths. A copy of the revocation shall be delivered to the person designated in the affidavit. If a parent attempting to revoke a relinquishment under this subsection has knowledge that a suit for termination of the parent-child relationship has been filed based on the parent's affidavit of relinquishment of parental rights, the parent shall file a copy of the revocation with the clerk of the court.

(h) The affidavit may not contain terms for limited post-termination contact between the child and the parent whose parental rights are to be relinquished as a condition of the relinquishment of parental rights.

(Acts 1995, 74th Leg., ch. 20, §1, effective April 20, 1995. Amended by Acts 1995, 74th Leg., ch. 751, §69, effective September 1, 1995; by Acts 1997, 75th Leg., ch. 561, §9, effective September 1, 1997; Acts 2003, 78th Leg., ch. 561, §3, effective September 1, 2003.)

§161.1035. Revocability of affidavits that fail to state their irrevocability

An affidavit of relinquishment of parental rights or affidavit of waiver of interest in a child that fails to state that the relinquishment or waiver is irrevocable for a stated time is:

(1) revocable only if the revocation is made before the 11th day after the date the affidavit is executed; and

(2) irrevocable on or after the 11th day after the date the affidavit is executed.

(Acts 1997, 75th Leg., ch. 561, §10, effective September 1, 1997.)

§161.104. Rights of designated managing conservator pending modification or termination of order

A person, licensed child-placing agency, or authorized agency designated managing conservator of a child in an irrevocable or unrevoked affidavit of relinquishment has a right to possession of the child superior to the right of the person executing the affidavit, the right to consent to medical, surgical, dental, and psychological treatment of the child, and the rights and duties given by Chapter 153 to a possessory conservator until such time as these rights and duties are modified or terminated by court order.

(Acts 1995, 74th Leg., ch. 20, §1, effective April 20, 1995. Amended by Acts 1995, 74th Leg., ch. 751, §70, effective September 1, 1995.)

§161.105. Affidavit of status of child for child with no presumed father

(a) If the child has no presumed father, an affidavit shall be:

(1) signed by the mother, whether or not a minor;

(2) witnessed by two credible persons; and

(3) verified before a person authorized to take oaths.

(b) The affidavit must:

(1) state that the mother is not and has not been married to the alleged father of the child;

(2) state that the mother and alleged father have not attempted to marry under the laws of this state or another state or nation;

(3) state that paternity has not been established under the laws of any state or nation; and

(4) contain one of the following, as applicable:

(A) the name and whereabouts of a man alleged to be the father;

(B) the name of an alleged father and a statement that the affiant does not know the whereabouts of the father;

(C) a statement that an alleged father has executed an acknowledgment of paternity under Chapter 160 and an affidavit of relinquishment of parental rights under this chapter and that both affidavits have been filed with the court; or

(D) a statement that the name of an alleged father is unknown.

(c) The affidavit of status of child may be executed at any time after the first trimester of the pregnancy of the mother.

(Acts 1995, 74th Leg., ch. 20, §1, effective April 20, 1995. Amended by Acts 1999, 76th Leg., ch. 556, §40, effective September 1, 1999.)

§161.106. Man may sign affidavit of waiver of interest in child

(a) A man may sign an affidavit disclaiming any interest in a child and waiving notice or the service of citation in any suit filed or to be filed affecting the parent-child relationship with respect to the child.

(b) The affidavit may be signed before the birth of the child.

(c) The affidavit shall be:

(1) signed by the man, whether or not a minor;

(2) witnessed by two credible persons; and

(3) verified before a person authorized to take oaths.

(d) The affidavit may contain a statement that the affiant does not admit being the father of the child or having had a sexual relationship with the mother of the child.

(e) An affidavit of waiver of interest in a child may be used in a suit in which the affiant attempts to establish an interest in the child. The affidavit may not be used in a suit brought by another person, licensed child-placing agency, or authorized agency to establish the affiant's paternity of the child.

(f) A waiver in an affidavit under this section that designates the Department of Protective and Regulatory Services or a licensed child-placing agency to serve as the managing conservator is irrevocable. A waiver in any other affidavit under this section is revocable unless it expressly provides that it is irrevocable for a stated period not to exceed 60 days after the date of execution.

(g) A waiver in an affidavit under this section that fails to state that the waiver is irrevocable for a stated time is revocable as provided by Section 161.1035.

(h) An affidavit under this section that contains a waiver that is revocable must contain:

(1) a statement in boldfaced type concerning the right of the person who executed the affidavit to revoke the affidavit only if the revocation is made before the 11th day after the date the affidavit is executed; and

(2) the name and address of the person to whom the revocation is to be delivered.

(i) A copy of the affidavit shall be provided to the person who executed the affidavit at the time the person signs the affidavit.

(j) To revoke a waiver, the person who executed the affidavit must sign a statement witnessed by two credible persons and verified before a person authorized to take oaths. A copy of the revocation shall be delivered to the person designated in the affidavit of waiver of interest in a child. If a person attempting to revoke an affidavit under this subsection has knowledge that a suit for termination of the parent-child relationship based on the person's waiver of interest in a child has been filed, the person shall file a copy of the revocation with the clerk of the court.

(Acts 1995, 74th Leg., ch. 20, §1, effective April 20, 1995. Amended by Acts 1997, 75th Leg., ch. 561, §11, effective September 1, 1997.)

§161.107. Department's efforts to locate missing parent or relative

(a) In this section:

(1) "Parent" means a parent whose parent-child relationship with a child has not been terminated.

(2) "Relative" means a parent, grandparent, or adult sibling or child.

(b) If a parent of the child has not been personally served in a suit in which the Department of Protective and Regulatory Services seeks termination, the department must make a diligent effort to locate that parent.

(c) If a parent has not been personally served and cannot be located, the department shall make a diligent effort to locate a relative of the missing parent to give the relative an opportunity to request appointment as the child's managing conservator.

(d) If the department is not able to locate a missing parent or a relative of that parent and sufficient information is available concerning the physical whereabouts of the parent or relative, the department shall request the state agency designated to administer a statewide plan for child support to use the parental locator service established under 42 U.S.C. Section 653 to determine the location of the missing parent or relative.

(e) The department shall be required to provide evidence to the court to show what actions were taken by the department in making a diligent effort to locate the missing parent and relative of the missing parent.

(Acts 1995, 74th Leg., ch. 20, §1, effective April 20, 1995. Amended by Acts 1995, 74th Leg., ch. 751, §71, effective September 1, 1995.)

§161.108. Mother may authorize release of child from hospital before execution of affidavit

(a) Before or at the time an affidavit of relinquishment of parental rights under Section 161.103 is executed, the mother of a newborn child may authorize the release of the child from the hospital or birthing center to a licensed child-placing agency, the Department of Protective and Regulatory Services, or another designated person.

(b) A release under this section must be:

(1) executed in writing;

(2) witnessed by two credible adults; and

(3) verified before a person authorized to take oaths.

(c) A hospital or birthing center shall comply with the terms of a release executed under this section without requiring a court order.
(Acts 1997, 75th Leg., ch. 561, §12, effective September 1, 1997.)

§161.109. Paternity registry certificate must be filed with court before termination

(a) If an affidavit of status of child as provided by this chapter states that the father of the child is unknown and no probable father is known, a certificate from the bureau of vital statistics signed by the registrar that a diligent search has been made of the paternity registry maintained by the bureau and that a registration has not been found pertaining to the father of the child in question must be filed with the court before a trial on the merits in the suit for termination may be held.

(b) In a proceeding to terminate parental rights in which the alleged or probable father has not been personally served with citation or signed an affidavit of relinquishment or an affidavit of waiver of interest, the court may not terminate the parental rights of the alleged or probable father, whether known or unknown, unless a certificate from the bureau of vital statistics signed by the registrar states that a diligent search has been made of the paternity registry maintained by the bureau and that a filing or registration has not been found pertaining to the father of the child in question.
(Acts 1997, 75th Leg., ch. 561, §12, effective September 1, 1997.)

c. Hearing and Order

§161.2011. Parent may request continuance until criminal charges are resolved

(a) A parent whose rights are subject to termination in a suit affecting the parent-child relationship and against whom criminal charges are filed that directly relate to the grounds for which termination is sought may file a motion requesting a continuance of the final trial in the suit until the criminal charges are resolved. The court may grant the motion only if the court finds that a continuance is in the best interest of the child. Notwithstanding any continuance granted, the court shall conduct status and permanency hearings with respect to the child as required by Chapter 263 and shall comply with the dismissal date under Section 263.401.

(b) Nothing in this section precludes the court from issuing appropriate temporary orders as authorized in this code.

(c) The court in which a suit to terminate the parent-child relationship is pending may render an order denying a parent access to a child if the parent is indicted for criminal activity that constitutes a ground for terminating the parent-child relationship under Section 161.001. The denial of access under this section shall continue until the date the criminal charges for which the parent was indicted are resolved and the court renders an order providing for access to the child by the parent.
(Acts 1997, 75th Leg., ch. 1022, §61, effective September 1, 1997. Amended by Acts 2001, 77th Leg., ch. 1090, §3, effective September 1, 2001.)

§161.202. Court shall give preferential setting to termination matters

In a termination suit, after a hearing, the court shall grant a motion for a preferential setting for a final hearing on the merits filed by a party to the suit or by the amicus attorney or attorney ad litem for the child and shall give precedence to that hearing over other civil cases if:

(1) termination would make the child eligible for adoption; and

(2) discovery has been completed or sufficient time has elapsed since the filing of the suit for the completion of all necessary and reasonable discovery if diligently pursued.
(Acts 1995, 74th Leg., ch. 20, §1, effective April 20, 1995. Amended by Acts 2001, 77th Leg., ch. 133, §5, effective September 1, 2001.)

§161.2021. Parents are to provide medical history

(a) In a termination suit, the court shall order each parent before the court to provide information regarding the medical history of the parent and the parent's ancestors.

(b) A parent may comply with the court's order under this section by completing the medical history report form adopted by the Department of Family and Protective Services under Section 161.1031.

(c) If the Department of Family and Protective Services is a party to the termination suit, the information provided under this section must be maintained in the department records relating to the child and made available to persons with whom the child is placed.
(Acts 2005, 79th Leg., ch. 1258, §2, effective September 1, 2005.)

§161.203. Court must approve dismissal of suit to terminate parental rights

A suit to terminate may not be dismissed nor may a nonsuit be taken unless the dismissal or nonsuit is approved by the court. The dismissal or nonsuit approved by the court is without prejudice.
(Acts 1995, 74th Leg., ch. 20, §1, effective April 20, 1995. Amended by Acts 2001, 77th Leg., ch. 1090, §4, effective September 1, 2001.)

§161.204. Court may terminate parental rights of man who signed affidavit of waiver of interest if in child's best interests

In a suit for termination, the court may render an order terminating the parent-child relationship between a child and a man who has signed an affidavit of waiver of interest in the child, if the termination is in the best interest of the child.
(Acts 1995, 74th Leg., ch. 20, §1, effective April 20, 1995. Amended by Acts 2001, 77th Leg., ch. 1090, §5, effective September 1, 2001.)

§161.205. Judicial alternatives to termination of parental rights

If the court does not order termination of the parent-child relationship, the court shall:

(1) deny the petition; or

(2) render any order in the best interest of the child.

(Acts 1995, 74th Leg., ch. 20, §1, effective April 20, 1995. Amended by Acts 2001, 77th Leg., ch. 1090, §6, effective September 1, 2001.)

§161.206. Standard and consequences of order terminating parental rights: clear and convincing evidence, divests all legal rights except inheritance, grandparent access

(a) If the court finds by clear and convincing evidence grounds for termination of the parent-child relationship,1 it shall render an order terminating the parent-child relationship.

(b) Except as provided by Section 161.2061, an order terminating the parent-child relationship divests the parent and the child of all legal rights and duties with respect to each other, except that the child retains the right to inherit from and through the parent unless the court otherwise provides.

(c) Nothing in this chapter precludes or affects the rights of a biological or adoptive maternal or paternal grandparent to reasonable access under Chapter 153.

(Acts 1995, 74th Leg., ch. 20, §1, effective April 20, 1995. Amended by Acts 1995, 74th Leg., ch. 709, §2, effective September 1, 1995; Acts 1995, 74th Leg., ch. 751, §72, effective September 1, 1995; Acts 2003, 78th Leg., ch. 561, §1, effective September 1, 2003.)

§161.2061. Limited post-termination contact terms

(a) If the court finds it to be in the best interest of the child, the court may provide in an order terminating the parent-child relationship that the biological parent who filed an affidavit of voluntary relinquishment of parental rights under Section 161.103 shall have limited post-termination contact with the child as provided by Subsection (b) on the agreement of the biological parent and the Department of Protective and Regulatory Services.

(b) The order of termination may include terms that allow the biological parent to:

(1) receive specified information regarding the child;

(2) provide written communications to the child; and

(3) have limited access to the child.

(c) The terms of an order of termination regarding limited post-termination contact may be enforced only if the party seeking enforcement pleads and proves that, before filing the motion for enforcement, the party attempted in good faith to resolve the disputed matters through mediation.

(d) The terms of an order of termination under this section are not enforceable by contempt.

(e) The terms of an order of termination regarding limited post-termination contact may not be modified.

(f) An order under this section does not:

(1) affect the finality of a termination order; or

(2) grant standing to a parent whose parental rights have been terminated to file any action under this title other than a motion to enforce the terms regarding limited post-termination contact until the court renders a subsequent adoption order with respect to the child.

(Acts 2003, 78th Leg., ch. 561, §2, effective September 1, 2003.)

§161.2062. Termination order may not require limited post-termination contact between child and biological parent in an adoption order

(a) An order terminating the parent-child relationship may not require that a subsequent adoption order include terms regarding limited post-termination contact between the child and a biological parent.

(b) The inclusion of a requirement for post-termination contact described by Subsection (a) in a termination order does not:

(1) affect the finality of a termination or subsequent adoption order; or

(2) grant standing to a parent whose parental rights have been terminated to file any action under this title after the court renders a subsequent adoption order with respect to the child.

(Acts 2003, 78th Leg., ch. 561, §2, effective September 1, 2003.)

§161.207. Court shall appoint managing conservator following termination

(a) If the court terminates the parent-child relationship with respect to both parents or to the only living parent, the court shall appoint a suitable, competent adult, the Department of Protective and Regulatory Services, a licensed child-placing agency, or an authorized agency as managing conservator of the child. An agency designated managing conservator in an unrevoked or irrevocable affidavit of relinquishment shall be appointed managing conservator.

(b) The order of appointment may refer to the docket number of the suit and need not refer to the parties nor be accompanied by any other papers in the record.

(Acts 1995, 74th Leg., ch. 20, §1, effective April 20, 1995.)

§161.208. Court may appoint Department as managing conservator in some cases

If a parent of the child has not been personally served in a suit in which the Department of Protective and Regulatory Services seeks termination, the court that terminates a parent-child relationship may not appoint the Department of Protective and Regulatory Services as permanent managing conservator of the child unless the court determines that:

(1) the department has made a diligent effort to locate a missing parent who has not been personally served and a relative of that parent; and

(2) a relative located by the department has had a reasonable opportunity to request appointment as managing conservator of the child or the department has not been able to locate the missing parent or a relative of the missing parent.

(Acts 1995, 74th Leg., ch. 20, §1, effective April 20, 1995.)

§161.209. Copy of order of termination need not be mailed to parties

A copy of an order of termination rendered under Section 161.206 is not required to be mailed to parties as provided by Rules 119a and 239a, Texas Rules of Civil Procedure.
(Acts 1995, 74th Leg., ch. 20, §1, effective April 20, 1995.)

§161.210. Court may order sealing of file

The court, on the motion of a party or on the court's own motion, may order the sealing of the file, the minutes of the court, or both, in a suit for termination.
(Acts 1995, 74th Leg., ch. 20, §1, effective April 20, 1995.)

§161.211. Validity of termination order is not subject to direct or collateral attack after 6 months

(a) Notwithstanding Rule 329, Texas Rules of Civil Procedure, the validity of an order terminating the parental rights of a person who has been personally served or who has executed an affidavit of relinquishment of parental rights or an affidavit of waiver of interest in a child or whose rights have been terminated under Section 161.002(b) is not subject to collateral or direct attack after the sixth month after the date the order was signed.

(b) Notwithstanding Rule 329, Texas Rules of Civil Procedure, the validity of an order terminating the parental rights of a person who is served by citation by publication is not subject to collateral or direct attack after the sixth month after the date the order was signed.

(c) A direct or collateral attack on an order terminating parental rights based on an unrevoked affidavit of relinquishment of parental rights or affidavit of waiver of interest in a child is limited to issues relating to fraud, duress, or coercion in the execution of the affidavit.
(Acts 1997, 75th Leg., ch. 600, §1, effective September 1, 1997; Acts 1997, 75th Leg., ch. 601, §2, effective September 1, 1997; by Acts 1999, 76th Leg., ch. 1390, §19, effective September 1, 1999.)

---

d. Standard of Proof

Texas first extended the clear-and-convincing standard of proof to termination proceedings in In re G.M., 596 S.W.2d 846 (Tex. 1980). The Texas Supreme Court reasoned that the constitutional interests at stake in the termination of parental rights are no less compelling than the liberty interest in an involuntary commitment proceeding. *Id.* at 847. This standard of proof was codified in Texas Family Code §161.001 *supra*. Texas's adoption of the clear-and-convincing standard of proof, by case law, occurred two years before the United States Supreme Court reached the same result in Santosky v. Kramer, 45 U.S. 745 (1982).

Although *G.M.* and *Santosky* established the clear-and-convincing standard of proof in termination proceedings, neither decision indicated how appellate courts are to review findings based on that burden of proof.

The Texas Supreme Court resolved the issue in In re C.H., 89 S.W. 3d 17 (Tex. 2002), in which the Texas Supreme Court reviewed the termination of a father's parental rights. The father abandoned the mother during her pregnancy, provided no assistance to the child after his birth, had an extensive criminal history involving drugs and assaults, and had no concrete plan to care for the child. Adopting an enhanced standard of review, the state supreme court held that the appellate standard for reviewing termination findings is "whether the evidence is such that a factfinder could reasonably form a firm belief or conviction about the truth of the State's allegation." *Id.* at 26. The court remanded the case for determination under the announced standard. Subsequently, the mother relinquished her parental rights and the Texas Court of Appeals issued a memorandum stating there was enough evidence that the father was "incapable of child-rearing and that a reasonable jury could form a firm conviction or belief from all the evidence that termination of his parental rights would be in C.H.'s best interest" (In re C.H., 2003 WL 789179).

e. Right to Counsel

Under the Child Abuse Prevention and Treatment Act (CAPTA), 42 U.S.C. §5106a(b), states were required (to qualify for federal funding) to provide for the appointment of guardians ad litem for every child involved in child abuse or neglect proceedings. Despite the federal requirement, CAPTA did not require that states appoint attorneys as guardians ad litem.

Recent years have witnessed increasing demands for guidelines for guardians ad litem and lawyers who represent children. In 1996, the ABA House of Delegates approved guidelines for lawyers representing abused or neglected children. See American Bar Association, Standards of Practice for Lawyers Who Represent Children in Abuse and Neglect Cases (1996). See generally David R. Katner, Coming to Praise, Not to Bury, the New ABA Standards of Practice for Lawyers Who Represent Children in Abuse and Neglect Cases, 14 Geo. J. Legal Ethics 103 (2000). Note that the ABA's Standards of Practice for Lawyers Representing Children in Custody Cases, approved by the ABA in 2003, apply to all children in custody proceedings except abuse or neglect cases initiated by a governmental entity. See Linda D. Elrod, Raising the Bar for Lawyers Who Represent Children: ABA Standards of Practice for Custody Cases, 37 Fam. L.Q. 105 (2003).

The Supreme Court has held that the Due Process Clause does not require that an indigent be afforded counsel prior to termination of parental rights. Lassiter v. Dept. of Soc. Servs., 452 U.S. 18 (1991). Nonetheless, Texas statute provides that the court "shall appoint an attorney ad litem to represent the interests of an indigent parent . . . who responds in opposition to the termination" (Tex. Fam. Code §107.013(a)). Similarly, the court shall appoint representation for the child in a suit by a governmental agency for termination of the parent-child relationship (Tex. Fam. Code §107.012). Texas also requires that the court appoint a guardian ad litem to represent the best interests of a child in a suit by a governmental agency for termination of the parent-child relationship (Tex. Fam. Code §107.011).

Texas Family Code

§107.001. Definition of terms

In this chapter:

(1) "Amicus attorney" means an attorney appointed by the court in a suit, other than a suit filed by a governmental entity, whose role is to provide legal services necessary to assist the court in protecting a child's best interests rather than to provide legal services to the child.

(2) "Attorney ad litem" means an attorney who provides legal services to a person, including a child, and who owes to the person the duties of undivided loyalty, confidentiality, and competent representation.

(3) "Developmentally appropriate" means structured to account for a child's age, level of education, cultural background, and degree of language acquisition.

(4) "Dual role" means the role of an attorney who is appointed under Section 107.0125 to act as both guardian ad litem and attorney ad litem for a child in a suit filed by a governmental entity.

(5) "Guardian ad litem" means a person appointed to represent the best interests of a child. The term includes:

(A) a volunteer advocate appointed under Subchapter C;

(B) a professional, other than an attorney, who holds a relevant professional license and whose training relates to the determination of a child's best interests;

(C) an adult having the competence, training, and expertise determined by the court to be sufficient to represent the best interests of the child; or

(D) an attorney ad litem appointed to serve in the dual role.

(Acts 1995, 74th Leg., ch. 751, §15, effective September 1, 1995; Acts 1997, 75th Leg., ch. 1294, §1, effective September 1, 1997; Acts 2003, 78th Leg., ch. 262, §1, effective September 1, 2003.)

§107.002. Duties of guardian ad litem

(a) A guardian ad litem appointed for a child under this chapter is not a party to the suit but may:

(1) conduct an investigation to the extent that the guardian ad litem considers necessary to determine the best interests of the child; and

(2) obtain and review copies of the child's relevant medical, psychological, and school records as provided by Section 107.006.

(b) A guardian ad litem appointed for the child under this chapter shall:

(1) within a reasonable time after the appointment, interview:

(A) the child in a developmentally appropriate manner, if the child is four years of age or older;

(B) each person who has significant knowledge of the child's history and condition, including any foster parent of the child; and

(C) the parties to the suit;

(2) seek to elicit in a developmentally appropriate manner the child's expressed objectives;

(3) consider the child's expressed objectives without being bound by those objectives;

(4) encourage settlement and the use of alternative forms of dispute resolution; and

(5) perform any specific task directed by the court.

(c) A guardian ad litem appointed for the child under this chapter is entitled to:

(1) receive a copy of each pleading or other paper filed with the court in the case in which the guardian ad litem is appointed;

(2) receive notice of each hearing in the case;

(3) participate in case staffings by an authorized agency concerning the child;

(4) attend all legal proceedings in the case but may not call or question a witness or otherwise provide legal services unless the guardian ad litem is a licensed attorney who has been appointed in the dual role;

(5) review and sign, or decline to sign, an agreed order affecting the child; and

(6) explain the basis for the guardian ad litem's opposition to the agreed order if the guardian ad litem does not agree to the terms of a proposed order.

(d) The court may compel the guardian ad litem to attend a trial or hearing and to testify as necessary for the proper disposition of the suit.

(e) Unless the guardian ad litem is an attorney who has been appointed in the dual role and subject to the Texas Rules of Evidence, the court shall ensure in a hearing or in a trial on the merits that a guardian ad litem has an opportunity to testify regarding, and is permitted to submit a report regarding, the guardian ad litem's recommendations relating to:

(1) the best interests of the child; and

(2) the bases for the guardian ad litem's recommendations.

(f) In a nonjury trial, a party may call the guardian ad litem as a witness for the purpose of cross-examination regarding the guardian's report without the guardian ad litem being listed as a witness by a party. If the guardian ad litem is not called as a witness, the court shall permit the guardian ad litem to testify in the narrative.

(g) In a contested case, the guardian ad litem shall provide copies of the guardian ad litem's report, if any, to the attorneys for the parties as directed by the court, but not later than the earlier of:

(1) the date required by the scheduling order; or

(2) the 10th day before the date of the commencement of the trial.

(h) Disclosure to the jury of the contents of a guardian ad litem's report to the court is subject to the Texas Rules of Evidence.

(Acts 1995, 74th Leg., ch. 20, §1, effective September 1, 1995. Amended by Acts 1995, 74th Leg., ch. 943, §10, effective September 1, 1995; Acts 1997, 75th Leg., ch. 1294, §2, effective September 1, 1997; Acts 2003, 78th Leg., ch. 262, §1, effective September 1, 2003; Acts 2005, 79th Leg., ch. 172, §1, effective September 1, 2005.)

§107.003.Duties of attorney ad litem and amicus attorney

An attorney ad litem appointed to represent a child or an amicus attorney appointed to assist the court:

(1) shall:

(A) subject to Rules 4.02, 4.03, and 4.04, Texas Disciplinary Rules of Professional Conduct, and within a reasonable time after the appointment, interview:

(i) the child in a developmentally appropriate manner, if the child is four years of age or older;

(ii) each person who has significant knowledge of the child's history and condition, including any foster parent of the child; and

(iii) the parties to the suit;

(B) seek to elicit in a developmentally appropriate manner the child's expressed objectives of representation;

(C) consider the impact on the child in formulating the attorney's presentation of the child's expressed objectives of representation to the court;

(D) investigate the facts of the case to the extent the attorney considers appropriate;

(E) obtain and review copies of relevant records relating to the child as provided by Section 107.006;

(F) participate in the conduct of the litigation to the same extent as an attorney for a party;

(G) take any action consistent with the child's interests that the attorney considers necessary to expedite the proceedings;

(H) encourage settlement and the use of alternative forms of dispute resolution; and

(I) review and sign, or decline to sign, a proposed or agreed order affecting the child;

(2) must be trained in child advocacy or have experience determined by the court to be equivalent to that training; and

(3) is entitled to:

(A) request clarification from the court if the role of the attorney is ambiguous;

(B) request a hearing or trial on the merits;

(C) consent or refuse to consent to an interview of the child by another attorney;

(D) receive a copy of each pleading or other paper filed with the court;

(E) receive notice of each hearing in the suit;

(F) participate in any case staffing concerning the child conducted by an authorized agency; and

(G) attend all legal proceedings in the suit.

(Acts 1997, 75th Leg., ch. 1294, §3, effective September 1, 1997. Amended by Acts 2003, 78th Leg., ch. 262, §1, effective September 1, 2003; Acts 2005, 79th Leg., ch. 172, §2, effective September 1, 2005.)

§107.004. Other duties of attorney ad litem

(a) Except as otherwise provided by this chapter, the attorney ad litem appointed for a child shall, in a developmentally appropriate manner:

(1) advise the child;

(2) represent the child's expressed objectives of representation and follow the child's expressed objectives of representation during the course of litigation if the attorney ad litem determines that the child is competent to understand the nature of an attorney-client relationship and has formed that relationship with the attorney ad litem; and

(3) as appropriate, considering the nature of the appointment, become familiar with the American Bar Association's standards of practice for attorneys who represent children in abuse and neglect cases, the suggested amendments to those standards adopted by the National Association of Counsel for Children, and the American Bar Association's standards of practice for attorneys who represent children in custody cases.

(b) An attorney ad litem appointed for a child in a proceeding under Chapter 262 or 263 shall complete at least three hours of continuing legal education relating to child advocacy as described by Subsection (c) as soon as practicable after the attorney ad litem's appointment. An attorney ad litem is not required to comply with this subsection if the court finds that the attorney ad litem has experience equivalent to the required education.

(c) The continuing legal education required by Subsection (b) must:

(1) be low-cost and available to persons throughout this state, including on the Internet provided through the State Bar of Texas; and

(2) focus on the duties of an attorney ad litem in, and the procedures of and best practices for, a proceeding under Chapter 262 or 263.

(d) Except as provided by Subsection (e), an attorney ad litem appointed for a child in a proceeding under Chapter 262 or 263 shall meet before each court hearing with:

(1) the child, if the child is at least four years of age; or

(2) the individual with whom the child ordinarily resides, including the child's parent, conservator, guardian, caretaker, or custodian, if the child is younger than four years of age.

(e) An attorney ad litem appointed for a child in a proceeding under Chapter 262 or 263 is not required to comply with Subsection (d) before a hearing if the court finds at that hearing that the attorney ad litem has shown good cause why the attorney ad litem's compliance with that subsection is not feasible or in the best interest of the child.

(Acts 2003, 78th Leg., ch. 262, §1, effective September 1, 2003. Amended by Acts 2005, 79th Leg., ch. 172, §3, effective September 1, 2005; Acts 2005, 79th Leg., ch. 268, §1.04(a), effective September 1, 2005.)

§107.005. Other duties of amicus attorney

(a) Subject to any specific limitation in the order of appointment, an amicus attorney shall advocate the best interests of the child after reviewing the facts and circumstances of the case. Notwithstanding Subsection (b), in determining the best interests of the child, an amicus attorney is not bound by the child's expressed objectives of representation.

(b) An amicus attorney shall, in a developmentally appropriate manner:

(1) with the consent of the child, ensure that the child's expressed objectives of representation are made known to the court;

(2) explain the role of the amicus attorney to the child;

(3) inform the child that the amicus attorney may use information that the child provides in providing assistance to the court; and

(4) become familiar with the American Bar Association's standards of practice for attorneys who represent children in custody cases.

(c) An amicus attorney may not disclose confidential communications between the amicus attorney and the child unless the amicus attorney determines that disclosure is necessary to assist the court regarding the best interests of the child.

(Acts 2003, 78th Leg., ch. 262, §1, effective September 1, 2003. Amended by Acts 2005, 79th Leg., ch. 172, §4, effective September 1, 2005.)

§107.006. Court shall authorize the attorney ad litem, guardian ad litem, or amicus attorney access and information to the child

(a) Except as provided by Subsection (c), in conjunction with an appointment under this chapter, other than an appointment of an attorney ad litem for an adult or a parent, the court shall issue an order authorizing the attorney ad litem, guardian ad litem for the child, or amicus attorney to have immediate access to the child and any information relating to the child.

(b) Without requiring a further order or release, the custodian of any relevant records relating to the child, including records regarding social services, law enforcement records, school records, records of a probate or court proceeding, and records of a trust or account for which the child is a beneficiary, shall provide access to a person authorized to access the records under Subsection (a).

(c) A medical, mental health, or drug or alcohol treatment record of a child that is privileged or confidential under other law may be released to a person appointed under Subsection (a) only in accordance with the other law.

(Acts 1995, 74th Leg., ch. 943, §11, effective September 1, 1995. Amended by Acts 1997, 75th Leg., ch. 1294, §4, effective September 1, 1997; Acts 2003, 78th Leg., ch. 262, §1, effective September 1, 2003; Acts 2005, 79th Leg., ch. 172, §5, effective September 1, 2005.)

§107.007. Attorney privilege

(a) An attorney ad litem, an attorney serving in the dual role, or an amicus attorney may not:

(1) be compelled to produce attorney work product developed during the appointment as an attorney;

(2) be required to disclose the source of any information;

(3) submit a report into evidence; or

(4) testify in court except as authorized by Rule 3.08, Texas Disciplinary Rules of Professional Conduct.

(b) Subsection (a) does not apply to the duty of an attorney to report child abuse or neglect under Section 261.101.

(Acts 2003, 78th Leg., ch. 262, §1, effective September 1, 2003.)

§107.008. Factors in which an attorney ad litem may substitute for the child's judgment

(a) An attorney ad litem appointed to represent a child or an attorney appointed in the dual role may determine that the child cannot meaningfully formulate the child's objectives of representation in a case because the child:

(1) lacks sufficient maturity to understand and form an attorney-client relationship with the attorney;

(2) despite appropriate legal counseling, continues to express objectives of representation that would be seriously injurious to the child; or

(3) for any other reason is incapable of making reasonable judgments and engaging in meaningful communication.

(b) An attorney ad litem or an attorney appointed in the dual role who determines that the child cannot meaningfully formulate the child's expressed objectives of representation may present to the court a position that the attorney determines will serve the best interests of the child.

(c) If a guardian ad litem has been appointed for the child in a suit filed by a governmental entity requesting termination of the parent-child relationship or appointment of the entity as conservator of the child, an attorney ad litem who determines that the child cannot meaningfully formulate the child's expressed objectives of representation:

(1) shall consult with the guardian ad litem and, without being bound by the guardian ad litem's opinion or recommendation, ensure that the guardian ad litem's opinion and basis for any recommendation regarding the best interests of the child are presented to the court; and

(2) may present to the court a position that the attorney determines will serve the best interests of the child.

(Acts 2003, 78th Leg., ch. 262, §1, effective September 1, 2003. Amended by Acts 2005, 79th Leg., ch. 172, §6, effective September 1, 2005.)

§107.009. Immunity of guardian ad litem and attorney ad litem

(a) A guardian ad litem, an attorney ad litem, or an amicus attorney appointed under this chapter is not liable for civil damages arising from an action taken, a recommendation made, or an opinion given in the capacity of guardian ad litem, attorney ad litem, or amicus attorney.

(b) Subsection (a) does not apply to an action taken, a recommendation made, or an opinion given:

(1) with conscious indifference or reckless disregard to the safety of another;

(2) in bad faith or with malice; or

(3) that is grossly negligent or willfully wrongful.

(Acts 2003, 78th Leg., ch. 262, §1, effective September 1, 2003. Amended by Acts 2005, 79th Leg., ch. 172, §7, effective September 1, 2005.)

§107.010. Court may appoint an attorney ad litem for an incapacitated person

The court may appoint an attorney to serve as an attorney ad litem for a person entitled to service of citation in a suit if the court finds that the person is incapacitated. The attorney ad litem shall follow the person's expressed objectives of

representation and, if appropriate, refer the proceeding to the proper court for guardianship proceedings.
(Acts 2003, 78th Leg., ch. 262, §1, effective September 1, 2003.)

§107.011. Appointment of guardian ad litem

(a) Except as otherwise provided by this subchapter, in a suit filed by a governmental entity seeking termination of the parent-child relationship or the appointment of a conservator for a child, the court shall appoint a guardian ad litem to represent the best interests of the child immediately after the filing of the petition but before the full adversary hearing.

(b) The guardian ad litem appointed for a child under this section may be:

(1) a charitable organization composed of volunteer advocates or an individual volunteer advocate appointed under Subchapter C;

(2) an adult having the competence, training, and expertise determined by the court to be sufficient to represent the best interests of the child; or

(3) an attorney appointed in the dual role.

(c) The court may not appoint a guardian ad litem in a suit filed by a governmental entity if an attorney is appointed in the dual role unless the court appoints another person to serve as guardian ad litem for the child and restricts the role of the attorney to acting as an attorney ad litem for the child.

(d) The court may appoint an attorney to serve as guardian ad litem for a child without appointing the attorney to serve in the dual role only if the attorney is specifically appointed to serve only in the role of guardian ad litem. An attorney appointed solely as a guardian ad litem:

(1) may take only those actions that may be taken by a nonattorney guardian ad litem; and

(2) may not:

(A) perform legal services in the case; or

(B) take any action that is restricted to a licensed attorney, including engaging in discovery other than as a witness, making opening and closing statements, or examining witnesses.

(Acts 1995, 74th Leg., ch. 751, §15, effective September 1, 1995. Amended by Acts 2003, 78th Leg., ch. 262, §1, effective September 1, 2003.)

§107.012. Court shall appoint attorney ad litem for child in suit by government entity

In a suit filed by a governmental entity requesting termination of the parent-child relationship or to be named conservator of a child, the court shall appoint an attorney ad litem to represent the interests of the child immediately after the filing, but before the full adversary hearing, to ensure adequate representation of the child.
(Acts 1995, 74th Leg., ch. 751, §15, effective September 1, 1995. Amended by Acts 2003, 78th Leg., ch. 262, §1, effective September 1, 2003.)

§107.0125. Court may appoint an attorney to serve in the dual role

(a) In order to comply with the mandatory appointment of a guardian ad litem under Section 107.011 and the mandatory appointment of an attorney ad litem under Section 107.012, the court may appoint an attorney to serve in the dual role.

(b) If the court appoints an attorney to serve in the dual role under this section, the court may at any time during the pendency of the suit appoint another person to serve as guardian ad litem for the child and restrict the attorney to acting as an attorney ad litem for the child.

(c) An attorney appointed to serve in the dual role may request the court to appoint another person to serve as guardian ad litem for the child. If the court grants the attorney's request, the attorney shall serve only as the attorney ad litem for the child.

(d) Unless the court appoints another person as guardian ad litem in a suit filed by a governmental entity, an appointment of an attorney to serve as an attorney ad litem in a suit filed by a governmental entity is an appointment to serve in the dual role regardless of the terminology used in the appointing order.
(Acts 2003, 78th Leg., ch. 262, §1, effective September 1, 2003.)

§107.013. Court shall appoint attorney ad litem to represent parent

(a) In a suit filed by a governmental entity in which termination of the parent-child relationship is requested, the court shall appoint an attorney ad litem to represent the interests of:

(1) an indigent parent of the child who responds in opposition to the termination;

(2) a parent served by citation by publication;

(3) an alleged father who failed to register with the registry under Chapter 160 and whose identity or location is unknown; and

(4) an alleged father who registered with the paternity registry under Chapter 160, but the petitioner's attempt to personally serve citation at the address provided to the registry and at any other address for the alleged father known by the petitioner has been unsuccessful.

(b) If both parents of the child are entitled to the appointment of an attorney ad litem under this section and the court finds that the interests of the parents are not in conflict, the court may appoint an attorney ad litem to represent the interests of both parents.

(c) In a suit filed by a governmental entity requesting temporary managing conservatorship of a child, the court shall appoint an attorney ad litem to represent the interests of an indigent parent of the child who responds in opposition to the suit.
(Acts 1995, 74th Leg., ch. 751, §15, effective September 1, 1995. Amended by Acts 1997, 75th Leg., ch. 561, §3, effective September 1, 1997; Acts 2001, 77th Leg., ch. 821, §2.11, effective June 14, 2001; Acts 2003, 78th Leg., ch. 262, §1, effective September 1, 2003; Acts 2005, 79th Leg., ch. 268, §1.06, effective September 1, 2005.)

§107.015. Attorney ad litem is entitled to reasonable fees

(a) An attorney appointed under this chapter to serve as an attorney ad litem for a child, an attorney in the dual role, or an attorney ad litem for a parent is entitled to reasonable fees and expenses in the amount set by the court to be paid by the parents of the child unless the parents are indigent.

(b) If the court determines that one or more of the parties are able to defray the fees and expenses of an attorney ad litem or guardian ad litem for the child as determined by the reasonable and customary fees for similar services in the county of jurisdiction, the fees and expenses may be ordered paid by one or more of those parties, or the court may order one or more of those parties, prior to final hearing, to pay the sums into the registry of the court or into an account authorized by the court for the use and benefit of the payee on order of the court. The sums may be taxed as costs to be assessed against one or more of the parties.

(c) If indigency of the parents is shown, an attorney ad litem appointed to represent a child or parent in a suit filed by a governmental entity shall be paid from the general funds of the county according to the fee schedule that applies to an attorney appointed to represent a child in a suit under Title 3 as provided by Chapter 51. The court may not award attorney ad litem fees under this chapter against the state, a state agency, or a political subdivision of the state except as provided by this subsection.

(d) A person appointed as a guardian ad litem or attorney ad litem shall complete and submit to the court a voucher or claim for payment that lists the fees charged and hours worked by the guardian ad litem or attorney ad litem. Information submitted under this section is subject to disclosure under Chapter 552, Government Code.

(Acts 1995, 74th Leg., ch. 20, §1, effective April 20, 1995. Redesignated from Family Code §107.003 by Acts 1995, 74th Leg., ch. 751, §15, effective September 1, 1995. Amended by Acts 1999, 76th Leg., ch. 1390, §6, effective September 1, 1999; Acts 2003, 78th Leg., ch. 262, §1, effective September 1, 2003; Acts 2005, 79th Leg., ch. 268, §1.07, effective September 1, 2005.)

§107.016. Court may provide for continued representation by attorney ad litem or guardian ad litem

In a suit filed by a governmental entity in which termination of the parent-child relationship or appointment of the entity as conservator of the child is requested, an order appointing the Department of Protective and Regulatory Services as the child's managing conservator may provide for the continuation of the appointment of the guardian ad litem or attorney ad litem for the child for any period set by the court.

(Acts 1995, 74th Leg., ch. 751, §15, effective September 1, 1995. Amended by Acts 1997, 75th Leg., ch. 575, §6, effective September 1, 1997; Acts 2003, 78th Leg., ch. 262, §1, effective September 1, 2003.)

§107.017. Court may not appoint an amicus attorney in suit filed by government entity

The court may not appoint a person to serve as an amicus attorney in a suit filed by a governmental entity under this chapter.

(Acts 2003, 78th Leg., ch. 262, §1, effective September 1, 2003.)

§107.021. Court has discretion in appointments

(a) In a suit in which the best interests of a child are at issue, other than a suit filed by a governmental entity requesting termination of the parent-child relationship or appointment of the entity as conservator of the child, the court may appoint one of the following:

(1) an amicus attorney;

(2) an attorney ad litem; or

(3) a guardian ad litem.

(a-1) In a suit requesting termination of the parent-child relationship that is not filed by a governmental entity, the court shall, unless the court finds that the interests of the child will be represented adequately by a party to the suit whose interests are not in conflict with the child's interests, appoint one of the following:

(1) an amicus attorney; or

(2) an attorney ad litem.

(b) In determining whether to make an appointment under this section, the court:

(1) shall:

(A) give due consideration to the ability of the parties to pay reasonable fees to the appointee; and

(B) balance the child's interests against the cost to the parties that would result from an appointment by taking into consideration the cost of available alternatives for resolving issues without making an appointment;

(2) may make an appointment only if the court finds that the appointment is necessary to ensure the determination of the best interests of the child, unless the appointment is otherwise required by this code; and

(3) may not require a person appointed under this section to serve without reasonable compensation for the services rendered by the person.

(Acts 2003, 78th Leg., ch. 262, §1, effective September 1, 2003. Amended by Acts 2005, 79th Leg., ch. 172, §8, effective September 1, 2005.)

§107.022. Court is prohibited from some appointments in suits not filed by a governmental entity

In a suit other than a suit filed by a governmental entity requesting termination of the parent-child relationship or appointment of the entity as conservator of the child, the court may not appoint:

(1) an attorney to serve in the dual role; or

(2) a volunteer advocate to serve as guardian ad litem for a child unless the training of the volunteer advocate is designed for participation in suits other than suits filed by a governmental entity requesting termination of the parent-child relationship or appointment of the entity as conservator of the child.

(Acts 2003, 78th Leg., ch. 262, §1, effective September 1, 2003. Amended by Acts 2005, 79th Leg., ch. 172, §9, effective September 1, 2005.)

§107.023. Reasonable fees in suits not filed by a governmental entity

(a) In a suit other than a suit filed by a governmental entity requesting termination of the parent-child relationship or appointment of the entity as conservator of the child, in addition to the attorney's fees that may be awarded under Chapter 106, the following persons are entitled to reasonable fees and expenses in an amount set by the court and ordered to be paid by one or more parties to the suit:

(1) an attorney appointed as an amicus attorney or as an attorney ad litem for the child; and

(2) a professional who holds a relevant professional license and who is appointed as guardian ad litem for the child, other than a volunteer advocate.

(b) The court shall:

(1) determine the fees and expenses of an amicus attorney, an attorney ad litem, or a guardian ad litem by reference to the reasonable and customary fees for similar services in the county of jurisdiction;

(2) order a reasonable cost deposit to be made at the time the court makes the appointment; and

(3) before the final hearing, order an additional amount to be paid to the credit of a trust account for the use and benefit of the amicus attorney, attorney ad litem, or guardian ad litem.

(c) A court may not award costs, fees, or expenses to an amicus attorney, attorney ad litem, or guardian ad litem against the state, a state agency, or a political subdivision of the state under this part.

(d) The court may determine that fees awarded under this subchapter to an amicus attorney, an attorney ad litem for the child, or a guardian ad litem for the child are necessaries for the benefit of the child.

(Acts 2003, 78th Leg., ch. 262, §1, effective September 1, 2003. Amended by Acts 2005, 79th Leg., ch. 172, §10, effective September 1, 2005.)

§107.031. Court may appoint volunteer advocates on behalf of child

(a) In a suit filed by a governmental entity requesting termination of the parent-child relationship or appointment of the entity as conservator of the child, the court may appoint a charitable organization composed of volunteer advocates whose charter mandates the provision of services to allegedly abused and neglected children or an individual who has received the court's approved training regarding abused and neglected children and who has been certified by the court to appear at court hearings as a guardian ad litem for the child or as a volunteer advocate for the child.

(b) In a suit other than a suit filed by a governmental entity requesting termination of the parent-child relationship or appointment of the entity as conservator of the child, the court may appoint a charitable organization composed of volunteer advocates whose training provides for the provision of services in private custody disputes or a person who has received the court's approved training regarding the subject matter of the suit and who has been certified by the court to appear at court hearings as a guardian ad litem for the child or as a volunteer advocate for the child. A person appointed under this subsection is not entitled to fees under Section 107.023.

(c) A court-certified volunteer advocate appointed under this section may be assigned to act as a surrogate parent for the child, as provided by 20 U.S.C. Section 1415(b), if:

(1) the child is in the conservatorship of the Department of Family and Protective Services;

(2) the volunteer advocate is serving as guardian ad litem for the child; and

(3) a foster parent of the child is not acting as the child's parent under Section 29.015, Education Code.

(Acts 1995, 74th Leg., ch. 751, §15, effective September 1, 1995. Amended by Acts 1997, 75th Leg., ch. 1294, §6, effective September 1, 1997; Acts 1999, 76th Leg., ch. 430, §3, effective September 1, 1999; Acts 2003, 78th Leg., ch. 262, §1, effective September 1, 2003; Acts 2005, 79th Leg., ch. 172, §11, effective September 1, 2005.)

H. STATE'S RESPONSIBILITY TO PROVIDE SERVICES

Many states require that, before terminating parental rights, the state first must provide rehabilitation services to the parents (including reunification efforts), and that the parent must make reasonable progress toward the return of the child. To enable states to qualify for federal funding for administering foster care and adoption services, the Adoption Assistance and Child Welfare Act (AACWA) of 1980, 42 U.S.C. §§620 et seq., 670 et seq., provides that a state must make "reasonable efforts" to prevent the need to remove a child from the home and to facilitate the child's return as soon as possible. In 1997, Congress enacted the Adoption and Safe Families Act (ASFA) as a response to the concern that the policy of family preservation and reunification, as mandated by the AACWA, was exposing children to unnecessary risks. ASFA removed the "reasonable efforts" requirement in cases in which the child was the victim of aggravated circumstances and emphasized speedier termination of parental rights. 42 U.S.C. §671(a)(15)(D)(i), (ii), (iii). Texas has a similar provision, permitting a court to waive the "reasonable efforts" requirement in aggravated circumstances (Tex. Fam. Code §262.2015).

1. Services Generally

§262.2015. Court may waive service plan and reasonable-efforts requirement in aggravated circumstances

(a) The court may waive the requirement of a service plan and the requirement to make reasonable efforts to return the child to a parent and may accelerate the trial schedule to result in a final order for a child under the care of the department at an earlier date than provided by Subchapter D, Chapter 263, if the court finds that the parent has subjected the child to aggravated circumstances.

(b) The court may find under Subsection (a) that a parent has subjected the child to aggravated circumstances if:

(1) the parent abandoned the child without identification or a means for identifying the child;

(2) the child is a victim of serious bodily injury or sexual abuse inflicted by the parent or by another person with the parent's consent;

(3) the parent has engaged in conduct against the child that would constitute an offense under the following provisions of the Penal Code:

(A) Section 19.02 (murder);

(B) Section 19.03 (capital murder);

(C) Section 19.04 (manslaughter);

(D) Section 21.11 (indecency with a child);

(E) Section 22.011 (sexual assault);

(F) Section 22.02 (aggravated assault);

(G) Section 22.021 (aggravated sexual assault);

(H) Section 22.04 (injury to a child, elderly individual, or disabled individual);

(I) Section 22.041 (abandoning or endangering child);

(J) Section 25.02 (prohibited sexual conduct);

(K) Section 43.25 (sexual performance by a child); or

(L) Section 43.26 (possession or promotion of child pornography);

(4) the parent voluntarily left the child alone or in the possession of another person not the parent of the child for at least six months without expressing an intent to return and without providing adequate support for the child;

(5) the parent's parental rights with regard to another child have been involuntarily terminated based on a finding that the parent's conduct violated Section 161.001(1)(D) or (E) or a substantially equivalent provision of another state's law;

(6) the parent has been convicted for:

(A) the murder of another child of the parent and the offense would have been an offense under 18 U.S.C. Section 1111(a) if the offense had occurred in the special maritime or territorial jurisdiction of the United States;

(B) the voluntary manslaughter of another child of the parent and the offense would have been an offense under 18 U.S.C. Section 1112(a) if the offense had occurred in the special maritime or territorial jurisdiction of the United States;

(C) aiding or abetting, attempting, conspiring, or soliciting an offense under Subdivision (A) or (B); or

(D) the felony assault of the child or another child of the parent that resulted in serious bodily injury to the child or another child of the parent; or

(7) the parent's parental rights with regard to two other children have been involuntarily terminated.

(c) On finding that reasonable efforts to make it possible for the child to safely return to the child's home are not required, the court shall at any time before the 30th day after the date of the finding, conduct an initial permanency hearing under Subchapter D, Chapter 263. Separate notice of the permanency plan is not required but may be given with a notice of a hearing under this section.

(d) The Department of Protective and Regulatory Services shall make reasonable efforts to finalize the permanent placement of a child for whom the court has made the finding described by Subsection (c). The court shall set the suit for trial on the merits as required by Subchapter D, Chapter 263, in order to facilitate final placement of the child.

(Acts 1997, 75th Leg., ch. 1022, §79, effective September 1, 1997. Amended by Acts 1999, 76th Leg., ch. 1150, §21, effective September 1, 1999; Acts 1999, 76th Leg., ch. 1390, §40, effective September 1, 1999; Acts 2001, 77th Leg., ch. 849, §5, effective September 1, 2001; Acts 2005, 79th Leg., ch. 268, §1.35, effective September 1, 2005.)

§264.201. Objective of Departmental services

(a) When the department provides services directly or by contract to an abused or neglected child and the child's family, the services shall be designed to:

(1) prevent further abuse;

(2) alleviate the effects of the abuse suffered;

(3) prevent removal of the child from the home; and

(4) provide reunification services when appropriate for the return of the child to the home.

(b) The department shall emphasize ameliorative services for sexually abused children.

(c) The department shall provide or contract for necessary services to an abused or neglected child and the child's family without regard to whether the child remains in or is removed from the family home. If parental rights have been terminated, services may be provided only to the child.

(d) The services may include in-home programs, parenting skills training, youth coping skills, and individual and family counseling.

(e) The department may not provide and a court may not order the department to provide supervision for visitation in a child custody matter unless the department is a petitioner or intervener in the underlying suit.

(Acts 1995, 74th Leg., ch. 20, §1, effective April 20, 1995. Amended by Acts 1999, 76th Leg., ch. 1150, §28, effective September 1, 1999; Acts 1999, 76th Leg., ch. 1390, §49, effective September 1, 1999.)

§264.2015. Family group conferencing may be developed

The department may collaborate with the courts and other appropriate local entities to develop and implement family group conferencing as a strategy for promoting family preservation and permanency for children.

(Acts 2005, 79th Leg., ch. 268, §1.52, effective September 1, 2005.)

§264.202. Department shall define baseline of foster care services for abused children

(a) The department, with assistance from national organizations with expertise in child protective services, shall define a minimal baseline of in-home and foster care services for abused or neglected children that meets the professionally recognized standards for those services. The department shall attempt to provide services at a standard not lower than the minimal baseline standard.

(b) The department, with assistance from national organizations with expertise in child protective services, shall develop outcome measures to track and monitor the effectiveness of in-home and foster care services.
(Acts 1995, 74th Leg., ch. 20, §1, effective April 20, 1995.)

§264.205. Department shall develop swift adoption teams

(a) The department shall develop swift adoption teams to expedite the process of placing a child under the jurisdiction of the department for adoption. Swift adoption teams developed under this section shall, in performing their duties, attempt to place a child for adoption with an appropriate relative of the child.

(b) A swift adoption team shall consist of department personnel who shall operate under policies adopted by rule by the department. The department shall set priorities for the allocation of department resources to enable a swift adoption team to operate successfully under the policies adopted under this subsection.

(c) The department shall, using a system of measurement developed by the department, report to the legislature on the success of swift adoption teams in expediting the administrative procedures and the length of time in placing children for adoption. The report shall include recommendations by the department concerning legislation that would enable the department to further improve adoption placements. The department shall report under this section on or before December 1 of each even-numbered year.
(Acts 1995, 74th Leg., ch. 943, §9, effective September 1, 1995. Amended by Acts 2001, 77th Leg., ch. 306, §4, effective September 1, 2001.)

§264.206. Department shall begin promptly efforts to search for adoptive parents

(a) The department shall begin its efforts to locate qualified persons to adopt a child, including persons registered with the adoptive parent registry under Subchapter B, [Fam. Code §264.101] at the time the department's permanency plan for the child becomes the termination of the parent-child relationship and adoption of the child.

(b) The department shall report to the court in which the department petitions for termination of the parent-child relationship on the child's adoptability and the department's search for prospective adoptive parents for the child, including information relating to the department's efforts to work with licensed child-placing agencies.
(Acts 1997, 75th Leg., ch. 600, §19, effective September 1, 1997; Acts 1997, 75th Leg., ch. 1022, §94, effective September 1, 1997.)

§264.207. Department shall adopt policies for improvement of services

(a) The department shall adopt policies that provide for the improvement of the department's services for children and families, including policies that provide for conducting a home study within four months after the date an applicant is approved for an adoption and documenting the results of the home study within 30 days after the date the study is completed. The policies adopted under this section must:

(1) be designed to increase the accountability of the department to individuals who receive services and to the public; and

(2) assure consistency of services provided by the department in the different regions of the state.

(b) To accomplish the goals stated in Subsection (a), the department shall:

(1) establish time frames for the initial screening of families seeking to adopt children;

(2) provide for the evaluation of the effectiveness of the department's management-level employees in expeditiously making permanent placements for children;

(3) establish, as feasible, comprehensive assessment services in various locations in the state to determine the needs of children and families served by the department;

(4) emphasize and centralize the monitoring and promoting of the permanent placement of children receiving department services;

(5) establish goals and performance measures in the permanent placement of children;

(6) seek private licensed child-placing agencies to place a child in the department's managing conservatorship who has been available for permanent placement for more than 90 days;

(7) provide information to private licensed child-placing agencies concerning children under Subdivision (6);

(8) provide incentives for a private licensed child-placing agency that places a child, as defined by Section 162.301, under Subdivision (6);

(9) encourage foster parents to be approved by the department as both foster parents and adoptive parents;

(10) address failures by the department's service regions in making permanent placements for children in a reasonable time; and

(11) require the department's service regions to participate in the Texas Adoption Resources Exchange.
(Acts 1997, 75th Leg., ch. 600, §19, effective September 1, 1997; Acts 1997, 75th Leg., ch. 1022, §94, effective September 1, 1997.)

§264.208. Location of parents

(a) The department shall create a division staffed by personnel trained in locating parents and relatives of children throughout the state.

(b) The department shall use outside contractors and volunteer resources to the extent feasible to perform its responsibilities under this section.
(Acts 1999, 76th Leg., ch. 228, §3, effective September 1, 1999.)

§264.204. Funding for community organizations that respond to less serious cases

(a) The department shall administer a grant program to provide funding to community organizations, including faith-based or county organizations, to respond to:

(1) low-priority, less serious cases of abuse and neglect; and

(2) cases in which an allegation of abuse or neglect of a child was unsubstantiated but involved a family that has been previously investigated for abuse or neglect of a child.

(b) The executive commissioner shall adopt rules to implement the grant program, including rules governing the submission and approval of grant requests and the cancellation of grants.

(c) To receive a grant, a community organization whose grant request is approved must execute an interagency agreement or a contract with the department. The contract must require the organization receiving the grant to perform the services as stated in the approved grant request. The contract must contain appropriate provisions for program and fiscal monitoring.

(d) In areas of the state in which community organizations receive grants under the program, the department shall refer low-priority, less serious cases of abuse and neglect to a community organization receiving a grant under the program.

(e) A community organization receiving a referral under Subsection (d) shall make a home visit and offer family social services to enhance the parents' ability to provide a safe and stable home environment for the child. If the family chooses to use the family services, a case manager from the organization shall monitor the case and ensure that the services are delivered.

(f) If after the home visit the community organization determines that the case is more serious than the department indicated, the community organization shall refer the case to the department for a full investigation.

(g) The department may not award a grant to a community organization in an area of the state in which a similar program is already providing effective family services in the community.

(h) For purposes of this section, a case is considered to be a less serious case of abuse or neglect if:

(1) the circumstances of the case do not appear to involve a reasonable likelihood that the child will be abused or neglected in the foreseeable future; or

(2) the allegations in the report of child abuse or neglect:

(A) are general in nature or vague and do not support a determination that the child who is the subject of the report has been abused or neglected or will likely be abused or neglected; or

(B) if substantiated, would not be considered abuse or neglect under this chapter.

(Acts 2005, 79th Leg., ch. 268, §1.53, effective September 1, 2005.)

§264.2041. Promotion of cultural diversity

The department shall:

(1) develop and deliver cultural competency training to all service delivery staff;

(2) increase targeted recruitment efforts for foster and adoptive families who can meet the needs of children and youth who are waiting for permanent homes;

(3) target recruitment efforts to ensure diversity among department staff; and

(4) develop collaborative partnerships with community groups, agencies, faith-based organizations, and other community organizations to provide culturally competent services to children and families of every race and ethnicity.

(Acts 2005, 79th Leg., ch. 268, §1.54(a), effective September 1, 2005.)

2. Services for At-Risk Youth

§264.301. Services for at-risk youth

(a) The department shall operate a program to provide services for children in at-risk situations and for the families of those children.

(b) The services under this section may include:

(1) crisis family intervention;

(2) emergency short-term residential care;

(3) family counseling;

(4) parenting skills training;

(5) youth coping skills training;

(6) mentoring; and

(7) advocacy training.

(Acts 1995, 74th Leg., ch. 20, §1, effective April 20, 1995. Amended by Acts 1995, 74th Leg., ch. 262, § 58, effective January 1, 1996.)

§264.302. Early youth intervention services

(a) This section applies to a child who:

(1) is seven years of age or older and under 17 years of age; and

(2) has not had the disabilities of minority for general purposes removed under Chapter 31.

(b) The department shall operate a program under this section to provide services for children in at-risk situations and for the families of those children.

(c) The department may not provide services under this section to a child who has:

(1) at any time been referred to juvenile court for engaging in conduct that violates a penal law of this state of the grade of felony other than a state jail felony; or

(2) been found to have engaged in delinquent conduct under Title 3.

(d) The department may provide services under this section to a child who engages in conduct for which the child may be found by a court to be an at-risk child, without regard to whether the conduct violates a penal law of this state of the grade of felony other than a state jail felony, if the child was younger than 10 years of age at the time the child engaged in the conduct.

(e) The department shall provide services for a child and the child's family if a contract to provide services under this section is available in the county and the child is referred to the department as an at-risk child by:

(1) a court under Section 264.304;

(2) a juvenile court or probation department as part of a progressive sanctions program under Chapter 59;

(3) a law enforcement officer or agency under Section 52.03; or

(4) a justice or municipal court under Article 45.057, Code of Criminal Procedure.

(f) The services under this section may include:

(1) crisis family intervention;

(2) emergency short-term residential care for children 10 years of age or older;

(3) family counseling;

(4) parenting skills training;

(5) youth coping skills training;

(6) advocacy training; and

(7) mentoring.

(Acts 1995, 74th Leg., ch. 262, §58, effective January 1, 1996. Amended by Acts 1997, 75th Leg., ch. 1086, §30, effective September 1, 1997; Acts 1997, 75th Leg., ch. 575, §31, effective September 1, 1997; Acts 2001, 77th Leg., ch. 1514, §16, effective September 1, 2001.)

§264.303. Department may file civil action to request determination of at-risk child

(a) The department may file a civil action to request any district court or county court, other than a juvenile court, to determine that a child is an at- risk child. A person with whom the department contracts to provide services under Section 264.302 may file an action under this section if the department has approved the filing.

(b) Notice of the action must be provided to:

(1) the child;

(2) the parent, managing conservator, or guardian of the child; and

(3) any other member of the child's household who may be affected by an order of the court if the court finds that the child is an at-risk child.

(c) A person served with notice of the action may, but is not required, to file a written answer. Any answer must be filed before the hearing on the action begins.

(Acts 1995, 74th Leg., ch. 262, §58, effective January 1, 1996.)

§264.304. Court shall set hearing for determination of at-risk child

(a) Unless a later date is requested by the department, the court shall set a date and time for the hearing not later than 30 days after the date the action is filed.

(b) The court is the trier of fact at the hearing.

(c) The court shall determine that the child is an at-risk child if the court finds that the child has engaged in the following conduct:

(1) conduct, other than a traffic offense and except as provided by Subsection (d), that violates:

(A) the penal laws of this state; or

(B) the penal ordinances of any political subdivision of this state;

(2) the unexcused voluntary absence of the child on 10 or more days or parts of days within a six-month period or three or more days or parts of days within a four-week period from school without the consent of the child's parent, managing conservator, or guardian;

(3) the voluntary absence of the child from the child's home without the consent of the child's parent, managing conservator, or guardian for a substantial length of time or without intent to return;

(4) conduct that violates the laws of this state prohibiting driving while intoxicated or under the influence of intoxicating liquor (first or second offense) or driving while under the influence of any narcotic drug or of any other drug to a degree that renders the child incapable of safely driving a vehicle (first or second offense); or(5) conduct that evidences a clear and substantial intent to engage in any behavior described by Subdivisions (1)-(4).

(d) The court may not determine that a child is an at-risk child if the court finds that the child engaged in conduct violating the penal laws of this state of the grade of felony other than a state jail felony when the child was 10 years of age or older.

(Acts 1995, 74th Leg., ch. 262, §58, effective January 1, 1996.)

§264.305. Court may order services for at-risk child

(a) Except as provided by Subsection (b), if the court finds that the child is an at-risk child under Section 264.304, the court may order the child, the child's parent, managing conservator, or guardian or any other member of the child's household to participate in services provided by the department under Section 264.302 and contained in a plan approved by the court.

(b) The court may order an at-risk child to participate in services involving emergency short-term residential care only if the court finds that the child engaged in conduct described by Section 264.304(c)(1), (2), (3), or (4).

(c) An order rendered by a court under this section expires not later than six months after the date the order was rendered.

(Acts 1995, 74th Leg., ch. 262, §58, effective January 1, 1996.)

§264.306. Sanctions for failure to participate in services

(a) A child who violates a court order under Section 264.305 by failing to participate in services provided by the department engages in conduct indicating a need for supervision and the department shall refer the child to an appropriate juvenile authority for proceedings under Title 3 for that conduct.

(b) A parent, managing conservator, guardian, or other member of the child's household who violates a court order under Section 264.305 by failing to participate in services provided by the department is subject to contempt of court. The court may under its contempt powers impose a community service requirement.

(Acts 1995, 74th Leg., ch. 262, §58, effective January 1, 1996.)

XII. PARENT-CHILD RELATIONSHIP IN SPECIAL CONTEXTS

This chapter explores the parent-child relationship in special contexts. First, the chapter examines liability for children's tortious acts, rules applicable to minors' contracts and property issues, particularly minor's earnings and inheritance rights. Next, it explores the emancipation doctrine, the education context, and minor's rights to medical care (focusing on issues of consent). Finally, the chapter concludes with the subject of nonmarital children and the rules governing the adjudication of parentage.

A. INTRODUCTION

California Family Code

§6500. Definition of minor

A minor is an individual who is under 18 years of age. The period of minority is calculated from the first minute of the day on which the individual is born to the same minute of the corresponding day completing the period of minority.
(Stats. 1992 (A.B. 2650), ch. 162, §10, effective January 1, 1994.)

§6601. Minor may enforce rights in civil proceeding by guardian

A minor may enforce the minor's rights by civil action or other legal proceedings in the same manner as an adult, except that a guardian must conduct the action or proceedings.
(Stats. 1992 (A.B. 2650), ch. 162, §10, effective January 1, 1994.)

B. TORT LIABILITY

1. Negligence

A minor is liable for his or her torts (e.g., assault, battery, trespass, etc.). However, under the traditional rule, children have limited liability for acts of negligence. The traditional rule takes into account the minor's age and experience. See, e.g., Restatement (Second) Torts §283A (the child's standard of conduct is that of "a reasonable person of like age, intelligence and experience under like circumstances"). California subscribes to this traditional view. Weisbart v. Flohr, 67 Cal. Rptr. 114 (Ct. App. 1968) (finding a seven-year-old boy liable for injuries he inflicted on a neighbor child).

Contributory negligence by the plaintiff is normally a bar to recovery. Jurisdictions adopt different approaches when the contributorily negligent plaintiff is a child. The majority rule adopts an age-based standard of care for a child's contributory negligence. Similar to the Restatement rule on negligence, a child's capacity to be contributorily negligent depends on age, intelligence and experience in comparison with other children in similar circumstances. A minority of jurisdictions adopt a presumption based on age, holding that children below a certain age cannot be held contributorily negligent.

California follows the majority approach on contributory negligence. See, e.g., Pittman v. Pedro Petroleum Corp., 117 Cal. Rptr. 220 (Ct. App. 1974) (holding that thirteen-year-old boy who fell from ladder on an unenclosed oil well derrick was guilty of contributory negligence based on Restatement standard of conduct in evaluating child's negligence). See also Christian v. Goodwin, 10 Cal. Rptr. 507 (Ct. App. 1961) (holding that issue of contributory negligence of four year old who was hit by a car was a question for the jury).

§6600. Minor is civilly liable for his or her wrongs

A minor is civilly liable for a wrong done by the minor, but is not liable in exemplary damages unless at the time of the act the minor was capable of knowing that the act was wrongful.
(Stats. 1992 (A.B. 2650), ch. 162, §10, effective January 1, 1994.)

2. Parental Liability for Child's Acts: Negligent Supervision

Generally, a parent (or other person with responsibility for a child) is liable for property damage proximately caused by the negligent actions of the child, provided that the conduct can be reasonably attributed to the negligent failure to exercise parental duties. Some states have enacted special statutes regarding acts of malicious mischief, including acts of vandalism committed by children. See, e.g., Cal. Penal Code §594. If a minor is convicted of defacing property by means of graffiti, the court may impose punishment consisting of imprisonment or fine (*id.*). If the minor is personally unable to pay the fine, the parents may bear liability (although the court may waive such liability for "good cause") (Cal. Penal Code §594(d)). The court may also require the minor to clean, repair or replace the property; and also require the minor and parents to keep the property free of graffiti for up to one year (Cal. Penal Code §594(c)). The parent's participation will not be required "if the court deems this participation to be detrimental" to the child, or if the parent is a single parent with care of young children (*id.*).

For parental liability for children's acts of misconduct that damage school property, see §F4 *infra*.

California Penal Code

§594. Penalty for vandalism

(a) Every person who maliciously commits any of the following acts with respect to any real or personal property not his or her own, in cases other than those specified by state law, is guilty of vandalism:

(1) Defaces with graffiti or other inscribed material.

(2) Damages.

(3) Destroys.

Whenever a person violates this subdivision with respect to real property, vehicles, signs, fixtures, furnishings, or property belonging to any public entity, as defined by Section 811.2 of the Government Code, or the federal government, it shall be a permissive inference that the person neither owned the property nor had the permission of the owner to deface, damage, or destroy the property.

(b)(1) If the amount of defacement, damage, or destruction is four hundred dollars ($400) or more, vandalism is punishable by imprisonment in the state prison or in a county jail not exceeding one year, or by a fine of not more than ten thousand dollars ($10,000), or if the amount of defacement, damage, or destruction is ten thousand dollars ($10,000) or more, by a fine of not more than fifty thousand dollars ($50,000), or by both that fine and imprisonment.

(2)(A) If the amount of defacement, damage, or destruction is less than four hundred dollars ($400), vandalism is punishable by imprisonment in a county jail not exceeding one year, or by a fine of not more than one thousand dollars ($1,000), or by both that fine and imprisonment.

(B) If the amount of defacement, damage, or destruction is less than four hundred dollars ($400), and the defendant has been previously convicted of vandalism or affixing graffiti or other inscribed material under Section 594, 594.3, 594.4, 640.5, 640.6, or 640.7, vandalism is punishable by imprisonment in a county jail for not more than one year, or by a fine of not more than five thousand dollars ($5,000), or by both that fine and imprisonment.

(c) Upon conviction of any person under this section for acts of vandalism consisting of defacing property with graffiti or other inscribed materials, the court may, in addition to any punishment imposed under subdivision (b), order the defendant to clean up, repair, or replace the damaged property himself or herself, or order the defendant, and his or her parents or guardians if the defendant is a minor, to keep the damaged property or another specified property in the community free of graffiti for up to one year. Participation of a parent or guardian is not required under this subdivision if the court deems this participation to be detrimental to the defendant, or if the parent or guardian is a single parent who must care for young children.

(d) If a minor is personally unable to pay a fine levied for acts prohibited by this section, the parent of that minor shall be liable for payment of the fine. A court may waive payment of the fine, or any part thereof, by the parent upon a finding of good cause.

(e) As used in this section, the term "graffiti or other inscribed material" includes any unauthorized inscription, word, figure, mark, or design, that is written, marked, etched, scratched, drawn, or painted on real or personal property.

(f) The court may order any person ordered to perform community service or graffiti removal pursuant to paragraph (1) of subdivision (c) to undergo counseling.

(g) This section shall become operative on January 1, 2002.

(Stats. 1998 (A.B. 1897), ch. 851, §2, effective January 1, 2002; Stats. 1998 (S.B. 1229), ch. 852, §1.2, effective January 1, 2002; Stats. 1998 (A.B. 1386), ch. 853, §1.6, effective January 1, 2002. Amended by Stats. 1999 (S.B. 966), ch. 83, §145, effective January 1, 2002; Initiative Measure (Prop. 21, §12.5, approved March 7, 2000, effective January 1, 2002); Stats. 2000 (S.B. 1616), ch. 50, §2, effective January 1, 2002.)

C. CONTRACT

At common law, the contracts of a minor are voidable. The minor could enforce his or her contracts against another party. However, if another party attempted to enforce the contract against the minor, the minor could disaffirm the contract (i.e., assert a defense of infancy). Disaffirmance could occur at any time during minority or even within a reasonable time after the minor reached majority. The policy behind permitting minors to disaffirm contracts is to protect them from overreaching by adults and from their own immaturity.

Most jurisdictions, including California, still follow the common law rule permitting minors to disaffirm their contracts (e.g., Cal. Fam. Code §6710). Some courts and legislatures change the common law rule in limited situations (such as for minors who work in the motion picture industry). See, e.g., Shields v. Gross, 448 N.E.2d 108 (N.Y. Ct. App. 1983) (holding that a minor in the motion picture industry may not disaffirm the contract executed by her mother). On minors' entertainment contracts, see §C *infra*.

1. Capacity

California Family Code

§6700. Minor may make contracts subject to power of disaffirmance

Except as provided in Section 6701, a minor may make a contract in the same manner as an adult, subject to the power of disaffirmance under Chapter 2 (commencing with Section 6710), and subject to Part 1 (commencing with Section 300) of Division 3 (validity of marriage).

(Stats. 1992 (A.B. 2650), ch. 162, §10, effective January 1, 1994.)

§6701. Exceptions to minor's right to contract

A minor cannot do any of the following:

(a) Give a delegation of power.

(b) Make a contract relating to real property or any interest therein.

(c) Make a contract relating to any personal property not in the immediate possession or control of the minor.

(Stats. 1992 (A.B. 2650), ch. 162, §10, effective January 1, 1994.)

2. Disaffirmance

Some statutes protect an adult or entity against the possibility of a minor's disaffirming a contract. For example, contracts for necessaries may not be disaffirmed if those necessaries have been furnished already to the minor or the minor's family, and the minor entered into the contract while not under the "care of a parent or guardian able to provide for the minor or the minor's family" (Cal. Fam. Code §6712). Also, a minor cannot disaffirm an obligation that was entered into by statutory authority (Cal. Fam. Code §6711). Finally, the legislature has enacted special minors' entertainment contract statutes and has provided that these contracts cannot be disaffirmed (Cal. Fam. Code §6751). See §C3 *infra*.

§6710. Minor's right of disaffirmance

Except as otherwise provided by statute, a contract of a minor may be disaffirmed by the minor before majority or within a reasonable time afterwards or, in case of the minor's death within that period, by the minor's heirs or personal representative.

(Stats. 1992 (A.B. 2650), ch. 162, §10, effective January 1, 1994.)

§6711. Exception to minor's right of disaffirmance: contract made under express statutory authority

A minor cannot disaffirm an obligation, otherwise valid, entered into by the minor under the express authority or direction of a statute.

(Stats. 1992 (A.B. 2650), ch. 162, §10, effective January 1, 1994.)

§6712. Exception to minor's right of disaffirmance: contract for necessaries

A contract, otherwise valid, entered into during minority, may not be disaffirmed on that ground either during the actual minority of the person entering into the contract, or at any time thereafter, if all of the following requirements are satisfied:

(a) The contract is to pay the reasonable value of things necessary for the support of the minor or the minor's family.

(b) These things have been actually furnished to the minor or to the minor's family.

(c) The contract is entered into by the minor when not under the care of a parent or guardian able to provide for the minor or the minor's family.

(Stats. 1992 (A.B. 2650), ch. 162, §10, effective January 1, 1994.)

§6713. Minor cannot recover goods from bona fide purchaser

If, before the contract of a minor is disaffirmed, goods the minor has sold are transferred to another purchaser who bought them in good faith for value and without notice of the transferor's defect of title, the minor cannot recover the goods from an innocent purchaser.

(Stats. 1992 (A.B. 2650), ch. 162, §10, effective January 1, 1994.)

3. Minors' Entertainment Contracts

Statutes in California authorize the superior court to approve or disapprove minors' entertainment contracts. Such court-approved contracts for the "provision of artistic or creative services" are not subject to disaffirmance. Statute defines the relevant types of contracts and services (Cal. Fam. Code §6750). In addition, a parent's signature on the agreement does not validate an entertainment contract with a minor that has not received court approval. In fact, non court-approved agreements with parental signatures are disaffirmable by performers and may expose parents to liability based upon third parties' reliance. Bonnie E. Berry, Practice in a Minor Key, 25 L.A. Law. 28, 31 (May 2002).

Additional laws protect the financial interests of child performers. For example, California Family Code §§6752 and 6753 provide that a portion of the minor's earnings from entertainment contracts must be set aside in trust until the minor reaches majority (age 18). This law (called the "Coogan Law"), originally enacted in 1939, was prompted by the parental squandering of the fortune of child actor Jackie Coogan. The law was amended in January 2000 to provide that (1) a minimum of 15 percent of the minor's gross earnings must be set aside in trust regardless of whether the contract was court approved (Cal. Fam. Code §6752(b), Cal. Fam. Code §6752(c)(1)); (2) funds must be deposited in a timely manner (Cal. Fam. Code §6752(b)(4)); and, (3) the 15 percent must be set aside in an "account or other savings plan" (Cal. Fam. Code §6752(b)(1)), although part of such funds may be invested in equity securities (i.e., in broad-based index funds, government securities and bonds) (Cal. Fam. Code §6753(e)(3)).

§6750. Application to different types of contracts and services

(a) This chapter applies to the following contracts entered into between an unemancipated minor and any third party or parties on or after January 1, 2000:

(1) A contract pursuant to which aminor is employed or agrees to render artistic or creative services, either directly or through a third party, including, but not limited to, a personal services corporation (loan-out company), or through a casting agency. "Artistic or creative services" includes, but is not limited to, services as an actor, actress, dancer, musician, comedian, singer, stunt-person, voice-over artist, or other performer or entertainer, or as a songwriter, musical producer or arranger, writer, director,

producer, production executive, choreographer, composer, conductor, or designer.

(2) A contract pursuant to which aminor agrees to purchase, or otherwise secure, sell, lease, license, or otherwise dispose of literary, musical, or dramatic properties, or use of a person's likeness, voice recording, performance, or story of or incidents in his or her life, either tangible or intangible, or any rights therein for use in motion pictures, television, the production of sound recordings in any format now known or hereafter devised, the legitimate or living stage, or otherwise in the entertainment field.

(3) A contract pursuant to which aminor is employed or agrees to render services as a participant or player in a sport.

(b) (1) If a minor is employed or agrees to render services directly for any person or entity, that person or entity shall be considered the minor's employer for purposes of this chapter.

(2) If a minor's services are being rendered through a third-party individual or personal services corporation (loan-out company), the person to whom or entity to which that third party is providing the minor's services shall be considered the minor's employer for purposes of this chapter.

(3) If a minor renders services as an extra, background performer, or in a similar capacity through an agency or service that provides one or more of those performers for a fee (casting agency), the agency or service shall be considered the minor's employer for the purposes of this chapter.

(c) (1) For purposes of this chapter, the minor's "gross earnings" shall mean the total compensation payable to the minor under the contract or, if the minor's services are being rendered through a third-party individual or personal services corporation (loan-out company), the total compensation payable to that third party for the services of the minor.

(2) Notwithstanding paragraph (1), with respect to contracts pursuant to which a minor is employed or agrees to render services as a musician, singer, songwriter, musical producer, or arranger only, for purposes of this chapter, the minor's "gross earnings" shall mean the total amount paid to the minor pursuant to the contract, including the payment of any advances to the minor pursuant to the contract, but excluding deductions to offset those advances or other expenses incurred by the employer pursuant to the contract, or, if the minor's services are being rendered through a third-party individual or personal services corporation (loan-out company), the total amount payable to that third party for the services of the minor.

(Stats. 1992 (A.B. 2650), ch. 162, §10, effective January 1, 1994. Amended Stats 1999 (S.B. 1162), ch. 940, §2; Stats. 2003 (A.B. 210), ch. 667, §1.)

§6751. Court-approved entertainment contracts are not subject to disaffirmance

(a) A contract, otherwise valid, of a type described in Section 6750, entered into during minority, cannot be disaffirmed on that ground either during the minority of the person entering into the contract, or at any time thereafter, if the contract has been approved by the superior court in any county in which the minor resides or is employed or in which any party to the contract has its principal office in this state for the transaction of business.

(b) Approval of the court may be given on petition of any party to the contract, after such reasonable notice to all other parties to the contract as is fixed by the court, with opportunity to such other parties to appear and be heard.

(c) Approval of the court given under this section extends to the whole of the contract and all of its terms and provisions, including, but not limited to, any optional or conditional provisions contained in the contract for extension, prolongation, or termination of the term of the contract.

(d) For the purposes of any proceeding under this chapter, a parent or legal guardian, as the case may be, entitled to the physical custody, care, and control of the minor at the time of the proceeding shall be considered the minor's guardian ad litem for the proceeding, unless the court shall determine that appointment of a different individual as guardian ad litem is required in the best interests of the minor.

(Stats. 1992 (A.B. 2650), ch. 162, §10, effective January 1, 1994. Amended Stats 1999 (S.B. 1162), ch. 940, §3.)

§6752. Court shall require parent to place portion of minor's gross earnings in trust

(a) A parent or guardian entitled to the physical custody, care, and control of a minor who enters into a contract of a type described in Section 6750 shall provide a certified copy of the minor's birth certificate indicating the minor's minority to the other party or parties to the contract and in addition, in the case of a guardian, a certified copy of the court document appointing the person as the minor's legal guardian.

(b) (1) Notwithstanding any other statute, in an order approving a minor's contract of a type described in Section 6750, the court shall require that 15 percent of the minor's gross earnings pursuant to the contract be set aside by the minor's employer in trust, in an account or other savings plan, and preserved for the benefit of the minor in accordance with Section 6753.

(2) The court shall require that at least one parent or legal guardian, as the case may be, entitled to the physical custody, care, and control of the minor at the time the order is issued be appointed as trustee of the funds ordered to be set aside in trust for the benefit of the minor, unless the court shall determine that appointment of a different individual, individuals, entity, or entities as trustee or trustees is required in the best interest of the minor.

(3) Within 10 business days after commencement of employment, the trustee or trustees of the funds ordered to be set aside in trust shall provide the minor's employer with a true and accurate photocopy of the trustee's statement pursuant to Section 6753. Upon presentation of the trustee's statement offered pursuant to this subdivision, the employer shall provide the parent or guardian with a written acknowledgement of receipt of the statement.

(4) The minor's employer shall deposit or disburse the 15 percent of the minor's gross earnings pursuant to the contract within 15 business days after receiving a true and accurate copy of the trustee's statement pursuant to subdivision (c) of Section 6753, a certified copy of the minor's birth certificate, and, in the case of a guardian, a

certified copy of the court document appointing the person as the minor's guardian. Notwithstanding any other provision of law, pending receipt ofthese documents, the minor's employer shall hold, for the benefit of the minor, the 15 percent of the minor's gross earnings pursuant to the contract.

(5) When making the initial deposit of funds, the minor's employer shall provide written notification to the financial institution or company that the funds are subject to Section 6753. Upon receipt of the court order, the minor's employer shall provide the financial institution with a copy of the order.

(6) Once the minor's employer deposits the set aside funds pursuant to Section 6753, in trust, in an account or other savings plan, the minor's employer shall have no further obligation or duty to monitor or account for the funds. The trustee or trustees of the trust shall be the only individual, individuals, entity, or entities with the obligation or duty to monitor and account for those funds once they have been deposited by the minor's employer. The trustee or trustees shall do an annual accounting of the funds held in trust, in an account or other savings plan, in accordance with Sections 16062 and 16063 of the Probate Code.

(7) The court shall have continuing jurisdiction over the trust established pursuant to the order and may at any time, upon petition of the parent or legal guardian, the minor, through his or her guardian ad litem, or the trustee or trustees, on good cause shown, order that the trust be amended or terminated, notwithstanding the provisions of the declaration of trust. An order amending or terminating a trust may be made only after reasonable notice to the beneficiary and, if the beneficiary is then a minor, to the parent or guardian, if any, and to the trustee or trustees of the funds with opportunity for all parties to appear and be heard.

(8) A parent or guardian entitled to the physical custody, care, and control of the minor shall promptly notify the minor's employer in writing of any change in facts that affect the employer's obligation or ability to set aside the funds in accordance with the order, including, but not limited to, a change of financial institution or account number, or the existence of a new or amended order issued pursuant to paragraph (7) amending or terminating the employer's obligations underthis section. The written notification shall be accompanied by a true and accurate photocopy of the trustee's statement pursuant to Section 6753 and, if applicable, a true and accurate photocopy of the new or amended order.

(9) (A) If a parent, guardian, or trustee fails to provide the minor's employer with a true and accurate photocopy of the trustee's statement pursuant to Section 6753 within 180 days after the commencement of employment, the employer shall forward to The Actors' Fund of America 15 percent of the minor's gross earnings pursuant to the contract, together with the minor's name and, if known, the minor's social security number, birth date, last known address, telephone number, e-mail address, dates of employment, and title of the project on which the minor was employed, and shall notify the parent, guardian, or trustee of that transfer by certified mail to the last known address. Upon receipt of those forwarded funds, The Actors' Fund of America shall become the trustee of those funds and the minor's employer shall have no further obligation or duty to monitor or account for the funds.

(B) The Actors' Fund of America shall make its best efforts to notify the parent, guardian, or trustee of their responsibilities to provide a true and accurate photocopy of the trustee's statement pursuant to Section 6753, and in the case of a guardian, a certified copy of the court document appointing the person as the minor's legal guardian. Within 15 business days after receiving those documents, The Actors' Fund of America shall deposit or disburse the funds as directed by the trustee's statement. When making that deposit or disbursal of the funds, The Actors' Fund of America shall provide to the financial institution notice that the funds are subject to Section 6753 and a copy of each applicable order, and shall thereafter have no further obligation or duty to monitor or account for the funds.

(c) The Actors' Fund of America shall notify each beneficiary of his or her entitlement to the funds that it holds for the beneficiary within 60 days after the date on which its records indicated that the beneficiary has attained 18 years of age or the date on which it received notice that the minor has been emancipated, by sending that notice to the last known address for the beneficiary or, if it has no specific separate address for the beneficiary, to the beneficiary's parent or guardian.

(d) (1) Notwithstanding any other statute, for any minor's contract of a type described in Section 6750 that is not being submitted for approval by the court pursuant to Section 6751, or for which the court has issued a final order denying approval, 15 percent of the minor's gross earnings pursuant to the contract shall be set aside by the minor's employer in trust, in an account or other savings plan, and preserved for the benefit of the minor in accordance with Section 6753. At least one parent or legal guardian, as the case may be, entitled to the physical custody, care, and control of the minor, shall be the trustee of the funds set aside for the benefit of the minor, unless the court, upon petition by the parent or legal guardian, the minor, through his or her guardian ad litem, or the trustee or trustees of the trust, shall determine that appointment of a different individual, individuals, entity, or entities as trustee or trustees is required in the best interest of the minor.

(2) Within 10 business days of commencement after employment, a parent or guardian, as the case may be, entitled to the physical custody, care, and control of the minor shall provide the minor's employer with a true and accurate photocopy of the trustee's statement pursuant to Section 6753 and in addition, in the case of a guardian, a certified copy of the court document appointing the person as the minor's legal guardian. Upon presentation of the trustee's statement offered pursuant to this subdivision, the employer shall provide the parent or guardian with a written acknowledgement of receipt of the statement.

(3) The minor's employer shall deposit 15 percent of the minor's gross earnings pursuant to the contract within 15 business days of receiving the trustee's statement pursuant to Section 6753, or if the court denies approval of

the contract, within 15 business days of receiving a final order denying approval of the contract. Notwithstanding any other statute, pending receipt of the trustee's statement or the final court order, the minor's employer shall hold for the benefit of the minor the 15 percent of the minor's gross earnings pursuant to the contract. When making the initial deposit of funds, the minor's employer shall provide written notification to the financial institution or company that the funds are subject to Section 6753.

(4) Once the minor's employer deposits the set aside funds in trust, in an account or other savings plan pursuant to Section 6753, the minor's employer shall have no further obligation or duty to monitor or account for the funds. The trustee or trustees of the trust shall be the only individual, individuals, entity, or entities with the obligation or duty to monitor and account for those funds once they have been deposited by the minor's employer. The trustee or trustees shall do an annual accounting of the funds held in trust, in an account or other savings plan, in accordance with Sections 16062 and 16063 of the Probate Code.

(5) Upon petition of the parent or legal guardian, the minor, through his or her guardian ad litem, or the trustee or trustees of the trust, to the superior court in any county in which the minor resides or in which the trust is established, the court may at any time, on good cause shown, order that the trust be amended or terminated, notwithstanding the provisions of the declaration of trust. An order amending or terminating a trust may be made only after reasonable notice to the beneficiary and, if the beneficiary is then a minor, to the parent or guardian, if any, and to the trustee or trustees of the funds with opportunity for all parties to appear and be heard.

(6) A parent or guardian entitled to the physical custody, care, and control of the minor shall promptly notify the minor's employer in writing of any change in facts that affect the employer's obligation or ability to set aside funds for the benefit of the minor in accordance with this section, including, but not limited to, a change of financial institution or account number, or the existence of a new or amended order issued pursuant to paragraph (5) amending or terminating the employer's obligations under this section. The written notification shall be accompanied by a true and accurate photocopy of the trustee's statement and attachments pursuant to Section 6753 and, if applicable, a true and accurate photocopy of the new or amended order.

(7) (A) If a parent, guardian, or trustee fails to provide the minor's employer with a true and accurate photocopy of the trustee's statement pursuant to Section 6753, within 180 days after commencement of employment, the employer shall forward to The Actors' Fund of America the 15 percent of the minor's gross earnings pursuant to the contract, together with the minor's name and, if known, the minor's social security number, birth date, last known address, telephone number, e-mail address, dates of employment, and the title of the project on which the minor was employed, and shall notify the parent, guardian, or trustee of that transfer by certified mail to the last known address. Upon receipt of those forwarded funds, The Actors' Fund of America shall become the trustee of those funds and the minor's employer shall have no further obligation or duty to monitor or account for the funds.

(B) The Actors' Fund of America shall make best efforts to notify the parent, guardian, or trustee of their responsibilities to provide a true and accurate photocopy of the trustee's statement pursuant to Section 6753 and in the case of a guardian, a certified copy of the court document appointing the person as the minor's legal guardian. After receiving those documents, The Actors' Fund of America shall deposit or disburse the funds as directed by the trustee's statement, and in accordance with Section 6753, within 15 business days. When making that deposit or disbursal of the funds, The Actors' Fund of America shall provide notice to the financial institution that the funds are subject to Section 6753, and shall thereafter have no further obligation or duty to monitor or account for the funds.

(C) The Actors' Fund of America shall notify each beneficiary of his or her entitlement to the funds that it holds for the beneficiary, within 60 days after the date on which its records indicate that the beneficiary has attained 18 years of age or the date on which it received notice that the minor has been emancipated, by sending that notice to the last known address that it has for the beneficiary, or to the beneficiary's parent or guardian, where it has no specific separate address for the beneficiary.

(e) Where a parent or guardian is entitled to the physical custody, care, and control of a minor who enters into a contract of a type described in Section 6750, the relationship between the parent or guardian and the minor is a fiduciary relationship that is governed by the law of trusts, whether or not a court has issued a formal order to that effect. The parent or guardian acting in his or her fiduciary relationship, shall, with the earnings and accumulations of the minor under the contract, pay all liabilities incurred by the minor under the contract, including, but not limited to, payments for taxes on all earnings, including taxes on the amounts set aside under subdivisions (b) and (c) of this section, and payments for personal or professional services rendered to the minor or the business related to the contract. Nothing in this subdivision shall be construed to alter any other existing responsibilities of a parent or legal guardian to provide for the support of a minor child.

(f)(1) Except as otherwise provided in this subdivision, The Actors' Fund of America, as trustee of unclaimed set-aside funds, shall manage and administer those funds in the same manner as a trustee under the Probate Code. Notwithstanding the foregoing, The Actors' Fund of America is not required to open separate, segregated individual trust accounts for each beneficiary but may hold the set-aside funds in a single, segregated master account for all beneficiaries, provided it maintains accounting records for each beneficiary's interest in the master account.

(2) The Actors' Fund of America shall have the right to transfer funds from the master account, or from a beneficiary's segregated account to its general account in an amount equal to the beneficiary's balance. The Actors'

Fund of America shall have the right to use those funds transferred to its general account to provide programs and services for young performers. This use of the funds does not limit or alter The Actors' Fund of America's obligation to disburse the set-aside funds to the beneficiary, or the beneficiary's parent, guardian, trustee, or estate pursuant to this chapter.

(3)(A) Upon receiving a certified copy of the beneficiary's birth certificate, or United States passport, and a true and accurate photocopy of the trustee's statement pursuant to Section 6753, The Actors' Fund of America shall transfer the beneficiary's balance to the trust account established for the beneficiary.

(B) The Actors' Fund of America shall disburse the set-aside funds to a beneficiary who has attained 18 years of age, after receiving proof of the beneficiary's identity and a certified copy of the beneficiary's birth certificate or United States passport, or to a beneficiary who has been emancipated, after receiving proof of the beneficiary's identity and appropriate documentation evidencing the beneficiary's emancipation.

(C) The Actors' Fund of America shall disburse the set-aside funds to the estate of a deceased beneficiary after receiving appropriate documentation evidencing the death of the beneficiary and the claimant's authority to collect those funds on behalf of the beneficiary.

(g)(1) The beneficiary of an account held by The Actors' Fund of America pursuant to this section shall be entitled to receive imputed interest on the balance in his or her account for the entire period during which the account is held at a rate equal to the lesser of the federal reserve rate in effect on the last business day of the prior calendar quarter or the national average money market rate as published in the New York Times on the last Sunday of the prior calendar quarter, adjusted quarterly.

(2) The Actors' Fund of America may assess and deduct from the balance in the beneficiary's account reasonable management, administrative, and investment expenses, including beneficiary-specific fees for initial set up, account notifications and account disbursements, and a reasonably allocable share of management, administrative, and investment expenses of the master account. No fees may be charged to any beneficiary's account during the first year that the account is held by The Actors' Fund of America.

(3) Notwithstanding paragraph (2), the amount paid on any claim made by a beneficiary or the beneficiary's parent or guardian after The Actors' Fund of America receives and holds funds pursuant to this section may not be less than the amount of the funds received plus the imputed interest.

(h) Notwithstanding any provision of this chapter to the contrary, any minor's employer holding set-aside funds under this chapter, which funds remain unclaimed 180 days after the effective date hereof, shall forward those unclaimed funds to The Actors' Fund of America, along with the minor's name and, if known, the minor's social security number, birth date, last known address, telephone number, e-mail address, dates of employment, and the title of the project on which the minor was employed, and shall notify the parent, guardian, or trustee of that transfer by certified mail to the last known address. Upon receipt of those forwarded funds by The Actors' Fund of America, the minor's employer shall have no further obligation or duty to monitor or account for the funds.

(i) All funds received by The Actors' Fund of America pursuant to this section shall be exempt from the application of the Unclaimed Property Law (Title 10 (commencing with Section 1300) of Part 3 of the Code of Civil Procedure), including, but not limited to, Section 1510 of the Code of Civil Procedure.

(Stats. 1999 (S.B. 1162), ch. 940, §5. Amended by Stats. 2003 (S.B. 210), ch. 667, §2.)

§6753. Parent shall establish minor's trust at designated financial institution and may not withdraw funds without court order

(a) The trustee or trustees shall establish a trust account, that shall be known as a Coogan Trust Account, pursuant to this section at a bank, savings and loan institution, credit union, brokerage firm, or company registered under the Investment Company Act of 1940, that is located in the State of California, unless a similar trust has been previously established, for the purpose of preserving for the benefit of the minor the portion of the minor's gross earnings pursuant to paragraph (1) of subdivision (b) of Section 6752 or pursuant to paragraph (1) of subdivision (c) of Section 6752. The trustee or trustees shall establish the trust pursuant to this section within seven business days after the minor's contract is signed by the minor, the third-party individual or personal services corporation (loan-out company), and the employer.

(b) Except as otherwise provided in this section, prior to the date on which the beneficiary of the trust attains the age of 18 years or the issuance of a declaration of emancipation of the minor under Section 7122, no withdrawal by the beneficiary or any other individual, individuals, entity, or entities may be made of funds on deposit in trust without written order of the superior court pursuant to paragraph (7) of subdivision (b) or paragraph (5) of subdivision (c) of Section 6752. Upon reaching the age of 18 years, the beneficiary may withdraw the funds on deposit in trust only after providing a certified copy of the beneficiary's birth certificate to the financial institution where the trust is located.

(c) The trustee or trustees shall, within 10 business days after the minor's contract is signed by the minor, the third-party individual or personal services corporation (loan-out company), and the employer, prepare a written statement under penalty of perjury that shall include the name, address, and telephone number of the financial institution, the name of the account, the number of the account, the name of the minor beneficiary, the name of the trustee or trustees of the account, and any additional information needed by the minor's employer to deposit into the account the portion of the minor's gross earnings prescribed by paragraph (1) of subdivision (b) or paragraph (1) of subdivision (c) of Section 6752. The trustee or trustees shall attach to the written statement a true and accurate photocopy of any information received from the financial institution confirming the creation of the account, such as an account agreement, account terms, passbook, or other similar writings.

(d) The trust shall be established in California either with a financial institution that is and remains insured at all times by the Federal Deposit Insurance Corporation (FDIC), the Securities Investor Protection Corporation (SIPC), or the National Credit Union Share Insurance Fund (NCUSIF) or their respective successors, or with a company that is and remains registered under the Investment Company Act of 1940. The trustee or trustees of the trust shall be the only individual, individuals, entity, or entities with the obligation or duty to ensure that the funds remain in trust, in an account or other savings plan insured in accordance with this section, or with a company that is and remains registered under the Investment Company Act of 1940 as authorized by this section.

(e) Upon application by the trustee or trustees to the financial institution or company in which the trust is held, the trust funds shall be handled by thefinancial institution or company in one or more of the following methods:

(1) The financial institution or company may transfer funds to another account or other savings plan at the same financial institution or company, provided that the funds transferred shall continue to be held in trust, and subject to this chapter.

(2) The financial institution or company may transfer funds to another financial institution or company, provided that the funds transferred shall continue to be held in trust, and subject to this chapter and that the transferring financial institution or company has provided written notification to the financial institution or company to which the funds will be transferred that the funds are subject to this section and written notice of the requirements of this chapter.

(3) The financial institution or company may use all or a part of the funds to purchase, in the name of and for the benefit of the minor, (A) investment funds offered by a company registered under the Investment Company Act of 1940, provided that if the underlying investments are equity securities, the investment fund is a broad-based index fund or invests broadly across the domestic or a foreign regional economy, is not a sector fund, and has assets under management of at least two hundred fifty million dollars ($ 250,000,000); or (B) government securities and bonds, certificates of deposit, money market instruments, money market accounts, or mutual funds investing solely in those government securities and bonds, certificates, instruments, and accounts, that are available at the financial institution where the trust fund or other savings plan is held, provided that the funds shall continue to be held in trust and subject to this chapter, those purchases shall have a maturity date on or before the date upon which the minor will attain the age of 18 years, and any proceeds accruing from those purchases shall be redeposited into that account or accounts or used to further purchase any of those or similar securities, bonds, certificates, instruments, funds, or accounts.

(Stats. 1999 (S.B. 1162), ch. 940, §7. Amended by Stats. 2003 (S.B. 210), ch. 667, §3.)

D. PROPERTY

1. Earnings

A parent had a common law right to a child's services and earnings. Modern statutes of many jurisdictions, including California, incorporate this common law rule. See, e.g., Cal. Fam. Code §7500.

§7500. Parents are entitled to child's services and earnings

(a) The mother of an unemancipated minor child, and the father, if presumed to be the father under Section 7611, are equally entitled to the services and earnings of the child.

(b) If one parent is dead, is unable or refuses to take custody, or has abandoned the child, the other parent is entitled to the services and earnings of the child.

(c) This section shall not apply to any services or earnings of an unemancipated minor child related to a contract of a type described in Section 6750.

(Stats. 1993 (A.B. 1500), ch. 219, §162. Amended Stats. 1999 (S.B. 1162), ch. 940, §8.)

§7503. Minor's employer shall pay minor until parent gives notice

The employer of a minor shall pay the earnings of the minor to the minor until the parent or guardian entitled to the earnings gives the employer notice that the parent or guardian claims the earnings.

(Stats. 1993 (A.B. 1500), ch. 219, §166.)

§7504. Parents may relinquish control and earnings to child

The parent, whether solvent or insolvent, may relinquish to the child the right of controlling the child and receiving the child's earnings. Abandonment by the parent is presumptive evidence of that relinquishment.

(Stats. 1993 (A.B. 1500), ch. 219, §167.)

2. Appointment of a Guardian

A child may inherit property (e.g., stocks, bonds, cash, real estate). At common law, if a child inherited property, or was given property that required active management, a court appointed a "guardian of the child's estate." Today, many states (including California) follow the same rule.

A guardian may be of two types: "a guardian of the person" (who is charged with personal decisionmaking), or "a guardian of the estate or property" (who is charged with asset management).

California Probate Code

§1500. Parent may nominate a guardian of minor's person and/or minor's estate

Subject to Section 1502, a parent may nominate a guardian of the person or estate, or both, of a minor child in either of the following cases:

(a) Where the other parent nominates, or consents in writing to the nomination of, the same guardian for the same child.

(b) Where, at the time the petition for appointment of the guardian is filed, either (1) the other parent is dead or lacks legal capacity to consent to the nomination or (2) the consent of the other parent would not be required for an adoption of the child.

(Stats. 1990 (A.B. 759), ch. 79, §14, effective July 1, 1991.)

§1501. Parent may nominate guardian for particular property of minor

Subject to Section 1502, a parent or any other person may nominate a guardian for property that a minor receives from or by designation of the nominator (whether before, at the time of, or after the nomination) including, but not limited to, property received by the minor by virtue of a gift, deed, trust, will, succession, insurance, or benefits of any kind.

(Stats. 1990 (A.B. 759), ch. 79, §14, effective July 1, 1991.)

§1502. Parent may nominate a guardian in a petition, at hearing, or in writing

(a) A nomination of a guardian under this article may be made in the petition for the appointment of the guardian or at the hearing on the petition or in a writing signed either before or after the petition for the appointment of the guardian is filed.

(b) The nomination of a guardian under this article is effective when made except that a writing nominating a guardian under this article may provide that the nomination becomes effective only upon the occurrence of such specified condition or conditions as are stated in the writing, including but not limited to such conditions as the subsequent legal incapacity or death of the person making the nomination.

(c) Unless the writing making the nomination expressly otherwise provides, a nomination made under this article remains effective notwithstanding the subsequent legal incapacity or death of the person making the nomination.

(Stats. 1990 (A.B. 759), ch. 79, §14, effective July 1, 1991.)

§1510. A relative may petition for appointment of a guardian for a minor

(a) A relative or other person on behalf of the minor, or the minor if 12 years of age or older, may file a petition for the appointment of a guardian of the minor.

(b) The petition shall request that a guardian of the person or estate of the minor, or both, be appointed, shall specify the name and address of the proposed guardian and the name and date of birth of the proposed ward, and shall state that the appointment is necessary or convenient.

(c) The petition shall set forth, so far as is known to the petitioner, the names and addresses of all of the following:

(1) The parents of the proposed ward.

(2) The person having legal custody of the proposed ward and, if that person does not have the care of the proposed ward, the person having the care of the proposed ward.

(3) The relatives of the proposed ward within the second degree.

(4) In the case of a guardianship of the estate, the spouse of the proposed ward.

(5) Any person nominated as guardian for the proposed ward under Section 1500 or 1501.

(d) If the proposed ward is a patient in or on leave of absence from a state institution under the jurisdiction of the State Department of Mental Health or the State Department of Developmental Services and that fact is known to the petitioner, the petition shall state that fact and name the institution.

(e) The petition shall state, so far as is known to the petitioner, whether or not the proposed ward is receiving or is entitled to receive benefits from the Veterans Administration and the estimated amount of the monthly benefit payable by the Veterans Administration for the proposed ward.

(f) If the petitioner has knowledge of any pending adoption, juvenile court, marriage dissolution, domestic relations, custody, or other similar proceeding affecting the proposed ward, the petition shall disclose the pending proceeding.

(g) If the petitioners have accepted or intend to accept physical care or custody of the child with intent to adopt, whether formed at the time of placement or formed subsequent to placement, the petitioners shall so state in the guardianship petition, whether or not an adoption petition has been filed.

(h) If the proposed ward is or becomes the subject of an adoption petition, the court shall order the guardianship petition consolidated with the adoption petition.

(Stats. 1990 (A.B. 759), ch. 79, §14, effective July 1, 1991. Amended Stats. 1992 (S.B. 1445), ch. 1064, §1.)

§2105. Court may appoint joint guardians; special rules apply if custodial parent has terminal condition

(a) The court, in its discretion, may appoint for a ward or conservatee:

(1) Two or more joint guardians or conservators of the person.

(2) Two or more joint guardians or conservators of the estate.

(3) Two or more joint guardians or conservators of the person and estate.

(b) When joint guardians or conservators are appointed, each shall qualify in the same manner as a sole guardian or conservator.

(c) Subject to subdivisions (d) and (e):

(1) Where there are two guardians or conservators, both must concur to exercise a power.

(2) Where there are more than two guardians or conservators, a majority must concur to exercise a power.

(d) If one of the joint guardians or conservators dies or is removed or resigns, the powers and duties continue in the remaining joint guardians or conservators until further appointment is made by the court.

(e) Where joint guardians or conservators have been appointed and one or more are (1) absent from the state and unable to act, (2) otherwise unable to act, or (3) legally disqualified from serving, the court may, by order made with or without notice, authorize the remaining joint guardians or conservators to act as to all matters embraced within its order.

(f) If a custodial parent has been diagnosed as having a terminal condition, as evidenced by a declaration executed by a licensed physician, the court, in its discretion, may appoint the custodial parent and a person nominated by the custodial parent as joint guardians of the person of the minor. However, this appointment shall not be made over the objection of a noncustodial parent without a finding that the noncustodial parent's custody would be detrimental to the minor, as provided in Section 3041 of the Family Code. It is the intent of the Legislature in enacting the amendments to this subdivision adopted during the 1995-1996 Regular Session for a parent with a terminal condition to be able to make arrangements for the joint care, custody, and control of his or her minor children so as to minimize the emotional stress of, and disruption for, the minor children whenever the parent is incapacitated or upon the parent's death, and to avoid the need to provide a temporary guardian or place the minor children in foster care, pending appointment of a guardian, as might otherwise be required.

"Terminal condition," for purposes of this subdivision, means an incurable and irreversible condition that, without the administration of life-sustaining treatme-nt, will, within reasonable medical judgment, result in death.

(Stats. 1990 (A.B. 759), ch. 79, §14, effective July 1, 1991. Amended Stats. 1993 (S.B. 305), ch. 978, §2; Stats. 1995 (A.B. 1104), ch. 278, §1; Stats. 1999 (A.B. 891), ch. 658, §11, effective July 1, 2000.)

3. Intestate Portion of Parent's Estate

Traditionally, both legitimate and nonmarital children could inherit by intestate succession from their mother. (Intestate succession occurs when a decedent dies without a valid will.) However, only legitimate children could inherit from their father. The modern trend is toward minimizing differences in the treatment of nonmarital versus marital children for succession purposes.

The United States Supreme Court first liberalized the traditional rule in the late 1970s. In Trimble v. Gordon, 430 U.S. 762 (1977), the Court invalidated, on equal protection grounds, an Illinois statute providing that a nonmarital children could inherit from her mother but could only inherit from her father if two conditions were met: the parents married following her birth and if the father acknowledged the child. However, in Lalli v. Lalli, 439 U.S. 259 (1978), the Supreme Court upheld a New York statute that required a judicial order of filiation (order of paternity establishment) during the putative father's lifetime in order for a nonmarital child to inherit intestate from the father. The Supreme Court found that, unlike the statute in *Trimble*, the New York statute survived the intermediate level of review because the classification was substantially related to important state interests in the accurate and orderly disposition of estates. The cases may best be understood by virtue of the fact that the Court was satisfied with the proof of paternity in *Trimble* (judicial declaration) but not in *Lalli* (informal written acknowledgment).

California law provides that the portion of the intestate estate that does not pass to the decedent's surviving spouse, or to a surviving domestic partner, passes to the decedent's issue (i.e., lineal descendants) (Cal. Prob. Code §6402). Other takers succeed to the intestate estate if the decedent leaves no surviving issue (*id.*).

§6402. Children's share of their intestate parent's estate

Except as provided in Section 6402.5 [for distribution of real property in cases of a predeceased spouse who died not more than 15 years before the decedent, leaving no surviving spouse or issue], the part of the intestate estate not passing to the surviving spouse or surviving domestic partner, as defined in subdivision (b) of Section 37, under Section 6401, or the entire intestate estate if there is no surviving spouse or domestic partner, passes as follows:

(a) To the issue of the decedent, the issue taking equally if they are all of the same degree of kinship to the decedent, but if of unequal degree those of more remote degree take in the manner provided in Section 240.

(b) If there is no surviving issue, to the decedent's parent or parents equally.

(c) If there is no surviving issue or parent, to the issue of the parents or either of them, the issue taking equally if they are all of the same degree of kinship to the decedent, but if of unequal degree those of more remote degree take in the manner provided in Section 240.

(d) If there is no surviving issue, parent or issue of a parent, but the decedent is survived by one or more grandparents or issue of grandparents, to the grandparent or grandparents equally, or to the issue of those grandparents if there is no surviving grandparent, the issue taking equally if they are all of the same degree of kinship to the decedent, but if of unequal degree those of more remote degree take in the manner provided in Section 240.

(e) If there is no surviving issue, parent or issue of a parent, grandparent or issue of a grandparent, but the decedent is survived by the issue of a predeceased spouse, to that issue, the issue taking equally if they are all of the same degree of kinship to the predeceased spouse, but if of unequal degree those of more remote degree take in the manner provided in Section 240.

(f) If there is no surviving issue, parent or issue of a parent, grandparent or issue of a grandparent, or issue of a predeceased spouse, but the decedent is survived by next of kin, to the next of kin in equal degree, but where there are two or more collateral kindred in equal degree who claim through different ancestors, those who claim through the nearest ancestor are preferred to those claiming through an ancestor more remote.

(g) If there is no surviving next of kin of the decedent and no surviving issue of a predeceased spouse of the decedent, but the decedent is survived by the parents of a predeceased spouse or the issue of those parents, to the parent or parents equally, or to the issue of those parents if both are deceased, the issue taking equally if they are all of the same degree of kinship to the predeceased spouse, but if of unequal degree those of more remote degree take in the manner provided in Section 240.

(Stats. 1990 (A.B. 759), ch. 79, §14, effective July 1, 1991. Amended by Stats. 2002 (A.B. 2216), ch. 447, §2, effective July 1, 2003.)

4. California Uniform Transfer to Minors Act (CUTMA)

Although property may be held in a child's name, practical problems arise because adults may be reluctant to do business with minors (recall the disaffirmance power, *supra*). As a result, a minor's property typically is held in the name of a guardian, or in a trust, or is registered in the name of a custodian under a state Uniform Transfers to Minors Act (UTMA). All states have some form of UTMA or its predecessor, the Uniform Gift to Minors Act (UGMA). See, e.g., Cal. Prob. Code §§3900 et seq. (CUTMA). These statutory provisions permit certain property to be registered in the name of a custodian who has broad powers to manage the property without court supervision. Although not as flexible as a trust, gifts based on UTMA or UGMA are more easily transferred and the assets more easily administered.

§3900. Title

This part may be cited as the "California Uniform Transfers to Minors Act."

(Stats. 1990 (A.B. 759), ch. 79, §14, effective July 1, 1991.)

§3901. Definitions

In this part:

(a) "Adult" means an individual who has attained the age of 18 years.

(b) "Benefit plan" means an employer's plan for the benefit of an employee or partner.

(c) "Broker" means a person lawfully engaged in the business of effecting transactions in securities or commodities for the person's own account or for the account of others.

(d) "Conservator" means a person appointed or qualified by a court to act as general, limited, or temporary guardian of a minor's property or a person legally authorized to perform substantially the same functions.

(e) "Court" means the superior court.

(f) "Custodial property" means (1) any interest in property transferred to a custodian under this part and (2) the income from and proceeds of that interest in property.

(g) "Custodian" means a person so designated under Section 3909 or a successor or substitute custodian designated under Section 3918.

(h) "Financial institution" means a bank, trust company, savings institution, or credit union, chartered and supervised under state or federal law or an industrial loan company licensed and supervised under the laws of this state.

(i) "Legal representative" means an individual's personal representative or conservator.

(j) "Member of the minor's family" means the minor's parent, stepparent, spouse, grandparent, brother, sister, uncle, or aunt, whether of the whole or half blood or by adoption.

(k) "Minor" means:

(1) Except as provided in paragraph (2), an individual who has not attained the age of 18 years.

(2) When used with reference to the beneficiary for whose benefit custodial property is held or is to be held, an individual who has not attained the age at which the custodian is required under Sections 3920 and 3920.5 to transfer the custodial property to the beneficiary.

(l) "Person" means an individual, corporation, organization, or other legal entity.

(m) "Personal representative" means an executor, administrator, successor personal representative, or special administrator of a decedent's estate or a person legally authorized to perform substantially the same functions.

(n) "State" includes any state of the United States, the District of Columbia, the Commonwealth of Puerto Rico, and any territory or possession subject to the legislative authority of the United States.

(o) "Transfer" means a transaction that creates custodial property under Section 3909.

(p) "Transferor" means a person who makes a transfer under this part.

(q) "Trust company" means a financial institution, corporation, or other legal entity, authorized to exercise general trust powers.

(Stats. 1990 (A.B. 759), ch. 79, §14, effective July 1, 1991.)

§3902. Jurisdiction

(a) This part applies to a transfer that refers to this part in the designation under subdivision (a) of Section 3909 by which the transfer is made if at the time of the transfer, the transferor, the minor, or the custodian is a resident of this state or the custodial property is located in this state. The custodianship so created remains subject to this part despite a subsequent change in residence of a transferor, the minor, or the custodian, or the removal of custodial property from this state.

(b) A person designated as custodian under this part is subject to personal jurisdiction in this state with respect to any matter relating to the custodianship.

(c) A transfer that purports to be made and which is valid under the Uniform Transfers to Minors Act, the Uniform Gifts to Minors Act, or a substantially similar act, of another State is governed by the law of the designated state and may be executed and is enforceable in this state if at the time of the transfer, the transferor, the minor, or the custodian is a resident of the designated state or the custodial property is located in the designated state.

(Stats. 1990 (A.B. 759), ch. 79, §14, effective July 1, 1991.)

§3903. Person may nominate custodian upon condition

(a) A person having the right to designate the recipient of property transferable upon the occurrence of a future event may revocably nominate a custodian to receive the property for a minor beneficiary upon the occurrence of the event by naming the custodian followed in substance by the words:

"as custodian for ______________________________
(Name of Minor)
under the California Uniform Transfers to Minors Act."

The nomination may name one or more persons as substitute custodians to whom the property must be transferred, in the order named, if the first nominated custodian dies before the transfer or is unable, declines, or is ineligible to serve. The nomination may be made in a will, a trust, a deed, an instrument exercising a power of appointment, or in a writing designating a beneficiary of contractual rights which is registered with or delivered to the payor, issuer, or other obligor of the contractual rights.

(b) A custodian nominated under this section must be a person to whom a transfer of property of that kind may be made under subdivision (a) of Section 3909.

(c) The nomination of a custodian under this section does not create custodial property until the nominating instrument becomes irrevocable or a transfer to the nominated custodian is completed under Section 3909. Unless the nomination of a custodian has been revoked, upon the occurrence of the future event, the custodianship becomes effective, and the custodian shall enforce a transfer of the custodial property pursuant to Section 3909.

(Stats. 1990 (A.B. 759), ch. 79, §14, effective July 1, 1991.)

§3904. Person may make transfer to custodian by gift or exercise of power of appointment

A person may make a transfer by irrevocable gift to, or the irrevocable exercise of a power of appointment in favor of, a custodian for the benefit of a minor pursuant to Section 3909.

(Stats. 1990 (A.B. 759), ch. 79, §14, effective July 1, 1991.)

§3905. Person may make transfer to custodian as authorized by will or trust

(a) A personal representative or trustee may make an irrevocable transfer pursuant to Section 3909 to a custodian for the benefit of a minor as authorized in the governing will or trust.

(b) If the testator or settlor has nominated a custodian under Section 3903 to receive the custodial property, the transfer shall be made to that person.

(c) If the testator or settlor has not nominated a custodian under Section 3903, or all persons so nominated as custodian die before the transfer or are unable, decline, or are ineligible to serve, the personal representative or the trustee, as the case may be, shall designate the custodian from among those eligible to serve as custodian for property of that kind under subdivision (a) of Section 3909.

(Stats. 1990 (A.B. 759), ch. 79, §14, effective July 1, 1991.)

§3906. Requirements for transfer by fiduciary

(a) Subject to subdivision (c), a personal representative or trustee may make an irrevocable transfer to another adult or trust company as custodian for the benefit of a minor pursuant to Section 3909, in the absence of a will or under a will or trust that does not contain an authorization to do so.

(b) Subject to subdivision (c), a conservator may make an irrevocable transfer to another adult or trust company as custodian for the benefit of the minor pursuant to Section 3909.

(c) A transfer under subdivision (a) or (b) may be made only if all of the following requirements are satisfied:

(1) The personal representative, trustee, or conservator considers the transfer to be in the best interest of the minor.

(2) The transfer is not prohibited by or inconsistent with provisions of the applicable will, trust agreement, or other governing instrument. For the purposes of this subdivision, a spendthrift provision (such as that described in Section 15300) shall not prohibit or be inconsistent with the transfer.

(3) The transfer is authorized by the court if it exceeds ten thousand dollars ($ 10,000) in value; provided, however, that such court authorization shall not be required when the transfer is to a custodian who is either (A) a trust company or (B) an individual designated as a trustee by the terms of a trust instrument which does not require a bond.

(Stats. 1990 (A.B. 759), ch. 79, §14, effective July 1, 1991. Amended Stats. 1996 (A.B. 2751), ch. 862, §13.)

§3907. Obligor may make transfer to custodian for minor

(a) Subject to subdivisions (b) and (c), a person not subject to Section 3905 or 3906 who holds property of, or owes a liquidated debt to, a minor not having a conservator may make an irrevocable transfer to a custodian for the benefit of the minor pursuant to Section 3909.

(b) If a person having the right to do so under Section 3903 has nominated a custodian under that section to receive the custodial property, the transfer shall be made to that person.

(c) If no custodian has been nominated under Section 3903, or all persons so nominated as custodian die before the transfer or are unable, decline, or are ineligible to serve, a transfer under this section may be made to an adult member of the minor's family or to a trust company unless the property exceeds ten thousand dollars ($10,000) in value.

(Stats. 1990 (A.B. 759), ch. 79, §14, effective July 1, 1991.)

§3909. Manner of creation and transfer of custodial property

(a) Custodial property is created and a transfer is made whenever any of the following occurs:

(1) An uncertificated security or a certificated security in registered form is either:

(A) Registered in the name of the transferor, an adult other than the transferor, or a trust company, followed in substance by the words:

"as custodian for ________________________
(Name of Minor)
under the California Uniform Transfers to Minors Act."

(B) Delivered if in certificated form, or any document necessary for the transfer of an uncertificated security is delivered, together with any necessary endorsement to an adult other than the transferor or to a trust company as custodian, accompanied by an instrument in substantially the form set forth in subdivision (b).

(2) Money is paid or delivered, or a security held in the name of a broker, financial institution, or its nominee is transferred, to a broker or financial institution for credit to an account in the name of the transferor, an adult other than the transferor, or a trust company, followed in substance by the words:

"as custodian for ________________________
(Name of Minor)
under the California Uniform Transfers to Minors Act."

(3) The ownership of a life or endowment insurance policy or annuity contract is either:

(A) Registered with the issuer in the name of the transferor, an adult other than the transferor, or a trust company, followed in substance by the words:

"as custodian for ________________________
(Name of Minor)
under the California Uniform Transfers to Minors Act."

(B) Assigned in a writing delivered to an adult other than the transferor or to a trust company whose name in the assignment is followed in substance by the words:

"as custodian for ________________________
(Name of Minor)
under the California Uniform Transfers to Minors Act."

(4) An irrevocable exercise of a power of appointment or an irrevocable present right to future payment under a contract is the subject of a written notification delivered to the payor, issuer, or other obligor that the right is transferred to the transferor, an adult other than the transferor, or a trust company, whose name in the notification is followed in substance by the words:

"as custodian for ________________________
(Name of Minor)
under the California Uniform Transfers to Minors Act."

(5) An interest in real property is recorded in the name of the transferor, an adult other than the transferor, or a trust company, followed in substance by the words:

"as custodian for ________________________
(Name of Minor)
under the California Uniform Transfers to Minors Act."

(6) A certificate of title issued by a department or agency of a state or of the United States which evidences title to tangible personal property is either:

(A) Issued in the name of the transferor, an adult other than the transferor, or a trust company, followed in substance by the words:

"as custodian for ________________________
(Name of Minor)
under the California Uniform Transfers to Minors Act."

(B) Delivered to an adult other than the transferor or to a trust company, endorsed to that person followed in substance by the words:

"as custodian for ________________________
(Name of Minor)
under the California Uniform Transfers to Minors Act."

(7) An interest in any property not described in paragraphs (1) through (6) is transferred to an adult other than the transferor or to a trust company by a written instrument in substantially the form set forth in subdivision (b).

(b) An instrument in the following form satisfies the requirements of subparagraph (B) of paragraph (1) and paragraph (7) of subdivision (a):

"TRANSFER UNDER THE CALIFORNIA UNIFORM
TRANSFERS TO MINORS ACT

I, ________________________
(Name of Transferor or Name and Representative Capacity if a Fiduciary)

hereby transfer to ________________________
(Name of Custodian)

as custodian for ________________________
(Name of Minor)

under the California Uniform Transfers to Minors Act, the following:
(insert a description of the custodial property sufficient to identify it).
Dated: ______________, _____

____
(Signature)

________________________acknowledges receipt of the
(Name of Custodian)
property described above as custodian for the minor named above under the California Uniform Transfers to Minors Act.
Dated: ______________, _____

________________________"
(Signature of Custodian)

(c) A transferor shall place the custodian in control of the custodial property as soon as practicable.
(Stats. 1990 (A.B. 759), ch. 79, §14, effective July 1, 1991. Amended by Stats. 1991 (S.B. 271), ch. 1055, §17.)

§3910. Transfer may be made only for one minor

A transfer may be made only for one minor, and only one person may be the custodian. All custodial property held under this part by the same custodian for the benefit of the same minor constitutes a single custodianship.
(Stats. 1990 (A.B. 759), ch. 79, §14, effective July 1, 1991.)

§3911. Validity of transfer

(a) The validity of a transfer made in a manner prescribed in this part is not affected by any of the following:

(1) Failure of the transferor to comply with subdivision (c) of Section 3909.

(2) Designation of an ineligible custodian, except designation of the transferor in the case of property for which the transferor is ineligible to serve as custodian under subdivision (a) of Section 3909.

(3) Death or incapacity of a person nominated under Section 3903 or designated under Section 3909 as custodian, or the disclaimer of the office by that person.

(b) A transfer made pursuant to Section 3909 is irrevocable, and the custodial property is indefeasibly vested in the minor, but the custodian has all the rights, powers, duties, and authority provided in this part, and neither the minor nor the minor's legal representative has any right, power, duty, or authority with respect to the custodial property except as provided in this part.

(c) By making a transfer, the transferor incorporates in the disposition all the provisions of this part and grants to the custodian, and to any third person dealing with a person designated as custodian, the respective powers, rights, and immunities provided in this part.

(d) A person is not precluded from being a custodian for a minor under this part with respect to some property because the person is a conservator of the minor with respect to other property.

(e) A person who is the conservator of the minor is not precluded from being a custodian for a minor under this part because the custodial property has or will be transferred to the custodian from the guardianship estate of the minor. In such case, for the purposes of Section 3909, the custodian shall be deemed to be "an adult other than the transferor."

(f) In the cases described in subdivisions (d) and (e), with respect to the property transferred to the custodian, this part applies to the extent it would apply if the person to whom the custodial property is transferred were not and had not been a conservator of the minor.

(Stats. 1990 (A.B. 759), ch. 79, §14, effective July 1, 1991.)

§3912. Custodian's rights and duties

(a) A custodian shall do all of the following:

(1) Take control of custodial property.

(2) Register or record title to custodial property if appropriate.

(3) Collect, hold, manage, invest, and reinvest custodial property.

(b) In dealing with custodial property, a custodian shall observe the standard of care that would be observed by a prudent person dealing with property of another and is not limited by any other statute restricting investments by fiduciaries except that:

(1) If a custodian is not compensated for his or her services, the custodian is not liable for losses to custodial property unless they result from the custodian's bad faith, intentional wrongdoing, or gross negligence, or from the custodian's failure to maintain the standard of prudence in investing the custodial property provided in this section.

(2) A custodian, in the custodian's discretion and without liability to the minor or the minor's estate, may retain any custodial property received from a transferor.

(c) A custodian may invest in or pay premiums on life insurance or endowment policies on (1) the life of the minor only if the minor or the minor's estate is the sole beneficiary or (2) the life of another person in whom the minor has an insurable interest only to the extent that the minor, the minor's estate, or the custodian in the capacity of custodian, is the irrevocable beneficiary.

(d) A custodian at all times shall keep custodial property separate and distinct from all other property in a manner sufficient to identify it clearly as custodial property of the minor. Custodial property consisting of an undivided interest is so identified if the minor's interest is held as a tenant in common and is fixed. Custodial property subject to recordation is so identified if it is recorded, and custodial property subject to registration is so identified if it is either registered, or held in an account designated, in the name of the custodian, followed in substance by the words:

"as custodian for ______________________
(Name of Minor)
under the California Uniform Transfers to Minors Act."

(e) A custodian shall keep records of all transactions with respect to custodial property, including information necessary for the preparation of the minor's tax returns, and shall make them available for inspection at reasonable intervals by a parent or legal representative of the minor or by the minor if the minor has attained the age of 14 years.

(Stats. 1990 (A.B. 759), ch. 79, §14, effective July 1, 1991.)

§3914. Custodian may use custodial property "as advisable for use and benefit of minor"

(a) A custodian may deliver or pay to the minor or expend for the minor's benefit as much of the custodial property as the custodian considers advisable for the use and benefit of the minor, without court order and without regard to (1) the duty or ability of the custodian personally, or of any other person, to support the minor or (2) any other income or property of the minor which may be applicable or available for that purpose.

(b) On petition of an interested person or the minor if the minor has attained the age of 14 years, the court may order the custodian to deliver or pay to the minor or expend for the minor's benefit so much of the custodial property as the court considers advisable for the use and benefit of the minor.

(c) A delivery, payment, or expenditure under this section is in addition to, not in substitution for, and does not affect, any obligation of a person to support the minor.

(d) In lieu of the powers and duties described in subdivision (a), a transferor who is also the custodian may elect to govern his or her custodial powers and duties under this subdivision. If such election is made, the custodian shall not pay over to the minor for expenditure by the minor, and shall not expend for the minor's use or benefit, any part of the custodial property for any purpose prior to the time specified in Section 3920, except by order of the court upon a showing that the expenditure is necessary for the support, maintenance, or education of the minor. When the powers and duties of the custodian are governed by this subdivision, the transferor-custodian shall file with the clerk of the court a declaration in substantially the following form:

Declaration Under the California Uniform Transfers to Minors Act

I, ________________________

(Name of Transferor-Custodian)

as custodian for ______________

(Name of Minor)

under the California Uniform Transfers to Minors Act, hereby irrevocably elect to be governed under subdivision (d) of Section 3914 of the Probate Code in my custodial capacity over the following described property

____

____

(Description of Custodial Property)

I declare under penalty of perjury that the foregoing is true and correct.

Dated: ________________, _____

____

(Signature of Transferor-Custodian)

(Stats. 1990 (A.B. 759), ch. 79, §14, effective July 1, 1991.)

§3916. Third party is protected from liability in dealing with purported custodian

A third person in good faith and without court order may act on the instructions of, or otherwise deal with, any person purporting to make a transfer or purporting to act in the capacity of a custodian and, in the absence of knowledge, is not responsible for determining any of the following:

(a) The validity of the purported custodian's designation.

(b) The propriety of, or the authority under this part for, any act of the purported custodian.

(c) The validity or propriety under this part of any instrument or instructions executed or given either by the person purporting to make a transfer or by the purported custodian.

(d) The propriety of the application of any property of the minor delivered to the purported custodian.

(Stats. 1990 (A.B. 759), ch. 79, §14, effective July 1, 1991.)

§3917. Custodian's liability to third parties

(a) A claim based on

(1) a contract entered into by a custodian acting in a custodial capacity,

(2) an obligation arising from the ownership or control of custodial property, or

(3) a tort committed during the custodianship, may be asserted against the custodial property by proceeding against the custodian in the custodial capacity, whether or not the custodian or the minor is personally liable therefor.

(b) A custodian is not personally liable for either of the following:

(1) On a contract properly entered into in the custodial capacity unless the custodian fails to reveal that capacity and to identify the custodianship in the contract.

(2) For an obligation arising from control of custodial property or for a tort committed during the custodianship unless the custodian is personally at fault.

(c) A minor is not personally liable for an obligation arising from ownership of custodial property or for a tort committed during the custodianship unless the minor is personally at fault.

(Stats. 1990 (A.B. 759), ch. 79, §14, effective July 1, 1991.)

§3918. Nominee may decline to serve or resign; successor custodians

(a) A person nominated under Section 3903 or designated under Section 3909 as custodian may decline to serve by delivering a valid disclaimer under Part 8 (commencing with Section 260) of Division 2 to the person who made the nomination or to the transferor or the transferor's legal representative. If the event giving rise to a transfer has not occurred and no substitute custodian able, willing, and eligible to serve was nominated under Section 3903, the person who made the nomination may nominate a substitute custodian under Section 3903; otherwise the transferor or the transferor's legal representative shall designate a substitute custodian at the time of the transfer, in either case from among the persons eligible to serve as custodian for that kind of property under subdivision (a) of Section 3909. The custodian so designated has the rights of a successor custodian.

(b) A custodian at any time may designate a trust company or an adult other than a transferor under Section 3904 as successor custodian by executing and dating an instrument of designation before a subscribing witness other than the successor. If the instrument of designation does not contain or is not accompanied by the resignation of the custodian, the designation of the successor does not take effect until the custodian resigns, dies, becomes incapacitated, or is removed. The transferor may designate one or more persons as successor custodians to serve, in the designated order of priority, in case the custodian originally designated or a prior successor custodian is unable, declines, or is ineligible to serve or resigns, dies, becomes incapacitated, or is removed. The designation either (1) shall be made in the same transaction and by the same document by which the transfer is made or (2) shall be made by executing and dating a separate instrument of designation before a subscribing witness other than a successor as a part of the same transaction and contemporaneously with the execution of the document by which the transfer is made. The designation is made by setting forth the successor custodian's name, followed in substance by the words: "is designated [first, second, etc., where applicable] successor custodian." A successor custodian designated by the transferor may be a trust company or an adult other than a transferor under Section 3904. A successor custodian effectively designated by the transferor has priority over a successor custodian designated by a custodian.

(c) A custodian may resign at any time by delivering written notice to the minor if the minor has attained the age of 14 years and to the successor custodian and by delivering the custodial property to the successor custodian.

(d) If the transferor has not effectively designated a successor custodian, and a custodian is ineligible, dies, or becomes incapacitated without having effectively designated a successor and the minor has attained the age of 14 years, the minor may designate as successor custodian, in the manner prescribed in subdivision (b), an adult member of the minor's family, a conservator of the minor, or a trust company. If the minor has not attained the age of 14 years or fails to act within 60 days after the ineligibility, death, or incapacity, the conservator of the minor becomes successor custodian. If the minor has no conservator or the conservator declines to act, the transferor, the legal representative of the transferor or of the custodian, an adult member of the minor's family, or any other interested person may petition the court to designate a successor custodian.

(e) A custodian who declines to serve under subdivision (a) or resigns under subdivision (c), or the legal representative of a deceased or incapacitated custodian, as soon as practicable, shall put the custodial property and records in the possession and control of the successor custodian. The successor custodian by action may enforce the obligation to deliver custodial property and records and becomes responsible for each item as received.

(f) A transferor, the legal representative of a transferor, an adult member of the minor's family, a guardian of the person of the minor, the conservator of the minor, or the minor if the minor has attained the age of 14 years, may petition the court to remove the custodian for cause and to designate a successor custodian other than a transferor under Section 3904 or to require the custodian to give appropriate bond.

(g) At least 15 days before the hearing on a petition under subdivision (d) or (f), the petitioner shall serve notice by mail or personal delivery on each of the following persons:

(1) The minor.

(2) The parent or parents of the minor.

(3) The transferor.

(h) Upon consideration of the petition under subdivision (d) or (f), the court may grant the relief that the court finds to be in the best interests of the minor.

(Stats. 1990 (A.B. 759), ch. 79, §14, effective July 1, 1991. Amended Stats. 1992 (A.B. 2975), ch. 871, §7.)

§3919. Minor may petition for an accounting

(a) A minor who has attained the age of 14 years, the minor's guardian of the person or legal representative, an adult member of the minor's family, a transferor, or a transferor's legal representative may petition the court for any of the following:

(1) An accounting by the custodian or the custodian's legal representative.

(2) A determination of responsibility, as between the custodial property and the custodian personally, for claims against the custodial property unless the responsibility has been adjudicated in an action under Section 3917 to which the minor or the minor's legal representative was a party.

(b) A successor custodian may petition the court for an accounting by the predecessor custodian.

(c) The court, in a proceeding under this part or in any other proceeding, may require or permit the custodian or the custodian's legal representative to account.

(d) If a custodian is removed under subdivision (f) of Section 3918, the court shall require an accounting and order delivery of the custodial property and records to the successor custodian and the execution of all instruments required for transfer of the custodial property.

(e) The right to petition for an accounting shall continue for one year after the filing of a final accounting by the custodian or the custodian's legal representative and delivery of the custodial property to the minor or the minor's estate.

(Stats. 1990 (A.B. 759), ch. 79, §14, effective July 1, 1991.)

§3920. Custodian shall terminate custodianship upon child's reaching majority

The custodian shall transfer in an appropriate manner the custodial property to the minor or to the minor's estate upon the earlier of the following:

(a) The minor's attainment of 18 years of age unless the time of transfer of the custodial property to the minor is delayed under Section 3920.5 to a time after the time the minor attains the age of 18 years.

(b) The time specified in the transfer pursuant to Section 3909 if the time of transfer of the custodial property to the minor is delayed under Section 3920.5 to a time after the time the minor attains the age of 18 years.

(c) The minor's death.

(Stats. 1990 (A.B. 759), ch. 79, §14, effective July 1, 1991.)

§3920.5. Custodian may delay time to terminate custodianship if transfer specifies a later age

(a) Subject to the requirements and limitations of this section, the time for transfer to the minor of custodial property transferred under or pursuant to Section 3903, 3904, 3905, or 3906, may be delayed until a specified time after the time the minor attains the age of 18 years, which time shall be specified in the transfer pursuant to Section 3909.

(b) To specify a delayed time for transfer to the minor of the custodial property, the words

"as custodian for ______________________
(Name of Minor)
until age ______________________
(Age for Delivery of Property to Minor)
under the California Uniform Transfers to Minors Act"

shall be substituted in substance for the words

"as custodian for ______________________
(Name of Minor)
under the California Uniform Transfers to Minors Act" in making the transfer pursuant to Section 3909.

(c) The time for transfer to the minor of custodial property transferred under or pursuant to Section 3903 or 3905 may be delayed under this section only if the governing will or trust or nomination provides in substance that the custodianship is to continue until the time the minor attains a specified age, which time may not be later than the time the minor attains 25 years of age, and in that case the governing will or trust or nomination shall determine the time to be specified in the transfer pursuant to Section 3909.

(d) The time for transfer to the minor of custodial property transferred by the irrevocable exercise of a power of appointment under Section 3904 may be delayed under this section only if the transfer pursuant to Section 3909 provides in substance that the custodianship is to continue until the time the minor attains a specified age, which time may not be later than the time the minor attains 25 years of age.

(e) The time for transfer to the minor of custodial property transferred by irrevocable gift under Section 3904 may be delayed under this section only if the transfer pursuant to Section 3909 provides in substance that the custodianship is to continue until the time the minor attains a specified age, which time may not be later than the time the minor attains 21 years of age.

(f) The time for transfer to the minor of custodial property transferred by a trustee under Section 3906 may be delayed under this section only if the transfer pursuant to Section 3909 provides that the custodianship is to continue until a specified time not later than the time the minor attains 25 years of age or the time of termination of all present beneficial interests of the minor in the trust from which the custodial property was transferred, whichever is to occur first.

(g) If the transfer pursuant to Section 3909 does not specify any age, the time for the transfer of the custodial property to the minor under Section 3920 is the time when the minor attains 18 years of age.

(h) If the transfer pursuant to Section 3909 provides in substance that the duration of the custodianship is for a time longer than the maximum time permitted by this section for the duration of a custodianship created by that type of transfer, the custodianship shall be deemed to continue only until the time the minor attains the maximum age permitted by this section for the duration of a custodianship created by that type of transfer.

(Stats. 1990 (A.B. 759), ch. 79, §14, effective July 1, 1991. Amended Stats. 1996 (A.B. 2751), ch. 862, §14.)

§3921. Determination of venue

Subject to the power of the court to transfer actions and proceedings as provided in the Code of Civil Procedure, a petition filed under this part shall be heard and proceedings thereon held in the superior court in the proper county, which shall be determined as follows:

(a) If the minor resides in this state, in either of the following counties:

(1) Where the minor resides.

(2) Where the custodian resides.

(b) If the minor does not reside within this state, in any of the following counties:

(1) Where the transferor resides.

(2) Where the custodian resides.

(3)Where the estate of a deceased or legally incapacitated custodian is being administered.

(4) Where a parent of the minor resides.

(c) If neither the minor, nor the transferor, nor any parent resides within this state, and no estate of a deceased or legally incapacitated custodian is being administered within this state, in any county.

(Stats. 1990 (A.B. 759), ch. 79, §14, effective July 1, 1991.)

§3922. Application to particular transfers

This part applies to a transfer within the scope of Section 3902 made on or after January 1, 1985, if either of the following requirements is satisfied:

(a) The transfer purports to have been made under the California Uniform Gifts to Minors Act.

(b) The instrument by which the transfer purports to have been made uses in substance the designation "as custodian under the Uniform Gifts to Minors Act" or "as custodian under the Uniform Transfers to Minors Act" of any other state, and the application of this part is necessary to validate the transfer.

(Stats. 1990 (A.B. 759), ch. 79, §14, effective July 1, 1991.)

§3923. Application to transfers made prior to January 1, 1985

(a) As used in this section, "California Uniform Gifts to Minors Act" means former Article 4 (commencing with Section 1154) of Chapter 3 of Title 4 of Part 4 of Division 2 of the Civil Code.

(b) Any transfer of custodial property, as now defined in this part, made before January 1, 1985, is validated, notwithstanding that there was no specific authority in the California Uniform Gifts to Minors Act for the coverage of custodial property of that kind or for a transfer from that source at the time the transfer was made.

(c) This part applies to all transfers made before January 1, 1985, in a manner and form prescribed in the California Uniform Gifts to Minors Act, except insofar as the application impairs constitutionally vested rights.

(d) To the extent that this part, by virtue of subdivision (c), does not apply to transfers made in a manner prescribed in the California Uniform Gifts to Minors Act or to the powers, duties, and immunities conferred by transfers in that manner upon custodians and persons dealing with custodians, the repeal of the California Uniform Gifts to Minors Act does not affect those transfers or those powers, duties, and immunities.

(Stats. 1990 (A.B. 759), ch. 79, §14, effective July 1, 1991.)

§3925. Statute is not exclusive method for making gifts or transfers to minors

This part shall not be construed as providing an exclusive method for making gifts or other transfers to minors.

(Stats. 1990 (A.B. 759), ch. 79, §14, effective July 1, 1991.)

E. EMANCIPATION

The doctrine of emancipation ends certain disabilities of minority and releases parents from specific obligations to their minor children. Thus, it allows minors to free themselves from parental control before adulthood.

Many states have codified the criteria for emancipation. Under California's Emancipation of Minors Act, several factors (such as marriage, active duty in the armed forces, or a judicial declaration) emancipate a person under age 18 (Cal. Fam. Code §7002). Emancipation confers adult status for purposes of parental support, control over earnings; and, the capacity to enter into a binding contract, make a will, establish a residence, and enroll in school (*id.* at §7050)).

To obtain a judicial declaration of emancipation in California, the minor must petition and assert that he or she willingly lives apart from parents or guardian with the latter's consent (or acquiescence) and is managing his or her own financial affairs (Cal. Fam. Code §7120(b)). The court must grant the petition if it finds the minor has met these requirements and "that emancipation would not be contrary to the minor's best interest" (Cal. Fam. Code §7122(a)).

On the history of California's legislation, see Carol Sanger & Eleanor Willemsen, Minor Changes: Emancipating Children in Modern Times, 25 U. Mich. J.L. Reform 239, 250-263 (1992).

California Family Code

§7000. Title

This part may be cited as the Emancipation of Minors Law.
(Stats. 1992 (A.B. 2650), ch. 162, §10, effective January 1, 1994.)

§7001. Purpose

It is the purpose of this part to provide a clear statement defining emancipation and its consequences and to permit an emancipated minor to obtain a court declaration of the minor's status. This part is not intended to affect the status of minors who may become emancipated under the decisional case law that was in effect before the enactment of Chapter 1059 of the Statutes of 1978.
(Stats. 1992 (A.B. 2650), ch. 162, §10, effective January 1, 1994.)

§7002. Conditions of emancipation: marriage, active duty or obtain declaration

A person under the age of 18 years is an emancipated minor if any of the following conditions is satisfied:

(a) The person has entered into a valid marriage, whether or not the marriage has been dissolved.

(b) The person is on active duty with the armed forces of the United States.

(c) The person has received a declaration of emancipation pursuant to Section 7122.
(Stats. 1992 (A.B. 2650), ch. 162, §10, effective January 1, 1994.)

§7050. Emancipated minor shall be considered an adult for designated purposes

An emancipated minor shall be considered as being an adult for the following purposes:

(a) The minor's right to support by the minor's parents.

(b) The right of the minor's parents to the minor's earnings and to control the minor.

(c) The application of Sections 300 and 601 of the Welfare and Institutions Code.

(d) Ending all vicarious or imputed liability of the minor's parents or guardian for the minor's torts. Nothing in this section affects any liability of a parent, guardian, spouse, or employer imposed by the Vehicle Code, or any vicarious liability that arises from an agency relationship.

(e) The minor's capacity to do any of the following:

(1) Consent to medical, dental, or psychiatric care, without parental consent, knowledge, or liability.

(2) Enter into a binding contract or give a delegation of power.

(3) Buy, sell, lease, encumber, exchange, or transfer an interest in real or personal property, including, but not limited to, shares of stock in a domestic or foreign corporation or a membership in a nonprofit corporation.

(4) Sue or be sued in the minor's own name.

(5) Compromise, settle, arbitrate, or otherwise adjust a claim, action, or proceeding by or against the minor.

(6) Make or revoke a will.

(7) Make a gift, outright or in trust.

(8) Convey or release contingent or expectant interests in property, including marital property rights and any right of survivorship incident to joint tenancy, and consent to a transfer, encumbrance, or gift of marital property.

(9) Exercise or release the minor's powers as donee of a power of appointment unless the creating instrument otherwise provides.

(10) Create for the minor's own benefit or for the benefit of others a revocable or irrevocable trust.

(11) Revoke a revocable trust.

(12) Elect to take under or against a will.

(13) Renounce or disclaim any interest acquired by testate or intestate succession or by inter vivos transfer, including exercise of the right to surrender the right to revoke a revocable trust.

(14) Make an election referred to in Section 13502 of, or an election and agreement referred to in Section 13503 of, the Probate Code.

(15) Establish the minor's own residence.

(16) Apply for a work permit pursuant to Section 49110 of the Education Code without the request of the minor's parents.

(17) Enroll in a school or college.
(Stats. 1992 (A.B. 2650), ch. 162, §10, effective January 1, 1994.)

§7051. Emancipated minor has same rights and duties as an adult regarding insurance contracts

An insurance contract entered into by an emancipated minor has the same effect as if it were entered into by an adult and, with respect to that contract, the minor has the same rights, duties, and liabilities as an adult.
(Stats. 1992 (A.B. 2650), ch. 162, §10, effective January 1, 1994.)

§7052. Emacipated minor's rights regarding stock, memberships in nonprofit corporation, or other property

With respect to shares of stock in a domestic or foreign corporation held by an emancipated minor, a membership in a nonprofit corporation held by an emancipated minor, or other property held by an emancipated minor, the minor may do all of the following:

(a) Vote in person, and give proxies to exercise any voting rights, with respect to the shares, membership, or property.

(b) Waive notice of any meeting or give consent to the holding of any meeting.

(c) Authorize, ratify, approve, or confirm any action that could be taken by shareholders, members, or property owners.
(Stats. 1992 (A.B. 2650) ch. 162, §10, effective January 1, 1994.)

§7110. Legislative intent to simplify proceedings

It is the intent of the Legislature that proceedings under this part be as simple and inexpensive as possible. To that end, the Judicial Council is requested to prepare and distribute to the clerks of the superior courts appropriate forms for the proceedings that are suitable for use by minors acting as their own counsel.

(Stats. 1992 (A.B. 2650), ch. 162, §10, effective January 1, 1994.)

§7111. Effect of declaration of emancipation on minor's entitlement to benefits

The issuance of a declaration of emancipation does not entitle the minor to any benefits under Division 9 (commencing with Section 10000) of the Welfare and Institutions Code which would not otherwise accrue to an emancipated minor.

(Stats. 1992 (A.B. 2650), ch. 162, §10, effective January 1, 1994.)

§7120. Minor may petition court for a declaration of emancipation

(a) A minor may petition the superior court of the county in which the minor resides or is temporarily domiciled for a declaration of emancipation.

(b) The petition shall set forth with specificity all of the following facts:

(1) The minor is at least 14 years of age.

(2) The minor willingly lives separate and apart from the minor's parents or guardian with the consent or acquiescence of the minor's parents or guardian.

(3) The minor is managing his or her own financial affairs. As evidence of this, the minor shall complete and attach a declaration of income and expenses as provided in Judicial Council form FL-150.

(4) The source of the minor's income is not derived from any activity declared to be a crime by the laws of this state or the laws of the United States.

(Stats. 1992 (A.B. 2650), ch. 162, §10, effective January 1, 1994. Amended Stats. 1993 (A.B. 1500), ch. 219, §156; Stats. 2004 (A.B. 3079), ch. 811, §3.)

§7121. Notice to minor's parents or guardian

(a) Before the petition for a declaration of emancipation is heard, notice the court determines is reasonable shall be given to the minor's parents, guardian, or other person entitled to the custody of the minor, or proof shall be made to the court that their addresses are unknown or that for other reasons the notice cannot be given.

(b) The clerk of the court shall also notify thelocal child support agency of the county in which the matter is to be heard of the proceeding. If the minor is a ward of the court, notice shall be given to the probation department. If the child is a dependent child of the court, notice shall be given to the county welfare department.

(c) The notice shall include a form whereby the minor's parents, guardian, or other person entitled to the custody of the minor may give their written consent to the petitioner's emancipation. The notice shall include a warning that a court may void or rescind the declaration of emancipation and the parents may become liable for support and medical insurance coverage pursuant to Chapter 2 (commencing with Section 4000) of Part 2 of Division 9 and Sections 17400, 17402, 17404, and 17422.

(Stats. 1992 (A.B. 2650), ch. 162, §10, effective January 1, 1994. Amended Stats. 1993 (A.B. 1500), ch. 219, §157; Stats. 2003 (A.B. 1710), ch. 365, §1.)

§7122. Court shall grant petition if emancipation would not be contrary to best interests

(a) The court shall sustain the petition if it finds that the minor is a person described by Section 7120 and that emancipation would not be contrary to the minor's best interest.

(b) If the petition is sustained, the court shall forthwith issue a declaration of emancipation, which shall be filed by the clerk of the court.

(c) A declaration is conclusive evidence that the minor is emancipated.

(Stats. 1992 (A.B. 2650), ch. 162, §10, effective January 1, 1994. Amended by Stats. 2002 (S.B. 1316), ch. 784, §107.)

§7123. Minor has right to petition for a writ of mandate if petition is denied

(a) If the petition is denied, the minor has a right to file a petition for a writ of mandate.

(b) If the petition is sustained, the parents or guardian have a right to file a petition for a writ of mandate if they have appeared in the proceeding and opposed the granting of the petition.

(Stats. 1992 (A.B. 2650), ch. 162, §10, effective January 1, 1994.)

§7130. Declaration obtained by fraud is voidable; declaration may be rescinded for indigent minor

(a) A declaration of emancipation obtained by fraud or by the withholding of material information is voidable.

(b) A declaration of emancipation of a minor who is indigent and has no means of support is subject to rescission.

(Stats. 1992 (A.B. 2650), ch. 162, §10, effective January 1, 1994.)

§7131. Any person or agency may file petition to void declaration for fraud

A petition to void a declaration of emancipation on the ground that the declaration was obtained by fraud or by the withholding of material information may be filed by any person or by any public or private agency. The petition shall be filed in the court that made the declaration.

(Stats. 1992 (A.B. 2650), ch. 162, §10, effective January 1, 1994.)

§7132. Minor, minor's conservator or district attorney may file petition to rescind declaration for indigence

(a) A petition to rescind a declaration of emancipation on the ground that the minor is indigent and has no means of support may be filed by the minor declared emancipated, by the minor's conservator, or by the district attorney of the county in which the minor resides. The petition shall be filed in the county in which the minor or the conservator resides.

(b) The minor may be considered indigent if the minor's only source of income is from public assistance benefits. The court shall consider the impact of the rescission of the declaration of emancipation on the minor and shall find the rescission of the declaration of emancipation will not be contrary to the best interest of the minor before granting the order to rescind.

(Stats. 1992 (A.B. 2650), ch. 162, §10, effective January 1, 1994. Amended Stats. 1993 (A.B. 1500), ch. 219, §158.)

§7133. Notice to parents to nullify or rescind declaration of emancipation

(a) Before a petition under this article is heard, notice the court determines is reasonable shall be given to the minor's parents or guardian, or proof shall be made to the court that their addresses are unknown or that for other reasons the notice cannot be given.

(b) The notice to parents shall state that if the declaration of emancipation is voided or rescinded, the parents may be liable to provide support and medical insurance coverage for the child pursuant to Chapter 2 (commencing with Section 4000) of Part 2 of Division 9 of this code and Sections 11350, 11350.1, 11475.1, and 11490 of the Welfare and Institutions Code.

(c) No liability accrues to a parent or guardian not given actual notice, as a result of voiding or rescinding the declaration of emancipation, until that parent or guardian is given actual notice.

(Stats. 1992 (A.B. 2650), ch. 162, §10, effective January 1, 1994. Amended Stats. 1993 (A.B. 1500), ch. 219, §159.)

§7134. Court shall issue order voiding or rescinding declaration

If the petition is sustained, the court shall forthwith issue an order voiding or rescinding the declaration of emancipation, which shall be filed by the clerk of the court.

(Stats. 1992 (A.B. 2650), ch. 162, §10, effective January 1, 1994. Amended by Stats. 2002 (S.B. 1316), ch. 784, §108.)

§7135. Voiding or rescission of declaration does not alter contractual obligations or property rights

Voiding or rescission of the declaration of emancipation does not alter any contractual obligation or right or any property right or interest that arose during the period that the declaration was in effect.

(Stats. 1992 (A.B. 2650), ch. 162, §10, effective January 1, 1994.)

§7140. Minor's emancipated status shall be entered in Department of Motor Vehicles computer network and stated on ID card

On application of a minor declared emancipated under this chapter, the Department of Motor Vehicles shall enter identifying information in its law enforcement computer network, and the fact of emancipation shall be stated on the department's identification card issued to the emancipated minor.

(Stats. 1992 (A.B. 2650), ch. 162, §10, effective January 1, 1994.)

§7141. Person who relies on ID card has same rights as if minor were emancipated

A person who, in good faith, has examined a minor's identification card and relies on a minor's representation that the minor is emancipated, has the same rights and obligations as if the minor were in fact emancipated at the time of the representation.

(Stats. 1992 (A.B. 2650), ch. 162, §10, effective January 1, 1994.)

§7142. Public entities and public employees are protected in case of good faith reliance

No public entity or employee is liable for any loss or injury resulting directly or indirectly from false or inaccurate information contained in the Department of Motor Vehicles records system or identification cards as provided in this part.

(Stats. 1992 (A.B. 2650), ch. 162, §10, effective January 1, 1994.)

§7143. Court shall send notice to Department of Motor Vehicles if declaration of emancipation is voided or rescinded

If a declaration of emancipation is voided or rescinded, notice shall be sent immediately to the Department of Motor Vehicles which shall remove the information relating to emancipation in its law enforcement computer network. Any identification card issued stating emancipation shall be invalidated.

(Stats. 1992 (A.B. 2650), ch. 162, §10, effective January 1, 1994.)

F. EDUCATION

1. Exclusion for Lack of Immunization

California Education Code

§48216. School district shall exclude pupil who has not been immunized

(a) The county office of education or the governing board of the school district of attendance shall exclude any pupil who has not been immunized properly pursuant to Chapter 1 (commencing with Section 120325) of Part 2 of Division 105 of the Health and Safety Code.

(b) The governing board of the district shall notify the parent or guardian of the pupil that they have two weeks to supply evidence either that the pupil has been properly immunized, or that the pupil is exempted from the immunization requirement pursuant to Section 120365 or 120370 of the Health and Safety Code.

(c) The governing board of the district, in the notice, shall refer the parent or guardian of the pupil to the pupil's usual source of medical care to obtain the immunization, or if no usual source exists, either refer the parent or guardian to the county health department, or notify the parent or guardian that the immunizations will be administered at a school of the district.

(Stats. 1978, ch. 325, §2, as Ed C, §46010.5. Amended Stats. 1991, ch. 984, §8 (S.B. 407); Stats. 1994 (A.B. 2971), ch. 1172, §12; Stats. 1996 (S.B. 1497), ch. 1023, §38, effective September 29, 1996. Amended and renumbered by Stats. 1997 (S.B. 727), ch. 855, §10, effective July 1, 1998.)

California Health & Safety Code

§120335. Students must be fully immunized

(a) As used in Chapter 1 (commencing with Section 120325, but excluding Section 120380), and as used in Sections 120400, 120405, 120410, and 120415, the term "governing authority" means the governing board of each school district or the authority of each other private or public institution responsible for the operation and control of the institution or the principal or administrator of each school or institution.

(b) The governing authority shall not unconditionally admit any person as a pupil of any private or public elementary or secondary school, child care center, day nursery, nursery school, family day care home, or development center, unless prior to his or her first admission to that institution he or she has been fully immunized. The following are the diseases for which immunizations shall be documented:

(1) Diphtheria.

(2) Hemophilus influenza type b, except for children who have reached the age of four years and six months.

(3) Measles.

(4) Mumps, except for children who have reached the age of seven years.

(5) Pertussis (whooping cough), except for children who have reached the age of seven years.

(6) Poliomyelitis.

(7) Rubella.

(8) Tetanus.

(9) Hepatitis B for all children entering the institutions listed in this subdivision at the kindergarten level or below on or after August 1, 1997.

(10) Varicella (chickenpox), effective July 1, 2001. Persons already admitted into California public or private schools at the kindergarten level or above before July 1, 2001, shall be exempt from the varicella immunization requirement for school entry. This paragraph shall be operative only to the extent that funds for this purpose are appropriated in the annual Budget Act.

The department may adopt emergency regulations to implement this paragraph including, but not limited to, requirements for documentation and immunization status reports, in accordance with the rulemaking provisions of the Administrative Procedure Act (Chapter 3.5 (commencing with Section 11340) of Part 1 of Division 3 of Title 2 of the Government Code). The initial adoption of emergency regulations shall be deemed to be an emergency and considered by the Office of Administrative Law as necessary for the immediate preservation of the public peace, health and safety, or general welfare. Emergency regulations adopted pursuant to this paragraph shall remain in effect for no more than 180 days.

(11) Any other disease deemed appropriate by the department, taking into consideration the recommendations of the United States Public Health Services' Centers for Disease Control Immunization Practices Advisory Committee and the American Academy of Pediatrics Committee of Infectious Diseases.

(c) On and after July 1, 1999, the governing authority shall not unconditionally admit any pupil to the 7th grade level, nor unconditionally advance any pupil to the 7th grade level, of any of the institutions listed in subdivision (b) unless the pupil has been fully immunized against hepatitis B.

(d) The department may specify the immunizing agents which may be utilized and the manner in which immunizations are administered.

(Formerly §3381, added by Stats. 1977, ch. 1176, §2, effective September 30, 1977. Amended by Stats. 1979, ch. 435, p. 1560, §2; Stats. 1982, ch. 472, p. 2067, §1, effective July 10, 1982; Stats. 1992 (A.B. 2798), ch. 1300, §2; Stats. 1992 (A.B. 2294), ch. 1320, §2; Stats. 1995 (A.B. 1194), ch. 291, §1. Renumbered §120335 and amended by Stats. 1996 (S.B. 1497), ch. 1023, §179, effective September 29, 1996. Amended by Stats. 1997 (A.B. 381), ch. 882, §1; Stats. 1999 (S.B. 741), ch. 747, §2.)

§120365. Exemptions from immunizations if contrary to parents' beliefs

Immunization of a person shall not be required for admission to a school or other institution listed in Section 120335 if the parent or guardian or adult who has assumed responsibility for his or her care and custody in the case of a minor, or the person seeking admission if an emancipated minor, files with the governing authority a letter or affidavit stating that the immunization is contrary to his or her beliefs. However, whenever there is good cause to believe that the person has been exposed to one of the communicable diseases listed in subdivision (a) of Section 120325, that person may be temporarily excluded from the school or institution until the local health officer is satisfied that the person is no longer at risk of developing the disease.

(Stats. 1995 (S.B. 1360), ch. 415, §7.)

§120370. Exemptions from immunizations for purposes of child's health and safety

If the parent or guardian files with the governing authority a written statement by a licensed physician to the effect that the physical condition of the child is such, or medical

circumstances relating to the child are such, that immunization is not considered safe, indicating the specific nature and probable duration of the medical condition or circumstances that contraindicate immunization, that person shall be exempt from the requirements of Chapter 1 (commencing with Section 120325, but excluding Section 120380) and Sections 120400, 120405, 120410, and 120415 to the extent indicated by the physician's statement.
(Stats. 1995 (S.B. 1360), ch. 415, §7.)

2. Other Grounds for Suspension or Expulsion

California Education Code

§48900. Pupil may be suspended or expelled on the following grounds

A pupil may not be suspended from school or recommended for expulsion, unless the superintendent or the principal of the school in which the pupil is enrolled determines that the pupil has committed an act as defined pursuant to any of subdivisions (a) to (q), inclusive:

(a) (1) Caused, attempted to cause, or threatened to cause physical injury to another person.

(2) Willfully used force or violence upon the person of another, except in self-defense.

(b) Possessed, sold, or otherwise furnished any firearm, knife, explosive, or other dangerous object, unless, in the case of possession of any object of this type, the pupil had obtained written permission to possess the item from a certificated school employee, which is concurred in by the principal or the designee of the principal.

(c) Unlawfully possessed, used, sold, or otherwise furnished, or been under the influence of, any controlled substance listed in Chapter 2 (commencing with Section 11053) of Division 10 of the Health and Safety Code, an alcoholic beverage, or an intoxicant of any kind.

(d) Unlawfully offered, arranged, or negotiated to sell any controlled substance listed in Chapter 2 (commencing with Section 11053) of Division 10 of the Health and Safety Code, an alcoholic beverage, or an intoxicant of any kind, and either sold, delivered, or otherwise furnished to any person another liquid, substance, or material and represented the liquid, substance, or material as a controlled substance, alcoholic beverage, or intoxicant.

(e) Committed or attempted to commit robbery or extortion.

(f) Caused or attempted to cause damage to school property or private property.

(g) Stolen or attempted to steal school property or private property.

(h) Possessed or used tobacco, or any products containing tobacco or nicotine products, including, but not limited to, cigarettes, cigars, miniature cigars, clove cigarettes, smokeless tobacco, snuff, chew packets, and betel. However, this section does not prohibit use or possession by a pupil of his or her own prescription products.

(i) Committed an obscene act or engaged in habitual profanity or vulgarity.

(j) Unlawfully possessed or unlawfully offered, arranged, or negotiated to sell any drug paraphernalia, as defined in Section 11014.5 of the Health and Safety Code.

(k) Disrupted school activities or otherwise willfully defied the valid authority of supervisors, teachers, administrators, school officials, or other school personnel engaged in the performance of their duties.

(l) Knowingly received stolen school property or private property.

(m) Possessed an imitation firearm. As used in this section, "imitation firearm" means a replica of a firearm that is so substantially similar in physical properties to an existing firearm as to lead a reasonable person to conclude that the replica is a firearm.

(n) Committed or attempted to commit a sexual assault as defined in Section 261, 266c, 286, 288, 288a, or 289 of the Penal Code or committed a sexual battery as defined in Section 243.4 of the Penal Code.

(o) Harassed, threatened, or intimidated a pupil who is a complaining witness or a witness in a school disciplinary proceeding for the purpose of either preventing that pupil from being a witness or retaliating against that pupil for being a witness, or both.

(p) Unlawfully offered, arranged to sell, negotiated to sell, or sold the prescription drug Soma.

(q) Engaged in, or attempted to engage in, hazing as defined in Section 32050.

(r) A pupil may not be suspended or expelled for any of the acts enumerated in this section, unless that act is related to school activity or school attendance occurring within a school under the jurisdiction of the superintendent or principal or occurring within any other school district. A pupil may be suspended or expelled for acts that are enumerated in this section and related to school activity or attendance that occur at any time, including, but not limited to, any of the following:

(1) While on school grounds.

(2) While going to or coming from school.

(3) During the lunch period whether on or off the campus.

(4) During, or while going to or coming from, a school sponsored activity.

(s) A pupil who aids or abets, as defined in Section 31 of the Penal Code, the infliction or attempted infliction of physical injury to another person may suffer suspension, but not expulsion, pursuant to this section, except that a pupil who has been adjudged by a juvenile court to have committed, as an aider and abettor, a crime of physical violence in which the victim suffered great bodily injury or serious bodily injury shall be subject to discipline pursuant to subdivision (a).

(t) As used in this section, "school property" includes, but is not limited to, electronic files and databases.

(u) A superintendent or principal may use his or her discretion to provide alternatives to suspension or expulsion, including, but not limited to, counseling and an anger management program, for a pupil subject to discipline under this section.

(v) It is the intent of the Legislature that alternatives to suspension or expulsion be imposed against any pupil who is truant, tardy, or otherwise absent from school activities.
(Stats. 1983, ch. 498, §91, effective July 28, 1983. Amended Stats. 1984, ch. 23, §1, ch. 536, §1; Stats. 1985, ch. 318, §1; Stats. 1986, ch. 111, §1, ch. 1136, §1; Stats. 1987, ch. 383, §1; Stats. 1989, ch. 1306, §1; Stats. 1992 (S.B. 1930), ch. 909, §1; Stats. 1994 (A.B. 2543), ch. 1198, §5; Stats. 1995 (S.B. 966), ch. 972, §6; Stats. 1996 (A.B. 692), ch. 915, §1; Stats. 1997 (A.B. 412), ch. 637, §1. Amended Stats. 2001 (A.B. 653), ch. 484, §1. Amended Stats. 2002 (A.B. 662), ch. 151, §1; Stats. 2002 (A.B.1901), ch. 643, §1.5; Stats. 2003 (A.B. 1411), ch. 21, §2.)

§48900.2. Pupil may be suspended or expelled for sexual harassment

In addition to the reasons specified in Section 48900, a pupil may be suspended from school or recommended for expulsion if the superintendent or the principal of the school in which the pupil is enrolled determines that the pupil has committed sexual harassment as defined in Section 212.5.

For the purposes of this chapter, the conduct described in Section 212.5 must be considered by a reasonable person of the same gender as the victim to be sufficiently severe or pervasive to have a negative impact upon the individual's academic performance or to create an intimidating, hostile, or offensive educational environment. This section shall not apply to pupils enrolled in kindergarten and grades 1 to 3, inclusive.
(Stats. 1992 (S.B. 1930), ch. 909, §2 (S.B. 1930).)

§48900.3. Pupil may be suspended or expelled for participation in act of hate violence

In addition to the reasons set forth in Sections 48900 and 48900.2, a pupil in any of grades 4 to 12, inclusive, may be suspended from school or recommended for expulsion if the superintendent or the principal of the school in which the pupil is enrolled determines that the pupil has caused, attempted to cause, threatened to cause, or participated in an act of, hate violence, as defined in subdivision (e) of Section 233.
(Stats. 1994 (A.B. 2543), ch. 1198, §6. Amended Stats. 1999 (A.B. 1600), ch. 646, §25.)

§48900.4. Pupil may be suspended or expelled for engaging in harassment or intimidation

In addition to the grounds specified in Sections 48900 and 48900.2, a pupil enrolled in any of grades 4 to 12, inclusive, may be suspended from school or recommended for expulsion if the superintendent or the principal of the school in which the pupil is enrolled determines that the pupil has intentionally engaged in harassment, threats, or intimidation, directed against school district personnel or pupils, that is sufficiently severe or pervasive to have the actual and reasonably expected effect of materially disrupting classwork, creating substantial disorder, and invading the rights of either school personnel or pupils by creating an intimidating or hostile educational environment.
(Stats. 1994 (A.B. 2752), ch. 1017, §1. Amended Stats. 2002 (A.B. 1901), ch. 643, §2.)

§48900.5. Suspension shall be imposed as last resort

Suspension shall be imposed only when other means of correction fail to bring about proper conduct. However, a pupil, including an individual with exceptional needs, as defined in Section 56026, may be suspended for any of the reasons enumerated in Section 48900 upon a first offense, if the principal or superintendent of schools determines that the pupil violated subdivision (a), (b), (c), (d), or (e) of Section 48900 or that the pupil's presence causes a danger to persons or property or threatens to disrupt the instructional process.
(Stats. 1983, ch. 498, §91, effective July 28, 1983. Amended Stats. 1983, ch. 1302, §20, effective September 30, 1983; Stats. 1985, ch. 907, §1, effective September 23, 1985.)

§48900.6. School may require community service as alternate discipline

As part of or instead of disciplinary action prescribed by this article, the principal of a school, the principal's designee, the superintendent of schools, or the governing board may require a pupil to perform community service on school grounds or, with written permission of the parent or guardian of the pupil, off school grounds, during the pupil's nonschool hours. For the purposes of this section, "community service" may include, but is not limited to, work performed in the community or on school grounds in the areas of outdoor beautification, community or campus betterment, and teacher, peer, or youth assistance programs. This section does not apply if a pupil has been suspended, pending expulsion, pursuant to Section 48915. However, this section applies if the recommended expulsion is not implemented or is, itself, suspended by stipulation or other administrative action.
(Stats. 1993 (A.B. 1714), ch. 212, §1. Amended Stats. 1995 (S.B. 966), ch. 972, §7; Stats. 2000 (A.B. 2169), ch. 225, §1.)

§48900.7. Pupil may be suspended or expelled for making terroristic threats

(a) In addition to the reasons specified in Sections 48900, 48900.2, 48900.3, and 48900.4, a pupil may be suspended from school or recommended for expulsion if the superintendent or the principal of the school in which the pupil is enrolled determines that the pupil has made terroristic threats against school officials or school property, or both.

(b) For the purposes of this section, "terroristic threat" shall include any statement, whether written or oral, by a person who willfully threatens to commit a crime which will result in death, great bodily injury to another person, or property damage in excess of one thousand dollars ($1,000), with the specific intent that the statement is to be taken as a threat, even if there is no intent of actually carrying it out, which, on its face and under the circumstances in which it is made, is so unequivocal, unconditional, immediate, and specific as to convey to the person threatened, a gravity of

purpose and an immediate prospect of execution of the threat, and thereby causes that person reasonably to be in sustained fear for his or her own safety or for his or her immediate family's safety, or for the protection of school district property, or the personal property of the person threatened or his or her immediate family.
(Stats. 1997 (A.B. 307), ch. 405, §1.)

§48900.8. School district shall report pupils' suspensions and expulsions

For purposes of notification to parents, and for the reporting of expulsion or suspension offenses to the department, each school district shall specifically identify, by offense committed, in all appropriate official records of a pupil each suspension or expulsion of that pupil for the commission of any of the offenses set forth in Section 48900, 48900.2, 48900.3, 48900.4, 48900.7, or 48915.
(Stats. 1997 (A.B. 412), ch. 637, §2. Amended Stats. 2005 (S.B. 512), ch. 667, §33.)

3. Corporal Punishment in Schools

At common law, a "parental privilege to discipline" follows from the United States Supreme Court's rulings that parents have a constitutionally protected right to the care, custody and control of their children. See, e.g., Meyer v. Nebraska, 262 U.S. 390 (1923); Pierce v. Society of Sisters, 268 U.S. 510 (1925). However, the privilege is subject to limitations regarding the amount and type of force that may be used. Also, the privilege is delegable by the parent to a teacher or to some other person in loco parentis. Finally, many states have statutes that regulate corporal punishment in the schools.

California law prohibits the infliction of corporal punishment upon pupils by persons employed by, or engaged in, public schools (Cal. Educ. Code §49001). Corporal punishment is defined as "the willfull infliction of, or willfully causing the infliction of, physical pain on a pupil" (*id.* at §49001(a)).

California Education Code

§49000. Legislative findings

The Legislature finds and declares that the protection against corporal punishment, which extends to other citizens in other walks of life, should include children while they are under the control of the public schools. Children of school age are at the most vulnerable and impressionable period of their lives and it is wholly reasonable that the safeguards to the integrity and sanctity of their bodies should be, at this tender age, at least equal to that afforded to other citizens.
(Stats. 1986, ch. 1069, §2.)

§49001. Definition of corporal punishment

(a) For the purposes of this section "corporal punishment" means the willful infliction of, or willfully causing the infliction of, physical pain on a pupil. An amount of force that is reasonable and necessary for a person employed by or engaged in a public school to quell a disturbance threatening physical injury to persons or damage to property, for purposes of self-defense, or to obtain possession of weapons or other dangerous objects within the control of the pupil, is not and shall not be construed to be corporal punishment within the meaning and intent of this section. Physical pain or discomfort caused by athletic competition or other such recreational activity, voluntarily engaged in by the pupil, is not and shall not be construed to be corporal punishment within the meaning and intent of this section.

(b) No person employed by or engaged in a public school shall inflict, or cause to be inflicted corporal punishment upon a pupil. Every resolution, bylaw, rule, ordinance, or other act or authority permitting or authorizing the infliction of corporal punishment upon a pupil attending a public school is void and unenforceable.
(Stats. 1986, ch. 1069, §4.)

4. Parental Liability for Students' Misconduct

Statutes also establish parental liability for children's acts of misconduct that result in injury or death to any pupil or school employee (or volunteer), or damage to school property. See, e.g., Cal. Educ. Code §48904. On parental liability for child's property damage, see also §B2 *supra*.

§48904. Parent's liability for child's misconduct resulting in injury, death or damage

(a)(1) Notwithstanding Section 1714.1 of the Civil Code, the parent or guardian of any minor whose willful misconduct results in injury or death to any pupil or any person employed by, or performing volunteer services for, a school district or private school or who willfully cuts, defaces, or otherwise injures in any way any property, real or personal, belonging to a school district or private school, or personal property of any school employee, shall be liable for all damages so caused by the minor. The liability of the parent or guardian shall not exceed ten thousand dollars ($10,000). The parent or guardian shall also be liable for the amount of any reward not exceeding ten thousand dollars ($10,000) paid pursuant to Section 53069.5 of the Government Code. The parent or guardian of a minor shall be liable to a school district or private school for all property belonging to the school district or private school loaned to the minor and not returned upon demand of an employee of the district or private school authorized to make the demand. . . .

(b)(1) Any school district or private school whose real or personal property has been willfully cut, defaced, or otherwise injured, or whose property is loaned to a pupil and willfully not returned upon demand of an employee of the district or private school authorized to make the demand may, after affording the pupil his or her due process rights, withhold the grades, diploma, and transcripts of the pupil responsible for the damage until the pupil or the pupil's parent or guardian has paid for the damages thereto, as provided in subdivision (a).

(2) The school district or private school shall notify the parent or guardian of the pupil in writing of the pupil's alleged misconduct before withholding the pupil's grades, diploma, or transcripts pursuant to this subdivision. When the minor and parent are unable to pay for the damages, or to return the property, the school district or private school shall provide a program of voluntary work for the minor in lieu of the payment of monetary damages. Upon completion of the voluntary work, the grades, diploma, and transcripts of the pupil shall be released.

(3) The governing board of each school district or governing body of each private school shall establish rules and regulations governing procedures for the implementation of this subdivision. The procedures shall conform to, but are not necessarily limited to, those procedures established in this code for the expulsion of pupils.

(Stats. 1983, ch. 498, §91, effective July 28, 1983. Amended by Stats. 1984, ch. 482, §13, effective July 17, 1984; Stats. 1984, ch. 948, §1; Stats. 1992 (A.B. 3257), ch. 445, §1.)

5. Students' First Amendment Rights

In the civil rights era of the 1960s, the United States Supreme Court recognized that students have a right to freedom of expression in the context of political speech. However, students do not possess the same First Amendment rights as adults. Students' exercise of the right to free speech is subject to limitation based on the possibility of disruption of school authority. Tinker v. Des Moines Indep. Community Sch. Dist., 393 U.S. 504 (1969).

Following *Tinker*, the Supreme Court circumscribed students' rights to freedom of expression in the context of school-sponsored newspapers. In Hazelwood School District v. Kuhlmeier, 484 U.S. 260 (1988), the Supreme Court held that school officials actions' censoring articles in the school newspaper did not violate students' First Amendment rights when school officials exercise control of the content in student speech in *school-sponsored* activities provided that their actions are reasonably related to legitimate pedagogical goals. See also Bethel v. Fraser, 478 U.S. 675 (1986) (holding that school officials' actions suspending a student for a speech containing a sexual metaphor did not violate student's rights because the school's interest in inculcating proper values and maintaining a proper educational environment outweighed the student's First Amendment right).

Following *Hazelwood*, *supra*, many states considered legislation protecting the student press. See Rosemary C. Salomone, Free Speech and School Governance in the Wake of *Hazelwood*, 26 Ga. L. Rev. 253, 306-315 (1992).

California had such legislation even prior to *Hazelwood* that protected student expression "whether or not such publications or other means of expression are supported financially by the school or by use of school facilities" (Cal. Educ. Code §48907).

§48907. Students shall have right to freedom of speech and press

Students of the public schools shall have the right to exercise freedom of speech and of the press including, but not limited to, the use of bulletin boards, the distribution of printed materials or petitions, the wearing of buttons, badges, and other insignia, and the right of expression in official publications, whether or not such publications or other means of expression are supported financially by the school or by use of school facilities, except that expression shall be prohibited which is obscene, libelous, or slanderous. Also prohibited shall be material which so incites students as to create a clear and present danger of the commission of unlawful acts on school premises or the violation of lawful school regulations, or the substantial disruption of the orderly operation of the school.

Each governing board of a school district and each county board of education shall adopt rules and regulations in the form of a written publications code, which shall include reasonable provisions for the time, place, and manner of conducting such activities within its respective jurisdiction.

Student editors of official school publications shall be responsible for assigning and editing the news, editorial, and feature content of their publications subject to the limitations of this section. However, it shall be the responsibility of a journalism adviser or advisers of student publications within each school to supervise the production of the student staff, to maintain professional standards of English and journalism, and to maintain the provisions of this section.

There shall be no prior restraint of material prepared for official school publications except insofar as it violates this section. School officials shall have the burden of showing justification without undue delay prior to any limitation of student expression under this section.

"Official school publications" refers to material produced by students in the journalism, newspaper, yearbook, or writing classes and distributed to the student body either free or for a fee.

Nothing in this section shall prohibit or prevent any governing board of a school district from adopting otherwise valid rules and regulations relating to oral communication by students upon the premises of each school.

(Stats. 1983, ch. 498, §91, effective July 28, 1983.)

§48950. School districts shall not subject pupils to disciplinary sanctions for constitutionally protected speech

(a) School districts operating one or more high schools and private secondary schools shall not make or enforce any rule subjecting any high school pupil to disciplinary sanctions solely on the basis of conduct that is speech or other communication that, when engaged in outside of the campus, is protected from governmental restriction by the First Amendment to the United States Constitution or Section 2 of Article 1 of the California Constitution.

(b) Any pupil enrolled in a school that has made or enforced any rule in violation of subdivision (a) may commence a civil action to obtain appropriate injunctive and declaratory relief as determined by the court. Upon motion, a court may award attorney's fees to a prevailing plaintiff in a civil action pursuant to this section.

(c) This section does not apply to any private secondary school that is controlled by a religious organization, to the extent that the application of this section would not be consistent with the religious tenets of the organization.

(d) Nothing in this section prohibits the imposition of discipline for harassment, threats, or intimidation, unless constitutionally protected.

(e) Nothing in this section shall be construed to supersede, or otherwise limit or modify, the provisions of Section 48907.

(f) The Legislature finds and declares that free speech rights are subject to reasonable time, place, and manner regulations.

(Stats. 1992 (S.B. 1115), ch. 1363, §1.)

6. Students' Fourth Amendment Rights

The United States Supreme Court has held that the Fourth Amendment's prohibition against unreasonable searches and seizures applies to juveniles. However, the standard for searches of juveniles ("reasonable suspicion") is lower than that for adults ("probable cause"). New Jersey v. T.L.O., 469 U.S. 325 (1985). Thus, the law permits searches of juveniles that would be unconstitutional as applied to adults. Subsequently, the Supreme Court upheld the constitutionality of random drug testing of student athletes (Vernonia Sch. Dist. v. Acton, 515 U.S. 646 (1995)), and students who participate in competitive extracurricular activities (Board of Educ. of Indept. Sch. Dist. of Pottawatomie Cty. v. Earls, 536 U.S. 822 (2002)).

California law prohibits school employees from conducting searches of pupils that involve (1) searches of a body cavity manually or with an instrument or, (2) removing or arranging clothing to permit a visual inspection of the pupil's "underclothing, breast, buttocks, or genitalia" (Cal. Educ. Code §49050).

§49050. School employees shall not conduct body searches

No school employee shall conduct a search that involves:

(a) Conducting a body cavity search of a pupil manually or with an instrument.

(b) Removing or arranging any or all of the clothing of a pupil to permit a visual inspection of the underclothing, breast, buttocks, or genitalia of the pupil.

(Stats. 1988, ch. 1102, §1.)

§49051. Admissibility of evidence in subsequent juvenile or criminal proceedings

Nothing in this article shall be construed to affect the admissibility of evidence in subsequent juvenile or criminal proceedings.

(Stats. 1988, ch. 1102, §1.)

G. MEDICAL CARE

At common law, only a parent could give consent to medical treatment for a child. The child lacked capacity to consent. This rule of parental consent accorded with notions of family privacy, parental autonomy, and parental financial responsibility.

Some states provide that a minor (specifically, an unemancipated minor) may consent to medical treatment. In many jurisdictions, statutes permit the minor to consent to medical treatment in cases of venereal disease, alcohol or drug abuse, and pregnancy-related complications (but not necessarily abortion services). If the physician provides medical care to a minor without securing informed consent, the physician may be liable for battery (i.e., a touching without consent).

An emancipated minor (i.e., a minor who is living apart from parents and managing his or her financial affairs, or who is married, in the armed services, or has secured a judicial declaration of emancipation) may consent to medical treatment on the same terms as an adult.

Certain exceptions and limitations exist to the traditional requirement of parental consent. Under the common law rule (now codified in many states), physicians may provide medical treatment to a child without parental consent in the event of an emergency if a parent is unavailable and delay would endanger the child. The state also limits parental prerogatives to consent to their child's medical treatment by certain mandatory health requirements. For example, most states require children to undergo newborn testing and screening, compulsory immunizations prior to school attendance, and school screening procedures (e.g., hearing and eyesight screenings). Finally, another limitation on the rule of parental consent occurs in the area of child neglect. Based on common law and statute, parents have the duty to provide their child with necessary medical care. If the parents refuse to provide consent to medical treatment, they may be subject to criminal and/or civil liability, and also the juvenile court may declare the child neglected and then order the appropriate medical treatment.

California law permits a minor who is 16 years or older to apply to the court for authorization of medical or dental care in those cases in which a parent's consent is necessary but the parent is not available (Cal. Fam. Code §6911). Minors who are 15 years or older may consent to medical care themselves if they are living apart from their parents and financially independent (Cal. Fam. Code §6922). Finally, young minors (12 years or older) may give consent to mental health treatment or counseling, or residential shelter services (Cal. Fam. Code §6924), treatment for a communicable disease (Cal. Fam. Code §6926), medical care for rape treatment (Cal. Fam. Code §6927), and drug or alcohol treatment (Cal. Fam. Code §6929).

1. Generally

California Family Code

§6900. Definitions govern construction

Unless the provision or context otherwise requires, the definitions in this chapter govern the construction of this part.

(Stats. 1992 (A.B. 2650), ch. 162, §10, effective January 1, 1994.)

§6901. "Dental care"

"Dental care" means X-ray examination, anesthetic, dental or surgical diagnosis or treatment, and hospital care by a dentist licensed under the Dental Practice Act.

(Stats. 1992 (A.B. 2650), ch. 162, §10, effective January 1, 1994.)

§6902. "Medical care"

"Medical care" means X-ray examination, anesthetic, medical or surgical diagnosis or treatment, and hospital care under the general or special supervision and upon the advice of or to be rendered by a physician and surgeon licensed under the Medical Practice Act.

(Stats. 1992 (A.B. 2650), ch. 162, §10, effective January 1, 1994.)

§6903. "Parent or guardian"

"Parent or guardian" means either parent if both parents have legal custody, or the parent or person having legal custody, or the guardian, of a minor.

(Stats. 1992 (A.B. 2650), ch. 162, §10, effective January 1, 1994.)

§6910. Parent, guardian or relative caregiver may authorize medical or dental care

The parent, guardian, or caregiver of a minor who is a relative of the minor and who may authorize medical care and dental care under Section 6550, may authorize in writing an adult into whose care a minor has been entrusted to consent to medical care or dental care, or both, for the minor.

(Stats. 1992 (A.B. 2650), ch. 162, §10, effective January 1, 1994. Amended Stats. 1996 (S.B. 392), ch. 563, §2.)

2. Minor's Ability to Consent

§6911. Conditions for court authorization of consent for minor's medical or dental care

(a) Upon application by a minor, the court may summarily grant consent for medical care or dental care or both for the minor if the court determines all of the following:

(1) The minor is 16 years of age or older and resides in this state.

(2) The consent of a parent or guardian is necessary to permit the medical care or dental care or both, and the minor has no parent or guardian available to give the consent.

(b) No fee may be charged for proceedings under this section.

(Stats. 1992 (A.B. 2650), ch. 162, §10, effective January 1, 1994.)

§6920. Minor alone may consent to medical or dental care in some cases

Subject to the limitations provided in this chapter, notwithstanding any other provision of law, a minor may consent to the matters provided in this chapter, and the consent of the minor's parent or guardian is not necessary.

(Stats. 1992 (A.B. 2650), ch. 162, §10, effective January 1, 1994.)

§6921. Minor's consent may not be disaffirmed

A consent given by a minor under this chapter is not subject to disaffirmance because of minority.

(Stats. 1992 (A.B. 2650), ch. 162, §10, effective January 1, 1994.)

§6922. Conditions by which minor alone may consent to medical or dental care

(a) A minor may consent to the minor's medical care or dental care if all of the following conditions are satisfied:

(1) The minor is 15 years of age or older.

(2) The minor is living separate and apart from the minor's parents or guardian, whether with or without the consent of a parent or guardian and regardless of the duration of the separate residence.

(3) The minor is managing the minor's own financial affairs, regardless of the source of the minor's income.

(b) The parents or guardian are not liable for medical care or dental care provided pursuant to this section.

(c) A physician and surgeon or dentist may, with or without the consent of the minor patient, advise the minor's parent or guardian of the treatment given or needed if the physician and surgeon or dentist has reason to know, on the basis of the information given by the minor, the whereabouts of the parent or guardian.

(Stats. 1992 (A.B. 2650), ch. 162, §10, effective January 1, 1994.)

§6924. Young minors may give consent to mental health treatment or counseling or residential shelter services

(a) As used in this section:

(1) "Mental health treatment or counseling services" means the provision of mental health treatment or counseling on an outpatient basis by any of the following:

(A) A governmental agency.

(B) A person or agency having a contract with a governmental agency to provide the services.

(C) An agency that receives funding from community united funds.

(D) A runaway house or crisis resolution center.

(E) A professional person, as defined in paragraph (2).

(2) "Professional person" means any of the following:

(A) A person designated as a mental health professional in Sections 622 to 626, inclusive, of Article 8 of Subchapter 3 of Chapter 1 of Title 9 of the California Code of Regulations.

(B) A marriage and family therapist as defined in Chapter 13 (commencing with Section 4980) of Division 2 of the Business and Professions Code.

(C) A licensed educational psychologist as defined in Article 5 (commencing with Section 4986) of Chapter 13 of Division 2 of the Business and Professions Code.

(D) A credentialed school psychologist as described in Section 49424 of the Education Code.

(E) A clinical psychologist as defined in Section 1316.5 of the Health and Safety Code.

(F) The chief administrator of an agency referred to in paragraph (1) or (3).

(G) A marriage and family therapist registered intern, as defined in Chapter 13 (commencing with Section 4980) of Division 2 of the Business and Professions Code, while working under the supervision of a licensed professional specified in subdivision (f) of Section 4980.40 of the Business and Professions Code.

(3) "Residential shelter services" means any of the following:

(A) The provision of residential and other support services to minors on a temporary or emergency basis in a facility that services only minors by a governmental agency, a person or agency having a contract with a governmental agency to provide these services, an agency that receives funding from community funds, or a licensed community care facility or crisis resolution center.

(B) The provision of other support services on a temporary or emergency basis by any professional person as defined in paragraph (2).

(b) A minor who is 12 years of age or older may consent to mental health treatment or counseling on an outpatient basis, or to residential shelter services, if both of the following requirements are satisfied:

(1) The minor, in the opinion of the attending professional person, is mature enough to participate intelligently in the outpatient services or residential shelter services.

(2) The minor (A) would present a danger of serious physical or mental harm to self or to others without the mental health treatment or counseling or residential shelter services, or (B) is the alleged victim of incest or child abuse.

(c) A professional person offering residential shelter services, whether as an individual or as a representative of an entity specified in paragraph (3) of subdivision (a), shall make his or her best efforts to notify the parent or guardian of the provision of services.

(d) The mental health treatment or counseling of a minor authorized by this section shall include involvement of the minor's parent or guardian unless, in the opinion of the professional person who is treating or counseling the minor, the involvement would be inappropriate. The professional person who is treating or counseling the minor shall state in the client record whether and when the person attempted to contact the minor's parent or guardian, and whether the attempt to contact was successful or unsuccessful, or the reason why, in the professional person's opinion, it would be inappropriate to contact the minor's parent or guardian.

(e) The minor's parents or guardian are not liable for payment for mental health treatment or counseling services provided pursuant to this section unless the parent or guardian participates in the mental health treatment or counseling, and then only for services rendered with the participation of the parent or guardian. The minor's parents or guardian are not liable for payment for any residential shelter services provided pursuant to this section unless the parent or guardian consented to the provision of those services.

(f) This section does not authorize a minor to receive convulsive therapy or psychosurgery as defined in subdivisions (f) and (g) of Section 5325 of the Welfare and Institutions Code, or psychotropic drugs without the consent of the minor's parent or guardian.

(Stats. 1992 (A.B. 2650), ch. 162, §10, effective January 1, 1994. Amended Stats. 1993 (A.B. 1500), ch. 219, §155; Stats. 2000 (A.B. 2161), ch. 519, §1.)

§6925. Minor may consent to contraceptives or treatment of pregnancy

(a) A minor may consent to medical care related to the prevention or treatment of pregnancy.

(b) This section does not authorize a minor:

(1) To be sterilized without the consent of the minor's parent or guardian.

(2) To receive an abortion without the consent of a parent or guardian other than as provided in Section 123450 of the Health and Safety Code.

(Stats. 1992 (A.B. 2650), ch. 162, §10, effective January 1, 1994. Amended Stats. 1996 (S.B. 1497), ch. 1023, §46, effective September 29, 1996.)

§6926. Young minor may consent to treatment for communicable disease

(a) A minor who is 12 years of age or older and who may have come into contact with an infectious, contagious, or communicable disease may consent to medical care related to the diagnosis or treatment of the disease, if the disease or condition is one that is required by law or regulation adopted pursuant to law to be reported to the local health officer, or is a related sexually transmitted disease, as may be determined by the State Director of Health Services.

(b) The minor's parents or guardian are not liable for payment for medical care provided pursuant to this section.

(Stats. 1992 (A.B. 2650), ch. 162, §10, effective January 1, 1994.)

§6927. Young minor rape victim may consent to medical care and collection of evidence

A minor who is 12 years of age or older and who is alleged to have been raped may consent to medical care related to

the diagnosis or treatment of the condition and the collection of medical evidence with regard to the alleged rape.
(Stats. 1992 (A.B. 2650), ch. 162, §10, effective January 1, 1994.)

§6928. Minor victim of sexual assault may consent to medical care and collection of evidence

(a) "Sexually assaulted" as used in this section includes, but is not limited to, conduct coming within Section 261 [rape], 286 [sodomy], or 288a [oral copulation] of the Penal Code.

(b) A minor who is alleged to have been sexually assaulted may consent to medical care related to the diagnosis and treatment of the condition, and the collection of medical evidence with regard to the alleged sexual assault.

(c) The professional person providing medical treatment shall attempt to contact the minor's parent or guardian and shall note in the minor's treatment record the date and time the professional person attempted to contact the parent or guardian and whether the attempt was successful or unsuccessful. This subdivision does not apply if the professional person reasonably believes that the minor's parent or guardian committed the sexual assault on the minor.
(Stats. 1992 (A.B. 2650), ch. 162, §10, effective January 1, 1994.)

§6929. Young minor may consent to drug or alcohol treatment

(a) As used in this section:

(1) "Counseling" means the provision of counseling services by a provider under a contract with the state or a county to provide alcohol or drug abuse counseling services pursuant to Part 2 (commencing with Section 5600) of Division 5 of the Welfare and Institutions Code or pursuant to Division 10.5 (commencing with Section 11750) of the Health and Safety Code.

(2) "Drug or alcohol" includes, but is not limited to, any substance listed in any of the following:

(A) Section 380 or 381 of the Penal Code.

(B) Division 10 (commencing with Section 11000) of the Health and Safety Code.

(C) Subdivision (f) of Section 647 of the Penal Code.

(3) "LAAM" means levoalphacetylmethadol as specified in paragraph (10) of subdivision (c) of Section 11055 of the Health and Safety Code.

(4) "Professional person" means a physician and surgeon, registered nurse, psychologist, clinical social worker, marriage and family therapist, marriage and family therapist registered intern when appropriately employed and supervised pursuant to subdivision (f) of Section 4980.40 of the Business and Professions Code, psychological assistant when appropriately employed and supervised pursuant to Section 2913 of the Business and Professions Code, or associate clinical social worker when appropriately employed and supervised pursuant to Section 4996.18 of the Business and Professions Code.

(b) A minor who is 12 years of age or older may consent to medical care and counseling relating to the diagnosis and treatment of a drug- or alcohol-related problem.

(c) The treatment plan of a minor authorized by this section shall include the involvement of the minor's parent or guardian, if appropriate, as determined by the professional person or treatment facility treating the minor. The professional person providing medical care or counseling to a minor shall state in the minor's treatment record whether and when the professional person attempted to contact the minor's parent or guardian, and whether the attempt to contact the parent or guardian was successful or unsuccessful, or the reason why, in the opinion of the professional person, it would not be appropriate to contact the minor's parent or guardian.

(d) The minor's parent or guardian is not liable for payment for any care provided to a minor pursuant to this section, except that if the minor's parent or guardian participates in a counseling program pursuant to this section, the parent or guardian is liable for the cost of the services provided to the minor and the parent or guardian.

(e) This section does not authorize a minor to receive replacement narcotic abuse treatment, in a program licensed pursuant to Article 3 (commencing with Section 11875) of Chapter 1 of Part 3 of Division 10.5 of the Health and Safety Code, without the consent of the minor's parent or guardian.

(f) It is the intent of the Legislature that the state shall respect the right of a parent or legal guardian to seek medical care and counseling for a drug- or alcohol-related problem of a minor child when the child does not consent to the medical care and counseling, and nothing in this section shall be construed to restrict or eliminate this right.

(g) Notwithstanding any other provision of law, in cases where a parent or legal guardian has sought the medical care and counseling for a drug- or alcohol-related problem of a minor child, the physician shall disclose medical information concerning the care to the minor's parent or legal guardian upon his or her request, even if the minor child does not consent to disclosure, without liability for the disclosure.
(Stats. 1992 (A.B. 2650), ch. 162, §10, effective January 1, 1994. Amended Stats. 1995 (A.B. 1113), ch. 455, §1, effective September 5, 1995; Stats. 1996 (A.B. 2883), ch. 656 §1; Stats. 2002 (S.B. 2026), ch. 1013, §79; Stats. 2004 (A.B. 2182), ch. 59, §1.

3. Newborn Screening

California Health & Safety Code

§123975. Screening newborns for hearing loss

(a) The department, in consultation with selected representatives of participating neonatal intensive care units, shall establish a system to screen all newborns and infants for hearing loss as defined in subdivision (e) of Section 124116 and create and maintain a system of assessment and followup services for newborns and infants identified by the screening in approved neonatal intensive care units participating in the California Children's Services Program. Screening, assessment, followup services, and reporting of these services shall be provided in a manner consistent with Article 6.5 (commencing with Section 124115) of Chapter 3. This section shall not be applicable to a newborn child whose parent or guardian objects to the tests on the ground that the tests conflict with his or her religious beliefs or practices.

(b) It is the intent of the Legislature, in enacting this section, to ensure the establishment and maintenance of protocols and quality of standards.

(c) The department shall implement this section for newborns and infants in neonatal intensive care units participating in the California Children's Services Program.

(Stats. 1995, ch. 415 (S.B. 1360), §8. Amended by Stats. 1998, ch. 310 (A.B. 2780), §22, effective August 19, 1998.)

§124111. Establishment of Newborn Eye Pathology Screening Task Force

(a) The Newborn Eye Pathology Screening Task Force is established and shall advise the State Department of Health Services on the newborn eye pathology screening protocol.

(b) The task force shall be composed of the following 12 members:

(1) The Director of Health Services as a nonvoting ex officio member.

(2) The 11 voting members shall be appointed by the Director of Health Services as follows:

(A) One ophthalmologist with a background in or knowledge of providing services to infants with retinoblastoma.

(B) One pediatric ophthalmologist who sees general pediatric patients and is a designee of the American Association for Pediatric Ophthalmology and Strabismus.

(C) One academic pediatrician with a background in or knowledge of infant eye pathology screening.

(D) One parent representing families with a child with blindness or other ocular abnormalities affecting vision.

(E) One representative from the California Academy of Family Physicians.

(F) One representative recommended by the State Department of Health Services.

(G) One representative from the American Academy of Pediatrics, California District.

(H) One community pediatrician with a background in or experience with the routine instillation of dilating eye drops as part of red reflex screening.

(I) One nurse with a background in or knowledge of the current department program for the instillation of eye drops to prevent conjunctivitis.

(J) One retinal specialist with research experience in detecting the signs of treatable congenital eye disease.

(K) One optometrist with a background in or experience with pupil dilation in infants and red reflex screening for intraocular pathology.

(c) Task force members shall serve without compensation, but shall be reimbursed for necessary travel expenses incurred in the performance of the duties of the task force.

(Stats. 2000, ch. 325 (A.B. 2185), §2.)

§124112. Adoption of protocol to detect blindness in infants

(a) On or before June 30, 2002, the department shall adopt the protocol developed by the American Academy of Pediatrics to optimally detect the presence of treatable causes of blindness in infants by two months of age. If a protocol is not developed on or before June 30, 2002, the department, in consultation with representatives of the Newborn Eye Pathology Task Force, shall establish a protocol to optimally detect the presence of treatable causes of blindness in infants by two months of age on or before January 1, 2003.

(b) If the American Academy of Pediatrics develops a protocol to optimally detect the presence of treatable causes of blindness by two months of age after the adoption of the protocol developed by the department, the department shall conform its protocol to the protocol adopted by the American Academy of Pediatrics.

(c) Nothing in the section shall be construed to supersede the clinical judgment of the licensed health care provider.

(d) Any screening examination recommended pursuant to subdivision (a) shall not be conducted on a newborn if a parent or guardian of the newborn objects to the examination on the grounds that the examination conflicts with the religious beliefs or practices of the parent or guardian.

(Stats. 2000, ch. 325 (A.B. 2185), §2.)

§124115. Title

This article shall be known, and may be cited as, the Newborn and Infant Hearing Screening, Tracking and Intervention Act.

(Stats. 1998, ch. 310 (A.B. 2780), § 23, effective August 19, 1998.)

§124115.5. Legislative findings regarding detection of hearing loss

(a) The Legislature finds and declares all of the following:

(1) Hearing loss occurs in newborns more frequently than any other health condition for which newborn screening is currently required.

(2) Early detection of hearing loss, early intervention, and followup services before six months of age, have been demonstrated to be highly effective in facilitating the development of a child's health and communication and cognitive skills.

(3) The State of California supports the National Healthy People 2000 goals, which promote early identification of children with hearing loss.

(4) Children of all ages can receive reliable and valid screening for hearing loss in a costeffective manner.

(5) Appropriate screening and identification of newborns and infants with hearing loss will facilitate early intervention during this critical time for development of communication, and may, therefore, serve the public purposes of promoting the healthy development of children and reducing public expenditure for health care and special education and related services.

(b) The purposes of this article shall be to do all of the following:

(1) Provide early detection of hearing loss in newborns, as soon after birth as possible, to enable children who fail a hearing screening and their families and other caregivers to obtain needed confirmatory tests or multidisciplinary evaluation, or both, and intervention services, at the earliest opportunity.

(2) Prevent or mitigate delays of language and communication development that could lead to academic failures associated with late identification of hearing loss.

(3) Provide the state with the information necessary to effectively plan, establish, and evaluate a comprehensive system of appropriate services for parents with newborns and infants who have a hearing loss.

(Stats. 1998, ch. 310 (A.B. 2780), §23, effective August 19, 1998.)

§124116. Definitions

As used in this article:

(a) "Birth admission" means the time after birth that the newborn remains in the hospital nursery prior to discharge.

(b) "CCS" means the California Children's Services program administered through the State Department of Health Services.

(c) "Department" means the State Department of Health Services.

(d) "Followup services" means all of the following:

(1) All services necessary to diagnose and confirm a hearing loss.

(2) Ongoing audiological services to monitor hearing.

(3) Communication services, including, but not limited to, aural rehabilitation, speech, language, social, and psychological services.

(4) Necessary support of the infant and family.

(e) "Hearing loss" means a hearing loss of 30 decibels or greater in the frequency region important for speech recognition and comprehension in one or both ears (from 500 through 4000 Hz). However, as technology allows for changes to this definition through the detection of less severe hearing loss, the department may modify this definition by regulation.

(f) "Infant" means a child 29 days through 12 months old.

(g) "Intervention services" means the early intervention services described in Part C of the Individuals with Disabilities Education Act (20 U.S.C. Secs. 1475 et seq.).

(h) "Newborn" means a child less than 29 days old.

(i) "Newborn hearing screening services" means those hearing screening tests that are necessary to achieve the identification of all newborns and infants with a hearing loss.

(j) "Parent" means a natural parent, adoptive parent, or legal guardian of a child.

(Stats. 1998, ch. 310 (A.B. 2780), §23, effective August 19, 1998.)

§124116.5. Hearing screening program for newborns

(a)(1) Every CCS-approved general acute care hospital with licensed perinatal services in this state shall offer all parents of a newborn, upon birth admission, a hearing screening test for the identification of hearing loss, using protocols approved by the department or its designee. The department shall begin phasing in implementation of a comprehensive hearing screening program by CCS-approved general acute care hospitals with licensed perinatal services on or after July 1, 1999, and a 100 percent participation shall be achieved by December 31, 2002.

(2) In order to meet the department's certification criteria, a hospital shall be responsible for developing a screening program that provides competent hearing screening, utilizes appropriate staff and equipment for administering the testing, completes the testing prior to the newborn's discharge from a newborn nursery unit, refers infants with abnormal screening results, maintains and reports data as required by the department, and provides physician and familyparent education.

(b) A hearing screening test provided for pursuant to subdivision (a) shall be performed by a licensed physician, licensed registered nurse, licensed audiologist, or an appropriately trained individual who is supervised in the performance of the test by a licensed health care professional.

(Stats. 1998, ch. 310 (A.B. 2780), §23, effective August 19, 1998.)

§124117. Approval of hospitals as screening providers

The department or its designee shall approve hospitals for participation as newborn hearing screening providers. These facilities shall then receive payment from the department for the newborn hearing screening services provided to newborns and infants eligible for the Medi-Cal or CCS programs in accordance with this article.

(Stats. 1998, ch. 310 (A.B. 2780), §23, effective August 19, 1998.)

§124118. Department shall provide hospitals with information and technical assistance

The department or its designee shall provide every CCS-approved acute care hospital that has licensed perinatal services or a CCS-approved neonatal intensive care unit (NICU), or both, as specified in Section 123975, written information on the current and most effective means available to screen the hearing of newborns and infants, and shall provide technical assistance and consultation to these hospitals in developing a system of screening each newborn and infant receiving care at the facility. The information shall also include the mechanism for referral of newborns and infants with abnormal test results.

(Stats. 1998, ch. 310 (A.B. 2780), §23, effective August 19, 1998.)

§124119. Development of reporting and tracking system

(a) The department shall develop and implement a reporting and tracking system for newborns and infants tested for hearing loss.

(b) The system shall provide the department with information and data to effectively plan, establish, monitor, and evaluate the Newborn and Infant Hearing Screening,

Tracking and Intervention Program, including the screening and followup components, as well as the comprehensive system of services for newborns and infants who are deaf or hard-of-hearing and their families.

(c) Every CCS-approved acute care hospital with licensed perinatal services or CCS-approved NICU, or both, in this state shall report to the department or the department's designee information as specified by the department to be included in the department's reporting and tracking system.

(d) All providers of audiological follow up and diagnostic services provided under this article shall report to the department or the department's designee information as specified by the department to be included in the department's reporting and tracking system.

(e) The information compiled and maintained in the tracking system shall be kept confidential in accordance with Chapter 5 (commencing with Section 10850) of Part 1 of Division 9 of the Welfare and Institutions Code, the Information Practices Act of 1977 (Chapter 1 (commencing with Section 1798) of Title 1.8 of Part 4 of Division 3 of the Civil Code), and the applicable requirements and provisions of Part C of the federal Individuals with Disabilities Education Act (20 U.S.C. Secs. 1475 et seq.).

(f) Data collected by the tracking system obtained directly from the medical records of the newborn or infant shall be for the confidential use of the department and for the persons or public or private entities that the department determines are necessary to carry out the intent of the reporting and tracking system.

(g) A health facility, clinical laboratory, audiologist, physician, registered nurse, or any other officer or employee of a health facility or laboratory or employee of an audiologist or physician, shall not be criminally or civilly liable for furnishing information to the department or its designee pursuant to the requirements of this section.

(Stats. 1998, ch. 310 (A.B. 2780), §23, effective August 19, 1998.)

§124119.5. Parents shall be given information on community resources

Parents of all newborns and infants diagnosed with a hearing loss shall be provided written information on the availability of community resources and services for children with hearing loss, including those provided in accordance with the federal Individuals with Disabilities Education Act (20 U.S.C. Secs. 1400 et seq.), through the reporting and tracking system followup procedures. Information shall include listings of local and statewide nonprofit deaf and hard-of-hearing consumer-based organizations, parent support organizations affiliated with deafness, and programs offered through the State Department of Social Services, Office of Deaf Access, State Department of Developmental Services, and the State Department of Education.

(Stats. 1998, ch. 310 (A.B. 2780), §23, effective August 19, 1998.)

§124120. Department may conduct community outreach and awareness campaign

The department may conduct a community outreach and awareness campaign to inform medical providers, pregnant women, and the families of newborns and infants on the availability of the newborn hearing screening program and the value of early hearing testing. The outreach and awareness campaign shall be conducted by an independent contractor.

(Stats. 1998, ch. 310 (A.B. 2780), §23, effective August 19, 1998. Amended by Stats. 2002, ch. 1161 (A.B. 442), §14, effective September 30, 2002.)

§124120.5. Written consent of parent

A newborn hearing screening test shall not be performed without the written consent of the parent.

(Stats. 1998, ch. 310 (A.B. 2780), §23, effective August 19, 1998.)

§124975. Legislative findings regarding screening of hereditary disorders

The Legislature hereby finds and declares that:

(a) Each person in the State of California is entitled to health care commensurate with his or her health care needs, and to protection from inadequate health services not in the person's best interests.

(b) Hereditary disorders, such as sickle cell anemia, cystic fibrosis, and hemophilia, are often costly, tragic, and sometimes deadly burdens to the health and well-being of the citizens of this state.

(c) Detection through screening of hereditary disorders can lead to the alleviation of the disability of some hereditary disorders and contribute to the further understanding and accumulation of medical knowledge about hereditary disorders that may lead to their eventual alleviation or cure.

(d) There are different severities of hereditary disorders, that some hereditary disorders have little effect on the normal functioning of individuals, and that some hereditary disorders may be wholly or partially alleviated through medical intervention and treatment.

(e) All or most persons are carriers of some deleterious recessive genes that may be transmitted through the hereditary process, and that the health of carriers of hereditary disorders is substantially unaffected by that fact.

(f) Carriers of most deleterious genes should not be stigmatized and should not be discriminated against by any person within the State of California.

(g) Specific legislation designed to alleviate the problems associated with specific hereditary disorders may tend to be inflexible in the face of rapidly expanding medical knowledge, underscoring the need for flexible approaches to coping with genetic problems.

(h) State policy regarding hereditary disorders should be made with full public knowledge, in light of expert opinion and should be constantly reviewed to consider changing medical knowledge and ensure full public protection.

(i) The extremely personal decision to bear children should remain the free choice and responsibility of the individual, and should not be restricted by the state.

(j) Participation of persons in hereditary disorders programs in the State of California should be wholly voluntary, except for initial screening for phenylketonuria

(PKU) and other genetic disorders treatable through the California newborn screening program. All information obtained from persons involved in hereditary disorders programs in the state should be held strictly confidential.

(k) In order to minimize the possibility for the reoccurrence of abuse of genetic intervention in hereditary disorders programs, all programs offering screening programs for heredity disorders shall comply with the principles established in the Hereditary Disorders Act (Section 27). The Legislature finds it necessary to establish a uniform statewide policy for the screening for heredity disorder in the State of California.

(Stats. 1995, ch. 415 (S.B. 1360), §8.)

§124977. Fees

(a) It is the intent of the Legislature that, unless otherwise specified, the program carried out pursuant to this chapter be fully supported from fees collected for services provided by the program.

(b)(1) The department shall charge a fee to all payers for any tests or activities performed pursuant to this chapter. The amount of the fee shall be established by regulation and periodically adjusted by the director in order to meet the costs of this chapter. Notwithstanding any other provision of law, any fees charged for prenatal screening and followup services provided to persons enrolled in the Medi-Cal program, health care service plan enrollees, or persons covered by health insurance policies, shall be paid in full directly to the Genetic Disease Testing Fund, subject to all terms and conditions of each enrollee's or insured's health care service plan or insurance coverage, whichever is applicable, including, but not limited to, copayments and deductibles applicable to these services, and only if these copayments, deductibles, or limitations are disclosed to the subscriber or enrollee pursuant to the disclosure provisions of Section 1363.

(2) The department shall expeditiously undertake all steps necessary to implement the fee collection process, including personnel, contracts, and data processing, so as to initiate the fee collection process at the earliest opportunity.

(3) The director shall convene, in the most cost-efficient manner and using existing resources, a working group comprised of health insurance, health care service plan, hospital, consumer, and department representatives to evaluate newborn and prenatal screening fee billing procedures, and recommend to the department ways to improve these procedures in order to improve efficiencies and enhance revenue collections for the department and hospitals. In performing its duties, the working group may consider models in other states. The working group shall make its recommendations by March 1, 2005.

(4) Effective for services provided on and after July 1, 2002, the department shall charge a fee to the hospital of birth, or, for births not occurring in a hospital, to families of the newborn, for newborn screening and followup services. The hospital of birth and families of newborns born outside the hospital shall make payment in full to the Genetic Disease Testing Fund. The department shall not charge or bill Medi-Cal beneficiaries for services provided under this chapter.

(c)(1) The Legislature finds that timely implementation of changes in genetic screening programs and continuous maintenance of quality statewide services requires expeditious regulatory and administrative procedures to obtain the most cost-effective electronic data processing, hardware, software services, testing equipment, and testing and followup services.

(2) The expenditure of funds from the Genetic Disease Testing Fund for these purposes shall not be subject to Section 12102 of, and Chapter 2 (commencing with Section 10290) of Part 2 of Division 2 of, the Public Contract Code, or to Division 25.2 (commencing with Section 38070). The department shall provide the Department of Finance with documentation that equipment and services have been obtained at the lowest cost consistent with technical requirements for a comprehensive high-quality program.

(3) The expenditure of funds from the Genetic Disease Testing Fund for implementation of the Tandem Mass Spectrometry screening for fatty acid oxidation, amino acid, and organic acid disorders, and screening for congenital adrenal hyperplasia may be implemented through the amendment of the Genetic Disease Branch Screening Information System contracts and shall not be subject to Chapter 3 (commencing with Section 12100) of Part 2 of Division 2 of the Public Contract Code, Article 4 (commencing with Section 19130) of Chapter 5 of Part 2 of Division 5 of Title 2 of the Government Code, and any policies, procedures, regulations or manuals authorized by those laws.

(d) (1) The department may adopt emergency regulations to implement and make specific this chapter in accordance with Chapter 3.5 (commencing with Section 11340) of Part 1 of Division 3 of Title 2 of the Government Code. For the purposes of the Administrative Procedure Act, the adoption of regulations shall be deemed an emergency and necessary for the immediate preservation of the public peace, health and safety, or general welfare. Notwithstanding Chapter 3.5 (commencing with Section 11340) of Part 1 of Division 3 of Title 2 of the Government Code, these emergency regulations shall not be subject to the review and approval of the Office of Administrative Law. Notwithstanding Section 11346.1 and Section 11349.6 of the Government Code, the department shall submit these regulations directly to the Secretary of State for filing. The regulations shall become effective immediately upon filing by the Secretary of State. Regulations shall be subject to public hearing within 120 days of filing with the Secretary of State and shall comply with Sections 11346.8 and 11346.9 of the Government Code or shall be repealed.

(2) The Office of Administrative Law shall provide for the printing and publication of these regulations in the California Code of Regulations. Notwithstanding Chapter 3.5 (commencing with Section 11340) of Part 1 of Division 3 of Title 2 of the Government Code, the regulations adopted pursuant to this chapter shall not be repealed by the Office of Administrative Law and shall remain in effect until revised or repealed by the department.

(3) The Legislature finds and declares that the health and safety of California newborns is in part dependent on an effective and adequately staffed genetic disease program, the cost of which shall be supported by the fees generated by the program.

(Stats. 2000, ch. 803 (A.B. 2427), §2. Amended by Stats. 2002, ch. 1161 (A.B. 442), §15.5, effective September 30, 2002; Stats. 2004 (S.B. 1103), ch. 228, §6.2, effective August 16, 2004.)

§124980. Regulations for hereditary disorder programs

The director shall establish any regulations and standards for hereditary disorders programs as the director deems necessary to promote and protect the public health and safety. Standards shall include licensure of master level genetic counselors and doctoral level geneticists. Regulations adopted shall implement the principles established in this section. These principles shall include, but not be limited to, the following:

(a) The public, especially communities and groups particularly affected by programs on hereditary disorders, should be consulted before any regulations and standards are adopted by the department.

(b) The incidence, severity, and treatment costs of each hereditary disorder and its perceived burden by the affected community should be considered and, where appropriate, state and national experts in the medical, psychological, ethical, social, and economic effects or programs for the detection and management of hereditary disorders shall be consulted by the department.

(c) Information on the operation of all programs on hereditary disorders within the state, except for confidential information obtained from participants in the programs, shall be open and freely available to the public.

(d) Clinical testing procedures established for use in programs, facilities, and projects shall be accurate, provide maximum information, and the testing procedures selected shall produce results that are subject to minimum misinterpretation.

(e) No test or tests may be performed on any minor over the objection of the minor's parents or guardian, nor may any tests be performed unless the parent or guardian is fully informed of the purposes of testing for hereditary disorders and is given reasonable opportunity to object to the testing.

(f) No testing, except initial screening for phenylketonuria (PKU) and other diseases that may be added to the newborn screening program, shall require mandatory participation, and no testing programs shall require restriction of childbearing, and participation in a testing program shall not be a prerequisite to eligibility for, or receipt of, any other service or assistance from, or to participate in, any other program, except where necessary to determine eligibility for further programs of diagnoses of or therapy for hereditary conditions.

(g) Pretest and posttest counseling services for hereditary disorders shall be available through the program or a referral source for all persons determined to be or who believe themselves to be at risk for a hereditary disorder. Genetic counseling shall be provided by a physician, a certified advanced practice nurse with a genetics specialty, or other appropriately trained licensed health care professional and shall be nondirective, shall emphasize informing the client, and shall not require restriction of childbearing.

(h) All participants in programs on hereditary disorders shall be protected from undue physical and mental harm, and except for initial screening for phenylketonuria (PKU) and other diseases that may be added to newborn screening programs, shall be informed of the nature of risks involved in participation in the programs, and those determined to be affected with genetic disease shall be informed of the nature, and where possible the cost, of available therapies or maintenance programs, and shall be informed of the possible benefits and risks associated with these therapies and programs.

(i) All testing results and personal information generated from hereditary disorders programs shall be made available to an individual over 18 years of age, or to the individual's parent or guardian. If the individual is a minor or incompetent, all testing results that have positively determined the individual to either have, or be a carrier of, a hereditary disorder shall be given through a physician or other source of health care.

(j) All testing results and personal information from hereditary disorders programs obtained from any individual, or from specimens from any individual, shall be held confidential and be considered a confidential medical record except for information that the individual, parent, or guardian consents to be released, provided that the individual is first fully informed of the scope of the information requested to be released, of all of the risks, benefits, and purposes for the release, and of the identity of those to whom the information will be released or made available, except for data compiled without reference to the identity of any individual, and except for research purposes, provided that pursuant to Subpart A (commencing with Section 46.101) of Part 46 of Title 45 of the Code of Federal Regulations entitled "Basic HHS Policy for Protection of Human Subjects," the research has first been reviewed and approved by an institutional review board that certifies the approval to the custodian of the information and further certifies that in its judgment the information is of such potentially substantial public health value that modification of the requirement for legally effective prior informed consent of the individual is ethically justifiable.

(k) A physician providing information to patients on expanded newborn screening shall disclose to the parent the physician's financial interest, if any, in the laboratory to which the patient is being referred.

(l) An individual whose confidentiality has been breached as a result of any violation of the provisions of the Hereditary Disorders Act, as defined in subdivision (b) of Section 27, may recover compensatory and civil damages. Any person who negligently breaches the confidentiality of an individual tested under this article shall be subject to civil damages of not more than ten thousand dollars ($ 10,000), reasonable attorney's fees, and the costs of litigation. Any person who knowingly breaches the confidentiality of an individual tested under this article shall be subject to payment of compensatory damages, and in addition, may be subject to civil damages of fifty thousand dollars ($ 50,000), reasonable attorney's fees, and the costs of litigation, or imprisonment in the county jail of not more than one year. If the offense is committed under false pretenses, the person may be subject to a fine of not more than one hundred thousand dollars ($ 100,000), imprisonment in the county jail of not more than one year, or both. If the offense is committed with the intent to sell, transfer, or use individually identifiable health information for commercial advantage, personal gain, or malicious harm, the person may be subject to a fine of not more than two hundred fifty thousand dollars ($ 250,000), imprisonment in the county jail of not more than one year, or both.

(m) "Genetic counseling" as used in this section shall not include communications that occur between patients and appropriately trained and competent licensed health care professionals, such as physicians, registered nurses, and physicians assistants who are operating within the scope of their license and qualifications as defined by their licensing authority.

(Stats. 1995, ch. 415 (S.B. 1360), §8. Amended by Stats. 1998, ch. 897 (S.B. 1800), §1; Stats. 1999, ch. 83 (S.B. 966), §117; Stats. 2000, ch. 941 (S.B. 1364), §2; Stats. 2004 (S.B. 1103), ch. 228, §6.3, effective August 16, 2004.)

§125000. Detection of preventable heritable or congenital disorders

(a) It is the policy of the State of California to make every effort to detect, as early as possible, phenylketonuria and other preventable heritable or congenital disorders leading to mental retardation or physical defects.

The department shall establish a genetic disease unit, that shall coordinate all programs of the department in the area of genetic disease. The unit shall promote a statewide program of information, testing, and counseling services and shall have the responsibility of designating tests and regulations to be used in executing this program.

The information, tests, and counseling for children shall be in accordance with accepted medical practices and shall be administered to each child born in California once the department has established appropriate regulations and testing methods. The information, tests, and counseling for pregnant women shall be in accordance with accepted medical practices and shall be offered to each pregnant woman in California once the department has established appropriate regulations and testing methods. These regulations shall follow the standards and principles specified in Section 124980. The department may provide laboratory testing facilities or contract with any laboratory that it deems qualified to conduct tests required under this section. However, notwithstanding Section 125005, provision of laboratory testing facilities by the department shall be contingent upon the provision of funding therefor by specific appropriation to the Genetic Disease Testing Fund enacted by the Legislature. If moneys appropriated for purposes of this section are not authorized for expenditure to provide laboratory facilities, the department may nevertheless contract to provide laboratory testing services pursuant to this section and shall perform laboratory services, including, but not limited to, quality control, confirmatory, and emergency testing, necessary to ensure the objectives of this program.

(b) The department shall charge a fee for any tests performed pursuant to this section. The amount of the fee shall be established and periodically adjusted by the director in order to meet the costs of this section.

(c) The department shall inform all hospitals or physicians and surgeons, or both, of required regulations and tests and may alter or withdraw any of these requirements whenever sound medical practice so indicates. To the extent practicable, the department shall provide notice to hospitals and other payers in advance of any increase in the fees charged for the program.

(d) This section shall not apply if a parent or guardian of the newborn child objects to a test on the ground that the test conflicts with his or her religious beliefs or practices.

(e) The genetic disease unit is authorized to make grants or contracts or payments to vendors approved by the department for all of the following:

(1) Testing and counseling services.

(2) Demonstration projects to determine the desirability and feasibility of additional tests or new genetic services.

(3) To initiate the development of genetic services in areas of need.

(4) To purchase or provide genetic services from any sums as are appropriated for this purpose.

(f) The genetic disease unit shall evaluate and prepare recommendations on the implementation of tests for the detection of hereditary and congenital diseases, including, but not limited to, biotinidase deficiency and cystic fibrosis. The genetic disease unit shall also evaluate and prepare recommendations on the availability and effectiveness of preventative followup interventions, including the use of specialized medically necessary dietary products.

It is the intent of the Legislature that funds for the support of the evaluations and recommendations required pursuant to this subdivision, and for the activities authorized pursuant to subdivision (e), shall be provided in the annual Budget Act appropriation from the Genetic Disease Testing Fund.

(g) Health care providers that contract with a prepaid group practice health care service plan that annually has at least 20,000 births among its membership, may provide, without contracting with the department, any or all of the testing and counseling services required to be provided under this section or the regulations adopted pursuant thereto, if the services meet the quality standards and adhere to the regulations established by the department and the plan pays that portion of a fee established under this section that is directly attributable to the department's cost of administering the testing or counseling service and to any required testing or counseling services provided by the state for plan members. The payment by the plan, as provided in this subdivision, shall be deemed to fulfill any obligation the provider or the provider's patient may have to the department to pay a fee in connection with the testing or counseling service.

(h) The department may appoint experts in the area of genetic screening, including, but not limited to, cytogenetics, molecular biology, prenatal, specimen collection, and ultrasound to provide expert advice and opinion on the interpretation and enforcement of regulations adopted pursuant to this section. These experts shall be designated agents of the state with respect to their assignments. These experts shall receive no salary, but shall be reimbursed for expenses associated with the purposes of this section. All expenses of the experts for the purposes of this section shall be paid from the Genetic Disease Testing Fund.

(Stats. 1995, ch. 415 (S.B. 1360), §8. Amended by Stats. 1998, ch. 310 (A.B. 2780), §25, effective August 19, 1998; Stats. 2004 (S.B. 1103), ch. 664, §6.4, effective August 16, 2004.)

§125001. Establishment of genetic disease testing program

(a) The department shall establish a program for the development, provision, and evaluation of genetic disease testing, and may provide laboratory testing facilities or make grants to, contract with, or make payments to, any laboratory that it deems qualified and cost-effective to conduct testing or with any metabolic specialty clinic to provide necessary treatment with qualified specialists. The program shall provide genetic screening and followup services for persons who have the screening.

(b) The department shall expand statewide screening of newborns to include tandem mass spectrometry screening for fatty acid oxidation, amino acid, and organic acid disorders and congenital adrenal hyperplasia as soon as possible. The department shall provide information with respect to these disorders and available testing resources to all women receiving prenatal care and to all women admitted to a hospital for delivery. If the department is unable to provide this statewide screening by August 1, 2005, the department shall temporarily obtain these testing services through a competitive bid process from one or more public or private laboratories that meet the department's requirements for testing, quality assurance, and reporting. If the department determines that contracting for these services is more cost-effective, and meets the other requirements of this chapter, than purchasing the tandem mass spectrometry equipment themselves, the department shall contract with one or more public or private laboratories.

(c) The department shall report to the Legislature regarding the progress of the program on or before July 1, 2006. The report shall include the costs for screening, followup, and treatment as compared to costs and morbidity averted for each condition tested for in the program.

(Stats. 1998, ch. 1011 (S.B. 537), §1. Amended by Stats. 2000, ch. 803 (A.B. 2427), §3; Stats. 2004 (S.B. 1103), ch. 228, §6.5, effective August 16, 2004; Stats. 2004 (S.B. 142), ch. 687, §1; Stats. 2005 (S.B. 1108), ch. 22, §137.)

4. Tattoos

California law regulates body piercing and tattoing of minors by imposing liability on the practitioner. The former may not be performed in the absence of a parent or without written notarized parental authorization. However, the latter may not be performed upon a minor.

California Penal Code

§652. Criminal liability for body piercing of minors

(a) It shall be an infraction for any person to perform or offer to perform body piercing upon a person under the age of 18, unless the body piercing is performed in the presence of, or as directed by, a notarized writing by, the person's parent or guardian.

(b) This section does not apply to the body piercing of an emancipated minor.

(c) As used in this section, "body piercing" means the creation of an opening in the body of a human being for the purpose of inserting jewelry or other decoration, including but not limited to, the piercing of a, lip, tongue, nose, or eyebrow. "Body piercing" does not include the piercing of an ear.

(d) Neither the minor upon whom the body piercing was performed, nor the parent or guardian of that minor, nor any other minor is liable for punishment under this section.

(Stats. 2005, ch. 307 (A.B. 646), §2.)

§653. Criminal liability for tattoing minors

Every person who tattoos or offers to tattoo a person under the age of 18 years is guilty of a misdemeanor.

As used in this section, to "tattoo" means to insert pigment under the surface of the skin of a human being , by pricking with a needle or otherwise, so as to produce an indelible mark or figure visible through the skin.

This section is not intended to apply to any act of a licensed practitioner of the healing arts performed in the course of his practice.

(Stats. 1955, ch. 1422, p. 2590, §1.)

H. PATERNITY ESTABLISHMENT

All states have longstanding statutes that enable parents to legitimate their nonmarital (illegitimate) children. Because of the variations in statutory treatment, the National Conference of Commissioners on Uniform State Laws addressed (NCCUSL) illegitimacy on several occasions. NCCUSL developed the Uniform Illegitimacy Act in 1922, the Uniform Act on Blood Tests to Determine Paternity Act in 1952, and the Uniform Paternity Act in 1960. However, the Uniform Illegitimacy Act subsequently was withdrawn, and none of the other Acts was widely adopted. See Uniform Parentage Act (1973), Prefatory Note.

To remedy the lack of uniformity in state law, NCCUSL approved the Uniform Parentage Act (UPA) in 1973. The UPA was also necessary because the United States Supreme Court in the late 1960s and early 1970s rendered much of state law on illegitimacy either unconstitutional or subject to doubt. *Id.*

The original UPA deals with legitimation in two ways. First, it provides that the parent-child relationship extends to every child, regardless of the parents' marital status. Second, it addresses the ascertainment of paternity. Under the UPA, paternity may be established either by a civil suit or by the existence of facts giving rise to rebuttable presumptions of paternity. To identify the father, the UPA establishes presumptions that cover certain cases in which a particular man is the probable father. A rebuttable presumption of paternity may be based upon (1) the marriage of the child's parents plus the father's acknowledgment of paternity (UPA §4(3), (2) the father's openly receiving the child into his home (UPA §4(4), or (3) the father's acknowledgment of paternity with certain formalities (UPA §4(5)). (Recent amendments require that the man reside with the child for the first two years of the child's life for the "holding out" presumption to apply.)

The original UPA also briefly addressed reproductive technology (which was in its infancy at the time). Specifically, the UPA provided that if a wife is artificially inseminated with sperm of a sperm donor who is not her husband, her husband shall be treated as if he is the natural father of the ensuing child (UPA §5(a)). See generally Homer H. Clark Jr., The Law of Domestic Relations in the United States 172 (2d ed. 1988). (Recent amendments provide that both a married and unmarried couple are entitled to use assisted-reproductive technologies.)

The UPA was revised substantially in 2000 and amended in 2002. Scientific advances in paternity testing and the development of the new reproductive technologies since the time of the original UPA warranted a comprehensive revision of the Act. For provisions of the revised UPA and additional background on the Act, see Part III *infra*. On paternity issues, see also Chapter X *supra*.

1. Conclusive Presumption Concerning Child of a Marriage

At common law, a presumption of legitimacy operated on behalf of the child of a married woman. This presumption (irrebuttable, in many states) held that the mother's husband was the father of the child. See, e.g., Cal. Fam. Code §7540. Courts justified the presumption on the ground that it promoted marital harmony. Michael H. v. Gerald D., 491 U.S. 110 (1989) (sustaining an application of a prior version of California Family Code §7540 barring a natural father's paternity claim regarding a child who was conceived while the mother was married to another man).

Dissatisfaction with the United States Supreme Court's decision in *Michael H.* led the California legislature to amend its presumption of legitimacy to allow a presumed father who is not the child's mother's husband (or the child through a guardian ad litem) to move for blood tests within two years of the child's birth (Cal. Fam. Code §7541(b)).

California Family Code

§7540. Conclusive presumption of paternity for child born during marriage

Except as provided in Section 7541, the child of a wife cohabiting with her husband, who is not impotent or sterile, is conclusively presumed to be a child of the marriage.

(Stats. 1992 (A.B. 2650), ch. 162, §10, effective January 1, 1994 as, §7500. Renumbered by Stats. 1993 (A.B. 1500), ch. 219, §161.)

§7541. Husband, presumed father, guardian or mother may file motion for blood tests to determine paternity within two years of birth

(a) Notwithstanding Section 7540, if the court finds that the conclusions of all the experts, as disclosed by the evidence based on blood tests performed pursuant to Chapter 2 (commencing with Section 7550), are that the husband is not the father of the child, the question of paternity of the husband shall be resolved accordingly.

(b) The notice of motion for blood tests under this section may be filed not later than two years from the child's date of birth by the husband, or for the purposes of establishing paternity by the presumed father or the child through or by the child's guardian ad litem. As used in this subdivision, "presumed father" has the meaning given in Sections 7611 and 7612 [set forth in §H4 *infra*].

(c) The notice of motion for blood tests under this section may be filed by the mother of the child not later than two years from the child's date of birth if the child's biological father has filed an affidavit with the court acknowledging paternity of the child.

(d) The notice of motion for blood tests pursuant to this section shall be supported by a declaration under oath submitted by the moving party stating the factual basis for placing the issue of paternity before the court.

(e) Subdivision (a) does not apply, and blood tests may not be used to challenge paternity, in any of the following cases:

(1) A case that reached final judgment of paternity on or before September 30, 1980.

(2) A case coming within Section 7613.

(3) A case in which the wife, with the consent of the husband, conceived by means of a surgical procedure.

(Stats. 1992 (A.B. 2650), ch. 162, §10, effective January 1, 1994 as, §7501. Amended and renumbered by Stats. 1993 (A.B. 1500), ch. 219, §163. Amended Stats. 1998 (A.B. 2801), ch. 581, §18.)

2. Blood Tests to Determine Paternity

California adopted the Uniform Act on Blood Tests to Determine Paternity in 1953. The Act, approved by NCCUSL in 1952, was not widely adopted.

§7550. Title

This chapter may be cited as the Uniform Act on Blood Tests to Determine Paternity.

(Stats. 1992 (A.B. 2650), ch. 162, §10, effective January 1, 1994. Amended Stats. 1993 (A.B. 1500), ch. 219, §174.)

§7551. Court may order parties to submit to genetic tests

In a civil action or proceeding in which paternity is a relevant fact, the court may upon its own initiative or upon suggestion made by or on behalf of any person who is involved, and shall upon motion of any party to the action or proceeding made at a time so as not to delay the proceedings unduly, order the mother, child, and alleged father to submit to genetic tests. If a party refuses to submit to the tests, the court may resolve the question of paternity against that party or enforce its order if the rights of others and the interests of justice so require. A party's refusal to submit to the tests is admissible in evidence in any proceeding to determine paternity. For the purposes of this chapter, "genetic tests" means any genetic test that is generally acknowledged as reliable by accreditation bodies designated by the United States Secretary of Health and Human Services.

(Stats. 1992 (A.B. 2650), ch. 162, §10, effective January 1, 1994. Amended Stats. 1997 (A.B. 573), ch. 599, §36.)

§7551.5. Hospitals, agencies, welfare offices and courts shall facilitate genetic tests

All hospitals, local child support agencies, welfare offices, and family courts shall facilitate genetic tests for purposes of enforcement of this chapter. This may include having a health care professional available for purposes of extracting samples to be used for genetic testing.

(Stats. 1999 (S.B. 240), ch. 652, §6.)

§7552.5. Copy of blood test results shall be served on all parties

(a) A copy of the results of all genetic tests performed under Section 7552 or 7558 shall be served upon all parties, by any method of service authorized under Chapter 5 (commencing with Section 1010) of Title 14 of Part 2 of the Code of Civil Procedure except personal service, no later than 20 days prior to any hearing in which the genetic test results may be admitted into evidence. . . .

(b) The genetic test results shall be admitted into evidence at the hearing or trial to establish paternity, without the need for foundation testimony of authenticity and accuracy, unless a written objection to the genetic test results is filed with the court and served on all other parties, by any party no later than five days prior to the hearing or trial where paternity is at issue.

(c) If a written objection is filed with the court and served on all parties within the time specified in subdivision (b), experts appointed by the court shall be called by the court as witnesses to testify to their findings and are subject to cross-examination by the parties.

(d) If a genetic test reflects a paternity index of 100 or greater, the copy of the results mailed under subdivision (a) shall be accompanied with a voluntary declaration of paternity form, information prepared according to Section 7572.

(Stats. 1994 (A.B. 3804), ch. 1266, §3.7. Amended Stats. 1997 (A.B. 573), ch. 599, §38; Stats. 1999 (S.B. 240), ch. 652, §7.)

§7554. Effect of experts' views as to paternity based on test results

(a) If the court finds that the conclusions of all the experts, as disclosed by the evidence based upon the tests, are that the alleged father is not the father of the child, the question of paternity shall be resolved accordingly.

(b) If the experts disagree in their findings or conclusions, or if the tests show the probability of the alleged father's paternity, the question, subject to Section 352 of the Evidence Code, shall be submitted upon all the evidence, including evidence based upon the tests.

(Stats. 1992 (A.B. 2650), ch. 162, §10, effective January 1, 1994.)

§7555. Presumption of paternity based on blood tests is rebuttable

(a) There is a rebuttable presumption, affecting the burden of proof, of paternity, if the court finds that the paternity index, as calculated by the experts qualified as examiners of genetic markers, is 100 or greater. This presumption may be rebutted by a preponderance of the evidence.

(b) As used in this section:

(1) "Genetic markers" mean separate genes or complexes of genes identified as a result of genetic tests.

(2) "Paternity index" means the commonly accepted indicator used for denoting the existence of paternity. It expresses the relative strength of the test results for and against paternity. The paternity index, computed using results of various paternity tests following accepted statistical principles, shall be in accordance with the method of expression accepted at the International Conference on Parentage Testing at Airlie House, Virginia, May 1982, sponsored by the American Association of Blood Banks.

(Stats. 1992 (A.B. 2650), ch. 162, §10, effective January 1, 1994. Amended Stats. 1993 (A.B. 1500), ch. 219, §175. Amended Stats. 1997 (A.B. 573), ch. 599, §39.)

§7558. Child support agency may require parties to submit to genetic testing in some circumstances

(a) This section applies only to cases where support enforcement services are being provided by the local child support agency pursuant to Section 17400 .

(b) In any civil action or proceeding in which paternity is a relevant fact, and in which the issue of paternity is contested, the local child support agency may issue an administrative order requiring the mother, child, and the alleged father to submit to genetic testing if any of the following conditions exist:

(1) The person alleging paternity has signed a statement under penalty of perjury that sets forth facts that establish a reasonable possibility of the requisite sexual conduct between the mother and the alleged father.

(2) The person denying paternity has signed a statement under penalty of perjury that sets forth facts that establish a reasonable possibility of the nonexistence of the requisite sexual contact between the parties.

(3) The alleged father has filed an answer in the action or proceeding in which paternity is a relevant fact and has requested that genetic tests be performed.

(4) The mother and the alleged father agree in writing to submit to genetic tests.

(c) Notwithstanding subdivision (b), the local child support agency may not order an individual to submit to genetic tests if the individual has been found to have good cause for failure to cooperate in the determination of paternity pursuant to Section 11477 of the Welfare and Institutions Code.

(d) The local child support agency shall pay the costs of any genetic tests that are ordered under subdivision (b), subject to the county obtaining a court order for reimbursement from the alleged father if paternity is established under Section 7553.

(e) Nothing in this section prohibits any person who has been ordered by the local child support agency to submit to genetic tests pursuant to this section from filing a notice of motion with the court in the action or proceeding in which paternity is a relevant fact seeking relief from the local child support agency's order to submit to genetic tests. In that event, the court shall resolve the issue of whether genetic tests should be ordered as provided in Section 7551. If any person refuses to submit to the tests after receipt of the administrative order pursuant to this section and fails to seek relief from the court from the administrative order either prior to the scheduled tests or within 10 days after the tests are scheduled, the court may resolve the question of paternity against that person or enforce the administrative order if the rights of others or the interest of justice so require. Except as provided in subdivision (c), a person's refusal to submit to tests ordered by the local child support agency is admissible in evidence in any proceeding to determine paternity if a notice of motion is not filed within the timeframes specified in this subdivision.

(f) If the original test result creates a rebuttable presumption of paternity under Section 7555 and the result is contested, the local child support agency shall order an additional test only upon request and advance payment of the contestant.

(Stats. 1997 (A.B. 573), ch. 599, §40. Amended Stats. 2000 (A.B. 1358), ch. 808, §72, effective September 28, 2000.)

3. Establishment of Paternity by Voluntary Declaration

Another important development in paternity establishment was the transformation from judicial to voluntary establishment of paternity. Starting in 1992, a few states adopted voluntary paternity establishment programs that targeted mothers at birthing facilities. Paula Roberts, Paternity Establishment: An Issue for the 1990s, 26 Clearinghouse Rev. 1019, 1020 (1993). The success of these programs prompted Congress to include a requirement for all states to adopt in-hospital programs in the Omnibus Budget Reconciliation Act of 1993, 42 U.S.C. §666(a)(5)(C) (2000). The Personal Responsibility and Work Opportunity Reconciliation Act of 1996, 42 U.S.C. §666 (2000), expands the scope of such programs (for example, by establishing voluntary acknowledgments as legal findings subject to rescission within 50 days, and requires states to streamline their paternity procedures (such as by blood testing). See generally Paul K. Legler, The Coming Revolution in Child Support Policy: Implications of the 1996 Welfare Act, 30 Fam. L.Q. 449, 532-533 (1996).

The California provisions on voluntary establishment of paternity are set forth in California Family Code §§7570 et seq. The legislation provides that prior to an unmarried new mother's leaving a hospital, the person responsible for registering live births at the hospital shall provide her (and attempt to provide to the father whom she has identified) a "voluntary declaration of paternity." Hospital staff shall witness the parents' signatures on this declaration of paternity and then forward it to the Department of Child Support Services (DCSS) (Cal. Fam. Code §7571(a)). The declaration of paternity, if not signed at the hospital, may be completed by parents, notarized and mailed subsequently to DCSS (Cal. Fam. Code §7571(d)). Prenatal clinics and local child support agency offices shall also give prospective parents the opportunity to sign the voluntary declaration (Cal. Fam. Code §7571(e), (f)).

§7570. Legislative findings

The Legislature hereby finds and declares as follows:

(a) There is a compelling state interest in establishing paternity for all children. Establishing paternity is the first step toward a child support award, which, in turn, provides children with equal rights and access to benefits, including, but not limited to, social security, health insurance, survivors' benefits, military benefits, and inheritance rights. Knowledge of family medical history is often necessary for correct medical diagnosis and treatment. Additionally, knowing one's father is important to a child's development.

(b) A simple system allowing for establishment of voluntary paternity will result in a significant increase in the ease of establishing paternity, a significant increase in paternity establishment, an increase in the number of children who have greater access to child support and other benefits, and a significant decrease in the time and money required to establish paternity due to the removal of the need for a lengthy and expensive court process to determine and establish paternity and is in the public interest.

(Stats. 1993 (A.B. 1277), ch. 1240, §1.)

§7571. Declaration of paternity

(a) On and after January 1, 1995, upon the event of a live birth, prior to an unmarried mother leaving any hospital, the person responsible for registering live births under Section 102405 of the Health and Safety Code shall provide to the natural mother and shall attempt to provide, at the place of birth, to the man identified by the natural mother as the natural father, a voluntary declaration of paternity together with the written materials described in Section 7572. Staff in the hospital shall witness the signatures of parents signing a voluntary declaration of paternity and shall forward the signed declaration to the Department of Child Support Services within 20 days of the date the declaration was signed. A copy of the declaration shall be made available to each of the attesting parents.

(b) No health care provider shall be subject to any civil, criminal, or administrative liability for any negligent act or omission relative to the accuracy of the information provided, or for filing the declaration with the appropriate state or local agencies.

(c) The local child support agency shall pay the sum of ten dollars ($10) to birthing hospitals and other entities that provide prenatal services for each completed declaration of paternity that is filed with the Department of Child Support Services, provided that the local child support agency and the hospital or other entity providing prenatal services has entered into a written agreement that specifies the terms and conditions for the payment as required by federal law.

(d) If the declaration is not registered by the person responsible for registering live births at the hospital, it may be completed by the attesting parents, notarized, and mailed to the Department of Child Support Services at any time after the child's birth.

(e) Prenatal clinics shall offer prospective parents the opportunity to sign a voluntary declaration of paternity. In order to be paid for their services as provided in subdivision (c), prenatal clinics must ensure that the form is witnessed and forwarded to the Department of Child Support Services within 20 days of the date the declaration was signed.

(f) Declarations shall be made available without charge at all local child support agency offices, offices of local registrars of births and deaths, courts, and county welfare departments within this state. Staff in these offices shall witness the signatures of parents wishing to sign a voluntary declaration of paternity and shall be responsible for forwarding the signed declaration to the Department of Child Support Services within 20 days of the date the declaration was signed.

(g) The Department of Child Support Services, at its option, may pay the sum of ten dollars ($10) to local registrars of births and deaths, county welfare departments, or courts for each completed declaration of paternity that is witnessed by staff in these offices and filed with the Department of Child Support Services. In order to receive payment, the Department of Child Support Services and the entity shall enter into a written agreement that specifies the terms and conditions for payment as required by federal law. The Department of Child Support Services shall study the effect of the ten dollar ($10) payment on obtaining completed voluntary declaration of paternity forms and shall report to the Legislature on any recommendations to change the ten dollar ($10) optional payment, if appropriate, by January 1, 2000.

(h) The Department of Child Support Services and local child support agencies shall publicize the availability of the declarations. The local child support agency shall make the declaration, together with the written materials described in subdivision (a) of Section 7572, available upon request to any parent and any agency or organization that is required to offer parents the opportunity to sign a voluntary declaration of paternity. The local child support agency shall also provide qualified staff to answer parents' questions regarding the declaration and the process of establishing paternity.

(i) Copies of the declaration and any rescissions filed with the Department of Child Support Services shall be made available only to the parents, the child, the local child support agency, the county welfare department, the county counsel, the State Department of Health Services, and the courts.

(j) Publicly funded or licensed health clinics, pediatric offices, Head Start programs, child care centers, social services providers, prisons, and schools may offer parents the opportunity to sign a voluntary declaration of paternity. In order to be paid for their services as provided in subdivision (c), publicly funded or licensed health clinics, pediatric offices, Head Start programs, child care centers, social services providers, prisons, and schools shall ensure that the form is witnessed and forwarded to the Department of Child Support Services.

(k) Any agency or organization required to offer parents the opportunity to sign a voluntary declaration of paternity shall also identify parents who are willing to sign, but were unavailable when the child was born. The organization shall then contact these parents within 10 days and again offer the parent the opportunity to sign a voluntary declaration of paternity.

(Stats. 1993 (A.B. 1277), ch. 1240, §1. Amended Stats. 1994 (A.B. 2208), ch. 1269, §51. Amended Stats. 1996 (S.B. 1497), ch. 1023, §47, effective September 29, 1996 (ch. 1062 prevails), (A.B. 1832), ch. 1062, §4; Stats. 1997 (A.B. 573), ch. 599, §41; Stats. 1998 (A.B. 2803), ch. 485, §67, (A.B. 2169), ch. 858, §3 (ch. 858 prevails); Stats. 1999 (S.B. 240), ch. 652, §8. Amended Stats. 2001 (S.B. 1191), ch. 745, §44, effective October 12, 2001; Stats. 2001 (S.B. 943), ch. 755, §9, effective October 12, 2001.)

§7572. State shall provide written materials to help parents comply

(a) The Department of Child Support Services, in consultation with the State Department of Health Services, the California Association of Hospitals and Health Systems, and other affected health provider organizations, shall work cooperatively to develop written materials to assist providers and parents in complying with this chapter. This written material shall be updated periodically by the Department of Child Support Services to reflect changes in law, procedures, or public need.

(b) The written materials for parents which shall be attached to the form specified in Section 7574 and provided to unmarried parents shall contain the following information:

(1) A signed voluntary declaration of paternity that is filed with the Department of Child Support Services legally establishes paternity.

(2) The legal rights and obligations of both parents and the child that result from the establishment of paternity.

(3) An alleged father's constitutional rights to have the issue of paternity decided by a court; to notice of any hearing on the issue of paternity; to have an opportunity to present his case to the court, including his right to present and cross-examine witnesses; to have an attorney represent him; and to have an attorney appointed to represent him if he cannot afford one in a paternity action filed by a local child support agency.

(4) That by signing the voluntary declaration of paternity, the father is voluntarily waiving his constitutional rights.

(c) Parents shall also be given oral notice of the rights and responsibilities specified in subdivision (b). Oral notice may be accomplished through the use of audio or videotape programs developed by the Department of Child Support Services to the extent permitted by federal law.

(d) The Department of Child Support Services shall, free of charge, make available to hospitals, clinics, and other places of birth any and all informational and training materials for the program under this chapter, as well as the paternity declaration form. The Department of Child Support Services shall make training available to every participating hospital, clinic, local registrar of births and deaths, and other place of birth no later than June 30, 1999.

(e) The Department of Child Support Services may adopt regulations, including emergency regulations, necessary to implement this chapter.

(Stats. 1993 (A.B. 1277), ch. 1240, §1. Amended by Stats. 1994 (A.B. 2208), ch. 1269, §51.5; Stats. 1996 (A.B. 1832), ch. 1062, §5; Stats. 1997 (A.B. 573), ch. 599, §42; Stats. 1998 (A.B. 2803), ch. 485, §68; Stats. 1998 (A.B. 2169), ch. 858, §4; Stats. 1999 (S.B. 966), ch. 83, §53; Stats. 1999 (S.B. 240), ch. 652, §10.)

§7573. Voluntary declaration of paternity is conclusive and has effect of judgment

Except as provided in Sections 7575, 7576, and 7577, a completed voluntary declaration of paternity, as described in Section 7574, that has been filed with the Department of Child Support Services shall establish the paternity of a child and shall have the same force and effect as a judgment for paternity issued by a court of competent jurisdiction. The voluntary declaration of paternity shall be recognized as a basis for the establishment of an order for child custody, visitation, or child support.

(Stats. 1996 (A.B. 1832), ch. 1062, §6. Amended Stats. 1998 (A.B. 2169), ch. 858, §5. Amended Stats. 2000 (A.B. 1358), ch. 808, §73, effective September 28, 2000.)

§7574. Contents of declaration of paternity

(a) The voluntary declaration of paternity shall be executed on a form developed by the Department of Child Support Services in consultation with the State Department of Health Services, the California Family Support Council, and child support advocacy groups.

(b) The form described in subdivision (a) shall contain, at a minimum, the following:

(1) The name and the signature of the mother.

(2) The name and the signature of the father.

(3) The name of the child.

(4) The date of birth of the child.

(5) A statement by the mother that she has read and understands the written materials described in Section 7572, that the man who has signed the voluntary declaration of paternity is the only possible father, and that she consents to the establishment of paternity by signing the voluntary declaration of paternity.

(6) A statement by the father that he has read and understands the written materials described in Section 7572, that he understands that by signing the voluntary declaration of paternity he is waiving his rights as described in the written materials, that he is the biological father of the child, and that he consents to the establishment of paternity by signing the voluntary declaration of paternity.

(7) The name and the signature of the person who witnesses the signing of the declaration by the mother and the father.

(Stats. 1996 (A.B. 1832), ch. 1062, §8. Amended Stats. 2000 (A.B. 1358), ch. 808, §74, effective September 28, 2000.

4. Uniform Parentage Act

Below is the California version of the 1973 Uniform Parentage Act. The revised version of the Uniform Parentage Act (not yet adopted by California) is included in Part III in Selected Uniform Acts *infra*.

a. General Provisions

§7600. Title

This part may be cited as the Uniform Parentage Act.

(Stats. 1992 (A.B. 2650), ch. 162, §10, effective January 1, 1994.)

§7601. Definition of parent and child relationship

"Parent and child relationship" as used in this part means the legal relationship existing between a child and the child's natural or adoptive parents incident to which the law confers or imposes rights, privileges, duties, and obligations. The term includes the mother and child relationship and the father and child relationship.

(Stats. 1992 (A.B. 2650), ch. 162, §10, effective January 1, 1994.)

§7602. Relevance of parents' marital status

The parent and child relationship extends equally to every child and to every parent, regardless of the marital status of the parents.

(Stats. 1992 (A.B. 2650), ch. 162, §10, effective January 1, 1994.)

§7604. Court may order pendente lite relief (custody or visitation order) upon finding of parent-child relationship

A court may order pendente lite relief consisting of a custody or visitation order pursuant to Part 2 (commencing with Section 3020) of Division 8, if the court finds both of the following:

(a) Based on the tests authorized by Section 7541, a parent and child relationship exists pursuant to Section 7540.

(b) The custody or visitation order would be in the best interest of the child.

(Stats. 1992 (A.B. 2650), ch. 162, §10, effective January 1, 1994. Amended by Stats. 1993 (A.B. 1500), ch. 219, §175.5.)

§7604.5. Evidence of bills for pregnancy, childbirth and genetic testing

Notwithstanding any other provision of law, bills for pregnancy, childbirth, and genetic testing shall be admissible as evidence without third-party foundation testimony and shall constitute prima facie evidence of costs incurred for those services.

(Added by Stats. 1997 (A.B. 573), ch. 599, §44.)

b. Establishing Parent-Child Relationship

§7610. Method of establishment of parent-child relationship

The parent and child relationship may be established as follows:

(a) Between a child and the natural mother, it may be established by proof of her having given birth to the child, or under this part.

(b) Between a child and the natural father, it may be established under this part.

(c) Between a child and an adoptive parent, it may be established by proof of adoption.

(Stats. 1992 (A.B. 2650), ch. 162, §10, effective Jan. 1, 1994.)

§7611. Conditions for establishment of presumed fatherhood

A man is presumed to be the natural father of a child if he meets the conditions provided in Chapter 1 (commencing with Section 7540) or Chapter 3 (commencing with Section 7570) of Part 2 or in any of the following subdivisions:

(a) He and the child's natural mother are or have been married to each other and the child is born during the marriage, or within 300 days after the marriage is terminated by death, annulment, declaration of invalidity, or divorce, or after a judgment of separation is entered by a court.

(b) Before the child's birth, he and the child's natural mother have attempted to marry each other by a marriage solemnized in apparent compliance with law, although the attempted marriage is or could be declared invalid, and either of the following is true:

(1) If the attempted marriage could be declared invalid only by a court, the child is born during the attempted marriage, or within 300 days after its termination by death, annulment, declaration of invalidity, or divorce.

(2) If the attempted marriage is invalid without a court order, the child is born within 300 days after the termination of cohabitation.

(c) After the child's birth, he and the child's natural mother have married, or attempted to marry, each other by a marriage solemnized in apparent compliance with law, although the attempted marriage is or could be declared invalid, and either of the following is true:

(1) With his consent, he is named as the child's father on the child's birth certificate.

(2) He is obligated to support the child under a written voluntary promise or by court order.

(d) He receives the child into his home and openly holds out the child as his natural child.

(e) If the child was born and resides in a nation with which the United States engages in an Orderly Departure Program or successor program, he acknowledges that he is the child's father in a declaration under penalty of perjury, as specified in Section 2015.5 of the Code of Civil Procedure. This subdivision shall remain in effect only until January 1, 1997, and on that date shall become inoperative.

(f) The child is in utero after the death of the decedent and the conditions set forth in Section 249.5 of the Probate Code are satisfied.

(Stats. 1992 (A.B. 2650), ch. 162, §10, effective January 1, 1994. Amended by Stats. 1993 (A.B. 1500), ch. 291, §176. Amended by Stats. 1994 (A.B. 2208), ch. 1269, §53; Stats. 2004 (A.B. 1910), ch. 775, §1.)

§7612. Presumption as natural father is rebuttable; effect of conflicting presumptions

(a) Except as provided in Chapter 1 (commencing with Section 7540) and Chapter 3 (commencing with Section 7570) of Part 2 or in Section 20102, a presumption under Section 7611 is a rebuttable presumption affecting the burden of proof and may be rebutted in an appropriate action only by clear and convincing evidence.

(b) If two or more presumptions arise under Section 7611 which conflict with each other, the presumption which on the facts is founded on the weightier considerations of policy and logic controls.

(c) The presumption under Section 7611 is rebutted by a judgment establishing paternity of the child by another man.

(Stats. 1992 (A.B. 2650), ch. 162, §10, effective January 1, 1994. Amended by Stats. 1993 (A.B. 1500), ch. 219, §178. Amended by Stats. 1994 (A.B. 2208), ch. 1269, §54.)

§7613. Father of child conceived by artificial insemination

(a) If, under the supervision of a licensed physician and surgeon and with the consent of her husband, a wife is inseminated artificially with semen donated by a man not her husband, the husband is treated in law as if he were the natural father of a child thereby conceived. The husband's consent must be in writing and signed by him and his wife. The physician and surgeon shall certify their signatures and the date of the insemination, and retain the husband's consent as part of the medical record, where it shall be kept confidential and in a sealed file. However, the physician and surgeon's failure to do so does not affect the father and child relationship. All papers and records pertaining to the insemination, whether part of the permanent record of a court or of a file held by the supervising physician and surgeon or elsewhere, are subject to inspection only upon an order of the court for good cause shown.

(b) The donor of semen provided to a licensed physician and surgeon for use in artificial insemination of a woman

other than the donor's wife is treated in law as if he were not the natural father of a child thereby conceived.
(Stats. 1992, c. 162 (A.B. 2650), §10, effective January 1, 1994.)

§7614. Validity of written promise to furnish support for a child

(a) A promise in writing to furnish support for a child, growing out of a presumed or alleged father and child relationship, does not require consideration and, subject to Section 7632, is enforceable according to its terms.

(b) In the best interest of the child or the mother, the court may, and upon the promisor's request shall, order the promise to be kept in confidence and designate a person or agency to receive and disburse on behalf of the child all amounts paid in performance of the promise.
(Stats. 1992 (A.B. 2650), ch. 162, §10, effective January 1, 1994.)

c. Jurisdiction and Venue

§7620. Person who has sexual intercourse in state submits to personal jurisdiction

(a) A person who has sexual intercourse in this state thereby submits to the jurisdiction of the courts of this state as to an action brought under this part with respect to a child who may have been conceived by that act of intercourse.

(b) An action under this part shall be brought in one of the following:

(1) The county in which the child resides or is found.

(2) The county in which a licensed California adoption agency maintains an office if that agency brings the action.

(3) If the father is deceased, the county in which proceedings for probate of the estate of the father of the child have been or could be commenced.

(Stats. 1992 (A.B. 2650), ch. 162, §10, effective January 1, 1994. Amended Stats. 2003 (S.B. 182), ch. 251, §1; Stats. 2005 (S.B. 302), ch. 627, §1.)

d. Determination of Parent-Child Relationship

§7630. Parties who may bring action to determine existence or nonexistence of father and child relationship

(a) A child, the child's natural mother, a man presumed to be the child's father under subdivision (a), (b), or (c) of Section 7611, an adoption agency to whom the child has been relinquished or a prospective adoptive parent of the child, may bring an action as follows:

(1) At any time for the purpose of declaring the existence of the father and child relationship presumed under subdivision (a), (b), or (c) of Section 7611.

(2) For the purpose of declaring the nonexistence of the father and child relationship presumed under subdivision (a), (b), or (c) of Section 7611 only if the action is brought within a reasonable time after obtaining knowledge of relevant facts. After the presumption has been rebutted, paternity of the child by another man may be determined in the same action, if he has been made a party.

(b) Any interested party may bring an action at any time for the purpose of determining the existence or nonexistence of the father and child relationship presumed under subdivision (d) or (f) of Section 7611.

(c) An action to determine the existence of the father and child relationship with respect to a child who has no presumed father under Section 7611 or whose presumed father is deceased may be brought by the child or personal representative of the child, the Department of Child Support Services, the mother or the personal representative or a parent of the mother if the mother has died or is a minor, a man alleged or alleging himself to be the father, or the personal representative or a parent of the alleged father if the alleged father has died or is a minor.

(d) An action under subdivision (c) shall be consolidated with a proceeding pursuant to Section 7662 whenever a proceeding has been filed under Chapter 5 (commencing with Section 7660). The parental rights of the alleged natural father shall be determined as set forth in Section 7664. The consolidated action shall be heard in the court in which the Section 7662 proceeding is filed, unless the court in which the action under subdivision (c) is filed finds, by clear and convincing evidence, that transferring the action to the other court poses a substantial hardship to the petitioner. Mere inconvenience does not constitute a sufficient basis for a finding of substantial hardship. If the court determines there is a substantial hardship, the consolidated action shall be heard in the court in which the paternity action is filed.
(Stats. 1992 (A.B. 2650), ch. 162, §10, effective January 1, 1994. Amended by Stats. 2000 (A.B. 1358), ch. 808, §76, effective September 28, 2000; Stats. 2001 (A.B. 538), ch. 353, §1; Stats. 2003 (S.B. 182), ch. 251, §2; Stats. 2004 (A.B. 1910), ch. 775, §2; Stats. 2005 (S.B. 302), ch. 627, §2.)

§7631. Man who is not a presumed father may bring action if mother consents to adoption

Except as to cases coming within Chapter 1 (commencing with Section 7540) of Part 2, a man not a presumed father may bring an action for the purpose of declaring that he is the natural father of a child having a presumed father under Section 7611, if the mother relinquishes for, consents to, or proposes to relinquish for or consent to, the adoption of the child. An action under this section shall be brought within 30 days after (1) the man is served as prescribed in Section 7666 with a notice that he is or could be the father of the child or (2) the birth of the child, whichever is later. The commencement of the action suspends a pending proceeding in connection with the adoption of the child until a judgment in the action is final.
(Stats. 1992 (A.B. 2650), ch. 162, §10, effective January 1, 1994. Amended by Stats. 1993 (A.B. 1500), ch. 219, §178.5.)

§7632. Parties' agreement does not bar subsequent action

Regardless of its terms, an agreement between an alleged or presumed father and the mother or child does not bar an action under this chapter.

(Stats. 1992 (A.B. 2650), ch. 162, §10, effective January 1, 1994.)

§7633. Action may be brought before birth

An action under this chapter may be brought before the birth of the child.

(Stats. 1992 (A.B. 2650), ch. 162, §10, effective January 1, 1994.)

§7634. Child support agency may bring action

(a) The local child support agency may, in the local child support agency's discretion, bring an action under this chapter in any case in which the local child support agency believes it to be appropriate.

(b) The Department of Child Support Services may review the current practices of service of process used by the local child support agencies pursuant to subdivision (a), and may develop methods to increase the number of persons served using personal delivery.

(Stats. 1992 (A.B. 2650), ch. 162, §10, effective January 1, 1994. Amended by Stats. 2000 (A.B. 1358), ch. 808, §77, effective September 28, 2000; Stats. 2004 (A.B. 252), ch. 849, §2.)

§7635. Child 12 years and older shall be party to action; minors shall be represented

(a) The child may, if under the age of 12 years, and shall, if 12 years of age or older, be made a party to the action. If the child is a minor and a party to the action, the child shall be represented by a guardian ad litem appointed by the court. The guardian ad litem need not be represented by counsel if the guardian ad litem is a relative of the child.

(b) The natural mother, each man presumed to be the father under Section 7611, and each man alleged to be the natural father, may be made parties and shall be given notice of the action in the manner prescribed in Section 7666 and an opportunity to be heard.

(c) The court may align the parties.

(d) In any initial or subsequent proceeding under this chapter where custody of, or visitation with, a minor child is in issue, the court may, if it determines it would be in the best interest of the minor child, appoint private counsel to represent the interests of the minor child pursuant to Chapter 10 (commencing with Section 3150) of Part 2 of Division 8.

(Stats. 1992 (A.B. 2650), ch. 162, §10, effective January 1, 1994. Amended by Stats. 1994 (A.B. 2208), ch. 1269, §55.)

§7636. Effect of judgment or order is determinative; exception

The judgment or order of the court determining the existence or nonexistence of the parent and child relationship is determinative for all purposes except for actions brought pursuant to Section 270 [criminal nonsupport of child] of the Penal Code.

(Stats. 1992 (A.B. 2650), ch. 162, §10, effective January 1, 1994.)

§7637. Judgment or order of paternity may contain range of other provisions

The judgment or order may contain any other provision directed against the appropriate party to the proceeding, concerning the duty of support, the custody and guardianship of the child, visitation privileges with the child, the furnishing of bond or other security for the payment of the judgment, or any other matter in the best interest of the child. The judgment or order may direct the father to pay the reasonable expenses of the mother's pregnancy and confinement.

(Stats. 1992 (A.B. 2650), ch. 162, §10, effective January 1, 1994. Amended by Stats. 1993 (A.B. 1500), ch. 291, §179.)

§7638. Application for name change of child may be included with petition

The procedure in an action under this part to change the name of a minor or adult child for whom a parent and child relationship is established pursuant to Section 7636, upon application in accordance with Title 8 (commencing with Section 1275) of Part 3 of the Code of Civil Procedure shall conform to those provisions, except that the application for the change of name may be included with the petition filed under this part and except as provided in Sections 1277 and 1278 of the Code of Civil Procedure.

(Stats. 1992 (A.B. 2650), ch. 162, §10, effective January 1, 1994.)

§7639. Court shall order that new birth certificate be issued in some cases

If the judgment or order of the court is at variance with the child's birth certificate, the court shall order that a new birth certificate be issued as prescribed in Article 2 (commencing with Section 102725) of Chapter 5 of Part 1 of Division 102 of the Health and Safety Code.

(Stats. 1992 (A.B. 2650), ch. 162, §10, effective January 1, 1994. Amended by Stats. 1996 (S.B. 1497), ch. 1023, §48, effective September 29, 1996.)

§7640. Court may order payment of fees and costs

The court may order reasonable fees of counsel, experts, and the child's guardian ad litem, and other costs of the action and pretrial proceedings, including blood tests, to be paid by the parties, excluding any governmental entity, in proportions and at times determined by the court.

(Stats. 1992 (A.B. 2650), ch. 162, §10, effective January 1, 1994. Amended by Stats. 1994 (A.B. 2208), ch. 1269, §55.2.)

§7641. Parties who may enforce father's obligation

(a) If existence of the father and child relationship is declared, or paternity or a duty of support has been acknowledged or adjudicated under this part or under prior law, the obligation of the father may be enforced in the same or other proceedings by any of the following:

(1) The mother.

(2) The child.

(3) The public authority that has furnished or may furnish the reasonable expenses of pregnancy, confinement, education, support, or funeral.

(4) Any other person, including a private agency, to the extent the person has furnished or is furnishing these expenses.

(b) The court may order support payments to be made to any of the following:

(1) The mother.

(2) The clerk of the court.

(3) A person, corporation, or agency designated to administer the payments for the benefit of the child under the supervision of the court.

(c) Willful failure to obey the judgment or order of the court is a civil contempt of the court. All remedies for the enforcement of judgments, including imprisonment for contempt, apply.

(Stats. 1992 (A.B. 2650), ch. 162, §10, effective January 1, 1994.)

§7642. Court has continuing jurisdiction to modify or set aside judgment or order

The court has continuing jurisdiction to modify or set aside a judgment or order made under this part. A judgment or order relating to an adoption may only be modified or set aside in the same manner and under the same conditions as an order of adoption may be modified or set aside under Section 9100 or 9102.

(Stats. 1992 (A.B. 2650), ch. 162, §10, effective January 1, 1994. Amended by Stats. 1999 (A.B. 380), ch. 653, §11.)

§7643. Proceedings may be conducted in closed court

(a) Notwithstanding any other law concerning public hearings and records, a hearing or trial held under this part may be held in closed court without admittance of any person other than those necessary to the action or proceeding. Except as provided in subdivision (b), all papers and records, other than the final judgment, pertaining to the action or proceeding, whether part of the permanent record of the court or of a file in a public agency or elsewhere, are subject to inspection only in exceptional cases upon an order of the court for good cause shown.

(b) Papers and records pertaining to the action or proceeding that are part of the permanent record of the court are subject to inspection by the parties to the action and their attorneys.

(Stats. 1992 (A.B. 2650), ch. 162, §10, effective January 1, 1994.)

§7644. Action for custody and support may be based upon voluntary declaration of paternity

(a) Notwithstanding any other law, an action for child custody and support and for other relief as provided in Section 7637 may be filed based upon a voluntary declaration of paternity as provided in Chapter 3 (commencing with Section 7570) of Part 2.

(b) Except as provided in Section 7576, the voluntary declaration of paternity shall be given the same force and effect as a judgment of paternity entered by a court of competent jurisdiction. The court shall make appropriate orders as specified in Section 7637 based upon the voluntary declaration of paternity unless evidence is presented that the voluntary declaration of paternity has been rescinded by the parties or set aside as provided in Section 7575 of the Family Code.

(c) The Judicial Council shall develop the forms and procedures necessary to implement this section.

(Stats. 1994 (A.B. 3804), ch. 1266, §7. Amended by Stats. 1996 (A.B. 1832), ch. 1062, §14.)

e. Determination of Mother-Child Relationship

Occasionally, issues arise as to the determination of the mother-child relationship. The California Supreme Court recently addressed the issue of whether the provision of California's version of the Uniform Parentage Act (UPA) that deals with presumed fatherhood applies equally to mothers. In Elisa B. v. Superior Court, 33 Cal. Rptr.3d 46 (Cal. 2005), the county filed an action to establish whether a former same-sex partner was obligated to pay child support for a child whose mother was receiving public assistance. The California Supreme Court held that under the UPA, a child may have two parents, both of whom are women. The court also ruled that the former partner was a presumed parent under the UPA, that the presumption should not be rebutted in this case (because the former partner supported the mother's decision to seek artificial insemination, agreed to raise the twins, and held them out as hers), and therefore was obligated to pay child support.

See generally Melanie B. Jacobs, Micah Has One Mommy and One Legal Stranger: Adjudicating Maternity for Nonbiological Lesbian Coparents, 50 Buff. L. Rev. 341 (2002).

§7650. Any interested person may bring action to determine existence of mother-child relationship

(a) Any interested person may bring an action to determine the existence or nonexistence of a mother and child relationship. Insofar as practicable, the provisions of this part applicable to the father and child relationship apply.

(b) A woman is presumed to be the natural mother of a child if the child is in utero after the death of the decedent and the conditions set forth in Section 249.5 of the Probate Code are satisfied.

(Stats. 1992 (A.B. 2650), ch. 162, §10, effective January 1, 1994. Amended by Stats. 2004 (A.B. 1910), ch. 775, §2.3.)

The sections of the Uniform Parentage Act on termination of parental rights in adoption proceedings are found in Chapter IX *infra* on Adoption (Cal. Fam.

Code §§7600–7670). The Uniform Parentage Act also provides for temporary restraining orders restraining all parties, without the prior written consent of the other party or a court order, from removing from the state any minor child for whom the proceeding seeks to establish a parent-child relationship (Cal. Fam. Code §§7700 et seq.(omitted).

PART II

SELECTED FEDERAL STATUTES

SELECTED FEDERAL STATUTES

Below are selections from the Child Support Recovery Act (CSRA) (as amended by the Deadbeat Parents Punishment Act); Child Victims' and Child Witnesses' Rights Act; Defense of Marriage Act (DOMA); Family and Medical Leave Act (FMLA); Pregnancy Discrimination Act (PDA) (Title VII, Civil Rights Act of 1964); International Parenting Kidnapping Act (IPKA); and the Wiretap Act (Title III, Omnibus Crime Control Act).

Child Support Recovery Act

18 U.S.C. §228 (2000), as amended by the Deadbeat Parents Punishment Act, 18 U.S.C. §228(a)(3) (2000)

The Child Support Recovery Act (CSRA) criminalizes the willful failure to pay a past-due support obligation for a child who resides in another state. Congress amended the CSRA in 1998 with the enactment of the Deadbeat Parents Punishment Act which makes willful failure to pay a support obligation for a child in another state a felony, if the obligation remains unpaid for over two years or exceeds $10,000.

§228. Federal criminal liability for willful failure to pay child support obligation for child who resides in another state

(a) Offense. — Any person who —

(1) willfully fails to pay a support obligation with respect to a child who resides in another State, if such obligation has remained unpaid for a period longer than 1 year, or is greater than $5,000;

(2) travels in interstate or foreign commerce with the intent to evade a support obligation, if such obligation has remained unpaid for a period longer than 1 year, or is greater than $5,000; or

(3) willfully fails to pay a support obligation with respect to a child who resides in another State, if such obligation has remained unpaid for a period longer than 2 years, or is greater than $10,000; shall be punished as provided in subsection (c).

(b) Presumption. — The existence of a support obligation that was in effect for the time period charged in the indictment or information creates a rebuttable presumption that the obligor has the ability to pay the support obligation for that time period.

(c) Punishment. — The punishment for an offense under this section is —

(1) in the case of a first offense under subsection (a)(1), a fine under this title, imprisonment for not more than 6 months, or both; and

(2) in the case of an offense under paragraph (2) or (3) of subsection (a), or a second or subsequent offense under subsection (a)(1), a fine under this title, imprisonment for not more than 2 years, or both.

(d) Mandatory restitution. — Upon a conviction under this section, the court shall order restitution under section 3663A in an amount equal to the total unpaid support obligation as it exists at the time of sentencing.

(e) Venue. — With respect to an offense under this section, an action may be inquired of and prosecuted in a district court of the United States for —

(1) the district in which the child who is the subject of the support obligation involved resided during a period during which a person described in subsection (a) (referred to in this subsection as an "obliger") failed to meet that support obligation;

(2) the district in which the obliger resided during a period described in paragraph (1); or

(3) any other district with jurisdiction otherwise provided for by law.

(f) Definitions. — As used in this section —

(1) the term "Indian tribe" has the meaning given that term in section 102 of the Federally Recognized Indian Tribe List Act of 1994 (25 U.S.C. §479a);

(2) the term "State" includes any State of the United States, the District of Columbia, and any commonwealth, territory, or possession of the United States; and

(3) the term "support obligation" means any amount determined under a court order or an order of an administrative process pursuant to the law of a State or of an Indian tribe to be due from a person for the support and maintenance of a child or of a child and the parent with whom the child is living.

(Pub. L. 102-521, §2(a), October 25, 1992, 106 Stat. 340, and amended Pub. L. 104-294, Title VI, §607(l), October 11, 1996, 110 Stat. 3512; Pub. L. 105-187, §2, June 24, 1998, 112 Stat. 618.)

Child Victims' and Child Witnesses' Rights Act

18 U.S.C. §3509 (2000)

The Child Victims' and Child Witnesses' Rights Act, applicable to the federal courts, was enacted in the wake of the United States Supreme Court's decision in Maryland v. Craig, 497 U.S. 836 (1990) (holding that the right of confrontation does not prohibit a procedure by which a child victim testifies via one way closed-circuit television). The Act permits a child witness to testify by either two-way closed-circuit television or videotaped depositions. The Act also presumes the competency of child witnesses and allows the use of anatomically-correct dolls to assist the child in testifying.

§3509. Rights of child victims and child witnesses

(a) Definitions. — For purposes of this section—

(1) the term "adult attendant" means an adult described in subsection (i) who accompanies a child throughout the

judicial process for the purpose of providing emotional support;

(2) the term "child" means a person who is under the age of 18, who is or is alleged to be —

(A) a victim of a crime of physical abuse, sexual abuse, or exploitation; or

(B) a witness to a crime committed against another person;

(3) the term "child abuse" means the physical or mental injury, sexual abuse or exploitation, or negligent treatment of a child;

(4) the term "physical injury" includes lacerations, fractured bones, burns, internal injuries, severe bruising or serious bodily harm;

(5) the term "mental injury" means harm to a child's psychological or intellectual functioning which may be exhibited by severe anxiety, depression, withdrawal or outward aggressive behavior, or a combination of those behaviors, which may be demonstrated by a change in behavior, emotional response, or cognition;

(6) the term "exploitation" means child pornography or child prostitution;

(7) the term "multidisciplinary child abuse team" means a professional unit composed of representatives from health, social service, law enforcement, and legal service agencies to coordinate the assistance needed to handle cases of child abuse;

(8) the term "sexual abuse" includes the employment, use, persuasion, inducement, enticement, or coercion of a child to engage in, or assist another person to engage in, sexually explicit conduct or the rape, molestation, prostitution, or other form of sexual exploitation of children, or incest with children;

(9) the term "sexually explicit conduct" means actual or simulated —

(A) sexual intercourse, including sexual contact in the manner of genital-genital, oral-genital, anal-genital, or oral-anal contact, whether between persons of the same or of opposite sex; sexual contact means the intentional touching, either directly or through clothing, of the genitalia, anus, groin, breast, inner thigh, or buttocks of any person with an intent to abuse, humiliate, harass, degrade, or arouse or gratify sexual desire of any person;

(B) bestiality;

(C) masturbation;

(D) lascivious exhibition of the genitals or pubic area of a person or animal; or

(E) sadistic or masochistic abuse;

(10) the term "sex crime" means an act of sexual abuse that is a criminal act;

(11) the term "negligent treatment" means the failure to provide, for reasons other than poverty, adequate food, clothing, shelter, or medical care so as to seriously endanger the physical health of the child; and

(12) the term "child abuse" does not include discipline administered by a parent or legal guardian to his or her child provided it is reasonable in manner and moderate in degree and otherwise does not constitute cruelty.

(b) Alternatives to live in-court testimony. —

(1) Child's live testimony by 2-way closed circuit television. —

(A) In a proceeding involving an alleged offense against a child, the attorney for the Government, the child's attorney, or a guardian ad litem appointed under subsection (h) may apply for an order that the child's testimony be taken in a room outside the courtroom and be televised by 2-way closed circuit television. The person seeking such an order shall apply for such an order at least 5 days before the trial date, unless the court finds on the record that the need for such an order was not reasonably foreseeable.

(B) The court may order that the testimony of the child be taken by closed-circuit television as provided in subparagraph (A) if the court finds that the child is unable to testify in open court in the presence of the defendant, for any of the following reasons:

(i) The child is unable to testify because of fear.

(ii) There is a substantial likelihood, established by expert testimony, that the child would suffer emotional trauma from testifying.

(iii) The child suffers a mental or other infirmity.

(iv) Conduct by defendant or defense counsel causes the child to be unable to continue testifying.

(C) The court shall support a ruling on the child's inability to testify with findings on the record. In determining whether the impact on an individual child of one or more of the factors described in subparagraph (B) is so substantial as to justify an order under subparagraph (A), the court may question the minor in chambers, or at some other comfortable place other than the courtroom, on the record for a reasonable period of time with the child attendant, the prosecutor, the child's attorney, the guardian ad litem, and the defense counsel present.

(D) If the court orders the taking of testimony by television, the attorney for the Government and the attorney for the defendant not including an attorney pro se for a party shall be present in a room outside the courtroom with the child and the child shall be subjected to direct and cross-examination. The only other persons who may be permitted in the room with the child during the child's testimony are —

(i) the child's attorney or guardian ad litem appointed under subsection (h);

(ii) Persons necessary to operate the closed-circuit television equipment;

(iii) A judicial officer, appointed by the court; and

(iv) Other persons whose presence is determined by the court to be necessary to the welfare and well-being of the child, including an adult attendant.

The child's testimony shall be transmitted by closed circuit television into the courtroom for viewing and hearing by the defendant, jury, judge, and public. The defendant shall be provided with the means of private, contemporaneous communication with the defendant's attorney during the testimony. The closed circuit television transmission shall relay into the room in which the child is testifying the defendant's image, and the voice of the judge.

(2) Videotaped deposition of child. —

(A) In a proceeding involving an alleged offense against a child, the attorney for the Government, the child's attorney, the child's parent or legal guardian, or the guardian ad litem appointed under subsection (h) may apply for an order that a deposition be taken of the child's testimony and that the deposition be recorded and preserved on videotape.

(B)(i) Upon timely receipt of an application described in subparagraph (A), the court shall make a preliminary finding regarding whether at the time of trial the child is likely to be unable to testify in open court in the physical presence of the defendant, jury, judge, and public for any of the following reasons:

(I) The child will be unable to testify because of fear.

(II) There is a substantial likelihood, established by expert testimony, that the child would suffer emotional trauma from testifying in open court.

(III) The child suffers a mental or other infirmity.

(IV) Conduct by defendant or defense counsel causes the child to be unable to continue testifying.

(ii) If the court finds that the child is likely to be unable to testify in open court for any of the reasons stated in clause (i), the court shall order that the child's deposition be taken and preserved by videotape.

(iii) The trial judge shall preside at the videotape deposition of a child and shall rule on all questions as if at trial. The only other persons who may be permitted to be present at the proceeding are —

(I) the attorney for the Government;

(II) the attorney for the defendant;

(III) the child's attorney or guardian ad litem appointed under subsection (h);

(IV) persons necessary to operate the videotape equipment;

(V) subject to clause (iv), the defendant; and

(VI) other persons whose presence is determined by the court to be necessary to the welfare and well-being of the child.

The defendant shall be afforded the rights applicable to defendants during trial, including the right to an attorney, the right to be confronted with the witness against the defendant, and the right to cross-examine the child.

(iv) If the preliminary finding of inability under clause (i) is based on evidence that the child is unable to testify in the physical presence of the defendant, the court may order that the defendant, including a defendant represented pro se, be excluded from the room in which the deposition is conducted. If the court orders that the defendant be excluded from the deposition room, the court shall order that 2-way closed circuit television equipment relay the defendant's image into the room in which the child is testifying, and the child's testimony into the room in which the defendant is viewing the proceeding, and that the defendant be provided with a means of private, contemporaneous communication with the defendant's attorney during the deposition.

(v) Handling of videotape. — The complete record of the examination of the child, including the image and voices of all persons who in any way participate in the examination, shall be made and preserved on video tape in addition to being stenographically recorded. The videotape shall be transmitted to the clerk of the court in which the action is pending and shall be made available for viewing to the prosecuting attorney, the defendant, and the defendant's attorney during ordinary business hours.

(C) If at the time of trial the court finds that the child is unable to testify as for a reason described in subparagraph (B)(i), the court may admit into evidence the child's videotaped deposition in lieu of the child's testifying at the trial. The court shall support a ruling under this subparagraph with findings on the record.

(D) Upon timely receipt of notice that new evidence has been discovered after the original videotaping and before or during trial, the court, for good cause shown, may order an additional videotaped deposition. The testimony of the child shall be restricted to the matters specified by the court as the basis for granting the order.

(E) In connection with the taking of a videotaped deposition under this paragraph, the court may enter a protective order for the purpose of protecting the privacy of the child.

(F) The videotape of a deposition taken under this paragraph shall be destroyed 5 years after the date on which the trial court entered its judgment, but not before a final judgment is entered on appeal including Supreme Court review. The videotape shall become part of the court record and be kept by the court until it is destroyed.

(c) Competency examinations. —

(1) Effect on Federal Rules of Evidence. — Nothing in this subsection shall be construed to abrogate rule 601 of the Federal Rules of Evidence.

(2) Presumption. — A child is presumed to be competent.

(3) Requirement of written motion. — A competency examination regarding a child witness may be conducted by the court only upon written motion and offer of proof of incompetency by a party.

(4) Requirement of compelling reasons. — A competency examination regarding a child may be conducted only if the court determines, on the record, that

compelling reasons exist. A child's age alone is not a compelling reason.

(5) Persons permitted to be present. — The only persons who may be permitted to be present at a competency examination are —

(A) the judge;

(B) the attorney for the Government;

(C) the attorney for the defendant;

(D) a court reporter; and

(E) persons whose presence, in the opinion of the court, is necessary to the welfare and well-being of the child, including the child's attorney, guardian ad litem, or adult attendant.

(6) Not before jury. — A competency examination regarding a child witness shall be conducted out of the sight and hearing of a jury.

(7) Direct examination of child. — Examination of a child related to competency shall normally be conducted by the court on the basis of questions submitted by the attorney for the Government and the attorney for the defendant including a party acting as an attorney pro se. The court may permit an attorney but not a party acting as an attorney pro se to examine a child directly on competency if the court is satisfied that the child will not suffer emotional trauma as a result of the examination.

(8) Appropriate questions. — The questions asked at the competency examination of a child shall be appropriate to the age and developmental level of the child, shall not be related to the issues at trial, and shall focus on determining the child's ability to understand and answer simple questions.

(9) Psychological and psychiatric examinations. — Psychological and psychiatric examinations to assess the competency of a child witness shall not be ordered without a showing of compelling need.

(d) Privacy protection. —

(1) Confidentiality of information. —

(A) A person acting in a capacity described in subparagraph (B) in connection with a criminal proceeding shall —

(i) keep all documents that disclose the name or any other information concerning a child in a secure place to which no person who does not have reason to know their contents has access; and

(ii) disclose documents described in clause (i) or the information in them that concerns a child only to persons who, by reason of their participation in the proceeding, have reason to know such information.

(B) Subparagraph (A) applies to —

(i) all employees of the Government connected with the case, including employees of the Department of Justice, any law enforcement agency involved in the case, and any person hired by the Government to provide assistance in the proceeding;

(ii) employees of the court;

(iii) the defendant and employees of the defendant, including the attorney for the defendant and persons hired by the defendant or the attorney for the defendant to provide assistance in the proceeding; and

(iv) members of the jury.

(2) Filing under seal. — All papers to be filed in court that disclose the name of or any other information concerning a child shall be filed under seal without necessity of obtaining a court order. The person who makes the filing shall submit to the clerk of the court —

(A) the complete paper to be kept under seal; and

(B) the paper with the portions of it that disclose the name of or other information concerning a child redacted, to be placed in the public record.

(3) Protective orders. —

(A) On motion by any person the court may issue an order protecting a child from public disclosure of the name of or any other information concerning the child in the course of the proceedings, if the court determines that there is a significant possibility that such disclosure would be detrimental to the child.

(B) A protective order issued under subparagraph (A) may —

(i) provide that the testimony of a child witness, and the testimony of any other witness, when the attorney who calls the witness has reason to anticipate that the name of or any other information concerning a child may be divulged in the testimony, be taken in a closed courtroom; and

(ii) provide for any other measures that may be necessary to protect the privacy of the child.

(4) Disclosure of information. — This subsection does not prohibit disclosure of the name of or other information concerning a child to the defendant, the attorney for the defendant, a multidisciplinary child abuse team, a guardian ad litem, or an adult attendant, or to anyone to whom, in the opinion of the court, disclosure is necessary to the welfare and well-being of the child.

(e) Closing the courtroom. — When a child testifies the court may order the exclusion from the courtroom of all persons, including members of the press, who do not have a direct interest in the case. Such an order may be made if the court determines on the record that requiring the child to testify in open court would cause substantial psychological harm to the child or would result in the child's inability to effectively communicate. Such an order shall be narrowly tailored to serve the Government's specific compelling interest.

(f) Victim impact statement. — In preparing the presentence report pursuant to rule 32(c) of the Federal Rules of Criminal Procedure, the probation officer shall request information from the multidisciplinary child abuse team and other appropriate sources to determine the impact of the offense on the child victim and any other children who may have been affected. A guardian ad litem appointed under subsection (h) shall make every effort to obtain and report information that accurately expresses the child's and the family's views concerning the child's victimization. A guardian ad litem shall use forms that permit the child to express the child's views concerning the personal consequences of the child's victimization, at a level and in a form of communication commensurate with the child's age and ability.

(g) Use of multidisciplinary child abuse teams. —

(1) In general. — A multidisciplinary child abuse team shall be used when it is feasible to do so. The court shall work with State and local governments that have established multidisciplinary child abuse teams designed to assist child victims and child witnesses, and the court and the attorney for the Government shall consult with the multidisciplinary child abuse team as appropriate.

(2) Role of multidisciplinary child abuse teams. — The role of the multidisciplinary child abuse team shall be to provide for a child services that the members of the team in their professional roles are capable of providing, including —

(A) medical diagnoses and evaluation services, including provision or interpretation of x-rays, laboratory tests, and related services, as needed, and documentation of findings;

(B) telephone consultation services in emergencies and in other situations;

(C) medical evaluations related to abuse or neglect;

(D) psychological and psychiatric diagnoses and evaluation services for the child, parent or parents, guardian or guardians, or other caregivers, or any other individual involved in a child victim or child witness case;

(E) expert medical, psychological, and related professional testimony;

(F) case service coordination and assistance, including the location of services available from public and private agencies in the community; and

(G) training services for judges, litigators, court officers nd others that are involved in child victim and child witness cases, in handling child victims and child witnesses.

(h) Guardian ad litem. —

(1) In general. — The court may appoint a guardian ad litem for a child who was a victim of, or a witness to, a crime involving abuse or exploitation to protect the best interests of the child. In making the appointment, the court shall consider a prospective guardian's background in, and familiarity with, the judicial process, social service programs, and child abuse issues. The guardian ad litem shall not be a person who is or may be a witness in a proceeding involving the child for whom the guardian is appointed.

(2) Duties of guardian ad litem. — A guardian ad litem may attend all the depositions, hearings, and trial proceedings in which a child participates, and make recommendations to the court concerning the welfare of the child. The guardian ad litem may have access to all reports, evaluations and records, except attorney's work product, necessary to effectively advocate for the child. (The extent of access to grand jury materials is limited to the access routinely provided to victims and their representatives.) A guardian ad litem shall marshal and coordinate the delivery of resources and special services to the child. A guardian ad litem shall not be compelled to testify in any court action or proceeding concerning any information or opinion received from the child in the course of serving as a guardian ad litem.

(3) Immunities. — A guardian ad litem shall be presumed to be acting in good faith and shall be immune from civil and criminal liability for complying with the guardian's lawful duties described in paragraph (2).(i) Adult attendant. — A child testifying at or attending a judicial proceeding shall have the right to be accompanied by an adult attendant to provide emotional support to the child. The court, at its discretion, may allow the adult attendant to remain in close physical proximity to or in contact with the child while the child testifies. The court may allow the adult attendant to hold the child's hand or allow the child to sit on the adult attendant's lap throughout the course of the proceeding. An adult attendant shall not provide the child with an answer to any question directed to the child during the course of the child's testimony or otherwise prompt the child. The image of the child attendant, for the time the child is testifying or being deposed, shall be recorded on videotape.

(j) Speedy trial. — In a proceeding in which a child is called to give testimony, on motion by the attorney for the Government or a guardian ad litem, or on its own motion, the court may designate the case as being of special public importance. In cases so designated, the court shall, consistent with these rules, expedite the proceeding and ensure that it takes precedence over any other. The court shall ensure a speedy trial in order to minimize the length of time the child must endure the stress of involvement with the criminal process. When deciding whether to grant a continuance, the court shall take into consideration the age of the child and the potential adverse impact the delay may have on the child's well-being. The court shall make written findings of fact and conclusions of law when granting a continuance in cases involving a child.

(k) Stay of civil action. — If, at any time that a cause of action for recovery of compensation for damage or injury to the person of a child exists, a criminal action is pending which arises out of the same occurrence and in which the child is the victim, the civil action shall be stayed until the end of all phases of the criminal action and any mention of the civil action during the criminal proceeding is prohibited. As used in this subsection, a criminal action is pending until its final adjudication in the trial court.

(l) Testimonial aids. — The court may permit a child to use anatomical dolls, puppets, drawings, mannequins, or any other demonstrative device the court deems appropriate for the purpose of assisting a child in testifying.

(Pub. L. 101-647, Title II, §225(a), November 29, 1990, 104 Stat. 4798, and amended Pub. L. 103-322, Title XXXIII, §§330010(6), (7), 330011(e), 330018(b), September 13, 1994, 108 Stat. 2143, 2145, 2149; Pub. L. 104-294, Title VI, §605(h), October 11, 1996, 110 Stat. 3510.)

Defense of Marriage Act (DOMA)

1 U.S.C. §7 (2000) & 28 U.S.C. 1738(c) (2000)

Congress enacted the Defense of Marriage Act (DOMA) in 1996 in response to Baehr v. Lewin, 852

P.2d 44 (Haw. 1993) (holding that the denial of marriage licenses to same-sex couples implicates the Hawaii state constitution's equal protection clause which explicitly bars sex-based discrimination).

DOMA has two parts. First, the Act provides, for the first time, a federal definition of the terms "marriage" and "spouse" (for purposes of federal benefits) by specifying that marriage is a union of a man and a woman; the term "spouse" refers only to a person of the opposite sex. Second, the Act specifies that states are not required to give effect to same-sex marriages under the Full Faith and Credit Clause of the U.S. Constitution. DOMA rests on Congress's power (in art. IV, §1 of the United States Constitution) to implement the Full Faith and Credit Clause.

§7. Definition of "marriage" and "spouse"

In determining the meaning of any Act of Congress, or of any ruling, regulation, or interpretation of the various administrative bureaus and agencies of the United States, the word "marriage" means only a legal union between one man and one woman as husband and wife, and the word "spouse" refers only to a person of the opposite sex who is a husband or a wife.*(Pub. L. 104-199, §3(a), September 21, 1996, 110 Stat. 2419.)*

§1738C. Effect of public acts, records or judicial proceedings respecting same-sex relationships that are treated as marriage under state law

No State, territory, or possession of the United States, or Indian tribe, shall be required to give effect to any public act, record, or judicial proceeding of any other State, territory, possession, or tribe respecting a relationship between persons of the same sex that is treated as a marriage under the laws of such other State, territory, possession, or tribe, or a right or claim arising from such relationship.*(Pub. L. 104-199, §2(a), September 21, 1996, 110 Stat. 2419.)*

Family and Medical Leave Act (FMLA)

29 U.S.C. §§2601, 2611, 2612, 2614 (2000)

The Family and Medical Leave Act became law in 1993 after a lengthy battle. The Act allows eligible employees to take up to a total of twelve weeks of leave annually for the following reasons: (1) the birth of the employee's child and to care for such child, (2) the placement of a child with the employee for adoption or foster care, (3) the need to care for an immediate family member who has a "serious health condition," or (4) the employee's personal "serious health condition" that renders the employee unable to perform the functions of employment.

§2601. Congressional findings and purposes

(a) Findings. Congress finds that—

(1) the number of single-parent households and two-parent households in which the single parent or both parents work is increasing significantly;

(2) it is important for the development of children and the family unit that fathers and mothers be able to participate in early childrearing and the care of family members who have serious health conditions;

(3) the lack of employment policies to accommodate working parents can force individuals to choose between job security and parenting;

(4) there is inadequate job security for employees who have serious health conditions that prevent them from working for temporary periods;

(5) due to the nature of the roles of men and women in our society, the primary responsibility for family caretaking often falls on women, and such responsibility affects the working lives of women more than it affects the working lives of men; and

(6) employment standards that apply to one gender only have serious potential for encouraging employers to discriminate against employees and applicants for employment who are of that gender.

(b) Purposes. It is the purpose of this Act—

(1) to balance the demands of the workplace with the needs of families, to promote the stability and economic security of families, and to promote national interests in preserving family integrity;

(2) to entitle employees to take reasonable leave for medical reasons, for the birth or adoption of a child, and for the care of a child, spouse, or parent who has a serious health condition;

(3) to accomplish the purposes described in paragraphs (1) and (2) in a manner that accommodates the legitimate interests of employers;

(4) to accomplish the purposes described in paragraphs (1) and (2) in a manner that, consistent with the Equal Protection Clause of the Fourteenth Amendment, minimizes the potential for employment discrimination on the basis of sex by ensuring generally that leave is available for eligible medical reasons (including maternity-related disability) and for compelling family reasons, on a gender-neutral basis; and

(5) to promote the goal of equal employment opportunity for women and men, pursuant to such clause.

§2611. Definitions

As used in this subchapter:

(1) Commerce. The terms "commerce" and "industry or activity affecting commerce" mean any activity, business, or industry in commerce or in which a labor dispute would hinder or obstruct commerce or the free flow of commerce, and include "commerce" and any "industry affecting commerce", as defined in paragraphs (1) and (3) of section 142 of this title.

(2) Eligible employee.

(A) In general. The term "eligible employee" means an employee who has been employed —

(i) for at least 12 months by the employer with respect to whom leave is requested under section 2612 of this title; and

(ii) for at least 1,250 hours of service with such employer during the previous 12-month period.

(B) Exclusions. The term "eligible employee" does not include —

(i) any Federal officer or employee covered under subchapter V of chapter 63 of Title 5; or

(ii) any employee of an employer who is employed at a worksite at which such employer employs less than 50 employees if the total number of employees employed by that employer within 75 miles of that worksite is less than 50.

(C) Determination. For purposes of determining whether an employee meets the hours of service requirement specified in subparagraph (A)(ii), the legal standards established under section 207 of this title shall apply.

(3) Employ; employee; State. The terms "employ", "employee", and "State" have the same meanings given such terms in subsections (c), (e), and (g) of section 203 of this title.

(4) Employer.

(A) In general. The term "employer" —

(i) means any person engaged in commerce or in any industry or activity affecting commerce who employs 50 or more employees for each working day during each of 20 or more calendar workweeks in the current or preceding calendar year;

(ii) includes —

(I) any person who acts, directly or indirectly, in the interest of an employer to any of the employees of such employer; and

(II) any successor in interest of an employer;

(III) includes any "public agency", as defined in section 203(x) of this title; and

(IV) includes the General Accounting Office and the Library of Congress.

(B) Public agency. For purposes of subparagraph (A)(iii), a public agency shall be considered to be a person engaged in commerce or in an industry or activity affecting commerce.

(5) Employment benefits. The term "employment benefits" means all benefits provided or made available to employees by an employer, including group life insurance, health insurance, disability insurance, sick leave, annual leave, educational benefits, and pensions, regardless of whether such benefits are provided by a practice or written policy of an employer or through an "employee benefit plan", as defined in section 1002(3) of this title.

(6) Health care provider. The term "health care provider" means —

(A) a doctor of medicine or osteopathy who is authorized to practice medicine or surgery (as appropriate) by the State in which the doctor practices; or

(B) any other person determined by the Secretary to be capable of providing health care services.

(7) Parent. The term "parent" means the biological parent of an employee or an individual who stood in loco parentis to an employee when the employee was a son or daughter.

(8) Person. The term "person" has the same meaning given such term in section 203(a) of this title.

(9) Reduced leave schedule. The term "reduced leave schedule" means a leave schedule that reduces the usual number of hours per workweek, or hours per workday, of an employee.

(10) Secretary. The term "Secretary" means the Secretary of Labor.

(11) Serious health condition. The term "serious health condition" means an illness, injury, impairment, or physical or mental condition that involves —

(A) inpatient care in a hospital, hospice, or residential medical care facility; or

(B) continuing treatment by a health care provider.

(12) Son or daughter. The term "son or daughter" means a biological, adopted, or foster child, a stepchild, a legal ward, or a child of a person standing in loco parentis, who is —

(A) under 18 years of age; or

(B) 18 years of age or older and incapable of self-care because of a mental or physical disability.

(13) Spouse. The term "spouse" means a husband or wife, as the case may be.

(Pub. L. 103-3, Title I, §101, February 5, 1993, 107 Stat. 7; Pub. L. 104-1, Title II, §202(c)(1)(A), January 23, 1995, 109 Stat. 9.)

§2612. Nature of leave requirement

(a) In general.

(1) Entitlement to leave. Subject to section 2613 of this title, an eligible employee shall be entitled to a total of 12 workweeks of leave during any 12-month period for one or more of the following:

(A) Because of the birth of a son or daughter of the employee and in order to care for such son or daughter.

(B) Because of the placement of a son or daughter with the employee for adoption or foster care.

(C) In order to care for the spouse, or a son, daughter, or parent, of the employee, if such spouse, son, daughter, or parent has a serious health condition.

(D) Because of a serious health condition that makes the employee unable to perform the functions of the position of such employee.

(2) Expiration of entitlement. The entitlement to leave under subparagraphs (A) and (B) of paragraph (1) for a birth or placement of a son or daughter shall expire at the end of the 12-month period beginning on the date of such birth or placement.

(b) Leave taken intermittently or on reduced leave schedule.

(1) In general. Leave under subparagraph (A) or (B) of subsection (a)(1) of this section shall not be taken by an employee intermittently or on a reduced leave schedule unless the employee and the employer of the employee agree otherwise. Subject to paragraph (2), subsection (e)(2) of this section, and section 2613(b)(5) of this title, leave under subparagraph (C) or (D) of subsection (a)(1) of this section may be taken intermittently or on a reduced leave schedule when medically necessary. The taking of leave intermittently or on a reduced leave schedule pursuant to this paragraph shall not result in a reduction in

the total amount of leave to which the employee is entitled under subsection (a) of this section beyond the amount of leave actually taken.

(2) Alternative position. If an employee requests intermittent leave, or leave on a reduced leave schedule, under subparagraph (C) or (D) of subsection (a)(1) of this section, that is foreseeable based on planned medical treatment, the employer may require such employee to transfer temporarily to an available alternative position offered by the employer for which the employee is qualified and that —

(A) has equivalent pay and benefits; and

(B) better accommodates recurring periods of leave than the regular employment position of the employee.

(c) Unpaid leave permitted. Except as provided in subsection (d) of this section, leave granted under subsection (a) may consist of unpaid leave. Where an employee is otherwise exempt under regulations issued by the Secretary pursuant to section 213(a)(1) of this title, the compliance of an employer with this subchapter by providing unpaid leave shall not affect the exempt status of the employee under such section.

(d) Relationship to paid leave.

(1) Unpaid leave. If an employer provides paid leave for fewer than 12 workweeks, the additional weeks of leave necessary to attain the 12 workweeks of leave required under this subchapter may be provided without compensation.

(2) Substitution of paid leave.

(A) In general. An eligible employee may elect, or an employer may require the employee, to substitute any of the accrued paid vacation leave, personal leave, or family leave of the employee for leave provided under subparagraph (A), (B), or (C) of subsection (a)(1) of this section for any part of the 12-week period of such leave under such subsection.

(B) Serious health condition. An eligible employee may elect, or an employer may require the employee, to substitute any of the accrued paid vacation leave, personal leave, or medical or sick leave of the employee for leave provided under subparagraph (C) or (D) of subsection (a)(1) of this section for any part of the 12-week period of such leave under such subsection, except that nothing in this subchapter shall require an employer to provide paid sick leave or paid medical leave in any situation in which such employer would not normally provide any such paid leave.

(e) Foreseeable leave.

(1) Requirement of notice. In any case in which the necessity for leave under subparagraph (A) or (B) of subsection (a)(1) of this section is foreseeable based on an expected birth or placement, the employee shall provide the employer with not less than 30 days' notice, before the date the leave is to begin, of the employee's intention to take leave under such subparagraph, except that if the date of the birth or placement requires leave to begin in less than 30 days, the employee shall provide such notice as is practicable.

(2) Duties of employee. In any case in which the necessity for leave under subparagraph (C) or (D) of subsection (a)(1) of this section is foreseeable based on planned medical treatment, the employee —

(A) shall make a reasonable effort to schedule the treatment so as not to disrupt unduly the operations of the employer, subject to the approval of the health care provider of the employee or the health care provider of the son, daughter, spouse, or parent of the employee, as appropriate; and

(B) shall provide the employer with not less than 30 days' notice, before the date the leave is to begin, of the employee's intention to take leave under such subparagraph, except that if the date of the treatment requires leave to begin in less than 30 days, the employee shall provide such notice as is practicable.

(f) Spouses employed by same employer. In any case in which a husband and wife entitled to leave under subsection (a) of this section are employed by the same employer, the aggregate number of workweeks of leave to which both may be entitled may be limited to 12 workweeks during any 12-month period, if such leave is taken —

(1) under subparagraph (A) or (B) of subsection (a)(1) of this section; or

(2) to care for a sick parent under subparagraph (C) of such subsection.

(Pub. L. 103-3, Title I, §102, February 5, 1993, 107 Stat. 9.)

§2614. Employment and benefits protection

(a) Restoration to position

(1) In general. Except as provided in subsection (b) of this section, any eligible employee who takes leave under section 2612 of this title for the intended purpose of the leave shall be entitled, on return from such leave —

(A) to be restored by the employer to the position of employment held by the employee when the leave commenced; or

(B) to be restored to an equivalent position with equivalent employment benefits, pay, and other terms and conditions of employment.

(2) Loss of benefits. The taking of leave under section 2612 of this title shall not result in the loss of any employment benefit accrued prior to the date on which the leave commenced.

(3) Limitations. Nothing in this section shall be construed to entitle any restored employee to —

(A) the accrual of any seniority or employment benefits during any period of leave; or

(B) any right, benefit, or position of employment other than any right, benefit, or position to which the employee would have been entitled had the employee not taken the leave.

(4) Certification. As a condition of restoration under paragraph (1) for an employee who has taken leave under section 2612(a)(1)(D) of this title, the employer may have a uniformly applied practice or policy that requires each such employee to receive certification from the health care provider of the employee that the employee is able to resume work, except that nothing in this paragraph shall supersede a valid State or local law or a collective bargaining agreement that governs the return to work of such employees.

(5) Construction. Nothing in this subsection shall be construed to prohibit an employer from requiring an employee on leave under section 2612 of this title to report periodically to the employer on the status and intention of the employee to return to work.

(b) Exemption concerning certain highly compensated employees.

(1) Denial of restoration. An employer may deny restoration under subsection (a) of this section to any eligible employee described in paragraph (2) if—

(A) such denial is necessary to prevent substantial and grievous economic injury to the operations of the employer;

(B) the employer notifies the employee of the intent of the employer to deny restoration on such basis at the time the employer determines that such injury would occur; and

(C) in any case in which the leave has commenced, the employee elects not to return to employment after receiving such notice.

(2) Affected employees. An eligible employee described in paragraph (1) is a salaried eligible employee who is among the highest paid 10 percent of the employees employed by the employer within 75 miles of the facility at which the employee is employed.

(c) Maintenance of health benefits.

(1) Coverage. Except as provided in paragraph (2), during any period that an eligible employee takes leave under section 2612 of this title, the employer shall maintain coverage under any "group health plan" (as defined in section 5000(b)(1) of Title 26) for the duration of such leave at the level and under the conditions coverage would have been provided if the employee had continued in employment continuously for the duration of such leave.

(2) Failure to return from leave. The employer may recover the premium that the employer paid for maintaining coverage for the employee under such group health plan during any period of unpaid leave under section 2612 of this title if—

(A) the employee fails to return from leave under section 2612 of this title after the period of leave to which the employee is entitled has expired; and

(B) the employee fails to return to work for a reason other than—

(i) the continuation, recurrence, or onset of a serious health condition that entitles the employee to leave under subparagraph (C) or (D) of section 2612(a)(1) of this title; or

(ii) other circumstances beyond the control of the employee.

(3) Certification.

(A) Issuance. An employer may require that a claim that an employee is unable to return to work because of the continuation, recurrence, or onset of the serious health condition described in paragraph (2)(B)(i) be supported by—

(i) a certification issued by the health care provider of the son, daughter, spouse, or parent of the employee, as appropriate, in the case of an employee unable to return to work because of a condition specified in section 2612(a)(1)(C) of this title; or

(ii) a certification issued by the health care provider of the eligible employee, in the case of an employee unable to return to work because of a condition specified in section 2612(a)(1)(D) of this title.

(B) Copy. The employee shall provide, in a timely manner, a copy of such certification to the employer.

(C) Sufficiency of certification.

(i) Leave due to serious health condition of employee. The certification described in subparagraph (A)(ii) shall be sufficient if the certification states that a serious health condition prevented the employee from being able to perform the functions of the position of the employee on the date that the leave of the employee expired.

(ii) Leave due to serious health condition of family member. The certification described in subparagraph (A)(i) shall be sufficient if the certification states that the employee is needed to care for the son, daughter, spouse, or parent who has a serious health condition on the date that the leave of the employee expired.

(Pub. L. 103-3, Title I, §104, February 5, 1993, 107 Stat. 12.)

Pregnancy Discrimination Act

42 U.S.C. §2000e(k) (2000)

The Pregnancy Discrimination Act of 1978, 42 U.S.C. §2000e(k) (2000), amends the definitional section of Title VII of the Civil Rights Act of 1964, 42 U.S.C. §2000e-2 (2000), that prohibits, inter alia, sex discrimination in employment.

§2000e. Definitions

For the purposes of this subchapter —

(a) The term "person" includes one or more individuals, governments, governmental agencies, political subdivisions, labor unions, partnerships, associations, corporations, legal representatives, mutual companies, joint- stock companies, trusts, unincorporated organizations, trustees, trustees in cases under Title 11, or receivers.

(b) The term "employer" means a person engaged in an industry affecting commerce who has fifteen or more employees for each working day in each of twenty or more calendar weeks in the current or preceding calendar year, and any agent of such a person, but such term does not include (1) the United States, a corporation wholly owned by the Government of the United States, an Indian tribe, or any department or agency of the District of Columbia subject by statute to procedures of the competitive service (as defined in section 2102 of Title 5), or (2) a bona fide private membership club (other than a labor organization) which is exempt from taxation under section 501(c) of Title 26, except that during the first year after March 24, 1972, persons having fewer than twenty-five employees (and their agents) shall not be considered employers.

(c) The term "employment agency" means any person regularly undertaking with or without compensation to procure employees for an employer or to procure for employees opportunities to work for an employer and includes an agent of such a person.

(d) The term "labor organization" means a labor organization engaged in an industry affecting commerce, and any agent of such an organization, and includes any organization of any kind, any agency, or employee representation committee, group, association, or plan so engaged in which employees participate and which exists for the purpose, in whole or in part, of dealing with employers concerning grievances, labor disputes, wages, rates of pay, hours, or other terms or conditions of employment, and any conference, general committee, joint or system board, or joint council so engaged which is subordinate to a national or international labor organization.

(e) A labor organization shall be deemed to be engaged in an industry affecting commerce if (1) it maintains or operates a hiring hall or hiring office which procures employees for an employer or procures for employees opportunities to work for an employer, or (2) the number of its members (or, where it is a labor organization composed of other labor organizations or their representatives, if the aggregate number of the members of such other labor organization) is (A) twenty-five or more during the first year after March 24, 1972, or (B) fifteen or more thereafter, and such labor organization —

(1) is the certified representative of employees under the provisions of the National Labor Relations Act, as amended [29 U.S.C.A. §§151 et seq.], or the Railway Labor Act, as amended [45 U.S.C.A. §§151 et seq.];

(2) although not certified, is a national or international labor organization or a local labor organization recognized or acting as the representative of employees of an employer or employers engaged in an industry affecting commerce; or

(3) has chartered a local labor organization or subsidiary body which is representing or actively seeking to represent employees of employers within the meaning of paragraph (1) or (2); or

(4) has been chartered by a labor organization representing or actively seeking to represent employees within the meaning of paragraph (1) or (2) as the local or subordinate body through which such employees may enjoy membership or become affiliated with such labor organization; or

(5) is a conference, general committee, joint or system board, or joint council subordinate to a national or international labor organization, which includes a labor organization engaged in an industry affecting commerce within the meaning of any of the preceding paragraphs of this subsection.

(f) The term "employee" means an individual employed by an employer, except that the term "employee" shall not include any person elected to public office in any State or political subdivision of any State by the qualified voters thereof, or any person chosen by such officer to be on such officer's personal staff, or an appointee on the policy making level or an immediate adviser with respect to the exercise of the constitutional or legal powers of the office. The exemption set forth in the preceding sentence shall not include employees subject to the civil service laws of a State government, governmental agency or political subdivision. With respect to employment in a foreign country, such term includes an individual who is a citizen of the United States.

(g) The term "commerce" means trade, traffic, commerce, transportation, transmission, or communication among the several States; or between a State and any place outside thereof; or within the District of Columbia, or a possession of the United States; or between points in the same State but through a point outside thereof.

(h) The term "industry affecting commerce" means any activity, business, or industry in commerce or in which a labor dispute would hinder or obstruct commerce or the free flow of commerce and includes any activity or industry "affecting commerce" within the meaning of the Labor-Management Reporting and Disclosure Act of 1959 [29 U.S.C.A. §§401 et seq.], and further includes any governmental industry, business, or activity.

(i) The term "State" includes a State of the United States, the District of Columbia, Puerto Rico, the Virgin Islands, American Samoa, Guam, Wake Island, the Canal Zone, and Outer Continental Shelf lands defined in the Outer Continental Shelf Lands Act [43 U.S.C.A. §§1331 et seq.].

(j) The term "religion" includes all aspects of religious observance and practice, as well as belief, unless an employer demonstrates that he is unable to reasonably accommodate to an employee's or prospective employee's religious observance or practice without undue hardship on the conduct of the employer's business.

(k) The terms "because of sex" or "on the basis of sex" include, but are not limited to, because of or on the basis of pregnancy, childbirth, or related medical conditions; and women affected by pregnancy, childbirth, or related medical conditions shall be treated the same for all employment-related purposes, including receipt of benefits under fringe benefit programs, as other persons not so affected but similar in their ability or inability to work, and nothing in section 2000e-2(h) of this title shall be interpreted to permit otherwise. This subsection shall not require an employer to pay for health insurance benefits for abortion, except where the life of the mother would be endangered if the fetus were carried to term, or except where medical complications have arisen from an abortion: Provided, That nothing herein shall preclude an employer from providing abortion benefits or otherwise affect bargaining agreements in regard to abortion.

(l) The term "complaining party" means the Commission, the Attorney General, or a person who may bring an action or proceeding under this subchapter.

(m) The term "demonstrates" means meets the burdens of production and persuasion.

(n) The term "respondent" means an employer, employment agency, labor organization, joint labor-management committee controlling apprenticeship or other training or retraining program, including an on-the-job training program, or Federal entity subject to section 2000e-16 of this title.

(Pub. L. 88-352, Title VII, §701, July 2, 1964, 78 Stat. 253; Pub. L. 89-554, §8(a), September 6, 1966, 80 Stat. 662; Pub. L. 92-261, §2, March 24, 1972, 86 Stat. 103; Pub. L. 95-555, §1, October 31, 1978, 92 Stat. 2076; Pub. L. 95-598, Title III, §330, November 6, 1978, 92 Stat. 2679; Pub. L. 99-514, §2, October 22, 1986, 100 Stat. 2095; Pub. L. 102-166, Title I, §§104, 109(a), November 21, 1991, 105 Stat. 1074, 1077.)

Title VII of the Civil Rights Act of 1964

42 U.S.C. §2000e-2 (2000)

"Unlawful employment practices"

(a) Employer practices. —It shall be an unlawful employment practice for an employer —

(1) to fail or refuse to hire or to discharge any individual, or otherwise to discriminate against any individual with respect to his compensation, terms, conditions, or privileges of employment, because of such individual's race, color, religion, sex, or national origin; or

(2) to limit, segregate, or classify his employees or applicants for employment in any way which would deprive or tend to deprive any individual of employment opportunities or otherwise adversely affect his status as an employee, because of such individual's race, color, religion, sex, or national origin.

(b) Employment agency practices. —It shall be an unlawful employment practice for an employment agency to fail or refuse to refer for employment, or otherwise to discriminate against, any individual because of his race, color, religion, sex, or national origin, or to classify or refer for employment any individual on the basis of his race, color, religion, sex, or national origin.

(c) Labor organization practices. —It shall be an unlawful employment practice for a labor organization —

(1) to exclude or to expel from its membership, or otherwise to discriminate against, any individual because of his race, color, religion, sex, or national origin;

(2) to limit, segregate, or classify its membership or applicants for membership, or to classify or fail or refuse to refer for employment any individual, in any way which would deprive or tend to deprive any individual of employment opportunities, or would limit such employment opportunities or otherwise adversely affect his status as an employee or as an applicant for employment, because of such individual's race, color, religion, sex, or national origin; or

(3) to cause or attempt to cause an employer to discriminate against an individual in violation of this section.

(d) Training programs. — It shall be an unlawful employment practice for any employer, labor organization, or joint labor-management committee controlling apprenticeship or other training or retraining, including on-the-job training programs to discriminate against any individual because of his race, color, religion, sex, or national origin in admission to, or employment in, any program established to provide apprenticeship or other training.

(e) Businesses or enterprises with personnel qualified on basis of religion, sex, or national origin; educational institutions with personnel of particular religion. — Notwithstanding any other provision of this subchapter,

(1) it shall not be an unlawful employment practice for an employer to hire and employ employees, for an employment agency to classify, or refer for employment any individual, for a labor organization to classify its membership or to classify or refer for employment any individual, or for an employer, labor organization, or joint labor-management committee controlling apprenticeship or other training or retraining programs to admit or employ any individual in any such program, on the basis of his religion, sex, or national origin in those certain instances where religion, sex, or national origin is a bona fide occupational qualification reasonably necessary to the normal operation of that particular business or enterprise, and

(2) it shall not be an unlawful employment practice for a school, college, university, or other educational institution or institution of learning to hire and employ employees of a particular religion if such school, college, university, or other educational institution or institution of learning is, in whole or in substantial part, owned, supported, controlled, or managed by a particular religion or by a particular religious corporation, association, or society, or if the curriculum of such school, college, university, or other educational institution or institution of learning is directed toward the propagation of a particular religion.

(f) Members of Communist Party or Communist-action or Communist-front organizations — As used in this subchapter, the phrase "unlawful employment practice" shall not be deemed to include any action or measure taken by an employer, labor organization, joint labor-management committee, or employment agency with respect to an individual who is a member of the Communist Party of the United States or of any other organization required to register as a Communist-action or Communist-front organization by final order of the Subversive Activities Control Board pursuant to the Subversive Activities Control Act of 1950 [50 U.S.C.A. §§781 et seq.].

(g) National security. — Notwithstanding any other provision of this subchapter, it shall not be an unlawful employment practice for an employer to fail or refuse to hire and employ any individual for any position, for an employer to discharge any individual from any position, or for an employment agency to fail or refuse to refer any individual for employment in any position, or for a labor organization to fail or refuse to refer any individual for employment in any position, if —

(1) the occupancy of such position, or access to the premises in or upon which any part of the duties of such position is performed or is to be performed, is subject to any requirement imposed in the interest of the national security of the United States under any security program in effect pursuant to or administered under any statute of the United States or any Executive order of the President; and

(2) such individual has not fulfilled or has ceased to fulfill that requirement.

(h) Seniority or merit system; quantity or quality of production; ability tests; compensation based on sex and authorized by minimum wage provisions. — Notwithstanding any other provision of this subchapter, it shall not be an unlawful employment practice for an employer to apply different standards of compensation, or different terms, conditions, or privileges of employment pursuant to a bona fide seniority or merit system, or a system which measures earnings by quantity or quality of production or to employees who work in different locations, provided that such differences are not the result of an intention to discriminate because of race, color, religion, sex, or national origin, nor shall it be an unlawful employment practice for an employer to give and to act upon the results of any professionally developed ability test provided that such test, its administration or action upon the results is not designed, intended or used to discriminate because of race, color, religion, sex or national origin. It shall not be an unlawful employment practice under this subchapter for any employer to differentiate upon the basis of sex in determining the amount of the wages or compensation paid or to be paid to employees of such employer if such differentiation is authorized by the provisions of section 206(d) of Title 29.

(i) Businesses or enterprises extending preferential treatment to Indians. —Nothing contained in this subchapter shall apply to any business or enterprise on or near an Indian reservation with respect to any publicly announced employment practice of such business or enterprise under which a preferential treatment is given to any individual because he is an Indian living on or near a reservation.

(j) Preferential treatment not to be granted on account of existing number or percentage imbalance. — Nothing contained in this subchapter shall be interpreted to require any employer, employment agency, labor organization, or joint labor-management committee subject to this subchapter to grant preferential treatment to any individual or to any group because of the race, color, religion, sex, or national origin of such individual or group on account of an imbalance which may exist with respect to the total number or percentage of persons of any race, color, religion, sex, or national origin employed by any employer, referred or classified for employment by any employment agency or labor organization, admitted to membership or classified by any labor organization, or admitted to, or employed in, any apprenticeship or other training program, in comparison with the total number or percentage of persons of such race, color, religion, sex, or national origin in any community, State, section, or other area, or in the available work force in any community, State, section, or other area.

(k) Burden of proof in disparate impact cases.

(1)(A) An unlawful employment practice based on disparate impact is established under this subchapter only if—

(i) a complaining party demonstrates that a respondent uses a particular employment practice that causes a disparate impact on the basis of race, color, religion, sex, or national origin and the respondent fails to demonstrate that the challenged practice is job related for the position in question and consistent with business necessity; or

(ii) the complaining party makes the demonstration de scribed in subparagraph (C) with respect to an alternative employment practice and the respondent refuses to adopt such alternative employment practice.

(B)(i) With respect to demonstrating that a particular employment practice causes a disparate impact as described in subparagraph (A)(i), the complaining party shall demonstrate that each particular challenged employment practice causes a disparate impact, except that if the complaining party can demonstrate to the court that the elements of a respondent's decisionmaking process are not capable of separation for analysis, the decisionmaking process may be analyzed as one employment practice.

(ii) If the respondent demonstrates that a specific employment practice does not cause the disparate impact, the respondent shall not be required to demonstrate that such practice is required by business necessity.

(C)(i) The demonstration referred to by subparagraph (A)(ii) shall be in accordance with the law as it existed on June 4, 1989, with respect to the concept of "alternative employment practice".

(ii) A demonstration that an employment practice is required by business necessity may not be used as a defense against a claim of intentional discrimination under this subchapter.

(iii) Notwithstanding any other provision of this subchapter, a rule barring the employment of an individual who currently and knowingly uses or possesses a controlled substance, as defined in schedules I and II of section 102(6) of the Controlled Substances Act (21 U.S.C. §802(6)), other than the use or possession of a drug taken under the supervision of a licensed health care professional, or any other use or possession authorized by the Controlled Substances Act [21 U.S.C.A. §§801 et seq.] or any other provision of Federal law, shall be considered an unlawful employment practice under this subchapter only if such rule is adopted or applied with an intent to discriminate because of race, color, religion, sex, or national origin.

(l) Prohibition of discriminatory use of test scores. — It shall be an unlawful employment practice for a respondent, in connection with the selection or referral of applicants or candidates for employment or promotion, to adjust the scores of, use different cutoff scores for, or otherwise alter the results of, employment related tests on the basis of race, color, religion, sex, or national origin.

(m) Impermissible consideration of race, color, religion, sex, or national origin in employment practices. —Except as otherwise provided in this subchapter, an unlawful employment practice is established when the complaining party demonstrates that race, color, religion, sex, or national origin was a motivating factor for any employment practice, even though other factors also motivated the practice.

(n) Resolution of challenges to employment practices implementing litigated or consent judgments or orders

(1)(A) Notwithstanding any other provision of law, and except as provided in paragraph (2), an employment practice that implements and is within the scope of a litigated or consent judgment or order that resolves a claim of employment discrimination under the Constitution or Federal civil rights laws may not be challenged under the circumstances described in subparagraph (B).

(B) A practice described in subparagraph (A) may not be challenged in a claim under the Constitution or Federal civil rights laws —

(i) by a person who, prior to the entry of the judgment or order described in subparagraph (A), had —

(I) actual notice of the proposed judgment or order sufficient to apprise such person that such judgment or order might adversely affect the interests and legal rights of such person and that an opportunity was available to present objections to such judgment or order by a future date certain; and

(II) a reasonable opportunity to present objections to such judgment or order; or

(ii) by a person whose interests were adequately represented by another person who had previously challenged the judgment or order on the same legal grounds and with a similar factual situation, unless there has been an intervening change in law or fact.

(2) Nothing in this subsection shall be construed to —

(A) alter the standards for intervention under rule 24 of the Federal Rules of Civil Procedure or apply to the rights of parties who have successfully intervened pursuant to such rule in the proceeding in which the parties intervened;

(B) apply to the rights of parties to the action in which a litigated or consent judgment or order was entered, or of members of a class represented or sought to be represented in such action, or of members of a group on whose behalf relief was sought in such action by the Federal Government;

(C) prevent challenges to a litigated or consent judgment or order on the ground that such judgment or order was obtained through collusion or fraud, or is transparently invalid or was entered by a court lacking subject matter jurisdiction; or

(D) authorize or permit the denial to any person of the due process of law required by the Constitution.

(3) Any action not precluded under this subsection that challenges an employment consent judgment or order described in paragraph (1) shall be brought in the court, and if possible before the judge, that entered such judgment or order. Nothing in this subsection shall preclude a transfer of such action pursuant to section 1404 of Title 28.

(Pub. L. 88-352, Title VII, §703, July 2, 1964, 78 Stat. 255; Pub. L. 92-261, §8(a), (b), March 24, 1972, 86 Stat. 109; Pub. L. 102-166, Title I, §§105(a), 106, 107(a), 108, November 21, 1991, 105 Stat. 1074-1076.)

International Parenting Kidnapping Act (IPKA)

18 U.S.C. §1204 (2000)

Congress enacted the International Parenting Kidnapping Act in 1993 to address international child abduction. IPKA makes it a federal felony for a parent wrongfully to remove or retain a child outside the United States. The IPKA permits several affirmative defenses: if the defendant has been granted custody or visitation by a court acting pursuant to the Uniform Child Custody Jurisdiction Act; or is fleeing from domestic violence; or had court-ordered custody and failed to return the child because of circumstances beyond the defendant's control, provided that the defendant made reasonable attempts to notify the other parent.

§1204. International parental kidnapping

(a) Whoever removes a child from the United States or retains a child (who has been in the United States) outside the United States with intent to obstruct the lawful exercise of parental rights shall be fined under this title or imprisoned not more than 3 years, or both.

(b) As used in this section —

(1) the term "child" means a person who has not attained the age of 16 years; and

(2) the term "parental rights", with respect to a child, means the right to physical custody of the child —

(A) whether joint or sole (and includes visiting rights); and

(B) whether arising by operation of law, court order, or legally binding agreement of the parties.

(c) It shall be an affirmative defense under this section that —

(1) the defendant acted within the provisions of a valid court order granting the defendant legal custody or visitation rights and that order was obtained pursuant to the Uniform Child Custody Jurisdiction Act and was in effect at the time of the offense;

(2) the defendant was fleeing an incidence or pattern of domestic violence;

(3) the defendant had physical custody of the child pursuant to a court order granting legal custody or visitation rights and failed to return the child as a result of circumstances beyond the defendant's control, and the defendant notified or made reasonable attempts to notify the other parent or lawful custodian of the child of such circumstances within 24 hours after the visitation period had expired and returned the child as soon as possible.

(d) This section does not detract from The Hague Convention on the Civil Aspects of International Parental Child Abduction, done at The Hague on October 25, 1980.

(Pub. L. 103-173, §2(a), December 2, 1993, 107 Stat. 1998.)

Wiretap Act, Title III, Omnibus Crime Control Act

18 U.S.C. §§2510 et seq. (2000)

Congress enacted Title III (known as the "Wiretap Act") to protect individuals from nonconsensual interception of wire or oral communications. With certain exceptions (e.g., law enforcement officers by court order), the Act imposes civil and criminal liability by the creation of a new tort, a new crime, and evidentiary rules excluding use of the contents. The United States Supreme Court has not yet reconciled the split in the federal courts of appeal concerning the existence of interspousal civil or criminal liability under the Act. Many states have enacted statutes similar to the federal law.

§2510. Definitions

As used in this chapter [18 USCS §§2510 et seq.] —

(1) "wire communication" means any aural transfer made in whole or in part through the use of facilities for the transmission of communications by the aid of wire, cable, or other like connection between the point of origin and the point of reception (including the use of such connection in a switching station) furnished or operated by any person engaged in providing or operating such facilities for the transmission of interstate or foreign communications or communications affecting interstate or foreign commerce;

(2) "oral communication" means any oral communication uttered by a person exhibiting an expectation that such communication is not subject to interception under circumstances justifying such expectation, but such term does not include any electronic communication;

(3) "State" means any State of the United States, the District of Columbia, the Commonwealth of Puerto Rico, and any territory or possession of the United States;

(4) "intercept" means the aural or other acquisition of the contents of any wire, electronic, or oral communication through the use of any electronic, mechanical, or other device.

(5) "electronic, mechanical, or other device" means any device or apparatus which can be used to intercept a wire, oral, or electronic communication other than —

(A) any telephone or telegraph instrument, equipment or facility, or any component thereof,

(i) furnished to the subscriber or user by a provider of wire or electronic communication service in the ordinary course of its business and being used by the subscriber or user in the ordinary course of its business or furnished by such subscriber or user for connection to the facilities of such service and used in the ordinary course of its business; or

(ii) being used by a provider of wire or electronic communication service in the ordinary course of its business, or by an investigative or law enforcement officer in the ordinary course of his duties;

(B) a hearing aid or similar device being used to correct subnormal hearing to not better than normal;

(6) "person" means any employee, or agent of the United States or any State or political subdivision thereof, and any individual, partnership, association, joint stock company, trust, or corporation;

(7) "Investigative or law enforcement officer" means any officer of the United States or of a State or political subdivision thereof, who is empowered by law to conduct investigations of or to make arrests for offenses enumerated in this chapter [18 USCS §§2510 et seq.], and any attorney authorized by law to prosecute or participate in the prosecution of such offenses;

(8) "contents", when used with respect to any wire, oral, or electronic communication, includes any information concerning the substance, purport, or meaning of that communication;

(9) "Judge of competent jurisdiction" means —

(A) a judge of a United States district court or a United States court of appeals; and

(B) a judge of any court of general criminal jurisdiction of a State who is authorized by a statute of that State to enter orders authorizing interceptions of wire, oral, or electronic communications;

(10) "communication common carrier" shall have the same meaning which is given the term "common carrier" by section 153(h) of title 47 of the United States Code;

(11) "aggrieved person" means a person who was a party to any intercepted wire, oral, or electronic communication or a person against whom the interception was directed;

(12) "electronic communication" means any transfer of signs, signals, writing, images, sounds, data, or intelligence of any nature transmitted in whole or in part by a wire, radio, electromagnetic, photoelectronic or photooptical system that affects interstate or foreign commerce, but does not include —

(A) any wire or oral communication;

(B) any communication made through a tone-only paging device;

(C) any communication from a tracking device (as defined in section 3117 of this title); or

(D) electronic funds transfer information stored by a financial institution in a communications system used for the electronic storage and transfer of funds;

(13) "user" means any person or entity who —

(A) uses an electronic communication service; and

(B) is duly authorized by the provider of such service to engage in such use;

(14) "electronic communications system" means any wire, radio, electromagnetic, photo-optical or photoelectronic facilities for the transmission of wire or electronic communications, and any computer facilities or related electronic equipment for the electronic storage of such communications;

(15) "electronic communication service" means any service which provides to users thereof the ability to send or receive wire or electronic communications;

(16) "readily accessible to the general public" means, with respect to a radio communication, that such communication is not —

(A) scrambled or encrypted;

(B) transmitted using modulation techniques whose essential parameters have been withheld from the public with the intention of preserving the privacy of such communication;

(C) carried on a subcarrier or other signal subsidiary to a radio transmission;

(D) transmitted over a communication system provided by a common carrier, unless the communication is a tone only paging system communication; or

(E) transmitted on frequencies allocated under part 25, subpart D, E, or F of part 74, or part 94 of the Rules of the Federal Communications Commission, unless, in the case of a communication transmitted on a frequency allocated under part 74 that is not exclusively allocated to broadcast auxiliary services, the communication is a two-way voice communication by radio;

(F) [Deleted]

(17) "electronic storage" means —

(A) any temporary, intermediate storage of a wire or electronic communication incidental to the electronic transmission thereof; and

(B) any storage of such communication by an electronic communication service for purposes of backup protection of such communication;

(18) "aural transfer" means a transfer containing the human voice at any point between and including the point of origin and the point of reception;

(19) "foreign intelligence information", for purposes of section 2517(6) of this title, means —

(A) information, whether or not concerning a United States person, that relates to the ability of the United States to protect against —

(i) actual or potential attack or other grave hostile acts of a foreign power or an agent of a foreign power;

(ii) sabotage or international terrorism by a foreign power or an agent of a foreign power; or

(iii) clandestine intelligence activities by an intelligence service or network of a foreign power or by an agent of a foreign power; or

(B) information, whether or not concerning a United States person, with respect to a foreign power or foreign territory that relates to —

(i) the national defense or the security of the United States; or

(ii) the conduct of the foreign affairs of the United States;

(20) "protected computer" has the meaning set forth in section 1030; and

(21) "computer trespasser" —

(A) means a person who accesses a protected computer without authorization and thus has no reasonable expectation of privacy in any communication transmitted to, through, or from the protected computer; and

(B) does not include a person known by the owner or operator of the protected computer to have an existing contractual relationship with the owner or operator of the protected computer for access to all or part of the protected computer.

(Pub. L. 90-351, Title III, §802, June 19, 1968, 82 Stat. 212; October. 21, 1986, Pub. L. 99-508, Title I, §101(a), (c)(1)(A), (4) 100 Stat. 1848, 1851. Amended October 25, 1994, Pub. L. 103-414, Title II, §§202(a), 203, 108 Stat. 4290, 4291; April 24, 1996, Pub. L. 104-132, Title VII, Subtitle B, §731, 110 Stat. 1303; October 26, 2001, Pub. L. 107-56, Title II, §§203(b)(2), 209(1), and 217(1), 115 Stat. 280, 283, 291; December 28, 2001, Pub. L. 107-108, Title III, §314(b), 115 Stat. 1402.)

§2511. Prohibition on the interception and disclosure of wire, oral, or electronic communications

(1) Except as otherwise specifically provided in this chapter [18 USCS §§2510 et seq.] any person who —

(a) intentionally intercepts, endeavors to intercept, or procures any other person to intercept or endeavor to intercept, any wire, oral, or electronic communication;

(b) intentionally uses, endeavors to use, or procures any other person to use or endeavor to use any electronic, mechanical, or other device to intercept any oral communication when —

(i) such device is affixed to, or otherwise transmits a signal through, a wire, cable, or other like connection used in wire communication; or

(ii) such device transmits communications by radio, or interferes with the transmission of such communication; or

(iii) such person knows, or has reason to know, that such device or any component thereof has been sent through the mail or transported in interstate or foreign commerce; or

(iv) such use or endeavor to use

(A) takes place on the premises of any business or other commercial establishment the operations of which affect interstate or foreign commerce; or

(B) obtains or is for the purpose of obtaining information relating to the operations of any business or other commercial establishment the operations of which affect interstate or foreign commerce; or

(v) such person acts in the District of Columbia, the Commonwealth of Puerto Rico, or any territory or possession of the United States;

(c) intentionally discloses, or endeavors to disclose, to any other person the contents of any wire, oral, or electronic communication, knowing or having reason to know that the information was obtained through the interception of a wire, oral, or electronic communication in violation of this subsection;

(d) intentionally uses, or endeavors to use, the contents of any wire, oral, or electronic communication, knowing or having reason to know that the information was obtained through the interception of a wire, oral, or electronic communication in violation of this subsection; or

(e)(i) intentionally discloses, or endeavors to disclose, to any other person the contents of any wire, oral, or electronic communication, intercepted by means authorized by sections 2511(2)(a)(ii), 2511(2)(b)-(c), 2511(2)(e), 2516, and 2518 of this chapter,

(ii) knowing or having reason to know that the information was obtained through the interception of such a communication in connection with a criminal investigation,

(iii) having obtained or received the information in connection with a criminal investigation, and

(iv) with intent to improperly obstruct, impede, or interfere with a duly authorized criminal investigation, shall be punished as provided in subsection (4) or shall be subject to suit as provided in subsection (5).

(2)(a)(i) It shall not be unlawful under this chapter [18 USCS §§2510 et seq.] for an operator of a switchboard, or an officer, employee, or agent of a provider of wire or electronic communication service, whose facilities are used in the transmission of a wire or electronic communication, to intercept, disclose, or use that communication in the normal course of his employment while engaged in any activity which is a necessary incident to the rendition of his service or to the protection of the rights or property of the provider of that service, except that a provider of wire communication service to the public shall not utilize service observing or random monitoring except for mechanical or service quality control checks.

(ii) Notwithstanding any other law, providers of wire or electronic communication service, their officers, employees, and agents, landlords, custodians, or other persons, are authorized to provide information, facilities, or technical assistance to persons authorized by law to intercept wire, oral, or electronic communications or to conduct electronic surveillance, as defined in section 101 of the Foreign Intelligence Surveillance Act of 1978 [50 USCS §1801] if such provider, its officers, employees, or agents, landlord, custodian, or other specified person, has been provided with —

(A) a court order directing such assistance signed by the authorizing judge, or

(B) a certification in writing by a person specified in section 2518(7) of this title or the Attorney General of the United States that no warrant or court order is required by law, that all statutory requirements have been met, and that the specified assistance is required,

setting forth the period of time during which the provision of the information, facilities, or technical assistance is authorized and specifying the information, facilities, or technical assistance required. No provider of wire or electronic communication service, officer, employee, or agent thereof, or landlord, custodian, or other specified person shall disclose the existence of any interception or surveillance or the device used to accomplish the interception or surveillance with respect to which the person has been furnished an order or certification under this subparagraph, except as may otherwise be required by legal process and then only after prior notification to the Attorney General or to the principal prosecuting attorney of a State or any political subdivision of a State, as may be appropriate. Any such disclosure, shall render such person liable for the civil damages provided for in section 2520. No cause of action shall lie in any court against any provider of wire or electronic communication service, its officers, employees, or agents, landlord, custodian, or other specified person for providing information, facilities, or assistance in accordance with the terms of a court order or certification under this chapter [18 USCS §§2510 et seq.].

(b) It shall not be unlawful under this chapter [18 USCS §§2510 et seq.] for an officer, employee, or agent of the Federal Communications Commission, in the normal course of his employment and in discharge of the monitoring responsibilities exercised by the Commission in the enforcement of chapter 5 of title 47 [47 USCS §§151 et seq.] of the United States Code, to intercept a wire or electronic communication, or oral communication transmitted by radio, or to disclose or use the information thereby obtained.

(c) It shall not be unlawful under this chapter [18 USCS §§2510 et seq.] for a person acting under color of law to intercept a wire, oral, or electronic communication, where such person is a party to the communication or one of the parties to the communication has given prior consent to such interception.

(d) It shall not be unlawful under this chapter [18 USCS §§2510 et seq.] for a person not acting under color of law to intercept a wire, oral, or electronic communication where such person is a party to the communication or where one of the parties to the communication has given prior consent to such interception unless such communication is intercepted for the purpose of committing any criminal or tortious act in violation of the Constitution or laws of the United States or of any State.

(e) Notwithstanding any other provision of this title or section 705 or 706 of the Communications Act of 1934 [47 USCS §605 or 606], it shall not be unlawful for an officer, employee, or agent of the United States in the normal course of his official duty to conduct electronic surveillance, as defined in section 101 of the Foreign Intelligence Surveillance Act of 1978 [50 USCS §1801], as authorized by that Act [50 USCS §§1801 et seq.].

(f) Nothing contained in this chapter or chapter 121 or 206 of this title [18 USCS §§2510 et seq., or 2701 et seq., or 3121 et seq.], or section 705 of the Communications Act of 1934 [47 USCS §605], shall be deemed to affect the acquisition by the United States Government of foreign intelligence information from international or foreign communications, or foreign intelligence activities conducted in accordance with otherwise applicable Federal law involving a foreign electronic communications system, utilizing a means other than electronic surveillance as defined in section 101 of the Foreign Intelligence Surveillance Act of 1978 [50 USCS §1801], and procedures in this chapter or chapter 121 or 206 of this title [18 USCS §§2510 et seq., or 2701 et seq., or 3121 et seq.] and the Foreign Intelligence Surveillance Act of 1978 [50 USCS §§1801 et seq.] shall be the exclusive means by which electronic surveillance, as defined in section 101 of such Act [50 USCS §1801], and the interception of domestic wire, oral, and electronic communications may be conducted.

(g) It shall not be unlawful under this chapter [18 USCS §§2510 et seq.] or chapter 121 of this title [18 USCS §§2701 et seq.] for any person —

(i) to intercept or access an electronic communication made through an electronic communication system that is configured so that such electronic communication is readily accessible to the general public;

(ii) to intercept any radio communication which is transmitted —

(I) by any station for the use of the general public, or that relates to ships, aircraft, vehicles, or persons in distress;

(II) by any governmental, law enforcement, civil defense, private land mobile, or public safety communications system, including police and fire, readily accessible to the general public;

(III) by a station operating on an authorized frequency within the bands allocated to the amateur, citizens band, or general mobile radio services; or

(IV) by any marine or aeronautical communications system;

(iii) to engage in any conduct which —

(I) is prohibited by section 633 of the Communications Act of 1934 [47 USCS §553]; or

(II) is excepted from the application of section 705(a) of the Communications Act of 1934 [47 USCS §605(a)] by section 705(b) of that Act [47 USCS §605(b)];

(iv) to intercept any wire or electronic communication the transmission of which is causing harmful interference to any lawfully operating station or consumer electronic equipment, to the extent necessary to identify the source of such interference; or

(v) for other users of the same frequency to intercept any radio communication made through a system that utilizes frequencies monitored by individuals engaged in the provision or the use of such system, if such communication is not scrambled or encrypted.

(h) It shall not be unlawful under this chapter [18 USCS §§2510 et seq.] —

(i) to use a pen register or a trap and trace device (as those terms are defined for the purposes of chapter 206 (relating to pen registers and trap and trace devices) of this title) [18 USCS §§3121 et seq.]; or

(ii) for a provider of electronic communication service to record the fact that a wire or electronic communication was initiated or completed in order to protect such provider, another provider furnishing service toward the completion of the wire or electronic communication, or a user of that service, from fraudulent, unlawful or abusive use of such service.

(i) It shall not be unlawful under this chapter [18 USCS §§2510 et seq.] for a person acting under color of law to intercept the wire or electronic communications of a computer trespasser transmitted to, through, or from the protected computer, if —

(i) the owner or operator of the protected computer authorizes the interception of the computer trespasser's communications on the protected computer;

(ii) the person acting under color of law is lawfully engaged in an investigation;

(iii) the person acting under color of law has reasonable grounds to believe that the contents of the computer trespasser's communications will be relevant to the investigation; and

(iv) such interception does not acquire communications other than those transmitted to or from the computer trespasser.

(3)(a) Except as provided in paragraph (b) of this subsection, a person or entity providing an electronic communication service to the public shall not intentionally divulge the contents of any communication (other than one to such person or entity, or an agent thereof) while in transmission on that service to any person or entity other than an addressee or intended recipient of such communication or an agent of such addressee or intended recipient.

(b) A person or entity providing electronic communication service to the public may divulge the contents of any such communication —

(i) as otherwise authorized in section 2511(2)(a) or 2517 of this title;

(ii) with the lawful consent of the originator or any addressee or intended recipient of such communication;

(iii) to a person employed or authorized, or whose facilities are used, to forward such communication to its destination; or

(iv) which were inadvertently obtained by the service provider and which appear to pertain to the commission of a crime, if such divulgence is made to a law enforcement agency.

(4)(a) Except as provided in paragraph (b) of this subsection or in subsection (5), whoever violates subsection (1) of this section shall be fined under this title or imprisoned not more than five years, or both.

(b) If the offense is a first offense under paragraph (a) of this subsection and is not for a tortious or illegal purpose or for purposes of direct or indirect commercial advantage or private commercial gain, and the wire or electronic communication with respect to which the offense under paragraph (a) is a radio communication that is not scrambled, encrypted, or transmitted using modulation techniques the essential parameters of which have been withheld from the public with the intention of preserving the privacy of such communication, then —

(i) if the communication is not the radio portion of a cellular telephone communication, a cordless telephone communication that is transmitted between the cordless telephone handset and the base unit, a public land mobile radio service communication or a paging service communication, and the conduct is not that described in subsection (5), the offender shall be fined under this title or imprisoned not more than one year, or both; and

(ii) if the communication is the radio portion of a cellular telephone communication, a cordless telephone communication that is transmitted between the cordless telephone handset and the base unit, a public land mobile radio service communication or a paging service communication, the offender shall be fined under this title.

(c) Conduct otherwise an offense under this subsection that consists of or relates to the interception of a satellite transmission that is not encrypted or scrambled and that is transmitted —

(i) to a broadcasting station for purposes of retransmission to the general public; or

(ii) as an audio subcarrier intended for redistribution to facilities open to the public, but not including data transmissions or telephone calls,

is not an offense under this subsection unless the conduct is for the purposes of direct or indirect commercial advantage or private financial gain.

(5)(a)(i) If the communication is —

(A) a private satellite video communication that is not scrambled or encrypted and the conduct in violation of this chapter [18 USCS §§2510 et seq.] is the private viewing of that communication and is not for a tortious or illegal purpose or for purposes of direct or indirect commercial advantage or private commercial gain; or

(B) a radio communication that is transmitted on frequencies allocated under subpart D of part 74 of the rules of the Federal Communications Commission that is not scrambled or encrypted and the conduct in violation of this chapter [18 USCS §§2510 et seq.] is not for a tortious or illegal purpose or for purposes of direct or indirect commercial advantage or private commercial gain,

then the person who engages in such conduct shall be subject to suit by the Federal Government in a court of competent jurisdiction.

(ii) In an action under this subsection —

(A) if the violation of this chapter [18 USCS §§2510 et seq.] is a first offense for the person under paragraph (a) of subsection (4) and such person has not been found liable in a civil action under section 2520 of this title, the Federal Government shall be entitled to appropriate injunctive relief; and

(B) if the violation of this chapter [18 USCS §§2510 et seq.] is a second or subsequent offense under paragraph (a) of subsection (4) or such person has been found liable in any prior civil action under section 2520, the person shall be subject to a mandatory $500 civil fine.

(b) The court may use any means within its authority to enforce an injunction issued under paragraph (ii)(A), and shall impose a civil fine of not less than $500 for each violation of such an injunction.

(Pub. L. 90-351, Title III, §802, June 19, 1968, 82 Stat. 213; July 29, 1970, Pub. L. 91-358, Title II, §211(a), 84 Stat. 654; October 25, 1978, Pub. L. 95-511, Title II, §201(a)-(c), 92 Stat. 1796; October 30, 1984, Pub. L. 98-549, §6(b)(2), (3), 98 Stat. 2804; October 21, 1986, Pub. L. 99-508, Title I, §§101(b), (c)(1), (5), (6), (d), (f)(1), 102, 100 Stat. 1848, 1853. Amended September 13, 1994, Pub. L. 103-322, Title XXXII, Subtitle I, §320901, Title XXXIII, §330016(1)(G), 108 Stat. 2123, 2147; October 25, 1994, Pub. L. 103-414, Title II, §§202(b), 204, 205, 108 Stat. 4290, 4291; October 11, 1996, Pub. L. 104-294, Title VI, §604(b)(42), 110 Stat. 3509; October 26, 2001, Pub. L. 107-56, Title II, §§204, 217(2), 115 Stat. 281, 291.)

§2512. Prohibition on the manufacture, distribution, possession, and advertising of communication intercepting devices

(1) Except as otherwise specifically provided in this chapter [18 USCS §§2510 et seq.], any person who intentionally —

(a) sends through the mail, or sends or carries in interstate or foreign commerce, any electronic, mechanical, or other device, knowing or having reason to know that the design of such device renders it primarily useful for the purpose of the surreptitious interception of wire, oral, or electronic communications;

(b) manufactures, assembles, possesses, or sells any electronic, mechanical, or other device, knowing or having reason to know that the design of such device renders it primarily useful for the purpose of the surreptitious interception of wire, oral, or electronic communications, and that such device or any component thereof has been or will be sent through the mail or transported in interstate or foreign commerce; or

(c) places in any newspaper, magazine, handbill, or other publication any advertisement of —

(i) any electronic, mechanical, or other device knowing or having reason to know that the design of such device renders it primarily useful for the purpose of the surreptitious interception of wire, oral, or electronic communications; or

(ii) any other electronic, mechanical, or other device, where such advertisement promotes the use of such device for the purpose of the surreptitious interception of wire, oral, or electronic communications, knowing or having reason to know that such advertisement will be sent through the mail or transported in interstate or foreign commerce, shall be fined under this title or imprisoned not more than five years, or both.

(2) It shall not be unlawful under this section for —

(a) a provider of wire or electronic communication service or an officer, agent, or employee of, or a person under contract with, such a provider, in the normal course of the business of providing that wire or electronic communication service, or

(b) an officer, agent, or employee of, or a person under contract with, the United States, a State, or a political subdivision thereof, in the normal course of the activities of the United States, a State, or a political subdivision thereof, to send through the mail, send or carry in interstate or foreign commerce, or manufacture, assemble, possess, or sell any electronic, mechanical, or other device knowing or having reason to know that the design of such device renders it primarily useful for the purpose of the surreptitious interception of wire, oral, or electronic communications.

(3) It shall not be unlawful under this section to advertise for sale a device described in subsection (1) of this section if the advertisement is mailed, sent, or carried in interstate or foreign commerce solely to a domestic provider of wire or electronic communication service or to an agency of the United States, a State, or a political subdivision thereof which is duly authorized to use such device.

(Pub. L. 90-351, Title III, §802, June 19, 1968, 82 Stat. 214; October 21, 1986, Pub. L. 99-508, Title I, §101(c)(1), (7), (f)(2), 100 Stat. 1851. Amended September 13, 1994, Pub. L. 103-322, Title XXXIII, §§330016(1)(L), 330022, 108 Stat. 2147, 2150; October 11, 1996, Pub. L. 104-294, Title VI, §604(b)(45), 110 Stat. 3509; November 21, 1997, Pub. L. 105-112, §2, 111 Stat. 2273.)

§2513. Authority to confiscate communication intercepting devices

Any electronic, mechanical, or other device used, sent, carried, manufactured, assembled, possessed, sold, or advertised in violation of section 2511 or section 2512 of this chapter may be seized and forfeited to the United States. All provisions of law relating to

(1) the seizure, summary and judicial forfeiture, and condemnation of vessels, vehicles, merchandise, and baggage for violations of the customs laws contained in title 19 of the United States Code,

(2) the disposition of such vessels, vehicles, merchandise, and baggage or the proceeds from the sale thereof,

(3) the remission or mitigation of such forfeiture,

(4) the compromise of claims, and

(5) the award of compensation to informers in respect of such forfeitures, shall apply to seizures and forfeitures incurred, or alleged to have been incurred, under the provisions of this section, insofar as applicable and not inconsistent with the provisions of this section; except that such duties as are imposed upon the collector of customs or any other person with respect to the seizure and forfeiture of vessels, vehicles, merchandise, and baggage under the provisions of the customs laws contained in title 19 of the United States Code shall be performed with respect to seizure and forfeiture of electronic, mechanical, or other intercepting devices under this section by such officers, agents, or other persons as may be authorized or designated for that purpose by the Attorney General.

(Pub. L. 90-351, Title III, §802, June 19, 1968, 82 Stat. 215; October 21, 1986, Pub. L. 99-508, Title I, §101(c), 100 Stat. 1851.)

§2515. Prohibition of admissibility of intercepted wire or oral communications

Whenever any wire or oral communication has been intercepted, no part of the contents of such communication and no evidence derived therefrom may be received in evidence in any trial, hearing, or other proceeding in or before any court, grand jury, department, officer, agency, regulatory body, legislative committee, or other authority of the United States, a State, or a political subdivision thereof if the disclosure of that information would be in violation of this chapter [18 USCS §§2510 et seq.].

(Pub. L. 90-351, Title III, §802, June 19, 1968, 82 Stat. 216.)

§2520. Recovery of civil damages for violations

(a) In general. Except as provided in section 2511(2)(a)(ii), any person whose wire, oral, or electronic communication is intercepted, disclosed, or intentionally used in violation of this chapter [18 USCS §§2510 et seq.] may in a civil action recover from the person or entity, other than the United States, which engaged in that violation such relief as may be appropriate.

(b) Relief. In an action under this section, appropriate relief includes —

(1) such preliminary and other equitable or declaratory relief as may be appropriate;

(2) damages under subsection (c) and punitive damages in appropriate cases; and

(3) a reasonable attorney's fee and other litigation costs reasonably incurred.

(c) Computation of damages.

(1) In an action under this section, if the conduct in violation of this chapter [18 USCS §§2510 et seq.], is the private viewing of a private satellite video communication that is not scrambled or encrypted or if the communication is a radio communication that is transmitted on frequencies allocated under subpart D of part 74 of the rules of the Federal Communications Commission that is not scrambled or encrypted and the conduct is not for a tortious or illegal purpose or for purposes of direct or indirect commercial advantage or private commercial gain, then the court shall assess damages as follows:

(A) If the person who engaged in that conduct has not previously been enjoined under section 2511(5) and has not been found liable in a prior civil action under this section, the court shall assess the greater of the sum of actual damages suffered by the plaintiff, or statutory damages of not less than $50 and not more than $500.

(B) If, on one prior occasion, the person who engaged in that conduct has been enjoined under section 2511(5) or has been found liable in a civil action under this section, the court shall assess the greater of the sum of actual damages suffered by the plaintiff, or statutory damages of not less than $100 and not more than $1000.

(2) In any other action under this section, the court may assess as damages whichever is the greater of —

(A) the sum of the actual damages suffered by the plaintiff and any profits made by the violator as a result of the violation; or

(B) statutory damages of whichever is the greater of $100 a day for each day of violation or $10,000.

(d) Defense. A good faith reliance on —

(1) a court warrant or order, a grand jury subpoena, a legislative authorization, or a statutory authorization;

(2) a request of an investigative or law enforcement officer under section 2518(7) of this title; or

(3) a good faith determination that section 2511(3) of this title permitted the conduct complained of; is a complete defense against any civil or criminal action brought under this chapter [18 USCS §§2510 et seq.] or any other law.

(e) Limitation. A civil action under this section may not be commenced later than two years after the date upon which the claimant first has a reasonable opportunity to discover the violation.

(f) Administrative discipline. If a court or appropriate department or agency determines that the United States or any of its departments or agencies has violated any provision of this chapter [18 USCS §§2510 et seq.], and the court or appropriate department or agency finds that the circumstances surrounding the violation raise serious questions about whether or not an officer or employee of the United States acted willfully or intentionally with respect to the violation, the department or agency shall, upon receipt of a true and correct copy of the decision and findings of the court or appropriate department or agency promptly initiate a proceeding to determine whether disciplinary action against the officer or employee is warranted. If the head of the department or agency involved determines that disciplinary action is not warranted, he or she shall notify the Inspector General with jurisdiction over the department or agency concerned and shall provide the Inspector General with the reasons for such determination.

(g) Improper disclosure is violation. Any willful disclosure or use by an investigative or law enforcement officer or governmental entity of information beyond the extent permitted by section 2517 is a violation of this chapter [18 USCS §§2510 et seq.] for purposes of section 2520(a).

(Pub. L. 90-351, Title III, §802, June 19, 1968, 82 Stat. 223; July 29, 1970, Pub. L. 91-358, Title II, §211(c), 84 Stat. 654; October 21, 1986, Pub. L. 99-508, Title I, §103, 100 Stat. 1854. Amended October 26, 2001, Pub. L. 107-56, Title II, §223(a), 115 Stat. 293.)

§2521. Attorney General may enjoin illegal interception

Whenever it shall appear that any person is engaged or is about to engage in any act which constitutes or will constitute a felony violation of this chapter [18 USCS §§2510 et seq.], the Attorney General may initiate a civil action in a district court of the United States to enjoin such violation. The court shall proceed as soon as practicable to the hearing and determination of such an action, and may, at any time before final determination, enter such a restraining order or prohibition, or take such other action, as is warranted to prevent a continuing and substantial injury to the United States or to any person or class of persons for whose protection the action is brought. A proceeding under this section is governed by the Federal Rules of Civil Procedure, except that, if an indictment has been returned against the respondent, discovery is governed by the Federal Rules of Criminal Procedure.

(Pub. L. 99-508, Title I, §110(a), October 21, 1986, 100 Stat. 1859.)

PART III

SELECTED UNIFORM ACTS

Selected Uniform Acts

Below are reprinted several uniform acts with selected commentary: the revised Uniform Adoption Act (approved by NCUSL in 1994), the revised Uniform Parentage Act (approved by NCCUSL in 2000 and amended in 2002), the Uniform Premarital Agreement Act (approved by NCCUSL in 1983), and Child Witness Testimony by Alternative Methods Act (approved by NCCUSL in August 2002).

UNIFORM ADOPTION ACT (1994)

TABLE OF CONTENTS

Prefatory Note

The guiding principle of the Uniform Adoption Act is a desire to promote the welfare of children and, particularly, to facilitate the placement of minor children who cannot be raised by their original parents with adoptive parents who can offer them stable and loving homes. The Act is premised on a belief that adoption offers significant legal, economic, social and psychological benefits not only for children who might otherwise be homeless, but also for parents who are unable to care for their children, for adults who want to nurture and support children, and for state governments ultimately responsible for the well-being of children.

The Act aims to be a comprehensive and uniform state adoption code that: (1) is consistent with relevant federal constitutional and statutory law; (2) delineates the legal requirements and consequences of different kinds of adoption; (3) promotes the integrity and finality of adoptions while discouraging "trafficking" in minors; (4) respects the choices made by the parties to an adoption about how much confidentiality or openness they prefer in their relations with each other, subject, however, to judicial protection of the adoptee's welfare; and (5) promotes the interest of minor children in being raised by individuals who are committed to, and capable of, caring for them.

The most striking characteristic of contemporary adoptions is the variety of contexts in which they occur. Of the 130,000 or more adoptions that are granted each year, over half are adoptions of minor children by stepparents or relatives. Perhaps another 15 to 20% or more are of older children, many of whom have previously been shunted back and forth between their birth families and foster care. Many of these children come to their adoptive parents with serious psychological or physical problems that will require years of treatment and loving parental attention. Approximately 7,000 to 10,000 adoptions of foreign born children occur annually despite the intricate web of domestic and foreign regulations that adoptive parents have to contend with in order to complete their families. In recent years, no more than 25 to 30% of all adoptions involve infants adopted by unrelated adults. For an analysis of the limited data available on different kinds of adoptions and an overview of contemporary adoption practice, see Adoption vol. 3 Future of Children (Packard Fdn, 1993).

At present, the legal process of adoption is complicated not only by the different kinds of children who are adopted and the different kinds of people who seek to adopt, but also by an extraordinarily confusing system of state, federal, and international laws and regulations. Despite allegedly common goals, state adoption laws are not and never have been uniform, and there now appear to be more inconsistencies than ever from one state to another. There are no clear answers to such basic questions as who may place a child for adoption, whose consent is required and when is consent final, how much money can be paid to whom and for what, how much information can or should be shared between birth and adoptive families, what makes an individual suitable as an adoptive parent, and what efforts are needed to encourage the permanent placement of minority children and other children with special needs who languish in foster care. Hundreds of thousands of children in this country need permanent homes, and hundreds of thousands of adults have at least some interest in adoption but are often discouraged by the confusing laws and procedures as well as by high financial and emotional costs.

To reduce this confusion — which confounds consensual adoptions and not only the relatively small number that are contested — the National Conference of Commissioners on Uniform State Laws has approved a Uniform Adoption Act to enable the States to respond more flexibly and reasonably to the changing social, economic and constitutional character of contemporary adoption practice.

In examining virtually every aspect of adoption practice, the Drafting Committee was assisted by its Reporter, Law Professor Joan Heifetz Hollinger, the principal author and editor of Adoption Law and Practice 2 vol. (Matthew Bender Co., 1988, Supp. 1989-1994), representatives from the Family Law Section of the American Bar Association, and dozens of advisers representing a wide array of professional and citizens organizations. After extensive discussion of the Act at five successive Annual Meetings, the Conference overwhelmingly approved it as a Uniform Act in August 1994.

The Act meets the changing psychosocial and economic aspects of contemporary adoptions by addressing the many different kinds of adoption that now occur and the different functions they serve. Adoptions may be characterized according to the kind of individuals being adopted — minors or adults, born in this country or foreign born, with or without special needs, with or without siblings. They may also be characterized according to the kind of individuals who are adopting — married couples, single individuals, stepparents, individuals previously related or unrelated to an adoptee. Another way to characterize adoptions is according to the type of placement — direct placement by a birth parent with an adoptive parent selected by the birth parent with or without the assistance of a lawyer or an agency, or placement by a public or private agency that has acquired custody of a minor from a birth parent through a voluntary relinquishment or an involuntary termination of parental rights. A fourth way to characterize adoptions is by the nature of the proceeding — contested or uncontested.

The Act goes beyond existing statutory laws to create a coherent framework for legitimizing and regulating both direct-placement and agency-supervised adoptions. The Act will facilitate the completion of consensual adoptions and expedite the resolution of contested adoptions. By promoting the integrity and finality of adoptions, the Act will serve the interests of children in establishing and maintaining legal ties to the individuals who are committed to, and capable of, parenting them. More specifically:

(1) The Act protects minor children against unnecessary separation from their birth parents, against placement with unsuitable adoptive parents, and against harmful delays in determination of their legal status.

(2) The Act protects birth parents from unwarranted termination of their parental rights. Minor children may not be adopted without parental consent or appropriate grounds for dispensing with parental consent. The Act attempts to ensure that a decision by a birth parent to relinquish a minor child and consent to the child's adoption is informed and voluntary. Once that decision is made, however, and expressed before a judge or another individual who is not implicated in any actual or potential conflict of interest with the birth parent, the decision is final and, with very few exceptions, irrevocable.

Involuntary as well as voluntary termination proceedings conform to constitutional standards of due process, but an individual's biological ties to a child are not alone sufficient to bestow full parental rights on that individual. The Act protects the parental status of biological parents who have actually functioned as a child's parents.

(3) The Act protects adoptive parents and adopted children by providing them with whatever information is reasonably available at the time of placement about the child's background, including health, genetic, and social history, and by providing access in later years to updated medical information.

(4) The Act discourages unlawful placement activities within and across state and national boundaries by keeping track of minor children once they have been placed for adoption, distinguishing between lawful and unlawful adoption-related expenses and activities, insisting that agencies, lawyers, and other providers of professional services explain their adoption-related services and fees to people considering adoption, requiring judicial approval of adoption-related expenses, and imposing sanctions against unlawful activities.

(5) The Act encourages different kinds of people to adopt. No one may be categorically excluded from being considered as an adoptive parent. Nonetheless, preplacement (except in stepparent adoptions and when waived by a court for good cause) as well as post-placement evaluations of prospective adoptive parents are required, whether initiated by an agency or directly by a birth parent, in order to determine the suitability of particular individuals to be adoptive parents.

(6) Individuals who have served as a minor child's foster or de facto parents are given standing to seek to adopt the child, subject to the particular child's needs. Agencies receiving public funds are required actively to recruit prospective adoptive parents for children who are considered difficult to place because of their age, health, race, ethnicity, or other special needs. The Act prohibits the delay or denial of a child's adoptive placement solely on the basis of racial or ethnic factors. A child's guardian ad litem as well as other interested persons may seek equitable and other appropriate relief against discriminatory placement activities.

(7) The Act requires expedited hearings for contested adoptions and the appointment of a guardian ad litem for minor children whose well-being is threatened by protracted or contested proceedings. During a proceeding, courts are authorized and encouraged to make interim custody arrangements to protect minors against detrimental disruptions of stable custodial environments. Good faith efforts must be made to notify any parent or alleged parent whose rights have not previously been relinquished or terminated of the pendency of an adoption of the parent's child.

(8) The Act clarifies the relationship to adoption proceedings of the Uniform Child Custody Jurisdiction Act, the federal Parental Kidnapping Prevention Act, and the Interstate Compact on the Placement of Children. The Act supports the finality of adoption decrees by strictly limiting the time for appeals or other challenges and by presuming that a final order terminating parental rights or granting an adoption is valid. A final adoption may not be challenged by anyone for any reason more than six months after the order is entered. Even if a challenge is begun within that time, the adoption may not be set aside unless the challenger proves with clear and convincing evidence that the adoption is contrary to the child's best interests.

(9) The Act permits mutually agreed-upon communication between birth and adoptive families before and after an adoption is final. It also ensures that, except for consensual contacts, the privacy and autonomy of adoptive and birth families will be fully protected. The Act's mutual consent registry is a "user friendly" approach to the issue of whether and when to release identifying information among birth parents, adoptees, and other members of an adoptee's birth and adoptive families. This balanced and uniform procedure can be the basis of a national interstate network for the consensual disclosure of identifying information.

(10) The Act clarifies the legal and economic consequences of different types of adoption so that, within these formal structures, the emotional and psychological aspects of adoptive parent and child relationships can flourish.

[ARTICLE] 1. GENERAL PROVISIONS

§1-101. Definitions

In this [Act]:

(1) "Adoptee" means an individual who is adopted or is to be adopted.

(2) "Adult" means an individual who has attained 18 years of age.

(3) "Agency" means a public or private entity, including the department, that is authorized by the law of this State to place individuals for adoption.

(4) "Child" means a minor or adult son or daughter, by birth or adoption.

(5) "Court," with reference to a court of this State, means the [appropriate court].

(6) "Department" means the [department of social services, or health services, or children's services].

(7) "Guardian" means an individual, other than a parent, appointed by an appropriate court as general guardian or guardian of the person of a minor.

(8) "Legal custody" means the right and duty to exercise continuing general supervision of a minor as authorized by law. The term includes the right and duty to protect, educate, nurture, and discipline the minor and to provide the minor with food, clothing, shelter, medical care, and a supportive environment.

(9) "Minor" means an individual who has not attained 18 years of age.

(10) "Parent" means an individual who is legally recognized as a mother or father or whose consent to the adoption of a minor is required under Section 2-401(a)(1). The term does not include an individual whose parental relationship to a child has been terminated judicially or by operation of law.

(11) "Person" means an individual, corporation, limited liability company, business trust, estate, trust, partnership, association, agency, joint venture, government, governmental subdivision or instrumentality, public corporation, or any other legal or commercial entity.

(12) "Physical custody" means the physical care and supervision of a minor.

(13) "Place for adoption" means to select a prospective adoptive parent for a minor and transfer physical custody of the minor to the prospective adoptive parent.

(14) "Relative" means a grandparent, great grandparent, sibling, first cousin, aunt, uncle, great-aunt, great-uncle, niece, or nephew of an individual, whether related to the individual by the whole or the half blood, affinity, or adoption. The term does not include an individual's stepparent.

(15) "Relinquishment" means the voluntary surrender to an agency by a minor's parent or guardian, for purposes of the minor's adoption, of the rights of the parent or guardian with respect to the minor, including legal and physical custody of the minor.

(16) "State" means a State of the United States, the District of Columbia, the Commonwealth of Puerto Rico, or any territory or insular possession subject to the jurisdiction of the United States.

(17) "Stepparent" means an individual who is the spouse or surviving spouse of a parent of a child but who is not a parent of the child.

Comment

"Child" is defined as a son or daughter by birth or adoption because biological and adopted children may be adults as well as minors and because the legal consequences of adoption are not limited to adoptees who are minors. The relationship of "parent and child" referred to in the Act is not limited to the rights and duties that exist between a parent and a child under the age of 18. This relationship includes the legal rights and duties that exist between a parent and a child of any age.

"Legal custody" is distinguished from "physical custody" because a person with whom a minor is actually living may not be the same or the only person who has the legal right to make decisions about the minor's care or the legal responsibility to provide that care. This distinction is important, for example, in determining who has the legal authority to place a minor for adoption. See Section 2-101.

"Parent" is defined to include any legally recognized mother or father — anyone recognized in this State or elsewhere as having the legal status of mother or father. Also included in the term are the women and men, other than a minor's guardian, whose consent to the adoption of a minor is required by the Act — these are the women and men who are probably recognized by most States as legal mothers or fathers. Excluded from the term "parent" are women and men whose status as legal mothers or fathers has been terminated in a judicial proceeding or "by operation of law," as, for example, is the fate in most States of egg or sperm donors who are not intended social parents. Also excluded are women or men who may be candidates for the legal designation of mother or father but who have not yet been recognized as such — for example, an alleged father who is not married to a birth mother, or a prospective adoptive parent who hopes to become a legally recognized parent but must await judicial approval of the proposed adoption. The Act does not refer to a child's parents at birth as the "natural" parents because to do so might imply that it is "unnatural" to be an adoptive parent. Moreover, the increasing use of artificial insemination, in vitro fertilization, embryo transfers, and other forms of "assisted conception" to create children makes it all the more difficult to know who is the most likely candidate for the designation of "natural" parent.

"Place for adoption" is defined as encompassing both the selection of a prospective adoptive parent and the transfer of a minor's physical custody to this individual. Article 2, Part 1, recognizes two kinds of adoptive placements: (1) direct placement, and (2) placement by an agency.

§1-102. Who may adopt or be adopted

Subject to this [Act], any individual may adopt or be adopted by another individual for the purpose of creating the relationship of parent and child between them.

Comment

No one is categorically excluded by the Act from being considered as a prospective adoptee or as a prospective adoptive parent. Determinations concerning the availability and suitability of individuals to become each other's adoptive parent or child are to be made on the basis of the particular needs and characteristics of each individual. A specific minor will not become available for adoption, for example, unless the parents of the minor consent to a direct adoptive placement, relinquish their parental rights to an agency, or have their parental rights terminated by a court. A specific individual will not be entitled to adopt a minor unless the individual is favorably evaluated as suitable to adopt, obtains custody of a minor from a person authorized to place the minor for adoption, and is permitted to adopt by a court upon a finding that the adoption is in the minor's best interests. Marital status, like other general characteristics such as race, ethnicity, religion, or age, does not preclude an individual from adopting, but, if a prospective adoptive parent is married, his or her spouse has to join in the petition. See Section 3-301.

§1-103. Name of adoptee after adoption

The name of an adoptee designated in a decree of adoption takes effect as specified in the decree.

§1-104. Legal relationship between adoptee and adoptive parent after adoption

After a decree of adoption becomes final, each adoptive parent and the adoptee have the legal relationship of parent and child and have all the rights and duties of that relationship.

Comment

Sections 1-104 through 1-106 state the most generally accepted legal consequences of adoption: (1) the adoptee becomes in all respects the child of the new adoptive parents; (2) except for the circumstances referred to in Section 1-105, any rights and duties of the adoptee's former parents (i.e., former adoptive or presumed parents as well as birth parents) which have not previously been terminated — are terminated; and (3) the adoptee retains any right or benefit acquired before the decree of adoption becomes final. See Section 3-706 to determine when the decree becomes final.

The Act defers to the State's probate and other laws for determining how an adoptee's status as the child of the adoptive parents affects their rights to intestate succession and inheritance by, from, and through each other, as well as the adoptee's rights to support, to be a beneficiary of any donative disposition, including class gifts, and to receive wrongful death proceeds, survivor's benefits, educational, insurance, medical, and other third party or public benefits.

§1-105. Legal relationship between adoptee and former parent after

Except as otherwise provided in Section 4-103, when a decree of adoption becomes final:

(1) the legal relationship of parent and child between each of the adoptee's former parents and the adoptee terminates, except for a former parent's duty to pay arrearages for child support; and

(2) any previous court order for visitation or communication with an adoptee terminates.

Comment

Except in an adoption by a stepparent, the consequences of an adoption are generally to terminate all aspects of the relationship of parent and child between the adoptee and the adoptee's former legal parents, including the rights of the adoptee and the adoptee's former parents to inheritance or intestate succession by, from, and through each other. Because the adoptee is no longer the legal "child" of a birth parent, the adoptee is similarly no longer the grandchild of a former grandparent, the sibling of a former sibling, and so on. The Act defers to the State's probate laws for the consequences of an adoption for class gifts and other donative dispositions in an instrument executed before or after the adoption becomes final by an adoptee or an adoptee's former parent or relative. See Section 4-103 for the consequences of an adoption by a stepparent.

Except in an adoption by a stepparent, the Act terminates any previous order for visitation or communication with an adoptee but leaves to other law of the State whether agreements for post-adoption visitation or communication are enforceable in a separate civil action. Nonetheless, Section 3-707(c) provides that the validity of an adoption cannot be challenged for failure to comply with such an agreement. Therefore, an agreement for post-adoption visitation or communication, while not prohibited by the Act, has no effect on the fundamental consequence of an adoption, which is to terminate the parental relationship between the child and the former parents and to create the relationship of parent and child in all respects between the adoptive parents and the adopted child.

§1-106. Other rights of adoptee

A decree of adoption does not affect any right or benefit vested in the adoptee before the decree becomes final.

§1-107. Proceedings subject to Indian child welfare act

A proceeding under this [Act] which pertains to an Indian child, as defined in the Indian Child Welfare Act, 25 U.S.C. Sections 1901 et seq., is subject to that Act.

§1-108. Recognition of adoption in another

A decree or order of adoption issued by a court of any other State which is entitled to full faith and credit in this State, or a decree or order of adoption entered by a court or administrative entity in another country acting pursuant to that country's law or to any convention or treaty on intercountry adoption which the United States has ratified, has the same effect as a decree or order of adoption issued by a court of this State. The rights and obligations of the parties as to matters within the jurisdiction of this State must be determined as though the decree or order were issued by a court of this State.

[ARTICLE] 2. ADOPTION OF MINORS

Prefatory Comment

By its own terms and in accordance with Section 5-101, this article applies to the adoption of unemancipated minors and in accordance with Section 5-101 to incompetent adults by unrelated individuals and by relatives. Article 5 applies to the adoption of adults and emancipated minors and Article 4 applies to the adoption of minors by their stepparents or other individuals who, with the consent of the custodial parent and the court, are permitted to adopt under Article 4.

Unlike many current adoption statutes, the Act defines "place for adoption," Section 1-101(13); specifies the individuals or entities who may place a minor and states the other prerequisites for a valid placement, Part 1 of this article; and provides sanctions for unlawful placement activities, Article 7. The Act recognizes a legitimate role for various providers of professional services in connection with an adoption and requires that they disclose the nature of their services and their fee schedules to birth parents and prospective adopters. See Section 2-102(e) for direct placements and Section 2-103(a) for placements by agencies. The Act provides, however, that the only persons who may actually select an adoptive parent and authorize a transfer of the minor's physical custody are a parent with legal and physical custody of a minor, a guardian with specific judicial authorization to place a minor, or an agency with legal custody of a minor and authorization from a parent, a guardian, or a court to place the minor for adoption.

[PART] 1. PLACEMENT OF MINOR FOR ADOPTION

§2-101. Who may place minor for adoption

(a) The only persons who may place a minor for adoption are:

(1) a parent having legal and physical custody of the minor, as provided in subsections (b) and (c);

(2) a guardian expressly authorized by the court to place the minor for adoption;

(3) an agency to which the minor has been relinquished for purposes of adoption; or

(4) an agency expressly authorized to place the minor for adoption by a court order terminating the relationship between the minor and the minor's parent or guardian.

(b) Except as otherwise provided in subsection (c), a parent having legal and physical custody of a minor may place the minor for adoption, even if the other parent has not executed a consent or a relinquishment or the other parent's relationship to the minor has not been terminated.

(c) A parent having legal and physical custody of a minor may not place the minor for adoption if the other parent has legal custody or a right of visitation with the minor and that parent's whereabouts are known, unless that parent agrees in writing to the placement or, before the placement, the parent who intends to place the minor sends notice of the intended placement by certified mail to the other parent's last known address.

(d) An agency authorized under this [Act] to place a minor for adoption may place the minor for adoption, even if only one parent has executed a relinquishment or has had his or her parental relationship to the minor terminated.

Comment

Subsection (a) specifies the persons who may "select a prospective adoptive parent for a minor and transfer physical custody of the minor to the prospective adoptive parent," as provided in the definition of "place for adoption" in Section 1-101(13). To protect minors against careless or unsupervised adoptive placements, a guardian, defined in the Act as a "general guardian or guardian of the person of a minor," Section 1-101(7), is not authorized to place the minor for adoption unless expressly authorized to do so by a court pursuant to the State's guardianship laws. Such authority is not likely to be granted unless the child's parents are deceased or otherwise incapacitated or have had their parental rights terminated.

Subsection (b) allows an "at risk" placement by one parent if that parent has both legal and physical custody of the child, and subsection (d) allows an "at risk" placement by an agency. The risk, which is generally thought to be low, is that the consent, relinquishment, or termination of the rights of the other parent will not occur and, as a result, the adoption will not be completed. The advantage of this kind of placement is that the child will be transferred to the home that is most likely to become the permanent adoptive home and will be spared an interlude in one or more foster homes. Before accepting custody of the child, the prospective adoptive parents must have a favorable preplacement evaluation, Part 2 of this article

(unless waived by a court for good cause), will be informed of the risks of the placement, and must have agreed in writing to provide medical and other care and support for the child pending execution of the requisite consents or relinquishments. See Section 2-102(d).

Subsection (c) provides that when both parents share legal custody, or one parent has legal custody and the other has a right of visitation, the parent having legal and physical custody cannot place a child without the other parent's written permission or without notifying the other parent of the intended placement. This provision is much less likely to affect the parents of an infant than of an older child when the parents — whether divorced or never married to each other — are subject to a court order for custody and visitation. One parent will be discouraged from attempting to place the child for adoption when the other parent maintains an actual and not simply de jure relationship to the child. If that parent can object to the placement while it is being contemplated, instead of after it has been made, the child can be spared the disruption of being shifted from one custodial environment to another. Nonetheless, if that parent does object or does not reply to the notice, and the parent who intends to place the child believes there are sufficient grounds to terminate the rights of the other parent — for example, a consistent failure to support and communicate with the child — the prospective adoptive parents can go ahead and file a petition for adoption. See Section 3-301. In conjunction with that petition, the parent who has selected the prospective adopters can file a petition to terminate the other parent's relationship to the child. See Section 3-501(1). If a custodial parent wants his or her spouse to adopt the child, a "placement" as contemplated by this part is not required and the parent and stepparent may commence an adoption proceeding under Article 4, in which case the status of the other parent will be determined during the pendency of that proceeding.

§2-102. Direct placement for adoption by parent or guardian

(a) A parent or guardian authorized to place a minor directly for adoption may place the minor only with a prospective adoptive parent for whom a favorable preplacement evaluation has been prepared pursuant to Sections 2-201 through 2-206 or for whom a preplacement evaluation is not required under Section 2-201(b) or (c).

(b) A parent or guardian shall personally select a prospective adoptive parent for the direct placement of a minor. Subject to [Article] 7, the parent or guardian may be assisted by another person, including a lawyer, health-care provider, or agency, in locating or transferring legal and physical custody of the minor to a prospective adoptive parent.

(c) A prospective adoptive parent shall furnish a copy of the preplacement evaluation to the parent or guardian and may provide additional information requested by the parent or guardian. The evaluation and any additional information must be edited to exclude identifying information, but information identifying a prospective adoptive parent need not be edited if the individual agrees to its disclosure. Subject to [Article] 7, a prospective adoptive parent may be assisted by another person in locating a minor who is available for adoption.

(d) If a consent to a minor's adoption is not executed at the time the minor is placed for adoption, the parent or guardian who places the minor shall furnish to the prospective adoptive parent a signed writing stating that the transfer of physical custody is for purposes of adoption and that the parent or guardian has been informed of the provisions of this [Act] relevant to placement for adoption, consent, relinquishment, and termination of parental rights. The writing must authorize the prospective adoptive parent to provide support and medical and other care for the minor pending execution of the consent within a time specified in the writing. The prospective adoptive parent shall acknowledge in a signed writing responsibility for the minor's support and medical and other care and for returning the minor to the custody of the parent or guardian if the consent is not executed within the time specified.

(e) A person who provides services with respect to direct placements for adoption shall furnish to an individual who inquires about the person's services a written statement of the person's services and a schedule of fees.

Comment

Consistent with the prevailing law in all but a few States, the Act recognizes and protects the right of a child's parent to select adoptive parents for the child and to transfer physical custody of the child directly to the prospective parents. As of 1994, only Connecticut, Delaware, and Massachusetts continued to bar direct placement as defined in this Act. Even these States, however, allow agencies to make "identified" placements in which a birth parent participates in the selection of an adoptive parent.

In contrast to prevailing practice in most States, the Act requires a preplacement evaluation for direct parental placements (unless waived by a court for good cause) — often referred to as "private" or "independent" placements — as well as for placements made by agencies. In order to reduce the risks to children of being "distributed" to "strangers" whose parental capacities are unknown, birth parents or guardians of a minor who make a direct placement must limit their choice of adoptive parents to individuals who have had a favorable preplacement evaluation. An individual who places a minor with someone who has not had a favorable evaluation is subject to a civil penalty. See Section 7-101.

Although a birth parent or guardian may be "assisted" by others when making a direct placement, the parent or guardian must personally select a prospective adoptive parent on the basis of the information contained in the preplacement evaluation and any additional information provided at the parent's or guardian's request. Moreover, a

person who assists in a direct placement may not charge a "finder's" fee or any similar fee for securing a placement, a consent, or a relinquishment. See Sections 7-101 and 7-102. Fees may be charged for lawful professional services rendered during an adoption. All service-providers must disclose in advance the nature of their services and their fees, subsection (e). See, also, Comment to Section 2-103.

The parent or guardian and the prospective adoptive parents may determine for themselves whether to share identifying information and whether to meet each other at the time of placement or at some later time.

Subsection (d) is consistent with the Act's requirement that an adoption based on a direct placement cannot be completed until at least three events occur: a parent or guardian has to place a minor with prospective adopters, the parent or guardian has to execute a consent to the proposed adoption, and the other parent's rights, if not previously terminated, have to be voluntarily or involuntarily terminated. Although they are not the only prerequisites for a valid adoption, these events are essential for an adoption begun through a direct placement.

It is not always possible for a consent to be executed before a child's physical custody is transferred to a prospective adoptive parent. In a direct placement of an infant, for example, the birth mother may release the infant to the prospective adopters from the hospital at least several days before she executes her consent. See Part 3 of this article.

To provide for a minor's care in the interlude between the transfer of physical custody and the execution of a consent, the individual who places the minor has to authorize the prospective adoptive parent to care for the minor pending the execution of the consent. The written authorization should specifically mention medical care so that, pursuant to many States' laws and the Employee Retirement Income Security Act (ERISA), 29 U.S.C.A. §1169, upon completion of the adoption, the adoptee can be deemed a covered dependent under the adoptive parent's group health insurance plan from the date of placement and not simply from the date the decree becomes final. The authorization may also enable an adoptee with special needs to qualify for federal or state medical assistance programs.

A placement authorization should also indicate when the consent is likely to be executed, and include an acknowledgment by the prospective adoptive parents that, if the parent or guardian who placed the minor decides not to execute the consent at the specified time, the parent or guardian may immediately reclaim physical custody of the child. If the individual who placed the child neither consents nor refuses to consent at the specified time, but simply disappears, the prospective adoptive parents have the option of (1) reporting the disappearance to the department for possible action under the State's child protection laws or (2) filing a petition to adopt under Article 3, Part 3 along with a petition to terminate the parent's rights under Article 3, Part 5 or the guardian's right to withhold consent. See Section 2-402(b).

§2-103. Placement for adoption by agency

(a) An agency authorized to place a minor for adoption shall furnish to an individual who inquires about its services a written statement of its services, including the agency's procedure for selecting a prospective adoptive parent for a minor and a schedule of its fees.

(b) An agency that places a minor for adoption shall authorize in writing the prospective adoptive parent to provide support and medical and other care for the minor pending entry of a decree of adoption. The prospective adoptive parent shall acknowledge in writing responsibility for the minor's support and medical and other care.

(c) Upon request by a parent who has relinquished a minor child pursuant to [Part] 4, the agency shall promptly inform the parent as to whether the minor has been placed for adoption, whether a petition for adoption has been granted, denied, or withdrawn, and, if the petition was not granted, whether another placement has been made.

Comment

Agencies are required to disclose to birth parents, guardians, and prospective adoptive parents the agencies' fee schedules and their policies concerning "closed" or "open" adoptions, the role of birth parents in selecting adoptive parents, and the extent to which the agencies feel bound to honor a birth parent's request for adoptive parents with particular characteristics. It is anticipated that in formulating regulations to implement the Act, the States will draft sample forms for agencies, lawyers, social workers, and other adoption-service providers to report, advertise, and account for their services and fees. See, e.g., Michigan's required "public information forms" for adoption service providers, Mich. P.A. 209 of 1994, Sec. 14.

The Comment to Section 2-102 on the importance of a written authorization to prospective adoptive parents to provide medical care for an adoptee is also relevant to subsection (b) of this section.

Subsection (c) responds to the desire of many birth parents who voluntarily relinquish a child to be informed whether and when the child is adopted.

§2-104. Preferences for placement when agency places minor

(a) An agency may place a minor for adoption only with an individual for whom a favorable preplacement evaluation has been prepared pursuant to Sections 2-201 through 2-206. Placement must be made:

(1) if the agency has agreed to place the minor with a prospective adoptive parent selected by the parent or guardian, with the individual selected by the parent or guardian;

(2) if the agency has not so agreed, with an individual selected by the agency in accordance with the best interest of the minor.

(b) In determining the best interest of the minor under subsection (a)(2), the agency shall consider the following individuals in order of preference:

(1) an individual who has previously adopted a sibling of the minor and who makes a written request to adopt the minor;

(2) an individual with characteristics requested by a parent or guardian, if the agency agrees to comply with the request and locates the individual within a time agreed to by the parent or guardian and the agency;

(3) an individual who has had physical custody of the minor for six months or more within the preceding 24 months or for half of the minor's life, whichever is less, and makes a written request to adopt the minor;

(4) a relative with whom the minor has established a positive emotional relationship and who makes a written request to adopt the minor; and

(5) any other individual selected by the agency.

(c) Unless necessary to comply with a request under subsection (b)(2), an agency may not delay or deny a minor's placement for adoption solely on the basis of the minor's race, national origin, or ethnic background. A guardian ad litem of a minor or an individual with a favorable preplacement evaluation who makes a written request to an agency to adopt the minor may maintain an action or proceeding for equitable relief against an agency that violates this subsection.

(d) If practicable and in the best interest of minors who are siblings, an agency shall place siblings with the same prospective adoptive parent selected in accordance with subsections (a) through (c).

(e) If an agency places a minor pursuant to subsection (a)(2), an individual described in subsection (b)(3) may commence an action or proceeding within 30 days after the placement to challenge the agency's placement. If the individual proves by a preponderance of the evidence that the minor has substantial emotional ties to the individual and that an adoptive placement of the minor with the individual would be in the best interest of the minor, the court shall place the minor with the individual.

§2-105. Recruitment of adoptive parents by agency

An agency receiving public funds pursuant to Title IV-E of the federal Adoption Assistance and Child Welfare Act, 42 U.S.C. §§ 670 et seq., or pursuant to [the State's adoption subsidy program], shall make a diligent search for and actively recruit prospective adoptive parents for minors in the agency's custody who are entitled to funding from those sources and who are difficult to place for adoption because of a special need as described in [the applicable law on minors with special needs]. The department shall prescribe the procedure for recruiting prospective adoptive parents pursuant to this section.

§2-106. Disclosure of information on background

(a) As early as practicable before a prospective adoptive parent accepts physical custody of a minor, a person placing the minor for adoption shall furnish to the prospective adoptive parent a written report containing all of the following information reasonably available from any person who has had legal or physical custody of the minor or who has provided medical, psychological, educational, or similar services to the minor:

(1) a current medical and psychological history of the minor, including an account of the minor's prenatal care, medical condition at birth, any drug or medication taken by the minor's mother during pregnancy, any subsequent medical, psychological, or psychiatric examination and diagnosis, any physical, sexual, or emotional abuse suffered by the minor, and a record of any immunizations and health care received while in foster or other care;

(2) relevant information concerning the medical and psychological history of the minor's genetic parents and relatives, including any known disease or hereditary predisposition to disease, any addiction to drugs or alcohol, the health of the minor's mother during her pregnancy, and the health of each parent at the minor's birth; and

(3) relevant information concerning the social history of the minor and the minor's parents and relatives, including:

(i) the minor's enrollment and performance in school, results of educational testing, and any special educational needs;

(ii) the minor's racial, ethnic, and religious background, tribal affiliation, and a general description of the minor's parents;

(iii) an account of the minor's past and existing relationship with any individual with whom the minor has regularly lived or visited; and

(iv) the level of educational and vocational achievement of the minor's parents and relatives and any noteworthy accomplishments;

(4) information concerning a criminal conviction of a parent for a felony, a judicial order terminating the parental rights of a parent, and a proceeding in which the parent was alleged to have abused, neglected, abandoned, or otherwise mistreated the minor, a sibling of the minor, or the other parent;

(5) information concerning a criminal conviction or delinquency adjudication of the minor; and

(6) information necessary to determine the minor's eligibility for state or federal benefits, including subsidies for adoption and other financial, medical, or similar assistance.

(b) Before a hearing on a petition for adoption, the person who placed a minor for adoption shall furnish to the prospective adoptive parent a supplemental written report containing information required by subsection (a) which was unavailable before the minor was placed for adoption but becomes reasonably available to the person after the placement.

(c) The court may request that a respondent in a proceeding under [Article] 3, [Part] 5, supply the information required by this section.

(d) A report furnished under this section must indicate who prepared the report and, unless confidentiality has been waived, be edited to exclude the identity of any individual who furnished information or about whom information is reported.

(e) Information furnished under this section may not be used as evidence in any civil or criminal proceeding against an individual who is the subject of the information.

(f) The department shall prescribe forms designed to obtain the specific information sought under this section and shall furnish the forms to a person who is authorized to place a minor for adoption or who provides services with respect to placements for adoption.

Comment

The provisions requiring any person who places a minor for adoption to provide prospective adoptive parents, preferably before placement, with whatever information is "reasonably available" about a minor's medical, psychological, and social history, are among the Act's most significant contributions to the improvement of contemporary adoption practice. These provisions will encourage the development of protocols — like those being drafted by the American Academy of Pediatrics in cooperation with child welfare agencies and attorneys — for collecting information in a non-intrusive manner that respects individual privacy. These provisions will also encourage better training of medical personnel, social workers, and genetic counselors who are called upon to assist prospective adoptive parents in evaluating the needs of minor adoptees. See, Marianne Blair, Lifting the Genealogical Veil: A Blueprint for Legislative Reform, 70 N.C. L. Rev 681 (1992). In addition, the provisions in Article 6 for maintaining, updating, and disclosing nonidentifying information respond to the growing awareness that many birth parents are too young to have much medical history to report at the time of placement, but may develop conditions later on which adoptive families may want disclosed to them.

Although most States now require that some nonidentifying background information be furnished to adoptive parents, the statutes are not uniform. They vary greatly with respect to the type of information sought, procedures, timing, administrative oversight, duties of care, and rules on confidentiality. Very few statutes require that the information be furnished before placement, when it can have the most beneficial effect on the ability of prospective adoptive parents to make informed decisions about whether to adopt a particular child. Hardly any statutes refer to genetic history and, until quite recently, most adoption service providers had no training at all in how to collect or evaluate genetic information or health histories so that the information is not unduly alarming to the prospective parents.

This section also protects against the random disclosure of confidential information and the use in civil or criminal proceedings of any information compiled pursuant to this section against an individual who is the subject of the information. For example, a parent's disclosure of drug addiction will not be admissible evidence in any proceeding involving the parent's alleged violation of other laws.

The reports required by this section must be included and retained in the permanent court records of the adoption proceeding. See Section 3-305(a)(7) and Article 6.

Article 7 provides sanctions and permits individual causes of action for unauthorized disclosures of information and for breaches of the statutory duty to provide information that is "reasonably available." See, e.g., Burr v. Bd. of Co. Comm., 491 N.E.2d 1101 (Ohio 1986) (public agency intentionally misrepresented biological family history, leaving adoptive parents unprepared for the child's later development of multiple neurological disorders); Gibbs v. Ernst, 615 A.2d 851 (Pa. App. 1993) (agency liable for failures to disclose child's history of physical and sexual abuse, leaving adoptive parents unprepared to deal with child's uncontrollably violent behavior); Blair, Liability for Misconduct in Disclosure of Health-Related Information, ch. 16, Adoption Law and Practice (J.H. Hollinger, ed. 1988-1994).

§2-107. Interstate placement

An adoption in this State of a minor brought into this State from another State by a prospective adoptive parent, or by a person who places the minor for adoption in this State, is governed by the laws of this State, including this [Act] and the Interstate Compact on the Placement of Children.

§2-108. Intercountry placement

An adoption in this State of a minor brought into this State from another country by a prospective adoptive parent, or by a person who places the minor for adoption in this State, is governed by this [Act], subject to any convention or treaty on intercountry adoption which the United States has ratified and any relevant federal law.

§2-201. Preplacement evaluation required

(a) Except as otherwise provided in subsections (b) and (c), only an individual for whom a current, favorable written preplacement evaluation has been prepared may accept custody of a minor for purposes of adoption. An evaluation is current if it is prepared or updated within the 18 months next preceding the placement of the minor with the individual for adoption. An evaluation is favorable if it contains a finding that the individual is suited to be an adoptive parent, either in general or for a particular minor.

(b) A court may excuse the absence of a preplacement evaluation for good cause shown, but the prospective adoptive parent so excused must be evaluated during the pendency of the proceeding for adoption.

(c) A preplacement evaluation is not required if a parent or guardian places a minor directly with a relative of the minor for purposes of adoption, but an evaluation of the relative is required during the pendency of a proceeding for adoption.

Comment

The Act requires that individuals who want to adopt be evaluated so that: (1) questions about their suitability to be adoptive parents can be addressed and (2) persons authorized to place minors for adoption can determine who is suitable as a prospective parent for a specific minor. The provisions governing preplacement evaluations in this part are compatible with ICPC requirements for interstate placements and are based to a large extent on analogous provisions in the Arizona, Florida, Michigan, New York, and Washington statutes.

Although an increasing number of States require preplacement evaluations for direct as well as for agency placements, most States require only post-placement evaluations — typically called "home studies" — for direct placement adoptions. By requiring a preplacement evaluation for direct as well as agency adoptions, the Act will have a substantial and beneficial effect on direct placements. There is no credible evidence that adoptive parents with whom a child has been placed directly by a birth parent are any less capable as parents than adoptive parents selected by public or private agencies. Nonetheless, more widespread use of preplacement evaluations will alleviate concerns about whether direct placements pose any risks to children.

Under some circumstances, a waiver of the preplacement evaluation may be warranted, especially if a refusal to grant a waiver is more harmful than beneficial to a minor. For example, if an agency has placed a minor with a foster parent during the pendency of a child protection proceeding and, after the minor's parents' rights are terminated, the agency wants the foster parent to adopt the minor, this agency "placement" should not be invalid simply because the transfer of physical custody to the foster parent occurs before a pre-adoptive evaluation. This situation would constitute "good cause" for a waiver under subsection (b). Another "good cause" situation might arise if a woman who intends to place her newborn for adoption gives birth prematurely, and the prospective adopter selected by the birth mother has not had a chance to complete an evaluation. This may justify a waiver combined with a court order for a prompt post-placement evaluation. By contrast, if circumstances indicate that an individual has ample opportunity to obtain a preplacement evaluation, but intentionally waits until the last minute and then seeks a waiver, the request for a waiver should be denied. See, e.g., In re Adoption of Male Infant A., 150 Misc.2d 893, 578 N.Y.S.2d 988 (1991).

Subsection (c) dispenses with the requirement of a preplacement evaluation when a minor is placed directly with a relative. When a parent leaves a child with a relative, without any formal transfer of custody or clear understanding of what the "leaving" means, and the relative is later permitted to petition to adopt the child, it is certainly appropriate to assess the relative's suitability as an adoptive parent during the adoption proceeding. It is not feasible, however, to require that the evaluation be completed before the parent leaves the child with the relative.

[PART] 2. PREPLACEMENT EVALUATION

§2-202. Preplacement evaluator

(a) Only an individual qualified by [a state-approved licensing, certifying, or other procedure] to make a preplacement evaluation may do so.

(b) An agency from which an individual is seeking to adopt a minor may require the individual to be evaluated by its own qualified employee or independent contractor, even if the individual has received a favorable preplacement evaluation from another qualified evaluator.

§2-203. Timing and content of preplacement evaluation

(a) An individual requesting a preplacement evaluation need not have located a prospective minor adoptee when the request is made, and the individual may request more than one evaluation.

(b) A preplacement evaluation must be completed within 45 days after it is requested. An evaluator shall expedite an evaluation for an individual who has located a prospective adoptee.

(c) A preplacement evaluation must be based upon a personal interview and visit at the residence of the individual being evaluated, personal interviews with others who know the individual and may have information relevant to the evaluation, and the information required by subsection (d).

(d) A preplacement evaluation must contain the following information about the individual being evaluated:

(1) age and date of birth, nationality, racial or ethnic background, and any religious affiliation;

(2) marital status and family history, including the age and location of any child of the individual and the identity of and relationship to anyone else living in the individual's household;

(3) physical and mental health, and any history of abuse of alcohol or drugs;

(4) educational and employment history and any special skills;

(5) property and income, including outstanding financial obligations as indicated in a current credit report or financial statement furnished by the individual;

(6) any previous request for an evaluation or involvement in an adoptive placement and the outcome of the evaluation or placement;

(7) whether the individual has been charged with having committed domestic violence or a violation of [the State's child protection statute], and the disposition of the charges, or whether the individual is subject to a court order restricting the individual's right to custody or visitation with a child;

(8) whether the individual has been convicted of a crime other than a minor traffic violation;

(9) whether the individual has located a parent interested in placing a minor with the individual for adoption and, if so, a brief description of the parent and the minor; and

(10) any other fact or circumstance that may be relevant in determining whether the individual is suited to be an adoptive parent, including the quality of the environment in the individual's home and the functioning of other children in the individual's household.

(e) An individual being evaluated must submit to fingerprinting and sign a release permitting the evaluator to obtain from an appropriate law enforcement agency any record indicating that the individual has been convicted of a crime other than a minor traffic violation.

(f) An individual being evaluated shall, at the request of the evaluator, sign any release necessary for the evaluator to obtain information required by subsection (d).

§2-204. Determining suitability to be adoptive parent

(a) An evaluator shall assess the information required by Section 2-203 to determine whether it raises a specific concern that placement of any minor, or a particular minor, in the home of the individual would pose a significant risk of harm to the physical or psychological well-being of the minor.

(b) If an evaluator determines that the information assessed does not raise a specific concern, the evaluator shall find that the individual is suited to be an adoptive parent. The evaluator may comment about any factor that in the evaluator's opinion makes the individual suited in general or for a particular minor.

(c) If an evaluator determines that the information assessed raises a specific concern, the evaluator, on the basis of the original or any further investigation, shall find that the individual is or is not suited to be an adoptive parent. The evaluator shall support the finding with a written explanation.

§2-205. Filing and copies of preplacement evaluation

(a) If a preplacement evaluation contains a finding that an individual is suited to be an adoptive parent, the evaluator shall give the individual a signed copy of the evaluation. At the individual's request, the evaluator shall furnish a copy of the evaluation to a person authorized under this [Act] to place a minor for adoption and, unless the individual requests otherwise, edit the copy to exclude identifying information.

(b) If a preplacement evaluation contains a finding that an individual is not suited to be an adoptive parent of any minor, or a particular minor, the evaluator shall immediately give a signed copy of the evaluation to the individual and to the department. The department shall retain for 10 years the copy and a copy of any court order concerning the evaluation issued pursuant to Section 2-206 or 2-207.

(c) An evaluator shall retain for two years the original of a completed or incomplete preplacement evaluation and a list of every source for each item of information in the evaluation.

(d) An evaluator who conducted an evaluation in good faith is not subject to civil liability for anything contained in the evaluation.

§2-206. Review of evaluation

(a) Within 90 days after an individual receives a preplacement evaluation with a finding that he or she is not suited to be an adoptive parent, the individual may petition a court for review of the evaluation.

(b) If the court determines that the petitioner has failed to prove suitability by a preponderance of the evidence, it shall order that the petitioner not be permitted to adopt a minor and shall send a copy of the order to the department to be retained with the copy of the original evaluation. If, at the time of the court's determination, the petitioner has custody of a minor for purposes of adoption, the court shall make an appropriate order for the care and custody of the minor.

(c) If the court determines that the petitioner has proved suitability, the court shall find the petitioner suitable to be an adoptive parent and the petitioner may commence or continue a proceeding for adoption of a minor. The court shall send a copy of its order to the department to be retained with the copy of the original evaluation.

§2-207. Action by department

If, before a decree of adoption is issued, the department learns from an evaluator or another person that a minor has been placed for adoption with an individual who is the subject of a preplacement evaluation on file with the department containing a finding of unsuitability, the department shall immediately review the evaluation and investigate the circumstances of the placement and may request that the individual return the minor to the custody of the person who placed the minor or to the department. If the individual refuses to return the minor, the department shall immediately commence an action or proceeding to remove the minor from the home of the individual pursuant to [the State's child protection statute] and, pending a hearing, the court shall make an appropriate order for the care and custody of the minor.

[PART] 3. TRANSFER OF PHYSICAL CUSTODY OF MINOR BY HEALTH-CARE FACILITY FOR PURPOSES OF ADOPTION

§2-301. "Health-care facility" defined

In this [part], "health-care facility" means a hospital, clinic, or other facility authorized by this State to provide services related to birth and neonatal care.

§2-302. Authorization to transfer physical custody

(a) A health-care facility shall release a minor for the purpose of adoption to an individual or agency not otherwise legally entitled to the physical custody of the minor if, in the presence of an employee authorized by the health-care facility, the woman who gave birth to the minor signs an authorization of the transfer of physical custody.

(b) An authorized employee in whose presence the authorization required under subsection (a) is signed shall attest the signing in writing.

§2-303. Reports to department

(a) No later than 72 hours after a release pursuant to Section 2-302, a health-care facility that releases a minor for purposes of adoption shall transmit to the department a copy of the authorization required by Section 2-302 and shall report:

(1) the name, address, and telephone number of the person who authorized the release;

(2) the name, address, and telephone number of the person to whom physical custody was transferred; and

(3) the date of the transfer.

(b) No later than 30 days after a release pursuant to Section 2-302, the person to whom physical custody of a minor was transferred shall report to the department which, if any, of the following has occurred:

(1) the filing of a petition for adoption with the name and address of the petitioner;

(2) the acquisition of custody of the minor by an agency and the name and address of the agency;

(3) the return of the minor to a parent or other person having legal custody and the name and address of the parent or other person; or

(4) the transfer of physical custody of the minor to another individual and the name and address of the individual.

§2-304. Action by department

(a) If the department receives a report required under Section 2-303(a) from a health-care facility, but does not receive the report required under Section 2-303(b) within 45 days after the transfer of a minor, the department shall immediately investigate to determine the whereabouts of the minor.

(b) If none of the dispositions listed in Section 2-303(b)(1) through (3) has occurred, or the minor has been transferred to an individual described in Section 2-303(b)(4) who has not filed a petition to adopt, the department shall immediately take appropriate action to remove the minor from the individual to whom the minor has been transferred.

(c) The department may also review and investigate compliance with Sections 2-101 through 2-106 and may maintain an action in the [appropriate] court to compel compliance.

[PART] 4. CONSENT TO AND RELINQUISHMENT FOR ADOPTION

§2-401. Persons whose consent required

(a) Unless consent is not required or is dispensed with by Section 2-402, in a direct placement of a minor for adoption by a parent or guardian authorized under this [Act] to place the minor, a petition to adopt the minor may be granted only if consent to the adoption has been executed by:

(1) the woman who gave birth to the minor and the man, if any, who:

(i) is or has been married to the woman if the minor was born during the marriage or within 300 days after the marriage was terminated or a court issued a decree of separation;

(ii) attempted to marry the woman before the minor's birth by a marriage solemnized in apparent compliance with law, although the attempted marriage is or could be declared invalid, if the minor was born during the attempted marriage or within 300 days after the attempted marriage was terminated;

(iii) has been judicially determined to be the father of the minor, or has signed a document that has the effect of establishing his parentage of the minor, and:

(A) has provided, in accordance with his financial means, reasonable and consistent payments for the support of the minor and has visited or communicated with the minor; or

(B) after the minor's birth, but before the minor's placement for adoption, has married the woman who gave birth to the minor or attempted to marry her by a marriage solemnized in apparent compliance with law, although the attempted marriage is or could be declared invalid; or

(iv) has received the minor into his home and openly held out the minor as his child;

(2) the minor's guardian if expressly authorized by a court to consent to the minor's adoption; or

(3) the current adoptive or other legally recognized mother and father of the minor.

(b) Unless consent is not required under Section 2-402, in a placement of a minor for adoption by an agency authorized under this [Act] to place the minor, a petition to adopt the minor may be granted only if consent to the adoption has been executed by:

(1) the agency that placed the minor for adoption; and

(2) any individuals described in subsection (a) who have not relinquished the minor.

(c) Unless the court dispenses with the minor's consent, a petition to adopt a minor who has attained 12 years of age may be granted only if, in addition to any consent required by subsections (a) and (b), the minor has executed an informed consent to the adoption.

Comment

As a general rule, both parents of a minor child must consent to their child's adoption. Nonetheless, although a birth mother's consent is nearly always required — except as stated in Section 2-402 — consent is not required from some of the men who may be the child's father. In accord with federal and state constitutional decisions since the early 1970s on the status of unwed fathers in adoption proceedings, the Act distinguishes the men who manifest "parenting behavior," and have therefore earned the right to withhold consent from a proposed adoption of their children, from the men who fail to perform parental duties and may therefore be denied the right to veto a proposed adoption. In specifying precisely which men are

entitled to consent and which men are merely entitled to notice of a proposed adoption, this section is influenced by, but departs from, the definition of "presumed father" in the Uniform Parentage Act, 9B ULA 298.

Special attention has been given to the thwarted father and the balance between his rights and the interests of the child. A thwarted father is a man who has been prevented from meeting his parenting responsibilities (a)(1)(iii) or (iv), because the mother did not tell him of the pregnancy or birth, lied about her plans for the child, disappeared after the child's birth, named another man as the father, or was married to another man in a State that maintains a version of the conclusive presumption of paternity upheld by a plurality of the U.S. Supreme Court in Michael H. v. Gerald D., 491 U.S. 110 (1989), or because the State, acting through its licensed agency, placed the child with prospective adoptive parents before he was aware of his child's existence or could assume parenting responsibilities; Lehr v. Robertson, 463 U.S. 248 (1983).

A thwarted father may be able to assert parental rights during the pendency of the adoption proceeding or in response to a petition to terminate his parental relationship to a minor. See Article 3, Part 5. A thwarted father may succeed in blocking an adoption if he not only can prove a "compelling reason" for not having performed parental duties but successfully defends against an effort by the prospective adoptive parents, the birth mother, or an agency to prove that termination of a thwarted father's rights is necessary to avoid detriment or a risk of substantial harm to the child. See Section 3-504(d) and (e). A person may not challenge an adoption decree more than six months after it is issued, even if the person was thwarted in his ability to assume parenting responsibilities.

The Act is consistent with U.S. Supreme Court decisions on the status of fathers in custody and stepparent adoption proceedings. The Court has not **ruled that all biological fathers have a constitutionally protected right to withhold consent to a proposed adoption of their child; Quilloin v. Walcott, 434 U.S. 246 (1978) (equal protection clause not violated by State's rule that unwed father who has "never shouldered any significant responsibility" for the care of his child, despite opportunities to do so, cannot veto the child's adoption by the mother's husband). Only those unwed biological fathers who perform parental duties and actively participate in childrearing are entitled to the same rights as is the birth mother to consent to, or to veto, an adoption; Caban v. Mohammed, 441 U.S. 380 (1979) (equal protection clause violated by state law that gives unwed mothers but not unwed fathers who support and care for their child a right to block an adoption). See, also, Stanley v. Illinois, 405 U.S. 645 (1972) (due process clause offended by denial of parental fitness hearing to unwed father who wanted custody of the three children he had both "sired and raised"). Although this Act is generally protective of the interests of unwed fathers in receiving notice of a proposed adoption, it is not unconstitutional to deny notice to unwed fathers who do not perform parental duties and who have not taken certain formal steps to acknowledge their paternity; Lehr v. Robertson, 463 U.S. 248 (1983). Moreover, the Court has ruled that not all biological fathers have a protected "liberty interest" in their biological offspring; Michael H. v. Gerald D., 491 U.S. 110 (1989) (upholding the legitimacy of a child's "unitary family" of birth mother and her husband against the desire of a biological father, not married to the mother, to establish his paternity and claim visitation rights).**

With respect to consent from an adoptee, the Act follows the prevailing practice in most States. Consent is required from adoptees who have attained a certain age — subsection (c) says 12 or older — subject to the court's discretion to waive the consent of an adoptee. See Section 2-402(b). When a minor adoptee's consent is required, it is in addition to the consent of the parents or guardian or agency, and without the minor's consent or sufficient justification for waiving it, the adoption cannot be granted.

When an agency is authorized by the Act to place a minor for adoption, the agency's consent is required in lieu of the consent of a parent or guardian who has relinquished the minor to the agency for adoption, and in lieu of the consent of any parent whose status has been legally terminated.

The consent of a minor's guardian is not required unless the court that appointed the guardian expressly authorizes the guardian to consent to the minor's adoption.

§2-402. Persons whose consent not required

(a) Consent to an adoption of a minor is not required of:

(1) an individual who has relinquished the minor to an agency for purposes of adoption;

(2) an individual whose parental relationship to the minor has been judicially terminated or determined not to exist;

(3) a parent who has been judicially declared incompetent;

(4) a man who has not been married to the woman who gave birth to the minor and who, after the conception of the minor, executes a verified statement denying paternity or disclaiming any interest in the minor and acknowledging that his statement is irrevocable when executed;

(5) the personal representative of a deceased parent's estate; or

(6) a parent or other person who has not executed a consent or a relinquishment and who fails to file an answer or make an appearance in a proceeding for adoption or for termination of a parental relationship within the requisite time after service of notice of the proceeding.

(b) The court may dispense with the consent of:

(1) a guardian or an agency whose consent is otherwise required upon a finding that the consent is being withheld contrary to the best interest of a minor adoptee; or

(2) a minor adoptee who has attained 12 years of age upon a finding that it is not in the best interest of the minor to require the consent.

Comment

Subsection (a)(2) deprives an individual whose parental rights in a specific child have been terminated pursuant either to the State's general termination statute or to Article 3, Part 5 of the right to veto the child's adoption.

Subsection (a)(3) provides that the consent of a mentally incompetent parent is not required. Upon an appropriate judicial determination that a parent is mentally incompetent and incapable of caring for a minor child, a guardian, or a conservator, is likely to be appointed to act in place of the parent. The task of this guardian or conservator is to protect the parent, and is not necessarily to perform parental responsibilities with respect to the parent's child. The Act provides that if another individual is to act in lieu of the parent for purposes of placing a minor child for adoption, that individual must be appointed by a court as the general guardian or guardian of the person of the child and must be specifically authorized by the court to place the minor for adoption and to consent to the minor's adoption. A guardian or conservator appointed to handle an incompetent parent's affairs is NOT entitled to place the minor or consent to an adoption.

Subsection (a)(4) is applicable to situations in which an alleged father wants to avoid any responsibility for a minor who may be his child, but is unwilling to execute a formal consent or relinquishment because that would require an admission of paternity. If this man executes a statement either denying paternity or disclaiming any interest in the child, his consent to the child's adoption is not required and he will not have to be notified of the adoption proceeding. A "disclaimer of any interest" allows a man to remain noncommittal on the issue of his paternity. This statement may be executed at any time, either before or after the child's birth, and is final and irrevocable. If a birth mother later consents to her child's adoption, or relinquishes the child to an agency, and an alleged father has executed a disclaimer, the adoption can proceed expeditiously. Alternatively, if the mother decides to retain custody of her child, she can later seek child support from the man who signed this "disclaimer" by bringing an action to establish his paternity. The disclaimer should not be allowed to serve as a defense against an "involuntary" paternity and child support action. Because a man who executes a disclaimer under this subsection is an individual whose legal status as a parent is not established, he is not included in the definition of "parent" in Section 1-101(10). Nonetheless, if he is, in fact, the biological father, the person who places the minor for adoption should attempt to learn his health and social history. See Section 1-106.

Subsection (b) is applicable to those rare situations in which an agency or guardian objects to an adoption after having placed the minor with a prospective adoptive parent. Because neither the agency nor the guardian has the benefit of a presumption of parental fitness, their consent can be dispensed with upon a showing by a preponderance of the evidence that the consent is being withheld contrary to the best interest of the minor. The prospective adoptive parents would have the burden of persuasion.

§2-403. Individuals who may relinquish minor

A parent or guardian whose consent to the adoption of a minor is required by Section 2-401 may relinquish to an agency all rights with respect to the minor, including legal and physical custody and the right to consent to the minor's adoption.

§2-404. Time and prerequisites for execution of consent or relinquishment

(a) A parent whose consent to the adoption of a minor is required by Section 2-401 may execute a consent or a relinquishment only after the minor is born. A parent who executes a consent or relinquishment may revoke the consent or relinquishment within 192 hours after the birth of the minor.

(b) A guardian may execute a consent to the adoption of a minor or a relinquishment at any time after being authorized by a court to do so.

(c) An agency that places a minor for adoption may execute its consent at any time before or during the hearing on the petition for adoption.

(d) A minor adoptee whose consent is required may execute a consent at any time before or during the hearing on the petition for adoption.

(e) Before executing a consent or relinquishment, a parent must have been informed of the meaning and consequences of adoption, the availability of personal and legal counseling, the consequences of misidentifying the other parent, the procedure for releasing information about the health and other characteristics of the parent which may affect the physical or psychological well-being of the adoptee, and the procedure for the consensual release of the parent's identity to an adoptee, an adoptee's direct descendant, or an adoptive parent pursuant to [Article] 6. The parent must have had an opportunity to indicate in a signed document whether and under what circumstances the parent is or is not willing to release identifying information, and must have been informed of the procedure for changing the document at a later time.

Comment

This section is consistent with the rule in every State that a birth parent's consent or relinquishment is not valid or final until some time

after a child is born. Many States provide that a valid consent may not be executed until at least 12, 24, 48, or, more typically, 72 hours after the child is born. Even the few States, like Washington or Alabama, which permit a consent to be executed before a child's birth, provide that the consent is not final (i.e., it remains revocable) until at least 48 hours after the birth or until confirmed in a formal termination proceeding. Most States provide that a consent or relinquishment is revocable for at least some period of time after being executed, but there are substantial and confusing differences from one State to another with respect to these time periods and with respect to the consequences of revocation for the parent, the child, and the prospective adoptive parent. This Act accommodates the interests of birth parents in not being pressured into making decisions they will later regret with the interests of minors and prospective adoptive parents in having an expeditious resolution of their status.

The Act responds to the needs of birth parents, and especially birth mothers, who are fully prepared shortly after a child's birth to execute an informed decision concerning the child's adoption. The Act also responds to the needs of birth parents who want more time to consider their decision.

This section provides that a consent to a direct placement for adoption, or a relinquishment to an agency, may be executed at any time after a child's birth, but may be absolutely revoked for up to 192 hours (8 days) after the birth. If executed more than 192 hours after birth, a consent or relinquishment is not revocable except for a limited time on the basis of fraud or duress and under the specific circumstances set forth in Sections 2-408 and 2-409. Of course, no parent is required to sign a consent or relinquishment at any time. Moreover, a parent who, before executing a consent, makes a direct placement, pursuant to Part 1 of this article, or authorizes the release of a new born from a birthing center, pursuant to Part 1 of this article, may decide to not execute the consent and to exercise her right to reclaim custody of the child.

Before executing a consent or relinquishment, parents must be offered personal counseling, as well as separate legal representation — minor parents must have separate representation — and must be given information about the meaning and consequences of adoptive placements, consents, relinquishments, and other aspects of an adoption. The parents should be informed that a prospective adoptive parent or an agency may pay for the legal or psychological counseling. See Sections 7-103 and 7-104. A birth parent, especially the birth mother, should also be warned about the consequences of not naming, or misidentifying, the other parent. To avoid even the appearance of a conflict of interest, a consent or relinquishment has to be executed before a "neutral" individual, who has to attest to the apparent validity of the consent or relinquishment. See Section 2-405. This individual also has to confirm that prospective adoptive parents in a direct placement, or an agency to whom a minor is relinquished, accepted the consent or relinquishment and acknowledged its consequences. See Section 2-405. The comprehensive content of the consent or relinquishment is also intended to protect the parent against any misunderstanding concerning a proposed adoption. See Section 2-406.

In some States, the Department of Social Services will develop informational material for dissemination to birth parents who are considering consenting to the adoption of their child or relinquishing their child for adoption. In other States, private as well as public adoption service-providers will develop and disseminate appropriate materials. The Act defers to each State's own decisions about what mix of public and private resources can best produce pamphlets, forms, and other materials to respond to the Act's goal of ensuring that consents or relinquishments are well informed as well as voluntary. Some States will insist, as they already do, that birth parents have separate legal counsel; others will leave that issue to be determined by the parties themselves. Some States may mandate other kinds of counseling instead of simply insisting that it be available and permitting the adoptive parents to pay for it.

This section treats birth mothers and fathers equally: neither can execute a consent until after their child is born. Nonetheless, an unwed or alleged father who is certain that he wants to eschew responsibility for the child, even before the child is born, can execute a disclaimer of parental interest under Section 2-402(a)(4).

The provisions of subsection (e) are based on what is a routine aspect of adoption practice in some States: parents are asked to provide information about their health and social history, told how to update this information in later years, and informed of the existence of the mutual consent registry. They are given an opportunity to record their preferences for withholding or releasing their identities to adoptive parents at any time or directly to adoptees when they are 18 or older. They are also informed that any preference indicated at the time may later be changed. Any document signed by a parent pursuant to this subsection becomes part of the court's permanent record and is filed with the registry established by Article 6.

§2-405. Procedure for execution of consent or relinquishment

(a) A consent or relinquishment executed by a parent or guardian must be signed or confirmed in the presence of:

(1) a judge of a court of record;

(2) an individual whom a judge of a court of record designates to take consents or relinquishments;

(3) an employee other than an employee of an agency to which a minor is relinquished whom an agency designates to take consents or relinquishments;

(4) a lawyer other than a lawyer who is representing an adoptive parent or the agency to which a minor is relinquished;

(5) a commissioned officer on active duty in the military service of the United States, if the individual executing the consent or relinquishment is in military service; or

(6) an officer of the foreign service or a consular officer of the United States in another country, if the individual executing the consent or relinquishment is in that country.

(b) A consent executed by a minor adoptee must be signed or confirmed in the presence of the court in the proceeding for adoption or in a manner the court directs.

(c) A parent who is a minor is competent to execute a consent or relinquishment if the parent has had access to counseling and has had the advice of a lawyer who is not representing an adoptive parent or the agency to which the parent's child is relinquished.

(d) An individual before whom a consent or relinquishment is signed or confirmed under subsection (a) shall certify in writing that he or she orally explained the contents and consequences of the consent or relinquishment, and to the best of his or her knowledge or belief, the individual executing the consent or relinquishment:

(1) read or was read the consent or relinquishment and understood it;

(2) signed the consent or relinquishment voluntarily and received or was offered a copy of it;

(3) was furnished the information and afforded an opportunity to sign the document described by Section 2-404(e);

(4) received or was offered counseling services and information about adoption; and

(5) if a parent who is a minor, was advised by a lawyer who is not representing an adoptive parent or the agency to which the parent's child is being relinquished, or, if an adult, was informed of the right to have a lawyer who is not representing an adoptive parent or an agency to which the parent's child is being relinquished.

(e) A prospective adoptive parent named or describe in a consent to the adoption of a minor shall sign a statement indicating an intention to adopt the minor, acknowledging an obligation to return legal and physical custody of the minor to the minor's parent if the parent revokes the consent within the time specified in Section 2-404(a), and acknowledging responsibility for the minor's support and medical and other care if the consent is not revoked.

(f) If an agency accepts a relinquishment, an employee of the agency shall sign a statement accepting the relinquishment, acknowledging its obligation to return legal and physical custody of the child to the minor's parent if the parent revokes the relinquishment within the time indicated in Section 2-404(a), and acknowledging responsibility for the minor's support and medical and other care if the relinquishment is not revoked.

(g) An individual before whom a consent or a relinquishment is signed or confirmed shall certify having received the statements required by subsections (e) and (f).

(h) A consent by an agency to the adoption of a minor in the agency's legal custody must be executed by the head or an individual authorized by the agency and must be signed or confirmed under oath in the presence of an individual authorized to take acknowledgments.

(i) A consent or relinquishment executed and signed or confirmed in another State or country is valid if in accordance with this [Act] or with the law and procedure prevailing where executed.

§2-406. Content of consent or relinquishment

(a) A consent or relinquishment required from a parent or guardian must be in writing and contain, in plain English or, if the native language of the parent or guardian is a language other than English, in that language:

(1) the date, place, and time of the execution of the consent or relinquishment;

(2) the name, date of birth, and current mailing address of the individual executing the consent or relinquishment;

(3) the date of birth and the name or pseudonym of the minor adoptee;

(4) if a consent, the name, address, and telephone and telecopier numbers of the lawyer representing the prospective adoptive parent with whom the individual executing the consent has placed or intends to place the minor for adoption;

(5) if a relinquishment, the name, address, and telephone and telecopier numbers of the agency to which the minor is being relinquished; and

(6) specific instructions as to how to revoke the consent or relinquishment and how to commence an action to set it aside.

(b) A consent must state that the parent or guardian executing the document is voluntarily and unequivocally consenting to the transfer of legal and physical custody to, and the adoption of the minor by, a specific adoptive parent whom the parent or guardian has selected.

(c) A relinquishment must state that the individual executing the relinquishment voluntarily consents to the permanent transfer of legal and physical custody of the minor to the agency for the purposes of adoption.

(d) A consent or relinquishment must state:

(1) an understanding that after the consent or relinquishment is signed or confirmed in substantial compliance with Section 2-405, it is final and, except under a circumstance stated in Section 2-408 or 2-409, may not be revoked or set aside for any reason, including the failure of an adoptive parent to permit the individual executing the consent or relinquishment to visit or communicate with the minor adoptee;

(2) an understanding that the adoption will extinguish all parental rights and obligations the individual executing the consent or relinquishment has with respect to the minor adoptee, except for arrearages of child support, and will remain valid whether or not any agreement for visitation or communication with the minor adoptee is later performed;

(3) that the individual executing the consent or relinquishment has:

(i) received a copy of the consent or relinquishment;

(ii) received or been offered counseling services and information about adoption which explains the meaning and consequences of an adoption;

(iii) been advised, if a parent who is a minor, by a lawyer who is not representing an adoptive parent or the agency to which the minor adoptee is being relinquished, or, if an adult, has been informed of the right to have a lawyer who is not representing an adoptive parent or the agency;

(iv) been provided the information and afforded an opportunity to sign the document described in Section 2-404(e); and

(v) been advised of the obligation to provide the information required under Section 2-106;

(4) that the individual executing the consent or relinquishment has not received or been promised any money or anything of value for the consent or the relinquishment, except for payments authorized by [Article] 7;

(5) that the minor is not an Indian child as defined in the Indian Child Welfare Act, 25 U.S.C. Sections 1901 et seq.;

(6) that the individual believes the adoption of the minor is in the minor's best interest; and

(7) if a consent, that the individual who is consenting waives further notice unless the adoption is contested, appealed, or denied.

(e) A relinquishment may provide that the individual who is relinquishing waives notice of any proceeding for adoption, or waives notice unless the adoption is contested, appealed, or denied.

(f) A consent or relinquishment may provide for its revocation if:

(1) another consent or relinquishment is not executed within a specified period;

(2) a court decides not to terminate another individual's parental relationship to the minor; or

(3) in a direct placement for adoption, a petition for adoption by a prospective adoptive parent, named or described in the consent, is denied or withdrawn.

§2-407. Consequences of consent or relinquishment

(a) Except under a circumstance stated in Section 2-408, a consent to the adoption of a minor which is executed by a parent or guardian in substantial compliance with Sections 2-405 and 2-406 is final and irrevocable, and:

(1) unless a court orders otherwise to protect the welfare of the minor, entitles the prospective adoptive parent named or described in the consent to the legal and physical custody of the minor and imposes on that individual responsibility for the support and medical and other care of the minor;

(2) terminates any duty of a parent who executed the consent with respect to the minor, except for arrearages of child support; and

(3) terminates any right of a parent or guardian who executed the consent to object to the minor's adoption by the prospective adoptive parent and any right to notice of the proceeding for adoption unless the adoption is contested, appealed, or denied.

(b) Except under a circumstance stated in Section 2-409, a relinquishment of a minor to an agency which is executed by a parent or guardian in substantial compliance with Sections 2-405 and 2-406 is final and irrevocable and:

(1) unless a court orders otherwise to protect the welfare of the minor, entitles the agency to the legal custody of the minor until a decree of adoption becomes final;

(2) empowers the agency to place the minor for adoption, consent to the minor's adoption, and delegate to a prospective adoptive parent responsibility for the support and medical and other care of the minor;

(3) terminates any duty of the individual who executed the relinquishment with respect to the minor, except for arrearages of child support; and

(4) terminates any right of the individual who executed the relinquishment to object to the minor's adoption and, unless otherwise provided in the relinquishment, any right to notice of the proceeding for adoption.

Comment

This section specifies the general legal consequences of a consent or relinquishment and is consistent with the Act's intention to keep track of a minor and assign responsibility for the minor's care and support throughout the adoption process. If executed in substantial compliance with this part, either document is final and irrevocable except under limited circumstances and entitles the prospective adoptive parents in a direct placement and the agency in an agency placement to the custody of the minor and requires them to provide support and care for the minor. The section also specifies the extent to which further notice of the adoption proceeding is or is not waived by a consent or relinquishment.

§2-408. Revocation of consent

(a) In a direct placement of a minor for adoption by a parent or guardian, a consent is revoked if:

(1) within 192 hours after the birth of the minor, a parent who executed the consent notifies in writing the prospective adoptive parent, or the adoptive parent's lawyer, that the parent revokes the consent, or the parent complies with any other instructions for revocation specified in the consent; or

(2) the individual who executed the consent and the prospective adoptive parent named or described in the consent agree to its revocation.

(b) In a direct placement of a minor for adoption by a parent or guardian, the court shall set aside the consent if the individual who executed the consent establishes:

(1) by clear and convincing evidence, before a decree of adoption is issued, that the consent was obtained by fraud or duress;

(2) by a preponderance of the evidence before a decree of adoption is issued that, without good cause shown, a

petition to adopt was not filed within 60 days after the minor was placed for adoption; or

(3) by a preponderance of the evidence, that a condition permitting revocation has occurred, as expressly provided for in the consent pursuant to Section 2-406.

(c) If the consent of an individual who had legal and physical custody of a minor when the minor was placed for adoption or when the consent was executed is revoked, the prospective adoptive parent shall immediately return the minor to the individual's custody and move to dismiss a proceeding for adoption or termination of the individual's parental relationship to the minor. If the minor is not returned immediately, the individual may petition the court named in the consent for appropriate relief. The court shall hear the petition expeditiously.

(d) If the consent of an individual who had legal and physical custody of a minor when the minor was placed for adoption or the consent was executed is set aside under subsection (b)(1), the court shall order the return of the minor to the custody of the individual and dismiss a proceeding for adoption.

(e) If the consent of an individual who had legal and physical custody of a minor when the minor was placed for adoption or the consent was executed is set aside under subsection (b)(2) or (3) and no ground exists under [Article] 3, [Part] 5, for terminating the relationship of parent and child between the individual and the minor, the court shall dismiss a proceeding for adoption and order the return of the minor to the custody of the individual unless the court finds that return will be detrimental to the minor.

(f) If the consent of an individual who did not have physical custody of a minor when the minor was placed for adoption or when the consent was executed is revoked or set aside and no ground exists under [Article] 3, [Part] 5, for terminating the relationship of parent and child between the individual and the minor, the court shall dismiss a proceeding for adoption and issue an order providing for the care and custody of the minor according to the best interest of the minor.

Comment

This section and Section 2-409 deal with the circumstances under which a consent or relinquishment is revoked or may be set aside. Revocation of a consent to a direct placement may occur, without judicial action, under two circumstances. First, a birth parent who executes consent before the minor is 192 hours old can decide to revoke within those 192 hours, subsection (a)(1). This right to revoke is absolute and requires the prospective adoptive parents or their attorney to return the infant to the parent if the infant had been placed with them. It is not lawful for a prospective adopter to retain custody of the infant after a parent has revoked under subsection (a)(1). If the infant is not returned, the birth parent may petition a court for relief, subsection (c). Second is when the parent and the prospective adopter mutually agree to revoke the consent and not proceed with the proposed adoption.

Any other effort to set aside a consent requires judicial action. Until a decree of adoption is issued, a consent will be set aside if the parent proves by clear and convincing evidence that it was obtained by fraud or duress. If a consent by a parent who previously had custody is set aside for this reason, the court shall order the child returned to the parent and dismiss the adoption proceeding. A finding of fraud or duress is tantamount to a finding that a valid consent never existed and therefore the parent has never agreed to the adoption of the child and the would-be adoptive parents have no basis for retaining custody of the child. The adoption proceeding must come to an end.

Actions to set aside consents for other reasons have less certain outcomes. Even if a parent establishes by a preponderance of the evidence that one or more of the contingencies specified in the consent has occurred — for example, the other parent's rights have not been terminated — it does not automatically follow that the parent is entitled to the legal or physical custody of the minor. The Act provides that the court has to take into account the minor's circumstances at the time a consent is set aside. Even though an adoption proceeding may have to be dismissed, the court has to make an order for the minor's care and custody. In making this order, this court must consider not only the status of the birth parent but also the needs and interests of the minor. It is therefore possible under some circumstances for the individuals who sought to adopt the minor to end up with custody of the minor. Much will depend on the relationship between the minor's birth parents, the length of time the minor has been out of their custody, whether independent grounds exist for terminating the rights of either birth parent, the recommendation of the minor's guardian ad litem [appointed in any contested proceeding, Section 3-201], the willingness of the would-be adopters to retain custody even if an adoption is not granted.

Most importantly, the Act does not treat a minor as an object that "belongs" to a parent or would-be parent and has to be shifted back and forth in the event "ownership" rights are changed or reinstated. The fact that a birth parent's status as a legal parent may be restored or recognized upon the setting aside of a consent or a relinquishment is not tantamount to a determination that the minor must be placed in that parent's custody. In the relatively atypical cases where a set-aside is warranted, the likely outcome is that the minor will end up in a parent's custody. Nonetheless, in the event of a set-aside, this Act requires the court to make an independent determination with respect to the minor's custody. That determination ultimately depends on what the court decides is not detrimental to the minor, subsection (e), or is in the minor's best interests, subsection (f). See, also, the consequences of dismissing a proceeding for adoption for other reasons. See Section 3-704.

§2-409. Revocation of relinquishment

(a) A relinquishment is revoked if:

(1) within 192 hours after the birth of the minor, a parent who executed the relinquishment gives written notice to the agency that accepted it, that the parent revokes the relinquishment, or the parent complies with any other instructions for revocation specified in the relinquishment; or

(2) the individual who executed the relinquishment and the agency that accepted it agree to its revocation.

(b) The court shall set aside a relinquishment if the individual who executed the relinquishment establishes:

(1) by clear and convincing evidence, before a decree of adoption is issued, that the relinquishment was obtained by fraud or duress; or

(2) by a preponderance of the evidence, that a condition permitting revocation has occurred, as expressly provided for in the relinquishment pursuant to Section 2-406.

(c) If a relinquishment by an individual who had legal and physical custody of a minor when the relinquishment was executed is revoked, the agency shall immediately return the minor to the individual's custody and move to dismiss a proceeding for adoption. If the minor is not returned immediately, the individual may petition the court named in the relinquishment for appropriate relief. The court shall hear the petition expeditiously.

(d) If a relinquishment by an individual who had legal and physical custody of a minor when the relinquishment was executed is set aside under subsection (b)(1), the court shall dismiss a proceeding for adoption and order the return of the minor to the custody of the individual.

(e) If a relinquishment by an individual who had legal and physical custody of a minor when the relinquishment was executed is set aside under subsection (b)(2) and no ground exists under [Article] 3, [Part] 5, for terminating the relationship of parent and child between the individual and the minor, the court shall dismiss a proceeding for adoption and order the return of the minor to the custody of the individual unless the court finds that return will be detrimental to the minor.

(f) If a relinquishment by an individual who did not have physical custody of a minor when the relinquishment was executed is revoked or set aside and no ground exists under [Article] 3, [Part] 5, for terminating the relationship of parent and child between the individual and the minor, the court shall dismiss a proceeding for adoption and shall issue an order providing for the care and custody of the minor according to the best interest of the minor.

[ARTICLE] 3. GENERAL PROCEDURE FOR ADOPTION OF MINORS

[PART] 1. JURISDICTION AND VENUE

Prefatory Comment

This Act provides jurisdictional provisions for adoption that are consistent with the jurisdictional provisions of the Uniform Child Custody Jurisdiction Act (UCCJA), but with modifications to address the distinctive characteristics of adoption proceedings and to reduce judicial uncertainty about how to apply the UCCJA "home state" and "significant connection" standards to adoptions. Under the UCCJA, §2, a "custody determination" is a "court decision and court orders and instructions providing for the custody of a child, including visitation rights," but not including child support orders. A "custody proceeding" includes proceedings in which "a custody determination is one of several issues, such as an action for divorce or separation, and includes child neglect and dependency proceedings." Moreover, the full faith and credit provisions of the federal Parental Kidnapping Prevention Act (PKPA), 28 U.S.C.A. §§1738A et seq., which affect "custody determinations" made pursuant to the UCCJA, should also apply to decrees or orders issued under this Act, but are not clearly applicable to a State's final decrees of adoption. The PKPA definition of "custody determination" is "a judgment, decree, or other order providing for the custody or visitation of a child, and includes permanent and temporary orders, and initial orders and modifications," 28 U.S.C.A. §1738A(b)(3). Although adoptions are not excluded from this definition, they are not specifically included.

Even without the benefit of the clarifications proposed by this Act, nearly all of the state appellate courts that have faced the question of whether adoption proceedings are within the scope of the UCCJA and the PKPA have answered, "yes." See, e.g., In re Adoption of Child by T.W.C., 270 N.J. Super. 225, 636 A.2d 1083 (1994); In re Adoption of Baby Girl B., 867 P.2d 1074 (Kan. App. 1994); In re Baby Girl Clausen, 502 N.W.2d 649 (Mich. 1993); Torres v. Mason, 848 P.2d 592 (Or. 1993); In re Brandon S., 507 N.W.2d 94 (Wis. 1993); In re Zachariah Nathaniel K., 6 Cal. App. 4th 1025, 8 Cal. Rptr. 2d 423 (1992); Rogers v. Platt, 199 Cal. App. 3d 1204, 245 Cal. Rptr. 532 (1988) and 641 F. Supp. 381 (D.D.C. 1986), *rev'd on other grounds,* 814 F.2d 683 (D.C.Cir. 1987); Gainey v. Olivo, 373 S.E.2d 4 (Ga. 1988), followed by Ga. Code Ann. §19-9-42(3) (expressly including adoption proceedings in the definition of "custody proceeding"); Souza v. Superior Ct., 193 Cal. App.3d 1304, 238 Cal. Rptr. 892 (1987) (UCCJA & PKPA apply to stepparent adoptions); Foster v. Stein, 183 Mich. App. 424, 454 N.W.2d 244 (1990); In re Adoption of B.E.W.G., 549 A.2d 1286 (Pa. Super. Ct. 1988); In re Adoption of K.C.P., 432 So.2d 620 (Fla. Ct. App. 1983) (Florida adoption proceeding violated UCCJA because custody proceedings with respect to minor were pending in New York).

Although these and many other decisions treat adoptions as custody determinations within the UCCJA and PKPA, they manifest considerable uncertainty about precisely how to fit adoptions into the existing jurisdictional pegs. Section 3-101 reduces this uncertainty by including "prospective

adoptive parent" in the list of individual's whose caregiving relationship to a minor can establish a basis for exercising jurisdiction. Subsection (a)(1) departs from the basic "home state" provision of the UCCJA to accommodate the special circumstances of an adoptive placement of an infant born in one State with prospective adoptive parents who live in another State. It does this by allowing prospective adoptive parents who live in State A and have had custody of an infant under the age of six months from soon after the infant was born in State B — but not from the exact moment of birth — to commence an adoption proceeding in State A without waiting an additional six months. This subsection therefore enables the prospective parents to comply in State A with the requirement that an adoption petition be filed within 30 days after placement. See Section 3-302. It is also consistent with the UCCJA/PKPA goal of having a proceeding that affects a child's status heard in the forum with reliable information about the child's future care.

Section 3-101 also departs from the UCCJA "home state" and "significant connection" plus "substantial evidence" provisions in order to clarify the circumstances under which an adoption proceeding may be commenced by prospective adoptive parents in the State where the agency that placed the minor is located, subsection (a)(3), or in a State other than one that issued a previous visitation or custody order with respect to the minor, subsection (c).

§3-101. Jurisdiction

(a) Except as otherwise provided in subsections (b) and (c), a court of this State has jurisdiction over a proceeding for the adoption of a minor commenced under this [Act] if:

(1) immediately before commencement of the proceeding, the minor lived in this State with a parent, a guardian, a prospective adoptive parent, or another person acting as parent, for at least six consecutive months, excluding periods of temporary absence, or, in the case of a minor under six months of age, lived in this State from soon after birth with any of those individuals and there is available in this State substantial evidence concerning the minor's present or future care;

(2) immediately before commencement of the proceeding, the prospective adoptive parent lived in this State for at least six consecutive months, excluding periods of temporary absence, and there is available in this State substantial evidence concerning the minor's present or future care;

(3) the agency that placed the minor for adoption is located in this State and it is in the best interest of the minor that a court of this State assume jurisdiction because:

(i) the minor and the minor's parents, or the minor and the prospective adoptive parent, have a significant connection with this State; and

(ii) there is available in this State substantial evidence concerning the minor's present or future care;

(4) the minor and the prospective adoptive parent are physically present in this State and the minor has been abandoned or it is necessary in an emergency to protect the minor because the minor has been subjected to or threatened with mistreatment or abuse or is otherwise neglected; or

(5) it appears that no other State would have jurisdiction under prerequisites substantially in accordance with paragraphs (1) through (4), or another State has declined to exercise jurisdiction on the ground that this State is the more appropriate forum to hear a petition for adoption of the minor, and it is in the best interest of the minor that a court of this State assume jurisdiction.

(b) A court of this State may not exercise jurisdiction over a proceeding for adoption of a minor if at the time the petition for adoption is filed a proceeding concerning the custody or adoption of the minor is pending in a court of another State exercising jurisdiction substantially in conformity with [the Uniform Child Custody Jurisdiction Act] or this [Act] unless the proceeding is stayed by the court of the other State.

(c) If a court of another State has issued a decree or order concerning the custody of a minor who may be the subject of a proceeding for adoption in this State, a court of this State may not exercise jurisdiction over a proceeding for adoption of the minor unless:

(1) the court of this State finds that the court of the State which issued the decree or order:

(i) does not have continuing jurisdiction to modify the decree or order under jurisdictional prerequisites substantially in accordance with [the Uniform Child Custody Jurisdiction Act] or has declined to assume jurisdiction to modify the decree or order; or

(ii) does not have jurisdiction over a proceeding for adoption substantially in conformity with subsection (a)(1) through (4) or has declined to assume jurisdiction over a proceeding for adoption; and

(2) the court of this State has jurisdiction over the proceeding.

§3-102. Venue

A petition for adoption of a minor may be filed in the court in the [county] in which a petitioner lives, the minor lives, or an office of the agency that placed the minor is located.

[PART] 2. GENERAL PROCEDURAL PROVISIONS

§3-201. Appointment of lawyer or guardian ad litem

(a) In a proceeding under this [Act] which may result in the termination of a relationship of parent and child, the court shall appoint a lawyer for any indigent, minor, or incompetent individual who appears in the proceeding and whose parental relationship to a child may be terminated, unless the court finds that the minor or incompetent individual has sufficient financial means to hire a lawyer, or the indigent individual declines to be represented by a lawyer.

(b) The court shall appoint a guardian ad litem for a minor adoptee in a contested proceeding under this [Act] and may appoint a guardian ad litem for a minor adoptee in an uncontested proceeding.

§3-202. No right to jury

A proceeding under this [Act] for adoption or termination of a parental relationship must be heard by the court without a jury.

§3-203. Confidentiality of proceedings

Except for a proceeding pursuant to [Article] 7, a civil proceeding under this [Act] must be heard in closed court.

§3-204. Custody during pendency of proceeding

In order to protect the welfare of the minor, the court shall make an interim order for custody of a minor adoptee according to the best interest of the minor in a contested proceeding under this [Act] for adoption or termination of a parental relationship and may make an interim order for custody in an uncontested proceeding.

§3-205. Removal of adoptee from state

Before a decree of adoption is issued, a petitioner may not remove a minor adoptee for more than 30 consecutive days from the State in which the petitioner resides without the permission of the court, if the minor was placed directly for adoption, or, if an agency placed the minor for adoption, the permission of the agency.

[PART] 3. PETITION FOR ADOPTION OF MINOR

§3-301. Standing to petition to adopt

(a) Except as otherwise provided in subsection (c), the only individuals who have standing to petition to adopt a minor under this [article] are:

(1) an individual with whom a minor has been placed for adoption or who has been selected as a prospective adoptive parent by a person authorized under this [Act] to place the minor for adoption; or

(2) an individual with whom a minor has not been placed for adoption or who has not been selected or rejected as a prospective adoptive parent pursuant to [Article] 2, [Parts] 1 through 3, but who has had physical custody of the minor for at least six months immediately before seeking to file a petition for adoption and is allowed to file the petition by the court for good cause shown.

(b) The spouse of a petitioner must join in the petition unless legally separated from the petitioner or judicially declared incompetent.

(c) A petition for adoption of a minor stepchild by a stepparent may be filed under [Article] 4 and a petition for adoption of an emancipated minor may be filed under [Article] 5.

§3-302. Time for filing petition

Unless the court allows a later filing, a prospective adoptive parent with standing under Section 3-301(a)(1) shall file a petition for adoption no later than 30 days after a minor is placed for adoption with that individual.

§3-303. Caption of petition

The caption of a petition for adoption of a minor must contain the name of or a pseudonym for the minor adoptee. The caption may not contain the name of the petitioner.

§3-304. Content of petition

(a) A petition for adoption of a minor must be signed and verified by the petitioner and contain the following information or state why any of the information omitted is not contained in the petition:

(1) the full name, age, and place and duration of residence of the petitioner;

(2) the current marital status of the petitioner, including the date and place of any marriage, the date of any legal separation or divorce, and the date of any judicial determination that a petitioner's spouse is incompetent;

(3) that the petitioner has facilities and resources to provide for the care and support of the minor;

(4) that a preplacement evaluation containing a finding that the petitioner is suited to be an adoptive parent has been prepared or updated within the 18 months next preceding the placement, or that the absence of a preplacement evaluation has been excused by a court for good cause shown or is not required under Section 2-201;

(5) the first name, sex, and date, or approximate date, and place of birth of the minor adoptee and a statement that the minor is or is not an Indian child as defined in the Indian Child Welfare Act, 25 U.S.C. Sections 1901 et seq.;

(6) the circumstances under which the petitioner obtained physical custody of the minor, including the date of placement of the minor with the petitioner for adoption and the name of the agency or the name or relationship to the minor of the individual that placed the minor;

(7) the length of time the minor has been in the custody of the petitioner and, if the minor is not in the physical custody of the petitioner, the reason why the petitioner does not have custody and the date and manner in which the petitioner intends to obtain custody;

(8) a description and estimate of the value of any property of the minor;

(9) that any law governing interstate or intercountry placement was complied with;

(10) the name or relationship to the minor of any individual who has executed a consent or relinquishment to the adoption or a disclaimer of paternal interest, and the name or relationship to the minor of any individual whose consent or relinquishment may be required, but whose parental relationship has not been terminated, and any fact or circumstance that may excuse the lack of consent;

(11) that a previous petition by the petitioner to adopt has or has not been made in any court, and its disposition; and

(12) a description of any previous court order or pending proceeding known to the petitioner concerning custody of or visitation with the minor and any other fact known to the petitioner and needed to establish the jurisdiction of the court.

(b) The petitioner shall request in the petition:

(1) that the petitioner be permitted to adopt the minor as the petitioner's child;

(2) that the court approve the full name by which the minor is to be known if the petition is granted; and

(3) any other relief sought by the petitioner.

§3-305. Required documents

(a) Before the hearing on a petition for adoption, the following must be filed:

(1) a certified copy of the birth certificate or other record of the date and place of birth of the minor adoptee;

(2) any consent, relinquishment, or disclaimer of paternal interest with respect to the minor that has been executed, and any written certifications required by Section 2-405(d) and (g) from the individual before whom a consent or relinquishment was executed;

(3) a certified copy of any court order terminating the rights and duties of the minor's parents or guardian;

(4) a certified copy of each parent's or former parent's marriage certificate, decree of divorce, annulment, or dissolution, or agreement or decree of legal separation, and a certified copy of any court order determining the parent's or former parent's incompetence;

(5) a certified copy of any existing court order or the petition in any pending proceeding concerning custody of or visitation with the minor;

(6) a copy of the preplacement evaluation and of the evaluation during the pendency of the proceeding for adoption;

(7) a copy of any report containing the information required by Section 2-106;

(8) a document signed pursuant to Section 2-404(e);

(9) a certified copy of the petitioner's marriage certificate, decree of divorce, annulment, or dissolution, or agreement or decree of legal separation, and a certified copy of any court order determining the incompetence of the petitioner's spouse;

(10) a copy of any agreement with a public agency to provide a subsidy for the benefit of a minor adoptee with a special need;

(11) if an agency placed the minor adoptee, a verified document from the agency stating:

(i) the circumstances under which it obtained custody of the minor for purposes of adoption;

(ii) that it complied with any provision of law governing an interstate or intercountry placement of the minor;

(iii) the name or relationship to the minor of any individual whose consent is required, but who has not executed a consent or a relinquishment or whose parental relationship has not been terminated, and any fact or circumstance that may excuse the lack of consent or relinquishment; and

(iv) whether it has executed its consent to the proposed adoption and whether it waives notice of the proceeding; and

(12) the name and address, if known, of any person who is entitled to receive notice of the proceeding for adoption.

(b) If an item required by subsection (a) is not available, the person responsible for furnishing the item shall file an affidavit explaining its absence.

[PART] 4. NOTICE OF PENDENCY OF PROCEEDING

§3-401. Service of notice

(a) Unless notice has been waived, notice of a proceeding for adoption of a minor must be served, within 20 days after a petition for adoption is filed, upon:

(1) an individual whose consent to the adoption is required under Section 2-401, but notice need not be served upon an individual whose parental relationship to the minor or whose status as a guardian has been terminated;

(2) an agency whose consent to the adoption is required under Section 2-401;

(3) an individual whom the petitioner knows is claiming to be or who is named as the father or possible father of the minor adoptee and whose paternity of the minor has not been judicially determined, but notice need not be served upon a man who has executed a verified statement, as described in Section 2-402(a)(4), denying paternity or disclaiming any interest in the minor;

(4) an individual other than the petitioner who has legal or physical custody of the minor adoptee or who has a right of visitation with the minor under an existing court order issued by a court in this or another State;

(5) the spouse of the petitioner if the spouse has not joined in the petition; and

(6) a grandparent of a minor adoptee if the grandparent's child is a deceased parent of the minor and, before death, the deceased parent had not executed a consent or relinquishment or the deceased parent's parental relationship to the minor had not been terminated.

(b) The court shall require notice of a proceeding for adoption of a minor to be served upon any person the court finds, at any time during the proceeding, is:

(1) a person described in subsection (a) who has not been given notice;

(2) an individual who has revoked a consent or relinquishment pursuant to Section 2-408(a) or 2-409(a) or is attempting to have a consent or relinquishment set aside pursuant to Section 2-408(b) or 2-409(b); or

(3) a person who, on the basis of a previous relationship with the minor adoptee, a parent, an alleged parent, or the petitioner, can provide information that is relevant to the proposed adoption and that the court in its discretion wants to hear.

§3-402. Content of notice

A notice required by Section 3-401 must use a pseudonym for a petitioner or any individual named in the petition for adoption who has not waived confidentiality and must contain:

(1) the caption of the petition;

(2) the address and telephone number of the court where the petition is pending;

(3) a concise summary of the relief requested in the petition;

(4) the name, mailing address, and telephone number of the petitioner or petitioner's lawyer;

(5) a conspicuous statement of the method of responding to the notice of the proceeding for adoption and the consequences of failure to respond; and

(6) any statement required by [other applicable law or rule].

§3-403. Manner and effect of service

(a) Personal service of the notice required by Section 3-401 must be made in a manner appropriate under [the rules of civil procedure for the service of process in a civil action in this State] unless the court otherwise directs.

(b) Except as otherwise provided in subsection (c), a person who fails to respond to the notice within 20 days after its service may not appear in or receive further notice of the proceeding for adoption.

(c) An individual who is a respondent in a petition to terminate the relationship of parent and child pursuant to [Part] 5 which is served upon the individual with the notice required by Section 3-401 may not appear in or receive further notice of the proceeding for adoption or for termination unless the individual responds to the notice as required by Section 3-504.

§3-404. Investigation and notice to unknown father

(a) If, at any time in a proceeding for adoption or for termination of a relationship of parent and child under [Part] 5, the court finds that an unknown father of a minor adoptee may not have received notice, the court shall determine whether he can be identified. The determination must be based on evidence that includes inquiry of appropriate persons in an effort to identify an unknown father for the purpose of providing notice.

(b) The inquiry required by subsection (a) must include whether:

(1) the woman who gave birth to the minor adoptee was married at the probable time of conception of the minor, or at a later time;

(2) the woman was cohabiting with a man at the probable time of conception of the minor;

(3) the woman has received payments or promises of support, other than from a governmental agency, with respect to the minor or because of her pregnancy;

(4) the woman has named any individual as the father on the birth certificate of the minor or in connection with applying for or receiving public assistance; and

(5) any individual has formally or informally acknowledged or claimed paternity of the minor in a jurisdiction in which the woman resided during or since her pregnancy, or in which the minor has resided or resides, at the time of the inquiry.

(c) If inquiry pursuant to subsection (b) identifies as the father of the minor an individual who has not received notice of the proceeding, the court shall require notice to be served upon him pursuant to Section 3-403 unless service is not possible because his whereabouts are unknown.

(d) If, after inquiry pursuant to subsection (b), the court finds that personal service cannot be made upon the father of the minor because his identity or whereabouts is unknown, the court shall order publication or public posting of the notice only if, on the basis of all information available, the court determines that publication or posting is likely to lead to receipt of notice by the father. If the court determines that publication or posting is not likely to lead to receipt of notice, the court may dispense with the publication or posting of a notice.

(e) If, in an inquiry pursuant to this section, the woman who gave birth to the minor adoptee fails to disclose the identity of a possible father or reveal his whereabouts, she must be advised that the proceeding for adoption may be delayed or subject to challenge if a possible father is not given notice of the proceeding, that the lack of information about the father's medical and genetic history may be detrimental to the adoptee, and that she is subject to a civil penalty if she knowingly misidentified the father.

Comment

This section is consistent with the notice requirements of the Uniform Putative and Unknown Fathers Act (UPUFA). It reflects a desire to provide notice of a proceeding under this Act for adoption or termination of a parent-child relationship to any alleged or possible father of a minor adoptee. The court must conduct an inquiry to determine whether an alleged father can be identified and located for the purpose of providing notice to him. This inquiry would include an examination of any putative father registry in a State where the alleged father might have been during the mother's pregnancy or at the time of the minor's birth. Nonetheless, this section does not require efforts to provide notice which are not likely to result in its actual receipt. Notice by publication or posting may be used only as directed by the court, and the court may direct it only when the father is likely to see or receive it.

This section protects the right of the adoptee's birth mother to remain silent in response to a request to name the father or to reveal his whereabouts. Women often have good reasons — for example, fear of abuse — for not naming a father. Moreover, birth mothers might be dissuaded from placing their children for adoption if they believed they would be punished for failure to name the father. See, e.g., Evans v. So. Car. DSS, 399 S.E.2d 156 (So. Car. 1990) (alleged father's due process rights are not violated by permitting mother to refuse to disclose his name); In re Karen A.B., 513 A.2d 770 (Del. 1986) (mother's refusal to name alleged father should not be allowed to delay adoption proceeding to detriment of child); Augusta Co. DSS v. Unnamed Mother, 348 S.E.2d 26 (Va. Ct. App. 1986) (mother may refuse to name alleged father, but "fair play" for father requires that court have discretion to attempt notice by publication).

A refusal by a mother to name a possible father of her child will make it more difficult, if not impossible, to serve him with notice of the adoption or termination proceedings, or to compile background information about him and his family as called for by Section 2-106. Although the mother's refusal leaves the adoption more

susceptible to challenge during the six month period after an order or decree is issued under the Act, Section 3-707, the interest in protecting the mother's decision to remain silent and the inability to punish a mother's refusal without placing the minor at even greater risk of harm outweighs the father's "right" to notice and the minor's interest in learning who the father is. If the father is aware of the mother's pregnancy and the child's birth, he has ample opportunity to acknowledge his paternity, assume parental responsibilities, and make his identity and whereabouts known in order to receive notice and participate in an adoption proceeding. If he does nothing to assert his parental rights and is not a "thwarted" father, he will not be entitled to participate in the adoption proceeding.

Nonetheless, the court or any individual asked to inquire about the father should explain to the mother why the name and whereabouts of the father are important for the adoptee, the prospective adoptive parents, and the integrity and finality of the adoption. The mother should be specifically advised that if the father is in any of the armed services, the Soldiers' and Sailors' Civil Relief Act allows a proceeding (including, perhaps, a proceeding to terminate his parental rights) to be stayed if, during the father's period of service, or within 60 days thereafter, it appears that he was prejudiced by reason of military service in presenting a defense, 50 App. U.S.C.A., §521. The mother should also be warned that she may be liable for a civil penalty if she names a "bogus father" with an intent to deceive the actual father, an agency, or a prospective adoptive parent. See Section 7-105(e).

§3-405. Waiver of notice

(a) A person entitled to receive notice required under this [Act] may waive the notice before the court or in a consent, relinquishment, or other document signed by the person.

(b) Except for the purpose of moving to revoke a consent or relinquishment on the ground that it was obtained by fraud or duress, a person who has waived notice may not appear in the proceeding for adoption.

[PART] 5. PETITION TO TERMINATE RELATIONSHIP BETWEEN PARENT AND CHILD

Prefatory Comment

The action authorized by Article 3, Part 5 has the same effect as an action under the State's general child protection statutes to terminate the rights of a parent of a minor child. In most States, the grounds for termination are physical or sexual abuse, neglect, abandonment, failure to support, and persistent failures to improve an already shaky parent-child relationship. Part 5 supplements the State's general termination statute by providing for an action, within the proceeding for adoption, to terminate the parental relationship between a minor and a parent whose voluntary consent or relinquishment cannot be obtained when the minor is the subject of a proceeding for adoption. Unlike an action to terminate under the typical child protection laws, which can be brought only by the State or the department, an action to terminate under Part 5 may be brought by a parent or guardian who has selected a prospective adoptive parent for a minor, by a prospective adoptive parent, or by an agency that is placing the minor. Although any of these persons may maintain the action, a desire for confidentiality may dictate that the parent or guardian or the agency file the action rather than the prospective adoptive parent.

§3-501. Authorization

A petition to terminate the relationship between a parent or an alleged parent and a minor child may be filed in a proceeding for adoption under this [Act] by:

(1) a parent or a guardian who has selected a prospective adoptive parent for a minor and who intends to place, or has placed, the minor with that individual;

(2) a parent whose spouse has filed a petition under [Article] 4 to adopt the parent's minor child;

(3) a prospective adoptive parent of the minor who has filed a petition to adopt under this [article] or [Article] 4; or

(4) an agency that has selected a prospective adoptive parent for the minor and intends to place, or has placed, the minor with that individual.

§3-502. Timing and content of petition

(a) A petition under this [part] may be filed at any time after a petition for adoption has been filed under this [article] or [Article] 4 and before entry of a decree of adoption.

(b) A petition under this [part] must be signed and verified by the petitioner, be filed with the court, and state:

(1) the name or pseudonym of the petitioner;

(2) the name of the minor;

(3) the name and last known address of the parent or alleged parent whose parental relationship to the minor is to be terminated;

(4) the facts and circumstances forming the basis for the petition and the grounds on which termination of a parental relationship is sought;

(5) if the petitioner is a prospective adoptive parent, that the petitioner intends to proceed with the petition to adopt the minor if the petition to terminate is granted; and

(6) if the petitioner is a parent, a guardian, or an agency, that the petitioner has selected the prospective adoptive parent who is the petitioner in the proceeding for adoption.

Comment

A petition to terminate under this part may be filed simultaneously with the petition for adoption or at any time during the pendency of the adoption proceeding. Consistent with Sections 3-301 and 3-

302, prompt filing is encouraged to avoid extensive delays in resolving the status of the adoptee. The petition for adoption should be served, if service is possible, at the same time as service of the petition to terminate and notice of the hearing of the termination petition. See Section 3-503.

An action to terminate parental rights is appropriate in almost any case where an adoption petition is filed after one parent has voluntarily relinquished a child, consented to the child's adoption in a direct placement, or has had his or her parental rights terminated, but the other parent has not executed a voluntary consent or relinquishment. For example, in an adoptive placement by an agency, the agency is permitted under the Act (Article 2, Part 1) to place a child after one parent has relinquished parental rights to the agency, but before the status of the other parent is determined. If the agency makes an at-risk placement, it should move expeditiously under this part to terminate the rights of the parent whose status is not determined. Alternatively, the agency could proceed under the State's general termination laws if it preferred not to place a child or allow prospective adoptive parents to file an adoption petition until the status of both birth parents was clarified.

In a direct placement, one parent with legal and physical custody of a child can place the child with prospective adoptive parents, albeit subject to the exception in Section 2-101(c). Direct placement by one parent often occurs before the status of the other parent is determined, and most frequently occurs when an unwed mother places a child before the status of the biological or alleged father is determined. This part permits the parent who makes a direct placement or the prospective adoptive parent to file a petition to terminate the rights of the other parent or alleged parent, either before or after the adoptive parent assumes physical custody of the adoptee, if a petition for adoption has been previously filed or is filed at the same time as the petition to terminate. See Comments to Section 3-301.

§3-503. Service of petition and notice

(a) A petition to terminate under this [part] and a notice of hearing on the petition must be served upon the respondent, with notice of the proceeding for adoption, in the manner prescribed in Sections 3-403 and 3-404.

(b) The notice of a hearing must inform the respondent of the method for responding and that:

(1) the respondent has a right to be represented by a lawyer and may be entitled to have a lawyer appointed by the court; and

(2) failure to respond within 20 days after service and, in the case of an alleged father, failure to file a claim of paternity within 20 days after service unless a claim of paternity is pending, will result in termination of the relationship of parent and child between the respondent and the minor unless the proceeding for adoption is dismissed.

§3-504. Grounds for terminating relationship

(a) If the respondent is served with a petition to terminate under this [part] and the accompanying notice and does not respond and, in the case of an alleged father, file a claim of paternity within 20 days after the service unless a claim of paternity is pending, the court shall order the termination of any relationship of parent and child between the respondent and the minor unless the proceeding for adoption is dismissed.

(b) If, under Section 3-404, the court dispenses with service of the petition upon the respondent, the court shall order the termination of any relationship of parent and child between the respondent and the minor unless the proceeding for adoption is dismissed.

(c) If the respondent responds and asserts parental rights, the court shall proceed with the hearing expeditiously. If the court finds, upon clear and convincing evidence, that one of the following grounds exists, and, by a preponderance of the evidence, that termination is in the best interest of the minor, the court shall terminate any relationship of parent and child between the respondent and the minor:

(1) in the case of a minor who has not attained six months of age at the time the petition for adoption is filed, unless the respondent proves by a preponderance of the evidence a compelling reason for not complying with this paragraph, the respondent has failed to:

(i) pay reasonable prenatal, natal, and postnatal expenses in accordance with the respondent's financial means;

(ii) make reasonable and consistent payments, in accordance with the respondent's financial means, for the support of the minor;

(iii) visit regularly with the minor; and

(iv) manifest an ability and willingness to assume legal and physical custody of the minor, if, during this time, the minor was not in the physical custody of the other parent;

(2) in the case of a minor who has attained six months of age at the time a petition for adoption is filed, unless the respondent proves by a preponderance of the evidence a compelling reason for not complying with this paragraph, the respondent, for a period of at least six consecutive months immediately preceding the filing of the petition, has failed to:

(i) make reasonable and consistent payments, in accordance with the respondent's means, for the support of the minor;

(ii) communicate or visit regularly with the minor; and

(iii) manifest an ability and willingness to assume legal and physical custody of the minor, if, during this time, the minor was not in the physical custody of the other parent;

(3) the respondent has been convicted of a crime of violence or of violating a restraining or protective order, and the facts of the crime or violation and the respondent's behavior indicate that the respondent is unfit to maintain a relationship of parent and child with the minor;

(4) the respondent is a man who was not married to the minor's mother when the minor was conceived or born and is not the genetic or adoptive father of the minor; or

(5) termination is justified on a ground specified in [the State's statute for involuntary termination of parental rights].

(d) If the respondent proves by a preponderance of the evidence that he or she had a compelling reason for not complying with subsection (c)(1) or (2) and termination is not justified on a ground stated in subsection (c)(3) through (5), the court may terminate the relationship of parent and child between the respondent and a minor only if it finds, upon clear and convincing evidence, that one of the following grounds exists, and, by a preponderance of the evidence, that termination is in the best interest of the minor:

(1) if the minor is not in the legal and physical custody of the other parent, the respondent is not able or willing promptly to assume legal and physical custody of the minor, and to pay for the minor's support, in accordance with the respondent's financial means;

(2) if the minor is in the legal and physical custody of the other parent and a stepparent, and the stepparent is the prospective adoptive parent, the respondent is not able or willing promptly to establish and maintain contact with the minor and to pay for the minor's support, in accordance with the respondent's financial means;

(3) placing the minor in the respondent's legal and physical custody would pose a risk of substantial harm to the physical or psychological well-being of the minor because the circumstances of the minor's conception, the respondent's behavior during the mother's pregnancy or since the minor's birth, or the respondent's behavior with respect to other minors, indicates that the respondent is unfit to maintain a relationship of parent and child with the minor; or

(4) failure to terminate the relationship of parent and child would be detrimental to the minor.

(e) In making a determination under subsection (d)(4), the court shall consider any relevant factor, including the respondent's efforts to obtain or maintain legal and physical custody of the minor, the role of other persons in thwarting the respondent's efforts to assert parental rights, the respondent's ability to care for the minor, the age of the minor, the quality of any previous relationship between the respondent and the minor and between the respondent and any other minor children, the duration and suitability of the minor's present custodial environment, and the effect of a change of physical custody on the minor.

Comment

To satisfy constitutional due process requirements, parental rights of a presumptively "fit" parent cannot be terminated involuntarily except on proof of specified grounds by clear and convincing evidence, Santosky v. Kramer, 455 U.S. 745 (1982). Generally, the grounds for termination have to be serious failures to perform parental responsibilities — sufficiently serious to overcome the presumption of fitness. The Act supplements the grounds for terminating parental rights that are in the child protection laws of most States. This section emphasizes failures by a parent or alleged parent to assume or maintain the parental duties of support, visitation, and communication. The section also focuses on the respondent's behavior with respect to the minor adoptee, the other parent, or other minors which suggests that the respondent is not fit to establish or maintain a parental relationship.

Under subsection (c)(1), a respondent father's rights may be terminated on the basis of his behavior prior to the minor adoptee's birth, including a failure to manifest an ability or willingness to assume parental duties, unless he can prove a "compelling reason" for his failure. State courts have found it constitutionally permissible to terminate a father's status for pre-birth "abandonment" of an unwed mother whom the father knew was pregnant. See, e.g., In re Adoption of Doe, 543 So.2d 741 (Fla. 1989) (unwed father's failure to support mother during pregnancy when he knew of pregnancy, and had the means to pay for some of her birth-related expenses, justifies the termination of his parental rights even though he filed an affidavit of paternity after the child was born); In re Baby Girl K., 335 N.W.2d. 846 (Wis. 1983), appeal dismissed, 104 S.Ct. 1262 (father's pre-birth neglect of mother and refusal to pay for prenatal care can be evidence of failure to assume parental responsibilities, and can justify termination of parental rights); Doe v. Attorney W., 210 So.2d 1312 (Miss. 1982) (father's rights terminated on basis of abandonment of unborn child).

Under subsection (c)(2), a parent of a child who is six months or older when the adoption petition is filed may have parental rights terminated for failure to maintain a substantial relationship with the child for six or more months before the petition was filed. This "no support and no visitation or communication" ground for termination is most likely to arise in the context of stepparent adoptions, but can arise in other contexts as well. This Act permits termination after six consecutive months of failure to support and visit, absent a compelling reason for the failure. Although state courts have generally upheld the constitutionality of this ground for terminating parental rights, they have often done so with respect to statutes that require 1-2 years of failures to support or communicate. See the many cases cited in Ch. 2 Adoption Law and Practice (J.H. Hollinger, ed., 1988-1994).

If, under subsection (c)(1) or (2), the respondent sustains the burden of proving a compelling reason for not performing the requisite parental duties, the petitioner may still attempt to prove by clear and convincing evidence one of the grounds listed in subsection (d). For example, a respondent father may avoid having his rights terminated under (c)(1) by proving that he had no reason to know of the minor's birth or expected birth or that he was "thwarted" in his efforts to assume parental duties by the mother, an agency, the prospective adoptive

parent, or another person. At that point, the petitioner may request termination of the father's status under subsection (d)(3) or (4). Although the father is "excused" for his earlier failures to perform parental duties, the fact remains that he has not performed them and has not had any prior relationship with the minor except for their biological connection. In this situation, it is not unconstitutional for the father's assertion of parental rights to be balanced against the risks of substantial harm or the actual detriment to the minor which may occur if the father's rights are not terminated. See, e.g., the U.S. Supreme Court cases cited in the Comment to Section 2-401 and: In re Appeal in Pima County Juvenile Severance Action no. 2-114487, 876 P.2d 1121 (Ariz. 1994) (rights of a father who fails to grasp parental "opportunity quickly, diligently, and persistently" may be terminated if court finds that it is in the child's best interest, even if the father's failure is understandable due to the mother's efforts to thwart him); In re Baby Boy C., 581 A.2d 1141 (D.C.App. 1990) (a presumptively fit thwarted father's right to veto a proposed adoption may nonetheless be overcome by clear and convincing evidence that it is in the best interest of the minor for the adoption to proceed); In re Raquel Marie X., 76 N.Y.2d 387, 559 N.Y.S.2d 855 (1990) (unwed father who is physically unable to develop custodial relationship with newborn child, because mother and child are living with mother's husband, is entitled to veto his child's adoption by "strangers" if he acts promptly to establish a legal and emotional bond to his child); In re Robert O., 80 N.Y.2d 254, 590 N.Y.S.2d 37 (1992) ("promptness is measured in terms of the baby's life, not by the onset of the father's awareness"). But see, In re Kelsey S., 823 P.2d 1216 (Cal. 1992) (unwed thwarted father who, once he is or should be aware of child's birth, has "sufficiently and timely demonstrated a full commitment to his parental role" can veto proposed adoption even if he may not be entitled to the child's custody); In re Doe, 638 N.E.2d 181 (Ill. 1994), *reh'g denied* July 1994, *cert.denied,* U.S. Sup. Ct. Nov. 1994 (unwed father who was prevented from demonstrating parental interest within 30 days of child's birth because of birth mother's lies has not lost his "preemptive right" to veto the child's adoption "wholly apart from any consideration of the so-called best interests of the child").

Under this Act, the needs and well-being of a minor must be considered independently of the claims of any other individual to a possessory interest in the minor. Subsections (d)(3) and (4) permit such an inquiry under the special circumstances of a mother or father whose rights cannot be terminated under subsection (c) but who, despite proving a compelling reason for prior failures, has nonetheless not had an actual ongoing relationship with the minor. The court is allowed to terminate the rights of a "thwarted" parent upon finding clear and convincing evidence that giving the respondent custody of the minor would "pose a risk of substantial harm to the physical or psychological well-being of the minor,"(d)(3), or that "failure to terminate would be detrimental to the minor," (d)(4), based on the factors listed in subsection (e). Only upon finding a risk of substantial harm or actual detriment to the minor can the court go on to consider whether termination would also be in the minor's best interests.

In determining for how long and for what purposes the potential interests of a thwarted biological father should be protected, this Act balances: (1) the birth mother's interest in placing her child for adoption without interference from a man whom she believes has no genuine interest in the child, (2) the minor's interest in remaining with suitable prospective adopters with whom the minor may already have bonded, (3) the minor's interest in being raised by biological parents, especially if, in addition to the biological connection, there is also evidence of the father's parental capacity, (4) the efforts by the birth mother or others to interfere wrongfully with the father's efforts to grasp his parental opportunities, and 5) society's interest in protecting minors against "legal limbo" and detrimental disruptions of custodial environments in which they are thriving. See also, Comments to Section 2-401.

Subsection (c)(3) permits termination for serious and violent offenses by one parent against another. The child protection laws of many States permit termination of a parent's rights on the ground that the parent was physically or sexually abusive to a minor, including the parent's other children. However, only a few States provide that a father's rape or murder of his child's mother justifies terminating his parental rights. See, e.g., Maine, Pennsylvania. This subsection is based in part on Justice Scalia's suggestion in fn. 4 of his opinion in Michael H. v. Gerald D., 491 U.S. 110 (1989), that a biological father who raped a child's mother would not have a constitutionally protected "liberty interest" in parenting the child "begotten by rape."

§3-505. Effect of order granting petition

An order issued under this [part] granting the petition:

(1) terminates the relationship of parent and child between the respondent and the minor, except an obligation for arrearages of child support;

(2) extinguishes any right the respondent had to withhold consent to a proposed adoption of the minor or to further notice of a proceeding for adoption; and

(3) is a final order for purposes of appeal.

§3-506. Effect of order denying petition

(a) If the court denies the petition to terminate a relationship of parent and child, the court shall dismiss the proceeding for adoption and shall determine the legal and physical custody of the minor according to the criteria stated in Section 3-704.

(b) An order issued under this [part] denying a petition to terminate a relationship of parent and child is a final order for purposes of appeal.

Comment

This section contains an important reminder that, if the court has to dismiss an adoption proceeding because it has denied a petition to terminate a parental relationship, it also must decide who will have legal and physical custody of the minor. There is no "automatic" answer to the question of where the minor shall live after an adoption proceeding is dismissed. In making its custody determination, the court is to follow the guidelines in Section 3-704, which, in turn, refer to the criteria set forth in Section 2-408 or 2-409 with respect to the revocation or setting aside of a consent or relinquishment. Under some circumstances, the individuals who had hoped to adopt the minor, as well as one or both birth parents or an agency will be able to seek custody of the minor. See Comments to Section 3-704.

[PART] 6. EVALUATION OF ADOPTEE AND PROSPECTIVE ADOPTIVE PARENT

§3-601. Evaluation during proceeding for adoption

(a) After a petition for adoption of a minor is filed, the court shall order that an evaluation be made by an individual qualified under Section 2-202.

(b) The court shall provide the evaluator with copies of the petition for adoption and of the items filed with the petition.

§3-602. Content of evaluation

(a) An evaluation must be based on a personal interview with the petitioner in the petitioner's residence and observation of the relationship between the minor adoptee and the petitioner.

(b) An evaluation must be in writing and contain:

(1) an account of any change in the petitioner's marital status or family history, physical or mental health, home environment, property, income, or financial obligations since the filing of the preplacement evaluation;

(2) all reasonably available information concerning the physical, mental, and emotional condition of the minor adoptee which is not included in any report on the minor's health, genetic, and social history filed in the proceeding for adoption;

(3) copies of any court order, judgment, decree, or pending legal proceeding affecting the minor adoptee, the petitioner, or any child of the petitioner;

(4) a list of the expenses, fees, or other charges incurred, paid, or to be paid, and anything of value exchanged or to be exchanged, in connection with the adoption;

(5) any behavior or characteristics of the petitioner which raise a specific concern, as described in Section 2-204(a), about the petitioner or the petitioner's home; and

(6) a finding by the evaluator concerning the suitability of the petitioner and the petitioner's home for the minor adoptee and a recommendation concerning the granting of the petition for adoption.

§3-603. Time and filing of evaluation

(a) The evaluator shall complete a written evaluation and file it with the court within 60 days after receipt of the court's order for an evaluation, unless the court for good cause allows a later filing.

(b) If an evaluation produces a specific concern, as described in Section 2-204(a), the evaluation must be filed immediately, and must explain why the concern poses a significant risk of harm to the physical or psychological well-being of the minor.

(c) An evaluator shall give the petitioner a copy of an evaluation when filed with the court and for two years shall retain a copy and a list of every source for each item of information in the evaluation.

[PART] 7. DISPOSITIONAL HEARING; DECREE OF ADOPTION

§3-701. Time for hearing on petition

The court shall set a date and time for hearing the petition, which must be no sooner than 90 days and no later than 180 days after the petition for adoption has been filed, unless the court for good cause sets an earlier or later date and time.

§3-702. Disclosure of fees and charges

At least 10 days before the hearing:

(1) the petitioner shall file with the court a signed and verified accounting of any payment or disbursement of money or anything of value made or agreed to be made by or on behalf of the petitioner in connection with the adoption, or pursuant to [Article] 7. The accounting must include the date and amount of each payment or disbursement made, the name and address of each recipient, and the purpose of each payment or disbursement;

(2) the lawyer for a petitioner shall file with the court an affidavit itemizing any fee, compensation, or other thing of value received by, or agreed to be paid to, the lawyer incidental to the placement and adoption of the minor;

(3) the lawyer for each parent of the minor or for the guardian of the minor shall file with the court an affidavit itemizing any fee, compensation, or other thing of value received by, or agreed to be paid to, the lawyer incidental to the placement and adoption of the minor;

(4) if an agency placed the minor for adoption, the agency shall file with the court an affidavit itemizing any fee, compensation, or other thing of value received by the

agency for, or incidental to, the placement and adoption of the minor; and

(5) if a guardian placed the minor for adoption, the guardian shall file with the court an affidavit itemizing any fee, compensation, or other thing of value received by the guardian for, or incidental to, the placement and adoption of the minor.

§3-703. Granting petition for adoption

(a) The court shall grant a petition for adoption if it determines that the adoption will be in the best interest of the minor, and that:

(1) at least 90 days have elapsed since the filing of the petition for adoption unless the court for good cause shown waives this requirement;

(2) the adoptee has been in the physical custody of the petitioner for at least 90 days unless the court for good cause shown waives this requirement;

(3) notice of the proceeding for adoption has been served or dispensed with as to any person entitled to receive notice under [Part] 4;

(4) every necessary consent, relinquishment, waiver, disclaimer of paternal interest, or judicial order terminating parental rights, including an order issued under [Part] 5, has been obtained and filed with the court;

(5) any evaluation required by this [Act] has been filed with and considered by the court;

(6) the petitioner is a suitable adoptive parent for the minor;

(7) if applicable, any requirement of this [Act] governing an interstate or intercountry placement for adoption has been met;

(8) the Indian Child Welfare Act, 25 U.S.C. Sections 1901 et seq., is not applicable to the proceeding or, if applicable, its requirements have been met;

(9) an accounting and affidavit required by Section 3-702 have been reviewed by the court, and the court has denied, modified, or ordered reimbursement of any payment or disbursement that is not authorized by [Article] 7 or is unreasonable or unnecessary when compared with the expenses customarily incurred in connection with an adoption;

(10) the petitioner has received each report required by Section 2-106; and

(11) any document signed pursuant to Section 2-404(e) concerning the release of a former parent's identity to the adoptee after the adoptee attains 18 years of age has been filed with the court.

(b) Notwithstanding a finding by the court that an activity prohibited by this [Act] has occurred, if the court makes the determinations required by subsection (a), the court shall grant the petition for adoption and report the violation to the appropriate authorities.

(c) Except as otherwise provided in [Article] 4, the court shall inform the petitioner and any other individual affected by an existing order for visitation or communication with the minor adoptee that the decree of adoption terminates any existing order for visitation or communication.

Comment

A judicial determination that a proposed adoption will be in the best interest of the minor adoptee is an essential — and ultimately the most important — prerequisite to the granting of the adoption. This determination is made in conjunction with a determination that all the other substantive and procedural requirements stated in subsection (a) have been satisfied. Among the most important of these are parental consents or relinquishments or, in lieu of these, disclaimers of parental interest or termination orders, and, in some circumstances, an agency's consent, a guardian's consent or relinquishment, or an adoptee's consent. Although a "substantial compliance" standard is not expressly stated in this section, the Act does not mandate absolute compliance with every provision. For example, consents or relinquishments executed in substantial compliance with Sections 2-405 and 2-406 are considered valid, many opportunities exist for obtaining, for good cause shown, exceptions to the Act's requirements, and other specific requirements are to be construed reasonably in order to serve the needs of minor adoptees.

Subsection (b) enables the court, notwithstanding serious irregularities in the placement, to grant an adoption upon the court's determination that the adoption is in the minor's best interests and that the other requirements under subsection (a) have been met. If the court grants the adoption but suspects that one or more provisions of the Act have been violated, the alleged violations should be referred to the appropriate authorities for imposition of the sanctions set forth in Article 7 or other applicable laws.

Violations of the Act should be addressed, but not at the expense of the minor adoptee's well-being. See, e.g., Yopp v. Batt, 467 N.W.2d 868 (Neb. 1991) (despite a possible violation of licensing requirements for adoptive placements, adoption granted because in best interests of minor); In re Adoption of Daniel C.D., N.Y.L.J. Nov. 12, 1986, p.14, col.1 (Bx. Surr. 1986) (adoption approved despite excessive fees charges by agency operating in another State); In re Adoption of a Child by I.T., 164 N.J. Super. 476, 397 A.2d 341 (1978) (adoption approved because "innocent" adoptive parents and child should not suffer as result of lawyer's failure to follow ICPC procedures). Nonetheless, the court may determine that the violations are so serious, or cast so many aspersions on the character of the adoptive parents, that the adoption is not in the minor's best interests and should be denied. See, e.g., Adoption of P.E.P., 407 S.E.2d 505 (N.C. 1991) (adoption set aside because of blatant violations by lawyer and adoptive parents of statute prohibiting payments for child-placing).

§3-704. Denial of petition for adoption

If a court denies a petition for adoption, it shall dismiss the proceeding and issue an appropriate order for the legal and physical custody of the minor. If the reason for the denial is that a consent or relinquishment is revoked or set aside pursuant to Section 2-408 or 2-409, the court shall determine the minor's custody according to the criteria stated in those sections. If the petition for adoption is denied for any other reason, the court shall determine the minor's custody according to the best interest of the minor.

Comment

If the court determines that a petition for adoption should be denied, the court is then responsible for determining who should have custody of the minor. In making this determination or in making an analogous determination upon denying a petition to terminate under Part 5, the court should consider the factors in Section 2-408 or 2-409, if relevant to the reasons for the denial, and should otherwise consider the minor's best interests. In some circumstances, it may be appropriate to return the minor to one or both birth parents or to a relative; in other cases, an agency should receive custody; in still other cases, the individuals who had hoped to adopt may be granted custody even though they cannot become the legal adoptive parents. See, e.g, Adoption of Kelsey S., 823 P.2d 1216 (Cal. 1992) (even if thwarted father has a right to withhold his consent to an adoption, the question of the child's custody remains to be decided); Lemley v. Barr, 343 S.E.2d 101 (W.Va. 1986) (even though UCCJA requires W. Va. courts to recognize Ohio order invalidating birth parent's consent, best interests hearing should be held to determine child's custody); Sorentino v. Fam. Ch. Soc., 378 A.2d 18 (1977) (even after birth parents' rights are vindicated, circumstances may warrant a hearing on whether transfer of custody from prospective adopters would pose risk of serious harm to child).

§3-705. Decree of adoption

(a) A decree of adoption must state or contain:

(1) the original name of the minor adoptee, if the adoption is by a stepparent or relative and, in all other adoptions, the original name or a pseudonym;

(2) the name of the petitioner for adoption;

(3) whether the petitioner is married or unmarried;

(4) whether the petitioner is a stepparent of the adoptee;

(5) the name by which the adoptee is to be known and when the name takes effect;

(6) information to be incorporated into a new birth certificate to be issued by the [State Registrar of Vital Records], unless the petitioner or an adoptee who has attained 12 years of age requests that a new certificate not be issued;

(7) the adoptee's date and place of birth, if known, or in the case of an adoptee born outside the United States, as determined pursuant to subsection (b);

(8) the effect of the decree of adoption as stated in Sections 1-104 through 1-106; and

(9) that the adoption is in the best interest of the adoptee.

(b) In determining the date and place of birth of an adoptee born outside the United States, the court shall:

(1) enter the date and place of birth as stated in the birth certificate from the country of origin, the United States Department of State's report of birth abroad, or the documents of the United States Immigration and Naturalization Service;

(2) if the exact place of birth is unknown, enter the information that is known and designate a place of birth according to the best information known with respect to the country of origin;

(3) if the exact date of birth is unknown, determine a date of birth based upon medical evidence as to the probable age of the adoptee and other evidence the court considers appropriate; and

(4) if documents described in paragraph (1) are not available, determine the date and place of birth based upon evidence the court finds appropriate to consider.

(c) Unless a petitioner requests otherwise and the former parent agrees, the decree of adoption may not name a former parent of the adoptee.

(d) Except for a decree of adoption of a minor by a stepparent which is issued pursuant to [Article] 4, a decree of adoption of a minor must contain a statement that the adoption terminates any order for visitation or communication with the minor that was in effect before the decree is issued.

(e) A decree that substantially complies with the requirements of this section is not subject to challenge solely because one or more items required by this section are not contained in the decree.

§3-706. Finality of decree

A decree of adoption is a final order for purposes of appeal when it is issued and becomes final for other purposes upon the expiration of the time for filing an appeal, if no appeal is filed, or upon the denial or dismissal of any appeal filed within the requisite time.

§3-707. Challenges to decree

(a) An appeal from a decree of adoption or other appealable order issued under this [Act] must be heard expeditiously.

(b) A decree or order issued under this [Act] may not be vacated or annulled upon application of a person who waived notice, or who was properly served with notice pursuant to this [Act] and failed to respond or appear, file an answer, or file a claim of paternity within the time allowed.

(c) The validity of a decree of adoption issued under this [Act] may not be challenged for failure to comply with an agreement for visitation or communication with an adoptee.

(d) A decree of adoption or other order issued under this [Act] is not subject to a challenge begun more than six months after the decree or order is issued. If a challenge is brought by an individual whose parental relationship to an adoptee is terminated by a decree or order under this [Act], the court shall deny the challenge, unless the court finds by clear and convincing evidence that the decree or order is not in the best interest of the adoptee.

§3-801. Report of adoption

(a) Within 30 days after a decree of adoption becomes final, the clerk of the court shall prepare a report of adoption on a form furnished by the [State Registrar of Vital Records] and certify and send the report to the [Registrar]. The report must include:

(1) information in the court's record of the proceeding for adoption which is necessary to locate and identify the adoptee's birth certificate or, in the case of an adoptee born outside the United States, evidence the court finds appropriate to consider as to the adoptee's date and place of birth;

(2) information in the court's record of the proceeding for adoption which is necessary to issue a new birth certificate for the adoptee and a request that a new certificate be issued, unless the court, the adoptive parent, or an adoptee who has attained 12 years of age requests that a new certificate not be issued; and

(3) the file number of the decree of adoption and the date on which the decree became final.

(b) Within 30 days after a decree of adoption is amended or vacated, the clerk of the court shall prepare a report of that action on a form furnished by the [Registrar] and shall certify and send the report to the [Registrar]. The report must include information necessary to identify the original report of adoption, and shall also include information necessary to amend or withdraw any new birth certificate that was issued pursuant to the original report of adoption.

[PART] 8. BIRTH CERTIFICATE

Comment

Sections 3-801 and 3-802 are a modified version of the relevant sections on adoptees' birth certificates contained in the Revised Model State Vital Statistics Act, as drafted by the U.S. Dept. of Health and Human Services and a committee of State Registrars of Vital Records. This part provides for the issuance of a new birth certificate once an adoption is final, unless the court, the adoptive parents, or an adoptee aged 12 or older, requests that a new certificate not be issued. The new certificate will retain the original date and place of birth of the adoptee, but will substitute the names of the adoptive parents for the names of the individuals listed as the parents at birth. The certificate will contain any additional information required by state regulation. This deference to state regulation allows for differences among the States with regard to such matters as including a special "mark" or "symbol" indicating that an original certificate has been replaced by the new certificate or that the parents listed on the new certificate are parents by adoption and not by birth. Most States do not permit the use of marks or symbols that would distinguish the birth certificates of adoptees from those of biological children.

§3-802. Issuance of new birth certificate

(a) Except as otherwise provided in subsection (d), upon receipt of a report of adoption prepared pursuant to Section 3-801, a report of adoption prepared in accordance with the law of another State or country, a certified copy of a decree of adoption together with information necessary to identify the adoptee's original birth certificate and to issue a new certificate, or a report of an amended adoption, the [Registrar] shall:

(1) issue a new birth certificate for an adoptee born in this State and furnish a certified copy of the new certificate to the adoptive parent and to an adoptee who has attained 12 years of age;

(2) forward a certified copy of a report of adoption for an adoptee born in another State to the [Registrar] of the State of birth;

(3) issue a certificate of foreign birth for an adoptee adopted in this State and who was born outside the United States and was not a citizen of the United States at the time of birth, and furnish a certified copy of the certificate to the adoptive parent and to an adoptee who has attained 12 years of age;

(4) notify an adoptive parent of the procedure for obtaining a revised birth certificate through the United States Department of State for an adoptee born outside the United States who was a citizen of the United States at the time of birth; or

(5) in the case of an amended decree of adoption, issue an amended birth certificate according to the procedure in paragraph (1) or (3) or follow the procedure in paragraph (2) or (4).

(b) Unless otherwise specified by the court, a new birth certificate issued pursuant to subsection (a)(1) or (3) or an amended certificate issued pursuant to subsection (a)(5) must include the date and place of birth of the adoptee, substitute the name of the adoptive parent for the name of the individual listed as the adoptee's parent on the original birth certificate, and contain any other information prescribed by [the State's vital records law or regulations].

(c) The [Registrar] shall substitute the new or amended birth certificate for the original birth certificate in the [Registrar's] files. The original certificate and all copies of the certificate in the files of the [Registrar] or any other custodian of vital records in the State must be sealed and are not subject to inspection until 99 years after the adoptee's date of birth, but may be inspected as provided in this [Act].

(d) If the court, the adoptive parent, or an adoptee who has attained 12 years of age requests that a new or amended birth certificate not be issued, the [Registrar] may not issue a new or amended certificate for an adoptee pursuant to subsection (a), but shall forward a certified copy of the report of adoption or of an amended decree of adoption for an adoptee who was born in another State to the appropriate office in the adoptee's State of birth.

(e) Upon receipt of a report that an adoption has been vacated, the [Registrar] shall:

(1) restore the original birth certificate for an individual born in this State to its place in the files, seal any new or amended birth certificate issued pursuant to subsection (a), and not allow inspection of a sealed certificate except upon court order or as otherwise provided in this [Act];

(2) forward the report with respect to an individual born in another State to the appropriate office in the State of birth; or

(3) notify the individual who is granted legal custody of a former adoptee after an adoption is vacated of the procedure for obtaining an original birth certificate through the United States Department of State for a former adoptee born outside the United States who was a citizen of the United States at the time of birth.

(f) Upon request by an individual who was listed as a parent on a child's original birth certificate and who furnishes appropriate proof of the individual's identity, the [Registrar] shall give the individual a noncertified copy of the original birth certificate.

[ARTICLE] 4. ADOPTION OF MINOR STEPCHILD BY STEPPARENT

Prefatory Comment

A stepparent who seeks to adopt a minor stepchild under this article has to deal with fewer as well as somewhat different legal requirements than does an individual who seeks to adopt an unrelated minor. These differences are justified because in the typical stepparent adoption, the minor has been living with the stepparent and the stepparent's spouse (the minor's custodial parent), and the adoption merely formalizes a de facto parent-child relationship. The minor is not physically transferred to a new and "strange" custodial environment, but remains in the household where the minor may have already lived for some time. When a stepparent adopts, an evaluation of the stepparent's suitability as an adoptive parent and an accounting of adoption-related expenses is less important than in the adoption-by-strangers scenario because (1) the minor's custodial parent has in effect "selected" the adoptive stepparent on the basis of personal knowledge; (2) the custodial parent is not subject to a pre- or post-placement evaluation under existing adoption or custody laws; (3) a denial of the petition to adopt is not likely to alter the existing custodial arrangement; (4) the expense and hassle of undergoing an evaluation or home-study may be disproportionate to any benefit for the minor which might result from an evaluation, but, see Comment to Section 4-111; and (5) the concerns about unlawful payments to birth parents or intermediaries which are expressed about other types of adoptions are arguably not present in stepparent adoptions, although, in fact, "pay-offs" to noncustodial parents may occur with some frequency in the form of private agreements not to seek child support arrears from the noncustodial parent.

Although data on the number of adoptions completed in this country each year are unreliable, it is estimated that well over half of the adoptions that do occur are by stepparents. This is not surprising given that: (1) remarriages account for nearly 46% of all marriages entered into in 1990, compared to 31% in 1970; (2) more than 1 million children are involved in a divorce each year; (3) in several million families, at least one spouse has had an out-of-wedlock child before getting married; and (4) nearly 7 million children live in stepfamilies, and these children are approximately 15% of all children under 18 living in two parent families. What is surprising is that, although stepparent adoptions represent more than 50% of all adoptions, they occur in only a small percentage of the "blended" households headed by a custodial parent and a stepparent. This small percentage may be due, at least in part, to dissatisfaction with the ways in which existing adoption laws are applied to adoptions by stepparents. Typically, the custodial parent is allowed to retain his or her parental status, the adoptive stepparent acquires the status of a legal parent, and the noncustodial parent's relationship to the child is cut off for most purposes. An exception occurs in those States that, like this Act, follow the approach of the Uniform Probate Code (UPC) and permit the child to continue to inherit from and through the former noncustodial parent. For stepfamilies in which a child maintains emotional ties to a noncustodial parent or to the noncustodial parent's family, the traditional approach of completely severing all ties to the noncustodial parent and that parent's family is not necessarily beneficial for the child, and is not always preferred by the parents or the stepparent. The growing body of literature on stepfamilies, while acknowledging that children often thrive in "blended" families, also points to the persistence of friction between children and stepparents and to the desire of many children to maintain contact with noncustodial parents and grandparents with whom they had a prior relationship.

Instead of treating the procedures for stepparent adoptions merely as exceptions to the more general rules pertaining to other adoptions, this Act, and particularly this article, takes an affirmative approach to stepparent adoptions. By allowing post-adoption visitation by noncustodial former parents, siblings, or grandparents, this article may encourage an increase in the number of stepparent adoptions in proportion to the total number of blended families. This would give more children the advantage of living in a household with two legal parents (custodial parent and adoptive stepparent), while not depriving these children of access to their noncustodial parent's family — assuming that such access would not be detrimental to the child. Moreover, if the traditional

rule of "complete severance" between adoptive and biological families is subject to some exceptions in the context of stepparent adoptions, it might be possible to avoid the bitterness that is often attendant upon efforts to terminate the rights of noncustodial parents, and more consensual adoptions might result.

§4-101. Other provisions applicable to adoption of stepchild

Except as otherwise provided by this [article], [Article] 3 applies to an adoption of a minor stepchild by a stepparent.

§4-102. Standing to adopt minor stepchild

(a) A stepparent has standing under this [article] to petition to adopt a minor stepchild who is the child of the stepparent's spouse if:

(1) the spouse has sole legal and physical custody of the child and the child has been in the physical custody of the spouse and the stepparent during the 60 days next preceding the filing of a petition for adoption;

(2) the spouse has joint legal custody of the child with the child's other parent and the child has resided primarily with the spouse and the stepparent during the 12 months next preceding the filing of the petition;

(3) the spouse is deceased or mentally incompetent, but before dying or being judicially declared mentally incompetent, had legal and physical custody of the child, and the child has resided primarily with the stepparent during the 12 months next preceding the filing of the petition; or

(4) an agency placed the child with the stepparent pursuant to Section 2-104.

(b) For good cause shown, a court may allow an individual who does not meet the requirements of subsection (a), but has the consent of the custodial parent of a minor to file a petition for adoption under this [article]. A petition allowed under this subsection must be treated as if the petitioner were a stepparent.

(c) A petition for adoption by a stepparent may be joined with a petition under [Article] 3, [Part] 5, to terminate the relationship of parent and child between a minor adoptee and the adoptee's parent who is not the stepparent's spouse.

Comment

In addition to permitting individuals who are within the formal definition of "stepparent" to adopt a minor stepchild under this article, Section 4-102 allows an individual who is a de facto stepparent, but is not, or is no longer, married to the custodial parent, to adopt as if he or she were a de jure stepparent. To file a petition under this article, the de facto stepparent or "second parent" has to have the consent of the court and the custodial parent, whose parental rights will not be terminated by an adoption under this article. In addition, for the court to grant the petition, the other requirements of this article have to be met, including the court's determination that the adoption is in the minor adoptee's best interests. See, e.g., Adoption of B.L.V.B., 628 A.2d 1271 (Vt. 1993) (de facto stepmother allowed to adopt her unmarried partner's biological children because it "serves no legitimate state interest" to deny the children "the security of a legally recognized relationship with their second parent"). See similar analysis in Matter of Evan, 153 Misc.2d 844, 583 N.Y.S.2d 997 (Surr. 1992).

If a stepchild's noncustodial parent refuses to consent to the proposed stepparent adoption or cannot be located, an adoption petition under this article may be joined with a petition under Article 3, Part 5, to terminate the parent-child relationship with the noncustodial parent. In most cases, the termination petition will allege that the noncustodial parent has failed to support and visit or communicate with the child for at least six months before the stepparent files the adoption petition, Section 3-504(c)(2), or that, even if the noncustodial parent had a compelling reason for failing to pay support and visit in the past, he is unlikely to perform these duties in the future, Section 3-504(d)(2). Of course, the stepparent and the custodial parent may also seek to prove any of the other grounds stated in Section 3-504 for terminating the noncustodial parent's rights.

§4-103. Legal consequences of adoption of stepchild

(a) Except as otherwise provided in subsections (b) and (c), the legal consequences of an adoption of a stepchild by a stepparent are the same as under Sections 1-103 through 1-106.

(b) An adoption by a stepparent does not affect:

(1) the relationship between the adoptee and the adoptee's parent who is the adoptive stepparent's spouse or deceased spouse;

(2) an existing court order for visitation or communication with a minor adoptee by an individual related to the adoptee through the parent who is the adoptive stepparent's spouse or deceased spouse;

(3) the right of the adoptee or a descendant of the adoptee to inheritance or intestate succession through or from the adoptee's former parent; or

(4) A court order or agreement for visitation or communication with a minor adoptee which is approved by the court pursuant to Section 4-113.

(c) Failure to comply with an agreement or order is not a ground for challenging the validity of an adoption by a stepparent.

§4-104. Consent to adoption

Unless consent is not required under Section 2-402, a petition to adopt a minor stepchild may be granted only if consent to the adoption has been executed by a stepchild who has attained 12 years of age; and

(1) the minor's parents as described in Section 2-401(a);

(2) the minor's guardian if expressly authorized by a court to consent to the minor's adoption; or

(3) an agency that placed the minor for adoption by the stepparent.

§4-105. Content of consent by stepparent's spouse

(a) A consent executed by a parent who is the stepparent's spouse must be signed or confirmed in the presence of an individual specified in Section 2-405, or an individual authorized to take acknowledgements.

(b) A consent under subsection (a) must be in writing, must contain the required statements described in Section 2-406(a)(1) through (3) and (d)(3) through (6), may contain the optional statements described in Section 2-406(f), and must state that:

(1) the parent executing the consent has legal and physical custody of the parent's minor child and voluntarily and unequivocally consents to the adoption of the minor by the stepparent;

(2) the adoption will not terminate the parental relationship between the parent executing the consent and the minor child; and

(3) the parent executing the consent understands and agrees that the adoption will terminate the relationship of parent and child between the minor's other parent and the minor, and will terminate any existing court order for custody, visitation, or communication with the minor, but:

(i) the minor and any descendant of the minor will retain rights of inheritance from or through the minor's other parent;

(ii) a court order for visitation or communication with the minor by an individual related to the minor through the parent executing the consent, or an agreement or order concerning another individual which is approved by the court pursuant to Section 4-113 survives the decree of adoption, but failure to comply with the terms of the order or agreement is not a ground for revoking or setting aside the consent or the adoption; and

(iii) the other parent remains liable for arrearages of child support unless released from that obligation by the parent executing the consent and by a governmental entity providing public assistance to the minor.

(c) A consent may not waive further notice of the proceeding for adoption of the minor by the stepparent.

§4-106. Content of consent by minor's other parent

(a) A consent executed by a minor's parent who is not the stepparent's spouse must be signed or confirmed in the presence of an individual specified in Section 2-405.

(b) A consent under subsection (a) must be in writing, must contain the required statements described in Section 2-406(a)(1) through (3) and (d)(3) through (6), may contain the optional statements described in Section 2-406(f), and must state that:

(1) the parent executing the consent voluntarily and unequivocally consents to the adoption of the minor by the stepparent and the transfer to the stepparent's spouse and the adoptive stepparent of any right the parent executing the consent has to legal or physical custody of the minor;

(2) the parent executing the consent understands and agrees that the adoption will terminate his or her parental relationship to the minor and will terminate any existing court order for custody, visitation, or communication with the minor, but:

(i) the minor and any descendant of the minor will retain rights of inheritance from or through the parent executing the consent;

(ii) a court order for visitation or communication with the minor by an individual related to the minor through the minor's other parent, or an agreement or order concerning another individual which is approved by the court pursuant to Section 4-113 survives the decree of adoption, but failure to comply with the terms of the order or agreement is not a ground for revoking or setting aside the consent or the adoption; and

(iii) the parent executing the consent remains liable for arrearages of child support unless released from that obligation by the other parent and any guardian ad litem of the minor and by a governmental entity providing public assistance to the minor; and

(3) the parent executing the consent has provided the adoptive stepparent with the information required by Section 2-106.

(c) A consent under subsection (a) may waive notice of the proceeding for adoption of the minor by the stepparent unless the adoption is contested, appealed, or denied.

§4-107. Content of consent by other persons

(a) A consent executed by the guardian of a minor stepchild or by an agency must be in writing and signed or confirmed in the presence of the court, or in a manner the court directs, and:

(1) must state the circumstances under which the guardian or agency obtained the authority to consent to the adoption of the minor by a stepparent;

(2) must contain the statements required by Sections 4-104 and 4-105, except for any that can be made only by a parent of the minor; and

(3) may waive notice of the proceeding for adoption, unless the adoption is contested, appealed, or denied.

(b) A consent executed by a minor stepchild in a proceeding for adoption by a stepparent must be signed or confirmed in the presence of the court or in a manner the court directs.

§4-108. Petition to adopt

(a) A petition by a stepparent to adopt a minor stepchild must be signed and verified by the petitioner and contain the following information or state why any of the information is not contained in the petition:

(1) the information required by Section 3-304(a) (1), (3), (5), and (8) through (12) and (b);

(2) the current marital status of the petitioner, including the date and place of marriage, the name and date and place of birth of the petitioner's spouse and, if the spouse is deceased, the date, place, and cause of death and, if the spouse is incompetent, the date on which a court declared the spouse incompetent;

(3) the length of time the minor has been residing with the petitioner and the petitioner's spouse and, if the minor is not in the physical custody of the petitioner and the petitioner's spouse, the reason why they do not have custody and when they intend to obtain custody; and

(4) the length of time the petitioner's spouse or the petitioner has had legal custody of the minor and the circumstances under which legal custody was obtained.

§4-109. Required documents

(a) After a petition to adopt a minor stepchild is filed, the following must be filed in the proceeding:

(1) any item required by Section 3-305(a) which is relevant to an adoption by a stepparent; and

(2) a copy of any agreement to waive arrearages of child support.

(b) If any of the items required by subsection (a) is not available, the person responsible for furnishing the item shall file an affidavit explaining its absence.

§4-110. Notice of pendency of proceeding

(a) Within 30 days after a petition to adopt a minor stepchild is filed, the petitioner shall serve notice of the proceeding upon:

(1) the petitioner's spouse;

(2) any other person whose consent to the adoption is required under this [article];

(3) any person described in Section 3-401(a)(3), (4), and (6) and (b); and

(4) the parents of the minor's parent whose parental relationship will be terminated by the adoption unless the identity or the whereabouts of those parents are unknown.

§4-111. Evaluation of stepparent

(a) After a petition for adoption of a minor stepchild is filed, the court may order that an evaluation be made by an individual qualified under Section 2-202 to assist the court in determining whether the proposed adoption is in the best interest of the minor.

(b) The court shall provide an evaluator with copies of the petition for adoption and of the items filed with the petition.

(c) Unless otherwise directed by the court, an evaluator shall base the evaluation on a personal interview with the petitioner and the petitioner's spouse in the petitioner's residence, observation of the relationship between the minor and the petitioner, personal interviews with others who know the petitioner and may have information relevant to the examination, and any information received pursuant to subsection (d).

(d) An evaluation under this section must be in writing and contain the following:

(1) the information required by Section 2-203(d) and (e);

(2) the information required by Section 3-602(b)(2) through (5); and

(3) the finding required by Section 3-602(b)(6).

(e) An evaluator shall complete an evaluation and file it with the court within 60 days after being asked for the evaluation under this section, unless the court allows a later filing.

(f) Section 3-603(b) and (c) apply to an evaluation under this section.

§4-112. Dispositional hearing; decree of adoption

Sections 3-701 through 3-707 apply to a proceeding for adoption of a minor stepchild by a stepparent, but the court may waive the requirements of Section 3-702.

§4-113. Visitation agreement and order

(a) Upon the request of the petitioner in a proceeding for adoption of a minor stepchild, the court shall review a written agreement that permits another individual to visit or communicate with the minor after the decree of adoption becomes final, which must be signed by the individual, the petitioner, the petitioner's spouse, the minor if 12 years of age or older, and, if an agency placed the minor for adoption, an authorized employee of the agency.

(b) The court may enter an order approving the agreement only upon determining that the agreement is in the best interest of the minor adoptee. In making this determination, the court shall consider:

(1) the preference of the minor, if the minor is mature enough to express a preference;

(2) any special needs of the minor and how they would be affected by performance of the agreement;

(3) the length and quality of any existing relationship between the minor and the individual who would be entitled to visit or communicate, and the likely effect on the minor of allowing this relationship to continue;

(4) the specific terms of the agreement and the likelihood that the parties to the agreement will cooperate in performing its terms;

(5) the recommendation of the minor's guardian ad litem, lawyer, social worker, or other counselor; and

(6) any other factor relevant to the best interest of the minor.

(c) In addition to any agreement approved pursuant to subsections (a) and (b), the court may approve the continuation of an existing order or issue a new order permitting the minor adoptee's former parent, grandparent, or sibling to visit or communicate with the minor if:

(1) the grandparent is the parent of a deceased parent of the minor or the parent of the adoptee's parent whose parental relationship to the minor is terminated by the decree of adoption;

(2) the former parent, grandparent, or sibling requests that an existing order be permitted to survive the decree of adoption or that a new order be issued; and

(3) the court determines that the requested visitation or communication is in the best interest of the minor.

(d) In making a determination under subsection (c)(3), the court shall consider the factors listed in subsection (b) and any objections to the requested order by the adoptive stepparent and the stepparent's spouse.

(e) An order issued under this section may be enforced in a civil action only if the court finds that enforcement is in the best interest of a minor adoptee.

(f) An order issued under this section may not be modified unless the court finds that modification is in the best interest of a minor adoptee and:

(1) the individuals subject to the order request the modification; or

(2) exceptional circumstances arising since the order was issued justify the modification.

(g) Failure to comply with the terms of an order approved under this section or with any other agreement for visitation or communication is not a ground for revoking, setting aside, or otherwise challenging the validity of a consent, relinquishment, or adoption pertaining to a minor stepchild, and the validity of the consent, relinquishment, and adoption is not affected by any later action to enforce, modify, or set aside the order or agreement.

Comment

This section permits a petitioner in a proceeding to adopt under this article to ask the court to approve an agreement for post-adoption visitation or communication with the adoptee by another individual. Subsection (b) lists the factors the court must consider in determining whether the agreement is in the best interests of the adoptee.

Subsection (c) permits an adoptee's former parent (i.e., the noncustodial parent), grandparent, or sibling to seek a court order for post-adoption visitation or communication with the adoptee over the objection of the custodial parent and the adoptive stepparent. The court cannot issue an order unless it considers the factors listed in subsection (b) and determines that, despite the objections, it would be in the best interests of the adoptee.

In addition to being enforceable in a civil action, visitation or communication orders approved under this section may be modified under "exceptional circumstances." As is indicated elsewhere in the Act, however, failure to abide by an agreement or order for post-adoption visitation\communication is not a basis for challenging the validity of a consent, relinquishment, or adoption.

[ARTICLE] 5. ADOPTION OF ADULTS AND EMANCIPATED MINORS

§5-101. Who may adopt adult or emancipated minor

(a) An adult may adopt another adult or an emancipated minor pursuant to this [article], but:

(1) an adult may not adopt his or her spouse; and

(2) an incompetent individual of any age may be adopted only pursuant to [Articles] 2, 3, and 4.

(b) An individual who has adopted an adult or emancipated minor may not adopt another adult or emancipated minor within one year after the adoption unless the prospective adoptee is a sibling of the adoptee.

Comment

An adoption of an adult, like an adoption of a minor, may serve different interests. It may provide formal recognition of a de facto relationship that has existed for many years — for example, when an individual has been reared by someone other than a parent, but a proceeding for adoption has never been initiated. It may be a belated adoption by a stepparent in a situation in which a child's noncustodial parent never consented to the proposed stepparent adoption. When the noncustodial parent dies, or the child reaches his 18th birthday, the noncustodial parent can no longer block the adoption by the stepparent.

An adoption of an adult may also occur simply to provide the adoptive parent with a legal heir to inherit the adoptive parent's estate. As long as the adults intend to create a parent-child relationship between each other, the adoption should be permitted. If a relationship other than that of parent and child is intended, the adoption may be denied. See, e.g., In re Robert Paul, 471 N.E.2d 424 (N.Y. 1984) (adoption by homosexual adult of his male lover disapproved because of desire to circumvent marriage laws and lack of genuine parent-child relationship).

This article covers the adoption of competent adults and emancipated minors. Emancipated minors are included because they are presumed to be sufficiently "adult" to be adopted without the benefit of the additional protections of Articles 2, 3, and 4. The term "emancipated" has the meaning it has in the State where the petition for adoption is filed. Because the proposed adoption of an incompetent adult should be subject to more concerns about "best interests" than are provided in this article, the Act requires that an adoption of an incompetent adult be handled pursuant to Article 2 (Adoption of Minors), Article 3 (General Adoption Procedure), and, if relevant, Article 4 (Adoption by Stepparent).

§5-102. Legal consequences of adoption

The legal consequences of an adoption of an adult or emancipated minor are the same as under Sections 1-103 through 1-106, but the legal consequences of adoption of an adult stepchild by an adult stepparent are the same as under Section 4-103.

§5-103. Consent to adoption

(a) Consent to the adoption of an adult or emancipated minor is required only of:

(1) the adoptee;

(2) the prospective adoptive parent; and

(3) the spouse of the prospective adoptive parent, unless they are legally separated, or the court finds that the spouse is not capable of giving consent or is withholding consent contrary to the best interest of the adoptee and the prospective adoptive parent.

(b) The consent of the adoptee and the prospective adoptive parent must:

(1) be in writing and be signed or confirmed by each of them in the presence of the court or an individual authorized to take acknowledgments;

(2) state that they agree to assume toward each other the legal relationship of parent and child and to have all of the rights and be subject to all of the duties of that relationship; and

(3) state that they understand the consequences the adoption may have for any right of inheritance, property, or support each has.

(c) The consent of the spouse of the prospective adoptive parent:

(1) must be in writing and be signed or confirmed in the presence of the court or an individual authorized to take acknowledgments;

(2) must state that the spouse:

(i) consents to the proposed adoption; and

(ii) understands the consequences the adoption may have for any right of inheritance, property, or support the spouse has; and

(3) may contain a waiver of any proceeding for adoption.

§5-104. Jurisdiction and venue

(a) The court has jurisdiction over a proceeding for the adoption of an adult or emancipated minor under this [article] if a petitioner lived in this State for at least 90 days immediately preceding the filing of a petition for adoption.

(b) A petition for adoption may be filed in the court in the [county] in which a petitioner lives.

§5-105. Petition for adoption

(a) A prospective adoptive parent and an adoptee under this [article] must jointly file a petition for adoption.

(b) The petition must be signed and verified by each petitioner and state:

(1) the full name, age, and place and duration of residence of each petitioner;

(2) the current marital status of each petitioner, including the date and place of marriage, if married;

(3) the full name by which the adoptee is to be known if the petition is granted;

(4) the duration and nature of the relationship between the prospective adoptive parent and the adoptee;

(5) that the prospective adoptive parent and the adoptee desire to assume the legal relationship of parent and child and to have all of the rights and be subject to all of the duties of that relationship;

(6) that the adoptee understands that a consequence of the adoption will be to terminate the adoptee's relationship as the child of an existing parent, but if the adoptive parent is the adoptee's stepparent, the adoption will not affect the adoptee's relationship with a parent who is the stepparent's spouse, but will terminate the adoptee's relationship to the adoptee's other parent, except for the right to inherit from or through that parent;

(7) the name and last known address of any other individual whose consent is required;

(8) the name, age, and last known address of any child of the prospective adoptive parent, including a child previously adopted by the prospective adoptive parent or his or her spouse, and the date and place of the adoption; and

(9) the name, age, and last known address of any living parent or child of the adoptee.

(c) The petitioners shall attach to the petition:

(1) a certified copy of the birth certificate or other evidence of the date and place of birth of the adoptee and the prospective adoptive parent, if available; and

(2) any required consent that has been executed.

§5-106. Notice and time of hearing

(a) Within 30 days after a petition for adoption is filed, the petitioners shall serve notice of hearing the petition upon any individual whose consent to the adoption is required under Section 5-103, and who has not waived notice, by sending a copy of the petition and notice of hearing to the individual at the address stated in the petition, or according to the manner of service provided in Section 3-403.

(b) The court shall set a date and time for hearing the petition, which must be at least 30 days after the notice is served.

§5-107. Dispositional hearing

(a) Both petitioners shall appear in person at the hearing unless an appearance is excused for good cause shown. In the latter event an appearance may be made for either or both of them by a lawyer authorized in writing to make the appearance, or a hearing may be conducted by telephone or other electronic medium.

(b) The court shall examine the petitioners, or the lawyer for a petitioner not present in person, and shall grant the petition for adoption if it determines that:

(1) at least 30 days have elapsed since the service of notice of hearing the petition for adoption;

(2) notice has been served, or dispensed with, as to any person whose consent is required under Section 5-103;

(3) every necessary consent, waiver, document, or judicial order has been obtained and filed with the court;

(4) the adoption is for the purpose of creating the relationship of parent and child between the petitioners and the petitioners understand the consequences of the relationship; and

(5) there has been substantial compliance with this [Act].

§5-108. Decree of adoption

(a) A decree of adoption issued under this [article] must substantially conform to the relevant requirements of Section 3-705 and appeals from a decree, or challenges to it, are governed by Sections 3-706 and 3-707.

(b) The court shall send a copy of the decree to each individual named in the petition at the address stated in the petition.

(c) Within 30 days after a decree of adoption becomes final, the clerk of the court shall prepare a report of the adoption for the [State Registrar of Vital Records], and, if the petitioners have requested it, the report shall instruct the [Registrar] to issue a new birth certificate to the adoptee, as provided in [Article] 3, [Part] 8.

Comment

Like any other adoption, the adoption of an adult terminates the adoptee's legal relationship to former parents and relatives, subject to the exception for adoption by a stepparent. Former parents and former family members may want to include the adoptee in their testamentary or other donative dispositions. Efforts by a former relative, for example, to include the adoptee in a class gift to "the child, heir, or issue" of the adoptee's former parent would no longer suffice under the laws of most States because, except for an adoption by a stepparent, the adoptee would not be considered the child, heir, or issue of the former parent for purposes of construing class gifts. Once the adoption is final, a specific reference to the adoptee will be necessary in order for a former parent or former family member to make a gift, bequest, or devise to the adoptee.

In the interest of protecting the private decision of the parties to an adult adoption, the Act does not require notice of the proceeding to other individuals who may be affected by the adoption except the adoptive parent's spouse. Nonetheless, the adoptee's own children and former parents should have an opportunity to adjust their economic affairs, including their testamentary plans, to take account of the adoption. Hence, this section requires that copies of the decree of adoption be sent to the adoptee's children and former parents.

The adoption also creates a new status for the adoptee with respect to the family of the adoptive parent. Some of these individuals may want to exclude the adoptee from a class gift or other donative disposition. This section, however, only requires that copies of the decree be sent to other children of the adoptive parent, not to other members of the adoptive parent's family, except his or her spouse. This means that an adoptive parent's own parent, sibling, aunt, uncle, etc. will have to learn about the adoption informally and decide whether to excise the new adult adoptee from their donative dispositions.

[ARTICLE] 6. RECORDS OF ADOPTION PROCEEDING: RETENTION, CONFIDENTIALITY, AND ACCESS

Prefatory Comment

The Act, and especially this article, is consistent with the law of every State with respect to: (1) the confidentiality of adoption proceedings, (2) the confidentiality of all records pertaining to the proceeding after an adoption becomes final, (3) the sealing of the court records of the adoption proceeding, (4) the basic procedure for sealing an adoptee's original birth certificate and issuing a new one to reflect the adoptive parent's legal parentage, and (5) the availability of a limited exception to the general rule of confidentiality through a judicial finding of "good cause." In contrast to most States, however, which require the permanent sealing of court records, the Act provides for the opening of sealed records after 99 years.

With respect to nonidentifying information about an adoptee's medical and social history, the Act is consistent with the goals of most modern statutes in encouraging the collection and release of this information to adoptive parents and adoptees at age 18 upon request. However, the Act is more comprehensive than many of these statutes and establishes careful procedures for compiling, maintaining, releasing, and updating nonidentifying information. The Act also authorizes civil and criminal penalties, as well as private actions for damages or equitable relief, for unwarranted failures to disclose information that should be disclosed and for unauthorized disclosure of confidential information. See Sections 7-105 and 7-106.

With respect to identifying information, the Act allows the consensual disclosure of identities through a mutual consent registry. This procedure recognizes and protects the rights of birth parents or adoptees who choose to remain unidentified as well as the interests of those who wish to disclose their identities. If one birth parent and an adoptee (at age 18 or older) or the adoptive parent of an adoptee under 18 register a willingness to disclose their identities, the identifying information must be disclosed. If there is no mutual consent, the Act allows a suit for disclosure of identifying information for good cause. Over half of the States have some form of mutual consent registry [e.g., Fla. Stat. Ann. §63.162 et seq.; Idaho Code §39-259A; La. Rev. St. Ann. §9:40.91.999; Ohio Rev. Code Ann. §3107.39 et seq.; Tex. Hum. Res. Code Ann. Tit. 2D, ch. 49]. Several States have no registry and disclose identities only by court order [e.g., D.C. Code §16-311; Montana Code Ann. §40-8-126 and 50-15-206; New Jersey].

For States that choose an approach different from the one taken in the Act, there are two existing alternatives. The first is to authorize a confidential intermediary who seeks out the individual who is the object of a search and requests permission for the disclosure of the individual's identity; [e.g., Ariz Code §134 (d); Mich. Comp. Laws Ann. 710.68b; N.D. Cent. Code §14-15-16; Wash. Rev. Code §26.33.343; Wis. Stat. Ann. §48.93]. The second is to provide original birth certificates to an adult adoptee upon request [e.g., Alaska St. §18.50.500 (to adoptee at age 18 or older); Ka. Code Ann. §65-2423 (to adoptee at age 18 or older adopted adult); Wash. Rev. Code Ann. §26.33.345 (for adoptions finalized after Sept. 1993, to adoptee at age 18 or older, unless birth parent has filed nondisclosure request)].

§6-101. Records defined

Unless the context requires otherwise, for purposes of this [article], "records" includes all documents, exhibits, and data pertaining to an adoption.

§6-102. Records confidential, court records sealed

(a) All records, whether on file with the court, or in the possession of an agency, the [Registrar of Vital Records or Statistics], a lawyer, or another provider of professional services in connection with an adoption, are confidential and may not be inspected except as provided in this [Act].

(b) During a proceeding for adoption, records are not open to inspection except as directed by the court.

(c) Within 30 days after a decree of adoption becomes final, the clerk of the court shall send to the [Registrar], in addition to the report of adoption required by Section 3-801, a certified copy of any document signed pursuant to Section 2-404(e) and filed in the proceeding for adoption.

(d) All records on file with the court must be retained permanently and sealed for 99 years after the date of the adoptee's birth. Sealed records and indices of the records are not open to inspection by any person except as provided in this [Act].

(e) Any additional information about an adoptee, the adoptee's former parents, and the adoptee's genetic history that is submitted to the court within the 99-year period, must be added to the sealed records of the court. Any additional information that is submitted to an agency, lawyer, or other professional provider of services within the 99-year period must be kept confidential.

§6-103. Release of nonidentifying information

(a) An adoptive parent or guardian of an adoptee, an adoptee who has attained 18 years of age, an emancipated adoptee, a deceased adoptee's direct descendant who has attained 18 years of age, or the parent or guardian of a direct descendant who has not attained 18 years of age may request the court that granted the adoption or the agency that placed the adoptee for adoption, to furnish the nonidentifying information about the adoptee, the adoptee's former parents, and the adoptee's genetic history that has been retained by the court or agency, including the information required by Section 2-106.

(b) The court or agency shall furnish the individual who makes the request with a detailed summary of any relevant report or information that is included in the sealed records of the court or the confidential records of the agency. The summary must exclude identifying information concerning an individual who has not filed a waiver of confidentiality with the court or agency. The department or the court shall prescribe forms and a procedure for summarizing any report or information released under this section.

(c) An individual who is denied access to nonidentifying information to which the individual is entitled under this [article] or Section 2-106 may petition the court for relief.

(d) If a court receives a certified statement from a physician which explains in detail how a health condition may seriously affect the health of the adoptee or a direct descendant of the adoptee, the court shall make a diligent effort to notify an adoptee who has attained 18 years of age, an adoptive parent or guardian of an adoptee who has not attained 18 years of age, or a direct descendant of a deceased adoptee that the nonidentifying information is available and may be requested from the court.

(e) If a court receives a certified statement from a physician which explains in detail why a serious health condition of the adoptee or a direct descendant of the adoptee should be communicated to the adoptee's genetic parent or sibling to enable them to make an informed reproductive decision, the court shall make a diligent effort to notify those individuals that the nonidentifying information is available and may be requested from the court.

(f) If the [Registrar] receives a request or any additional information from an individual pursuant to this section, the [Registrar] shall give the individual the name and address of the court or agency having the records, and if the court or agency is in another State, shall assist the individual in locating the court or agency. The [Registrar] shall prescribe a reasonable procedure for verifying the identity, age, or other relevant characteristics of an individual who requests or furnishes information under this section.

§6-104. Disclosure of identifying information

(a) Except as otherwise provided in this [article], identifying information about an adoptee's former parent, an adoptee, or an adoptive parent which is contained in records, including original birth certificates, required by this [Act] to be confidential or sealed, may not be disclosed to any person.

(b) Identifying information about an adoptee's former parent must be disclosed by the [Registrar] to an adoptee who has attained 18 years of age, an adoptive parent or guardian of an adoptee who has not attained 18 years of age, a deceased adoptee's direct descendant who has attained 18 years of age, or the parent or guardian of a direct descendant who has not attained 18 years of age if one of these individuals requests the information and:

(1) the adoptee's former parent or, if the former parent is deceased or has been judicially declared incompetent, an adult descendant of the former parent authorizes the disclosure of his or her name, date of birth, or last known address, or other identifying information, either in a document signed pursuant to Section 2-404(e) and filed in the proceeding for adoption or in another signed document filed with the court, an agency, or the [Registrar]; or

(2) the adoptee's former parent authorizes the disclosure of the requested information only if the adoptee, adoptive parent, or direct descendant agrees to release similar identifying information about the adoptee, adoptive parent, or direct descendant and this individual authorizes the disclosure of the information in a signed document kept by the court, an agency, or the [Registrar].

(c) Identifying information about an adoptee or a deceased adoptee's direct descendant must be disclosed by the [Registrar] to an adoptee's former parent if that individual requests the information and:

(1) an adoptee who has attained 18 years of age, an adoptive parent or guardian of an adoptee who has not attained 18 years of age, a deceased adoptee's direct descendant who has attained 18 years of age, or the parent or guardian of a direct descendant who has not attained 18 years of age authorizes the disclosure of the requested information in a signed document kept by the court, an agency, or the [Registrar]; or

(2) one of the individuals listed in paragraph (1) authorizes the disclosure of the requested information only if the adoptee's former parent agrees to release similar information about himself or herself, and the former parent authorizes the disclosure of the information in a signed document kept by the court, an agency, or the [Registrar].

(d) Identifying information about an adult sibling of an adoptee who has attained 18 years of age must be disclosed by the [Registrar] to an adoptee if the sibling is also an adoptee and both the sibling and the adoptee authorize the disclosure.

(e) Subsection (d) does not permit disclosure of a former parent's identity unless that parent has authorized disclosure under this [Act].

§6-105. Action for disclosure of information

(a) To obtain information not otherwise available under Section 6-103 or 6-104, an adoptee who has attained 18 years of age, an adoptee who has not attained 18 years of age and has the permission of an adoptive parent or guardian, an adoptive parent or guardian of an adoptee who has not attained 18 years of age, a deceased adoptee's direct descendant who has attained 18 years of age, the parent or guardian of a direct descendant who has not attained 18 years of age, or an adoptee's former parent may file a petition in the court to obtain information about another individual described in this section which is contained in records, including original birth certificates, required by this [Act] to be confidential or sealed.

(b) In determining whether to grant a petition under this section, the court shall review the sealed records of the relevant proceeding for adoption and shall make specific findings concerning:

(1) the reason the information is sought;

(2) whether the individual about whom information is sought has filed a signed document described in Section 2-404(e) or 6-104 requesting that his or her identity not be disclosed, or has not filed any document;

(3) whether the individual about whom information is sought is alive;

(4) whether it is possible to satisfy the petitioner's request without disclosing the identity of another individual;

(5) the likely effect of disclosure on the adoptee, the adoptive parents, the adoptee's former parents, and other members of the adoptee's original and adoptive families; and

(6) the age, maturity, and expressed needs of the adoptee.

(c) The court may order the disclosure of the requested information only upon a determination that good cause exists for the release based on the findings required by subsection (b) and a conclusion that:

(1) there is a compelling reason for disclosure of the information; and

(2) the benefit to the petitioner will be greater than the harm to any other individual of disclosing the information.

§6-106. Statewide registry

The [Registrar] shall:

(1) establish a statewide confidential registry for receiving, filing, and retaining documents requesting, authorizing, or not authorizing, the release of identifying information;

(2) prescribe and distribute forms or documents on which an individual may request, authorize, or refuse to authorize the release of identifying information;

(3) devise a procedure for releasing identifying information in the [Registrar's] possession upon receipt of an appropriate request and authorization;

(4) cooperate with registries in other States to facilitate the matching of documents filed pursuant to this [article] by individuals in different States; and

(5) announce and publicize to the general public the existence of the registry and the procedure for the consensual release of identifying information.

§6-107. Release of original birth certificate

(a) In addition to any copy of an adoptee's original birth certificate authorized for release by a court order issued pursuant to Section 6-105, the [Registrar] shall furnish a copy of the original birth certificate upon the request of an adoptee who has attained 18 years of age, the direct descendant of a deceased adoptee, or an adoptive parent or guardian of an adoptee who has not attained 18 years of age, if the individual who makes the request furnishes a consent to disclosure signed by each individual who was named as a parent on the adoptee's original birth certificate.

(b) When 99 years have elapsed after the date of birth of an adoptee whose original birth certificate is sealed under this [Act], the [Registrar] shall unseal the original certificate and file it with any new or amended certificate that has been issued. The unsealed certificates become public information in accordance with any statute or regulation applicable to the retention and disclosure of records by the [Registrar].

§6-108. Certificate of adoption

Upon the request of an adoptive parent or an adoptee who has attained 18 years of age, the clerk of the court that entered a decree of adoption shall issue a certificate of adoption which states the date and place of adoption, the date of birth of the adoptee, the name of each adoptive parent, and the name of the adoptee as provided in the decree.

§6-109. Disclosure authorized in course of employment

This [article] does not preclude an employee or agent of a court, agency, or the [Registrar] from:

(1) inspecting permanent, confidential, or sealed records for the purpose of discharging any obligation under this [Act];

(2) disclosing the name of the court where a proceeding for adoption occurred, or the name of an agency that placed an adoptee, to an individual described in Sections 6-103 through 6-105, who can verify his or her identity; or

(3) disclosing nonidentifying information contained in confidential or sealed records in accordance with any other applicable state or federal law.

§6-110. Fee for services

A court, an agency, or the [Registrar] may charge a reasonable fee for services, including copying services, it performs pursuant to this [article].

[ARTICLE] 7. PROHIBITED AND PERMISSIBLE ACTIVITIES IN CONNECTION WITH ADOPTION

§7-101. Prohibited activities in placement

(a) Except as otherwise provided in [Article] 2, [Part] 1:

(1) a person, other than a parent, guardian, or agency, as specified in Sections 2-101 through 2-103, may not place a minor for adoption or advertise in any public medium that the person knows of a minor who is available for adoption;

(2) a person, other than an agency or an individual with a favorable preplacement evaluation, as required by Sections 2-201 through 2-207, may not advertise in any public medium that the person is willing to accept a minor for adoption;

(3) an individual, other than a relative or stepparent of a minor, who does not have a favorable preplacement evaluation or a court-ordered waiver of the evaluation, or who has an unfavorable evaluation, may not obtain legal or physical custody of a minor for purposes of adoption; and

(4) a person may not place or assist in placing a minor for adoption with an individual, other than a relative or stepparent, unless the person knows that the individual has a favorable preplacement evaluation or a waiver pursuant to Section 2-201.

(b) A person who violates subsection (a) is liable for a [civil penalty] not to exceed [$5,000] for the first violation, and not to exceed [$10,000] for each succeeding violation in an action brought by the [appropriate official]. The court may enjoin from further violations any person who violates subsection (a) and shall inform any appropriate licensing authority or other official of the violation.

Comment

This section authorizes civil penalties, injunctive relief, and other sanctions against persons engaged in unlawful placement activities. Those subject to liability under this section include a person who attempts to place a minor without authority under Section 2-101 to do so, a person other than an agency or an individual with a favorable preplacement evaluation who advertises for an adoptable child, an individual who has an unfavorable evaluation or has not sought an evaluation and who attempts to obtain custody of an adoptable child, and a person who places a minor with an individual whom the person knows does not have a favorable evaluation or a waiver. Prospective adoptive parents with a favorable evaluation may advertise their interest in finding an adoptable child. Similarly, persons authorized to place a minor — birth parents, guardians with placement authority, agencies with legal and physical custody of minors — may advertise their willingness to place minor children for adoption.

§7-102. Unlawful payments related to adoption

(a) Except as otherwise provided in Sections 7-103 and 7-104, a person may not pay or give or offer to pay or give to any other person, or request, receive, or accept any money or anything of value, directly or indirectly, for:

(1) the placement of a minor for adoption;

(2) the consent of a parent, a guardian, or an agency to the adoption of a minor; or

(3) the relinquishment of a minor to an agency for the purpose of adoption.

(b) The following persons are liable for a [civil penalty] not to exceed [$5,000] for the first violation, and not to exceed [$10,000] for each succeeding violation in an action brought by the [appropriate official]:

(1) a person who knowingly violates subsection (a);

(2) a person who knowingly makes a false report to the court about a payment prohibited by this section or authorized by Section 7-103 or 7-104; and

(3) a parent or guardian who knowingly receives or accepts a payment authorized by Section 7-103 or 7-104 with the intent not to consent to an adoption or to relinquish a minor for adoption.

(c) The court may enjoin from further violations any person described in subsection (b) and shall inform any appropriate licensing authority or other official of the violation.

Comment

This section authorizes civil penalties, injunctive relief, and other sanctions against persons who knowingly accept or make payments, directly or indirectly, for a placement, consent, or relinquishment — in other words, payments that are, or appear to be, for the "purchase" of a child. Most States have similar provisions. These sanctions are also available against a person who knowingly makes a false report about adoption-related payments or who acts fraudulently by knowingly accepting a legitimate adoption-related payment, as listed in Section 7-103 or 7-104, with the intent of not consenting to the proposed adoption.

§7-103. Lawful payments related to adoption

(a) Subject to the requirements of Sections 3-702 and 3-703 for an accounting and judicial approval of fees and charges related to an adoption, an adoptive parent, or a person acting on behalf of an adoptive parent, may pay for:

(1) the services of an agency in connection with an adoption;

(2) advertising and similar expenses incurred in locating a minor for adoption;

(3) medical, hospital, nursing, pharmaceutical, travel, or other similar expenses incurred by a mother or her minor child in connection with the birth or any illness of the minor;

(4) counseling services for a parent or a minor for a reasonable time before and after the minor's placement for adoption;

(5) living expenses of a mother for a reasonable time before the birth of her child and for no more than six weeks after the birth;

(6) expenses incurred in ascertaining the information required by Section 2-106;

(7) legal services, court costs, and travel or other administrative expenses connected with an adoption, including any legal services performed for a parent who consents to the adoption of a minor or relinquishes the minor to an agency;

(8) expenses incurred in obtaining a preplacement evaluation and an evaluation during the proceeding for adoption; and

(9) any other service the court finds is reasonably necessary.

(b) A parent or a guardian, a person acting on the parent's or guardian's behalf, or a provider of a service listed in subsection (a), may receive or accept a payment authorized by subsection (a). The payment may not be made contingent on the placement of a minor for adoption, relinquishment of the minor, or consent to the adoption. If the adoption is not completed, a person who is authorized to make a specific payment by subsection (a) is not liable for that payment unless the person has agreed in a signed writing with a provider of a service to make the payment regardless of the outcome of the proceeding for adoption.

Comment

Subsection (a) specifies the adoption-related fees and charges that an adoptive parent may lawfully pay, subject to the judicial accounting and approval provisions of Sections 3-702 and 3-703. In addition to expenses incurred for preplacement and postplacement evaluations, legal and psychological counseling for themselves, and expenses for locating an adoptable child, the adoptive parents are permitted to pay the medical costs incurred in connection with a child's birth, living and counseling expenses of the birth mother for reasonable periods of time, and the legal expenses incurred by a birth parent who consents to the adoption or relinquishes a minor child to an agency.

Under subsection (b), payments cannot be made contingent on a birth parent's performance of any promise to place a minor, consent to an adoption, or relinquish the minor. If an adoption is not completed, adoptive parents who have made payments during the proceeding are not entitled to reimbursement or restitution, but they do not have to make additional payments to service providers unless they have agreed to do so regardless of the outcome of the adoption proceeding.

§7-104. Charges by agency

Subject to the requirements of Sections 3-702 and 3-703 for an accounting and judicial approval of fees and charges related to an adoption, an agency may charge or accept a fee or other reasonable compensation from a prospective adoptive parent for:

(1) medical, hospital, nursing, pharmaceutical, travel, or other similar expenses incurred by a mother or her minor child in connection with the birth or any illness of the minor;

(2) a percentage of the annual cost the agency incurs in locating and providing counseling services for minor adoptees, parents, and prospective parents;

(3) living expenses of a mother for a reasonable time before the birth of a child and for no more than six weeks after the birth;

(4) expenses incurred in ascertaining the information required by Section 2-106;

(5) legal services, court costs, and travel or other administrative expenses connected with an adoption, including the legal services performed for a parent who relinquishes a minor child to the agency;

(6) preparation of a preplacement evaluation and an evaluation during the proceeding for adoption; and

(7) any other service the court finds is reasonably necessary.

§7-105. Failure to disclose information

(a) A person, other than a parent, who has a duty to furnish the nonidentifying information required by Section 2-106, or authorized for release under [Article] 6, and who intentionally refuses to provide the information is subject to a [civil penalty] not to exceed [$5,000] for the first violation, and not to exceed [$10,000] for each succeeding violation in an action brought by the [appropriate official]. The court may enjoin the person from further violations of the duty to furnish nonidentifying information.

(b) An employee or agent of an agency, the court, or the [State Registrar of Vital Records] who intentionally destroys any information or report compiled pursuant to Section 2-106, or authorized for release under [Article] 6, is guilty of a [misdemeanor] [punishable upon conviction by a fine of not more than [$] or imprisonment for not more than [ ], or both].

(c) In addition to the penalties provided in subsections (a) and (b), an adoptive parent, an adoptee, or any person who is the subject of any information required by Section 2-106, or authorized for release under [Article] 6, may maintain an action for damages or equitable relief against a person, other than a parent who placed a minor for adoption, who fails to perform the duties required by Section 2-106 or [Article] 6.

(d) A prospective adoptive parent who knowingly fails to furnish information or knowingly furnishes false information to an evaluator preparing an evaluation pursuant to [Article] 2, [Part] 2 or [Article] 3, [Part] 6, with the intent to deceive the evaluator, is guilty of a [misdemeanor] [punishable upon conviction by a fine of not more than [$] or imprisonment for not more than [ ], or both].

(e) An evaluator who prepares an evaluation pursuant to [Article] 2, [Part] 2 or [Article] 3, [Part] 6 and who knowingly omits or misrepresents information about the individual being evaluated with the intent to deceive a person authorized under this [Act] to place a minor for adoption is guilty of a [misdemeanor] [punishable upon conviction by a fine of not more than [$] or imprisonment for not more than [ ], or both].

(f) A parent of a minor child who knowingly misidentifies the minor's other parent with an intent to deceive the other parent, an agency, or a prospective adoptive parent is subject to a [civil penalty] not to exceed [$5,000] in an action brought by the [appropriate official].

Comment

The civil penalties authorized in subsection (a) for an intentional refusal to provide nonidentifying information and the criminal penalties authorized in subsection (b) for an intentional destruction of this information are consistent with the Act's requirement that adoptive parents and adoptees be provided with as much relevant information as is reasonably available about the medical, genetic, and social history of adoptees and their biological families; Section 2-106 and Article 6. These sanctions can be imposed against agencies, lawyers, evaluators, and other providers of professional services who fail to perform their responsibilities according to a generally acceptable standard of care. Subsection (d) authorizes criminal sanctions against a prospective adoptive parent who knowingly furnishes false information during an evaluation with the intent to deceive the evaluator.

The Act's requirement that agencies, parents, lawyers, and others involved in an adoption must provide background information that is "reasonably available" is intended to create a statutory duty to use reasonable efforts to obtain the information and to disclose the information that is collected to prospective adoptive parents. In addition to the civil penalties for a breach of the statutory duty, subsection (c) allows adoptive parents and adoptees to maintain an action for damages or equitable relief for failures to provide reasonably available background information or perform the statutory duties set forth in Article 6. The best way for adoption-service providers to avoid liability under this section is to pass along to adoptive families the nonidentifying information they have compiled and not withhold information, as many agencies and lawyers routinely did before the 1980s.

Birth parents are generally exempt from the sanctions in this section lest they be deterred from consenting or relinquishing because of a possible criminal penalty for failing to disclose their medical or social histories. The Act's goal is to facilitate adoptions, not to impede them by punishing parents. Nonetheless, subsection (f) authorizes a civil penalty against a birth parent who knowingly withholds the name of the other parent with an intent to deceive prospective adoptive parents or an agency. This provision may serve to warn birth parents about the harmful consequences for their children of failing to tell the truth. One such consequence may be the belated discovery by the other parent of an adoption proceeding, followed by an effort by that parent to contest the adoption, thus plunging the parties into litigation with an uncertain outcome.

§7-106. Unauthorized disclosure of information

(a) Except as authorized in this [Act], a person who furnishes or retains a report or records pursuant to this [Act] may not disclose any identifying or nonidentifying information contained in the report or records.

(b) A person who knowingly gives or offers to give or who accepts or agrees to accept anything of value for an unauthorized disclosure of identifying information made confidential by this [Act] is guilty of a [misdemeanor] [punishable upon conviction by a fine of not more than [$] or imprisonment for not more than [ ], or both,] for the first violation and of a [felony] [punishable upon conviction by a fine of not more than [$] or imprisonment for not more than [ ], or both,] for each succeeding violation.

(c) A person who knowingly gives or offers to give or who accepts or agrees to accept anything of value for an unauthorized disclosure of nonidentifying information made confidential by this [Act] is subject to a [civil penalty] not to exceed [$5,000] for the first violation, and not to exceed [$10,000] for each succeeding violation in an action brought by the [appropriate official].

(d) A person who makes a disclosure, that the person knows is unauthorized, of identifying or nonidentifying information from a report or record made confidential by this [Act] is subject to a [civil penalty] not to exceed [$2,500] for the first violation, and not to exceed [$5,000] for each succeeding violation in an action brought by the [appropriate official].

(e) The court may enjoin from further violations any person who makes or obtains an unauthorized disclosure and shall inform any appropriate licensing authority or other official of the violation.

(f) In addition to the penalties provided in subsections (b) through (e), an individual who is the subject of any of the information contained in a report or records made confidential by this [Act] may maintain an action for damages or equitable relief against any person who makes or obtains, or is likely to make or obtain, an unauthorized disclosure of the information.

(g) Identifying information contained in a report or records required by this [Act] to be kept confidential or sealed may not be disclosed under any other law of this State.

§7-107. Action by department

The department may review and investigate compliance with this [Act] and may maintain an action in the [appropriate court] to compel compliance.

[ARTICLE] 8. Miscellaneous provisions

§8-101. Uniformity of application and construction

This [Act] shall be applied and construed to effectuate its general purpose to make uniform the law with respect to the subject of this [Act] among the States enacting it.

§8-102. Short title

This [Act] may be cited as the Uniform Adoption Act (1994).

§8-103. Severability clause

If any provision of this [Act] or its application to any person or circumstance is held invalid, the invalidity does not affect other provisions or application of this [Act] which can be given effect without the invalid provision or application, and to this end the provisions of this [Act] are severable.

§8-104. Effective date

This [Act] takes effect on ______.

§8-105. Repeals

The following acts and parts of acts are repealed:

(1) ____________.
(2) ____________.
(3) ____________.

§8-106. Transitional provisions

A proceeding for adoption commenced before the effective date of this [Act] may be completed under the law in effect at the time the proceeding was commenced.

UNIFORM CHILD ABDUCTION PREVENTION ACT (2006)

TABLE OF CONTENTS

Prefatory Note

Child abduction is a serious problem both in scope and effect. A study commissioned by the Office of Juvenile Justice and Delinquency Prevention estimated that 262,100 children were abducted in 1999; 203,900 (78 per cent) of them were abducted by a parent or family member; approximately 1000 of the abductions were international. The purpose of the Uniform Child Abduction Prevention Act is to deter both predecree and postdecree domestic and international child abductions by parents, persons acting on behalf of a parent or others. Family abductions may be preventable through the identification of risk factors and the imposition of appropriate preventive measures.

The Uniform Child Abduction Prevention Act is premised on the general principle that preventing an abduction is in a child's best interests. Abducted children may suffer long-lasting harm. Federal law recognizes that parental abduction is harmful to children. Child abductions can occur before or after entry of a child-custody determination. This Act allows the court to impose abduction prevention measures at any time.

Many abductions occur before a court has had the opportunity to enter a child-custody determination. Children at the center of custody disputes are at the highest risk for potential abductions. Jurisdictional laws help deter abductions by specifying the proper state to handle custody litigation. The Uniform Child Custody Jurisdiction Act sets out four concurrent bases for jurisdiction. Congress passed the Parental Kidnapping Prevention Act of 1980 to deter abductions, discourage interstate conflicts, and promote cooperation between states about custody matters by resolving jurisdictional conflicts. The Parental Kidnapping Prevention Act prioritizes the state in which the child has lived for six months preceding the filing of the petition (the home state) as the place for custody litigation and prohibits a second state from assuming jurisdiction if there is

an action pending in the state that has proper jurisdiction. The Uniform Child Custody Jurisdiction and Enforcement Act, now in 45 jurisdictions, also prioritizes home state jurisdiction notwithstanding the child's absence. Jurisdictional laws do not provide prevention measures for abduction.

Post-decree abductions often occur because the existing child-custody determinations lack sufficient protective provisions to prevent an abduction. An award of joint physical custody without a designation of specific times; a vague order granting "reasonable visitation"; or the lack any restrictions on custody and visitation make orders hard to enforce. The awareness of abduction risk factors and preventive measures available can reduce the threat of abduction by giving the court the tools to make the initial child-custody determination clearer, more specific, and more easily enforceable.

If an abduction occurs after a child-custody determination, all states have enforcement remedies. Forty-six jurisdictions use the procedures in Article 3 of the Uniform Child Custody Jurisdiction and Enforcement Act. In addition, courts can punish abductors for contempt and allow tort actions for custodial interference. Several federal laws help locate missing children and criminalize international parental kidnapping. While there is no federal law criminalizing interstate parental kidnapping, there is a mechanism for apprehending persons who violate state parental kidnapping laws and travel across state lines. When enacting the Parental Kidnapping Prevention Act, Congress declared that the Unlawful Flight to Avoid Prosecution provision applies to cases involving parental kidnapping and interstate or international flight to avoid prosecution. While every state criminally forbids custodial interference by parents or relatives of the child, the laws differ as to the elements of the offenses, the punishments given, and whether a child-custody determination must exist for a violation to occur.

If the abduction is international, the Hague Convention on the Civil Aspects of International Child Abduction, currently in effect between the United States and fifty-five countries, facilitates the return of an abducted child to the child's habitual residence. Many countries, however, have not ratified the Hague Convention on the Civil Aspects of International Child Abduction, the United States has not accepted all nations' accessions, and some countries that have ratified do not comply with the treaty obligations.

This Act is civil law and complements existing state law. This Act does not limit, contradict, or supercede the Uniform Child Custody Jurisdiction and Enforcement Act or the Uniform Child Custody Jurisdiction Act. This Act is not meant to prevent a legitimate relocation action filed in accordance with the law of the state having jurisdiction to make a child-custody determination nor to prevent a victim of domestic violence from escaping abuse.

The Uniform Child Abduction Prevention Act applies to predecree and intrastate cases, to emergency situations, and to cases in which risk factors exist and the current child-custody determination lacks abduction prevention measures. Only three states have enacted comprehensive child abduction prevention statutes; two other states include provisions to reduce the risk of abduction. This Act will fill a void in the majority of states by identifying circumstances indicating a risk of abduction and providing measures to prevent the abduction of children, predecree or postdecree.

§1. Short title

This [act] may be cited as the Uniform Child Abduction Prevention Act.

§2. Definitions

In this [act]:

(1) "Abduction" means the wrongful removal or wrongful retention of a child.

(2) "Child" means an unemancipated individual who is less than 18 years of age.

(3) "Child-custody determination" means a judgment, decree, or other order of a court providing for the legal custody, physical custody, or visitation with respect to a child. The term includes a permanent, temporary, initial, and modification order.

(4) "Child-custody proceeding" means a proceeding in which legal custody, physical custody, or visitation with respect to a child is at issue. The term includes a proceeding for divorce, dissolution of marriage, separation, neglect, abuse, dependency, guardianship, paternity, termination of parental rights, or protection from domestic violence.

(5) "Court" means an entity authorized under the law of a state to establish, enforce, or modify a child-custody determination.

(6) "Petition" includes a motion or its equivalent.

(7) "Record" means information that is inscribed on a tangible medium or that is stored in an electronic or other medium and is retrievable in perceivable form.

(8) "State" means a state of the United States, the District of Columbia, Puerto Rico, the United States Virgin Islands, or any territory or insular possession subject to the jurisdiction of the United States. The term includes a federally recognized Indian tribe or nation.

(9) "Travel document" means records relating to a travel itinerary, including travel tickets, passes, reservations for transportation, or accommodations. The term does not include a passport or visa.

(10) "Wrongful removal" means the taking of a child that breaches rights of custody or visitation given or recognized under the law of this state.

(11) "Wrongful retention" means the keeping or concealing of a child that breaches rights of custody or visitation given or recognized under the law of this state.

Comment

To the extent possible, the definitions track the Uniform Child Custody Jurisdiction and Enforcement Act. The definition of a child as a person under age 18 is the same as in Section 102(2) of the Uniform Child Custody Jurisdiction and Enforcement Act. State law determines when a child becomes emancipated before age 18. This Act is limited to the abduction of minors even though the risk of abduction may apply to a disabled adult who has an appointed adult guardian.

The definition of "child-custody determination" is the same as the definition in Section 102(3) of the Uniform Child Custody Jurisdiction and Enforcement Act. This Act uses the traditional terminology of "custody" and "visitation" because that is the language used in the Uniform Child Custody Jurisdiction and Enforcement Act although local terminology may differ. The definition of a child-custody proceeding differs insignificantly from Section 102(4) of the Uniform Child Custody Jurisdiction and Enforcement Act.

The definition of abduction covers wrongful removal or wrongful retention. The definition is broad enough to encompass not only an abduction committed by either parent or a person acting on behalf of the parent but also other abductions. Generally both parents have the right to companionship and access to their child unless a court states otherwise. Abductions can occur against an individual or other entity with custody rights, as well as against an individual with visitation or access rights. A parent with joint legal or physical custody rights, by operation of law, court order, or legally binding agreement, commits an abduction by wrongfully interfering with the other parent's rights. A removal or retention of a child can be "wrongful" predecree or postdecree. An abduction is wrongful where it is in breach of an existing "child-custody determination" or, if predecree, in violation of rights attributed to a person by operation of law. The term "breaches rights of custody" tracks Article 3 of the Hague Convention on the Civil Aspects of International Child Abduction.

§3. Cooperation and communication among courts

Sections [110], [111], and [112] of [insert citation to the provisions of the Uniform Child Custody Jurisdiction and Enforcement Act or its equivalent in the state] apply to cooperation and communications among courts in proceedings under this [act].

Comment

It is possible, even likely, that abduction situations will involve more than one state. Thus, there is a need for mechanisms for communication among courts, for testimony to be obtained quickly by means other than physical presence, and for cooperation between courts in different states. Sections 110, 111, and 112 of the Uniform Child Custody Jurisdiction and Enforcement Act provide mechanisms to deal with these issues. States that do not have the Uniform Child Custody Jurisdiction and Enforcement Act may want to include these provisions or use some similar provision of existing state law.

§4. Actions for abduction prevention measures

(a) A court on its own motion may order abduction prevention measures in a child- custody proceeding if the court finds that the evidence establishes a credible risk of abduction of the child.

(b) A party to a child-custody determination or another individual or entity having a right under the law of this state or any other state to seek a child-custody determination for the child may file a petition seeking abduction prevention measures to protect the child under this [act].

(c) A prosecutor or public authority designated under [insert citation to Section 315 of the Uniform Child Custody Jurisdiction and Enforcement Act or applicable law of this state] may seek a warrant to take physical custody of a child under Section 9 or other appropriate prevention measures.

Comment

An abduction may occur before a child-custody proceeding has commenced, after the filing but before entry of a child-custody determination, or in violation of an existing child-custody determination. To obtain abduction prevention measures, either the court on its own may impose the measures or a party to a child custody proceeding or an individual or entity having the right to seek custody may file a petition seeking abduction prevention measures.

A court hearing a child custody case may determine that the evidence shows a credible risk of abduction. Therefore, even without a party filing a petition under this Act, the court on its own motion can impose appropriate abduction prevention measures. Usually, however, a parent who fears that the other parent or family members are preparing to abduct the child will file a petition in an existing custody dispute. An individual or other entity, such as the state child welfare agency, which has a right to lawful custody may file a petition alleging a risk of abduction and seeking prevention measures with respect to a child who is not yet the subject of a child-custody determination.

The Act allows a prosecutor or public authority designated in Section 315 of the Uniform Child Custody Jurisdiction and Enforcement Act to seek a warrant under Section 9 of this Act if there is an imminent risk of wrongful removal.

§5. Jurisdiction

(a) A petition under this [act] may be filed only in a court that has jurisdiction to make a child-custody determination with respect to the child at issue under [insert citation to Uniform Child Custody Jurisdiction and Enforcement Act or the Uniform Child Custody Jurisdiction Act].

(b) A court of this state has temporary emergency jurisdiction under [insert citation to Section 204 of the Uniform Child Custody Jurisdiction and Enforcement Act or Section 3(a)(3) of the Uniform Child Custody Jurisdiction Act] if the court finds a credible risk of abduction.

Comment

This Act complements, but does not limit, contradict, or supercede the Uniform Child Custody Jurisdiction and Enforcement Act, 9 U.L.A. Part I 657 (1999), or the Uniform Child Custody Jurisdiction Act, 9 U.L.A. Part I 115 (1988). A court must have jurisdiction sufficient to make an initial child-custody determination, a modification, or temporary emergency jurisdiction to issue prevention measures under this Act.

The Parental Kidnapping Prevention Act prioritizes the child's home state as the primary jurisdictional basis; prohibits a court in one state from exercising jurisdiction if a valid custody proceeding is already pending in another state; and requires that states give full faith and credit to sister state decrees made in accordance with its principles. The Uniform Child Custody Jurisdiction and Enforcement Act follows the Parental Kidnapping Prevention Act.

A court has temporary emergency jurisdiction under the Uniform Child Custody Jurisdiction and Enforcement Act only if the child has been abandoned or it is necessary in an emergency to protect the child because the child, or a sibling or parent of the child, is subjected to or threatened with mistreatment or abuse. This Act equates a credible risk of abduction with threatened mistreatment or abuse for emergency jurisdiction purposes.

If a state would be able to exercise emergency jurisdiction under Section 204 the Uniform Child Custody Jurisdiction and Enforcement Act, it can do so even if another court has issued a child-custody determination and has continuing exclusive jurisdiction. The reference to Section 204 brings in all of its provisions that include communication, length of time of temporary orders, and the like.

Under Section 208 of the Uniform Child Custody Jurisdiction and Enforcement Act, if a court has jurisdiction because a person seeking to invoke its jurisdiction has engaged in unjustifiable conduct, the court shall decline to exercise its jurisdiction. However, as the comment to Section 208 explains, domestic violence victims should not be charged with unjustifiable conduct for conduct that occurred in the process of fleeing domestic violence. Domestic violence also shall be considered in a court's inconvenient forum analysis under Section 207(b)(1) of the Uniform Child Custody Jurisdiction and Enforcement Act.

§6. Contents of petition

A petition under this [act] must be verified and include a copy of any existing child-custody determination, if available. The petition must specify the risk factors for abduction, including the relevant factors described in Section 7. Subject to [insert citation to Section 209(e) of the Uniform Child Custody Jurisdiction and Enforcement Act or cite the law of this state providing for the confidentiality of procedures, addresses, and other identifying information], if reasonably ascertainable, the petition must contain:

(1) the name, date of birth, and gender of the child;

(2) the customary address and current physical location of the child;

(3) the identity, customary address, and current physical location of the respondent;

(4) a statement of whether a prior action to prevent abduction or domestic violence has been filed by a party or other individual or entity having custody of the child, and the date, location, and disposition of the action;

(5) a statement of whether a party to the proceeding has been arrested for a crime related to domestic violence, stalking, or child abuse or neglect, and the date, location, and disposition of the case; and

(6) any other information required to be submitted to the court for a child-custody determination under [insert citation to Section 209 of the Uniform Child Custody Jurisdiction and Enforcement Act or applicable law of this state].

Comment

The contents of the petition follow those for pleadings under Section 209 of the Uniform Child Custody Jurisdiction and Enforcement Act. The information is made subject to state law on the protection of names or identifying information in certain cases. A number of states have enacted laws relating to the protection of victims in domestic violence and child abuse cases by keeping confidential the victims' names, addresses, and other information. These procedures must be followed if the state law requires their applicability. If a state does not protect names and addresses, then a provision similar to Section 209(e) of the Uniform Child Custody Jurisdiction and Enforcement Act should be added. That provision reads:

> **If a party alleges in an affidavit or a pleading under oath that the health, safety, or liberty of a party or child would be jeopardized by disclosure of identifying information, the information must be sealed and may not be disclosed to the other party or the public unless the court orders the disclosure to be made after a hearing in which the court takes into consideration the health, safety, or liberty of the party or child**

and determines that the disclosure is in the interest of justice.

The requirement for information on domestic violence or child abuse is to alert the court to the possibility that a batterer or abuser is attempting to use the Act. Domestic violence underlies large numbers of parental kidnapping. One study found that approximately one half of abductors had been violent toward the other parent during the marriage or relationship. Some batterers abduct their children during or after custody litigation; others abduct before initiating legal proceedings. The court should not allow a batterer to use this Act to gain temporary custody or additional visitation in an uncontested hearing. A person who has committed domestic violence or child abuse poses a risk of harm to the child. Such a person, however, may still seek relief in a contested hearing where the issues can be fully examined by the court. In order to screen for domestic violence or child abuse, the petition requires disclosure of all relevant information and the court can inquire about domestic violence at any hearing.

Notice and opportunity to be heard should be given according to the law of the state and may be by publication if other means are not effective. See Section 108(a) of the Uniform Child Custody Jurisdiction and Enforcement Act.

§7. Factors to determine risk of abduction

(a) In determining whether there is a credible risk of abduction of a child, the court shall consider any evidence that the petitioner or respondent:

(1) has previously abducted or attempted to abduct the child;

(2) has threatened to abduct the child;

(3) has recently engaged in activities that may indicate a planned abduction, including:

(A) abandoning employment;

(B) selling a primary residence;

(C) terminating a lease;

(D) closing bank or other financial management accounts, liquidating assets, hiding or destroying financial documents, or conducting any unusual financial activities;

(E) applying for a passport or visa or obtaining travel documents for the respondent, a family member, or the child; or

(F) seeking to obtain the child's birth certificate or school or medical records;

(4) has engaged in domestic violence, stalking, or child abuse or neglect;

(5) has refused to follow a child-custody determination;

(6) lacks strong familial, financial, emotional, or cultural ties to the state or the United States;

(7) has strong familial, financial, emotional, or cultural ties to another state or country;

(8) is likely to take the child to a country that:

(A) is not a party to the Hague Convention on the Civil Aspects of International Child Abduction and does not provide for the extradition of an abducting parent or for the return of an abducted child;

(B) is a party to the Hague Convention on the Civil Aspects of International Child Abduction but:

(i) the Hague Convention on the Civil Aspects of International Child Abduction is not in force between the United States and that country;

(ii) is noncompliant according to the most recent compliance report issued by the United States Department of State; or

(iii) lacks legal mechanisms for immediately and effectively enforcing a return order under the Hague Convention on the Civil Aspects of International Child Abduction;

(C) poses a risk that the child's physical or emotional health or safety would be endangered in the country because of specific circumstances relating to the child or because of human rights violations committed against children;

(D) has laws or practices that would:

(i) enable the respondent, without due cause, to prevent the petitioner from contacting the child;

(ii) restrict the petitioner from freely traveling to or exiting from the country because of the petitioner's gender, nationality, marital status, or religion; or

(iii) restrict the child's ability legally to leave the country after the child reaches the age of majority because of a child's gender, nationality, or religion;

(E) is included by the United States Department of State on a current list of state sponsors of terrorism;

(F) does not have an official United States diplomatic presence in the country; or

(G) is engaged in active military action or war, including a civil war, to which the child may be exposed;

(9) is undergoing a change in immigration or citizenship status that would adversely affect the respondent's ability to remain in the United States legally;

(10) has had an application for United States citizenship denied;

(11) has forged or presented misleading or false evidence on government forms or supporting documents to obtain or attempt to obtain a passport, a visa, travel documents, a Social Security card, a driver's license, or other government-issued identification card or has made a misrepresentation to the United States government;

(12) has used multiple names to attempt to mislead or defraud; or

(13) has engaged in any other conduct the court considers relevant to the risk of abduction.

(b) In the hearing on a petition under this [act], the court shall consider any evidence that the respondent believed in good faith that the respondent's conduct was necessary to avoid imminent harm to the child or respondent and any other evidence that may be relevant to whether the respondent may be permitted to remove or retain the child.

Comment

The list of risk factors constitutes a summary of the wide variety of types of behaviors and characteristics that researchers have found to be present. The risk factors are based on research that has been done during the last twelve years. Research also shows that abducting parents dismiss the value of the other parent in the child's life; have young children or children vulnerable to influence; and often have the support of their family and others. Parents who have made credible threats to abduct a child or have a history are particularly high risk especially when accompanied by other factors, such as quitting a job, selling a home, and moving assets. *See* Janet Johnston & Linda Girdner, *Family Abductors: Descriptive Profiles and Preventative Interventions* (U.S. Dep't of Justice, OJJDP 2001 NCJ 182788); ABA, Early Identification of Risk Factors for Parental Abduction (NCJ185026). The more of these factors that are present, the more likely the chance of an abduction. However, the mere presence of one or more of these factors does not mean that an abduction will occur just as the absence of these factors does not guarantee that no abduction will occur. Some conduct described in the factors can be done in conjunction with a relocation petition, which would negate an inference that the parent is planning to abduct the child.

International abductions pose more obstacles to return of a child than do abductions within the United States. Courts should consider evidence that the respondent was raised in another country and has family support there, has a legal right to work in a foreign country and has the ability to speak that foreign language. There are difficulties associated with securing return of children from countries that are not treaty partners under the Hague Convention on the Civil Aspects of Child Abduction or are not compliant with the Convention. Compliance Reports are available at the United States Department of State website or may be obtained by contacting the Office of Children's Issues in Department of State.

Courts should be particularly sensitive to the importance of preventive measures where there is an identified risk of a child being removed to countries that are guilty of human rights violations, including arranged marriages of children, child labor, lack of child abuse laws, female genital mutilation, sexual exploitation, any form of child slavery, torture, and the deprivation of liberty. These countries pose potentially serious obstacles to return of a child and pose the possibility of harm.

Courts need to be sensitive to domestic violence issues. Batterers often abduct their children before as well as during and after custody litigation. However, courts also need to be aware of the dynamics of domestic violence. Rather than a vindictive reason for taking the child, a victim fleeing domestic violence may be attempting to protect the victim and the child. Almost half of the parents in one parental kidnapping study were victims of domestic violence and half of the parents who were contemplating abducting their children were motivated by the perceived need to protect their child from physical, sexual, and emotional abuse. Geoffrey L. Greif & Rebecca L. Hegar, When Parents Kidnap: The Families Behind the Headlines 8 (1993). Some of the risk factors involve the same activities that might be undertaken by a victim of domestic violence who is trying to relocate or flee to escape violence. If the evidence shows that the parent preparing to leave is fleeing domestic violence, the court must consider that any order restricting departure or transferring custody may pose safety issues for the respondent and the child, and therefore, should be imposed only when the risk of abduction, the likely harm from the abduction, and the chances of recovery outweigh the risk of harm to the respondent and the child.

The Uniform Child Custody Jurisdiction and Enforcement Act recognizes that domestic violence victims should be considered. The Comment to Section 208 of the Uniform Child Custody Jurisdiction and Enforcement Act (Jurisdiction Declined by Reason of Conduct) states that "Domestic violence victims should not be charged with unjustifiable conduct for conduct that occurred in the process of fleeing domestic violence, even if their conduct is technically illegal. An inquiry must be made whether the flight was justified under the circumstances of the case."

§8. Provisions and measures to prevent abduction

(a) If a petition is filed under this [act], the court may enter an order that must include:

(1) the basis for the court's exercise of jurisdiction;

(2) the manner in which notice and opportunity to be heard were given to the persons entitled to notice of the proceeding;

(3) a detailed description of each party's custody and visitation rights and residential arrangements for the child;

(4) a provision stating that a violation of the order may subject the party in violation to civil and criminal penalties; and

(5) identification of the child's country of habitual residence at the time of the issuance of the order.

(b) If, at a hearing on a petition under this [act] or on the court's own motion, the court after reviewing the evidence finds a credible risk of abduction of the child, the court shall enter an abduction prevention order. The order must include the provisions required by subsection (a) and measures and conditions, including those in subsections (c), (d), and (e), that are reasonably calculated to prevent abduction of the child, giving due consideration to the custody and visitation rights of the parties. The court shall consider the age of the child, the potential harm to the child from an abduction, the legal and practical difficulties of returning the child to the jurisdiction if abducted, and the reasons for the potential abduction, including evidence of domestic violence, stalking, or child abuse or neglect.

(c) An abduction prevention order may include one or more of the following:

(1) an imposition of travel restrictions that require that a party traveling with the child outside a designated geographical area provide the other party with the following:

(A) the travel itinerary of the child;

(B) a list of physical addresses and telephone numbers at which the child can be reached at specified times; and

(C) copies of all travel documents;

(2) a prohibition of the respondent directly or indirectly:

(A) removing the child from this state, the United States, or another geographic area without permission of the court or the petitioner's written consent;

(B) removing or retaining the child in violation of a child-custody determination;

(C) removing the child from school or a child-care or similar facility; or

(D) approaching the child at any location other than a site designated for supervised visitation;

(3) a requirement that a party register the order in another state as a prerequisite to allowing the child to travel to that state;

(4) with regard to the child's passport:

(A) a direction that the petitioner place the child's name in the United States Department of State's Child Passport Issuance Alert Program;

(B) a requirement that the respondent surrender to the court or the petitioner's attorney any United States or foreign passport issued in the child's name, including a passport issued in the name of both the parent and the child; and

(C) a prohibition upon the respondent from applying on behalf of the child for a new or replacement passport or visa;

(5) as a prerequisite to exercising custody or visitation, a requirement that the respondent provide:

(A) to the United States Department of State Office of Children's Issues and the relevant foreign consulate or embassy, an authenticated copy of the order detailing passport and travel restrictions for the child;

(B) to the court:

(i) proof that the respondent has provided the information in subparagraph (A); and

(ii) an acknowledgment in a record from the relevant foreign consulate or embassy that no passport application has been made, or passport issued, on behalf of the child;

(C) to the petitioner, proof of registration with the United States Embassy or other United States diplomatic presence in the destination country and with the Central Authority for the Hague Convention on the Civil Aspects of International Child Abduction, if that Convention is in effect between the United States and the destination country, unless one of the parties objects; and

(D) a written waiver under the Privacy Act, 5 U.S.C. Section 552a [as amended], with respect to any document, application, or other information pertaining to the child authorizing its disclosure to the court and the petitioner; and

(6) upon the petitioner's request, a requirement that the respondent obtain an order from the relevant foreign country containing terms identical to the child-custody determination issued in the United States.

(d) In an abduction prevention order, the court may impose conditions on the exercise of custody or visitation that:

(1) limit visitation or require that visitation with the child by the respondent be supervised until the court finds that supervision is no longer necessary and order the respondent to pay the costs of supervision;

(2) require the respondent to post a bond or provide other security in an amount sufficient to serve as a financial deterrent to abduction, the proceeds of which may be used to pay for the reasonable expenses of recovery of the child, including reasonable attorneys fees and costs if there is an abduction; and

(3) require the respondent to obtain education on the potentially harmful effects to the child from abduction.

(e) To prevent imminent abduction of a child, a court may:

(1) issue a warrant to take physical custody of the child under Section 9 or the law of this state other than this [act];

(2) direct the use of law enforcement to take any action reasonably necessary to locate the child, obtain return of the child, or enforce a custody determination under this [act] or the law of this state other than this [act]; or

(3) grant any other relief allowed under the law of this state other than this [act].

(f) The remedies provided in this [act] are cumulative and do not affect the availability of other remedies to prevent abduction.

Comment

This act provides courts with a choice of remedies. Ideally the court will choose the least restrictive measures and conditions to maximize opportunities for continued parental contact while minimizing the opportunities for abduction. The most restrictive measures should be used when there have been prior custody violations and overt threats to take the child; when the child faces substantial potential harm from an abducting parent who may have serious mental or personality disorder, history of abuse or violence or no prior relationship with the child; or when the obstacles to recovering the child are formidable due to countries not cooperating and enforcing orders from the United States, not being signatories to the Hague Convention on the Civil Aspects of International Child Abduction or non-compliant. Section 8 lists the possible prevention measures categorized as travel restrictions, conditions on the exercise of custody and visitation, and urgent measures when abduction is imminent or in progress.

If a person files a petition under this Act, even if the court decides not to order restrictive measures or impose conditions, the court may clarify and make more specific the existing child-

custody determination. To enter an abduction prevention order, the court must have jurisdiction to make a child-custody determination even if it is emergency jurisdiction. The court should set out the basis for the court's exercise of jurisdiction. The more apparent on the face of the document that the court issuing the order had proper jurisdiction, the more likely courts in other states and countries are to recognize it as valid. The court should also include a statement showing that the parties were properly served and given adequate notice. This makes it apparent on the face of the order that due process was met. *See* Sections 108 and 205 of the Uniform Child Custody Jurisdiction and Enforcement Act. States do not require personal jurisdiction to make a child-custody determination.

The court may make an existing child-custody order clearer and more specific. Vague orders are difficult to enforce without additional litigation. The term "reasonable visitation" can lead to conflicts between the parents and make it difficult for law enforcement officers to know if the order is being violated. The court may specify the dates and times for each party's custody and visitation, including holidays, birthdays, and telephone or Internet contact. Because joint custody arrangements create special enforcement problems, the court should ensure that the order specifies the child's residential placement at all times. Whenever possible, the residential arrangements should represent the parents' agreement. However, to prevent abductions, it is important for the court order to be specific as to the residential arrangements for the child. If there is a threat of abduction, awarding sole custody to one parent makes enforcement easier.

The court may also include language in the prevention order to highlight the importance of both parties complying with the court order by including in bold language: "VIOLATION OF THIS ORDER MAY SUBJECT THE PARTY IN VIOLATION TO CIVIL AND CRIMINAL PENALTIES."

Because every abduction case may be a potential international abduction case, the prevention order should identify the place of habitual residence of a child. Although the Hague Convention on the Civil Aspects of International Child Abduction does not define "habitual residence" and the determination is made by the court in the country hearing a petition for return of a child, a statement in the child-custody determination or prevention order may help. A typical statement reads:

> The State of ___________, United States of America, is the habitual residence of the minor children within the meaning of the Hague Convention on the Civil Aspects of International Child Abduction.

If the court finds a credible risk of abduction, this Act provides numerous measures to prevent an abduction. Courts can require a party traveling outside a specified geographical area to provide the other party with all relevant information about where the child will be and how to contact the child. The court can impose travel restrictions prohibiting the respondent from leaving the United States or a specific geographical area; from removing the child from school, day care or other facilities, and can restrict contact other than as specified in the order. The court may also impose passport restrictions and require the respondent to provide assurances and safeguards as a condition of traveling with the child.

The court may also choose to impose restrictions on custody or visitation. The most common, and one of the most effective, restrictions is supervised visitation. Visitation should remain supervised until the court decides the threat of abduction has passed. In addition, the court may require the posting of a bond sufficient to serve both as a deterrent and as a source of funds for the cost of the return of the child. If domestic violence is present, the court may want to order the abusive person to obtain education, counseling or attend a batterers' intervention and prevention program.

Because of international abduction cases are the most complex and difficult, reasonable restrictions to prevent such abductions are necessary. If a credible risk of international abduction of the child exists, passport controls and travel restrictions may be indispensable. It may be advantageous in some cases to obtain a "mirror" or reciprocal order. Before exercising rights, the respondent would need to get a custody order from the country to which the respondent will travel that recognizes both the United States order and the court's continuing jurisdiction. The foreign court would need to agree to order return of the child if the child was taken in violation of the court order. This potentially expensive and time consuming remedy should only be ordered when likely to be of assistance. Because the foreign court may subsequently modify its order, problems can arise.

The court may do whatever is necessary to prevent an abduction, including using the warrant procedure under this act or under the law of the state. Many law enforcement officers are unclear about their role in responding to parental kidnapping cases. One study showed that 70 percent of law enforcement agencies reported that they did not have written policies and procedures governing child abduction cases. A provision in the custody order directing law enforcement officer to "accompany and assist" a parent to recover an abducted child may be useful but is not included in this Act. The language tracks Section 316 of the Uniform Child Custody Jurisdiction and Enforcement Act that authorizes law enforcement to take any lawful action reasonably necessary to locate a child or a party and assist a prosecutor or appropriate public official in obtaining return of a child or enforcing a child-custody determination.

The remedies provided in this Act are intended to supplement and complement existing law.

§9. Warrant to take physical custody of child

(a) If a petition under this [act] contains allegations, and the court finds that there is a credible risk that the child is imminently likely to be wrongfully removed, the court may issue an ex parte warrant to take physical custody of the child.

(b) The respondent on a petition under subsection (a) must be afforded an opportunity to be heard at the earliest possible time after the ex parte warrant is executed, but not later than the next judicial day unless a hearing on that date is impossible. In that event, the court shall hold the hearing on the first judicial day possible.

(c) An ex parte warrant under subsection (a) to take physical custody of a child must:

(1) recite the facts upon which a determination of a credible risk of imminent wrongful removal of the child is based;

(2) direct law enforcement officers to take physical custody of the child immediately;

(3) state the date and time for the hearing on the petition; and

(4) provide for the safe interim placement of the child pending further order of the court.

(d) If feasible, before issuing a warrant and before determining the placement of the child after the warrant is executed, the court may order a search of the relevant databases of the National Crime Information Center system and similar state databases to determine if either the petitioner or respondent has a history of domestic violence, stalking, or child abuse or neglect.

(e) The petition and warrant must be served on the respondent when or immediately after the child is taken into physical custody.

(f) A warrant to take physical custody of a child, issued by this state or another state, is enforceable throughout this state. If the court finds that a less intrusive remedy will not be effective, it may authorize law enforcement officers to enter private property to take physical custody of the child. If required by exigent circumstances, the court may authorize law enforcement officers to make a forcible entry at any hour.

(g) If the court finds, after a hearing, that a petitioner sought an ex parte warrant under subsection (a) for the purpose of harassment or in bad faith, the court may award the respondent reasonable attorney's fees, costs, and expenses.

(h) This [act] does not affect the availability of relief allowed under the law of this state other than this [act].

Comment

This section authorizes issuance of a warrant in an emergency situation, such as an allegation that the respondent is preparing to abduct the child to a foreign country and is on the way to the airport. The harm is the credible risk of imminent removal. If the court finds such a risk, the court should temporarily waive the notice requirements and issue a warrant to take physical custody of the child. Immediately after the warrant is executed, the respondent is to receive notice of the proceedings. This section mirrors Section 311 of the Uniform Child Custody Jurisdiction and Enforcement Act on warrants to pick up a child which are available when there is an existing child-custody determination. In many states, the term used in civil cases is "writ of attachment."

The court should hear the testimony of the petitioner or another witness before issuing the warrant. The testimony may be heard in person, by telephone, or by any other means acceptable under local law, which may include video conferencing or use of other technology.

Domestic violence includes "family" violence. Because some batterers may try to use the warrant procedure to prevent victims and the children from escaping domestic violence or child abuse, the court should check relevant state and national databases to see if either the petitioner or respondent's name is listed or if relevant information exists that has not been disclosed before issuing the warrant and ordering placement. Lundy Bancroft & Jay G. Silverman, The Batterer as Parent: Addressing the Impact of Domestic Violence on Family Dynamics 73, 75 (2002)(indicating that most parental abductions take place in the context of a history of domestic violence because threatening to take the child from the mother is a form of control).

Some courts have computer terminals on the bench and a database search takes seconds. Courts without computer access can seek the assistance of law enforcement. Unless impracticable, the court should conduct a search of all person databases of the National Crime Information Center system, including the protection order file, the historical protection order file, the warrants file, the sex offender registry, and the persons on supervised release file. In addition, it is recommended that courts run searches in the National Law Enforcement Telecommunication System in the petitioner's state of birth, current state of residence, and other recent states of residence. Civil courts are authorized by statute and National Crime Information Center policy to have access to information in several files for domestic violence and stalking cases. Because child abduction involves family members and can harm children, and violence between the parents is often a factor leading to child abduction, cases in which a parent alleges a risk of wrongful removal should permit access to the relevant databases.

The court should also view comparable state databases, such as the state department of social service registry of persons found to have abused or neglected children. If the petitioner or respondent are listed for a reason related to a crime of domestic or family violence, the court may refuse to issue a warrant or order any appropriate placement authorized under the laws of the state. The warrant must provide for the placement of a child pending the hearing. Temporary placement will most often be with the petitioner unless the database check reveals the petitioner is a likely or known abuser.

The court must state the reasons for issuance of the warrant. The warrant can be enforced by law

enforcement officers wherever the child is found in the state. The warrant may authorize entry upon private property to pick up the child if no less intrusive means are possible. In extraordinary cases, the warrant may authorize law enforcement to make a forcible entry at any hour. This section also authorizes law enforcement officers to enforce out of state warrants.

Section 9 applies only to wrongful removals, not wrongful retentions. It does not hinder a court from issuing any other immediate ex parte relief to prevent a wrongful removal or retention as may be allowed under law other than this act.

§10. Duration of abduction prevention order

An abduction prevention order remains in effect until the earliest of:

(1) the time stated in the order;

(2) the emancipation of the child;

(3) the child's attaining 18 years of age; or

(4) the time the order is modified, revoked, vacated, or superseded by a court with jurisdiction under [insert citation to Sections 201 through 203 of the Uniform Child Custody Jurisdiction and Enforcement Act or Section 3 of the Uniform Child Custody Jurisdiction Act and applicable law of this state].

§11. Uniformity of application of construction

In applying and construing this uniform act, consideration must be given to the need to promote uniformity of the law with respect to its subject matter among states that enact it.

§12. Relation to Electronic Signatures in Global and National Commerce Act

This [act] modifies, limits, and supersedes the federal Electronic Signatures in Global and National Commerce Act, 15 U.S.C. Section 7001, et seq., but does not modify, limit, or supersede Section 101(c) of the act, 15 U.S.C. Section 7001(c), or authorize electronic delivery of any of the notices described in Section 103(b) of that act, 15 U.S.C. Section 7003(b).

§13. Effective date

This [act] takes effect on .

UNIFORM CHILD WITNESS TESTIMONY BY ALTERNATIVE METHODS ACT (2002)

TABLE OF CONTENTS

§1. Short title

This [Act] may be cited as the Uniform Child Witness Testimony by Alternative Methods Act.

§2. Definitions

In this [Act]:

(1) "Alternative method" means a method by which a child witness testifies which does not include all of the following:

(A) having the child testify in person in an open forum;

(B) having the child testify in the presence and full view of the finder of fact and presiding officer; and

(C) allowing all of the parties to be present, to participate, and to view and be viewed by the child.

(2) "Child witness" means an individual under the age of [13] who has been or will be called to testify in a proceeding.

(3) "Criminal proceeding" means a trial or hearing before a court in a prosecution of a person charged with violating a criminal law of this State or a [insert term for a juvenile delinquency proceeding] involving conduct that if engaged in by an adult would constitute a violation of a criminal law of this State.

(4) "Noncriminal proceeding" means a trial or hearing before a court or an administrative agency of this State having judicial or quasi-judicial powers, other than a criminal proceeding.

Comment

In litigation to which the Act should apply, Sections 2(3) and (4) define criminal and noncriminal proceedings broadly. In these sections, the word "court" embraces both jury and non-jury actions. Section 2(3) defining criminal proceeding also includes a juvenile delinquency proceeding or comparable proceeding involving conduct that if engaged in by an adult would constitute a violation of the criminal law of the state. An alternative method by which a child testifies in a juvenile proceeding involving such conduct is no less important than in an adult criminal proceeding. See In re Gault, 387 U.S. 1 (1967); In re Winship, 397 U.S. 358 (1970).

In noncriminal proceedings, the Act may be invoked in civil cases generally, in juvenile and family law proceedings, subject to the provisions of

Section 3, and in administrative proceedings. In the context of physical or sexual abuse, the impact upon and risks to a child testifying in the courtroom in civil cases for damages, in juvenile proceedings and in family law proceedings are potentially as real as in criminal prosecutions. Similarly, the testimony of a child by an alternative method may also, for instance, be appropriate in an administrative proceeding to revoke the license of a day care center.

"Child witness" is defined in Section 2(2) as an individual under the age of a bracketed [13] who is competent to testify and is called to testify in the proceeding. The Act thereby accommodates the diverse approaches to age currently recognized among the several states for taking the testimony of a child by an alternative method. For example, while in Georgia the taking of testimony by closed-circuit television applies to a child ten years of age or younger (Ga. Code Ann. §17-8-55) and in Florida the age is under sixteen years (Fla. Stat. Ann. §92.54). The approach in the Act is based upon a recommendation that the maximum age should be thirteen.

The term "child witness" in Section 2(2) includes both a child who is a party to a proceeding and one who is merely called to testify as a witness.

Finally, as to the taking of the testimony of a child by an alternative method, the term is defined broadly in Section 2(1) to mean not only alternative methods currently recognized among the several states for taking the testimony of a child, such as audio visual recordings to be later presented in the courtroom, closed-circuit television which is transmitted directly to the courtroom, and room arrangements that avoid direct confrontation between a witness and a particular party or the finder of fact, but also other similar methods either currently employed or through technology yet to be developed or recognized in the future.

§3. Applicability

This [Act] applies to the testimony of a child witness in a criminal or noncriminal proceeding. However, this [Act] does not preclude, in a noncriminal proceeding, any other procedure permitted by law for a child witness to testify [, or in a [*insert the term for a juvenile delinquency proceeding*] involving conduct that if engaged in by an adult would constitute a violation of a criminal law of this State, testimony by a child witness in a closed forum as [authorized or required] by [*cite the law of this State that permits or requires closed juvenile hearings*]].

Comment

Section 3 provides that in noncriminal proceedings the Act does not preclude the use of other recognized state procedures for taking the testimony of a child by an alternative method. For example, in Delaware in custody and visitation cases the court is authorized to "interview the child in chambers to ascertain the child's wishes as to his or her custodian." Del. Code Ann. Tit. 13, §724. There are twenty states that have statutes similar to the Delaware statute. In addition, there are also a number of states in which a similar procedure is authorized by court rule or decisional law. See, for example, the Davidson County Juvenile Court Rules in Tennessee and the North Dakota case of Ryan v. Flemming, 533 N.W.2d 920 (N.D. 1995), authorizing a trial judge to interview a child in chambers. Section 3 also accommodates the law of eight states (and perhaps other states when children under 12 years of age are involved) authorizing or requiring a closed forum in juvenile proceedings in which criminal law violations are at issue. Thus, the Act preserves the right to utilize existing closed court procedures in an adopting state but, at the same time, also preserves the use of the other alternative method procedures provided for by the Act. The Act does not apply to or govern the taking or use of evidence obtained through discovery depositions or other discovery methods or devices authorized and regulated by the Rules of Civil or Criminal Procedure of the enacting jurisdiction.

As a legislative note, it should be observed that the bracketed material in Section 3 should be omitted in enacting states that require or substantially require an open forum in juvenile proceedings in which criminal law violations are at issue.

§4. Hearing whether to allow testimony by alternative method

(a) The presiding officer in a criminal or noncriminal proceeding may order a hearing to determine whether to allow a child witness to testify by an alternative method. The presiding officer, for good cause shown, shall order the hearing upon motion of a party, a child witness, or an individual determined by the presiding officer to have sufficient standing to act on behalf of the child.

(b) A hearing to determine whether to allow a child witness to testify by an alternative method must be conducted on the record after reasonable notice to all parties, any nonparty movant, and any other person the presiding officer specifies. The child's presence is not required at the hearing unless ordered by the presiding officer. In conducting the hearing, the presiding officer is not bound by rules of evidence except the rules of privilege.

Comment

Sections 4(a) and (b) set forth the procedures for instituting and conducting the hearing to determine whether an alternative method for taking the testimony of the child should be authorized. The hearing authorized in Section 4 is in the nature of a preliminary hearing or a hearing on a motion in limine to determine only whether the testimony of the child should be taken by an alternative method. The Uniform Rules of Evidence (1999), Rule 104(d) and the Federal Rules of Evidence, Rule 104(c)

provide for conducting a hearing on a preliminary matter out of the presence of the jury if the interests of justice require. The Section 4 hearing is a separate and distinct hearing from the proceeding defined in Sections 2(3) and (4) in which, upon order of the presiding officer, the testimony is actually presented by an alternative method. See also Sections 7 and 8, *infra*. The hearing under Section 4 may, in the discretion of the presiding officer, be conducted in an *in camera* proceeding.

The term "presiding officer" is used in this Act to broadly describe the person under whose supervision and jurisdiction the proceeding is being conducted. It includes a judge in whose court the case is being heard, a quasi-judicial officer, or an administrative law judge or hearing officer, depending upon the nature of the case and the type of proceeding in which the testimony of a child is sought or presented by an alternative method.

The hearing under Section 4 is initiated upon the motion of a party, the child witness, an interested individual with sufficient connection to the child to be a proper person to seek to protect the child's best interests, or the presiding officer *sua sponte,* all as set forth in Section 4(a).

It is also required under Section 4(b) that reasonable notice be given to all parties, a nonparty movant, or other appropriate person. The child's presence at the hearing is not required unless ordered by the presiding officer. The presiding officer should consider the factors enumerated in Section 6 of the Act, *infra,* in determining whether the child should be present at the hearing.

In conducting the hearing under Section 4, the presiding officer is not bound by the rules of evidence except for the rules of privilege, for example, as set forth in Rule 104(a) of the Uniform Rules of Evidence (1999) or Rule 104(a) of the Federal Rules of Evidence. At the same time, if, as provided in Rule 104(b) of the Uniform Rules, "there is a factual basis to support a good faith belief that a review of the allegedly privileged material is necessary, the court [or presiding officer], in making its determination, may review the material outside the presence of any other person."

Finally, Section 4(b) also provides that the hearing to determine whether an alternative method for the presenting of the testimony of the child is to be permitted shall be conducted on the record. It is also expected that a transcript of the record of the hearing will be made available to the public and news media to the same extent as in similar motions in any other judicial or quasi-judicial proceeding, subject, of course, to the presiding officer's authority, as in any other case, to balance constitutional and privacy interests and seal from public view sensitive information that should be protected. See Press-Enterprise Co. v. Superior Court, 478 U.S. 1 (1986).

§5. Standards for determining whether child witness may testify by alternative method

(a) In a criminal proceeding, the presiding officer may allow a child witness to testify by an alternative method only in the following situations:

(1) The child may testify otherwise than in an open forum in the presence and full view of the finder of fact if the presiding officer finds by clear and convincing evidence that the child would suffer serious emotional trauma that would substantially impair the child's ability to communicate with the finder of fact if required to testify in the open forum.

(2) The child may testify other than face-to-face with the defendant if the presiding officer finds by clear and convincing evidence that the child would suffer serious emotional trauma that would substantially impair the child's ability to communicate with the finder of fact if required to be confronted face-to-face by the defendant.

(b) In a noncriminal proceeding, the presiding officer may allow a child witness to testify by an alternative method if the presiding officer finds by a preponderance of the evidence that allowing the child to testify by an alternative method is necessary to serve the best interests of the child or enable the child to communicate with the finder of fact. In making this finding, the presiding officer shall consider:

(1) the nature of the proceeding;

(2) the age and maturity of the child;

(3) the relationship of the child to the parties in the proceeding;

(4) the nature and degree of emotional trauma that the child may suffer in testifying; and

(5) any other relevant factor.

Comment

Section 5 sets forth the standards that must be applied by the presiding officer in determining whether to allow the child to testify by an alternative method. Sections 5(a)(1) and (2) prescribe the standards that must be applied in criminal proceedings. In the case of face-to-face confrontation, Section 5(a)(2) comports with the essence of the holding of the Supreme Court of the United States in Maryland v. Craig, 497 U.S. 836 (1990), that the presenting of the testimony by an alternative method is necessary to protect the welfare of the child witness and that the child would suffer serious emotional stress and be traumatized to the extent the child could not reasonably be expected to communicate in the courtroom or the personal presence of a party. The Act does not attempt to define the method or methods by which face-to-face confrontation may be avoided. Closed-circuit television projected directly into the courtroom, video-taped testimony presented in the courtroom or room arrangements or equipment that shield the witness from the defendant [or the finder of fact in the case of Section 5(a)(1)] have been used with varying degrees of approval by the courts. See Maryland v. Craig, 497 U.S. 836 (1990); Coy v. Iowa, 487 U.S. 1012 (1988). The word "defendant" in Section 5(a)(2) is intended to include and incorporate the word respondent or other similar term, if any, that may be used to denote the accused in a juvenile delinquency proceeding included in Section 2(3).

Sections 5(a)(1) and (2) establish the standard of "clear and convincing evidence" (highly probably true) as the standard that must be met in determining whether to permit the presentation of testimony of a child by an alternative method. The standard of persuasion in criminal cases currently varies throughout the several states. However, there are at least four states that apply the clear and convincing evidence standard of persuasion in determining whether to permit the presentation of a child's testimony by an alternative method. These are: Alaska (Reutter v. State, 886 P.2d 1298 (Alaska Ct. App. 1994)); Arkansas (Ark. Code Ann. §16-43-1001); California (Cal. Penal Code §1347); Connecticut (Conn. Gen. Stat. §54-86g); and New York (N.Y. Crim. Proc. Law §65.10). Of these, the Alaska decision in Reutter seems most persuasive because of the court's reliance on *Maryland v. Craig, supra.* In *Craig,* the Supreme Court did not address the issue other than to require specific evidence and an express finding that the probable effect of the defendant's presence on the child witness would significantly impair the ability of the child to testify accurately. See Maryland v. Craig, 497 U.S. at 855-856. In *Reutter*, the court held that the preponderance of evidence standard was insufficient to meet the requirements of *Craig*. See Reutter v. State, 886 P.2d at 1308. Therefore, given the criminal nature of the proceedings under Sections 5(a)(1) and (2) and the persuasiveness of *Reutter*, it seems appropriate that any state adopting the Act should conform to the clear and convincing evidence standard of persuasion even though there are at least two jurisdictions which follow the preponderance of evidence standard of persuasion. See Thomas v. People, 803 P.2d 144 (Colo. 1990); United States v. Carrier, 9 F.3d 867 (10th Cir. 1993).

Section 5(b) sets forth the standards that must be applied in noncriminal proceedings to determine whether to permit an alternative method for presenting the testimony of a child. In these proceedings the Act sets forth the alternative standards of "best interests of the child" or to "enable the child to communicate with the finder of fact." However, unlike criminal proceedings, the standard of persuasion is only that the presiding officer must find by a preponderance of the evidence (more probably true than not) "that allowing the child to testify by an alternative method is necessary to protect the best interests of the child or enable the child to communicate with the finder of fact." Given the civil nature of these proceedings and the fact that the preponderance of evidence standard generally applies to civil proceedings, this lesser standard of persuasion is appropriate for noncriminal proceedings. Sections 5(b)(1) through (5) set forth a non-exclusive list of factors that the presiding officer may consider in making this determination.

§6. Factors for determining whether to permit alternative method

If the presiding officer determines that a standard under Section 5 has been met, the presiding officer shall determine whether to allow a child witness to testify by an alternative method and in doing so shall consider:

(1) alternative methods reasonably available;

(2) available means for protecting the interests of or reducing emotional trauma to the child without resort to an alternative method;

(3) the nature of the case;

(4) the relative rights of the parties;

(5) the importance of the proposed testimony of the child;

(6) the nature and degree of emotional trauma that the child may suffer if an alternative method is not used; and

(7) any other relevant factor.

Comment

If the presiding officer determines under Section 5 that the standards for permitting the use of an alternative method for the presentation of the testimony of a child witness have been met, then the presiding officer shall consider the factors set forth in Section 6 in deciding whether to allow the presentation of a child witness' testimony by an alternative method.

§7. Order regarding testimony by alternative method

(a) An order allowing or disallowing a child witness to testify by an alternative method must state the findings of fact and conclusions of law that support the presiding officer's determination.

(b) An order allowing a child witness to testify by an alternative method must:

(1) state the method by which the child is to testify;

(2) list any individual or category of individuals allowed to be in, or required to be excluded from, the presence of the child during the testimony;

(3) state any special conditions necessary to facilitate a party's right to examine or cross-examine the child;

(4) state any condition or limitation upon the participation of individuals present during the testimony of the child;

(5) state any other condition necessary for taking or presenting the testimony.

(c) The alternative method ordered by the presiding officer may be no more restrictive of the rights of the parties than is necessary under the circumstances to serve the purposes of the order.

Comment

Section 7 provides expressly for the issuance of an order either allowing or disallowing the

presentation of the testimony of a child witness by an alternative method. First, Section 7(a) requires a statement of the findings of fact and conclusions of law that support the presiding officer's determination. Second, Section 7(b) specifies the conditions under which the testimony is to be presented if an alternative method is to be ordered. Third, Section 7(c) requires that the alternative method be no more restrictive of the rights of the parties than is necessary to serve the purposes of presenting the testimony by an alternative method. In this connection, it should also be observed that the Act does not expressly provide for a priority in the alternative methods that may be ordered by the presiding officer. Nevertheless, in complying with Section 7(c), the importance of the examination or cross-examination of the child witness as provided in Section 8 strongly suggests that the alternative method authorized would normally include only video-taped testimony, closed-circuit television, or shielding the child witness in the courtroom from a face-to-face confrontation with the defendant or other party against whom the testimony is being offered.

§8. Right of party to examine child witness

An alternative method ordered by the presiding officer must permit a full and fair opportunity for examination or cross-examination of the child witness by each party.

Comment

Section 8 ensures that the requirements of the Sixth Amendment right of confrontation will be met in criminal proceedings and, when applicable, preserves the right of examination and cross-examination of the child witness in noncriminal proceedings. However, Section 8 does not impact upon other state noncriminal proceedings where limitations are placed upon the right to examine or cross-examine the child witness through the interviewing of a child in chambers, or some other recognized *in camera* examination of the child witness. See Comment to Section 3, *supra.* When the testimony of a child witness is presented by an alternative method as permitted under this Act, such testimony becomes part of the trial or hearing record like any other evidence presented to the finder of fact.

§9. Uniformity of application and construction

In applying and construing this Uniform Act, consideration must be given to the need to promote uniformity of the law with respect to its subject matter among states that enact it.

§10. Severability clause

If any provision of this [Act] or the application to any person or circumstance is held invalid, the invalidity does not affect other provisions or applications of this [Act] which can be given effect without the invalid provision or application, and to this end the provisions of this [Act] are severable.

§11. Effective date

This [Act] takes effect [ ].

§12. Repeals

The following acts and parts of acts are repealed:

(1) . . .
(2) . . .

UNIFORM PARENTAGE ACT (2000) (as amended in 2002)

TABLE OF CONTENTS

Article 4. Registry of paternity

Article 5. Genetic testing

Article 6. Proceeding to adjudicate parentage

Article 7. Child of assisted reproduction

Prefatory Note

The National Conference of Commissioners on Uniform State Laws has addressed the subject of parentage throughout the 20th Century. In 1922, the Conference promulgated the "Uniform Illegitimacy Act," followed by the "Uniform Blood Tests To Determine Paternity Act" in 1952, the "Uniform Paternity Act" in 1960, and certain provisions in the "Uniform Probate Code" in 1969. The "Uniform Illegitimacy Act" was withdrawn by the Conference and none of the other Acts were widely adopted. As of June 1973, the Blood Tests to Determine Paternity Act had been enacted in nine states, the "Uniform Paternity Act" in four, and the "Uniform Probate Code" in five.

The most important uniform act addressing the status of the nonmarital child was the Uniform Parentage Act approved in 1973 [hereinafter referred to as UPA (1973)]. As of December 2000, UPA (1973) was in effect in 19 states stretching from Delaware to California; in addition, many other states have enacted significant portions of it. Among the many notable features of this landmark Act was the declaration that all children should be treated equally without regard to marital status of the parents. In addition, the Act established a set of rules for presumptions of parentage, shunned the term "illegitimate," and chose instead to employ the term "child with no presumed father."

UPA (1973) had its genesis in a law review article, Harry D. Krause, A Proposed Uniform Act on Legitimacy, 44 Tex. L. Rev. 829 (1966); see also Krause, Equal Protection for the Illegitimate, 65 Mich. L. Rev. 477 (1967). Professor Krause followed with a pathfinding book, Illegitimacy: Law and Social Policy (1971), and then went on to serve as the reporter for UPA (1973). When work on the Act began, the notion of substantive legal equality of children regardless of the marital status of their parents seemed revolutionary. Even though the Conference had put itself on record in favor of equal rights of support and inheritance in the Paternity Act and the Probate Code, the law of many states continued to differentiate very significantly in the legal treatment of marital and nonmarital children. A series of United States Supreme Court decisions invalidating state inheritance, custody, and tort laws that disadvantaged out-of-wedlock children provided the both the impetus and a receptive climate for the Conference to promulgate UPA (1973).

Case law has not always reached consistent results in construing UPA (1973). Moreover, widely differing treatment on subjects not dealt with by the Act has been common. For example, California courts have held that a nonmarital father does not have standing to sue an intact family to assert his rights of fatherhood. Another UPA (1973) state, Colorado, has declared that under its state constitution the father may not be denied such rights. Texas, which has adopted many of the provisions of UPA (1973), reached much the same conclusion. Similarly, a judgment's binding effect on the child or on others seeking to claim a benefit of the judgment or to attack the judgment collaterally is confused in the case law. Adding to the confusion is the fact that UPA (1973) is entirely silent regarding the relationship between a divorce and a determination of parentage. Finally, the incredible scientific advances in parentage testing since 1973 warrant a thoroughgoing revision of the Act.

Beginning in the 1980s, states began to adopt paternity registries in an attempt to deal with the risk of a man's subsequent claim of paternity after the mother relinquishes a child for adoption. Although at that time the Conference rejected a paternity registry as a solution, it promulgated the Uniform Putative and Unknown Fathers Act in 1988 (UPUFA) to deal with the rights of such men. However, UPUFA has not been enacted by any state. In 1988 the Conference also adopted the Uniform Status of Children of Assisted Conception Act (USCACA). Assisted reproduction and gestational agreements became commonplace in the 1990s,

long after the promulgation of UPA (1973). The USCACA resembled a model act more than a uniform act because it provided two opposing options regarding "gestational agreements." To date, only two states have enacted USCACA, each choosing a different option.

The promulgation of the Uniform Parentage Act in 2000, as amended in 2002, is now the official recommendation of the Conference on the subject of parentage. This Act relegates to history all of the earlier uniform acts dealing with parentage, to wit, UPA (1973), UPUFA (1988), and USCACA (1988). The amendments of 2002 are the end-result of objections lodged by the American Bar Association Section of Individual Rights and Responsibilities and the ABA Committee on the Unmet Legal Needs of Children, based on the view that in certain respects the 2000 version did not adequately treat a child of unmarried parents equally with a child of married parents. Because equal treatment of nonmarital children was a hallmark of the 1973 Act, the objections caused the drafters of the 2000 version to reconsider certain sections of the Act. Through extended discussion and a meeting of representatives of all the entities involved, a determination was made that the objections had merit. As a result of this process, the amendments shown in this Act were presented by mail ballot to the Commissioners and unanimously approved in November 2002.

In brief outline, UPA (2002) is structured as follows: Article 1. General Provisions, adds many new definitions to clarify the participants in determinations of parentage and adapt the Act to recent scientific developments. Article 2. Parent-Child Relationship, will look familiar to past users of UPA (1973) because it continues a number of the 1973 provisions with little or no change, while eliminating the ambiguous term "natural" to describe a genetic parent. Article 3. Voluntary Acknowledgment of Paternity, is entirely new and is driven by federal mandates that states provide simplified nonjudicial means to establish paternity, especially for newborns and young children. Article 4. Registry of Paternity, is entirely new and incorporates a tightly integrated registry law to deal with the rights of a man who is neither an acknowledged, presumed or adjudicated father. A primary goal of this article is to facilitate adoption proceedings. Article 5. Genetic Testing, comprehensively covers that subject in ten separate sections (the 1973 Act had one section on the subject). Article 6. Proceeding to Adjudicate Parentage, sets forth the parties to, and the procedures for, adjudicating parentage and challenging acknowledgments, presump-tions, and judgments. Article 7. Child of Assisted Reproduction, recodifies USCACA (1988), but applies its provisions to nonmarital as well as marital children born as a result of assisted reproductive technologies. The bracketed Article 8. Gestational Agreement, is based upon USCACA (1988), but follows only the option that permits enforcement of a gestational agreement. Moreover, the Act makes a number of important changes in that option.

UPA (1973) contained a number of other substantive provisions, including those applicable to child support and custody. These subjects are omitted from UPA (2002) because other state law adequately provides for them.

Finally, Uniform Parentage Act (2002) is consistent with the provisions of two other uniform acts of great significance, namely the Uniform Interstate Family Support Act [UIFSA (1996) and UIFSA (2001)] and the Uniform Child Custody Jurisdiction and Enforcement Act [UCCJEA (1997)].

ARTICLE 1. GENERAL PROVISIONS

A word about the drafting convention of the Conference that appears throughout this Act.

Brackets in the statutory text are inserted to warn legislative draftsmen in the several states that the suggested language is likely to be subject to local variation. For example, a State may not refer to UPA (2000) as an "[Act]," but may label it as a "chapter," "title," etc. Often times the brackets flag terminology that is known to vary greatly, e.g., [petition], or is clearly subject to local option, e.g., [30 days].

§101. Short title

This [Act] may be cited as the Uniform Parentage Act.

§102. Definitions

In this [Act]:

(1) "Acknowledged father" means a man who has established a father-child relationship under [Article] 3.

(2) "Adjudicated father" means a man who has been adjudicated by a court of competent jurisdiction to be the father of a child.

(3) "Alleged father" means a man who alleges himself to be, or is alleged to be, the genetic father or a possible genetic father of a child, but whose paternity has not been determined. The term does not include:

(A) a presumed father;

(B) a man whose parental rights have been terminated or declared not to exist; or

(C) a male donor.

(4) "Assisted reproduction" means a method of causing pregnancy other than sexual intercourse. The term includes:

(A) intrauterine insemination;

(B) donation of eggs;

(C) donation of embryos;

(D) in-vitro fertilization and transfer of embryos; and

(E) intracytoplasmic sperm injection.

(5) "Child" means an individual of any age whose parentage may be determined under this [Act].

(6) "Commence" means to file the initial pleading seeking an adjudication of parentage in [the appropriate court] of this State.

(7) "Determination of parentage" means the establishment of the parent-child relationship by the signing of a valid acknowledgment of paternity under [Article] 3 or adjudication by the court.

(8) "Donor" means an individual who produces eggs or sperm used for assisted reproduction, whether or not for consideration. The term does not include:

(A) a husband who provides sperm, or a wife who provides eggs, to be used for assisted reproduction by the wife;

(B) a woman who gives birth to a child by means of assisted reproduction [, except as otherwise provided in [Article] 8]; or

(C) a parent under Article 7 [or an intended parent under Article 8].

(9) "Ethnic or racial group" means, for purposes of genetic testing, a recognized group that an individual identifies as all or part of the individual's ancestry or that is so identified by other information.

(10) "Genetic testing" means an analysis of genetic markers to exclude or identify a man as the father or a woman as the mother of a child. The term includes an analysis of one or a combination of the following:

(A) deoxyribonucleic acid; and

(B) blood-group antigens, red-cell antigens, human-leukocyte antigens, serum enzymes, serum proteins, or red-cell enzymes.

[(11) "Gestational mother" means an adult woman who gives birth to a child under a gestational agreement.]

(12) "Man" means a male individual of any age.

(13) "Parent" means an individual who has established a parent-child relationship under Section 201.

(14) "Parent-child relationship" means the legal relationship between a child and a parent of the child. The term includes the mother-child relationship and the father-child relationship.

(15) "Paternity index" means the likelihood of paternity calculated by computing the ratio between:

(A) the likelihood that the tested man is the father, based on the genetic markers of the tested man, mother, and child, conditioned on the hypothesis that the tested man is the father of the child; and

(B) the likelihood that the tested man is not the father, based on the genetic markers of the tested man, mother, and child, conditioned on the hypothesis that the tested man is not the father of the child and that the father is of the same ethnic or racial group as the tested man.

(16) "Presumed father" means a man who, by operation of law under Section 204, is recognized as the father of a child until that status is rebutted or confirmed in a judicial proceeding.

(17) "Probability of paternity" means the measure, for the ethnic or racial group to which the alleged father belongs, of the probability that the man in question is the father of the child, compared with a random, unrelated man of the same ethnic or racial group, expressed as a percentage incorporating the paternity index and a prior probability.

(18) "Record" means information that is inscribed on a tangible medium or that is stored in an electronic or other medium and is retrievable in perceivable form.

(19) "Signatory" means an individual who authenticates a record and is bound by its terms.

(20) "State" means a State of the United States, the District of Columbia, Puerto Rico, the United States Virgin Islands, or any territory or insular possession subject to the jurisdiction of the United States.

(21) "Support-enforcement agency" means a public official or agency authorized to seek:

(A) enforcement of support orders or laws relating to the duty of support;

(B) establishment or modification of child support;

(C) determination of parentage; or

(D) location of child-support obligors and their income and assets.

Comment

Four separate definitions of "father" are provided by the Act to account for the permutations of a man who may be so classified. Subsection (1), "acknowledged father," directly responds to a 1996 federal mandate encouraging states to adopt nonjudicial means for a man to identify himself as the father of a child in order to achieve an early determination of paternity. The term "acknowledged father" is given a relatively narrow meaning, rather than the broader definition previously accorded to the term. Only a man who acknowledges paternity of a child in accordance with the formal requirements established in Article 3 qualifies as an "acknowledged father." Because the mother of the child must concur in the formal acknowledgment, the federal mandate declares that the states must treat the action as which is the equivalent of an adjudication of paternity.

Subsection (2), "adjudicated father," although self-defining, presents a policy choice reached by the Conference that contested parentage matters are reserved for courts to resolve. The definition is limited to judicial adjudication of parentage, rather than providing for an alternative of administrative determination of parentage.

Subsection (3), "alleged father," is derived from the UPUFA §1(1), although much of the terminology has been changed. A man who is asserted to be, or asserts himself to be or possibly to be, the father of a child is the primary target of the Uniform Parentage Act.

Subsection (16), "presumed father," is more fully defined by the factual circumstances establishing a presumption of paternity in §204, infra.

Closely related to the definitions of "father," Subsection (12) is derived from the UPUFA §1(1). Defining "man" to include all male humans eliminates the connotation of adulthood, thereby

satisfying the obvious need for the Act to cover under-age progenitors. Although objection to calling a 14-year-old father a "man" was raised when UPUFA was considered by the Conference, for purposes of procreation such a teen-age boy is a man.

Note that a wide variety of other terms historically employed to identify the male parent are not defined in this section. Specifically, the term "putative father" has been replaced by the broader term "alleged father." According to Webster's, "putative" means "commonly accepted or supposed." Clearly, many "alleged fathers" do not fit that definition. Further, UPUFA chose the term "biological father" over more ambiguous "natural father." Because one woman may be the genetic mother of a child while another woman is the gestational mother, for consistency the term "genetic father" was substituted for "biological." Definitions are not supplied for such terms as "unknown father, legal father, real father, and the like," either because the term is self-defining or because it is ambiguous.

Subsection (8) was amended in 2002 to clarify that an individual who becomes a parent through assisted reproduction as provided in Article 7 is not a "donor." Similarly, if bracketed Article 8, Gestational Agreement, is enacted, an individual who is an intended parent through the procedure implemented in that article is not a "donor." No substantive change is intended by this clarification.

Subsection (9), "ethnic or racial group," relates to an individual only for purposes of genetic testing. The genetic tests themselves do not determine the race or ethnic group of the individual. Rather, if a tested individual is not excluded, his race or ethnic group provided is used in the paternity calculations because those calculations give the most conservative result, that is, those most favoring non-paternity.

Subsection (10), "genetic testing," contemplates that paternity testing must be broadly defined to include all of the traditional genetic tests, such as blood types and HLA (Human Leukocyte Antigen), as well as newer DNA technologies. In the past the term "blood test" was commonly applied to paternity testing. However, this usage actually referred to the sample collected; in fact, the tests were genetic tests performed on blood samples. The Act uses the scientific term "deoxyribonucleic acid." This is to accommodate the changes in technology used to evaluate the DNA. Early DNA testing involved RFLP technology (Restriction Fragment Length Polymorphism), followed by PCR techniques (Polymerase Chain Reaction); these may be replaced by newer technology, such as SNP (Single Nucleotide Polymorphisms). The type of DNA technology to be employed is best left to scientific bodies, such as accreditation agencies, see §503(a), *infra*.

Subsection (11), "gestational mother," is derived from USCACA (1988) '1(4), which employed the now-discarded term "surrogate mother" to define the same factual circumstances dealt with in bracketed Article 8, Gestational Agreement, *infra*. For purposes of this Act, a woman giving birth to her own genetic child, a.k.a. "birth mother," is distinguished from a "gestational mother." The former is both a gestational and genetic mother, while the latter also gives birth to a child, who may or may not be her genetic child. In the Act the term "gestational mother" is narrowly defined to restrict it to a situation in which a woman gives birth to a child pursuant to a gestational agreement validated under Article 8. If Article 8 is not enacted, this definition should be omitted from the Act. The 2002 amendment providing that the gestational mother must be an adult corrects a drafting oversight.

A 2002 amendment deleted former subsection (12), "intended parents," as adopted in UPA 2000. That term is now employed exclusively in bracketed Article 8, and thus is no longer appropriate as a definition for the Act.

Subsection (14), "parent-child relationship," is derived from UPA (1973) §1. A wide variety of the rights and duties flowing to and from parents and children are found in many other laws of this state.

Subsection (15), "paternity index," defines a complex scientific and mathematical concept. Note that the definition includes statistical measures of the mother and tested man. The tested man may be an alleged father, or any other potential biological father. In fact, under appropriate circumstances Article 5 provides for testing without samples from the mother or the alleged father. In these cases the expert statistically reconstructs the missing potential mother or biological father from genetic testing of samples from their relatives. Therefore the definition is correct even in cases involving a missing parent.

Subsection (18) is derived from the Uniform Electronic Transactions Act §102(13), which establishes a standard for either paper or electronic record keeping.

§103. Scope of [act]; choice of law

(a) This [Act] applies to every determination of parentage in this State.

(b) The court shall apply the law of this State to adjudicate the parent-child relationship. The applicable law does not depend on:

(1) the place of birth of the child; or

(2) the past or present residence of the child.

(c) This [Act] does not create, enlarge, or diminish parental rights or duties under other law of this State.

[(d) This [Act] does not authorize or prohibit an agreement between a woman and a man and another woman intended parents in which the woman relinquishes all rights as a parent of a child conceived by means of assisted reproduction, and which provides that the man and other woman intended parents become the parents of the child. If a birth results under such an agreement and the agreement is unenforceable under [the law of this State], the parent-child relationship is determined as provided in [Article] 2.]

Comment

The new UPA conforms to the requirement of 42 U.S.C. §666(a)(5)(A), that a state must provide that parentage proceedings be available at any time before a child attains 18 years of age or suffer the potential penalty of forfeiture of the federal funds that subsidize child support enforcement by the state. . . .

Subsection (a) was amended in 2002 in response to objections that the phrase "governs every determination of parentage" was excessively broad and could conflict with other state laws, such as those governing probate issues.

Subsection (b) is derived from the UIFSA (1996) §303 and UPA (1973) §8(b). This section simplifies choice of law principles; the local court is directed to apply local law. If in fact this state is an inappropriate forum, dismissal for forum non-conveniens may be appropriate.

Subsection (d) is bracketed. If a state enacts Article 8, Gestational Agreement, this subsection should be omitted. If a state does not enact Article 8, this subsection should be included to make clear that this Act does not affect other law of the jurisdiction on the subject, if any. The 2002 amendment employs consistent language in order to treat married and unmarried couples alike with regard to parentage issues, and reflects the terminology in Articles 2, 7, and bracketed Article 8.

§104. Court of this state

The [designate] court is authorized to adjudicate parentage under this [Act].

§105. Protection of participants

Proceedings under this [Act] are subject to other law of this State governing the health, safety, privacy, and liberty of a child or other individual who could be jeopardized by disclosure of identifying information, including address, telephone number, place of employment, social security number, and the child's day-care facility and school.

§106. Determination of maternity

Provisions of this [Act] relating to determination of paternity apply to determinations of maternity.

ARTICLE 2. PARENT-CHILD RELATIONSHIP

§201. Establishment of parent-child relationship

(a) The mother-child relationship is established between a woman and a child by:

(1) the woman's having given birth to the child [, except as otherwise provided in [Article] 8];

(2) an adjudication of the woman's maternity; [or]

(3) adoption of the child by the woman [; or

(4) an adjudication confirming the woman as a parent of a child born to a gestational mother if the agreement was validated under [Article] 8 or is enforceable under other law].

(b) The father-child relationship is established between a man and a child by:

(1) an unrebutted presumption of the man's paternity of the child under Section 204;

(2) an effective acknowledgment of paternity by the man under [Article] 3, unless the acknowledgment has been rescinded or successfully challenged;

(3) an adjudication of the man's paternity;

(4) adoption of the child by the man; [or]

(5) the man's having consented to assisted reproduction by a woman under [Article] 7 which resulted in the birth of the child [; or

(6) an adjudication confirming the man as a parent of a child born to a gestational mother if the agreement was validated under [Article] 8 or is enforceable under other law].

Comment

Subsection (b)(5) and bracketed subsections (a)(4) and (b)(6) reflect the fact that Article 7 provides that both a married and an unmarried couple are entitled to assisted reproductive technologies in order to become parents and, if bracketed Article 8 is enacted, to enter into a gestational agreement. If a state enacts Article 8, Gestational Agreement, the brackets should be removed. If a state does not enact Article 8, the bracketed subsections should be omitted.

§202. No discrimination based on marital status

A child born to parents who are not married to each other has the same rights under the law as a child born to parents who are married to each other.

Comment

From a legal and social policy perspective, this is one of the most significant substantive provisions of the Act, reaffirming the principle that regardless of the marital status of the parents, children and parents have equal rights with respect to each other. As discussed in the Prefatory Note, *supra*, U.S. Supreme Court decisions and lower federal and state court decisions require equal treatment of marital and nonmarital children without regard to the circumstances of their birth. . . .

§203. Consequences of establishment of parentage

Unless parental rights are terminated, a parent-child relationship established under this [Act] applies for all purposes, except as otherwise specifically provided by other law of this State.

§204. Presumption of paternity

(a) A man is presumed to be the father of a child if:

(1) he and the mother of the child are married to each other and the child is born during the marriage;

(2) he and the mother of the child were married to each other and the child is born within 300 days after the marriage is terminated by death, annulment, declaration of invalidity, or divorce [, or after a decree of separation];

(3) before the birth of the child, he and the mother of the child married each other in apparent compliance with law, even if the attempted marriage is or could be declared invalid, and the child is born during the invalid marriage or within 300 days after its termination by death, annulment, declaration of invalidity, or divorce [, or after a decree of separation];

(4) after the birth of the child, he and the mother of the child married each other in apparent compliance with law, whether or not the marriage is or could be declared invalid, and he voluntarily asserted his paternity of the child, and:

(A) the assertion is in a record filed with [state agency maintaining birth records];

(B) he agreed to be and is named as the child's father on the child's birth certificate; or

(C) he promised in a record to support the child as his own.

(5) for the first two yeats of the child's life, he resided in the same household with the child and openly held out the child as his own.

(b) A presumption of paternity established under this section may be rebutted only by an adjudication under [Article] 6.

Comment

A network of presumptions was established by UPA (1973) for application to cases in which proof of external circumstances indicate a particular man to be the probable father. The simplest of these is also the best known — birth of a child during the marriage between the mother and a man. When promulgated in 1973 the contemporaneous commentary noted that:

While perhaps no one state now includes all these presumptions in its law, the presumptions are based on existing presumptions of 'legitimacy' in state laws and do not represent a serious departure. Novel is that they have been collected under one roof. All presumptions of paternity are rebuttable in appropriate circumstances. Uniform Parentage Act (1973), Prefatory Note, 9B U.L.A. 379 (2001).

After amendments adopted in 2002, the Uniform Parentage Act retains all but one of the original presumptions of paternity contained in UPA §4 (1973). Originally the 2000 version of the new Act limited presumptions of paternity to those related to marriage. The objection by the ABA Steering Committee on the Unmet Legal Needs of Children and the Section of Individual Rights and Responsibilities that this could result in differential treatment of children born to unmarried parents resulted in the revision to this section.

Subsection (1) deals with a child born during a marriage; subsection (2) deals with a child conceived during marriage but born after its termination; subsection (3) deals with a child conceived or born during an invalid marriage; and, subsection (4) deals with a child born before a valid or invalid marriage, accompanied by other facts indicating the husband is the father.

Added by amendment in 2002, subsection (5), is a significant revision of UPA §4(4) (1973), which created a presumption of paternity if a man "receives the child into his home and openly holds out the child as his natural child . . . ." Because there was no time frame specified in the 1973 Act, the language fostered uncertainty about whether the presumption could arise if the receipt of the child into the man's home occurred for a short time or took place long after the child's birth. To more fully serve the goal of treating nonmarital and marital children equally, the "holding out" presumption is restored, subject to an express durational requirement that the man reside with the child for the first two years of the child's life. This mirrors the presumption applied to a married man established by §607, *infra*. Once this presumption arises, it is subject to attack only under the limited circumstances set forth in §607 for challenging a marital presumption, and is similarly subject to the estoppel principles of §608.

One presumption found in UPA (1973) is not repeated in the new Act. Former UPA §4(5) created a presumption of paternity if the man "acknowledges his paternity of the child in a writing filed with [named agency] [and] . . . the mother . . . does not dispute the acknowledgment within a reasonable time . . . ." This presumption was eliminated because it conflicts with Article 3, Voluntary Acknowledgment of Paternity, under which a valid acknowledgment establishes paternity rather than a presumption of paternity.

Finally, subsection (b) is a complete rewrite of UPA (1973) §4(b). The requirement that a presumption "may be rebutted . . . only by clear and convincing evidence" was eliminated from the Act. The same fate was accorded the statement that: "If two or more presumptions arise which conflict with each other, the presumption which on the facts is founded on the weightier considerations of policy and logic controls." Nowadays the existence of modern genetic testing obviates this old approach to the problem of conflicting presumptions when a court is to determine paternity. Nowadays, genetic testing makes it possible in most cases to resolve competing claims to paternity. Moreover, courts may use the estoppel principles in §608 in appropriate circumstances to deny requests for genetic testing in the interests of preserving a child's ties to the presumed or acknowledged father who openly held himself out as the child's father regardless of whether he is in fact the genetic father.

ARTICLE 3. VOLUNTARY ACKNOWLEDGMENT OF PATERNITY

Prefatory Note

Voluntary acknowledgment of paternity has long been an alternative to a contested paternity suit. Under UPA (1973) §4, the inclusion of a man's name on the child's birth certificate created a presumption of paternity, which could be rebutted. In order to improve the collection of child support, especially from unwed fathers, the U.S. Congress mandated a fundamental change in the acknowledgment procedure. The Personal Responsibility and Work Opportunity Reconciliation Act of 1996 (PRWORA, also known as the Welfare Reform Act) conditions receipt of federal child support enforcement funds on state enactment of laws that greatly strengthen the effect of a man's voluntary acknowledgment of paternity, 42 U.S.C. '666(a)(5)(C). . . . In brief, it provides that a valid, unrescinded, unchallenged acknowledgment of paternity is to be treated as equivalent to a judicial determination of paternity.

Because in many respects the federal Act is nonspecific, the new UPA contains clear and comprehensive procedures to comply with the federal mandate. Primary among the factual circumstances that Congress did not take into account was that a married woman may consent to an acknowledgement of paternity by a man who may indeed be her child's genetic father, but is not her husband. Under the new UPA, the mother's husband is the presumed father of the child, see §204, supra. By ignoring the real possibility that the child will have both an acknowledged father and a presumed father, Congress left it to the states to sort out which of the men should be recognized as the legal father.

Further, PRWORA does not require that a man acknowledging paternity must assert genetic paternity of the child. Section 301 is designed to prevent circumvention of adoption laws by requiring a sworn assertion of genetic parentage of the child.

Sections 302 through 305 clarify that if a child has a presumed father, that man must file a denial of paternity in conjunction with another man's acknowledgment of paternity in order for the acknowledgement to be valid. If the presumed father is unwilling to cooperate, or his whereabouts are unknown, a court proceeding is necessary to resolve the issue of parentage.

Congress also directed that the acknowledgment can be "rescinded" within a particular timeframe, and subsequently can be "challenged"—without stating a timeframe. Those procedures are dealt with in §§307-309.

Finally, the related issue of issuance or revision of birth certificates is left to other state law.

§301. Acknowledgment of paternity

The mother of a child and a man claiming to be the father of the child may sign an acknowledgment of paternity with intent to establish the man's paternity.

Comment

PRWORA does not explicitly require that a man acknowledging parentage necessarily is asserting his genetic parentage of the child. In order to prevent circumvention of adoption laws, §301 corrects this omission by requiring a sworn assertion of genetic parentage of the child. A 2002 amendment provides that a man who signs an acknowledgment of paternity declares that he is the genetic father of the child. Thus both the man and the mother acknowledge his paternity, under penalty of perjury, without requiring the parents to spell out the details of their sexual relations. Further, the amended language also takes into account a situation in which a man, who is unable to have sexual intercourse with his partner, may still have contributed to the conception of the child through the use of his own sperm. Henceforth, a man in that situation will be able to recognize legally his paternity through the voluntary acknowledgment procedure.

§302. Execution of acknowledgment of paternity

(a) An acknowledgment of paternity must:

(1) be in a record;

(2) be signed, or otherwise authenticated, under penalty of perjury by the mother and by the man seeking to establish his paternity;

(3) state that the child whose paternity is being acknowledged:

(A) does not have a presumed father, or has a presumed father whose full name is stated; and

(B) does not have another acknowledged or adjudicated father;

(4) state whether there has been genetic testing and, if so, that the acknowledging man's claim of paternity is consistent with the results of the testing; and

(5) state that the signatories understand that the acknowledgment is the equivalent of a judicial adjudication of paternity of the child and that a challenge to the acknowledgment is permitted only under limited circumstances and is barred after two years.

(b) An acknowledgment of paternity is void if it:

(1) states that another man is a presumed father, unless a denial of paternity signed or otherwise authenticated by the presumed father is filed with the [agency maintaining birth records];

(2) states that another man is an acknowledged or adjudicated father; or

(3) falsely denies the existence of a presumed, acknowledged, or adjudicated father of the child.

(c) A presumed father may sign or otherwise authenticate an acknowledgment of paternity.

Comment

The federal statute cited above provides that receipt of the federal subsidy by a state for its child support enforcement program is contingent on state enactment of laws establishing specific procedures for voluntary acknowledgment of paternity. This deceptively simple principle proved difficult to implement.

Problems most notably include fact situations in which the mother of the child is married to someone other than the man who intends to acknowledge his paternity. With an acknowledgment the child would then have both an acknowledged father and a presumed father. To deal with this circumstance, many states have passed laws allowing the presumed father to sign a denial of paternity, which must be filed as part of the acknowledgment. This Act adopts this common sense solution; otherwise the acknowledgment would have no legal consequence because it cannot affect the legal rights of the presumed father.

At least two other provisions of this section warrant special emphasis. Subsection (a)(2) requires that the acknowledgment be "signed, or otherwise authenticated, under penalty of perjury," just as income tax returns and many other government documents require. Clearly, the potential punishment for false swearing is substantial, and the benefits from avoiding the complication of requiring witnesses and a notary are significant in this context. Mandating greater formality would greatly discourage the in-hospital signatures so earnestly desired in 42 U.S.C. §666(a)(5)(C)(ii). . . .

Similarly, in an attempt to ensure full disclosure and avoid false swearing, subsection (a)(4) requires that the results of genetic testing, if any, be reported along with confirmation that the acknowledgment is consistent with the results of that testing. This provision is also designed to avoid a possible subversion of the requirements for an adoption. A would-be "father" whose parentage of a child has been excluded by genetic testing may not validly sign an acknowledgment once that fact has been established.

§303. Denial of paternity

A presumed father may sign a denial of his paternity. The denial is valid only if:

(1) an acknowledgment of paternity signed, or otherwise authenticated, by another man is filed pursuant to Section 305;

(2) the denial is in a record, and is signed, or otherwise authenticated, under penalty of perjury; and

(3) the presumed father has not previously:

(A) acknowledged his paternity, unless the previous acknowledgment has been rescinded pursuant to Section 307 or successfully challenged pursuant to Section 308; or

(B) been adjudicated to be the father of the child.

§304. Rules for acknowledgment and denial of paternity

(a) An acknowledgment of paternity and a denial of paternity may be contained in a single document or may be signed in counterparts, and may be filed separately or simultaneously. If the acknowledgement and denial are both necessary, neither is valid until both are filed.

(b) An acknowledgment of paternity or a denial of paternity may be signed before the birth of the child.

(c) Subject to subsection (a), an acknowledgment of paternity or denial of paternity takes effect on the birth of the child or the filing of the document with the [agency maintaining birth records], whichever occurs later.

(d) An acknowledgment of paternity or denial of paternity signed by a minor is valid if it is otherwise in compliance with this [Act].

§305. Effect of acknowledgment or denial of paternity

(a) Except as otherwise provided in Sections 307 and 308, a valid acknowledgment of paternity filed with the [agency maintaining birth records] is equivalent to an adjudication of paternity of a child and confers upon the acknowledged father all of the rights and duties of a parent.

(b) Except as otherwise provided in Sections 307 and 308, a valid denial of paternity by a presumed father filed with the [agency maintaining birth records] in conjunction with a valid acknowledgment of paternity is equivalent to an adjudication of the nonpaternity of the presumed father and discharges the presumed father from all rights and duties of a parent.

§306. No filing fee

The [agency maintaining birth records] may not charge for filing an acknowledgment of paternity or denial of paternity.

§307. Proceeding for rescission

A signatory may rescind an acknowledgment of paternity or denial of paternity by commencing a proceeding to rescind before the earlier of:

(1) 60 days after the effective date of the acknowledgment or denial, as provided in Section 304; or

(2) the date of the first hearing, in a proceeding to which the signatory is a party, before a court to adjudicate an issue relating to the child, including a proceeding that establishes support.

Comment

This section reflects a decision by NCCUSL to require a judicial adjudicatory process to rescind a voluntary acknowledgment of paternity. The federal statute, 42 U.S.C. '666(a)(5)(c)(D)(ii), does not prescribe the method for the rescission. . . .

§308. Challenge after expiration of period for rescission

(a) After the period for rescission under Section 307 has expired, a signatory of an acknowledgment of paternity or denial of paternity may commence a proceeding to challenge the acknowledgment or denial only:

(1) on the basis of fraud, duress, or material mistake of fact; and

(2) within two years after the acknowledgment or denial is filed with the [agency maintaining birth records].

(b) A party challenging an acknowledgment of paternity or denial of paternity has the burden of proof.

§309. Procedure for rescission or challenge

(a) Every signatory to an acknowledgment of paternity and any related denial of paternity must be made a party to a proceeding to rescind or challenge the acknowledgment or denial.

(b) For the purpose of rescission of, or challenge to, an acknowledgment of paternity or denial of paternity, a signatory submits to personal jurisdiction of this State by signing the acknowledgment or denial, effective upon the filing of the document with the [agency maintaining birth records].

(c) Except for good cause shown, during the pendency of a proceeding to rescind or challenge an acknowledgment of paternity or denial of paternity, the court may not suspend the legal responsibilities of a signatory arising from the acknowledgment, including the duty to pay child support.

(d) A proceeding to rescind or to challenge an acknowledgment of paternity or denial of paternity must be conducted in the same manner as a proceeding to adjudicate parentage under [Article] 6.

(e) At the conclusion of a proceeding to rescind or challenge an acknowledgment of paternity or denial of paternity, the court shall order the [agency maintaining birth records] to amend the birth record of the child, if appropriate.

§310. Ratification barred

A court or administrative agency conducting a judicial or administrative proceeding is not required or permitted to ratify an unchallenged acknowledgment of paternity.

§311. Full faith and credit

A court of this State shall give full faith and credit to an acknowledgment of paternity or denial of paternity effective in another State if the acknowledgment or denial has been signed and is otherwise in compliance with the law of the other State.

Comment

PRWORA requires states "to give full faith and credit to such an affidavit [of acknowledgment of paternity] signed in any other State according to its procedures.", *Id.* And, §666(a)(5)(D)(ii) provides that a "signed voluntary acknowledgment is considered a legal finding of paternity . . . ." In sum, federal law requires that an acknowledgment of paternity has the same status as a "judgment," 28 U.S.C. §1738, a "child custody determination," 28 U.S.C. §1738A, and a "child support order," 28 U.S.C. §1738B. This section implements these mandates.

§312. Forms for acknowledgment and denial of paternity

(a) To facilitate compliance with this [article], the [agency maintaining birth records] shall prescribe forms for the acknowledgment of paternity and the denial of paternity.

(b) A valid acknowledgment of paternity or denial of paternity is not affected by a later modification of the prescribed form.

§313. Release of information

The [agency maintaining birth records] may release information relating to the acknowledgment of paternity or denial of paternity to a signatory of the acknowledgment or denial and to courts and [appropriate state or federal agencies] of this or another State.

§314. Adoption of rules

The [agency maintaining birth records] may adopt rules to *implement this [article].]

ARTICLE 4. REGISTRY OF PATERNITY
PART 1. GENERAL PROVISIONS

§401. Establishment of registry

A registry of paternity is established in the [agency maintaining the registry].

§402. Registration for notification

(a) Except as otherwise provided in subsection (b) or Section 405, a man who desires to be notified of a proceeding for adoption of, or termination of parental rights regarding, a child that he may have fathered must register in the registry of paternity before the birth of the child or within 30 days after the birth.

(b) A man is not required to register if [:

(1)] a father-child relationship between the man and the child has been established under this [Act] or other law [; or

(2) the man commences a proceeding to adjudicate his paternity before the court has terminated his parental rights].

(c) A registrant shall promptly notify the registry in a record of any change in the information registered. The [agency maintaining the registry] shall incorporate all new information received into its records but need not affirmatively seek to obtain current information for incorporation in the registry.

§403. Notice of proceeding

Notice of a proceeding for the adoption of, or termination of parental rights regarding, a child must be given to a registrant who has timely registered. Notice must be given in a manner prescribed for service of process in a civil action.

§404. Termination of parental rights: child under one year of age

The parental rights of a man who may be the father of a child may be terminated without notice if:

(1) the child has not attained one year of age at the time of the termination of parental rights;

(2) the man did not register timely with the [agency maintaining the registry]; and

(3) the man is not exempt from registration under Section 402.

§405. Termination of parental rights: child at least one year of age

(a) If a child has attained one year of age, notice of a proceeding for adoption of, or termination of parental rights regarding, the child must be given to every alleged father of the child, whether or not he has registered with the [agency maintaining the registry].

(b) Notice must be given in a manner prescribed for service of process in a civil action.

PART 2. OPERATION OF REGISTRY

§411. Required form

The [agency maintaining the registry] shall prepare a form for registering with the agency. The form must require the signature of the registrant. The form must state that the form is signed under penalty of perjury. The form must also state that:

(1) a timely registration entitles the registrant to notice of a proceeding for adoption of the child or termination of the registrant's parental rights;

(2) a timely registration does not commence a proceeding to establish paternity;

(3) the information disclosed on the form may be used against the registrant to establish paternity;

(4) services to assist in establishing paternity are available to the registrant through the support-enforcement agency;

(5) the registrant should also register in another State if conception or birth of the child occurred in the other State;

(6) information on registries of other States is available from [appropriate state agency or agencies]; and

(7) procedures exist to rescind the registration of a claim of paternity.

§412. Furnishing of information; confidentiality

(a) The [agency maintaining the registry] need not seek to locate the mother of a child who is the subject of a registration, but the [agency maintaining the registry] shall send a copy of the notice of registration to a mother if she has provided an address.

(b) Information contained in the registry is confidential and may be released on request only to:

(1) a court or a person designated by the court;

(2) the mother of the child who is the subject of the registration;

(3) an agency authorized by other law to receive the information;

(4) a licensed child-placing agency;

(5) a support-enforcement agency;

(6) a party or the party's attorney of record in a proceeding under this [Act] or in a proceeding for adoption of, or for termination of parental rights regarding, a child who is the subject of the registration; and

(7) the registry of paternity in another State.

§413. Penalty for releasing information

An individual commits a [appropriate level misdemeanor] if the individual intentionally releases information from the registry to another individual or agency not authorized to receive the information under Section 412.

§414. Rescission of registration

A registrant may rescind his registration at any time by sending to the registry a rescission in a record signed or otherwise authenticated by him, and witnessed or notarized.

§415. Untimely registration

If a man registers more than 30 days after the birth of the child, the [agency] shall notify the registrant that on its face his registration was not filed timely.

§416. Fees for registry

(a) A fee may not be charged for filing a registration or a rescission of registration.

(b) [Except as otherwise provided in subsection (c), the] [The] [agency maintaining the registry] may charge a reasonable fee for making a search of the registry and for furnishing a certificate.

[(c) A support-enforcement agency [is] [and other appropriate agencies, if any, are] not required to pay a fee authorized by subsection (b).]

PART 3. SEARCH OF REGISTRIES

§421. Search of appropriate registry

(a) If a father-child relationship has not been established under this [Act] for a child under one year of age, a [petitioner] for adoption of, or termination of parental rights regarding, the child, must obtain a certificate of search of the registry of paternity.

(b) If a [petitioner] for adoption of, or termination of parental rights regarding, a child has reason to believe that the conception or birth of the child may have occurred in another State, the [petitioner] must also obtain a certificate of search from the registry of paternity, if any, in that State.

§422. Certificate of search of registry

(a) The [agency maintaining the registry] shall furnish to the requester a certificate of search of the registry on request of an individual, court, or agency identified in Section 412.

(b) A certificate provided by the [agency maintaining the registry] must be signed on behalf of the [agency] and state that:

(1) a search has been made of the registry; and

(2) a registration containing the information required to identify the registrant:

(A) has been found and is attached to the certificate of search; or

(B) has not been found.

(c) A [petitioner] must file the certificate of search with the court before a proceeding for adoption of, or termination of parental rights regarding, a child may be concluded.

§423. Admissibility of registered information

A certificate of search of the registry of paternity in this or another State is admissible in a proceeding for adoption of, or termination of parental rights regarding, a child and, if relevant, in other legal proceedings.

ARTICLE 5. GENETIC TESTING

§501. Scope of article

This [article] governs genetic testing of an individual to determine parentage, whether the individual:

(1) voluntarily submits to testing; or

(2) is tested pursuant to an order of the court or a support-enforcement agency.

§502. Order for testing

(a) Except as otherwise provided in this [article] and [Article] 6, the court shall order the child and other designated individuals to submit to genetic testing if the request for testing is supported by the sworn statement of a party to the proceeding:

(1) alleging paternity and stating facts establishing a reasonable probability of the requisite sexual contact between the individuals; or

(2) denying paternity and stating facts establishing a possibility that sexual contact between the individuals, if any, did not result in the conception of the child.

(b) A support-enforcement agency may order genetic testing only if there is no presumed, acknowledged, or adjudicated father.

(c) If a request for genetic testing of a child is made before birth, the court or support-enforcement agency may not order in-utero testing.

(d) If two or more men are subject to court-ordered genetic testing, the testing may be ordered concurrently or sequentially.

§503. Requirements for genetic testing

(a) Genetic testing must be of a type reasonably relied upon by experts in the field of genetic testing and performed in a testing laboratory accredited by:

(1) the American Association of Blood Banks, or a successor to its functions;

(2) the American Society for Histocompatibility and Immunogenetics, or a successor to its functions; or

(3) an accrediting body designated by the federal Secretary of Health and Human Services.

(b) A specimen used in genetic testing may consist of one or more samples, or a combination of samples, of blood, buccal cells, bone, hair, or other body tissue or fluid. The specimen used in the testing need not be of the same kind for each individual undergoing genetic testing.

(c) Based on the ethnic or racial group of an individual, the testing laboratory shall determine the databases from which to select frequencies for use in calculation of the probability of paternity. If there is disagreement as to the testing laboratory's choice, the following rules apply:

(1) The individual objecting may require the testing laboratory, within 30 days after receipt of the report of the test, to recalculate the probability of paternity using an ethnic or racial group different from that used by the laboratory.

(2) The individual objecting to the testing laboratory's initial choice shall:

(A) if the frequencies are not available to the testing laboratory for the ethnic or racial group requested, provide the requested frequencies compiled in a manner recognized by accrediting bodies; or

(B) engage another testing laboratory to perform the calculations.

(3) The testing laboratory may use its own statistical estimate if there is a question regarding which ethnic or racial group is appropriate. If available, the testing laboratory shall calculate the frequencies using statistics for any other ethnic or racial group requested.

(d) If, after recalculation using a different ethnic or racial group, genetic testing does not rebuttably identify a man as the father of a child under Section 505, an individual who has been tested may be required to submit to additional genetic testing.

§504. Report of genetic testing

(a) A report of genetic testing must be in a record and signed under penalty of perjury by a designee of the testing laboratory. A report made under the requirements of this [article] is self-authenticating.

(b) Documentation from the testing laboratory of the following information is sufficient to establish a reliable chain of custody that allows the results of genetic testing to be admissible without testimony:

(1) the names and photographs of the individuals whose specimens have been taken;

(2) the names of the individuals who collected the specimens;

(3) the places and dates the specimens were collected;

(4) the names of the individuals who received the specimens in the testing laboratory; and

(5) the dates the specimens were received.

§505. Genetic testing results; rebuttal

(a) Under this [Act], a man is rebuttably identified as the father of a child if the genetic testing complies with this [article] and the results disclose that:

(1) the man has at least a 99 percent probability of paternity, using a prior probability of 0.50, as calculated by using the combined paternity index obtained in the testing; and

(2) a combined paternity index of at least 100 to 1.

(b) A man identified under subsection (a) as the father of the child may rebut the genetic testing results only by other genetic testing satisfying the requirements of this [article] which:

(1) excludes the man as a genetic father of the child; or

(2) identifies another man as the possible father of the child.

(c) Except as otherwise provided in Section 510, if more than one man is identified by genetic testing as the possible father of the child, the court shall order them to submit to further genetic testing to identify the genetic father.

§506. Costs of genetic testing

(a) Subject to assessment of costs under [Article] 6, the cost of initial genetic testing must be advanced:

(1) by a support-enforcement agency in a proceeding in which the support-enforcement agency is providing services;

(2) by the individual who made the request;

(3) as agreed by the parties; or

(4) as ordered by the court.

(b) In cases in which the cost is advanced by the support-enforcement agency, the agency may seek reimbursement from a man who is rebuttably identified as the father.

§507. Additional genetic testing

The court or the support-enforcement agency shall order additional genetic testing upon the request of a party who contests the result of the original testing. If the previous genetic testing identified a man as the father of the child under Section 505, the court or agency may not order additional testing unless the party provides advance payment for the testing.

§508. Genetic testing when specimens not available

(a) Subject to subsection (b), if a genetic-testing specimen is not available from a man who may be the father of a child, for good cause and under circumstances the court considers to be just, the court may order the following individuals to submit specimens for genetic testing:

(1) the parents of the man;

(2) brothers and sisters of the man;

(3) other children of the man and their mothers; and

(4) other relatives of the man necessary to complete genetic testing.

(b) Issuance of an order under this section requires a finding that a need for genetic testing outweighs the legitimate interests of the individual sought to be tested.

§509. Deceased individual

For good cause shown, the court may order genetic testing of a deceased individual.

§510. Identical brothers

(a) The court may order genetic testing of a brother of a man identified as the father of a child if the man is commonly believed to have an identical brother and evidence suggests that the brother may be the genetic father of the child.

(b) If each brother satisfies the requirements as the identified father of the child under Section 505 without consideration of another identical brother being identified as the father of the child, the court may rely on nongenetic evidence to adjudicate which brother is the father of the child.

§511. Confidentiality of genetic testing

(a) Release of the report of genetic testing for parentage is controlled by [applicable state law].

(b) An individual who intentionally releases an identifiable specimen of another individual for any purpose other than that relevant to the proceeding regarding parentage without a court order or the written permission of the individual who furnished the specimen commits a [appropriate level misdemeanor].

ARTICLE 6. PROCEEDING TO ADJUDICATE PARENTAGE

PART 1. NATURE OF PROCEEDING

§601. Proceeding authorized

A civil proceeding may be maintained to adjudicate the parentage of a child. The proceeding is governed by the [rules of civil procedure].

§602. Standing to maintain proceeding

Subject to [Article] 3 and Sections 607 and 609, a proceeding to adjudicate parentage may be maintained by:

(1) the child;

(2) the mother of the child;

(3) a man whose paternity of the child is to be adjudicated;

(4) the support-enforcement agency [or other governmental agency authorized by other law];

(5) an authorized adoption agency or licensed child-placing agency; [or]

(6) a representative authorized by law to act for an individual who would otherwise be entitled to maintain a proceeding but who is deceased, incapacitated, or a minor [; or

(7) an intended parent under [Article] 8].

Comment

This section grants standing to a broad range of individuals and agencies to bring a parentage proceeding. But, several limitations on standing to

sue are contained within the Act. Article 3 details the procedures involved in a voluntary acknowledgment of parentage. Sections 607 and 609 establish the ground rules for proceedings involving children with, and without, a presumed father. Article 8 regulates parentage determinations arising from a gestational agreement.

§603. Parties to proceeding

The following individuals must be joined as parties in a proceeding to adjudicate parentage:

(1) the mother of the child; and

(2) a man whose paternity of the child is to be adjudicated.

§604. Personal jurisdiction

(a) An individual may not be adjudicated to be a parent unless the court has personal jurisdiction over the individual.

(b) A court of this State having jurisdiction to adjudicate parentage may exercise personal jurisdiction over a nonresident individual, or the guardian or conservator of the individual, if the conditions prescribed in [Section 201 of the Uniform Interstate Family Support Act] are fulfilled.

(c) Lack of jurisdiction over one individual does not preclude the court from making an adjudication of parentage binding on another individual over whom the court has personal jurisdiction.

Comment

Although custody and visitation proceedings are considered to be status adjudications, and therefore do not require personal jurisdiction over both parents, subsection (a) confirms the long-standing view that paternity proceedings require personal jurisdiction.

Subsection (b) incorporates the long-arm provision for establishing personal jurisdiction over an absent respondent set forth in UIFSA (1996), which is in effect in every state.

Subsection (c) makes the best of a situation in which an adjudication will almost inevitably be incomplete because not all the necessary parties are subject to the personal jurisdiction of the court. The most likely scenario for this unfortunate circumstance is one in which the mother and alleged father of the child are subject to the court's jurisdiction, but the mother's absent husband is not. Even if the husband's whereabouts are known, if both the forum court and the court of his residence lack jurisdiction over all three parties, there still is no court with power to bind all of them to a parentage determination.

Subsection (c) takes the common sense approach that a court should not be dissuaded from making a parentage decision, even if it cannot bind all appropriate parties. In the scenario described above, binding the mother and alleged father to a decision of the man's parentage may not technically bind the husband (the presumed father), but more than likely it will end litigation on the subject.

§605. Venue

Venue for a proceeding to adjudicate parentage is in the [county] of this State in which:

(1) the child resides or is found;

(2) the [respondent] resides or is found if the child does not reside in this State; or

(3) a proceeding for probate or administration of the presumed or alleged father's estate has been commenced.

§606. No limitation: child having no presumed, acknowledged, or adjudicated father

A proceeding to adjudicate the parentage of a child having no presumed, acknowledged, or adjudicated father may be commenced at any time, even after:

(1) the child becomes an adult, but only if the child initiates the proceeding; or

(2) an earlier proceeding to adjudicate paternity has been dismissed based on the application of a statute of limitation then in effect.

Comment

. . . The new UPA directs that an individual whose parentage has not been determined has a civil right to determine his or her own parentage, which should not be subject to limitation except when an estate has been closed. Accordingly, if the action is initiated by the child this section allows a proceeding to adjudicate parentage after the child has reached the age of majority. Such a proceeding is the exclusive province of the child, however. This limitation prohibits the filing of an intrusive proceeding by an individual claiming to be a parent of an adult child, or by a legal stranger. There appear to be no reported problems encountered in states without a statute of limitations for such actions.

§607. Limitation: child having presumed father

(a) Except as otherwise provided in subsection (b), a proceeding brought by a presumed father, the mother, or another individual to adjudicate the parentage of a child having a presumed father must be commenced not later than two years after the birth of the child.

(b) A proceeding seeking to disprove the father-child relationship between a child and the child's presumed father may be maintained at any time if the court determines that:

(1) the presumed father and the mother of the child neither cohabited nor engaged in sexual intercourse with each other during the probable time of conception; and

(2) the presumed father never openly held out the child as his own.

Comment

This section deals with difficult issues. First, it establishes the right of a mother or a presumed marital or nonmarital father to challenge the presumption of his paternity established by ‘ 204. Second, it clarifies the right of a third-party male to

claim paternity of a child who has an existing presumed father.

UPA (1973) §6(a) places a "[five-year] limitation on the time in which a proceeding may be brought "for the purpose of declaring the non-existence of the father and child relationship presumed under [the Act]." At that time, the comment noted that:

> **Ten states have denied standing to a man claiming to be the father when the mother was married to another at the time of the child's birth. In some of these states, even though a presumed father may seek to rebut his presumed paternity, a third-party male will be denied standing to raise that same issue.**

As of the year 2000, the right of an "outsider" to claim paternity of a child born to a married woman varies considerably among the states. Thirty-three states allow a man alleging himself to be the father of a child with a presumed father to rebut the marital presumption. Some states have granted this right through legislation, while in other states case law has recognized the alleged father's right to rebut the presumption and establish his paternity. In some states, there is both statutory and common law support for the standing of a man alleging himself to be the father to assert his paternity of a child born to a married woman. Not that long ago, some states imposed an absolute bar on a man commencing a proceeding to establish his paternity if state law provides a statutory presumption of the paternity of another man. See Michael H. v. Gerald D., 491 U.S. 110 (1989). It is increasingly clear that those days are coming to an end.

The new UPA attempts to establish a middle ground on these exceedingly complex issues. Subsection (a) establishes a two-year limitation for rebutting the presumption of paternity established under §204 if the mother and presumed father were cohabiting at the time of conception. The presumption of paternity may be attacked by the mother, the presumed father, or a third-party male during this limited period; thereafter the presumption is immune from attack by any of those individuals except as provided in subsection (b).

The reverse fact situation is also clear; a presumption of paternity may be challenged at any time if the mother and the presumed father were not cohabiting and did not engage in sexual intercourse at the probable time of conception and the presumed father never openly held out the child as his own.

Under the fact circumstances described in subsection (b), nonpaternity of the presumed father is generally assumed by all the parties as a practical matter. It is inappropriate for the law to assume a presumption known by all those concerned to be untrue.

§608. Authority to deny motion for genetic testing

(a) In a proceeding to adjudicate the parentage of a child having a presumed father or to challenge the paternity of a child having an acknowledged father under circumstances described in Section 607, the court may deny a motion seeking an order for genetic testing of the mother, the child, and the presumed father if the court determines that:

(1) the conduct of the mother or the presumed father estops that party from denying parentage; and

(2) it would be inequitable to disprove the father-child relationship between the child and the presumed father.

(b) In determining whether to deny a motion seeking an order for genetic testing under this section, the court shall consider the best interest of the child, including the following factors:

(1) the length of time between the proceeding to adjudicate parentage and the time that the presumed or acknowledged father was placed on notice that he might not be the genetic father;

(2) the length of time during which the presumed or acknowledged father has assumed the role of father of the child;

(3) the facts surrounding the presumed or acknowledged father's discovery of his possible nonpaternity;

(4) the nature of the relationship between the child and the presumed or acknowledged father;

(5) the age of the child;

(6) the harm that may result to the child if presumed or acknowledged paternity is successfully disproved;

(7) the nature of the relationship between the child and any alleged father;

(8) the extent to which the passage of time reduces the chances of establishing the paternity of another man and a child-support obligation in favor of the child; and

(9) other factors that may affect the equities arising from the disruption of the father-child relationship between the child and the presumed father or the chance of other harm to the child.

(c) In a proceeding involving the application of this section, a minor or incapacitated child must be represented by a guardian ad litem.

(d) Denial of a motion seeking an order for genetic testing must be based on clear and convincing evidence.

(e) If the court denies a motion seeking an order for genetic testing, it shall issue an order adjudicating the presumed father to be the father of the child.

Comment

This section incorporates the doctrine of paternity by estoppel, which extends equally to a child with a presumed father or an acknowledged father. In appropriate circumstances, the court may deny genetic testing and find the presumed or acknowledged father to be the father of the child. The most common situation in which estoppel should be applied arises when a man knows that a child is not, or may not be, his genetic child, but the man has affirmatively accepted his role as child's father and both the mother and the child have relied

on that acceptance. Similarly, the man may have relied on the mother's acceptance of him as the child's father and the mother is then estopped to deny the man's presumed parentage.

Subsection (b) delineates the standards for denying genetic testing. Subsection (c) requires the child to be independently represented. Subsection (d) requires an elevated standard of proof before the order for genetic testing can be denied.

Because §607 places a two-year limitation on challenging the presumption of parentage, the application of this section should be applied in those meritorious cases in which the best interest of the child compels the result and the conduct of the mother and presumed or acknowledged father is clear.

§609. Limitation: child having acknowledged or adjudicated father

(a) If a child has an acknowledged father, a signatory to the acknowledgment of paternity or denial of paternity may commence a proceeding seeking to rescind the acknowledgement or denial or challenge the paternity of the child only within the time allowed under Section 307 or 308.

(b) If a child has an acknowledged father or an adjudicated father, an individual, other than the child, who is neither a signatory to the acknowledgment of paternity nor a party to the adjudication and who seeks an adjudication of paternity of the child must commence a proceeding not later than two years after the effective date of the acknowledgment or adjudication.

(c) A proceeding under this section is subject to the application of the principles of estoppel established in Section 608.

§610. Joinder of proceedings

(a) Except as otherwise provided in subsection (b), a proceeding to adjudicate parentage may be joined with a proceeding for adoption, termination of parental rights, child custody or visitation, child support, divorce, annulment, [legal separation or separate maintenance,] probate or administration of an estate, or other appropriate proceeding.

(b) A [respondent] may not join a proceeding described in subsection (a) with a proceeding to adjudicate parentage brought under [the Uniform Interstate Family Support Act].

§611. Proceeding before birth

A proceeding to determine parentage may be commenced before the birth of the child, but may not be concluded until after the birth of the child. The following actions may be taken before the birth of the child:

(1) service of process;

(2) discovery; and

(3) except as prohibited by Section 502, collection of specimens for genetic testing.

§612. Child as party; representation

(a) A minor child is a permissible party, but is not a necessary party to a proceeding under this [article].

(b) The court shall appoint an [attorney ad litem] to represent a minor or incapacitated child if the child is a party or the court finds that the interests of the child are not adequately represented.

PART 2. SPECIAL RULES FOR PROCEEDING TO ADJUDICATE PARENTAGE

§621. Admissibility of results of genetic testing; expenses

(a) Except as otherwise provided in subsection (c), a record of a genetic-testing expert is admissible as evidence of the truth of the facts asserted in the report unless a party objects to its admission within [14] days after its receipt by the objecting party and cites specific grounds for exclusion. The admissibility of the report is not affected by whether the testing was performed:

(1) voluntarily or pursuant to an order of the court or a support-enforcement agency; or

(2) before or after the commencement of the proceeding.

(b) A party objecting to the results of genetic testing may call one or more genetic-testing experts to testify in person or by telephone, videoconference, deposition, or another method approved by the court. Unless otherwise ordered by the court, the party offering the testimony bears the expense for the expert testifying.

(c) If a child has a presumed, acknowledged, or adjudicated father, the results of genetic testing are inadmissible to adjudicate parentage unless performed:

(1) with the consent of both the mother and the presumed, acknowledged, or adjudicated father; or

(2) pursuant to an order of the court under Section 502.

(d) Copies of bills for genetic testing and for prenatal and postnatal health care for the mother and child which are furnished to the adverse party not less than 10 days before the date of a hearing are admissible to establish:

(1) the amount of the charges billed; and

(2) that the charges were reasonable, necessary, and customary.

§622. Consequences of declining genetic testing

(a) An order for genetic testing is enforceable by contempt.

(b) If an individual whose paternity is being determined declines to submit to genetic testing ordered by the court, the court for that reason may adjudicate parentage contrary to the position of that individual.

(c) Genetic testing of the mother of a child is not a condition precedent to testing the child and a man whose paternity is being determined. If the mother is unavailable or declines to submit to genetic testing, the court may order the testing of the child and every man whose paternity is being adjudicated.

§623. Admission of paternity authorized

(a) A [respondent] in a proceeding to adjudicate parentage may admit to the paternity of a child by filing a pleading to that effect or by admitting paternity under penalty of perjury when making an appearance or during a hearing.

(b) If the court finds that the admission of paternity satisfies the requirements of this section and finds that there is no reason to question the admission, the court shall issue an order adjudicating the child to be the child of the man admitting paternity.

§624. Temporary order

(a) In a proceeding under this [article], the court shall issue a temporary order for support of a child if the order is appropriate and the individual ordered to pay support is:

(1) a presumed father of the child;

(2) petitioning to have his paternity adjudicated;

(3) identified as the father through genetic testing under Section 505;

(4) an alleged father who has declined to submit to genetic testing;

(5) shown by clear and convincing evidence to be the father of the child; or

(6) the mother of the child.

(b) A temporary order may include provisions for custody and visitation as provided by other law of this State.

PART 3. HEARINGS AND ADJUDICATION

§631. Rules for adjudication of paternity

The court shall apply the following rules to adjudicate the paternity of a child:

(1) The paternity of a child having a presumed, acknowledged, or adjudicated father may be disproved only by admissible results of genetic testing excluding that man as the father of the child or identifying another man as the father of the child.

(2) Unless the results of genetic testing are admitted to rebut other results of genetic testing, a man identified as the father of a child under Section 505 must be adjudicated the father of the child.

(3) If the court finds that genetic testing under Section 505 neither identifies nor excludes a man as the father of a child, the court may not dismiss the proceeding. In that event, the results of genetic testing, and other evidence, are admissible to adjudicate the issue of paternity.

(4) Unless the results of genetic testing are admitted to rebut other results of genetic testing, a man excluded as the father of a child by genetic testing must be adjudicated not to be the father of the child.

§632. Jury prohibited

The court, without a jury, shall adjudicate paternity of a child.

§633. Hearings; inspection of records

(a) On request of a party and for good cause shown, the court may close a proceeding under this [article].

(b) A final order in a proceeding under this [article] is available for public inspection. Other papers and records are available only with the consent of the parties or on order of the court for good cause.

§634. Order on default

The court shall issue an order adjudicating the paternity of a man who:

(1) after service of process, is in default; and

(2) is found by the court to be the father of a child.

§635. Dismissal for want of prosecution

The court may issue an order dismissing a proceeding commenced under this [Act] for want of prosecution only without prejudice. An order of dismissal for want of prosecution purportedly with prejudice is void and has only the effect of a dismissal without prejudice.

§636. Order adjudicating parentage

(a) The court shall issue an order adjudicating whether a man alleged or claiming to be the father is the parent of the child.

(b) An order adjudicating parentage must identify the child by name and date of birth.

(c) Except as otherwise provided in subsection (d), the court may assess filing fees, reasonable attorney's fees, fees for genetic testing, other costs, and necessary travel and other reasonable expenses incurred in a proceeding under this [article]. The court may award attorney's fees, which may be paid directly to the attorney, who may enforce the order in the attorney's own name.

(d) The court may not assess fees, costs, or expenses against the support-enforcement agency of this State or another State, except as provided by other law.

(e) On request of a party and for good cause shown, the court may order that the name of the child be changed.

(f) If the order of the court is at variance with the child's birth certificate, the court shall order [agency maintaining birth records] to issue an amended birth registration.

§637. Binding effect of determination of parentage

(a) Except as otherwise provided in subsection (b), a determination of parentage is binding on:

(1) all signatories to an acknowledgement or denial of paternity as provided in [Article] 3; and

(2) all parties to an adjudication by a court acting under circumstances that satisfy the jurisdictional requirements of [Section 201 of the Uniform Interstate Family Support Act].

(b) A child is not bound by a determination of parentage under this [Act] unless:

(1) the determination was based on an unrescinded acknowledgment of paternity and the acknowledgement is consistent with the results of genetic testing;

(2) the adjudication of parentage was based on a finding consistent with the results of genetic testing and the consistency is declared in the determination or is otherwise shown; or

(3) the child was a party or was represented in the proceeding determining parentage by an [attorney ad litem].

(c) In a proceeding to dissolve a marriage, the court is deemed to have made an adjudication of the parentage of a child if the court acts under circumstances that satisfy the jurisdictional requirements of [Section 201 of the Uniform Interstate Family Support Act], and the final order:

(1) expressly identifies a child as a "child of the marriage," "issue of the marriage," or similar words indicating that the husband is the father of the child; or

(2) provides for support of the child by the husband unless paternity is specifically disclaimed in the order.

(d) Except as otherwise provided in subsection (b), a determination of parentage may be a defense in a subsequent proceeding seeking to adjudicate parentage by an individual who was not a party to the earlier proceeding.

(e) A party to an adjudication of paternity may challenge the adjudication only under law of this State relating to appeal, vacation of judgments, or other judicial review.

ARTICLE 7. CHILD OF ASSISTED REPRODUCTION

Prefatory Note

During the last thirty years, medical science has developed a wide array of assisted reproductive technology, often referred to as ART, which have enabled childless individuals and couples to become parents. Thousands of children are born in the United States each year as the result of ART. If a married couple uses their own eggs and sperm to conceive a child born to the wife, the parentage of the child is straightforward. The wife is the mother — by gestation and genetics, the husband is the father — by genetics and presumption. Also, insofar as the Uniform Parentage Act is concerned, neither parent fits the definition of a "donor."

Current state laws and practices are not so straightforward, however. If a woman gives birth to a child conceived using sperm from a man other than her husband, she is the mother and her husband, if any, is the presumed father. However, the man who provided the sperm might assert his biological paternity, or the husband might seek to rebut the martial presumption of paternity by proving through genetic testing that he is not the genetic father. As was the case in UPA (1973), it is necessary for the new Act to clarify definitively the parentage of a child born under these circumstances.

Similarly, assisted reproduction may involve the eggs from a woman other than the mother — perhaps using the intended father's sperm, perhaps not. In either event, the new Act makes a policy decision to clearly exclude the egg donor from claiming maternity. Theoretically, it is even possible that absent appropriate legislation the mother could attempt to deny maternity based on her lack of genetic relationship.

Finally, many couples employ a common ART procedure that combines sperm and eggs to form a pre-zygote that is then frozen for future use. If the couple later divorces, or one of them dies, absent legislation there are no clear rules for determining the parentage of a child resulting from a pre-zygote implanted after divorce or after the death of the would-be father. Disposition of such pre-zygotes, or even issues of their "ownership," create not only broad publicity, but also are problems on which courts need guidance.

§701. Scope of article

This [article] does not apply to the birth of a child conceived by means of sexual intercourse [, or as the result of a gestational agreement as provided in [Article] 8].

§702. Parental status of donor

A donor is not a parent of a child conceived by means of assisted reproduction.

Comment

If a child is conceived as the result of assisted reproduction, this section clarifies that a donor (whether of sperm or egg) is not a parent of the resulting child. The donor can neither sue to establish parental rights, nor be sued and required to support the resulting child. In sum, donors are eliminated from the parental equation.

The new UPA does not deal with many of the complex and serious legal problems raised by the practice of assisted reproduction. Issues such as ownership and disposition of embryos, regulation of the medical procedures, insurance coverage, etc., are left to other statutes or to the common law. Only the issue of parentage falls within the purview of this Act. This was also the case in UPA (1973), which wholly deferred speaking on the subject except to ensure the husband's paternal responsibility when he gave his consent to what was then called "artificial insemination" of his wife (now known in the scientific community as "intrauterine insemination"). The commentary to UPA (1973) stated: "It was thought useful, however, to single out and cover . . . at least one fact situation that occurs frequently."

The new UPA goes well beyond that narrow view; it governs the parentage issues in all cases in which the birth mother is also the woman who intends to parent the child. It also ensures that if the mother is a married woman, her husband will be the

father of the child if he gives his consent to assisted reproduction by his wife, regardless of which aspect of ART is utilized. UPA (1973) §5(b) specified that a male donor would not be considered the father of a child born of artificial insemination if the sperm was provided to a licensed physician for use in artificial insemination of a married woman other than the donor's wife. The new Act does not continue the requirement that the donor provide the sperm to a licensed physician. Further, this section of the new UPA does not limit a donor's statutory exemption from becoming a legal parent of a child resulting from ART to a situation in which the donor provides sperm for assisted reproduction by a married woman. This requirement is not realistic in light of present ART practices and the constitutional protections of the procreative rights of unmarried as well as married women. Consequently, this section shields all donors, whether of sperm or eggs, (§102 (8), supra), from parenthood in all situations in which either a married woman or a single woman conceives a child through ART with the intent to be the child's parent, either by herself or with a man, as provided in sections 703 and 704.

If a married woman bears a child of assisted reproduction using a donor's sperm, the donor will not be the father in any event. Her husband will be the father unless and until the husband's lack of consent to the assisted reproduction is proven within two years of his learning of the birth, see §705, infra. This provides certainty of nonparentage for prospective donors.

The comment to now-withdrawn USCACA §4(a) states that "nonparenthood is also provided for those donors who provide sperm for assisted reproduction by unmarried women." Under those circumstances — called a "relatively rare situation" in the 1988 comment — Athe child would have no legally recognized father." This result is retained in the new UPA, although the frequency of unmarried women using assisted reproduction appears to have grown significantly since 1988.

§703. Paternity of child of assisted reproduction

If a man who provides sperm for, or consents to, assisted reproduction by a woman as provided in Section 704 with the intent to be the parent of her child, is a parent of the resulting child.

Comment

The father-child relationship is created between a man and the resulting child if the man provides sperm for, or consents to, assisted reproduction by a woman with the intent to be the parent of her child, see §704, infra. This provision reflects the concern for the best interests of nonmarital as well as marital children of assisted reproduction demonstrated throughout the Act. Given the dramatic increase in the use of ART in the United States during the past decade, it is crucial to clarify the parentage of all of the children born as a result of modern science.

§704. Consent to assisted reproduction

(a) Consent by a woman, and a man who intends to be a parent of a child born to the woman by assisted reproduction must be in a record signed by the woman and the man. This requirement does not apply to a donor.

(b) Failure of a man to sign a consent required by subsection (a), before or after birth of the child, does not preclude a finding of paternity if the woman and the man, during the first two years of the child's life resided together in the same household with the child and openly held out the child as their own.

Comment

Subsection (a) requires that a man, whether married or unmarried, who intends to be a parent of a child must consent in a record to all forms of assisted reproduction covered by this article. The amendment clarifies that the requirement of consent does not apply to a male or a female donor.

Subsection (b) provides that even if a husband, or an unmarried man who intends to be a parent of the child, did not consent to assisted reproduction, he may nonetheless be found to be the father of a child born through that means if he and the mother openly hold out the child as their own. This principle is taken from the Uniform Probate Code §2-114(c) (1993), which provides that neither "natural parent" nor kindred may inherit from or through a child "unless that natural parent has openly treated the child as his [or hers], and has not refused to support the child." The "holding out" requirement substitutes evidence of the parties' conduct after the child is born for the requirement of formal consent in a record to prospective assisted reproduction. The "Anon-support" phrase in ' 2-114(c) was not carried forward in subsection (b) (and the term "natural parent" has been replaced by more accurate terminology).

§705. Limitation on husband's dispute of paternity

(a) Except as otherwise provided in subsection (b), the husband of a wife who gives birth to a child by means of assisted reproduction may not challenge his paternity of the child unless:

(1) within two years after learning of the birth of the child he commences a proceeding to adjudicate his paternity; and

(2) the court finds that he did not consent to the assisted reproduction, before or after birth of the child.

(b) A proceeding to adjudicate paternity may be maintained at any time if the court determines that:

(1) the husband did not provide sperm for, or before or after the birth of the child consent to, assisted reproduction by his wife;

(2) the husband and the mother of the child have not cohabited since the probable time of assisted reproduction; and

(3) the husband never openly held out the child as his own.

(c) The limitation provided in this section applies to a marriage declared invalid after assisted reproduction

§706. Effect of dissolution of marriage or withdrawal of consent

(a) If a marriage is dissolved before placement of eggs, sperm, or embryos, the former spouse is not a parent of the resulting child unless the former spouse consented in a record that if assisted reproduction were to occur after a divorce, the former spouse would be a parent of the child.

(b) The consent of a woman or a man to assisted reproduction may be withdrawn by that individual in a record at any time before placement of eggs, sperm, or embryos. An individual who withdraws consent under this section is not a parent of the resulting child.

Comment

This section is entirely new to the Parentage Act, but its logic is derived from the policy stated in §707, infra. Subsection (a) applies only to married couples and posits that if there is to be no liability for a child conceived by assisted reproduction after death, then there should be no liability for a child conceived or implanted after divorce. If a former wife proceeds with assisted reproduction after a divorce, the former husband is not the legal parent of the resulting child unless he had previously consented in a record to post-divorce assisted reproduction. If such were the case, subsection (b) provides a mechanism for him to withdraw that consent, i.e., by so stating in a record (presumably to be filed with the laboratory in which the sperm or embryos are stored).

An amendment in 2002 extends a similar right to an unmarried man. Although there is no automatic cancellation of consent via divorce in the unmarried context, the man may withdraw his consent to ART before the woman conceives or is implanted, and thereby avoid being determined to be the legal parent of the resulting child.

In either fact scenario, a child born through assisted reproduction accomplished after consent has been voided by divorce or withdrawn in a record will have a legal mother under §201(a)(1). However, the child will have a genetic father, but not a legal father. In this instance, intention, rather than biology, is the controlling factor. The section is intended to encourage careful drafting of assisted reproduction agreements. The attorney and the parties themselves should discuss the issue and clarify their intent before a problem arises.

This Act does not attempt to resolve issues as to control of frozen embryos following dissolution of marital or nonmarital relationships. As indicated in the prefatory note, those matters are left to other state laws.

§707. Parental status of deceased individual

If an individual who consented in a record to be a parent by assisted reproduction a spouse dies before placement of eggs, sperm, or embryos, the deceased individual is not a parent of the resulting child unless the deceased spouse consented in a record that if assisted reproduction were to occur after death, the deceased individual would be a parent of the child.

Comment

Absent consent in a record, the death of an individual whose genetic material is subsequently used either in conceiving an embryo or in implanting an already existing embryo into a womb ends the potential legal parenthood of the deceased. This section is designed primarily to avoid the problems of intestate succession which could arise if the posthumous use of a person's genetic material leads to the deceased being determined to be a parent. Of course, an individual who wants to explicitly provide for such children in his or her will may do so.

ARTICLE 8. GESTATIONAL AGREEMENT

Prefatory Note

The longstanding shortage of adoptable children in this country has led many would-be parents to enlist a gestational mother (previously referred to as a "surrogate mother") to bear a child for them. As contrasted with the assisted reproduction regulated by Article 7, which involves the would-be parent or parents and most commonly one and sometimes two anonymous donors, the gestational agreement (previously known as a surrogacy agreement) provided in this article is designed to involve at least three parties; the intended mother and father and the woman who agrees to bear a child for them through the use of assisted reproduction (the gestational mother). Additional people may be involved. For example, if the proposed gestational mother is married, her husband, if any, must be included in the agreement to dispense with his presumptive paternity of a child born to his wife. Further, an egg donor or a sperm donor, or both, may be involved, although neither will be joined as a party to the agreement. Thus, by definition, a child born pursuant to a gestational agreement will need to have maternity as well as paternity clarified.

The subject of gestational agreements was last addressed by the National Conference of

Commissioners on Uniform State Laws in 1988 with the adoption of the Uniform Status of Children of Assisted Conception Act (USCACA). Because some Commissioners believed that such agreements should be prohibited, while others believed that such agreements should be allowed, but regulated, USCACA offered two alternatives on the subject; either to regulate such activities through a judicial review process or to void such contracts. As might have been predicted, the only two states to enact USCACA selected opposite options; Virginia chose to regulate such agreements, while North Dakota opted to void them.

In the years since the promulgation of USCACA (and virtual de facto rejection of that Act), approximately one-half of the states developed statutory or case law on the issue. Of those, about one-half recognized such agreements, and the other half rejected them. A survey in December, 2000, revealed a wide variety of approaches: eleven states allow gestational agreements by statute or case law; six states void such agreements by statute; eight states do not ban agreements per se, but statutorily ban compensation to the gestational mother, which as a practical matter limits the likelihood of agreement to close relatives; and two states judicially refuse to recognize such agreements. In states rejecting gestational agreements, the legal status of children born pursuant to such an agreement is uncertain. If gestational agreements are voided or criminalized, individuals determined to become parents through this method will seek a friendlier legal forum. This raises a host of legal issues. For example, a couple may return to their home state with a child born as the consequence of a gestational agreement recognized in another state. This presents a full faith and credit question if their home state has a statute declaring gestational agreements to be void or criminal.

Despite the legal uncertainties, thousands of children are born each year pursuant to gestational agreements. One thing is clear; a child born under these circumstances is entitled to have its status clarified. Therefore, NCCUSL once again ventured into this controversial subject, withdrawing USCACA and substituting bracketed Article 8 of the new UPA. The article incorporates many of the USCACA provisions allowing validation and enforcement of gestational agreements, along with some important modifications. The article is bracketed because of a concern that state legislatures may decide that they are still not ready to address gestational agreements, or that they want to treat them differently from what Article 8 provides. States may omit this article without undermining the other provisions of the UPA (2002).

Article 8's replacement of the USCACA terminology, "surrogate mother," by "gestational mother" is important. First, labeling a woman who bears a child a "surrogate" does not comport with the dictionary definition of the term under any construction, to wit: "a person appointed to act in the place of another" or "something serving as a substitute." The term is especially misleading when "surrogate" refers to a woman who supplies both "egg and womb," that is, a woman who is a genetic as well as gestational mother. That combination is now typically avoided by the majority of ART practitioners in order to decrease the possibility that a genetic\gestational mother will be unwilling to relinquish her child to unrelated intended parents. Further, the term "surrogate" has acquired a negative connotation in American society, which confuses rather than enlightens the discussion.

In contrast, term "gestational mother" is both more accurate and more inclusive. It applies to both a woman who, through assisted reproduction, performs the gestational function without being genetically related to a child, and a woman is both the gestational and genetic mother. The key is that an agreement has been made that the child is to be raised by the intended parents. The latter practice has elicited disfavor in the ART community, which has concluded that the gestational mother's genetic link to the child too often creates additional emotional and psychological problems in enforcing a gestational agreement.

The new UPA treats entering into a gestational agreement as a significant legal act that should be approved by a court, just as an adoption is judicially approved. The procedure established generally follows that of USCACA, but departs from its terms in several important ways. First, nonvalidated gestational agreements are unenforceable (not void), thereby providing a strong incentive for the participants to seek judicial scrutiny. Second, there is no longer a requirement that at least one of the intended parents would be genetically related to the child born of the gestational agreement. Third, individuals who enter into nonvalidated gestational agreements and later refuse to adopt the resulting child may be liable for support of the child.

Although legal recognition of gestational agreements remains controversial, the plain fact is that medical technologies have raced ahead of the law without heed to the views of the general public — or legislators. Courts have recently come to acknowledge this reality when forced to render decisions regarding collaborative reproduction, noting that artificial insemination, gestational carriers, cloning and gene splicing are part of the present, as well as of the future. One court predicted that even if all forms of assisted reproduction were outlawed in a particular state, its courts would still be called upon to decide on the identity of the lawful

parents of a child resulting from those procedures undertaken in less restrictive states. This court noted:

> **Again we must call on the Legislature to sort out the parental rights and responsibilities of those involved in artificial reproduction. No matter what one thinks of artificial insemination, traditional and gestational surrogacy (in all of its permutations) and — as now appears in the not-too-distant future, cloning and even gene splicing — courts are still going to be faced with the problem of determining lawful parentage. A child cannot be ignored. Even if all the means of artificial reproduction were outlawed with draconian criminal penalties visited on the doctors and parties involved, courts would still be called upon to decide who the lawful parents are and who — other than the taxpayers — is obligated to provide maintenance and support for the child. These cases will not go away. Again we must call on the Legislature to sort out the parental rights and responsibilities of those involved in artificial reproduction . . . . Courts can continue to make decisions on an ad hoc basis without necessarily imposing some grand scheme . . . . Or, the Legislature can act to impose a broader order which, even though it might not be perfect on a case-by-case basis, would bring some predictability to those who seek to make use of artificial reproductive techniques. Buzzanca v. Buzzanca, 72 Cal. Rptr. 2d 280 (Cal. Ct. App. 1998).**

§801. Gestational agreement authorized

(a) A prospective gestational mother, her husband if she is married, a donor or the donors, and the intended parents may enter into a written agreement providing that:

(1) the prospective gestational mother agrees to pregnancy by means of assisted reproduction;

(2) the prospective gestational mother, her husband if she is married, and the donors relinquish all rights and duties as the parents of a child conceived through assisted reproduction; and

(3) the intended parents become the parents of the child.

(b) The man and the woman who are the intended parents must both be parties to the gestational agreement.

(c) A gestational agreement is enforceable only if validated as provided in Section 803.

(d) A gestational agreement does not apply to the birth of a child conceived by means of sexual intercourse.

(e) A gestational agreement may provide for payment of consideration.

(f) A gestational agreement may not limit the right of the gestational mother to make decisions to safeguard her health or that of the embryos or fetus.

Comment

The previous uniform act on this subject, USCACA, proposed two alternatives, one of which was to declare that gestational agreements were void. Subsection (a) rejects that approach. The scientific state of the art and the medical facilities providing the technological capacity to utilize a woman other than the woman who intends to raise the child to be the gestational mother, guarantee that such agreements will continue to be written. Subsection (a) recognizes that certainty and initiates a procedure for its regulation by a judicial officer. This section permits all of the individuals directly involved in the procedure to enter into a written agreement; this includes the intended parents, the gestational mother, and her husband, if she is married. In addition, if known donors are involved, they also must sign the agreement. The agreement must provide that the intended parents will be the parents of any child born pursuant to the agreement while all of the others (gestational mother, her husband, if any, and the donors, as appropriate) relinquish all parental rights and duties.

Under subsection (b), a valid gestational agreement requires that the man and woman who are the intended parents, whether married or unmarried, to be parties to the gestational agreement. This reflects the Act's comprehensive concern for the best interest of nonmarital as well as marital children born as the result of a gestational agreement. Throughout UPA the goal is to treat marital and nonmarital children equally.

Subsection (c) provides that in order to be enforceable, the agreement must be validated by the appropriate court under '803.

Subsection (e) is intended to shield gestational agreements that include payment of the gestational mother from challenge under "baby-selling" statutes that prohibit payment of money to the birth mother for her consent to an adoption.

Subsection (f) is intended to acknowledge that the gestational mother, as a pregnant woman, has a constitutionally-recognized right to decide issues regarding her prenatal care. In other words, the intended parents have no right to demand that the gestational mother undergo any particular medical regimen at their behest.

§802. Requirements of petition

(a) The intended parents and the prospective gestational mother may commence a proceeding in the [appropriate court] to validate a gestational agreement.

(b) A proceeding to validate a gestational agreement may not be maintained unless:

(1) the mother or the intended parents have been residents of this State for at least 90 days;

(2) the prospective gestational mother's husband, if she is married, is joined in the proceeding; and

(3) a copy of the gestational agreement is attached to the [petition].

§803. Hearing to validate gestational agreement

(a) If the requirements of subsection (b) are satisfied, a court may issue an order validating the gestational agreement and declaring that the intended parents will be the parents of a child born during the term of the of the agreement.

(b) The court may issue an order under subsection (a) only on finding that:

(1) the residence requirements of Section 802 have been satisfied and the parties have submitted to the jurisdiction of the court under the jurisdictional standards of this [Act];

(2) unless waived by the court, the [relevant child-welfare agency] has made a home study of the intended parents and the intended parents meet the standards of suitability applicable to adoptive parents;

(3) all parties have voluntarily entered into the agreement and understand its terms;

(4) adequate provision has been made for all reasonable health-care expense associated with the gestational agreement until the birth of the child, including responsibility for those expenses if the agreement is terminated; and

(5) the consideration, if any, paid to the prospective gestational mother is reasonable.

Comment

This pre-conception authorization process for a gestational agreement is roughly analogous to prevailing adoption procedures in place in most states. Just as adoption contemplates the transfer of parentage of a child from the birth parents to the adoptive parents, a gestational agreement involves the transfer from the gestational mother to the intended parents. The Act is designed to protect the interests of the child to be born under the gestational agreement as well as the interests of the gestational mother and the intended parents.

In contrast to USCACA (1988) '1(3), there is no requirement that at least one of the intended parents be genetically related to the child born of a gestational agreement. Similarly, the likelihood that the gestational mother will also be the genetic mother is not directly addressed in the new Act, while USCACA (1988) apparently assumed that such a fact pattern would be typical. Experience with the intractable problems caused by such a combination has dissuaded the majority of fertility laboratories from following that practice. See In re Matter of Baby M., 537 A.2d 1227 (N.J. 1988).

This section seeks to protect the interests of the child in several ways. The major protection of the child is the authorization procedure itself. The Act requires closely supervised gestational arrangements to ensure the security and well being of the child. Once a petition has been filed, subsection (a) permits — but does not require — the court to validate a gestational agreement. If it validates, the court must declare that the intended parents will be the parents of any child born pursuant to, and during the term of, the agreement.

Subsection (b) requires the court to make five separate findings before validating the agreement. Subsection (b)(1) requires the court to ensure that the 90-day residency requirement of §802 has been satisfied and that it has jurisdiction over the parties;

Under subsection (b)(2), the court will be informed of the results of a home study of the intended parents who must satisfy the suitability standards required of prospective adoptive parents.

The interests of all the parties are protected by subsection (b)(3), which is designed to protect the individuals involved from the possibility of overreaching or fraud. The court must find that all parties consented to the gestational agreement with full knowledge of what they agreed to do, which necessarily includes relinquishing the resulting child to the intended parents who are obligated to accept the child.

The requirement of assurance of health-care expenses until birth of the resulting child imposed by subsection (b)(4) further protects the gestational mother.

Finally, subsection (b)(5) mandates that the court find that compensation of the gestational mother, if any, is reasonable in amount.

Section 803, spells out detailed requirements for the petition and the findings that must be made before an authorizing order can be issued, but nowhere states the consequences of violations of the rules. Because of the variety of types of violations that could possibly occur, a bright-line rule concerning the effect of such violations is inappropriate. The consequences of a failure to abide by the rules of this section are left to a case-by-case determination. A court should be guided by the Act's intention to permit gestational agreements and the equities of a particular situation. Note that §806 provides a period for termination of the agreement and vacating of the order. The discovery of a failure to abide by the rules of §803 would certainly provide an occasion for terminating the agreement. On the other hand, if a failure to abide by the rules of §803 is discovered by a party during a time when §806 termination is permissible, failure to seek termination might be an appropriate reason to estop the party from later seeking to overturn or ignore the §803 order.

§804. Inspection of records

The proceedings, records, and identities of the individual parties to a gestational agreement under this [article] are subject to inspection under the standards of confidentiality applicable to adoptions as provided under other law of this State.

§805. Exclusive, continuing jurisdiction

Subject to the jurisdictional standards of [Section 201 of the Uniform Child Custody Jurisdiction and Enforcement Act], the court conducting a proceeding under this [article] has exclusive, continuing jurisdiction of all matters arising out of the gestational agreement until a child born to the gestational mother during the period governed by the agreement attains the age of 180 days.

§806. Termination of gestational agreement

(a) After issuance of an order under this [article], but before the prospective gestational mother becomes pregnant by means of assisted reproduction, the prospective gestational mother, her husband, or either of the intended parents may terminate the gestational agreement by giving written notice of termination to all other parties.

(b) The court for good cause shown may terminate the gestational agreement.

(c) An individual who terminates a gestational agreement shall file notice of the termination with the court. On receipt of the notice, the court shall vacate the order issued under this [article]. An individual who does not notify the court of the termination of the agreement is subject to appropriate sanctions.

(d) Neither a prospective gestational mother nor her husband, if any, is liable to the intended parents for terminating a gestational agreement pursuant to this section.

§807. Parentage under validated gestational agreement

(a) Upon birth of a child to a gestational mother, the intended parents shall file notice with the court that a child has been born to the gestational mother within 300 days after assisted reproduction. Thereupon, the court shall issue an order:

(1) confirming that the intended parents are the parents of the child ;

(2) if necessary, ordering that the child be surrendered to the intended parents; and

(3) directing the [agency maintaining birth records] to issue a birth certificate naming the intended parents as parents of the child.

(b) If the parentage of a child born to a gestational mother is alleged not to be the result of assisted reproduction, the court shall order genetic testing to determine the parentage of the child.

(c) If the intended parents fail to file notice required under subsection (a), the gestational mother or the appropriate State agency may file notice with the court that a child has been born to the gestational mother within 300 days after assisted reproduction. Upon proof of a court order issued pursuant to Section 803 validating the gestational agreement, the court shall order the intended parents are the parents of the child and are financially responsible for the child.

§808. Gestational agreement: effect of subsequent marriage

After the issuance of an order under this [article], subsequent marriage of the gestational mother does not affect the validity of a gestational agreement, her husband's consent to the agreement is not required, and her husband is not a presumed father of the resulting child.

§809. Effect of nonvalidated gestational agreement

(a) A gestational agreement, whether in a record or not, that is not judicially validated is not enforceable.

(b) If a birth results under a gestational agreement that is not judicially validated as provided in this [article], the parent-child relationship is determined as provided in [Article] 2.

(c) Individuals who are parties to a nonvalidated gestational agreement as intended parents may be held liable for support of the resulting child, even if the agreement is otherwise unenforceable. The liability under this subsection includes assessing all expenses and fees as provided in Section 636.]

ARTICLE 9. MISCELLANEOUS PROVISIONS

§901. Uniformity of application and construction

In applying and construing this Uniform Act, consideration must be given to the need to promote uniformity of the law with respect to its subject matter among States that enact it.

§902. Severability clause

If any provision of this [Act] or its application to an individual or circumstance is held invalid, the invalidity does not affect other provisions or applications of this [Act] which can be given effect without the invalid provision or application, and to this end the provisions of this [Act] are severable.

§903. Time of taking effect

This [Act] takes effect on __________.

§904. Repeal

The following acts and parts of acts are repealed:

(1) [Uniform Act on Paternity, 1960]

(2) [Uniform Parentage Act, 1973]

(3) [Uniform Putative and Unknown Fathers Act, 1988]

(4) [Uniform Status of Children of Assisted Conception Act, 1988]

(5) [other inconsistent statutes]

§905. Transitional provision

A proceeding to adjudicate parentage which was commenced before the effective date of this [Act] is governed by the law in effect at the time the proceeding was commenced.

Uniform Premarital Agreement Act Prefatory Note

The number of marriages between persons previously married and the number of marriages between persons each of whom is intending to continue to pursue a career is steadily increasing. For these and other reasons, it is becoming more and more common for persons contemplating marriage to seek to resolve by agreement certain issues presented by the forthcoming marriage. However, despite a lengthy legal history for these premarital agreements, there is a substantial uncertainty as to the enforceability of all, or a portion, of the provisions of these agreements and a significant lack of uniformity of treatment of these agreements among the states. The problems caused by this uncertainty and nonuniformity are greatly exacerbated by the mobility of our population. Nevertheless, this uncertainty and nonuniformity seem reflective not so much of basic policy differences between the states but rather a result of spasmodic, reflexive responses to varying factual circumstances at different times. Accordingly, uniform legislation conforming to modern social policy that provides both certainty and sufficient flexibility to accommodate different circumstances would appear to be both a significant improvement and a goal realistically capable of achievement.

This Act is intended to be relatively limited in scope. Section 1 defines a "premarital agreement" as "an agreement between prospective spouses made in contemplation of marriage and to be effective upon marriage." Section 2 requires that a premarital agreement be in writing and signed by both parties. Section 4 provides that a premarital agreement becomes effective upon the marriage of the parties. These sections establish significant parameters. That is, the Act does not deal with agreements between persons who live together but who do not contemplate marriage or who do not marry. Nor does the Act provide for postnuptial or separation agreements or with oral agreements.

On the other hand, agreements that are embraced by the Act are permitted to deal with a wide variety of matters and Section 3 provides an illustrative list of those matters, including spousal support, which can properly be dealt with in a premarital agreement.

Section 6 is the key operative section of the Act and sets forth the conditions under which a premarital agreement is not enforceable. An agreement is not enforceable if the party against whom enforcement is sought proves that (a) he or she did not execute the agreement voluntarily, or that (b) the agreement was unconscionable when it was executed and, before execution of the agreement, he or she (1) was not provided a fair and reasonable disclosure of the property or financial obligations of the other party, (2) did not voluntarily and expressly waive, in writing, any right to disclosure of the property or financial obligations of the other party beyond the disclosure provided, and (3) did not have, or reasonably could not have had, an adequate knowledge of the property and financial obligations of the other party.

Even if these conditions are not proven, if a provision of a premarital agreement modifies or eliminates spousal support, and that modification or elimination would cause a party to be eligible for support under a program of public assistance at the time of separation, marital dissolution, or death, a court is authorized to order the other party to provide support to the extent necessary to avoid that eligibility.

These sections form the heart of the Act; the remaining sections deal with more tangential issues. Section 5 prescribes the manner in which a premarital agreement may be amended or revoked; Section 7 provides for very limited enforcement where a marriage is subsequently determined to be void; and Section 8 tolls any statute of limitations applicable to an action asserting a claim for relief under a premarital agreement during the parties' marriage.

§1. Definitions

As used in this Act:

(1) "Premarital agreement" means an agreement between prospective spouses made in contemplation of marriage and to be effective upon marriage.

(2) "Property" means an interest, present or future, legal or equitable, vested or contingent, in real or personal property, including income and earnings.

§2. Formalities

A premarital agreement must be in writing and signed by both parties. It is enforceable without consideration.

Comment

This section restates the common requirement that a premarital agreement be reduced to writing and signed by both parties (see Ariz. Rev. Stats. §25201; Ark. Stats. §55310; Cal. Civ. C. §5134; 13 Dela. Code 1974 §301; Idaho Code §32917; Ann. Laws Mass. ch. 209, §25; Minn. Stats. Ann. §519.11;

Montana Rev. C. §36123; New Mex. Stats. Ann. 1978 §4024; Ore. Rev. Stats. §108.140; Vernon's Texas Codes Ann. §5.44; Vermont Stats. Ann. Title 12, §181). Many states also require other formalities, including notarization or an acknowledgment (see, e.g., Arizona, Arkansas, California, Idaho, Montana, New Mexico) but may then permit the formal statutory requirement to be avoided or satisfied subsequent to execution (see In re Marriage of Cleveland, 76 Cal. App. 3d 357 (1977) (premarital agreement never acknowledged but "proved" by sworn testimony of parties in dissolution proceeding)). This Act dispenses with all formal requirements except a writing signed by both parties. Although the section is framed in the singular, the agreement may consist of one or more documents intended to be part of the agreement and executed as required by this section.

Section 2 also restates what appears to be the almost universal rule regarding the marriage as consideration for a premarital agreement (see, e.g., Ga. Code §20303; Barnhill v. Barnhill, 386 So. 2d 749 (Ala. Civ. App. 1980); Estate of Gillilan v. Estate of Gillilan, 406 N.E. 2d 981 (Ind. App. 1980); Friedlander v. Friedlander, 494 P.2d 208 (Wash. 1972); but cf. Wilson v. Wilson, 170 A. 2d 679, 685 (Me. 1961)). The primary importance of this rule has been to provide a degree of mutuality of benefits to support the enforceability of a premarital agreement. A marriage is a prerequisite for the effectiveness of a premarital agreement under this Act (see Section 4). This requires that there be a ceremonial marriage. Even if this marriage is subsequently determined to have been void, Section 7 may provide limits of enforceability of an agreement entered into in contemplation of that marriage. Consideration as such is not required and the standards for enforceability are established by Sections 6 and 7. Nevertheless, this provision is retained here as a desirable, if not essential, restatement of the law. On the other hand, the fact that marriage is deemed to be consideration for the purpose of this Act does not change the rules applicable in other areas of law (see, e.g., 26 U.S.C.A. §2043 (release of certain marital rights not treated as consideration for federal estate tax), 2512; Merrill v. Fahs, 324 U.S. 308, rehearing denied 324 U.S. 888 (release of marital rights in premarital agreement not adequate and full consideration for purposes of federal gift tax).

Finally, a premarital agreement is a contract. As required for any other contract, the parties must have the capacity to contract to enter into a binding agreement. Those persons who lack the capacity to contract but who under other provisions of law are permitted to enter into a binding agreement may enter into a premarital agreement under those other provisions of law.

§3. Content

(a) Parties to a premarital agreement may contract with respect to:

(1) the rights and obligations of each of the parties in any of the property of either or both of them whenever and wherever acquired or located;

(2) the right to buy, sell, use, transfer, exchange, abandon, lease, consume, expend, assign, create a security interest in, mortgage, encumber, dispose of, or otherwise manage;

(3) the disposition of property upon separation, marital dissolution, death, or the occurrence or nonoccurrence of any other event;

(4) the modification or elimination of spousal support;

(5) the making of a will, trust, or other arrangement to carry out the provisions of the agreement;

(6) the ownership rights in and disposition of the death benefit from a life insurance policy;

(7) the choice of law governing the construction of the agreement; and

(8) any other matter, including their personal rights and obligations, not in violation of public policy or a statute imposing a criminal penalty.

(b) The right of a child to support may not be adversely affected by a premarital agreement.

Comment

Section 3 permits the parties to contract in a premarital agreement with respect to any matter listed and any other matter not in violation of public policy or any statute imposing a criminal penalty. The matters are intended to be illustrative, not exclusive. Paragraph (4) of subsection (a) specifically authorizes the parties to deal with spousal support obligations. There is a split in authority among the states as to whether a premarital agreement may control the issue of spousal support. A few states do not permit a premarital agreement to control this issue (see, e.g., In re Marriage of Winegard, 278 N.W.2d 505 (Iowa 1979); Fricke v. Fricke, 42 N.W.2d 500 (Wis. 1950)). However, the better view and growing trend is to permit a premarital agreement to govern this matter if the agreement and the circumstances of its execution satisfy certain standards (see, e.g., Newman v. Newman, 653 P.2d 728 (Colo. Sup. Ct. 1982); Parniawski v. Parniawski, 359 A.2d 719 (Conn. 1976); Volid v. Volid, 286 N.E. 2d 42 (Ill. 1972); Osborne v. Osborne, 428 N.E. 2d 810 (Mass. 1981); Hudson v. Hudson, 350 P.2d 596 (Okla. 1960); Unander v. Unander, 506 P.2d 719 (Ore. 1973)) (see Sections 7 and 8).

Paragraph (8) of subsection (a) makes clear that the parties may also contract with respect to other matters, including personal rights and

obligations, not in violation of public policy or a criminal statute. Hence, subject to this limitation, an agreement may provide for such matters as the choice of abode, the freedom to pursue career opportunities, the upbringing of children, and so on. However, subsection (b) of this section makes clear that an agreement may not adversely affect what would otherwise be the obligation of a party to a child.

§4. Effect of Marriage

A premarital agreement becomes effective upon marriage.

§5. Amendment, Revocation

After marriage, a premarital agreement may be amended or revoked only by a written agreement signed by the parties. The amended agreement or the revocation is enforceable without consideration.

§6. Enforcement

(a) A premarital agreement is not enforceable if the party against whom enforcement is sought proves that:

(1) that party did not execute the agreement voluntarily; or

(2) the agreement was unconscionable when it was executed and, before execution of the agreement, that party:

(i) was not provided a fair and reasonable disclosure of the property or financial obligations of the other party;

(ii) did not voluntarily and expressly waive, in writing, any right to disclosure of the property or financial obligations of the other party beyond the disclosure provided; and

(iii) did not have, or reasonably could not have had, an adequate knowledge of the property or financial obligations of the other party.

(b) If a provision of a premarital agreement modifies or eliminates spousal support and that modification or elimination causes one party to the agreement to be eligible for support under a program of public assistance at the time of separation or marital dissolution, a court, notwithstanding the terms of the agreement, may require the other party to provide support to the extent necessary to avoid that eligibility.

(c) An issue of unconscionability of a premarital agreement shall be decided by the court as a matter of law.

Comment

This section sets forth the conditions that must be proven to avoid the enforcement of a premarital agreement. If prospective spouses enter into a premarital agreement and their subsequent marriage is determined to be void, the enforceability of the agreement is governed by Section 7.

The conditions stated under subsection (a) are comparable to concepts that are expressed in the statutory and decisional law of many jurisdictions. Enforcement based on disclosure and voluntary execution is perhaps most common (see, e.g., Ark. Stats. §55309; Minn. Stats. Ann. §519.11; In re Kaufmann's Estate, 171 A. 2d 48 (Pa. 1961) (alternate holding)). However, knowledge or reason to know, together with voluntary execution, may also be sufficient (see, e.g., Tenn. Code Ann. §36606; Barnhill v. Barnhill, 386 So. 2d 749 (Ala. Civ. App. 1980); Del Vecchio v. Del Vecchio, 143 So. 2d 17 (Fla. 1962); Coward v. Coward, 582 P. 2d 834 (Or. App. 1978); but see Matter of Estate of Lebsock, 618 P.2d 683 (Colo. App. 1980)) and so may a voluntary, knowing waiver (see Hafner v. Hafner, 295 N.W. 2d 567 (Minn. 1980)). In each of these situations, it should be underscored that execution must have been voluntary (see Lutgert v. Lutgert, 338 So. 2d 1111 (Fla. 1976); see also 13 Dela. Code 1974 §301 (10-day waiting period)). Finally, a premarital agreement is enforceable if enforcement would not have been unconscionable at the time the agreement was executed (cf. Hartz v. Hartz, 234 A.2d 865 (Md. 1967) (premarital agreement upheld if no disclosure but agreement was fair and equitable under the circumstances)).

The test of "unconscionability" is drawn from §306 of the Uniform Marriage and Divorce Act (UMDA) (see Ferry v. Ferry, 586 S.W. 2d 782 (Mo. 1979); see also Newman v. Newman, 653 P.2d 728 (Colo. Sup. Ct. 1982) (maintenance provisions of premarital agreement tested for unconscionability at time of marriage termination)). The following discussion set forth in the Commissioner's Note to §306 of the UMDA is equally appropriate here:

> **Subsection (b) undergirds the freedom allowed the parties by making clear that the terms of the agreement respecting maintenance and property disposition are binding upon the court unless those terms are found to be unconscionable. The standard of unconscionability is used in commercial law, where its meaning includes protection against onesidedness, oppression, or unfair surprise (see §2302, Uniform Commercial Code), and in contract law. . . . It has been used in cases respecting divorce settlements or awards. Bell v. Bell, 371 P.2d 773, 150 Colo. 174 (1962) ("this division of property is manifestly unfair, inequitable and unconscionable"). Hence the**

act does not introduce a novel standard unknown to the law. In the context of negotiations between spouses as to the financial incidents of their marriage, the standard includes protection against overreaching, concealment of assets, and sharp dealing not consistent with the obligations of marital partners to deal fairly with each other.

In order to determine whether the agreement is unconscionable, the court may look to the economic circumstances of the parties resulting from the agreement, and any other relevant evidence such as the conditions under which the agreement was made, including the knowledge of the other party. If the court finds the agreement not unconscionable, its terms respecting property division and maintenance may not be altered by the court at the hearing. (Commissioner's Note, §306, Uniform Marriage and Divorce Act.)

Nothing in Section 6 makes the absence of assistance of independent legal counsel a condition for the unenforceability of a premarital agreement. However, lack of that assistance may well be a factor in determining whether the conditions stated in Section 6 may have existed (see, e.g., Del Vecchio v. Del Vecchio, 143 So.2d 17 (Fla. 1962)).

Even if the conditions stated in subsection (a) are not proven, if a provision of a premarital agreement modifies or eliminates spousal support, subsection (b) authorizes a court to provide very limited relief to a party who would otherwise be eligible for public welfare (see, e.g., Osborne v. Osborne, 428 N.E. 2d 810 (Mass. 1981) (dictum); Unander v. Unander, 506 P.2d 719 (Ore. 1973) (dictum)).

No special provision is made for enforcement of provisions of a premarital agreement relating to personal rights and obligations. However, a premarital agreement is a contract and these provisions may be enforced to the extent that they are enforceable under otherwise applicable law (see Avitzur v. Avitzur, 459 N.Y.S. 2d 572 (Ct. App.).

Section 6 is framed in a manner to require the party who alleges that a premarital agreement is not enforceable to bear the burden of proof as to that allegation. The statutory law conflicts on the issue of where the burden of proof lies (contrast Ark. Stats. §55313; 31 Minn. Stats. Ann. §519.11 with Vernon's Texas Codes Ann. §5.45). Similarly, some courts have placed the burden on the attacking spouse to prove the invalidity of the agreement. Linker v. Linker, 470 P.2d 921 (Colo. 1970); Matter of Estate of Benker, 296 N.W. 2d 167 (Mich. App. 1980); In re Kauffmann's Estate, 171 A.2d 48 (Pa. 1961). Some have placed the burden on those relying on the agreement to prove its validity. Hartz v. Hartz, 234 A.2d 865 (Md. 1967). Finally, several have adopted a middle ground by stating that a premarital agreement is presumptively valid but if a disproportionate disposition is made for the wife, the husband bears the burden of proof of showing adequate disclosure. (Del Vecchio v. Del Vecchio, 143 So.2d 17 (Fla. 1962); Christians v. Christians, 44 N.W.2d 431 (Iowa 1950); In re Neis' Estate, 225 P.2d 110 (Kans. 1950); Truitt v. Truitt's Adm'r, 162 S.W. 2d 31 (Ky. 1942); In re Estate of Strickland, 149 N.W. 2d 344 (Neb. 1967); Kosik v. George, 452 P.2d 560 (Or. 1969); Friedlander v. Friedlander, 494 P.2d 208 (Wash. 1972).

§7. Enforcement: Void Marriage

If a marriage is determined to be void, an agreement that would otherwise have been a premarital agreement is enforceable only to the extent necessary to avoid an inequitable result.

§8. Limitations of Actions

Any statute of limitations applicable to an action asserting a claim for relief under a premarital agreement is tolled during the marriage of the parties to the agreement. However, equitable defenses limiting the time for enforcement, including laches and estoppel, are available to either party.

§9. Application and Construction

This [Act] shall be applied and construed to effectuate its general purpose to make uniform the law with respect to the subject of this [Act] among states enacting it.

§10. Short Title

This [Act] may be cited as the Uniform Premarital Agreement Act.

§11. Severability

If any provision of this [Act] or its application to any person or circumstance is held invalid, the invalidity does not affect other provisions or applications of this [Act] which can be given effect without the invalid provision or application, and to this end the provisions of this [Act] are severable.

§12. Time of Taking Effect

This [Act] takes effect ______________________ and applies to any premarital agreement executed on or after that date.

§13. Repeal

The following acts and parts of acts are repealed:

(a)
(b)
(c)

PART IV

AMERICAN LAW INSTITUTE, PRINCIPLES OF THE LAW OF FAMILY DISSOLUTION: ANALYSIS AND RECOMMENDATIONS (2000)

American Law Institute, Principles of the Law of Family Dissolution: Analysis and Recommendations (2000) [Selected Principles and Commentary]

Below are selected ALI Principles (and selected commentary) on the topics of child custody (Chapter 2), division of property upon dissolution and compensatory spousal payments (Chapters 4 and 5) and domestic partners (Chapter 6). The remaining sections of the ALI Principles (including Commentary, Illustrations and Reporter's Notes) may be found in the American Law Institute, Principles of the Law of Family Dissolution: Analysis and Recommendations (Matthew Bender & Co., 2002).[1]

Chapter 2. The Allocation of Custodial and Decisionmaking Responsibility for Children

Topic 1. Scope, Objectives, Definitions, and Parties.

§2.01 Scope of Chapter 2.

This Chapter sets forth Principles governing the allocation of custodial and decisionmaking responsibility for a minor child when the parents do not live together.

§2.02 Objectives; best interests of the child defined

(1) The primary objective of Chapter 2 is to serve the child's best interests, by facilitating all of the following:

(a) parental planning and agreement about the child's custodial arrangements and upbringing;

(b) continuity of existing parent-child attachments;

(c) meaningful contact between the child and each parent;

(d) caretaking relationships by adults who love the child, know how to provide for the child's needs, and place a high priority on doing so;

(e) security from exposure to conflict and violence;

(f) expeditious, predictable decisionmaking and the avoidance of prolonged uncertainty respecting arrangements for the child's care and control.

(2) A secondary objective of Chapter 2 is to achieve fairness between the parents.

 The complete text of the Principles of the Law of Family Dissolution: Analysis and Recommendations is now available on the ALI website at *www.ali.org* or by calling ALI at 1-800-253-6397.

Comment

a. In general. **This section sets forth general criteria defining the child's best interests. More specific criteria are set forth in other sections of Chapter 2. See §2.08 (allocation of custodial responsibility), §2.09 (allocation of decisionmaking authority), §2.10 (dispute resolution), §2.11 (limiting factors), §2.12 (prohibited factors), §2.17 (the relocation of a parent), and §2.18 (allocation of responsibility to individuals other than legal parents).**

b. The child's best interests and fairness to parents. **Paragraph (1) states the Chapter's primary objective as serving the child's best interests. The priority of the child's interests over those of the competing adults is premised on the assumption that when a family breaks up, children are usually the most vulnerable parties and thus most in need of the law's protection.**

Fairness to the parents when it can also be achieved, however, is another objective of Chapter 2. Fairness to parents is not only a valid objective in itself, but it is intertwined with the child's interests. The Chapter assumes that without confidence in the basic fairness of the rules, parents are more likely to engage in strategic, resentful or uncooperative behavior, from which children may suffer; conversely, when parents believe that the rules are fair, they are more likely to invest themselves in their children and to act fairly toward others. Accordingly, when more than one rule could be expected to serve the interests of children equally well, or when the impact of the alternative rules upon children is uncertain, Chapter 2 adopts the rule most likely to produce results that achieve the greatest fairness between parents.

Acceptance of the rules governing the allocation of responsibility for children also depends on the consistency between these rules and society's basic values, such as freedom of religion, the ability to relocate geographically, and equal treatment based on race and sex. Respect for these values necessarily informs what is considered beneficial to children, as well as what is fair to adults. Chapter 2 incorporates these values implicitly in the design of these Principles and through express limitations on the factors that can be considered in applying the Principles.

c. Securing Chapter 2's objectives through determinate standards. **While the best-interests-of-the-child test expresses the appropriate priority in favor of the interests of the child, and while it provides the flexibility that permits a court to reach what it believes is the best result in an individual case, it has long been criticized for its indeterminacy. To apply the test, courts must often choose between specific values and views about childrearing. For example, a court may need to choose between a parent who provides greater emotional security for the child and one who emphasizes intellectual stimulation, or between a home life emphasizing the values of conformance and obedience and an upbringing that encourages creativity and challenge to authority. One parent may be deeply religious while the other parent has no religious faith. The parents may use different disciplinary styles, have different attitudes about sex education, or disagree about the need for bedtime routines. When the only guidance for the court is what best serves the child's interests, the court must rely on its own value judgments, or upon experts who have their own theories of what is good for children and what is effective parenting.**

The indeterminacy of the best-interests test makes it often difficult for parents to predict the outcome of a case. This difficulty encourages strategic or manipulative behavior that is usually adverse to the child's interests. For example, a parent may make custodial demands for strategic purposes to pressure the other parent into financial or other compromises that are unfair and do not serve the child's interests, or to force into litigation a case that could have been settled if the result were more predictable. A parent may attempt to leave the other out of decisions respecting the child, or to influence the child, the child's teachers, and others to see the other parent in a negative light. A parent uncertain of a case's outcome is more likely to hire experts whose job it will be, in part, to highlight the flaws of the other parent in custody reports or in courtroom testimony.

More determinate custody standards can help reduce these difficulties. More determinate standards, however, are not necessarily better standards. Favoring a parent because of his or her sex, or religion, for example, may produce relatively certain, predictable results, but not acceptable ones. Moreover, even when a determinate standard conforms to broadly held views about what is good for children, it can intrude — just as indeterminate standards do — on matters concerning a child's upbringing that this society generally leaves up to parents themselves, and standardize child-rearing arrangements in a way that unnecessarily curtails diversity and cultural pluralism.

The question for rule-makers is not whether the law in this area should require determinacy or permit unbridled judicial discretion. It is, rather, what blend of determinacy and discretion produces the best combination of predictable and acceptable results, and what substantive values are most appropriately reflected in the mix. This Chapter attempts to achieve this equilibrium through structured decisionmaking criteria that limit judicial discretion and at the same time express widely held societal commitments to children and to family diversity.

Some authorities argue for a focus on avoiding harm to the child — the-least-detriment-to-the-child standard — rather than on affirmatively serving the child's best interests. There are certain advantages to such a focus, which implicitly concedes that the law is limited in its ability to ensure good outcomes for children. However, a least-detriment standard is no more determinate than a best-interests standard, and thus could not be expected to avoid its difficulties. Moreover, in setting a modest goal, a least-detriment standard may set the sights of parents too low, when the law should be trying to stimulate their best efforts on behalf of their children. For this reason, Chapter 2 attempts to clarify and refine the best-interests standard rather than to eliminate it.

d. Parental planning and agreement. **The law is limited in its ability to secure the welfare of children. Even if there were consensus on what parenting practices were best for children, parents cannot be made to love their children, nor can they be supervised in all of their encounters with them. However, the law can attempt to stimulate, or at least not inhibit, the motivations of parents to do well by their children. One of the ways it can do this is by respecting the decisions parents have made about their children in the past and by encouraging their planning for their children's future.**

Chapter 2's reliance on past caretaking in allocating custodial responsibility respects decisions parents have made about their children in the past. See §2.08(1). In requiring parenting plans, the Chapter encourages parents to plan for their children's future. See §2.05. The limits the Chapter places on the court's discretion to reject voluntary and informed agreements by the parents further affirms parental autonomy and situates responsibility in those assumed by Chapter 2, as a general matter, to be in the best position to decide what is in the child's best interests. See §§2.06 and 2.16(1).

e. Continuity of existing parent-child attachments. **While Chapter 2 attempts to avoid unnecessary value judgments about what is best for children, it accepts and builds on certain principles of child welfare about which there is clear consensus. One of these principles, recognized in Paragraph 1(b), is that the continuity of existing parent-child attachments after the break-up of a family unit is a factor critical to the child's well-being. Such attachments are thought to affect the child's sense of identity and later ability to trust and to form healthy relationships.**

It is sometimes difficult to evaluate the strength of a child's various attachments or to weigh the importance of the child's attachments against other factors that are relevant to the child's welfare. Chapter 2's priority on the past division of caretaking responsibilities recognizes these difficulties by assuming that the strength of the child's various attachments correspond roughly to the share of responsibility a party has assumed for the child's past caretaking. See §2.08(1). . . .

§2.03 Definitions

For purposes of this Chapter, the following definitions apply.

(1) Unless otherwise specified, a *parent* is either a legal parent, a parent by estoppel, or a de facto parent.

(a) A *legal parent* is an individual who is defined as a parent under other state law.

(b) A *parent by estoppel* is an individual who, though not a legal parent,

(i) is obligated to pay child support under Chapter 3; or

(ii) lived with the child for at least two years and

(A) over that period had a reasonable, good-faith belief that he was the child's biological father, based on marriage to the mother or on the actions or representations of the mother, and fully accepted parental responsibilities consistent with that belief, and

(B) if some time thereafter that belief no longer existed, continued to make reasonable, good-faith efforts to accept responsibilities as the child's father; or

(iii) lived with the child since the child's birth, holding out and accepting full and permanent responsibilities as parent, as part of a prior co-parenting agreement with the child's legal parent (or, if there are two legal parents, both parents) to raise a child together each with full parental rights and responsibilities, when the court finds that recognition of the individual as a parent is in the child's best interests; or

(iv) lived with the child for at least two years, holding out and accepting full and permanent responsibilities as a parent, pursuant to an agreement with the child's parent (or, if there are two legal parents, both parents), when the court finds that recognition of the individual as a parent is in the child's best interests.

(C) A *de facto parent* is an individual other than a legal parent or a parent by estoppel who, for a significant period of time not less than two years,

(i) lived with the child and,

(ii) for reasons primarily other than financial compensation, and with the agreement of a legal parent to form a parent-child relationship, or as a result of a complete failure or inability of any legal parent to perform caretaking functions,

(A) regularly performed a majority of the caretaking functions for the child, or

(B) regularly performed a share of caretaking functions at least as great as that of the parent with whom the child primarily lived.

(2) A *parenting plan* is a set of provisions for allocation of custodial responsibility and decisionmaking responsibility on behalf of a child and for resolution of future disputes between the parents.

(3) *Custodial responsibility* refers to physical custodianship and supervision of a child. It usually includes, but does not necessarily require, residential or overnight responsibility.

(4) *Decisionmaking responsibility* refers to authority for making significant life decisions on behalf of the child, including decisions about the child's education, spiritual guidance, and health care.

(5) *Caretaking functions* are tasks that involve interaction with the child or that direct, arrange, and supervise the interaction and care provided by others. Caretaking functions include but are not limited to all of the following:

(a) satisfying the nutritional needs of the child, managing the child's bedtime and wake-up routines, caring for the child when sick or injured, being attentive to the child's personal hygiene needs including washing, grooming, and dressing, playing with the child and arranging for recreation, protecting the child's physical safety, and providing transportation;

(b) directing the child's various developmental needs, including the acquisition of motor and language skills, toilet training, self-confidence, and maturation;

(c) providing discipline, giving instruction in manners, assigning and supervising chores, and performing other tasks that attend to the child's needs for behavioral control and self-restraint;

(d) arranging for the child's education, including remedial or special services appropriate to the child's needs and interests, communicating with teachers and counselors, and supervising homework;

(e) helping the child to develop and maintain appropriate interpersonal relationships with peers, siblings, and other family members;

(f) arranging for health-care providers, medical follow-up, and home health care;

(g) providing moral and ethical guidance;

(h) arranging alternative care by a family member, babysitter, or other child-care provider or facility, including investigation of alternatives, communication with providers, and supervision of care.

(6) *Parenting functions* are tasks that serve the needs of the child or the child's residential family. Parenting functions include caretaking functions, as defined in Paragraph (5), and all of the following additional functions:

(a) providing economic support;

(b) participating in decisionmaking regarding the child's welfare;

(c) maintaining or improving the family residence, including yard work, and house cleaning;

(d) doing and arranging for financial planning and organization, car repair and maintenance, food and clothing purchases, laundry and dry cleaning, and other tasks supporting the consumption and savings needs of the household;

(e) performing any other functions that are customarily performed by a parent or guardian and that are important to a child's welfare and development.

(7) *Domestic violence* is the infliction of physical injury, or the creation of a reasonable fear thereof, by a parent or a present or former member of the child's household, against the child or another member of the household. Reasonable action taken by an individual for self-protection, or the protection of another individual, is not domestic violence.

Comment

a. Legal parent. **This Chapter uses the term "legal parent" to refer to any individual recognized as a parent under other state law. Individuals defined as parents under state law ordinarily include biological parents, whether or not they are or ever have been married to each other, and adoptive parents. In some states, an individual may be a parent also by virtue of an unrebutted legal presumption, such as the presumption that a husband is the father of his wife's child. An individual is not a parent under Paragraph (1)(a) if, under applicable state law, the individual's status as parent has been terminated. . . .**

b. Parent by estoppel. **An individual who is not a legal parent may be a parent by estoppel under Paragraph (1)(b). A parent by estoppel is an individual who, even though not a legal parent, has acted as a parent under certain specified circumstances which serve to estop the legal parent from denying the individual's status as a parent. While these circumstances typically contain a component of reliance by the individual claiming parent status, the goal of the Chapter is to protect the parent-child relationship presumed to have developed under these various circumstances rather than reliance itself. Accordingly, the requirements in §2.03(1)(b) focus on function, rather than on detrimental reliance.**

A parent by estoppel is afforded all of the privileges of a legal parent under this Chapter, including standing to bring an action and the right to have notice of and participate in an action brought by another under §2.04, the benefit of the presumptive allocation of custodial time provided for in §2.08(1)(a), the advantage of the presumption in favor of a joint allocation of decisionmaking responsibility afforded by §2.09(2), the right of access to school and health records specified in §2.09(4), and priority over a de facto parent and a nonparent in the allocation of primary custodial responsibility under §2.18.

(i) Individual who is obligated to pay child support. **Four circumstances may create parent-by-estoppel status under §2.03(1)(b). First, when a parent obtains a child-support order against another under Chapter 3, the parent is estopped under §2.03(1)(b)(1) from denying that the other individual is a parent when that individual seeks an allocation of custodial responsibility under Chapter 3. Most individuals upon whom a child-support obligation is imposed under Chapter 3 are legal parents. However, §3.03 permits the imposition of a child-support obligation upon other individuals when a court determines that their prior conduct estops them from denying the obligation. For example, a stepfather who undertook to replace a child's biological father by supporting the child and otherwise assuming responsibility for the child may be estopped, under some circumstances, from denying an obligation for child support when the marriage underlying the stepparent relationship ends. . . . When this happens and a child-support order is issued against the stepfather under §3.03. §2.03(1)(b)(I) provides that legal parent is, in turn, estopped from denying the supporting parent status as parent under Chapter 2. . . .**

(ii) Individual who had reasonable, good-faith belief he was the child's father. **A man is a parent by estoppel if he lived with the child and fully accepted parental responsibilities for the child for at least two years, in the reasonable, good-faith belief that he was the child's biological father. See Paragraph (1)(b)(ii). Paragraph (1)(b)(ii) applies only to men, based on the assumption that a woman virtually always knows if she is a child's mother, whereas a man may be unsure, or misled, about his parentage. Estoppel principles are not likely to be helpful when there are mistakes over maternity, such as might occur when conception occurs outside the womb or when babies are switched at birth. These situations are not covered by this Chapter.**

Because Chapter 2 treats a parent by estoppel the same as a legal parent, it is important to limit the category to the most appropriate cases. The objective requirements in Paragraph (1)(b)(ii) that a man have lived with the child for at least two years and fully accepted responsibilities as a parent during that period are designed to identify those parent-child relationships most important to preserve through allocations of responsibility under Chapter 2.

To determine whether the requirements of Paragraph (1)(b)(ii) are met, the full range of parenting functions performed by the adult in question are relevant, not just the caretaking functions. In this sense, the definition is more generous than the definition of de facto parent in Paragraph (1)(c) and Comment *c*, below. The parent-by-estoppel definition is more strict, however, in requiring that the man have had a reasonable, good-faith belief that he was the parent. When this reasonable good faith exists, the individual is seeking status based not solely on his functioning as a parent, but on the combination of the parental functions performed and the expectations of the parties. As is the case with a de

facto parent, the necessary indications of a commitment to the child must have existed for a period of at least two years, assuring that the commitment is serious, longterm, and significant.

A man's good-faith belief that he was the child's legal father may be based on a number of different factors. Marriage to the child's mother is perhaps the most common circumstance. In some states, marriage to the child's mother at the time the child is born is sufficient to establish that a man is the child's legal father; in most states it will create a presumption to that effect. If an individual is a legal parent under state law by virtue of such rules, he or she is a legal parent under Paragraph (1)(a). Under Paragraph (1)(b)(ii), it may reasonably be inferred, absent evidence to the contrary and even without an applicable presumption, that a man who was married to the child's mother when the child was born had a reasonable, good-faith belief that he was the child's biological father.

Another way a man can establish the reasonable, good-faith belief required by Paragraph (1)(b)(ii) is by establishing that he had sexual intercourse with the mother at the approximate time of conception, and that the mother made subsequent statements or otherwise engaged in conduct that affirmed his paternity of the child.

In some circumstances a man who had a good-faith belief that he was the child's father and who lived with the child for two years or more may learn that he is not the child's father before an action for custodial responsibility or decisionmaking authority under Chapter 2 is initiated. In such a circumstance, a man remains a parent by estoppel as long as he continues to accept responsibilities as the child's father after learning the truth, or makes reasonable efforts to do so. See Paragraph (1)(b)(ii)(B). . . .

(iii) Individual who is a co-parent since the child's birth, pursuant to a co-parenting agreement with the legal parent(s). **An individual may also be a parent by estoppel on the basis of a co-parenting agreement with the child's legal parent or parents, when that individual has lived with the child since the child was born, holding himself or herself out as the child's parent and accepting the responsibilities thereof. See Paragraph (1)(b)(iii). This Paragraph combines functional criteria with an agreement that the individual in question will act fully and permanently as parent.**

This Paragraph contemplates the situation of two cohabiting adults who undertake to raise a child together, with equal rights and responsibilities as parents. Adoption is the clearer, and thus preferred, legal avenue for recognition of such parent-child relationships, but adoption is sometimes not legally available or possible, especially if the one of the adults is still married to another, or if the adults are both women, or both men. Neither the unavailability of adoption nor the failure to adopt when adoption would have been available forecloses parent-by-estoppel status. However, the failure to adopt when adoption was available may be relevant to whether an agreement was intended.

A formal, written agreement is not required to create a parent-by-estoppel status under Paragraph (1)(b)(iii), but the absence of formalities may also affect the factfinder's determination of whether an agreement was made. The factfinder must determine whether, given the circumstances, the actions of the individual seeking status as parent and those of the legal parent or parents are sufficiently clear and unambiguous to indicate that a parent status was understood by all of them. The factfinder's determination should not turn upon whether the parties are of the same sex or different sexes, or even whether the parties are married, since these factors do not bear on whether a family relationship is intended. As a practical matter, however, the less traditional the arrangement, the greater assistance a formal agreement may be in clarifying the parties' intentions.

Paragraph (1)(b)(iii) requires the agreement of the child's legal parent or parents. Sometimes the child has only one legal parent. When there are two legal parents, each parent must agree. Agreement may be implied from the circumstances. See Comment *iv*, below.

An individual may not be a parent by estoppel under this Paragraph if the agreement provides for less than a full assumption of the responsibilities as a parent. An agreement for visitation only, or one that specifically excludes obligations for financial support or for caretaking responsibility, does not serve as the basis for recognition as a parent by estoppel. However, in appropriate circumstances, an agreement under which a legal parent gives up some parental rights and obligations but reserves others may have some effect. . . .

Parent-by-estoppel status is created under this Paragraph only when the court determines that the status is in the child's best interests. This inquiry should focus primarily on the benefits and costs of participation by another individual, as a parent, in the proceedings and in the child's life. Ordinarily, if an individual meets the criteria of Paragraph (1)(b)(iii) (or Paragraph (1)(b)(iv)), the court would be expected to find that parent-by-estoppel status is in the child's best interests. The case for recognition of an additional parent is weaker if a child already has two (or more) parents, although this factor is not dispositive, particularly if one of the child's legal parents has formed no significant parental relationship with the child. Other relevant factors include the extent of the involvement of the various parties in the child's life and the strength of their respective emotional bonds to the child. . . .

(iv) Individual who is a co-parent for at least two years, by agreement with the legal parent(s). **Some co-parenting arrangements arise not from an undertaking by the couple before the child's birth, but afterwards, when the legal parent or parents agree** to the assumption of the responsibilities of parenthood by another. These arrangements may give rise to parent-by-estoppel status only when the individual in question lived with the child for two years and more, holding out and accepting full and permanent responsibilities as a parent, with the agreement of the child's legal parent or parents. See Paragraph (1)(b)(iv). As with Paragraph (1)(b)(iii), this Paragraph applies only when the court determines that the creation of parent-by-estoppel status is in the child's best interests. See Comment *iii*, above.

One circumstance contemplated by this Paragraph is the marriage of a man to a woman who is pregnant with another man's child, with the understanding that he will serve as the child's father. If the understanding continues for two years or more, with the man living with the child and accepting full responsibilities as the child's parent, he could be a parent by estoppel under Paragraph (1)(b)(iv).

Marriage is not essential to the creation of parental status under Paragraph (1)(b)(iv), although it may make it easier to persuade a factfinder of the individual's full and permanent commitment to the child. Likewise, it is not essential that the two adults are of different sexes; a same-sex couple might also undertake to have permanent joint parenting rights and responsibilities and thereby create parent-by-estoppel status under this Paragraph.

Paragraph (1)(b)(iv) requires the agreement of each of the child's legal parents. As is the case under Paragraph (1)(b)(iii), sometimes the child has only one legal parent. If the child has two legal parents, both parents must agree. A parent cannot be estopped from denying parent status to an individual who has functioned as such, if that parent did not earlier agree to the arrangement giving rise to the estoppel. Agreement, however, may be implied from the circumstances. For example, the legal father who knows that his child is being raised by the mother and her husband and who fails to visit or support the child has, by this conduct, communicated his acceptance of this arrangement and is estopped from later denying parental status to the stepfather. In contrast, the legal father who acknowledges the stepfather's role but who continues to exercise his own parental rights and responsibilities has not agreed to stepfather's status as the child's parent. . .

c. De facto parent. Occasionally an individual who is not a legal parent under state law, does not have a child-support obligation, did not have the good-faith belief that he was the child's parent, did not hold himself or herself out as the child's parent, did not have an agreement with the legal parent to serve as a co-parent, and otherwise does not meet the requirements of a parent by estoppel, may nonetheless have functioned as the child's primary parent. Such individual may be a de facto parent under Paragraph (1)(c).

The requirements for becoming a de facto parent are strict, to avoid unnecessary and inappropriate intrusion into the relationships between legal parents and their children. The individual must have lived with the child for a significant period of time (not less than two years), and acted in the role of a parent for reasons primarily other than financial compensation. The legal parent or parents must have agreed to the arrangement, or it must have arisen because of a complete failure or inability of any legal parent to perform caretaking functions. In addition, the individual must have functioned as a parent either by (a) having performed the majority share of caretaking functions for the child, or (b) having performed a share of caretaking functions that is equal to or greater than the share assumed by the legal parent with whom the child primarily lives.

As is the case with an individual seeking to be a parent by estoppel under Paragraph (1)(b)(iii) or Paragraph (1)(b)(iv), the best course of action for an individual who expects legal recognition as a de facto parent would be formal adoption, if available under applicable state law. Failure to adopt the child when it would have been possible is some evidence, although not dispositive, that the legal parent did not agree to the formation of the de facto parent relationship.

(i) Residence requirement. Like an individual seeking recognition of a parent by estoppel under Paragraph (1)(b)(ii), (iii), or (iv), an individual seeking recognition as a de facto parent must have lived with the child. See Paragraph (1)(c)(i). This requirement is especially important, since the de facto parent category might otherwise include neighbors, nonresidential relatives, or hired babysitters on whom parents have relied for regular caretaking functions, and whose recognition as parents, as a general matter, would be highly undesirable. In requiring that an individual seeking recognition as a de facto parent have previously lived with the child, Paragraph (1)(c) is intended to cover those individuals most likely to have engaged with the child in the role of a family member and to exclude those outsiders the parents may have called upon to assist them in caring for their child in an auxiliary role. . . .

(ii) Exclusion of relationships motivated by financial compensation. To qualify as a de facto parent, an adult must have performed caretaking functions "for reasons primarily other than financial compensation." See Paragraph (1)(c)(ii). The law grants parents responsibility for their children based, in part, on the assumption that they are motivated by love and loyalty, and thus are likely to act in the child's best interests. The same motivations cannot be assumed on the part of adults who have provided caretaking functions primarily for financial reasons. Thus, relationships to children formed by babysitters and other paid caretakers are not recognized under Paragraph (1)(c). Relationships with foster parents are also generally excluded, both because of the financial compensation involved and because inclusion of foster parents would undermine the integrity of a state-run system designed to provide temporary, rather than indefinite, care for children.

The requirement that an individual have performed caretaking functions primarily for nonfinancial reasons does not rule out caretakers who may qualify for financial assistance to care for the child but whose caretaking role was not motivated primarily by that assistance. Thus, for example, family members who take children into their homes primarily out of family affinity may be de facto parents even if, as a result of taking a child into their home, they are able to qualify for welfare benefits, foster-care payments, or other forms of financial assistance. . . .

(iii) Agreement of a parent to the de facto parent relationship. **Like a parent-by-estoppel status, a de facto parent relationship cannot arise by accident, in secrecy, or as a result of improper behavior. The agreement requirement of Paragraph (1)(c)(ii) limits de facto parent status, in most circumstances, to those individuals whose relationship to the child has arisen with knowledge and agreement of the legal parent. Although agreement may be implied by the circumstances, it requires an affirmative act or acts by the legal parent demonstrating a willingness and an expectation of shared parental responsibilities. Agreement is not established by the mere delegation of babysitting duties to a roommate or an adult partner. Retention of authority over matters of the child's care, such as discipline, manifests an absence of agreement to the formation of a de facto parent relationship.**

The only circumstance in which a de facto parent may be recognized without the agreement of a legal parent is when there has been a total failure or inability by the legal parent to care for the child. This circumstance exists only when a parent is absent, or virtually absent, from the child's life, such as when a parent has abandoned the child or has been imprisoned or institutionalized. While some of these circumstances may be considered beyond the control of the legal parent, they function in the same way to permit to develop the kind of long-term, substitute parent-child relationship that this Chapter seeks to recognize. . . .

(iv) Length of caretaking relationship. **To qualify as a de facto parent, an adult must have assumed caretaking functions for a significant period of time, not less than two years. The two-year minimum is intended to establish a threshold that readily will screen out potential claimants who have only temporary relationships with a child. In some cases, a period longer than two years may be required in order to establish that an individual has the kind of relationship that warrants recognition. The length of time that constitutes a significant period will depend on many circumstances, including the age of the child, the frequency of contact, and the intensity of the relationship. For a child under the age of six whose caretaking needs are quite significant, a two-year period in which the adult in question has performed the clear majority of caretaking functions is likely to qualify as significant. A longer period may be required for school-aged children, and an even longer period if the child is an adolescent.**

In addition to the time-period requirement set forth in Paragraph (1)(c), a de facto parent, in order to have standing to initiate an action, must have resided with the child within the six-month period prior to the commencement of the action or maintained or attempted to maintain the relationship since no longer living with the child. See §2.04(l)(c). This additional standing requirement is justified by the fact that the status of a de facto parent is based on an individual's functioning as a parent, and it is assumed that the importance of this role diminishes as the period of functioning as a parent becomes more remote in time. . . .

(v) Share of caretaking functions. **To be a de facto parent, the individual must have functioned as a parent in one of two alternative ways. The first alternative is to have performed the majority share of caretaking functions for the child. What constitutes a caretaking function is defined in Paragraph (5). See Comment *g*, below, and §2.08, Comment *c*.**

The second way to satisfy the caretaking-functions requirement is to have performed a share of caretaking functions that was equal to or greater than that performed by the parent with whom the child primarily lived. An individual who is sharing caretaking responsibility equally with a child's only other parent will meet this criterion. So will an individual who is sharing caretaking responsibility for a child whose parents live in different households, if the child lives primarily in the household in which that individual also lives and the individual performs at least as much caretaking responsibility as the parent in that household. An equal sharing of caretaking duties with a parent who is not providing the primary home for the child is insufficient to satisfy this criterion. . . .

d. Parenting plan. **A parenting plan sets forth provisions for the allocation of responsibility for a child, including custodial arrangements and decisionmaking responsibility. It also includes mechanisms for resolving subsequent disputes that may arise between the parents. The required components of a parenting plan are set forth in §2.05. Criteria for each of these components are set forth in §§2.06 to 2.12.**

e. Custodial responsibility. **This Chapter replaces the traditional terminology of "custody" and "visitation," as well as the more specific labels "sole," "joint," and "shared" custody, with the**

single term "custodial responsibility." This substitution is intended to avoid the win-lose conceptualization suggested by the more conventional terminology of "custody" and "visitation," and to reinforce the reality that not only primary responsibility for the child but all other forms of physical responsibility are also important, and custodial in nature. While any beneficial effects of this shift in terminology on people's perceptions of parenthood cannot be measured, it is assumed that the unified concept of custodial responsibility has some potential to strengthen the usual expectation that both parents have responsibility regardless of the proportion of time each spends with the child, and that neither parent is a mere "visitor". . .

f. Decisionmaking responsibility. **Decisionmaking responsibility is the Chapter's term for what most states call "legal custody." It encompasses the authority to make significant decisions delegated to parents over their minor children as a matter of law, such as those relating to health care, education, permission to marry, and to enlist in the military. The definition leaves open the possibility of adding other areas that, in individual cases, are significant life decisions for the child. Whether the child will attend a religious school or boarding school, pursue school sports, travel alone abroad, work in a resort away from home for the summer, or buy an expensive car are examples of other significant life decisions for which it might be appropriate to allocate decisionmaking responsibility. . . .**

g. Parenting and caretaking functions. **This Chapter recognizes two overlapping sets of functions that parents serve. Parenting functions encompass a broad category of responsibilities and chores related to the child's upbringing and to support of the family and household. These include not only caretaking functions, discussed in more detail below, but also other functions relating to the maintenance of the child and the child's family, such as financial support, purchase and care of clothing, food shopping, and care and upkeep of the family residence, automobile, and yard. See §2.03(6).**

Caretaking functions are the subset of parenting functions that involve the direct delivery of day-to-day care and supervision to the child. These functions include physical supervision, feeding, grooming, discipline, transportation, direction of the child's intellectual and emotional development, and arrangement of the child's peer activities, medical care, and education. See Paragraph (5). Because caretaking functions involve tasks relating directly to a child's care and upbringing, it is assumed that they are likely to have a special bearing on the strength and quality of the adult's relationship with the child. For this reason, the Chapter makes each parent's share of past caretaking functions central to the allocation of custodial responsibility at divorce. See §2.08(1). While caretaking functions have greater significance for the allocation of custodial responsibility, parenting functions are relevant to other matters, including the guaranteed minimum allocation of custodial responsibility allowed in §2.08(1)(a), the presumed allocation of joint decisionmaking responsibility in §2.09(2), and other issues.

The distinction between parenting and caretaking functions is not intended to suggest different degrees of commitment by parents to a child. Rather, it recognizes that different types of involvement in the child's life are relevant in different ways to the various allocation issues addressed by the Chapter. . . .

h. Domestic violence. **The Principles of this Chapter require that when a parent commits domestic violence affecting the safety of another parent or the child, special measures must be taken to protect family members. See §2.11; see also §2.05(2)(f) (parenting plan requires description of circumstances involving domestic violence); §2.05(3) (court must have screening process for identifying domestic violence); §2.06(2) (requiring hearing on parental agreement when there is credible information that child abuse or domestic violence has occurred); §2.07(2) (requiring mediators involved in dispute resolution to screen for domestic violence); and §2.07(3) (precluding involuntary, face-to-face mediation).**

Paragraph (7) defines domestic violence as the infliction of physical injury, or of reasonable fear thereof, between family members or members of a household, past or present. The definition does not include emotional abuse, even though this form of abuse can be very harmful to an individual and coercive, because of the difficulty of distinguishing it from the emotional turmoil produced in many intimate relationships, particularly in the circumstances surrounding family dissolution. Taking advantage of the emotional vulnerability of a parent, however, may be a reason for the court to decide that a parental agreement is not voluntary, and thus not entitled to deference. See §§2.06(1)(a) and 2.16(1). See also §2.07(2) (requiring individuals providing mediation services to screen not only for domestic violence, but also for other conditions or circumstances that may impede a party's capacity to participate in the mediation process).

Physical injury, or reasonable fear thereof, may be established by various means. To facilitate proof in cases in which a criminal action has already been successfully prosecuted, states may designate crimes involving physical injury or the threat thereof against the domestic victim, that are presumed to meet the definition of domestic violence. These crimes may include assault, battery, kidnapping, malicious mischief, reckless endangerment, sexual assault, rape, and stalking, among others. The existence of domestic violence may also be established by credible testimony

thereof, or by proof of violation of a domestic-violence protection order when adequate notice and opportunity to be heard were properly afforded respondent.

Domestic violence sometimes involves responsive actions between the parents. Responsive acts of violence do not necessarily cancel each other out. The definition of domestic violence in Paragraph (7) excludes a reasonable, defensive act to another individual's aggression, such as action reasonably taken for self-protection or for the protection of another individual.

Similarly, in some situations of mutual domestic violence, one parent's physical aggression is substantially more extreme, or dangerous, than the other's. While both aggressions may satisfy the definition of domestic violence, the measures necessary to protect a victim of domestic violence required by §2.11 must be commensurate with the severity of the violence. . . .

§2.04 Parties to an action under this chapter

(1) All of the following individuals should be given a right to bring an action under this Chapter, and to be notified of and participate as a party in an action filed by another:

(a) a legal parent of the child, as defined in §2.03(l)(a);

(b) a parent by estoppel, as defined in §2.03(l)(b);

(c) a de facto parent of the child, as defined in §2.03(l)(c), who has resided with the child within the six-month period prior to the filing of the action or who has consistently maintained or attempted to maintain the parental relationship since residing with the child;

(d) a biological parent who is not a legal parent but who has an agreement with a legal parent under which he or she reserved some parental rights or responsibilities;

(e) an individual allocated custodial responsibility or decisionmaking responsibility regarding the child under an existing parenting plan.

(2) In exceptional cases, a court should have discretion to grant permission to intervene, under such terms as it establishes, to other individuals or public agencies whose participation in the proceedings under this Chapter it determines is likely to serve the child's best interests, but such individuals should not have standing to initiate an action under this Chapter.

Topic 2. Parenting Plan

§2.05 Parenting plan: proposed, temporary, and final

(1) An individual seeking a judicial allocation of custodial responsibility or decisionmaking responsibility under this Chapter should be required to file with the court a proposed parenting plan containing proposals for each of the provisions specified in Paragraph (5). Individuals should be allowed to file a joint plan.

(2) Each parenting plan filed under Paragraph (1) should be required to be supported by an affidavit containing, to the extent known or reasonably discoverable by the filing individual or individuals, all of the following:

(a) the name and address of any individual who has a right to participate in the action under §2.04;

(b) the name, address, and length of co-residence of any individuals with whom the child has lived for one year or more, or in the case of a child less than one year old, any individuals with whom the child has lived for any significant period of time since birth;

(c) a description of the past allocation of caretaking and other parenting functions performed by each individual identified under Paragraph (2)(a) or (2)(b), including at a minimum during the 24 months preceding the filing of an action under this Chapter;

(d) a description of the employment and child-care schedules of any individual seeking an allocation of custodial responsibility, and any expected changes to these schedules in the future;

(e) a schedule of the child's school and extracurricular activities;

(f) a description of any of the limiting factors specified in §2.11 that are present in the case, including any restraining orders to prevent child abuse or domestic violence, with case number and issuing court;

(g) financial information required to be disclosed under Chapter 3;

(h) a description of the known areas of agreement and disagreement with any other parenting plan submitted in the case.

The court should maintain the confidentiality of information required to be filed under this section if the individual providing the information demonstrates a reasonable fear of child abuse or domestic violence and disclosure of the information would increase safety risks.

(3) The court should have a process to identify cases in which there is credible information that child abuse, as defined by state law, or domestic violence as defined in §2.03(7), has occurred. The process should include assistance for possible victims of domestic violence in complying with Paragraph (2), referral to appropriate resources for safe shelter, counseling, safety planning, information regarding the potential impact of domestic violence on children, and information regarding civil and criminal remedies for domestic violence. The process should include a system for ensuring the court review mandated in §2.06(2) when there is credible information that child abuse or domestic violence has occurred.

(4) Prior to a decision on a final parenting plan and upon motion of a party, the court may order a temporary allocation of custodial responsibility or decisionmaking responsibility as the court determines is in the child's best interests, considering the factors in §§2.08 and 2.09. A temporary allocation order ordinarily should not preclude access to the child by a parent who has been exercising a reasonable share of parenting functions. Upon credible information of one or more of the circumstances set forth in §2.11(l) and pending adjudication of the underlying facts, the court should issue a temporary order limiting or denying access to the child as required by that section, in order to protect the child or other family member.

(5) After consideration of any proposed parenting plans submitted in the case and any evidence presented in support

thereof, the court should order a parenting plan that is consistent with the provisions of §§2.08-2.12 and contains the following provisions:

(a) a provision for the child's living arrangements and for each parent's custodial responsibility, which should include either

(i) a custodial schedule that designates in which parent's home each minor child will reside on given days of the year; or

(ii) a formula or method for determining such a schedule in sufficient detail that, if necessary, the schedule can be enforced in a subsequent proceeding.

(b) an allocation of decisionmaking responsibility as to significant matters reasonably likely to arise with respect to the child; and

(c) a provision consistent with §2.07 for resolution of disputes that arise under the plan, and a provision establishing remedies for violations of the plan.

(6) The court may provide in the parenting plan for how issues relating to a party's future relocation will be resolved, and it may provide for future modifications of the parenting plan if specified contingencies occur.

(7) Expedited procedures should facilitate the prompt issuance of a parenting plan.

Comment

a. In general. **The parenting plan is a core concept of this Chapter. This section requires parents to file a parenting plan in order to encourage them to anticipate their children's needs and make arrangements for them. Although courts will still be called upon to resolve conflicts between some parents, the parenting-plan requirement locates responsibility for the welfare of the child in the first instance in parents rather than in courts. If the parents reach agreement on how their children's needs will be met, §2.06 requires the court ordinarily to accept and order that plan. Even when the parents cannot agree, the requirement that courts consider each of their proposed plans gives each of the parents an incentive to produce a thoughtful and rational plan.**

The parenting-plan concept presupposes a diverse range of childrearing arrangements, and rejects any pre-established set of statutory choices about what arrangements are best for children. Rules that favor sole custody with visitation, joint custody, or some other specified arrangement express particular preferences about what is best for children, but they do not reflect the preferences, experiences, or welfare of all families. The parenting-plan requirement allows parents to customize their arrangements to take account of the family's own actual circumstances; if they cannot agree, other rules in the Chapter retain the focus on the family's actual experience, through its patterns of past caretaking. See §2.08(1). . . .

e. Order allocating custodial responsibility. **Paragraph 5(a) requires that a court-ordered parenting plan allocate custodial responsibility for the child. Custodial responsibility is defined in §2.03(3). The custodial arrangements should include either a schedule for each parent's access to the child or a method for determining such a schedule, with sufficient specificity that the court or third-party decisionmaker can enforce the order if necessary. A method may involve decisionmaking by a third party or another nonjudicial mechanism for dispute resolution. See also Comment g and §2.10. An order for "reasonable" access is not specific enough unless a method is specified for interpreting the provision in the event of future disputes.**

f. Order allocating decisionmaking responsibility. **Paragraph (5)(b) requires an allocation of decisionmaking responsibility relating to significant matters the parents or the court reasonably anticipate arising with respect to the child, such as the child's health and education. Limits on the court's authority to settle disputes concerning a child's religious upbringing are addressed in §2.09 and §2.12. Matters not covered by §2.09 constitute day-to-day decisionmaking and follow custodial responsibility. See §2.09(3). . . .**

Not all potential issues of decisionmaking responsibility must be resolved in the parenting plan. Some assessment must be made of those likely to arise, which should be resolved, and those that are not likely to arise. Efforts to resolve detailed hypothetical questions in advance may provoke unnecessary parental conflict. . . . The parents, of course, are free to settle any issues they wish on their own, in a jointly submitted parenting plan. A court, however, should not address potentially inflammatory issues that appear unlikely to arise. It may also defer unresolved issues that may arise to a mechanism for dispute resolution specified in the parenting plan. See Paragraph (5)(c) and §2.10.

g. Provisions for resolving future disputes. **Paragraph (5)(c) requires that a parenting plan address how disputes that may arise under the plan will be resolved. Such provisions should minimize the need for future judicial involvement. They may entail mediation or a designated arbitrator or decisionmaker who has the authority, when the parents disagree, to assess a child's circumstances and resolve the disagreement. Such provisions may also provide a mechanism for periodic review of the child's circumstances to anticipate and prevent future disputes. Any procedure for dispute resolution is subject to the limits set forth in §2.07 and §2.10, including those relating to judicial review.**

h. Discretionary provisions relating to relocation of one of the parents. **Paragraph (6) gives the court discretion to anticipate and resolve future disputes relating to the relocation of one of the parents. These provisions can either set forth in advance the consequences of a relocation or require a procedure to be followed in the event of a relocation.**

If a plan does not resolve matters relating to a parent's relocation, these matters must be resolved under 2.17, which provides a default rule. Provisions relating to relocation, like any other provisions of the parenting plan, are subject to modification under the rules set forth in §§2.15 and 2.16. . . .

§2.06 Parental Agreements

(1) The court should order provisions of a parenting plan agreed to by the parents, unless the agreement

(a) is not knowing or voluntary, or

(b) would be harmful to the child.

(2) The court, on any basis it deems sufficient, may conduct an evidentiary hearing to determine whether there is a factual basis under Paragraph (1) to find that the court should not be bound by an agreement. If credible information is presented to the court that child abuse as defined by state law or domestic violence as defined by §2.03(7) has occurred, the court should hold a hearing and, if the court determines that child abuse or domestic violence has occurred, it should order appropriate protective measures under §2.11.

(3) If the court rejects an agreement, in whole or in part, under the standards set forth in Paragraph (1), it should allow the parents the opportunity to negotiate another agreement.

Comment

a. Deference to private agreements. **The law in most jurisdictions grants courts, as part of their *parens patriae* authority, the authority to review a private agreement at divorce to determine whether it serves the child's interests. This section takes a more deferential view toward an agreement parents make about their children, requiring the court to adopt an agreement to which the parents have agreed at the time of the hearing, except when the agreement is not knowing or voluntary or when it would harm the child.**

This section, like §7.09, is subject to standard contract-law principles not inconsistent with the section. Most of the principles addressing basic issues of contract formation, such as the capacity of the parties to contract, are not specifically addressed in these sections and thus must be derived from other applicable law.

This section does not govern agreements made during or before marriage, although such agreements may sometimes be relevant to an allocation of custodial and decisionmaking responsibility. See §§2.08(1)(e) and 2.09(1)(e).

The approach to parental agreements taken in these Principles assumes that courts have neither the time nor the resources to give meaningful review to all parental agreements. Even if greater time and resources were available, court review is unlikely to uncover concrete evidence that the agreement is not in the interests of the child, particularly in the face of a united front by the parents, or to lead to a better agreement than the agreement the parents have reached on their own. This section also assumes that a plan to which parents agree is more likely to succeed than one that has been ordered by the court over the objection of one or both parents.

The obligation to defer to parental agreements applies whether the agreement covers all matters to be resolved between the parents or only some of them. If the court finds part, or the whole, of the agreement to be unacceptable under the Paragraph (1) standards, Paragraph (3) requires the court to allow parents an opportunity to renegotiate the agreement. . . .

b. When the agreement is not knowing or voluntary. **Contract law requires mutual assent to an agreement for it to be enforceable. Requirements of knowing and voluntary consent are viewed more strictly in the family-law setting than in the commercial context because of the greater opportunities that tend to exist in the family-dissolution setting for manipulation, advantage taking, and coercion. Although this section takes a more deferential stance toward parental agreements than is generally taken under prevailing law, a court still may determine that the agreement should not be enforced because the parties failed to consent to it. . . .**

c. Harm to the child. **The court also should not defer to a parental agreement if it finds that the agreement is harmful to the child. See Paragraph (1)(b). This standard is different from traditional law which, as a formal matter at least, expects courts in every case to determine affirmatively if an agreement is in the child's best interests.**

This section does not rule out any particular type of agreement as per se harmful. Most problematic in principle is one parent's waiver of the other parent's child-support obligation, in exchange for the latter agreeing not to seek custodial access to the child. Agreements involving child support are subject to the Principles set forth in Chapter 3, which do not allow the approval of an agreement if it provides for substantially less child support than would otherwise be awarded, unless the court determines that the child-support terms are consistent with the interests of the child. . . .

Previous abuse by a parent to whom a significant amount of custodial responsibility has been allocated in the agreement is another circumstance that may lead a court to conclude that the agreement would be harmful to the child. . . .

§2.07 Court-ordered services

(1) The court may inform the parents, or require them to be informed, about any of the following:

(a) how to prepare a parenting plan;

(b) the impact of family dissolution on children and how the needs of children facing family dissolution can best be met;

(c) the impact of conflict and domestic violence on children, and the availability of resources for addressing these issues;

(d) mediation or other nonjudicial procedures designed to help them reach agreement.

(2) A mediator should screen for domestic violence and for other conditions or circumstances that may impede a party's capacity to participate in the mediation process. If there is credible evidence of such circumstances, the mediation should not occur, unless reasonable steps are taken both

(a) to ensure meaningful consent of each party to participate in the mediation and to any results reached through the mediation process; and

(b) to protect the safety of the victim.

(3) The court should not compel any services under Paragraph (1) that would require a parent to have a face-to-face meeting with the other parent.

(4) A mediator should not be allowed to make a recommendation to the court in a case in which the mediator has provided mediation services.

(5) A mediator should not be allowed to reveal information that a parent has disclosed during mediation under a reasonable expectation of confidentiality, except such information as is necessary to factfinding under §2.06 or §2.11.

(6) A court should be prohibited from ordering services authorized under Paragraph (1) unless available at no cost or at a cost that is reasonable in light of the financial circumstances of each parent. When one parent' ability to pay for such services is significantly greater than the other', the court should have discretion to order that parent to pay some or all of the expenses of the other.

§2.08 Allocation of custodial responsibility

(1) Unless otherwise resolved by agreement of the parents under §2.06, the court should allocate custodial responsibility so that the proportion of custodial time the child spends with each parent approximates the proportion of time each parent spent performing caretaking functions for the child prior to the parents'separation or, if the parents never lived together, before the filing of the action, except to the extent required under §2.11 or necessary to achieve one or more of the following objectives:

(a) to permit the child to have a relationship with each parent which, in the case of a legal parent or a parent by estoppel who has performed a reasonable share of parenting functions, should be not less than a presumptive amount of custodial time set by a uniform rule of statewide application;

(b) to accommodate the firm and reasonable preferences of a child who has reached a specific age, set by a uniform rule of statewide application;

(c) to keep siblings together when the court finds that doing so is necessary to their welfare;

(d) to protect the child' welfare when the presumptive allocation under this section would harm the child because of a gross disparity in the quality of the emotional attachment between each parent and the child or in each parent's demonstrated ability or availability to meet the child's needs;

(e) to take into account any prior agreement, other than one under §2.06, that would be appropriate to consider in light of the circumstances as a whole, including the reasonable expectations of the parties, the extent to which they could have reasonably anticipated the events that occurred and their significance, and the interests of the child;

(f) to avoid an allocation of custodial responsibility that would be extremely impractical or that would interfere substantially with the child' need for stability in light of economic, physical, or other circumstances, including the distance between the parents' residences, the cost and difficulty of transporting the child, each parent's and the child's daily schedules, and the ability of the parents to cooperate in the arrangement;

(g) to apply the Principles set forth in §2.17(4) if one parent relocates or proposes to relocate at a distance that will impair the ability of a parent to exercise the presumptive amount of custodial responsibility under this section;

(h) to avoid substantial and almost certain harm to the child.

(2) In determining the proportion of caretaking functions each parent previously performed for the child under Paragraph (1), the court should not consider the division of functions arising from temporary arrangements after the parents'separation, whether those arrangements are consensual or by court order. The court may take into account information relating to the temporary arrangements in determining other issues under this section.

(3) If the court is unable to allocate custodial responsibility under Paragraph (1) because there is no history of past performance of caretaking functions, as in the case of a newborn, or because the history does not establish a sufficiently clear pattern of caretaking, the court should allocate custodial responsibility based on the child's best interests, taking into account the factors and considerations that are set forth in this Chapter, preserving to the extent possible this section's priority on the share of past caretaking functions each parent performed.

(4) In determining how to schedule the custodial time allocated to each parent, the court should take account of economic, physical, and other practical circumstances, such as those listed in Paragraph (1)(f).

Comment

a. In general. **This section states the criteria for allocating custodial responsibility between parents when they have not reached their own agreement about this allocation. These criteria also establish** the bargaining context for parents seeking agreement.

Custodial responsibility refers to physical control of and access to the child, or what traditionally has been called child custody. See §2.03(3). This term refers to the child's living arrangements, including with whom the child lives and when, and any periods of time during which another person is scheduled by the court to have caretaking responsibility for the child.

Paragraph (1) establishes the general rule that the proportion of custodial responsibility allocated each parent should approximate the proportion of caretaking functions each parent exercised prior to their separation or, if they never lived together, prior to the filing of the action. The exceptions set forth in this section are, for the most part, quite specific. First, when a parent had a caretaking role so minimal that the allocation based on past caretaking would not allow for sufficient contact for that parent to have a meaningful relationsehip with the child, Paragraph (1)(a) requires the court to order an allocation sufficient to allow such a relationship. In the case of a parent who has exercised a reasonable share of parenting functions, which includes such things as providing financial support for the child, see §2.03(6), the amount of this allocation is determined according to presumptive guidelines, established in a uniform rule of statewide application.

Second, under Paragraph (1)(b), the court should accommodate the firm preferences of a child who has reached a specific age. This age should be set forth in a uniform rule of statewide application.

Third, under Paragraph (1)(c), the court should depart from the allocation of custodial responsibility based on past caretaking when keeping the child's siblings together is necessary for their welfare.

Fourth, Paragraph (1)(d) requires a departure from the allocation based on past caretaking to protect the child's welfare when there is a gross disparity in the quality of the emotional attachments between each parent and the child or in each parent's demonstrated ability or availability to meet a child's needs.

Fifth, Paragraph (1)(e) requires a court to give effect to a prior agreement of the parents when the circumstances as a whole, including the reasonable expectations of the parents and the interests of the child, make it appropriate to do so.

Sixth, Paragraph (1)(f) requires the court to take into account the impracticality, or the impact on the child's stability, of various practical circumstances, including the parents' financial resources, the location of their residences, their, schedules and the schedule of the child, and their ability to cooperate.

Seventh, Paragraph (1)(g) provides for a departure from the past caretaking, standard that is made necessary by a parent's actual or pending relocation, in accordance with the considerations relevant to modifications of a parenting plan when a parent relocates, which are set forth in §2.17.

All provisions in this section are subject to the requirements of §2.11, requiring limitations to protect the child and the child's parent from domestic violence and other serious parental failures.

Paragraph (2) limits the weight to be given to temporary custodial arrangement. Evidence of the adjustment of the child or the parent to a temporary arrangement may be considered in resolving some issues relevant to the child's welfare, but the proportion of caretaking functions assumed by each parent during this period is not taken into account in determining what share of past caretaking functions each parent performed under Paragraph (1).

In some cases, custodial responsibility cannot be allocated under Paragraph (1). The prior division of caretaking functions does not provide a basis for an allocation under Paragraph (1) if, for example, parents who equally shared past caretaking functions agree that the child should live primarily with one parent but are unable to agree who should be that parent. The factor will also be inapplicable in cases involving newborns, or when caretaking patterns have changed too significantly or too often over time. See also Paragraph (1)(f) and §2.17(4)(c). In such cases, Paragraph (3) provides that the court make the allocation decision in accordance with the traditional, more open-ended best interests-of-the-child test. All of the factors referred to in this section may be relevant to this test and, in applying the test, the priority on the past division caretaking functions should be preserved to the extent possible.

Once the parents' respective shares of custodial responsibility have been established, Paragraph (4) provides for consideration of practical factors in determining the scheduling of custodial time.

b. Rationale for reliance on past caretaking. The ideal standard for determining a child's custodial arrangements is one that both yields predictable and easily adjudicated results and also consistently serves the child's best interests. While the best-interests-of-the-child test may appear well suited to this objective, the test is too subjective to produce predictable results. Its unpredictability encourages strategic bargaining and prolonged litigation. The indeterminacy of the test also draws the court into comparisons between parenting styles and values that are matters of parental autonomy not appropriate for judicial resolution. See §2.02, Comment *c*.

The allocation of custodial responsibility presumed in Paragraph (1) yields more predictable and more easily adjudicated results, thereby advancing the best interests of children in most cases without infringing on parental autonomy. It assumes that the division of past caretaking functions correlates well with other factors associated with the child's best interests, such as the quality of each parent's emotional attachment to the child and the parents' respective parenting abilities. It requires factfinding that is less likely than the traditional best-interests test to require expert testimony about such matters as the child's emotional state or developmental needs, the parents' relative abilities, and the strength of their emotional relationships to the child. Avoiding expert testimony is desirable because such testimony, within an adversarial context, tends to focus on the weaknesses of each parent and thus undermines the spirit of cooperation and compromise necessary to successful post-divorce custodial arrangements; therapists are better used in the divorce context to assist parents in making plans to deal constructively with each other and their children at separation.

Some parents will disagree over how caretaking roles were previously divided, making the past division of caretaking functions itself a potential litigation issue. The difficulties in applying the standard, however, must be evaluated in light of the available alternatives. While each parent's share of past caretaking will in some cases be disputed, these functions encompass specific tasks and responsibilities about which concrete evidence is available and thus offer greater determinacy than more qualitative standards, such as parental competence, the strength of the parent-child emotional bond or — as the general standard simply puts it — the child's best interests. These qualitative criteria are future-oriented and highly subjective, whereas how the parents divided caretaking responsibilities in the past is a concrete question of historical fact, like other questions courts are accustomed to resolving.

Fashioning arrangements based on patterns of past caretaking is calculated to preserve the greatest degree of stability in the child's life. This is not to say that the child's life will stay the same after separation. Before separation, caretaking functions are often exercised by the parents together, or at frequently interspersed intervals. These functions must be handled differently once the parents live separately. In addition, the parents' separation may make it necessary for them to change their work schedules and rearrange other obligations. The inevitability of such changes, however, makes it all the more desirable that there be stability as to those matters the court can affect, especially the child's relationships with the primary caretaker.

The reliance on past caretaking is also designed to correspond reasonably parties' actual expectations, sometimes better than their own stated at divorce. This is because expectations and preferences are often at divorce by feelings of loss, anxiety, guilt, and anger — feelings that tend not only to cloud a parent's judgment and ability to make decisions on behalf of the child, but also to exaggerate the amount of responsibility a parent wants to assume for a child, or the objections he or she has to the other parent's level of involvement in the child's life. The way the parents chose to divide responsibility when the family lived together anchors the negotiations in their own lived experience rather than in unrealistic or emotion-based aspirations about the future. . . .

c. Measuring past caretaking functions. The relevant shares of past caretaking functions to be measured under this section are those exercised while the parents lived together or, if they never lived together, before the filing of the action. The standard does not incorporate other parenting functions that are not caretaking functions. See §2.03(5) and (6). It also does not encompass functions performed after their separation, unless the parents have otherwise agreed. See §2.08(2) and Comment *m*.

A parent's proportion of past caretaking functions is measured primarily by the time spent performing the functions. Any different measure, even if it is otherwise reasonable, would only reintroduce the kinds of qualitative disputes that the caretaking-functions factor is intended to reduce. Significant disparities in the level of initiative and investment between the parents would be appropriate only when there is a demonstrated disparity in parenting abilities that is so substantial that consideration of it is required to prevent harm to the child's welfare. See Paragraph (1)(d) and Comment *h*.

In the majority of cases, only a rough approximation of each parent's share of past caretaking is necessary. For example, when a "traditional" homemaker parent has spent a much larger proportion of time caring for the child than the other, that parent ordinarily will be allocated primary custodial responsibility for the child subject only to the presumptive allocation of custodial time to the other parent necessary to satisfy Paragraph (1)(a). See Comment *e*. If this allocation exceeds the parent's share of past caretaking responsibilities, there is no reason for him or her to litigate those shares more precisely.

Parents who shared responsibility for their child more or less equally also are unlikely to have reason to dispute the exact proportions of time each parent spent performing caretaking functions, since the more nearly equal past caretaking has been, the more the practical factors relating to work schedules and the location of the parents' respective homes and school determine the details of the arrangements. See Paragraphs (1)(f) and (4); §2.20.

While a precise accounting of the responsibilities assumed for caretaking functions is often not required, when measurements are necessary they should be based on the parents' actual performance of caretaking functions. They should not be based on unsupported assumptions, especially those arising from a parent's sex or work status. . . .

The most difficult circumstance for ascertaining the parents' respective shares of past caretaking functions is when the division of caretaking functions has changed substantially over time. When an arrangement that lasted a long time is followed by a more recent arrangement of much shorter duration, the longer arrangement usually warrants priority; a different result would give too little consideration to the caretaking functions likely to have been most significant to the child, and would provide an incentive for parents to engage in strategic behavior close in time to, and in anticipation of, a separation. By the same token, a substantial change in caretaking patterns that has endured for a significant period ordinarily should take precedence over a long-past caretaking pattern. It would be difficult to reduce these guidelines to a mathematical formula, given the variety of circumstances such guidelines would have to address, including the child's age, the relative lengths of each prior caretaking arrangement, and the relative involvement of each parent in caretaking. When changes over time have been sufficiently complex or difficult to measure, the court must allocate custodial responsibility without the aid of the caretaking functions factor. See Paragraph (3) and Comment *n*.

Sometimes there is no history of past performance of caretaking functions, as is the case with a newborn child. In such a case, it is not possible to allocate custodial responsibility according to past practices, and the dispute must be resolved under the best-interests test. See Paragraph (3). . . .

f. Child's preferences. **Giving great weight to the preferences of a child at his or her parents' divorce can raise significant difficulties. Children may feel responsible for the outcome of a custody dispute if they believe they have participated in its resolution, whatever that might be. Children whose preferences are followed may feel responsible for the consequences, whether that be their own unhappiness or that of a parent. Children whose preferences are not followed may come to believe that the court considered them unimportant, or ineffective.**

In addition, the child's preference can be unreliable, short-sighted or irrational. It can also be difficult to ascertain, as the child may have conflicted feelings, or be subject to pressure by one or both parents, or wish to mislead the interviewer. . . .

For these reasons, Paragraph (1)(b) provides for a departure from the division of custodial time otherwise warranted by the past division of caretaking functions only to accommodate the preferences of a child who has attained a specified, mature age, and only when the child's preferences are firm and within the bounds of reason. This accommodation assumes that the preferences of older children are more likely to conform to their best interests than those of younger children, and thus that these preferences may be appropriate to consider along with the past caretaking roles of the parents. This qualification to the past caretaking standard also acknowledges that it is often unrealistic to expect a court-ordered arrangement to work well when an older child is firmly opposed to it.

So that the rule can be easily administered, the age at which a child's preferences should matter under Paragraph (1)(b) should be set forth in a uniform rule in each jurisdiction. Since maturity develops gradually rather than all at once upon attaining a certain age, no single age will either identify all mature minors or exclude all immature ones. The rule-maker could reasonably choose the age of 11, 12, 13, or even 14 as the appropriate age, in accord with its views about maturity and childhood.

When a child attains the age specified by the uniform state rule at a time after a parenting plan has been ordered, the original plan may be later modified to accommodate the child's firm and reasonable preferences. This modification can be ordered under §2.16(2)(c), without meeting the more rigorous standards of §2.15.

The preferences of children who do not meet the age specified in the rule of statewide application are not relevant in applying Paragraph (1). When custodial responsibility is not allocated under Paragraph (1), however, the court must resort to the more open-ended best-interests-of-the-child test, under Paragraph (3). . . . Under this test, even the preferences of young children may provide evidence of the child's best interests, as good as other evidence relevant under this standard. The weight to be given these preferences should depend on indicators of its reliability, including the child's age and maturity level, and the quality of the reasons given for it.

Generally speaking, the preferences of a child, even when relevant, should not be directly solicited. The risks of involving children in disputes for which they may feel personally responsible may be diminished by ascertaining their preferences indirectly. . . . Paragraph (1)(b) assumes that in most cases, children with firm preferences will find a way to make those preferences known without significant effort by those involved in the case.

j. When otherwise appropriate allocation of custodial responsibility would be extremely impractical or would substantially interfere with child's need for stability. **Some custodial arrangements that would otherwise be appropriate under Paragraph (1) may be extremely impractical, or substantially interfere with a child's needed stability. Custodial arrangements involving substantially equal amounts of custodial responsibility and no primary custodial home pose particular challenges. When the difficulties of making an arrangement consistent with past caretaking patterns are so substantial as to compromise the child's welfare,**

Paragraph (1)(f) provides for departure from the otherwise appropriate arrangement.

The practical circumstances to be accounted for under Paragraph (1)(f) include the location of the parents' residences, as well as their daily schedules, flexibility, and ability to manage a particular arrangement without excessive conflict. In addition, the parents' economic circumstances, while not otherwise relevant to how custodial responsibility is allocated (see §§2.12(1)(f) and 2.15(3)(a)), are relevant in determining whether a particular custodial arrangement is feasible. Factors relating to the child, including his or her daily schedule, activities, and individual needs, also affect the practicality of a custodial arrangement. . . .

§2.09 Allocation of significant decisionmaking responsibility

(1) Unless otherwise resolved by agreement of the parents under §2.06, the court should allocate responsibility for making significant life decisions on behalf of the child, including decisions regarding the child's education and health care, to one parent or to two parents jointly, in accordance with the child's best interests, in light of the following:

(a) the allocation of custodial responsibility under §2.08;

(b) the level of each parent's participation in past decisionmaking on behalf of the child;

(c) the wishes of the parents;

(d) the level of ability and cooperation the parents have demonstrated in past decisionmaking on behalf of the child;

(e) a prior agreement, other than one agreed to under §2.06, that would be appropriate to consider under the circumstances as a whole including the reasonable expectations of the parents and the interests of the child;

(f) the existence of any limiting factors, as set forth in §2.11.

(2) The court should presume that an allocation of decisionmaking responsibility jointly to each legal parent or parent by estoppel who has been exercising a reasonable share of parenting functions is in the child's best interests. The presumption is overcome if there is a history of domestic violence or child abuse, or if it is shown that joint allocation of decisionmaking responsibility is not in the child's best interests.

(3) Unless otherwise provided or agreed by the parents, a parent should have sole responsibility for day-to-day decisions for the child while the child is in that parent's custodial care and control, including emergency decisions affecting the health and safety of the child.

(4) Even if not allocated decisionmaking responsibility under this section, any legal parent and any parent by estoppel should have access to the child's school and health-care records to which legal parents have access by other law, except insofar as access is not in the best interests of the child or when the provision of such information might endanger an individual who has been the victim of child abuse or domestic violence.

§2.10 Criteria for parenting plan — dispute resolution

(1) Unless otherwise resolved by agreement of the parents under §2.06, and subject to the limitations set forth in §2.07, the court should include in the parenting plan a process for resolving future disputes that will serve the child's best interests in light of the following:

(a) the parents' present wishes regarding future dispute resolution;

(b) circumstances, including but not limited to financial circumstances, that may affect the parents' ability to participate in a prescribed process for dispute resolution;

(c) the existence of any limiting factor set forth in §2.11.

(2) The court may order a nonjudicial process of dispute resolution, by designating with particularity the person or organization to conduct the process or the method for selecting such a person or organization.

(3) The disposition of a dispute through a nonjudicial process of dispute resolution that was ordered by the court without prior parental agreement is subject to de novo judicial review. However, if the parents have agreed in a parenting plan or by agreement thereafter to a binding resolution of future disputes by nonjudicial process, a decision resulting from such process is binding upon the parents, unless the court finds it will result in harm to the child or is the result of fraud, misconduct, corruption, or other serious irregularity in the dispute-resolution process.

§2.11 Criteria for parenting plan — limiting factors

(1) If either of the parents so requests, or upon receipt of credible information that such conduct has occurred, the court should determine promptly whether a parent who would otherwise be allocated responsibility under a parenting plan has done any of the following:

(a) abused, neglected, or abandoned a child, as defined by state law;

(b) inflicted domestic violence, or allowed another to inflict domestic violence, as defined in §2.03(7);

(c) abused drugs, alcohol, or another substance in a way that interferes with the parent's ability to perform caretaking functions;

(d) interfered persistently with the other parent's access to the child, except in the case of actions taken with a reasonable, good-faith belief that they are necessary to protect the safety of the child or the interfering parent or another family member, pending adjudication of the facts underlying that belief which the interfering parent should be required to initiate as soon as reasonably possible.

(2) If a parent is found to have engaged in any activity specified by Paragraph (1), the court should impose limits that are reasonably calculated to protect the child, child's parent, or other member of the household from harm. The limitations available to the court to consider include, but are not restricted to, the following:

(a) an adjustment, including a reduction or the elimination, of the custodial responsibility of a parent;

(b) supervision of the custodial time between a parent and the child;

(c) exchange of the child between parents through an intermediary, or in a protected setting;

(d) restraints on a parent's communication with or proximity to the other parent or the child;

(e) a requirement that a parent abstain from possession or consumption of alcohol or nonprescribed drugs while exercising custodial responsibility and within a specified period immediately preceding such exercise;

(f) denial of overnight custodial responsibility;

(g) restrictions on the presence of specific persons while a parent is with the child;

(h) a requirement that a parent post a bond to secure return of the child following a period in which the parent is exercising custodial responsibility or to secure other performance required by the court;

(i) a requirement that a parent complete a treatment program for perpetrators of domestic violence, for drug or alcohol abuse, or for other behavior addressed in this section;

(j) any other constraints or conditions that the court deems necessary to provide for the safety of the child, a child's parent, or any other person whose safety immediately affects the child's welfare.

(3) If a parent is found to have engaged in any activity specified in Paragraph (1), the court should not allocate custodial responsibility or decisionmaking responsibility to that parent without making special written findings under §1.02 that the child, other parent, or other household member can be adequately protected from harm by the limits imposed under Paragraph (2). A parent found to have engaged in the behavior specified in Paragraph (1) should have the burden of proving that an allocation of custodial responsibility or decisionmaking responsibility to that parent will not endanger the child, other parent, or other household member.

§2.12 Criteria for parenting plan — prohibited factors

(1) In issuing orders under this Chapter, the court should not consider any of the following factors:

(a) the race or ethnicity of the child, a parent, or other member of the household;

(b) the sex of a parent or the child;

(c) the religious practices of a parent or the child, except to the minimum degree necessary to protect the child from severe and almost certain harm or to protect the child's ability to practice a religion that has been a significant part of the child's life;

(d) the sexual orientation of a parent;

(e) the extramarital sexual conduct of a parent, except upon a showing that it causes harm to the child;

(f) the parents' relative earning capacities or financial circumstances, except the court may take account of the degree to which the combined financial resources of the parents set practical limits on the custodial arrangements.

(2) Nothing in this section should preclude the court's consideration of a parent's ability to care for the child, including meeting the child's needs for a positive self-image.

Comment

a. In general. **This section prohibits decisionmaking based on race, ethnicity, sex, religion, sexual orientation, extramarital sexual conduct, or the parents' financial circumstances, except in very limited circumstances. Historically, courts have sometimes taken these factors into account in custody determinations. Insofar as the decision rules of the Chapter rely on concrete standards to which these prohibited factors are irrelevant, the section is redundant. See, e.g., §2.08(1) and §2.17(4)(a). The best-interests test has been retained, however, in circumstances in which these concrete standards are inappropriate, or cannot be applied. See, e.g., §2.08(3) and §2.17(4)(b) and (c). Section 2.12 ensures that in applying these more open-ended standards, decisionmaking is not based on any of the prohibited factors.**

All stereotypes should be avoided in decisionmaking under this Chapter, including those based on many factors not covered by this section such as disability, age, intelligence level, personality, and appearance. The section singles out race, ethnicity, sex, religion, sexual orientation, extramarital conduct, and financial circumstances because these factors historically have created the most troublesome distortions in judgments about what is best for a child, and thus require the greatest vigilance to avoid.

The section does not preclude consideration of a parent's ability to meet a child's needs, which is relevant to many determinations under this Chapter. See, e.g., §2.08(1)(d) and §2.08(3). A child's needs may include such factors as positive self-esteem and a healthy sense of identity, which may sometimes relate to the child's race, ethnicity, sex, religion, or sexual orientation. In cases in which matters of this sort would otherwise be relevant under the Chapter, Paragraph (2) clarifies that the section does not preclude their consideration.

b. Race and ethnicity. **The Supreme Court has held that the Equal Protection Clause of the Fourteenth Amendment to the U.S. Constitution prohibits use of a parent's race as a determinative factor in custody decisions. Palmore v. Sidoti, 466 U.S. 429 (1984). *Palmore* concerned a motion for a change in custody brought by a father who claimed that his daughter would be psychologically damaged and stigmatized by the remarriage of her white custodial mother to a black man. The Supreme Court acknowledged the "risk that a child living with a stepparent of a different race may be subject to a variety of pressures and stresses not present if the child were living with parents of the same racial or ethnic origin," 466 U.S. at 433. Nonetheless, the Court held that "private biases and the possible injury they might inflict" are not permissible considerations. Id. "Private biases may be outside the reach of the law, but the law cannot, directly or indirectly, give them effect." Id.**

While racial prejudice has no place in custody decisions, many believe that a child's positive sense of his or her racial identity depends on being raised by a parent of the same race. It is especially tempting to assume that a child who is a member of a stigmatized race is best off when raised by a parent with the same racial identity.

In accordance with this assumption, some states have allowed or even preferred race matching in foster-care and adoption placements. Whether or not a race-based preference is appropriate in these contexts, this section states the principle that race has no appropriate part to play in resolving disputes between the parents of a biracial child. A child shares the race of each biological parent. The very act of identifying a child with the race of one parent—usually the one belonging to the more stigmatized race—contributes to the racial subordination of which it is a response. Moreover, each parent can contribute to a child's sense of a positive racial identity, regardless of his or her own racial identity, and regardless of whether he or she has primary custodial responsibility. In any event, it cannot be assumed that the parent whose racial identity is most closely identified with that of the child is better suited to nurturing a healthy racial identity than the other parent.

The prohibition of consideration of race does not preclude consideration of a parent's greater capacity to nurture a child's self-esteem, including a positive, racial identity. See Paragraph (2). Capacity to meet a child's needs that are related to his or her race does not concern race, in the prohibited sense, but a parent's abilities, which are relevant under §2.08(1)(d) and §2.08(3). A higher capacity for nurturing a child's self-esteem, however, is not established merely by showing the closest racial identity with the child. . . .

c. Sex. Attitudes about appropriate gender roles and differences between men and women have been pervasive in family law. In 19th-century England, fathers had an absolute right to the custody and earnings of their children. While fathers' rights were paramount in colonial America, by the 19th century custody awards were justified in accordance with the child's best interests. This focus for a time favored the innocent party to a divorce but gradually led to presumptions and preferences favoring mothers, especially mothers of young children.

The tender-years presumption and maternal-preference rules have been eliminated almost entirely from state statutes, but implicit bias is still sometimes evident. The assumption that mothers do, and should, provide most of the care of children leads to a custody bias against fathers in favor of mothers. At the same time, an implicit maternal bias also gives rise to expectations about mothers that, when disappointed, may cause women to be judged more negatively than fathers for the same conduct, and fathers to be overly rewarded for parenting conduct that exceeds the rather modest expectations set for them.

Paragraph (1)(b) prohibits consideration of the sex of the parent or the child as a general rule. It disallows both explicit discrimination based on sex, and the implicit evaluation of the behaviors and abilities of mothers and fathers according to different sets of expectations based on their sex. It provides that neither parent should be penalized for acting according to, or outside of, traditional gender-role expectations. For example, a mother who works and puts her child in day care should not be evaluated as putting her career above the welfare of her children when a father who works while his children are in day care is considered a responsible provider. Likewise, a mother who has an extramarital affair should not be deemed less fit than a father who has such an affair; and a mother should not be judged more negatively because she is easily "overwrought," while a father's temper is overlooked as ordinary or understandable. The prohibition against sex-based determination in Paragraph (1)(b) requires courts to be on guard against these types of stereotype-based judgments.

Some people believe that the healthy development of a child's gender identity is aided by a strong relationship with the same-sex parent, who can provide a model for the child's own behavior and self-definition. Even if it were shown that the parent of the same sex as the child had something unique to offer the child, however, sex is not an appropriate basis for the allocation of custodial responsibility for the child. First, sensitivity to the child's emotional needs has no inevitable relationship to the sex of the parent; some daughters have closer and healthier relationships to their fathers and some sons relate better to their mothers. Second, having a positive influence on a child is not the exclusive province of the parent with whom the child primarily lives. A father can influence and direct his son even if the child lives most of the time with his mother; a mother, likewise, can guide her daughter's maturation process even if she lives primarily with her father. Finally, the sex-modeling rationale presupposes a set of attitudes that are themselves, to some significant extent, the product of gender role stereotyping. While parents themselves are free to engrain gender-role stereotypes, the state is not.

Paragraph (1)(b) does not preclude consideration of a parent's ability to meet a child's needs, which might relate to her sense of gender identity and self-image. See Paragraph (2). The parent's sex, however, is not relevant in determining this ability. . . .

d. Religion. Paragraph (1)(c) prohibits decisionmaking based on the religious practices of the child or parent, except to the minimum degree necessary to protect a child from severe and almost certain harm, or to protect the child's ability to practice a religion to which the child has made a substantial commitment. This prohibition recognizes the constitutional importance of an individual's ability to freely exercise his or her religion, which combines with a parent's constitutionally protected interest in child-rearing to form a strong barrier to judicial consideration of religion in custody decisions. Under this section, custodial and decisionmaking responsibility for the child ordinarily will be allocated without regard to a parent's religion or religious practices.

The nature of religious faith makes it difficult to apply the exception for severe and almost certain harm to the child. A religious practice considered harmful by one parent may be considered necessary to eternal salvation by the other parent. A determination that one parent's religious practices will harm a child unavoidably intrudes on that parent's religious exercise. Nonetheless, harm that is sufficiently clear, significant, and certain should not be ignored altogether because of the presence of religious considerations. In deciding whether the potential harm is significant and certain enough, physical harm that would be recognized by a state's abuse and neglect statutes would ordinarily suffice, as would substantial interference with the relationship between the child and the other parent.

The issue of harm can arise when each parent wishes to expose the child to a different, conflicting religion. One parent may wish to limit the religious practices of the other parent when that parent is with the child, out of concern that those practices are distressing to the child, perhaps even inhibiting the child's ability to develop a coherent religious perspective. Paragraph (1)(c) precludes such limits. The confusion that exposure to different, even conflicting, religions can be expected to cause in some children is a harm, like many others (including any harm to children when married parents attempt to raise their children in two different religions), as to which the law is ill-equipped to save children. Taking this confusion into account would require courts to make comparative judgments between religions, which the U.S. Constitution prohibits. It would also require setting enforceable limits on a parent's religious practices when with the child. The approach taken by Paragraph (1)(c) reflects a realism about what courts can be expected to accomplish with respect to the spiritual health of children when the parents disagree about a child's religious upbringing.

Some parents anticipate disputes over the religious upbringing of their children by agreement at the time of divorce. Generally, parental agreements made in the context of a separation are favored by these Principles. See §2.06. Separation agreements concerning religion raise special enforcement problems that warrant special caution. In particular, First Amendment considerations prohibit courts from becoming entangled in adjudications concerning compliance with religious rules, or unduly interfering with the parent's free-exercise rights. Courts should not enforce contract provisions requiring a parent to follow through on a contractual obligation to engage, or forbear from engaging, in a religious practice, those necessitating interpretation of the requirements of a particular religion, or those whose obligations cannot be readily and objectively determined by the court without unnecessary entanglement in religious matters or intrusion into a parent's free-exercise rights.

When the agreement was made outside the setting of a divorce, it is not enforceable as such, although it may be taken into account when appropriate in light of the circumstances as a whole, including the reasonable expectations of the parents and the interests of the child-subject to the cautions listed above. See §2.08(1)(e) . . . ; §2.09(1)(e). . . .

The exception in Paragraph (1)(c) for children who have made a substantial commitment to the practice of a particular religion is intended to apply to those children who have experienced an upbringing for a substantial period in a particular religious tradition and have developed their own identity in, or allegiance to, that religion. The section recognizes that at some point in the development of a religious identity, a child may acquire his or her own interest in religious freedom that warrants consideration along with the parents' interests. . . .

e. Sexual orientation. Consideration of a parent's sexual orientation is prohibited by Paragraph (1)(d). Sexual orientation is a factor to which prejudicial attitudes and stereotypes historically have attached. While some raise moral objections to homosexuality, the scientific evidence has not established that homosexual parent is inferior as a parent. It has not been shown that a homosexual parent is more likely to molest his or her child, or that a child raised by a homosexual parent is less well adjusted. Given this, consideration of a parent's sexual orientation would amount to decisionmaking based on conjecture and stereotype.

It may be assumed that the societal prejudice that attends homosexuality can be a source of distress for the child of a homosexual parent. The degree of any stress, however, does not appear to depend upon the amount of custodial responsibility the parent is assigned. Moreover, it has not been shown that less contact with a homosexual parent makes coming to terms with that parent's sexual identity any easier. Consideration of homosexuality as a negative factor in how parental responsibility is allocated may even reinforce the shame and stigma of that status, making the child's acceptance of the parent more difficult. In any event, societal prejudice is generally not a legitimate basis for making custody decisions.

In some cases, a child's own homosexuality may be an important dimension of the child's experience, and the parent's ability to address that dimension may be significant to the child's welfare.

Paragraph (2) clarifies that consideration of this ability is not ruled out by this section. . . .

f. Extramarital sexual conduct. **Sexual misconduct has also been a factor on which courts in custody cases sometimes relied unduly. Paragraph (1)(e) prohibits consideration of extramarital sexual conduct by a parent, unless it is shown that the conduct causes harm to the child.**

In accordance with the general approach of this section against overreliance on factors that are grounded in prejudice and bias, Paragraph (1)(e) prohibits the court from presuming harm based on the extramarital relationship of a parent. Even a child's awareness of such a relationship, or dislike of the individual with whom a parent has developed an intimate relationship, should not justify inferences relating to the child's welfare or parental fitness; children cannot be protected from every source of unhappiness and unease. To prevent courts from exaggerating the significance of parental practices of which they disapprove, the section allows consideration of sexual misconduct only when there is a showing of harm. Specific harm must be shown, although the standard is not as rigorous as the severe and almost certain harm standard applied to restrictions on consideration of religious practices. See Paragraph (1)(c).

Paragraph (1)(e) applies equally to homosexual and heterosexual conduct. While a small number of states criminalize certain homosexual behaviors, these laws (like those criminalizing certain homosexual and heterosexual behaviors) are rarely enforced and do not authorize consequences relating to a parent's access to a child.

Even when sexual conduct may be considered because it is shown to be harmful to a child, this does not mean that the factor should be dispositive. In allocating custodial responsibility, for example, the parents' respective shares of past caretaking determine their shares of custodial time, unless one of the exceptions set forth in §2.08 applies. Even in cases in which the court is allocating custodial responsibility under the best-interests test, the priority on the past performance of caretaking functions is retained. See §2.08(3). Thus, in cases in which the caretaking functions exercised by one parent were more substantial than the other, that factor should still be the dominant consideration. . . .

g. Financial circumstances. **Few doubt that a child's welfare is affected by the amount of financial resources available to help raise the child. Given fair child-support rules, however, this factor should not be used as a basis for allocating custodial and decisionmaking responsibility for the child. Allocation of these responsibilities depends on qualitative factors, measured in the first instance in this Chapter through past performance of caretaking functions. Taking account of the parents' financial circumstances undermines the priority on actual caretaking patterns, tending to favor the parent with the greater investment in human capital and, correspondingly, to disfavor the parent who has made the heavier investment in caretaking.**

Paragraph (1)(f) prohibits consideration of disparities in the financial circumstances of the parents with one limited exception. The exception recognizes that in some circumstances the total financial resources of the parents place limits on the feasibility of alternative custodial arrangements, such as arrangements involving equal allocations of custodial time, or arrangements involving frequent long-distance travel. . .

Topic 3. Fact Finding

§2.13 Court-ordered investigation; appointment of guardian ad litem or lawyer for the child

(1) The court may order a written investigation or evaluation to assist it in determining any issue relevant to proceedings under this Chapter. The court should specify the scope of the investigation or evaluation and the authority of the investigator or evaluator.

(2) The court may appoint a guardian ad litem to represent the child's interests. The court should specify the terms of the appointment, including the guardian's role, duties, and scope of authority.

(3) The court may appoint a lawyer to represent the child if the child is competent to direct the terms of the representation and the court has a reasonable basis for finding that the appointment would be helpful in resolving the issues of the case. The court may also appoint a lawyer to represent the guardian ad litem appointed under Paragraph (2). The court should specify the terms of the appointment, including the lawyer's role, duties, and scope of authority.

(4) When substantial allegations of domestic violence as defined by §2.03(7) or child abuse or child neglect as defined by existing state law have been made or when there is credible information that domestic violence or child abuse or neglect has occurred, the court should order an investigation under Paragraph (1) or appoint a guardian ad litem or an attorney under Paragraph (2) or (3), unless the court is satisfied that the information adequate to evaluate the allegations will be secured without such an order or appointment.

(5) Subject to whatever restrictions on disclosure may exist under other state law or §2.09(4), the court may require the child, parent, or other person having information about the child or parent to provide information to a person or agency appointed under this section.

(6) A party should be allowed to cross-examine an investigator, evaluator, or guardian ad litem who submits a report, evidence, or recommendations to the court. A lawyer appointed under Paragraph (3) should not be a witness in the proceedings, except as allowed under standards applicable in other civil proceedings.

(7) Appointments, investigations, evaluations services, or tests should not be ordered under this section unless at no cost to the persons involved, or at a cost that is reasonable in light of the financial resources of the parents. When one parent's

ability to pay is significantly greater than the other's, the court should allocate the costs between them equitably.

Comment

a. In general. **There are three basic models of child representation. The factfinder model uses a neutral person or agency who investigates the child's circumstances and presents to the court facts and evaluations deemed relevant to the proceedings. The child-protection model uses an intermediary who furthers the child's interests through either factfinding, advocacy, or some combination of the two. The attorney-client model is based on an attorney-client relationship, with the child as client directing the terms of the representation by the lawyer.**

This section allows the court to act in accordance with any one of these three models. Paragraph (1) authorizes the court to order an investigation or an evaluation of the child or the parents or their circumstances. Paragraph (2) permits the appointment of a guardian ad litem who, at the court's discretion, may serve in an investigatory capacity, an advocacy role, or both. Paragraph (3) permits appointment of a lawyer to serve as independent counsel to the child or the guardian ad litem.

b. No general duty of appointment. **There is an appealing case to be made for ordering an independent investigation or evaluation, or for appointing a guardian or an attorney for the child, in every dispute involving a child. Children are the innocent victims of family disruption, usually unable to protect or advocate effectively for themselves. Parents can be distracted at the time of separation or divorce, their judgments clouded by their own problems. The purpose of a court-ordered investigation or evaluation is to ensure that the court be able to make its decisions under this Chapter based on complete information. A guardian or lawyer for the child can act as a buffer against bad decisionmaking by parents and ensure that the child's best interests receive focused attention.**

Despite these potential benefits, the measures permitted by this section present some significant difficulties. First, court-ordered investigations or evaluations and the appointment of an advocate for the child can constitute undesirable and inappropriate intrusions on the authority of parents. Ideally, parents make good arrangements for their children on their own, by agreement. Courts should not presume that they cannot do so, or distrust them when they try. See §2.06. Indeed, the presence of outside investigators, evaluators, and child representatives may relieve pressure on parents to keep the interests of the child paramount. When someone else has been assigned to protect the child's interests, a parent may feel released from that responsibility and more at liberty to protect his or her own interests. This effect is the opposite of what these Principles are attempting to achieve.

Second, the effort to obtain better information about, or representation for, the child can have a negative effect on the proceedings themselves. While the appointment of a separate representative for the child may sometimes ameliorate the level of conflict generated in the proceedings, it often only heightens conflict. Even the presence of an independent investigator or evaluator can intensify the strategic behavior of parents, who may seek advantage through alliance with he investigator or evaluator rather than a collaborative solution with each other. Investigators and representatives can also be expensive for the parents, whose financial resources often are already stretched as a result of the divorce.

In addition, it should not be assumed that an independent, court-ordered investigation or evaluation will assure an outcome for a child that is "best," in some objective or neutral sense. Disagreements about the best interests of children among child advocates and among academic and clinical professionals are hard to explain apart from the value judgments and policy commitments that underlie them. See §2.02, Comment *c*.

Because of these difficulties, this section does not require a court-ordered investigation or evaluation or the appointment of a guardian ad litem or attorney in every case. It gives the court discretion to make such an order or appointment when the court has concerns about whether the child's welfare can be protected by the parties before the court. The court's discretion should be guided by the overall goals of the Chapter. . . .

§2.14 Interview of the child by the court

The court should have discretion to interview the child, or direct another person to interview the child, in order to obtain information relevant to the issues of the case. Counsel for a parent or for the child should be permitted to propose questions to the court that may be asked of the child.

Topic 4. Modification of Parenting Plan

§2.15 Modification upon showing of changed circumstances or harm

(1) Except as provided in Paragraph (2), in §2.16 or in §2.17, a court may modify a court-ordered parenting plan if it finds, on the basis of facts that were not known or have arisen since the entry of the prior order and were not anticipated therein, that a substantial change has occurred in the circumstances of the child or of one or both parents and that a modification is necessary to the child's welfare.

(2) Even if a substantial change of circumstances has not occurred, a court may modify a parenting plan if it finds that the plan arrangements are not working as contemplated and in some specific way cause harm to the child.

(3) Unless the parents have agreed otherwise, none of the following circumstances is sufficient to justify a significant modification of a parenting plan except where harm to the child is shown:

(a) circumstances resulting in an involuntary loss of income, by loss of employment or otherwise, affecting the parent's economic status;

(b) a parent's remarriage or cohabitation;

(c) a parent's choice of reasonable caretaking arrangements for the child, including the child's placement in day care.

(4) For purposes of Paragraph (1), the onset or significant worsening of any limiting factor defined in §2.11(l) constitutes a substantial change of circumstances under this section.

Comment

a. In general. **Rules for modifying a parenting plan must balance the benefits of stability against the costs of rigidity. On the one hand, changes in caretaking arrangements, or even the possibility that such changes will be made, promotes insecurity and instability in parenting arrangements. On the other hand, an inflexible approach to modification can perpetuate arrangements that have proven unsatisfactory or reduce a parent's incentive to agree to modified arrangements that would benefit the child. Given the risks, no approach to this issue is without difficulty.**

This Chapter resolves the tension with a layered set of rules that recognize the need for stability in most circumstances, along with the desirability of flexibility in certain specified situations and the inappropriateness of modification others. As a general rule, significant judicial modification of a permanent parenting plan is allowed under this section only upon a showing of (1) a substantial change in the circumstances on which the parenting plan was based at makes modification necessary to the child's welfare, excluding changes in economic or marital status, or in caretaking arrangements; or (2) harm to the child. Modification is more readily available, under a less strict standard, in four specific circumstances: (1) changes agreed to by the parents, (2) changes in the actual arrangements under which the child has been receiving care without objection by the parent opposing the modification; (3) minor modifications in the plan; (4) the attainment of the age specified in a uniform rule of statewide application under §2.08(1)(b) of a child who has a firm and reasonable preference for a different residential arrangement. See §2.16. Other special rules are designed to strike a balance between stability and flexibility in a child's residential arrangements in the particular context of a parent's relocation. See §2.17. . .

§2.16 Modification without showing of changed circumstances

(1) The court should modify a parenting plan in accordance with a parental agreement, unless it finds that the agreement is not knowing or voluntary, or would be harmful to the child.

(2) The court may modify a parenting plan without a showing of changed circumstances otherwise required by §2.15(1) if the modification is in the child's best interests and

(a) reflects the de facto arrangement under which the child has been receiving care, without parental objection, for the six months preceding filing of the petition for modification, provided the arrangement is not the result of a parent's acquiescence resulting from domestic violence or from other conditions or circumstances that impeded the parent's capacity to give meaningful consent;

(b) constitutes a minor modification in the plan;

(c) is necessary to accommodate the firm preferences of a child who has attained the age specified pursuant to §2.08(1)(b); or

(d) is necessary to change a parenting plan that was based on an agreement that the court would not have ordered under §2.06 had the court been aware of the circumstances at the time the plan was ordered, if modification is sought under this section within six months of the issuance of the parenting plan.

§2.17 Relocation of a parent

(1) The relocation of a parent constitutes a substantial change in circumstances under §2.15(1) only when the relocation significantly impairs either parent's ability to exercise responsibilities the parent has been exercising or attempting to exercise under the parenting plan.

(2) Unless otherwise ordered by the court, a parent who has responsibility under a parenting plan who changes, or intends to change, residences for more than 90 days should give a minimum of 60 days' advance notice, or the earliest notice practicable under the circumstances, to any other parent with responsibility under the same parenting plan. Notice should include all of the following:

(a) the intended date of the relocation,

(b) the address of the intended new residence,

(c) the specific reasons for the intended relocation,

(d) a proposal for how custodial responsibility should be modified, if necessary, in light of the intended move.

A court may consider a failure to comply with the notice requirements of this section without good cause as a factor in determining whether the relocation is in good faith under Paragraph (4), and as a basis for awarding reasonable expenses and reasonable attorney's fees attributable to such failure.

(3) When changed circumstances are shown under Paragraph (1), if practical the court should revise the parenting plan to accommodate the relocation without changing the proportion of custodial responsibilities each parent is exercising.

(4) When a relocation constituting changed circumstances under Paragraph (1) renders it impractical to maintain the same proportion of custodial responsibility to each parent, the court should modify the parenting plan in accordance with the child's best interests, as defined in §2.08 and §2.09, and in accordance with the following principles:

(a) The court should allow a parent who has been exercising the clear majority of custodial responsibility to relocate with the child if that parent shows that the relocation is for a valid purpose, in good faith, and to a location that is reasonable in light of the purpose.

(i) For purposes of this Paragraph, what is a "clear majority" of custodial responsibility should be established through a rule of statewide application.

(ii) For purposes of this Paragraph, the court should recognize any of the following purposes for a relocation as valid: (1) to be close to significant family or other sources of support, (2) to address significant health problems, (3) to protect the safety of the child or another member of the child's household from a significant risk of harm, (4) to pursue a significant employment or educational opportunity, (5) to be with one's spouse or domestic partner who lives in, or is pursuing a significant employment or educational opportunity in, the new location, (6) to significantly improve the family's quality of life. The relocating parent should have the burden of proving the validity of any other purpose.

(iii) The court should find that a move for a valid purpose is reasonable unless its purpose is shown to be substantially achievable without moving, or by moving to a location that is substantially less disruptive of the other parent's relationship to the child.

(b) If a parent who has been exercising the clear majority of custodial responsibility does not establish that the purpose for that parent's relocation is valid, in good faith, and to a location that is reasonable in light of the purpose, the court should order the plan modifications most consistent with the child's best interests. Among the modifications the court should consider is a reallocation of primary custodial responsibility, effective if and when the relocation occurs, but such a reallocation should not be ordered if the relocating parent demonstrates that the child's best interests would be served by the child's relocation with the parent.

(c) If neither parent has been exercising a clear majority of custodial responsibility for the child, the court should modify the plan in accordance with the child's best interests, taking into account all relevant factors including the effects of the relocation on the child.

(d) The court should deny the request of a parent for a reallocation of custodial responsibility to enable the parent to relocate with the child if the parent has been exercising substantially less custodial responsibility for the child than the other parent, unless the relocating parent demonstrates that the reallocation is necessary to prevent harm to the child.

(e) The court should minimize the impairment to parent-child relationship caused by a parent's relocation through alternative arrangements for the exercise of custodial responsibility appropriate to the parents' resources and circumstances and the developmental level of the child.

Comment

a. In general. **The relocation of a parent, or both parents, is a circumstance that frequently follows divorce. The ability to change one's area of residence is an important individual right. So is having access to one's child. When two parents have been exercising continuing care and responsibility for a child, the relocation of one of them puts these two interests in sometimes irreconcilable conflict.**

In resolving the conflict between parents when one or both of them wish to relocate, courts have used a variety of tests, none of which is fully satisfactory. Some tests attach little value to the relocating parent's needs; others ignore what may amount to substantial consequences to the nonmoving parent. Balancing tests leave courts to pin their own value on the competing interests in an individual case, making objectivity and consistency extremely difficult.

This section treats any relocation that significantly impairs the exercise of a parent's custodial responsibility as a substantial change in circumstances, thereby justifying review of the custodial arrangements. See Paragraph (1). Upon review, if the relocating parent has been exercising the clear majority of custodial responsibility for the child, that parent is allowed to relocate with the child without a specific showing of the benefits to the child, as long as the relocation is for a valid purpose, in good faith, and to a location that is reasonable in light of the purpose. See Paragraph (4)(a). If the purpose for the modification is not valid or the location not reasonable and the nonmoving parent is willing and fit to assume primary custodial responsibility, the court may reallocate primary custodial responsibility to the nonrelocating parent, unless it finds that the child's interests would be best served by remaining with the relocating parent. See Paragraph (4)(b). Likewise, if the parents have been sharing custodial responsibility more or less equally, past caretaking patterns are not dispositive, and the court may modify the custodial arrangements under the best-interests test. See Paragraph (4)(c). Finally, a parent who has been exercising substantially less custodial responsibility for the child than the other parent may not relocate with the child, unless that parent demonstrates that the relocation is necessary to prevent harm to the child. See Paragraph (4)(d). Whatever effects a relocation may have on the allocation of primary custodial responsibility, the court should attempt to minimize the effects of a relocation through alternative arrangements that are consistent with the parents' resources and the child's needs. See Paragraph (4)(e). . . .

Topic 5. Allocations of Responsibility to Individuals Other than Legal Parents

§2.18 Allocations of responsibility to individuals other than legal parents

(1) The court should allocate responsibility to a legal parent, a parent by estoppel, or a de facto parent as defined in §2.03, in accordance with the same standards set forth in §§2.08 through 2.12, except that

(a) it should not allocate the majority of custodial responsibility to a de facto parent over the objection of a legal parent or a parent by estoppel who is fit and willing to assume the majority of custodial responsibility unless

(i) the legal parent or parent by estoppel has not been performing a reasonable share of parenting functions, as defined in §2.03(6), or

(ii) the available alternatives would cause harm to the child; and

(b) it should limit or deny an allocation otherwise to be made if, in light of the number of other individuals to be allocated responsibility, the allocation would be impractical in light of the objectives of this Chapter.

(2) A court should not allocate responsibility to an individual who is not a legal parent, a parent by estoppel, or a de facto parent, over a parent's objection, if that parent is fit and willing to care for the child, unless any of the following circumstances exist:

(a) the individual is a grandparent or other relative who has developed a significant relationship with the child and

(i) the parent objecting to the allocation has not been performing a reasonable share of parenting functions for the child; and

(ii) if there is another legal parent or parent by estoppel, that parent is unable or unwilling to care for the child, or consents to the allocation;

(b) the individual is a biological parent of the child who is not the child's legal parent but who has an agreement with a legal parent under which the individual retained some parental rights or responsibilities;

(c) the available alternatives would cause harm to the child.

Topic 6. Enforcement of Parenting Plans

§2.19 Enforcement of parenting plans

(1) If, upon a complaint from an individual with responsibility under a parenting plan, the court finds that another individual intentionally and without good cause violated a provision of a court-ordered parenting plan, it should enforce the remedies specified in the plan or, if no remedies are specified or they are inadequate, it should find that the plan has been violated and order an appropriate remedy, which may include one or more of the following:

(a) in the case of interference with the exercise of custodial responsibility for a child by the other parent, an award of substitute time for that parent to make up for time missed with the child;

(b) in the case of missed time by a parent, an award of costs in recognition of lost opportunities by the other parent, child-care costs, and other reasonable expenses in connection with the missed time;

(c) a modification of the plan, if the requirements for a modification are met under §2.15, §2.16, or §2.17;

(d) an order that the parent who violated the plan obtain appropriate counseling;

(e) an award of court costs, reasonable attorney's fees, and any other reasonable expenses in enforcing the plan;

(f) any other appropriate remedy.

(2) Except as provided in a jointly submitted plan that has been ordered by the court, the court should treat obligations established in a parenting plan as independent obligations, and it should not recognize as a defense to an action under this section by one parent that the other parent failed to meet obligations under a parenting plan or child-support order.

(3) A court may treat an agreement between parents to depart from a parenting plan as a defense to a claim that the plan has been violated, even though the agreement was not made part of a court order, but only as to acts or omissions consistent with the agreement that occur before the agreement is disaffirmed by either parent.

Chapter 4. Division of Property upon Dissolution

Topic 1. Introductory Provisions

§4.01 Scope of Chapter 4

(1) This Chapter sets forth principles for dividing property between spouses at the dissolution of their marriage.

(2) The enforceability of agreements between spouses or prospective spouses concerning the division of their property is governed by Chapter 7 and not by this Chapter.

§4.02 Objective of Principles Governing the Division of Property

The objective of this Chapter is to allocate property by principles

(1) that respect both spousal ownership rights in their property and the equitable claims that each spouse has on the property in consequence of their marital relationship;

(2 that facilitate the satisfaction of obligations the spouses have under Chapter 3 to support their children and under Chapter 5 to share equitably in the financial losses arising from the dissolution of their marriage; and

(3) that are consistent and predictable in appli-cation.

Topic 2. Definition and Characterization of Property

§4.03 Definition of marital and separate property

(1) Property acquired during marriage is marital property, except as otherwise expressly provided in this Chapter.

(2) Inheritances, including bequests and devises, and gifts from third parties, are the separate property of the acquiring spouse even if acquired during marriage.

(3) Property received in exchange for separate property is separate property even if acquired during marriage.

(4) Property acquired during marriage but after the parties have commenced living apart pursuant to either a written separation agreement or a judicial decree, is the separate property of the acquiring spouse unless the agreement or decree specifies otherwise.

(5) For the purpose of this section "during marriage" means after the commencement of marriage and before the filing and service of a petition for dissolution (if that petition ultimately results in a decree dissolving the marriage), unless there are facts, set forth in written findings of the trial court (§1.02), establishing that use of another date is necessary to avoid a substantial injustice.

(6) Property acquired during a relationship between the spouses that immediately preceded their marriage, and which was a domestic-partner relationship as defined by §6.03, is treated as if it were acquired during the marriage.

§4.04 Income from and appreciation of separate property

(1) Both income during marriage from separate property, and the appreciation in value during marriage of separate property, are marital property to the extent the underlying asset is subsequently recharacterized as marital property, pursuant to §4.12.

(2) Both income during marriage from separate property, and the appreciation in value during marriage of separate property, are marital property to the extent the income or appreciation is attributable to either spouse's labor during marriage, pursuant to §4.05.

(3) Income from and appreciation of separate property are separate property if they are not marital property under Paragraph (1) or (2).

§4.05 Enhancement of separate property by marital labor

(1) A portion of any increase in the value of separate property is marital property whenever either spouse has devoted substantial time during marriage to the property's management or preservation.

(2) The increase in value of separate property over the course of the marriage is measured by the difference between the market value of the property when acquired, or at the beginning of the marriage, if later, and the market value of the property when sold, or at the end of the marriage, if sooner.

(3) The portion of the increase in value that is martial property under Paragraph (1) is the difference between the actual amount by which the property has increased in value, and the amount by which capital of the same value would have increased over the same time period if invested in assets of relative safety requiring little management.

§4.06 Property acquired in exchange for marital and separate property

(1) Property acquired during marriage in exchange for other property is presumed to be marital property.

(a) The presumption of Paragraph (1) is rebutted by evidence that the consideration for the acquired property included a spouse's separate property.

(b) If the presumption is rebutted, the acquired property consists of marital- and separate-property shares in proportion to the value of the marital and separate property for which it was exchanged.

(2) Property acquired on credit during marriage is presumed to be marital property.

(a) The presumption of Paragraph (2) is rebutted by evidence that the down payment, or any payments that reduce the loan's principal balance, were made from a spouse's separate property.

(b) If the presumption is rebutted as described in Paragraph (2)(a), the acquired property consists of marital and separate shares in proportion to the value of the marital and separate property that was applied to the down payment or to reduce the debt. Payments not shown to have been made from separate property are treated as having been made from marital property.

(c) The presumption of Paragraph (2) is rebutted by evidence that neither spouse has personal liability for the loan and that, under the terms of the loan instrument and governing law, the creditor's sole recourse for nonpayment is against one spouse's separate property.

(d) If the presumption is rebutted as described in Paragraph (2)(c),

(i) the acquired property is the separate property of the spouse who owns the separate property that the creditor may reach, except that

(ii) if either the down payment, or reductions in the principal balance of the loan, were made from marital property, the acquired property consists of marital and separate shares in proportion to the value of the marital and separate property that was applied to the debt or down payment. Any payments not shown to have been made from separate property are treated as having been made from marital property.

(3) Property acquired on credit before marriage is presumed to be the separate property of the acquiring spouse, except that the acquired property is marital property to the extent the principal balance of the loan is reduced with payments made from marital property.

(4) Any presumption under this section is also rebutted by evidence that the spouses shared an intention concerning the characterization of the property that is inconsistent with the presumption.

§4.07 Earning capacity and goodwill

(1) Spousal earning capacity, spousal skills, and earnings from post-dissolution spousal labor, are not marital property.

(2) Occupational licenses and educational degrees are not marital property.

(3) Business goodwill and professional goodwill earned during marriage are marital property to the extent they have value apart from the value of spousal earning capacity, spousal skills, or post-dissolution spousal labor.

(a) Evidence of an increment during marriage in the market value of business or professional goodwill establishes the existence of divisible marital property in that amount except to the extent that market value includes the value of post-dissolution spousal labor.

(b) Business or professional goodwill that is not marketable is nevertheless marital property to the extent a value can be established for it that does not include the value of spousal earning capacity, spousal skills, or post-dissolution spousal labor.

§4.08 Deferred or contingent earnings and wage substitutes

(1) Property earned by labor performed during marriage is marital property whether received before, during, or after the marriage. Property earned by labor not performed during marriage is the separate property of the laboring spouse even if received during marriage.

(a) Vested pension rights are marital property to the extent they are earned during the marriage.

(b) Contingent returns on labor performed during marriage, including unvested pension rights, choices in action, and compensation contingent on post-dissolution events, are marital property to the extent they are earned during the marriage.

(2) Benefits received as compensation for a loss take their character from the asset they replace.

(a) Insurance proceeds and personal-injury recoveries are marital property to the extent that entitlement to them arises from the loss of a marital asset, including income that the beneficiary-spouse would have earned during the marriage. The dissolution court may make a reasonable allocation of an undifferentiated award between its marital- and separate-property components.

(b) Disability pay and workers' compensation payments are marital property to the extent they replace income or benefits the recipient would have earned during the marriage but for the qualifying disability or injury.

(3) Where the value of the marital-property portion of a spouse's entitlement to future payments can be determined at dissolution, the court may include it in reckoning the worth of the marital property assigned to each spouse. Where the value of the future payments is not known at the time of dissolution, where their receipt is contingent on future events or not reasonably assured, or where for other reasons it is not equitable under the circumstances to include their value in the property assigned at the time of dissolution, the court may decline to do so, and instead either

(a) fix the spouses' respective shares in such future payments if and when received, or,

(b) if it is not possible to fix their share at the time of dissolution, reserve jurisdiction to make an appropriate order at the earliest practical date.

Topic 3. Allocation of Property on Dissolution of Marriage

§4.09 Division of marital property generally

(1) Except as provided in Paragraph (2) of this section, marital property and marital debts are divided at dissolution so that the spouses receive net shares equal in value, although not necessarily identical in kind.

(2) The spouses are allocated net shares of the marital property or debts that are unequal in value if, and only if, one or more of the following is true:

(a) Pursuant to §5.10, §5.11, or §5.14, the court compensates a spouse for a loss recognized in Chapter 5, in whole or in part, with an enhanced share of the marital property.

(b) Pursuant to §4.10, the court allows one spouse an enhanced share of the marital property because the other spouse previously made an improper disposition of some portion of it.

(c) Marital debts exceed marital assets, and it is just and equitable to assign the excess debt unequally, because of a significant disparity in the spouses' financial capacity, their participation in the decision to incur the debt, or their consumption of the goods or services that the debt was incurred to acquire.

(d) Debt has been incurred to finance a spouse's education, in which case it is treated as the separate obligation of the spouse whose education it financed.

(3) When a "deferred-sale-of-family-residence order" is made under §3.11, any resulting enhancement in the residential parent's property share is additional child support, whether or not it is recognized as such in the formal child-support award, and therefore no adjustment is required under this section to offset it.

§4.10 Financial misconduct as grounds for unequal division of marital property

(1) If one spouse, without the other spouse's consent, has made gifts of marital property to third parties that are substantial relative to the total value of the marital property at the time of the gift, the court should augment the other spouse's share of the remaining marital property by one-half of the value of such gifts. This Paragraph applies only to gifts made after a date that is set by counting back, from the date on which the dissolution petition is served, a fixed period of time specified in a rule of statewide application.

(2) If marital property is lost, expended, or destroyed through the intentional misconduct of one spouse, the court should augment the other spouse's share of the remaining marital property by one-half the value of the lost or destroyed property. This Paragraph applies only to misconduct after a date that is set by counting back, from the date on which the dissolution petition is served, a fixed period of time specified in a rule of statewide application.

(3) If marital property is lost or destroyed through the negligence of one spouse, the court should augment the other spouse's share of the remaining marital property by one-half the value of the lost or destroyed property. This Paragraph applies only to negligence that took place after service of the dissolution petition.

(4) If a spouse is entitled to a remedy under Paragraph (1) or (2), or would have been entitled to a remedy had concealed or conveyed property not been recovered, the court should enlarge that spouse's share of the marital property by an

amount sufficient to offset all reasonable costs, including professional fees, which that spouse incurred to establish or remedy the improper concealment or conveyance, whenever the court also finds that the other spouse's concealment or conveyance either

(a) had the purpose of denying the first spouse his or her share of the marital property at dissolution, or

(b) was undertaken with knowledge that such denial was its likely effect.

(5) Paragraphs (1), (2), and (3) may be applied to gifts, misconduct, or neglect that occurred prior to the date specified in the statewide rule required under those sections, if facts set forth in written findings of the trial court (§1.02) establish that their application to the earlier incidents is necessary to avoid a substantial injustice.

(6) If there is insufficient marital property for an adjustment in its allocation to provide the appropriate remedy under this section, the court may achieve an equivalent result by

(a) making an award to one spouse of some portion of the other's separate property, as allowed under §4.11, or, if the available separate property is also inadequate for this purpose,

(b) requiring one spouse to make equitable reimbursement to the other in such installment payments as the court judges equitable in light of the financial capacity and other obligations of the spouse making reimbursement.

§4.11 Separate property

(1) In every dissolution of marriage, all separate property should be assigned to its owner, except that when there is insufficient marital property to permit the reimbursement that would otherwise be required under §4.10, the court may reassign the spouses' separate property in order to achieve the equivalent result.

(2) Separate property that is recharacterized as marital property under §4.12 is allocated between the spouses under §4.09 and not under this section.

§4.12 Recharacterization of separate property as marital property at the dissolution of long-term marriage

(1) In marriages that exceed a minimum duration specified in a rule of statewide application, a portion of the separate property that each spouse held at the time of their marriage should be recharacterized at dissolution as marital property.

(a) The percentage of separate property that is recharacterized as marital property under Paragraph (1) should be determined by the duration of the marriage, according to a formula specified in a rule of statewide application.

(b) The formula should specify a marital duration at which the full value of the separate property held by the spouses at the time of their marriage is recharacterized at dissolution as marital property.

(2) A portion of separate property acquired by each spouse during marriage should be recharacterized at dissolution as marital property if, at the time of dissolution, both the marital duration, and the time since the property's acquisition (the "holding period"), exceed the minimum length specified for each in a rule of statewide application.

(a) The percentage of separate property that is re-characterized as marital property under Paragraph (2) should be determined by a formula, specified in a rule of statewide application, that takes into account both the marital duration and the holding period of the property in question.

(b) The formula should specify a marital duration and holding period at which the full value of the property is recharacterized at dissolution as marital property.

(3) For the purpose of this section, any appreciation in the value of separate property, or income from it, that would otherwise itself be separate property, is treated as having been acquired at the same time as the underlying asset, and any asset acquired in exchange for separate property is treated as having been acquired as of the time its predecessor asset was acquired.

(4) A spouse should be able to avoid the application of this section to gifts or inheritances received during marriage by giving written notice of that intention to the other spouse within a time period following the property's receipt that is specified in a rule of statewide application.

(5) The provision of a will or deed of gift specifying that a bequest or gift is not subject to claims under this section should be given effect.

(6) This section should not apply to separate property if, as set forth in written findings of the trial court (§1.02), preservation of the property's separate character is necessary to avoid substantial injustice.

Comment

a. General Rationale. **This section gives spouses in long-term marriages a share, at dissolution, in one another's separate property. According to the principle set forth in Paragraph (1)(a), that share increases with the length of their marriage. The share begins at zero in the marriage's earliest years. Serious inequities could result in the short-term marriage if the rule were otherwise. As the marriage lengthens, however, the equities change. After many years of marriage, spouses typically do not think of their separate-property assets as separate, even if they would be so classified under the technical property rules. Both spouses are likely to believe, for example, that such assets will be available to provide for their joint retirement, for a medical crisis of either spouse, or for other personal emergencies. The longer the marriage, the more likely it is that the spouses will have made decisions about their employment or the use of their marital assets that are premised in part on such expectations about the separate property of both spouses. If the marriage ends with the death of the wealthier spouse, the common law has traditionally provided the remedy of a forced share for survivors not otherwise provided for. The 1990 revision of the Uniform Probate Code gradually enlarges the spouse's forced share with the**

duration of the marriage according to a mechanical formula. Section 4.12 of these Principles provides an analogous remedy when the marriage ends with dissolution rather than death.

States that distinguish between marital and separate property generally do not have provisions under which the character of separate property changes with the passage of time. However, some states make no distinction between separate and marital property, and permit their courts to award any property owned by either spouse to the other. In practice, it appears that the longer the marital duration, the more likely are courts in these states to allocate a portion of one spouse's premarital or inherited property to the other spouse. This section reaches a similar result. . . .

Chapter 5. Compensatory Spousal Payments

Topic 1. Introductory Provisions

§5.01 Scope

(1) This Chapter sets forth the principles that govern financial claims between spouses arising in the dissolution of their marriage, other than claims for a share in their property or for support of their children.

(2) The enforceability of agreements between spouses or prospective spouses concerning financial claims otherwise arising under this Chapter is governed by Chapter 7 and not by this Chapter.

(3) The enforcement of judgments is not within the scope of this Chapter, but an order for periodic payments rendered pursuant to the principles set forth in this Chapter should be enforceable by all of the remedies available for enforcement of child-support awards.

§5.02 Objective

(1) The objective of this Chapter is to allocate financial losses that arise at the dissolution of a marriage according to equitable principles that are consistent and predictable in application.

(2) Losses are allocated under this Chapter without regard to marital misconduct, but nothing in this Chapter is intended to foreclose a spouse from bringing a claim recognized under other law for injuries arising from conduct that occurred during the marriage.

(3) Equitable principles of loss recognition and allocation should take into account all of the following:

(a) The loss of earning capacity arising from a spouse's disproportionate share of caretaking responsibilities for children or other persons to whom the spouses have a moral obligation;

(b) Losses that arise from the changes in life opportunities and expectations caused by the adjustments individuals ordinarily make over the course of a long marital relationship;

(c) Disparities in the financial impact of a short marital relationship on the spouses' post-divorce lives, as compared to their situation prior to marriage;

(d) The primacy of the income earner's claim to benefit from the fruits of his or her own labor, as compared to claims of a former spouse.

Comment

a. Compensation for losses rather than meeting needs. **The division of one household into two typically creates financial losses for the spouses. Without reallocation, these losses are not likely to fall equitably as between them. Such equitable reallocation is therefore the principal objective of this Chapter. The division of property and the provision of child support already reallocate some of the financial losses arising from divorce, but in many divorces there are additional financial losses that these remedies do not address. Not all of these additional losses give rise to claims between the spouses for compensation, but equity requires that many do. This Chapter identifies these compensable financial losses.**

The measurement of compensable losses arising at dissolution requires defining the baseline against which to judge the claimant's financial status at dissolution. The sections that follow in Topics 2 and 3 generally adopt the marital living standard as the appropriate baseline in longer marriages, and each spouse's, premarital living standard as the appropriate baseline in shorter marriages. The divorced person may find himself or herself worse off than during the marriage, but better off than before it. In that case, the choice of baseline determines whether the same objective situation is seen as a loss or a gain. For the same reason, a principle that compensates a spouse for loss of the marital living standard could instead be said to protect the gain in living standard that spouse obtained from the marriage. The choice of language is of course less important than the underlying rule it describes. That rule, as implemented in this Chapter, ties the degree of protection against loss of marital living standard to two factors primarily: the marriage's duration (§5.04) and the duration of the period during which the claimant was the primary caretaker of the marital children (§5.05). Because losses are shared, the compensable loss is not equal to the entire loss of living standard in many cases. Losses other than the marital living standard may be compensable without regard to the marital duration or the duration of the caretaking period. Section 5.03 lists the compensable losses and identifies the section that addresses each in detail. The rationale for the selection and measurement of each compensable loss is provided in the identified section.

Counterparts can be found in the existing law of alimony (or as many states now call it, "maintenance") for each of the losses recognized in this Chapter. But, because the modern law of

alimony has no coherent rationale, its application varies considerably both among and within jurisdictions. Early in the no-fault reform era, one influential formulation described alimony as an award meant to provide support for the spouse in "need" who is "unable to support himself through appropriate employment." Uniform Marriage and Divorce Act, §308(a)(1) and (2). With time, it has become apparent that this conception of alimony's purpose has two principal difficulties. There is first the failure to provide any satisfactory explanation for placing the obligation to support needy individuals on their former spouses rather than on their parents, their children, their friends, or society in general. The absence of any explanation for requiring an individual to meet the needs of a former spouse leads inevitably to the second problem, the law's historic inability to provide any consistent principle for determining when, and to what extent, a former spouse is "in need." We cannot choose among the many possible definitions of need if we do not know the reason for imposing the obligation to meet it. Some judicial opinions find the alimony claimant in "need" only if unable to provide for her basic necessities, others if the claimant is unable to support himself at a moderate middle-class level, and still others whenever the claimant is unable to sustain the living standard enjoyed during the marriage even if it was lavish. Some opinions suggest that the measure the claimant's need will vary with the identity of his former spouse or the length of his marriage.

These results cannot be harmonized if need is retained as the central concept, for there is nothing to explain why its definition should vary among these cases. The inference is that the explanation for alimony is something other than the relief of need. The gradual realization of this point can be seen in the great number of modern decisions allowing alimony awards without requiring need as the court itself would define it, and in other decisions terminating alimony awards despite the claimant's continued need.

The principal conceptual innovation of this Chapter is therefore to recharacterize the remedy it provides as *compensation for loss* rather than *relief of need.* A spouse frequently seems in need at the conclusion of a marriage because its dissolution imposes a particularly severe loss on him or her. The intuition that the former spouse has an obligation to meet that need arises from the perception that the need results from the unfair allocation of the financial losses arising from the marital failure. This perception explains why we have alimony, and why all alimony claims cannot be adjudicated by reference to a single standard of need. If the payment's justification is not relief of need but the equitable reallocation of the losses arising from the marital failure, then need is not an appropriate eligibility requirement for the award. While many persons who have suffered an inequitable financial loss will be in need, others will not, and the remainder will vary in their degree of need. At the same time, some formerly married individuals may find themselves in need for reasons unrelated to the marriage and its subsequent dissolution. In that case, there may be no basis for imposing a special obligation to meet that need on their former spouses.

This recharacterization of the remedy requires replacing the terms "alimony" and "maintenance," which are both associated historically with relief of need. The term "compensatory payment" or "compensatory award" is therefore employed instead. This change in terms should not obscure the fact that the advantage derived from grounding compensatory payments on a principle of *loss* rather than *need* is less the alteration of existing practices than the explanation of them. The categories of compensable loss bear a close factual relationship to fact patterns that often yield alimony awards in existing law. But focusing on loss permits more coherent definition of the cases qualifying for compensatory payments than is possible in a system judging all claims on the single but ill-defined goal of relieving need. The shift in analysis from *need* to *loss* thus facilitates more precise rules of adjudication, with a correspondingly reduced disparity of result. See Comment *d.*

Equally important, recharacterizing the award's purpose from the relief of need to the equitable allocation of loss transforms the claimant's petition from a plea for help to, a claim of entitlement. Although conceptual confusion over the grounds for alimony has undoubtedly contributed to mistaken judgments in both directions, inadequate or missing awards have been the more frequent problem. This failure of alimony has created pressure to expand the relief available through the division of property so as to reach claims for which that remedy is ill-suited. Reconceptualizing alimony as compensatory payments for losses arising from the marriage and its failure establishes it as an entitlement providing a more reliable remedy for the divorce-related financial claims.

b. Limitation to financial losses. This Chapter provides for the equitable allocation of the financial losses arising from divorce. Divorce also imposes emotional losses and emotional gains, but these Principles do not recognize these as an element of awards. The reasons for this exclusion are pragmatic as well, as principled. The pains and joys that individuals find from divorce are no commensurable with its financial costs, so that there is no method for determining the extent to which compensation for a financial loss should be reduced or enlarged to reflect nonfinancial gains or losses. Any effort to consider the emotional consequences of divorce would also require evaluation of the parties' marital conduct. A spouse may experience relief or even joy from having terminated an oppressive marriage, but we presumably would not wish to reduce that spouse's financial claims by assigning monetary value to these emotional gains. So also if joy came from the freedom to pursue an intimate relationship with a third person that had begun during the marriage, unless we distinguish the cases on grounds of fault. These same examples could of course be offered with the genders reversed. The point is nonetheless the same: To include consideration of emotional losses and gains would require a more general examination of marital misconduct, which this section rejects. See Comment e.

Similar reasoning requires exclusion of the emotional loss sometimes borne by the noncustodial spouse who suffers estrangement from the marital children. Here, too, there is no common scale on which to weigh this estrangement and the spouses' financial losses. Moreover, the equitable weight of the noncustodial spouse's claim may depend upon whether the estrangement results from the custodial arrangement or the claimant's own conduct, yet that distinction would result in many of the same difficulties that counsel against marital fault adjudications. Finally, the parent's emotional disengagement from the marital children may have benefits as well as burdens, and the noncustodial spouse's emotional loss could not be considered in isolation from these other emotional consequences of the custodial arrangements. Taking full account of the emotional effects would require the court to gauge the net emotional outcome for each parent, and then compare them to one another. These Principles therefore exclude claims of emotional loss by the noncustodial parent, just as other nonfinancial losses are excluded.

c. Limitation to losses arising from dissolution. The remedies provided by section aim at an equitable allocation of the losses that are realized when one household is divided into two. They are not meant to provide compensation for inequities in the spousal give and take during the marriage. Divorcing individuals are likely to believe that the allocation of resources and responsibilities during their marriage was unfair. It would seem certain that some are correct. But the divorce law cannot provide general relief for unfair conduct in marriage. Married couples spend their funds on many joint consumption items — homes, vacations, automobiles, entertainment, meals — the value of which are impossible to locate between the spouses even though some will have been purchased primarily for their utility to one spouse, others for their utility to the other. The same is true of all activities during marriage that affect both spouses.

The no-fault divorce law of most states gives spouses the legal power to terminate the marriage unilaterally. In principle, this power makes it impossible for either spouse to impose an inequitable arrangement on the other, at least in the long term. In practice, this may not be true. Parties may be bound together by nonlegal ties that keep persons in unhappy relationships. There is little the law can do to alter that. The law can, however, ensure that parties are not bound to exploitative relationships by legal rules that place on them an unfair share of the losses that would arise if they divorce. A no-fault divorce law therefore requires concurrent remedies providing an equitable reallocation of those losses.

d. Consistency and predictability in application. The vague standards governing alimony in most existing law yields inconsistent and unpredictable adjudication. The analogous problem for child-support awards was resolved by the widespread adoption of child-support guidelines. Although alimony guidelines have been employed in some states, they have not been widely adopted. Alimony is more resistant to guidelines because marriage does not alone establish an alimony obligation, in the way that parenthood alone establishes a child-support obligation. The benefits of predictability and consistency that can achieved with guidelines therefore require the prior establishment of a coherent rationale for requiring the award and accompanying rules for identifying eligible claimants. Satisfaction of these requirements, and thus achievement of the objective of consistency and predictability, is facilitated by reconceptualizing the award as compensation for loss rather than as relief of need. See Comment *a*.

e. Exclusion of marital misconduct. Paragraph (2) excludes consideration of marital misconduct in the equitable allocation of the financial losses arising at dissolution. This is consistent with the position of the Uniform Marriage and Divorce Act and of approximately half of the states. Nonfinancial losses are not compensable at dissolution in any event, see Comment *b*, and financial losses are compensable without regard to whether they arise from the other spouse's misconduct. In most states, individuals may bring tort actions to recover for physical and emotional losses arising from the intentional or negligent conduct of their spouse, and the exclusion of marital misconduct from consideration in dissolution proceedings does not bar such tort claims. For a more complete statement of the rationale underlying the exclusion of marital misconduct from dissolution proceedings, see Chapter 1, Topic 2.

f. Factors to consider in an equitable allocation of losses. Paragraph (3) sets out four essential components of an equitable allocation of the financial losses at dissolution. The first three identify categories of financial losses that an equitable system must consider. When one of the spouses leaves the labor market, in whole or in part, to care for children or other persons for whom both spouses are morally responsible, a loss in

earning capacity may result with effects that linger after dissolution. These losses are addressed more fully in §§5.05 and 5.12. The second component, identified in Paragraph (3)(b), focuses on the consequence of a long-term relationship itself, whether or not it includes children. Over the course of a long marriage, people make adjustments to accommodate their life together, and these adjustments often have a financial impact on them that continues even after their relationship ends. This component of an equitable loss allocation is addressed more fully in §5.04. Finally, Paragraph (3)(c) recognizes that a short marital relationship may, in some cases, have a very different financial impact on one spouse than on the other. Sections 5.15 and 5.13 identify two such cases in which equitable considerations require a financial adjustment between the spouses.

Paragraphs (3)(a), (3)(b), and (3)(c) only identify three general circumstances in which equitable considerations may require a remedy. The commentary to the sections referenced above elaborates upon the rationale for a remedy in each case, identifies more precisely the circumstances under which a remedy is required, and provides an appropriate method for setting the remedy's amount.

Common to these sections is the conviction that, as marriages lengthen, continuing obligations between former spouses depend less on explicit agreement and promise than on their relationship itself, molded by them jointly, with consequences for them and their children. Marriages can give rise to duties that continue even though the marriage itself has been terminated on the petition of one or both spouses. A principal objective of this Chapter is therefore to identify the nature of those duties and the precise contours of the financial obligations arising from them that survive the marriage's dissolution. Paragraph (3)(d) is relevant in determining the limits of the financial obligations arising from these duties. The legal duties that spouses acquire toward one another over time cannot give rise to obligations so demanding as to place the obligor in less favorable circumstances than the obligee. The primacy of an individual's claim to the fruits of his or her own labors survives even the longest relationships, and necessarily limits that individual's responsibility to a former spouse. This principle operates even in fashioning the contours of the legal obligation to one's children, and helps explain why the law allows the income-earner to retain some disproportionate benefit from his earnings, as compared to the children. Legally enforced obligations to a former spouse can be no greater than to one's children. . . .

§5.03 Kinds of compensatory awards

(1) Compensatory awards should allocate equitably between the spouses certain financial losses that either or both may incur at dissolution when the family is divided into separate economic units.

(2) The following compensable losses are recognized in Topic 2 of this Chapter:

(a) In a marriage of significant duration, the loss in living standard experienced at dissolution by the spouse who has less wealth or earning capacity (§5.04).

(b) An earning-capacity loss incurred during marriage but continuing after dissolution and arising from one spouse's disproportionate share, during marriage, of the care of the marital children or of the children of either spouse (§5.05).

(c) An earning-capacity loss incurred during marriage and continuing after dissolution, and arising from the care provided by one spouse to a sick, elderly, or disabled third party, in fulfillment of a moral obligation of the other spouse or of both spouses jointly (§5.12).

(3) The following compensable losses are recognized in Topic 3 of this Chapter:

(a) The loss either spouse incurs when the marriage is dissolved before that spouse realizes a fair return from his or her investment in the other spouse's earning capacity (§5.15).

(b) An unfairly disproportionate disparity between the spouses in their respective abilities to recover their premarital living standard after the dissolution of a short marriage (§5.13).

(4) A spouse may qualify for more than one kind of compensatory award, but duplicate compensation should not be provided for any loss, and

(a) as provided in §§5.04, 5.05, and 5.12, the combined value of all Topic 2 awards cannot exceed the maximum award that could be made under §5.04 alone in any dissolution involving spouses with similar incomes; and

(b) as provided in §§5.15 and 5.13, awards are not available under Topic 3 to an individual whose aggregate entitlement under Topic 2 is substantial.

Topic 2. Entitlements Based on the Parties' Disparate Financial Capacity

§5.04 Compensation for loss of marital living standard

(1) A person married to someone with significantly greater wealth or earning capacity is entitled at dissolution to compensation for a portion of the loss in the standard of living he or she would otherwise experience, when the marriage was of sufficient duration that equity requires that some portion of the loss be treated as the spouses' joint responsibility.

(2) Entitlement to an award under this section should be determined by a rule of statewide application under which a presumption of entitlement arises in marriages of specified duration and spousal-income disparity.

(3) The value of the award made under this section should be determined by a rule of statewide application that sets a presumptive award of periodic payments calculated by applying a specified percentage to the difference between the incomes the spouses are expected to have after dissolution. This percentage is referred to in this Chapter as the *durational factor*, and should increase with the duration of the marriage until it reaches a maximum value set by the rule.

(4) The presumptions established under this section should govern unless there are facts, set forth in written findings of the trial court (§1.02), establishing that the presumption's application to the case before the court would yield a substantial injustice. An award may be made under this section in cases where no presumption of entitlement arises, if facts not present at the dissolution of most marriages of similar duration and income levels establish that a substantial injustice will result if there is no compensation, and those facts are set forth in written findings of the trial court (§1.02).

(5) The duration of an award of periodic payments made under this section should be determined as provided in §5.06. Subsequent modification of the award's amount or duration is allowed as provided under §§5.07, 5.08, and 5.09. An award of periodic payments that would otherwise arise under this section may be replaced, in whole or in part, by a single lump-sum payment, as provided in §5.10.

(6) In determining the duration of a marriage for the purpose of this section, the court should include any period immediately preceding the formal marriage during which the parties lived together as domestic partners, as defined in §6.03.

§5.05 Compensation for primary caretaker's residual loss in earning capacity

(1) A spouse should be entitled at dissolution to compensation for the earning-capacity loss arising from his or her disproportionate share during marriage of the care of the marital children, or of the children of either spouse.

(2) Entitlement to an award under this section should be determined by a rule of statewide application under which a presumption of entitlement arises at the dissolution of a marriage in which

(a) there are or have been marital children, or children of either spouse;

(b) while under the age of majority the children have lived with the claimant (or with both spouses, when the claim is against the stepparent of the children), for a minimum period specified in the rule; and

(c) the claimant's earning capacity at dissolution is substantially less than that of the other spouse.

(3) A presumption of entitlement governs in the absence of a determination by the trial court that the claimant did not provide substantially more than half of the total care that both spouses together provided for the children.

(4) The value of an award under this section should be determined by a rule of statewide application under which a presumption arises that the award shall require a set of periodic payments in an amount calculated by applying a percentage, called the *child-care durational factor*, to the difference between the incomes the spouses are expected to have at dissolution.

(a) The rule of statewide application should specify a value for the child-care durational factor that increases with the duration of the *child-care period*, which is the period during which the claimant provided significantly more than half of the total care that both spouses together provided for the children.

(b) The child-care period equals the entire period during which minor children of the marriage, or of the spouse against whom the claim is made, lived in the same household as the claimant, unless a shorter period is established by the evidence. In the case of stepchildren of the spouse against whom the claim is made, the child-care period equals the entire period during which the minor children lived in the same household as both spouses, unless a shorter period is established by the evidence.

(5) A claimant may be entitled to both an award under this section and an award under §5.04, but in no case shall the combined value of the child-care durational factor, and the durational factor employed to determine the presumed award under §5.04, exceed the maximum value allowed for the §5.04 durational factor alone.

(6) The presumed value of the award, as set under Paragraph (4), should govern unless there are facts, set forth in the written findings of the trial court (§1.02), establishing that the presumption's application to the case before the court would yield a substantial injustice.

(7) The duration of an award of periodic payments made under this section should be determined as provided in §5.06. Subsequent modification of the award's amount or duration is allowed as provided under §§5.07, 5.08, and 5.09. An award of periodic payments that would otherwise arise under this section may be replaced, in whole or in part, by a single lump-sum payment, as provided in §5.10.

§5.06 Duration of award of periodic payments under §§5.04 and 5.05

(1) An award of periodic payments made pursuant to §5.04 or §5.05 may have a term that is fixed or indefinite, according to a rule of statewide application under which a presumption arises

(a) that the term is indefinite when the age of the obligee, and the length of the marriage, are both greater than a minimum value specified in the rule; and, when this presumption does not apply,

(b) that the term is fixed at a duration equal, for awards under §5.04, to the length of the marriage multiplied by a factor specified in the rule and, for awards under §5.05, to the length of the child-care period multiplied by a factor specified in the rule.

(2) The term set by the presumption should govern in the absence of written findings of the trial court (§1.02) that show either

(a) that the term specified in the court's order is less likely than the presumed term to require subsequent modification or extension; or

(b) that the presumption's application to the particular case will yield a substantial injustice.

(3) An award of periodic payments, whether fixed or indefinite in term, may be modified, terminated, or extended as provided in §§5.07, 5.08, and 5.09.

(4) In determining the duration of a marriage for the purpose of this section, the court should include any period immediately preceding the formal marriage during which the parties lived together as domestic partners, as defined in §6.03.

§5.07 Automatic termination of awards made under §§5.04 and 5.05

An obligation to make periodic payments imposed under §5.04 or §5.05 ends automatically at the remarriage of the obligee or at the death of either party, without regard to the award's term as fixed in the decree, unless either

(1) the original decree provides otherwise, or

(2) the court makes written findings (§1.02) establishing that termination of the award would work a substantial injustice because of facts not present in most cases to which this section applies.

§5.08 Judicial modification of awards made under §§5.04 and 5.05

(1) The size of the periodic payments previously ordered under §5.04 or §5.05 should be modified if any of the following circumstances exists:

(a) the income of either the obligee or obligor is far below the level upon which the existing award was based, and the living standards of the spouses are therefore substantially more or substantially less disparate than contemplated by the prior order;

(b) the loss for which the award provides compensation is substantially smaller than was expected when the prior award was made because of an increase in the obligee's income;

(c) at the time of the prior order, the obligor's income, upon which the prior award was based, was less than it had been earlier in the marriage, but has since increased substantially.

(2) The amount of the periodic payments awarded under §5.04 or §5.05 may be adjusted to reflect significant changes in the cost of living that adversely affect the obligee, but only to the extent the income of the obligor has increased proportionately.

(3) The modified award is determined by applying the principles set forth in §5.04 or §5.05 to the changed circumstances. Circumstances that would justify departure from the presumptions that ordinarily govern at the time of an initial decree are also cause, if they later arise, for allowing or denying a petition for modification.

(4) The duration of a fixed-term award may be extended if both

(a) the existing decree is based upon a duration shorter than that called for by the governing presumption, and

(b) the circumstances as they actually occur are substantially inconsistent with those expected when the shorter duration was chosen.

§5.09 Effect of obligee's cohabitation

(1) An obligation to make periodic payments under §5.04 or §5.05 is terminated, without regard to its duration as fixed in the decree, when the obligor shows that the obligee established a domestic-partner relationship with a third person, unless either

(a) the original decree provides otherwise, or

(b) the court makes written findings (§1.02) establishing that termination of the award would work a substantial injustice.

(2) An obligor seeking termination of periodic payments under Paragraph (1) must show the obligee's establishment of a domestic-partner relationship with a third person by proof of any of the following:

(a) a court in another proceeding determined in a final order that the obligee established a domestic-partner relationship, as defined in §6.03;

(b) the obligee maintained a common household with the third person and their common child, as defined in §6.03, for the cohabitation parenting period set under §6.03(2);

(c) the obligee maintained a common household with the third person for the cohabitation period set under §6.03(3), unless the obligee rebuts the resulting presumption of a domestic partnership, as provided under §6.03(3);

(d) for a significant period of time, the obligee and the third person shared a primary residence and a life together as a couple, as those terms are defined in §6.03(6) and (7).

(3) An obligation to make periodic payments under §5.04 or §5.05 is suspended when the obligor shows that the obligee maintained a "common household," as defined in §6.03, with another person (who may be the obligor), for a continuous period, specified in a rule of statewide application, of at least three months, unless either

(a) the original decree provides otherwise, or

(b) the obligee shows that he or she and the other person do not share "a life together as a couple," as defined in §6.03(7).

(4) An obligation suspended under Paragraph (3) should be reinstated for any remaining portion of its original term, if the obligee shows that the relationship upon which the suspension was based has ended, unless the obligor shows, under Paragraph (2), that the relationship, before ending, endured long enough to become a domestic partnership.

§5.10 Form of award under §§5.04 and 5.05

(1) Except as provided in Paragraphs (2) and (3) of this section, a compensatory award made pursuant to §5.04 or §5.05 should be for monthly payments in the amount determined under those sections, to continue for the duration determined under §5.06.

(2) Where equity requires, the court may provide that an award made under either §5.04 or §5.05 may take any of the following forms:

(a) periodic payments in periods other than monthly, or for a different amount and term, than the monthly payments otherwise required, so long as the entire set of payments is of equal value to those that would have otherwise been ordered under Paragraph (1);

(b) an enhancement of the obligee's share of the marital property, pursuant to §4.09, equivalent in value to the monthly payments that would otherwise be ordered;

(c) a single payment of equivalent value to the monthly payments that would otherwise be ordered, where the obligor has sufficient resources from which to make such a payment;

(d) a combination of the foregoing that in the aggregate are equivalent in value to the monthly payments that would otherwise be ordered under Paragraph (1).

(3) In comparing the values of different forms of payment, the court should consider, insofar as possible, the chance that an award of periodic payments will later be modified in amount or duration under §5.07, §5.08, or §5.09.

§5.11 Compensation for the residual loss of earning capacity arising from the care of third parties

(1) A spouse is entitled at dissolution to compensation for an earning-capacity loss arising from the care provided during marriage to a sick, elderly, or disabled third party, in fulfillment of a moral obligation of the other spouse or of both spouses jointly. An award is allowed only to a claimant whose earning capacity at divorce is substantially less than that of the other spouse.

(2) The claimant under this section has the burden of persuading the factfinder that an earning-capacity loss has been incurred, that it arose from such care, and that it has not been substantially restored by the time of dissolution. The value of any award under this section should be established by a statewide rule under which the presumptive amount of the award is calculated by rules analogous to those implementing §5.05.

(3) The form of an award made under this section, and the duration and modifiability of required periodic payments, should be governed by rules analogous to those adopted for awards made pursuant to §5.05.

Topic 3. Entitlements Not Based on the Parties' Disparate Financial Capacity

§5.12 Compensation for contributions to the other spouse's education or training

(1) A spouse is entitled at divorce to reimbursement for the financial contributions made to the other spouse's education or training when all of the following are shown:

(a) the claimant provided funds for the tuition or other direct costs of the other spouse's education or training, or provided the principal financial support of the family while the other spouse acquired the education or training;

(b) the education or training was completed within a specified number of years, set in a rule of statewide application, immediately preceding the filing of the petition for dissolution;

(c) the education or training for which reimbursement is sought substantially enhanced the obligor's earning capacity.

(2) No award may be made under this section against a spouse:

(a) who is entitled to an award under §5.04 or §5.05; or

(b) who would have been entitled to an award under those sections but for the enhancement of his or her earning capacity from education or training described in Paragraphs (1)(a), (1)(b), and (1)(c).

(3) If both spouses qualify for reimbursement under this section, their claims are netted against one another.

(4) The award allowed under this section is calculated by

(a) adding the obligor's share of the family living expenses during the period of education or training to the obligor's direct educational costs, to determine the obligor's total education or training costs;

(b) subtracting from the total costs the income of the obligor during that period, the amount of any debts then incurred that remain outstanding at the time of divorce and that are assigned to the obligor, and expenditures made during that period from the obligor's separate property; and

(c) adjusting the difference for changes in the real value of the dollar between the time when the education was obtained and the time of divorce.

(5) An award under this section is nonmodifiable and takes the form fixed under §5.14.

§5.13 Restoration of premarital living standard after a short marriage

(1) At the dissolution of a marriage in which neither spouse qualifies for an award under §5.04 or §5.05 because the marriage is childless and of short duration, the court may make an award to correct an inequitable disparity that would otherwise exist in the extent to which the spouses are able at dissolution to recover their respective premarital living standards.

(2) A disparity between the spouses in the extent to which each is able at dissolution to recover his or her premarital living standard is inequitable if the disparity arises because

(a) during marriage, or in anticipation of it, one spouse made significant expenditures from separate assets, or gave up specific educational or occupational opportunities; and

(b) the assets were expended, or the opportunities forgone, to allow the other spouse's pursuit of similar opportunities without undue disruption of the marital life, to facilitate the couple's bearing or adoption of children, or to serve some other purpose that the spouses then agreed was important to their marital life; and

(c) at the time of dissolution, the expended assets are largely unrecoverable, or the lost opportunities leave the claimant with an earning capacity that is significantly less than it was before the marriage.

(3) The value of an award under this section should be for half the amount necessary to allow the obligee to recover his or her premarital living standard, unless facts set forth in written findings of the trial court (§1.02) establish that equity requires a different award, in light of the duration of the marriage and of the parties' relative financial circumstances at dissolution.

(4) Where the loss arises from the obligee's forgone educational or occupational opportunities, an award of transitional assistance that allows the obligee a reasonable chance to recover the lost opportunity, or its equivalent, satisfies this section.

(5) An award made under this section may be for either a lump sum, or for periodic payments for a fixed term and amount, as is equitable and practical under the circumstances, and is in either event not modifiable.

§5.14 Form of award under §§5.12 and 5.13

An award made under §§5.12 and 5.13 may take any of the following forms:

(1) an enhanced share of the marital property, pursuant to §4.09;

(2) a lump-sum payment made by the obligor from his separate property;

(3) where neither (a) nor (b) is possible without imposing unreasonable hardship on the obligor, a set term of monthly payments of equivalent value. An award in the form of monthly payments is not modifiable and is unaffected by the death or remarriage of either party.

Chapter 6. Domestic Partners

Topic 1. Scope and Objectives

§6.01 Scope

(1) This Chapter governs the financial claims of domestic partners against one another at the termination of their relationship. For the purpose of defining relationships to which this Chapter applies, domestic partners are two persons of the same or opposite sex, not married to one another, who for a significant period of time share a primary residence and a life together as a couple, as determined by §6.03.

(2) A contract between domestic partners that

(i) waives or limits claims that would otherwise arise under this Chapter or

(ii) provides remedies not provided by this Chapter, is enforceable according to its terms and displaces any inconsistent claims under this Chapter, so long as it satisfies the requirements of Chapter 7 for the enforcement of agreements.

(3) Nothing in this Chapter forecloses contract claims between persons who have no claims under this Chapter, but who have formed a contract that is enforceable under applicable law.

(4) Claims for custodial and decisionmaking responsibilities, and for child support, are governed by Chapters 2 and 3, and not by this Chapter.

(5) Claims arise under this Chapter from any period during which one or both of the domestic partners were married to someone else only to the extent that they do not compromise the marital claims of a domestic partner's spouse.

§6.02 Objectives of the rules governing termination of the relationship of domestic partners

(1) The primary objective of Chapter 6 is fair distribution of the economic gains and losses incident to termination of the relationship of domestic partners by

(a) allocating property according to principles that respect both individual ownership rights and equitable claims that each partner has on the property in consequence of the relationship, and that are consistent and predictable in application; and

(b) allocating financial losses that arise at the termination of the relationship according to equitable principles that are consistent and predictable in application. Equitable principles of loss recognition and allocation should take into account

(i) loss of earning capacity arising from a partner's disproportionate share of caretaking responsibilities for children or other persons to whom the partners have a moral obligation;

(ii) losses that arise from the changes in life opportunities and expectations caused by the adjustments individuals ordinarily make over the course of a long relationship;

(iii) disparities in the financial impact of a short relationship on the partners' postseparation lives, as compared to their lives before the relationship; and

(iv) the primacy of the income earner's claim to benefit from the fruits of his or her own labor, as compared to the claims of a domestic partner.

(2) The secondary objective of Chapter 6 is protection of society from social-welfare burdens that should be borne, in whole or in part, by individuals.

Comment

a. The basis of this Chapter. **A complete treatment of family dissolution cannot limit itself to relationships entered according to the procedures and ceremonies required to create a lawful marriage. Although society's interests in the orderly administration of justice and the stability of families are best served when the formalities of marriage are observed, a rapidly increasing percentage of Americans form domestic relationships without such formalities. Few of these couples make explicit contracts to govern their relationship or its termination. Most states have responded to this reality with principles drawn from the law of contract. Some have applied expansive notions of implied agreement and have also resorted to a variety of equitable doctrines. By these devices, they allow their courts to provide remedies when a domestic relationship dissolves, whether or not it has been created pursuant to an explicit agreement.**

. . .

Domestic partners fail to marry for diverse reasons. Among others, some have been unhappy in prior marriages and therefore wish to avoid the form of marriage even as they enjoy its substance with a domestic partner. Some begin a casual relationship that develops slowly into a durable union, by which time a formal marriage ceremony may seem awkward or even unnecessary, for many Americans entertain the widespread, albeit erroneous, belief that the mere passage of time transforms cohabitation into common-law marriage. Failure to marry may reflect group mores; some ethnic and social groups have a substantially lower incidence of marriage and a substantially higher incidence of informal domestic relationships than do others. Failure to marry may also reflect strong social or economic inequality between the partners, which allows the stronger partner to resist the weaker partner's preference for marriage. Finally,

there are domestic partners who are not allowed to marry each other under state law because they, are of the same sex, although they are otherwise eligible to marry and would marry one another if the law allowed them to do so. In all these cases, the absence of formal marriage may have little or no bearing on the character of the parties' domestic relationship and on the equitable considerations that underlie claims between lawful spouses at the dissolution of a marriage.

This Chapter is premised on the familiar principle that legal rights and obligations may arise from the conduct of parties with respect to one another, even though they have created no formal document or agreement setting forth such an undertaking. The implementation of this principle requires careful definition of the domestic relationships that give rise to such obligations. Domestic relationships that satisfy the criteria of §6.03 closely resemble marriages in function, and their termination therefore poses the same social and legal issues as does the dissolution of a marriage. For that reason, this Chapter applies most of the Principles set out in Chapters 4 and 5 to the dissolution of domestic relationships. The application of these Principles to domestic relationships, and the exceptions to such application, are addressed in §§6.04, 6.05, and 6.06.

The Chapter does not impose all the consequences of recognition as domestic partners on every couple that falls within its definition because domestic partners may, by agreement, avoid the rules that this Chapter would otherwise apply. However, the freedom to contract with respect to a domestic relationship is not unlimited. It is subject, under traditional law as well as under Chapter 7, to some limitations not generally applicable to other contracts. Nevertheless, under §6.01, domestic partners have the same opportunity to contract out of the usual rules as do marital partners. This Chapter may thus be understood as a set of default rules that apply to domestic partners who do not provide explicitly for a different set of rules. The default rules are, in effect, a contract imposed by law on parties who do not set forth their agreement to some different set of rules. The law of marriage and divorce can, of course, be similarly understood. For marital partners who do not make another agreement, entry into formal marriage subjects them to the law of marriage and divorce. For domestic partners who do not make another agreement, their course of conduct over a period of years subjects them to parallel rules set forth in this Chapter.

b. The objectives of this Chapter. **The most important objective of this Chapter is just resolution of the economic claims of parties who qualify as Chapter 6 domestic partners. The Chapter also advances, as a secondary objective, the fair allocation of responsibilities between individuals and society. Fairness vis-a-vis society requires that individuals closely implicated in the economic circumstances of persons with whom they lived as domestic partners assume some economic responsibility for those circumstances. . . .**

It is not an objective (or a likely effect) of this Chapter to encourage parties to enter a nonmarital relationship as an alternative to marriage. On the contrary, to the extent that some individuals avoid marriage in order to avoid responsibilities to a partner, this Chapter reduces the incentive to avoid marriage because it diminishes the effectiveness of that strategy. Under this Chapter, one may avoid such obligations in long-term nonmarital relationships only as one may avoid them in marriage, by entering enforceable agreements so providing. Nor are domestic relationships likely to provide a satisfactory alternative to marriage for those otherwise inclined to marry, because informal domestic relationships are not generally recognized by third parties, including governments, which often make marriage advantageous under various regulatory and benefit schemes. . . .

Topic 2. Whether Persons Are Domestic Partners

§6.03 Determination that persons are domestic partners

(1) For the purpose of defining relationships to which this Chapter applies, domestic partners are two persons of the same or opposite sex, not married to one another, who for a significant period of time share a primary residence and a life together as a couple.

(2) Persons are domestic partners when they have maintained a common household, as defined in Paragraph (4), with their common child, as defined in Paragraph (5), for a continuous period that equals or exceeds a duration, called the *cohabitation parenting period*, set in a rule of statewide application.

(3) Persons not related by blood or adoption are presumed to be domestic partners when they have maintained a common household, as defined in Paragraph (4), for a continuous period that equals or exceeds a duration, called the *cohabitation period*, set in a rule of statewide application. The presumption is rebuttable by evidence that the parties did not share life together as a couple, as defined by Paragraph (7).

(4) Persons *maintain a common household* when they share a primary residence only with each other and family members; or when, if they share a household with other unrelated persons, they jointly, rather than as individuals, with respect to management of the household.

(5) Persons have a *common child* when each is either the child's legal parent or parent by estoppel, as defined by §2.03.

(6) When the requirements of Paragraph (2) or (3) are not satisfied, a person asserting a claim under this Chapter bears the burden of proving that for a significant period of time the parties shared a primary residence and a life together as a couple, as defined in Paragraph (7). Whether a period of time is significant is determined in light of all the Paragraph (7) circumstances of the parties' relationship and, particularly, the

extent to which those circumstances wrought change in the life of one or both parties.

(7) Whether persons share a life together as a couple is determined by reference to all the circumstances, including:

(a) the oral or written statements or promises made to one another, or representations jointly made to third parties, regarding their relationship;

(b) the extent to which the parties intermingled their finances;

(c) the extent to which their relationship fostered the parties' economic interdependence, or the economic dependence of one party upon the other;

(d) the extent to which the parties engaged in conduct and assumed specialized or collaborative roles in furtherance of their life together;

(e) the extent to which the relationship wrought change in the life of either or both parties;

(f) the extent to which the parties acknowledged responsibilities to each other, as by naming the other the beneficiary of life insurance or of a testamentary instrument, or as eligible to receive benefits under an employee-benefit plan;

(g) the extent to which the parties' relationship was treated by the parties as qualitatively distinct from the relationship either party had with any other person;

(h) the emotional or physical intimacy of the parties' relationship;

(i) the parties' community reputation as a couple;

(j) the parties' participation in a commitment ceremony or registration as a domestic partnership;

(k) the parties' participation in a void or voidable marriage that, under applicable law, does not give rise to the economic incidents of marriage;

(l) the parties' procreation of, adoption of, or joint assumption of parental functions toward a child;

(m) the parties' maintenance of a common household, as defined by Paragraph (4).

Topic 3. Consequences of a Determination That Persons are Domestic Partners

§6.04 Domestic-partnership property defined

(1) Except as provided in Paragraph (3) of this section, property is domestic-partnership property if it would be marital property under Chapter 4, had the domestic partners been married to one another during the domestic-partnership period.

(2) The domestic-partnership period

(a) starts when the domestic partners began sharing a primary residence, unless either partner shows that the parties did not begin sharing life together as a couple until a later date, in which case the domestic-partnership period starts on that later date, and

(b) ends when the parties ceased sharing a primary residence.

For the purpose of this Paragraph, parties who are the biological parents of a common child began sharing life together as a couple no later than the date on which their common child was conceived.

(3) Property that would be recharacterized as marital property under §4.12 if the parties had been married, is not domestic-partnership property.

§6.05 Allocation of domestic-partnership property

Domestic-partnership property should be divided according to the principles set forth for the division of marital property in §4.09 and §4.10.

§6.06 Compensatory payments

(1) Except as otherwise provided in this section,

(a) a domestic partner is entitled to compensatory payments on the same basis as a spouse under Chapter 5, and

(b) wherever a rule implementing a Chapter 5 principle makes the duration of the marriage a relevant factor, the application of that principle in this Chapter should instead employ the duration of the domestic-partnership period, as defined in §6.04(2).

(2) No claim arises under this section against a domestic partner who is neither a legal parent nor a parent by estoppel (as defined in §2.03) of a child whose care provides the basis of the claim.

GLOSSARY OF TERMS

This glossary gives definitions for key terms and concepts used in Family Law Code, Selected States, and ALI Principles.

Abortifacient: This herb, product or implement is used to induce an abortion. See also "Comstock laws."

Abrogation: This procedure is the annulment of an adoption by adoptive parents. Despite a concern with the negative impact on the adoptee, courts permit abrogation in some cases (e.g., when the adoptive parents are victims of fraud, such as on the part of an agency).

Absolute divorce: English law, historically, distinguished between "absolute divorce" (our modern idea of divorce) and "divorce a mensa et thoro" (i.e., a legal separation which did not permit the parties to remarry). Absolute divorce was not granted in England until 1857. In contrast, by the nineteenth century in America, all the northern colonies granted judicial divorces.

Abstinence-based sex education: School programs that encourage abstinence (refraining from sexual relations) while also including instruction on contraception and disease prevention. Abstinence-based sex education received a boost from federal welfare reform legislation in 1996 that allocated money to states that adopt educational programs teaching the social, psychological and health gains from abstaining from sexual activity. See "Personal Responsibility and Work Opportunity Reconciliation Act."

Adoption: In this legal process, the adoptive parent(s) assume(s) all legal rights and obligations in relation to an adoptee and, thereby, terminates all rights and obligations of the biological parents. The process may also be used in many jurisdictions to adopt an adult (e.g., for inheritance purposes).

Adultery: Adultery, i.e., the act of engaging in sexual relations with someone other than one's legal spouse, is both a criminal act and a fault-based ground for divorce in some jurisdictions.

Affinity: Affinity (to be distinguished from "consanguinity" which refers to relationships by blood) involves a relationship created by law (e.g., step-relationships, in-law relationships). A marriage between persons who are related by affinity may be invalid depending on the jurisdiction. See also "Consanguinity."

Alienation of affections: This tort claim is based on a third party's intentional interference with the marital relationship. It was only available to husbands at common law.

Alimony: Alimony was the term formerly used to signify payments from one spouse (traditionally the husband) to the other for support either pending the divorce litigation ("alimony pendente lite") or following the divorce. Modern usage has replaced the term with the gender-neutral "spousal support" and "maintenance." Gender-based statutes prescribing that husbands shall pay wives alimony violate Equal Protection. Orr v. Orr, 440 U.S. 268 (1979).

American Law Institute (ALI): The American Law Institute is an organization of prominent judges, lawyers and law professors, organized in 1923, to promote clarification and simplification of the law and to improve its administration. Among the ALI projects are the Restatements of the Law that address many subjects. Since 1989, the ALI has been involved in a project (published as "Principles of the Law of Family Dissolution: Analysis and Recommendations") to reform family law by clarifying its underlying principles and making policy recommendations.

Annulment: This judicial declaration (sometimes called "a judgment of nullity") specifies that no marriage occurred because of the existence of some impediment. An annulment declares a marriage *void ab initio,* unlike a divorce, which terminates a valid marriage. Annulments were more common during the fault-based era when divorce was difficult to obtain.

Antenuptial agreement: See "Premarital agreement."

Anti-heart balm legislation: These state statutes (sometimes called "Heart Balm Acts") abolished claims, such as breach of promise and alienation of affections, because of their sexist, out-dated and extortionate nature..

Antimiscegenation statutes: These laws, which were declared unconstitutional on Equal Protection grounds in Loving v. Virginia, 388 U.S. 1 (1967), prohibited interracial marriages.

Antinepotism policies: These policies, which were originally enacted to prevent public officials from conferring employment on unqualified relatives, prevent a spouse's employer from employing the other spouse (hence, sometimes called "no-spousal employment" policies).

Arbitration: This dispute resolution process (commonly used in the labor context) is sometimes resorted to by marital parties to permit a third party, chosen by the parties, to serve as a decisionmaker.

Artificial insemination: This reproductive technique, originally used in humans to combat male infertility, results in the introduction of a man's sperm into a woman's uterus.

Assisted conception: This contemporary term refers to such methods of new reproductive technology to combat infertility, as in vitro fertilization, embryo transplants, and surrogacy.

Babyselling: This criminal offense punishes the payment or acceptance of money or other consideration in exchange for the adoption of a child. Some courts and commentators analogize surrogacy to this practice.

Battered child syndrome: This medical condition, discovered by radiologists in the 1960s, refers to injuries to children which are in various stages of healing and inflicted by parents who provide inconsistent causal explanations.

Battered woman's syndrome: This syndrome, discovered by psychologist Lenore Walker, describes the nature of the abuse suffered by long-term victims of battering. The modern trend is the acceptance of the admissibility of this evidence to establish a defense in spousal homicide cases.

Best interests of the child: This criteria, based on a concern with child welfare, is the subjective standard for custody and adoption decisions. Many factors (race, religion, sexual orientation, domestic violence, disability) enter into the determination of the child's best interests.

Bigamy: This criminal offense involves being married to more than one spouse at one time, i.e., contracting a second marriage without having terminated legally the prior marriage.

Bilateral divorce: This type of divorce proceeding, in which personal jurisdiction exists over *both* spouses, permits a court to settle property issues incident to the divorce (not just the marriage termination).

Breach of promise to marry: This cause of action, now abolished by many states, permits the imposition of tort liability for the violation of a promise by one person to marry the other.

Capacity: A marriage may be annulled for lack of capacity, i.e., the ability to understand and fulfill a marriage contract. Statutory requirements for capacity include: the parties must be of opposite sexes; married to only one spouse at a time; not related, and, above the statutorily defined age. These requirements are distinguished from "state of mind" restrictions, which require that the parties marry voluntarily, without fraud or duress.

Central registry: This database of reported cases of suspected child abuse, established by many states, was intended originally to ascertain the incidence and nature of abuse, to assist professionals to determine whether a child has been previously abused, and to keep track of persons suspected of abuse. Recently, social services agencies use these registries to preclude individuals with abusive propensities from working in child care.

Cloning: In this biotechnological process, a woman's egg is stripped of its nucleus (containing DNA) and injected with DNA that is obtained from another person's nonreproductive cell. After exposure to growth factors, the egg divides into the beginning stages of an embryo. Currently, a distinction exists between "reproductive cloning" and "nonreproductive or therapeutic cloning" for stem-cell research to treat human diseases. The latter process involves harvesting stem cells from early embryos and exposing them to growth factors, which causes them to differentiate into other, more adult cells.

Cohabitation: Cohabitation is the state of living together without being formally married, and is generally thought to include sexual intercourse. It is one of several requisite elements of a common law marriage. See also "Common law marriage."

Common law marriage: This form of marriage, followed by approximately a dozen states, requires heterosexual couples to enter into a present agreement to be married, to cohabit for a period of time in a jurisdiction which recognizes common law marriages (although the time may be quite brief), and to hold themselves out as husband and wife. Common law marriage, since it is a valid marriage, must be dissolved by death or divorce before the parties may enter into a subsequent marriage with other parties.

Community property: Under this marital property regime based on a partnership model, a husband and wife who reside in a community property jurisdiction are regarded (as of the date of the marriage) as the respective owners of an undivided one-half interest in all property which was acquired following the marriage. Community property is distinct from "separate property." (See "separate property.") Whereas a few community property states require an equal division of the community property, others follow a regime of equitable distribution. Further, statutes in some community property jurisdictions give their courts authority to include separate property in equitable distribution whereas other community property states exclude separate property.

Comstock laws: These state and federal laws banned the circulation and importation of "obscene" materials through the national mail at the end of the nineteenth century. "Obscene" materials were defined to include articles for preventing conception, producing abortion, or other immoral purposes.

Conciliation: This form of alternative dispute resolution consists of marital counseling that is entered into with the object of reconciliation. In the fault era, some states established court-connected conciliation services, which now provide mediation services.

Conditional gift: This present, often an engagement ring, is given by a donor on the condition that the donee will perform a future act (such as undergo a marriage). The theory underlying a conditional gift is that if the act, upon which the gift is conditioned, does not occur, then the donee must return the gift.

Confidential marriage: A procedural variation permitted in some jurisdictions, similar to proxy or common law marriage, which permits a marriage to be entered into without the necessity of fulfilling all the usual requirements (e.g., dispensing with blood tests).

Consanguinity: This term denotes a blood relationship between two persons, such as parent-child, brother-sister, uncle-niece, etc. It is distinguishable from affinity relationships (relations created by law). Almost all jurisdictions have incest statutes that provide criminal sanctions for marriage or sexual intercourse between persons related by consanguinity. In addition, civil restrictions prevent persons thus related from obtaining a marriage license.

Consortium: The cause of action for "loss of consortium" consists of tortious interference by a third party with a spouse's rights to the services, companionship, affection, and sexual relations, of the other spouse. The action was available first only to husbands, but later extended to wives.

Criminal conversation: Under this common law tort, a husband might seek damages against another man for the latter's interference with the marital relationship. Unlike the tort of alienation of affections, criminal conversation required proof of the tortfeasor's sexual intercourse with the wife.

Cruelty: This fault-based ground for divorce consists of a course of conduct that is so severe as to create an adverse effect on plaintiff's physical or mental well-being. Although early courts required actual or threatened physical violence, courts subsequently permitted mental cruelty to suffice.

Cryopreservation: This mode of assisted conception, which involves the preservation of embryos by the freezing process, poses issues about the property rights that attach to genetic material.

Custodial responsibility: The term used by the American Law Institute's Principles of the Law of Family Dissolution for the concept of physical custody. See also "Decisionmaking responsibility."

Decisionmaking responsibility: The term used by the American Law Institute's Principles of the Law of Family Dissolution for the concept of legal custody. See also "Custodial responsibility."

De facto parent: As used by the American Law Institute's Principles of the Law of Family Dissolution, a de facto parent is a person, other than a legal parent or parent by estoppel, who has regularly performed an equal or greater share of caretaking as the parent with whom the child primarily lived, lived with the child for a significant period (not less than two years), and acted as a parent for non-financial reasons (and with the agreement of a legal parent) or as a result of a complete failure or inability of any legal parent to perform caretaking functions. ALI Principles, *supra,* §2.03(1)(c). See also "Parent by estoppel."

Dispositional hearing: This second stage of a juvenile court proceeding, such as for abuse or neglect (following the first adjudicatory stage) determines the appropriate placement for the child (i.e., with a relative, foster care, return to the home).

Dissolution: The word "divorce," with its gender-based stereotypes and stigma has been replaced with this more modern usage.

Domestic partnership legislation: Legislation, which has been enacted in a few states (and several local communities), that extends a limited degree of legal protection to same-sex couples. It generally requires a public registration of the partnership by the couple.

Domicile: This legal concept is a prerequisite for the assertion of jurisdiction in many family law matters, such as marriage, divorce, custody or adoption. At common law, a married woman acquired the domicile of her husband. Domicile includes: physical presence plus intent to remain permanently. Although the term generally is distinguishable from "residence" (because a person has only one domicile but may have many temporary residences), some states' durational residency requirements for divorce often are construed so as to be indistinguishable from "domicile." See also "Durational residency requirements."

Dual representation: Commentators and courts criticize this practice of having one attorney represent both spouses in a divorce proceeding as resulting in an inherent conflict of interest. The practice is also referred to as "multiple representation."

Due process, procedural: According to this constitutional guarantee (under the Fourteenth Amendment), the government may infringe upon life, liberty, or property only if it does so by a procedure that provides adequate notice and an opportunity to be heard before the decision is rendered.

Due process, substantive: According to this constitutional guarantee (under the Fourteenth Amendment), the government may infringe certain fundamental rights (those rights inherent in the concept of "liberty") based only upon a strong justification that survives strict scrutiny.

Durational residency requirements: Durational residency requirements require a divorce petitioner to be a state resident for a specific period of time, varying from a minimum of six weeks to one year. Some states impose durational residency requirements either instead of, or in addition to, a domiciliary requirement. The Supreme Court in Sosna v. Iowa, 419 U.S. 393 (1975), held that these state requirements are constitutional.

Emancipation: This procedure releases a minor from parental care and control. Thus, it enables a child to acquire, for example, the right to retain earnings and to make decisions regarding medical care. Emancipation may occur, expressly, such as by parental consent or, implicitly, such as by acts of parental abandonment. At common law, marriage or service in the armed forces resulted in emancipation. A minor may also secure emancipation judicially.

Embryo transplant: In this method of assisted conception, a fertilized embryo is implanted in the uterus of a woman who may be a surrogate mother.

Equal protection: This guarantee, under the Fourteenth Amendment, prohibits the government from denying equal protection under the law. This requirement has been interpreted as meaning that the government must treat alike those persons who are similarly situated.

Equitable adoption: By resort to this equitable remedy, courts effectuate an adoption (or effectuate the consequences of an adoption) in cases in which a legal adoption never occurred. The process is sometimes referred to as "virtual adoption." Many cases arise when an adoptive parent dies and the adoptee seeks a determination of inheritance rights. Courts generally apply equitable adoption by resort to either contract theory or estoppel theory.

Estoppel: This doctrine was relevant in the fault-based era when many courts refused to recognize foreign divorces. Such divorces might be protected by means of the estoppel doctrine. That is, a spouse who goes to a foreign country and secures a foreign divorce could be estopped from denying its validity subsequently.

Ex parte divorce: In an ex parte or unilateral divorce, a court has jurisdiction over only one spouse. This enables the court to terminate the marriage but not to adjudicate the financial incidents of the marriage (i.e., property, spousal support).

Family and Medical Leave Act (FMLA): Congress enacted this legislation to provide employees with gender-neutral leave for reasons of childbirth, adoption, or illness. It provides for three months unpaid leave for employers of over 50 employees to care for infants or seriously ill family members.

Fault-based divorce: This doctrine permitted divorce to the "innocent" spouse, thereby placing blame for the marital breakdown on the "guilty" spouse who had committed a marital wrong. Traditional fault-based grounds for divorce included cruelty, adultery, and desertion, etc. Traditional fault-based defenses include recrimination, condonation, and connivance. Prior to the late 1960s when the movement for no-fault divorce emerged, fault-based divorce was the only type of divorce permitted in the United States.

Freedom of Access to Clinic Entrances Act (FACE): Congress enacted this legislation in 1994 to penalize the use of force, threat of force, or physical obstruction to the entrance of abortion clinics. The legislation was enacted in response to violent protests at abortion clinics that reduced women's access to abortion. Many states have enacted similar legislation.

Free Exercise clause: This First Amendment provision prohibits government from interfering with the individual's exercise of his or her religion (religious beliefs or religious conduct).

Full Faith and Credit clause: This constitutional provision (Article IV, §1) provides that a state shall give full faith and credit to "the public acts, records and judicial proceedings" of other states. The doctrine was especially important in the fault-based era to give effect to divorce decrees granted by other states that had jurisdiction over at least one of the marital parties. The clause is also important today in terms of the controversial issue of same-sex marriage: The clause would appear to dictate that a state must recognize same-sex marriage if validly contracted in another state. No state yet recognizes such marriages.

Fundamental right: For equal protection purposes, fundamental rights are rights that are either explicitly or implicitly guaranteed by the Constitution. For substantive due process purposes, fundamental rights are those rights that are "deeply rooted in our history and traditions" (according to Griswold v. Connecticut, 381 U.S. 479 (1965)), and may or may not be explicitly enumerated.

Guardian ad litem: This individual, who may or may not be an attorney (depending on the jurisdiction), represents a child who is the subject of a child abuse and neglect proceeding or custody dispute.

Heart balm acts: See "Anti-heart balm legislation."

Heart balm suit: These causes of action provide tort liability for such claims as: breach of promise to marry and alienation of affections. Many states have abolished, or circumscribed recovery for, these actions. See also "Anti-heart balm legislation."

Illegitimate: This term for a child who is born out of wedlock, i.e., to parents who are not married, has been replaced by the less stigmatizing term "nonmarital child."

Incest: Incest signifies marriage or sexual intercourse between persons who are related by consanguinity or affinity. Incest constitutes both a criminal offense and a civil restriction on marriage.

Incompatibility: This was an early no-fault ground for divorce, which eliminated proof of fault

Independent adoption: This form of adoption is the placement of children with adoptive parents by private (i.e., not state) persons or agencies. Because of the unlicensed nature of the practice, it is the subject of public policy concerns.

Intermediate scrutiny: The middle-tier test used by courts to review possibly unconstitutional legislative classifications. The test is used by the U.S. Supreme Court for gender-based classifications (among others), although some states use strict scrutiny for gender-based classifications.

Interspousal immunity: This common law doctrine precluded one marital partner from recovering in tort from the other. The preclusion was based on the rationale that the partners constituted one legal entity, and also that judicial intervention would disturb marital harmony. The majority of courts have abolished the doctrine for intentional and negligent torts.

Interspousal wiretapping: This practice involves electronic surveillance by one spouse of the other within the marital home. The federal courts are divided about whether liability attaches for interspousal wiretapping under Title III of the Omnibus Crime Control Act.

Intestate succession: An "intestate" is a person who dies without a will. Adopted children generally lose the right to inherit from a biological parent who dies intestate because the adoption terminates the child's former relationship with the biological parent(s). In addition, inheritance law, traditionally, also precluded nonmarital children from inheriting from their father (but not their mother) by intestate succession. The Supreme Court has declared this policy a violation of equal protection in some situations (e.g., Trimble v. Gordon, 430 U.S. 762 (1977)).

In-vitro fertilization (IVF): In this method of assisted conception, an ova is removed surgically from a woman and subsequently placed in a laboratory medium with sperm. The resultant embryo is then implanted either in the ova donor or a surrogate mother.

Irreconcilable differences: This no-fault ground for divorce (sometimes termed "irretrievable breakdown") specifies that the marriage is broken, but does not place blame on either party.

Joint custody: Joint custody (technically joint legal custody) is a custody arrangement, based on the rationale that children need frequent and continuing contact with both parents following divorce, which confers legal responsibility upon both parents for major childrearing decisions regarding the child's upbringing, health, welfare, and education. "Joint legal custody" is distinguishable from "joint physical custody." That is, parents may share joint legal custody, although the children may reside primarily with one parent.

Judgment of nullity: See "Annulment."

Level of scrutiny: This term refers to the appropriate test that courts use to evaluate laws or legislative classifications that burden constitutional rights. The three tests include: minimal scrutiny (the rational basis test), intermediate scrutiny (substantially related to an important governmental objective), or strict scrutiny (necessary to a compelling interest).

Lex loci: The rule of lex loci (Latin for "law of the place") holds that a marriage that is valid in the place where it was performed is valid everywhere. The major exception to the rule is when a marriage is contrary to public policy.

Licensure: One of the formalities that states require for entry into marriage. Specifically, states require that parties who desire to marry procure a marriage license, often by applying to a county clerk. The clerk may refuse to issue the license if the information provided by the parties reveals that they are ineligible to marry. See also "Solemnization."

Living separate and apart: This no-fault ground for divorce refers to a physical separation and intention to dissolve a marriage. Courts do not always require that the spouses actually reside in separate homes.

Maiden name: This term describes a woman's surname at birth. Traditionally, by custom, a woman gave up her maiden name upon marriage and adopted her husband's surname. Modern social mores have resulted in more women retaining their maiden (or "birth") names.

Maintenance: This modern term, used to describe the financial support given by one spouse to the other following divorce, has replaced the former term "alimony."

Marital rape: This act (also called "spousal rape"), which was not recognized as a criminal offense until recently by several states, consists of a husband forcing his wife to have sexual intercourse with him against her will.

Maternity leave: This policy provides women with a temporary leave from employment for the purposes of pregnancy or childbirth. See also "Family and Medical Leave Act"; "Pregnancy Discrimination Act."

Mediation: Divorce mediation is a process by which the parties themselves, with the help of a third-party mediator, resolve their disputes. Unlike in arbitration, the parties do not cede their authority to a neutral third party to resolve their dispute, but rather make their own agreements with the mediator serving as a facilitator. Some jurisdictions make mediation mandatory (e.g., California for custody and visitation disputes).

Meretricious: This form of relationship (signifying a "sham" marriage) often refers to unmarried heterosexual couples living together.

Minimal scrutiny: This test is the lowest level of scrutiny that is used by courts to review legislative classifications. It requires only that the challenger prove that the classification is not rationally related to any permissible governmental purpose. Almost any classification can survive minimal scrutiny on the theory that a legislature must have had a sound reason to enact a given law.

Necessaries: These are items (e.g., food, shelter, medical care) that are deemed by courts to be necessary for basic sustenance. At common law, a husband was responsible for the necessaries of his wife and children and could be charged for payment of necessaries even without the husband's consent.

Ne exeat: An equity writ that restrains a person from leaving or removing property from the jurisdiction; often used to restrain a parent from removing a child from the jurisdiction.

No-fault divorce: This form of divorce largely eliminates the importance of finding one spouse at fault for the breakdown of the marriage. After first being enacted in California in 1968, it has now been adopted, in one form or another, by all jurisdictions. However, no-fault divorce does not have the same meaning in all jurisdictions: some states permit no-fault divorce only if both parties consent whereas other states permit it even if only one party desires it. Further, some states define "no fault" to mean that the parties have "irreconcilable differences" but other states define it to signify a marital breakdown that results in the parties physically living apart for a statutorily defined period of time.

Nonmarital child: This modern term is used to describe a child whose parents are not married to each other. The term eliminates the stigma of such traditional terms as "illegitimate," or "out-of-wedlock."

***No-spousal employment policies*:** See "Antinepotism policies."

Nuclear family: This traditional family was composed of husband and wife and their coresident children. It is now decreasing in importance with the rising incidence of divorce and the growth of alternative family forms.

Open adoption: In this modern form of adoption, the biological parents of a child who is placed for adoption are aware of the identity of the adoptive parents. Similarly, the adopted child is aware of the identity of the biological parents. Occasionally, the biological and adoptive parents may enter into an agreement regarding the adoption such that the biological parent(s) continues to play some role (e.g., visitation) in the child's life.

Out-of-wedlock: See "Illegitimate."

Palimony: This term refers to a lawsuit, award, or agreement, by a member of an unmarried couple that seeks "quasi-spousal support," similar to alimony (hence the name "palimony"). Such claims became popular in the wake of Marvin v. Marvin, (557 P.2d 106 (Cal. 1976)), which held that unmarried couples may enter into express contracts (unless the consideration for these contracts rests on the exchange of sexual services) and implied contracts as well.

Parens patriae: This Latin term (literally "parent of the country") signifies that the state is responsible for the welfare of its vulnerable citizens (such as children). The concept is often invoked when courts assert jurisdiction over abused and neglect children.

Parent by estoppel: As used by the American Law Institute's Principles of the Law of Family Dissolution, a parent by estoppel is a person who acts as a parent in circumstances that would estop the child's legal parent from denying the claimant's parental status. The status may be created when an individual: (1) is obligated for child support, or (2) has lived with the child for at least two years and has a reasonable belief that he is the father, or (3) has had an agreement with the child's legal parent since birth (or for at least two years) to serve as a co-parent provided that recognition of parental status would serve the child's best interests. ALI Principles §2.03(1)(b), *supra.* See also "De facto parent."

Parental privilege to discipline: This right, based on constitutional principles derived from Meyer v. Nebraska, 262 U.S. 390 (1923), and Pierce v. Soc'y of Sisters, 268 U.S. 510 (1925) permits parents to discipline their children as part of their protected Fourteenth Amendment "liberty interest" in raising their children as they see fit. However, by statute in many jurisdictions, the force used to administer discipline must be reasonable and for purposes of correction.

Parenting plan: Developments in an increasing number of jurisdictions require divorcing parents who seek custody to file a written agreement by which the parents specify the allocation of physical and legal custody and the method for the resolution of future disputes. The American Law Institute's Principles of the Law of Family Dissolution requires parties seeking custody determinations to submit a parenting plan. See ALI Principles, *supra,* §§2.05, 2.06.

Partial birth abortion: An abortion in the late stage of pregnancy (in or after the fifth month). In Stenberg v. Carhart, 530 U.S. 914 (2000), the United States Supreme Court held that the Nebraska statute banning partial birth abortion was unconstitutional because it lacked any exception for preservation of the mother's health.

Personal Responsibility and Work Opportunity Reconciliation Act (PRWORA): Federal welfare reform legislation enacted by Congress in 1996. PRWORA required all states to adopt the Uniform Interstate Family Support Act to facilitate interstate child support enforcement; requires the establishment and maintenance of statewide case registries for collection and disbursement of support payments; expands the federal Parent Locator Service, requires states to adopt improved procedures for child support enforcement (such as mandatory income withholding); established a conditional work program (Temporary Assistance for Needy Families Program) to replace Aid to Dependent Children; addresses teen pregnancy by prohibiting states from providing benefits to unwed teen mothers unless the young women meet certain conditions, and monitoring states' progress in teen pregnancy prevention efforts; and requires states to expand services relating to paternity establishment with the goal of increasing collection of child support payments.

Polygamy: The criminal offense of having *more than two* spouses at one time, as distinct from "bigamy," which means having two spouses at one time, and "monogamy," which means having only one spouse. Civil restrictions prevent an individual who is validly married from obtaining a license to marry (again) without terminating the prior marriage.

Postminority (sometimes "postmajority") support: This form of child support, after a child reaches the age of majority (18 in most jurisdictions), may be ordered by a court, for example, to require a noncustodial parent to pay for the child's college expenses.

Preemption: This doctrine holds that federal statutes preclude operation of state law on a given subject according to congressional intent.

Pregnancy Discrimination Act: This amendment to Title VII of the Civil Rights Act of 1964 was enacted by Congress in 1978 to address employment discrimination against pregnant employees. The Act analogizes pregnancy to a disability by mandating that an employer shall provide the same benefits for pregnant employees as the employer provides to disabled employees. Feminists have criticized the Act for its outmoded treatment of pregnancy as a disability. See also "Family and Medical Leave Act."

Premarital agreement: This contract (also called an "antenuptial" or "prenuptial" agreement), which is executed by prospective spouses, establishes the parties' property rights in the event of death or dissolution.

Presumption of legitimacy: Courts often apply this presumption, which holds that the husband of a married woman is the natural father of any child to whom she gives birth at any time during the marriage. The presumption is based on a desire not to interfere with family harmony. The presumption raises potential problems in the surrogacy situation because the surrogate's husband may acquire thereby parental rights to the child; surrogacy agreements must overcome this presumption.

Private ordering: This principle signifies the ability of the divorcing parties to resolve matters of property and support themselves without judicial intervention. The practice has been on the increase since the 1960s, triggered by considerable dissatisfaction with traditional dispute resolution processes. The ALI Principles of the Law of Family Dissolution give considerable deference to private ordering in custody decisionmaking.

Putative spouse doctrine: This doctrine protects the property rights upon death or dissolution of an "innocent" spouse by upholding the validity of a marriage provided that that spouse has a good faith belief in the validity of the marriage. The doctrine is distinguishable from common law marriage because, in the putative spouse situation, the parties have undergone a marriage ceremony that at least one spouse believes has resulted in a valid marriage.

Recordation: This aspect of the process of getting married follows the solemnization of the marriage. The person who officiates at the wedding signs the marriage certificate and submits it to the county clerk. Recordation occurs when the county clerk registers the marriage so that it becomes part of the public record.

Rehabilitation: Under this modern principle of dissolution, a spouse is awarded only enough property (and/or support) to permit her to become self-supporting. Thus, a court may award a dependent wife enough funds to enable her to obtain education or training to begin a new career or take up a career that she abandoned upon the marriage.

Relation back doctrine: This doctrine has the effect of rendering a marriage that has been nullified judicially to be considered void from inception. As a result, the doctrine may result in reinstatement of a benefit, for example, that was lost because of the relationship.

Religious (or racial) matching provisions: These provisions, applicable to adoption, provide that the religion (or race) of the adoptive parents shall match that of the adopted child, whenever possible. The constitutionality of these provisions has been upheld.

Separate property: This term, as used in community property jurisdictions, signifies property that is acquired by a spouse prior to the marriage and property acquired after the marriage by either spouse by gift, devise or bequest. Statutes in some community property jurisdictions give courts authority to include separate property in equitable distribution, whereas other community property jurisdictions exclude separate property. See also "Community property."

Separation agreement: This agreement, which is entered into by spouses who have decided to separate (and, usually, to terminate their marriage as well), addresses the financial incidents of the divorce (property, spousal support, etc). It is sometimes referred to as a "settlement agreement."

Settlement agreement: See "Separation agreement."

Solemnization: One of the formalities that states require for entry into marriage. All states require solemnization of marriage by an authorized person before witnesses (subject to some exceptions), although no specific form of ceremony is prescribed. See also "Licensure."

Spousal support: This modern term is used to describe the financial support provided by one spouse to the other following the termination of a marriage. Traditionally, it was referred to as "alimony."

Strict scrutiny: This is the highest level of judicial examination that is used to determine the constitutionality of a regulation or act. The test requires that the regulation or act must be necessary to a compelling state interest to be upheld. This level of scrutiny is applied to racial qualifications and also to determine whether a fundamental constitutional right has been violated. The Supreme Court has not applied strict scrutiny to sex-based discrimination, although some state courts do so.

Subsidized adoption: This policy provides state funds to facilitate the placement of children with special needs, i.e., those children who are hard to place due to their age, race, or background.

Substantially related to an important governmental interest: This is the intermediate level of scrutiny that the Supreme Court has determined (in Craig v. Boren, 429 U.S. 190 (1976)) is applicable to review sex-based discrimination. Although higher than the rational basis test, this test is not as rigorous as the strict scrutiny test.

Summary dissolution: This divorce procedure, authorized by statute in many jurisdictions, permits termination of marriage in a relatively short period of time. It often obviates the need for an appearance. Some states provide for the procedure if both parties consent, have no children, have no real property and few debts, and the marriage is of short duration.

Summary seizure: This disposition, which is sometimes ordered by courts in child abuse and neglect cases, provides for the removal of a child from an abusive home without notice to a parent or parents. Removal of the child, prior to a full hearing, is permitted based on the state's concern that the child is being endangered by immediate or threatened harm. Courts and commentators have expressed constitutional concerns about vagueness in such statutes and the arbitrary nature of the practice.

Surrogate motherhood: This method of assisted conception consists of a contractual agreement that specifies that a woman agrees to be artificially inseminated with the semen of a man who is not her husband, to carry the ensuing fetus to term, and to surrender the child, at birth, to the biological father. Many jurisdictions have held such agreements to be violative of public policy. The most famous surrogacy case is In re Baby M, 537 A.2d 1227 (N.J. 1988).

Therapeutic abortion: This type of abortion is undertaken to safeguard the mother's mental or physical health. The liberalization of state abortion restrictions began in the 1960s when many jurisdictions adopted the American Law Institute (ALI)'s Model Penal Code provisions liberalizing abortion for pregnancies resulting from rape or incest, those involving a deformed fetus, and, for therapeutic abortions.

Transracial adoption: This type of adoption, formerly known as "interracial adoption," refers to an adoption of a child by parents of a different race. Today, it is a highly controversial practice.

Trimester framework: These guidelines for abortion were established in Roe v. Wade, 410 U.S. 113 (1973) (holding that the woman does not have an absolute right to an abortion but that the right to an abortion is limited by legitimate state interests). In *Roe*, the United States Supreme Court held that, due to the constitutionally protected right to an abortion, the state may not interfere with the abortion decision during the first trimester. However, during the second trimester, the state may regulate abortion in the interest of maternal health. And, after viability, the state may regulate, and even proscribe, abortion in the interests of the protection of potential life. The trimester framework was replaced with the undue burden standard by the U.S. Supreme Court in Planned Parenthood of Southeastern Pennsylvania v. Casey, 505 U.S. 833 (1992). See "Undue burden."

Undue burden: This standard by which to evaluate state abortion restrictions was announced by the U.S. Supreme Court in Planned Parenthood v. Casey, 505 U.S. 833 (1992). Only those regulations that impose an "undue burden" on the woman's abortion decision will be subject to strict scrutiny. The Court defines undue burden as the placement of a substantial obstacle in a woman's path. The *Casey* Court determines that neither the informed consent requirement nor the 24-hour waiting period create undue burdens, although spousal notification policies do.

Uniform Law Commissioners: The National Conference of Commissioners on Uniform State Laws (NCCUSL) is an organization that was founded 111 years ago and consists of more than 300 lawyers, judges, and law professors, appointed by the states as well as by the District of Columbia, Puerto Rico, and the Virgin Islands. The organization drafts model laws that promote uniformity and works toward their enactment in state legislatures.

Unilateral divorce: See "Ex parte divorce."

Vagueness: This shortcoming renders a classification unconstitutional because the classification fails to alert people as to the specific conduct that is prohibited. That is, the classification constitutes a violation of due process under the Fourteenth Amendment.

Viability: The point at which the fetus is potentially able to live outside the womb. According to Roe v. Wade, 410 U.S. 113 (1973), the Supreme Court stated that subsequent to viability, the state may regulate and even proscribe abortion except to preserve the life or health of the mother. In Planned Parenthood v. Casey, 505 U.S. 833 (1992), however, the Court downplayed somewhat the importance of viability. Although reaffirming a woman's right to obtain a previability abortion, *Casey* allows states to impose regulations throughout pregnancy provided that such regulations do not impose an undue burden.

Void marriage: States have substantive requirements regarding capacity that determine marriage validity (restrictions about incest, bigamy, same-sex marriages etc.). The presence of any of these substantive defects renders a marriage "void," i.e., invalid from its inception.

Voidable marriage: In addition to states' substantive restrictions regarding capacity, jurisdictions also have state of mind requirements for entry into a valid marriage. Unlike substantive defects that render a marriage void, a defect concerning state of mind renders a marriage "voidable." For example, the existence of fraud or duress vitiates consent and makes the marriage voidable at the request of the injured party.

Waiting period: Many states impose a waiting period (often three to five days) between the time the applicants apply for the license and its issuance to deter hasty marriages. Some states impose a waiting period before a woman may have an abortion. See Planned Parenthood of Southeastern Pennsylvania v. Casey, 505 U.S. 833 (1992) (holding that the 24-hour waiting period of the Pennsylvania abortion statute did not impose an undue burden).

Wrongful abortion: A suit on behalf of parents alleging that but for the defendant-physician's negligence (e.g., regarding incorrect diagnosis of genetic defects), the parents would *not* have aborted the fetus.

Wrongful adoption: This doctrine enables an adoptive parent to recover tort damages (similar to an action for misrepresentation) from an adoption agency that fails to disclose fully information about a child's biological parents or prior history.

Wrongful birth: A suit on behalf of the parents of a disabled child in which the plaintiffs allege that the negligence of the defendants (in terms of the performance of prenatal testing or genetic counseling) deprived the parents of the right to make the decision to terminate the pregnancy because of the likelihood that the child would be born physically or mentally disabled. Many jurisdictions recognize wrongful birth actions although few recognize wrongful life actions. See also "Wrongful life."

Wrongful conception: A claim on behalf of parents of an unexpected child alleging that the conception resulted from negligent sterilization procedures or a defective contraceptive product.

Wrongful life: A suit on behalf of a *child* for negligent failure to prevent the birth of a child born with some impairment. Thus, the plaintiff is claiming that because of the defendant's negligence, the child is forced to live such an unbearable life that it would have been better had the child never been born.

TABLE OF CASES

TABLE OF STATUTES

INDEX

Abbreviations

CAL. CIV.	California Civil Code
CAL. CIV. PROC.	California Code of Civil Procedure
CAL. EDUC.	California Education Code
CAL. FAM.	California Family Code
CAL. GOVT.	California Government Code
CAL. HEALTH & SAFETY	California Health & Safety Code
CAL. LAB.	California Labor Code
CAL. PENAL	California Penal Code
CAL. PROB.	California Probate Code
CAL. REV. & TAX.	California Revenue and Taxation Code
CAL. RULES OF COURT	California Rules of Court
CAL. UNEMP. INS.	California Unemployment Insurance Code
CAL. WELF. & INST.	California Welfare & Institutions Code
HAW. REV. STAT.	Hawaii Revised Statutes
MASS. CONST.	Massachusetts Constitution
MASS. GEN. LAWS	Massachusetts General Laws
N.Y. CIV. PRAC. LAWS AND RULES	New York Civil Practice Laws and Rules
N.Y. CIV. RIGHTS	New York Civil Rights Law
N.Y. CODE PROF. RESP.	New York Code of Professional Responsibility
N.Y. CONST.	New York Constitution
N.Y. CRIM. PROC.	New York Criminal Procedure Law
N.Y. DOM. REL.	New York Domestic Relations Law
N.Y. FAM. CT.	New York Family Court Act
N.Y. GEN. OBLIG.	New York General Obligations Law
N.Y. RULES OF COURT Policies	New York Rules of Court Standards & Administrative
N.Y. SOC. SERV.	New York Social Services Law
TEX. CONST.	Texas Constitution
TEX. CRIM. PROC.	Texas Criminal Procedure Code
TEX. EDUC.	Texas Education Code
TEX. FAM.	Texas Family Code
TEX. HEALTH & SAFETY	Texas Health & Safety Code
TEX. HUM. RES.	Texas Human Resources Code
TEX. INS.	Texas Insurance Code
TEX. LAB.	Texas Labor Code
TEX. PENAL	Texas Penal Code
TEX. R. EVID.	Texas Rules of Evidence
TEX. TAX	Texas Tax Code

References are to code sections, rules, and pages. Page references are in *italics*.